college accounting

a practical approach

Jeffrey Slater
North Shore Community College

Brian Zwicker
Grant MacEwan University (Instructor Emeritus)

canadian twelfth edition

PEARSON

Toronto

Acquisitions Editor: Megan Farrell
Sponsoring Editor: Kathleen McGill
Marketing Manager: Claire Varley
Developmental Editor: Karen Townsend
Program Manager: Patricia Ciardullo
Project Manager: Jessica Hellen
Media Editor: Nicole Mellow
Media Producer: Olga Avdyeyeva
Production Services: Sapna Rastogi and Vasundhara Sawhney, Cenveo Publisher Services
Permissions Project Manager: Joanne Tang
Text Permissions Research: Khalid Shakshir, Electronic Publishing Services
Cover and Interior Designer: Anthony Leung
Cover Image: GettyImages

Credits and acknowledgments of material borrowed from other sources and reproduced, with permission, in this textbook appear on the appropriate page.

10 9 8 7 6 5 4 3 2 1 [EB]

Library and Archives Canada Cataloguing in Publication

Slater, Jeffrey, 1947-, author
College accounting : a practical approach / Jeffrey Slater, Brian Zwicker. – Canadian twelfth edition.

Includes index.
ISBN 978-0-13-313323-3 (pbk.)

I. Zwicker, Brian, 1944-, author II. Title.

HF5636.S53 2014 657'.044 C2013-904779-4

PEARSON

ISBN 978-0-13-313323-3

For Darien and Laura

Brief Contents

Contents

AVAILABLE ON MyAccountingLab

Preface

Welcome to the Canadian twelfth edition of *College Accounting: A Practical Approach* by Jeffrey Slater and Brian Zwicker. In this edition, we introduce several important changes that will greatly enhance the student learning experience while allowing for highly organized and efficient class leadership. In most revisions, even one of the changes we have included in this edition would be a standout event, but several very positive alterations make the Canadian twelfth edition another significant regeneration in the long and respected history of *College Accounting*. At the same time, we have maintained the many features that have helped make *College Accounting* a classroom favourite for more than 25 years.

NEW TO THE CANADIAN TWELFTH EDITION

Improving on MyAccountingLab! Added with the last revision, we have made many changes to ensure that the MAL continues to meet student and instructor needs. The MAL platform—an online homework presentation and assessment tool—has been designed, tested, and used in various textbooks published by Pearson in North America for many years. The addition of MAL to any text is a carefully considered venture mainly because of the effort required by all involved. The result is well worth the investment because MAL provides student and instructor access to a considerable set of resources that will greatly expand and enhance the teaching and learning of accounting. Through MAL, instructors integrate technology into their course design and students gain a valuable supplemental resource. MAL can also be used in the student assessment process, if desired. However, the biggest benefit may well be the large quantity and high quality of review material available to students who need additional practice and assistance in the learning of accounting.

Another Change to the Chapter Order. A modified chapter order has become necessary in the Canadian twelfth edition. Previously, the topic of special journals was designed so that a single chapter made it easier for students to grasp the concept of a special journal more easily and completely. This approach also delayed to a later chapter the topic of taxes, which helped students to really understand how special journals work without clouding the issue with Canadian taxes such as PST, GST, and HST at the same time.

This change was carefully investigated for the previous edition, and unanimous approval given by reviewers for the change. What became apparent was that the new chapter, while otherwise excellent, took a lot longer for students to cover/master. Accordingly, that previous chapter, which covered all special journals, has now been split into two chapters. This will benefit all involved, especially since it allowed a bit more room to cover an alternate method for recording credit memos and multicolumn Sales Journals—a worthwhile addition.

The number of chapters in the text itself has been reduced. There are now thirteen chapters in the actual text, plus several in electronic format. The electronic format can be easily incorporated into a more challenging course design. Custom Publishing allows any qualifying institution to have a custom version published just for their students. Chapters from the previous edition, and, indeed from a number of previous editions, can easily be added to the custom volume. If interested, please contact your PearsonEd representative for details.

New "Quick Review" Feature. Designed to give students a self-paced and structured alternative to retaining the main points of each chapter, the new feature will be found to be yet another way to improve the learning of accounting. In addition to assisting students with learning the subject matter, the Quick Review also permits each student to assess their progress in each chapter, and thereby focus more intensely on areas they find they may need to work on.

"Need Help?" Continued. Many of our reviewers pointed out that students needed more explanation and practice material with the basics. The "Need Help?" feature is our major response to these requests. The first five chapters now include the "Need Help?" sections, with each of the self-review quizzes near the end of each learning unit. It is like having a private tutoring session with the authors, as student questions are anticipated and step-by-step guidance is given as the solution is laid out in logical order. This feature should greatly extend student retention, especially for those students who benefit from detailed and exacting repetition.

Several reviewers also called for additional explanatory material on the subject of debits and credits, mentioning that some students just do not "get it" the first (or, indeed, the second) time around. This edition also includes a "Need Help?" feature on debits and credits, drawing on material used for decades by the Canadian author in classroom settings. While there is no objective evidence that it helps with understanding this sometimes troublesome topic, the number of smiles around the classroom following the "nautical" example does suggest that it works—sometimes very well. This new feature is included, logically enough, in Chapter 2.

Accounting Cycle Tutorial (ACT). Online practice and review of the accounting cycle can greatly extend student retention of the details of this fundamental topic. Margin logos direct students to the appropriate ACT section and material, which provides online practice, application, and review. ACT is provided for the chapters that cover this topic in depth.

MAJOR FEATURES MAINTAINED AND EXPANDED

In addition to the above major additions and changes, the Canadian twelfth edition has retained and in many cases improved upon the pedagogy that has made *College Accounting* a classic. Here are some details:

Includes 19 chapters! In addition to the 13 chapters published in the text itself, six additional chapters are available from MyAccountingLab for those institutions that need to incorporate them into their course design. The additional chapters are:

- Chapter 14—Accounting for Bad Debts. Adapted with minor changes from the eleventh edition of *College Accounting*
- Chapter 15—Accounting for Property, Plant, Equipment, and Intangible Assets. Adapted with minor changes from the eleventh edition of *College Accounting*
- Chapter 16—Statement of Cash Flows. Adapted with minor changes from the eleventh edition of *College Accounting*
- Chapter 17—Analyzing Financial Statements. Updated from an earlier edition of *College Accounting*
- Chapter 18—Notes Receivable and Payable. Updated from an earlier edition of *College Accounting*

- Chapter 19—Accounting for Merchandise Inventory. Adapted with minor changes from an earlier edition of *College Accounting*

These auxiliary chapters will assist instructors who need to extend their students' education while keeping the text's price under control. In general, the chapters continued from an earlier Canadian edition retain many of the features adopters have come to appreciate. Because they are adapted from a high-quality source, they are of considerable assistance in selected circumstances.

Expanded Coverage of Banking Trends. This material was already the best available in Canada but has been further upgraded, and in places completely rewritten, to alter the basic information so it is as current and meaningful as possible. Additional problem material has been developed and will be appreciated by any instructor who aims to provide students with plenty of practice in this vital area.

Condensed Chapter Openers. Feedback has been consistent in maintaining that the chapter openers are not thoroughly appreciated by students—in fact most students do not read them at all. The new edition takes this into account.

Continuing Problem. A continuing problem runs through all chapters, asking students to apply skills to the business scenario set in the Big Picture. It is based on the Precision Computer Centre. Reviewers have reported success in having some, or all, of the continuing problem completed using accounting software.

Payroll Chapters. Chapters 9 and 10 (formerly 8 and 9) have been rewritten where necessary to reflect the latest laws and taxation deduction rules in effect in Canada, and updated forms are shown as well. Because the topic of special journals now covers multi-column Sales Journals, it has also been possible to include a discussion and illustration of how sales commissions are handled in Payroll. At the request of a number of reviewers, a special comprehensive payroll problem has been added near the end of Chapter 10. This should provide an excellent resource for courses that stress the complete knowledge of the payroll process.

GST and HST Accounting. These taxes are a reality in Canada. The essential details of how to account for GST and HST are covered in Chapter 11. This chapter has been designed to accommodate instructors who choose to emphasize this topic, and textbook examples and problem material using HST have been strengthened. Plenty of material using PST still exists in the text for those situations where HST is not yet a marketplace reality. A small section dealing with the Quick Method of accounting for GST/HST has been added for the twelfth edition at the request of some reviewers.

Subway Boxes. The real-world accounting issues facing franchise owners and corporate staff are presented in boxed features based on research of the internationally known company. Discussion questions tie the boxes to chapter concepts.

Check Figures. Brief mention of key amounts or other hints in the margins continue to provide quick feedback for students to monitor progress in all A, B, and C problems.

Coverage of Perpetual Inventory. Both merchandise inventory and special journals are discussed. An appendix uses the general journal approach to teach entries for a merchandise company using perpetual inventory, while an appendix to Chapter 11 available on MyAccountingLab shows how all the special journals in Chapters 6, 7 and 11 would look in a perpetual system. The related appendix to Chapter 13, also available on MyAccountingLab, shows how a worksheet for a merchandise company would look in a perpetual inventory system. Auxiliary Chapter 19 extends this coverage in a very complete way, where the bulk of the material is directed to perpetual inventory issues.

Extensive End-of-Chapter Framework. Each chapter offers extensive learning aids, including:

- Discussion Questions/Classroom Demonstration Exercises
- Mini Exercises
- Exercises—Now with two sets to choose from!
- Problem sets A, B, and C (as well as set D in the Instructor's Resource Manual)
- Continuing Problem: a cumulative problem that runs through Chapters 1 to 13, asking students to work through the entire business cycle for Precision Computer Centre
- Simulations available in selected chapters: students will benefit from completing the extended and realistic cases presented at the end of Chapters 5, 11, and 13. The case at the end of Chapter 5 can also be completed using computer software if deemed appropriate.

THE SLATER/ZWICKER PACKAGE

The text is just the starting point. Because the needs of Canadian instructors are very high on our priority list, we have taken certain other steps designed to maximize instructor effectiveness and efficiency. These steps include the provision of an Instructor's Resource Manual, Instructor's Solution Manual, PowerPoint Presentation and Pearson Canada TestGen (a computerized test bank). We also offer the complete Canadianization of the *Study Guide with Working Papers*. We invested many hours to ensure the highest quality possible, and we hope it shows in increased clarity, accuracy, and consistency.

INSTRUCTOR'S SUPPLEMENTS

- **Instructor's Solutions Manual.** This manual provides answers to discussion questions and solutions to exercises, mini exercises, problems, practice problems, classroom demonstration exercises, and a guide to discussion of ethical issues.
- **Instructor's Resource Manual.** The Instructor's Resource Manual (IRM) includes Class Quizzes and Class Activities, both designed to reinforce key points introduced in the text; Lesson Outlines designed for a variety of classroom situations; Typical Student Misconceptions that identify common errors gathered from almost 50 years of combined teaching experience; and Teaching Tips to help students remember and absorb textbook material. In addition, Lecture Notes provide a useful check to ensure nothing critical is overlooked during classroom preparation, and Business-World Notes take students beyond the accounting textbook by providing a glimpse of what takes place in the real world. The IRM is also available online as a download.
- **PowerPoint Presentation.** These slide presentations pair key points covered in the chapters with figures from the textbook to provoke effective classroom discussion.
- **Pearson TestGen.** The Pearson TestGen provides testing software that enables instructors to view and edit existing questions, add questions, generate tests, and distribute those tests in a variety of formats. Powerful search and sort functions make it easy to locate questions and arrange them in any order desired. TestGen

also enables instructors to administer tests on a local area network, have the tests graded electronically, and have the results prepared in electronic or printed reports.

TestGen is compatible with Windows and Macintosh operating systems and is available online for download. The question content has been significantly altered as well to provide a larger set of questions from which to choose tests and quizzes, etc.

CourseSmart for Instructors. CourseSmart goes beyond traditional expectations—providing instant, online access to the textbooks and course materials you need at a lower cost for students. And even as students save money, you can save time and hassle with a digital eTextbook that allows you to search for the most relevant content at the very moment you need it. Whether it's evaluating textbooks or creating lecture notes to help students with difficult concepts, CourseSmart can make life a little easier. See how when you visit **www.coursesmart.com/instructors**.

Technology Specialists. Pearson's Technology Specialists work with faculty and campus course designers to ensure that Pearson technology products, assessment tools, and online course materials are tailored to meet your specific needs. This highly qualified team is dedicated to helping schools take full advantage of a wide range of educational resources, by assisting in the integration of a variety of instructional materials and media formats. Your local Pearson Canada sales representative can provide you with more details on this service program.

FOR STUDENTS

Study Guide with Working Papers. This publication has undergone all necessary revisions and enhancements. It contains forms for the quiz at the end of each learning unit in the chapter, for all exercises and mini exercises, for the problems (A, B, and C) at the end of each chapter, and for the practice-set problems that follow Chapters 5, 8, and 13. In addition, all worksheets are treated as foldouts—an appreciated enhancement by all accounts. At the end of each chapter of the *Study Guide with Working Papers*, there is a summary practice test designed to prepare students for in-class exams. It consists of fill-in-the-blank questions, a matching question, and true/false questions. Like previous editions, the *Study Guide with Working Papers* is a completely Canadian publication. Many changes have been made to help ensure that each student's experience is as effective and efficient as possible.

MyAccountingLab. MyAccountingLab delivers proven results in helping individual students succeed. It provides engaging experiences that personalize, stimulate, and measure learning for each student. MyAccountingLab is the portal to an array of learning tools for all learning styles—practice questions with guided solutions are only the beginning. MyAccountingLab provides a rich suite of learning tools, including:

- Static and algorithmic exercises and problems from the textbook
- Help Me Solve It question-specific interactive coaching
- An online, interactive Accounting Cycle Tutorial
- A dynamic eText with links to media assets
- Self-review animations in Chapters 1–5

CourseSmart for Students. CourseSmart provides instant, online access to the textbooks and course materials you need at a lower cost. With instant access from any computer and the ability to search your text, you'll find the content you need quickly, no matter where you are. See all the benefits at **www.coursesmart.com/students**.

ACKNOWLEDGMENTS

The task of publishing a Canadian edition of any textbook is a challenging venture. In this case it helped to be working from an outstanding original and with an outstanding team.

Thanks are certainly due to the many helpful folks at Pearson Canada, including Acquisitions Editor Megan Farrell, Sponsoring Editor Kathleen McGill, Developmental Editor Karen Townsend, Project Manager Jessica Hellen, Marketing Manager Claire Varley, and Production Editors Sapna Rastogi and Vasundhara Sawhney of Cenveo Publisher Services. Special thanks to copy editor Cat Haggert for her diligence and hard work.

Thanks are also due to the following reviewers who provided valuable criticism and suggestions during the development of the manuscript:

Frieda Ambroziak Georgian College; Allan Bray, Saskatchewan Institute of Applied Science and Technology; Carmen Burt, Okanagan College; Grace Credico Lethbridge College; Tina M. Dean, College of the North Atlantic; Imelda Engels, College of the Rockies; Denise Dodson NSCC; Ken Hartford, St. Clair College; Pat Humphreys, Medicine Hat College; Teresa Kisilevich Okanagan College; Ferne Mac Lennan NSCC; Michael Malkoun, St. Clair College; Joe Mariani, Algonquin College; Jennifer Moorlag Yukon College; Shawn Richards Humber College; Laurie A. Schmit SIAST Woodland; Dawn Sturt College of New Caledonia; Barrie Tober Niagara College; and Don Woolridge, College of the North Atlantic.

The *Study Guide with Working Papers* as well as the Solutions Manual were created by Pat Tuttle, whose skills with the software used are substantial. Pat cheerfully took on several other tasks as well and generally made the whole process run quite smoothly.

A special thanks to Imelda Engels, who very kindly allowed the use (with modifications) of the comprehensive payroll project she used very successfully with her students at the College of the Rockies in Cranbrook, B.C.

Despite the best efforts of so many talented people, it is inevitable that a few errors will persist. I accept responsibility for them and would appreciate your help in identifying them so that they can be totally eliminated in future printings. With so much material now available online, it is possible to update many important documents without waiting for a revised printing, so please take the time to contact me if you spot anything that needs to be improved.

Brian Zwicker
Edmonton, Alberta
email me at: brian@bzwicker.ca

CHAPTER 1

Accounting Concepts and Procedures

AN INTRODUCTION

LEARNING OBJECTIVES

- **LO 1** Defining and listing the functions of accounting (p. 4)
- **LO 2** Recording transactions in the basic accounting equation (p. 7)
- **LO 3** Seeing how revenue, expenses, and withdrawals expand the basic accounting equation (p. 13)
- **LO 4** Preparing an income statement, a statement of owner's equity, and a balance sheet (p. 20)

THE BIG PICTURE

Businesses small and large sell billions of dollars of goods and services every day. The business must keep track of each of these sales for income tax reasons as well as good business practice. When you purchase an item at your local grocery store or online from Amazon.ca, accounting surrounds each transaction.

When you buy an item from Amazon.ca, such as a set of headphones, you keep track of the purchase, often using your PayPal account or credit card. Amazon.ca also keeps track of the sale in a special account they call their Revenue account. Starting with this chapter, you will see how all companies record these transactions and prepare reports, which can be read and understood by interested parties.

Accounting is the language of business, and learning about this important topic can have huge positive consequences for you. Whether you want to own and run your own company or work for some larger concern, knowledge of accounting is an important skill to have. This chapter begins to teach you about this central business topic.

Many corporate executives feel that Sarbanes-Oxley is too strict and costly to implement. In Canada, our new legislation is seen as less objectionable—possibly because our laws did not require as much of a change as in the United States.

During the past few years, you could pick up almost any newspaper and read stories about financial scandals. In the United States, the events related to WorldCom and Enron are good examples, while here in Canada, Nortel Networks Corporation has created headlines. Were these companies "cooking the books"? With jail sentences of up to 25 years for some of the corporate officers convicted of unlawful activities, the answer is clearly—yes! In the United States, a federal statute called the **Sarbanes-Oxley Act** was passed into law to help prevent future attempts to defraud the public. In Canada, the Ontario Securities Commission has created National Policies (Numbers 58-102—which gave birth to the Canadian Public Accountability Board—and 58-201) that cover much the same thing. Both countries are attempting to increase the focus on internal controls, the role and responsibility of auditors, and increased penalties for business fraud to improve the accuracy and reliability of published accounting reports.

Accounting is the language of business; it provides information to managers, owners, investors, governmental agencies, and others inside and outside the organization. Accounting provides answers and insights to questions like these:

- Should I invest in Amazon.com?
- Is Subway's cash balance sufficient?
- Will Internet companies show a good return in the future?
- Can General Motors Canada pay its debt obligations?
- What percentage of IBM's marketing budget is for e-business? How does this compare with the competition? What is the overall financial condition of IBM?

The Internet is creating many new opportunities and challenges for all forms of business organizations.

Smaller businesses also need answers to their financial questions:

- Did business increase enough over the last year to warrant hiring a new assistant?
- Should we spend more money to design, produce, and send out new brochures in an effort to create more business?
- What role should the Internet play in our business?

Accounting is as important to individuals as it is to businesses; it answers questions like:

- Should I take out a loan for a new car or wait until I can afford to pay cash?
- Would my money work better in a chartered bank or in a credit union savings plan?

Accounting is the process that analyzes, records, classifies, summarizes, reports, and interprets financial information for decision-makers—whether individuals, small businesses, large corporations, or governmental and not-for-profit agencies—in a timely fashion. It is important that students understand the "whys" of the accounting process. Just knowing the mechanics is not enough.

CATEGORIES OF BUSINESS ORGANIZATION

There are three main categories of business organization: (1) sole proprietorship, (2) partnership, and (3) corporation. Let's define each of them and look at their advantages and disadvantages. This information also appears in Table 1-1 and

TABLE 1-1 Types of Business Organization

	Sole Proprietorship	Partnership	Corporation
Ownership	Business owned by one person	Business owned by more than one person	Business owned by shareholders
Formation	Easy to form	Easy to form	More difficult to form
Liability	Owner could lose personal assets to meet obligations of business	Partners could lose personal assets to meet obligations of partnership	Limited personal risk; shareholders' loss is usually limited to their investment in the company
Closing	Ends with death of owner or closing of business	Ends with death of a partner or exit of a partner	Can continue indefinitely

is more extensively discussed in one of the auxiliary chapters now appearing on MyAccountingLab.

Sole Proprietorship

A **sole proprietorship** is a business that has one owner. That person is both the owner and the manager of the business. One advantage of a sole proprietorship is that the owner makes all the decisions for the business. One disadvantage is that if the business cannot pay its obligations, the business owner must pay them. This means that the owner could lose some personal assets (e.g., house or savings).

Sole proprietorships are easy to form. They end if the business closes or when the owner dies.

Partnership

A **partnership** is a form of business ownership that has at least two owners (partners). Each partner acts as an owner of the company. This is an advantage because the partners can share the decision-making and the risks of the business. A disadvantage is that, as in a sole proprietorship, the partners' personal assets could be lost if the partnership cannot meet its obligations.

Partnerships are easy to form, but may rely on legal advice to create a workable agreement. They end when a partner dies or leaves the partnership.

Corporation

eBay is an example of a corporation.

A **corporation**, such as Canadian Tire, is a business owned by shareholders. The corporation may have only a few shareholders or it may have many shareholders. The shareholders are not personally liable for the corporation's debts, and they usually do not have input into the business decisions.

Corporations are more difficult to form than sole proprietorships or partnerships. Corporations can exist indefinitely.

CLASSIFYING ORGANIZATIONS BY ACTIVITY

Whether we are looking at a sole proprietorship, a partnership, or a corporation, the business can be classified by what the business does to earn money. Companies are categorized as service, merchandising, or manufacturing businesses (see Table 1-2 for examples of each type).

TABLE 1-2 Examples of Service, Merchandising, and Manufacturing Businesses

Service Businesses	Merchandising Businesses	Manufacturing Businesses
eBay	Sears	Mattel
Jane's Painting Co.	Eddie Bauer	General Motors
Dr. Wheeler, M.D.	The Bay	Intel
H&R Block	Amazon.com	Bombardier

CAREERS IN ACCOUNTING

There are many career opportunities in accounting. They vary according to the amount of education and experience required. You should note that while a lot of routine accounting work is now done using computers, this has not lessened the need for all kinds of accounting personnel.

Accounting Clerks: Accounting clerks perform most of a business's record-keeping functions. Sometimes, accounting clerks perform specific functions and are given a title that relates to these functions. *Payroll clerk* and *accounts payable clerk* are examples of such titles. Accounting clerks may perform their work manually or by computer.

Accounting clerks generally are required to have completed at least a one-semester accounting course and have some computer skills.

Bookkeepers: Bookkeepers are sometimes called "general bookkeepers" or "full-charge bookkeepers." That is because they do general accounting work, perform some summarizing and analyzing of accounting information, and supervise the accounting clerks. In some companies, they also may help managers and owners interpret accounting information. The size of the company determines the bookkeeper's responsibility.

Usually, bookkeepers need one or two years of accounting training and experience as an accounting clerk. Some computer knowledge is necessary too.

Accountants: Accountants plan, summarize, analyze, report, and interpret accounting information. Other responsibilities include assisting the owners and managers of the business in making financial decisions and supervising other accounting personnel.

Generally, accountants need a college diploma in accounting. They also may need additional professional credentials.

Accountants fall into three general classifications: public accountants, private accountants, and non-profit accountants. (The opportunities in these categories are discussed in the following sections for each classification.)

A local cab company is a good example of a **service company** because it provides a service. The first part of this book focuses on service businesses.

Stores like Sears and Target sell products. They are called merchandising companies. **Merchandising companies** can either make and sell their own products or sell products that are made by other suppliers. Companies like Intel and General Motors that only make products and sell to other companies (often called retailers or dealers) are called **manufacturing companies**.

Definition of Accounting

LO 1

Defining and listing the functions of accounting

Accounting (also called the **accounting process**) is a system that measures the activities of a business in financial terms. It provides reports and financial statements that show how the various transactions the business undertook (e.g., buying and selling goods) affected the business. It does this by performing the following functions:

- **Analyzing:** Looking at what happened and how the business was affected
- **Recording:** Putting the information into the accounting system
- **Classifying:** Grouping all of the same activities (e.g., all purchases) together
- **Summarizing:** Creating totals by category and/or date, which are used in the next two functions

- **Reporting:** Issuing the reports that tell the results of the previous functions
- **Interpreting:** Examining the reports to determine how the various pieces of information they contain relate to each other

The system communicates the reports and financial statements to people who are interested in the information, such as the business's decision-makers, investors, creditors, governmental agencies (e.g., Canada Revenue Agency), and so on.

As you can see, a lot of people use these reports. A set of procedures and guidelines exists to make sure that everyone prepares and interprets the reports the same way.

Canadian accountants rely on a set of **generally accepted accounting principles** (abbreviated as GAAP) to guide them in the process of preparing financial reports for business entities. To study these in detail usually takes a complete course.

Types of Accountants

Public Accountants: Public accountants provide services to clients for a fee. They may work alone or work for an accounting firm. Two professional accounting bodies are chiefly concerned with public accounting in Canada: the Certified General Accountants Association and the Canadian Institute of Chartered Accountants. (All professional groups have provincial identities as well.) Membership is restricted to those who have passed a challenging set of qualifying examinations and who have served a period of training in various accounting positions. These professional accountants perform many accounting tasks, but they also provide advice on taxation, perform audits, and consult on many aspects of business operations.

Private Accountants (Managerial Accountants): The main difference between public accountants and private accountants is that most private accountants work for a single business. A business may employ one accountant or it may have many.

Private accountants who pass an examination prepared by the Society of Management Accountants of Canada will become Certified Management Accountants (CMAs). Those who pass the exam given by the Institute of Internal Auditors can become Certified Internal Auditors (CIAs).

There are many opportunities in private accounting. Private accountants may manage the accounting system, prepare reports and financial statements, prepare budgets, or determine certain costs (e.g., the cost of producing a new product). Some large firms have their own tax accountants and internal auditors.

Non-Profit (Governmental) Accountants: Non-profit accounting is used by governmental agencies and non-profit agencies such as religious organizations, hospitals, and charitable organizations. These entities use accountants to prepare budgets and keep records.

It is important to know that some non-profit agencies do make money. These agencies can keep their non-profit classifications if they keep the profit in the agency. Also, accounting procedures are very similar to procedures for profit-seeking businesses.

As this book is being completed, it is becoming a certainty that three of the professional accounting bodies are joining forces to create a single accounting desigination. Soon, all CAs, CGAs and CMAs will use the designation CPA.

International Accounting Rules Come to Canada

Companies that have their shares listed on stock exchanges must now adhere to a set of international accounting rules. **International Financial Reporting Standards (IFRS)** have been adopted by a large number of countries, and Canada has joined their ranks. The United States has yet to adopt the IFRS but may well do so in the next few years. The important thing to know is that only Canada's largest companies need to pay attention to the IFRS, because small- and medium-sized companies are exempt (although any company can use the new rules if it chooses to do so). Furthermore, Canadian accounting standards were already very advanced, and because of that fact, in many areas, Canada's rules were already in agreement with the international ones.

Most students who use this textbook should not worry too much about IFRS. Just be aware that the new rules exist, and if ever you decide to pursue a career in accounting, it is then that you will need to understand how IFRS really work and how they are applied.

Difference Between Bookkeeping and Accounting

Confusion often arises concerning the difference between bookkeeping and accounting. **Bookkeeping** is the recording (record-keeping) function of the accounting process; a bookkeeper enters accounting information in the company's books. An accountant takes that information and prepares the financial reports that are used to analyze the company's financial position. Accounting involves many complex activities. Often, it includes the preparation of tax and financial reports, budgeting, and analyses of financial information.

Today, computers are used for routine bookkeeping operations that used to take weeks or months to complete. Basic accounting knowledge is needed even though computers can help with routine tasks.

LEARNING UNIT 1-1

The Accounting Equation

ASSETS, LIABILITIES, AND EQUITIES

Let's begin our study of accounting concepts and procedures by looking at a small business: Catherine Hall's law practice. Catherine decided to open her practice at the end of August 2016. She consulted her accountant, Todd Amark, before she made her decision. Todd told her some important things before she made this decision. First, he told her the new business would be considered a separate **business entity** whose finances had to be kept separate and distinct from Catherine's personal finances. The accountant went on to say that all transactions can be analyzed using the basic accounting equation: Assets = Liabilities + Owner's Equity.

Catherine had never heard of the basic accounting equation. She listened carefully as Todd explained the terms used in the equation and how the equation works.

Assets

Cash, land, supplies, office equipment, buildings, and other things of value *owned* by a firm are called **assets**.

Equities

The rights or financial claims to the assets are called **equities**. Equities belong to those who supply the assets. If you are the only person to supply assets to the firm, you have the sole right or financial claim to them. For example, if you supply the law firm with $5,000 in cash and $4,000 in office equipment, your equity in the firm is $9,000.

Relationship Between Assets and Equities

The relationship between assets and equities is:

Assets	=	**Equities**
(Total value of items *owned* by a business)		(Total claims *against* the assets)

The total dollar value of the assets of the law firm will be equal to the total dollar value of the financial claims to those assets; that is, equal to the total dollar value of the equities.

The total dollar value is broken down on the left-hand side of the equation to show the specific items of value owned by the business and on the right-hand side to show the types of claims against the assets owned.

Liabilities

A firm may have to borrow money to buy more assets; when this occurs, it means the firm is *buying assets on account* (buy now, pay later). Suppose Catherine's law firm purchases a desk for $400 on account from Joe's Stationery, and the store is willing to wait 10 days for payment. The law firm has created a **liability**: an obligation to pay that comes due in the future. Joe's Stationery is called the **creditor**. This liability—the amount owed to Joe's Stationery—gives the store the right, or the financial claim, to $400 of the law firm's assets. When Joe's Stationery is paid, the store's rights to the assets of the law firm will end since the obligation has been paid off.

Basic Accounting Equation

To better understand the various claims to a business's assets, accountants divide equities into two parts. The claims of creditors—outside persons or businesses—are labelled *liabilities*. The claims of the business's owner are labelled **owner's equity**. Let's see how the accounting equation looks now. It can be rewritten as follows:

Assets = **Equities**

1. Liabilities: rights of creditors
2. Owner's equity: rights of owner

Assets = Liabilities + Owner's Equity

LO 2 Recording transactions in the basic accounting equation

The total value of all the assets of a firm equals the combined total value of the financial claims of the creditors (liabilities) and the claims of the owner (owner's equity). This is known as the **basic accounting equation**. The basic accounting equation provides a basis for understanding the accounting system of a business. The equation is used to record business transactions in a logical and orderly way that shows their impact on the company's assets, liabilities, and owner's equity.

Importance of Creditors

Another way of presenting the basic accounting equation is:

Assets − Liabilities = Owner's Equity

This form of the equation stresses the importance of creditors. The owner's rights to the business's assets are determined after the rights of the creditors are subtracted. In other words, creditors have first claim on assets. If a firm has no liabilities—and therefore no creditors—the owner has the total rights to assets. Another term for the owner's current investment, or equity, in the business's assets is **capital**.

As Catherine Hall's law firm engages in business transactions (paying bills, serving clients, and so on), changes will take place in the assets, liabilities, and owner's equity (capital). Let's analyze some of these transactions.

The term *cash* in accounting includes currency and cheques on hand as well as bank accounts. In this textbook, *cash account* will usually mean the balance in the company's bank account.

Transaction A: **Aug. 26: Catherine invests $7,000 in cash and $800 worth of office equipment into the business.**

On August 26, Catherine withdraws $7,000 from her personal bank account and deposits the money in the law firm's newly opened bank account. She also invests $800 worth of office equipment in the business. She plans to be open for business on September 1. With the help of her accountant, Catherine begins to prepare the accounting records for the business. We put this information into the basic accounting equation as follows:

In our analyses, assume that any number without a sign in front of it is a + amount.

ASSETS	= LIABILITIES	+ OWNER'S EQUITY
Cash + Office Equipment	=	**C. Hall, Capital**
$7,000 + $800	=	$7,800

$7,800 = $7,800

Note: Capital is part of owner's equity; it is not an asset.

Note that the total value of the assets, cash, and office equipment—$7,800—is equal to the combined total value of liabilities (none, so far) and owner's equity ($7,800). Remember, Catherine Hall has supplied all the cash and office equipment, so she has the sole financial claim to the assets. Note that the heading "C. Hall, Capital" is written under the owner's equity heading. The $7,800 is Catherine's investment, or equity, in the firm's assets.

Transaction B: **Aug. 27: Law practice buys office equipment for cash, $900.**

From the initial investment of $7,000 cash, the law firm buys $900 worth of office equipment (such as a desk). **Equipment** lasts a long time, while **supplies** (such as pens) tend to be used up relatively quickly.

	ASSETS	= LIABILITIES	+ OWNER'S EQUITY
	Cash + Office Equipment	=	**C. Hall, Capital**
BEGINNING BALANCE	$7,000 + $ 800	=	$7,800
TRANSACTION	−900 + 900		
ENDING BALANCE	$6,100 + $1,700	=	$7,800

$7,800 = $7,800

Shift in Assets

As a result of the last transaction, the law office has less cash but has increased its amount of office equipment. This is called a **shift in assets**—the makeup of the assets has changed, but the total of the assets remains the same.

Suppose you go food shopping at the supermarket with $100 and spend $60. As you leave the store, you have two assets, food and money. The composition of the assets has been *shifted*—you have more food and less money than you did—but the *total* of the assets has not increased or decreased. The total value of the food, $60, plus the cash, $40, is still $100. When you borrow money from the bank, on the other hand, you have an increase in cash (an asset) and an increase in liabilities; overall there is an increase in assets, not just a shift.

The accounting equation can remain in balance even if only one side is affected. The key point to remember is that the left-hand-side total of assets must always equal the right-hand-side total of liabilities and owner's equity.

Transaction C: Aug. 30: Business buys additional office equipment on account, $400.

The law firm purchases an additional $400 worth of chairs and desks from Wilmington Company. Instead of demanding cash right away, Wilmington agrees to deliver the equipment and to allow up to 60 days for the law practice to pay the invoice (bill).

This liability, or obligation to pay in the future, has some interesting effects on the basic accounting equation. Wilmington Company has accepted as payment a partial claim against the assets of the law practice. This claim exists until the law firm pays the bill. This unwritten promise to pay the creditor is a liability called **accounts payable**.

	ASSETS		= LIABILITIES	+ OWNER'S EQUITY
	Cash	+ Office Equipment	= Accounts Payable	C. Hall, Capital
BEGINNING BALANCE	$6,100	+ $1,700	=	$7,800
TRANSACTION		+400	= +$400	
ENDING BALANCE	$6,100	+ $2,100	= $ 400	+ $7,800
		$8,200	= $8,200	

When this information is analyzed, we can see that the law practice has increased what it owes (accounts payable) as well as what it owns (office equipment) by $400. The law practice gains $400 in an asset but has an obligation to pay Wilmington Company at a future date.

The owner's equity remains unchanged. This transaction results in an increase of total assets from $7,800 to $8,200.

Finally, note that after each transaction the basic accounting equation remains in balance.

LEARNING UNIT 1-1 REVIEW

AT THIS POINT you should be able to:

- List the functions of accounting. (pp. 4–5)
- Define and explain the differences between sole proprietorships, partnerships, and corporations. (p. 3)
- Describe the various types of accountants in Canada. (p. 4)
- Compare and contrast bookkeeping and accounting. (p. 6)
- Explain the role of the computer as an accounting tool. (p. 6)
- State the purpose of the accounting equation. (pp. 6–7)
- Explain the difference between liabilities and owner's equity. (p. 7)
- Define capital. (p. 7)
- Explain the difference between a shift in assets and an increase in assets. (p. 8)

To test your understanding of this material, complete Self-Review Quiz 1-1. The blank forms you need are in the *Study Guide with Working Papers* for Chapter 1. The solution to the quiz follows the quiz here in the text. If you have difficulty doing the problems, review Learning Unit 1-1 and the solution to the quiz. You might also check the text's website for helpful student aids. Your instructor will provide details.

Keep in mind that learning accounting is like learning to type—the more you practise, the better you become. You will not be an expert in one day. Be patient. It will all come together.

Self-Review Quiz 1-1

(The blank forms you need are on page 1-1 of the *Study Guide with Working Papers.*)

Record the following transactions in the basic accounting equation:

1. Gracie Ryan invests $17,000 to begin a real estate office.
2. The real estate office buys $600 worth of computer equipment for cash.
3. The real estate office buys $500 worth of additional computer equipment on account.

Solution to Self-Review Quiz 1-1

	ASSETS		=	LIABILITIES	+ OWNER'S EQUITY
	Cash	+ Computer Equipment	=	Accounts Payable	+ Gracie Ryan, Capital
1.	+$17,000				+$17,000
BALANCE	17,000		=		17,000
2.	−600	+$600			
BALANCE	16,400	+ 600	=		17,000
3.		500		+$500	
ENDING BALANCE	$16,400	+ $ 1,100	=	$500	+ $17,000

$17,500 = $17,500

NEED HELP?

Let's review first: The left side of the accounting equation shows what is owned by the business and the right side of the equation shows who supplied those assets to a business. Now let's look at the transactions in the solution:

Transaction 1: In your head you must say to yourself, "What did the business get and how did it get it?" The business is getting or increasing its cash by $17,000 and that cash is being supplied by Gracie Ryan. Think of Gracie as increasing her rights in the business since she is supplying cash. Keep in mind that capital does not mean cash. Instead it is what the owner supplies to the business. (Gracie may in the future supply other items to the business.)

So the end result is to put $17,000 on the left side of the equation under cash and put $17,000 under Gracie Ryan, Capital, on the right side. The sum of the left side must equal the sum on the right side.

Transaction 2: Here we are NOT looking at the personal finances of Gracie. You must focus on the business. What did the business get and who supplied it to the business?

In this transaction the business is getting $600 of computer equipment by using some of its cash. IT IS SHIFTING ITS ASSETS: MORE EQUIPMENT FOR LESS CASH. Note that capital is not affected since Gracie has not supplied anything new to the business. Note that the right side of the equation is not touched, but the equation still remains in balance. We are just rearranging the composition of the assets.

Transaction 3: Now the business is getting more equipment but is not paying cash. The equipment is being supplied by a creditor called Accounts Payable. Hopefully in the future the business will be able to pay the creditor back the $500 that it owes. The end result is that the business now has $1,100 in equipment. Note that capital is not affected since no new investments were made by Gracie into the business.

SUMMARY

At the end of these three transactions this company is made up of two assets, Cash $16,400 and Computer Equipment $1,100. The total of the assets was supplied by creditors $500 and the owner, Gracie Ryan, Capital, $17,000. The sum of the left side must equal the sum of the right side.

LEARNING UNIT 1-2

The Balance Sheet

The balance sheet shows the company's financial position as of a particular date. (In our example, that date is at the end of August.)

In the first learning unit, the transactions for Catherine Hall's law office were recorded in the accounting equation. The transactions we recorded occurred before the law firm opened for business. A report, called a **balance sheet** or **statement of financial position**, can show the position of the company before it started operating. The balance sheet is a formal report that presents the information from the ending balances of both sides of the accounting equation. Think of the balance sheet as a snapshot of the business's financial position as of a particular date.

Let's look at the balance sheet of Catherine Hall's law practice for August 31, 2016, shown in Figure 1-1. The figures in the balance sheet come from the ending balances of the accounting equation for the law practice as shown in Learning Unit 1-1.

Note in Figure 1-1 that the assets owned by the law practice appear on the left-hand side and that liabilities and owner's equity appear on the right-hand side. Both sides equal $8,200. This *balance* between left and right gives the balance sheet its name.

POINTS TO REMEMBER IN PREPARING A BALANCE SHEET

The Heading

Do you remember the three elements that make up a balance sheet? They are assets, liabilities, and owner's equity.

The heading of the balance sheet provides the following information:

- The company name: Catherine Hall, Barrister and Solicitor
- The name of the report: Balance Sheet
- The date at which the report is prepared: August 31, 2016

Figure 1-1
The Balance Sheet

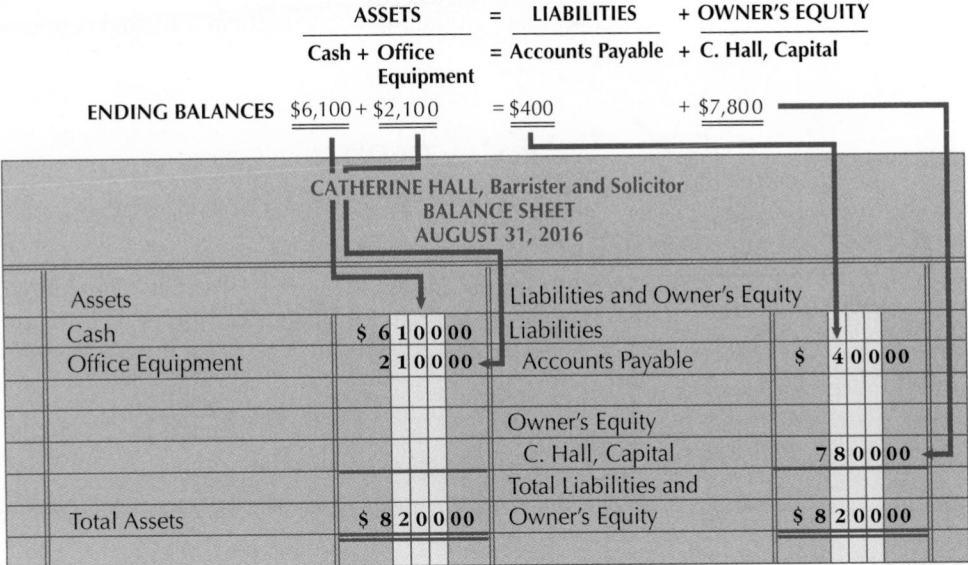

	ASSETS	=	LIABILITIES	+ OWNER'S EQUITY
	Cash + Office Equipment	=	Accounts Payable	+ C. Hall, Capital
ENDING BALANCES	$6,100 + $2,100	=	$400	+ $7,800

CATHERINE HALL, Barrister and Solicitor
BALANCE SHEET
AUGUST 31, 2016

Assets		Liabilities and Owner's Equity	
Cash	$ 6 1 0 0 00	Liabilities	
Office Equipment	2 1 0 0 00	Accounts Payable	$ 4 0 0 00
		Owner's Equity	
		C. Hall, Capital	7 8 0 0 00
		Total Liabilities and	
Total Assets	$ 8 2 0 0 00	Owner's Equity	$ 8 2 0 0 00

Use of the Dollar Sign

Note that the dollar sign is not repeated every time a figure appears. As shown in the balance sheet for Catherine Hall's law practice, it is usually placed to the left of each column's top figure and to the left of the column's total.

Distinguishing the Total

CATHERINE HALL, Barrister and Solicitor
BALANCE SHEET
AUGUST 31, 2016

Assets	
Cash	$ 6 1 0 0 00
Office Equipment	2 1 0 0 00
Total Assets	$ 8 2 0 0 00

A single line means the numbers above it have been added or subtracted.

A double line indicates a total.

When adding numbers down a column, use a single line before the total and a double line beneath it. A single line means that the numbers above it have been added or subtracted. A double line indicates a total. It is important to align the numbers in the column; many errors occur because these figures are not lined up. These rules are the same for all accounting reports.

This balance sheet gives Catherine the information she needs to see the law firm's financial position before it opens for business. This information does not tell her, however, whether the firm will make a profit.

LEARNING UNIT 1-2 REVIEW

AT THIS POINT you should be able to:

- Define and state the purpose of a balance sheet. (p. 11)
- Identify and define the elements making up a balance sheet. (p. 11)
- Show the relationship between the accounting equation and the balance sheet. (p. 11)
- Prepare a balance sheet in proper form from information provided. (p. 11)
- Place dollar signs correctly in a formal report. (p. 12)

Self-Review Quiz 1-2

(The blank forms you need are on page 1-2 of the *Study Guide with Working Papers.*)

The date is November 30, 2016. Use the following information to prepare in proper form a balance sheet for Janning Company:

Accounts Payable	$30,000
Cash	8,000
A. Janning, Capital	9,000
Office Equipment	31,000

Quiz Tip

The heading of a balance sheet answers the questions *Who, What,* and *When.* November 30, 2016 is the particular date.

Solution to Self-Review Quiz 1-2

JANNING COMPANY
BALANCE SHEET
NOVEMBER 30, 2016

Assets		Liabilities and Owner's Equity	
Cash	$ 8 0 0 0 00	Liabilities	
Office Equipment	31 0 0 0 00	Accounts Payable	$30 0 0 0 00
		Owner's Equity	
		A. Janning, Capital	9 0 0 0 00
		Total Liabilities and	
Total Assets	$39 0 0 0 00	Owner's Equity	$39 0 0 0 00

Capital does not mean cash. The capital amount is the owner's current investment of assets in the business.

NEED HELP?

Let's review first: A photo of your family as of a particular date is like a balance sheet. It gives you a history of your family as of a particular date. The balance sheet is a formal report that lists assets, liabilities, and owner's equity for a business as of a particular date.

Before making the report, identify whether each item is an asset, a liability, or owner's equity. Accounts payable is a liability. Cash is an asset, or something of value owned by the business. A. Janning, Capital, is owner's equity, or what the owner is supplying to the business.

The heading of a balance sheet answers three questions:

Who? Janning Company

What report? Balance Sheet

When? November 30, 2016

The left side of the balance sheet lists the assets: cash, and office equipment.

The right side lists who supplies the assets to the business: creditors (accounts payable) or the owner, A. Janning, Capital. Use single rules to add and double rules for totals. The sum of the left side must equal the sum of the right side.

LEARNING UNIT 1-3

The Accounting Equation Expanded: Revenue, Expenses, and Withdrawals

LO 3 Seeing how revenue, expenses, and withdrawals expand the basic accounting equation

As soon as Catherine Hall's office opened, she began performing legal services for her clients and earning revenue for the business. At the same time, as a part of doing business, she incurred various expenses, such as rent. See Figure 1-2 for an example of how these activities affect owner's equity.

When Catherine asked her accountant how these transactions fitted into the accounting equation, he began by defining some terms.

KEY TERMS IN THE ACCOUNTING EQUATION

When revenue is earned, it is recorded as an increase in owner's equity and an increase in assets.

Revenue A service company earns **revenue** when it provides services to its clients and gives them a bill. Catherine's law firm earned revenue when she provided legal services to her clients for legal fees. When revenue is earned, owner's equity is increased. In effect, revenue is a subdivision of owner's equity.

Figure 1-2
Owner's Equity

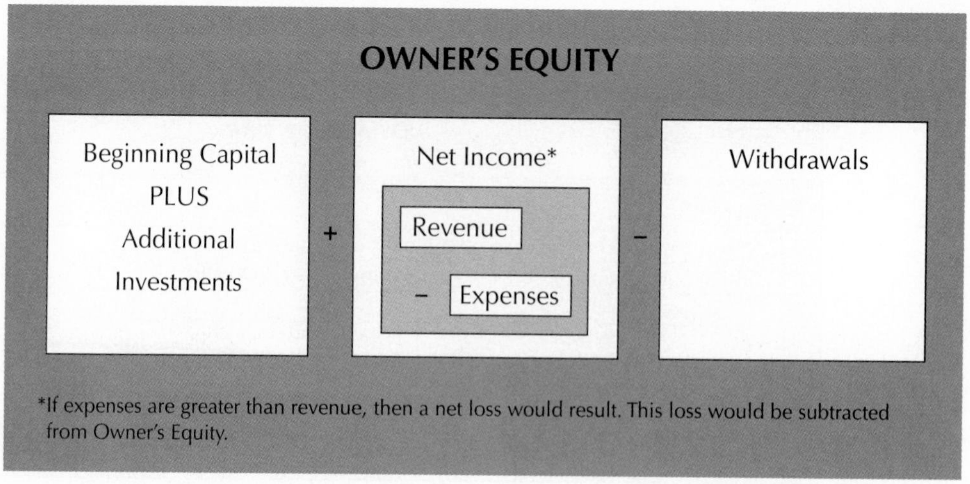
OWNER'S EQUITY
Beginning Capital PLUS Additional Investments
+
Net Income*
Revenue
– Expenses
–
Withdrawals
*If expenses are greater than revenue, then a net loss would result. This loss would be subtracted from Owner's Equity.

Assets are increased. The increase is in the form of cash if the client pays right away. If the client promises to pay in the future, the increase is called **accounts receivable**. When revenue is earned, the transaction is recorded as an increase in revenue and an increase in assets (either as cash and/or as accounts receivable, depending on whether it was paid right away or will be paid in the future).

> ***Accounts receivable*** **is an asset. The law firm expects to receive amounts owed by clients at a later date.**

> ***Remember:*** **Accounts receivable results from earning revenue when cash is not yet received.**

Expenses A business's **expenses** are the costs the company incurs in carrying on operations in its effort to create revenue. Expenses are also a subdivision of owner's equity; when expenses are incurred, they *decrease* owner's equity. Expenses can be paid for in cash or they can be charged.

> **Record an expense when it is incurred, whether it is paid then or is to be paid later.**

Net Income/Net Loss When revenue totals more than expenses, **net income** is the result; when expenses total more than revenue, **net loss** is the result.

Withdrawals At some point, Catherine Hall may need to withdraw cash or other assets from the business to pay living or other personal expenses that do not relate to the business. We will record these transactions in an account called **withdrawals**. Sometimes this account is called the *owner's drawing account*. The withdrawals account is a subdivision of owner's equity that records payments to the owner not related to the business. Withdrawals decrease owner's equity.

> **Withdrawals are not the same as salary. Catherine's law firm is not incorporated and hence cannot pay her a salary.**

It is important to remember the difference between expenses and withdrawals. Expenses relate to business operations; withdrawals are the result of personal needs outside the normal operations of the business.

Now let's analyze the September transactions for Catherine Hall's law firm using an **expanded accounting equation** that includes withdrawals, revenues, and expenses.

EXPANDED ACCOUNTING EQUATION

Transaction D: **Sept. 1–30: Provided legal services for cash, $3,000.**

Transactions A, B, and C were discussed earlier when the law office was being formed in August. See Learning Unit 1-1.

In the law firm's first month of operation, a total of $3,000 in cash was received for legal services performed. In the accounting equation, the asset Cash is increased by $3,000. Revenue is also increased by $3,000, resulting in an increase in owner's equity.

	ASSETS			=	LIABILITIES	+	OWNER'S EQUITY		
	Cash	+ Accts. Rec.	+ Office Equip.	=	Accts. Pay.	+ C. Hall, Capital	− C. Hall, Withdr.	+ Revenue	− Expenses
BAL. FWD.	$6,100		+$ 2,100	=	$ 400	+ $7,800			
TRANS.	+3,000							+ $3,000	
END. BAL.	$9,100		+$ 2,100	=	$ 400	+ $7,800		+ $3,000	
			$11,200	=	$11,200				

A revenue column was added to the basic accounting equation. Amounts are recorded in the revenue column when they are earned. They are also recorded in the assets columns, under Cash and/or under Accounts Receivable. Do not think of revenue as an asset. It is part of owner's equity. It is the revenue that creates an inward flow of cash and accounts receivable.

***Transaction E:* Sept. 1–30: Provided legal services on account, $4,000.**

	ASSETS			=	LIABILITIES	+	OWNER'S EQUITY		
	Cash	+ Accts. Rec.	+ Office Equip.	=	Accts. Pay.	+ C. Hall, Capital	− C. Hall, Withdr.	+ Revenue	− Expenses
BAL. FWD.	$9,100		+$ 2,100	=	$ 400	+ $7,800		+ $3,000	
TRANS.		+ $4,000						+ $4,000	
END. BAL.	$9,100	+ $4,000	+$ 2,100	=	$ 400	+ $7,800		+ $7,000	
			$15,200	=	$15,200				

Catherine's law practice also performed legal work on account for $4,000. Her firm did not receive the cash for these earned legal fees; it accepted an unwritten promise from these clients that payment would be made in the future.

During September, some of Catherine's clients who had received services and promised to pay in the future decided to reduce what they owed the practice by $700 when their bills came due. This is shown as follows on the expanded accounting equation.

***Transaction F:* Sept. 1–30: Received $700 cash as partial payment of previous services performed on account.**

	ASSETS			=	LIABILITIES	+	OWNER'S EQUITY		
	Cash	+ Accts. Rec.	+ Office Equip.	=	Accts. Pay.	+ C. Hall, Capital	− C. Hall, Withdr.	+ Revenue	− Expenses
BAL. FWD.	$ 9,100	+ $4,000	+$ 2,100	=	$ 400	+ $7,800		+ $7,000	
TRANS.	+700	−700							
END. BAL.	$9,800	+ $3,300	+$ 2,100	=	$ 400	+ $7,800		+ $7,000	
			$15,200	=	$15,200				

The law firm increased the asset Cash by $700 and decreased another asset, Accounts Receivable, by $700. The *total* of assets does not change. The right-hand side of the expanded accounting equation has not been touched because the total on the left-hand side of the equation has not changed. The revenue was recorded when it was earned, and the *same revenue cannot be recorded twice.* This transaction analyzes the situation *after* the revenue has been previously earned and recorded. Transaction F shows a shift in assets—increased cash and reduced accounts receivable.

Transaction G: **Sept. 1–30: Paid salaries expense, $600.**

	ASSETS			= LIABILITIES +		OWNER'S EQUITY		
	Cash	**+ Accts. Rec.**	**+ Office Equip.**	**= Accts. Pay.**	**+ C. Hall, Capital**	**− C. Hall, Withdr.**	**+ Revenue**	**− Expenses**
BAL. FWD.	$9,800	+ $3,300	+$ 2,100	= $ 400	+ $7,800		+ $7,000	
TRANS.	**−600**							**+ $600**
END. BAL.	$9,200	+ $3,300	+$ 2,100	= $ 400	+ $7,800		+ **$7,000**	− $600
			$14,600	= $14,600				

While her law firm cannot pay Catherine a salary, it can legally pay a salary (or wages) to any employee. This $600 was not paid to Catherine.

As expenses increase, they decrease owner's equity. This incurred expense of $600 reduces the cash by $600. Although the expense was paid, the total of our expenses to date has *increased* by $600. Keep in mind that owner's equity decreases as expenses increase, so the accounting equation remains in balance.

Transaction H: **Sept. 1–30: Paid rent expense, $700.**

	ASSETS			= LIABILITIES +		OWNER'S EQUITY		
	Cash	**+ Accts. Rec.**	**+ Office Equip.**	**= Accts. Pay.**	**+ C. Hall, Capital**	**− C. Hall, Withdr.**	**+ Revenue**	**− Expenses**
BAL. FWD.	$ 9,200	+ $3,300	+$ 2,100	= $ 400	+ $7,800		+ $7,000	− $ 600
TRANS.	**−700**							**+700**
END. BAL.	$8,500	+ $3,300	+$ 2,100	= $ 400	+ $7,800		+ $7,000	− $1,300
			$13,900	= $13,900				

During September, the practice incurred rent expenses of $700. This rent was not paid in advance; it was paid when it came due. The payment of rent reduces the asset Cash by $700 and increases the expenses of the firm, resulting in a decrease in owner's equity. The firm's expenses are now $1,300.

Transaction I: Sept. 1–30: Incurred advertising expenses of $300, to be paid next month.

	ASSETS			=	LIABILITIES +	OWNER'S EQUITY			
	Cash	+ Accts. Rec.	+ Office Equip.	=	Accts. Pay.	+ C. Hall, Capital	− C. Hall, Withdr.	+ Revenue	− Expenses
BAL. FWD.	$8,500	+ $3,300	+$ 2,100	=	$ 400	+ $7,800		+ $7,000	− $1,300
TRANS.					+300				+300
END. BAL.	$8,500	+ $3,300	+$ 2,100	=	$ 700	+ $7,800		+ $7,000	− $1,600
			$13,900	=	$13,900				

Catherine ran an ad in the local newspaper and incurred an expense of $300. This increase in expenses caused a corresponding decrease in owner's equity. Since Catherine has not paid the newspaper for the advertising yet, her firm owes $300. Thus the firm's liabilities (Accounts Payable) increase by $300. Eventually, when the bill comes in and is paid, both Cash and Accounts Payable will be decreased.

Transaction J: Sept. 1–30: Catherine withdrew $200 for personal use.

	ASSETS			=	LIABILITIES +	OWNER'S EQUITY			
	Cash	+ Accts. Rec.	+ Office Equip.	=	Accts. Pay.	+ C. Hall, Capital	− C. Hall, Withdr.	+ Revenue	− Expenses
BAL. FWD.	$8,500	+ $3,300	+$ 2,100	=	$ 700	+ $7,800		+ $7,000	− $1,600
TRANS.	−200						+ $200		
END. BAL.	$8,300	+ $3,300	+$ 2,100	=	$ 700	+ $7,800	$200	+ $7,000	− $1,600
			$13,700	=	$13,700				

By taking $200 for personal use, Catherine has *increased* her withdrawals from the business by $200 and decreased the asset Cash by $200. Note that, as withdrawals increase, the owner's equity will *decrease*. Keep in mind that a withdrawal is *not* a business expense. It is a subdivision of owner's equity that records money or other assets an owner withdraws from the business for *personal* use.

Subdivision of Owner's Equity

Take a moment to review the subdivisions of owner's equity:

- As capital increases, owner's equity increases (see transaction A).
- As withdrawals increase, owner's equity decreases (see transaction J).
- As revenue increases, owner's equity increases (see transaction D).
- As expenses increase, owner's equity decreases (see transaction G).

Catherine Hall's Expanded Accounting Equation

The following is a summary of the expanded accounting equation for Catherine Hall's law firm. The + or – sign in front of a transaction indicates whether the account is increased or decreased by that transaction.

Catherine Hall
Barrister and Solicitor
Expanded Accounting Equation: A Summary

	ASSETS					=	LIABILITIES +				OWNER'S EQUITY				
	Cash	+	Accts. Rec.	+	Office Equip.	=	Accts. Pay.	+	C. Hall, Capital	–	C. Hall, Withdr.	+	Revenue	–	Expenses
A.	+$7,000				+$800	=			+$7,800						
BALANCE	7,000			+	800	=			7,800						
B.	–900				+900										
BALANCE	6,100			+	1,700	=			7,800						
C.					+400	=	+$400								
BALANCE	6,100			+	2,100	=	400	+	7,800						
D.	+3,000												+$3,000		
BALANCE	9,100			+	2,100	=	400	+	7,800			+	3,000		
E.			+$4,000										+4,000		
BALANCE	9,100	+	4,000	+	2,100	=	400	+	7,800			+	7,000		
F.	+700		–700												
BALANCE	9,800	+	3,300	+	2,100	=	400	+	7,800			+	7,000		
G.	–600														+$600
BALANCE	9,200	+	3,300	+	2,100	=	400	+	7,800			+	7,000	–	600
H.	–700														+700
BALANCE	8,500	+	3,300	+	2,100	=	400	+	7,800			+	7,000	–	1,300
I.							+300								+300
BALANCE	8,500	+	3,300	+	2,100	=	700	+	7,800			+	7,000	–	1,600
J.	–200										+$200				
END. BAL.	$8,300	+	$ 3,300	+	$ 2,100	=	$700	+	$ 7,800	–	$200	+	$7,000	–	$1,600
			$13,700			=			$13,700						

LEARNING UNIT 1-3 REVIEW

AT THIS POINT you should be able to:

- Define and explain the difference between revenue and expenses. (pp. 13–14)
- Define and explain the difference between net income and net loss. (p. 14)
- Explain the subdivision of owner's equity. (pp. 14–17)
- Explain the effects of withdrawals, revenue, and expenses on owner's equity. (pp. 16–17)
- Record transactions in an expanded accounting equation and balance the basic accounting equation as a means of checking the accuracy of your calculations. (p. 17)

Self-Review Quiz 1-3

(The blank forms you need are on page 1-2 of the *Study Guide with Working Papers.*)

Record the following transactions in the expanded accounting equation for the Bing Company. Note that all titles have a beginning balance.

1. Received cash revenue, $4,000.
2. Billed customers for services rendered, $6,000.
3. Received a bill for telephone expenses (to be paid next month), $125.
4. Bob Bing withdrew cash for personal use, $500.
5. Received $1,000 from customers in partial payment for services performed in transaction 2.

Quiz Tip

Think of expenses and withdrawals as *increasing*. As they increase, they will reduce the owner's rights. For example, in transaction 4, withdrawals increased by $500, resulting in total withdrawals increasing from $800 to $1,300. This represents a decrease in owner's equity.

Solution to Self-Review Quiz 1-3

	ASSETS					=	LIABILITIES	+	OWNER'S EQUITY						
	Cash	+	Accts. Rec.	+	Cleaning Equip.	=	Accts. Pay.	+	B. Bing, Capital	−	B. Bing, Withdr.	+	Revenue	−	Expenses
BEG. BAL.	$ 9,000	+	$ 2,500	+	$6,500	=	$1,000	+	$11,800	−	$ 800	+	$ 8,000	−	$2,000
1.	+4,000												+4,000		
BALANCE	13,000	+	2,500	+	6,500	=	1,000	+	11,800	−	800	+	12,000	−	2,000
2.			+6,000										+6,000		
BALANCE	13,000	+	8,500	+	6,500	=	1,000	+	11,800	−	800	+	18,000	−	2,000
3.							+125								+125
BALANCE	13,000	+	8,500	+	6,500	=	1,125	+	11,800	−	800	+	18,000	−	2,125
4.	−500										+500				
BALANCE	12,500	+	8,500	+	6,500	=	1,125	+	11,800	−	1,300	+	18,000	−	2,125
5.	+1,000		−1,000												
END. BAL.	$13,500		$ 7,500		$6,500	=	$1,125	+	$11,800	−	$ 1,300	+	$18,000	−	$2,125
			$ 27,500			=					$27,500				

NEED HELP?

Let's review first: You record revenue only when it is earned. What can the business get? Cash, of course, but also customers' promises to pay later, which are recorded as Accounts Receivable. Revenue is not an asset but does provide an inward flow of assets into the business. Revenue is part of owner's equity. Think of expenses as always increasing in a business. The end result will be a decrease in owner's equity. Expenses are recorded when they happen and can be paid for by cash or charged as Accounts Payable.

Withdrawals work just like expenses, but they represent personal withdrawals by the owner. Expenses and withdrawals are not recorded together. Each has a separate title.

Transaction 1: The company has done the work. It now records revenue of $4,000 in the revenue column (put numbers in this column only when we do the work). This time the inward flow from the revenue is all in the form of cash of $4,000.

Transaction 2: This time the company does the work but is not getting the cash. It is receiving promises that it will be paid in the future. You record the $6,000 in the revenue column because you did the work. The inward flow from this revenue is not cash but promises called Accounts Receivable. Thus, the Accounts Receivable column is increased by $6,000.

Transaction 3: An expense has happened and should be recorded whether money is paid or not. The expenses for telephone have INCREASED by $125, resulting in the total expenses rising to $2,125. As expenses in a business rise, the end result is a reduction in owner's equity.

Since the expense was charged, the $125 is recorded under Accounts Payable because the expense will be paid in the future. At this point this telephone expense has created a liability. Remember that an expense is not a liability.

Transaction 4: This transaction relates to a personal transaction and does not affect any expenses in the business. Bob Bing takes $500 cash from the business. Think of Bob as gaining the $500, but in reality his owner's rights will be reduced. This is shown by a $500 gain under withdrawals, which now results in a total of $1,300 (a reduction to owner's equity) and a decrease to cash. Note that expenses are not affected since this is a personal transaction.

Transaction 5: No new work is done, so we do not record any new revenue. Here customers are paying part of what they owe. The result is that company cash increased by $1,000 and Accounts Receivable is reduced by $1,000. This is a shift in assets: more cash, less accounts receivable.

SUMMARY

Note the four subdivisions of owner's equity: Capital, Withdrawals, Revenues, and Expenses. As capital and revenue increase, owner's equity will increase. As expenses and withdrawals increase, owner's equity will decrease. Revenue is not an asset. Rather, it provides assets in the form of cash and/or accounts receivable. Record revenue only when work is done and billed. Record expenses only when they happen, whether or not cash is received.

LEARNING UNIT 1-4

Preparing Financial Reports

LO 4

Preparing an income statement, a statement of owner's equity, and a balance sheet

Catherine Hall would like to be able to find out whether her firm is making a profit, so she asks her accountant whether he can measure the firm's financial performance on a monthly basis. Her accountant replies that there are a number of financial reports that he can prepare, such as the income statement, which shows how well the law firm has performed over a specific period of time. The accountant can use the information in the income statement to prepare other reports.

THE INCOME STATEMENT

The income statement is prepared from data found in the revenue and expense columns of the expanded accounting equation.

An **income statement** is an accounting report that shows business results in terms of revenue and expenses. If revenues are greater than expenses, the report shows net income. If expenses are greater than revenues, the report shows net loss. An income statement can cover any number of months up to 12. It does not usually cover more than one year. The report shows the result of all revenues and expenses throughout the entire period and not just as of a specific date. The income statement for Catherine Hall's law firm is shown in Figure 1-3.

Points to Remember in Preparing an Income Statement

Heading The heading of an income statement tells the same three things as all other accounting reports: the company's name, the name of the report, and the period of time the report covers (or the date of preparation).

Locate the dollar signs used in the Income Statement. They are shown at the top of each column and in the total.

The Set-Up As you can see on the income statement, the inside column of numbers ($600, $700, and $300) is used to subtotal all expenses ($1,600) before subtracting them from revenue ($7,000 − $1,600 = $5,400).

Operating expenses may be listed in alphabetical order, in order of largest amounts to smallest, or in a set order established by the accountant.

Figure 1-3
The Income Statement

CATHERINE HALL, Barrister and Solicitor INCOME STATEMENT FOR THE MONTH ENDED SEPTEMBER 30, 2016		
Revenue:		
Legal Fees		$7 000 00
Operating Expenses:		
Salaries Expense	$600 00	
Rent Expense	700 00	
Advertising Expense	300 00	
Total Operating Expenses		1 600 00
Net Income		$5 400 00

Note that withdrawals are not shown in the Income Statement. They are not an expense.

THE STATEMENT OF OWNER'S EQUITY

As we said, the income statement is a business report that shows business results in terms of revenue and expenses. However, how does net income or net loss affect owner's equity? To find that out, we have to look at another category of report, the statement of owner's equity.

The **statement of owner's equity** shows for a certain period of time what changes occurred in Catherine Hall, Capital. The statement of owner's equity is shown in Figure 1-4.

If this statement of owner's equity is omitted, the information will be included in the owner's equity section of the balance sheet.

The capital of Catherine Hall can be

Increased by: Owner Investment
Net Income (Revenue greater than Expenses)

Decreased by: Owner Withdrawals
Net Loss (Expenses greater than Revenue)

Remember, a withdrawal is *not* a business expense and thus is not involved in the calculation of net income or net loss on the income statement. It appears on the statement of owner's equity. The statement of owner's equity summarizes the effects of all the subdivisions of owner's equity (revenue, expenses, withdrawals) on beginning capital. The ending capital figure ($13,000) will be the beginning figure in the next statement of owner's equity.

Suppose that Catherine's law firm had operated at a loss in the month of September. Instead of net income, there was a net loss and an additional investment of $700 was made on September 15. The statement on the next page shows how it would look if this had happened.

Figure 1-4
Statement of Owner's Equity

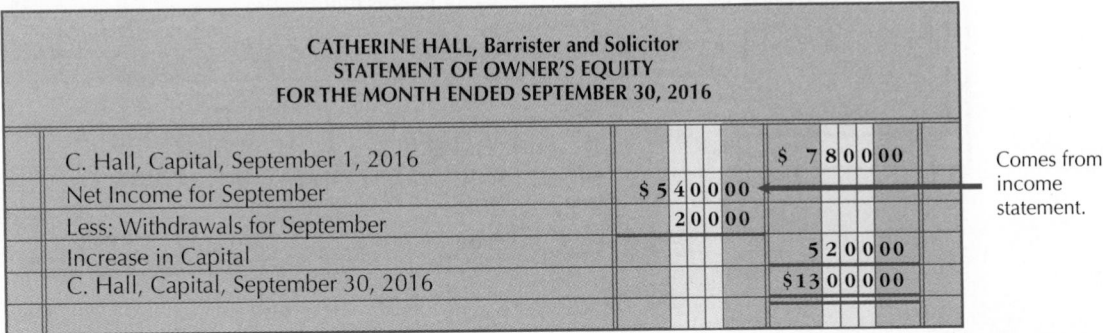

CATHERINE HALL, Barrister and Solicitor STATEMENT OF OWNER'S EQUITY FOR THE MONTH ENDED SEPTEMBER 30, 2016		
C. Hall, Capital, September 1, 2016		$ 7 800 00
Net Income for September	$5 400 00	
Less: Withdrawals for September	200 00	
Increase in Capital		5 200 00
C. Hall, Capital, September 30, 2016		$13 000 00

Comes from income statement.

This statement is for illustration only, and is not directly related to the set of transactions shown earlier.

CATHERINE HALL, Barrister and Solicitor
STATEMENT OF OWNER'S EQUITY
FOR THE MONTH ENDED SEPTEMBER 30, 2016

C. Hall, Capital, September 1, 2016		$7,800.00
Additional Investment, September 15, 2016		700.00
		$8,500.00
Less: Net Loss for September	$400.00	
Withdrawals for September	200.00	
Decrease in Capital		600.00
C. Hall, Capital, September 30, 2016		$7,900.00

THE BALANCE SHEET

Now let's look at how to prepare a balance sheet from the expanded accounting equation (see Figure 1-5). As you can see, the asset accounts (Cash, Accounts Receivable, and Office Equipment) appear on the left side of the balance sheet. Accounts Payable and C. Hall, Capital appear on the right side. Notice that the $13,000 of capital can be calculated within the accounting equation or read from the statement of owner's equity.

MAIN ELEMENTS OF THE INCOME STATEMENT, THE STATEMENT OF OWNER'S EQUITY, AND THE BALANCE SHEET

In this chapter, we have discussed three financial reports: the income statement, the statement of owner's equity, and the balance sheet. (There is a fourth report, called the cash flow statement, that is covered in Auxiliary Chapter 16 of this textbook.) Let us review the elements of the expanded accounting equation that go into each report and the usual order in which the reports are prepared. Figure 1-5 presents a diagram of the balance sheet and the accounting equation. Table 1-3 summarizes what information goes on each report.

CATHERINE HALL, Barrister and Solicitor
BALANCE SHEET
SEPTEMBER 30, 2016

Assets		Liabilities and Owner's Equity	
Cash	$ 8,300.00	Liabilities	
Accounts Receivable	3,300.00	Accounts Payable	$ 700.00
Office Equipment	2,100.00	Owner's Equity	
		C. Hall, Capital	13,000.00
		Total Liabilities and	
Total Assets	$13,700.00	Owner's Equity	$13,700.00

$13,000 comes from ending capital figure on statement of owner's equity.

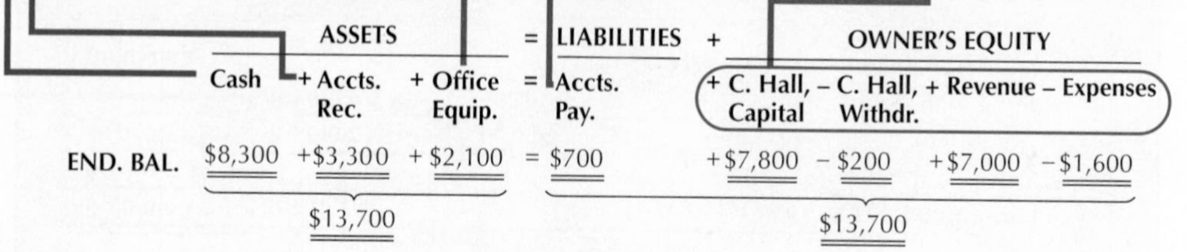

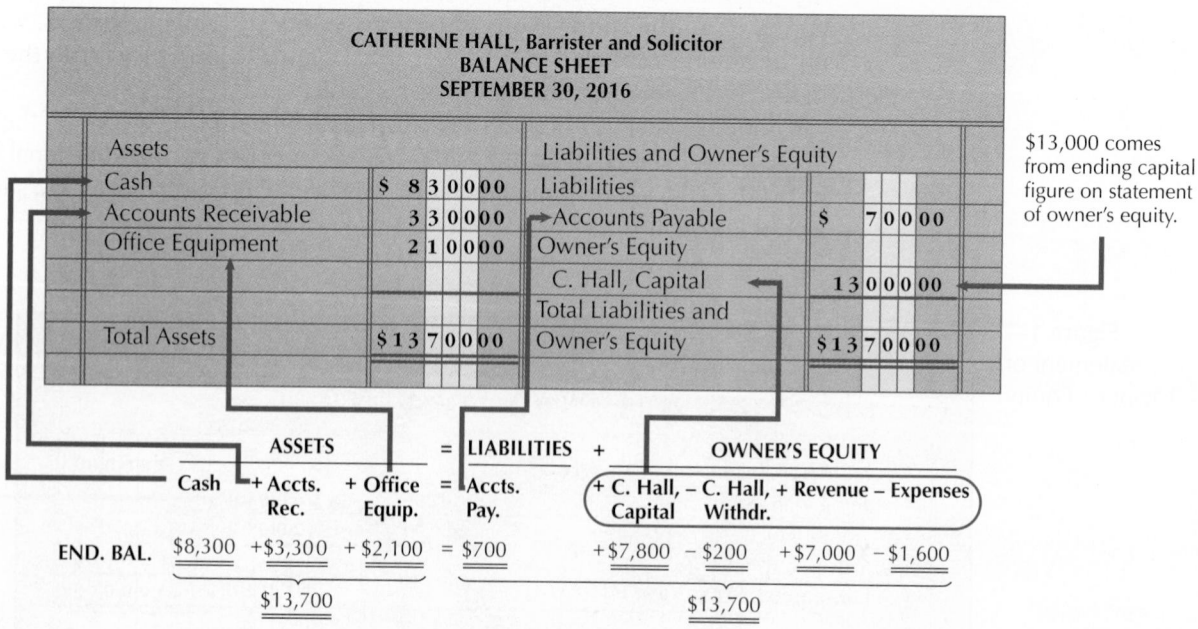

Figure 1-5 The Balance Sheet and the Accounting Equation

- The income statement is prepared first; it includes revenues and expenses and shows net income or net loss. This net income or net loss is used to update the next report, the statement of owner's equity.
- The statement of owner's equity is prepared second; it includes beginning capital and any additional investments, the net income or net loss shown on the income statement, withdrawals, and the total, which is the **ending capital**.
- The balance sheet is prepared last; it includes the final balances of each of the elements listed in the accounting equation under Assets and Liabilities. The balance in Capital comes from the statement of owner's equity.

TABLE 1-3 What Goes on Each Financial Report

	Income Statement	Statement of Owner's Equity	Balance Sheet
Assets			X
Liabilities			X
Capital (beginning)		X	
Additional Investments		X	
Capital (ending)		X	X
Withdrawals		X	
Revenues	X		
Expenses	X		
Net Income (Loss)	X	X	

LEARNING UNIT 1-4 REVIEW

AT THIS POINT you should be able to:

- Define and state the purpose of the income statement, the statement of owner's equity, and the balance sheet. (pp. 20–22)
- Discuss why the income statement should be prepared first. (p. 23)
- Calculate a new figure for capital on the statement of owner's equity and balance sheet. (pp. 21–22)
- Compare and contrast these three financial reports. (pp. 22–23)
- Show what happens on a statement of owner's equity if there is a net loss. (p. 22)

Self-Review Quiz 1-4

(The blank forms you need are on pages 1-3 and 1-4 of the *Study Guide with Working Papers.*)

From the following balances for Rusty Realty, prepare:

2. Income statement for month ended November 30, 2017
3. Statement of owner's equity for the month ended November 30, 2017
4. Balance sheet as of November 30, 2017

Cash	$40,000	R. Rusty, Withdrawals	1,000
Accounts Receivable	13,700	Commissions Earned	15,000
Office Furniture	14,900	Rent Expense	2,000
Accounts Payable	9,000	Advertising Expense	1,500
R. Rusty, Capital, November 1, 2017	50,000	Salaries Expense	900

Solution to Self-Review Quiz 1-4

Quiz Tip

Note that the inside column is used only for subtotalling.

RUSTY REALTY INCOME STATEMENT FOR THE MONTH ENDED NOVEMBER 30, 2017		
Revenue:		
Commissions Earned		$ 15,000.00
Operating Expenses:		
Rent Expense	$ 2,000.00	
Advertising Expense	1,500.00	
Salaries Expense	900.00	
Total Operating Expenses		4,400.00
Net Income		$ 10,600.00

Subtotal Columns

Quiz Tip

The Net Income from the income statement is used to help build the statement of owner's equity.

RUSTY REALTY STATEMENT OF OWNER'S EQUITY FOR THE MONTH ENDED NOVEMBER 30, 2017		
R. Rusty, Capital, November 1, 2017		$ 50,000.00
Net Income for November	$ 10,600.00	
Less: Withdrawals for November	1,000.00	
Increase in Capital		9,600.00
R. Rusty, Capital, November 30, 2017		$ 59,600.00

Quiz Tip

The new figure for Capital, from the statement of owner's equity, is used as the Capital figure on the balance sheet.

RUSTY REALTY BALANCE SHEET NOVEMBER 30, 2017			
Assets		Liabilities and Owner's Equity	
Cash	$ 40,000.00	Liabilities	
Accounts Receivable	13,700.00	Accounts Payable	$ 9,000.00
Office Furniture	14,900.00		
		Owner's Equity	
		R. Rusty, Capital	59,600.00
		Total Liabilities and	
Total Assets	$ 68,600.00	Owner's Equity	$ 68,600.00

NEED HELP?

Let's review first: The first formal report is the income statement, which is made up of only revenues and expenses. This report shows how a company is performing for a specific period of time. The second report is the statement of the owner's equity. This report shows how capital has changed from its beginning balance. The net income is added to the beginning balance less any personal withdrawals resulting in a new figure for capital, which will be placed in the balance sheet. This third report, the balance sheet, is made up of assets, liabilities, and the new figure for capital. The balance sheet shows the history of the company as of a particular date.

The Income Statement: Commissions earned is the revenue for Rusty Realty. It is entered to the right since it is the only revenue. The inside column is used for a subtotal if there is more than one source of revenue.

Rent, Advertising, and Salaries are expenses that are listed on the income statement. Note that we use the inside column to subtotal them and then list the final figure as total operating expenses of $4,400 in the right column. The difference between revenue ($15,000) and the total operating expenses ($4,400) results in a net income of $10,600. Keep in mind that net income is not cash. Remember that some revenue may not have resulted in cash and some of the expenses may not have been paid for in cash.

Statement of Owner's Equity: The beginning balance of R. Rusty, Capital is $50,000. We place this to the right because it is one number. We then use the inside column to add net income from the income statement ($10,600) and subtract any withdrawals ($1,000) to get an increase in Capital of $9,600, which is placed in the right column. This figure is then added to beginning capital to arrive at R. Rusty, Capital (ending) of $59,600.

Balance Sheet: All the assets are listed on the left (cash, accounts receivable, and office furniture), for a total of $68,600. The liability of $9,000 for accounts payable is listed on the right and will be added to the new figure for R. Rusty, Capital of $59,600 from the statement of owner's equity.

SUMMARY

The income statement lists out revenue and expenses. No withdrawals are found on this report. The statement of owner's equity will show how capital changes by net income, net loss, and/or withdrawals. The balance shows the new history of the company's assets, liabilities, and a new figure for capital.

A Fresh Start

Preparing Financial Statements ❹ (20 min)

"Hey, Stan the man!" a loud voice boomed. "I never thought I'd see you making sandwiches!" Stan Hernandez stopped layering lettuce in a foot-long submarine sandwich and grinned at his old college buddy, Ron.

"Neither did I. But then again," said Stan, "I never thought I'd own a profitable business either." That night, catching up on their lives over dinner, Stan told Ron how he became the proud owner of a Subway sandwich restaurant. "After working like crazy at Xellent Media for five years and *finally* making it to marketing manager, then wham . . . I got laid off," said Stan. "That very day I was having my lunch at the local Subway as usual, when . . . "

"Hmmm, wait a minute! I did notice you've lost quite a bit of weight," Ron interrupted and began to compare him to Jared Fogle, the young man who lost weight on a diet of Subway sandwiches.

"Right!" Stan quipped, "Not only was I laid off, but I was 'downsizing!' *Anyway*, I was eating a Sweet Onion Chicken Teriyaki sub when I opened up an *Entrepreneur* magazine someone had left on the table—right to the headline 'Subway Named #1 Franchise in All Categories for 17th Time in 23 Years.'"

To make a foot-long submarine sandwich story short, Stan realized his long-time dream of being his own boss by owning a business with a proven product and highly successful business model. When you look at Stan's restaurant, you are really seeing two businesses. While Stan is the sole proprietor of his business, he operates under an agreement with Subway head office. Subway supplies the business know-how and support (like training at Subway University, national advertising, and gourmet bread recipes). Stan supplies capital (his $15,000 investment fee) and his food preparation, management, and elbow grease. Subway and Stan operate interdependent businesses, and both rely on accounting information for their success.

Subway, in business since 1965, has grown dramatically over the years and now has over 33,000 locations in 92 countries. It has even surpassed McDonald's in the number of locations in the United States and Canada. To manage this enormous service business requires very careful control of each of its stores.

At a Subway regional office, Mariah Washington, a field consultant for Stan's territory, monitors Stan's restaurant closely. In addition to making monthly visits to check whether Stan is complying with Subway's model in everything from décor to uniforms to food quality and safety, she also looks closely at Stan's weekly sales and inventory reports. When Stan's sales go up, Subway's do too, because each Subway franchisee, like Stan, pays Subway, the franchiser, a percentage of sales in the form of royalties.

Why does headquarters require accounting reports? Accounting reports give the information both Stan and the company need to make business decisions in a number of vital areas. For example:

- Before Stan could buy his Subway restaurant, the company needed to know how much cash Stan had, the value of his assets, and the amount of his liabilities (such as credit card debt). Stan prepared a personal balance sheet to give them this information.
- Stan must have the right amount of supplies on hand. If he has too few, he can't make the sandwiches. If he has too much for the amount he expects to sell, items like sandwich meats and bread dough may spoil. The inventory report tells Mariah what supplies are on hand. In combination with the sales report, it also alerts Mariah to potential red flags. If Stan is reporting that he is using far too much bread dough for the number of sandwiches he is selling, then there is a problem.
- Although Subway does not require its restaurant owners to report operating costs and profit information, Subway gives them the option and most franchisees choose to report. Information on profitability helps Mariah and Stan make decisions like whether and when to remodel or buy new equipment.

So that its restaurant owners can make business decisions in a timely manner, Subway requires them to submit the weekly sales and inventory report to headquarters electronically every Thursday by 2 p.m. Stan has his latest report in mind as he makes a move to pay the bill for his dinner with Ron. "We had a great week. Let me get this," he says. "Thanks, Stan the Man. I'm going to keep in touch because I may just be ready for a business opportunity of my own!"

DISCUSSION QUESTIONS

1. What makes Stan a sole proprietor?
2. Why are Stan and Subway interdependent businesses?
3. Why did Stan have to share his personal balance sheet with Subway? Do you think most interdependent businesses do this?
4. What does Subway learn from Stan's weekly sales and inventory reports?

Chapter Assignments

DEMONSTRATION PROBLEM

Michael Brown opened his law office on June 1, 2016. During the first month of operations, Michael conducted the following transactions:

(The blank forms you need are on pages 1-5 and 1-6 of the *Study Guide with Working Papers.*)

1. Invested $6,000 in cash into the law practice.
2. Paid $600 for office equipment.
3. Purchased additional office equipment on account, $1,000.
4. Received cash for performing legal services for clients, $2,000.
5. Paid part-time salaries, $800.
6. Performed legal services for clients on account, $1,000.
7. Paid rent, $1,200.
8. Withdrew $500 from his law practice for personal use.
9. Received $500 from clients in partial payment for legal services performed, transaction 6.

Assignment
Record these transactions in the expanded accounting equation.
Prepare the financial statements at June 30 for Michael Brown, Barrister and Solicitor.

Solution to Demonstration Problem

	ASSETS			= LIABILITIES +		OWNER'S EQUITY			
A.	Cash	+ Accts. Rec.	+ Office Equip.	=	Accts. Pay.	+ M. Brown, Capital	− M. Brown, Withdr.	+ Legal Fees	− Expenses
1.	+$6,000					+$6,000			
BAL.	6,000			=		6,000			
2.	−600		+$600						
BAL.	5,400		+ 600	=		+ 6,000			
3.			+1,000		+$1,000				
BAL.	5,400		+ 1,600	=	1,000	+ 6,000			
4.	+2,000							+$2,000	
BAL.	7,400		+ 1,600	=	1,000	+ 6,000		+ 2,000	
5.	−800								+$800
BAL.	6,600		+ 1,600	=	1,000	+ 6,000		+ 2,000	− 800
6.		+$1,000						+1,000	
BAL.	6,600	+ 1,000	+ 1,600	=	1,000	+ 6,000		+ 3,000	− 800
7.	−1,200								+1,200
BAL.	5,400	+ 1,000	+ 1,600	=	1,000	+ 6,000		+ 3,000	− 2,000
8.	−500						+$500		
BAL.	4,900	+ 1,000	+ 1,600	=	1,000	+ 6,000	− 500	+ 3,000	− 2,000
9.	+500	−500							
END. BAL.	$5,400	+ $ 500	+ $1,600	=	$1,000	+ $6,000	− $500	+ $3,000	− $2,000
			$7,500	=	$7,500				

Solution Tips to Expanded Accounting Equation

- **Transaction 1:** The business increased its Cash by $6,000. Owner's Equity (capital) increased when Michael supplied the cash to the business.
- **Transaction 2:** A shift in assets occurred when the equipment was purchased. The business lowered its Cash by $600, and a new column—Office Equipment—was increased for the $600 of equipment that was bought. The amount of capital is not touched because the owner did not supply any new funds.
- **Transaction 3:** When creditors supply $1,000 of additional equipment, the business Accounts Payable shows the debt. The business increased what it *owes* the creditors.
- **Transaction 4:** Legal Fees, a subdivision of Owner's Equity, is increased when the law firm provides a service even if no money is received. The service provides an inward flow of $2,000 to Cash, an asset. Remember that Legal Fees are *not* an asset. As Legal Fees increase, Owner's Equity increases.
- **Transaction 5:** The salary paid by Michael's law office shows an $800 increase in Expenses and a corresponding decrease in Owner's Equity as well as a decrease in Cash.
- **Transaction 6:** Michael did the work and earned the $1,000. That $1,000 is recorded as revenue. This time the Legal Fees create an inward flow of assets called Accounts Receivable for $1,000. Remember that Legal Fees are not an asset. They are a subdivision of Owner's Equity.
- **Transaction 7:** The $1,200 rent expense reduces Owner's Equity as well as Cash.
- **Transaction 8:** Withdrawals are for personal use. Here the business decreases Cash by $500 while Michael's withdrawals increase $500. Withdrawals decrease the Owner's Equity.

- **Transaction 9:** This transaction does not reflect new revenue in the form of Legal Fees. It is only a shift in assets: more Cash and less Accounts Receivable.

Solution Tips to Financial Statements

B-1. The income statement lists only revenues and expenses for a period of time. The inside column is for subtotalling. Withdrawals are not listed here.

B-2. The statement of owner's equity takes the net income figure of $1,000 and adds it to beginning capital less any withdrawals. This new capital figure of $6,500 will go on the balance sheet. This statement shows changes in capital for a period of time.

B-3. The $5,400, $500, $1,600, and $1,000 came from the totals of the expanded accounting equation. The capital figure of $6,500 came from the statement of owner's equity. This balance sheet reports assets, liabilities, and a new figure for capital at a specific date.

B-1. MICHAEL BROWN, BARRISTER AND SOLICITOR
INCOME STATEMENT
FOR THE MONTH ENDED JUNE 30, 2016

Revenue:		
Legal Fees		$3,000
Operating Expenses:		
Salaries Expense	$ 800	
Rent Expense	1,200	
Total Operating Expenses		2,000
Net Income		$1,000

B-2. MICHAEL BROWN, BARRISTER AND SOLICITOR
STATEMENT OF OWNER'S EQUITY
FOR THE MONTH ENDED JUNE 30, 2016

Michael Brown, Capital, June 1, 2016		$6,000
Net income for June	$1,000	
Less withdrawals for June	500	
Increase in Capital		500
Michael Brown, Capital, June 30, 2016		$6,500

B-3. MICHAEL BROWN, BARRISTER AND SOLICITOR
BALANCE SHEET
JUNE 30, 2016

Assets		**Liabilities and Owner's Equity**	
Cash	$5,400	Liabilities	
Accounts Receivable	500	Accounts Payable	$1,000
Office Equipment	1,600	Owner's Equity	
		M. Brown, Capital	$6,500
Total Assets	$7,500	Total Liabilities and Owner's Equity	$7,500

SUMMARY OF KEY POINTS

Learning Unit 1-1

1. The functions of accounting involve analyzing, recording, classifying, summarizing, reporting, and interpreting financial information.
2. A sole proprietorship is a business owned by one person. A partnership is a business owned by two or more persons. A corporation is a business owned by shareholders.
3. Different specialists in accounting have made it possible to serve the needs of many different business entities in Canada. CAs, CGAs, and CMAs have somewhat different training and experience, but will in the future all use the designation CPA instead.
4. Bookkeeping is the recording part of accounting.
5. The computer is a tool to use in the accounting process.
6. Assets = Liabilities + Owner's Equity is the basic accounting equation that helps in analyzing business transactions.
7. Liabilities represent amounts owed to creditors, while capital represents what is invested by the owner.
8. Capital does not mean cash. Capital is the owner's current investment. The owner could have invested in equipment that was purchased before the new business was started.
9. In a shift of assets, the composition of assets changes, but the total value of assets does not change. For example, if a bill is paid by a customer, the firm increases cash (an asset) but decreases accounts receivable (an asset), so there is no overall increase in assets; total assets remain the same. When you borrow money from a bank, you have an increase in cash (an asset) and an increase in liabilities; overall there is an increase in assets, not just a shift.

Learning Unit 1-2

1. The balance sheet is a report written as of a particular date. It lists the assets, liabilities, and owner's equity of a business. The heading of the balance sheet answers the questions *Who, What,* and *When* (as of a specific date).
2. The balance sheet is a formal report of a financial position.

Learning Unit 1-3

1. Revenue generates an inward flow of assets. Expenses generate an outward flow of assets or a potential outward flow. Revenue and expenses are subdivisions of owner's equity. Revenue is not an asset.
2. When revenue totals more than expenses, net income is the result; when expenses total more than revenue, net loss is the result.
3. Owner's equity can be subdivided into four elements: capital, withdrawals, revenue, and expenses.
4. Withdrawals decrease owner's equity; revenue increases owner's equity; expenses decrease owner's equity. A withdrawal is not a business expense; it is for personal use.

Learning Unit 1-4

1. The income statement is a report written for a specific period of time that lists earned revenue and expenses incurred to produce the earned revenue. The net income or net loss will be used in the statement of owner's equity.

2. The statement of owner's equity reveals the causes of a change in capital. This report lists additional investments in the company, net income (or net loss), and withdrawals. The ending figure for capital will be used on the balance sheet.
3. The balance sheet uses the ending balances of assets and liabilities from the accounting equation and the capital from the statement of owner's equity.
4. The income statement should be prepared first because the information on it relating to net income or net loss is used to prepare the statement of owner's equity, which in turn provides information about capital for the balance sheet. In this way, each document builds upon information provided by the previous report.

KEY TERMS

Accounting A system that measures a business's activities in financial terms, provides written reports and financial statements about those activities, and communicates these reports to decision-makers and others (p. 4)

Accounting process See *Accounting* (p. 4)

Accounts payable Amounts owed to creditors that result from the purchase of goods or services on account; a liability (p. 9)

Accounts receivable Amounts to be paid by customers resulting from sales of goods and/or services on credit; an asset (p. 14)

Assets Properties (resources) of value owned by a business (cash, supplies, equipment, land, and so on) (p. 6)

Balance sheet A report, as of a particular date, that shows the amount of assets owned by a business as well as the amount of claims (liabilities and owner's equity) against these assets (p. 11)

Basic accounting equation Assets = Liabilities + Owner's Equity (p. 7)

Bookkeeping The recording function of the accounting process (p. 6)

Business entity In accounting, it is assumed that a business is separate and distinct from the personal assets of the owner. Each unit or entity requires separate accounting functions. (p. 6)

Capital The owner's investment of equity in the company (p. 7)

Corporation A type of business organization that is owned by shareholders. Usually, shareholders are not personally liable for the corporation's debts. (p. 3)

CPA The new professional accounting designation to be used in Canada (p. 5)

Creditor Someone who has a claim to assets (p. 7)

Ending capital Beginning Capital + Additional Investments + Net Income − Withdrawals = Ending Capital. *Or:* Beginning Capital + Additional Investments − Net Loss − Withdrawals = Ending Capital (p. 23)

Equipment Assets acquired to be used in business activities, usually with an expected life of two to ten years (p. 8)

Equities The financial claim of creditors (liabilities) and owners (owner's equity) who supply the assets and expenses to a firm (p. 6)

Expanded accounting equation Assets = Liabilities + Capital − Withdrawals + Revenue − Expenses (p. 14)

Expense Cost incurred in running a business by consuming goods or services in producing revenue; a subdivision of owner's equity. When expenses increase, there is a decrease in owner's equity. (p. 14)

Generally accepted accounting principles (GAAP) The procedures and guidelines that must be followed during the accounting process (p. 5)

Income statement An accounting report that details the performance of a firm (revenue minus expenses) for a specific period of time (p. 20)

International Financial Reporting Standards (IFRS) Adopted in Canada effective January 1, 2010, for companies listing their shares on a stock exchange. May be adapted by other Canadian companies as well, but is optional (p. 5)

Liability An obligation that comes due in the future. A liability increases the financial rights or claims of creditors to assets. (p. 7)

Manufacturing companies Businesses that make a product and sell it to their customers; they may also make and sell their own products (p. 4)

Merchandising companies Businesses that buy a product from a manufacturing company, distributor, or wholesaler to sell to their customers (p. 4)

Net income When revenue totals more than expenses, the result is net income (p. 14)

Net loss When expenses total more than revenue, the result is net loss (p. 14)

Owner's equity Rights or financial claims to the assets of a business by the owner (in the accounting equation, assets minus liabilities) (p. 7)

Partnership A form of business organization that has at least two owners. The partners are usually personally liable for the partnership's debts. (p. 3)

Revenue An amount earned by performing services for customers or selling goods to customers. Revenue increases cash and/or accounts receivable. It is a subdivision of owner's equity—as revenue increases, owner's equity increases. (p. 13)

Sarbanes-Oxley Act Legislation passed in the United States that attempts to prevent the presentation of false or misleading financial statements by public companies (p. 1)

Service company Business that provides a service (p. 4)

Shift in assets A shift that occurs when the composition of the assets has changed, but the total of the assets remains the same (p. 8)

Sole proprietorship A business that has one owner. The owner is personally liable for paying the business's debts. (p. 3)

Statement of financial position Another name for a balance sheet (p. 11)

Statement of owner's equity A financial report that reveals the change in capital. The ending figure for capital is then placed on the balance sheet. (p. 21)

Supplies One type of asset acquired by a firm. A supply item is temporarily treated as an asset until it is consumed, when its value is transferred to expense. Sometimes if it is not a significant amount it is treated as an expense when purchased—both treatments are possible. (p. 8)

Withdrawals A subdivision of owner's equity that records money or other assets an owner withdraws from a business for personal use (p. 14)

Quick Review

The following Tips are from Learning Units 1-1 to 1-4. Answer the Assess Your Progress questions and use the How Did You Do? at the bottom of the page to see how you well you know the material. The Quick Review provides tips before each Assess Your Progress to help you avoid common accounting errors.

LU 1-1 The Accounting Equation

Tips: After a transaction is recorded in the accounting equation, the sum of all the assets must equal the total of all the liabilities and owner's equity.

Assess Your Progress

Answer true or false to the following statements:

1. Capital is cash.
2. Accounts Payable is a liability.
3. A shift in assets means liabilities will increase.
4. Assets – Liabilities = Owner's Equity.
5. Assets represent what is owned by the business.

LU 1-2 The Balance Sheet

Tips: The balance sheet is a formal report listing assets, liabilities, and owner's equity as of a particular date.

Assess Your Progress

Answer true or false to the following statements:

1. Cash is a liability.
2. Office Equipment is an asset.
3. Accounts Payable is listed under assets.
4. Capital is listed under liabilities.
5. A heading of a financial report is required to have a date or period of time covered.

LU 1-3 The Expanded Accounting Equation

Tips: Revenue is recorded when earned even if cash is not received. Expenses are recorded when they happen (incurred) whether they are paid or to be paid later.

Assess Your Progress

Answer true or false to the following statements:

1. Revenue is an asset.
2. Withdrawals increase owner's equity.
3. As expenses go down, owner's equity goes down.
4. An advertising bill incurred but unpaid is recorded as an increase in Advertising Expense and a decrease in liability.
5. Revenue inflows can only be in the form of cash.

LU 1-4 Financial Reports

Tips: Net income from the income statement is used to update the statement of owner's equity. The ending figure for capital on the statement of owner's equity is the one used to update the balance sheet.

Assess Your Progress

Answer true or false to the following statements:

1. Net income occurs when expenses are greater than revenue.
2. Withdrawals will reduce owner's capital on the income statement.
3. The balance sheet lists assets, liabilities, and expenses.
4. Withdrawals are listed on the income statement.
5. Assets are listed on the income statement.

How Did You Do? Answers to the Assess Your Progress Questions

LU 1-1

1. False—Capital represents the owner's claim to the assets.
2. True.
3. False—A shift in assets means liabilities will stay the same.
4. True.
5. True.

LU 1-2

1. False—Cash is an asset.
2. True.
3. False—Accounts Payable is listed under liabilities.
4. False—Capital is listed under owner's equity.
5. True.

LU 1-3

1. False—Revenue is part of owner's equity.
2. False—Withdrawals decrease owner's equity.
3. False—As expenses go down, owner's equity goes up.
4. False—An advertising bill incurred but unpaid is recorded as an increase in Advertising Expense and an increase in liability.
5. False—Revenue inflows can be in the form of cash and/or accounts receivable.

LU 1-4

1. False—Net income occurs when expenses are less than revenue.
2. False—Withdrawals will reduce owner's capital on the statement of owner's equity.
3. False—Expenses are listed on the income statement.
4. False—Withdrawals are listed on the statement of owner's equity.
5. False—Assets are listed on the balance sheet.

BLUEPRINT OF FINANCIAL REPORTS

❶ Income Statement

Measuring performance

Revenue		XXX
Less: Operating expenses:		
Expense 1	XXX	
Expense 2	XX	
Expense 3	XX	XXX
Net Income		XXX

❷ Statement of Owner's Equity

Calculating new figure for Capital

Beginning Capital		XXX
Additional Investments		XXX
Total Investments		XXX
Net Income (or Loss)	XXX	
Less: Withdrawals	XXX	
Change in Capital		XXX
Ending Capital		XXX

❸ Balance Sheet

Showing where we now stand

Assets		Liabilities and Owner's Equity	
Asset 1	XXX	Liabilities	XXX
Asset 2	XXX	Owner's Equity	
Asset 3	XXX	Ending Capital	XXX
		Total Liabilities +	
Total Assets	XXX	Owner's Equity	XXX

QUESTIONS, CLASSROOM DEMONSTRATION EXERCISES, EXERCISES, AND PROBLEMS

Discussion Questions and Critical Thinking/Ethical Case

1. What are the functions of accounting?
2. Define, compare, and contrast sole proprietorships, partnerships, and corporations.
3. How are businesses classified?
4. What is the relationship of bookkeeping to accounting?
5. List the three elements of the basic accounting equation.
6. Define capital.
7. The total of the left-hand side of the accounting equation must equal the total of the right-hand side. True or false? Please explain.
8. A balance sheet tells a company where it is going and how well it will perform. True or false? Please explain.
9. Revenue is an asset. True or false? Please explain.
10. Into what categories is owner's equity subdivided?
11. A withdrawal is a business expense. True or false? Please explain.
12. As expenses increase, they cause owner's equity to increase. Defend or reject.
13. What does an income statement show?
14. The statement of owner's equity calculates only ending withdrawals. True or false? Please explain.
15. Paul Kloss, accountant for Lowe & Co., travelled to Vancouver on company business. His total expenses came to $350. Paul felt that since the trip extended over the weekend, he could pad his expense account with an additional $100 of expenses. After all, weekends represent his own time, not the company's. What would you do? Write your specific recommendations to Paul.

Classroom Demonstration Exercises

(The blank forms you need are on page 1-7 of the *Study Guide with Working Papers.*)

Classifying Accounts

Preparing to record transactions
❷ (5 min)

1. Classify each of the following items as an asset (A), liability (L), or part of owner's equity (OE).

a. Apple iPod ______
b. Accounts Receivable ______
c. Accounts Payable ______
d. Cash ______
e. B. James, Capital ______
f. Kodak Digital Camera ______

The Accounting Equation

Accounting equation details
❷ (5 min)

2. Complete:

a. ____________: rights of the creditors.
b. ____________ are the total value of items owned by a business.
c. ____________ ____________ is an unwritten promise to pay a creditor.

Shift versus Increase in Assets

Recording transactions in the basic accounting equation
❷ (5 min)

3. Identify which transaction below results in a shift in assets (S) and which transaction causes an increase in assets (I).

a. Jay's Internet Cafe bought computer equipment on account ____________.
b. Eastern Tile Co. bought office equipment for cash ____________.

The Balance Sheet

Preparing a balance sheet
❷ ❹ (5 min)

4. From the following, calculate what would be the total of assets on the balance sheet.

B. Fleese, Capital	$18,000
Computer Equipment	4,000
Accounts Payable	6,000
Cash	12,000

The Accounting Equation Expanded

Expanding the basic accounting equation
❷ (5 min)

5. Identify with a ✔ which of the following are subdivisions of owner's equity.

a. Vehicles _____
b. Accounts Receivable _____
c. J. Penny, Capital _____
d. Advertising Expense _____
e. Accounts Payable _____
f. Taxi Fees Earned _____
g. J. Penny, Withdrawals _____
h. Computer Equipment _____

Identifying Assets

Steps in the recording of transactions
❷ (5 min)

6. Identify with a ✔ which of the following are *not* assets.

a. DVD Player _____
b. Accounts Receivable _____
c. Accounts Payable _____
d. Grooming Fees Earned _____

The Accounting Equation Expanded

Revenue and expenses expand the basic accounting equation
❸ (5 min)

7. Which of the following statements are false?

a. _____ Revenue provides only outward flows of cash.
b. _____ Revenue is a subdivision of assets.
c. _____ Revenue provides an inward flow of cash and/or accounts receivable.
d. _____ Expenses are part of total assets.

Preparing Financial Statements

Expanded accounting equation details are used to prepare financial statements
❹ (5 min)

8. Indicate whether the following items would appear on the income statement (IS), statement of owner's equity (OE), or balance sheet (BS).

a. ______ Tutoring Fees Earned
b. ______ Office Equipment
c. ______ Accounts Receivable
d. ______ Supplies on Hand
e. ______ Legal Fees Earned
f. ______ Advertising Expense
g. ______ J. Earl, Capital (Beginning)
h. ______ Accounts Payable

Preparing Financial Statements

Financial statements
❹ (5 min)

9. Indicate next to each comment whether it refers to the income statement (IS), statement of owner's equity (OE), or balance sheet (BS).

a. ______ Withdrawals found on it
b. ______ Lists total of all assets
c. ______ Statement that is prepared last
d. ______ Statement listing net income

Exercises

Set A

(The forms you need are on pages 1-8 and 1-9 of the *Study Guide with Working Papers.*)

The accounting equation
❷ (5 min)

1-1A. Complete the following table:

	Assets	=	Liabilities	+	Owner's Equity
a.	$19,000	=	?	+	$4,000
b.	?	=	$6,000	+	$9,000
c.	$10,000	=	$4,000	+	?

Recording transactions in the accounting equation
❷ (5 min)

1-2A. Record the following transactions in the basic accounting equation:

Assets = Liabilities + Owner's Equity

Treat each transaction separately.

a. Ralph invests $8,000 in his company.
b. The company buys equipment for cash, $600.
c. The company buys equipment on account, $900.

Preparing a balance sheet
❷ ❹ (10 min)

1-3A. From the following, prepare a balance sheet for Range Co.'s Cleaners at the end of November 2016: Cash, $50,000; Equipment, $7,000; Accounts Payable, $14,000; B. Range, Capital.

Recording transactions in the expanded accounting equation
❸ (15 min)

1-4A. Record the following transactions in the expanded accounting equation. The running balance may be omitted for simplicity.

ASSETS			= LIABILITIES +	OWNER'S EQUITY			
Cash	+ Accounts Receivable	+ Computer Equipment	= Accounts Payable	+ B. Bell, Capital	− B. Bell, Withdrawals	+ Revenue	− Expenses

a. B. Bell invested $60,000 in Bell's Computer Company.
b. Bought computer equipment on account, $7,000.
c. Paid personal telephone bill from company bank account, $200.
d. Received cash for services rendered, $14,000.
e. Billed customers for services rendered for the month, $30,000.
f. Paid current rent expense, $4,000.
g. Paid supplies expense, $1,500.

Preparing the income statement, statement of owner's equity, and balance sheet
❹ (20 min)

1-5A. From the following account balances for June 2016, prepare in proper form (a) an income statement, (b) a statement of owner's equity, and (c) a balance sheet for French Realty.

Cash	$3,310	S. French, Withdrawals	40
Accounts Receivable	1,490	Professional Fees	2,900
Office Equipment	6,700	Salaries Expense	500
Accounts Payable	2,000	Utilities Expense	360
S. French, Capital, June 1, 2016	8,000	Rent Expense	500

Exercises

Set B

(The forms you need are on pages 1-8 and 1-9 of the *Study Guide with Working Papers*)

The accounting equation
❷ (5 min)

1-1B. Complete the following table:

	Assets	=	Liabilities	+	Owner's Equity
a.	$15,000	=	?	+	$6,000
b.	?	=	$8,000	+	$11,000
c.	$14,000	=	$5,000	+	?

Recording transactions in the accounting equation
❷ (5 min)

1-2B. Record the following transactions in the basic accounting equation:

Assets = Liabilities + Owner's Equity

Treat each transaction separately.

a. Ralph invests $12,000 in his company.
b. The company buys equipment for cash, $2,000.
c. The company buys equipment on account, $3,500.

Preparing a balance sheet
❷ ❹ (10 min)

1-3B. From the following, prepare a balance sheet for Range Co.'s Cleaners at the end of November 2016: Cash, $20,000; Equipment, $16,000; Accounts Payable, $12,000; B. Range, Capital.

Record transactions in the expanded accounting equation
❸ (15 min)

1-4B. Record the following transactions in the expanded accounting equation. The running balance may be omitted for simplicity.

ASSETS			= LIABILITIES +	OWNER'S EQUITY			
Cash	**+ Accounts Receivable**	**+ Computer Equipment**	**= Accounts Payable**	**+ B. Bell, Capital**	**− B. Bell, Withdrawals**	**+ Revenue**	**− Expenses**

a. B. Bell invested $40,000 in Bell's Computer Company.
b. Bought computer equipment on account, $8,000.
c. Paid personal telephone bill from company bank account, $150.
d. Received cash from services rendered, $12,000.
e. Billed customers for services rendered for the month, $25,000.
f. Paid current rent expense, $3,000.
g. Paid supplies expense, $900.

Preparing the income statement, statement of owner's equity, and balance sheet
❹ (20 min)

1-5B. From the following account balances for June 2016, prepare in proper form (a) an income statement, (b) a statement of owner's equity, and (c) a balance sheet for French Realty.

Cash	$4,650	S. French, Withdrawals	640
Accounts Receivable	2,600	Professional Fees	5,600
Office Equipment	8,500	Salaries Expense	800
Accounts Payable	4,000	Utilities Expense	760
S. French, Capital, June 1, 2016	9,000	Rent Expense	650

Group A Problems

(The forms you need are on pages 1-10 to 1-16 of the *Study Guide with Working Papers.*)

The accounting equation
❷ (15 min)

Check Figure
Total Assets $25,000

1A-1. Mia Anabelle, who lives in Winnipeg, decided to open Mia's Nail Spa. Mia completed the following transactions:

A. Invested $20,000 cash from her personal bank account into the business.

B. Bought equipment for cash, $4,000.

C. Bought additional equipment on account, $6,000.

D. Paid $1,000 cash to reduce what was owed from Transaction C.

Based on the above information, record these transactions in the basic accounting equation.

Preparing a balance sheet
❷ ❹ (10 min)

Check Figure
Total Assets $52,000

1A-2. Bill See is the accountant for See's Internet Service. His task is to construct a balance sheet from the following information, as of September 30, 2017, in proper form. Could you help him?

Building	$20,000	Cash	18,000
Accounts Payable	15,000	Equipment	14,000
B. See, Capital	37,000		

Recording transactions in the expanded accounting equation
❸ (20 min)

Check Figure
Total Assets $17,340

1A-3. At the end of November, Rick Fox of Corner Brook decided to open his own desktop publishing business. Analyze the following transactions he completed by recording their effects in the expanded accounting equation.

a. Invested $12,000 in his desktop publishing business.

b. Bought new office equipment on account, $4,000.

c. Received cash for desktop publishing services rendered, $500.

d. Performed desktop publishing services on account, $2,100.

e. Paid part-time secretary's salary, $650.

f. Paid office supplies expense for the month, $210.

g. Rent expense for office due but not yet paid, $900.

h. Rick Fox withdrew cash for personal use, $400.

Preparing the income statement, statement of owner's equity, and balance sheet
❹ (30 min)

Check Figure
Total Assets $3,385

1A-4. Jane West, owner of West's Stencilling Service in Grande Prairie, has requested that you prepare from the following balances (a) an income statement for June 2017, (b) a statement of owner's equity for June, and (c) a balance sheet as of June 30, 2017.

Cash	$2,300	Stencilling Fees	3,000
Accounts Receivable	400	Advertising Expense	110
Equipment	685	Repair Expense	25
Accounts Payable	310	Travel Expense	250
J. West, Capital, June 1, 2017	1,200	Supplies Expense	190
J. West, Withdrawals	300	Rent Expense	250

Comprehensive problem
❷ ❸ ❹ (45 min)

Check Figure
Total Assets Nov. 30 $12,915

1A-5. Jill Martin of Regina opened Martin's Catering Service. As her accountant, analyze the transactions listed below and present in proper form:

1. The analysis of the transactions by utilizing the expanded accounting equation
2. A balance sheet showing the position of the firm before opening on November 1, 2016

3. An income statement for the month of November
4. A statement of owner's equity for November
5. A balance sheet as of November 30, 2016

2016		
Oct.	28	Jill Martin invested $8,000 in the catering business from her personal savings account.
	29	Bought equipment for cash from Munroe Co., $900.
	30	Bought additional equipment on account from Ryan Co., $1,800.
	31	Paid $1,000 to Ryan Co. as partial payment of the October 30 transaction.

(You should now prepare your balance sheet as of October 31, 2016.)

Nov.	1	Catered a graduation and immediately collected cash, $2,900.
	4	Paid salaries of employees, $720.
	8	Prepared desserts for customers on account, $300.
	11	Received $100 cash as partial payment of November 8 transaction.
	15	Paid telephone bill, $75.
	18	Jill paid her home electricity bill from the company's bank account, $90.
	19	Catered a wedding and received cash, $1,800.
	25	Bought additional equipment on account, $400.
	28	Rent expense due but not yet paid, $600.
	29	Paid supplies expense, $400.

Group B Problems

(The forms you need are on pages 1-10 to 1-16 of the *Study Guide with Working Papers.*)

The accounting equation
❷ (15 min)

Check Figure

Total Assets $16,700

1B-1. Mia Anabelle of Winnipeg began a new business called Mia's Nail Spa. The following transactions resulted:

A. Mia invested $16,000 cash from her personal bank account into the salon.
B. Bought equipment on account, $1,500.
C. Paid $800 cash to reduce what was owed from Transaction B.
D. Purchased additional equipment for cash, $3,000.

Record these transactions in the basic accounting equation.

Preparing a balance sheet
❷ ❹ (15 min)

Check Figure

Total Assets $84,000

1B-2. Bill See has asked you to prepare a balance sheet as of September 30, 2017, for See's Internet Service of Halifax. Assist Bill.

B. See, Capital	$24,000
Accounts Payable	60,000
Equipment	40,000
Building	28,000
Cash	16,000

Recording transactions in the expanded accounting equation
❸ (20 min)

1B-3. Rick Fox of Corner Brook decided to open his own desktop publishing company at the end of November. Analyze the following transactions by recording their effects in the expanded accounting equation.

Check Figure

Total Assets $14,505

A. Rick Fox invested $9,000 in the desktop publishing business.
B. Purchased new office equipment on account, $3,000.
C. Received cash for desktop publishing services rendered, $1,290.
D. Paid part-time secretary's salary, $625.
E. Billed customers for desktop publishing services rendered, $2,690.
F. Paid rent expense for the month, $500.
G. Rick withdrew cash for personal use, $350.
H. Advertising expense due but not yet paid, $100.

Preparing an income statement, statement of owner's equity, and balance sheet
❹ (30 min)

Check Figure

Total Assets $3,723

1B-4. Jane West, owner of West's Stencilling Service in Grande Prairie, has requested that you prepare from the following balances (a) an income statement for June 2017, (b) a statement of owner's equity for June, and (c) a balance sheet as of June 30, 2017.

Cash	$2,043	Stencilling Fees	1,098
Accounts Receivable	1,140	Advertising Expense	135
Equipment	540	Repair Expense	45
Accounts Payable	45	Travel Expense	90
J. West, Capital, June 1, 2017	3,720	Supplies Expense	270
J. West, Withdrawals	360	Rent Expense	240

Comprehensive problem
❷ ❸ ❹ (45 min)

Check Figure

Total Assets Nov. 30 $17,200

1B-5. Jill Martin of Regina opened Martin's Catering Service. As her accountant, analyze the transactions listed below and present the following information in proper form:

1. The analysis of the transactions using the expanded accounting equation
2. A balance sheet showing the financial position of the firm before opening on November 1, 2016
3. An income statement for the month of November
4. A statement of owner's equity for November
5. A balance sheet as of November 30, 2016

2016		
Oct.	28	Jill Martin invested $9,500 in the catering business.
	29	Bought equipment on account from Munroe Co., $1,200.
	30	Bought equipment for cash from Ryan Co., $1,500.
	31	Paid $600 to Munroe Co. as partial payment of the October 29 transaction.
Nov.	1	Catered a business luncheon and immediately collected cash, $2,400.
	4	Paid salaries of employees, $580.
	8	Provided catering services to Northwest Community College on account, $4,500.
	11	Received from Northwest Community College $2,000 cash as partial payment of November 8 transaction.
	15	Paid telephone bill, $95.
	18	Jill paid her home mortgage with a company cheque, $825.
	19	Provided catering services and received cash, $1,800.
	25	Bought additional equipment on account, $500.
	28	Rent expense due but not yet paid, $750.
	29	Paid supplies expense, $600.

Group C Problems

(The forms you need are on pages 1-17 to 1-23 of the *Study Guide with Working Papers.*)

The accounting equation
❷ (15 min)

Check Figure
Total Assets $12,500

1C-1. Ruth Jones began a new business called RJ Graphics, located in Moncton. The following transactions resulted:

A. Ruth invested $10,500 cash from her personal bank account in the graphics company.
B. Bought computer equipment on account, $4,500.
C. Paid $2,500 cash to reduce what was owed from Transaction B.
D. Purchased software for cash, $3,800.

Record these transactions in the basic accounting equation.

Preparing a balance sheet
❷ ❹ (15 min)

Check Figure
Total Assets $83,000

1C-2. Lewis Loh has asked you to prepare a balance sheet as of April 30, 2016, for Loh's Database Service of Orillia.

Lewis Loh, Capital	$49,000	Building	34,000
Accounts Payable	34,000	Cash	23,000
Equipment	26,000		

Recording transactions in the expanded accounting equation
❸ (25 min)

Check Figure
Total Assets $16,658

1C-3. Leroy Greene of Vancouver decided to open his own training services company at the end of October. Analyze the following transactions by recording their effects in the expanded accounting equation.

A. Leroy invested $9,000 in the company.
B. Purchased new office equipment on account, $4,250.
C. Received cash for services rendered, $2,350.
D. Paid secretary's salary, $800.
E. Billed customers for training services rendered, $3,650.
F. Paid rent expense for the month, $600.
G. Leroy withdrew cash for personal use, $1,000.
H. Advertising expense was due but as yet unpaid, $400.
I. Repair to office equipment paid, $192.

Preparing an income statement, statement of owner's equity, and balance sheet
❹ (35 min)

Check Figure
Total Assets $8,776

1C-4. Jennifer Pace, owner of Jennifer's Fashion Service (located in Dorval), has requested that you prepare from the following balances (a) an income statement for July 2016, (b) a statement of owner's equity for July, and (c) a balance sheet as of July 31, 2016.

Cash	$1,524	Advertising Expense	635
Accounts Receivable	3,672	Repair Expense	387
Equipment	3,580	Travel Expense	1,690
Accounts Payable	1,830	Supplies Expense	262
Jennifer Pace, Capital, July 1, 2016	6,430	Rent Expense	440
Jennifer Pace, Withdrawals	710	Office Expenses	175
Consulting Fees Earned	4,815		

Comprehensive problem
❷ ❸ ❹ (50 min)

Check Figure
Total Assets May 31 $27,722

1C-5. Howard McGraw of Windsor opened First City Surveying Service. As his accountant, analyze the transactions listed and present to Howard the following information, in proper form:

1. The analysis of the transactions using the expanded accounting equation
2. A balance sheet showing the financial position of the firm before opening on May 1, 2016

3. An income statement for the month of May
4. A statement of owner's equity for May
5. A balance sheet as of May 31, 2016

2016		
Apr.	23	Howard invested $17,000 in the surveying business.
	26	Bought equipment on account from Chapman & Co., $4,750.
	29	Bought equipment for cash from Majestic Co., $2,895.
	30	Paid $2,375 to Chapman & Co. as partial payment of the April 26 transaction.
May	2	Surveyed a new business location and immediately collected cash, $2,350.
	3	Paid salaries of employees, $975.
	10	Provided surveying services to City Community College on account, $4,950.
	13	Received from City Community College $2,500 cash as partial payment of the May 10 transaction.
	14	Paid telephone bill, $104.
	17	Howard paid his home mortgage from the company's bank account, $1,043.
	21	Provided surveying services and received cash, $1,825.
	24	Bought additional equipment on account from Jensen Bros., $2,415.
	27	Paid rent expense for the month, $825.
	28	Paid supplies expense, $246.
	31	Advertising bill received but not yet paid, $410.

On-the-Job Training

(The forms you need are on pages 1-24 to 1-25 of the *Study Guide with Working Papers.*)

Recording and reporting transactions
❸ ❹ (20 min)

T-1. You have just been hired to prepare, if possible, an income statement for the year ended December 31, 2015, for Roger's Window Washing Company. The problem is that Roger kept only the following records (on the back of a piece of cardboard).

Assume that Roger's Window Washing Company records all revenues when earned and all expenses when incurred.

You feel that it is part of your job to tell Roger how to organize his records better. What would you tell him?

Money in:

Window cleaning	*$11,376*
My investment	*1,200*
Loan from brother-in-law	*4,000*

Money out:

Salaries	*$5,080*
Withdrawals	*6,200*
Supplies expense	*1,400*

What I owe or they owe me

A. People that work for me but I still owe salaries to $1,800
B. Owe bank interest of $300
C. Work done but clients still owe me $2,900
D. Advertising bill due but not paid $95

Preparing accurate balance sheets
❷ ❹ (30 min)

T-2. While Jon Lune was on a business trip, he asked Abby Slowe, the bookkeeper for Lune Co., to try to complete a balance sheet for the year ended December 31, 2016. Abby, who had been on the job only two months, submitted the following:

LUNE CO.
FOR THE YEAR ENDED DECEMBER 31, 2016

Building	$44600 00	Accounts Payable	$127604 00
Land	72935 00	Accounts Receivable	104337 00
Notes Payable	75328 00	Auto	14268 00
Cash	10016 00	Desks	6825 00
J. Lune, Capital	?	Total Equity	$250034 00

1. Help Abby fix as well as complete the balance sheet.
2. What written recommendations would you make about the bookkeeper? Should she be retained?
3. Suppose that (a) Jon Lune invested an additional $20,000 in cash as well as additional desks with a value of $8,000 and (b) Lune Co. bought an auto for $6,000 paying $2,000 down and issuing a note for the balance. Prepare an updated balance sheet. Assume that these two transactions occurred on January 4.

CONTINUING PROBLEM

Preparing financial statements from the expanded accounting equation
❸ ❹ (45 min)

The following problem will continue from one chapter to the next, carrying the balances forward from month to month. Each chapter will focus on the learning experience of the chapter and add additional information as the business grows. The necessary forms are provided on pages 1-26 to 1-28 of the *Study Guide with Working Papers*.

Assignment

1. Set up an expanded accounting equation spreadsheet using the following accounts:

Assets	Liabilities	Owner's Equity
Cash	Accounts Payable	T. Freedman, Capital
Supplies		T. Freedman, Withdrawals
Computer Shop Equipment		Service Revenue
Office Equipment		Expenses (notate type)

2. Analyze and record each transaction in the expanded accounting equation.

3. Prepare the financial statements for Precision Computer Centre for the period ending May 31.

Tony Freedman decided to begin his own computer service business on May 2, 2016. He named the business the Precision Computer Centre. During the month of May, Tony conducted the following business transactions:

(a) Invested $4,500 of his savings into the business.
(b) Paid $1,200 (cheque No. 201) for a computer from Multi Systems, Inc.
(c) Paid $600 (cheque No. 202) for office equipment from Office Furniture, Inc.
(d) Set up a new account with Staples and purchased $250 in office supplies on credit.
(e) Paid May rent, $400 (cheque No. 203).
(f) Repaired a system for a customer; collected $250.
(g) Collected $200 for system upgrade labour charge from a customer.
(h) Electric bill due at May 31 but unpaid, $85.
(i) Received $1,200 for services performed on Taylor Golf computers.
(j) Tony withdrew $100 (cheque No. 204) to take his wife Carol out in celebration of opening the new business. ***Note:*** The business is too small to worry about GST (or HST) and PST is not applicable either. Tony's company may on occasion pay some GST or HST, but these details are not used in any transactions until a later chapter.

CHAPTER 2

Debits and Credits

ANALYZING AND RECORDING BUSINESS TRANSACTIONS

LEARNING OBJECTIVES

- **LO 1** Recording transactions in T accounts according to the rules of debit and credit (p. 51)
- **LO 2** Setting up and organizing a chart of accounts (p. 52)
- **LO 3** Preparing a trial balance (p. 63)
- **LO 4** Preparing financial statements from a trial balance (p. 64)

Do you ever wonder how a shop will know if cash taken in at the register will equal the sales at the end of the day? If you go to Subway and purchase a sub, how will Subway know that the money collected for your sale will equal the amount in the register at day's end? In this chapter, we learn how businesses small and large are required to use the accounting equation to ensure this balance. By following the rules associated with the accounting equation, investors and creditors who review financial statements can have confidence that businesses like Subway are accurately reporting their financial activities.

In Chapter 1, we used the expanded accounting equation to document the financial transactions performed by Catherine Hall's law firm. Remember how long it was: the cash column had a long list of pluses and minuses, and there was no quick system of recording and summarizing the increases and decreases of cash or other items. Can you imagine the problem Canadian Tire or Tim Hortons would have if they used the expanded accounting equation to track the thousands of business transactions they do each day?

Let's look at the problem a little more closely. Every business transaction is recorded in the accounting equation under a specific **account**. There are different accounts for each of the subdivisions of the accounting equation—there are asset accounts, liability accounts, expense accounts, revenue accounts, and so on. What is needed is a way to record the increases and decreases in specific account *categories* and yet keep them together in one place. The answer is the **standard account** form (see Figure 2-1). A standard account is a formal account that includes columns for date, explanation, posting reference (PR), debit, and credit. Each account has a separate form and all transactions affecting that account are recorded on the form. All the business's account forms (which often are referred to as *ledger*

Figure 2-1
The Standard Account Form

Account Title							Account No.
Date	Item	PR	Debit	Date	Item	PR	Credit

The standard account form is the source of the T account's shape.

accounts) are then placed in a **ledger**. Each page of the ledger contains one account. The ledger may be in the form of a bound or a loose-leaf book. If computers are used, the ledger may be part of a computer printout. For simplicity's sake, in this chapter, we will use the **T account** form, which got its name because it looks like the letter T. Generally, T accounts are used for classroom demonstration purposes.

LEARNING UNIT 2-1

The T Account

Each T account contains three basic parts:

1 Title of Account	
2 **Left side**	**Right side** 3

Debit defined

1. The *left* side of any T account
2. An amount entered on the left side of any account is said to be *debited* to an account.

All T accounts have this structure. In accounting, the left side of any T account is called the **debit** side.

At this point, for you, the word *debit* in accounting means a position, the left side of an account. Don't think of it as good (+) or bad (−).

Left side **Dr. (debit)**	

Credit defined

1. The *right* side of any T account
2. An amount entered on the right side of an account is said to be *credited* to an account.

Amounts entered on the left side of any account are said to be *debited* to an account. The word *debit* is from the Latin *debere*; the abbreviation for debit is Dr.

The right side of any T account is called the **credit** side.

	Right side **Cr. (credit)**

Amounts entered on the right side of an account are said to be *credited* to an account. The word *credit* is from the Latin *credere;* the abbreviation for credit is Cr.

At this point, do not associate the definitions of debit and credit with the words *increase* and *decrease.* Think of debit or credit as indicating only a *position* (left side or right side) of a T account.

NEED HELP?

Most of the jobs or professions in society use a terminology that includes unique terms. This is true for many of our non-business tasks as well. Take golf, for example. There are many unique golf terms in constant use, such as "par," "eagle," and (all too often) "bogie," and you only need to listen to a televised golf competition to hear them.

Many people enjoy sailing as a hobby, and there are thousands of mariners who work in the shipping industry. As you might expect, these people have developed certain terms or abbreviations that have a distinct meaning for them.

If during a sailing competition a sailor shouts, "Hard to port!" it does not mean turn around and head for shore, and it certainly has nothing to do with an expensive, sweet, strong wine! In the context of sailing, "port" simply means "left." If a right turn is wanted, you say, "Starboard." This same terminology has been adopted in the airline industry as well.

So it has always been a puzzle why some accounting students have difficulty with the terms "debit" and "credit." There should be no puzzle here; the terms are used in a manner unique to bookkeeping, and all students of accounting need to familiarize themselves with what the terms mean and how they are used. This should not take long, but possibly because the words do have a more general meaning in society, it can be confusing at first. But if you want to get a good foothold in this field, it is essential to quickly master the use of these terms.

This chapter explains the terms clearly, and students should make an effort to ensure they know what each term means. It might help to remember that, just as in sailing, "port" means "left" and so it is with bookkeeping. "Debit" also means "left" ("on the left," actually). And also, just as "starboard" means "right" in sailing, "credit" also means "right" ("on the right"). While it is true that the word "credit" has other meanings, these should be ignored when you are learning about bookkeeping and accounting.

Good luck with mastering these two terms!

BALANCING AN ACCOUNT

No matter which individual account is being balanced, the procedure will be the same.

Dollar signs are not used in standard accounts or T accounts. However, dollar signs are used in formal financial reports.

	Dr.	Cr.
Entries →	**4,000**	**300**
	500	**400**
Footings →	4,500	700
Ending Balance →	3,800	

Footings aid in balancing an account. The ending balance is the difference between the footings.

In the "real" world, the T account would also include the date of the transaction. The date would appear to the left of the entry, as shown below.

Note that on the debit (left) side, the amounts add up to $4,500. On the credit (right) side, the amounts add up $700. The $4,500 and the $700 written in small type are called **footings**. Footings help in calculating the new (or ending) balance. The **ending balance** ($3,800) is placed on the debit or left side, since the total of the debit side is greater than that of the credit side.

If the total were greater on the credit side, that is the side the ending balance would be on.

		Dr.	Cr.	
	4/2	**4,000**	**300**	**4/3**
	4/20	**500**	**400**	**4/25**
Footings		4,500	700	
Balance		3,800		

Remember, the ending balance does not tell us anything about increase or decrease. It tells us only that we have an ending balance of $3,800 on the debit side.

LEARNING UNIT 2-1 REVIEW

AT THIS POINT you should be able to:

- Define ledger. (p. 48)
- State the purpose of a T account. (p. 48)
- Identify the three parts of a T account. (p. 48)
- Define debit. (p. 48)
- Define credit. (p. 48)
- Explain footings and calculate the balance of an account. (p. 49)

Self-Review Quiz 2-1

(The blank forms you need are on page 2-1 of the *Study Guide with Working Papers.*)

Respond True or False to the following:

1.

Dr.	Cr.
3,000	200
200	600

The balance of the account is $2,400 Cr.

2. A credit always means increase.

3. A debit is the left side of any account.

4. A ledger can be prepared manually or by computer.

5. Footings replace the need for debits and credits.

Quiz Tip

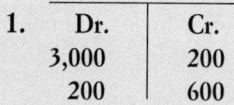

Dr. + Dr. ⟶ Add to get Dr. balance.

Cr. + Cr. ⟶ Add to get Cr. balance.

Dr. – Cr. ⟶ Subtract to get balance for the larger side.

Solutions to Self-Review Quiz 2-1

1. False **2.** False **3.** True **4.** True **5.** False

NEED HELP?

Let's review first: Debit does not mean good or bad. Instead, it represents a position, the left side of any account. Credit does not mean good or bad either. It represents a position, the right side of any account.

1. It is false because if you add the two debits of 3,000 and 200 you get 3,200 on the debit, or left side. A Dr. + Dr. = Debit balance. Now if you add the credit side of 200 and 600 you get a balance of 800 on the credit side. A Cr. + Cr. = Credit balance. To find the ending balance we take 3,200 less the 800 to arrive at a balance that is still larger on the DEBIT side by 2,400.

2. A credit is a position. It is the right side of any account.

3. Yes, the debit is always the left-hand side of any account. It does not mean good or bad.

4. Years ago the ledger, a group of accounts, was prepared manually; however, today most ledgers are updated by computer software.

5. Footings are used to total the debits and total the credits. The smaller total is deducted from the larger total to arrive at a new balance. Think of footings as the totals of a column.

LEARNING UNIT 2-2

Recording Business Transactions: Debits and Credits

Can you get a queen in checkers? Is there a fourth down in the CFL? In a baseball game, does a runner rounding first base skip second base and run over the pitcher's mound to get to third? No—most of us don't do such things because we follow the rules of the game. Usually we learn the rules first and reflect on the reasons for them afterward. The same is true in accounting.

Instead of first trying to understand all the rules of debit and credit and how they were developed in accounting, it will be easier to learn the rules by "playing the game."

T-ACCOUNT ENTRIES FOR ACCOUNTING IN THE ACCOUNTING EQUATION

Have patience. Learning the rules of debit and credit is like learning to play any game—the more you play, the easier it becomes. Table 2-1 shows the rules for the side on which you enter an increase or a decrease for each of the separate accounts in the accounting equation. For example, an increase is entered on the debit side in the asset account but on the credit side for a liability account.

It might be easier to visualize these rules of debit and credit if we look at them in the T account form, using + to show increase and − to show decrease.

ASSETS		=	LIABILITIES		+	OWNER'S EQUITY										
					+	Capital		−	Withdrawals		+	Revenue		−	Expenses	
Dr.	Cr.		Dr.	Cr.		Dr.	Cr.		Dr.	Cr.		Dr.	Cr.		Dr.	Cr.
+	−		−	+		−	+		+	−		−	+		+	−

Rules for Assets Work in the Opposite Direction to Those for Liabilities

When you look at the equation, you can see that the rules for assets work in the opposite direction to those for liabilities. That is, for assets, the increases appear on the debit side and the decreases are shown on the credit side; the opposite is true for liabilities. As for owner's equity, the rules for withdrawals and expenses, which

Be sure to follow the rules of debit and credit when recording accounts. They were designed to keep the accounting equation in balance.

LO 1

Recording transactions in T accounts according to the rules of debit and credit

TABLE 2-1 Rules of Debit and Credit

Account Category	Increase (Normal Balance)	Decrease
Assets	Debit	Credit
Liabilities	Credit	Debit
Owner's Equity:		
Capital	Credit	Debit
Withdrawals	Debit	Credit
Revenue	Credit	Debit
Expenses	Debit	Credit

decrease owner's equity, work in the opposite direction to the rules for capital and revenue, which *increase* owner's equity.

Assets		+	Withdrawals		+	Expenses		=	Liabilities		+	Capital		+	Revenue	
Dr.	Cr.		Dr.	Cr.		Dr.	Cr.		Dr.	Cr.		Dr.	Cr.		Dr.	Cr.
+	−		+	−		+	−		−	+		−	+		−	+

Normal Balance	
Dr.	Cr.
Assets	Liabilities
Expenses	Capital
Withdrawals	Revenue

This setup may help you understand that the rules for withdrawals and expenses are just the opposite of the rules for capital and revenue.

A **normal balance of an account** is the side that increases by the rules of debit and credit. For example, the balance of cash is a debit balance because an asset is increased by a debit. We will discuss normal balances further in Chapter 3.

Balancing the Equation

It is important to remember that any amount(s) entered on the debit side of a T account or accounts also must be on the credit side of another T account or accounts. This ensures that the total amount added to the debit side will equal the total amount added to the credit side, thereby keeping the accounting equation in balance.

The chart of accounts aids in locating and identifying accounts quickly.

Chart of Accounts

Our job is to analyze Catherine Hall's business transactions—the transactions we looked at in Chapter 1—using a system of accounts guided by the rules of debits and credits that will summarize increases and decreases of individual accounts in the ledger. The goal is to prepare an income statement, statement of owner's equity, and balance sheet for Catherine Hall. Sound familiar? If this system works, the rules of debits and credits and the use of accounts will give us the same answers as in Chapter 1 but with greater ease, and faster, too!

LO 2

Setting up and organizing a chart of accounts

Balance Sheet Accounts

Large companies may have four digits assigned to each title, and sometimes up to 24 or more digits (e.g., Exxon).

Catherine's accountant developed what is called a **chart of accounts**. The chart of accounts is a numbered list of all of the business's accounts. It allows accounts to be located quickly. In Catherine's business, for example, 100s are assets, 200s are liabilities, and so on. As you can see in Table 2-2, each separate asset and liability has its own number. Note that the chart may be expanded as the business grows.

TABLE 2-2 Chart of Accounts for Catherine Hall, Barrister and Solicitor

Balance Sheet Accounts	
Assets	**Liabilities**
111 Cash	211 Accounts Payable
112 Accounts Receivable	
121 Office Equipment	**Owner's Equity**
	311 Catherine Hall, Capital
	312 Catherine Hall, Withdrawals
Income Statement Accounts	
Revenue	**Expenses**
411 Legal Fees	511 Salaries Expense
	512 Rent Expense
	513 Advertising Expense

THE ACCOUNTING ANALYSIS: FIVE STEPS

Steps to analyze and record transactions.

Steps 1 and 2 will come from the chart of accounts. Remember the rules of debit and credit tell us only on which side to place information. Whether the debit or credit represents increases or decreases depends on the account category:

- Assets, Expenses, and Withdrawals are increased with a debit
- Liabilities, Owner's Equity, and Revenue are increased with a credit

Think of a business transaction as an exchange—you get something and you give up or part with something.

We will analyze the transactions in Catherine Hall's law firm using a teaching device called a *transaction analysis chart*. (Keep in mind that the transaction analysis chart is not a part of any formal accounting system.) There are five steps in analyzing each business transaction:

Step 1: Determine which accounts are affected. *Examples:* cash, accounts payable, rent expense. A transaction always affects at least two accounts.

Step 2: Determine which categories the accounts belong to—assets, liabilities, capital, withdrawals, revenue, or expenses. *Example:* Cash is an asset.

Step 3: Determine whether the accounts increase or decrease. *Example:* If you receive cash, that account is increasing.

Step 4: What do the rules of debits and credits say (Table 2-1)?

Step 5: What does the T account look like? Place amounts in the accounts on either the left or right side depending on the rules in Table 2-1.

This is how the five-step analysis looks in chart form:

1 Accounts Affected	2 Category	3 ↓ or ↑ (decrease) (increase)	4 Rules of Dr. and Cr.	5 Appearance of T Accounts

Let us emphasize a major point: *Do not try to debit or credit an account until you have gone through the first four steps of the transaction analysis.*

APPLYING THE TRANSACTION ANALYSIS TO CATHERINE HALL'S LAW PRACTICE

Note that in column 3 of the chart, there can be any combination of arrows, as long as the sum of the debits equals the sum of the credits in the T accounts in column 5.

Transaction A: **Aug. 26: Catherine Hall invests $7,000 cash and $800 worth of office equipment in the business.**

1 Accounts Affected	2 Category	3 ↓ ↑	4 Rules of Dr. and Cr.	5 Appearance of T Accounts
Cash	Asset	↑	Dr.	Cash 111 (A) 7,000 |
Office Equipment	Asset	↑	Dr.	Office Equipment 121 (A) 800 |
C. Hall, Capital	Owner's Equity	↑	Cr.	C. Hall, Capital 311 | 7,800 (A)

Note again that every transaction affects at least two T accounts, and the total amount added to the debit side(s) must equal the total amount added to the credit side(s) of the T accounts for each transaction.

Analysis of Transaction A

Step 1: Which accounts are affected? The law firm receives cash and office equipment, so three accounts are involved: cash, office equipment, and C. Hall, Capital. These account titles come from the chart of accounts.

Step 2: Which categories do these accounts belong to? Cash and office equipment are assets; C. Hall, Capital, is owner's equity.

Step 3: Are the accounts increasing or decreasing? The cash and office equipment, both assets, are increasing in the business. The rights or claims of C. Hall, Capital, are also increasing since Catherine invested money and office equipment in the business.

Step 4: What do the rules say? According to the rules of debit and credit, an increase in assets (cash and office equipment) is a debit. An increase in capital is a credit. Note that the total dollar amount of debits will equal the total dollar amount of credits when the T accounts are updated in column 5.

Step 5: What does the T account look like? The amounts for cash and office equipment are entered on the debit side. The amount for C. Hall, Capital, goes on the credit side.

Double-entry bookkeeping system: **The total of all debits is equal to the total of all credits.**

A transaction that involves more than one credit or more than one debit is called a **compound entry**. This first transaction of Catherine Hall's law firm is a compound entry; it involves a debit of $7,000 to Cash and a debit of $800 to Office Equipment (as well as a credit of $7,800 to C. Hall, Capital).

There is a name for this double-entry analysis of transactions, where two or more accounts are affected and the total of debits equals the total of credits. It is called **double-entry bookkeeping**. This double-entry system helps in checking the recording of business transactions.

As we continue, the explanations will be brief, but do not forget to apply the five steps in analyzing and recording each business transaction.

Transaction B: **Aug. 27: Law practice bought office equipment for cash, $900.**

1 Accounts Affected	2 Category	3 ↓ ↑	4 Rules of Dr. and Cr.	5 T Account Update
Office Equipment	Asset	↑	Dr.	Office Equipment 121 Dr.: (A) 800; (B) 900
Cash	Asset	↓	Cr.	Cash 111 Dr.: (A) 7,000 — Cr.: 900 (B)

Analysis of Transaction B

Step 1: The law firm paid cash for the office equipment it received. The accounts involved in the transaction are Cash and Office Equipment.

Step 2: The accounts belong to these categories: Office Equipment is an asset account; Cash is an asset account.

Step 3: The asset account Office Equipment is increasing. The asset account Cash is decreasing—it is being reduced to buy the office equipment.

Step 4: An increase in the asset account Office Equipment is a debit; a decrease in the asset account Cash is a credit.

Step 5: When the amounts are placed in the T accounts, the amount for office equipment goes on the debit side and the amount for cash on the credit side.

Transaction C: **Aug. 30: Bought more office equipment on account, $400.**

1 Accounts Affected	2 Category	3 ↓ ↑	4 Rules of Dr. and Cr.	5 T Account Update
Office Equipment	Asset	↑	Dr.	Office Equipment 121 Dr.: (A) 800; (B) 900; (C) 400
Accounts Payable	Liability	↑	Cr.	Accounts Payable 211 Cr.: 400 (C)

Analysis of Transaction C

Step 1: The law firm receives office equipment by promising to pay in the future. An obligation or liability account, Accounts Payable, is created.

Step 2: Office Equipment is an asset. Accounts Payable is a liability.

Step 3: The asset account Office Equipment is increasing; the liability account Accounts Payable is increasing because the amount the firm owes is going up.

Step 4: An increase in the asset account, Office Equipment, is a debit. An increase in the liability account, Accounts Payable, is a credit.

Step 5: Enter the amount for office equipment on the debit side of the T account. The amount for accounts payable goes on the credit side.

Transaction D: **Sept. 1–30: Provided legal services for cash, $3,000.**

1 Accounts Affected	2 Category	3 ↓ ↑	4 Rules of Dr. and Cr.	5 T Account Update
Cash	Asset	↑	Dr.	Cash 111 Dr.: (A) 7,000; (D) 3,000 | Cr.: 900 (B)
Legal Fees	Revenue	↑	Cr.	Legal Fees 411 Cr.: 3,000 (D)

Analysis of Transaction D

Step 1: The firm has earned revenue from legal services and receives $3,000 in cash.

Step 2: Cash is an asset account. Legal fees is a revenue account.

Step 3: Cash, an asset account, is increasing. Legal fees, or revenue, is also increasing.

Step 4: An increase in cash, an asset, is debited. An increase in legal fees, or revenue, is credited.

Step 5: Enter the amount for cash on the debit side of the T account. Enter the amount for legal fees on the credit side.

Transaction E: **Sept. 1–30: Provided legal services on account, $4,000.**

1 Accounts Affected	2 Category	3 ↓ ↑	4 Rules of Dr. and Cr.	5 T Account Update
Accounts Receivable	Asset	↑	Dr.	Accounts Receivable 112 (E) 4,000 |
Legal Fees	Revenue	↑	Cr.	Legal Fees 411 | 3,000 (D) | 4,000 (E)

Analysis of Transaction E

Step 1: The law practice has earned revenue but has not yet received payment (cash). The amounts owed by these clients are called *accounts receivable*. Revenue is earned at the time the legal services are provided, whether payment is received then or will be received sometime in the future.

Step 2: Accounts Receivable is an asset account. Legal Fees is a revenue account.

Step 3: The Accounts Receivable account is increasing because the law practice has increased the amount owed to it for legal fees that have been earned but not paid. The Legal Fees account, or revenue, is increasing.

Step 4: An increase in the asset account, Accounts Receivable, is a debit. An increase in revenue is a credit.

Step 5: Enter the amount for Accounts Receivable on the debit side of the T account. The amount for Legal Fees goes on the credit side.

Transaction F: **Sept. 1–30: Received $700 cash from clients for services rendered previously on account.**

1 Accounts Affected	2 Category	3 ↓ ↑	4 Rules of Dr. and Cr.	5 T Account Update
Cash	Asset	↑	Dr.	Cash 111 (A) 7,000 | 900 (B) (D) 3,000 | (F) 700 |
Accounts Receivable	Asset	↓	Cr.	Accounts Receivable 112 (E) 4,000 | 700 (F)

Analysis of Transaction F

Step 1: The law firm collects $700 in cash from previous revenue earned. Since the revenue is recorded at the time it is earned and not when the payment is received, in this transaction, we are concerned only with the payment, which affects the Cash and Accounts Receivable accounts.

Step 2: Cash is an asset account. Accounts Receivable is an asset account.

Step 3: Since clients are paying what is owed, cash (asset) is increasing and the amount owed (accounts receivable) is decreasing (the total amount owed by clients to Catherine Hall is going down). This transaction results in a shift in assets, more cash for less accounts receivable.

Step 4: An increase in the Cash account, an asset, is a debit. A decrease in the Accounts Receivable account, an asset, is a credit.

Step 5: Enter the amount for Cash on the debit side of the T account. The amount for Accounts Receivable goes on the credit side.

Transaction G: **Sept. 1–30: Paid salaries expense, $600.**

1 Accounts Affected	2 Category	3 ↓ ↑	4 Rules of Dr. and Cr.	5 T Account Update
Salaries Expense	Expense	↑	Dr.	Salaries Expense 511 (G) 600 |
Cash	Asset	↓	Cr.	Cash 111 (A) 7,000 | 900 (B) (D) 3,000 | 600 (G) (F) 700 |

Analysis of Transaction G

Step 1: The law firm pays $600 worth of salaries expense by cash.

Step 2: Salaries Expense is an expense account. Cash is an asset account.

Step 3: The salaries expense of the law firm is increasing, which results in a decrease in cash available.

Step 4: An increase in Salaries Expense, an expense account, is a debit. A decrease in Cash, an asset account, is a credit.

Step 5: Enter the amount for Salaries Expense on the debit side of the T account. The amount for Cash goes on the credit side.

Transaction H: **Sept. 1–30: Paid rent expense, $700.**

1 Accounts Affected	2 Category	3 ↓ ↑	4 Rules of Dr. and Cr.	5 T Account Update
Rent Expense	Expense	↑	Dr.	Rent Expense 512 (H) 700 |
Cash	Asset	↓	Cr.	Cash 111 (A) 7,000 | 900 (B) (D) 3,000 | 600 (G) (F) 700 | 700 (H)

Analysis of Transaction H

Step 1: The law firm's rent expenses are paid in cash.

Step 2: Rent is an expense. Cash is an asset.

Step 3: The rent expense increases the expenses, and the payment for the rent expense decreases the cash.

Step 4: An increase in Rent Expense, an expense account, is a debit. A decrease in Cash, an asset account, is a credit.

Step 5: Enter the amount for Rent Expense on the debit side of the T account. Place the amount for Cash on the credit side.

Transaction I: **Sept. 1–30: Received a bill for advertising expense (to be paid next month), $300.**

1 Accounts Affected	2 Category	3 ↓ ↑	4 Rules of Dr. and Cr.	5 T Account Update
Advertising Expense	Expense	↑	Dr.	Advertising Expense 513 Dr.: (I) 300
Accounts Payable	Liability	↑	Cr.	Accounts Payable 211 Cr.: 400 (C) 300 (I)

Analysis of Transaction I

Step 1: The advertising bill has come in and payment is due but has not yet been made. Therefore, the accounts involved here are Advertising Expense and Accounts Payable; the expense has created a liability.

Step 2: Advertising Expense is an expense account. Accounts Payable is a liability account.

Step 3: Both the expense and the liability are increasing.

Step 4: An increase in an expense is a debit. An increase in a liability is a credit.

Step 5: Enter the amount for the Advertising Expense account on the debit side of the T account. Enter the amount for the Accounts Payable account on the credit side.

Transaction J: **Sept. 1–30: Hall withdrew cash for personal use, $200.**

1 Accounts Affected	2 Category	3 ↓ ↑	4 Rules of Dr. and Cr.	5 T Account Update
C. Hall, Withdrawals	Owner's Equity (Withdrawals)*	↑	Dr.	**C. Hall, Withdrawals 312** (J) 200 |
Cash	Asset	↓	Cr.	**Cash 111** (A) 7,000 | 900 (B) (D) 3,000 | 600 (G) (F) 700 | 700 (H) | 200 (J)

*Withdrawals are actually a subcategory of Owner's Equity and act as a contra account—that is, as the Withdrawals account increases, the Owner's Equity account decreases.

Analysis of Transaction J

Withdrawals are always increased by debits.

Step 1: Catherine Hall withdraws cash from the business for *personal* use. This withdrawal is not a business expense.

Step 2: This transaction affects the Withdrawals and Cash accounts.

Step 3: Catherine has increased what she has withdrawn from the business for personal use. The business cash has been decreased.

Step 4: An increase in withdrawals is a debit. A decrease in cash is a credit. (*Remember:* Withdrawals go on the statement of owner's equity; expenses go on the income statement.)

Step 5: Enter the amount for C. Hall, Withdrawals, on the debit side of the T account. The amount for Cash goes on the credit side.

SUMMARY OF TRANSACTIONS FOR CATHERINE HALL

ASSETS = LIABILITIES + CAPITAL − WITHDRAWALS + REVENUE − EXPENSES

ASSETS	=	LIABILITIES	+	CAPITAL	−	WITHDRAWALS	+	REVENUE	−	EXPENSES
Cash 111 (A) 7,000 | 900 (B) (D) 3,000 | 600 (G) (F) 700 | 700 (H) | 200 (J)	=	**Accounts Payable 211** | 400 (C) | 300 (I)	+	**C. Hall, Capital 311** | 7,800 (A)	−	**C. Hall, Withdrawals 312** (J) 200 |	+	**Legal Fees 411** | 3,000 (D) | 4,000 (E)	−	**Salaries Expense 511** (G) 600 |
Accounts Receivable 112 (E) 4,000 | 700 (F)									−	**Rent Expense 512** (H) 700 |
Office Equipment 121 (A) 800 | (B) 900 | (C) 400 |									−	**Advertising Expense 513** (I) 300 |

LEARNING UNIT 2-2 REVIEW

AT THIS POINT you should be able to:

- State the rules of debit and credit. (p. 51)
- List the five steps of a transaction analysis. (p. 53)
- Show how to fill out a transaction analysis chart. (p. 53)
- Explain double-entry bookkeeping. (p. 54)

Self-Review Quiz 2-2

(The blank forms you need are on pages 2-1 and 2-2 of the *Study Guide with Working Papers.*)

King Company uses the following accounts from its chart of accounts: Cash (111), Accounts Receivable (112), Equipment (121), Accounts Payable (211), Jamie King, Capital (311), Jamie King, Withdrawals (312), Professional Fees (411), Utilities Expense (511), and Salaries Expense (512).

Record the following transactions in transaction analysis charts.

A. Jamie King invested $1,000 cash and equipment worth $700 from his personal assets into the business.
B. Billed clients for services rendered, $12,000.
C. Utilities bill due but as yet unpaid, $150.
D. Jamie King withdrew cash for personal use, $120.
E. Paid salaries expense, $250.

Quiz Tip

Column 1 titles must come from the chart of accounts. The order doesn't matter as long as the total of all debits equals the total of all credits.

Solution to Self-Review Quiz 2-2

A.

1 Accounts Affected	2 Category	3 ↓ ↑	4 Rules of Dr. and Cr.	5 T Account Update
Cash	Asset	↑	Dr.	Cash 111 (A) 1,000 |
Equipment	Asset	↑	Dr.	Equipment 121 (A) 700 |
Jamie King, Capital	Capital	↑	Cr.	Jamie King, Capital 311 | 1,700 (A)

B.

1 Accounts Affected	2 Category	3 ↓ ↑	4 Rules of Dr. and Cr.	5 T Account Update
Accounts Receivable	Asset	↑	Dr.	Accounts Receivable 112 (B) 12,000 |
Professional Fees	Revenue	↑	Cr.	Professional Fees 411 | 12,000 (B)

C.

1 Accounts Affected	2 Category	3 ↓ ↑	4 Rules of Dr. and Cr.	5 T Account Update
Utilities Expense	Expense	↑	Dr.	Utilities Expense 511 (C) 150 |
Accounts Payable	Liability	↑	Cr.	Accounts Payable 211 | 150 (C)

D.

1 Accounts Affected	2 Category	3 ↓ ↑	4 Rules of Dr. and Cr.	5 T Account Update
Jamie King, Withdrawals	Owner's Equity (Withdrawals)	↑	Dr.	Jamie King, Withdrawals 312 (D) 120 |
Cash	Asset	↓	Cr.	Cash 111 (A) 1,000 | 120 (D)

E.

Think of expenses as always increasing.

1 Accounts Affected	2 Category	3 ↓ ↑	4 Rules of Dr. and Cr.	5 T Account Update
Salaries Expense	Expense	↑	Dr.	Salaries Expense 512 (E) 250 |
Cash	Asset	↓	Cr.	Cash 111 (A) 1,000 | 120 (D) | 250 (E)

NEED HELP?

Let's review first: Make up a note card of the rules of debit and credit from Table 2-1. You will notice that assets, withdrawals, and expenses increase when you put amounts on the left, or debit, side of these accounts. The accounting system balances because liabilities, capital, and revenue increase when you put amounts on the right, or credit, side of these accounts. The increase side of any account will represent its normal balance. Think of a chart of accounts as a roadmap to all account titles a company will use. ALL ACCOUNTS AFFECTED MUST COME FROM THE CHART OF ACCOUNTS.

Transaction A: In column 1 all titles must come from the chart of accounts. The order listed does not matter as long as the sum of the left side equals the sum of the right side. In this transaction we see that accounts affected include cash, equipment, and Jamie King, Capital. Cash and equipment are assets, while capital is categorized as capital. Remember that the six category choices are as follows:

assets

liabilities

capital

withdrawals

revenue

expenses

The cash and equipment in the business are increasing (thus arrows up), and because the owner, Jamie King, supplied them Capital rights are increasing. Assets are increased by putting amounts on the debit side and capital is increased by putting amounts on the credit side.

Transaction B: Here we do the work but do not get the money. We see from the chart of accounts that revenue is called Professional Fees and amounts owed by customers are called Accounts Receivable. Revenue for King Co. is going up and customers owe the company more money. Increase in an asset is a debit and increase in revenue is a credit.

Transaction C: Here we record utilities expense before it is paid. The expenses have increased for King Co., and it has increased what it owes the utility company. An increase in an expense is a debit and an increase in a liability is a credit. Here an expense has created a liability.

Transaction D: This is not a business expense since this is a personal withdrawal of cash by the owner, Jamie King. Withdrawals are increasing since King is taking the withdrawal but the business is lowering its cash from the withdrawal. An increase in withdrawal is a debit and a decrease in cash is a credit. Note the "dr" in the middle of "withdrawal." A withdrawals account always increases by a debit.

Transaction E: In this transaction the business has another expense increasing and is paying for it using cash. The end result is that expense increases on the debit side and cash, which is an asset, decreases on the credit side. Remember that we record expenses when they happen whether they are paid or not. Here they were paid. In transaction C they were not paid.

SUMMARY

The mind process charts are a great way to organize your information before deciding what to debit or credit. Column 1 must come from the chart of accounts. In the category column you have six choices: assets, liabilities, capital, revenue, withdrawals, and expenses. The arrows tell you if the business accounts are increasing or decreasing. Note in column 5 that if an account is repeated, a running summary of all transactions is accumulated in the account.

LEARNING UNIT 2-3

The Trial Balance and Preparation of Financial Statements

Let us look at all the transactions we have discussed for Catherine Hall's business, arranged by T account and recorded using the rules of debit and credit.

ASSETS = LIABILITIES + CAPITAL − WITHDRAWALS + REVENUE − EXPENSES

Cash 111

(A) 7,000	900 (B)
(D) 3,000	600 (G)
(F) 700	700 (H)
	200 (J)
10,700	2,400 ← Footings
8,300 ← Ending Balance	

= **Accounts Payable 211**

	400 (C)
	300 (I)
	700

\+ **C. Hall, Capital 311**

	7,800 (A)

− **C. Hall, Withdrawals 312**

(J) 200	

\+ **Legal Fees 411**

	3,000 (D)
	4,000 (E)
	7,000

− **Salaries Expense 511**

(G) 600	

− **Rent Expense 512**

(H) 700	

− **Advertising Expense 513**

(I) 300	

Accounts Receivable 112

(E) 4,000	700 (F)
3,300	

Office Equipment 121

(A) 800	
(B) 900	
(C) 400	
2,100	

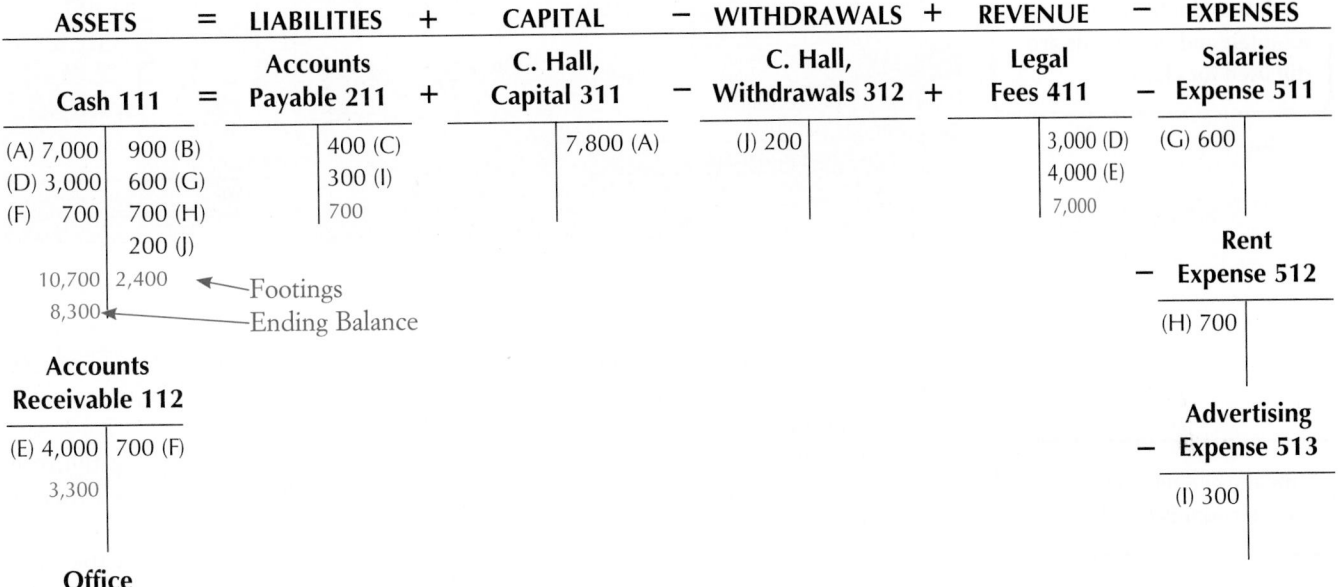

This grouping of accounts is much easier to use than the expanded accounting equation because all of the transactions that affect a particular account are in one place.

As we saw in Learning Unit 2-2, when all the transactions are recorded in the accounts, the total of all the debits should be equal to the total of all the credits. (If they are not equal, the accountant must go back and find the error by checking the numbers and adding every column again.)

LO 3 Preparing a trial balance

THE TRIAL BALANCE

Footings are used to indicate or obtain the balance of any T account that has more than one entry. If all entries in the account are on one side, the total *is* the footing. If there are entries on both sides of the account, the balance is obtained by subtracting the smaller total (footing) from the larger. For example, look at the Cash account above. The footing for the debit side is $10,700 and the footing for the credit side is $2,400. Since the debit side is larger, we subtract $2,400 from $10,700 to arrive at an *ending balance* of $8,300. Now look at the Rent Expense account. There is no need for a footing because there is only one entry. The amount itself is the ending balance. When the ending balance has been found for every account, we should be able to show that the total of all debits equals the total of all credits.

The ending balances are used to prepare a **trial balance**. The trial balance is not a financial report, although it is used to prepare financial reports. The trial balance lists all of the accounts with their balances in the same order as they appear in the chart of accounts. It proves the accuracy of the ledger.

Footings are used to indicate or obtain the balance of any T account. They are not needed if there is only one entry in the account.

As mentioned earlier, the ending balance of cash, $8,300, is a *normal balance* because it is on the side that increases the asset account.

Figure 2-2
Trial Balance for Catherine Hall's Law Firm

CATHERINE HALL, Barrister and Solicitor
TRIAL BALANCE
SEPTEMBER 30, 2016

	Dr.	Cr.
Cash	8 300 00	
Accounts Receivable	3 300 00	
Office Equipment	2 100 00	
Accounts Payable		700 00
C. Hall, Capital		7 800 00
C. Hall, Withdrawals	200 00	
Legal Fees		7 000 00
Salaries Expense	600 00	
Rent Expense	700 00	
Advertising Expense	300 00	
Totals	15 500 00	15 500 00

Since this is not a formal report, there is no need to use dollar signs; however, the single and double lines under subtotals and final totals are still used for clarity.

In the ideal situation, businesses would take a trial balance every day. The large number of transactions most businesses conduct each day makes this impractical. Instead, trial balances are prepared periodically.

Only the ending balance of each account is listed.

Keep in mind that the figure for capital might not be the beginning figure if any additional investment has taken place during the period. You can tell this by looking at the capital account in the ledger.

A more detailed discussion of the trial balance will be provided in the next chapter. For now, notice the heading, how the accounts are listed, the debits in the left column, the credits in the right, and the fact that the total of debits is equal to the total of credits.

A trial balance for Catherine Hall's firm's accounts is shown in Figure 2-2.

PREPARING FINANCIAL STATEMENTS

LO 4 Preparing financial statements from a trial balance

The trial balance is used to prepare the financial statements. The diagram in Figure 2-3 shows how financial statements can be prepared from a trial balance. Financial statements do not have debit or credit columns. The left column in the income statement and the statement of owner's equity is used only to subtotal numbers. If there were more than one liability, we would have two columns on the right-hand side of the balance sheet, one to subtotal the liabilities (inside column) and the total of the liabilities in the right column.

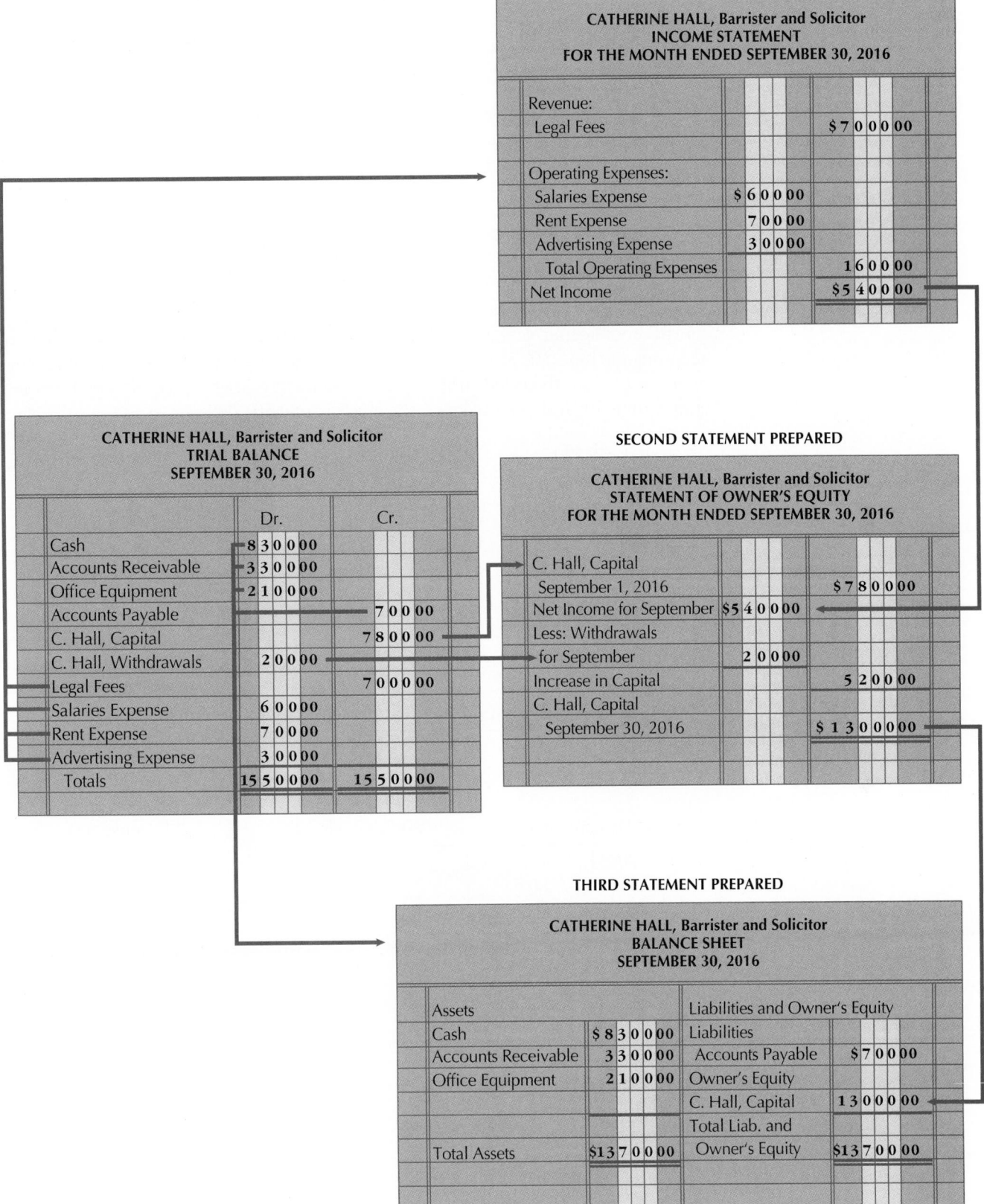

FIRST STATEMENT PREPARED

CATHERINE HALL, Barrister and Solicitor
INCOME STATEMENT
FOR THE MONTH ENDED SEPTEMBER 30, 2016

Revenue:		
Legal Fees		$7 000 00
Operating Expenses:		
Salaries Expense	$600 00	
Rent Expense	700 00	
Advertising Expense	300 00	
Total Operating Expenses		1 600 00
Net Income		$5 400 00

CATHERINE HALL, Barrister and Solicitor
TRIAL BALANCE
SEPTEMBER 30, 2016

	Dr.	Cr.
Cash	8 300 00	
Accounts Receivable	3 300 00	
Office Equipment	2 100 00	
Accounts Payable		700 00
C. Hall, Capital		7 800 00
C. Hall, Withdrawals	200 00	
Legal Fees		7 000 00
Salaries Expense	600 00	
Rent Expense	700 00	
Advertising Expense	300 00	
Totals	15 500 00	15 500 00

SECOND STATEMENT PREPARED

CATHERINE HALL, Barrister and Solicitor
STATEMENT OF OWNER'S EQUITY
FOR THE MONTH ENDED SEPTEMBER 30, 2016

C. Hall, Capital		
September 1, 2016		$7 800 00
Net Income for September	$5 400 00	
Less: Withdrawals		
for September	200 00	
Increase in Capital		5 200 00
C. Hall, Capital		
September 30, 2016		$ 13 000 00

THIRD STATEMENT PREPARED

CATHERINE HALL, Barrister and Solicitor
BALANCE SHEET
SEPTEMBER 30, 2016

Assets		Liabilities and Owner's Equity	
Cash	$ 8 300 00	Liabilities	
Accounts Receivable	3 300 00	Accounts Payable	$700 00
Office Equipment	2 100 00	Owner's Equity	
		C. Hall, Capital	13 000 00
		Total Liab. and	
Total Assets	$13 700 00	Owner's Equity	$13 700 00

Figure 2-3 Steps in Preparing Financial Statements from a Trial Balance

LEARNING UNIT 2-3 REVIEW

AT THIS POINT you should be able to:

- Explain the role of footings. (p. 63)
- Prepare a trial balance from a set of accounts. (p. 64)
- Prepare financial statements from a trial balance. (p. 65)

Self-Review Quiz 2-3

(The blank forms you need are on pages 2-2 to 2-4 of the *Study Guide with Working Papers.*)

As the bookkeeper of Pam's Hair Salon, you are to prepare from the following accounts on June 30, 2017: (1) a trial balance as of June 30; (2) an income statement for the month ended June 30; (3) a statement of owner's equity for the month ended June 30; and (4) a balance sheet as of June 30, 2017.

Cash 111	
4,500	300
2,000	100
1,000	1,200
300	1,300
	2,600
7,800	5,500
2,300	

Accounts Payable 211	
300	700
	400

Salon Fees 411	
	3,500
	1,000
	4,500

Accounts Receivable 121	
1,000	300
700	

Pam Jay, Capital 311	
	4,000*

Rent Expense 511	
1,200	

Salon Equipment 131	
700	

Pam Jay, Withdrawals 321	
100	

Salon Supplies Expense 521	
1,300	

Salaries Expense 531	
2,600	

*No additional investments.

Solution to Self-Review Quiz 2-3

❶

PAM'S HAIR SALON
TRIAL BALANCE
JUNE 30, 2017

	Dr.	Cr.
Cash	2300 00	
Accounts Receivable	700 00	
Salon Equipment	700 00	
Accounts Payable		400 00
Pam Jay, Capital		4000 00
Pam Jay, Withdrawals	100 00	
Salon Fees		4500 00
Rent Expense	1200 00	
Salon Supplies Expense	1300 00	
Salaries Expense	2600 00	
Totals	8900 00	8900 00

❷

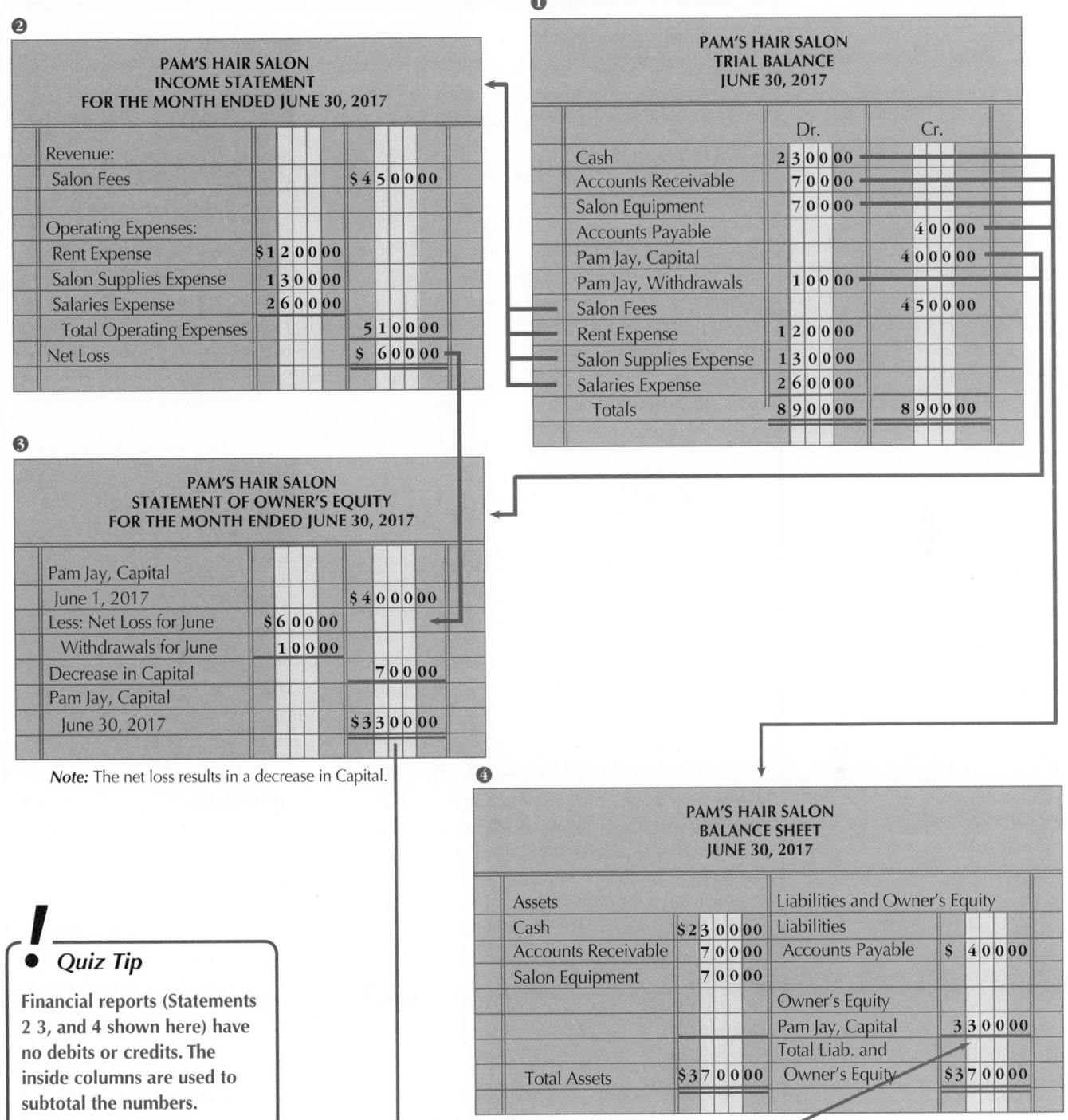

PAM'S HAIR SALON
INCOME STATEMENT
FOR THE MONTH ENDED JUNE 30, 2017

Revenue:		
Salon Fees		$4500 00
Operating Expenses:		
Rent Expense	$1200 00	
Salon Supplies Expense	1300 00	
Salaries Expense	2600 00	
Total Operating Expenses		5100 00
Net Loss		$ 600 00

❸

PAM'S HAIR SALON
STATEMENT OF OWNER'S EQUITY
FOR THE MONTH ENDED JUNE 30, 2017

Pam Jay, Capital		
June 1, 2017		$4000 00
Less: Net Loss for June	$600 00	
Withdrawals for June	100 00	
Decrease in Capital		700 00
Pam Jay, Capital		
June 30, 2017		$3300 00

Note: The net loss results in a decrease in Capital.

❹

PAM'S HAIR SALON
BALANCE SHEET
JUNE 30, 2017

Assets		Liabilities and Owner's Equity	
Cash	$2300 00	Liabilities	
Accounts Receivable	700 00	Accounts Payable	$ 400 00
Salon Equipment	700 00		
		Owner's Equity	
		Pam Jay, Capital	3300 00
		Total Liab. and	
Total Assets	$3700 00	Owner's Equity	$3700 00

!

Quiz Tip

Financial reports (Statements 2 3, and 4 shown here) have no debits or credits. The inside columns are used to subtotal the numbers.

NEED HELP?

Let's review first: The trial balance is a list of accounts and their ending balances. Each account will have either a debit or credit balance (but not both). When a trial balance is complete, the total of all the debits must equal the total of all the credits. When preparing a trial balance, you list assets, liabilities, capital, withdrawals, revenue, and expenses.

Trial balance: After you have taken the balance of the Cash account in the ledger, it has a debit balance of 2,300 (we added the debits, we added the credits, and we took the difference between them, which resulted in 2,300 more on the left side). For Accounts Receivable 1,000 less 300 leaves us with a 700 debit balance. Salon Equipment has one number so that is the balance (700 debit). Once Accounts Payable is balanced it is 400 larger on the credit side (700–300). The only other account that needs footing is Salon Fees, so the 3,500 and 1,000 are added together for a credit balance of 4,500. Once each balance is listed, the sum on the left (8,900) does indeed equal the sum on the right (8,900). Each ending balance for Pam's Hair Salon ends up on the normal balance side.

	Dr.	Cr.
Cash	x	
Acc. Rec.	x	
Salon Equip.	x	
Acc. Pay.		x
Pam Jay, Cap.		x
Pam Jay, Withd.	x	
Salon Fees		x
Rent Exp.	x	
Salon Supp. Exp.	x	
Salaries Exp.	x	

Note that titles on the trial balance are not indented.

Income Statement: Once the trial balance is complete, the first report to make is the income statement, which is made up of only revenue and expense. Remember that there are no debits or credits on financial reports. All we are taking are the ending balances of each title from the trial balance. For the income statement, we list salon fees as the revenue and then list the three expense titles in the inside column. Total operating expenses are then subtracted from the salon fees to arrive at a net loss. Here revenue is less than operating expenses ($4,500–$5,100).

Statement of Owner's Equity: The second report to prepare is the statement of owner's equity, which shows how to calculate a new figure for capital. Note that in this case, the net loss of $600 is ADDED to the $100 from Pam Jay, Withdrawals, resulting in a decrease of $700 to capital. The new figure for capital is $3,300 ($4,000–$700).

Balance Sheet: The third report is the balance sheet, which lists out each asset, liability, and the new figure for Pam Jay, Capital. This report shows that as of June 30 total assets is $3,700 and total liabilities and owner's equity is $3,700. Remember that the ending figure for capital comes from the statement of owner's equity.

SUMMARY

The trial balance is a list of ending balances of ledger accounts. These balances are used to prepare the three financial reports. Financial reports have no debits or credits. The inside columns are used to subtotal numbers. Revenue and expenses go on the income statement. Withdrawals and either net income or net loss go on the statement of owner's equity to calculate a new figure for capital. The balance sheet is a list of assets, liabilities, and the new amount for ending capital. Remember that the trial balance has debit or credits, not the financial reports.

When Stan took the big leap from being an employee to a Subway owner, the thing that terrified him most was not the part about managing people—that was one of his strengths as a marketing manager. Why, at Xellent Media, 40 sales reps reported to him! No, Stan was terrified of having to manage the accounts. Subway restaurant owners have so many accounts to deal with—food costs, payroll, rent, utilities, supplies, advertising, promotion, wages, and, biggest of all, cash. It's critical for owners to keep debits and credits straight. If not, both they and Subway could lose a lot of money, quickly.

SUBWAY

DEBITS ON THE LEFT

Recording transactions accurately ❷ (20 min)

While Stan got some intense training in accounting and bookkeeping at Subway University, he still felt shaky about doing his own books. When he confided his fears to Mariah Washington, his field consultant, she suggested he hire an accountant. "You need to play to your strengths," said Mariah. "More and more owners are using accountants, and almost all owners of multiple franchises do. In fact, some accountants actually specialize in handling Subway accounts for these multi-restaurant owners."

Even though Stan decided to hire his cousin, Lila, to do his accounting, he still needs to feed her the right data so she can calculate his T accounts. Like many small business owners, Stan enters data into an accounting software program such as Sage 50®, which he then uploads to his accountant, who edits it and reviews it for accuracy. Several times in the beginning, Stan mistakenly debited both cash and supplies when he paid for orders of paper cups, bread dough, and other supplies.

Lila urged Stan to review the rules for recording debits and credits. She even told him to practise for a while using a paper ledger. "On the computer, debits and credits are not as visible as they are with your paper system. Since you enter only the payables, the computer does the other side of the balance sheet. So you have to bone up on debits and credits to ensure that your Sage 50® data is correct."

DISCUSSION QUESTIONS

1. Why is the Cash account so important in Stan's business?
2. Why do you think that most owners of the larger restaurants use accountants to do their books instead of doing the books themselves?
3. Is the difference between debits and credits important to Subway restaurant owners who don't do their own books?

Chapter Assignments

DEMONSTRATION PROBLEM

The chart of accounts of Mel's Delivery Service includes the following: Cash, 111; Accounts Receivable, 112; Office Equipment, 121; Delivery Trucks, 122; Accounts Payable, 211; Mel Free, Capital, 311; Mel Free, Withdrawals, 312; Delivery Fees Earned, 411; Advertising Expense, 511; Gas Expense, 512; Salaries Expense, 513; and Telephone Expense, 514. The following transactions resulted for Mel's Delivery Service during the month of July 2017:

The blank forms you need are on pages 2-5 through 2-7 of the *Study Guide with Working Papers*.

A. Mel invested $10,000 in the business from his personal savings account.
B. Bought delivery truck on account, $17,000.
C. Advertising bill received but unpaid, $700.
D. Bought office equipment for cash, $1,200.
E. Received cash for delivery services rendered, $15,000.
F. Paid salaries expense, $3,000.
G. Paid gas expense for company trucks, $1,250.

H. Billed customers for delivery services rendered, $4,000.
I. Paid telephone bill, $300.
J. Received $3,000 as partial payment of transaction H.
K. Mel paid home telephone bill from company chequebook, $150.

Assignment

As Mel's newly employed accountant, you must do the following:

1. Set up T accounts in a ledger.
2. Record transactions in the T accounts. (Place the letter of the transaction next to the entry.)
3. Foot and take the balance of each account where appropriate.
4. Prepare a trial balance at the end of July.
5. Prepare from the trial balance, in proper form, (a) an income statement for the month of July, (b) a statement of owner's equity, and (c) a balance sheet as of July 31, 2017.

Solution to Demonstration Problem

1, 2, 3. **GENERAL LEDGER**

Cash 111

(A) 10,000	1,200 (D)
(E) 15,000	3,000 (F)
(J) 3,000	1,250 (G)
	300 (I)
	150 (K)
28,000	5,900
22,100	

Accounts Payable 211

	17,000 (B)
	700 (C)
	17,700

Advertising Expense 511

(C) 700	

Accounts Receivable 112

(H) 4,000	3,000 (J)
1,000	

Mel Free, Capital 311

	10,000 (A)

Gas Expense 512

(G) 1,250	

Office Equipment 121

(D) 1,200	

Mel Free, Withdrawals 312

(K) 150	

Salaries Expense 513

(F)	3,000

Delivery Trucks 122

(B) 17,000	

Delivery Fees Earned 411

	15,000 (E)
	4,000 (H)
	19,000

Telephone Expense 514

(I) 300	

Solution Tips to Recording Transactions

A.	Cash	A	↑	Dr.
	Mel Free, Capital	Cap.	↑	Cr.

B.	Delivery Trucks	A	↑	Dr.
	Accts. Payable	L	↑	Cr.

C.	Advertising Expense	Exp.	↑	Dr.
	Accts. Payable	L	↑	Cr.

D.	Office Equipment	A	↑	Dr.
	Cash	A	↓	Cr.

E.	Cash	A	↑	Dr.
	Del. Fees Earned	Rev.	↑	Cr.

F.	Salaries Expense	Exp.	↑	Dr.
	Cash	A	↓	Cr.

G.	Gas Expense	Exp.	↑	Dr.
	Cash	A	↓	Cr.

H.	Accts. Receivable	A	↑	Dr.
	Del. Fees Earned	Rev.	↑	Cr.

I.	Tel. Expense	Exp.	↑	Dr.
	Cash	A	↓	Cr.

J.	Cash	A	↑	Dr.
	Accts. Receivable	A	↓	Cr.

K.	Mel Free, Withdr.	Withdr.	↑	Dr.
	Cash	A	↓	Cr.

4.

Mel's Delivery Service
Trial Balance
July 31, 2017

	Dr.	Cr.
Cash	22,100	
Accounts Receivable	1,000	
Office Equipment	1,200	
Delivery Trucks	17,000	
Accounts Payable		17,700
Mel Free, Capital		10,000
Mel Free, Withdrawals	150	
Delivery Fees Earned		19,000
Advertising Expense	700	
Gas Expense	1,250	
Salaries Expense	3,000	
Telephone Expense	300	
Totals	46,700	46,700

Solution Tips to Taking the Balance of an Account and Preparation of a Trial Balance

3. Footings: Cash — Add left side, $28,000. Add right side, $5,900. Take difference, $22,100, and write on side that is larger.

   Accounts Payable — Add $17,000 + $700 and write on same side. Total is $17,700.

4. Trial balance is a list of the ledger's ending balances. The list is in the same order as the chart of accounts. Each title has only one number listed, either as a debit or credit balance.

Figure 2-4 Financial Reports

5(a)

MEL'S DELIVERY SERVICE
INCOME STATEMENT
FOR THE MONTH ENDED JULY 31, 2017

Revenue:		
Delivery Fees Earned		$19,000.00
Operating Expenses:		
Advertising Expense	$700.00	
Gas Expense	1,250.00	
Salaries Expense	3,000.00	
Telephone Expense	300.00	
Total Operating Expenses		5,250.00
Net Income		$13,750.00

(b)

MEL'S DELIVERY SERVICE
STATEMENT OF OWNER'S EQUITY
FOR THE MONTH ENDED JULY 31, 2017

Mel Free, Capital		
July 1, 2017		$10,000.00
Net Income for July	$13,750.00	
Less Withdrawals for July	150.00	
Increase in Capital		$13,600.00
Mel Free, Capital		
July 31, 2017		$23,600.00

(c)

MEL'S DELIVERY SERVICE
BALANCE SHEET
JULY 31, 2017

Assets		Liabilities and Owner's Equity	
Cash	$22,100.00	Liabilities	
Accounts Receivable	1,000.00	Accounts Payable	$17,700.00
Office Equipment	1,200.00		
Delivery Trucks	17,000.00		
		Owner's Equity	
		Mel Free, Capital	23,600.00
		Total Liab. and	
Total Assets	$41,300.00	Owner's Equity	$41,300.00

Solution Tips to Preparing Financial Statements from a Trial Balance

			Trial Balance	
			Dr.	Cr.
Balance Sheet	<	Assets	X	
		Liabilities		X
Statement of Equity	<	Capital		X
		Withdrawals	X	
Income Statement	<	Revenues		X
		Expenses	X	
			XX	XX

Net income of $13,750 on the income statement goes on the statement of owner's equity.

Ending capital of $23,600 on the statement of owner's equity goes on the balance sheet as the new figure for capital.

Note: Financial statements do not show debits or credits. The inside column is used for subtotalling.

SUMMARY OF KEY POINTS

Learning Unit 2-1

1. A T account is a simplified version of a standard account.
2. A ledger is a group of accounts.
3. A debit is the left-hand position (side) of an account and a credit is the right-hand position (side) of an account.
4. A footing is the total of one side of an account. The ending balance is the difference between the footings on the left and right sides.

Learning Unit 2-2

1. A chart of accounts for a company lists the account titles and their numbers.
2. The transaction analysis chart is a teaching device, not to be confused with standard accounting procedures.
3. A compound entry is a transaction involving more than one debit or credit.

Learning Unit 2-3

1. In double-entry bookkeeping, the recording of each business transaction affects two or more accounts, and the total of debits equals the total of credits.
2. A trial balance is a list of the ending balances of all accounts, listed in the same order as on the chart of accounts.
3. Any additional investments during the period will result in having a figure for capital in the trial balance different from the beginning figure for capital in the statement of owner's equity.
4. There are *no* debit or credit columns on the three financial statements.

KEY TERMS

Account An accounting device used in bookkeeping to record increases and decreases of business transactions relating to individual assets, liabilities, capital, withdrawals, revenue, and expenses (p. 47)

Chart of accounts A numbering system of accounts that lists the account titles and account numbers to be used by a company (p. 52)

Compound entry A transaction involving more than one debit or credit (p. 54)

Credit The right-hand side of any account. A number entered on the right side of any account is said to be credited to that account. (p. 48)

Debit The left-hand side of any account. A number entered on the left side of any account is said to be debited to that account. (p. 48)

Double-entry bookkeeping An accounting system in which the recording of each transaction affects two or more accounts, and the total of the debits is equal to the total of the credits (p. 54)

Ending balance The difference between footings in a T account (p. 49)

Footings The totals of each of the two sides of a T account (p. 49)

Ledger A group of accounts that records data from business transactions (p. 48)

Normal balance of an account The side of an account that increases by the rules of debit and credit (p. 52)

Standard account A formal account that includes columns for date, explanation, posting reference, and debit and credit amounts (p. 47)

T account A skeleton version of a standard account, used for demonstration purposes (p. 48)

Trial balance A list of the ending balances of all the accounts in a ledger. The total of the debits should equal the total of the credits. (p. 63)

QUICK REVIEW

The following Tips are from Learning Units 2-1 to 2-3. Answer the Assess Your Progress questions and use the How Did You Do? at the bottom of the page to see how well you know the material. The Quick Review provides tips before each Assess Your Progress to help you avoid common accounting errors.

LU 2-1 The T Account

Tips: Think of "debit" or "credit" as only indicating a position (left or right). To balance an account, total the left (debit) side and the right (credit) side and take the difference between the two totals. This ending balance is placed on the side that is greater. Do not think at this point of "debit" or "credit" as being good or bad. They simply indicate a position, left or right.

Assess Your Progress

Answer true or false to the following statements:

1. A number entered on the left side of an account is said to be credited to the account.
2. Debits always are positive.
3. Footings are always a credit balance.
4. "Credit" always means the number should be put on the right side.
5. A ledger does not use debits or credits.

LU 2-2 Recording Business Transactions: Debits and Credits

Tips: Assets, withdrawals, and expenses will increase on the debit side, while liabilities, capital, and revenues will increase on the credit side. The normal balance of an account is on the side that increases it. The goal of each transaction is for the sum of the left side to equal the sum of the right side. Compound entries result when three or more accounts affect a transaction.

Assess Your Progress

Answer true or false to the following statements:

1. Rules for debit and credit work in the opposite direction as capital and revenue.
2. An increase in an asset always is a debit.
3. Withdrawals increase with a credit.
4. After a transaction is recorded it can have only one debit and one credit.
5. An unpaid bill results in a debit to a liability and a credit to an expense.

LU 2-3 The Trial Balance and Preparation of Financial Statements

Tips: A trial balance is a list of the accounts in the ledger with their ending balances. Each account can only have a debit or credit balance. A trial balance will list assets, liabilities, capital, withdrawals, revenue, and expenses. When the financial statements are prepared, there are no debits or credits on the financial reports. It is the ending balance of each account that is listed. The inside columns of financial reports are used for subtotalling.

Assess Your Progress

Answer true or false to the following statements:

1. Withdrawals are usually a credit balance on the trial balance.
2. A balance sheet will list only debit accounts.
3. The balance sheet is always prepared before the income statement.
4. Subtotalling is only used on the trial balance.
5. The beginning balance of capital is shown on the balance sheet.

How Did You Do? Answers to the Assess Your Progress

LU 2-1

1. False – A number entered on the left side of an account is said to be debited to the account.
2. False – Debits are on the left-hand side of the account.
3. False – Whether or not footings are a credit balance depends on which side is larger after balancing.
4. True.
5. False – A ledger does use debits and credits.

LU 2-2

1. False – Rules for debit and credit work in the same direction as capital and revenue.
2. True.
3. False – Withdrawals increase with a debit.
4. False – After a transaction is recorded it can have more than one debit or credit as long as the total of debits equals the total of credits.
5. False – An unpaid bill results in a debit to expense and a credit to liability.

LU 2-3

1. False – Withdrawals are usually a debit balance on the trial balance.
2. False - Balance sheet numbers result from the ending balance of both debit and credit accounts.
3. False – Prepared after the income statement.
4. False – Subtotalling is used in preparing financial reports; the trial balance is not a financial report.
5. False – The ending figure for capital is shown on the balance sheet.

BLUEPRINT FOR PREPARING FINANCIAL STATEMENTS FROM A TRIAL BALANCE

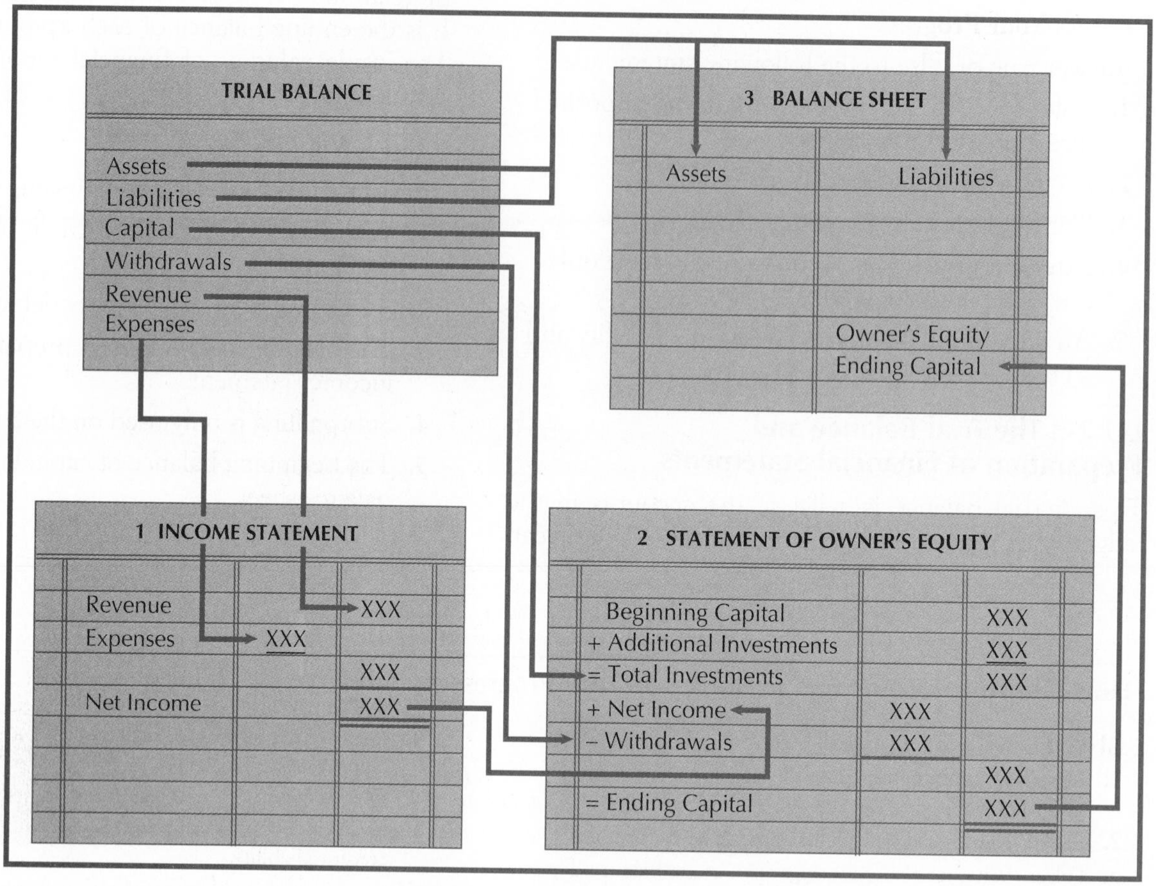

QUESTIONS, CLASSROOM DEMONSTRATION EXERCISES, EXERCISES, AND PROBLEMS

Discussion Questions and Critical Thinking/Ethical Case

1. Define a ledger.
2. Why is the left-hand side of an account called a debit?
3. Footings are used in balancing all accounts. True or false? Please explain.
4. What is the end product of the accounting process?
5. What do we mean when we say that a transaction analysis chart is a teaching device?
6. What are the five steps of the transaction analysis chart?
7. Explain the concept of double-entry bookkeeping.
8. A trial balance is a formal report. True or false? Please explain.
9. Why are there no debit or credit columns on financial reports?
10. Compare the financial statements prepared from the expanded accounting equation with those prepared from a trial balance.

11. Audrey Flet, the bookkeeper of ALN Co., was scheduled to leave on a three-week vacation at 5:00 on Friday. She couldn't get the company's trial balance to balance. At 4:30, she decided to put in fictitious figures to make it balance. Audrey told herself she would fix it when she got back from her vacation. Was Audrey right or wrong to do this? Why?

Classroom Demonstration Exercises

(The blank forms you need are on page 2-8 of the *Study Guide with Working Papers.*)

The T Account

Balancing T accounts
❶ ❷ (5 min)

1. For the following, foot and balance each account.

Cash 110

9/5	12,000	800	9/7
9/9	6,000		

C. Clark, Capital 311

		6,000	6/9
		4,000	9/3
		1,000	9/7

Transaction Analysis

Analyzing transactions
❶ (5 min)

2. Complete the following:

Account	Category	↑	↓	Normal Balance
A. Accounts Payable	Liability	Cr.	Dr.	Cr.
B. Taxable Fees Earned				
C. Accounts Receivable				
D. M. Blanc, Capital				
E. M. Blanc, Withdrawals				
F. Prepaid Advertising				
G. Rent Expense				

Analyzing and recording transactions
❷ (5 min)

Transaction Analysis

3. Record the following transaction in the transaction analysis chart: Provided bookkeeping services for $2,500, receiving $600 cash with the remainder to be paid next month.

Accounts Affected	Category	↓ ↑	Rules of Dr. and Cr.	T Accounts

Preparing a trial balance
❸ (5 min)

Trial Balance

4. Rearrange the following titles in the order in which they would appear in a trial balance:

J. Joy, Withdrawals	Hair Salon Fees Earned
Accounts Receivable	Utility Expense
Cash	Salary Expense
J. Joy, Capital	Advertising Expense
Office Equipment	Accounts Payable

Preparing financial statements from a trial balance
❹ (10 min)

Trial Balance/Financial Statements

5. For the following trial balance, identify the statement in the following list in which each title will appear:

- Income Statement (IS)
- Statement of Owner's Equity (OE)
- Balance Sheet (BS)

Bernie Co.
Trial Balance
November 20, 2015

		Dr.	Cr.
A. _____	Cash	500	
B. _____	Accounts Receivable	200	
C. _____	Computer Equipment	600	
D. _____	Accounts Payable		900
E. _____	L. Bernard, Capital		240
F. _____	L. Bernard, Withdrawals	250	
G. _____	Legal Fees Earned		1,000
H. _____	Director's Fees Earned		500
I. _____	Wage Expense	300	
J. _____	Supplies Expense	700	
K. _____	Internet Advertising Expense	90	
	TOTALS	2,640	2,640

Exercises

Set A

(The blank forms you need are on pages 2-9 and 2-10 of the *Study Guide with Working Papers.*)

Preparing a chart of accounts
1 (10 min)

2-1A. From the following titles, prepare a chart of accounts using the same numbering system as used in this chapter.

Panasonic HD Television	Legal Fees
Salary Expense	L. Jones, Capital
Accounts Payable	Cash
Accounts Receivable	Advertising Expense
Repair Expense	L. Jones, Withdrawals

Accounts, categories, rules, and the reports on which they appear
1 (5 min)

2-2A. Record the following transaction in the transaction analysis chart: Sandy Pointer bought a new piece of computer equipment for $19,000, paying $3,000 down and agreeing to pay the balance in 30 days.

Preparing a chart of accounts
1 (5 min)

2-3A. Complete the following table. For each account listed on the left, indicate the category to which it belongs, whether increases and decreases in the account are marked on the debit or credit side, and in which financial report the account appears. A sample is provided.

Accounts Affected	Category	↑	↓	Appears on Which Financial Report
Supplies	Asset	Dr.	Cr.	Balance Sheet
Legal Fees Earned				
P. Rey, Withdrawals				
Accounts Payable				
Salaries Expense				
Auto				

Rules of debits and credits
1 (20 min)

2-4A. Given the following accounts, complete the table by inserting the appropriate number next to each individual transaction to indicate which account is debited and which account is credited.

1. Cash
2. Accounts Receivable
3. Equipment
4. Accounts Payable
5. B. Baker, Capital
6. B. Baker, Withdrawals
7. Plumbing Fees Earned
8. Salaries Expense
9. Advertising Expense
10. Supplies Expense

Transaction	Rules Dr.	Rules Cr.
A. Paid salaries expense.	8	1
B. Bob paid personal utilities bill from company bank account.		
C. Advertising bill was received but not yet paid.		
D. Received cash from plumbing fees.		
E. Paid supplies expense.		
F. Bob invested additional equipment in the business.		
G. Billed customers for plumbing services rendered.		
H. Received one-half the balance from transaction G.		
I. Bought equipment on account.		

Preparing financial statements
❹ (20 min)

2-5A. From the following trial balance of Hall's Cleaners, prepare the following:

- Income statement
- Statement of owner's equity
- Balance sheet

HALL'S CLEANERS
TRIAL BALANCE
JULY 31, 2016

	Dr.	Cr.
Cash	55000	
Equipment	69200	
Accounts Payable		45500
J. Hall, Capital		80000
J. Hall, Withdrawals	19800	
Cleaning Fees		45800
Salaries Expense	16000	
Utilities Expense	11300	
Totals	171300	171300

Exercises

Set B

(The forms you need are on pages 2-9 and 2-10 of the Study *Guide with Working Papers.*)

Preparing a chart of accounts
❹ (10 min)

2-1B. From the following titles, prepare a chart of accounts using the same numbering system as used in this chapter.

Oppo Blu-ray Player	Legal Fees
Cash	L. Jones, Capital
Accounts Payable	Office Assistance Expense
Accounts Receivable	Cleaning Expense
Rent Expense	L. Jones, Withdrawals

Accounts, categories, rules, and the reports on which they appear
❶ (5 min)

2-2B. Record the following transaction in the transaction analysis chart: Sandy Pointer bought a new piece of computer equipment for $21,000, paying $5,000 down and agreeing to pay the balance in 30 days.

Preparing a chart of accounts
❶ (5 min)

2-3B. Complete the following table. For each account listed on the left, indicate the category to which it belongs, whether increases and decreases in the account are marked on the debit or credit side, and in which financial report the account appears. A sample is provided.

Accounts Affected	Category	↑	↓	Appears on Which Financial Report
Supplies	Asset	Dr.	Cr.	Balance Sheet
Legal Fees Earned				
P. Rey, Withdrawals				
Cash				
Accounts Receivable				
Rent Expense				

Rules of debits and credits
❶ (20 min)

2-4B. Given the following accounts, complete the table by inserting the appropriate number next to each individual transaction to indicate which account is debited and which account is credited.

1. Cash
2. Accounts Receivable
3. Equipment
4. Accounts Payable
5. B. Baker, Capital
6. B. Baker, Withdrawals
7. Plumbing Fees Earned
8. Salaries Expense
9. Advertising Expense
10. Supplies Expense

Transaction	Rules Dr.	Rules Cr.
A. Paid rent expense.		
B. Bob withdrew money from company bank account.		
C. Cleaning bill was received but not yet paid.		
D. Received cash from plumbing fees.		
E. Rendered plumbing services on account.		
F. Bob purchased additional equipment on account.		
G. Bought supplies on account.		
H. Received one-half the balance from transaction E.		
I. Bob contributed additional equipment to the business.		

Preparing financial statements
❹ (20 min)

2-5B. From the following trial balance of Hall's Cleaners, prepare the following:

- Income statement
- Statement of owner's equity
- Balance sheet

HALL'S CLEANERS
TRIAL BALANCE
JULY 31, 2016

	Dr.	Cr.
Cash	750 00	
Equipment	645 00	
Accounts Payable		525 00
J. Hall, Capital		700 00
J. Hall, Withdrawals	245 00	
Cleaning Fees		748 00
Salaries Expense	250 00	
Utilities Expense	83 00	
Totals	1973 00	1973 00

Group A Problems

(The forms you need are on pages 2-11 to 2-16 of the *Study Guide with Working Papers.*)

Using a transaction analysis chart
❶ (20 min)

Check Figure

	Cash		
(A)	21,000	400	(F)
(D)	1,400		

2A-1. The following transactions occurred in the opening and operation of Bill's Delivery Service of Charlottetown:

A. Bill O'Brien opened the delivery service by investing $21,000 from his personal savings account.

B. Purchased used delivery trucks on account, $9,000.

C. Rent expense was due but unpaid, $900.

D. Received cash for services rendered, $1,400.

E. Billed a client on account, $150.

F. Bill withdrew cash for his personal use, $400.

Complete the transaction analysis chart in the *Study Guide with Working Papers.* The chart of accounts includes Cash; Accounts Receivable; Delivery; Accounts Payable; Bill O'Brien, Capital; Bill O'Brien, Withdrawals; Delivery Fees Earned; and Rent Expense.

Recording transactions in ledger accounts
❶ (20 min)

Check Figure

	Cash		
(A)	20,000	90	(D)
(C)	900	400	(E)
		1,000	(G)

2A-2. Bernie Pillows opened a consulting company in Fairview and the following transactions resulted:

A. Bernie invested $20,000 in the consulting business.

B. Bought office equipment on account, $5,000.

C. Received cash for consulting work that it completed for a client, $900.

D. Bernie paid a personal bill from the company bank account, $90.

E. Paid advertising expense for the month, $400.

F. Rent expense for the month was due but not yet paid, $1,400.

G. Paid $1,000 as partial payment of what was owed from the transaction in B.

As Bernie's accountant, analyze and record the transactions in T account form. Set up the T accounts on the basis of the chart of accounts on page 83. Enter each transaction in the appropriate T account and label it with the letter of the transaction.

Chart of Accounts

Assets
Cash 111
Office Equipment 121

Liabilities
Accounts Payable 211

Owner's Equity
Bernie Pillows, Capital 311
Bernie Pillows, Withdrawals 312

Revenue
Consulting Fees Earned 411

Expenses
Advertising Expense 511
Rent Expense 512

Preparing a trial balance from the T accounts
❸ (20 min)

2A-3. From the following T accounts of Barry's Cleaning Service of Yarmouth, (a) record and foot the balances on the appropriate pages in the *Study Guide with Working Papers*, and (b) prepare a trial balance in proper form for May 31, 2016.

Check Figure
Trial Balance Total $16,100

Cash 111

(A)	7,000	200	(D)
(G)	3,500	200	(E)
		400	(F)
		200	(H)
		900	(I)

Accounts Payable 211

(D)	200	1,300	(C)

Fees Earned 411

		8,000	(B)

Accounts Receivable 112

(B)	8,000	3,500	(G)

Barry Joy, Capital 311

		7,000	(A)

Rent Expense 511

(F)	400		

Office Equipment 121

(C)	1,300		
(H)	200		

Barry Joy, Withdrawals 312

(I)	900		

Utilities Expense 512

(E)	200		

Preparing financial reports from the trial balance
❹ (40 min)

2A-4. From the trial balance of Grace Lantz, Barrister and Solicitor, of Winnipeg, prepare (a) an income statement for the month of May, (b) a statement of owner's equity for the month ended May 31, and (c) a balance sheet as of May 31, 2017.

Check Figure
Total Assets $6,400

GRACE LANTZ, Barrister and Solicitor
TRIAL BALANCE
MAY 31, 2017

	Dr.	Cr.
Cash	5 0 0 0 00	
Accounts Receivable	6 5 0 00	
Office Equipment	7 5 0 00	
Accounts Payable		4 3 0 0 00
Salaries Payable		6 7 5 00
G. Lantz, Capital		1 2 7 5 00
G. Lantz, Withdrawals	3 0 0 00	
Revenue from Legal Fees		2 3 5 0 00
Utilities Expense	3 0 0 00	
Rent Expense	4 5 0 00	
Salaries Expense	1 1 5 0 00	
Totals	8 6 0 0 00	8 6 0 0 00

Comprehensive problem
❶ ❸ ❹ (60 min)

2A-5. The chart of accounts for Angel's Delivery Service of Flin Flon is as follows:

Chart of Accounts

Assets
Cash 111
Accounts Receivable 112
Office Equipment 121
Delivery Trucks 122

Liabilities
Accounts Payable 211

Owner's Equity
Alice Angel, Capital 311
Alice Angel, Withdrawals 312

Revenue
Delivery Fees Earned 411

Expenses
Advertising Expense 511
Gas Expense 512
Salaries Expense 513
Telephone Expense 514

Check Figure
Trial Balance Total $38,100

Angel's Delivery Service completed the following transactions during the month of March 2016:

A. Alice Angel invested $16,000 in the delivery service from her personal savings account.
B. Bought delivery trucks on account, $18,000.
C. Bought office equipment for cash, $600.
D. Paid advertising expense, $250.
E. Collected cash for delivery services rendered, $2,600.
F. Paid drivers' salaries, $900.
G. Paid gas expense for trucks, $1,200.
H. Performed delivery services for a customer on account, $800.
I. Telephone expense was due but not yet paid, $700.
J. Received $300 as partial payment of transaction H.
K. Alice Angel withdrew cash for personal use, $300.

As Alice's newly employed accountant, you must:

1. Set up T accounts in a ledger.
2. Record transactions in the T accounts. (Place the letter of the transaction next to the entry.)
3. Foot the T accounts where appropriate.
4. Prepare a trial balance at the end of March 2016.
5. Prepare from the trial balance, in proper form, (a) an income statement for the month of March, (b) a statement of owner's equity for the month of March, and (c) a balance sheet as of March 31, 2016.

Group B Problems

(The forms you need are on pages 2-11 to 2-16 of the *Study Guide with Working Papers.*)

Using a transaction analysis chart
❷ (20 min)

Check Figure

Cash	
2,500	275
1,200	

2B-1. Bill O'Brien decided to open a delivery service in Charlottetown. Record the following transactions in the transaction analysis charts:

A. Bill invested $2,500 in the delivery service from his personal savings account.

B. Purchased a delivery truck on account, $900.

C. Rent expense was due but unpaid, $250.

D. Performed delivery services for cash, $1,200.

E. Billed clients for deliveries rendered, $700.

F. Bill paid his home heating bill using a company cheque, $275.

The chart of accounts for the delivery service includes Cash; Accounts Receivable; Delivery Truck; Accounts Payable; Bill O'Brien, Capital; Bill O'Brien, Withdrawals; Fees Earned; and Rent Expense.

Recording transactions in ledger accounts
❶ (20 min)

Check Figure

Cash			
(A)	20,000	200	(D)
(C)	1,200	600	(E)
		400	(G)

2B-2. Bernie Pillows established a new consulting company in Fairview. Record the following transactions for Bernie in T account form. Label each entry with the letter of the transaction.

A. Bernie invested $20,000 in the consulting business from his personal bank account.

B. Bought office equipment on account, $6,000.

C. Company rendered consulting to Jensen Corp. and received cash, $1,200.

D. Bernie withdrew cash for personal use, $200.

E. Paid advertising expense, $600.

F. Rent expense was due but not yet paid, $500.

G. Paid $400 in partial payment of transaction B.

The chart of accounts includes Cash, 111; Office Equipment, 121; Accounts Payable, 211; Bernie Pillows, Capital, 311; Bernie Pillows, Withdrawals, 312; Consulting Fees Earned, 411; Advertising Expense, 511; and Rent Expense, 512.

Preparing a trial balance from the T accounts
❸ (20 min)

Check Figure
Trial Balance Total $20,000

2B-3. From the following T accounts of Barry's Cleaning Service of Yarmouth, (a) record and foot the balances on the appropriate pages in the *Study Guide with Working Papers,* and (b) prepare a trial balance for May 31, 2016.

Cash 111	
(A) 10,000	4,000 (C)
(F) 4,000	310 (D)
(G) 2,000	50 (E)
	600 (H)

Accounts Receivable 112	
(G) 2,000	

Office Equipment 121	
(B) 2,000	
(C) 4,000	

Accounts Payable 211	
	2,000 (B)

Barry Joy, Capital 311	
	10,000 (A)

Barry Joy, Withdrawals 312	
(H) 600	

Fees Earned 411	
	4,000 (F)
	4,000 (G)

Rent Expense 511	
(D) 310	

Utilities Expense 512	
(E) 50	

Preparing financial statements from the trial balance
❹ (40 min)

2B-4. From the trial balance of Grace Lantz, Barrister and Solicitor, of Winnipeg, prepare (a) an income statement for the month of May, (b) a statement of owner's equity for the month ended May 31, and (c) a balance sheet as of May 31, 2017.

> ***Check Figure***
>
> **Total Assets $10,800**

GRACE LANTZ, Barrister and Solicitor
TRIAL BALANCE
MAY 31, 2017

	Dr.	Cr.
Cash	6 000 00	
Accounts Receivable	2 400 00	
Office Equipment	2 400 00	
Accounts Payable		200 00
Salaries Payable		600 00
G. Lantz, Capital		4 000 00
G. Lantz, Withdrawals	2 000 00	
Revenue from Legal Fees		9 800 00
Utilities Expense	100 00	
Rent Expense	300 00	
Salaries Expense	1 400 00	
Totals	14 600 00	14 600 00

Comprehensive problem
❶ ❸ ❹ (60 min)

2B-5. The chart of accounts of Angel's Delivery Service of Flin Flon includes the following: Cash, 111; Accounts Receivable, 112; Office Equipment, 121; Delivery Trucks, 122; Accounts Payable, 211; Alice Angel, Capital, 311; Alice Angel, Withdrawals, 312; Delivery Fees Earned, 411; Advertising Expense, 511; Gas Expense, 512; Salaries Expense, 513; and Telephone Expense, 514. The following transactions resulted from Angel's Delivery Service during the month of March 2016:

> ***Check Figure***
>
> **Trial Balance Total $84,300**

A. Alice invested $40,000 in the business from her personal savings account.

B. Bought delivery trucks on account, $25,000.

C. Advertising bill was received but not yet paid, $800.

D. Bought office equipment for cash, $2,500.

E. Received cash for delivery services rendered, $13,000.

F. Paid salaries expense, $1,850.

G. Paid gas expense for company trucks, $750.

H. Billed customers for delivery services rendered, $5,500.

I. Paid telephone bill, $400.

J. Received $1,600 as partial payment of transaction H.

K. Alice paid her home telephone bill with a company cheque, $88.

As Alice's newly employed accountant, you must:

1. Set up T accounts in a ledger.
2. Record transactions in the T accounts. (Place the letter of the transaction next to the entry.)
3. Foot the T accounts where appropriate.
4. Prepare a trial balance at the end of March 2016.
5. Prepare from the trial balance, in proper form, (a) an income statement for the month of March, (b) a statement of owner's equity for the month ended March 31, and (c) a balance sheet as of March 31, 2016.

Group C Problems

(The forms you need are on pages 2-17 to 2-21 of the *Study Guide with Working Papers.*)

Using a transaction analysis chart
❶ (20 min)

Check Figure

	Cash		
(A)	3,500	175	(F)
(D)	2,100		

2C-1. Jack James decided to open an editing service in Vernon. Record the following transactions in the transaction analysis charts:

A. Jack invested $3,500 in the editing service from his personal savings account.

B. Purchased office equipment on account, $1,875.

C. Rent expense was due but not yet paid, $425.

D. Performed editing services for cash, $2,100.

E. Billed clients for editing services provided, $1,490.

F. Jack paid a home repair bill from the company bank account, $175.

The chart of accounts for the business includes Cash; Accounts Receivable; Office Equipment; Accounts Payable; Jack James, Capital; Jack James, Withdrawals; Editing Fees Earned; and Rent Expense.

Recording transactions in ledger accounts
❶ (20 min)

Check Figure

	Cash		
(A)	14,000	364	(D)
(C)	3,250	725	(E)
		2,750	(G)

2C-2. Val McIntyre of Halifax established a graphics company. Record the following transactions for Val in T account form. Label each entry with the letter of the transaction.

A. Val McIntyre invested $14,000 in the business from her personal bank account.

B. Bought computer equipment on account, $5,500.

C. Business rendered service to Portias Corp. and received cash, $3,250.

D. Val McIntyre withdrew cash for personal use, $364.

E. Paid advertising expense, $725.

F. Rent expense was due but not yet paid, $615.

G. Paid $2,750 in partial payment of transaction B.

The chart of accounts includes Cash, 111; Office Equipment, 121; Accounts Payable, 211; Val McIntyre, Capital, 311; Val McIntyre, Withdrawals, 312; Graphics Fees Earned, 411; Advertising Expense, 511; and Rent Expense, 512.

Preparing a trial balance from the T accounts
❸ (20 min)

2C-3. From the following T accounts of Linda's Consulting Service of Taber, (a) record and foot the balances on the appropriate pages in the *Study Guide with Working Papers*, and (b) prepare a trial balance for October 31, 2017.

> ***Check Figure***
> **Trial Balance Total $14,000**

Cash 111

(A)	6,000	4,000	(B)
(F)	3,500	340	(D)
(G)	3,000	150	(E)
		600	(H)

Accounts Receivable 112

(G)	1,000		

Equipment 121

(B)	4,000		
(C)	500		

Accounts Payable 211

		500	(C)

Linda Miyagawa, Capital 311

		6,000	(A)

Linda Miyagawa, Withdrawals 312

(H)	600		

Fees Earned 411

		3,500	(F)
		4,000	(G)

Rent Expense 511

(D)	340		

Utilities Expense 512

(E)	150		

Preparing financial statements from the trial balance
❹ (40 min)

2C-4. From the trial balance shown below for Glenda Shaver, an architect from Peterborough, prepare (a) an income statement for the month of June, (b) a statement of owner's equity for the month ended June 30, and (c) a balance sheet as of June 30, 2017.

> ***Check Figure***
> **Total Assets $9,740**

GLENDA SHAVER, Architect
TRIAL BALANCE
JUNE 30, 2017

	Dr.	Cr.
Cash in Bank	2200 00	
Accounts Receivable	1075 00	
Supplies	265 00	
Equipment	6200 00	
Accounts Payable		620 00
Glenda Shaver, Capital		5600 00
Glenda Shaver, Withdrawals	950 00	
Fees Earned		6715 00
Rent Expense	1200 00	
Advertising Expense	480 00	
Utilities Expense	565 00	
Totals	12935 00	12935 00

Comprehensive problem
❶ ❸ ❹ (70 min)

Check Figure

Trial Balance Total $57,650

2C-5. The chart of accounts of Clara's Design Service of Montreal includes the following: Cash, 111; Accounts Receivable, 112; Office Equipment, 121; Design Equipment, 122; Accounts Payable, 211; Clara Benson, Capital, 311; Clara Benson, Withdrawals, 312; Design Fees Earned, 411; Advertising Expense, 511; Repair Expense, 512; Salaries Expense, 513; and Telephone Expense, 514. The following transactions occurred for Clara's Design Service during the month of March 2017:

A. Clara invested $33,000 in the business from her personal savings account.
B. Bought design equipment on account, $14,000.
C. Advertising bill was received but not yet paid, $1,150.
D. Bought office equipment for cash, $3,300.
E. Received cash for design services rendered, $5,900.
F. Paid salaries expense, $1,720.
G. Paid repair expense for design equipment, $320.
H. Billed customers for design services rendered, $4,300.
I. Paid telephone bill, $150.
J. Received $2,000 as partial payment of transaction H.
K. Clara paid home telephone bill from company bank account, $66.
L. Paid $700 on the bill received in transaction C.

As Clara's newly employed accountant, your task is to:

1. Set up T accounts in a ledger.
2. Record transactions in the T accounts. (Place the letter of the transaction next to the entry.)
3. Foot the T accounts where appropriate.
4. Prepare a trial balance for the end of March 2017.
5. Prepare from the trial balance, in proper form, (a) an income statement for the month of March, (b) a statement of owner's equity for the month ended March 31, and (c) a balance sheet as of March 31, 2017.

On-the-Job Training

(The forms you need are on pages 2-22 and 2-23 of the *Study Guide with Working Papers.*)

Preparing a trial balance from accurate transactions
❸ (20 min)

T-1. Andy Leaf is a careless bookkeeper. He is having a terrible time getting his trial balance to balance. Andy has asked for your assistance in preparing a correct trial balance. The following is the incorrect trial balance.

RANCH COMPANY TRIAL BALANCE JUNE 30, 2017		
	Dr.	Cr.
Cash	510 00	
Accounts Receivable		635 00
Office Equipment	260 00	
Accounts Payable	10 00	
Wages Payable	10 00	
H. Clo, Capital	635 00	
H. Clo, Withdrawals	1440 00	
Professional Fees		2240 00
Rent Expense		240 00
Advertising Expense	25 00	
Totals	2890 00	3115 00

Facts you have discovered:

- Debits to the Cash account were $2,640; credits to the Cash account were $2,150.
- Amy Hall paid $15, but this was not updated in Accounts Receivable.
- A purchase of office equipment for $105 on account was never recorded in the ledger.
- Revenue was understated in the ledger by $180.

Show how the trial balance will indeed balance once these are corrected. Tell Ranch Company how it can avoid this problem in the future. Write out your recommendations.

Preparing accurate transaction records ensures the trial balance will be correct
3 (20 min)

T-2. Cookie Mejias, owner of Mejias Company, asked her bookkeeper how each of the following situations will affect the totals of the trial balance and individual ledger accounts.

- An $850 payment for a desk was recorded as a debit to Office Equipment, $85, and a credit to Cash, $85.
- A payment of $300 to a creditor was recorded as a debit to Accounts Payable, $300, and a credit to Cash, $100.
- An Accounts Receivable collection of $400 was recorded as a debit to Cash, $400, and a credit to C. Mejias, Capital, $400.
- The payment of a liability of $400 was recorded as a debit to Accounts Payable, $40, and a credit to Supplies, $40.
- A purchase of equipment for $800 was recorded as a debit to Supplies, $800, and a credit to Cash, $800.
- A payment of $95 to a creditor was recorded as a debit to Accounts Payable, $95, and a credit to Cash, $59.

What did the bookkeeper tell Cookie? Which accounts were overstated and which were understated? Which were correct? Explain in writing how mistakes can be avoided in the future.

Recording transactions in T accounts; preparing a trial balance; and preparing financial statements from the trial balance
❶❸❹ (60 min)

CONTINUING PROBLEM

The Precision Computer Centre created its chart of accounts as follows:

Chart of Accounts
as of May 1, 2016

Assets

1000	Cash
1020	Accounts Receivable
1025	Prepaid Rent
1030	Supplies
1080	Computer Shop Equipment
1090	Office Equipment

Liabilities

2000	Accounts Payable

Owner's Equity

3000	T. Freedman, Capital
3010	T. Freedman, Withdrawals

Revenue

4000	Service Revenue

Expenses

5010	Advertising Expense
5020	Rent Expense
5030	Utilities Expense
5040	Phone Expense
5050	Supplies Expense
5060	Insurance Expense
5070	Postage Expense

You will use this chart of accounts to complete the Continuing Problem.

The following problem continues from Chapter 1. The balances as of May 31 have been brought forward in your *Study Guide with Working Papers* on pages 2-24 to 2-25. Additional transactions in June were:

(k) Received the phone bill for the month of May, $155.
(l) Paid $150 (cheque No. 205) for insurance for the month.
(m) Paid $200 (cheque No. 206) of the amount due from transaction (d) in Chapter 1.
(n) Paid advertising expense for the month, $1,400 (cheque No. 207).
(o) Billed a client (Jeannine Sparks) for services rendered, $850.
(p) Collected $900 for services rendered—a cash sale.
(q) Paid the electric bill in full for the month of May (cheque No. 208—transaction (h), Chapter 1), $85.
(r) Paid cash (cheque No. 209) for $50 in stamps.
(s) Purchased $200 worth of supplies from Computer Connection on account.

Assignment

1. Set up T accounts in a ledger.
2. Record the transactions (k) through (s) in the appropriate T accounts.
3. Foot the T accounts where appropriate.
4. Prepare a trial balance at the end of June 2016.
5. From the trial balance, prepare an income statement, a statement of owner's equity, and a balance sheet for the two months ending June 30, 2016.

CHAPTER 3

Beginning the Accounting Cycle

JOURNALIZING, POSTING, AND THE TRIAL BALANCE

LEARNING OBJECTIVES

- LO 1 Journalizing—analyzing and recording business transactions into a journal (p. 93)
- LO 2 Posting—transferring information from a journal to a ledger (p. 102)
- LO 3 Preparing a trial balance (p. 110)

WestJet owns and operates a very successful fleet of aircraft—mostly, if not entirely, made up of Boeing 737s. Many factors go into ensuring that each customer enjoys a flight that meets or exceeds his or her expectations. One of the important tasks that WestJet completes each night is to prepare each aircraft for the flights scheduled for the next day. To ensure this happens without any errors or mistakes, the airline uses a number of checklists. As a task is completed, the task is "checked off" by an employee who initials the list, taking personal responsibility for that procedure.

Like all other businesses, WestJet must ensure that its accounting records are maintained properly over a period of time. To guarantee that this is done properly, the company follows a set of steps, similar to a checklist, that in accounting is known as the **accounting cycle.** Once one cycle is completed (usually called a fiscal year), another one begins. Learning the accounting procedures needed during an accounting cycle will help you understand how a business like WestJet maintains accurate and dependable accounting records. This chapter begins the explanation of the accounting cycle.

The normal accounting procedures that are performed over a period of time are called the **accounting cycle**. The accounting cycle takes place in a period of time called an **accounting period**. An accounting period is the period of time covered by the income statement. Although it can be any time period up to one year (e.g., one month or three months), most businesses use a one-year accounting period. The year can be either a **calendar year** (January 1 through December 31) or a fiscal year.

A **fiscal year** is an accounting period that runs for any 12 consecutive months, so it can be the same as a calendar year. A business can choose any fiscal year that is convenient. For example, some retailers may decide to end their fiscal year when inventories and business activity are at a low point, such as after the Christmas season. This is called a **natural business year**. Using a natural business year allows the business to count its year-end inventory when it is easiest to do so.

This chapter covers steps 1 to 4 of the accounting cycle.

LO 1

Journalizing—analyzing and recording business transactions into a journal

Businesses would not be able to operate successfully if they prepared financial statements only at the end of their calendar or fiscal year. That is why most businesses prepare **interim reports** on a monthly, quarterly, or semi-annual basis and companies whose shares are traded on stock exchanges are required to produce these reports quarterly for reporting on stock exchanges.

In this chapter, as well as in Chapters 4 and 5, we will follow Brenda Clark's new business, Clark's Desktop Publishing Services. We will follow the normal accounting procedures that the business performs over a period of time. Clark has chosen to use a fiscal period of January 1 to December 31.

LEARNING UNIT 3-1

Analyzing and Recording Business Transactions in a Journal: Steps 1 and 2 of the Accounting Cycle

THE GENERAL JOURNAL

A business uses a journal to record transactions in chronological order. A ledger accumulates information from a journal. The journal and the ledger are in two different books.

Journal—book of original entry
Ledger—book of final entry

Journal—from the French word *jour: day* (chronological)

Chapter 2 taught us how to analyze and record business transactions in T accounts, or ledger accounts. However, recording a debit in an account on one page of the ledger and recording the corresponding credit on a different page of the ledger can make it difficult to find errors. It would be much easier if all of the business's transactions were located in the same place. That is the function of the **journal** or **general journal**. Transactions are entered in the journal in chronological order (January 1, 8, 15, etc.) and then this recorded information is used to update the ledger accounts. In computerized accounting, a journal may be recorded on disk or in **cloud computing**; the accounting files may be stored off site, and accessed over the Internet.

We will use a general journal, the simplest form of a journal, to record the transactions of Clark's Desktop Publishing Services. A transaction (debit[s] + credit[s]) that has been analyzed and recorded in a journal is called a **journal entry**. The process of recording the journal entry in the journal is called **journalizing**.

The journal is called the **book of original entry** since it contains the first formal information about the business transactions. The ledger is known as the **book of final entry** because the information it contains has been transferred from the journal. Like the ledger, the journal may be a bound or loose-leaf book. Each of the journal pages looks like the one in Figure 3-1. The pages of the journal are numbered consecutively from page 1. Keep in mind that the journal and the ledger are separate books. Also note that both journals and ledgers exist in computerized accounting although they look different from the manual formats.

Relationship Between the Journal and the Chart of Accounts

The accountant must refer to the business's chart of accounts for the account name that is to be used in the journal. Every company has its own "unique" chart of accounts.

The chart of accounts for Clark's Desktop Publishing Services appears below. By the end of Chapter 5, we will have discussed each of these accounts.

Note that we will continue to use transaction analysis charts as a teaching aid in the journalizing process.

Journalizing the Transactions of Clark's Desktop Publishing Services

Certain formalities must be followed in making journal entries: The date of the transaction must be recorded. The debit portion of the transaction is recorded first. The credit portion of a transaction is indented about 1 centimetre and placed

Figure 3-1
The General Journal

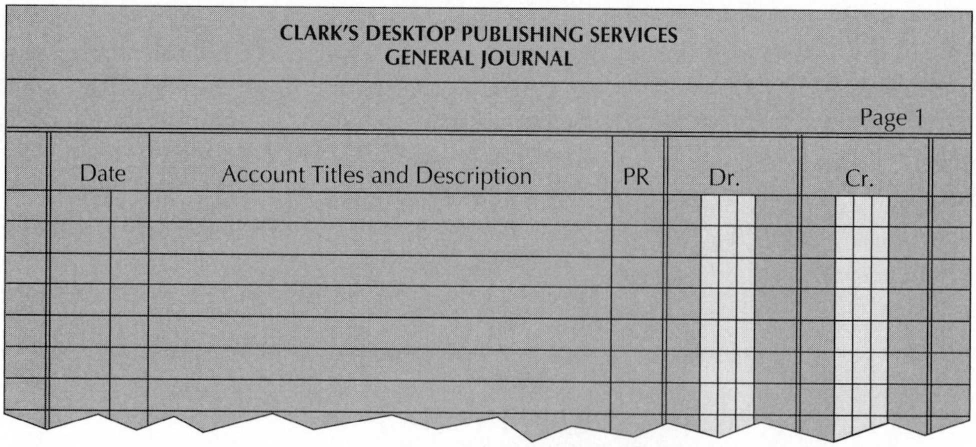

Clark's Desktop Publishing Services
Chart of Accounts

Assets (100–199)
111 Cash
112 Accounts Receivable
114 Office Supplies on hand
115 Prepaid Rent
121 Desktop Publishing Equipment
122 Accumulated Depreciation, Desktop Publishing Equipment

Liabilities (200–299)
211 Accounts Payable
212 Salaries Payable

Owner's Equity (300–399)
311 Brenda Clark, Capital
312 Brenda Clark, Withdrawals
313 Income Summary

Revenue (400–499)
411 Desktop Publishing Fees

Expenses (500–599)
511 Office Salaries Expense
512 Advertising Expense
513 Telephone Expense
514 Office Supplies Expense
515 Rent Expense
516 Depreciation Expense, Desktop Publishing Equipment

below the debit line(s). The explanation of the journal entry follows immediately after the credit and about 2 centimetres from the date column. A one-line space follows each transaction and explanation. This makes the journal easier to read, and there is less chance of mixing transactions. Finally, as always, the total amount of debits must equal the total amount of credits. The same format is used for each of the entries in the journal.

May 1, 2016: Brenda Clark began the business by investing $10,000 in cash.

1 Accounts Affected	2 Category	3 ↑ ↓	4 Rules of Dr. and Cr.
Cash	Asset	↑	Dr.
Brenda Clark, Capital	Owner's Equity	↑	Cr.

For now the PR (posting reference) column is blank; we will discuss it later.

CLARK'S DESKTOP PUBLISHING SERVICES GENERAL JOURNAL					
					Page 1
Date		Account Titles and Description	PR	Dr.	Cr.
2016 May	1	Cash		10 000 00	
		Brenda Clark, Capital			10 000 00
		Initial investment of cash by owner			

Let's now look at the structure of this journal entry. The entry contains the following information:

1. Year of the journal entry — 2016
2. Month of the journal entry — May
3. Day of the journal entry — 1
4. Name(s) of account(s) debited — Cash
5. Name(s) of account(s) credited — Brenda Clark, Capital
6. Explanation of transaction — Initial investment of cash by owner
7. Amount of debit(s) — $10,000
8. Amount of credit(s) — $10,000

Note that in this compound entry we have one debit and two credits—but the total amount of debits equals the total amount of credits.

May 1: Purchased desktop publishing equipment from Ben Co. for $6,000, paying $1,000 and promising to pay the balance within 30 days.

1 Accounts Affected	2 Category	3 ↑ ↓	4 Rules of Dr. and Cr.
Desktop Publishing Equipment	**Asset**	↑	**Dr.**
Cash	**Asset**	↓	**Cr.**
Accounts Payable	**Liability**	↑	**Cr.**

A journal entry that includes three or more accounts is called a compound journal entry.

This transaction affects three accounts. When a journal entry has more than two accounts, it is called a **compound journal entry**.

	1	Desktop Publishing Equipment		6 000 00	
		Cash			1 000 00
		Accounts Payable			5 000 00
		Purchase of equipment from Ben Co.			

In this entry, only the day is entered in the date column. That is because the year and month were entered at the top of the page from the first transaction. There is no need to repeat this information until a new page is needed or a change of month occurs.

May 1: Rented office space, paying $1,200 in advance for the first three months.

1 Accounts Affected	2 Category	3 ↑ ↓	4 Rules of Dr. and Cr.
Prepaid Rent	**Asset**	↑	**Dr.**
Cash	**Asset**	↓	**Cr.**

> **Rent paid in advance is an asset.**

In this transaction, Clark gains an asset called prepaid rent and gives up an asset, cash. The prepaid rent does not become an expense until it expires.

	1	Prepaid Rent		1 2 0 0 00	
		Cash			1 2 0 0 00
		Rent paid in advance (3 months)			

May 3: Purchased office supplies from Norris Co. on account, $600.

1 Accounts Affected	2 Category	3 ↑ ↓	4 Rules of Dr. and Cr.
Office Supplies on hand	**Asset**	↑	**Dr.**
Accounts Payable	**Liability**	↑	**Cr.**

> **Supplies may be debited directly to the expense account as a matter of convenience.**

Remember, supplies are an asset when they are purchased. Once they are used up or consumed in the operation of business, they become an expense.

	3	Office Supplies on hand		6 0 0 00	
		Accounts Payable			6 0 0 00
		Purchase of supplies on account			
		from Norris Co.			

May 7: Completed sales promotion pieces for a client and immediately collected $3,000.

1 Accounts Affected	2 Category	3 ↑ ↓	4 Rules of Dr. and Cr.
Cash	**Asset**	↑	**Dr.**
Desktop Publishing Fees	**Revenue**	↑	**Cr.**

	7	Cash		3 000 00	
		Desktop Publishing Fees			3 000 00
		Cash received for services rendered			

May 10: Paid office salaries, $650.

1 Accounts Affected	2 Category	3 ↑ ↓	4 Rules of Dr. and Cr.
Office Salaries Expense	Expense	↑	Dr.
Cash	Asset	↓	Cr.

	10	Office Salaries Expense		650 00	
		Cash			650 00
		Payment of office salaries			

Remember, expenses are recorded when they are incurred, no matter when they are paid.

May 17: Bill received from Al's News Co. but not paid.

1 Accounts Affected	2 Category	3 ↑ ↓	4 Rules of Dr. and Cr.
Advertising Expense	Expense	↑	Dr.
Accounts Payable	Liability	↑	Cr.

	17	Advertising Expense		250 00	
		Accounts Payable			250 00
		Bill received but not paid from			
		Al's News Co.			

Keep in mind that as withdrawals *increase,* owner's equity *decreases.*

May 20: Paid personal mortgage installment, $625.

1 Accounts Affected	2 Category	3 ↑ ↓	4 Rules of Dr. and Cr.
Brenda Clark, Withdrawals	Owner's Equity (Withdrawals)	↑	Dr.
Cash	Asset	↓	Cr.

	20	Brenda Clark, Withdrawals		625 00	
		Cash			625 00
		Personal withdrawal of cash			

Reminder: **Revenue is recorded when it is earned, no matter when the cash is actually received.**

May 22: Billed Morris Company for a sophisticated desktop publishing job, $5,000.

1 Accounts Affected	2 Category	3 ↑ ↓	4 Rules of Dr. and Cr.
Accounts Receivable	Asset	↑	Dr.
Desktop Publishing Fees	Revenue	↑	Cr.

	22	Accounts Receivable		5000 00	
		Desktop Publishing Fees			5000 00
		Billed Morris Co. for fees earned			

May 24: Paid office salaries, $650.

1 Accounts Affected	2 Category	3 ↑ ↓	4 Rules of Dr. and Cr.
Office Salaries Expense	Expense	↑	Dr.
Cash	Asset	↓	Cr.

Note: **Since we are on page 2 of the journal, the year and month are repeated.**

CLARK'S DESKTOP PUBLISHING SERVICES
GENERAL JOURNAL

Page 2

Date		Account Titles and Description	PR	Dr.	Cr.
2016 May	24	Office Salaries Expense		650 00	
		Cash			650 00
		Payment of office salaries			

May 28: Paid half the amount owed for desktop publishing equipment purchased May 1 from Ben Co., $2,500.

1 Accounts Affected	2 Category	3 ↑ ↓	4 Rules of Dr. and Cr.
Accounts Payable	**Liability**	↓	**Dr.**
Cash	**Asset**	↓	**Cr.**

	28	Accounts Payable	250000	
		Cash		250000
		Paid half the amount owed Ben Co.		

May 29: Received and paid telephone bill, $220.

1 Accounts Affected	2 Category	3 ↑ ↓	4 Rules of Dr. and Cr.
Telephone Expense	**Expense**	↑	**Dr.**
Cash	**Asset**	↓	**Cr.**

	29	Telephone Expense	22000	
		Cash		22000
		Paid telephone bill		

This concludes the journal transactions of Clark's Desktop Publishing Services. (See pages 104 and 105 for a summary of all the transactions.)

LEARNING UNIT 3-1 REVIEW

AT THIS POINT you should be able to:

- Explain the purpose of the accounting cycle. (p. 92)
- Define and explain the relationship of the accounting period to the income statement. (p. 92)
- Compare and contrast a calendar year and a fiscal year. (p. 92)
- Explain the term "natural business year." (p. 92)
- Explain the function of interim reports. (p. 93)
- Define and state the purpose of a journal. (p. 93)
- Compare and contrast a book of original entry and a book of final entry. (p. 93)
- Differentiate between a chart of accounts and a journal. (p. 93)
- Explain a compound entry. (pp. 95–96)
- Journalize business transactions. (pp. 94–95)

Self-Review Quiz 3-1

(The blank forms you need are on pages 3-1 and 3-2 of the *Study Guide with Working Papers.*)

The following are the transactions of Lowe's Repair Service. Journalize the transactions in proper form. The chart of accounts includes Cash; Accounts Receivable; Prepaid Rent; Repair Supplies; Repair Equipment; Accounts Payable; A. Lowe, Capital; A. Lowe, Withdrawals; Repair Fees Earned; Salaries Expense; Advertising Expense; and Supplies Expense.

2015		
June	1	A. Lowe invested $7,000 cash and $5,000 worth of repair equipment in the business.
	1	Paid two months' rent in advance, $1,200.
	4	Bought repair supplies from Melvin Co. on account, $600. (These supplies have not yet been consumed or used up.)
	15	Performed repair work, received $600 in cash, and had to bill Doe Co. for remaining balance of $300.
	18	A. Lowe paid his home telephone bill, $50, using a company cheque.
	22	Advertising bill for $400 from Jones Co. was received, but payment was not due yet. (Advertising has already appeared in the newspaper.)
	25	Paid salaries, $1,400.

Quiz Tip

All titles for the debits and credits come from the chart of accounts. Debits are against the date column and credits are indented. The description is indented further. The PR column is left blank in the journalizing process.

Solution to Self-Review Quiz 3-1

LOWE'S REPAIR SERVICE
GENERAL JOURNAL

Page 1

Date		Account Titles and Description	PR*	Dr.	Cr.
2015 June	1	Cash		7 0 0 0 00	
		Repair Equipment		5 0 0 0 00	
		A. Lowe, Capital			12 0 0 0 00
		Owner investment			
	1	Prepaid Rent		1 2 0 0 00	
		Cash			1 2 0 0 00
		Rent paid in advance (2 months)			
	4	Repair Supplies		6 0 0 00	
		Accounts Payable			6 0 0 00
		Purchase of supplies on account			
	15	Cash		6 0 0 00	
		Accounts Receivable		3 0 0 00	
		Repair Fees Earned			9 0 0 00
		Performed repairs			
	18	A. Lowe, Withdrawals		5 0 00	
		Cash			5 0 00
		Personal withdrawal			
	22	Advertising Expense		4 0 0 00	
		Accounts Payable			4 0 0 00
		Advertising bill			
	25	Salaries Expense		1 4 0 0 00	
		Cash			1 4 0 0 00
		Paid salaries			

*Note that the PR column is left blank in the journalizing process.

NEED HELP?

Let's review first: When recording transactions into a general journal, the debit(s) will be against the date column and the credit(s) will be indented. These titles will come from the chart of accounts. The explanation line will then be indented below the last credit entry. The sum of the left side (Dr.) must equal the sum of the right side (Cr.) for each transaction.

Here are the mind process charts for each transaction. Be sure to remember that the accounts affected come from the chart of accounts. You have six categories:assets, liabilities, capital, withdrawals, revenues, and expenses. You must ask yourself what the company is getting and how it is getting it. Remember to think of expenses and withdrawals as increasing, resulting in a decrease to owner's equity.

June 1	Cash	Asset	↑	Dr.
	Repair Equip.	Asset	↑	Dr.
	A. Lowe, Cap.	Capital	↑	Cr.

Debits are listed first against the date column and credits are indented. This is an investment by the owner. The month is written because the month starts a new page.

1	Prepaid Rent	Asset	↑	Dr.
	Cash	Asset	↓	Cr.

This is a shift in assets, more rent paid in advance by cash. Note that the month is not repeated.

4	Repair Supplies	Asset	↑	Dr.
	Accounts Pay.	Liability	↑	Cr.

This is an example of buy now and pay later. Supplies will not be an expense until they are used up, and are initially debited to this asset account.

15	Cash	Asset	↑	Dr.
	Acc. Receiv.	Asset	↑	Dr.
	Rep. Fees Earn.	Revenue	↑	Cr.

Here we did the work and got some money as well as a promise that the customer will pay later. Note how the two debits are against the date column and the credit is indented.

18	A. Lowe, Withdr.	Withdr.	↑	Dr.
	Cash	Asset	↓	Cr.

The owner increases her withdrawals for personal use and the end result is that the business has less cash.

22	Advertising Exp.	Expense	↑	Dr.
	Accounts	Pay. Liability	↑	Cr.

An expense has been incurred but is not paid for. This expense has created a liability. Think of expenses as always increasing.

25	Salaries Exp.	Expense	↑	Dr.
	Cash	Asset	↓	Cr.

Here the expense is increasing and it is being paid for in cash.

LEARNING UNIT 3-2

Posting to the Ledger: Step 3 of the Accounting Cycle

LO 2

Posting—transferring information from a journal to a ledger

The **general journal** serves a particular purpose: it puts every transaction that the business makes in one place. There are things it cannot do, however. For example, if you were asked to find the balance of the Cash account from the general journal, you would have to go through the entire journal and look for only the cash entries. Then you would have to add up the debits and the credits for the Cash account (separately) and determine the difference between the two totals.

What we really need to do to find balances of accounts is transfer the information from the journal to the **general ledger**. This is called **posting**. In the general ledger, we will accumulate an ending balance for each account so that we can prepare financial statements.

POSTING

Footings are not needed in three-column accounts.

In Chapter 2, we used the T account form to make our ledger entries. T accounts are very simple, but they are not used in the real business world. They are used only for demonstration purposes. In practice, accountants often use a **three-column account** form that includes a column for each account's running balance. Figure 3-2 shows a standard three-column account (all the details are made up). We will use that format in the text from now on to illustrate general ledger accounts.

Figure 3-2
Three-Column Account

GENERAL LEDGER

Accounts Payable — Account No. 211

Date		Explanation	PR	Debit	Credit	Dr. or Cr.	Balance
2016 May	1		GJ1		5000 00	Cr.	5000 00
	3		GJ1		600 00	Cr.	5600 00
	17		GJ1		250 00	Cr.	5850 00
	28		GJ2	2500 00		Cr.	3350 00

Now let's look at how to post the transactions of Clark's Desktop Publishing Services from its journal. The diagram in Figure 3-3 shows how to post the cash line from the journal to the ledger. The steps in the posting process are numbered and illustrated in the figure.

Step 1: In the Cash account in the ledger, record the date (May 1, 2016) and the amount of the entry ($10,000).

Step 2: Record the page number of the journal "GJ1" in the posting reference (PR) column of the Cash account.

Step 3: Calculate the new balance of the account. You keep a running balance in each account as you would in your chequebook. To do this, you take the present balance in the account on the previous line and add or subtract the transaction as necessary to arrive at your new balance. The balances are defined as either a debit or credit amount by placing either Dr. or Cr. in the Dr. or Cr. column next to the balance column.

Step 4: Record the account number of Cash (111) in the posting reference (PR) column of the journal. This is called **cross-referencing**.

The same sequence of steps occurs for each line in the journal. In a manual system like Clark's, the debits and credits in the journal may be posted in the order in which they were recorded, or all the debits may be posted first and then all the credits. If Clark used a computer system, the program would post at the press of a menu button.

Using Posting References

The posting references (PR) are very helpful. In the journal, the PR column tells us which transactions have or have not been posted and also to which accounts they have been posted. In the ledger, the posting reference leads us back to the original transaction in its entirety so that we can see why the debit or credit was recorded and what other accounts were affected. (It leads us back to the original transaction by identifying the journal and the page in the journal from which the information came.)

Figure 3-3
How to Post from Journal to Ledger

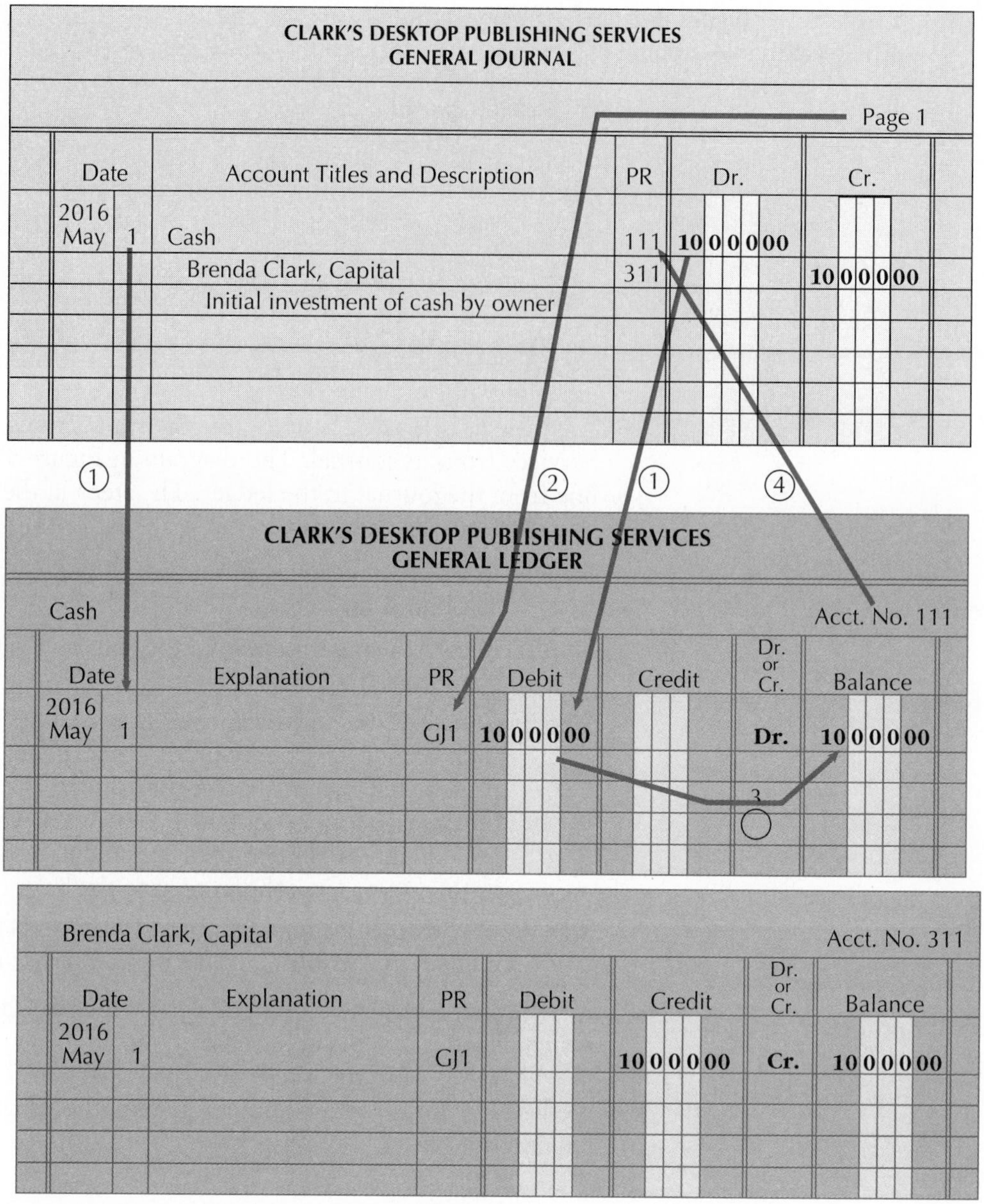

LEARNING UNIT 3-2 REVIEW

AT THIS POINT you should be able to:

- State the purpose of posting. (p. 102)
- Discuss the advantages of the three-column account. (p. 102)
- Identify the elements to be posted. (p. 103)
- From journalized transactions, post to the general ledger. (p. 103)

Self-Review Quiz 3-2

(The forms you need are on pages 3-3 to 3-6 of the *Study Guide with Working Papers.*)

The following are the journalized transactions of Clark's Desktop Publishing Services. Your task is to post information to the ledger. The ledger in your workbook has all the account titles and numbers that were used from the chart of accounts.

CLARK'S DESKTOP PUBLISHING SERVICES
GENERAL JOURNAL

Page 1

Date		Account Titles and Description	PR	Dr.	Cr.
2016 May	1	Cash		10 000 00	
		Brenda Clark, Capital			10 000 00
		Initial investment of cash by owner			
	1	Desktop Publishing Equipment		6 000 00	
		Cash			1 000 00
		Accounts Payable			5 000 00
		Purchase of equipment from Ben Co.			
	1	Prepaid Rent		1 200 00	
		Cash			1 200 00
		Rent paid in advance (3 months)			
	3	Office Supplies on hand		600 00	
		Accounts Payable			600 00
		Purchase of supplies on account from Norris Co.			
	7	Cash		3 000 00	
		Desktop Publishing Fees			3 000 00
		Cash received for services rendered			
	10	Office Salaries Expense		650 00	
		Cash			650 00
		Payment of office salaries			
	17	Advertising Expense		250 00	
		Accounts Payable			250 00
		Bill received but not paid from Al's News Co.			
	20	Brenda Clark, Withdrawals		625 00	
		Cash			625 00
		Personal withdrawal of cash			
	22	Accounts Receivable		5 000 00	
		Desktop Publishing Fees			5 000 00
		Billed Morris Co. for fees earned			

CLARK'S DESKTOP PUBLISHING SERVICES
GENERAL JOURNAL

Page 2

Date		Account Titles and Description	PR	Dr.	Cr.
2016 May	24	Office Salaries Expense		650 00	
		Cash			650 00
		Payment of office salaries			
	28	Accounts Payable		2500 00	
		Cash			2500 00
		Paid half the amount owed Ben Co.			
	29	Telephone Expense		220 00	
		Cash			220 00
		Paid telephone bill			

Posting references

Solution to Self-Review Quiz 3-2

Remember: The PR column remains empty until the entries have been posted.

CLARK'S DESKTOP PUBLISHING SERVICES
GENERAL JOURNAL

Page 1

Date		Account Titles and Description	PR	Dr.	Cr.
2016 May	1	Cash	111	10000 00	
		Brenda Clark, Capital	311		10000 00
		Initial investment of cash by owner			
	1	Desktop Publishing Equipment	121	6000 00	
		Cash	111		1000 00
		Accounts Payable	211		5000 00
		Purchase of equipment from Ben Co.			
	1	Prepaid Rent	115	1200 00	
		Cash	111		1200 00
		Rent paid in advance (3 months)			
	3	Office Supplies on Hand	114	600 00	
		Accounts Payable	211		600 00
		Purchase of supplies on account from Norris Co.			
	7	Cash	111	3000 00	
		Desktop Publishing Fees	411		3000 00
		Cash received for services rendered			
	10	Office Salaries Expense	511	650 00	
		Cash	111		650 00
		Payment of office salaries			

Date		Account Titles and Description	PR	Dr.	Cr.
	17	Advertising Expense	512	250 00	
		Accounts Payable	211		250 00
		Bill received from Al's News Co. but not paid			
	20	Brenda Clark, Withdrawals	312	625 00	
		Cash	111		625 00
		Personal withdrawal of cash			
	22	Accounts Receivable	112	5000 00	
		Desktop Publishing Fees	411		5000 00
		Billed Morris Co. for fees earned			

CLARK'S DESKTOP PUBLISHING SERVICES
GENERAL JOURNAL

Page 2

Date		Account Titles and Description	PR	Dr.	Cr.
2016 May	24	Office Salaries Expense	511	650 00	
		Cash	111		650 00
		Payment of office salaries			
	28	Accounts Payable	211	2500 00	
		Cash	111		2500 00
		Paid half the amount owed Ben Co.			
	29	Telephone Expense	513	220 00	
		Cash	111		220 00
		Paid telephone bill			

Posting to ledger accounts

CLARK'S DESKTOP PUBLISHING SERVICES
PARTIAL GENERAL LEDGER

Cash — Acct. No. 111

Date		Explanation	PR	Debit	Credit	Dr. or Cr.	Balance
2016 May	1		GJ1	10000 00		Dr.	10000 00
	1		GJ1		1000 00	Dr.	9000 00
	1		GJ1		1200 00	Dr.	7800 00
	7		GJ1	3000 00		Dr.	10800 00
	10		GJ1		650 00	Dr.	10150 00
	20		GJ1		625 00	Dr.	9525 00
	24		GJ2		650 00	Dr.	8875 00
	28		GJ2		2500 00	Dr.	6375 00
	29		GJ2		220 00	Dr.	6155 00

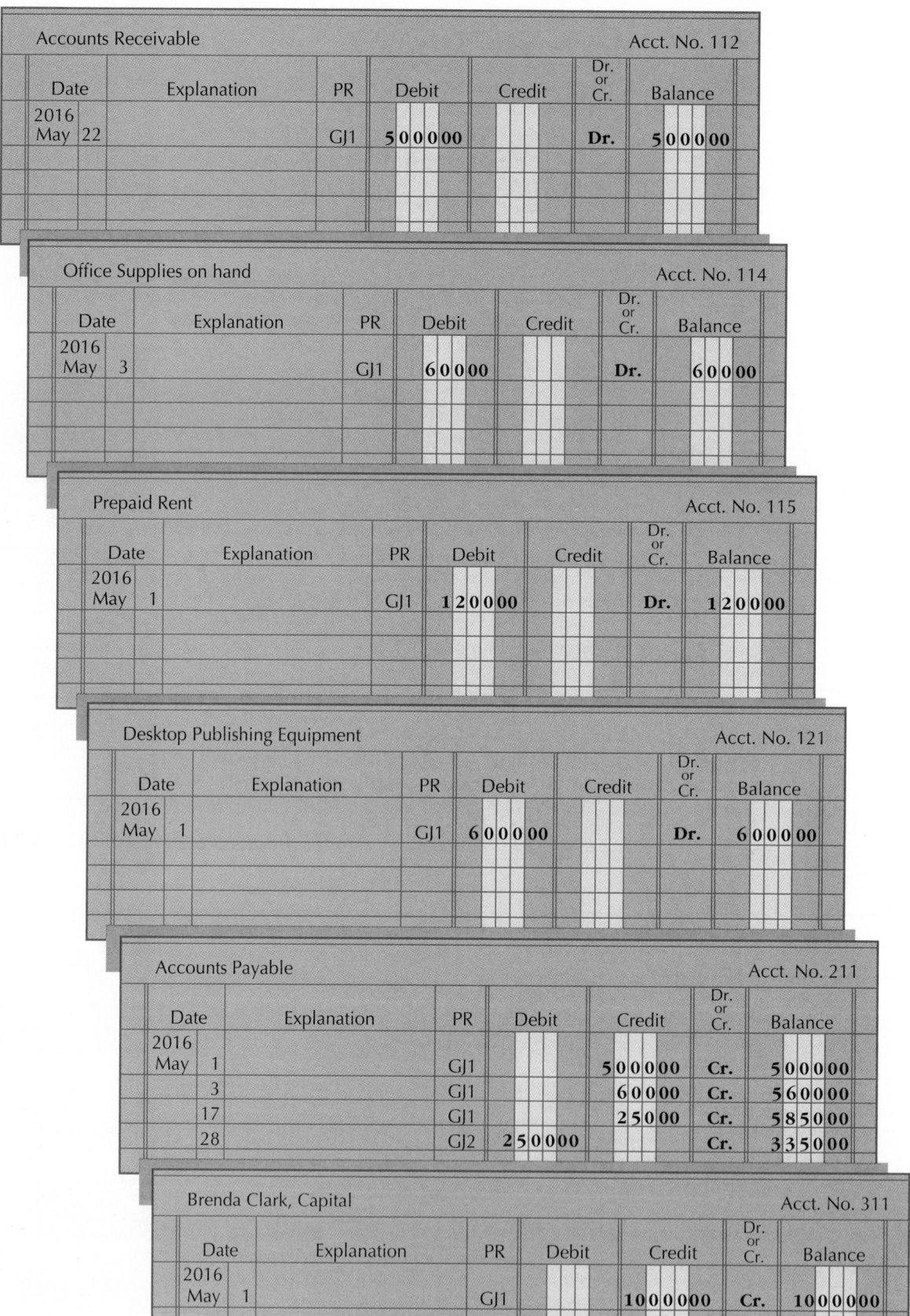

Accounts Receivable — Acct. No. 112

Date		Explanation	PR	Debit	Credit	Dr. or Cr.	Balance
2016 May	22		GJ1	5 000 00		Dr.	5 000 00

Office Supplies on hand — Acct. No. 114

Date		Explanation	PR	Debit	Credit	Dr. or Cr.	Balance
2016 May	3		GJ1	600 00		Dr.	600 00

Prepaid Rent — Acct. No. 115

Date		Explanation	PR	Debit	Credit	Dr. or Cr.	Balance
2016 May	1		GJ1	1 200 00		Dr.	1 200 00

Desktop Publishing Equipment — Acct. No. 121

Date		Explanation	PR	Debit	Credit	Dr. or Cr.	Balance
2016 May	1		GJ1	6 000 00		Dr.	6 000 00

Accounts Payable — Acct. No. 211

Date		Explanation	PR	Debit	Credit	Dr. or Cr.	Balance
2016 May	1		GJ1		5 000 00	Cr.	5 000 00
	3		GJ1		600 00	Cr.	5 600 00
	17		GJ1		250 00	Cr.	5 850 00
	28		GJ2	2 500 00		Cr.	3 350 00

Brenda Clark, Capital — Acct. No. 311

Date		Explanation	PR	Debit	Credit	Dr. or Cr.	Balance
2016 May	1		GJ1		10 000 00	Cr.	10 000 00

Brenda Clark, Withdrawals — Acct. No. 312

Date		Explanation	PR	Debit	Credit	Dr. or Cr.	Balance
2016							
May	20		GJ1	625 00		Dr.	625 00

Desktop Publishing Fees — Acct. No. 411

Date		Explanation	PR	Debit	Credit	Dr. or Cr.	Balance
2016							
May	7		GJ1		3000 00	Cr.	3000 00
	22		GJ1		5000 00	Cr.	8000 00

Office Salaries Expense — Acct. No. 511

Date		Explanation	PR	Debit	Credit	Dr. or Cr.	Balance
2016							
May	10		GJ1	650 00		Dr.	650 00
	24		GJ2	650 00		Dr.	1300 00

Advertising Expense — Acct. No. 512

Date		Explanation	PR	Debit	Credit	Dr. or Cr.	Balance
2016							
May	17		GJ1	250 00		Dr.	250 00

Telephone Expense — Acct. No. 513

Date		Explanation	PR	Debit	Credit	Dr. or Cr.	Balance
2016							
May	29		GJ2	220 00		Dr.	220 00

! *Quiz Tip*

The PR column in the ledger tells from which part of the journal the information came. The PR column in the journal (the last to be filled in) tells to what account number in the ledger the information was posted.

NEED HELP?

Let's review first: The PR column of the journal will show to which account information has been posted. The PR column in the ledger accounts shows from which page of the journal the information came. When updating ledger accounts, two debits added equals a debit balance. Two credits added would be a credit balance. If you have a debit and a credit, take the difference between them; whichever side is larger is the balance (be it a debit or credit).

Partial General Ledger:

Cash: There are nine postings from the journal to the Cash account. GJ1 means that posting came from the general journal, page 1. In the second line, the credit of 1,000 is subtracted from the debit balance in line 1 (10,000) to show a new balance of 9,000 in line 2. In line 3 the 1,200 credit is then subtracted from the 9,000 debit for a current balance of 7,800. Normally the balance is on the side that causes it to increase. Thus cash is normally a debit balance.

Accounts Payable: In this account, the first three postings were credits from the general journal. Note that the month is written only once. Since all three are credits, we add them together, arriving at a credit balance of 5,850. On May 28 a debit of 2,500 is posted and we take the difference between a 5,850 credit balance and a 2,500 debit balance to arrive at a 3,350 ending credit balance.

Office Salaries Expense: Note that here we have two debit postings, so they are added together to arrive at a 1,300 debit balance.

SUMMARY

Posting is copying from the journal to the ledger. The ledger will accumulate information in the form of debits and credits. The last line in the balance column will show whether it is a debit or credit balance. The general journal does not show a running balance like the ledger accounts do.

LEARNING UNIT 3-3

Preparing the Trial Balance: Step 4 of the Accounting Cycle

LO 3 Preparing a trial balance

Did you notice in Self-Review Quiz 3-2 that each account had a running balance figure? Did you know the normal balance of each account in Clark's ledger? As we discussed in Chapter 2, the list of the individual accounts with their balances taken from the ledger is called a **trial balance**.

The trial balance shown in Figure 3-4 was developed from the ledger accounts of Clark's Desktop Publishing Services that were posted and balanced in Self-Review Quiz 3-2. If the information is journalized or posted incorrectly, the trial balance will not be correct.

There are some things the trial balance will not show:

The totals of a trial balance can balance and yet be incorrect.

- The capital figure on the trial balance may not be the beginning capital figure. For instance, if Brenda Clark had made additional investments during the period, the additional investment would have been journalized and posted to the capital account. The only way to tell whether the capital balance on the trial balance is the original balance is to check the ledger capital account to see whether any additional investments were made. This will be important when we make financial reports.

CLARK'S DESKTOP PUBLISHING SERVICES
TRIAL BALANCE
MAY 31, 2016

	Debit	Credit
Cash	6 155 00	
Accounts Receivable	5 000 00	
Office Supplies on hand	600 00	
Prepaid Rent	1 200 00	
Desktop Publishing Equipment	6 000 00	
Accounts Payable		3 350 00
Brenda Clark, Capital		10 000 00
Brenda Clark, Withdrawals	625 00	
Desktop Publishing Fees		8 000 00
Office Salaries Expense	1 300 00	
Advertising Expense	250 00	
Telephone Expense	220 00	
Totals	21 350 00	21 350 00

The trial balance lists the accounts in the same order as in the ledger. The $6,155 figure for cash came from the ledger.

Figure 3-4 The Trial Balance

- There is no guarantee that transactions have been properly recorded. For example, the following errors would remain undetected: (1) a transaction that may have been omitted in the journalizing process; (2) a transaction incorrectly analyzed and recorded in the journal; (3) a journal entry journalized or posted twice; and (4) a journal entry posted to an incorrect account.

WHAT TO DO IF A TRIAL BALANCE DOESN'T BALANCE

The trial balance of Clark's Desktop Publishing Services shows that the total of debits is equal to the total of credits. However, what happens if the trial balance is in balance, but the correct amount is not recorded in each ledger account? Accuracy in the journalizing and posting process will help ensure that no errors are made.

Even if there is an error, the first rule is "Don't panic." Everyone makes mistakes and there are accepted ways of correcting them. Once an entry has been made in ink, correcting an error must always show that the entry has been changed and who changed it. Sometimes the change has to be explained.

SOME COMMON MISTAKES

Correcting the trial balance: what to do if your trial balance doesn't balance.

Using an adding machine that prints amounts on a paper roll can be very helpful in spotting errors. Remember to clear the machine before each series of amounts is entered.

If the trial balance does not balance, the cause could be something relatively simple. Here are some common errors and how they can be fixed:

- If the difference (the amount you are off) is 10, 100, 1,000, and so on, there probably is a mathematical error.
- If the difference is equal to an individual account balance in the ledger, the amount could have been omitted. It is also possible that the figure was not posted from the general journal.
- Divide the difference by 2; then check to see if a debit should have been a credit and vice versa in the ledger or the trial balance. *Example:* \$150 difference ÷ 2 = \$75. This means that you may have placed \$75 as a debit to an account instead of a credit or vice versa.
- If the difference is evenly divisible by 9, a slide or a transposition may have occurred. A **slide** is an error resulting from adding or deleting zeros in writing numbers. For example, \$4,175.00 may have been copied as \$41.75. A **transposition** is the accidental rearrangement of the digits of a number. For example, \$4,175 might have been accidentally written as \$4,157.
- Compare the balances in the trial balance with the ledger accounts to check for copying errors.
- Recompute balances in each ledger account.
- Trace all postings from journal to ledger.

If you cannot find the error after you have done all of this, take a break. Then start all over again.

MAKING A CORRECTION BEFORE POSTING

Before posting, error correction is straightforward. Simply draw a line through the incorrect entry in the journal, write the correct information above the line, and write your initials near the change.

Correcting an Error in an Account Title The following illustration shows an error and its correction in an account title:

		1	Desktop Publishing Equipment		6000 00	
			Cash			1000 00
			Accounts Payable amp ~~Accounts Receivable~~			5000 00
			Purchase of equipment from Ben Co.			

Correcting a Numerical Error Numbers are handled the same way as account titles, as the next change, from 520 to 250, shows:

		17	Advertising Expense		250 00	
			Accounts Payable			amp 250 00 ~~520 00~~
			Bill from Al's News			

Correcting an Entry Error If a number has been entered in the wrong column, a straight line is drawn through it, and the number is then written in the correct column:

		1	Desktop Publishing Equipment		6000 00	
			Cash			1000 00
			Accounts Payable		amp ~~5000 00~~	5000 00
			Purchase of equipment from Ben Co.			

MAKING A CORRECTION AFTER POSTING

It is also possible to correct an amount that is correctly entered in the journal but posted incorrectly to the ledger of the proper account. The first step is to draw a line through the error and write the correct figure above it. The next step is to change the running balance to reflect the corrected posting. Here, too, a line is drawn through the balance and the corrected balance is written above it. Both changes must be initialled.

Desktop Publishing Fees — Acct. No. 411

Date		Explanation	PR	Debit	Credit	Dr. or Cr.	Balance
2016 May	7		GJ1		3000 00	Cr.	3000 00
	22		GJ1		amp 5000 00 ~~500 00~~	Cr.	8000 00 amp ~~3500 00~~

CORRECTING AN ENTRY POSTED TO THE WRONG ACCOUNT

Drawing a line through an error and writing the correction above it is possible when a mistake has occurred within the proper account, but when an error involves a posting to the wrong account, the journal must include a correction accompanied by an explanation. In addition, the correct information must be posted to the appropriate ledger accounts.

Suppose, for example, that as a result of tracing postings from journal entries to ledger accounts, you find that a $180 telephone bill was incorrectly debited as an advertising expense. The following illustration shows how this is done.

Step 1: The error is corrected by making a new entry in the journal, dated with the date when the correction is entered, and the correction is explained.

GENERAL JOURNAL Page 3

Date		Account Titles and Description	PR	Dr.	Cr.
2016					
May	29	Telephone Expense	513	18000	
		Advertising Expense	512		18000
		To correct error in which			
		Advertising Expense was debited			
		for charges to Telephone Expense			

Step 2: The Advertising Expense ledger account is also corrected, by posting the new entry.

Advertising Expense Acct. No. 512

Date		Explanation	PR	Debit	Credit	Dr. or Cr.	Balance
2016							
May	17			17500		Dr.	17500
	23			18000		Dr.	35500
	29	*Correcting entry*	GJ3		18000	Dr.	17500

Step 3: The Telephone Expense ledger account is corrected.

Telephone Expense Acct. No. 513

Date		Explanation	PR	Debit	Credit	Dr. or Cr.	Balance
2016							
May	29		GJ3	18000		Dr.	18000

LEARNING UNIT 3-3 REVIEW

AT THIS POINT you should be able to:

- Prepare a trial balance from a ledger, which uses three-column accounts. (p. 110)
- Analyze and correct a trial balance that doesn't balance. (p. 111)
- Correct journal and posting errors. (pp. 111–113)

Self-Review Quiz 3-3

(The blank forms you need are on page 3-7 of the *Study Guide with Working Papers.*)

1.

Interoffice Memo

TO: Al Vincent

FROM: Professor Jones

RE: Trial Balance

You have submitted to me an incorrect trial balance. Could you please rework and turn it in to me before next Friday?

Note: Individual amounts look okay.

A. RICE
TRIAL BALANCE
OCTOBER 31, 2017

	Dr.	Cr.
Cash		8 0 6 0 00
Operating Expenses		1 7 0 0 00
A. Rice, Withdrawals		4 0 0 00
Service Revenue		5 4 0 0 00
Equipment	5 0 0 0 00	
Accounts Receivable	3 5 4 0 00	
Accounts Payable	2 0 0 0 00	
Supplies	3 0 0 00	
A. Rice, Capital		1 1 6 0 0 00

2. An $8,000 debit to Office Equipment was mistakenly journalized and posted on June 9, 2017, to Office Supplies. Prepare the appropriate journal entry to correct this error.

Quiz Tip

Items in a trial balance are listed in the same order as in the ledger or the chart of accounts. Expect each account to have its normal balance (either debit or credit).

Solution to Self-Review Quiz 3-3

1.

A. RICE
TRIAL BALANCE
OCTOBER 31, 2017

	Dr.	Cr.
Cash	8 0 6 0 00	
Accounts Receivable	3 5 4 0 00	
Supplies	3 0 0 00	
Equipment	5 0 0 0 00	
Accounts Payable		2 0 0 0 00
A. Rice, Capital		1 1 6 0 0 00
A. Rice, Withdrawals	4 0 0 00	
Service Revenue		5 4 0 0 00
Operating Expenses	1 7 0 0 00	
Totals	1 9 0 0 0 00	1 9 0 0 0 00

2.

GENERAL JOURNAL					Page 4
Date		Account Titles and Description	PR	Dr.	Cr.
2017 June	9	Office Equipment		800000	
		Office Supplies			800000
		To correct error in which Office Supplies			
		was debited for purchase of			
		Office Equipment			

NEED HELP?

Let's review first: Items in a trial balance are listed in the same order as in the ledger or the chart of accounts. Expect each account to have its normal balance (either a debit or a credit). No title in the trial balance can have both a debit and credit balance.

List the ending balance of each ledger account (last number listed in the balance columns) and list them in the order of the ledger. They should follow this pattern:

Assets	Dr.
Liabilities	Cr.
Capital	Cr.
Withdrawals	Dr.
Revenues	Cr.
Expenses	Dr.

When complete, the total of all debits will equal the total of the credits. In this case the total is 19,000.

SUMMARY

The trial balance lists the accounts in the same order as the ledger. Be sure to refer to the learning unit for what to do if the trial balance does not balance. It could be a posting mistake or just a math error.

Chapter Assignments

DEMONSTRATION PROBLEM: STEPS 1–4 OF THE ACCOUNTING CYCLE

(The blank forms you need are on pages 3-8 to 3-10 of the *Study Guide with Working Papers.*)

In March, Abby's Employment Agency had the following transactions:

2016 Mar.	1	Abby Todd invested $5,000 cash in the new employment agency.
	4	Bought equipment for cash, $200.
	5	Earned employment fee commission, $200, but payment from Blue Co. will not be received until June.
	7	Paid wages expense, $300.
	8	Abby paid her home utility bill from the company chequebook, $75.
	11	Placed Rick Wool at DVD Corporation, receiving $1,200 cash.

Mar. 15 Paid cash for supplies, $200.
28 Telephone bill received but not paid, $180.
29 Advertising bill received but not paid, $400.

The chart of accounts includes Cash, 111; Accounts Receivable, 112; Supplies, 131; Equipment, 141; Accounts Payable, 211; A. Todd, Capital, 311; A. Todd, Withdrawals, 321; Employment Fees Earned, 411; Wage Expense, 511; Telephone Expense, 521; and Advertising Expense, 531.

Your task is to:

a. Set up a ledger based on the chart of accounts.
b. Journalize (all page 1) and post transactions.
c. Prepare a trial balance for March 31.

Solution to Demonstration Problem

a.

Cash 111

Date		PR	Debit	Credit	Dr. or Cr.	Balance
2016						
Mar	1	GJ1	5000 00		Dr.	5000 00
	4	GJ1		200 00	Dr.	4800 00
	7	GJ1		300 00	Dr.	4500 00
	8	GJ1		75 00	Dr.	4425 00
	11	GJ1	1200 00		Dr.	5625 00
	15	GJ1		200 00	Dr.	5425 00

Accounts Receivable 112

Date		PR	Debit	Credit	Dr. or Cr.	Balance
2016						
Mar	5	GJ1	200 00		Dr.	200 00

Supplies on hand 131

Date		PR	Debit	Credit	Dr. or Cr.	Balance
2016						
Mar	15	GJ1	200 00		Dr.	200 00

Equipment 141

Date		PR	Debit	Credit	Dr. or Cr.	Balance
2016						
Mar	4	GJ1	200 00		Dr.	200 00

Accounts Payable 211

Date		PR	Debit	Credit	Dr. or Cr.	Balance
2016						
Mar	28	GJ1		180 00	Cr.	180 00
	29	GJ1		400 00	Cr.	580 00

A. Todd, Capital 311

Date		PR	Debit	Credit	Dr. or Cr.	Balance
2016						
Mar	1	GJ1		5000 00	Cr.	5000 00

A. Todd, Withdrawals 321

Date		PR	Debit	Credit	Dr. or Cr.	Balance
2016						
Mar	8	GJ1	75 00		Dr.	75 00

Employment Fees Earned 411

Date		PR	Debit	Credit	Dr. or Cr.	Balance
2016						
Mar	5	GJ1		200 00	Cr.	200 00
	11	GJ1		1200 00	Cr.	1400 00

Wage Expense 511

Date		PR	Debit	Credit	Dr. or Cr.	Balance
2016						
Mar	7	GJ1	300 00		Dr.	300 00

Telephone Expense 521

Date		PR	Debit	Credit	Dr. or Cr.	Balance
2016						
Mar	28	GJ1	180 00		Dr.	180 00

Advertising Expense 531

Date		PR	Debit	Credit	Dr. or Cr.	Balance
2016						
Mar	29	GJ1	400 00		Dr.	400 00

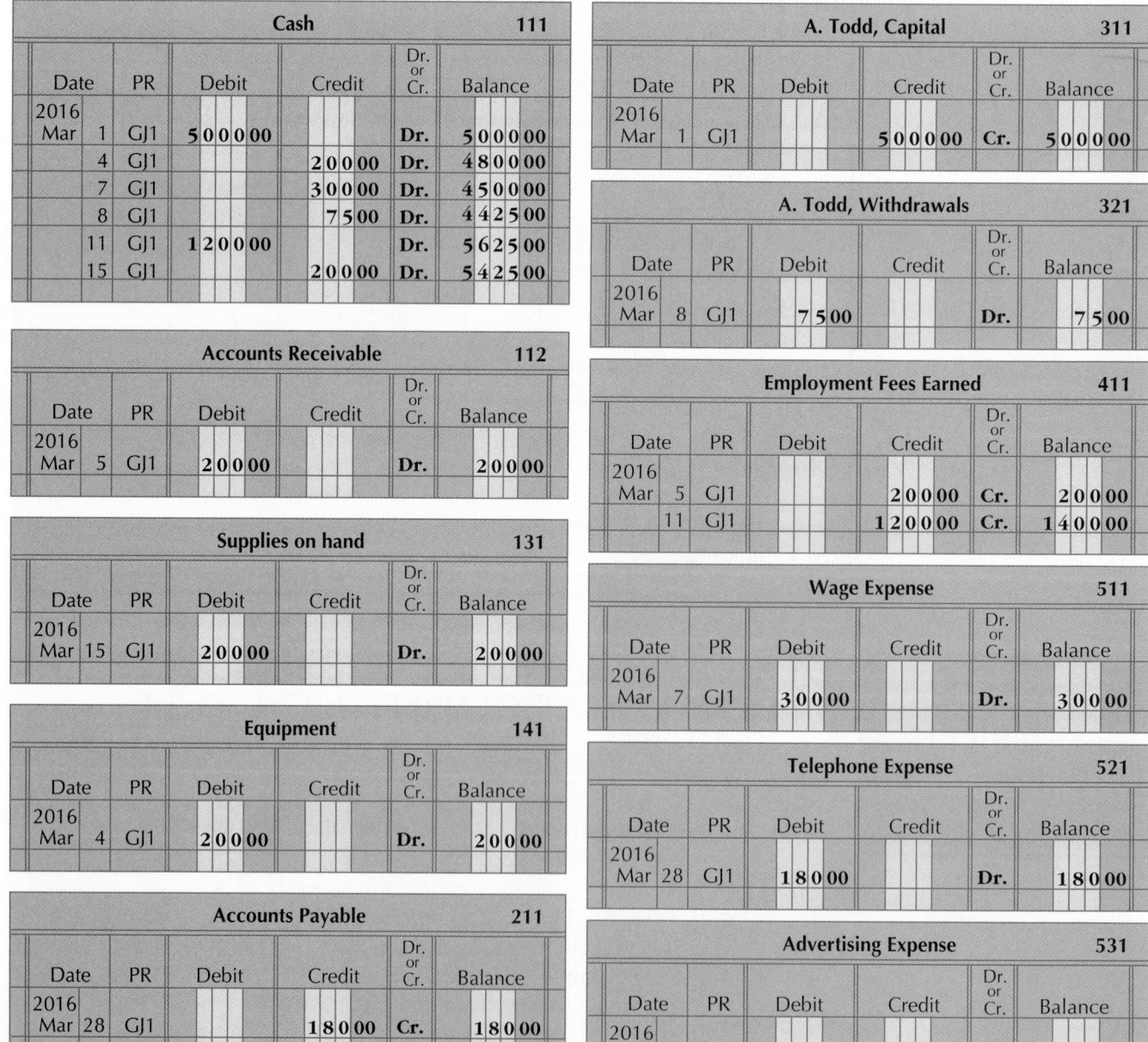

Figure 3-5 General Ledger

b.

Figure 3-6
Journal Entries and Post References

ABBY'S EMPLOYMENT AGENCY

Page 1

Date		Account Titles and Description	PR	Dr.	Cr.
2016 Mar	1	Cash	111	500000	
		A. Todd, Capital	311		500000
		Owner investment			
	4	Equipment	141	20000	
		Cash	111		20000
		Bought equipment for cash			
	5	Accounts Receivable	112	20000	
		Employment Fees Earned	411		20000
		Fees on account from Blue Co.			
	7	Wage Expense	511	30000	
		Cash	111		30000
		Paid wages			
	8	A. Todd, Withdrawals	321	7500	
		Cash	111		7500
		Personal withdrawals			
	11	Cash	111	120000	
		Employment Fees Earned	411		120000
		Cash fees			
	15	Supplies on hand	131	20000	
		Cash	111		20000
		Bought supplies for cash			
	28	Telephone Expense	521	18000	
		Accounts Payable	211		18000
		Telephone bill owed			
	29	Advertising Expense	531	40000	
		Accounts Payable	211		40000
		Advertising bill received			

Solution Tips to Journalizing

1. When journalizing, the PR column is not filled in.
2. Write the name of the debit against the date column. Indent credits and list them below debits. Be sure total debits for each transaction equal total credits.
3. Skip a line after each transaction.

March 1	Cash	A	↑	Dr.	$5,000
	A. Todd, Capital	O.E.	↑	Cr.	$5,000
4	Equipment	A	↑	Dr.	$ 200
	Cash	A	↓	Cr.	$ 200
5	Accts. Receivable	A	↑	Dr.	$ 200
	Empl. Fees Earned	Rev.	↑	Cr.	$ 200
7	Wages Expense	Exp.	↑	Dr.	$ 300
	Cash	A	↓	Cr.	$ 300
8	A. Todd, Withdrawals	O.E.	↑	Dr.	$ 75
	Cash	A	↓	Cr.	$ 75
11	Cash	A	↑	Dr.	$1,200
	Empl. Fees Earned	Rev.	↑	Cr.	$1,200
15	Supplies on hand	A	↑	Dr.	$ 200
	Cash	A	↓	Cr.	$ 200
28	Telephone Expense	Exp.	↑	Dr.	$ 180
	Accounts Payable	L	↑	Cr.	$ 180
29	Advertising Expense	Exp.	↑	Dr.	$ 400
	Accounts Payable	L	↑	Cr.	$ 400

Solution Tips to Posting

The PR column in the ledger Cash account tells you from which page journal information came. After the ledger Cash account is posted, account number 111 is put in the PR column of the journal for cross-referencing.

Note how we keep a running balance in the Cash account. A $5,000 debit balance and a $200 credit entry result in a new debit balance of $4,800.

Figure 3-7 c.

ABBY'S EMPLOYMENT AGENCY
TRIAL BALANCE
MARCH 31, 2016

	Dr.	Cr.
Cash	5 4 2 5 00	
Accounts Receivable	2 0 0 00	
Supplies on hand	2 0 0 00	
Equipment	2 0 0 00	
Accounts Payable		5 8 0 00
A. Todd, Capital		5 0 0 0 00
A. Todd, Withdrawals	7 5 00	
Employment Fees Earned		1 4 0 0 00
Wage Expense	3 0 0 00	
Telephone Expense	1 8 0 00	
Advertising Expense	4 0 0 00	
Totals	6 9 8 0 00	6 9 8 0 00

Solution Tip to Trial Balance

The trial balance lists the ending balance of each title in the order in which they appear in the ledger. The total of 6,980 on the left equals 6,980 on the right.

SUMMARY OF KEY POINTS

Learning Unit 3-1

1. The accounting cycle is a sequence of accounting procedures that are usually performed during an accounting period.
2. An accounting period is the time period for which the income statement is prepared. The time period can be any period up to one year.
3. A calendar year is from January 1 to December 31. The fiscal year is any 12-month period. A fiscal year could be a calendar year but does not have to be.
4. Interim reports are statements that are usually prepared for a portion of the business's calendar or fiscal year (e.g., a month or a quarter).
5. A general journal is a book that records transactions in chronological order. Here debits and credits are shown together on one page. It is the book of original entry.
6. The ledger is a collection of accounts where information is accumulated from the postings of the journal. The ledger is the book of final entry.
7. Journalizing is the process of recording journal entries.

8. The chart of accounts provides the specific titles of accounts to be entered in the journal.
9. When journalizing, the posting reference (PR) column is left blank.
10. A compound journal entry occurs when more than two accounts are affected in the journalizing process of a business transaction.

Learning Unit 3-2

1. Posting is the process of transferring information from the journal to the ledger.
2. The journal and ledger contain the same information but in a different form.
3. The three-column ledger account keeps a running balance of an account.
4. The normal balance of an account will be located on the side that increases according to the rules of debits and credits. For example, the normal balances of liabilities occur on the credit side.
5. The mechanical process of posting requires care in accurately transferring dates, posting references, titles, and amounts.

Learning Unit 3-3

1. A trial balance is a list of the individual accounts with their balances.
2. A trial balance can balance but be incorrect. For example, an entire journal entry may not have been posted.
3. If a trial balance doesn't balance, check for errors in addition, omission of postings, slides, transpositions, copying errors, and so on.
4. Specific procedures should be followed in making corrections in journals and ledgers.

KEY TERMS

Accounting cycle For each accounting period, the process that begins with the analyzing and recording of business transactions into a journal and ends with the completion of a post-closing trial balance (to be described in Chapter 5) (p. 92)

Accounting period The period of time for which an income statement is prepared (p. 92)

Book of final entry A ledger that receives information about business transactions from a book of original entry—a journal (p. 93)

Book of original entry A book that records the first formal information about business transactions—a journal (p. 93)

Calendar year January 1 to December 31 (p. 92)

Cloud Computing Data files are kept on an offsite computer, and accessed using the Internet (p. 93)

Compound journal entry A journal entry that affects more than two accounts (p. 95)

Cross-referencing Adding the account number of the ledger account that was updated to the PR column of the journal, and inserting the journal page on the ledger account (p. 103)

Fiscal year The 12-month period a business chooses for its accounting year (p. 92)

General journal The simplest form of a journal, which records information from transactions in chronological order as they occur, linking the debit and credit parts of transactions (pp. 93, 102)

General ledger A collection of accounts that includes all those needed to contain the individual balances that show up on any of the financial statements (asset accounts, liability and equity accounts, revenue accounts, and expense accounts) (p. 102)

Interim reports Financial reports that are prepared for a month, quarter, or some other portion of the fiscal year (p. 93)

Journal A listing of business transactions in chronological order, with the debit and credit parts of transactions on one page (p. 93)

Journal entry The transaction (debits and credits) that is recorded in a journal once it is analyzed (p. 93)

Journalizing The process of recording a transaction entry in the journal (p. 93)

Natural business year A business's fiscal year that ends at the same time as a slow seasonal period begins (p. 92)

Posting The transferring, copying, or recording of information from a journal to a ledger (p. 102)

Slide The error of adding or deleting zeros when a number is written; for example, 79,200 → 7,920 (p. 111)

Three-column account A running balance account that records debits and credits, has a column for an ending balance (debit or credit), and replaces the standard two-column account we used earlier (p. 102)

Transposition The accidental rearrangement of the digits of a number; for example, 152 for 125 (p. 111)

Trial balance An informal listing of the ledger accounts and their balances that aids in proving the equality of debits and credits (p. 110)

QUICK REVIEW

The following Tips are from Learning Units 3-1 to 3-3. Answer the Assess Your Progress questions and use the How Did You Do? at the bottom of the page to see how well you know the material. The Quick Review provides tips before each Assess Your Progress to help you avoid common accounting errors.

LU 3-1 Analyzing and Recording Business Transactions into a Journal: Steps 1 and 2 of the Accounting Cycle

Tips: When journalizing transactions, be sure to use the Chart of Accounts. It provides the specific titles you will use for either debit(s) or credit(s). You will not use the Chart of Accounts for the explanations in the journal. In the journal, the debit portion of the transaction is listed first, followed by the credit portion. Remember that these titles come from the Chart of Accounts. The total of all debits must equal the total of all credits for each individual transaction.

Assess Your Progress

Answer true or false to the following statements:

1. The ledger is the book of original entry.
2. Compound journal entries must have no more than three credits.
3. Billing a company for services on account would result in a debit to cash.
4. When you journalize, the PR column must be completed.
5. Rent paid in advance is an expense.

LU 3-2 Posting to the Ledger: Step 3 of the Accounting Cycle

Tips: Posting is transferring information from the journal to the ledger. The ledger accounts keep a running balance of each title, while the journal does not. Cross-referencing helps to fill in the PR column of the journal to show the account number that was posted from that line. With computer software, today's posting could be just a click away.

Assess Your Progress

Answer true or false to the following statements:

1. Posting can only be done manually.
2. Posting means transferring information from the ledger to the journal.
3. Cross-referencing means the PR column in the ledger is up to date.
4. Posting can only be done once a month.
5. Posting results in information being accumulated in the journal.

LU 3-3 Preparing the Trial Balance: Step 4 of the Accounting Cycle

Tips: The trial balance is listed in the same order as the general ledger. Only one balance is shown for each account in the trial balance. Keep in mind that the trial balance could be in balance and still be incorrect due to posting twice, missing transactions, or analyzing them incorrectly.

Assess Your Progress

Answer true or false to the following statements:

1. The trial balance is in the same order as the journal.
2. A trial balance can have two balances for some accounts.
3. Slides and transpositions can help locate errors in the trial balance.
4. If a journal entry is posted, no corrections can be made.
5. Account titles that have credit balances are indented.

How Did You Do? Answers to the Assess Your Progress Questions

LU 3-1

1. False—The ledger is the book of final entry.
2. False—Compound journal entries must have more than two accounts.
3. False—Billing a company for services on account would result in a debit to accounts receivable.
4. False—When you post, the PR column is completed.
5. False—Rent paid in advance is an asset.

LU 3-2

1. False—Posting can be done by computer.
2. False—Posting means transferring information from the journal to the ledger.
3. False—Cross-referencing means the PR column is updated in the journal.
4. False—Posting can be done at various times.
5. False—Posting results in information being accumulated in the ledger.

LU 3-3

1. False—The trial balance is in the same order as the ledger.
2. False—A trial balance can have only one balance per title.
3. True.
4. False—If a journal entry is posted, corrections can still be made.
5. False—All account titles are listed with no indentations.

BLUEPRINT OF FIRST FOUR STEPS OF THE ACCOUNTING CYCLE

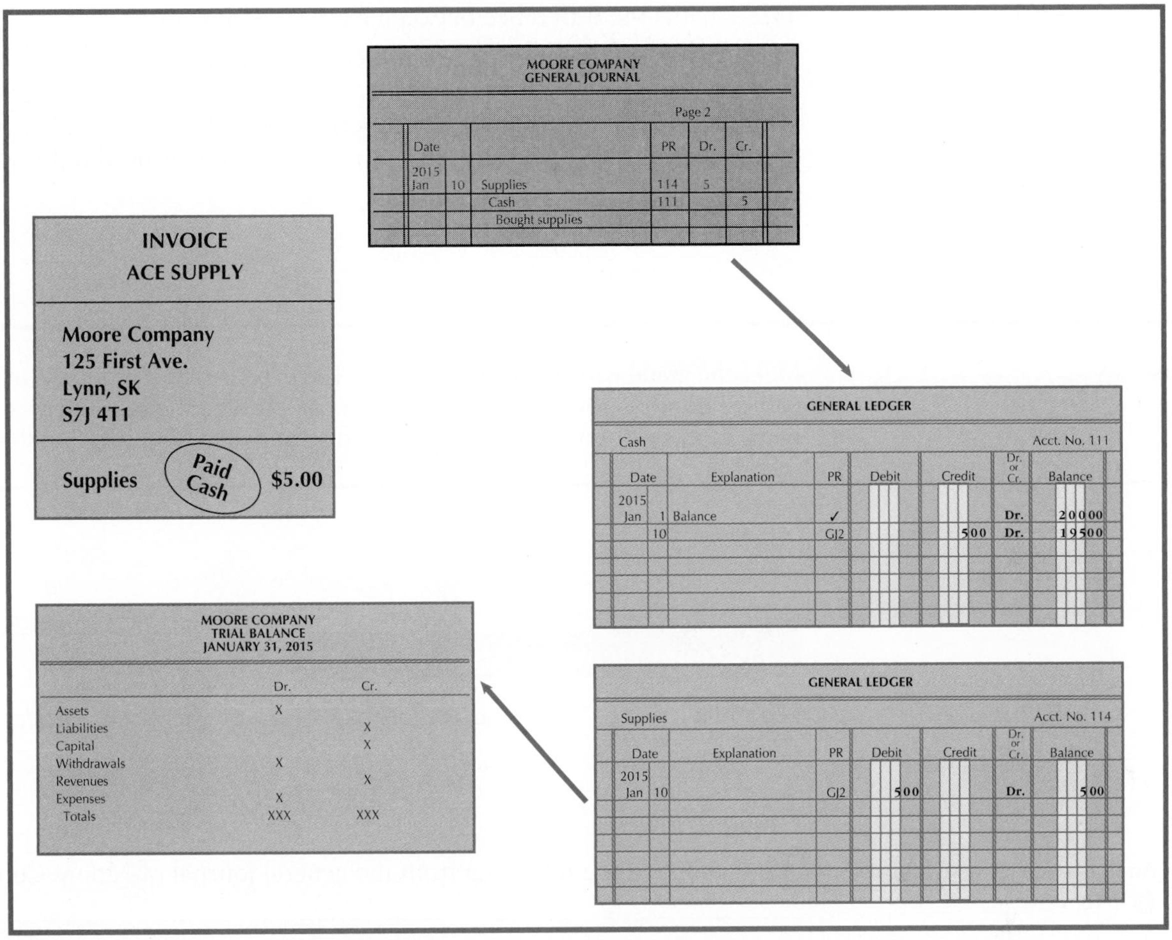

QUESTIONS, CLASSROOM DEMONSTRATION EXERCISES, EXERCISES, AND PROBLEMS

Discussion Questions and Critical Thinking/Ethical Case

1. Explain the concept of the accounting cycle.
2. An accounting period is based on the balance sheet. Agree or disagree.
3. Compare and contrast a calendar year versus a fiscal year.
4. What are interim reports?
5. Why is the ledger called the book of final entry?
6. How do transactions get “linked” in a general journal?
7. What is the relationship of the chart of accounts to the general journal?
8. What is a compound journal entry?
9. Posting means updating the journal. Agree or disagree. Please comment.
10. The side that decreases an account is the normal balance. True or false?

11. The PR column of a general journal is the last item to be filled in during the posting process. Agree or disagree.
12. Discuss the concept of cross-referencing.
13. What is the difference between a transposition and a slide?
14. Jay Simons, the accountant of See Co., wanted to buy a new computer software package for his general ledger. He couldn't do it because all funds were frozen for the rest of the fiscal period. Jay called his friend at Joor Industries and asked whether he could copy its software. Why should or shouldn't Jay do that?

MyAccountingLab

Make the grade with MyAccountingLab! The exercises and problems marked with ● can be found on MyAccountingLab. You can practise them as often as you want, and many of them feature step-by-step guided solutions to help you find the right answer.

Classroom Demonstration Exercises

(The blank forms you need are on page 3-11 of the *Study Guide with Working Papers.*)

General Journal

Analyzing the general journal
❶ (5 min)

1. Complete the following from the general journal of Moore Company.

MOORE COMPANY
GENERAL JOURNAL
Page 1

Date		Account Titles and Description	PR	Dr.	Cr.
2015					
Nov.	19	Cash		900000	
		Equipment		1000000	
		B. Moore, Capital			1900000
		Initial investment by owner			

a. Year of journal entry
b. Month of journal entry
c. Day of journal entry
d. Name(s) of account(s) debited
e. Name(s) of account(s) credited
f. Explanation of transaction
g. Amount of debit(s)
h. Amount of credit(s)
i. Page of journal

General Journal

Explanation of transactions
❶ (5 min)

2. Provide the explanation for each of these general journal entries.

GENERAL JOURNAL						Page 4
Date		Account Titles and Descriptions	PR	Debit	Credit	
2015 June	11	Cash		17 000 00		
		Office Equipment		26 000 00		
		B. Blue, Capital			43 000 00	
		(A)				
	15	Cash		40 00		
		Accounts Receivable		70 00		
		Legal Fees Earned			110 00	
		(B)				
	22	Salary Expense		40 00		
		Cash			40 00	
		(C)				

Posting and Balancing

Balancing general ledger accounts
❷ (5 min)

3. Balance this three-column account. What function does the PR column serve? When will Account 111 be used in the journalizing and posting process?

Name: Cash — Account No. 111

Date		Explanation	PR	Debit	Credit	Dr. or Cr.	Balance
2015 May	1		GJ1	19 00			
	4		GJ1	9 00			
	11		GJ2		6 00		
	14		GJ3	2 00			

The Trial Balance

Preparing an accurate trial balance
❸ (15 min)

4. The following trial balance was prepared *incorrectly.*

Lee Company
Trial Balance
October 31, 2017

	Dr.	Cr.
D. Lee, Capital	30	
Equipment	112	
Rent Expense		17
Advertising Expense		3
Accounts Payable		108
Taxi Fare Income	16	
Cash	17	
D. Lee, Withdrawals		5
Totals	**175**	**133**

a. Rearrange the accounts in the proper order.

b. Calculate the total of the trial balance. (Small numbers are used intentionally so that you can do the calculations in your head.) Assume that each account has a normal balance.

Correcting Entry

When a trial balance does not balance
❸ (5 min)

5. On June 2, 2017, a telephone expense for $210 was debited to Repair Expense. On July 11, 2017, this error was found. Prepare the correcting journal entry. When would a correcting entry *not* be needed?

Exercises

Set A

(The forms you need are on pages 3-12 to 3-16 of the *Study Guide with Working Papers.*)

Analyzing the general journal
❶ (5 min)

3-1A. Prepare journal entries for the following transactions that occurred during October:

2017

Oct.	3	Janet Wills invested $70,000 cash and $6,000 worth of equipment in her new business.
	6	Purchased building for $40,000 on account.
	13	Purchased a truck from Lowell Co. for $16,000 cash.
	17	Bought supplies from Lee Co. on account, $900.

Preparing journal entries
❶ (10 min)

3-2A. Record the following in the general journal of Reggie's Auto Repair Shop.

2016

Jan.	4	Reggie Long invested $16,000 cash in the auto repair shop.
	7	Paid $7,000 for auto repair equipment.
	8	Bought auto repair equipment for $6,000 on account from Lowell Co.
	15	Received $900 for repair fees earned.
	18	Billed Sullivan Co. $900 for services rendered.
	22	Reggie withdrew $300 for personal use.

Posting
❷ (10 min)

3-3A. Post the following transactions to the ledger of King Company. The partial ledger of King Company includes Cash, 111; Equipment, 121; Accounts Payable, 211; and A. King, Capital, 311. Please use three-column accounts in the posting process.

GENERAL JOURNAL

Page 4

Date		Account Titles and Description	PR	Dr.	Cr.
2015 April	6	Cash		17 000 00	
		A. King, Capital			17 000 00
		Cash investment			
	13	Equipment		8 000 00	
		Cash			3 000 00
		Accounts Payable			5 000 00
		Purchase of equipment			

Journalizing, posting, and preparing a trial balance
❶ ❷ ❸ (20 min)

3-4A. From the following transactions for Lowe Company for the month of July, (a) prepare journal entries (assume that it is page 1 of the journal), (b) post to the ledger (use three-column account style), and (c) prepare a trial balance.

2017
July

4 Joan Lowe invested $6,000 in the business.
7 Bought equipment on account, $800 from Lax Co.
15 Billed Friend Co. for services rendered, $4,000.
18 Received $5,000 cash for services rendered.
25 Paid salaries expense, $1,800.
28 Joan withdrew $400 for personal use.

A partial chart of accounts includes: Cash, 111; Accounts Receivable, 112; Equipment, 121; Accounts Payable, 211; J. Lowe, Capital, 311; J. Lowe, Withdrawals, 312; Fees Earned, 411; Salaries Expense, 511.

Correcting the trial balance
❸ (15 min)

3-5A. You have been hired to correct the following trial balance that has been recorded improperly from the ledger to the trial balance.

SUN CO.
TRIAL BALANCE
MARCH 31, 2015

	Dr.	Cr.
Accounts Payable	300000	
A. Sun, Capital		650000
A. Sun, Withdrawals		30000
Services Earned		570000
Concessions Earned	250000	
Rent Expense	140000	
Salaries Expense	350000	
Miscellaneous Expense		130000
Cash	1000000	
Accounts Receivable		120000
Totals	2040000	1500000

Correcting entry
❶ (10 min)

3-6A. On February 5, 2016, Mike Sullivan made the following journal entry to record the purchase of office equipment priced at $1,400 on account. This transaction had not yet been posted when the error was discovered. Make the appropriate correction.

GENERAL JOURNAL

Date		Account Titles and Description	PR	Dr.	Cr.
2016 Feb.	5	Office Equipment		80000	
		Accounts Payable			80000
		Purchase of office equipment on account			

Exercises

Set B

(The forms you need are on pages 3-12 and 3-16 of the *Study Guide with Working Papers.*)

Preparing journal entries
❶ (10 min)

3-1B. Prepare journal entries for the following transactions that occurred during October:

2017 Oct.	3	Janet Wills invested $90,000 cash and $8,000 worth of equipment in her new business.
	6	Purchased building for $50,000 on account.
	13	Purchased a truck from Lowell Co. for $26,000 cash.
	17	Bought supplies from Lee Co. on account, $800.

Preparing journal entries
❶ (10 min)

3-2B. Record the following in the general journal of Reggie's Auto Repair Shop.

2016 Jan.	4	Reggie Long invested $21,000 cash in the auto repair shop.
	7	Paid $9,000 for auto repair equipment.
	8	Bought auto repair equipment for $5,000 on account from Lowell Co.
	15	Received $1,200 for repair fees earned.
	18	Billed Sullivan Co. $980 for services rendered.
	22	Reggie withdrew $500 for personal use.

Posting
❶ (10 min)

3-3B. Post the following transactions to the ledger of King Company. The partial ledger of King Company includes Cash, 111; Equipment, 121; Accounts Payable, 211; and A. King, Capital, 311. Please use three-column accounts in the posting process.

GENERAL JOURNAL — Page 4

Date		Account Titles and Description	PR	Dr.	Cr.
2015 April	6	Cash		17 000 00	
		A. King, Capital			17 000 00
		Cash investment			
	13	Equipment		8 000 00	
		Cash			3 000 00
		Accounts Payable			5 000 00
		Purchase of equipment			

Journalizing, posting, and preparing a trial balance
❶ ❷ ❸ (20 min)

3-4B. From the following transactions for Lowe Company for the month of July, (a) prepare journal entries (assume that it is page 1 of the journal), (b) post to the ledger (use three-column account style), and (c) prepare a trial balance.

2017
July
4 Joan Lowe invested $7,000 in the business.
7 Bought equipment on account, $900 from Lax Co.
15 Billed Friend Co. for services rendered, $4,600.
18 Received $3,000 cash for services rendered.
25 Paid salaries expense, $1,600.
28 Joan withdrew $500 for personal use.

A partial chart of accounts includes: Cash, 111; Accounts Receivable, 112; Equipment, 121; Accounts Payable, 211; J. Lowe, Capital, 311; J. Lowe, Withdrawals, 312; Fees Earned, 411; Salaries Expense, 511.

Correcting the trial balance
❸ (15 min)

3-5B. You have been hired to correct the following trial balance that has been recorded improperly from the ledger to the trial balance.

SUN CO.
TRIAL BALANCE
MARCH 31, 2015

	Dr.	Cr.
Accounts Payable	300000	
A. Sun, Capital		650000
A. Sun, Withdrawals		30000
Services Earned		570000
Concessions Earned	250000	
Rent Expense	140000	
Salaries Expense	350000	
Miscellaneous Expense		130000
Cash	1000000	
Accounts Receivable		120000
Totals	2040000	1500000

Correcting entry
❶ (10 min)

3-6B. On February 5, 2016, Mike Sullivan made the following journal entry to record the purchase of equipment priced at $1,600 on account. This transaction had not yet been posted when the error was discovered. Make the appropriate correction.

GENERAL JOURNAL

Date		Account Titles and Description	PR	Dr.	Cr.
2016 Feb.	5	Office Equipment		80000	
		Accounts Payable			80000
		Purchase of office equipment on account			

Journalizing
❶ (30 min)

Group A Problems

(The forms you need are on pages 3-17 to 3-26 of the *Study Guide with Working Papers.*)

3A-1. Jack Lang operates Jack's Cleaning Service in Victoria. As the bookkeeper, you have been requested to journalize the following transactions:

2016		
Aug.	1	Paid rent for two months in advance, $9,000.
	6	Purchased cleaning equipment on account from Ryan's Supply House, $4,000.
	12	Purchased cleaning supplies from Lee's Wholesale for $900 cash.
	15	Received $1,900 cash from cleaning fees earned.
	19	Jack withdrew $900 for his personal use.
	22	Advertising bill was received from *Sagnicton News* but was still unpaid, $400.
	23	Paid hydro expense, $90.
	26	Paid salaries expense, $700.
	29	Performed cleaning services for $2,100; however, payment will not be received until October.
	29	Paid Ryan's Supply House half the amount owed from August 6 transaction.

Check Figure

August 22

Dr. Advertising Expense $400
Cr. Accounts Payable $400

Your task is to journalize the above transactions. The chart of accounts for Jack's Cleaning Service is as follows:

Chart of Accounts

Assets	**Owner's Equity**
111 Cash	311 Jack Lang, Capital
112 Accounts Receivable	312 Jack Lang, Withdrawals
114 Prepaid Rent	
116 Cleaning Supplies	
120 Office Equipment	**Revenue**
121 Cleaning Equipment	411 Cleaning Fees Earned
Liabilities	**Expenses**
211 Accounts Payable	511 Advertising Expense
	512 Hydro Expense
	514 Salaries Expense

Comprehensive problem: journalizing, posting, and preparing a trial balance
❶ ❷ ❸ (45 min)

3A-2. On June 2, 2017, Betty Rice opened Betty's Art Studio in Toronto. The following transactions occurred in June:

2017		
June	2	Betty Rice invested $12,000 in the art studio.
	3	Paid three months' rent in advance, $1,200.
	4	Purchased $600 worth of equipment from Astor Co. on account.
	6	Received $900 cash for art training workshop for teachers.
	9	Purchased $400 worth of art supplies for cash.
	10	Billed Lester Co. $2,100 for group art lessons for its employees.
	10	Paid salaries of assistants, $600.
	16	Betty withdrew $200 from the business for her personal use.
	27	Paid electrical expense, $140.
	30	Paid telephone bill for June, $210.

Check Figure

Trial Balance Total $15,600

Required

a. The ledger is already set up for you based on the Chart of Accounts.

b. Journalize (using journal page 1) and post the June transactions.

c. Prepare a trial balance as of June 30, 2017.

The chart of accounts for Betty's Art Studio is as follows:

Chart of Accounts

Assets	**Owner's Equity**
111 Cash	311 Betty Rice, Capital
112 Accounts Receivable	312 Betty Rice, Withdrawals
114 Prepaid Rent	
121 Art Supplies	**Revenue**
131 Equipment	411 Art Fees Earned
Liabilities	**Expenses**
211 Accounts Payable	511 Electrical Expense
	521 Salaries Expense
	531 Telephone Expense

Comprehensive problem: journalizing, posting, and preparing a trial balance
❶ ❷ ❸ (45 min)

3A-3. The following transactions occurred in June 2015 for A. French Placement Agency of Fredericton:

2015		
June	1	A. French invested $9,000 cash in the placement agency.
	1	Bought equipment on account from Hook Co., $2,000.
	4	Earned placement fees of $1,600, but payment will not be received until July.
	5	A. French withdrew $100 for his personal use.
	11	Placed a client on a local TV show, receiving $600 cash.
	15	Bought supplies on account from Lyon Co., $500.
	28	Paid telephone bill for June, $160.
	28	Paid wages expense, $300.
	29	Advertising bill from Shale Co. was received but not yet paid, $900.

Check Figure

Trial Balance Total $14,600

The chart of accounts for A. French Placement Agency is as follows:

Chart of Accounts

Assets	**Owner's Equity**
111 Cash	311 A. French, Capital
112 Accounts Receivable	321 A. French, Withdrawals
131 Supplies	
141 Equipment	**Revenue**
	411 Placement Fees Earned
Liabilities	
211 Accounts Payable	**Expenses**
	511 Wages Expense
	521 Telephone Expense
	531 Advertising Expense

Required

a. The ledger is already set up for you based on the Chart of Accounts.

b. Journalize (page 1) and post the June transactions.

c. Prepare a trial balance as of June 30, 2015.

Group B Problems

(The forms you need are on pages 3-17 to 3-26 of the *Study Guide with Working Papers.*)

Journalizing
1 (30 min)

Check Figure

April 22
Dr. Advertising Expense $75
Cr. Accounts Payable $75

3B-1. In April 2016, Jack Lang opened a new cleaning service in Victoria. Please assist him by journalizing the following business transactions:

2016

Apr. 1 Jack Lang invested $6,000 worth of cleaning equipment as well as $3,000 cash in the new business.

2 Purchased cleaning supplies on account from Rex Co., $500.

9 Purchased office equipment on account from Ross Stationery, $400.

12 Jack paid his home telephone bill from the company bank account, $60.

19 Received $600 cash for cleaning services performed.

22 Advertising bill was received but not yet paid, $75.

23 Hydro bill was received but not yet paid, $90.

26 Performed cleaning services for Eastgate School, $700; however, payment will not be received until May.

29 Paid salaries expense, $400.

30 Paid Ross Stationery half the amount owed from April 9 transaction.

The chart of accounts for Jack's Cleaning Service includes: Cash, 111; Accounts Receivable, 112; Prepaid Rent, 114; Cleaning Supplies, 116; Office Equipment, 120; Cleaning Equipment, 121; Accounts Payable, 211; Jack Lang, Capital, 311; Jack Lang, Withdrawals, 312; Cleaning Fees Earned, 411; Advertising Expense, 511; Hydro Expense, 512; and Salaries Expense, 514.

Comprehensive problem: journalizing, posting, and preparing a trial balance
❶ ❷ ❸ (45 min)

Check Figure

Trial Balance Total $9,620

3B-2. In June, the following transactions occurred for Betty's Art Studio of Toronto:

2017		
June	2	Betty Rice invested $6,000 in the art studio.
	2	Paid four months' rent in advance, $1,200.
	3	Purchased art supplies on account from A.J.K., $700.
	6	Purchased equipment on account from Reese Company, $900.
	9	Received $1,300 cash for art training program provided to Northwest Community College.
	10	Billed Long Co. for art lessons provided, $600.
	13	Betty withdrew $400 from the art studio to buy a new power saw for her home.
	16	Paid salaries expense, $400.
	27	Paid telephone bill, $118.
	30	Electricity bill was received but not yet paid, $120.

Required

a. The ledger is already set up for you based on the Chart of Accounts.

b. Journalize (all page 1) and post the June transactions.

c. Prepare a trial balance as of June 30, 2017.

Chart of accounts includes: Cash, 111; Accounts Receivable, 112; Prepaid Rent, 114; Art Supplies, 121; Equipment, 131; Accounts Payable, 211; Betty Rice, Capital, 311; Betty Rice, Withdrawals, 312; Art Fees Earned, 411; Electrical Expense, 511; Salaries Expense, 521; Telephone Expense, 531.

Comprehensive problem: journalizing, posting, and preparing a trial balance
❶ ❷ ❸ (45 min)

Check Figure

Trial Balance Total $9,385

3B-3. In June, A. French Placement Agency of Fredericton had the following transactions:

2015		
June	1	A. French invested $6,000 in the new placement agency.
	4	Bought equipment for cash, $350.
	5	Earned placement fee commission, $2,100, but payment from Avon Co. will not be received until July.
	8	Paid wages expense, $400.
	11	A. French paid his home utility bill using a company cheque, $69.
	12	Placed Jay Diamond on a national TV show, receiving $900 cash.
	15	Paid cash for supplies, $350.
	28	Telephone bill was received but not yet paid, $185.
	29	Advertising bill was received but not yet paid, $200.

The chart of accounts includes: Cash, 111; Accounts Receivable, 112; Supplies, 131; Equipment, 141; Accounts Payable, 211; A. French, Capital, 311; A. French, Withdrawals, 321; Placement Fees Earned, 411; Wages Expense, 511; Telephone Expense, 521; Advertising Expense, 531.

Required

a. The ledger is already set up for you based on the Chart of Accounts.

b. Journalize (all page 1) and post transactions.

c. Prepare a trial balance for June 30, 2015.

Group C Problems

(The forms you need are on pages 3-27 to 3-36 of the *Study Guide with Working Papers.*)

Journalizing
1 (40 min)

3C-1. In March, Etta Standforth opened a financial planning centre in downtown Calgary. Please assist her by journalizing the following business transactions:

Check Figure

March 21
Dr. Advertising Expense $495
Cr. Accounts Payable $495

2015		
Mar.	2	Etta Standforth invested $4,500 worth of computer equipment as well as $9,000 cash in the new business.
	6	Purchased computer supplies on account from Carry Co., $355.
	9	Purchased office equipment on account from A-One Stationery, $1,895.
	13	Etta paid her home telephone bill from the company bank account, $55.
	20	Received $1,875 cash for financial planning services performed.
	21	Advertising bill was received but not yet paid, $495.
	23	Cleaning bill was received but not yet paid, $95.
	27	Performed financial planning services for Harriet Corp., $2,725; however, payment will not be received until April.
	28	Paid salaries expense, $2,100.
	29	Paid A-One Stationery half the amount owed from March 9 transaction, $947.50.
	30	Received bill for repairs on equipment, $250—to be paid in April.

The chart of accounts for the company includes: Cash, 111; Accounts Receivable, 112; Prepaid Rent, 114; Computer Supplies, 116; Office Equipment, 120; Computer Equipment, 121; Accounts Payable, 211; Etta Standforth, Capital, 311; Etta Standforth, Withdrawals, 312; Planning Fees Earned, 411; Advertising Expense, 511; Salaries Expense, 512; Repairs Expense, 513; and Cleaning Expense, 514.

Comprehensive problem: journalizing, posting, and preparing a trial balance
❶ ❷ ❸ (50 min)

Check Figure

Trial Balance Total $29,115

3C-2. In July, the following transactions occurred for Rodger's Fitness Training Studio of Sydney:

2017		
July	2	Rodger Baldwin invested $16,200 in the studio.
	3	Paid three months' rent in advance, $1,650.
	4	Purchased supplies on account from Marlin Supplies, $640.
	7	Purchased equipment on account from Brinkley Company, $8,300.
	8	Received $2,100 cash for fitness training program provided to Anne Webber Dance Group.
	11	Billed Short Co. for lessons provided, $1,400.
	14	Rodger withdrew $759 from the studio to buy a new stereo for his apartment.
	15	Paid salaries expense, $1,350.
	28	Paid telephone bill for studio, $160.
	29	Electricity bill was received but not yet paid, $150.
	31	Advertising bill was received from *City Newspaper* but not yet paid, $325.

Required

a. The ledger is already set up for you based on the Chart of Accounts.

b. Journalize (all page 1) and post the July transactions.

c. Prepare a trial balance as of July 31, 2017.

Chart of accounts includes: Cash, 111; Accounts Receivable, 112; Prepaid Rent, 114; Supplies, 121; Equipment, 131; Accounts Payable, 211; Rodger Baldwin, Capital, 311; Rodger Baldwin, Withdrawals, 321; Fees Earned, 411; Advertising Expense, 511; Electrical Expense, 515; Salaries Expense, 521; Telephone Expense, 531.

Comprehensive problem: journalizing, posting, and preparing a trial balance
❶ ❷ ❸ (50 min)

Check Figure

Trial Balance total $19,830

3C-3. In June, Matt Nepoose Investigative Agency of Thunder Bay had the following transactions:

2016		
June	3	Matt Nepoose invested $15,000 in the new agency.
	4	Bought equipment for cash, $5,100.
	7	Earned investigative fee, $3,200, but payment from client will not be received until later.
	10	Matt paid his home water and gas bill from the company bank account, $107.
	11	Located missing spouse, received $975 cash.
	14	Paid cash for supplies, $270.
	18	Paid wages expense, $1,100.
	25	Received half of the fee earned on June 7, $1,600.
	27	Telephone bill was received but not yet paid, $130.
	28	Advertising bill was received but not yet paid, $525.

The chart of accounts includes: Cash, 111; Accounts Receivable, 112; Supplies, 131; Equipment, 141; Accounts Payable, 211; M. Nepoose, Capital, 311; M. Nepoose, Withdrawals, 321; Investigative Fees Earned, 411; Wages Expense, 511; Telephone Expense, 521; Advertising Expense, 531.

Required

a. The ledger is already set up for you based on the Chart of Accounts.

b. Journalize (all page 1) and post transactions.

c. Prepare a trial balance for June 30, 2016.

On-the-Job Training

(The forms you need are on pages 3-37 to 3-38 of the *Study Guide with Working Papers.*)

Correcting the trial balance
3 (30 min)

T-1. Paul Regan, bookkeeper of Hampton Co., has been up half the night trying to get his trial balance to balance. His results are shown below.

Ken Small, the accountant, compared Paul's amounts in the trial balance with those in the ledger, recomputed each account balance, and compared postings. Ken found the 10 errors listed below the trail balance.

HAMPTON CO.
TRIAL BALANCE
JUNE 30, 2016

	Dr.	Cr.
Office Sales		5720 00
Cash	3260 00	
Accounts Receivable	5660 00	
Office Equipment	8400 00	
Accounts Payable		4160 00
D. Hole, Capital		11560 00
D. Hole, Withdrawals		700 00
Wages Expense	2600 00	
Rent Expense	940 00	
Utilities Expense	26 00	
Office Supplies	120 00	
Prepaid Rent	180 00	

1. $200 debit to D. Hole, Withdrawals, was posted as a credit.
2. Hole, Withdrawals, was listed on the trial balance as a credit.
3. A Note Payable account with a credit balance of $2,400 was not listed on the trial balance.
4. The pencilled footings for Accounts Payable were debits of $5,320 and credits of $8,800.
5. A debit of $180 to Prepaid Rent was not posted.
6. The entry for office supplies bought for $60 was posted as a credit to Office Supplies.
7. A debit of $120 to Accounts Receivable was not posted.
8. A cash payment of $420 was credited to Cash for $240.

9. The pencilled footing of the credits to Cash was overstated by $400.
10. Utilities Expense of $260 was listed in the trial balance as $26.

Assist Paul Regan by preparing a correct trial balance. What advice could you give Ken about Paul? Explain the situation to Paul. Put your answers in writing.

Errors in recording transactions and their relationship to the trial balance
3 (20 min)

T-2. Lauren Oliver, an accountancy lab tutor, is having a debate with some of her assistants. They are trying to find out how each of the following five unrelated situations would affect the trial balance:

1. $5 debit to Cash in the ledger was not posted.
2. $10 debit to Computer Supplies was debited to Computer Equipment.
3. An $8 debit to Wages Expense was debited twice to the account.
4. A $4 debit to Computer Supplies was debited to Computer Sales.
5. $35 credit to Accounts Payable was posted as a $53 credit.

Indicate to Lauren the effect that each situation will have on the trial balance. If a situation will have no effect, indicate that fact. Put in writing how each of these situations could be avoided in the future.

CONTINUING PROBLEM

Preparing financial statements after journalizing, posting, and preparing a trial balance
❶ ❷ ❸ (45 min)

Tony's computer centre is picking up in business, so he has decided to expand his bookkeeping system to a general journal/ledger system. The balances from June have been forwarded to the ledger accounts. The forms are in the *Study Guide with Working Papers*, pages 3-39 to 3-44.

Assignment

1. Use the chart of accounts provided in Chapter 2 (page 91) to record the transactions illustrated by the following documents.

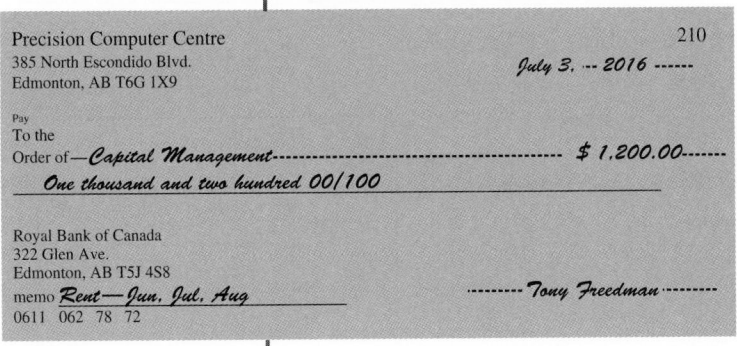

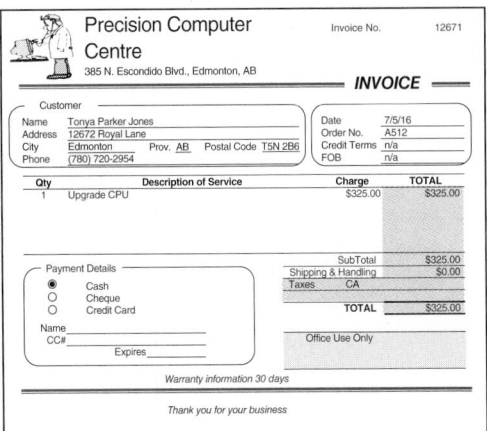

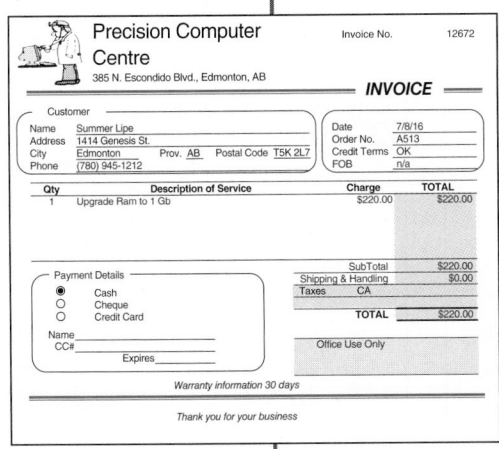

Precision Computer Centre
385 North Escondido Blvd.
Edmonton, AB T6G 1X9
210
July 3, --- 2016 ------

Pay To the Order of—*Capital Management*------------------ *$ 1,200.00*------
One thousand and two hundred 00/100

Royal Bank of Canada
322 Glen Ave.
Edmonton, AB T5J 4S8
memo *Rent—Jun, Jul, Aug* --------*Tony Freedman*--------
0611 062 78 72

Precision Computer Centre
385 N. Escondido Blvd., Edmonton, AB
Invoice No. 12671
INVOICE

Customer
Name: Tonya Parker Jones
Address: 12672 Royal Lane
City: Edmonton Prov. AB Postal Code T5N 2B6
Phone: (780) 720-2954

Date: 7/5/16
Order No.: A512
Credit Terms: n/a
FOB: n/a

Qty	Description of Service	Charge	TOTAL
1	Upgrade CPU	$325.00	$325.00

SubTotal $325.00
Shipping & Handling $0.00
Taxes CA
TOTAL $325.00

Payment Details: ◉ Cash ○ Cheque ○ Credit Card
Name ______ CC# ______ Expires ______
Office Use Only
Warranty information 30 days
Thank you for your business

Precision Computer Centre
385 N. Escondido Blvd., Edmonton, AB
Invoice No. 12672
INVOICE

Customer
Name: Summer Lipe
Address: 1414 Genesis St.
City: Edmonton Prov. AB Postal Code T5K 2L7
Phone: (780) 945-1212

Date: 7/8/16
Order No.: A513
Credit Terms: OK
FOB: n/a

Qty	Description of Service	Charge	TOTAL
1	Upgrade Ram to 1 Gb	$220.00	$220.00

SubTotal $220.00
Shipping & Handling $0.00
Taxes CA
TOTAL $220.00

Payment Details: ◉ Cash ○ Cheque ○ Credit Card
Name ______ CC# ______ Expires ______
Office Use Only
Warranty information 30 days
Thank you for your business

Precision Computer Centre
385 North Escondido Blvd.
Edmonton, AB T6G 1X9
211
July 10, --- 2016 ------

Pay To the Order of—*West Bell Canada* ------------------ *$ 155.00*------
One hundred and fifty five 00/100

Royal Bank of Canada
322 Glen Ave.
Edmonton, AB T5J 4S8
memo *May phone bill transaction (k) Chpt. 2* --------*Tony Freedman*--------
0611 062 78 72

Refer back to Chapter 2, transaction (k).

Jeannine Sparks
1919 Sierra St.
Edmonton, AB T6H 3J5
251
July 12, --2016------

Pay To the Order of—*Precision Computer Centre* ------------------ *$ 850.00*------
Eight Hundred and Fifty dollars 00/100

First National Bank
322 Cardiff Ave.
Edmonton, AB T5J 3E6
memo *Computer Fixed, Transaction (o) Chpt. 2* -------*Jeannine Sparks*--------
0822 062 78 27

Refer back to Chapter 2, transaction (o).

Precision Computer Centre
385 North Escondido Blvd.
Edmonton, AB T6G 1X9
212
July 15, --- 2016 ------

Pay To the Order of—*Computer Connection* ------------------ *$ 200.00*------
Two hundred dollars and 00/100

Royal Bank of Canada
322 Glen Ave.
Edmonton, AB T5J 4S8
memo *Account due from transaction (s) Chpt. 2* --------*Tony Freedman*--------
0611 062 78 72

Refer back to Chapter 2, transaction (s).

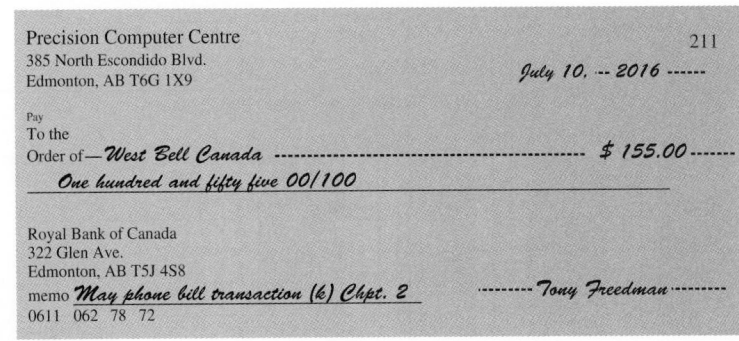

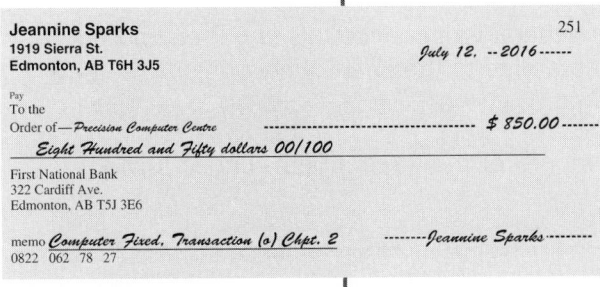

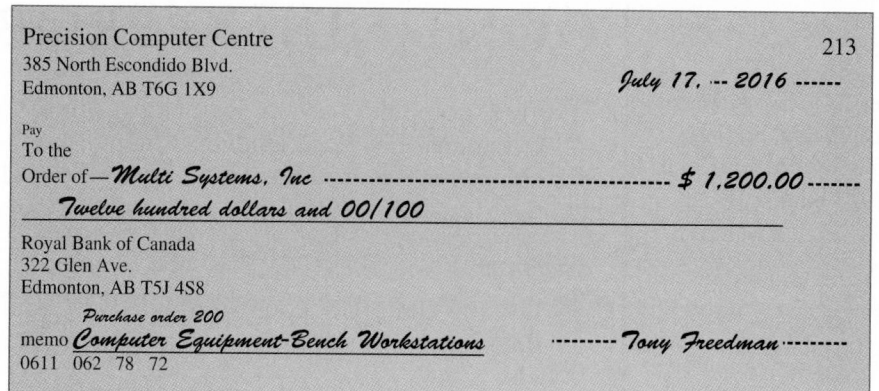

Precision Computer Centre
385 North Escondido Blvd.
Edmonton, AB T6G 1X9

213

July 17, -- 2016 ------

Pay
To the
Order of—*Multi Systems, Inc* -- *$ 1,200.00* ------

Twelve hundred dollars and 00/100

Royal Bank of Canada
322 Glen Ave.
Edmonton, AB T5J 4S8

Purchase order 200
memo *Computer Equipment-Bench Workstations* -------- *Tony Freedman* --------

0611 062 78 72

Purchased computer shop equipment.

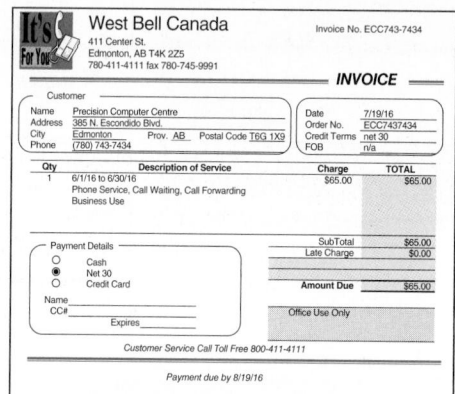

West Bell Canada
411 Center St.
Edmonton, AB T4K 2Z5
780-411-4111 fax 780-745-9991

Invoice No. ECC743-7434

INVOICE

Customer
Name: Precision Computer Centre
Address: 385 N. Escondido Blvd.
City: Edmonton Prov. AB Postal Code T6G 1X9
Phone: (780) 743-7434

Date: 7/19/16
Order No.: ECC7437434
Credit Terms: net 30
FOB: n/a

Qty	Description of Service	Charge	TOTAL
1	6/1/16 to 6/30/16 Phone Service, Call Waiting, Call Forwarding Business Use	$65.00	$65.00

Payment Details
○ Cash
◉ Net 30
○ Credit Card
Name ________
CC# ________
Expires ________

SubTotal	$65.00
Late Charge	$0.00
Amount Due	$65.00

Office Use Only

Customer Service Call Toll Free 800-411-4111

Payment due by 8/19/16

City Electric
1515 Industrial Blvd.
Edmonton, AB T6K 1L7
780-745-1999 fax 780-754-6622

Invoice No. A60692443

INVOICE

Customer
Name: Precision Computer Centre
Address: 385 N. Escondido Blvd.
City: Edmonton Prov. AB Postal Code T6G 1X9
Phone: (780) 743-7434

Date: 7/24/16
Order No.: 385-66725-9045
Credit Terms: net 30
FOB: n/a

Qty	Description of Service	Charge	TOTAL
1	6/1/16 to 6/30/16 Baseline Allowance 241 kWh @ 1270	$95.00	$95.00

Payment Details
○ Cash
◉ Net 30
○ Credit Card
Name ________
CC# ________
Expires ________

SubTotal	$95.00
Late Charge	$0.00
Amount Due	$95.00

Office Use Only

Questions? Please Call: 1-800-411-7227

Payment due by 8/22/16

Precision Computer Centre
385 N. Escondido Blvd., Edmonton, AB

Invoice No. 12673

INVOICE

Customer
Name: Mike Hammer
Address: 300 Carisbad Dr.
City: Edmonton Prov. AB Postal Code T5N 2B6
Phone: (780) 720-2199

Date: 7/26/16
Order No.: A514
Credit Terms: n/a
FOB: n/a

Qty	Description of Service	Charge	TOTAL
1	add video card	$140.00	$140.00

Payment Details
◉ Cash
○ Cheque
○ Credit Card
Name ________
CC# ________
Expires ________

SubTotal	$140.00
Shipping & Handling	$0.00
Taxes CA	
TOTAL	$140.00

Office Use Only

Warranty information 30 days

Thank you for your business

Precision Computer Centre
385 N. Escondido Blvd., Edmonton, AB

Invoice No. 12674

INVOICE

Customer
Name: Dr. Anthony Pitale
Address: 229 Diamond Rich Ave.
City: Edmonton Prov. AB Postal Code T5K 2L7
Phone: (780) 729-2777

Date: 7/30/16
Order No.: A515
Credit Terms: net 15 days
FOB: n/a

Qty	Description of Service	Charge	TOTAL
1	Set up Network Server	$2,600.00	$2,600.00

Payment Details
○ Cash/Cheque
◉ Net 15 days
○ Credit Card
Name ________
CC# ________
Expires ________

SubTotal	$2,600.00
Shipping & Handling	$0.00
Taxes CA	
TOTAL	$2,600.00

Office Use Only

Warranty information 30 days

Thank you for your business

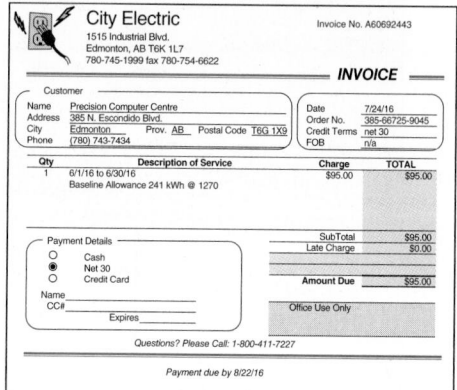

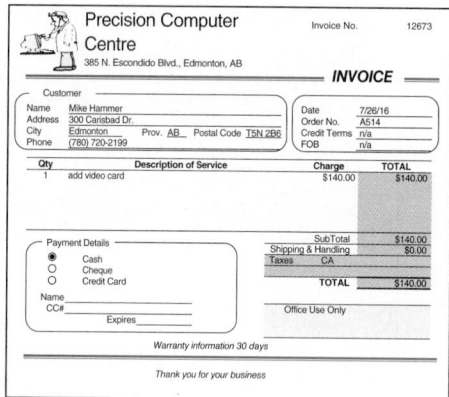

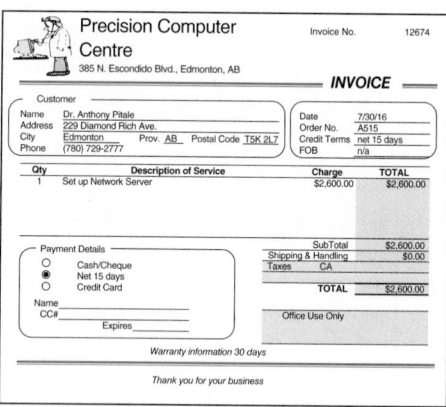

2. Post all transactions to the general ledger accounts (the Prepaid Rent account No. 1025 has been added to the chart of accounts).
3. Prepare a trial balance for July 31, 2016.
4. Prepare the financial statements for the three months ended July 31, 2016.

CHAPTER 4

The Accounting Cycle Continued

PREPARING WORKSHEETS AND FINANCIAL STATEMENTS

LEARNING OBJECTIVES

- **LO 1** Making adjustments for prepaid rent, office supplies, depreciation on equipment, and accrued salaries (p. 143)
- **LO 2** Preparing an adjusted trial balance on the worksheet (p. 149)
- **LO 3** Completing the income statement and balance sheet sections of the worksheet (p. 152)
- **LO 4** Preparing financial statements from the worksheet (p. 156)

Designing a new product for today's marketplace is a complex task. Products like hybrid or electric cars or an ultrabook computer take years to be completely ready for the market, and even then are sometimes subject to recalls. Whether it is tires on a car or laptop batteries, it seems not a week goes by without news of yet another recall of some complicated device. To help design these complex products, engineers and scientists use powerful computer software to keep everything organized and moving forward.

Accountants also use something similar to keep themselves organized when producing financial statements. A worksheet allows accountants to manage the process of moving from a trial balance to finished financial statements in an orderly and managed way. Most such worksheets are best done on a computer these days, but the essence of the tool is described and illustrated in this chapter. Completing this chapter will aid you in understanding the logical flow of the accounting process and also help you to better understand how financial statements are produced.

In the accompanying diagram, steps 1–4 show the steps of the accounting cycle that were completed for Clark's Desktop Publishing Services in the last chapter. This chapter continues the cycle with steps 5 and 6, the preparation of a worksheet and the three financial statements.

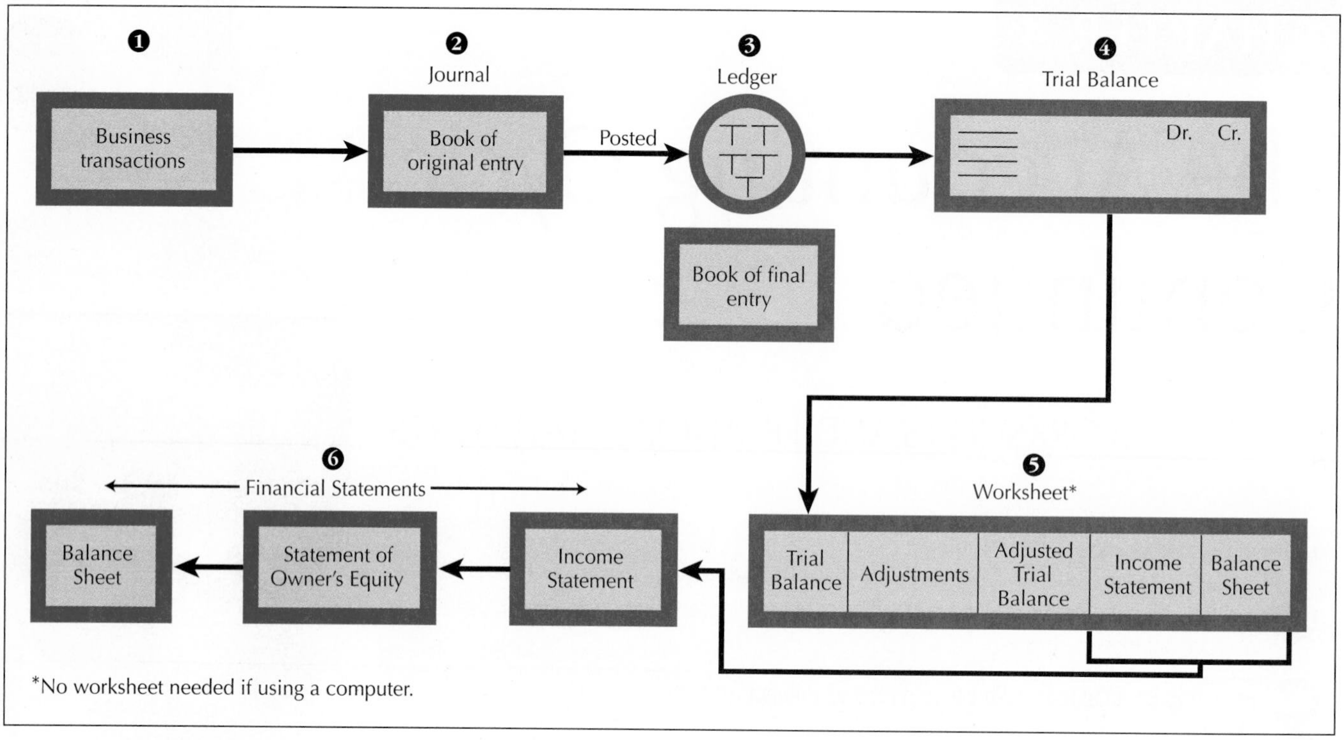

The worksheet is not a formal report, so no dollar signs appear on it. Because it is a ruled form, there are no commas either.

An accountant uses a **worksheet** to organize and check data before preparing the financial reports necessary to complete the accounting cycle. The most important function of the worksheet is to allow the accountant to find and correct errors before financial statements are prepared. In a way, a worksheet acts as the accountant's scratch pad. No one sees the worksheet once the formal reports are prepared. The beginning of a sample worksheet is shown in Figure 4-1.

CLARK'S DESKTOP PUBLISHING SERVICES
WORKSHEET
FOR THE MONTH ENDED MAY 31, 2016

Account Titles	Trial Balance		Adjustments		Adjusted Trial Balance		Income Statement	
	Dr.	Cr.	Dr.	Cr.	Dr.	Cr.	Dr.	Cr.
Cash	6155 00							
Accounts Receivable	5000 00							
Office Supplies	600 00							
Prepaid Rent	1200 00							
Desktop Publishing Equipment	6000 00							
Accounts Payable		3350 00						
Brenda Clark, Capital		10000 00						
Brenda Clark, Withdrawals	625 00							
Desktop Publishing Fees		8000 00						
Office Salaries Expense	1300 00							
Advertising Expense	250 00							
Telephone Expense	220 00							
	21350 00	21350 00						

Figure 4-1 Sample Worksheet—Started, with Trial Balance

LEARNING UNIT 4-1

Step 5 of the Accounting Cycle: Preparing a Worksheet

> As is true for all accounting statements, the heading includes the name of the company, the name of the report, the date, and the accounting period covered.

The accounts listed on the far left of the worksheet are taken from the ledger. The rest of the worksheet has five sections: trial balance, adjustments, adjusted trial balance, income statement, and balance sheet. Each of these sections is divided into debit and credit columns. Refer often to the special overlays in Figure 4-5 (see page 148b) as you study this learning unit. The transparencies illustrating the completion of a worksheet can be very useful to your understanding of the process.

THE TRIAL BALANCE SECTION

> Worksheets can be completed using spreadsheet software such as Excel. If your worksheets are carefully designed, several types of errors can be prevented.

We discussed how to prepare a trial balance in Chapter 3. Some companies prepare a separate trial balance; others, such as Clark's Desktop Publishing Services, prepare the trial balance directly on the worksheet. Every account in the ledger that has a balance is entered in the trial balance. It is not common to include account numbers in the Trial Balance, although this could be done if the accountant thought it helpful. Additional titles from the ledger are added as they are needed. (We will show this later.)

THE ADJUSTMENTS SECTION

> **LO 1** Making adjustments for prepaid rent, office supplies, depreciation on equipment, and accrued salaries

Chapters 1 to 3 discussed transactions that occurred with outside suppliers and companies. In a real business, inside transactions also occur during the accounting cycle. These transactions must be recorded too. At the end of the worksheet process, the accountant will have all of the business's accounts up to date and ready to be used to prepare the formal financial statements. By analyzing each of Clark's accounts on the worksheet, the accountant will be able to identify specific accounts that must be **adjusted** to bring them up to date. The accountant for Clark's Desktop Publishing Services needs to adjust the following accounts:

A. Office Supplies
B. Prepaid Rent
C. Desktop Publishing Equipment
D. Office Salaries Expense

Let's look at how to analyze and adjust each of these accounts.

A. Adjusting the Office Supplies Account

> The adjustment for supplies deals with the amount of supplies used up.

On May 31, the accountant found out that the company had only $100 worth of office supplies on hand. When the company originally purchased the $600 worth of office supplies, they were considered an asset. However, as the supplies get used up, they become an expense.

- Office supplies available, $600
- Office supplies left or on hand as of May 31, $100
- Office supplies used up in the operation of the business for the month of May, $500

As a result, the asset Office Supplies on the trial balance is too high (it should be $100, not $600). At the same time, if we don't show the additional expense of supplies used, the company's *net income* will be too high.

If Clark's accountant does not adjust the trial balance to reflect the change, the company's net income would be too high on the income statement and both sides (assets and owner's equity) of the balance sheet also would be too high.

> Adjustments affect both the income statement and the balance sheet.
>
> **Office Supplies Expense 514**
>
> | Dr. | Cr. |
> |---|---|
> | 500 | |
>
> This is supplies used up.
>
> **Office Supplies 114**
>
> | Dr. | Cr. |
> |---|---|
> | 600 | 500 |
> | 100 | |
>
> This is supplies on hand.

Now let's look at the adjustment for office supplies in terms of the transaction analysis chart.

Accounts Affected	Category	↑ ↓	Rules
Office Supplies Expense	Expense	↑	Dr.
Office Supplies	Asset	↓	Cr.

Will go on income statement. (Dr.)

Will go on balance sheet. (Cr.)

For our discussion, the letter A is used to code the Office Supplies adjustment because it is the first adjustment.

The Office Supplies Expense account comes from the Chart of Accounts on page 94. Since it is not listed in the trial balance account titles, it must be listed below the trial balance. Let's see how we enter this adjustment on the worksheet.

Note: All accounts listed below the trial balance will be *increasing*.

Place $500 in the debit column of the adjustments section on the same line as Office Supplies Expense. Place $500 in the credit column of the adjustments section on the same line as Office Supplies. The numbers in the adjustment column show what is used, *not* what is on hand.

CLARK'S DESKTOP PUBLISHING SERVICES
WORKSHEET
FOR THE MONTH ENDED MAY 31, 2016

Account Titles	Trial Balance Dr.	Trial Balance Cr.	Adjustments Dr.	Adjustments Cr.
Cash	6 1 5 5 00			
Accounts Receivable	5 0 0 0 00			
Office Supplies	6 0 0 00			(A) 5 0 0 00
Prepaid Rent	1 2 0 0 00			
Desktop Publishing Equipment	6 0 0 0 00			
Accounts Payable		3 3 5 0 00		
Brenda Clark, Capital		10 0 0 0 00		
Brenda Clark, Withdrawals	6 2 5 00			
Desktop Publishing Fees		8 0 0 0 00		
Office Salaries Expense	1 3 0 0 00			
Advertising Expense	2 5 0 00			
Telephone Expense	2 2 0 00			
	21 3 5 0 00	21 3 5 0 00		
Office Supplies Expense			(A) 5 0 0 00	

A decrease in Office Supplies, $500

An increase in Office Supplies Expense, $500

The Office Supplies Expense account indicates the amount of supplies used up. It is listed below other trial balance accounts since it was not on the original trial balance.

B. Adjusting the Prepaid Rent Account

Back on May 1, Clark's Desktop Publishing Services paid three months' rent in advance. The accountant realized that the rent expense would be $400 per month ($1,200 ÷ 3 months = $400).

Remember, when rent expense is paid in advance, it is considered an asset called *prepaid rent.* When the asset, prepaid rent, begins to expire or be used up, it becomes an expense. Now it is May 31, and one month's prepaid rent has become an expense.

A debit will increase the account Office Supplies Expense; a credit will reduce the asset account Office Supplies.

Adjusting Prepaid Rent: On page 110 the trial balance showed a figure for Prepaid Rent of $1,200. The amount of rent *expired* is the adjustment figure used to update Prepaid Rent and Rent Expense.

Rent Expense 515

400	

Prepaid Rent 115

1,200	400
800	

Take this one slowly.

Original cost of $6,000 for desktop publishing equipment remains *unchanged* after adjustments.

How is this handled? Should the account be $1,200, or is there really only $800 of prepaid rent left as of May 31? What do we need to do to bring prepaid rent to the "true" balance? The answer is that we must increase Rent Expense by $400 and decrease Prepaid Rent by $400.

Without this adjustment, the expenses for Clark's Desktop Publishing Services for May will be too low, and the asset Prepaid Rent will be too high. If unadjusted amounts were used in the formal reports, the net income shown on the income statement would be too high, and both sides (assets and owner's equity) would be too high on the balance sheet.

In terms of our transaction analysis chart, the adjustment would look like this:

Will go on income statement.

Accounts Affected	Category	↑ ↓	Rules
Rent Expense	Expense	↑	Dr.
Prepaid Rent	Asset	↓	Cr.

Will go on balance sheet.

Like the Office Supplies Expense account, the Rent Expense account comes from the chart of accounts on page 94.

The worksheet on page 146 shows how to enter an adjustment to Prepaid Rent.

C. Adjusting the Desktop Publishing Equipment Account for Depreciation

The life of the asset affects how it is adjusted. The two accounts we discussed above, Office Supplies and Prepaid Rent, involved things that are used up relatively quickly. Equipment—like desktop publishing equipment—is expected to last much longer. Also, it is expected to help produce revenue over a longer period. That is why accountants treat it differently. The balance sheet reports the **historical cost**, or original cost, of the equipment. The original cost also is reflected in the ledger. The adjustment shows how the cost of the equipment is allocated (spread) to the income statement over its expected useful life. This spreading is called **depreciation**. To depreciate the equipment, we have to figure out how much of its cost is "used up" each month. Then we have to keep a running total of how that depreciation mounts up over time. Canada Revenue Agency has a specific set of rules (called **Capital Cost Allowance** rules), which tell how businesses in Canada may depreciate their assets for tax purposes. For accounting reports, however, different methods can be used to calculate depreciation. We will use the simplest method—straight-line depreciation—to calculate the depreciation of Clark's Desktop Publishing Services' equipment. Under the straight-line method, equal amounts are taken over successive periods of time. There are several other methods of calculating depreciation, but these are not covered in this chapter, but an appendix chapter covers the topic in detail.

The Rent Expense is the second account to be adjusted. We label it B as a reference for our discussion.

Rent Expense is listed below other trial balance accounts since it was not on the original trial balance.

Again, note that accounts listed below the trial balance are always increasing.

CLARK'S DESKTOP PUBLISHING SERVICES
WORKSHEET
FOR THE MONTH ENDED MAY 31, 2016

Account Titles	Trial Balance Dr.	Trial Balance Cr.	Adjustments Dr.	Adjustments Cr.
Cash	6155 00			
Accounts Receivable	5000 00			
Office Supplies	600 00			(A) 500 00
Prepaid Rent	1200 00			(B) 400 00
Desktop Publishing Equipment	6000 00			
Accounts Payable		3350 00		
Brenda Clark, Capital		10000 00		
Brenda Clark, Withdrawals	625 00			
Desktop Publishing Fees		8000 00		
Office Salaries Expense	1300 00			
Advertising Expense	250 00			
Telephone Expense	220 00			
	21350 00	21350 00		
Office Supplies Expense			(A) 500 00	
Rent Expense			(B) 400 00	

A decrease in Prepaid Rent, $400

An increase in Rent Expense, $400

The calculation of depreciation for the year for Clark's Desktop Publishing Services is as follows:

$$\frac{\text{Cost of Equipment} - \text{Residual Value}}{\text{Estimated Years of Usefulness}}$$

Assume equipment has a five-year life.

Desktop publishing equipment has an expected life of approximately five years. At the end of that time, the property's value is called its "residual value." Think of **residual value** as the estimated value of the equipment at the end of the fifth year. For Clark, the equipment has an estimated residual value of $1,200.

$$\frac{\$6{,}000 - \$1{,}200}{5 \text{ Years}} = \frac{\$4{,}800}{5} = \$960 \text{ depreciation per year}$$

Clark's will record $960 of depreciation each year.

Our trial balance is for one month, so we must determine the adjustment for that month:

$$\frac{\$960}{12 \text{ Months}} = \$80 \text{ depreciation per month}$$

Depreciation is an expense reported on the income statement.

This $80 is known as *Depreciation Expense* and will be shown on the income statement.

Next, we have to create a new account that can keep a running total of the depreciation amount apart from the original cost of the equipment. That account is called **Accumulated Depreciation**.

Accumulated Depreciation

Dr.	Cr.
–	+

is a contra-asset account found on the balance sheet.

The Accumulated Depreciation account shows the amount of depreciation that has been taken or accumulated over a period of time. This is a **contra-asset account**; it has a normal balance opposite that of an asset such as equipment. Accumulated Depreciation will summarize, accumulate, or build up the amount of depreciation that is taken on the desktop publishing equipment over its estimated useful life.

This is how it would look on a partial balance sheet of Clark's Desktop Publishing Services.

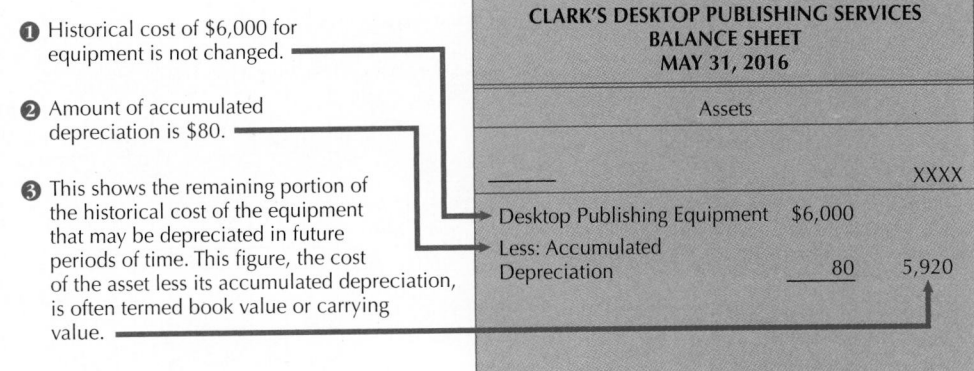

At the end of June the accumulated depreciation will be $160, but historical cost will stay at $6,000.

Important point: Book value is not the same as market value.

❶ Historical cost of $6,000 for equipment is not changed.

❷ Amount of accumulated depreciation is $80.

❸ This shows the remaining portion of the historical cost of the equipment that may be depreciated in future periods of time. This figure, the cost of the asset less its accumulated depreciation, is often termed book value or carrying value.

CLARK'S DESKTOP PUBLISHING SERVICES BALANCE SHEET MAY 31, 2016		
Assets		
____		XXXX
Desktop Publishing Equipment	$6,000	
Less: Accumulated Depreciation	80	5,920

Recording depreciation as an expense does not mean that there is any current payment of cash.

Let's summarize the key points before going on to enter the adjustment on the worksheet:

1. Depreciation Expense goes on the income statement, which results in:
   a. An increase in total expenses
   b. A decrease in net income
2. Accumulated Depreciation is a contra-asset account found on the balance sheet next to its related equipment account.
3. The original cost of equipment is not reduced; it stays the same until the equipment is sold or retired.
4. Each month, the amount in the Accumulated Depreciation account grows larger, while the cost of the equipment remains the same.
5. Businesses may reduce their income tax expense by deducting Capital Cost Allowance (CCA). This CCA is similar to depreciation, and some smaller businesses may use CCA values for their depreciation expense.

Now, let's analyze the adjustment on the transaction analysis chart.

Depreciation Expense, Desktop Publishing Equip. 516	
80	

Accumulated Depreciation, Desktop Publishing Equip. 122	
	80

Will go on income statement.

Accounts Affected	Category	↑ ↓	Rules
Depreciation Expense, Desktop Publishing Equipment	Expense	↑	Dr.
Accumulated Depreciation, Desktop Publishing Equipment	Asset (Contra)	↑	Cr.

Will go on balance sheet.

Note that the original cost of the equipment on the worksheet has *not* been changed ($6,000).

Remember, the original cost of the equipment never changes: the equipment account is not included among the affected accounts because the original cost of equipment remains the same. When the Accumulated Depreciation increases (as a credit), the equipment's **book value** decreases.

The worksheet on page 148 shows how we enter the adjustment for depreciation of desktop publishing equipment.

CLARK'S DESKTOP PUBLISHING SERVICES
WORKSHEET
FOR THE MONTH ENDED MAY 31, 2016

Account Titles	Trial Balance Dr.	Trial Balance Cr.	Adjustments Dr.	Adjustments Cr.
Cash	6155 00			
Accounts Receivable	5000 00			
Office Supplies	600 00			(A) 500 00
Prepaid Rent	1200 00			(B) 400 00
Desktop Publishing Equipment	6000 00			
Accounts Payable		3350 00		
Brenda Clark, Capital		10000 00		
Brenda Clark, Withdrawals	625 00			
Desktop Publishing Fees		8000 00		
Office Salaries Expense	1300 00			
Advertising Expense	250 00			
Telephone Expense	220 00			
	21350 00	21350 00		
Office Supplies Expense			(A) 500 00	
Rent Expense			(B) 400 00	
Depreciation Exp., DTP Equip.			(C) 80 00	
Accum. Depn., DTP Equip.				(C) 80 00

An increase in Depreciation Expense, Desktop Publishing Equipment

An increase in Accumulated Depreciation, Desktop Publishing Equipment

The third account to be adjusted is assigned the letter C.

Because this is a new business, neither account had a previous balance. Therefore, neither is listed in the account titles of the trial balance. We need to list both accounts below Rent Expense in the account titles section. On the worksheet, put $80 in the debit column of the adjustments section on the same line as Depreciation Expense, DTP Equipment, and put $80 in the credit column of the adjustments section on the same line as Accumulated Depreciation, DTP Equipment.

Next month (June in our example), accumulated depreciation will appear listed in the original trial balance.

Next month, on June 30, a further $80 would be entered under Depreciation Expense, and Accumulated Depreciation would show a balance of $160. Remember, Clark's was a new company in May, so no previous depreciation was taken.

Now let's look at the last adjustment for Clark's Desktop Publishing Services.

Accumulated Depreciation	
Dr.	Cr.
	History of amount of depreciation taken to date

D. Adjusting the Accrued Salaries Account

Adjusting salaries

Clark's Desktop Publishing Services paid $1,300 in Office Salaries Expense (see the trial balance of any previous worksheet in this chapter). The last salary cheques for the month were paid on May 25. How can we update this account to show the salary expense as of May 31?

John Murray worked for Clark's on May 28, 29, 30, and 31, but his next paycheque is not due until June 8. John earned $350 for these four days. Is the $350 an expense to Clark's in May, when it was earned, or in June when it is due and is paid?

Month shown is for illustration only. It may not agree with any particular year.

May

S	M	T	W	T	F	S
		1	2	3	4	5
6	7	8	9	10	11	12
13	14	15	16	17	18	19
20	21	22	23	24	25	26
27	28	29	30	31		

CLARK'S DESKTOP PUBLISHING SERVICES WORKSHEET FOR THE MONTH ENDED MAY 31, 2016				
	Adjusted Trial Balance		Income Statement	
Account Titles	Dr.	Cr.	Dr.	Cr.
Cash	6155 00			
Accounts Receivable	5000 00			
Office Supplies	100 00			
Prepaid Rent	800 00			
Desktop Publishing Equipment	6000 00			
Accounts Payable		3350 00		
Brenda Clark, Capital		10000 00		
Brenda Clark, Withdrawals	625 00			
Desktop Publishing Fees		8000 00		8000 00
Office Salaries Expense	1650 00		1650 00	
Advertising Expense	250 00		250 00	
Telephone Expense	220 00		220 00	
Office Supplies Expense	500 00		500 00	
Rent Expense	400 00		400 00	
Amortization Expense, DTP Equipment	80 00		80 00	
Accumulated Amortization, DTP Equipment		80 00		
Accrued Salaries		350 00		
	21780 00	21780 00	3100 00	8000 00
Net Income			4900 00	
			8000 00	8000 00

8,000
− 3,100
4,900 → Net Income

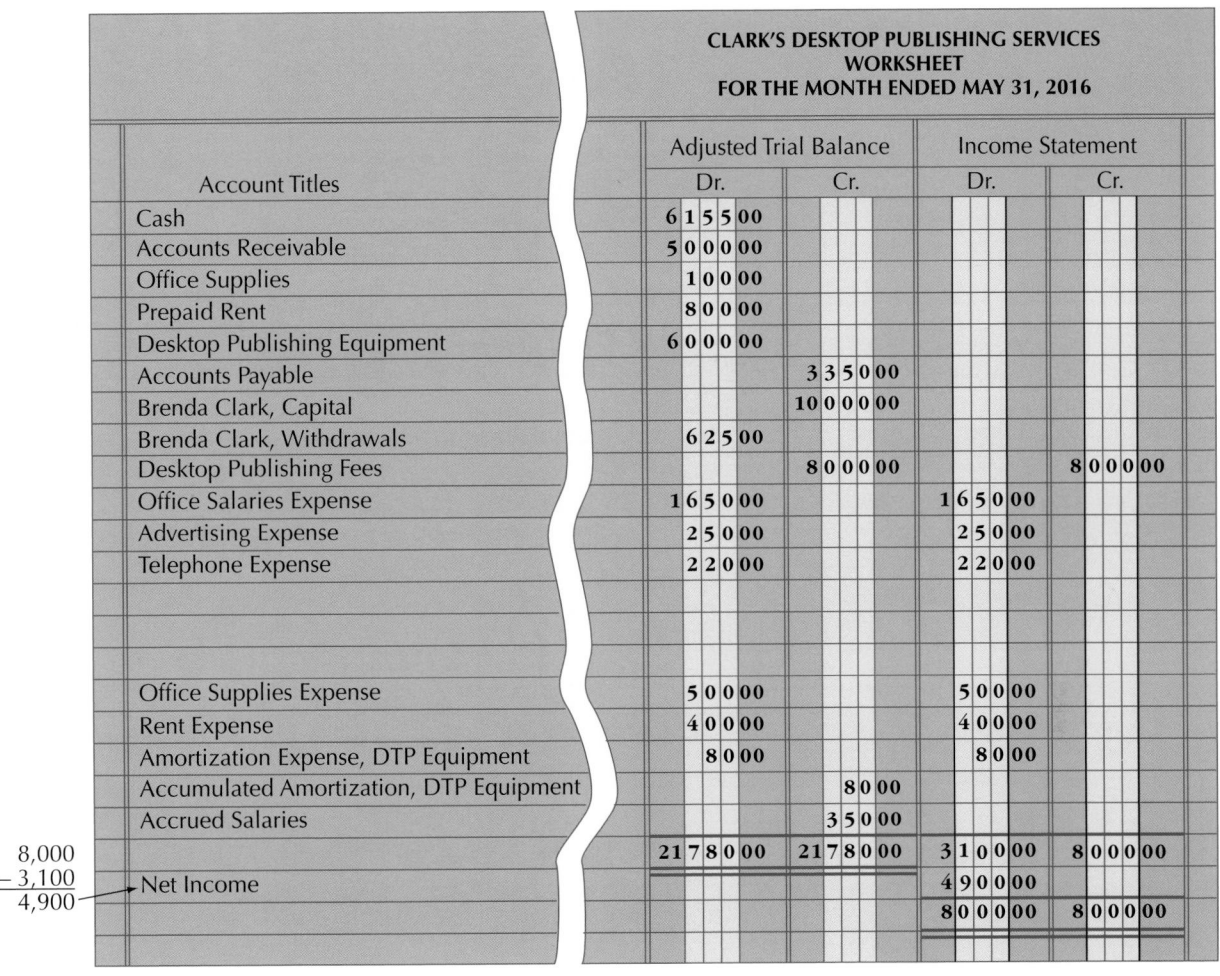

Figure 4-4 The Income Statement Section of the Worksheet

Remember: **The ending figure for capital is *not* on the worksheet.**

To see whether additional investments occurred for the period, you must check the capital account in the ledger.

The amounts come from the adjusted trial balance except the $4,900, which was carried over from the income statement section.

THE BALANCE SHEET SECTION

To fill out the balance sheet section of the worksheet, the following are carried over from the adjusted trial balance section: assets, contra-assets, liabilities, capital, and withdrawals. The net income is brought over to the credit column of the balance sheet so the two columns balance. This net income will be added to the figure for capitalization on the statement of owner's equity.

Let's now look at the completed worksheet in Figure 4-5 to see how the balance sheet section is completed. The base worksheet here provides the trial balance. When Overlay No. 1 is placed over the base worksheet, we can see all the adjustments and the adjusted trial balance. Overlay No. 2 provides the income statement items and also the balance sheet items. Finally, Overlay No. 3 totals the income statement and balance sheet columns, determines the difference, enters the difference appropriately in each statement, and totals the columns again. Note how the net income of $4,900 is brought over to the credit column of the worksheet. The figure for capital is also in the credit column, while the figure for withdrawals is in the debit column. By placing the net income in the credit column, both sides total $18,680. If a net loss were to occur, it would be placed in the debit column of the balance sheet.

Now that we have completed the worksheet, we can go on to the three financial statements. But let's summarize our progress first.

CLARK'S DESKTOP PUBLISHING SERVICES
WORKSHEET
FOR THE MONTH ENDED MAY 31, 2016

Account Titles	Trial Balance		Adjustments		Adjusted Trial Balance		Income Statement		Balance Sheet	
	Dr.	Cr.	Dr.	Cr.	Dr.	Cr.	Dr.	Cr.	Dr.	Cr.
Cash	6 1 5 5 00									
Accounts Receivable	5 0 0 0 00									
Office Supplies	6 0 0 00									
Prepaid Rent	1 2 0 0 00									
Desktop Publishing Equipment	6 0 0 0 00									
Accounts Payable		3 3 5 0 00								
Brenda Clark, Capital		10 0 0 0 00								
Brenda Clark, Withdrawals	6 2 5 00									
Desktop Publishing Fees		8 0 0 0 00								
Office Salaries Expense	1 3 0 0 00									
Advertising Expense	2 5 0 00									
Telephone Expense	2 2 0 00									
	21 3 5 0 00	21 3 5 0 00								

Figure 4-5 Sample Worksheet

Flip to Overlay No. 1—Adjustments A, B, C, and D

An expense can be incurred without being paid as long as it has helped in creating earned revenue for a period of time.

Think back to Chapter 1 when we first discussed revenue and expenses. We noted then that revenue is recorded when it is earned, not when the payment is received, and expenses are recorded when they are incurred, not when they are actually paid. This principle will be discussed further in a later chapter; for now, it is enough to remember that we record revenue and expenses when they occur because we want to match earned revenue with the expenses that resulted in earning those revenues. In this case, by working those four days, John Murray created some revenue for Clark's in May. Therefore, the office salaries expense must be shown in May—the month in which the revenue was earned.

The results are:

- Office Salaries Expense is increased by $350. This unpaid and unrecorded expense for salaries for which payment is not yet due is called **Accrued Salaries**. Sometimes, accrued salaries is also called **Salaries Payable**. In effect, we now show the true expense for salaries ($1,650 instead of $1,300):

Office Salaries Expense	
1,300	
350	

- The second result is that accrued salaries is increased by $350. Clark's has created a liability called Accrued Salaries, meaning that the firm owes money for salaries. When the firm pays John Murray, it will reduce its liability, Accrued Salaries, as well as decrease its cash.

In terms of the transaction analysis chart, the following would be done:

Accounts Affected	Category	↑ ↓	Rules
Office Salaries Expense	Expense	↑	Dr.
Accrued Salaries	Liability	↑	Cr.

How the adjustment for accrued salaries is entered on the worksheet is shown at the top of page 150.

The account Office Salaries Expense is already listed in the account titles, so $350 is placed in the debit column of the adjustments section on the same line as Office Salaries Expense. However, because the Accrued Salaries is not listed in the account titles, the account title Accrued Salaries is added below the trial balance, below Accumulated Depreciation, DTP Equipment. Also, $350 is placed in the credit column of the adjustments section on the same line as Accrued Salaries.

Now that we have finished all the adjustments that we intended to make, we total the adjustments section, as shown in Figure 4-2.

THE ADJUSTED TRIAL BALANCE SECTION

LO 2

Preparing an adjusted trial balance on the worksheet

The adjusted trial balance is the next section on the worksheet. To fill it out, we must summarize the information in the trial balance and adjustments sections, as shown in Figure 4-3.

Note that when the numbers are brought across from the trial balance to the adjusted trial balance, two debits will be added together and two credits will be added together. If the numbers include a debit and a credit, take the difference between the two and place it on the side that has the larger figure. The total debits must always equal the total credits on the adjusted trial balance.

Now that we have completed the adjustments and adjusted trial balance sections of the worksheet, it is time to move on to the income statement and the

The Accrued Salaries account is coded D because it is the fourth account to be adjusted.

Remember, all accounts added below the trial balance are increasing.

CLARK'S DESKTOP PUBLISHING SERVICES
WORKSHEET
FOR THE MONTH ENDED MAY 31, 2016

Account Titles	Trial Balance Dr.	Trial Balance Cr.	Adjustments Dr.	Adjustments Cr.
Cash	6155 00			
Accounts Receivable	5000 00			
Office Supplies	600 00			(A) 500 00
Prepaid Rent	1200 00			(B) 400 00
Desktop Publishing Equipment	6000 00			
Accounts Payable		3350 00		
Brenda Clark, Capital		10000 00		
Brenda Clark, Withdrawals	625 00			
Desktop Publishing Fees		8000 00		
Office Salaries Expense	1300 00		(D) 350 00	
Advertising Expense	250 00			
Telephone Expense	220 00			
	21350 00	21350 00		
Office Supplies Expense			(A) 500 00	
Rent Expense			(B) 400 00	
Depreciation Exp., DTP Equip.			(C) 80 00	
Accum. Depn., DTP Equip.				(C) 80 00
Accrued Salaries				(D) 350 00

An increase in Office Salaries Expense, $350

An increase in Accrued Salaries, $350

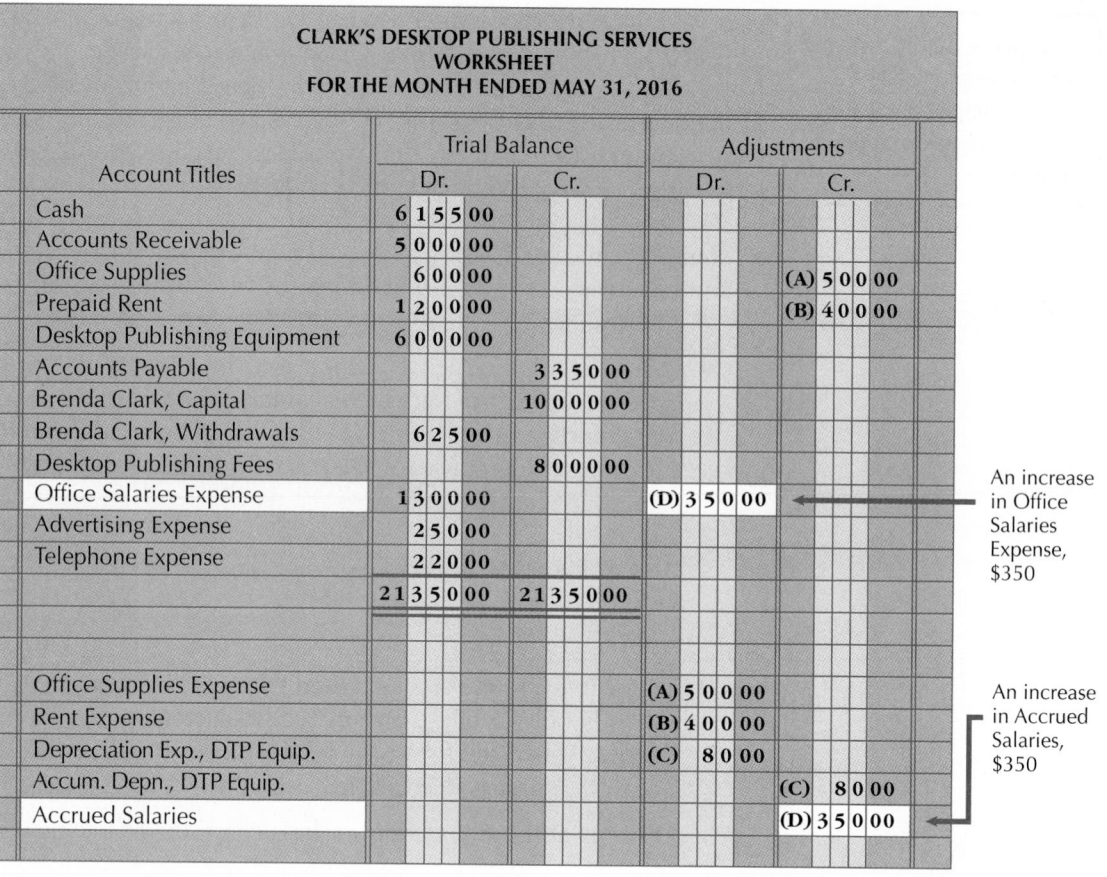

Figure 4-2
The Adjustments Section of the Worksheet

CLARK'S DESKTOP PUBLISHING SERVICES
WORKSHEET
FOR THE MONTH ENDED MAY 31, 2016

Account Titles	Trial Balance Dr.	Trial Balance Cr.	Adjustments Dr.	Adjustments Cr.
Cash	6155 00			
Accounts Receivable	5000 00			
Office Supplies	600 00			(A) 500 00
Prepaid Rent	1200 00			(B) 400 00
Desktop Publishing Equipment	6000 00			
Accounts Payable		3350 00		
Brenda Clark, Capital		10000 00		
Brenda Clark, Withdrawals	625 00			
Desktop Publishing Fees		8000 00		
Office Salaries Expense	1300 00		(D) 350 00	
Advertising Expense	250 00			
Telephone Expense	220 00			
	21350 00	21350 00		
Office Supplies Expense			(A) 500 00	
Rent Expense			(B) 400 00	
Depreciation Expense, DTP Equip.			(C) 80 00	
Accum. Depn., DTP Equip.				(C) 80 00
Accrued Salaries				(D) 350 00
			1330 00	1330 00

CLARK'S DESKTOP PUBLISHING SERVICES WORKSHEET FOR THE MONTH ENDED MAY 31, 2016						
	Trial Balance		Adjustments		Adjusted Trial Balance	
Account Titles	Dr.	Cr.	Dr.	Cr.	Dr.	Cr.
Cash	6155 00				6155 00	
Accounts Receivable	5000 00				5000 00	
Office Supplies	600 00			(A) 500 00	100 00	
Prepaid Rent	1200 00			(B) 400 00	800 00	
Desktop Publishing Equipment	6000 00				6000 00	
Accounts Payable		3350 00				3350 00
Brenda Clark, Capital		10000 00				10000 00
Brenda Clark, Withdrawals	625 00				625 00	
Desktop Publishing Fees		8000 00				8000 00
Office Salaries Expense	1300 00		(D) 350 00		1650 00	
Advertising Expense	250 00				250 00	
Telephone Expense	220 00				220 00	
	21350 00	21350 00				
Office Supplies Expense			(A) 500 00		500 00	
Rent Expense			(B) 400 00		400 00	
Depreciation Exp., DTP Equip.			(C) 80 00		80 00	
Accum. Depn., DTP Equip.				(C) 80 00		80 00
Accrued Salaries				(D) 350 00		350 00
			1330 00	1330 00	21780 00	21780 00

If no adjustment is made, just carry over the amount from the trial balance on same side.

Supplies were $600, but we used up $500, leaving us with a $100 balance in supplies. *Note:* If there is a debit and a credit, take the *difference* between the two and place it on the side that has the larger figure.

Note: Equipment is *not* adjusted here.

Two debits are added together. If there were two credits, they also would have been added together and shown in the credit column.

Carry these amounts over to adjusted trial balance in the same positions.

Note: The total of the left (debit) must equal the total of the right (credit) ($21,780).

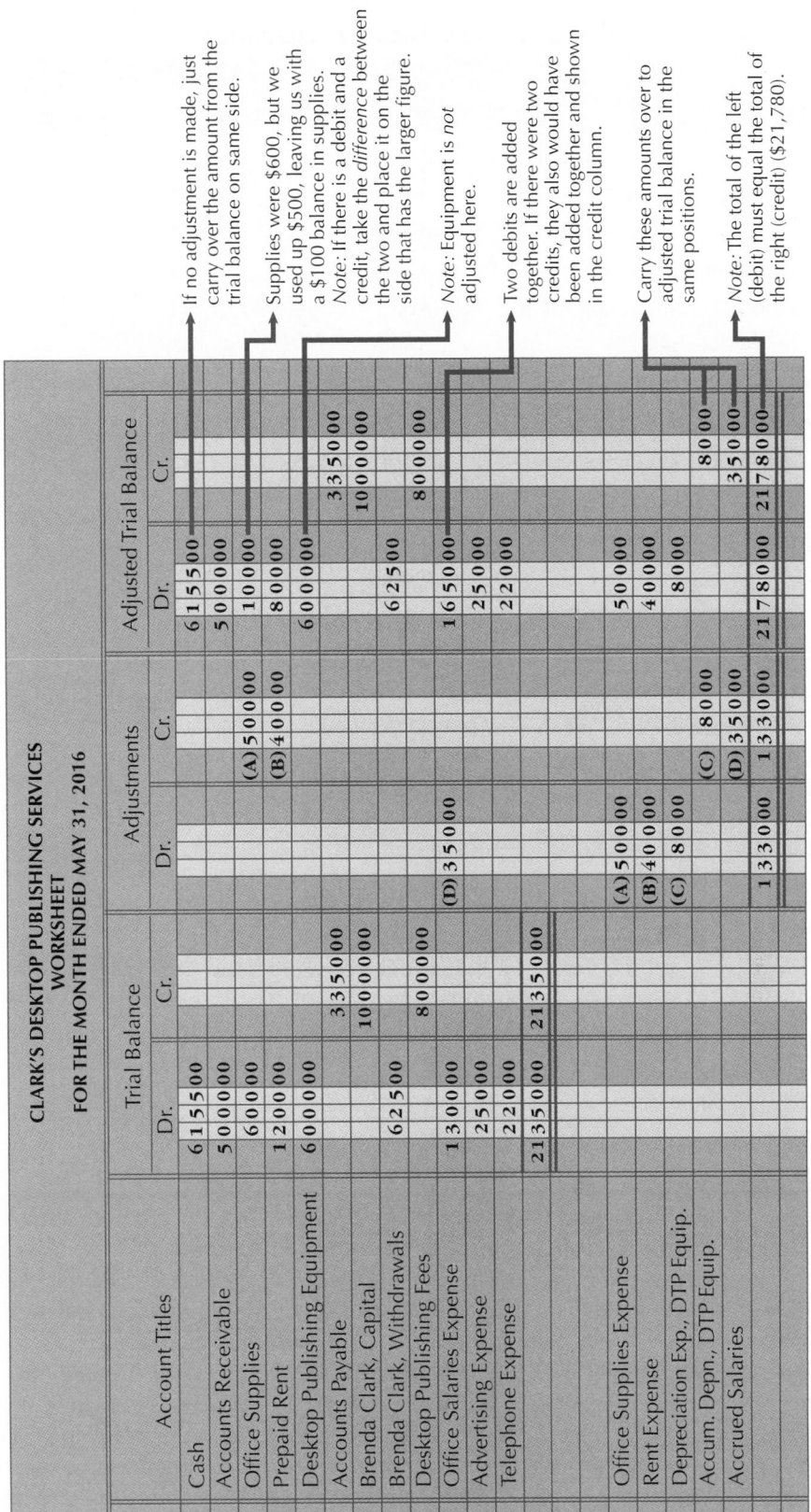

Figure 4-3 The Adjusted Trial Balance Section of the Worksheet

TABLE 4-1 Normal Balances and Account Categories

Account Title	Category	Normal Balance on Adjusted Trial Balance	Income Statement Dr.	Income Statement Cr.	Balance Sheet Dr.	Balance Sheet Cr.
Cash	Asset	Dr.			X	
Accounts Receivable	Asset	Dr.			X	
Office Supplies	Asset	Dr.			X	
Prepaid Rent	Asset	Dr.			X	
Desktop Publishing Equipment	Asset	Dr.			X	
Accounts Payable	Liability	Cr.				X
Brenda Clark, Capital	Owner's Equity	Cr.				X
Brenda Clark, Withdrawals	Owner's Equity	Dr.			X	
Desktop Publishing Fees	Revenue	Cr.		X		
Office Salaries Expense	Expense	Dr.	X			
Advertising Expense	Expense	Dr.	X			
Telephone Expense	Expense	Dr.	X			
Office Supplies Expense	Expense	Dr.	X			
Rent Expense	Expense	Dr.	X			
Depreciation Expense, DTP Equipment	Expense	Dr.	X			
Accumulated Depreciation, DTP Equipment	Asset (Contra)	Cr.				X
Accrued Salaries	Liability	Cr.				X

balance sheet sections. Before we do that, however, look at the chart shown in Table 4-1 above. This table should be used as a reference to help you fill out the next two sections of the worksheet.

Keep in mind that the numbers from the adjusted trial balance are carried over to one of the last four columns of the worksheet before the net income or net loss can be calculated.

LO 3

Completing the income statement and balance sheet sections of the worksheet

In the worksheet, net income is placed in the debit column of the income statement. Net loss goes in the credit column.

The difference between $3,100 Dr. and $8,000 Cr. indicates a net income of $4,900. Do not think of the Net Income as a Dr. or Cr. The $4,900 is placed in the debit column to balance the two columns at $8,000. Actually, the credit side is larger by $4,900.

THE INCOME STATEMENT SECTION

As shown in Figure 4-4, the income statement section lists only revenue and expenses from the adjusted trial balance. Note that Accumulated Depreciation and Accrued Salaries do not go on the income statement. Accumulated Depreciation is a contra-asset account found on the balance sheet. Accrued Salaries is a liability account also found on the balance sheet.

The revenue ($8,000) and all the individual expenses are listed in the income statement section. The revenue is placed in the credit column of the income statement section because it has a credit balance. The expenses have debit balances, so they are placed in the debit column of the income statement section. The following steps must be taken after the debits and credits are placed in the correct columns:

Step 1: Total the debits and the credits.
Step 2: Calculate the difference between the totals of the debit and credit columns and place this difference on the side with the smaller total.
Step 3: Total the two columns again.

The worksheet in Figure 4-4 shows that the label "Net Income" is added in the account title column on the same line as $4,900. When there is a net income, it will be placed in the debit column of the income statement section of the worksheet. If there is a net loss, it is placed in the credit column. The $8,000 total indicates that the two columns are in balance.

LEARNING UNIT 4-1 REVIEW

AT THIS POINT you should be able to:

- Define and explain the purpose of a worksheet. (p. 142)
- Explain the need as well as the process for adjustments. (pp. 143–145)
- Explain the concept of depreciation. (p. 145)
- Explain the difference between depreciation expense and accumulated depreciation. (p. 147)
- Prepare a worksheet from a trial balance and adjustment data. (p. 149)

Self-Review Quiz 4-1

From the accompanying trial balance and adjustment data, complete a worksheet for P. Logan Company for the month ended December 31, 2015. (You can use a blank foldout worksheet located at the end of the *Study Guide with Working Papers.*)

Note: The numbers used in this quiz may seem impossibly small, but we have done that on purpose, so that at this point you don't have to worry too much about arithmetic, just about preparing the worksheet correctly.

P. LOGAN COMPANY
TRIAL BALANCE
DECEMBER 31, 2015

	Dr.	Cr.
Cash	15 00	
Accounts Receivable	3 00	
Prepaid Insurance	3 00	
Store Supplies	5 00	
Store Equipment	6 00	
Accumulated Depreciation, Store Equipment		4 00
Accounts Payable		2 00
P. Logan, Capital		14 00
P. Logan, Withdrawals	3 00	
Revenue from Clients		25 00
Rent Expense	2 00	
Salaries Expense	8 00	
	45 00	45 00

Adjustment Data

a. Depreciation Expense, Store Equipment, $1

b. Insurance expired, $2

c. Supplies on hand, $1

d. Salaries owed but not paid to employees, $3

Solution to Self-Review Quiz 4-1

Don't adjust this line! Store Equipment always contains the historical cost.

P. LOGAN COMPANY
WORKSHEET
FOR THE MONTH ENDED DECEMBER 31, 2015

Account Titles	Trial Balance Dr.	Trial Balance Cr.	Adjustments Dr.	Adjustments Cr.	Adjusted Trial Balance Dr.	Adjusted Trial Balance Cr.	Income Statement Dr.	Income Statement Cr.	Balance Sheet Dr.	Balance Sheet Cr.
Cash	15 00				15 00				15 00	
Accounts Receivable	3 00				3 00				3 00	
Prepaid Insurance	3 00			(B) 2 00	1 00				1 00	
Store Supplies	5 00			(C) 4 00	1 00				1 00	
Store Equipment	6 00				6 00				6 00	
Accumulated Depreciation, Store Equipment		4 00		(A) 1 00		5 00				5 00
Accounts Payable		2 00				2 00				2 00
P. Logan, Capital		14 00				14 00				14 00
P. Logan, Withdrawals	3 00				3 00				3 00	
Revenue from Clients		25 00				25 00		25 00		
Rent Expense	2 00				2 00		2 00			
Salaries Expense	8 00		(D) 3 00		11 00		11 00			
	45 00	45 00								
Depreciation Expense, Store Equipment			(A) 1 00		1 00		1 00			
Insurance Expense			(B) 2 00		2 00		2 00			
Supplies Expense			(C) 4 00		4 00		4 00			
Accrued Salaries				(D) 3 00		3 00				3 00
			10 00	10 00	49 00	49 00	20 00	25 00	29 00	24 00
Net Income							5 00			5 00
							25 00	25 00	29 00	29 00

Note that Accumulated Depreciation is listed in the trial balance since this is not a new company. Store Equipment has already been depreciated $4 from an earlier period.

Quiz Tip

The adjustment for supplies worth $4 represents the amount *used up*. The *on-hand* amount of $1 ends up on the adjusted trial balance.

NEED HELP?

Let's review first: When completing a worksheet, we list the original trial balance, add adjustments, complete an adjusted trial balance, and then decide which titles go on the income statement and balance sheet. Since we do not have columns for statement of owner's equity, withdrawals and net income will be placed on the balance sheet columns to arrive at a new figure for capital. Remember, it is the old figure for capital that is placed on the worksheet.

Account title column: Any item not listed on the original trial balance will be listed below the trial balance. This will happen when we make adjustments. Note that when we list each title below the trial balance, it will be increasing in value.

Adjustment column: Depreciation

A. Depreciation:

In this adjustment Accumulated Depreciation is already listed on the trial balance so we only have to add Depreciation Expense below the trial balance. Here is the mind process chart for this adjustment:

Depn. Expense, St. Equip.	Expense	↑	Dr. $1
Acc. Depn., St. Equip.	Contra-asset	↑	Cr. $1

Note that the original cost of Store Equipment of $6 is not touched.

B. Insurance Expired:

In this adjustment, Prepaid Insurance is already listed on the trial balance, so we only have to add Insurance Expense below the trial balance. Here is the mind process chart for this adjustment:

Insurance Expense	Expense	↑	Dr. $2
Prepaid Insurance	Asset	↓	Cr. $2

Expired means used up and thus we use the amount of $2.

C. Supplies on Hand:

In this adjustment, we have to calculate the amount of supplies used up. We take the beginning amount of supplies of $5 less the amount on hand of $1 to equal the amount used up of $4. This is the amount of the adjustment. Since we have Office Supplies listed on the trial balance, we only have to add Supplies Expense below the trial balance. Here is the mind process chart for this adjustment:

Supplies Expense	Expense	↑	Dr. $4
Office Supplies	Asset	↓	Cr. $4

D. Salaries Owed:

In this adjustment, we have Salaries Expense already listed on the trial balance. Here we have to add Accrued Salaries below the trial balance. The following mind process chart shows the new expense that has been incurred but has not been paid:

Salaries Expense	Expense	↑	Dr. $3
Accrued Salaries	Liability	↑	Cr. $3

The sum of all the debits on the adjustments equals the sum of the credits.

Adjusted Trial Balance Columns: Accounts that were not adjusted or added below the trial balance have their balances carried over to the adjusted trial balance. Accounts that were adjusted will have their combined balances carried over to the adjusted trial balance.

For example, Salaries Expense is adjusted by adding the debit balance of $8 and the adjustment of $3 to equal an $11 debit balance on the adjusted trial balance. Every account in the adjusted trial balance will end up on the Income Statement or Balance Sheet columns of the worksheet.

Income Statement Columns: From the adjusted trial balance all revenues and expenses accounts are listed. Note that when we total the debit and credit columns, they do not equal each other until we calculate the difference between revenues and expenses. In this case, the ($5) difference will be added to the debit column of the income statement section so both columns will total $25.

Balance Sheet Columns: From the adjusted trial balance, assets and withdrawals will end up in the debit column. The old figures for capital, liabilities, and contra-assets are in the credit column. Note that the totals of the columns will not balance until a net income of $5 is placed under the $24. This is done because we use the old figure for capital on the worksheet, and there is no column on the worksheet for the statement of owner's equity.

SUMMARY

On the worksheet, accounts listed below the trial balance are increasing. Adjustments must be made for supplies used up. The original cost of equipment is never touched in the adjustment process. Capital is the old balance on the worksheet. Net income is the difference between revenue and expenses and is carried over to the credit column of the balance sheet. Net losses would be in opposite columns. Income statement columns and balance sheet columns will be out of balance by amount of Net Income.

LEARNING UNIT 4-2

Step 6 of the Accounting Cycle: Preparing the Financial Statements from the Worksheet

LO 4

Preparing financial statements from the worksheet

The formal financial statements can be prepared from the worksheet completed in Learning Unit 4-1. Before beginning, we must check that the entries on the worksheet are correct and in balance. To do this, we have to be sure that (1) all entries are recorded in the appropriate columns, (2) the correct amounts are entered in the proper places, (3) the addition is correct across the columns (i.e., from the trial balance to the adjusted trial balance to the financial reports), and (4) the columns are added correctly.

PREPARING THE INCOME STATEMENT

The first statement to be prepared for Clark's Desktop Publishing Services is the income statement. When preparing the income statement, it is important to remember that:

1. Every figure on the formal report is on the worksheet. Figure 4-6 shows where each of these figures goes on the income statement.
2. There are no debit or credit columns on the formal report.
3. The inside column on financial reports is used for subtotalling.
4. Withdrawals do not go on the income statement; they go on the statement of owner's equity.

Take a moment to look at the income statement in Figure 4-6. Note which items go where from the income statement section of the worksheet onto the formal report.

PREPARING THE STATEMENT OF OWNER'S EQUITY

Figure 4-7 is the statement of owner's equity for Clark's. The figure shows where on the worksheet the information comes from. It is important to remember that if there were additional investments, the figure on the worksheet for capital would

Account Titles	Income Statement Dr.	Income Statement Cr.
Cash		
Accounts Receivable		
Office Supplies		
Prepaid Rent		
Desktop Publishing Equipment		
Accounts Payable		
Brenda Clark, Capital		
Brenda Clark, Withdrawals		
Desktop Publishing Fees		8000 00
Office Salaries Expense	1650 00	
Advertising Expense	250 00	
Telephone Expense	220 00	
Office Supplies Expense	500 00	
Rent Expense	400 00	
Depn. Expense, DTP Equip.	80 00	
Accum. Depn., DTP Equip.		
Accrued Salaries		
	3100 00	8000 00
Net Income	4900 00	
	8000 00	8000 00

CLARK'S DESKTOP PUBLISHING SERVICES
INCOME STATEMENT
FOR THE MONTH ENDED MAY 31, 2016

Revenue:		
Desktop Publishing Fees		$8000 00
Operating Expenses:		
Office Salaries Expense	$1650 00	
Advertising Expense	250 00	
Telephone Expense	220 00	
Office Supplies Expense	500 00	
Rent Expense	400 00	
Depreciation Expense, DTP Equipment	80 00	
Total Operating Expenses		3100 00
Net Income		$4900 00

Figure 4-6 From Worksheet to Income Statement

CLARK'S DESKTOP PUBLISHING SERVICES
STATEMENT OF OWNER'S EQUITY
FOR THE MONTH ENDED MAY 31, 2016

Brenda Clark, Capital, May 1, 2016		$10000 00
Net Income for May	$4900 00	
Less: Withdrawals for May	625 00	
Increase in Capital		4275 00
Brenda Clark, Capital, May 31, 2016		$14275 00

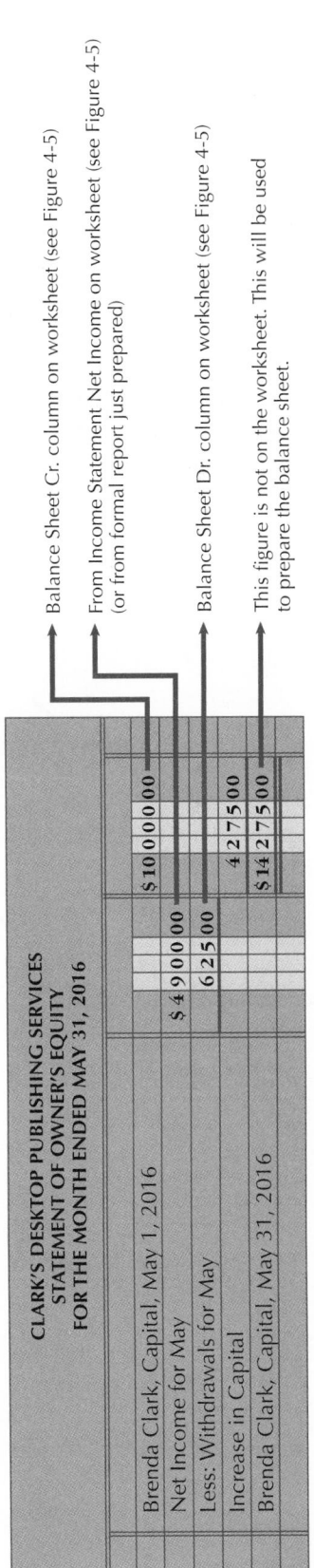

Balance Sheet Cr. column on worksheet (see Figure 4-5)

From Income Statement Net Income on worksheet (see Figure 4-5) (or from formal report just prepared)

Balance Sheet Dr. column on worksheet (see Figure 4-5)

This figure is not on the worksheet. This will be used to prepare the balance sheet.

Figure 4-7 Completing a Statement of Owner's Equity

not be the beginning figure for capital. Checking the ledger account for capital will tell you whether the amount is correct. Note how net income and withdrawals aid in calculating the new figure for capital.

PREPARING THE BALANCE SHEET

In preparing the balance sheet (page 159), remember that the balance sheet section totals on the worksheet ($18,680) do *not* usually match the totals on the formal balance sheet ($17,975). This occurs because information is grouped differently on the formal report. First, in the formal report, Accumulated Depreciation ($80) is subtracted from Desktop Publishing Equipment, reducing the balance. Second, Withdrawals ($625) are subtracted from Owner's Equity, reducing the balance further. These two reductions (−$80 + [−$625] = −$705) represent the difference between the worksheet and the formal version of the balance sheet ($17,975 − $18,680 = −$705). Figure 4-8 (page 159) shows how to prepare the balance sheet from the worksheet.

LEARNING UNIT 4-2 REVIEW

AT THIS POINT you should be able to:

- Prepare the three financial statements from a worksheet. (pp. 156–158)
- Explain why totals of the formal balance sheet don't match totals of balance sheet columns on the worksheet. (p. 158)

Self-Review Quiz 4-2

(The forms you need are located on pages 4-1 to 4-3 of the *Study Guide with Working Papers.*)

From the worksheet on page 154 for P. Logan, prepare (1) an income statement for December, (2) a statement of owner's equity, and (3) a balance sheet for December 31, 2015. No additional investments took place during the period.

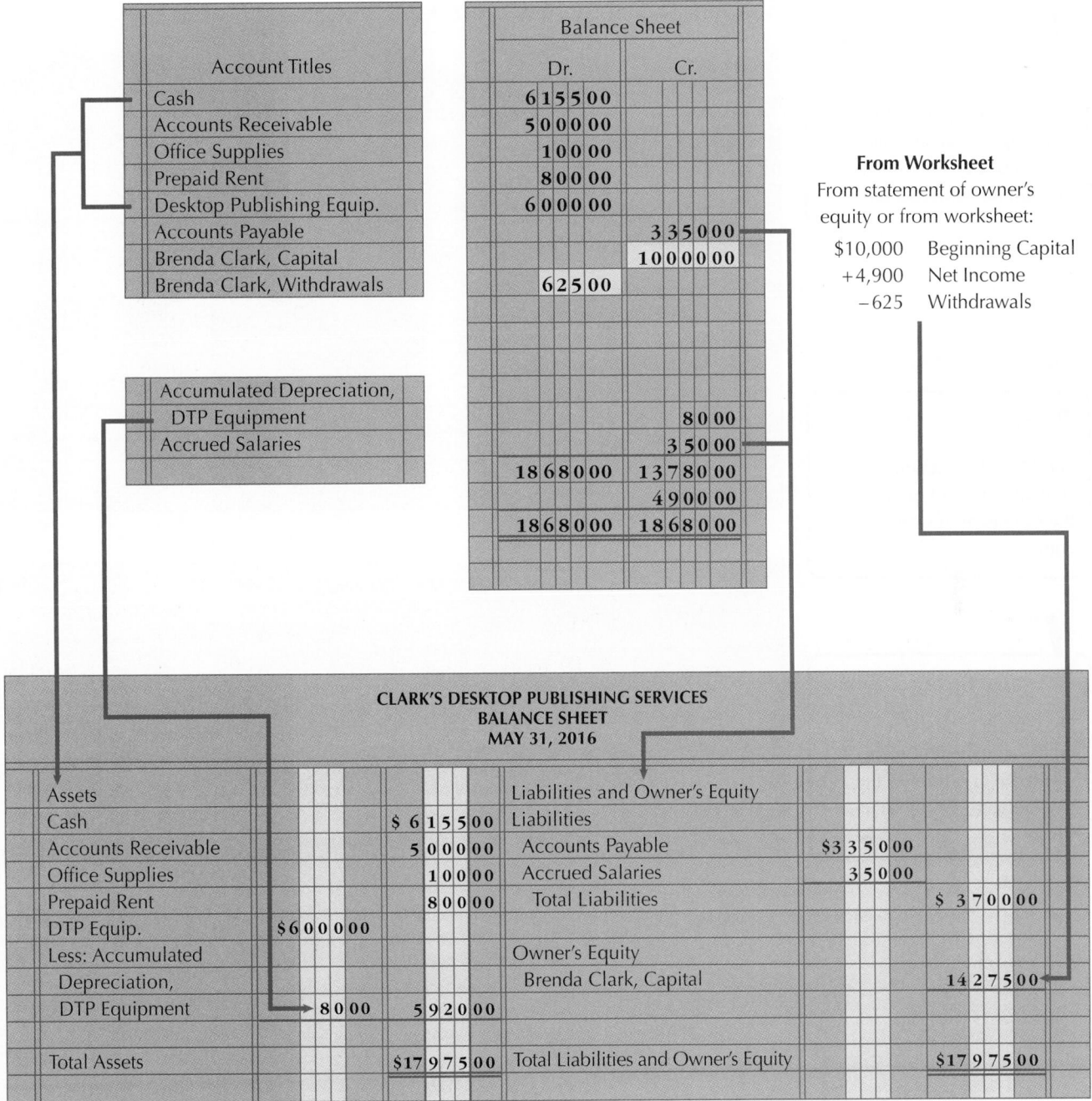

Account Titles	Balance Sheet Dr.	Balance Sheet Cr.
Cash	6155.00	
Accounts Receivable	5000.00	
Office Supplies	100.00	
Prepaid Rent	800.00	
Desktop Publishing Equip.	6000.00	
Accounts Payable		3350.00
Brenda Clark, Capital		10000.00
Brenda Clark, Withdrawals	625.00	
Accumulated Depreciation, DTP Equipment		80.00
Accrued Salaries		350.00
	18680.00	13780.00
		4900.00
	18680.00	18680.00

From Worksheet

From statement of owner's equity or from worksheet:

$10,000	Beginning Capital
+4,900	Net Income
−625	Withdrawals

CLARK'S DESKTOP PUBLISHING SERVICES
BALANCE SHEET
MAY 31, 2016

Assets			Liabilities and Owner's Equity		
Cash		$6155.00	Liabilities		
Accounts Receivable		5000.00	Accounts Payable	$3350.00	
Office Supplies		100.00	Accrued Salaries	350.00	
Prepaid Rent		800.00	Total Liabilities		$3700.00
DTP Equip.	$6000.00				
Less: Accumulated Depreciation, DTP Equipment	80.00	5920.00	Owner's Equity		
			Brenda Clark, Capital		14275.00
Total Assets		$17975.00	Total Liabilities and Owner's Equity		$17975.00

Figure 4-8 From Worksheet to Balance Sheet

Solution to Self-Review Quiz 4-2

> **Quiz Tip**
>
> The income statement is made up of revenue and expenses. Use the inside column for subtotalling.

P. LOGAN COMPANY
INCOME STATEMENT
FOR THE MONTH ENDED DECEMBER 31, 2015

Revenue:		
Revenue from Clients		$25 00
Operating Expenses:		
Rent Expense	$ 2 00	
Salaries Expense	11 00	
Depreciation Expense, Store Equipment	1 00	
Insurance Expense	2 00	
Supplies Expense	4 00	
Total Operating Expenses		20 00
Net Income		$ 5 00

> **Quiz Tip**
>
> The $5 on the income statement is used to update the statement of owner's equity.

P. LOGAN COMPANY
STATEMENT OF OWNER'S EQUITY
FOR THE MONTH ENDED DECEMBER 31, 2015

P. Logan, Capital, December 1, 2015		$14 00
Net Income for December	$5 00	
Less: Withdrawals for December	3 00	
Increase in Capital		2 00
P. Logan, Capital, December 31, 2015		$16 00

> **Quiz Tip**
>
> The ending capital figure on the statement of owner's equity ($16) is used as the capital figure on the balance sheet.

P. LOGAN COMPANY
BALANCE SHEET
DECEMBER 31, 2015

Assets			Liabilities and Owner's Equity		
Cash		$15 00	Liabilities		
Accounts Receivable		3 00	Accounts Payable	$2 00	
Prepaid Insurance		1 00	Accrued Salaries	3 00	
Store Supplies		1 00	Total Liabilities		$ 5 00
Store Equipment	$6 00		Owner's Equity		
Less Accumulated Depreciation, Store Equipment	5 00	1 00	P. Logan, Capital		16 00
Total Assets		$21 00	Total Liabilities and Owner's Equity		$21 00

NEED HELP?

Let's review first: There are no debits or credits on the formal financial statements. The three financial statements are made from the last four columns of the worksheet.

Income Statement: The income statement is made up of revenues and expenses. Use the inside column for subtotalling. All numbers found on the income statement are also found on the worksheet.

Statement of Owner's Equity: The net income of $5 is used from the income statement to update the statement of owner's equity. Note that $14 is the old figure from the worksheet. The increase in capital of $2 is not found on the worksheet. Logan's ending figure of $16 is not found on the worksheet.

Balance Sheet: Logan's ending figure of $16 from the statement of owner's equity is used as the capital figure on the balance sheet. Note under assets how the inside column is used to calculate store equipment less accumulated depreciation. Note that the totals of $21 from the balance sheet are not found on the worksheet. When the financial report is prepared there are no debits or credits.

SUMMARY

The worksheet is prepared in terms of debits and credits, but that is not the case for the formal financial statements. The inside column of the financial statements is for subtotalling. The worksheet uses the old figure for Capital while the balance sheet uses the figure from the statement of owner's equity for the new figure of Capital. Many of the numbers on the statement of owner's equity and balance sheet will not be found on the worksheet, since information is grouped differently on the formal report because there are no debits or credits on formal financial statements.

WHERE THE DOUGH GOES

Preparing adjustments for amotization, an adjusted trial balance, and balance sheet
1 2 3 (20 min)

No matter how harried Stan Hernandez feels as the owner of his own Subway restaurant, the aroma of his fresh-baked gourmet breads always perks him up. However, the sales generated by Subway's line of gourmet seasoned breads perk Stan up even more. Subway restaurants introduced freshly baked bread in 1983, a practice that made it stand out from other fast-food chains and helped build its reputation for made-to-order freshness. Since then, Subway franchisees have introduced many types of gourmet seasoned breads—such as Hearty Italian or Monterey Cheddar—according to a schedule determined by headquarters.

Stan was one month into the "limited-time promotion" for the chain's new Roasted Garlic seasoned bread when his bake oven started faltering. "The temperature controls just don't seem quite right," said his employee and sandwich artist, Rashid. "It's taking incrementally longer to bake the bread."

"This couldn't happen at a worse time," moaned Stan. "We're baking enough Roasted Garlic bread to keep a whole town of vampires away, but if we don't get it out of the oven fast enough, we'll keep our customers away!"

That very day Stan called his field consultant, Mariah, to discuss what to do about his bake oven. Mariah reminded Stan that his oven trouble illustrated the flip side of buying an existing store from a retired franchisee—having to repair or replace worn or old equipment. After receiving a rather expensive repair estimate and considering the age of the oven, Stan ultimately decided it would make sense for him to purchase a new one. Mariah concurred, saying, "At the rate your sales are going, Stan, you're going to need that roomier new model."

"Wow, do you realize how much this new bake oven is going to cost me?—$3,000!" Stan exclaimed while meeting with his cousin-turned-Subway-accountant, Lila Hernandez. "Yes, it's a lot to lay out, Stan," said Lila, "but you'll be depreciating the cost over a period of 10 years, which will help you at tax time. Let's do the adjustment on your worksheet so that you can see it."

The two of them were sitting in Stan's small office behind the Subway kitchen, and they pulled up this month's worksheet on Stan's computer program. Lila laughed, "I'm sure glad you started entering your worksheets on the computer again! The figures on those old ones were so doodled over and crossed out that I could barely decipher them! We may need your worksheets at tax time."

"Anything for you, *mi prima*," Stan said. "I may depreciate my bake oven, but my gratitude for your accounting skills only appreciates with time!"

DISCUSSION QUESTIONS

1. If you are using a straight-line method of depreciation and Stan's bake oven has a residual value of $1,000, how much depreciation will he account for each year, and what would be the adjustment for each month?
2. Where does Lila get the information on the useful life of Stan's bake oven and the estimate for its residual value? Why do you think she gets her information from this particular source?
3. Why is a clean worksheet helpful even after that month's statements have been prepared?

Chapter Assignments

DEMONSTRATION PROBLEM: STEPS 5 AND 6 OF THE ACCOUNTING CYCLE

(The blank forms you need are on pages 4-4 and 4-5 of the *Study Guide with Working Papers.*)

From the following trial balance and additional data, complete (1) a worksheet and (2) the three financial statements (numbers are intentionally small so you can concentrate on the theory).

Frost Company
Trial Balance
December 31, 2017

	Dr.	Cr.
Cash	14	
Accounts Receivable	4	
Prepaid Insurance	5	
Plumbing Supplies	3	
Plumbing Equipment	7	
Accumulated Depreciation, Plumbing Equipment		5
Accounts Payable		1
J. Frost, Capital		12
J. Frost, Withdrawals	3	
Plumbing Fees		27
Rent Expense	4	
Salaries Expense	5	
Totals	45	45

Adjustment Data

a. Insurance expired, $3

b. Plumbing supplies on hand, $1

c. Depreciation Expense, Plumbing Equipment, $1

d. Salaries owed but not paid to employees, $2

Solution Tips for Building a Worksheet

1. Adjustments

a.

Insurance Expense	**Expense**	↑	**Dr.**	**$3**
Prepaid Insurance	**Asset**	↓	**Cr.**	**$3**

Expired means used up.

b.

Plumbing Supplies Expense	**Expense**	↑	**Dr.**	**$2**
Plumbing Supplies	**Asset**	↓	**Cr.**	**$2**

$3 − $1 = $2 *used up*

c.

Depreciation Expense, Plumbing Equipment	**Expense**	↑	**Dr.**	**$1**
Accumulated Depreciation, Plumbing Equipment	**Contra-Asset**	↑	**Cr.**	**$1**

The original cost of equipment of $7 is not "touched."

d.

Salaries Expense	Expense	↑	Dr.	$2
Accrued Salaries	Liability	↑	Cr.	$2

2. Last four columns of worksheet are prepared from adjusted trial balance.
3. Capital of $12 is the old figure. Net income of $10 (revenue – expenses) is brought over to same side as capital on the balance sheet Cr. column to balance columns.

Frost Company
Income Statement
for the Month Ended December 31, 2017

Revenue:		
Plumbing Fees		$27
Operating Expenses:		
Rent Expense	$4	
Salaries Expense	7	
Insurance Expense	3	
Plumbing Supplies Expense	2	
Depreciation Expense, Plumbing Equipment	1	
Total Operating Expenses		17
Net Income		$10

Frost Company
Statement of Owner's Equity
for the Month Ended December 31, 2017

J. Frost, Capital, December 1, 2017		$12
Net Income for December	$10	
Less: Withdrawals for December	3	
Increase in Capital		7
J. Frost, Capital, December 31, 2017		$19

Frost Company
Balance Sheet
December 31, 2017

Assets			**Liabilities and Owner's Equity**		
Cash		$14	Liabilities:		
Accounts Receivable		4	Accounts Payable	$1	
Prepaid Insurance		2	Accrued Salaries	2	
Plumbing Supplies		1	Total Liabilities		$ 3
Plumbing Equipment	$7				
Less: Accum. Depn.	6	1	Owner's Equity:		
			J. Frost, Capital		19
Total Assets		$22	Total Liabilities and Owner's Equity		$22

Original cost not adjusted "used up" "on hand"

FROST COMPANY
WORKSHEET
FOR THE MONTH ENDED DECEMBER 31, 2017

Account Titles	Trial Balance Dr.	Trial Balance Cr.	Adjustments Dr.	Adjustments Cr.	Adjusted Trial Balance Dr.	Adjusted Trial Balance Cr.	Income Statement Dr.	Income Statement Cr.	Balance Sheet Dr.	Balance Sheet Cr.
Cash	14 00				14 00				14 00	
Accounts Receivable	4 00				4 00				4 00	
Prepaid Insurance	5 00			(A) 3 00	2 00				2 00	
Plumbing Supplies	3 00			(B) 2 00	1 00				1 00	
Plumbing Equipment	7 00				7 00				7 00	
Accumulated Depreciation, Plumbing Equipment		5 00		(C) 1 00		6 00				6 00
Accounts Payable		1 00				1 00				1 00
J. Frost, Capital		12 00				12 00				12 00
J. Frost, Withdrawals	3 00				3 00				3 00	
Plumbing Fees		27 00				27 00		27 00		
Rent Expense	4 00				4 00		4 00			
Salaries Expense	5 00		(D) 2 00		7 00		7 00			
	45 00	45 00								
Insurance Expense			(A) 3 00		3 00		3 00			
Plumbing Supplies Expense			(B) 2 00		2 00		2 00			
Depreciation Expense, Plumbing Equipment			(C) 1 00		1 00		1 00			
Accrued Salaries				(D) 2 00		2 00				2 00
			8 00	8 00	48 00	48 00	17 00	27 00	31 00	21 00
Net Income							10 00			10 00
							27 00	27 00	31 00	31 00

Solution Tips for Preparing Financial Statements from a Worksheet

Inside columns of the three financial statements are used for subtotalling. No debits or credits appear on the formal statements.

Statement	
Income Statement	From income statement columns of worksheet for revenue and expenses.
Statement of Owner's Equity	Beginning figure for Capital from the balance sheet Cr. column on the worksheet. Net Income from the income statement. Withdrawal figure from the balance sheet Dr. column on the worksheet.
Balance Sheet	Assets from the balance sheet Dr. column on the worksheet. Liabilities and Accumulated Depreciation from the balance sheet Cr. column on the worksheet. New figure for Capital from statement of owner's equity.

Note how Plumbing Equipment $7 and Accumulated Depreciation $6 are re-arranged on the formal balance sheet. The Total Assets of $22 is not on the worksheet. Remember, no debits or credits appear on formal statements.

SUMMARY OF KEY POINTS

Learning Unit 4-1

1. The worksheet is not a formal statement.
2. Adjustments update certain accounts so that they will be up to their latest balance before financial reports are prepared. Adjustments are the result of internal transactions.
3. Adjustments will affect both the income statement and the balance sheet.
4. Accounts listed *below* the account titles on the trial balance of the worksheet are *increasing*.
5. The original cost of a piece of equipment is not adjusted; historical cost is not lost.
6. Depreciation is the process of spreading the original cost of the asset over its expected useful life.
7. Accumulated depreciation is a contra-asset on the balance sheet that summarizes, accumulates, or builds up the amount of depreciation that an asset has accumulated.
8. Book value is the original cost less accumulated depreciation.
9. Accrued salaries are unpaid and unrecorded expenses that are accumulating but for which payment is not yet due.
10. Revenue and expenses go on income statement sections of the worksheet. Assets, contra-assets, liabilities, capital, and withdrawals go on balance sheet sections of the worksheet.

Learning Unit 4-2

1. The formal statements prepared from a worksheet do not have debit or credit columns.
2. Revenue and expenses go on the income statement. Beginning capital plus net income less withdrawals (or beginning capital minus net loss, less withdrawals) goes on the statement of owner's equity. Be sure to check the capital account in the ledger to see if any additional investments took place. Assets, contra-assets, liabilities, and the new figure for capital go on the balance sheet.

KEY TERMS

Accrued Salaries A liability account that records salaries that are earned by employees but are unpaid and unrecorded (and thus need to be recorded by an adjustment) and will not come due for payment until the next accounting period (p. 149)

Accumulated Depreciation A contra-asset account that summarizes or accumulates the amount of depreciation that has been taken on an asset (p. 146)

Adjusting The process of calculating the latest up-to-date balance of each account at the end of an accounting period (p. 143)

Book value Cost of equipment less accumulated depreciation (p. 147)

Capital Cost Allowance Another term for depreciation as defined in law by the *Income Tax Act* and administered by the Canada Revenue Agency (p. 145)

Contra-asset account An account that causes another related account to be restated or revalued. Its normal balance is a credit, which reduces the net asset value. (p. 146)

Depreciation The allocation (spreading) of the cost of an asset (such as an auto or equipment) over its expected useful life (p. 145)

Historical cost The actual cost of an asset at time of purchase (p. 145)

Residual value Book value of an asset after all the allowable depreciation has been deducted. Also, an estimate of disposal value at the end of an asset's useful life (p. 146)

Salaries Payable Sometimes used as an alternative term for accrued salaries. It is not as precise because, even though employees may have earned wages at the year (or month) end date, the amounts are often not actually payable until the next period. (p. 149)

Worksheet A columnar device used by accountants to aid them in completing the accounting cycle. It is not a formal statement. (p. 142)

QUICK REVIEW

The following Tips are from Learning Units 4-1 to 4-2. Answer the Assess Your Progress questions and use the How Did You Do? at the bottom of the page to see how well you know the material. The Quick Review provides tips before each Assess Your Progress to help you avoid common accounting errors.

LU 4-1 Step 5 of the Accounting Cycle: Preparing a Worksheet

Tips: When preparing adjustments on a worksheet, the accounts listed below the trial balance will always be increasing. In the adjustment for supplies, the adjustment is the amount of supplies used, not what is on hand. Keep in mind that for the adjustment for depreciation the original cost of the asset is not touched. The adjustment is an increase in Depreciation Expense and an increase in Accumulated Depreciation. Depreciation Expense goes on the income statement as an expense, and Accumulated Depreciation goes on the balance sheet as a contra-asset account. Keep in mind that the original costs of the asset and accumulated depreciation are both listed on the balance sheet.

Assess Your Progress

Answer true or false to the following statements:

1. A worksheet is a formal report.
2. Accumulated Depreciation is a contra-liability.
3. The adjustment for supplies is the amount of supplies on hand.
4. The normal balance of Accumulated Depreciation is a debit.
5. The old figure for Capital is on the worksheet, so Net Income must be brought over at the bottom to the balance sheet credit column so totals will balance.

LU 4-2 Step 6 of the Accounting Cycle: Preparing the Financial Statements from the Worksheet

Tips: The worksheet uses debits and credits; however, when the three formal financial statements are prepared they do not use debits and credits. The worksheet uses the beginning figure for Capital (no additional investment during the month), but when the financial statements are complete the formal balance sheet will list the figure for ending Capital from the statement of owner's equity.

Assess Your Progress

Answer true or false to the following statements:

1. Subtotalling is not used in preparing the formal financial statements from a worksheet.
2. Withdrawals are listed on the income statement.
3. Accumulated Depreciation is added to the cost of the asset on the balance sheet.
4. Debits are the inside column on the formal reports.
5. Totals on the formal balance sheet will match totals on the worksheet.

How Did You Do? Answers to the Assess Your Progress Questions

LU 4-1

1. False—A worksheet is an informal report.
2. False—Accumulated Depreciation is a contra-asset.
3. False—The adjustment for Supplies is the amount of supplies used up.
4. False—The normal balance of Accumulated Depreciation is a credit.
5. True.

LU 4-2

1. False—Subtotalling *is* used in preparing the formal financial statements from a worksheet.
2. False—Withdrawals are listed on the statement of owner's equity.
3. False—Accumulated Depreciation is subtracted from the cost of the asset on the balance sheet.
4. False—There are no debits or credits on financial statements.
5. False—Totals on formal reports do not match totals on the worksheet since there are no debits and credits on financial reports and subtotalling is used.

BLUEPRINT OF STEPS 5 AND 6 OF THE ACCOUNTING CYCLE

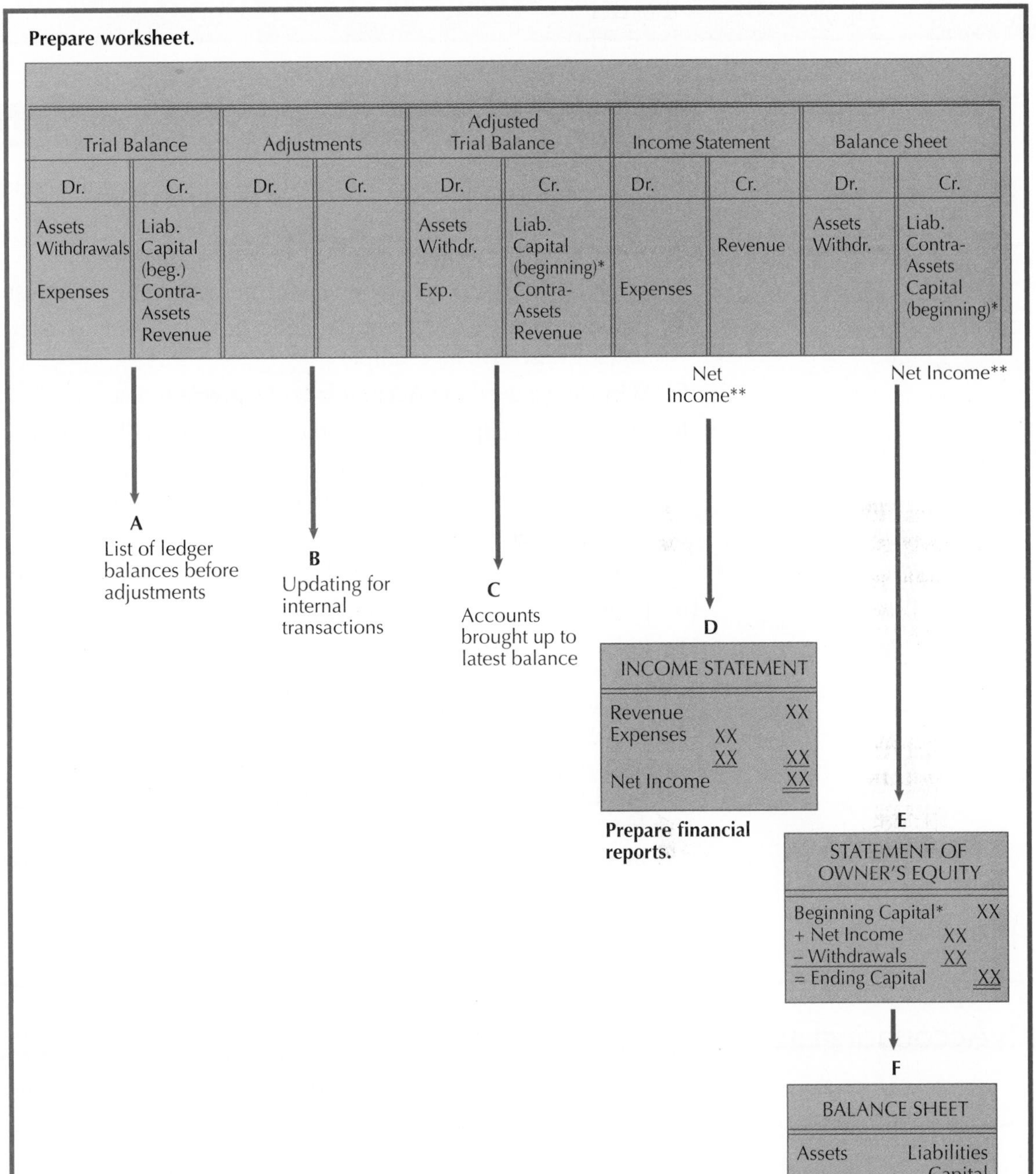

*No additional investment during the period.
**If net loss, record on Cr. side of income statement columns and Dr. side of balance sheet columns.

QUESTIONS, CLASSROOM DEMONSTRATION EXERCISES, EXERCISES, AND PROBLEMS

Discussion Questions and Critical Thinking/Ethical Case

1. Worksheets are required in every company's accounting cycle. Please agree or disagree and explain why.
2. What is the purpose of adjusting accounts?
3. What is the relationship of internal transactions to the adjusting process?
4. Explain how an adjustment can affect both the income statement and balance sheet. Please give an example.
5. Why do we need the Accumulated Depreciation account?
6. Depreciation expense goes on the balance sheet. True or false? Why?
7. Each month the cost of accumulated depreciation grows while the cost of equipment goes up. Agree or disagree. Defend your position.
8. Define accrued salaries.
9. Why don't the formal financial statements contain debit or credit columns?
10. Explain how the financial statements are prepared from the worksheet.
11. Janet Fox, President of Angel Co., went to a tax seminar. One of the speakers at the seminar advised the audience to put off showing expenses until next year because doing so would allow them to take advantage of a new tax law. When Janet returned to the office, she called in her accountant, Frieda O'Riley. She told Frieda to forget about making any adjustments for salaries in the old year so more expenses could be shown in the new year. Frieda told her that putting off these expenses would not follow generally accepted accounting principles. Janet said she should do it anyway. You make the call. Write your specific recommendations to Frieda.

MyAccountingLab

Make the grade with MyAccountingLab! The exercises and problems marked with ● can be found on MyAccountingLab. You can practise them as often as you want, and many of them feature step-by-step guided solutions to help you find the right answer.

Classroom Demonstration Exercises

(The blank forms you need are on pages 4-6 and 4-7 of the *Study Guide with Working Papers.*)

Adjustment for Supplies

Making adjustments for supplies
1 (5 min)

1. Before adjustment:

Office Supplies		Office Supplies Expense	
700			

Given

At year-end, an inventory of supplies shows $50.

Required

a. How much is the adjustment for office supplies?

b. Draw a transaction analysis box for this adjustment.

c. What will be the balance of office supplies on the adjusted trial balance?

Adjustment for Prepaid Rent

Making adjustments for prepaid rent
❶ (10 min)

2. Before adjustment:

Prepaid Rent	
1,200	

Rent Expense	

Given

At year-end, expired rent is $700.

Required

a. How much is the adjustment for Prepaid Rent?

b. Draw a transaction analysis box for this adjustment.

c. What will be the balance of Prepaid Rent on the adjusted trial balance?

Adjustment for Depreciation

Making adjustments for depreciation
❶ (10 min)

3. Before adjustment:

Equipment	
9,000	

Accumulated Depreciation, Equipment	
	2,000

Depreciation Expense, Equipment	

Given

For the current year, depreciation on equipment is $2,000.

Required

a. Which of the three T accounts is not affected?

b. Which title is a contra-asset?

c. Draw a transaction analysis box for this adjustment.

d. What will be the balance of each of these three accounts on the adjusted trial balance?

Adjustment for Accrued Salaries

Making adjustments for accrued salaries
❶ (10 min)

4. Before adjustment:

Salaries Expense	
1,400	

Accrued Salaries	

Given

Accrued Salaries, $300

Required

a. Draw a transaction analysis box for this adjustment.

b. What will be the balances of these two accounts on the adjusted trial balance?

Preparing worksheet sections
❷ ❸ (15 min)

Worksheet

5. From the following adjusted trial balance (ATB) titles on a worksheet of a lawyer, identify in which column each account will be listed in the last four columns of the worksheet.
(ID) Income statement, Dr. column
(IC) Income statement, Cr. column
(BD) Balance sheet, Dr. column
(BC) Balance sheet, Cr. column

ATB	ID	IC	BD	BC
a. Legal Fees	_______	_______	_______	_______
b. Accounts Payable	_______	_______	_______	_______
c. Cash	_______	_______	_______	_______
d. Prepaid Advertising	_______	_______	_______	_______
e. Accrued Salaries	_______	_______	_______	_______
f. Depreciation Expense	_______	_______	_______	_______
g. V., Capital	_______	_______	_______	_______
h. V., Withdrawals	_______	_______	_______	_______
i. Computer Supplies	_______	_______	_______	_______
j. Rent Expense	_______	_______	_______	_______
k. Supplies Payable	_______	_______	_______	_______
l. Advertising Expense	_______	_______	_______	_______
m. Accumulated Depreciation	_______	_______	_______	_______
n. Accrued Wages	_______	_______	_______	_______

Preparing financial statements from the worksheet
❸ ❹ (15 min)

6. From the following balance sheet (which was made from the worksheet and other financial statements), explain why the lettered numbers were not found on the worksheet. *Hint:* There are no debits or credits on the formal financial statements.

Laze Co.
Balance Sheet
December 31, 2015

Assets			**Liabilities and Owner's Equity**		
Cash		$ 6	Liabilities		
Accounts Receivable		2	Accounts Payable	$2	
Supplies		2	Accrued Salaries	1	
Equipment	$10		Total Liabilities		$ 3 (B)
Less: Accumulated			Owner's Equity		
Depreciation	4	6 (A)	H. Wells, Capital		13
			Total Liabilities and		
Total Assets		$16	Owner's Equity		$16

Exercises

Set A

(The blank forms you need are on pages 4-8 and 4-9 of the *Study Guide with Working Papers.*)

Categorizing accounts
4 (5 min)

4-1A. Complete the following table.

Account	Category	Normal Balance	Found on Which Financial Statement(s)
Accounts Payable			
Prepaid Rent			
Office Equipment			
Depreciation Expense			
B. Reel, Capital			
B. Reel, Withdrawals			
Office Supplies			
Accumulated Depreciation			

Reviewing adjustments and the transaction analysis charts
1 (10 min)

4-2A. Use transaction analysis charts to analyze the following adjustments:

a. Depreciation on equipment, $600
b. Rent expired, $400

Recording adjusting entries
1 (10 min)

4-3A. From the following adjustment data, calculate the adjustment amount and record appropriate debits or credits:

a. Supplies purchased, $700; Supplies on hand, $200
b. Store equipment, $12,000; Accumulated depreciation before adjustment, $900; Depreciation expense, $200

Preparing a wordsheet
2 3 (20 min)

4-4A. From the following trial balance and adjustment data, complete a worksheet for J. Trent as of December 31, 2017:

a. Depreciation expense, store equipment, $2.00
b. Insurance expired, $1.00
c. Store supplies on hand, $4.00
d. Wages owed but not paid, $5.00 (they are an expense in the old year)

J. TRENT
TRIAL BALANCE
DECEMBER 31, 2017

	Dr.	Cr.
Cash	9 00	
Accounts Receivable	2 00	
Prepaid Insurance	7 00	
Store Supplies	6 00	
Store Equipment	7 00	
Accumulated Depreciation, Store Equipment		2 00
Accounts Payable		4 00
J. Trent, Capital		17 00
J. Trent, Withdrawals	6 00	
Revenue from Clients		24 00
Rent Expense	4 00	
Wage Expense	6 00	
	47 00	47 00

Preparing financial statements from a worksheet
❹ (20 min)

4-5A. From the completed worksheet in Exercise 4-4A, prepare:

a. An income statement for December

b. A statement of owner's equity for December

c. A balance sheet as of December 31, 2017

Exercises

Set B

(The forms you need are on pages 4-8 and 4-9 of the *Study Guide with Working Papers*.)

Categorizing accounts
❹ (5 min)

4-1B. Complete the following table.

Account	Category	Normal Balance	Found on Which Financial Statement(s)
Cash			
Office Supplies			
Building			
Depreciation Expense			
B. Reel, Capital			
B. Reel, Withdrawals			
Prepaid Insurance			
Accrued Salaries			

4-2B. Use transaction analysis charts to analyze the following adjustments:

a. Depreciation on equipment, $800

b. Insurance premium expired, $300

Recording adjusting entries
❶ (10 min)

4-3B. From the following adjustment data, calculate the adjustment amount and record appropriate debits or credits:

a. Supplies purchased, $1,200; supplies on hand, $400

b. Store equipment, $17,000; accumulated depreciation before adjustment, $3,700; depreciation expense, $2,100

Preparing a worksheet
❷❸ (20 min)

4-4B. From the following trial balance and adjustment data, complete a worksheet for J. Trent as of December 31, 2017:

a. Depreciation expense, store equipment, $3.00

b. Insurance expired, $2.00

c. Store supplies on hand, $2.00

d. Wages owed but not paid, $6.00 (an expense of 2017)

J. TRENT TRIAL BALANCE DECEMBER 31, 2017		
	Dr.	Cr.
Cash	8 00	
Accounts Receivable	9 00	
Prepaid Insurance	6 00	
Store Supplies	6 00	
Store Equipment	24 00	
Accumulated Depreciation, Store Equipment		6 00
Accounts Payable		27 00
J. Trent, Capital		10 00
J. Trent, Withdrawals	8 00	
Revenue from Clients		38 00
Rent Expense	8 00	
Wage Expense	12 00	
	81 00	81 00

Preparing financial statements from a worksheet
❹ (20 min)

4-5B. From the completed worksheet in Exercise 4-4B, prepare:

a. An income statement for December

b. A statement of owner's equity for December

c. A balance sheet as of December 31, 2017

Group A Problems

(The blank forms you need are on pages 4-10 and 4-11 of the *Study Guide with Working Papers.*)

Completing a partial worksheet up to the adjusted trial balance
❶ ❷ (15 min)

Check Figure

Total, Adjusted Trial Balance $35,350

4A-1. The following is the trial balance for Jill's Fitness Centre of Etobicoke for December 31, 2016.

JILL'S FITNESS CENTRE TRIAL BALANCE DECEMBER 31, 2016		
	Debit	Credit
Cash	10 0 0 0 00	
Accounts Receivable	6 0 0 0 00	
Fitness Supplies	5 4 0 0 00	
Fitness Equipment	9 2 0 0 00	
Accumulated Depreciation, Fitness Equipment		7 0 0 0 00
J. Walsh, Capital		14 3 5 0 00
J. Walsh, Withdrawals	3 0 0 0 00	
Fitness Fees		13 3 0 0 00
Rent Expense	9 0 0 00	
Advertising Expense	1 5 0 00	
	34 6 5 0 00	34 6 5 0 00

Given
The following adjustment data on December 31:

a. Fitness supplies on hand, $900

b. Depreciation taken on fitness equipment, $700

Complete a partial worksheet up to the adjusted trial balance.

Completing a worksheet
❶ ❷ ❸ (30 min)

4A-2. The trial balance below is for Ling's Landscaping Service of Merritt for December 31, 2015.

> *Check Figure*
>
> **Net Income $654**

LING'S LANDSCAPING SERVICE
TRIAL BALANCE
DECEMBER 31, 2015

	Dr.	Cr.
Cash	4000 00	
Accounts Receivable	700 00	
Prepaid Rent	800 00	
Landscaping Supplies	742 00	
Landscaping Equipment	1400 00	
Accumulated Depreciation, Landscaping Equipment		1060 00
Accounts Payable		836 00
A. Ling, Capital		3250 00
Landscaping Revenue		4356 00
Heat Expense	400 00	
Advertising Expense	200 00	
Wages Expense	1260 00	
	9502 00	9502 00

Adjustment data to update the trial balance:

a. Rent expired, $600
b. Landscaping supplies on hand (remaining), $200
c. Depreciation expense, landscaping equipment, $300
d. Wages earned by workers but not paid and not due until January, $400

Required

Prepare a worksheet for Ling's Landscaping Service for the month of December.

Comprehensive problem
❶ ❷ ❸ ❹ (60 min)

4A-3. The following is the trial balance for Kevin's Moving Co. of Dartmouth.

> *Check Figure*
>
> **Net Income $2,140**

KEVIN'S MOVING CO.
TRIAL BALANCE
OCTOBER 31, 2017

	Dr.	Cr.
Cash	5000 00	
Prepaid Insurance	2500 00	
Moving Supplies	1200 00	
Moving Truck	11000 00	
Accumulated Depreciation, Moving Truck		9000 00
Accounts Payable		2768 00
K. Hoff, Capital		5442 00
K. Hoff, Withdrawals	1400 00	
Revenue from Moving		9000 00
Wages Expense	3712 00	
Rent Expense	1080 00	
Advertising Expense	318 00	
	26210 00	26210 00

Adjustment data to update trial balance:

a. Insurance expired, $700

b. Moving supplies on hand, $900

c. Depreciation on moving truck, $500

d. Wages earned but unpaid, $250

Required

1. Complete a worksheet for Kevin's Moving Co. for the month of October.

2. Prepare an income statement for October, a statement of owner's equity for October, and a balance sheet as of October 31, 2017.

Comprehensive problem
❶❷❸❹ (60 min)

4A-4. The following is a trial balance for Dick's Repair Service of Moose Jaw.

Check Figure

Net Income $1,830

DICK'S REPAIR SERVICE TRIAL BALANCE NOVEMBER 30, 2016		
	Dr.	Cr.
Cash	3 2 0 0 00	
Prepaid Insurance	4 0 0 0 00	
Repair Supplies	4 6 0 0 00	
Repair Equipment	3 0 0 0 00	
Accumulated Depreciation, Repair Equipment		7 0 0 00
Accounts Payable		5 5 7 0 00
D. Horn, Capital		3 8 0 0 00
Revenue from Repairs		7 0 0 0 00
Wages Expense	1 8 0 0 00	
Rent Expense	3 6 0 00	
Advertising Expense	1 1 0 00	
	17 0 7 0 00	17 0 7 0 00

Adjustment data to update the trial balance:

a. Insurance expired, $700

b. Repair supplies on hand, $3,000

c. Depreciation on repair equipment, $200

d. Wages earned but not yet paid, $400

Required

1. Complete a worksheet for Dick's Repair Service for the month of November.

2. Prepare an income statement for November, a statement of owner's equity for November, and a balance sheet as of November 30, 2016.

Group B Problems

(The blank forms you need are on pages 4-10 and 4-11 of the *Study Guide with Working Papers.*)

Completing a partial worksheet up to adjusted trial balance
❶❷ (15 min)

4B-1. For Jill's Fitness Centre of Etobicoke, complete a partial worksheet up to the adjusted trial balance using the following adjustment data and trial balance:

a. Fitness supplies on hand, $3,000

b. Depreciation taken on fitness equipment, $500

JILL'S FITNESS CENTRE TRIAL BALANCE DECEMBER 31, 2016		
	Dr.	Cr.
Cash	6000 00	
Accounts Receivable	2000 00	
Fitness Supplies	4200 00	
Fitness Equipment	8000 00	
Accumulated Depreciation, Fitness Equipment		4700 00
J. Walsh, Capital		16000 00
J. Walsh, Withdrawals	1000 00	
Fitness Fees		1400 00
Rent Expense	800 00	
Advertising Expense	100 00	
	22100 00	22100 00

> ***Check Figure***
>
> **Total, Adjusted Trial Balance $22,600**

Completing a worksheet
❶ ❷ ❸ (30 min)

4B-2. Given the following trial balance and adjustment data for Ling's Landscaping Service of Merritt, prepare a worksheet for the month of December.

LING'S LANDSCAPING SERVICE TRIAL BALANCE DECEMBER 31, 2015		
	Dr.	Cr.
Cash	396 00	
Accounts Receivable	284 00	
Prepaid Rent	400 00	
Landscaping Supplies	310 00	
Landscaping Equipment	1000 00	
Accumulated Depreciation, Landscaping Equipment		200 00
Accounts Payable		346 00
A. Ling, Capital		456 00
Landscaping Revenue		4680 00
Heat Expense	632 00	
Advertising Expense	1200 00	
Wages Expense	1460 00	
Total	5682 00	5682 00

> ***Check Figure***
>
> **Net Income $673**

Adjustment Data

a. Landscaping supplies on hand, $60
b. Rent expired, $150
c. Depreciation on landscaping equipment, $200
d. Wages earned but unpaid, $115

Comprehensive problem
❶ ❷ ❸ ❹ (60 min)

4B-3. Using the following trial balance and adjustment data for Kevin's Moving Co. of Dartmouth, prepare:

1. A worksheet for the month of October
2. An income statement for October, a statement of owner's equity for October, and a balance sheet as of October 31, 2017

Adjustment Data

a. Insurance expired, $600
b. Moving supplies on hand, $310

c. Depreciation on moving truck, $580

d. Wages earned but unpaid, $410

Check Figure

Net Loss $1,628

KEVIN'S MOVING CO. TRIAL BALANCE OCTOBER 31, 2017		
	Dr.	Cr.
Cash	3920 00	
Prepaid Insurance	3288 00	
Moving Supplies	1400 00	
Moving Truck	10658 00	
Accumulated Depreciation, Moving Truck		3660 00
Accounts Payable		1312 00
K. Hoff, Capital		17482 00
K. Hoff, Withdrawals	4240 00	
Revenue from Moving		8162 00
Wages Expense	5712 00	
Rent Expense	1080 00	
Advertising Expense	318 00	
	30616 00	30616 00

Comprehensive problem

❶ ❷ ❸ ❹ (60 min)

4B-4. As the bookkeeper of Dick's Repair Service in Moose Jaw, use the information that follows to prepare:

1. A worksheet for the month of November
2. An income statement for November, a statement of owner's equity for November, and a balance sheet as of November 30, 2016

Check Figure

Net Income $1,012

DICK'S REPAIR SERVICE TRIAL BALANCE NOVEMBER 30, 2016		
	Dr.	Cr.
Cash	3204 00	
Prepaid Insurance	4000 00	
Repair Supplies	770 00	
Repair Equipment	3106 00	
Accumulated Depreciation, Repair Equipment		650 00
Accounts Payable		1904 00
D. Horn, Capital		6258 00
Revenue from Repairs		5634 00
Wages Expense	1600 00	
Rent Expense	1560 00	
Advertising Expense	206 00	
	14446 00	14446 00

Adjustment Data

a. Insurance expired, $300

b. Repair supplies on hand, $170

c. Depreciation on repair equipment, $250

d. Wages earned but unpaid, $106

Group C Problems

(The forms you need are on pages 4-12 and 4-13 of the *Study Guide with Working Papers.*)

Completing a partial worksheet up to adjusted trial balance
❶ ❷ (15 min)

Check Figure

Total, Adjusted Trial Balance $21,511

4C-1. Please complete a partial worksheet up to the adjusted trial balance for CJ's Mountain Safety Training of Banff, using the following adjustment data and trial balance:

a. Supplies on hand, $1,605

b. Depreciation taken on equipment, $265

CJ'S MOUNTAIN SAFETY TRAINING
TRIAL BALANCE
DECEMBER 31, 2017

	Dr.	Cr.
Cash	12100 00	
Accounts Receivable	1370 00	
Supplies	2170 00	
Safety Equipment	3180 00	
Accumulated Depreciation, Safety Equipment		1060 00
Chris Janz, Capital		15416 00
Chris Janz, Withdrawals	700 00	
Fees Earned		4770 00
Rent Expense	900 00	
Advertising Expense	370 00	
Utilities Expense	456 00	
Totals	21246 00	21246 00

Completing a worksheet
❶ ❷ ❸ (30 min)

Check Figure

Net Income $3,690.25

4C-2. Given the following trial balance and adjustment data for The Debbie Rose Art Studio of Richmond, your task is to prepare a worksheet for the month of November, the first month of operations in a new fiscal year.

THE DEBBIE ROSE ART STUDIO
TRIAL BALANCE
NOVEMBER 30, 2015

	Dr.	Cr.
Cash	3813 00	
Accounts Receivable	2820 00	
Prepaid Rent	850 00	
Painting Supplies	921 00	
Studio Equipment	5985 00	
Accumulated Depreciation, Studio Equipment		1995 00
Accounts Payable		1788 00
Debbie Rose Allen, Capital		5828 00
Painting Revenue		7816 00
Advertising Expense	510 00	
Utilities Expense	278 00	
Wages Expense	2250 00	
Totals	17427 00	17427 00

Adjustment Data

a. Painting supplies on hand, $595.

b. Prepaid rent represents the first and last months' rent on a new office lease signed November 1, 2015.

c. Depreciation on studio equipment is based on straight-line, five-year life and a residual value of $480.

d. Wages earned but unpaid amounted to 24.5 hours at $10 per hour.

Comprehensive problem
❶ ❷ ❸ ❹ (60 min)

4C-3. Using the following trial balance and adjustment data for Vivian's Repair Co. of Windsor, prepare:

1. A worksheet for October
2. An income statement for October, a statement of owner's equity for October, and a balance sheet as of October 31, 2016

Adjustment Data

a. One-quarter of the prepaid insurance has expired.

b. Repair supplies on hand, $795.

c. Depreciation on repair equipment is based on the straight-line approach, with a 10-year life and a residual value of $1,200.

d. Depreciation on building is also straight-line, 50-year life, and no residual value.

e. Wages earned but unpaid amounted to 76 hours at $14 per hour at month-end.

Check Figure

Net Income $13,553.92

VIVIAN'S REPAIR CO.
TRIAL BALANCE
OCTOBER 31, 2016

	Dr.	Cr.
Cash	3 3 2 6 00	
Prepaid Insurance	1 3 8 9 00	
Repair Supplies	1 1 4 8 00	
Repair Equipment	8 4 6 0 00	
Building	50 0 0 0 00	
Accumulated Depreciation, Repair Equipment		3 9 5 2 00
Accumulated Depreciation, Building		12 5 0 0 00
Accounts Payable		2 7 2 4 00
Vivian Hunter, Capital		43 0 8 5 00
Vivian Hunter, Withdrawals	13 4 0 0 00	
Repair Fees Revenue		28 6 8 5 00
Wages Expense	10 8 9 0 00	
Utilities Expense	8 4 1 00	
Advertising Expense	1 4 9 2 00	
Totals	90 9 4 6 00	90 9 4 6 00

Comprehensive problem
❶ ❷ ❸ ❹ (45 min)

4C-4. As the bookkeeper of Maritime Internet Access Service of Amherst, use the information that follows to prepare:

1. A worksheet for August, the end of the first quarter in the current fiscal year
2. An income statement for August, a statement of owner's equity for August, and a balance sheet as of August 31, 2015

Adjustment Data

a. Two-thirds of the prepaid insurance remains prepaid at month-end.

b. Computer supplies on hand, $268.

c. Depreciation on computer equipment is based on the straight-line method, a four-year life, and residual value of $1,400.

d. Wages earned but unpaid amounted to 64 hours at $15 per hour at month-end.

e. Advertising bill received, not yet paid, $245.

MARITIME INTERNET ACCESS SERVICE
TRIAL BALANCE
AUGUST 31, 2015

	Dr.	Cr.
Cash	70800	
Prepaid Insurance	105000	
Computer Supplies	42600	
Computer Equipment	1148000	
Accumulated Depreciation, Computer Equipment		420000
Accounts Payable		84000
Lucy Northwest, Capital		288700
Lucy Northwest, Withdrawals	147800	
Revenue from Services Provided		1438500
Wages Expense	476000	
Rent Expense	148500	
Advertising Expense	92500	
Totals	2231200	2231200

Check Figure

Net Income $4,872.00

On-the-Job Training

(The blank forms you need are on pages 4-14 to 4-15 of the *Study Guide with Working Papers.*)

Preparing adjustments
❶ (20 min)

T-1.

TO: Hal Hogan, Bookkeeper

FROM: Pete Tennant, V. P.

RE: Adjustments for year ended December 31, 2016

Hal, here is the information you requested. Please supply me with the adjustments needed ASAP. Also, please put in writing why we need to do these adjustments.

Thanks

Attached to memo:

a. Insurance data:

Policy No.	*Date of Policy Purchase*	*Policy Length*	*Cost*
100	November 1 of previous year	4 years	$480
200	May 1 of current year	2 years	600
300	September 1 of current year	1 year	240

b. Rent data: Prepaid rent had a $500 balance at beginning of year. An additional $400 in rent was paid in advance in June. At year-end, $200 in rent had expired.

c. Revenue data: Accrued storage fees of $500 were earned but uncollected and unrecorded at year-end.

T-2.

> *Hint:* Unearned rent is a liability on the balance sheet.

Adjustments
❶ (30 min)

On Friday, Harry Swag's boss asks him to prepare a special report that is due on Monday at 8 a.m. Harry gathers the following material in his briefcase:

			December 31	
			2016	2017
Prepaid Advertising			$300	$600
Accrued Interest			150	350
Unearned Rent			500	300
Cash paid for:	Advertising	$1,900		
	Interest	1,500		
Cash received for:	Rent	2,300		

As his best friend, you want to help Harry show the amounts that are to be reported on the 2017 income statement for (a) Advertising Expense, (b) Interest Expense, and (c) Rent Fees Earned. Please explain in writing why unearned rent is considered a liability.

CONTINUING PROBLEM

At the end of July, Tony took a complete inventory of his supplies and found the following:

5 dozen ¼″ screws at a cost of $8 a dozen
2 dozen ½″ screws at a cost of $5 a dozen
2 cartons of computer inventory paper at a cost of $14 a carton
3 metres of coaxial cable at a cost of $4 per metre

After speaking to his accountant, he found that a reasonable depreciation amount for each of his long-term assets is as follows:

Computer purchased May 6, 2016	Depreciation $33 a month
Office equipment purchased May 16, 2013, 2016	Depreciation $10 a month
Computer workstations purchased July 17, 2016	Depreciation $20 a month

Tony uses the straight-line method of depreciation and declares no salvage value for any of the assets. If any long-term asset is purchased in the first 15 days of the month, he will charge depreciation for the full month. If an asset is purchased on the 16th of the month, or later, he will not charge depreciation in the month it was purchased.

July's rent has now expired.

Assignment

Use your trial balance from the completed problem in Chapter 3 and the above adjusting information to complete the worksheet for the three months ended July 31, 2016. From the worksheets, prepare the financial statements. (See pages 4-16 to 4-19 in your *Study Guide with Working Papers*.)

CHAPTER 5

The Accounting Cycle Completed

ADJUSTING, CLOSING, AND POST-CLOSING TRIAL BALANCE

LEARNING OBJECTIVES

By April 30 of each year, Canadian taxpayers must send in their completed tax forms to Revenue Canada. Sometimes it seems that it is a very short period of time before the process has to be repeated. It is an annual process of course, and our tax laws can be complicated.

Companies in business to earn a profit also must complete annual tax returns and pay income tax based on how much money they made during the previous year. Unlike individuals who must file by April 30 each year, businesses must complete and file their tax returns based on when their fiscal year ends. A business can choose to end their fiscal year whenever they prefer, but most end at the conclusion of a particular month, and often choose that month based on an analysis of how their business happens over a typical year. A company that specializes in selling ski equipment might choose to end their year in the summer months when major sales for the year are complete and the ordering process for the next busy season has not yet begun in earnest.

No matter when a business ends its fiscal year, the accounting cycle must be completed so that these businesses can report to the appropriate governmental agencies, like Revenue Canada, the Stock Exchange, and to investors and creditors.

Remember: **For ease of presentation, we are using a month as the accounting cycle for Clark's. In the business world, the cycle can be any time period but is usually one year.**

In Chapters 3 and 4, we completed these steps of the manual accounting cycle for Clark's Desktop Publishing Services:

Step 1: Business transactions occurred and generated source documents.
Step 2: Business transactions were analyzed and recorded in a journal.
Step 3: Information was posted or transferred from journal to ledger.
Step 4: A trial balance was prepared.
Step 5: A worksheet was completed.
Step 6: Financial statements were prepared.

This chapter covers the following steps, which will complete Clark's accounting cycle for the month of May:

Step 7: Journalizing and posting adjusting entries

Step 8: Journalizing and posting closing entries

Step 9: Preparing a post-closing trial balance

LEARNING UNIT 5-1

Journalizing and Posting Adjusting Entries: Step 7 of the Accounting Cycle

LO 1 Journalizing and posting adjusting entries

RECORDING JOURNAL ENTRIES FROM THE WORKSHEET

Purpose of adjusting entries

The information in the worksheet is up to date. The financial statements prepared from that information can give the business's management and other interested parties a good idea of where the business stands as of a particular date. The problem is that the worksheet is an informal report. The information concerning the adjustments has not been placed in the journal or posted to the ledger accounts. This means that the books are not up to date and ready for the next accounting cycle to begin. For example, the ledger shows $1,200 of prepaid rent (page 106), but the balance sheet we prepared in Chapter 4 shows an $800 balance. Essentially, the worksheet is a tool for preparing financial statements. Now we must use the adjustment columns of the worksheet as a basis for bringing the ledger up to date. We do this by **adjusting journal entries** (see Figure 5-1). Again, the updating must be done before the next accounting period starts. For Clark's Desktop Publishing Services, the next period begins on June 1.

At this point, many ledger accounts are *not up to date.*

Figure 5-1 shows the adjusting journal entries for Clark's taken from the adjustments section of the worksheet (see Figure 5-2). Once the adjusting journal entries are posted to the ledger, the accounts making up the financial statements that were prepared from the worksheet will correspond with the updated ledger. (Keep in mind that this is the same journal we have been using.) Let's look at some simplified T accounts to show how Clark's ledger looked before and after the adjustments were posted. Adjustments A and B are below. Adjustments C and D are on page 188.

Adjustments A to D in the adjustments section of the worksheet must be recorded in the journal and posted to the ledger.

Adjustment A

Before posting:

Office Supplies 114	
600	

Office Supplies Expense 514	

After posting:

Office Supplies 114	
600	500

Office Supplies Expense 514	
500	

Adjustment B

Before posting:

Prepaid Rent 115	
1,200	

Rent Expense 515	

After posting:

Prepaid Rent 115	
1,200	400

Rent Expense 515	
400	

Figure 5-1
Adjusting Journal Entries, After They Have Been Posted

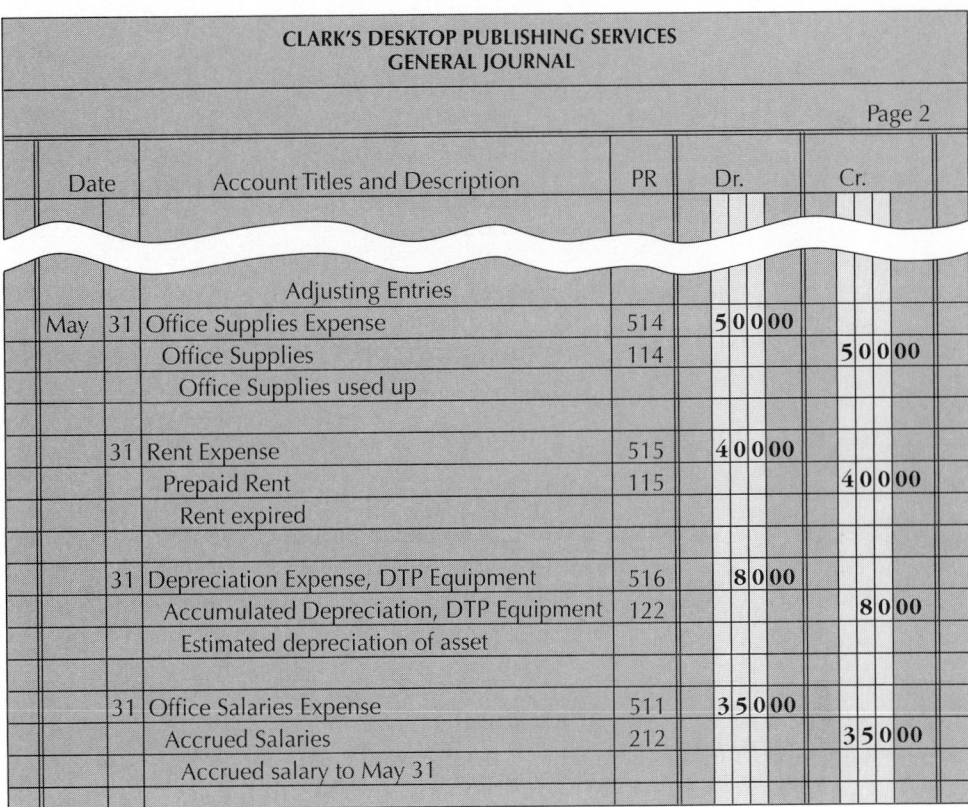

CLARK'S DESKTOP PUBLISHING SERVICES
GENERAL JOURNAL

Page 2

Date		Account Titles and Description	PR	Dr.	Cr.
		Adjusting Entries			
May	31	Office Supplies Expense	514	500 00	
		Office Supplies	114		500 00
		Office Supplies used up			
	31	Rent Expense	515	400 00	
		Prepaid Rent	115		400 00
		Rent expired			
	31	Depreciation Expense, DTP Equipment	516	80 00	
		Accumulated Depreciation, DTP Equipment	122		80 00
		Estimated depreciation of asset			
	31	Office Salaries Expense	511	350 00	
		Accrued Salaries	212		350 00
		Accrued salary to May 31			

Figure 5-2
Journalizing and Posting Adjustments from the Adjustments Section of the Worksheet

Account Titles	Trial Balance Dr.	Trial Balance Cr.	Adjustments Dr.	Adjustments Cr.
Cash	6155 00			
Accounts Receivable	5000 00			
Office Supplies	600 00			(A) 500 00
Prepaid Rent	1200 00			(B) 400 00
Desktop Publishing Equipment	6000 00			
Accounts Payable		3350 00		
Brenda Clark, Capital		10000 00		
Brenda Clark, Withdrawals	625 00			
Desktop Publishing Fees		8000 00		
Office Salaries Expense	1300 00		(D) 350 00	
Advertising Expense	250 00			
Telephone Expense	220 00			
	21350 00	21350 00		
Office Supplies Expense			(A) 500 00	
Rent Expense			(B) 400 00	
Depreciation Expense, DTP Equipment			(C) 80 00	
Accumulated Depreciation, DTP Equipment				(C) 80 00
Accrued Salaries				(D) 350 00
			1330 00	1330 00

Adjustment C

Before posting:

Desktop Publishing Equipment 121	
6,000	

Depreciation Expense, DTP Equipment 516	

Accumulated Depreciation, DTP Equipment 122	

After posting:

Desktop Publishing Equipment 121	
6,000	

Depreciation Expense, DTP Equipment 516	
80	

Accumulated Depreciation, DTP Equipment 122	
	80

This last adjustment shows the same balances for Depreciation Expense and Accumulated Depreciation. However, in subsequent adjustments, the Accumulated Depreciation balance will keep getting larger, but the debit to Depreciation Expense and the credit to Accumulated Depreciation will be the same. We will see why in a moment.

Adjustment D

Before posting:

Office Salaries Expense 511	
650	
650	

Accrued Salaries 212	

After posting:

Office Salaries Expense 511	
650	
650	
350	

Accrued Salaries 212	
	350

LEARNING UNIT 5-1 REVIEW

AT THIS POINT you should be able to:

- Define and state the purpose of adjusting entries. (p. 186)
- Journalize adjusting entries from the worksheet. (p. 187)
- Post journalized adjusting entries to the ledger. (p. 187)
- Compare specific ledger accounts before and after posting of the journalized adjusting entries. (pp. 186, 188)

Self-Review Quiz 5-1

(The blank forms you need are on pages 5-1 and 5-2 of the *Study Guide with Working Papers.*)

Turn to the worksheet of P. Logan Company (p. 154) and (1) journalize and post the adjusting entries and (2) compare the adjusted ledger accounts before and after the adjustments are posted. T accounts with beginning balances are provided in your *Study Guide*.

> **!** ***Quiz Tip***
>
> **These journal entries come from the adjustments column of the worksheet.**

Solution to Self-Review Quiz 5-1

GENERAL JOURNAL — Page 2

Date		Account Titles and Description	PR	Dr.	Cr.
		Adjusting Entries			
Dec.	31	Depreciation Expense, Store Equipment	511	1 00	
		Accumulated Depreciation, Store Equipment	122		1 00
		Estimated depreciation of equipment			
	31	Insurance Expense	516	2 00	
		Prepaid Insurance	116		2 00
		Insurance expired			
	31	Supplies Expense	514	4 00	
		Store Supplies	114		4 00
		Store Supplies used			
	31	Salaries Expense	512	3 00	
		Accrued Salaries	212		3 00
		Accrued salaries payable			

PARTIAL LEDGER

Before Posting

Depreciation Expense, Store Equipment 511	

Accumulated Depreciation, Store Equipment 122	
	4

Prepaid Insurance 116	
3	

Insurance Expense 516	

Store Supplies 114	
5	

Supplies Expense 514	

Salaries Expense 512	
8	

Accrued Salaries 212	

After Posting

Depreciation Expense, Store Equipment 511	
1	

Accumulated Depreciation, Store Equipment 122	
	4
	1

Prepaid Insurance 116	
3	2

Insurance Expense 516	
2	

Store Supplies 114	
5	4

Supplies Expense 514	
4	

Salaries Expense 512	
8	
3	

Accrued Salaries 212	
	3

NEED HELP?

Let's review first: Once the financial statements are prepared from the worksheet, our ledger is still not up to date. Information about the adjustments on the worksheet have not been journalized or posted to the ledger.

How to update the ledger with adjustments on the worksheet: Using the worksheet of Logan Company, go to the adjustments column and journalize the four adjusting entries. Once the adjustments are journalized, they must be posted to the ledger. When the postings are complete, the legder accounts for depreciation expense, accumulated depreciation, insurance expense, prepaid insurance, supplies expense, store supplies, accrued salaries, and salaries expense will have the latest, up-to-date balances, and the PR column is filled in with the correct account numbers.

SUMMARY

The ending balances in the ledger after posting adjustments will be the same amounts that were found on the adjusted trial balance.

LEARNING UNIT 5-2

Journalizing and Posting Closing Entries: Step 8 of the Accounting Cycle

LO 2

Journalizing and posting closing entries

To make recording of the next fiscal year's transactions easier, a mechanical step, called **closing**, is taken by the accountant at Clark's. Closing is used to end—or close off—the revenue, expense, and withdrawal accounts at the end of the fiscal year. The information needed to complete closing entries will be found in the income statement and balance sheet sections of the worksheet.

To make it easier to understand this process, we will first look at the difference between temporary (nominal) accounts and permanent (real) accounts.

Here is the expanded accounting equation that we used in an earlier chapter:

Assets = Liabilities + Capital − Withdrawals + Revenues − Expenses

Permanent accounts are found on the balance sheet.

Three of the items in that equation—assets, liabilities, and capital—are known as **real** or **permanent accounts** because their balances are carried over from one fiscal year to another. The other three items—withdrawals, revenue, and expenses—are called **nominal** or **temporary accounts** because their balances are not carried over from one fiscal year to another. Instead, their balances are set to zero at the beginning of each fiscal year. This allows us to accumulate new data about revenue, expenses, and withdrawals in the new fiscal year. The process of closing summarizes the effects of the temporary accounts on capital for that period by using **closing journal entries** and by posting them to the ledger. When the closing process is complete, the accounting equation will be reduced to:

After all closing entries are journalized and posted to the ledger, all temporary accounts have a zero balance in the ledger. Closing is a step-by-step process.

Assets = Liabilities + Ending Capital

If you look back at page 157 in Chapter 4, you will see that we have calculated the new capital on the balance sheet for Clark's Desktop Publishing Services to be $14,275. However, before the mechanical closing procedures are journalized and posted, the capital account of Brenda Clark in the ledger is only $10,000 (Chapter 3, page 108). Let's look now at how to journalize and post closing entries.

HOW TO JOURNALIZE CLOSING ENTRIES

There are four steps to be performed in journalizing closing entries:

An Income Summary is a temporary account located in the chart of accounts under Owner's Equity. It does not have a normal balance of a debit or a credit.

Step 1: Clear the revenue account balances and transfer them to Income Summary. **Income Summary** is a temporary account in the ledger needed for closing. At the end of the closing process, there will be a zero balance in Income Summary.

Revenue → Income Summary

Step 2: Clear the individual expense account balances and transfer them to Income Summary.

Expenses → Income Summary

Sometimes, closing the accounts is referred to as "clearing the accounts."

Step 3: Clear the balance in Income Summary and transfer it to Capital.

Income Summary → Capital

Step 4: Clear the balance in Withdrawals and transfer it to Capital.

Withdrawals → Capital

Figure 5-3 is a visual representation of these four steps. Keep in mind that this information must first be journalized and then posted to the appropriate ledger accounts. The worksheet presented in Figure 5-4 contains all the figures we will need for the closing process.

Figure 5-3
Four Steps in Journalizing Closing Entries

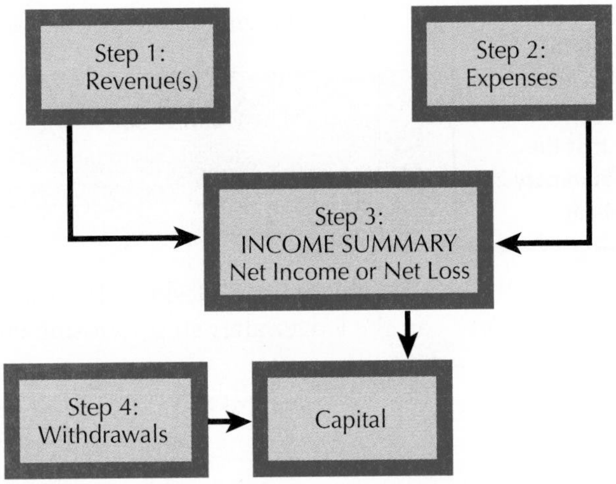

Figure 5-4
Closing Figures on the Worksheet

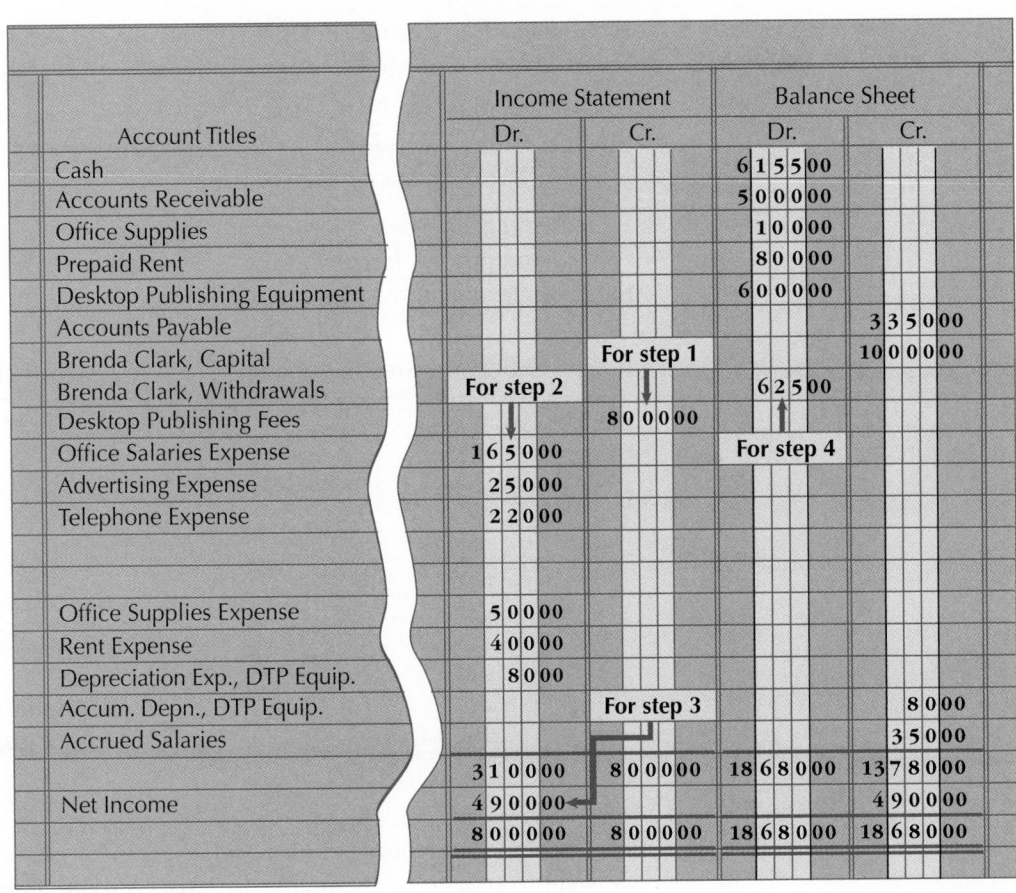

Account Titles	Income Statement Dr.	Income Statement Cr.	Balance Sheet Dr.	Balance Sheet Cr.
Cash			6155 00	
Accounts Receivable			5000 00	
Office Supplies			100 00	
Prepaid Rent			800 00	
Desktop Publishing Equipment			6000 00	
Accounts Payable				3350 00
Brenda Clark, Capital		For step 1		10000 00
Brenda Clark, Withdrawals	For step 2		625 00	
Desktop Publishing Fees		8000 00		
Office Salaries Expense	1650 00		For step 4	
Advertising Expense	250 00			
Telephone Expense	220 00			
Office Supplies Expense	500 00			
Rent Expense	400 00			
Depreciation Exp., DTP Equip.	80 00			
Accum. Depn., DTP Equip.		For step 3		80 00
Accrued Salaries				350 00
	3100 00	8000 00	18680 00	13780 00
Net Income	4900 00			4900 00
	8000 00	8000 00	18680 00	18680 00

Step 1: Clear Revenue Balance(s) and Transfer to Income Summary

Don't forget two goals of closing:

1. **Clear all temporary accounts in the ledger.**
2. **Update Capital to a new balance that reflects a summary of all the temporary accounts.**

Here is what is in the ledger before closing entries are journalized and posted:

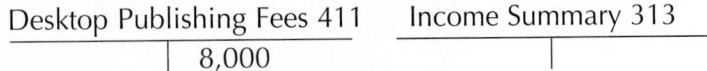

Desktop Publishing Fees 411		Income Summary 313	
	8,000		

The income statement section on the worksheet above shows that the Desktop Publishing Fees account has a credit balance of $8,000. To close or clear this to zero in the ledger, a debit of $8,000 is needed. However, if we add an amount to the debit side, we must also add a credit—so we add $8,000 on the credit side of the Income Summary account.

> **All numbers used in the closing process can be found on the worksheet in Figure 5-4. Note that the *account* Income Summary is *not* on the worksheet.**

The following is the journalized closing entry for step 1:

2016					
May	31	Desktop Publishing Fees	411	8000 00	
		Income Summary	313		8000 00
		To close income account			

This is what Desktop Publishing Fees and Income Summary should look like in the ledger after step 1 closing entries are journalized and posted:

Desktop Publishing Fees 411	
8,000	8,000
Closing	

Income Summary 313	
	8,000
	Revenue

Note that the revenue balance is cleared to zero and transferred to Income Summary, a temporary account also located in the ledger.

Step 2: Clear Individual Expense Balances and Transfer the Total to Income Summary

Here is what is in the ledger for each expense before step 2 closing entries are journalized and posted. Each expense is listed on the worksheet in the debit column of the income statement section as above.

Office Salaries Expense 511	
650	
650	
350	

Advertising Expense 512	
250	

Telephone Expense 513	
220	

Office Supplies Expense 514	
500	

Rent Expense 515	
400	

Depreciation Expense, DTP Equipment 516	
80	

The income statement section of the worksheet lists all the expenses as debits. If we want to reduce each expense to zero, each one must be credited.

The following is the journalized closing entry for step 2:

> **The $3,100 is the total of the expenses on the worksheet.**

	31	Income Summary	313	3100 00	
		Office Salaries Expense	511		1650 00
		Advertising Expense	512		250 00
		Telephone Expense	513		220 00
		Office Supplies Expense	514		500 00
		Rent Expense	515		400 00
		Depreciation Expense, DTP Equipment	516		80 00
		To close expense accounts			

This is what individual expense accounts and the Income Summary should look like in the ledger after step 2 closing entries are journalized and posted:

Office Salaries Expense 511

650	Closing 1,650
650	
350	

Advertising Expense 512

250	Closing 250

Telephone Expense 513

220	Closing 220

Office Supplies Expense 514

500	Closing 500

Rent Expense 515

400	Closing 400

Depreciation Expense 516

80	Closing 80

Remember: The worksheet is a tool. The accountant realizes that the information about the total of the expenses will be transferred to Income Summary.

Income Summary 313

Expenses	Revenue
Step 2 3,100	8,000 Step 1

Step 3: Clear Balance in Income Summary (Net Income) and Transfer It to Capital

This is how the Income Summary and Brenda Clark, Capital, accounts look before step 3:

Income Summary 313

3,100	8,000
	4,900

Brenda Clark, Capital 311

	10,000

Note that the balance of Income Summary (Revenue minus Expenses, or $8,000 – $3,100) is $4,900. That is the amount we must clear from the Income Summary account and transfer to the Brenda Clark, Capital, account.

The opposite would take place if the business had a net loss.

To transfer the balance of $4,900 from Income Summary (check the bottom of the debit column of the income statement section on the worksheet; see Figure 5-4) to Capital, it will be necessary to debit Income Summary for $4,900 (the difference between the revenue and the expenses) and credit or increase Capital of Brenda Clark with $4,900.

This is the journalized closing entry for step 3:

At the end of these three steps, Income Summary has a zero balance. If we had a net loss, the end result would be to decrease capital. The entry would be to debit Capital and credit Income Summary for the loss.

	31	Income Summary	313	490000	
		Brenda Clark, Capital	311		490000
		Net income closed to capital			

This is what the Income Summary and Brenda Clark, Capital, accounts will look like in the ledger after step 3 closing entries are journalized and posted:

Today's accounting software handles the closing process easily. However, accountants usually have to do step 4 separately.

Income Summary 313

Total of expenses →	3,100	8,000	← **Revenue**
Debit to close account →	4,900	4,900	← **Net income**

Brenda Clark, Capital 311

	10,000	
	4,900	**Net income**

Note that the $10,000 is a beginning balance since no additional investments were made during the period.

Step 4: Clear the Withdrawals Balance and Transfer It to Capital

Next, we must close the Withdrawals account. The Brenda Clark, Withdrawals, and Brenda Clark, Capital, accounts now look like this:

Brenda Clark, Withdrawals 312	
625	

Brenda Clark, Capital 311	
	10,000
	4,900

To bring the Withdrawals account to a zero balance and summarize its effect on Capital, we must credit Withdrawals and debit Capital.

Remember, withdrawals are a non-business expense and thus not transferred to Income Summary. The closing entry is journalized as follows:

	31	Brenda Clark, Capital	311	625 00	
		Brenda Clark, Withdrawals	312		625 00
		Close withdrawals into Capital			

At this point, the Brenda Clark, Withdrawals, and Brenda Clark, Capital, accounts would look like this in the ledger:

Brenda Clark, Withdrawals 312	
625	Closing 625

Brenda Clark, Capital 311	
625 Withdrawals	10,000 Beginning balance
	4,900 Net income

The four steps in closing the books

CLARK'S DESKTOP PUBLISHING SERVICES
GENERAL JOURNAL

Date		Account Title and Description	PR	Dr.	Cr.
2016					
May	31	Desktop Publishing Fees	411	8000 00	
		Income Summary	313		8000 00
		To close income account			
	31	Income Summary	313	3100 00	
		Office Salaries Expense	511		1650 00
		Advertising Expense	512		250 00
		Telephone Expense	513		220 00
		Office Supplies Expense	514		500 00
		Rent Expense	515		400 00
		Depreciation Expense, DTP Equipment	516		80 00
		To close expense accounts			
	31	Income Summary	313	4900 00	
		Brenda Clark, Capital	311		4900 00
		Net income closed to capital			
	31	Brenda Clark, Capital	311	625 00	
		Brenda Clark, Withdrawals	312		625 00
		Transfer withdrawals to capital			

Now let's look at a summary of the closing entries. The complete ledger for Clark's Desktop Publishing Services is shown in Figure 5-5 beginning on the next page.

Figure 5-5
Complete Ledger

CLARK'S DESKTOP PUBLISHING SERVICES
GENERAL LEDGER

Cash — Account No. 111

Date		Explanation	PR	Debit	Credit	Dr. or Cr.	Balance
2016 May	1		GJ1	10 000 00		Dr.	10 000 00
	1		GJ1		1 000 00	Dr.	9 000 00
	1		GJ1		1 200 00	Dr.	7 800 00
	7		GJ1	3 000 00		Dr.	10 800 00
	10		GJ1		650 00	Dr.	10 150 00
	20		GJ1		625 00	Dr.	9 525 00
	24		GJ2		650 00	Dr.	8 875 00
	28		GJ2		2 500 00	Dr.	6 375 00
	29		GJ2		220 00	Dr.	6 155 00

Accounts Receivable — Acct. No. 112

Date		Explanation	PR	Debit	Credit	Dr. or Cr.	Balance
2016 May	22		GJ1	5 000 00		Dr.	5 000 00

Office Supplies — Acct. No. 114

Date		Explanation	PR	Debit	Credit	Dr. or Cr.	Balance
2016 May	3		GJ1	600 00		Dr.	600 00
	31	Adjusting	GJ2		500 00	Dr.	100 00

Prepaid Rent — Acct. No. 115

Date		Explanation	PR	Debit	Credit	Dr. or Cr.	Balance
2016 May	1		GJ1	1 200 00		Dr.	1 200 00
	31	Adjusting	GJ2		400 00	Dr.	800 00

Desktop Publishing Equipment — Acct. No. 121

Date		Explanation	PR	Debit	Credit	Dr. or Cr.	Balance
2016 May	1		GJ1	6 000 00		Dr.	6 000 00

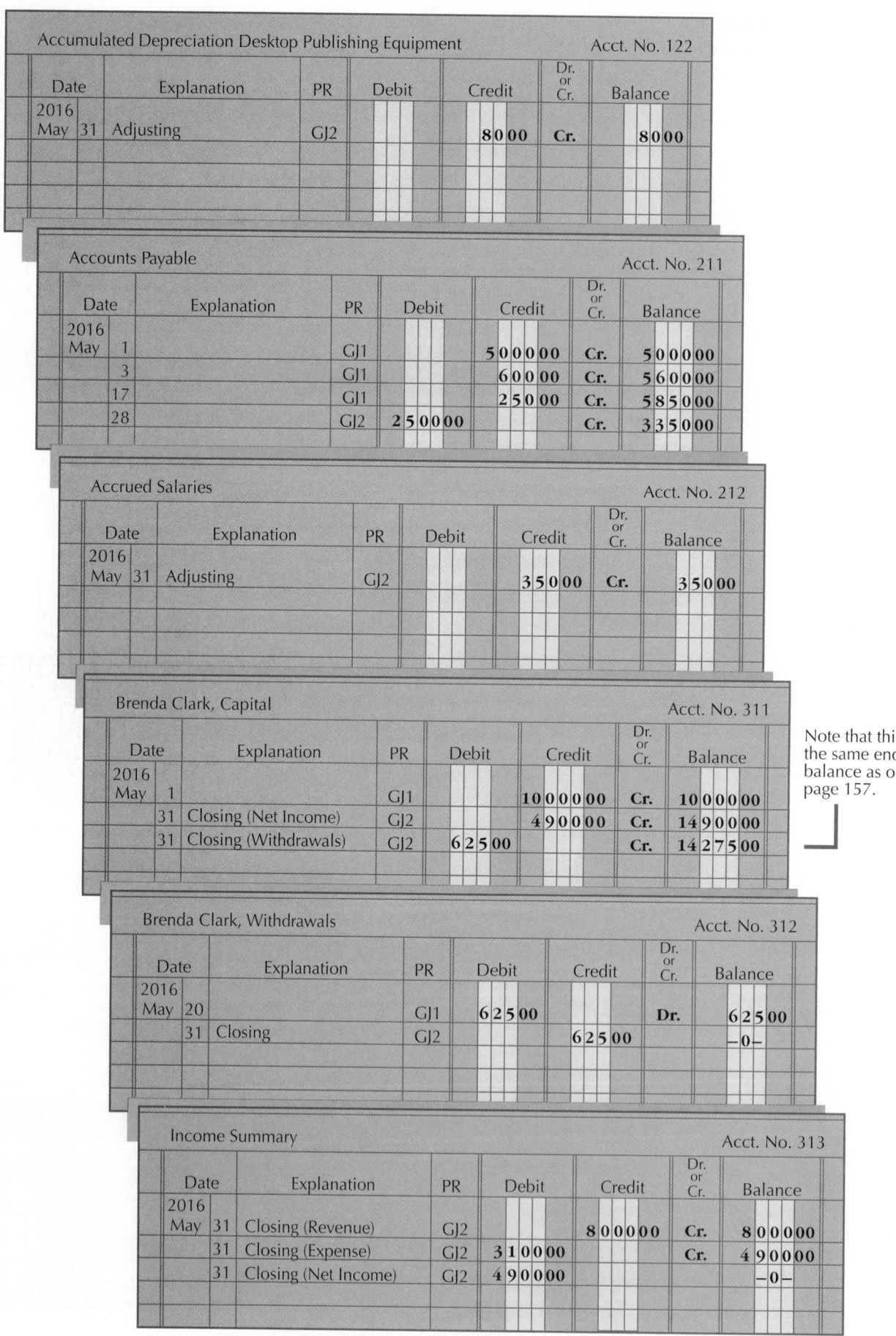

Accumulated Depreciation Desktop Publishing Equipment — Acct. No. 122

Date		Explanation	PR	Debit	Credit	Dr. or Cr.	Balance
2016							
May	31	Adjusting	GJ2		80 00	Cr.	80 00

Accounts Payable — Acct. No. 211

Date		Explanation	PR	Debit	Credit	Dr. or Cr.	Balance
2016							
May	1		GJ1		5 000 00	Cr.	5 000 00
	3		GJ1		600 00	Cr.	5 600 00
	17		GJ1		250 00	Cr.	5 850 00
	28		GJ2	2 500 00		Cr.	3 350 00

Accrued Salaries — Acct. No. 212

Date		Explanation	PR	Debit	Credit	Dr. or Cr.	Balance
2016							
May	31	Adjusting	GJ2		350 00	Cr.	350 00

Brenda Clark, Capital — Acct. No. 311

Date		Explanation	PR	Debit	Credit	Dr. or Cr.	Balance
2016							
May	1		GJ1		10 000 00	Cr.	10 000 00
	31	Closing (Net Income)	GJ2		4 900 00	Cr.	14 900 00
	31	Closing (Withdrawals)	GJ2	625 00		Cr.	14 275 00

Note that this is the same ending balance as on page 157.

Brenda Clark, Withdrawals — Acct. No. 312

Date		Explanation	PR	Debit	Credit	Dr. or Cr.	Balance
2016							
May	20		GJ1	625 00		Dr.	625 00
	31	Closing	GJ2		625 00		–0–

Income Summary — Acct. No. 313

Date		Explanation	PR	Debit	Credit	Dr. or Cr.	Balance
2016							
May	31	Closing (Revenue)	GJ2		8 000 00	Cr.	8 000 00
	31	Closing (Expense)	GJ2	3 100 00		Cr.	4 900 00
	31	Closing (Net Income)	GJ2	4 900 00			–0–

Desktop Publishing Fees — Acct. No. 411

Date		Explanation	PR	Debit	Credit	Dr. or Cr.	Balance
2016							
May	7		GJ1		3 000 00	Cr.	3 000 00
	22		GJ1		5 000 00	Cr.	8 000 00
	31	Closing	GJ2	8 000 00			–0–

Office Salaries Expense — Acct. No. 511

Date		Explanation	PR	Debit	Credit	Dr. or Cr.	Balance
2016							
May	10		GJ1	650 00		Dr.	650 00
	24		GJ2	650 00		Dr.	1 300 00
	31	Adjusting	GJ2	350 00		Dr.	1 650 00
	31	Closing	GJ2		1 650 00		–0–

Advertising Expense — Acct. No. 512

Date		Explanation	PR	Debit	Credit	Dr. or Cr.	Balance
2016							
May	17		GJ1	250 00		Dr.	250 00
	31	Closing	GJ2		250 00		–0–

Telephone Expense — Acct. No. 513

Date		Explanation	PR	Debit	Credit	Dr. or Cr.	Balance
2016							
May	29		GJ2	220 00		Dr.	220 00
	31	Closing	GJ2		220 00		–0–

Office Supplies Expense — Acct. No. 514

Date		Explanation	PR	Debit	Credit	Dr. or Cr.	Balance
2016							
May	31	Adjusting	GJ2	500 00		Dr.	500 00
	31	Closing	GJ2		500 00		–0–

Rent Expense							Acct. No. 515
Date		Explanation	PR	Debit	Credit	Dr. or Cr.	Balance
2016 May	31	Adjusting	GJ2	400 00		Dr.	400 00
	31	Closing	GJ2		400 00		–0–

Depreciation Expense, Desktop Publishing Equipment							Acct. No. 516
Date		Explanation	PR	Debit	Credit	Dr. or Cr.	Balance
2016 May	31	Adjusting	GJ2	80 00		Dr.	80 00
	31	Closing	GJ2		80 00		–0–

Note that the word "adjusting" or "closing" is written in the explanation column of individual ledgers, as, for example, in the one for Office Supplies. If the goals of closing have been achieved, only permanent accounts will have balances carried to the next fiscal year. All temporary accounts will have zero balances.

LEARNING UNIT 5-2 REVIEW

AT THIS POINT you should be able to:

- Define closing. (p. 190)
- Differentiate between temporary (nominal) and permanent (real) accounts. (p. 190)
- List the four mechanical steps of closing. (p. 190)
- Explain the role of the Income Summary account. (p. 190)
- Explain the role of the worksheet in the closing process. (p. 190)

Self-Review Quiz 5-2

(The blank forms you need are on pages 5-2 and 5-3 of the *Study Guide with Working Papers.*)

Go to the worksheet for P. Logan on page 154. Then (1) journalize and post the closing entries and (2) calculate the new balance for P. Logan, Capital.

Solution to Self-Review Quiz 5-3

Quiz Tip

- Revenue closed to Income Summary
- Each expense closed to Income Summary
- Net Income closed to Capital
- Withdrawals closed to Capital

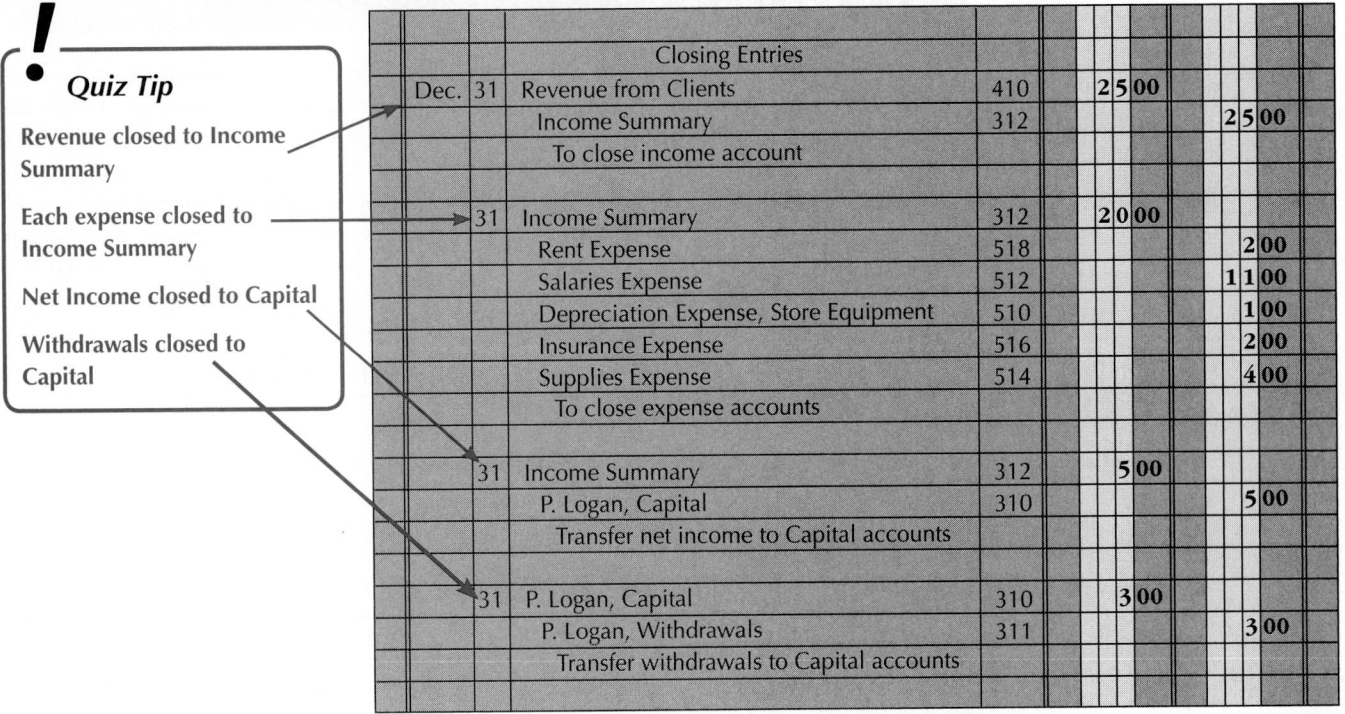

		Closing Entries			
Dec.	31	Revenue from Clients	410	25 00	
		Income Summary	312		25 00
		To close income account			
	31	Income Summary	312	20 00	
		Rent Expense	518		2 00
		Salaries Expense	512		11 00
		Depreciation Expense, Store Equipment	510		1 00
		Insurance Expense	516		2 00
		Supplies Expense	514		4 00
		To close expense accounts			
	31	Income Summary	312	5 00	
		P. Logan, Capital	310		5 00
		Transfer net income to Capital accounts			
	31	P. Logan, Capital	310	3 00	
		P. Logan, Withdrawals	311		3 00
		Transfer withdrawals to Capital accounts			

PARTIAL LEDGER

P. Logan, Capital 310

Dr.	Cr.
3	14
	5
	16

Revenue from Clients 410

Dr.	Cr.
25	25

Supplies Expense 514

Dr.	Cr.
4	4

P. Logan, Withdrawals 311

Dr.	Cr.
3	3

Depreciation Expense, Store Equipment 510

Dr.	Cr.
1	1

Insurance Expense 516

Dr.	Cr.
2	2

Income Summary 312

Dr.	Cr.
20	25
5	5

Salaries Expense 512

Dr.	Cr.
11	11

Rent Expense 518

Dr.	Cr.
2	2

P. Logan, Capital		$14
Net Income	$5	
Less: Withdrawals	3	
Increase in Capital		2
P. Logan, Capital (ending)		$16

Quiz Tip

No calculations are needed in the closing process. All numbers come from the worksheet. Income Summary is a temporary account in the ledger.

NEED HELP?

Let's review first: Why are closing entries necessary? In the ledger, we need to get the new balance in the Capital account. When financial statements were prepared, the ledger for Capital had only the old balance. Also, to get ready for the next accounting period, we must close all temporary accounts to zero so they will be ready to collect new data regarding revenues, expenses, and withdrawals. Without the closing process each year, financial statements would run into the next period and financial analysis would be difficult. Keep in mind that the Income Summary account that will be used in the closing process is a temporary account (I like to call it a storage area for revenues and expenses).

Why use the four steps to closing?

The four steps to closing when journalized and posted will do the following:

1. Clear all temporary accounts to zero.
2. Update the Capital account in the ledger to its new balance.

Steps to closing:

1. Close revenue account(s) to Income Summary.
2. Close each INDIVIDUAL expense to Income Summary.
3. Remove the balance in Income Summary (net income or net loss) and transfer it to the Capital account.
4. Close any withdrawals directly to Capital.

All the closing entries can be journalized directly from the last four columns of the worksheet. Each individual expense, along with the total of expenses, is found on the worksheet. Once these four closing entries are journalized and posted, all temporary accounts have a zero balance and P. Logan, Capital, now has an ending balance of $16. This is same amount of ending capital that was used to make the formal balance sheet.

SUMMARY

If you look at the T account in the solution you will see four numbers in Income Summary. Can you explain them?

20...this represents the total of all the expenses.

25...this represents the total revenue of all the revenues.

5 on the credit side...this is net income (25 – 20).

5 on the debit side...this comes from the third closing entry, which transfers the balance in Income Summary to Capital.

LEARNING UNIT 5-3

The Post-Closing Trial Balance: Step 9 of the Accounting Cycle and the Accounting Cycle Reviewed

LO 3 Preparing a post-closing trial balance

The post-closing trial balance helps prove the accuracy of the adjusting and closing process. It contains the true ending figure for capital.

PREPARING A POST-CLOSING TRIAL BALANCE

The last step in the accounting cycle is the preparation of a **post-closing trial balance** (sometimes called an opening trial balance), which lists only permanent accounts in the ledger and their balances after adjusting and closing entries have been posted. This post-closing trial balance aids in checking whether the ledger is in balance. It is important to do this checking because so many new postings go to the ledger from the adjusting and closing process.

The procedure for taking a post-closing trial balance is the same as for a trial balance except that since closing entries have closed all temporary accounts, the post-closing trial balance will contain only permanent accounts (balance sheet). Keep in mind, however, that adjustments have occurred.

THE ACCOUNTING CYCLE REVIEWED

Table 5-1 lists the steps that we completed in the manual accounting cycle for Clark's Desktop Publishing Services for the month of May.

Insight: Most companies journalize and post adjusting and closing entries only at the end of their fiscal year. A company that prepares interim reports may complete only the first six steps of the cycle. Worksheets allow the preparation of interim reports without the formal adjusting and closing of the books.

TABLE 5-1 Steps of the Manual Accounting Cycle

Step	Explanation
1. Business transactions occur and generate source documents.	Gathering source documents such as cash register tapes, sales tickets, bills, cheques, payroll cards, etc.
↓	↓
2. Analyze and record business transactions into a journal.	Entering transactions into the accounting system, called journalizing.
↓	↓
3. Post or transfer information from journal to ledger.	Copying the debits and credits of the journal entries into the ledger accounts.
↓	↓
4. Prepare a trial balance.	Summarizing each individual ledger account and listing these accounts and their balances to test for mathematical accuracy in recording transactions.
↓	↓
5. Prepare a worksheet.	Creating a multicolumn form that summarizes accounting information to complete the accounting cycle.
↓	↓
6. Prepare financial statements.	Producing the income statement, statement of owner's equity, and balance sheet from information in the worksheet.
↓	↓
7. Journalize and post adjusting entries.	Using figures in the adjustment columns of the worksheet to bring the ledger up to date.
↓	↓
8. Journalize and post closing entries.	Using figures in the income statement and balance sheet sections of worksheet to prepare the accounts to track the transactions in the next fiscal year.
↓	↓
9. Prepare a post-closing trial balance.	Proving the mathematical accuracy of the adjusting and closing process of the accounting cycle.

Insight: To prepare a financial report for April, the data needed can be obtained by subtracting the worksheet accumulated totals for the end of March from the worksheet prepared at the end of April. In this chapter, we chose a month that would show the completion of an entire cycle for Clark's Desktop Publishing Services.

LEARNING UNIT 5-3 REVIEW

AT THIS POINT you should be able to:

- Prepare a post-closing trial balance. (p. 200)
- Explain the relationship of interim reports to the accounting cycle. (p. 201)

Self-Review Quiz 5-3

(The blank forms you need are on page 5-3 of the *Study Guide with Working Papers.*)

From the ledger on pages 195-198, prepare a post-closing trial balance.

Solution to Self-Review Quiz 5-3

Quiz Tip

The post-closing trial balance contains only permanent accounts because all temporary accounts have been closed. All temporary accounts are summarized in the Capital account.

CLARK'S DESKTOP PUBLISHING SERVICES
POST-CLOSING TRIAL BALANCE
MAY 31, 2016

	Dr.	Cr.
Cash	6 1 5 5 00	
Accounts Receivable	5 0 0 0 00	
Office Supplies	1 0 0 00	
Prepaid Rent	8 0 0 00	
Desktop Publishing Equipment	6 0 0 0 00	
Accumulated Depreciation, Desktop Publishing Equipment		8 0 00
Accounts Payable		3 3 5 0 00
Accrued Salaries		3 5 0 00
Brenda Clark, Capital		14 2 7 5 00
	18 0 5 5 00	18 0 5 5 00

NEED HELP?

Let's review first: The post-closing trial balance contains only permanent accounts because all temporary accounts have been closed. All temporary accounts are summarized in the Capital account. Remember that Income Summary is a temporary account.

Post-Closing Trial Balance: Once all the closing entries have been journalized and posted, we can then prepare a post-closing trial balance. Since only permanent accounts are left after closing, the structure of the post-closing trial balance should look as follows:

Assets	Dr.
Contra-Assets	Cr.
Liabilities	Cr.
Ending Capital	Cr.

SUMMARY

To begin the next accounting cycle, only permanent accounts with balances are brought forward. In the new cycle, transactions will be journalized and posted. Adjustments will be made and new financial statements will be prepared. By the end of the cycle, all temporary accounts will be closed to get a new ending figure for capital in the ledger. The end result will be to prepare a new post-closing trial balance.

CLOSING TIME

Closing and balancing the books ❷ ❸ (20 min)

"You wait and see," Stan told his new sandwich artist Wanda Kurtz. "Everything will fall into place soon." Wanda had a tough time serving customers quickly enough, and Stan was in the middle of giving her a pep talk when the phone rang.

"I'll let the machine pick it up," Stan reassured Wanda, as he proceeded to train her in some crucial POS touch-screen manoeuvres.

"Stan!" an urgent voice came over the answering machine. "I think you've forgotten something!" Stan picked up the phone and said, "Lila, can I get back to you tomorrow? I'm in the middle of an important talk with Wanda." One of Stan's strong points as an employer was his ability to focus 100% on his employees' concerns. Yet, Lila simply would not wait.

"Stan," Lila said impatiently, "you absolutely must get me your worksheet by 12 noon tomorrow so that I can close your books," she insisted. "Tomorrow's the 31st of March and we close on the last day of the month!"

"*Ay caramba!*" Stan sighed. "Looks like I'm going to be up till the wee hours," he confided to Wanda when he put down the phone.

Although Subway company policy doesn't require a closing every month, closing the books is a key part of their accounting training for all new franchisees. By closing their books, business owners can clearly measure their net profit and loss for each period, separate from all other periods. This makes activities such as budgeting and comparing performance with similar businesses (or performance over time) possible.

At 9 a.m. the next day, an exhausted Stan opened the restaurant and emailed his worksheet to Lila. He was feeling quite pleased with himself—that is, until he heard Lila's urgent-sounding voice coming over the answering machine 30 minutes later.

"I've been over and over this," said Lila after Stan picked it up, "and I can't get it to balance. I know it's hard for you to do this during working hours, but I need you to go back over the figures."

Stan opened up his computer and pored over his worksheets. Errors are hard to find when closing the books and, unfortunately, there is no set way to detect errors and even no set place to start. Stan chose payroll because it is one of the largest expenses and because of the new hire.

At 11:45 he called Lila, who sounded both exasperated and relieved to hear from him. "I think I've got it! It looks like I messed up on adjusting the Salaries Expense account. I looked at the Payroll Register and compared the total of the Accrued Salaries account. It didn't match! When I hired Wanda Kurtz on the 26th, I should have increased both the Salaries Expense and the Accrued Salaries lines because she has accrued wages."

"Yes," said Lila. "Salaries Expense is a debit and Accrued Salaries is a credit and you skipped the payable. Great! With this adjusting entry in the general journal, the worksheet will balance.

Stan's sigh of relief turned into a big yawn and they both laughed. "I guess I just find it easier to hire people and train them than to account for them," said Stan.

DISCUSSION QUESTIONS

1. How would the adjustment be made if Wanda Kurtz received $7 per hour and worked 25 additional hours? Where do you place her accrued wages?
2. Stan bought three new Subway aprons and hats for Wanda Kurtz for $20 each but forgot to post it to the Uniforms account. How much will the closing balance be off? In what way will it be off?
3. Put yourself in Stan's shoes: What is the value of doing a monthly closing, no matter how much—or little—business you do?

Chapter Assignments

DEMONSTRATION PROBLEM: REVIEWING THE ACCOUNTING CYCLE

(The blank forms you need are on pages 5-4 to 5-10 of the *Study Guide with Working Papers.*)

From the following transactions for Rolo Company, complete the entire accounting cycle. The chart of accounts includes:

Assets
- 111 Cash
- 112 Accounts Receivable
- 114 Prepaid Rent
- 115 Office Supplies
- 121 Office Equipment
- 122 Accumulated Depreciation, Office Equipment

Liabilities
- 211 Accounts Payable
- 212 Accrued Salaries

Owner's Equity
- 311 R. Kern, Capital
- 312 R. Kern, Withdrawals
- 313 Income Summary

Revenue
- 411 Fees Earned

Expenses
- 511 Salaries Expense
- 512 Advertising Expense
- 513 Rent Expense
- 514 Office Supplies Expense
- 515 Depreciation Expense, Office Equipment

We will use unusually small numbers to simplify the calculations and to emphasize the theory.

2016		
Jan.	2	Rolo Kern invested $1,200 cash and $100 worth of office equipment to open Rolo Co.
	2	Paid rent for three months in advance, $300.
	3	Purchased office equipment on account, $50.
	4	Bought office supplies for cash, $40.
	8	Collected $400 for services rendered.
	11	Rolo paid his home electric bill from the company bank account, $20.
	14	Provided $100 worth of services to clients who will not pay until next month.
	15	Paid salaries, $60.
	18	Advertising bill for $70 was received but will not be paid until next month.

Adjustment Data on January 31

a. Supplies on hand, $6

b. Rent Expired, $100

c. Depreciation, Office Equipment, $20

d. Salaries Accrued, $50

Solutions to Demonstration Problem

Journalizing Transactions and Posting to Ledger, Rolo Company

General Journal — Page 1

Date		Account Titles and Description	PR	Dr.	Cr.
2016 Jan.	2	Cash	111	1 2 0 0 00	
		Office Equipment	121	1 0 0 00	
		R. Kern, Capital	311		1 3 0 0 00
		Initial investment			
	2	Prepaid Rent	114	3 0 0 00	
		Cash	111		3 0 0 00
		Rent paid in advance—3 months			
	3	Office Equipment	121	5 0 00	
		Accounts Payable	211		5 0 00
		Purchased equipment on account			
	4	Office Supplies	115	4 0 00	
		Cash	111		4 0 00
		Supplies purchased for cash			
	8	Cash	111	4 0 0 00	
		Fees Earned	411		4 0 0 00
		Services rendered			
	11	R. Kern, Withdrawals	312	2 0 00	
		Cash	111		2 0 00
		Personal payment of a bill			
	14	Accounts Receivable	112	1 0 0 00	
		Fees Earned	411		1 0 0 00
		Services rendered on account			
	15	Salaries Expense	511	6 0 00	
		Cash	111		6 0 00
		Paid salaries			
	18	Advertising Expense	512	7 0 00	
		Accounts Payable	211		7 0 00
		Advertising bill, but not paid			

Solution Tips to Journalizing and Posting Transactions

Jan. **2**	**Cash**	**Asset**	↑	**Dr.**	**$1,200**
	Office Equipment	**Asset**	↑	**Dr.**	**$ 100**
	R. Kern, Capital	**Capital**	↑	**Cr.**	**$1,300**

Jan. **2**	**Prepaid Rent**	**Asset**	↑	**Dr.**	**$ 300**
	Cash	**Asset**	↓	**Cr.**	**$ 300**

Jan. 3	Office Equipment Accounts Payable	Asset Liability	↑ ↑	Dr. Cr.	$ 50 $ 50

Jan. 4	Office Supplies Cash	Asset Asset	↑ ↓	Dr. Cr.	$ 40 $ 40

Jan. 8	Cash Fees Earned	Asset Revenue	↑ ↑	Dr. Cr.	$400 $400

Jan. 11	R. Kern, Withdrawals Cash	Owner's Equity (Withdr.) Asset	↑ ↓	Dr. Cr.	$ 20 $ 20

Jan. 14	Accounts Receivable Fees Earned	Asset Revenue	↑ ↑	Dr. Cr.	$100 $100

Jan. 15	Salaries Expense Cash	Expense Asset	↑ ↓	Dr. Cr.	$ 60 $ 60

Jan. 18	Advertising Expense Accounts Payable	Expense Liability	↑ ↑	Dr. Cr.	$ 70 $ 70

Note: All account titles come from the chart of accounts. When journalizing, the PR column of the general journal is blank. It is in the posting process that we update the ledger. The PR columns in the ledger accounts tell us from which journal page the information came. After posting to the account in the ledger, we fill in the PR column of the journal, which tells us to what account number the information was transferred.

COMPLETING THE WORKSHEET

See the worksheet on page 208.

Solution Tips to the Trial Balance and Completion of the Worksheet

After the posting process from the journal to the ledger is complete, we take the ending balance in each account and prepare a trial balance on the worksheet. If an account title has no balance, it is not listed on the trial balance. New titles on the worksheet will be added below the trial balance as needed.

ROLO COMPANY
WORKSHEET
FOR THE MONTH ENDED JANUARY 31, 2016

Account Titles	Trial Balance Dr.	Trial Balance Cr.	Adjustments Dr.	Adjustments Cr.	Adjusted Trial Balance Dr.	Adjusted Trial Balance Cr.	Income Statement Dr.	Income Statement Cr.	Balance Sheet Dr.	Balance Sheet Cr.
Cash	1 1 8 0 00				1 1 8 0 00				1 1 8 0 00	
Accounts Receivable	1 0 0 00				1 0 0 00				1 0 0 00	
Prepaid Rent	3 0 0 00			(B) 1 0 0 00	2 0 0 00				2 0 0 00	
Office Supplies	4 0 00			(A) 3 4 00	6 00				6 00	
Office Equipment	1 5 0 00				1 5 0 00				1 5 0 00	
Accounts Payable		1 2 0 00				1 2 0 00				1 2 0 00
R. Kern, Capital		1 3 0 0 00				1 3 0 0 00				1 3 0 0 00
R. Kern, Withdrawals	2 0 00				2 0 00				2 0 00	
Fees Earned		5 0 0 00				5 0 0 00		5 0 0 00		
Salaries Expense	6 0 00		(D) 5 0 00		1 1 0 00		1 1 0 00			
Advertising Expense	7 0 00				7 0 00		7 0 00			
	1 9 2 0 00	1 9 2 0 00								
Office Supplies Expense			(A) 3 4 00		3 4 00		3 4 00			
Rent Expense			(B) 1 0 0 00		1 0 0 00		1 0 0 00			
Depn. Expense, Office Equip.			(C) 2 0 00		2 0 00		2 0 00			
Accum. Depn., Office Equip.				(C) 2 0 00		2 0 00				2 0 00
Accrued Salaries				(D) 5 0 00		5 0 00				5 0 00
			2 0 4 00	2 0 4 00	1 9 9 0 00	1 9 9 0 00	3 3 4 00	5 0 0 00	1 6 5 6 00	1 4 9 0 00
Net Income							1 6 6 00			1 6 6 00
							5 0 0 00	5 0 0 00	1 6 5 6 00	1 6 5 6 00

The amount of office supplies on hand ($6) is *not* the adjustment. The amount used up needs to be calculated.

Office Supplies Expense	**Expense**	↑	**Dr.**	**$ 34**	**($40 − $6)**
Office Supplies	**Asset**	↓	**Cr.**	**$ 34**	

Expired

Rent Expense	**Expense**	↑	**Dr.**	**$100**	
Prepaid Rent	**Asset**	↓	**Cr.**	**$100**	

Do not touch original cost of equipment.

Depn. Exp., Office Equip.	**Expense**	↑	**Dr.**	**$ 20**	
Accum. Depn., Office Equip.	**Asset (Contra)**	↓	**Cr.**	**$ 20**	

Owed but not paid

Salaries Expense	**Expense**	↑	**Dr.**	**$ 50**	
Accrued Salaries	**Liability**	↑	**Cr.**	**$ 50**	

Note: This information is on the worksheet but has *not* been updated in the ledger. (This will occur when we journalize and post adjustments at the end of the cycle.)

Note that the last four columns of the worksheet come from numbers on the adjusted trial balance.

We move Net Income of $166 to the balance sheet credit column since the capital figure is the old one on the worksheet.

PREPARING THE FORMAL FINANCIAL STATEMENTS

ROLO COMPANY
INCOME STATEMENT
FOR THE MONTH ENDED JANUARY 31, 2016

Revenue:		
Fees Earned		$500.00
Operating Expenses:		
Salaries Expense	$110.00	
Advertising Expense	70.00	
Office Supplies Expense	34.00	
Rent Expense	100.00	
Depreciation Expense, Office Equipment	20.00	
Total Operating Expenses		334.00
Net Income		$166.00

ROLO COMPANY
STATEMENT OF OWNER'S EQUITY
FOR THE MONTH ENDED JANUARY 31, 2016

R. Kern, Capital, January 1, 2016		$1300.00
Net Income for January	$166.00	
Less: Withdrawals for January	20.00	
Increase in Capital		146.00
R. Kern, Capital, January 31, 2016		$1446.00

ROLO COMPANY BALANCE SHEET JANUARY 31, 2016					
Assets			Liabilities and Owner's Equity		
Cash		$1180 00	Liabilities:		
Accounts Receivable		100 00	Accounts Payable	$120 00	
Prepaid Rent		200 00	Accrued Salaries	50 00	
Office Supplies		6 00	Total Liabilities		$170 00
Office Equipment	$150 00		Owner's Equity:		
Less: Acc. Depn.	20 00	130 00	R. Kern, Capital		1446 00
			Total Liabilities and		
Total Assets		$1616 00	Owner's Equity		$1616 00

Solution Tips to Preparing the Financial Statements

The statements are prepared from the worksheet. (Many of the ledger accounts are not up to date.) The income statement lists revenue and expenses. The net income figure of $166 is used to update the statement of owner's equity. The statement of owner's equity calculates a new figure for Capital, $1,446 (Beginning Capital + Net Income – Withdrawals). This new figure is then listed on the balance sheet (Assets, Liabilities, and a new figure for Capital).

JOURNALIZING AND POSTING ADJUSTING AND CLOSING ENTRIES

See the journal at the top of page 211.

Solution Tips to Journalizing and Posting Adjusting and Closing Entries

ADJUSTMENTS

The adjustments from the worksheet are journalized (same journal) and posted to the ledger. Now ledger accounts will be brought up to date. Remember, we have already prepared the financial reports from the worksheet. Our goal now is to get the ledger up to date.

CLOSING

Note: Income Summary is a temporary account located in the ledger.

Where do I get my information for closing?

Goals

1. Adjust all temporary accounts in the ledger to zero balances.
2. Determine a new figure for capital in the ledger.

	Date		Account Titles and Description	PR	Dr.	Cr.
	General Journal					Page 2
			Adjusting Entries			
	2016 Jan.	31	Office Supplies Expense	514	34 00	
			Office Supplies	115		34 00
			Supplies used			
		31	Rent Expense	513	100 00	
			Prepaid Rent	114		100 00
			Rent expired			
		31	Depreciation Expense, Office Equipment	515	20 00	
			Accumulated Depreciation, Office Equip.	122		20 00
			Estimated Depreciation			
		31	Salaries Expense	511	50 00	
			Accrued Salaries	212		50 00
			Accrued salaries			
			Closing Entries			
Closing: Step 1 →		31	Fees Earned	411	500 00	
			Income Summary	313		500 00
			To close income accounts			
Step 2 →		31	Income Summary	313	334 00	
			Salaries Expense	511		110 00
			Advertising Expense	512		70 00
			Office Supplies Expense	514		34 00
			Rent Expense	513		100 00
			Depreciation Expense, Office Equipment	515		20 00
			To close expense accounts			
Step 3 →		31	Income Summary	313	166 00	
			R. Kern, Capital	311		166 00
			Net income closed to Capital			
Step 4 →		31	R. Kern, Capital	311	20 00	
			R. Kern, Withdrawals	312		20 00
			Close withdrawals into Capital			

Steps in the Closing Process

Step 1: Close revenue to Income Summary.

Step 2: Close individual expenses to Income Summary.

Step 3: Close balance of Income Summary to Capital. (This really is the net income figure on the worksheet.)

Step 4: Close balance of Withdrawals to Capital.

All the journal closing entries are posted. (No new calculations are needed since all figures are on the worksheet.) The result in the ledger is that all temporary accounts have a zero balance.

GENERAL LEDGER

Cash — Acct. No. 111

Date		Explanation	PR	Debit	Credit	Dr. or Cr.	Balance
2016							
Jan.	2		GJ1	120000		Dr.	120000
	2		GJ1		30000	Dr.	90000
	4		GJ1		4000	Dr.	86000
	8		GJ1	40000		Dr.	126000
	11		GJ1		2000	Dr.	124000
	15		GJ1		6000	Dr.	118000

Accounts Receivable — Acct. No. 112

Date		Explanation	PR	Debit	Credit	Dr. or Cr.	Balance
2016							
Jan.	14		GJ1	10000		Dr.	10000

Prepaid Rent — Acct. No. 114

Date		Explanation	PR	Debit	Credit	DR or Cr.	Balance
2016							
Jan.	2		GJ1	30000		Dr.	30000
	31	Adjustment	GJ2		10000	Dr.	20000

Office Supplies — Acct. No. 115

Date		Explanation	PR	Debit	Credit	Dr. or Cr.	Balance
2016							
Jan.	4		GJ1	4000		Dr.	4000
	31	Adjustment	GJ2		3400	Dr.	600

Office Equipment — Acct. No. 121

Date		Explanation	PR	Debit	Credit	Dr. or Cr.	Balance
2016							
Jan.	2		GJ1	10000		Dr.	10000
	3		GJ1	5000		Dr.	15000

Accumulated Depreciation, Office Equipment — Acct. No. 122

Date		Explanation	PR	Debit	Credit	Dr. or Cr.	Balance
2016							
Jan.	31	Adjustment	GJ2		2000	Cr.	2000

Accounts Payable — Acct. No. 211

Date		Explanation	PR	Debit	Credit	Dr. or Cr.	Balance
2016							
Jan.	3		GJ1		5000	Cr.	5000
	18		GJ1		7000	Cr.	12000

Accrued Salaries — Acct. No. 212

Date		Explanation	PR	Debit	Credit	Dr. or Cr.	Balance
2016							
Jan.	31	Adjustment	GJ2		5000	Cr.	5000

R. Kern, Capital — Acct. No. 311

Date		Explanation	PR	Debit	Credit	Dr. or Cr.	Balance
2016							
Jan.	2		GJ1		130000	Cr.	130000
	31	Closing	GJ2		16600	Cr.	146600
	31	Closing	GJ2	2000		Cr.	144600

R. Kern, Withdrawals — Acct. No. 312

Date		Explanation	PR	Debit	Credit	Dr. or Cr.	Balance
2016							
Jan.	12		GJ1	2000		Dr.	2000
	31	Closing	GJ2		2000		-0-

Income Summary — Acct. No. 313

Date		Explanation	PR	Debit	Credit	Dr. or Cr.	Balance
2016							
Jan.	31	Closing	GJ2		50000	Cr.	50000
	31	Closing	GJ2	33400		Cr.	16600
	31	Closing	GJ2	16600			-0-

Fees Earned — Acct. No. 411

Date		Explanation	PR	Debit	Credit	Dr. or Cr.	Balance
2016							
Jan.	8		GJ1		40000	Cr.	40000
	14		GJ1		10000	Cr.	50000
	31	Closing	GJ2	50000			-0-

Salaries Expense — Acct. No. 511

Date		Explanation	PR	Debit	Credit	Dr. or Cr.	Balance
2016							
Jan.	15		GJ1	6000		Dr.	6000
	31	Adjusting	GJ2	5000		Dr.	11000
	31	Closing	GJ2		11000		-0-

Advertising Expense — Acct. No. 512

Date		Explanation	PR	Debit	Credit	Dr. or Cr.	Balance
2016							
Jan.	18		GJ1	7000		Dr.	7000
	31	Closing	GJ2		7000		-0-

Rent Expense — Acct. No. 513

Date		Explanation	PR	Debit	Credit	Dr. or Cr.	Balance
2016							
Jan.	31	Adjusting	GJ2	10000		Dr.	10000
	31	Closing	GJ2		10000		-0-

Office Supplies Expense — Acct. No. 514

Date		Explanation	PR	Debit	Credit	Dr. or Cr.	Balance
2016							
Jan.	31	Adjusting	GJ2	3400		Dr.	3400
	31	Closing	GJ2		3400		-0-

Depreciation Expense, Office Equipment — Acct. No. 515

Date		Explanation	PR	Debit	Credit	Dr. or Cr.	Balance
2016							
Jan.	31	Adjusting	GJ2	2000		Dr.	2000
	31	Closing	GJ2		2000		-0-

These are all permanent accounts.

ROLO CO. POST-CLOSING TRIAL BALANCE JANUARY 31, 2016		
	Dr.	Cr.
Cash	1 1 8 0 00	
Accounts Receivable	1 0 0 00	
Prepaid Rent	2 0 0 00	
Office Supplies	6 00	
Office Equipment	1 5 0 00	
Accumulated Depreciation, Office Equipment		2 0 00
Accounts Payable		1 2 0 00
Accrued Salaries		5 0 00
R. Kern, Capital		1 4 4 6 00
	1 6 3 6 00	1 6 3 6 00

Solution Tips for the Post-Closing Trial Balance

The post-closing trial balance is a list of the ledger balances *after* adjusting and closing entries have been completed. Note the figure for capital $1,446 is the new figure.

Beginning Capital	$1,300
+ Net Income	166
− Withdrawals	20
= Ending Capital	$1,446

Next accounting period, we will enter new amounts in the Revenues, Expenses, and Withdrawals accounts. For now, the post-closing trial balance is made up only of permanent accounts.

SUMMARY OF KEY POINTS

Learning Unit 5-1

1. After formal financial reports have been prepared, the ledger still has not been brought up to date.
2. Information for journalizing adjusting entries comes from the adjustments section of the worksheet.

Learning Unit 5-2

1. Closing is a mechanical process that is completed before the accountant can record transactions for the next fiscal year.
2. Assets, Liabilities, and Capital are permanent (real) accounts; their balances are carried over from one fiscal year to another. Withdrawals, Revenue, and Expenses are nominal (temporary) accounts; their balances are *not* carried over from one fiscal year to another.
3. Income Summary is a temporary account in the general ledger and does not have a normal balance. It will summarize revenue and expenses and transfer the balance to capital. Withdrawals do not go into Income Summary because they are *not* business expenses.
4. All information for closing can be obtained from the worksheet.

5. When closing is complete, all temporary accounts in the ledger will have a zero balance, and all this information will be updated in the Capital account.
6. Closing entries are usually done only at year-end. Interim reports can be prepared from worksheets that are prepared monthly, quarterly, and so on.

Learning Unit 5-3

1. The post-closing trial balance is prepared from the ledger accounts after the adjusting and closing entries have been posted. Of course, it must balance!
2. The accounts on the post-closing trial balance are all permanent accounts.

KEY TERMS

Adjusting journal entries Journal entries that are needed to update specific ledger accounts to reflect correct balances at the end of an accounting period (p. 186)

Closing The process of bringing the balances of all revenue, expense, and withdrawal accounts to zero, ready for a new fiscal year (p. 190)

Closing journal entries Journal entries that are prepared to (a) reduce or clear all temporary accounts to a zero balance and (b) update capital to a new closing balance (p. 190)

Income Summary A temporary account in the ledger that summarizes revenue and expenses and transfers its balance (net income or net loss) to capital. It does not have a normal balance.(p. 190)

Nominal accounts See ***Temporary accounts*** (p. 190)

Permanent accounts Balances of accounts that are carried over to the next fiscal year; examples: assets, liabilities, capital (p. 190)

Post-closing trial balance The final step in the accounting cycle that lists only permanent accounts in the ledger and their balances after adjusting and closing entries have been posted (p. 200)

Real accounts See ***Permanent accounts*** (p. 190)

Temporary accounts Balances of accounts at the end of a fiscal year that are not carried over to the next fiscal year. These accounts—Revenue, Expenses, Withdrawals—help to provide a new or ending figure for capital to begin the next fiscal year. Keep in mind that Income Summary is also a temporary account. (p. 190)

QUICK REVIEW

The following Tips are from Learning Units 5-1 to 5-3. Answer the Assess Your Progress questions and use the How Did You Do? at the bottom of the page to see how well you know the material. The Quick Review provides tips before each Assess Your Progress to help you avoid common accounting errors.

LU 5-1 Journalizing and Posting Adjusting Entries: Step 7 of the Accounting Cycle

Tips: All adjustments can be journalized and posted from the adjustments section of the worksheet. Remember that all accounts listed below the original trial balance are increasing. The adjustment for supplies is the amount used up. The adjustment for rent is the amount of rent that has expired. The adjustment for depreciation does not affect the original cost of the asset. The adjustment for salaries shows a new expense creating a liability because it is not yet paid.

Assess Your Progress

Answer true or false to the following statements:

1. After the adjustment is posted, the Supplies ledger account shows the amount on hand.
2. After posting, Accumulated Depreciation has a debit balance.
3. Adjustments on a worksheet do not have to be journalized and posted.
4. After the adjustment is posted, Prepaid Rent shows the amount expired.
5. Depreciation Expense is a contra-asset.

LU 5-2 Journalizing and Posting Closing Entries: Step 8 of the Accounting Cycle

Tips: The goal of closing is to update the ledger for the next accounting cycle. All temporary accounts need to be cleared, and a new figure for capital results. In the process, Income Summary is a temporary account that helps close revenues and expenses to Capital. Withdrawals will be closed directly to Capital since it is not a business expense. When the closing process is complete, all temporary accounts will be closed. All information needed to do the closing can be found in the income statement and balance sheet sections of the worksheet.

Assess Your Progress

Answer true or false to the following statements:

1. Income Summary is a permanent account.
2. Income Summary is found on the worksheet.
3. Expenses are permanent accounts.
4. The balance in Income Summary is closed to the Cash account.
5. Income Summary has a normal debit balance.

LU 5-3 The Post-Closing Trial Balance: Step 9 of the Accounting Cycle and the Cycle Reviewed

Tips: The post-closing trial balance lists the accounts of the ledger after all closing entries have been posted. Only permanent accounts remain, and all temporary accounts now have a zero balance. The title "Income Summary" is used only in the closing process and thus never ends up on the post-closing trial balance.

Assess Your Progress

Answer true or false to the following statements:

1. Income Summary is listed on the post-closing trial balance.
2. Interim reports are always prepared each month.
3. Capital on the post-closing trial balance is the beginning balance for the next accounting cycle.
4. Accumulated Depreciation is a temporary account.
5. Supplies on the post-closing trial balance represent the amount of supplies used up.

How Did You Do? Answers to the Assess Your Progress Questions

LU 5-1

1. True.
2. False—After posting, Accumulated Depreciation has a credit balance.
3. False—Adjustments on a worksheet have to be journalized and posted.
4. False—After the adjustment is posted, Prepaid Rent shows the amount that has not expired yet.
5. False—Depreciation Expense is an expense.

LU 5-2

1. False—Income Summary is a temporary account.
2. False—Income Summary is not found on the worksheet.
3. False—Expenses are temporary accounts.
4. False—The balance in Income Summary is closed to Capital.
5. False—Income Summary has no normal balance.

LU 5-3

1. False—Income Summary is a temporary account and thus not listed on the post-closing trial balance since it is closed.
2. False—Interim reports are only optional and there is no set requirement for when and how often they are prepared.
3. True.
4. False—Accumulated Depreciation is a permanent account.
5. False—Supplies on the post-closing trial balance represents the amount of supplies on hand.

BLUEPRINT OF THE CLOSING PROCESS FROM THE WORKSHEET

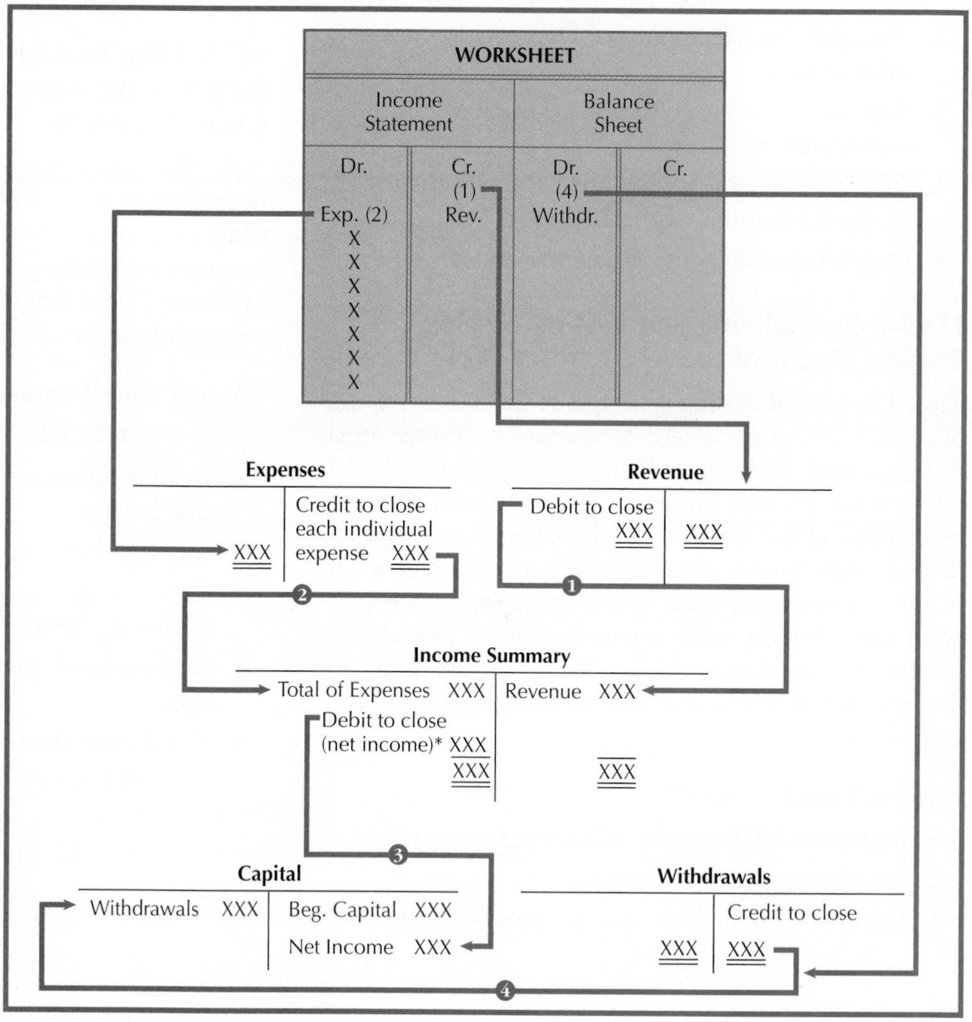

*If a net loss, it would require a credit to close.

The Closing Steps

1. Close revenue balances to Income Summary.
2. Close each *individual* expense and transfer the *total* of all expenses to Income Summary.
3. Transfer the balance in Income Summary (Net Income or Net Loss) to Capital.
4. Close Withdrawals to Capital.

QUESTIONS, CLASSROOM DEMONSTRATION EXERCISES, EXERCISES, AND PROBLEMS

Discussion Questions and Critical Thinking/Ethical Case

1. When a worksheet is completed, what balances are found in the general ledger?
2. Why must adjusting entries be journalized even though the formal reports have already been prepared?

3. "Closing slows down the recording of next year's transactions." Defend or reject this statement with supporting evidence.
4. What is the difference between temporary and permanent accounts?
5. What are the two major goals of the closing process?
6. List the four steps in closing.
7. What is the purpose of the Income Summary and where is it located?
8. How can a worksheet aid the closing process?
9. What accounts are usually listed on a post-closing trial balance?
10. Closing entries are always prepared once a month. Agree or disagree. Why?
11. Todd Silver is the purchasing agent for Moore Company. One of his suppliers, Gem Company, offers Todd a free vacation to France if he buys at least 75% of Moore's supplies from Gem Company. Todd, who is angry because Moore Company has not given him a raise in over a year, is considering the offer. Write out your recommendation to Todd.

MyAccountingLab

Make the grade with MyAccountingLab! The exercises and problems marked with ● can be found on MyAccountingLab. You can practise them as often as you want, and many of them feature step-by-step guided solutions to help you find the right answer.

Classroom Demonstration Exercises

(The blank forms you need are on pages 5-11 and 5-12 of the *Study Guide with Working Papers.*)

Journalizing and Posting Adjusting Entries

Posting adjusting entries
❶ (5 min)

1. Enter the beginning balances in the *Study Guide with Working Papers.* Post the following adjusting entries (be sure to cross-reference back to the journal) that came from the Adjustment columns of the worksheet.

General Journal — Page 3

Date		Account Titles and Description	PR	Dr.	Cr.
2015 Dec.	31	Insurance Expense		600	
		Prepaid Insurance			600
		Insurance expired			
	31	Supplies Expense		400	
		Store Supplies			400
		Supplies used			
	31	Depreciation Expense, Store Equipment		900	
		Accum. Depreciation, Store Equipment			900
		Estimated Depreciation			
	31	Salaries Expense		500	
		Accrued Salaries			500
		Accrued salaries			

LEDGER ACCOUNTS BEFORE ADJUSTING ENTRIES POSTED

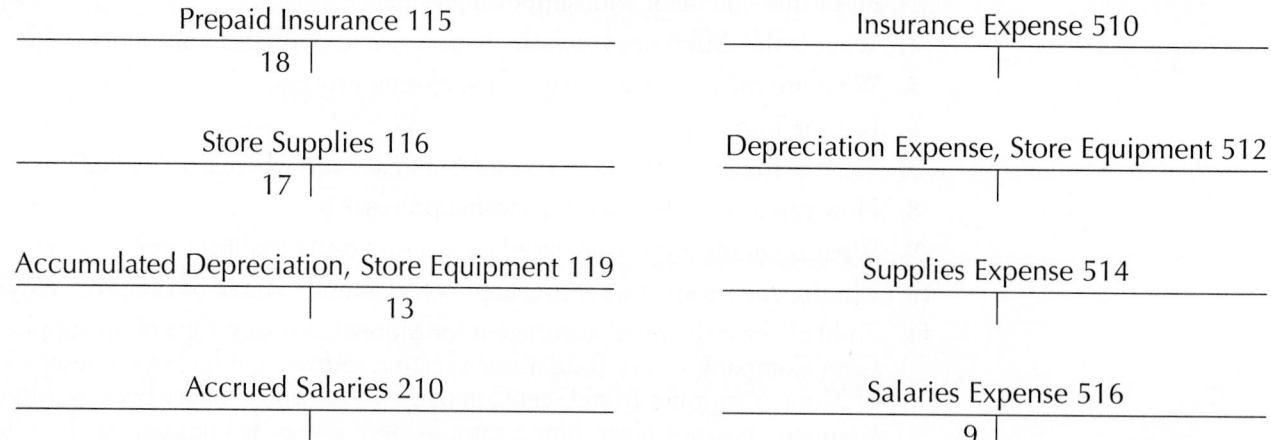

Prepaid Insurance 115	
18	

Insurance Expense 510	

Store Supplies 116	
17	

Depreciation Expense, Store Equipment 512	

Accumulated Depreciation, Store Equipment 119	
	13

Supplies Expense 514	

Accrued Salaries 210	

Salaries Expense 516	
9	

Closing Steps and Journalizing Closing Entries

Steps in the closing process
❷ (10 min)

2. Explain the four steps of the closing process given the following Dec. 31 ending balances, before closing:

Fees Earned	$ 200
Rent Expense	100
Advertising Expense	60
J. Rice, Capital	3,000
J. Rice, Withdrawals	15

Journalizing Closing Entries

Journalizing the closing entries from T accounts
❷ (15 min)

3. From the following accounts, journalize the closing entries (assume that December 31 is the closing date).

Mel Blanc, Capital 310	
	40

Gas Expense 510	
8	

Mel Blanc, Withdrawals 312	
7	

Advertising Expense 512	
12	

Income Summary 314	

Depreciation Expense, Taxi 516	
8	

Taxi Fare Income 410	
	39

Posting to Income Summary

The Income Summary account
❷ (10 min)

4. Draw a T account for Income Summary and post to it all entries from question 3 that affect it. Is Income Summary a temporary or permanent account?

Posting to Capital

The Capital account
❷ (10 min)

5. Draw a T account for Mel Blanc, Capital, and post to it all entries from question 3 that affect it. What is the final balance of the capital account?

Exercises

Set A

(The blank forms you need are on pages 5-13 and 5-14 of the *Study Guide with Working Papers.*)

Journalizing adjusting entries
❶ (1 min)

5-1A. From the adjustments section of a worksheet presented here, prepare adjusting journal entries for the end of December.

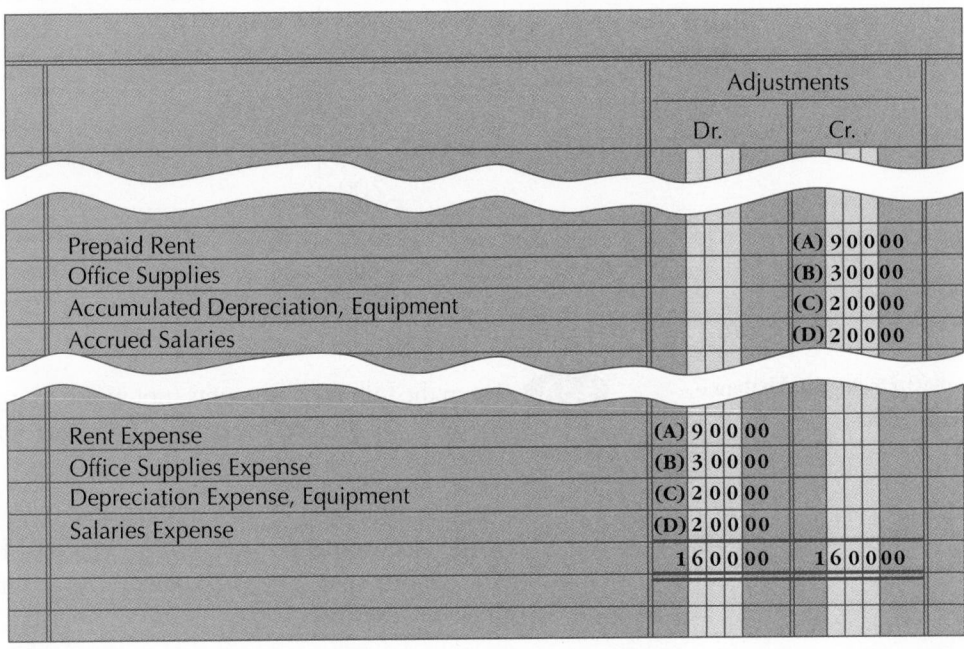

	Adjustments Dr.	Adjustments Cr.
Prepaid Rent		(A) 900 00
Office Supplies		(B) 300 00
Accumulated Depreciation, Equipment		(C) 200 00
Accrued Salaries		(D) 200 00
Rent Expense	(A) 900 00	
Office Supplies Expense	(B) 300 00	
Depreciation Expense, Equipment	(C) 200 00	
Salaries Expense	(D) 200 00	
	1600 00	1600 00

Temporary versus permanent accounts
❶ ❷ (10 min)

5-2A. Complete this table by placing an X in the correct column for each item.

	Temporary	*Permanent*	*Will Be Closed*
Example: **Accounts Receivable**		X	
1. Income Summary			
2. Jen Rich, Capital			
3. Salary Expense			
4. Jen Rich, Withdrawals			
5. Fees Earned			
6. Accounts Payable			
7. Cash			

Closing entries
❷ (5 min)

5-3A. From the following T accounts, journalize the four closing entries on December 31, 2015.

J. King, Capital	
	14,000

J. King, Withdrawals	
4,000	

Income Summary	

Fees Earned	
	33,000

Rent Expense	
5,000	

Wages Expense	
7,000	

Insurance Expense	
1,200	

Depreciation Expense, Office Equipment	
900	

Reconstructing closing entries
❷ (20 min)

5-4A. From the following posted T accounts, reconstruct the closing journal entries for December 31, 2017.

M. Foster, Capital	
Withdrawals 100	2,000 (Dec. 1)
	Net Income 700

Insurance Expense	
50	Closing 50

M. Foster, Withdrawals	
100	Closing 100

Wages Expense	
100	Closing 100

Income Summary	
Expenses 600	Revenue 1,300
700	

Rent Expense	
200	Closing 200

Salon Fees	
Closing 1,300	1,300

Depreciation Expense, Equipment	
250	Closing 250

Post-closing trial balance
❸ (20 min)

5-5A. From the following accounts (not in order), prepare a post-closing trial balance for Wey Co. on December 31, 2018. ***Note:*** These balances are *before* closing.

Accounts Receivable	18,875	P. Wey, Capital	63,450
Legal Library	14,250	P. Wey, Withdrawals	1,500
Office Equipment	59,700	Legal Fees Earned	12,000
Repair Expense	2,850	Accounts Payable	45,000
Salaries Expense	1,275	Cash	22,000

Exercises

Set B

(The forms you need are on pages 5-13 and 5-14 of the *Study Guide with Working Papers.*)

Journalizing adjusting entries
❶ (20 min)

5-1B. From the adjustments section of a worksheet presented here, prepare adjusting journal entries for the end of December.

	Adjustments Dr.	Adjustments Cr.
Prepaid Rent		(A) 700 00
Office Supplies		(B) 200 00
Accumulated Depreciation, Equipment		(C) 300 00
Accrued Salaries		(D) 400 00
Rent Expense	(A) 700 00	
Office Supplies Expense	(B) 200 00	
Depreciation Expense, Equipment	(C) 300 00	
Salaries Expense	(D) 400 00	
	1600 00	1600 00

Temporary versus permanent accounts
❶ ❷ (10 min)

5-2B. Complete this table by placing an X in the correct column for each item.

	Temporary	*Permanent*	*Will Be Closed*
Example: **Accounts Receivable**		X	
1. Store Supplies on Hand			
2. Accrued Salaries			
3. Jon Rich, Withdrawals			
4. Income Summary			
5. Commissions Earned			
6. Accounts Payable			
7. Accumulated Depreciation			

Closing entries
❷ (5 min)

5-3B. From the following T accounts, journalize the four closing entries on December 31, 2015.

J. King, Capital	
	23,000

Rent Expense	
6,000	

J. King, Withdrawals	
5,000	

Salaries Expense	
9,000	

Income Summary	

Insurance Expense	
800	

Fees Earned	
	46,000

Depreciation Expense, Office Equipment	
1,400	

Reconstructing closing entries
❷ (20 min)

5-4B. From the following posted T accounts, reconstruct the closing journal entries for December 31, 2017.

M. Foster, Capital	
Withdrawals 200	2,000 (Dec. 1)
	Net Income 950

Insurance Expense	
80	Closing 80

M. Foster, Withdrawals	
200	Closing 200

Wages Expense	
650	Closing 650

Income Summary	
Expense 1,250	Revenue 2,400
950	

Rent Expense	
220	Closing 220

Salon Fees	
Closing 2,400	2,400

Depreciation Expense, Office Equipment	
300	Closing 300

Post-closing trial balance
❸ (20 min)

5-5B. From the following accounts (not in order), prepare a post-closing trial balance for Wey Co. on December 31, 2018. ***Note:*** These balances are *before* closing.

Accounts Receivable	8,750	P. Wey, Capital	26,610
Legal Library	6,830	P. Wey, Withdrawals	2,500
Accum. Depn., O.E.	3,000	Cleaning Expense	1,000
Office Equipment	15,700	Legal Fees Earned	18,640
Repair Expense	1,240	Accounts Payable	5,200
Salaries Expense	3,200	Cash	8,230

Group A Problems

(The blank forms you need are on pages 5-15 to 5-30 of the *Study Guide with Working Papers.*)

Review of preparing a worksheet and journalizing adjusting and closing entries
❶ ❷ (40 min)

Check Figure
Net Income $14,600

5A-1. The following data is given for Debbie's Dance Studio of Vernon:

DEBBIE'S DANCE STUDIO
TRIAL BALANCE
JUNE 30, 2017

	Dr.	Cr.
Cash	4000000	
Accounts Receivable	700000	
Prepaid Insurance	40000	
Dance Supplies	150000	
Dance Equipment	1300000	
Accumulated Depreciation, Dance Equipment		1190000
Accounts Payable		2100000
D. Dee, Capital		1320000
D. Dee, Withdrawals	80000	
Dance Fees Earned		1980000
Salaries Expense	160000	
Telephone Expense	100000	
Advertising Expense	60000	
	6590000	6590000

Adjustment Data

a. Insurance expired, $300

b. Dance supplies on hand, $700

c. Depreciation on dance equipment, $500

d. Salaries earned by employees but not to be paid until July, $400

Required

1. Prepare a worksheet.

2. Journalize adjusting and closing entries.

Journalizing and posting adjusting and closing entries and preparing a post-closing trial balance
❶ ❷ ❸ (35 min)

5A-2. As the bookkeeper for Potter Cleaning Service, **a.** from the trial balance columns of the worksheet on page 224, enter the beginning balance of each account before adjustments in your working papers, **b.** journalize and post adjusting entries, **c.** journalize and post closing entries, and **d.** from the ledger (after all posting is complete), prepare a post-closing trial balance at March 31, 2016.

Check Figure (5A-2)

Post-Closing Trial Balance total $3,504

Comprehensive review of the entire accounting cycle, Chapters 1-5

❶ ❷ ❸ (150 min)

Check Figure

Net Income $15,780

5A-3. As the bookkeeper of Pete's Plowing of Fredericton, you have been asked to complete the entire accounting cycle for Pete from the following information (see the chart of accounts on page 225):

2015		
Jan.	3	Pete invested $7,000 cash and $6,000 worth of snow equipment in the plowing company.
	3	Paid rent in advance for garage space, $2,000.
	5	Purchased office equipment on account from Ling Corp., $7,200.
	6	Purchased snow supplies for $700 cash.
	9	Collected $15,000 from plowing local shopping centres.
	12	Pete Mack withdrew $1,000 from the business for personal use.
	20	Plowed North East Co. parking lots, payment not to be received until March, $5,000.
	26	Paid salaries to employees, $1,800.
	27	Paid Ling Corp. one-half amount owed for office equipment.
	30	Advertising bill was received from Bush Co. but will not be paid until March, $900.
	31	Paid telephone bill, $210.

Adjustment Data

a. Snow supplies on hand, $400

b. Rent expired, $600

c. Depreciation on office equipment, $120

$(\$7{,}200 \div 5 \text{ yr.} \rightarrow \frac{\$1{,}440}{12 \text{ mo.}} = \$120/\text{mo.})$

d. Depreciation on snow equipment,$100

$(\$6{,}000 \div 5 \text{ yr.} \rightarrow \frac{\$1{,}200}{12 \text{ mo.}} = \$100/\text{mo.})$

e. Accrued salaries, $190

POTTER CLEANING SERVICE
WORKSHEET
FOR THE MONTH ENDED MARCH 31, 2016

Account Titles	Trial Balance Dr.	Trial Balance Cr.	Adjustments Dr.	Adjustments Cr.	Adjusted Trial Balance Dr.	Adjusted Trial Balance Cr.	Income Statement Dr.	Income Statement Cr.	Balance Sheet Dr.	Balance Sheet Cr.
Cash	400 00				400 00				400 00	
Prepaid Insurance	520 00			(A) 180 00	340 00				340 00	
Cleaning Supplies	144 00			(B) 100 00	44 00				44 00	
Auto	2720 00				2720 00				2720 00	
Accum. Depreciation, Auto		860 00		(C) 150 00		1010 00				1010 00
Accounts Payable		224 00				224 00				224 00
B. Potter, Capital		540 00				540 00				540 00
B. Potter, Withdrawals	460 00				460 00				460 00	
Cleaning Fees		4680 00				4680 00		4680 00		
Salaries Expense	1440 00		(D) 160 00		1600 00		1600 00			
Telephone Expense	264 00				264 00		264 00			
Advertising Expense	196 00				196 00		196 00			
Gas Expense	160 00				160 00		160 00			
	6304 00	6304 00								
Insurance Expense			(A) 180 00		180 00		180 00			
Cleaning Supplies Expense			(B) 100 00		100 00		100 00			
Depreciation Expense, Auto			(C) 150 00		150 00		150 00			
Accrued Salaries				(D) 160 00		160 00				160 00
			590 00	590 00	6614 00	6614 00	2650 00	4680 00	3964 00	1934 00
Net Income							2030 00			2030 00
							4680 00	4680 00	3964 00	3964 00

Pete's Plowing
Chart of Accounts

Assets	Owner's Equity
111 Cash	311 Pete Mack, Capital
112 Accounts Receivable	312 Pete Mack, Withdrawals
114 Prepaid Rent	313 Income Summary
115 Snow Supplies	
121 Office Equipment	**Revenue**
122 Accumulated Depreciation, Office Equipment	411 Plowing Fees
123 Snow Equipment	**Expenses**
124 Accumulated Depreciation, Snow Equipment	511 Salaries Expense
	512 Advertising Expense
	513 Telephone Expense
Liabilities	514 Rent Expense
211 Accounts Payable	515 Snow Supplies Expense
212 Accrued Salaries	516 Depreciation Expense, Office Equipment
	517 Depreciation Expense, Snow Equipment

Group B Problems

(The blank forms you need are on pages 5-15 to 5-30 of the *Study Guide with Working Papers.*)

Review of preparing a worksheet and journalizing and closing entries
❶ ❷ (40 min)

5B-1.

To: Matt Kamimsk
From: Abbey Ellen
Re: Accounting Needs

Please prepare ASAP from the following information (attached) (1) a worksheet, along with (2) journalized adjusting and closing entries.

Check Figure

Net Income $3,530

DEBBIE'S DANCE STUDIO
TRIAL BALANCE
JUNE 30, 2017

	Dr.	Cr.
Cash	10 1 5 0 00	
Accounts Receivable	5 0 0 0 00	
Prepaid Insurance	7 0 0 00	
Dance Supplies	3 0 0 00	
Dance Equipment	12 9 5 0 00	
Accumulated Depreciation, Dance Equipment		4 0 0 0 00
Accounts Payable		5 7 5 0 00
D. Dee, Capital		15 1 5 0 00
D. Dee, Withdrawals	4 0 0 00	
Dance Fees Earned		5 2 0 0 00
Salaries Expense	4 5 0 00	
Telephone Expense	7 0 00	
Advertising Expense	8 0 00	
	30 1 0 0 00	30 1 0 0 00

Adjustment Data

a. Insurance expired, $100
b. Dance supplies on hand, $20
c. Depreciation on dance equipment, $200
d. Salaries earned by employees but not due to be paid until July, $490

Journalizing and posting adjusting and closing entries, and preparing a post-closing trial balance
❶❷❸ (35 min)

5B-2. As the bookkeeper for Potter Cleaning Service, **a.** from the trial balance columns of the worksheet on page 227, enter the beginning balance of each account in your working papers, **b.** journalize and post adjusting entries, **c.** journalize and post closing entries, and **d.** from the ledger (after all posting is complete), prepare a post-closing trial balance at March 31, 2016.

Check Figure **(5B-2)**

Post-Closing Trial Balance $3,294

Comprehensive review of entire accounting cycle, Chapters 1-5
❶❷❸ (150 min)

Check Figure

Net Income $9,610

5B-3. From the following transactions as well as additional data, complete the entire accounting cycle for Pete's Plowing of Fredericton (use the chart of accounts on page 225).

2015
Jan. 3 To open the business, Pete invested $8,000 cash and $9,600 worth of snow equipment.
3 Paid rent for five months in advance, $3,000.
5 Purchased office equipment on account from Russell Co., $6,000.
6 Bought snow supplies, $350.
9 Collected $7,000 for plowing during winter storm emergency.
12 Pete paid his home telephone bill using a company cheque, $70.
20 Billed Eastern Freight Co. for plowing fees earned but not to be received until March, $6,500.
23 Advertising bill was received from Jones Co. but will not be paid until next month, $350.
26 Paid salaries to employees, $1,800.
30 Paid Russell Co. one-half of amount owed for office equipment.
31 Paid telephone bill of company, $165.

Adjustment Data

a. Snow supplies on hand, $200
b. Rent expired, $600
c. Depreciation on office equipment ($6,000 ÷ 4 yr. → $1,500 ÷ 12 = $125), $125
d. Depreciation on snow equipment ($9,600 ÷ 2 yr. → $4,800 ÷ 12 = $400), $400
e. Salaries accrued, $300

Group C Problems

(The forms you need are on pages 5-31 to 5-47 of the *Study Guide with Working Papers.*)

Review of preparing a worksheet and journalizing adjusting and closing entries
❶❷ (40 min)

Check Figure

Net Income $16,340.00

5C-1.

TO: Peter George
FROM: Anthony Hoang
RE: Accounting Procedures

Please prepare from the following information (attached), (1) a worksheet, along with (2) journalized adjusting and closing entries for the year ending May 31, 2017.

POTTER CLEANING SERVICE
WORKSHEET
FOR THE MONTH ENDED MARCH 31, 2016

Account Titles	Trial Balance Dr.	Trial Balance Cr.	Adjustments Dr.	Adjustments Cr.	Adjusted Trial Balance Dr.	Adjusted Trial Balance Cr.	Income Statement Dr.	Income Statement Cr.	Balance Sheet Dr.	Balance Sheet Cr.
Cash	1 7 2 4 00				1 7 2 4 00				1 7 2 4 00	
Prepaid Insurance	3 5 0 00			(A) 2 0 0 00	1 5 0 00				1 5 0 00	
Cleaning Supplies	8 0 0 00			(B) 6 0 0 00	2 0 0 00				2 0 0 00	
Auto	1 2 2 0 00				1 2 2 0 00				1 2 2 0 00	
Accumulated Depreciation, Auto		6 6 0 00		(C) 1 5 0 00		8 1 0 00				8 1 0 00
Accounts Payable		6 7 4 00				6 7 4 00				6 7 4 00
B. Potter, Capital		2 4 8 0 00				2 4 8 0 00				2 4 8 0 00
B. Potter, Withdrawals	6 0 0 00				6 0 0 00				6 0 0 00	
Cleaning Fees		3 7 0 0 00				3 7 0 0 00		3 7 0 0 00		
Salaries Expense	2 0 0 0 00		(D) 1 7 5 00		2 1 7 5 00		2 1 7 5 00			
Telephone Expense	2 8 4 00				2 8 4 00		2 8 4 00			
Advertising Expense	2 7 6 00				2 7 6 00		2 7 6 00			
Gas Expense	2 6 0 00				2 6 0 00		2 6 0 00			
	7 5 1 4 00	7 5 1 4 00								
Insurance Expense			(A) 2 0 0 00		2 0 0 00		2 0 0 00			
Cleaning Supplies Expense			(B) 6 0 0 00		6 0 0 00		6 0 0 00			
Depreciation Expense, Auto			(C) 1 5 0 00		1 5 0 00		1 5 0 00			
Accrued Salaries				(D) 1 7 5 00		1 7 5 00				1 7 5 00
			1 1 2 5 00	1 1 2 5 00	7 8 3 9 00	7 8 3 9 00	3 9 4 5 00	3 7 0 0 00	3 8 9 4 00	4 1 3 9 00
Net Loss								2 4 5 00	2 4 5 00	
							3 9 4 5 00	3 9 4 5 00	4 1 3 9 00	4 1 3 9 00

Adjustment Data

a. Insurance expired, $510.75

b. Disposal supplies on hand, $723

c. Depreciation for the year on disposal equipment is based on the straight-line method, 12-year life, and a residual value of $1,225.

d. Depreciation for the year on building is also straight-line, 20-year life, and a residual value of $25,000

e. Wages earned by employees but not due to be paid until June amounted to 36 hours at $18/hour plus 30 hours at $24/hour.

ECO DOCUMENT DISPOSAL COMPANY
TRIAL BALANCE
MAY 31, 2017

	Debit	Credit
Cash	22 210 00	
Accounts Receivable	1 200 00	
Prepaid Insurance	681 00	
Disposal Supplies	1 542 00	
Disposal Equipment	11 740 00	
Accumulated Depreciation, Disposal Equipment		7 010 00
Building	48 000 00	
Accumulated Depreciation, Building		20 700 00
Accounts Payable		4 660 00
A. Hoang, Capital		48 681 00
A. Hoang, Withdrawals	16 742 00	
Disposal Fees Revenue		52 720 00
Wages Expense	28 240 00	
Utilities Expense	2 544 00	
Advertising Expense	872 00	
	133 771 00	133 771 00

Journalizing and posting adjusting and closing entries, and preparing a post-closing trial balance
❶❷❸ (35 min)

Check Figure (5C-2)

Post-Closing Trial Balance $30,845.63

5C-2. Refer to the worksheet for Chalke's Computer Repair Service of Brandon on page 229. The beginning balances (from the trial balance column) in each account are already entered in your working papers. **a.** Journalize and post adjusting and closing entries to each account in the ledger, and **b.** prepare from the ledger a post-closing trial balance at the end of November.

Comprehensive review of the entire accounting cycle, Chapters 1-5
❶❷❸ (175 min)

5C-3. From the following transactions as well as additional data, please complete the entire accounting cycle for Mike's Plumbing of Prince Albert (use a chart of accounts similar to the one on page 225).

2016

May 1 To open the business, Mike Quinlan invested $10,000 cash and $7,400 worth of plumbing equipment.

1 Paid rent for four months in advance, $1,980.

3 Purchased office equipment on account from MacKenzie Co., $3,800.

7 Bought plumbing supplies, $1,645.

8 Collected $3,600 for plumbing services provided.

9 Mike paid his home utility bill with a company cheque, $122.

10 Billed Western Construction Co. for plumbing fees earned but not to be received until later, $9,600.

14 Advertising bill was received from ABCD Radio Co. but is not to be paid until next month, $420.

21 Received cheque from Western Construction Co. in partial payment of transaction dated May 10, $4,800.

CHALKE'S COMPUTER REPAIR SERVICE
WORKSHEET
NOVEMBER 30, 2015

Account Titles	Trial Balance Dr.	Trial Balance Cr.	Adjustments Dr.	Adjustments Cr.	Adjusted Trial Balance Dr.	Adjusted Trial Balance Cr.	Income Statement Dr.	Income Statement Cr.	Balance Sheet Dr.	Balance Sheet Cr.
Cash	2,396.48			(A) 36.84	2,359.64				2,359.64	
Prepaid Insurance	714.56			(C) 238.19	476.37				476.37	
Accounts Receivable	5,277.42				5,277.42				5,277.42	
Repair Parts and Supplies	1,597.47			(D) 540.27	1,057.20				1,057.20	
Van	21,675.00				21,675.00				21,675.00	
Accumulated Depreciation, Van		8,103.65		(B) 347.40		8,451.05				8,451.05
Accounts Payable		3,802.60		(F) 243.00		4,045.60				4,045.60
Tricia Chalke, Capital		13,663.58				13,663.58				13,663.58
Tricia Chalke, Withdrawals	2,600.00				2,600.00				2,600.00	
Repair Revenue		16,458.70				16,458.70		16,458.70		
Advertising Expense	714.38		(F) 243.00		957.38		957.38			
Automotive Expense	2,345.51				2,345.51		2,345.51			
Cleaning Expense	375.00				375.00		375.00			
Miscellaneous Expense	178.14				178.14		178.14			
Postage and Office Expense	284.17				284.17		284.17			
Salaries Expense	3,870.40		(E) 420.00		4,290.40		4,290.40			
	41,998.53	41,998.53								
Insurance Expense			(C) 238.19		238.19		238.19			
Bank Charges Expense			(A) 36.84		36.84		36.84			
Depreciation Expense, Van			(B) 347.40		347.40		347.40			
Accrued Salaries				(E) 420.00		420.00				420.00
Supplies Expense			(D) 540.27		540.27		540.27			
			1,825.70	1,825.70	43,038.93	43,038.93	9,593.30	16,458.70	33,445.63	26,580.23
Net Income							6,865.40			6,865.40
							16,458.70	16,458.70	33,445.63	33,445.63

May 28 Paid MacKenzie Co. one-half of amount owed for office equipment, $1,900.
31 Paid telephone bill of company, $184.
31 Received bill from George's Cleaning to be paid in June, $215.
31 Paid salaries to employees, $4,100.

Adjusting Data

a. Plumbing supplies remaining at month-end were $328.

b. One month's rent expired in May.

c. Depreciation on office equipment uses the straight-line method, a life of five years, and a residual value of $500.

d. Depreciation of plumbing equipment also uses the straight-line method, a life of three years, and zero residual value.

e. Salaries accrued amounted to 20% of the salaries paid on May 31.

Check Figure

Net Income $5,388.44

On-the-Job Training

(The forms you need are on page 5-48 of the *Study Guide with Working Papers.*)

Analyzing financial information and completing the accounting cycle
❷ (15 min)

T-1. Carol Miller needs a loan from her local bank to help finance her business. She has submitted the following unadjusted trial balance to the bank. As the loan officer, you will be meeting with Carol tomorrow. Could you make some specific written suggestions to Carol regarding her loan report?

Cash in Bank	$ 770	
Accounts Receivable	1,480	
Office Supplies	3,310	
Equipment	7,606	
Accounts Payable		$ 684
C. Miller, Capital		8,000
Service Fees		17,350
Salaries	11,240	
Utilities Expense	842	
Rent Expense	360	
Insurance Expense	280	
Advertising Expense	146	
Totals	$26,034	$26,034

Closing entries
❷ (15 min)

T-2. Janet Smother is the new bookkeeper who replaced Dick Burns, owing to his sudden illness. Janet finds a note on her desk requesting that she close the books and supply the ending capital figure. Janet is upset since she can find only the following:

a. Revenue and expense accounts were all zero balance.

b. Income Summary

Income Summary	
14,360	19,300

c. Owner withdrew $8,000.

d. Owner's beginning capital was $34,400.

Could you help Janet accomplish her assignment? What written suggestions should Janet make to her supervisor so that this situation will not happen again?

Comprehensive problem: journalizing and posting adjusting and closing entries; and preparing a post-closing trial balance
❶ ❷ ❸ (60 min)

CONTINUING PROBLEM

Tony has decided to end the Precision Computer Centre's first year as of July 31, 2016. Below is an updated chart of accounts.

Assets

1000 Cash
1020 Accounts Receivable
1025 Prepaid Rent
1030 Supplies
1080 Computer Shop Equipment
1081 Accumulated Depreciation, Computer Shop Equipment
1090 Office Equipment
1091 Accumulated Depreciation, Office Equipment

Liabilities

2000 Accounts Payable

Owner's Equity

3000 T. Freedman, Capital
3010 T. Freedman, Withdrawals
3020 Income Summary

Revenue

4000 Service Revenue

Expenses

5010 Advertising Expense
5020 Rent Expense
5030 Utilities Expense
5040 Phone Expense
5050 Supplies Expense
5060 Insurance Expense
5070 Postage Expense
5080 Depreciation Expense, Computer Shop Equipment
5090 Depreciation Expense, Office Equipment

Assignment

(See pages 5-49 to 5-54 in your *Study Guide with Working Papers*.)

1. Journalize the adjusting entries from Chapter 4.
2. Post the adjusting entries to the ledger.
3. Journalize the closing entries.
4. Post the closing entries to the ledger.
5. Prepare a post-closing trial balance.

MINI PRACTICE SET

Sullivan Realty
Reviewing the Accounting Cycle Twice

Estimated time 5 hours

This comprehensive review problem requires you to complete the accounting cycle for Sullivan Realty twice. This will allow you to review Chapters 1 to 5 while reinforcing the relationships among all parts of the accounting cycle. By completing two cycles, you will see how the ending June balances in the ledger are used to accumulate data in July. (The blank forms you need are on pages 5-58 to 5-74 of the *Study Guide with Working Papers.*)

On June 1, John Sullivan opened a real estate office in Hamilton called Sullivan Realty. The following transactions were completed for the month of June. Note that facsimile documents have been provided to illustrate these events:

2016

#1, p. 233 → June 3 John Sullivan invested $20,000 cash in the real estate agency,
#2, p. 233 → along with $4,000 worth of office equipment.

3 Rented office space and paid three months' rent in advance, $3,000, cheque No. 601.

Sullivan Realty
Chart of Accounts

Assets

111	Cash
112	Accounts Receivable
114	Prepaid Rent
115	Office Supplies
121	Office Equipment
122	Accumulated Depreciation, Office Equipment
123	Automobile
124	Accumulated Depreciation, Automobile

Liabilities

211	Accounts Payable
212	Accrued Salaries

Owner's Equity

311	John Sullivan, Capital
312	John Sullivan, Withdrawals
313	Income Summary

Revenue

411	Commissions Earned

Expenses

511	Rent Expense
512	Salaries Expense
513	Gas Expense
514	Repairs Expense
515	Telephone Expense
516	Advertising Expense
517	Office Supplies Expense
518	Depreciation Expense, Office Equipment
519	Depreciation Expense, Automobile
524	Miscellaneous Expense

1.

CURRENT ACCOUNT DEPOSIT SLIP

ROYAL BANK

June 3, 2016
DATE

DEPOSITOR'S INITIALS	TELLER'S INITIALS
JS	PRL

CREDIT ACCOUNT OF

SULLIVAN REALTY

PLEASE LIST FOREIGN CHEQUES ON A SEPARATE DEPOSIT SLIP

VISA AND CHEQUES	VISA VOUCHER TOTAL	DETAILS	CASH (INCL COUPONS)
Sullivan	20,000.00	X 5	
		X 10	
		X 20	
		X 50	
		X 100	
		X	
		COIN	
		CANADIAN CASH TOTAL	
	20,000.00	VISA & CHQS	20,000.00
U.S. CHQS.		RATE	
U.S. CASH		RATE	
	NET DEPOSIT		20,000.00

COMPARED WITH ORIGINAL DEPOSIT SLIP AS TO TOTAL ONLY

I: 05337 123'498'6 51

2.

S

SULLIVAN REALTY
485 KING STREET WEST
HAMILTON, ONTARIO L9H 6W3
PHONE (905) 527-1223

601

June 3 2016

PAY TO THE ORDER OF Hamilton One Property Management Co. $ 3,000

~~~~~~ Three thousand ~~~~~~ 00/100 DOLLARS

THE ROYAL BANK OF CANADA
MAIN BRANCH
204 KING STREET WEST
HAMILTON, ONTARIO L9H 4Z9

SULLIVAN REALTY

FOR Rent – June–August 2016

PER John Sullivan

II"000601 I: 05337 123'498'6

	2016	
#3a & b, p. 234 →	June 4	Bought a company automobile. Cheque No. 602, $14,000.00
#4a & b, pp. 234 & 235 →	4	Purchased office supplies. Wrote cheque No. 603, $300.
#5, p. 235 →	5	Purchased additional office supplies on account, $150.
#6a & b, pp. 235 & 236 →	6	Sold a house and collected a $6,000 commission.
#7, p. 236 →	7	Paid gas bill for car, $22. Cheque No. 604.
#8, p. 236 →	14	Paid the salary of the part-time office secretary, $350. Cheque No. 605.
#9, p. 236 →	18	Sold a building lot and earned a commission, $6,500. Payment is to be received on July 9.
#10, p. 237 →	21	John Sullivan withdrew $1,000 from the business to pay personal expenses. Cheque No. 606.
#11a & b, p. 237 →	21	Sold a house and collected a $3,500 commission.
#12, p. 238 →	24	Paid gas bill for car. $25. Cheque No. 607.
#13a & b, p. 238 →	25	Paid $600 to repair automobile. Cheque No. 608.
#14, p. 238 →	28	Paid the salary of the part-time office secretary, $350. Cheque No. 609.
#15a & b, p. 239 →	28	Paid the June telephone bill, $510. Cheque No. 610.
#16, p. 240 →	28	Received advertising bill for June, $1,200. The bill is to be paid by July 5.
~~~~~~

3a.

AUTO CITY WEST

2674 King Street West
Hamilton, Ontario L9H 1A1
Phone (905) 527-9755; Fax (905) 527-9756

INVOICE

INVOICE NO. WEA1097
DATE: June 4/16
TERMS: Cash

To:
Sullivan Realty
485 King Street West
Hamilton, Ontario L9H 6W3

Ship To:
June 4/16
Pickup

QUANTITY	DESCRIPTION	UNIT PRICE	AMOUNT
1	ONLY 2008 Z75 4-Door Automatic	14,000	$14,000
		SUBTOTAL	14,000
		FREIGHT	
		TAX	
		TOTAL DUE	$14,000

Make all cheques payable to Auto City West

PAYMENT RECEIVED - Cheque #602 - Thank you

THANK YOU FOR YOUR BUSINESS!

3b.

SULLIVAN REALTY
485 KING STREET WEST
HAMILTON, ONTARIO L9H 6W3
PHONE (905) 527-1223

602

June 4 20*16*

PAY TO THE ORDER OF *Auto City West* $ *14,000.00*

Fourteen thousand *00* /100 DOLLARS

THE ROYAL BANK OF CANADA
MAIN BRANCH
204 KING STREET WEST
HAMILTON, ONTARIO L9H 4Z9

SULLIVAN REALTY

FOR *Automobile - Inv. WEA1097*

PER *John Sullivan*

⑈000602 ⑆: 05337 123'498'6

4a.

Office Depot

#53 Niagara Mall
Hamilton, Ontario L9H 1B1
Phone (905) 527-1233, Fax (905) 527-1234

INVOICE

DATE: Jun 4/16
NUMBER: D198795
TERMS: Cash

SOLD TO:
Sullivan Realty
485 King Street West
Hamilton, Ontario L9H 6W3

SHIPPED TO:
Sullivan Realty
485 King Street West

DATE	DESCRIPTION	UNIT PRICE	AMOUNT
Jun 4/16	Office supplies PAYMENT RECEIVED - CHQ #603 - THANK YOU		$300.00
		Subtotal	300.00
		Total	$300.00

Business Number: 115555559

PLEASE PAY THE ABOVE

THANK YOU FOR YOUR BUSINESS

4b.

SULLIVAN REALTY 485 KING STREET WEST HAMILTON, ONTARIO L9H 6W3 PHONE (905) 527-1223	603
	June 4 2016
PAY TO THE ORDER OF Office Depot	$ 300.00
~~ Three hundred ~~~~	00 /100 DOLLARS
THE ROYAL BANK OF CANADA MAIN BRANCH 204 KING STREET WEST HAMILTON, ONTARIO L9H 4Z9	SULLIVAN REALTY
FOR Office supplies	PER John Sullivan

⑈000603 ⑆: 05337 123'498'6

5.

Office Depot
#53 Niagara Mall
Hamilton, Ontario L9H 1B1
Phone (905) 527-1233, Fax (905) 527-1234

INVOICE

DATE: Jun 5/16
NUMBER: D198825
TERMS: net 30

SOLD TO:
Sullivan Realty
485 King Street West
Hamilton, Ontario L9H 6W3

SHIPPED TO:
Sullivan Realty
485 King Street West

DATE	DESCRIPTION	UNIT PRICE	AMOUNT
Jun 5/16	Office supplies		$150.00
		Subtotal	150.00
		Total	$150.00

Business Number: 115555559

PLEASE PAY THE ABOVE

THANK YOU FOR YOUR BUSINESS

6a.

CURRENT ACCOUNT DEPOSIT SLIP
ROYAL BANK

June 6, 2016
DATE

DEPOSITOR'S INITIALS	TELLER'S INITIALS
JS	MG

CREDIT ACCOUNT OF
SULLIVAN REALTY

PLEASE LIST FOREIGN CHEQUES ON A SEPARATE DEPOSIT SLIP

VISA AND CHEQUES		DETAILS	CASH (INCL COUPONS)
	VISA VOUCHER TOTAL		
H. Penchant	6,000 00	X 5	
		X 10	
		X 20	
		X 50	
		X 100	
		X	
		COIN	
		CANADIAN CASH TOTAL	
	6,000 00	VISA & CHQS	6,000 00
U.S. CHQS.		RATE	
U.S. CASH		RATE	
	NET DEPOSIT		6,000 00

⑆: 05337 123'498'6 51

COMPARED WITH ORIGINAL DEPOSIT SLIP AS TO TOTAL ONLY

6b.

SULLIVAN REALTY

COMMISSION REPORT — *Date* June 6, 2016

Name: Mr. and Mrs. Harold Penchant

Date	*Sales Description*	*Sales No.*	*Commission Amount*	
Jun 6/16	*Home at 44 Brookhaven Crescent*	*A1001*	*$6,000.00*	*Paid in full.*
C001		*Remarks:*		

7.

SULLIVAN REALTY
485 KING STREET WEST
HAMILTON, ONTARIO L9H 6W3
PHONE (905) 527-1223

604

June 7 20 16

PAY TO THE ORDER OF Anderson Petroleum Ltd. $ 22.00

~~~ Twenty-two ~~~~~~~~~ 00/100 DOLLARS

THE ROYAL BANK OF CANADA
MAIN BRANCH
204 KING STREET WEST
HAMILTON, ONTARIO L9H 4Z9

SULLIVAN REALTY

FOR Gas bill – June 7 PER John Sullivan

II"000604 I: 05337 123'498'6

8.

SULLIVAN REALTY
485 KING STREET WEST
HAMILTON, ONTARIO L9H 6W3
PHONE (905) 527-1223

605

June 14 20 16

PAY TO THE ORDER OF Pamela Dawson $ 350.00

~~~ Three hundred fifty ~~~~~~~~~~~ 00 /100 DOLLARS

THE ROYAL BANK OF CANADA
MAIN BRANCH
204 KING STREET WEST
HAMILTON, ONTARIO L9H 4Z9

SULLIVAN REALTY

FOR Salary – June 1-14 PER John Sullivan

II"000605 I: 05337 123'498'6

9.

SULLIVAN REALTY

COMMISSION REPORT — *Date* June 18, 2016

Name: East End Land Developers

Date	*Sales Description*	*Sales No.*	*Commission Amount*	
Jun 18/16	*Lot at 999 King Street East*	*A1002*	*$6,500.00*	
C002		*Remarks:* Payment due July 9, 2016		

10.

S SULLIVAN REALTY 485 KING STREET WEST HAMILTON, ONTARIO L9H 6W3 PHONE (905) 527-1223	606 June 21 20 16
PAY TO THE ORDER OF John Sullivan	$ 1,000.00
~~ One thousand ~~~~~~~~~~~~~~~~	00 /100 DOLLARS
THE ROYAL BANK OF CANADA MAIN BRANCH 204 KING STREET WEST HAMILTON, ONTARIO L9H 4Z9	SULLIVAN REALTY
FOR Withdrawal	PER John Sullivan
⑈000606 ⑆: 05337 123'498'6	

11a.

CURRENT ACCOUNT DEPOSIT SLIP
ROYAL BANK

June 21, 2016
DATE

DEPOSITOR'S INITIALS	TELLER'S INITIALS
PD	AS

CREDIT ACCOUNT OF

SULLIVAN REALTY

PLEASE LIST FOREIGN CHEQUES ON A SEPARATE DEPOSIT SLIP

VISA AND CHEQUES	VISA VOUCHER TOTAL	DETAILS	CASH (INCL COUPONS)
L. Harrison	3,500.00	X 5	
		X 10	
		X 20	
		X 50	
		X 100	
		X	
		COIN	
		CANADIAN CASH TOTAL	
	3,500.00	VISA & CHQS	3,500.00
U.S. CHQS.		RATE	
U.S. CASH		RATE	
NET DEPOSIT			3,500.00

⑆: 05337 123'498'6 51

COMPARED WITH ORIGINAL DEPOSIT SLIP AS TO TOTAL ONLY

11b.

SULLIVAN REALTY COMMISSION REPORT				*Date* June 21, 2016
Name: Ms Laura Harrison				
Date	***Sales Description***	***Sales No.***	***Commission Amount***	
Jun 21/16	*Home at 842 Alder Road*	*A1003*	*$3,500.00*	*Paid in full.*
C003		***Remarks:***		

12.

SULLIVAN REALTY
485 KING STREET WEST
HAMILTON, ONTARIO L9H 6W3
PHONE (905) 527-1223

607

June 24 20 16

PAY TO THE ORDER OF Anderson Petroleum Ltd. $ 25.00

~~~~ Twenty-five ~~~~~~~~~~ 00/100 DOLLARS

THE ROYAL BANK OF CANADA
MAIN BRANCH
204 KING STREET WEST
HAMILTON, ONTARIO L9H 4Z9

SULLIVAN REALTY

FOR Gas bill - June 24 PER John Sullivan

II"000607 I: 05337 123'498'6

13a.

AUTO CITY WEST

2674 King Street West
Hamilton, Ontario L9H 1A1
Phone (905) 527-9755; Fax (905) 527-9756

INVOICE

INVOICE NO. WES3750

DATE: June 25/16

TERMS: Cash

To:

Sullivan Realty
485 King Street West
Hamilton, Ontario L9H 6W3

Ship To:

Pickup

QUANTITY	DESCRIPTION	UNIT PRICE	AMOUNT
1	Only Z75 Air conditioning repair		$ 600.00

Make all cheques payable to Auto City West

SUBTOTAL	600.00
FREIGHT	
TAX	
TOTAL DUE	$ 600.00

PAYMENT RECEIVED - Cheque #608 - Thank you

THANK YOU FOR YOUR BUSINESS!

13b.

SULLIVAN REALTY
485 KING STREET WEST
HAMILTON, ONTARIO L9H 6W3
PHONE (905) 527-1223

608

June 25 20 16

PAY TO THE ORDER OF Auto City West $ 600.00

~~~~ Six hundred ~~~~~~~~~~~~~ 00 /100 DOLLARS

THE ROYAL BANK OF CANADA
MAIN BRANCH
204 KING STREET WEST
HAMILTON, ONTARIO L9H 4Z9

SULLIVAN REALTY

FOR Automobile repairs - Inv WES3750 PER John Sullivan

II"000608 I: 05337 123'498'6

14.

SULLIVAN REALTY
485 KING STREET WEST
HAMILTON, ONTARIO L9H 6W3
PHONE (905) 527-1223

609

June 28 20 16

PAY TO THE ORDER OF Pamela Dawson $ 350.00

~~~~ Three hundred fifty ~~~~~~~~~~~~ 00 /100 DOLLARS

THE ROYAL BANK OF CANADA
MAIN BRANCH
204 KING STREET WEST
HAMILTON, ONTARIO L9H 4Z9

SULLIVAN REALTY

FOR Salary - June 16-30

PER John Sullivan

⑈000609 ⑆: 05337 123'498'6

15a.

Phones Ontario

#2110 Steel Place
Hamilton, Ontario L9G 4B4
Phone (905) 529-7190
Fax (905) 529-0063

Your Statement

In Account with

SULLIVAN REALTY
485 KING STREET WEST
HAMILTON ON L9H 6W3

Account #09444 710-190

Payment received
July 2, 2016
Phones Ontario

Billing Period: June 1 to June 30

Payments/Adjustments/Deposits Details Opened account June 3, 2016. Thank you.	$0.00
Monthly rental and changes to service	510.00
Amount now. due Payment due after July 10, 2016 $522.75 **Total Due**	$510.00

15b.

SULLIVAN REALTY
485 KING STREET WEST
HAMILTON, ONTARIO L9H 6W3
PHONE (905) 527-1223

610

June 28 20 16

PAY TO THE ORDER OF Phones Ontario $ 510.00

~~~~ Five hundred ten ~~~~~~~~~~ 00/100 DOLLARS

THE ROYAL BANK OF CANADA
MAIN BRANCH
204 KING STREET WEST
HAMILTON, ONTARIO L9H 4Z9

SULLIVAN REALTY

FOR June phone bill

PER John Sullivan

⑈000610 ⑆: 05337 123'498'6

16.

City News

85 Main Street, Hamilton, Ontario L9H 0C0
Phone (905) 527-1030 Fax (905) 527-1031

INVOICE

SOLD TO:	Sullivan Realty 485 King Street West Hamilton ON L9H 6W3	**Invoice No.:** **Date:** **Due Date:**	4879 June 28, 2016 July 5, 2016

DATE	DESCRIPTION		AMOUNT
June 25/16	Advertising in City News during June 2016		$1,200.00
		SUBTOTAL	1,200.00
		TOTAL	$1,200.00

Business Number 944122338
MAKE ALL CHEQUES PAYABLE TO CITY NEWS.

Required Work for June

1. Journalize transactions and post to ledger accounts.
2. Prepare a trial balance in the first two columns of the worksheet and complete the worksheet using the following adjustment data:
   a. One month's rent had expired
   b. An inventory shows $50 worth of office supplies remaining
   c. Depreciation on office equipment, $100
   d. Depreciation on automobile, $200
3. Prepare a June income statement, statement of owner's equity, and balance sheet.
4. From the worksheet, journalize and post adjusting and closing entries (page 3 of journal).
5. Prepare a post-closing trial balance.

During July, Sullivan Realty completed these transactions:

	2016		
#17, p. 241	July	2	Paid for June office supplies purchased on account, $150. Cheque No. 611.
#18, p. 241		2	Purchased additional office supplies on account, $700.
#19, p. 242		2	Paid advertising bill for June. Cheque No. 612.
#20a & b, p. 242		4	Sold a house and collected a commission, $6,600.
#21, p. 242		5	Paid for gas for car, $29. Cheque No. 613.
#22, p. 243		9	Collected commission from sale of building lot on June 18.
#23, p. 243		12	Paid $300 to send employees to realtor's workshop. Cheque No. 614.
#24, p. 243		15	Paid the salary of the part-time office secretary, $350. Cheque No. 615.

#25, p. 244 → 16 Sold a house and earned a commission of $2,400. Commission to be received August 11.

#26a & b, p. 244 → 19 Sold a building lot and collected a commission of $7,000.

#27, p. 245 → 23 Sent a cheque for $40 to help sponsor a local road race to aid the poor. (This is not to be considered an advertising expense, but it is a business expense.) Cheque No. 616.

#28a & b, p. 245 → 26 Paid for repairs to automobile, $590. Cheque No. 617.

#29, p. 246 → 29 John Sullivan withdrew $1,800 from the business to pay personal expenses. Cheque No. 618.

#30, p. 246 → 31 Paid the salary of the part-time office secretary, $350. Cheque No. 619.

#31a & b, pp. 246 & 247 → July 31 Paid the July telephone bill, $236. Cheque No. 620.

#32, p. 247 → 31 Advertising bill for July was received, $1,400. The bill is to be paid in August.

17.

S

SULLIVAN REALTY
485 KING STREET WEST
HAMILTON, ONTARIO L9H 6W3
PHONE (905) 527-1223

611

July 2 20 16

PAY TO THE ORDER OF Office Depot $ 150.00

One hundred fifty 00 /100 DOLLARS

THE ROYAL BANK OF CANADA
MAIN BRANCH
204 KING STREET WEST
HAMILTON, ONTARIO L9H 4Z9

SULLIVAN REALTY

FOR Invoice #D198825 PER John Sullivan

⑈000611 ⑆: 05337 123'498'6

18.

Office Depot
#53 Niagara Mall
Hamilton, Ontario L9H 1B1
Phone (905) 527-1233, Fax (905) 527-1234

INVOICE

DATE: July 2/16
NUMBER: D1996035
TERMS: Cash

SOLD TO:
Sullivan Realty
485 King Street West
Hamilton, Ontario L9H 6W3

SHIPPED TO:
Sullivan Realty
485 King Street West

DATE	DESCRIPTION	UNIT PRICE	AMOUNT
July 2/16	Office supplies		$700.00
		Subtotal	700.00
		Total	$700.00

Business Number: 115555559

PLEASE PAY THE ABOVE

THANK YOU FOR YOUR BUSINESS

19.

SULLIVAN REALTY
485 KING STREET WEST
HAMILTON, ONTARIO L9H 6W3
PHONE (905) 527-1223

612

July 2 20 16

PAY TO THE ORDER OF City News $ 1,200.00

~~~ One thousand two hundred ~~~ 00 /100 DOLLARS

THE ROYAL BANK OF CANADA
MAIN BRANCH
204 KING STREET WEST
HAMILTON, ONTARIO L9H 4Z9

SULLIVAN REALTY

FOR Invoice #4879

PER John Sullivan

⑈000612 ⑆: 05337 123'498'6

20a.

SULLIVAN REALTY COMMISSION REPORT				Date July 4, 2016
Name: Mr. and Mrs. Andrew Tran				
Date	***Sales Description***	***Sales No.***	***Commission Amount***	
July 4/16	*Home at 1014 Cedar Lane*	*A1004*	*$6,600.00*	*Paid in full.*
C004		***Remarks:***		

20b.

CURRENT ACCOUNT DEPOSIT SLIP
ROYAL BANK

July 4, 2016
DATE

DEPOSITOR'S INITIALS	TELLER'S INITIALS
PD	MG

CREDIT ACCOUNT OF

SULLIVAN REALTY

PLEASE LIST FOREIGN CHEQUES ON A SEPARATE DEPOSIT SLIP

VISA AND CHEQUES	VISA VOUCHER TOTAL	DETAILS	CASH (INCL COUPONS)
A. Tran	6,6000 00	X 5	
		X 10	
		X 20	
		X 50	
		X 100	
		X	
		COIN	
		CANADIAN CASH TOTAL	
	6,600 00	VISA & CHQS	6,600 00
U.S. CHQS.		RATE	
U.S. CASH		RATE	
NET DEPOSIT			6,600 00

COMPARED WITH ORIGINAL DEPOSIT SLIP AS TO TOTAL ONLY

⑆: 05337 123'498'6 51

21.

SULLIVAN REALTY
485 KING STREET WEST
HAMILTON, ONTARIO L9H 6W3
PHONE (905) 527-1223

613

July 5 20 16

PAY TO THE ORDER OF Anderson Petroleum Ltd. $ 29.00

~~~ Twenty-nine ~~~ 00/100 DOLLARS

THE ROYAL BANK OF CANADA
MAIN BRANCH
204 KING STREET WEST
HAMILTON, ONTARIO L9H 4Z9

SULLIVAN REALTY

FOR Gas bill - July 5

PER John Sullivan

⑈000613 ⑆: 05337 123'498'6

22.

CURRENT ACCOUNT
DEPOSIT SLIP
ROYAL BANK

July 9, 2016
DATE

DEPOSITOR'S INITIALS	TELLER'S INITIALS
PD	MG

CREDIT ACCOUNT OF

SULLIVAN REALTY

PLEASE LIST FOREIGN CHEQUES ON A SEPARATE DEPOSIT SLIP

VISA AND CHEQUES		DETAILS	CASH (INCL COUPONS)
	VISA VOUCHER TOTAL		
East End		X 5	
Land		X 10	
Developers	6,500.00	X 20	
		X 50	
		X 100	
		X	
		COIN	
		CANADIAN CASH TOTAL	
	6,500 00	VISA & CHQS	6,500 00
U.S. CHQS.		RATE	
U.S. CASH		RATE	
	NET DEPOSIT		6,500 00

COMPARED WITH ORIGINAL DEPOSIT SLIP AS TO TOTAL ONLY

|: 05337 123'498'6 51

23.

S

SULLIVAN REALTY
485 KING STREET WEST
HAMILTON, ONTARIO L9H 6W3
PHONE (905) 527-1223

614

July 12 20 16

PAY TO THE ORDER OF Hamilton Realtors' Association $ 300.00

~~~~ Three hundred ~~~~~~~~~~~~ 00 /100 DOLLARS

THE ROYAL BANK OF CANADA
MAIN BRANCH
204 KING STREET WEST
HAMILTON, ONTARIO L9H 4Z9

SULLIVAN REALTY

FOR Workshop registration

PER John Sullivan

||"000614 |: 05337 123'498'6

24.

S

SULLIVAN REALTY
485 KING STREET WEST
HAMILTON, ONTARIO L9H 6W3
PHONE (905) 527-1223

615

July 15 20 16

PAY TO THE ORDER OF Pamela Dawson $ 350.00

~~~~ Three hundred fifty ~~~~~~~~~~~~ 00 /100 DOLLARS

THE ROYAL BANK OF CANADA
MAIN BRANCH
204 KING STREET WEST
HAMILTON, ONTARIO L9H 4Z9

SULLIVAN REALTY

FOR Salary - July 1-15

PER John Sullivan

||"000615 |: 05337 123'498'6

25.

SULLIVAN REALTY COMMISSION REPORT				*DATE* July 16, 2016
Name:	Mr. Hans Hollemeyer			
Date	*Sales Description*	*Sales No.*	*Commission Amount*	
July 16/16	*Home at RR2, Site 3*	*A1010*	*$2,400.00*	
C005		*Remarks:* Payment due August 11, 2016		

26a.

CURRENT ACCOUNT DEPOSIT SLIP
ROYAL BANK

July 19, 2016
DATE

DEPOSITOR'S INITIALS	TELLER'S INITIALS
PD	PRL

CREDIT ACCOUNT OF
SULLIVAN REALTY

PLEASE LIST FOREIGN CHEQUES ON A SEPARATE DEPOSIT SLIP

VISA AND CHEQUES		DETAILS	CASH (INCL COUPONS)
	VISA VOUCHER TOTAL		
B. Game	7,000 00	X 5	
		X 10	
		X 20	
		X 50	
		X 100	
		X	
		COIN	
		CANADIAN CASH TOTAL	
	7,000 00	VISA & CHQS	7,000 00
U.S. CHQS.		RATE	
U.S. CASH		RATE	
NET DEPOSIT			7,000 00

COMPARED WITH ORIGINAL DEPOSIT SLIP AS TO TOTAL ONLY

1: 05337 123'498'6 51

26b.

SULLIVAN REALTY COMMISSION REPORT				*Date* July 19, 2016
Name:	Mr. and Mrs. Benjamin Game			
Date	*Sales Description*	*Sales No.*	*Commission Amount*	
July 19/16	*Building lot at 5004 King St. E*	*A1005*	*$7,000.00*	*Paid in full.*
C006		*Remarks:*		

27.

SULLIVAN REALTY
485 KING STREET WEST
HAMILTON, ONTARIO L9H 6W3
PHONE (905) 527-1223

616

July 23 2016

PAY TO THE ORDER OF Mustard Seed Ministries $ 40.00

~~~ Forty ~~~~~~~~~~~~ 00/100 DOLLARS

THE ROYAL BANK OF CANADA
MAIN BRANCH
204 KING STREET WEST
HAMILTON, ONTARIO L9H 4Z9

SULLIVAN REALTY

FOR Aid to the poor

PER John Sullivan

⑈000616 ⑆: 05337 123'498'6

28a.

AUTO CITY WEST

2674 King Street West
Hamilton, Ontario L9H 1A1
Phone (905) 527-9755; Fax (905) 527-9756

INVOICE

INVOICE NO. WES3945

DATE: July 26/16

TERMS: Cash

To:
Sullivan Realty
485 King Street West
Hamilton, Ontario L9H 6W3

Ship To:
Pickup

QUANTITY	DESCRIPTION	UNIT PRICE	AMOUNT
	Z75 75,000 km maintenance		$ 590.00
		SUBTOTAL	590.00
		FREIGHT	
		TAX	
		TOTAL DUE	$ 590.00

Make all cheques payable to Auto City West

PAYMENT RECEIVED - Cheque #617 - Thank you

THANK YOU FOR YOUR BUSINESS!

28b.

SULLIVAN REALTY
485 KING STREET WEST
HAMILTON, ONTARIO L9H 6W3
PHONE (905) 527-1223

617

July 26 2016

PAY TO THE ORDER OF Auto City West $ 590.00

~~~ Five hundred ninety ~~~~~~~~~~~~ 00 /100 DOLLARS

THE ROYAL BANK OF CANADA
MAIN BRANCH
204 KING STREET WEST
HAMILTON, ONTARIO L9H 4Z9

SULLIVAN REALTY

FOR Automobile repairs - Inv. WES3945

PER John Sullivan

⑈000617 ⑆: 05337 123'498'6

29.

SULLIVAN REALTY
485 KING STREET WEST
HAMILTON, ONTARIO L9H 6W3
PHONE (905) 527-1223

618

July 29 20 16

PAY TO THE ORDER OF John Sullivan $ 1,800.00

~~~ One thousand eight hundred ~~~ 00 /100 DOLLARS

THE ROYAL BANK OF CANADA
MAIN BRANCH
204 KING STREET WEST
HAMILTON, ONTARIO L9H 4Z9

SULLIVAN REALTY

FOR Withdrawal PER John Sullivan

II"000618 I: 05337 123'498'6

30.

SULLIVAN REALTY
485 KING STREET WEST
HAMILTON, ONTARIO L9H 6W3
PHONE (905) 527-1223

619

July 31 20 16

PAY TO THE ORDER OF Pamela Dawson $ 350.00

~~~ Three hundred fifty ~~~ 00/100 DOLLARS

THE ROYAL BANK OF CANADA
MAIN BRANCH
204 KING STREET WEST
HAMILTON, ONTARIO L9H 4Z9

SULLIVAN REALTY

FOR Salary - July 16-31 PER John Sullivan

II"000619 I: 05337 123'498'6

31a.

Phones Ontario

#2110 Steel Place
Hamilton, Ontario L9G 4B4
Phone (905) 529-7190
Fax (905) 529-0063

Your Statement

In Account with SULLIVAN REALTY
485 KING STREET WEST
HAMILTON ON L9H 6W3

Account #09444 710-190

Payment received July 31, 2016 **Phones Ontario**

Billing Period: July 1 to July 31

Payments/Adjustments/Deposits Details	$510.00
Payment Received July 2. Thank you.	-510.00
Monthly rental and services	236.00
Total Due	$236.00

Amount now due
Payment due after August 9, 2016 $241.90

31b.

S

SULLIVAN REALTY
485 KING STREET WEST
HAMILTON, ONTARIO L9H 6W3
PHONE (905) 527-1223

620

July 31 20 16

PAY TO THE ORDER OF Phones Ontario $ 236.00

~~~ Two hundred thirty-six ~~~~~~~~~~ 00 /100 DOLLARS

THE ROYAL BANK OF CANADA
MAIN BRANCH
204 KING STREET WEST
HAMILTON, ONTARIO L9H 4Z9

SULLIVAN REALTY

FOR July phone bill

PER John Sullivan

⑈000620 ⑆: 05337 123'498'6

32.

City News

85 Main Street, Hamilton, Ontario L9H 0C0
Phone (905) 527-1030 Fax (905) 527-1031

INVOICE

SOLD TO: Sullivan Realty
485 King Street West
Hamilton ON L9H 6W3

Invoice No.: 5400
Date: July 30, 2016
Due Date: August 7, 2016

DATE	DESCRIPTION		AMOUNT
July 30/16	Advertising in City News during July 2016		$1,400.00
		SUBTOTAL	1,400.00
		TOTAL	$1,400.00

Business Number 944122338
MAKE ALL CHEQUES PAYABLE TO CITY NEWS.

Required Work for July

1. Journalize transactions in a general journal (pages 4 and 5) and post to ledger accounts.
2. Prepare a trial balance in the first two columns of the worksheet and complete the worksheet using the following adjustment data:
   a. One month's rent had expired.
   b. An inventory shows $90 worth of office supplies remaining.
   c. Depreciation on office equipment, $100
   d. Depreciation on automobile, $200
3. Prepare a July income statement, statement of owner's equity, and balance sheet.
4. From the worksheet, journalize and post adjusting and closing entries (page 6 of journal).
5. Prepare a post-closing trial balance.
~~~

CHAPTER 6

Special Journals

THE BASICS, PART 1

LEARNING OBJECTIVES

- **LO 1** Understanding the need for special journals as well as important factors that guide the design of a sales journal (p. 248)
- **LO 2** Entering transactions into the sales journal, recording to the accounts receivable sub-ledger, and posting to general ledger accounts (p. 253)
- **LO 3** Creating, recording, and posting a credit memorandum (p. 259)
- **LO 4** Recording transactions in the cash receipts journal (including payments from customers taking a cash discount), recording to the AR sub-ledger, posting to general ledger accounts, and preparing a schedule of accounts receivable (p. 265)

Having a single journal (the general journal) can work satisfactorily for a very small company, but is not very efficient. As soon as a business grows to the size where more than one bookkeeper is needed, the general journal does not work at all—except for certain specialized transactions, such as adjusting and closing entries at year end.

This chapter explains how a small business can more easily cope with recording transactions using Sales and Cash Received. Even if the business uses a computer and accounting software such as Sage 50®, students will greatly benefit from knowing how these two journals work and understanding their relationship with both the accounts receivable and the general ledger. The principles described in this chapter are not different when used in a computerized context.

Please be aware that we deliberately avoid the topic of taxes. Of course taxes on things bought and sold are an important reality in the business world, and Chapter 11 covers the necessary details quite thoroughly. For now, concentrate on learning the principles of how special journals work, and leave the topic of taxes for later.

LEARNING UNIT 6-1

Designing and Understanding Special Journals

LO 1

Understanding the need for special journals as well as important factors that guide the design of a sales journal

Thus far in our study of accounting, we have seen how a bookkeeper uses a general journal to record transactions for a business, and how the details recorded in that journal are transferred (or posted) to a general ledger. This was followed by studying how the information in the GL is used by an accountant to prepare financial statements. Finally, we have seen how the books of a business are closed each year to facilitate the recording of another year's worth of transactions. In other words, we know how the various steps in the accounting cycle are implemented. Nothing you will discover in this chapter and the next will change any of that, but to see a more realistic view of how the accounting cycle is actually implemented in a business setting, we must extend and expand some of the procedural details.

One fundamental truth that we must face is that the use of only a general journal is much too inefficient to be useful in any realistic, day-to-day setting. If a business were to use just this one journal, then all transactions that happen each day would need to be recorded there, and that in turn means that only a single bookkeeper could use the journal at any one time. Most businesses—even a small one—would have dozens or hundreds of individual transactions in a day, and a business like WestJet might have tens of thousands. Clearly, almost every business needs a much more efficient way to record transactions. Not only must the recording method be efficient, it must also allow for several individuals to work together in capturing the many transaction details that happen each day.

MAIN TYPES OF JOURNALS

Therefore, every reporting entity uses **special journals** to make the recording of business transactions efficient and "scalable," meaning the ability to accommodate any size of business, from the small to the gigantic. Most of the transactions entered into by a business fall into four types of journals:

- The Sales Journal. In this journal a business will record the credit transactions that take place with its customers.
- The Cash Receipts Journal. Here the business records all payments it receives—mostly perhaps from its customers, but occasionally from other sources as well.

  These two journals are covered in detail in this chapter.
- The Purchases Journal. This journal will include the details of all purchases made by a company from its suppliers, who are basically the companies that it buys goods and services from.
- The Cash Payments Journal. All cheques written by the company (or funds transferred electronically) are recorded here. Most payments might go to suppliers, but there are many other types of funds distributed as well, and these will also be included in this journal.

  Chapter 7 will describe the purchases and cash payments journals in detail.

OTHER JOURNALS

Inquiring students are probably wondering whether there any other journals that are used by a company. The answer is, Yes. Several other types of journals are often seen in a business environment. These might include a payroll journal as well as a number of others, but the four mentioned above are common to most businesses and hence form the foundation of our study of this important subject. As we go through the material in these two chapters, other special journals will be mentioned, but only limited details will be provided. For most students, mastery of the four most common journals will be sufficient for the majority of businesses. If a student does work for a business where more than the basic special journals are needed, it should be a minor matter to think through how they work. After all, the principles of special journals are the same for all.

When you study Chapters 9 and 10 dealing with payroll matters, the payroll journal will be illustrated. The majority of businesses have the need to pay their employees, and the payroll journal is a central feature in this part of the operations of most businesses.

FUNDAMENTALS OF CUSTOMER RELATIONS

Before we begin to look at the details of what a sales journal is and how it is used, it is useful to mention some of the realities of how a business relates to its customers. Only if we have an understanding of this important relationship can the bookkeeping details make total sense. Here are some of the factors that a business must keep in mind when designing and using a sales journal and a cash receipts journal:

1. Allowing a customer to purchase "on credit" (sometimes: "on account") can be a risky decision. The business hopes that each customer will pay on time and in the correct amount, but sometimes they pay quite slowly, and on occasion do not pay at all. Slow or non-payment of agreed-to invoices is a costly matter, and steps should be taken to minimize these events. Steps often taken by a business include:
   a. Investigating each possible customer's credit rating. Only a customer that can demonstrate a history of paying their debts in a reliable way should be considered for credit sales. This is a matter where a lot of good judgment is often necessary. Sometimes you encounter a new customer which has no rating at all, or a credit check may reveal that a given customer usually pays a bit slowly, but always pays in the end. Because there is also a cost to not making a sale (the lost margin on a sale that might take place if a customer's order is accepted), it then becomes a matter of judgment as to whether credit terms will be extended in a given case.
   b. One very common way that a seller can try and speed up collections from its customers is to offer a cash discount. Various incentives can be offered to each customer to reward them for paying promptly. One very common set of terms is to offer a discount (a **sales discount**) of 2% if an invoice is paid within 10 days (the **discount period**), otherwise the whole amount is due in 30 days (the **credit period**.) There are many such terms that can be used, and each company may select a different one that best suits their business model. Note that it is possible for each customer to be granted a different terms offer, but this is a little unusual, and throughout this chapter we will use the so-called "2% 10 days, net 30" just described.
   c. To make business dealings with customers go smoothly, but also to recognize that certain customers should pay a slightly different price, a seller will often use what is often called a **trade discount.** Each item sold is assigned a dollar value, sometimes referred to a "suggested list" or "retail price." When items are purchased in relatively low quantities by smaller customers, they are offered a trade discount of 30%. Larger customers who purchase more items at a time may be granted a more generous trade discount of 40%. Certain other categories of customers, such as governments or educational institutions, may have special discounts as well. The exact number and details will vary a lot between businesses, but the intent here is to accommodate the reality of the need for different sets of prices for selected customers, while at the same time having and maintaining only one master price list for all of the seller's products.

      As a practical matter, the use of trade discounts does not cause any bookkeeping or accounting issues at all, since sales are simply recorded at the actual selling price for any given customer. It is true that the per-unit prices are different for selected customers, but this is just a detail, and so we will not spend more time considering this particular matter.
   d. One very important business reality is that some person or persons must be placed in charge of collecting money owed by customers. It is important to take precautions before any credit sale takes place, but once the sale is recorded it becomes necessary to ensure that all monies owed are collected as promptly as possible. In this chapter we illustrate the preparation of a monthly list of amounts due from customers, and that list is one of the crucial reports that can be used to help ensure that amounts due are collected with as little delay as possible. Note that this is one of the main advantages that a computerized accounting system can have, since it is a trivial matter for a computer to produce lists of amounts owed at a moment's notice, and in differing levels of detail. We do not illustrate this

in the chapter, but all students should be aware of this important benefit of using a computer to record transactions.

e. To help out in the process of proper business management, a sales journal can be designed to capture many helpful details. The exact nature of the details tracked will differ between companies, but in the next Learning Unit we will show a couple of common ways that a sales journal can be customized to provide helpful information. The first modification will be to include extra columns for selected product groupings. This can help to track which products are selling well and which may need some incentives to sell better. The second of our illustrations will involve tracking sales by salesperson, which can lead to increased direct supervision over the people who deal with customers on a daily basis. This can have added advantages as well, such as allowing each salesperson to have a sales quota that they are expected to reach during a given period—or even allow for direct monetary rewards for performance, sometimes called a sales commission. We not only show how this might be designed into the sales journal, but will use this information to show how it relates to a payroll journal in Chapter 9.

LEARNING UNIT 6-1 REVIEW

AT THIS POINT you should be able to:

- State the names of at least five special journals. (p. 249)
- Discuss the factors that have a bearing on how a company sets up and monitors its credit sales. (pp. 250–251)
- Explain why cash discount terms are needed, and give an example of one. (p. 250)
- Explain what a trade discount is, how it is used, and its relation to bookkeeping. (p. 250)

Self-Review Quiz 6-1

(The forms you need are on page 6-1 of the *Study Guide with Working Papers.*)

Which of the following statements are true?

1. Recording sales transactions in a general journal is considered efficient.
2. Most businesses will use at least six types of journals (Note—tricky!)
3. Allowing customers to buy on credit can be risky.
4. Cash discounts are rarely used to speed up cash collections from customers.
5. Trade discounts cause challenges when recording customer invoices.

Solution to Self-Review Quiz 6-1

Numbers 2 and 3 are true. (Re.: number 2, remember that the general journal is also used.)

LEARNING UNIT 6-2

The Sales Journal and Accounts Receivable Subsidiary Ledger

Art's Clothing Company buys large quantities of various types of clothing at distributors' prices, and then sells the same items to its own customers at a higher price. Some would describe this company as a "distributor" while the company's customers might be known as "retailers" since they in turn sell to the general public. We will examine Art's Clothing Company to show how this business entity records its Sales, Sales Returns, and Cash Receipts transactions. As a reminder of how sales have been recorded up to this point, here are three journal entries that Art's would make in the absence of a sales journal:

ART'S CLOTHING COMPANY
GENERAL JOURNAL

April	2	Accounts Receivable, Hal's		80000	
		Sales			80000
		Sales on account			
	6	Accounts Receivable, Bevans		160000	
		Sales			160000
		Sales on account			
	19	Accounts Receivable, Roe		200000	
		Sales			200000
		Sales on account			

It is pretty obvious that these journal entries are not too efficient—especially if Art's records dozens or hundreds of such transactions in a month. Also bear in mind that Art's company will also have many other types of transactions (like Purchases and Payroll), and therefore it is true that as the company grows larger it would not be possible for a single bookkeeper to manage to record all of the transactions in the general journal—there would simply be too many!

SUBSIDIARY LEDGERS

In the same way that Art's Clothing Company needs more than just a general journal, the business needs more than just a general ledger. For example, so far in this text, the only title we have used for recording amounts owed to the seller has been Accounts Receivable. Art's could have replaced the Accounts Receivable title in the general ledger with the following list of customers that owe it money:

- Account Receivable, Bevans Company
- Account Receivable, Hal's Clothing
- Account Receivable, Mel's Department Store
- Account Receivable, Roe Company

As you can see, this would not be manageable if Art's had 1,000 or more credit customers. To solve this problem, Art's sets up a separate **accounts receivable subsidiary ledger**. Such a special ledger, often simply called a **subsidiary ledger**, contains a single type of account, such as "on account" or "credit" customers. A page is opened for each customer and the pages are usually arranged alphabetically by customer name.

Figure 6-1
Partial General Ledger and Accounts Receivable Subsidiary Ledger of Art's Clothing Company

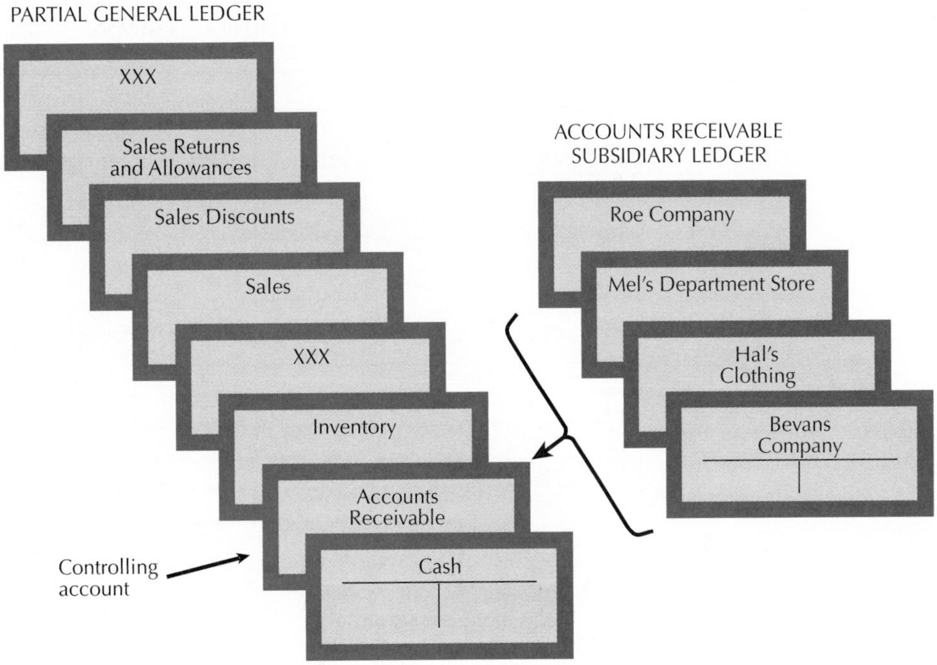

Proving: At the end of the month, the sum of the accounts receivable subsidiary ledger balances will equal the ending balance in Accounts Receivable, the controlling account in the general ledger.

The general ledger is _not_ in the same book as the accounts receivable subsidiary ledger.

Making sure that the total of all customer accounts agrees with the controlling account is often called reconciliation.

Figure 6-1 shows how the accounts receivable subsidiary ledger fits in with the general ledger. To clarify the difference in updating the general ledger versus the subsidiary ledger, we will *post* to the general ledger and *record* in the subsidiary ledger. The word "post" refers to information that is moved from the journal to the general ledger; the word "record" refers to information that is transferred from the journal into the individual customer's account in the subsidiary ledger.

The accounts receivable subsidiary ledger or any other subsidiary ledger can be in the form of a card file, a binder notebook, a formal, pre-printed ledger page or computer files on disks. It will not have page numbers, but each account may have a unique number to help identify it. The accounts receivable subsidiary ledger is organized alphabetically by customer name and address; new customers can be added and inactive customers deleted, once the balance in their account is zero.

When using an accounts receivable subsidiary ledger, Accounts Receivable in the general ledger is called the **controlling account** since it summarizes or controls the accounts receivable subsidiary ledger. At the end of the month, the total of the individual accounts in the accounts receivable ledger must equal the ending balance in Accounts Receivable in the general ledger.

Art's Clothing Company will use the following subsidiary ledgers:

Accounts receivable subsidiary ledger	Records money owed by credit customers
Accounts payable subsidiary ledger	Records money owed to creditors

Let's now look more closely at the sales journal, general ledger, and subsidiary ledger for Art's Wholesale Clothing Company to see how transactions are recorded in the special journal as well as posted and recorded to specific ledger accounts.

THE SALES JOURNAL

LO 2
Entering transactions into the sales journal, recording to the accounts receivable subledger, and posting to general ledger accounts

The **sales journal** for Art's Clothing Company records all sales made on account to customers. Figure 6-2 shows the sales journal at the end of the first month of operation, along with the recordings in the accounts receivable ledger and posting to the general ledger. Keep in mind that the reason the balances in the accounts receivable subsidiary ledger are *debit* balances is that the customers listed *owe* Art's Clothing Company money. For some companies, a sales journal would have multiple revenue account columns, and this is illustrated later in this chapter.

Figure 6-2
Sales Journal
Recording and Postings

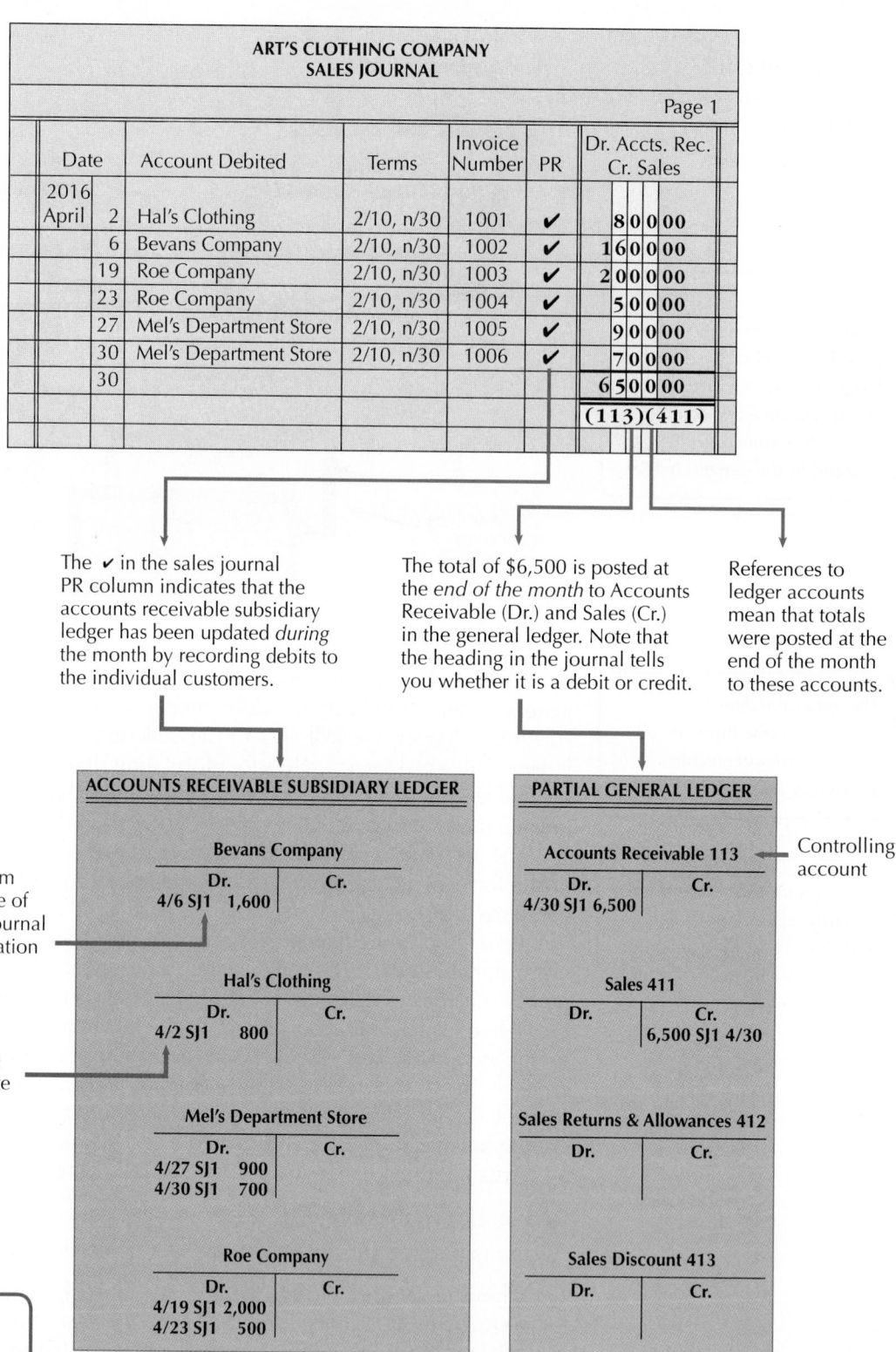

ART'S CLOTHING COMPANY
SALES JOURNAL

Page 1

Date		Account Debited	Terms	Invoice Number	PR	Dr. Accts. Rec. Cr. Sales
2016						
April	2	Hal's Clothing	2/10, n/30	1001	✔	800 00
	6	Bevans Company	2/10, n/30	1002	✔	1600 00
	19	Roe Company	2/10, n/30	1003	✔	2000 00
	23	Roe Company	2/10, n/30	1004	✔	500 00
	27	Mel's Department Store	2/10, n/30	1005	✔	900 00
	30	Mel's Department Store	2/10, n/30	1006	✔	700 00
	30					6500 00
						(113)(411)

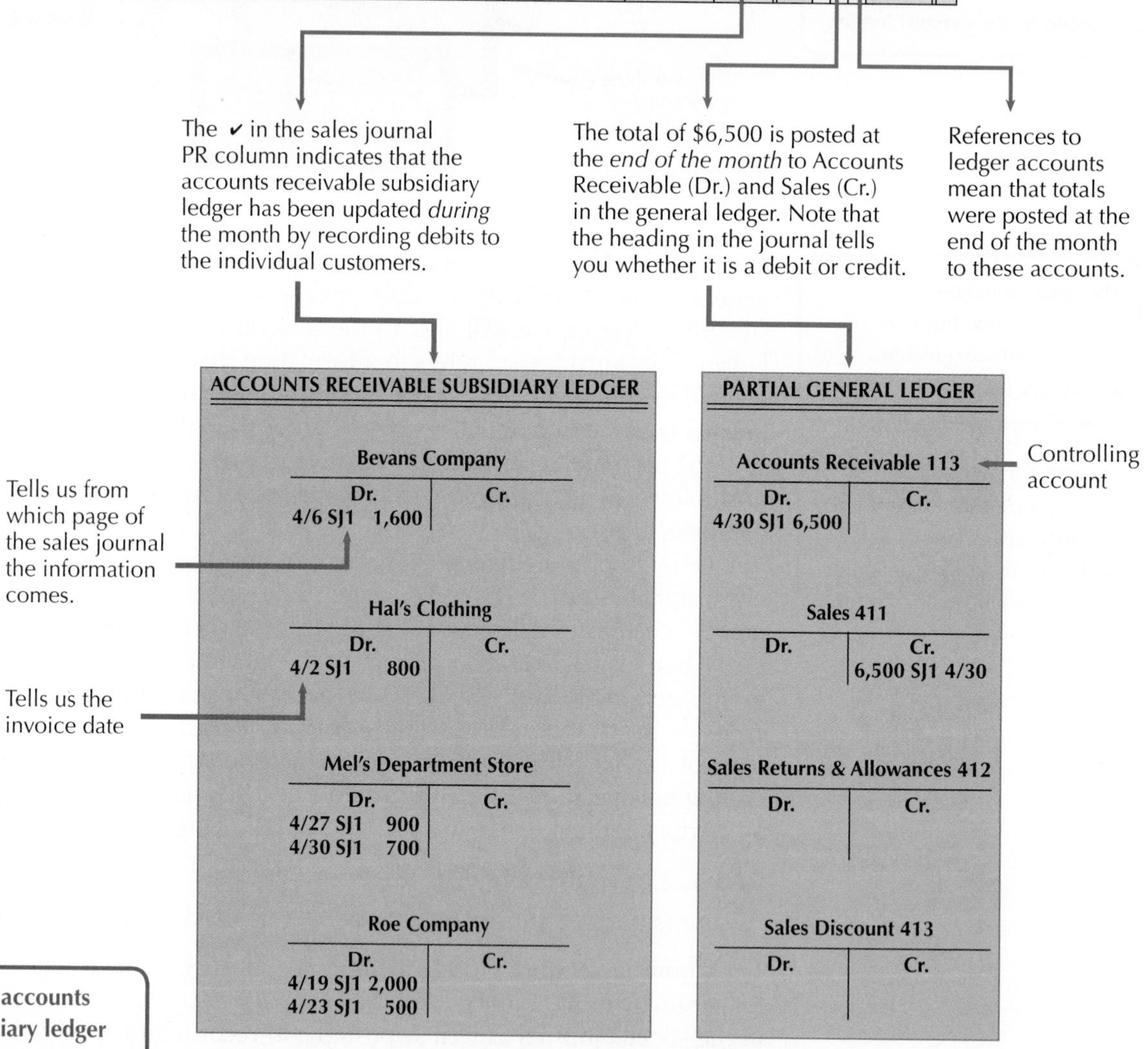

The ✔ in the sales journal PR column indicates that the accounts receivable subsidiary ledger has been updated *during* the month by recording debits to the individual customers.
The total of $6,500 is posted at the *end of the month* to Accounts Receivable (Dr.) and Sales (Cr.) in the general ledger. Note that the heading in the journal tells you whether it is a debit or credit.
References to ledger accounts mean that totals were posted at the end of the month to these accounts.
ACCOUNTS RECEIVABLE SUBSIDIARY LEDGER
Bevans Company
Dr.
Cr.
4/6 SJ1 1,600
Hal's Clothing
Dr.
Cr.
4/2 SJ1 800
Mel's Department Store
Dr.
Cr.
4/27 SJ1 900
4/30 SJ1 700
Roe Company
Dr.
Cr.
4/19 SJ1 2,000
4/23 SJ1 500
Tells us from which page of the sales journal the information comes.
Tells us the invoice date
PARTIAL GENERAL LEDGER
Accounts Receivable 113
Controlling account
Dr.
Cr.
4/30 SJ1 6,500
Sales 411
Dr.
Cr.
6,500 SJ1 4/30
Sales Returns & Allowances 412
Dr.
Cr.
Sales Discount 413
Dr.
Cr.

Recording in the accounts receivable subsidiary ledger occurs daily.

Hal's Clothing

Dr.	Cr.
4/2 SJ1 800	

✔ in the journal means accounts receivable subsidiary ledger has been updated.

Look at the first transaction listed in the sales journal. It shows that on April 2, Art's Clothing Company sold merchandise on account to Hal's Clothing for $800. The bill or **sales invoice** for this sale is shown in Figure 6-3.

Recording from the Sales Journal to the Accounts Receivable Subsidiary Ledger

As shown on the first line of the sales journal in Figure 6-2, the information on the invoice is recorded in the sales journal. However, *the PR column is left blank.* As soon as possible, we now update the accounts receivable subsidiary ledger. To do

Invoice number → Sales Invoice No. 1001

Art's Clothing Company
1528 Belle Avenue
Toronto, Ontario M5A 2L4

Name and address of customer → Sold to: Hal's Clothing
91 Century Avenue
Winnipeg, MB R2C 4X7

Date: April 2, 2016 ← Date of sale
Your purchase order No: 430
Ship via: Acme Truck Co.

Shipped to: Same
Credit terms → Terms: 2/10, n/30

Sold by: J.L.

Quantity	Description	Unit Price	Total
20	Men's dress shirts—code 16B	$20.00	$400.00
10	Ladies' designer jeans—code 18C	35.00	350.00
10	Baseball caps—code 22D	5.00	50.00
			$800.00

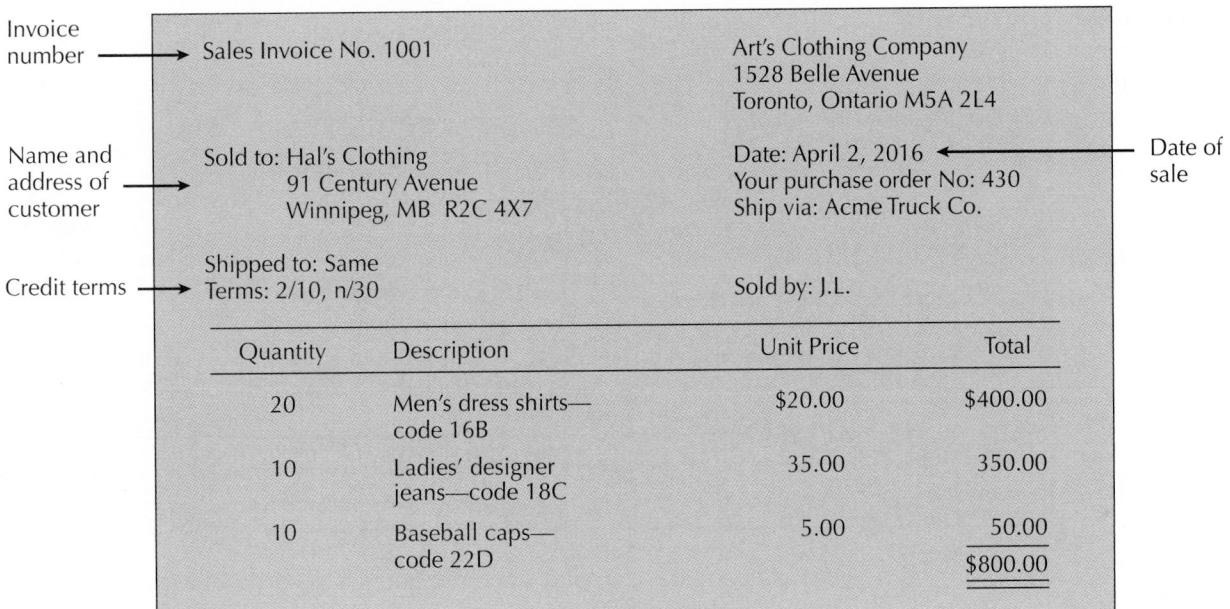

Figure 6-3 Sales Invoice

Recording to the general ledger occurs at end of month and uses the journal total:

Accounts Receivable 113

Dr.	Cr.
SJ1 4/30 6,500	

Sales 411

Dr.	Cr.
	6,500 4/30 SJ1

this, we pull out the Hal's Clothing file card and update it: The debit side must show the $800 owed to Art along with the date (April 2) and page of the sales journal (SJ1). Once that is done, place a ✔ in the posting reference column of the sales journal. The accounts receivable subsidiary ledger shows us Hal's outstanding balance at any moment in time. We do not have to go through all the invoices. Note that the sales journal needs only one line instead of the three lines that would have been required in a general journal.

Posting at the End of the Month from the Sales Journal to the General Ledger

The sales journal is totalled ($6,500) at the end of the month. Looking above, you can see that one heading of Art's sales journal is a debit to accounts receivable and a credit to sales. Therefore, at the end of the month, the $6,500 total is posted to Accounts Receivable (debit) *and* to Sales (credit) in the general ledger. In the general ledger, we record the date (4/30), the initials of the journal (SJ), the page of the sales journal (1), and the appropriate debit or credit ($6,500). Once the account in the general ledger is updated, we place below the totals in the sales journal the account numbers to which the information was posted (as in Figure 6-2, where these accounts are 113 and 411).

MULTICOLUMN SALES JOURNAL

Take a close look at the invoice shown above. Art's Clothing Company has decided that it is helpful to keep track of sales in three different categories:

- Men's clothing
- Ladies' clothing
- All other clothing

It is easy to see from invoice 1001 that $400 of the total was for sales of Men's clothing; $350 was for Ladies' clothing, and the balance, $50, was for Other. To keep track of the three categories of sales, Art's designed a Sales Journal with more columns. It looks like Figure 6-4.

Please note that all of the recordings to the customers' accounts are exactly the same as before when the single-column form of sales journal was used, and the

Figure 6-4
Multicolumn Sales Journal

ART'S CLOTHING COMPANY
SALES JOURNAL

Page 1

Date		Customer's Account	Invoice Number	PR	Invoice Total - Dr.	Men's Clothing Sales - Cr.	Ladies' Clothing Sales - Cr.	Other Sales - Cr.
2016 April	2	Hal's Clothing	1001	✔	800 00	400 00	350 00	50 00
	6	Bevans Company	1002	✔	1600 00	600 00	800 00	200 00
	19	Roe Company	1003	✔	2000 00	1100 00	750 00	150 00
	23	Roe Company	1004	✔	500 00	200 00	200 00	100 00
	27	Mel's Department Store	1005	✔	900 00	460 00	380 00	60 00
	29	Mel's Department Store	1006	✔	700 00	310 00	350 00	40 00
	30	Monthly Totals		✔	6500 00	3070 00	2830 00	600 00
					(113)	(411)	(412)	(413)

same check mark is added once the entry is recorded in the customer's account. The main change is there are now three postings to the Sales accounts in the general ledger (to the 411, 412, & 413 accounts) instead of a single posting (to account 411) as shown earlier. Notice that the journal correctly **cross-adds**, which means that the debit to account 113 is exactly offset by the three credit entries to the Sales accounts 411, 412, and 412. Cross-adding is also referred to as cross-footing or cross-balancing. The bookkeeper must ensure that the journal is correct at the end of each month; in other words, that $3,070 + $2,830 + $600 = $6,500.

If that mathematical accuracy is not checked routinely, then the general ledger is sure to become out of balance, and a lot of work will need to be done to correct the error(s).

MULTICOLUMN SALES JOURNAL WITH SALES BY SALESPERSON

Another worthwhile addition that Art's Clothing Company might choose to include in the sales journal is the detail of which salesperson is associated with which sale. Notice that Figure 6-3 shows that invoice 1001 to Hal's Clothing was sold by a person with the initials "J. L." Let's assume that these initials stand for Jean Lamont, one of three sales representatives that take care of sales to specific customers of Art's Clothing Company. The other two sales reps are Pat Kingston (P. K.) and Melody Chui (M. C.). Since Art's company wants to keep a record of which sales invoices are associated with a specific sales rep, then a simple way to accomplish that might be to add one extra column that can include the sales person's initials, as shown in Figure 6-5

Realize that in most cases a sales journal will contain many more entries than are shown here. We have kept the size small so as to emphasize the principles involved.

Please note that the total sales by salesperson are *not posted* to the general ledger. This is just a notation in the journal that might be useful to management in keeping track of how productive each salesperson has been in a given month. As we will see in Chapter 9, this information can also be used to calculate sales commissions, if that is in part how employees are paid.

Also worth noting is how handy it would be to have all of the sales for a given month included in an Excel spreadsheet. This would allow sales to be analyzed in a number of different ways quite quickly. It is actually rather common to find a company's sales listed in a spreadsheet on a monthly basis, and where this is done, the printed spreadsheet can be used as the sales journal. If a company uses a computer with typical accounting software, then the use of a spreadsheet is generally avoided, because most accounting software is capable of generating any analysis that is needed.

ART'S CLOTHING COMPANY SALES JOURNAL									
									Page 1
Date		Customer's Account	Sold By	Invoice Number	PR	Invoice Total - Dr.	Men's Clothing Sales - Cr.	Ladies' Clothing Sales - Cr.	Other Sales - Cr.
2016 April	2	Hal's Clothing	JL	1001	✔	800 00	400 00	350 00	50 00
	6	Bevans Company	MC	1002	✔	1600 00	600 00	800 00	200 00
	19	Roe Company	PK	1003	✔	2000 00	1100 00	750 00	150 00
	23	Roe Company	PK	1004	✔	500 00	200 00	200 00	100 00
	27	Mel's Department Store	JL	1005	✔	900 00	460 00	380 00	60 00
	29	Mel's Department Store	JL	1006	✔	700 00	310 00	350 00	40 00
	30	Monthly Totals			✔	6500 00	3070 00	2830 00	600 00
						(113)	(411)	(412)	(413)
Sales by Salesperson:									
			JL			2400 00			
			MC			1600 00			
			PK			2500 00			
		Total Sales				6500 00			

Figure 6-5 Multicolumn Sales Journal with Sales by Salesperson

LEARNING UNIT 6-2 REVIEW

AT THIS POINT you should be able to:

- Define and state the purposes of the accounts receivable subsidiary ledger. (pp. 252–253)
- Define and state the purpose of the controlling account, Accounts Receivable. (p. 253)
- Journalize, record, and post sales on account to a sales journal and its related accounts receivable and general ledgers. (pp. 254–255)
- Define and use a multicolumn Sales Journal to keep track of sales made in different categories. (pp. 255–256)
- Show how additional details can be added to a Sales Journal, and determine whether this memorandum-only information is posted to General Ledger accounts. (pp. 256–257)

Self-Review Quiz 6-2

(The forms you need are on page 6-1 of the *Study Guide with Working Papers.*)

Which of the following statements are false?

1. A Sales Journal can be customized for each company.
2. Special journals aid the division of labour.
3. The subsidiary ledger makes the general ledger less manageable.
4. The subsidiary ledger is separate from the general ledger.

!

Quiz Tip

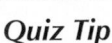

The normal balance of each account in the accounts receivable subsidiary ledger is a debit.

5. The controlling account is located in the accounts receivable subsidiary ledger.
6. The total(s) of a sales journal is (are) posted to the general ledger at the end of the month.
7. The accounts receivable subsidiary ledger is arranged in alphabetical order.
8. Transactions recorded into a sales journal are recorded weekly to the accounts receivable subsidiary ledger.

Solution to Self-Review Quiz 6-2

Numbers 3, 5, and 8 are false.

LEARNING UNIT 6-3

The Credit Memorandum

Merchandising businesses often use the **Sales Returns and Allowances** account to handle transactions involving returns or price adjustments of goods that have already been sold to customers on account. For example, if a customer returns the goods he has bought, that account will be credited for the amount charged for the goods returned; if a customer gets an allowance because the goods she purchased were damaged, that account will be credited for the amount of the allowance. In both of these examples, the company's net sales revenue decreases. That is why the account is called a contra-revenue account: Sales revenue decreases and its normal balance is a debit.

A credit memorandum *reduces* accounts receivable.

Companies usually handle sales returns and allowances by means of a **credit memorandum**. Credit memoranda inform customers that the amount of the goods returned or the amount allowed for damaged goods has been subtracted from (credited to) the customer's ongoing account with the company.

A sample credit memorandum from Art's Clothing Company appears in Figure 6-6. It shows that on April 12, credit memo No. 1 was issued to Bevans Company for defective merchandise that had been returned. (Figure 6-2 on page 254 shows that Art's Clothing Company sold Bevans Company $1,600 worth of merchandise on April 6.)

Sales Returns and Allowances	
Dr.	Cr.
+	−

A contra-revenue account

Let's assume that Art's has high-quality goods and does not expect many sales returns and allowances. On this assumption, no special journal for sales returns and allowances will be needed. Instead, any returns and allowances will be recorded in the general journal, and all postings and recordings will be done when journalized. Let's look at a transaction analysis chart before we journalize, record, and post this transaction.

Figure 6-6
Credit Memorandum

Art's Clothing Company
1528 Belle Avenue
Toronto, ON M5A 2L4

Credit Memorandum No. 1

Date: April 12, 2016

Credit to: Bevans Company
110 Aster Road
Amherst, NS B4H 3A5

We credit your account as follows:
Merchandise returned 60 model 8B men's dress gloves—$600

End result is that Bevans owes Art's Clothing Company less money.

Note that the Sales Returns and Allowances account is increasing, which in turn reduces sales revenue and reduces the amount owed by the customer (accounts receivable).

Accounts Affected	Category	↑ ↓	Rules
Sales Returns and Allowances	Revenue (Contra)	↑	Dr.
Accounts Receivable, Bevans Co.	Asset	↓	Cr.

LO 3

Creating, recording, and posting a credit memorandum

Remember, sales discounts are *not* taken on returns.

JOURNALIZING, RECORDING, AND POSTING THE CREDIT MEMORANDUM

The credit memorandum results in two postings to the general ledger and one recording in the accounts receivable subsidiary ledger (see Figure 6-7).

Note in the PR column next to Accounts Receivable, Bevans Co., that there is a diagonal line with the account number 113 above and a ✔ below. This is to show that the amount of $600 has been credited to Accounts Receivable, the controlling account in the general ledger, *and* credited to the account of Bevans Company in the accounts receivable subsidiary ledger.

Figure 6-7
Posting and Recording for the Credit Memorandum in the Subsidiary General Ledgers

Page 1

Date		Account Titles and Description	PR	Dr.	Cr.
2016 April	12	Sales Returns and Allowances	412	600 00	
		Accounts Receivable, Bevans Co.	113/✔		600 00
		Issued Credit Memo			

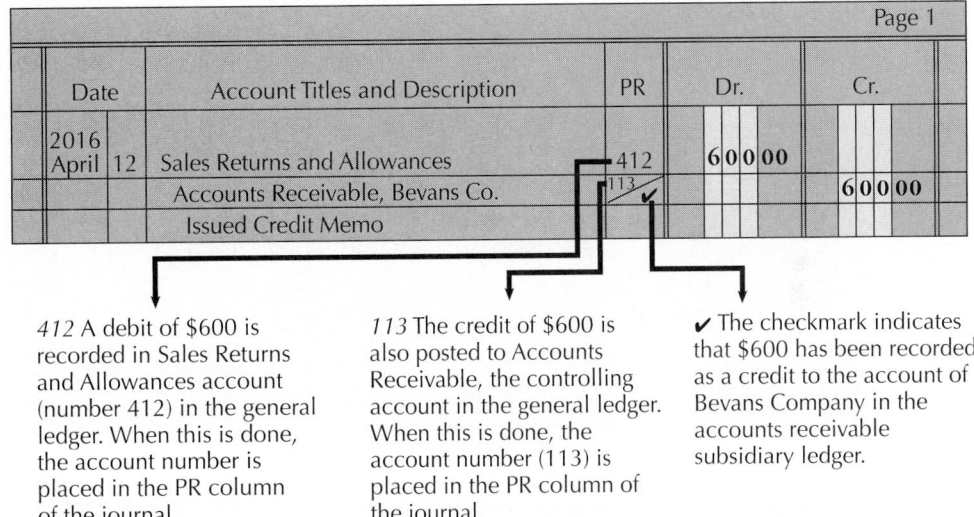

412 A debit of $600 is recorded in Sales Returns and Allowances account (number 412) in the general ledger. When this is done, the account number is placed in the PR column of the journal.

113 The credit of $600 is also posted to Accounts Receivable, the controlling account in the general ledger. When this is done, the account number (113) is placed in the PR column of the journal.

✔ The checkmark indicates that $600 has been recorded as a credit to the account of Bevans Company in the accounts receivable subsidiary ledger.

If the accountant for Art's Clothing Company decided to develop a special journal for sales returns and allowances, the entry for a credit memorandum such as the one we've been discussing would look like this:

SALES RETURNS AND ALLOWANCES JOURNAL

Date		Credit Memo No.	Account Credited	PR	Sales Returns and Allowances—Dr. Accounts Receivable—Cr.
2016 April	12	1	Bevans Company	✔	600 00

During the month, the subsidiary ledger is updated, and the total would be posted at the end of the month to the general ledger.

Accountants do not completely agree about the accounting method shown next, but if proper controls are in place, it can be a very efficient way to enter credit memoranda. Please bear in mind that a credit memo reduces a customer's account balance, so any such document must be properly approved (likely by the sales manager or credit manager) before it is entered into the company's records. If there is a concern with the method shown below, it is that it might be very easy to insert non-approved credit memos into the sales journal and thereby escape close scrutiny. However, if a responsible official looks over the details in the sales journal each period, there is little cause for concern.

The actual method is very simple: Just insert the credit memo on an appropriate row in the Sales Journal as a negative amount—usually shown by being in brackets. Mostly, the credit memos are included in date order, just like the invoices. Shown below is the sales journal you have already looked at, but now including details of CM No. 1:

ART'S CLOTHING COMPANY
SALES JOURNAL

Page 1

Date		Customer's Account	Invoice Number	PR	Invoice Total - Dr.	Men's Clothing Sales - Cr.	Ladies' Clothing Sales - Cr.	Other Sales - Cr.
2016								
April	2	Hal's Clothing	1001	✔	800 00	400 00	350 00	50 00
	6	Bevans Company	1002	✔	1600 00	600 00	800 00	200 00
	12	Bevans Company	CM1	✔	(600 00)	(600 00)		
	19	Roe Company	1003	✔	2000 00	1100 00	750 00	150 00
	23	Roe Company	1004	✔	500 00	200 00	200 00	100 00
	27	Mel's Department Store	1005	✔	900 00	460 00	380 00	60 00
	29	Mel's Department Store	1006	✔	700 00	310 00	350 00	40 00
	30	Monthly Totals—Note—These totals have changed due to the inclusion of CM-1.		✔	5900 00	2470 00	2830 00	600 00
					(113)	(411)	(412)	(413)

Notice that the journal still correctly cross-adds, which means that the debit to account 113 is exactly offset by the three credit entries to the Sales accounts 411, 412, and 412, although two of the amounts are now lower because of the inclusion of the credit memo. The bookkeeper must always ensure that the journal cross-adds at the end of each month—in other words, that $2,470 + $2,830 + $600 = $5,900.

LEARNING UNIT 6-3 REVIEW

AT THIS POINT you should be able to:

- Explain, journalize, post, and record a credit memorandum. (pp. 258–260)

Self-Review Quiz 6-3

(The forms you need are on pages 6-1 to 6-3 of the *Study Guide with Working Papers.*)

Journalize the following transactions in the sales journal or general journal for Moss Company. Record in the accounts receivable subsidiary ledger and post to general ledger accounts as appropriate. Use the same journal headings that we used for Art's Clothing Company. (All sales carry credit terms of 2/10, n/30.)

2015		
May	1	Sold merchandise on account to Jane Company, invoice No. 1, $600.
	4	Sold merchandise on account to Ralph Company, invoice No. 2, $2,500.
	18	Issued credit memo No. 1 to Jane Company for $200 for defective merchandise returned.

Quiz Tip

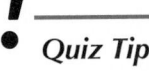

Total of accounts receivable subsidiary ledger, $400 + $2,500, does indeed equal the balance ($2,900) in the controlling account, Accounts Receivable, at the end of the month in the general ledger.

Solution to Self-Review Quiz 6-3

MOSS COMPANY
SALES JOURNAL

Page 1

Date		Account Debited	Terms	Invoice No.	PR	Dr. Accts. Rec. Cr. Sales
2015 May	1	Jane Company	2/10, n/30	1	✔	600 00
	4	Ralph Company	2/10, n/30	2	✔	2 500 00
	31					3 100 00
						(112) (411)

MOSS COMPANY
GENERAL JOURNAL

Page 1

Date		Account Titles and Description	PR	Dr.	Cr.
2015 May	18	Sales Returns and Allowances	412	200 00	
		Accounts Receivable, Jane Company	112/✔		200 00
		Issued credit memo #1			

PARTIAL GENERAL LEDGER

Accounts Receivable — Acct. No. 112

Date		Explanation	PR	Debit	Credit	Dr. or Cr.	Balance
2015							
May	18		GJ1		200 00	Cr.	200 00
	31		SJ1	3 100 00		Dr.	2 900 00

Controlling Account. Note the unusual balance of $200 (Cr.) because of the return. Why? Because the total of the sales journal is not posted until the end of the month.

Sales — Acct. No. 411

Date		Explanation	PR	Debit	Credit	Dr. or Cr.	Balance
2015							
May	31		SJ1		3 100 00	Cr.	3 100 00

Sales Returns and Allowances — Acct. No. 412

Date		Explanation	PR	Debit	Credit	Dr. or Cr.	Balance
2015							
May	18		GJ1	200 00		Dr.	200 00

ACCOUNTS RECEIVABLE LEDGER

NAME Jane Company
ADDRESS 1218 Broadview Avenue, Toronto, ON M5X 2A1

Date		Explanation	PR	Debit	Credit	Dr. Balance
2015						
May	1		SJ1	600 00		600 00
	18		GJ1		200 00	400 00

Customers owe Moss money and thus each account has a debit balance.

NAME Ralph Company
ADDRESS 1300 Marine Drive, West Vancouver, BC V6P 9B6

Date		Explanation	PR	Debit	Credit	Dr. Balance
2015						
May	4		SJ1	2 500 00		2 500 00

LEARNING UNIT 6-4

Cash Receipts Journal and Schedule of Accounts Receivable

Besides the sales journal, another special journal often used in a merchandising operation is the cash receipts journal. The **cash receipts journal** records the receipt of cash (or cheques) from any source. The number of columns a cash receipts journal will have depends on how frequently certain types of transactions occur. For example, in the cash receipts journal for Art's Clothing Company, the accountant has developed the headings shown in Figure 6-8. Below each heading is a description of the purpose of that column and when to update the accounts receivable ledger as well as the general ledger.

The following transactions occurred in April for Art's and affected the cash receipts journal:

2016

April	1	Art Newner invested $8,000 in the business.
	5	Received cheque from Hal's Clothing for payment of invoice No. 1001 less discount.
	15	Cash sales for first half of April, $900.
	16	Received cheque from Bevans Company in settlement of invoice No. 1002 less returns and discount.
	22	Received cheque from Roe Company for payment of invoice No. 1003 less discount.
	26	Sold store equipment, $500.
	30	Cash sales for second half of April, $1,200.

Figure 6-8 Cash Receipts Journal

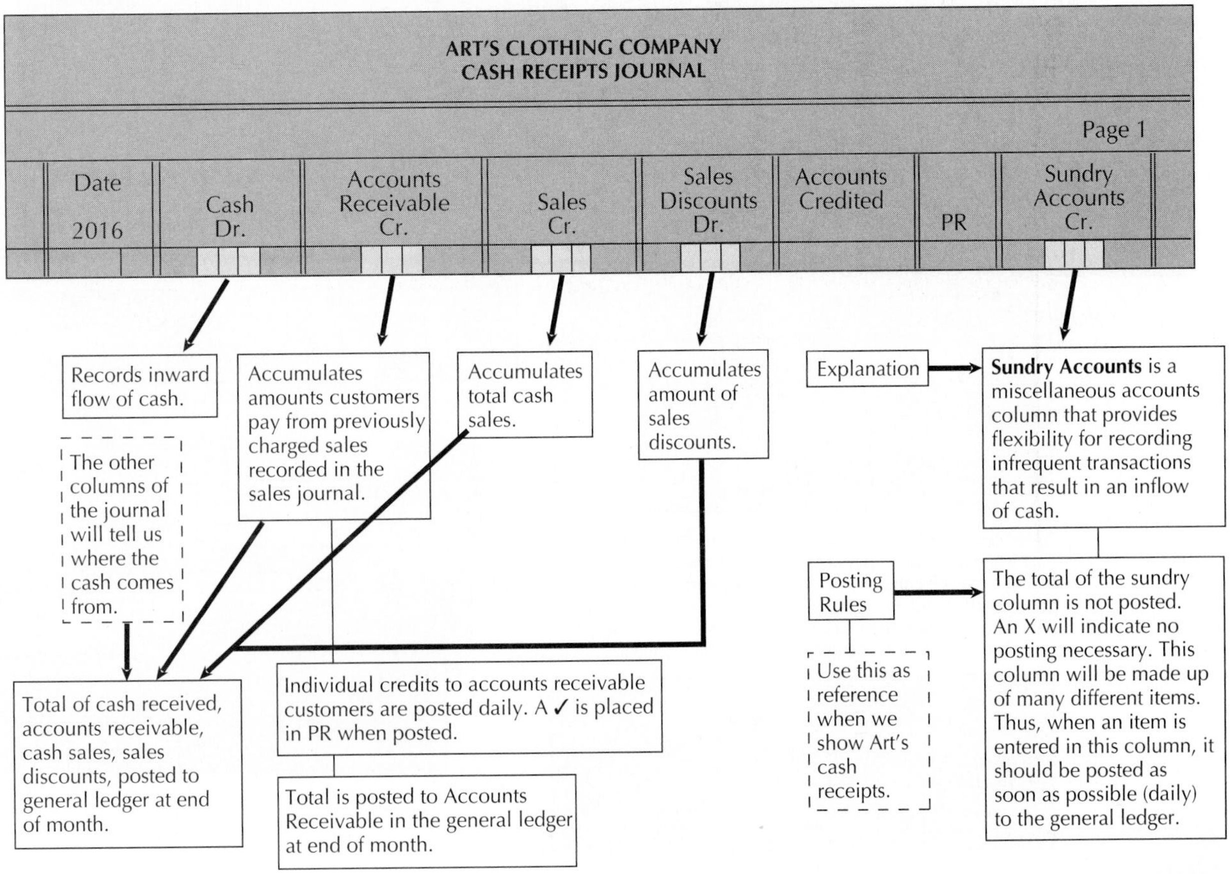

ART'S CLOTHING COMPANY
CASH RECEIPTS JOURNAL
Page 1
Date 2016
Cash Dr.
Accounts Receivable Cr.
Sales Cr.
Sales Discounts Dr.
Accounts Credited
PR
Sundry Accounts Cr.
Records inward flow of cash.
Accumulates amounts customers pay from previously charged sales recorded in the sales journal.
Accumulates total cash sales.
Accumulates amount of sales discounts.
Explanation
Sundry Accounts is a miscellaneous accounts column that provides flexibility for recording infrequent transactions that result in an inflow of cash.
The other columns of the journal will tell us where the cash comes from.
Posting Rules
The total of the sundry column is not posted. An X will indicate no posting necessary. This column will be made up of many different items. Thus, when an item is entered in this column, it should be posted as soon as possible (daily) to the general ledger.
Use this as reference when we show Art's cash receipts.
Total of cash received, accounts receivable, cash sales, sales discounts, posted to general ledger at end of month.
Individual credits to accounts receivable customers are posted daily. A ✓ is placed in PR when posted.
Total is posted to Accounts Receivable in the general ledger at end of month.

Figure 6-9 shows the completed cash receipts journal for the end of April, along with the recordings to the accounts receivable ledger and posting to the general ledger. Study the diagram; we will review it in a moment.

Figure 6-9 Cash Receipts Journal and Posting

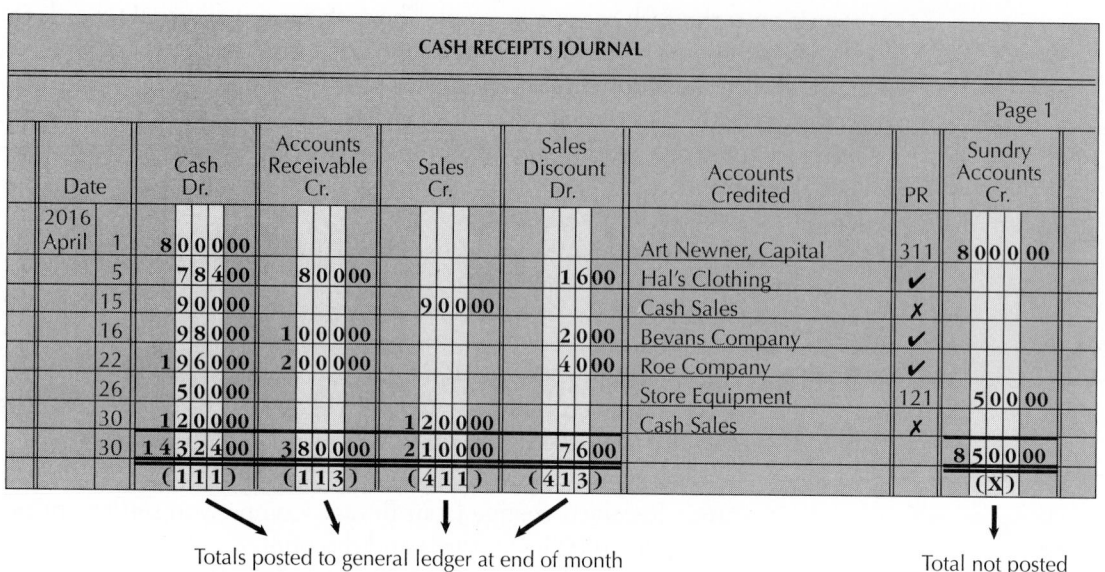

CASH RECEIPTS JOURNAL

Page 1

Date		Cash Dr.	Accounts Receivable Cr.	Sales Cr.	Sales Discount Dr.	Accounts Credited	PR	Sundry Accounts Cr.
2016 April	1	8 000 00				Art Newner, Capital	311	8 000 00
	5	784 00	800 00		16 00	Hal's Clothing	✓	
	15	900 00		900 00		Cash Sales	✗	
	16	980 00	1 000 00		20 00	Bevans Company	✓	
	22	1 960 00	2 000 00		40 00	Roe Company	✓	
	26	500 00				Store Equipment	121	500 00
	30	1 200 00		1 200 00		Cash Sales	✗	
	30	14 324 00	3 800 00	2 100 00	76 00			8 500 00
		(111)	(113)	(411)	(413)			(X)

Totals posted to general ledger at end of month

Total not posted

ACCOUNTS RECEIVABLE LEDGER

NAME Bevans Company
ADDRESS 110 Aster Road, Amherst, NS B4H 3A5

Date		Explanation	PR	Debit	Credit	Dr. Balance
2016 April	6		SJ1	1 600 00		1 600 00
	12		GJ1		600 00	1 000 00
	16		CRJ1		1 000 00	-0-

NAME Hal's Clothing
ADDRESS 91 Century Avenue, Winnipeg, MN R2C 4X7

Date		Explanation	PR	Debit	Credit	Dr. Balance
2016 April	2		SJ1	800 00		800 00
	5		CRJ1		800 00	-0-

NAME Mel's Department Store
ADDRESS 181 Foss Road, Fredericton, NB E3A 2N8

Date		Explanation	PR	Debit	Credit	Dr. Balance
2016 April	26		SJ1	900 00		900 00
			SJ1	700 00		1 600 00

NAME Roe Company
ADDRESS 18 Rantool Street, Regina, SK S4P 3J7

Date		Explanation	PR	Debit	Credit	Dr. Balance
2016 April	19		SJ1	2 000 00		2 000 00
	22		CRJ1		2 000 00	-0-
	23		SJ1	500 00		500 00

Note on accounts receivable: Very occasionally (because of an error, e.g., when a customer pays twice for the same invoice), a credit balance may be called for. Credit balances are opposite to the normal debit balance and are signified by placing the balance in brackets. For example, suppose that Hal's Clothing (see above) mistakenly paid its invoice twice. The account would then appear as follows:

NAME Hal's Clothing
ADDRESS 91 Century Avenue, Winnipeg, MN R2C 4X7

Date		Explanation	PR	Debit	Credit	Dr. Balance
2016 April	2		SJ1	800 00		800 00
	5		CRJ1		800 00	-0-
	10		CRJ1		800 00	(800 00)

PARTIAL GENERAL LEDGER

Cash — Acct. No. 111

Date		Explanation	PR	Debit	Credit	Dr. or Cr.	Balance
2016 April	30		CRJ1	14 324 00		Dr.	14 324 00

Accounts Receivable — Acct. No. 113

Date		Explanation	PR	Debit	Credit	Dr. or Cr.	Balance
2016 April	12		GJ1		600 00	Cr.	600 00
	30		SJ1	6 500 00		Dr.	5 900 00
	30		CRJ1		3 800 00	Dr.	2 100 00

Store Equipment — Acct. No. 121

Date		Explanation	PR	Debit	Credit	Dr. or Cr.	Balance
2016 April	1	Balance				Dr.	4 000 00
	26		CRJ1		500 00	Dr.	3 500 00

Art Newner, Capital — Acct. No. 311

Date		Explanation	PR	Debit	Credit	Dr. or Cr.	Balance
2016 April	1		CRJ1		8 000 00	Cr.	8 000 00

Sales — Acct. No. 411

Date		Explanation	PR	Debit	Credit	Dr. or Cr.	Balance
2016 April	30		SJ1		6 500 00	Cr.	6 500 00
	30		CRJ1		2 100 00	Cr.	8 600 00

Sales Returns and Allowances — Acct. No. 412

Date		Explanation	PR	Debit	Credit	Dr. or Cr.	Balance
2016 April	12		GJ1	600 00		Dr.	600 00

Sales Discounts — Acct. No. 413

Date		Explanation	PR	Debit	Credit	Dr. or Cr.	Balance
2016 April	30		CRJ1	76 00		Dr.	76 00

LO 4

Recording transactions in the cash receipts journal (including payments from customers taking a cash discount), recording to the AR sub-ledger, posting to general ledger accounts, and preparing a schedule of accounts receivable

JOURNALIZING, RECORDING, AND POSTING FROM THE CASH RECEIPTS JOURNAL

On April 5, Art's Clothing Company received a cheque from Hal's Clothing for payment of invoice No. 1 less discount. Remember, it was in the sales journal that this transaction was first recorded (Figure 6-2). At that time, we updated the accounts receivable ledger, indicating that Hal's Clothing owed Art's $800. Since Hal's Clothing is paying within the 10-day discount period, Art's Clothing Company offers a $16 sales discount ($800 × 0.02). (Remember, all credit sales carried terms of 2/10, n/30.)

Now, when payment is received, Art's Clothing Company updates the cash receipts journal (see page 264) by entering the date (April 5), cash debit of $784, sales discounts debit of $16, credit to accounts receivable of $800, and which account name (Hal's Clothing) is to be credited. The terms of sale indicate that Hal's Clothing is entitled to the discount and no longer owes Art's Clothing Company the $800 balance. *As soon as this line is entered into the cash receipts journal, Art's will update the ledger account of Hal's Clothing.* Note, in the accounts receivable ledger of Hal's Clothing, how the date (April 5), posting reference (CRJ1), and credit amount ($800) are recorded. The balance in the accounts receivable ledger is zero. The last step of this transaction is to go back to the cash receipts journal and put a ✔ in the posting reference column.

In studying this cash receipts journal, note that:

The last step is to put a check mark in the PR column of the cash receipts journal to show the accounts receivable ledger is up to date.

1. All totals of cash receipts in the journal columns except sundry were posted to the general ledger at the end of the month.
2. Art Newner, Capital, and Store Equipment were posted to the general ledger when entered in the sundry column. It is assumed that the equipment account had a beginning balance of $4,000 in the general ledger.
3. The cash sales were not posted when entered (hence the X to show no posting is needed). The sales and cash totals are posted at the end of the month.
4. A ✔ means information was recorded daily to the customer's account in the accounts receivable ledger.
5. The Accounts Credited column describes each transaction.

We can prove the accuracy of recording transactions of the cash receipts journal by totalling the columns with debit balances and the columns with credit balances. This cross-adding (or cross-footing or cross-balancing), is done before the totals are posted. Also, if a bookkeeper were using more than one page for the cash receipts journal, the balances on the bottom of one page would be brought forward to the top of the next page. This verifying of totals would result in less work when trying to find journalizing or posting errors at a later date. Let's see how to cross-foot the cash receipts journal of Art's Clothing Company (Figure 6-7).

Proving the cash receipts journal.

Debit Columns	**= Credit Columns**		
Cash + Sales Discounts	**= Accounts Receivable**	**+ Sales**	**+ Sundry**
$14,324 + $76	**= $3,800**	**+ $2,100**	**+ $8,500**
$14,400	**= $14,400**		

SCHEDULE OF ACCOUNTS RECEIVABLE

From Figure 6-9, let's list the customers that have an ending balance in the accounts receivable ledger of Art's Clothing Company. This listing is called a **schedule of accounts receivable**. The balance of the controlling account, Accounts Receivable ($2,100), in the general ledger (see p. 264) does indeed equal the sum of the individual customer balances in the accounts receivable ledger ($2,100), as shown below in the schedule of accounts receivable. The schedule of accounts receivable can help forecast potential cash inflows as well as better inform possible credit and collection decisions.

Schedule is listed in alphabetical order.

Art's Clothing Company Schedule of Accounts Receivable April 30, 2016	
Mel's Department Store	$1,600.00
Roe Company	500.00
Total Accounts Receivable	$2,100.00

One excellent idea that can assist with collections (by allowing a collections officer to focus on amounts that have been outstanding the longest) is a schedule of accounts receivable that is aged (called an **aged schedule of accounts receivable**).

The example shown below illustrates the simple principle involved (Figure 6-10). Needless to say, this schedule can be prepared manually, but is an automatic feature of all computer software. It can also be helpful to view the percentages for each category.

Figure 6-10. Schedule of Accounts Receivable

An Example Company
Schedule of Accounts Receivable
As of July 31, 2017

Customer	Outstanding Balance	0–30 Days	31–60 Days	61–90 Days	91 Days or More
Arrow Supply	1,400	900	500		
Carson Engineering	2,850	680	1,245	825	100
Gerrard Office Management	500				500
Harrowsmith Printing	4,360	2,300	2,060		
Markham Furnishers	3,875	640	2,100	1,135	
Jacobin and Company	1,340	140	700	500	
Marcell Outfitters	6,435	670	1,875	2,475	1,415
Turnbull Safety	2,750	2,750			
Williamson Consulting	4,375	2,450	1,585	240	100
Totals	27,885	10,530	10,065	5,175	2,115
Percentages		38%	36%	19%	8%

LEARNING UNIT 6-4 REVIEW

AT THIS POINT you should be able to:

- Journalize, record, and post, transactions using a cash receipts journal. (p. 265)
- Prepare a schedule of accounts receivable. (pp. 265–266)

Self-Review Quiz 6-4

(The forms you need are on pages 6-4 to 6-6 of the *Study Guide with Working Papers.*)

Journalize, cross-add, record, and post when appropriate, the following transactions into the cash receipts journal of Moore Co. Use the same headings as for Art's Clothing Company.

Accounts Receivable Ledger

Name	*Balance*	*Invoice No.*
Irene Welch	$500	1
Chantel Simard	200	2

Partial General Ledger

Account	*Account No.*	*Balance*
Cash	110	$600
Accounts Receivable	120	700
Store Equipment	130	600
Sales	410	700
Sales Discounts	420	—

2016

May 3 Received cheque from Irene Welch for invoice No. 1 less 2% discount.

7 Cash sales collected, $400.

14 Received cheque from Chantel Simard for invoice No. 2 less 2% discount.

20 Sold store equipment at cost, $300.

Solution to Self-Review Quiz 6-4

MOORE COMPANY
CASH RECEIPTS JOURNAL

Page 2

Date		Cash Dr.	Accounts Receivable Cr.	Sales Cr.	Sales Discounts Dr.	Description of Receipt	PR	Sundry Accounts Cr.
2016 May	3	490 00	500 00		10 00	Irene Welch	✔	
	7	400 00		400 00		Cash Sales	✗	
	14	196 00	200 00		4 00	Chantel Simard	✔	
	20	300 00				Store Equipment	130	300 00
	31	1 386 00	700 00	400 00	14 00			300 00
		(110)	(120)	(410)	(420)			(X)

Cross-adding: $1,400.00 = $1,400.00

Quiz Tip

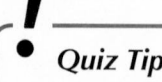

The total of the Sundry column is not posted; only individual amounts are posted to the general ledger.

Quiz Tip

Sum of all debits equals sum of all credits.

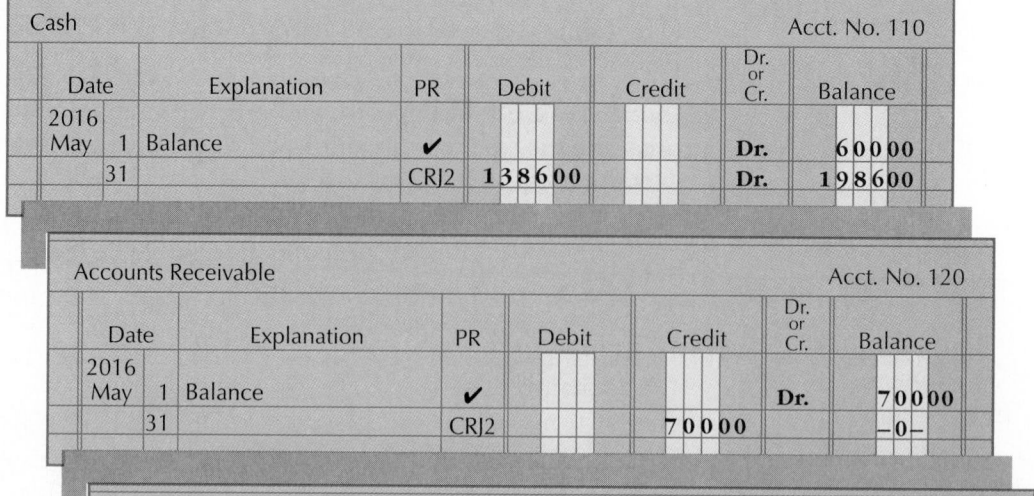

PARTIAL GENERAL LEDGER

Cash — Acct. No. 110

Date		Explanation	PR	Debit	Credit	Dr. or Cr.	Balance
2016 May	1	Balance	✔			Dr.	600 00
	31		CRJ2	1 386 00		Dr.	1 986 00

Accounts Receivable — Acct. No. 120

Date		Explanation	PR	Debit	Credit	Dr. or Cr.	Balance
2016 May	1	Balance	✔			Dr.	700 00
	31		CRJ2		700 00		–0–

Store Equipment — Acct. No. 130

Date		Explanation	PR	Debit	Credit	Dr. or Cr.	Balance
2016 May	1	Balance	✔			Dr.	600 00
	20		CRJ2		300 00	Dr.	300 00

Sales — Acct. No. 410

Date		Explanation	PR	Debit	Credit	Dr. or Cr.	Balance
2016 May	1	Balance	✔			Cr.	700 00
	31		CRJ2		400 00	Cr.	1 100 00

Sales Discounts — Acct. No. 420

Date		Explanation	PR	Debit	Credit	Dr. or Cr.	Balance
2016 May	31		CRJ2	14 00		Dr.	14 00

ACCOUNTS RECEIVABLE LEDGER

NAME Irene Welch
ADDRESS 10 Rong Road, Timmins, ON P4N 4M3

Date		Explanation	PR	Debit	Credit	Dr. Balance
2016 May	1	Balance	✔			500 00
	3		CRJ2		500 00	–0–

NAME Chantel Simard
ADDRESS 9017 Robitaille Road, Montreal, QC H1K 4R3

Date		Explanation	PR	Debit	Credit	Dr. Balance
2016 May	1	Balance	✔			200 00
	14		CRJ2		200 00	–0–

Chapter Assignments

COMPREHENSIVE DEMONSTRATION PROBLEM WITH SOLUTION TIPS

(Students please note that this Comprehensive Problem is part one of a two-part series, and many instructors will want you to complete this part of the problem at the same time as the balance of the problem at the same point in Chapter 7. It can be done at this point, but will have a more comprehensive feel to it if it is completed at the same time as part two in the next chapter. In any event, the forms you need are on pages 7-5 to 7-11 of the *Study Guide with Working Papers.*)

a. For the Walter Lantz Co. in July, 2016, journalize, record, and post the following transactions as needed to the sales, cash receipts, and general journals. All terms are 2/10, n/30.

b. Prepare a schedule of accounts receivable and accounts payable.

	2016		
CRJ	July	2	Walter Lantz invested $8,000 in the business.
SJ		4	Sold merchandise on account to Panda Co., invoice No. 1—$300.
SJ		5	Sold merchandise on account to Buzzard Co., invoice No. 2—$600.
CR		6	Cash sale—$400.
GJ		8	Issued credit memorandum No. 1 to Panda Co. for defective merchandise—$100.
CRJ		11	Received cheque from Panda Co. for invoice No. 1 less returns and discount.
CRJ		16	Cash sale—$500.
SJ		19	Sold merchandise on account to Panda Co.—$550, invoice No. 3.

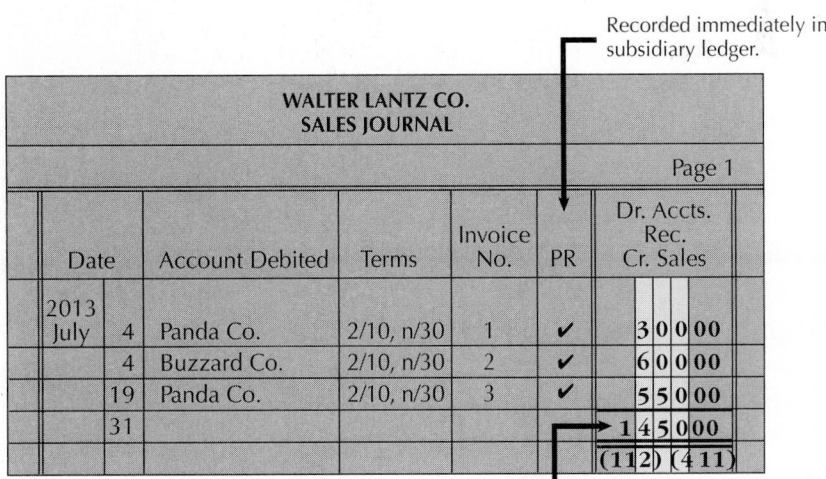

Recorded immediately in subsidiary ledger.

WALTER LANTZ CO.
SALES JOURNAL

Page 1

Date		Account Debited	Terms	Invoice No.	PR	Dr. Accts. Rec. Cr. Sales
2013 July	4	Panda Co.	2/10, n/30	1	✔	300 00
	4	Buzzard Co.	2/10, n/30	2	✔	600 00
	19	Panda Co.	2/10, n/30	3	✔	550 00
	31					1 450 00
						(112) (411)

Total posted at end of month to general ledger accounts.

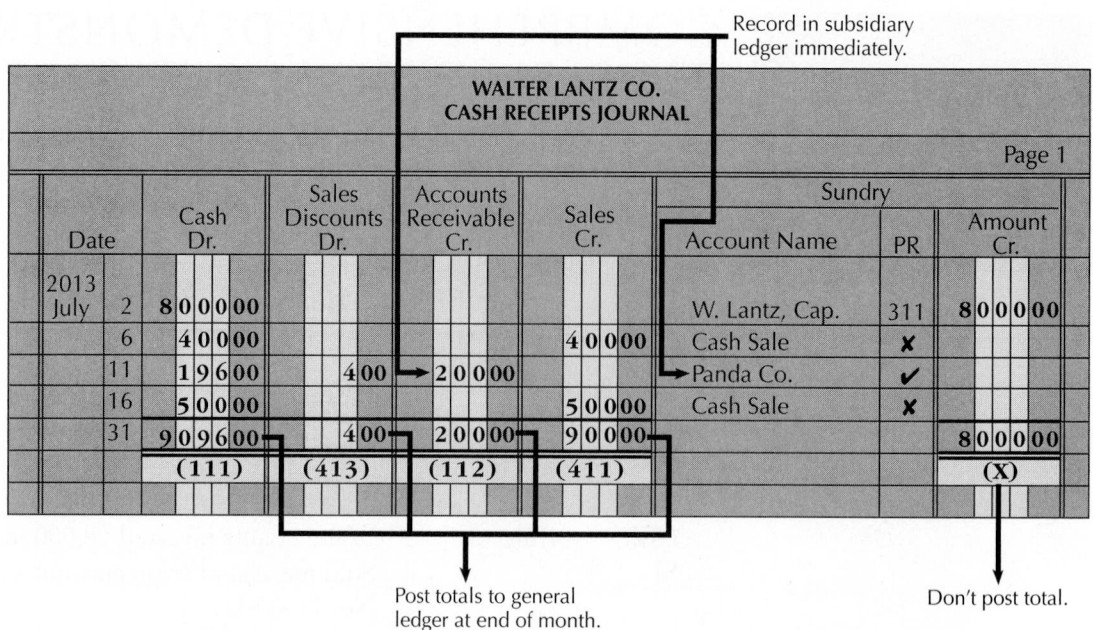

Record in subsidiary ledger immediately.

WALTER LANTZ CO.
CASH RECEIPTS JOURNAL

Page 1

Date		Cash Dr.	Sales Discounts Dr.	Accounts Receivable Cr.	Sales Cr.	Sundry Account Name	Sundry PR	Sundry Amount Cr.
2013 July	2	8000 00				W. Lantz, Cap.	311	8000 00
	6	400 00			400 00	Cash Sale	✗	
	11	196 00	4 00	200 00		Panda Co.	✓	
	16	500 00			500 00	Cash Sale	✗	
	31	9096 00	4 00	200 00	900 00			8000 00
		(111)	(413)	(112)	(411)			(X)

Post totals to general ledger at end of month.

Don't post total.

GENERAL JOURNAL Page 1

Date		Account Titles and Description	PR	Dr.	Cr.
2013 July	8	Sales Returns and Allowances	412	100 00	
		Accounts Receivable, Panda Co.	112/✓		100 00
		Issued credit memo			

Post immediately to general ledger.

Recorded immediately in subsidiary ledger.

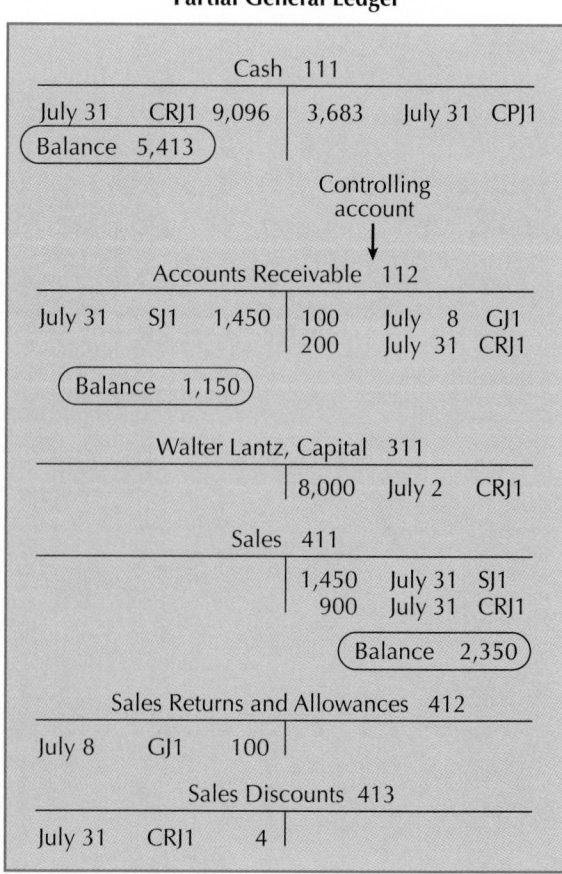

Accounts receivable subsidiary ledger usually contains accounts with debit balances

Accounts Receivable Subsidiary Ledger

Buzzard Co.

Date		PR	Debit	Credit	Dr. Balance
2013 July	5	SJ1	600 00		600 00

Panda Co.

Date		PR	Debit	Credit	Dr. Balance
2013 July	4	SJ1	300 00		300 00
	8	GJ1		100 00	200 00
	11	CRJ1		200 00	–0–
	19	SJ1	550 00		550 00

Partial General Ledger

Cash 111

July 31	CRJ1	9,096	3,683	July 31	CPJ1
Balance 5,413					

Controlling account

Accounts Receivable 112

July 31	SJ1	1,450	100	July 8	GJ1
			200	July 31	CRJ1
Balance 1,150					

Walter Lantz, Capital 311

			8,000	July 2	CRJ1

Sales 411

			1,450	July 31	SJ1
			900	July 31	CRJ1
			Balance 2,350		

Sales Returns and Allowances 412

July 8	GJ1	100			

Sales Discounts 413

July 31	CRJ1	4			

The controlling accounts for Accounts Receivable at the end of the month equal the sum of the accounts receivable subsidiary ledger.

WALTER LANTZ CO. SCHEDULE OF ACCOUNTS RECEIVABLE JULY 31, 2013	
Buzzard Co.	$ 600.00
Panda Co.	550.00
Total Accounts Receivable	$1150.00

SUMMARY OF KEY POINTS

Learning Unit 6-1

1. Special journals increase efficiency and allow multiple clerks to work on record-keeping at the same time.
2. This chapter describes and illustrates the sales journal and the cash receipts journal. The purchases journal and the cash payments journal are covered in the next chapter. Other journals are also possible.
3. Proper management of a company involves care in selecting which customers will have the right to buy goods and/or services on credit, and also requires that collections be monitored to minimize losses from uncollected sales.
4. Use of trade discounts is an effective way to avoid costly routine alterations to price lists and also allows for an easy way to recognize customer differences by adjusting the allowed trade discount to recognize special situations—like customer loyalty or size.

Learning Unit 6-2

1. The sales journal records details of sales to customers on account.
2. The accounts receivable subsidiary ledger replaces a single accounts receivable account in the general ledger with multiple accounts in a separate ledger.
3. The AR sub-ledger can be in the form of cards, paper in a binder, or a computer file—the principle is the same.
4. The sales journal can have one column or can have multiple columns if a company wants to keep details of sales by category or territory. Multiple-column journals must cross-add at period end.
5. A check mark in the Post. Ref. box means that the amount has been recorded to the customer's account in the AR sub-ledger.
6. Placing an account number underneath a column total at period end in a multiple-column journal means that total has been posted to the relevant GL account.

Learning Unit 6-3

1. When a credit memorandum is issued, the result is that Sales Returns and Allowances is increasing and Accounts Receivable is decreasing. When we record this in a general journal, we assume that all parts of the transaction will be posted to the general ledger and recorded in the subsidiary ledger when the entry is journalized.

2. A credit memo can also be recorded in a special journal if the volume warrants it.
3. A credit memo can also be entered into the sales journal as a negative amount, but more care and control may be needed.

Learning Unit 6-4

1. The cash receipts journal records receipt of cash from any source.
2. Post each item in the sundry column to record the credit part of a transaction that does not occur frequently. Never post the *total* of sundry. Post items in the sundry column to the general ledger when entered.
3. A ✔ in the posting reference column of the cash receipts journal means that the accounts receivable subsidiary ledger has been updated (recorded) with a credit.
4. An ✗ in the cash receipts journal posting reference column means no posting was necessary since the totals of these columns will be posted at the end of the month.
5. Cross-adding means proving that the total of debits and the total of credits are equal in the special journal, thus verifying the accuracy of recording.
6. A schedule of accounts receivable is a listing of the ending balances of customers in the accounts receivable subsidiary ledger. This total should be the same balance as found in the controlling account, Accounts Receivable, in the general ledger.
7. An aged schedule may be helpful in ensuring all accounts are collected at an early date.

KEY TERMS

Accounts receivable subsidiary ledger A book or file that contains the individual records of amounts owed by various credit customers, usually in alphabetical order (p. 252)

Aged schedule of accounts receivable A detailed list of all customer accounts showing how long each balance has been outstanding (p. 266)

Cash receipts journal A special journal that records all transactions involving the receipt of cash from any source (p. 263)

Controlling account (AR) The Accounts Receivable account in the general ledger, after postings are complete, shows the total amount of money owed to a firm. This figure is broken down in the accounts receivable subsidiary ledger, where it indicates specifically who owes the money. (p. 253)

Credit memorandum A piece of paper sent by the seller to a customer who has returned merchandise previously purchased on credit. The credit memorandum indicates to the customer that the seller is reducing the amount owed by the customer. (p. 258)

Credit period Length of time allowed for payment of goods sold on account (p. 250)

Cross-adding The process of proving that the total debit columns of a special journal are equal to the total columns of that journal; also referred to as cross-footing or cross-balancing (p. 255)

Discount period A period during which a customer can take a cash discount to encourage early payment of bills. The discount period is shorter than the credit period. (p. 250)

Sales discount Cash discount granted to customers for payments made within a specific period of time. A contra-revenue account is used to record sales discounts granted. (p. 250)

Sales invoice A bill sent to a customer reflecting a sale, usually on credit (p. 254)

Sales journal A special journal used to record only sales made on account. May have one column, or many (p. 253)

Sales Returns and Allowances A contra-revenue account that records price adjustments and allowances granted on merchandise that is defective and has been returned. It has a debit balance. (p. 258)

Schedule of accounts receivable A list of the customers, in alphabetical order, that have an outstanding balance in the accounts receivable subsidiary ledger. This total should be equal to the balance of the Accounts Receivable controlling account in the general ledger at the end of the month. (p. 265)

Special journal A journal used to record similar groups of transactions. *Example:* the sales journal, which records all sales on account (p. 249)

Subsidiary ledger A ledger that contains accounts of a single type. *Example:* the accounts receivable subsidiary ledger, which records all customers that purchase goods on account (p. 252)

Trade discount A device used to allow for one basic product price list but different selling prices for customers in different categories, such as size or loyalty (p. 250)

Sundry accounts Miscellaneous accounts column(s) in a special journal, which records transactions that do not occur often (p. 263)

QUICK REVIEW

The following Tips are from Learning Units 6-1 to 6-4. Answer the Assess Your Progress questions and use the How Did You Do? at the bottom of the page to see how well you know the material. The Quick Review provides tips before each Assess Your Progress to help you avoid common accounting errors.

LU 6-1 Designing and Understanding Special Journals

Tips: Special journals are used to make the record-keeping tasks of a business more efficient, and also allow more than one person to work on the company's records at the same time. One special journal is called the sales journal, and recorded here are credit sales to a company's customers. Several other special journals are commonly used by a business. This chapter describes the sales journal and the cash receipts journal, while the next chapter details the purchases journal and the cash payments journal. A company might have a need for other special journals as well—the payroll journal is one example.

Businesses need to control the process of selling on credit to customers, as well as the ultimate collection of monies owed. Controlling sales is often done by designating certain persons as sales managers—possibly one person for each territory or product line. To assist with collections, a cash discount can be used. It also helps to have some person or persons made responsible for effective collection of all monies owed. The sales journal can be designed to capture helpful information to help with these tasks.

Assess Your Progress

Answer true or false to the following statements:

1. Special journals allow more than one bookkeeper to work on a company's records.
2. A customer relations manager helps to manage the sales function.
3. Cash discounts cost money and should be avoided.
4. Having a lot of details about a company's sales helps in managing the company.
5. A trade discount applies to all customers equally.

LU 6-2 The Sales Journal and Accounts Receivable Subsidiary Ledger

Tips: Making a single journal entry in the general journal for every sale made by a company each period is very inefficient, and should be avoided if possible. Similarly, it is quite confusing to have a separate account in the general ledger for each customer. To help with these problems, most businesses use a sales journal and an accounts receivable subsidiary ledger. The controlling account, Accounts Receivable, in the general ledger will equal the sum of individual Accounts Receivable accounts in the subsidiary ledger at the end of the month. The normal balance of each account in the subsidiary ledger is a debit. A company's sales journal is a list of all invoices for a period, usually with several important details included, such as an invoice number, terms, and so on. A multiple-column sales journal can also contain extra columns—one for each desired category of sales. Some sales journals also include details regarding the identity of each salesperson. At the end of each period, the sales journal is totalled, and if it is multicolumned, the column totals must cross-add to prove that the debits equal the credits. These column totals are posted to the general ledger at period-end. Details of each invoice are recorded to each customer's account in the accounts receivable subsidiary ledger, which may be designed to capture other details as well, such as salesperson, terms, and more.

Assess Your Progress

Answer true or false to the following statements:

1. The controlling account is located in the subsidiary ledger.
2. A check mark in the posting reference column means the controlling account has been updated.
3. Accounts in subsidiary ledgers can be listed alphabetically.
4. All subsidiary ledgers consist of pages in a bound volume.
5. Details of sales by salesperson are always posted to the general ledger.

LU 6-3 The Credit Memorandum

Tips: Companies usually handle sales returns and allowances by means of a credit memorandum. When a credit memorandum is issued, Sales Returns and Allowances will increase with a debit, and an Accounts Receivable controlling account, as well as the specific customer's account in the subsidiary ledger, will be reduced by a credit. If the number of credit memos is large, a company might use a special journal to record them all. The chapter shows how a credit memo is recorded using the general journal, and this can work well if the number of credit memos is low. Some companies allow credit memos to be recorded as negative amounts in the sales journal. This is a very efficient way to record these documents, but added controls might be needed to help ensure that all such entries are legitimate.

Assess Your Progress

Answer true or false to the following statements:

1. A credit memorandum only affects the controlling account.
2. Sales discounts are taken on the original sale less any applicable credit memos.
3. Sales Returns and Allowances is a contra revenue account.
4. A company should always use the general journal to enter credit memos.
5. It is acceptable to enter credit memos as negative amounts in the sales journal.

LU 6-4 Cash Receipts Journal and Schedule of Accounts Receivable

Tips: All normal cash received by a business in a period should be entered in the cash receipts journal. Most of the amounts should come from customers, and any payments made by credit customers must be recorded to that customer's account. Some cash receipts from non-customers are received periodically, and the cash receipts journal has a sundry column to accommodate these unusual events. Sales discounts should never be allowed on sales returns, of course, and also should be subject to approval by the sales manager or credit manager, and then entered as part of each transaction on a separate row in the cash receipts journal. When all postings are done, the sum of the subsidiary ledger should equal the ending balance in the controlling account. It is the schedule of accounts receivable that lists each customer with its ending balance and proves this equality. To assist in effective collection of all amounts owed, the schedule of accounts receivable at period end can be constructed with additional detail, showing the length of time each amount making up each customer's total has been unpaid.

Assess Your Progress

Answer true or false to the following statements:

1. The schedule of accounts receivable lists debits first.
2. The normal balance of an Accounts Receivable account is a credit.
3. The controlling account does not match the total of the schedule of accounts receivable at the end of the month.
4. Sales Discounts is a contra-asset.
5. There are three possible ways to enter a credit memo.

How Did You Do: Answers to the Assess Your Progress Questions

LU 6-1

1. True.
2. False—Such person is usually called the sales manager.
3. False—on balance. True, they cost some money, but help save on bad debts in the long run.
4. True.
5. False—An advantage of trade discounts is that they can be altered for each customer.

LU 6-2

1. False—It is included in the general ledger.
2. False—A check mark means that the amount has been recorded to the customer account.
3. True—However, some companies may arrange things differently. Using account numbers is one example.
4. False—That is one way, but the accounts can be on cards or exist as files in a computer.
5. False—Details of sales by salesperson are not posted to the general ledger.

LU 6-3

1. False—A credit memorandum affects both the controlling account and the subsidiary ledger.
2. True.
3. True.
4. False—this is a good way, but a bit inefficient. A special journal is helpful when the number of CMs are large, or a CM can be entered into the sales journal as a negative amount.
5. True—so long as good controls are in place.

LU 6-4

1. False—There are no debits on the schedule of accounts receivable.
2. False—The normal balance of an accounts receivable account is a debit.
3. False—The controlling account must match the total of the schedule of accounts receivable at the end of the period.
4. False—Sales Discounts is a contra-revenue account.
5. True.

BLUEPRINT OF SALES AND CASH RECEIPT JOURNALS

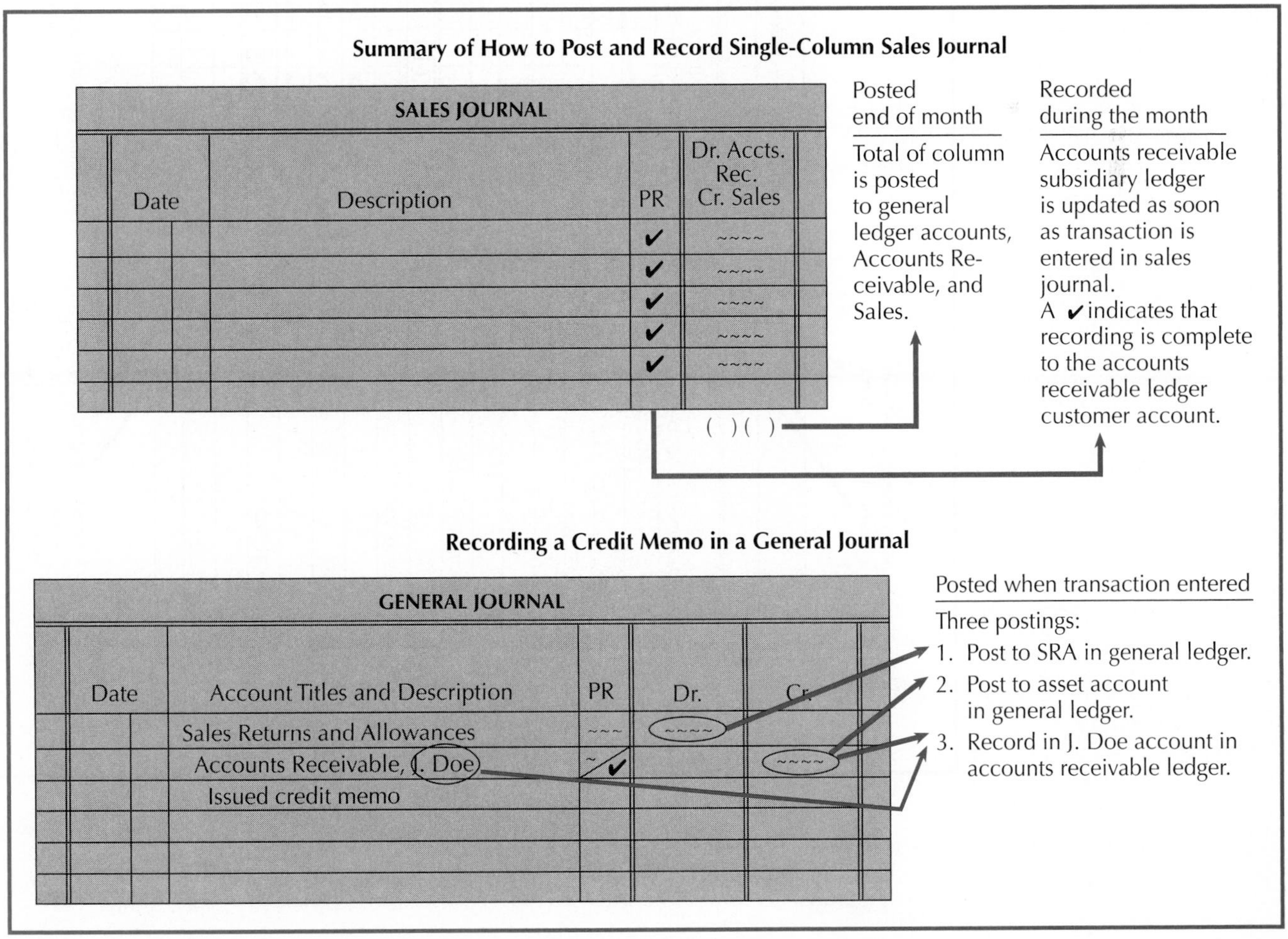

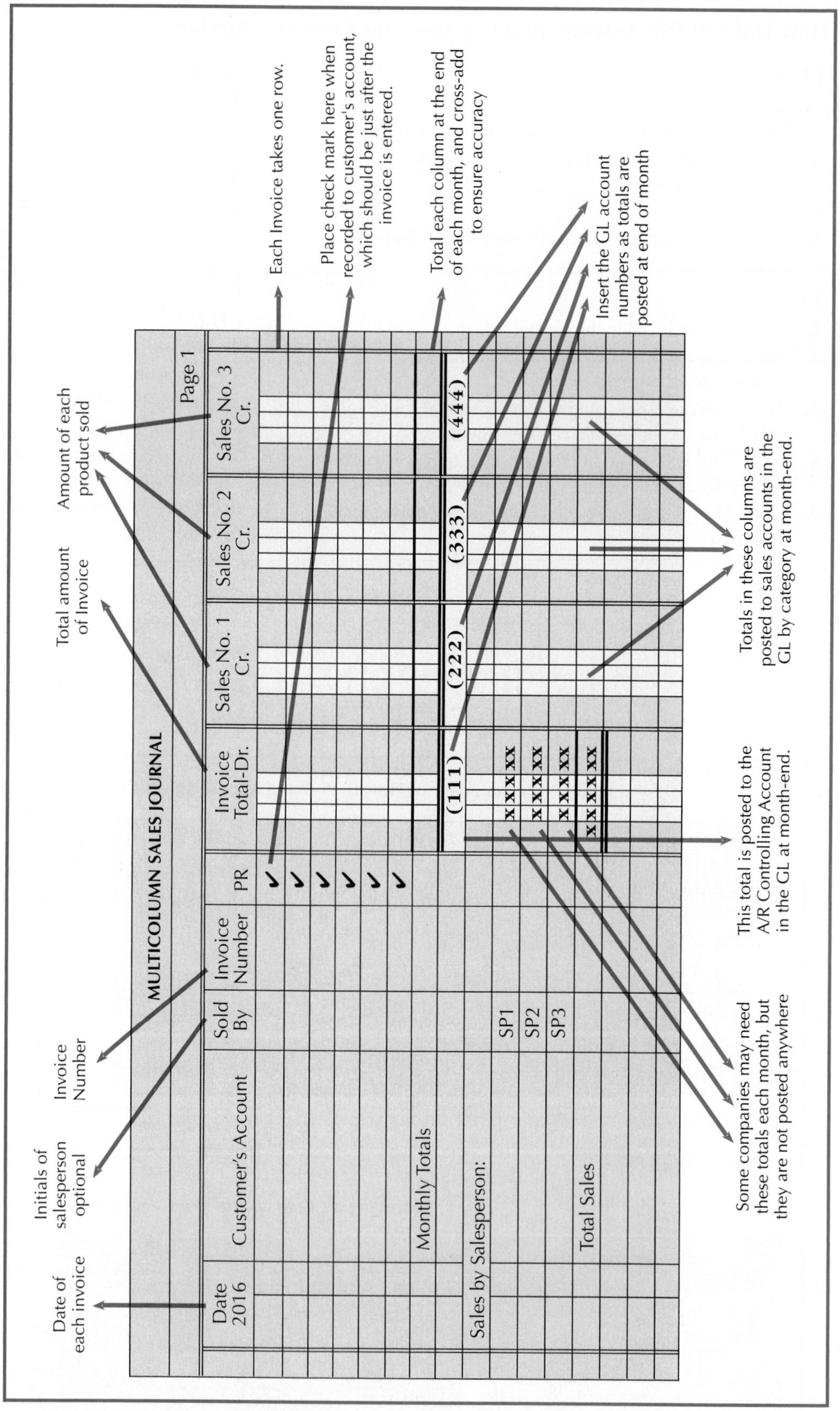
MULTICOLUMN SALES JOURNAL
Page 1
Date 2016
Customer's Account
Sold By
Invoice Number
PR
Invoice Total-Dr.
Sales No. 1 Cr.
Sales No. 2 Cr.
Sales No. 3 Cr.
Monthly Totals
(111)
(222)
(333)
(444)
Sales by Salesperson:
SP1
SP2
SP3
Total Sales
xxxxx
xxxxx
xxxxx
xxxxxx
Date of each invoice
Initials of salesperson optional
Invoice Number
Total amount of Invoice
Amount of each product sold
Each Invoice takes one row.
Place check mark here when recorded to customer's account, which should be just after the invoice is entered.
Total each column at the end of each month, and cross-add to ensure accuracy
Insert the GL account numbers as totals are posted at end of month
Totals in these columns are posted to sales accounts in the GL by category at month-end.
This total is posted to the A/R Controlling Account in the GL at month-end.
Some companies may need these totals each month, but they are not posted anywhere

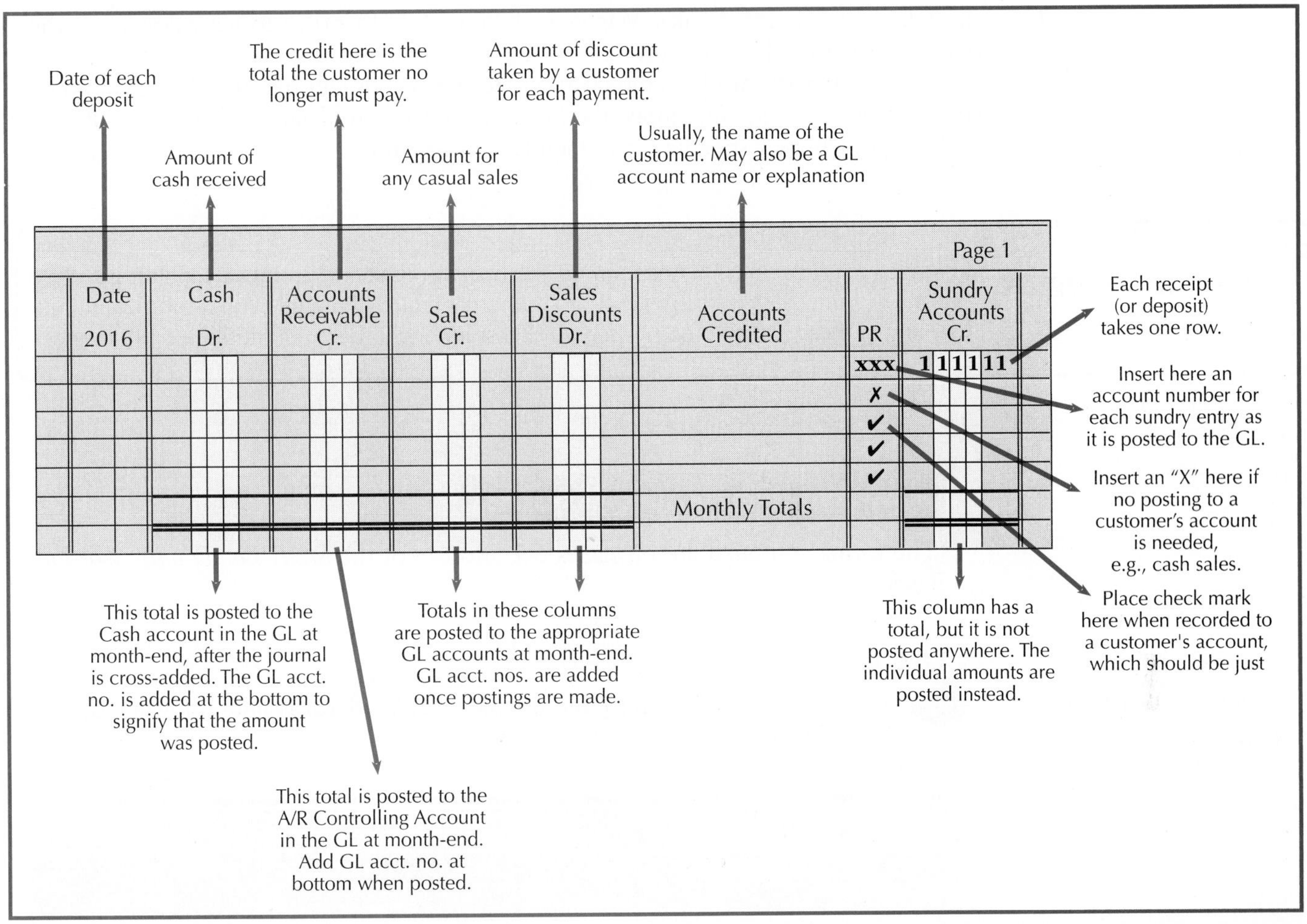
Date of each deposit
Amount of cash received
The credit here is the total the customer no longer must pay.
Amount for any casual sales
Amount of discount taken by a customer for each payment.
Usually, the name of the customer. May also be a GL account name or explanation
Page 1
Date 2016
Cash Dr.
Accounts Receivable Cr.
Sales Cr.
Sales Discounts Dr.
Accounts Credited
PR
Sundry Accounts Cr.
xxx
1 1 1 1 11
Monthly Totals
Each receipt (or deposit) takes one row.
Insert here an account number for each sundry entry as it is posted to the GL.
Insert an "X" here if no posting to a customer's account is needed, e.g., cash sales.
Place check mark here when recorded to a customer's account, which should be just
This total is posted to the Cash account in the GL at month-end, after the journal is cross-added. The GL acct. no. is added at the bottom to signify that the amount was posted.
Totals in these columns are posted to the appropriate GL accounts at month-end. GL acct. nos. are added once postings are made.
This column has a total, but it is not posted anywhere. The individual amounts are posted instead.
This total is posted to the A/R Controlling Account in the GL at month-end. Add GL acct. no. at bottom when posted.

QUESTIONS, CLASSROOM DEMONSTRATION EXERCISES, EXERCISES, AND PROBLEMS

Discussion Questions and Critical Thinking/Ethical Case

1. Explain the purpose of a contra-revenue account.
2. What is the normal balance of sales discounts?
3. Give two examples of contra-revenue accounts.
4. What is the difference between a discount period and a credit period?
5. Explain the terms (a) 2/10, n/30; (b) n/10, EOM.
6. If special journals are used, what purpose will a general journal serve?
7. Compare and contrast the controlling account Accounts Receivable with the accounts receivable subsidiary ledger.
8. Explain how to calculate net sales.
9. Why is the accounts receivable subsidiary ledger organized in alphabetical order?
10. What is an invoice? What purpose does it serve?
11. When a seller issues a credit memorandum, what accounts will be affected?
12. Explain the purpose of a schedule of accounts receivable.

13. Amy Jak is the National Sales Manager of Rowe Co. In order to get sales up to the projection for the old year, Amy asked the accountant to put the first two weeks of sales in January back into December. Amy told the accountant that this secret would be between them. Should Amy move the new sales into the old sales year? You make the call. Write down your specific recommendations to Amy.

Classroom Demonstration Exercises

(The forms you need are on pages 6-7 and 6-9 of the *Study Guide with Working Papers.*)

Overview

Recording transactions
❷ ❸ (6 min)

1. Complete the following table for Sales, Sales Returns and Allowances, and Sales Discounts:

Accounts Affected	Category	↑↓	Rules	Temporary or Permanent

Calculating Net Sales

Net sales
❷ ❸ (6 min)

2. Given the following, calculate net sales:

Gross sales	$30
Sales returns and allowances	8
Sales discounts	2

Sales Journal and General Journal

Sales transactions
❷ ❸ (10 min)

3. Beside each of the three transactions below the box, enter the number of any of the following six treatments that apply. (More than one number can be used.)

1. Journalize into the sales journal.
2. Record immediately to the subsidiary ledger.
3. Post totals from the sales journal at end of month to the general ledger.
4. Journalize in the general journal.
5. Record and post immediately to subsidiary and general ledgers.
6. Journalize into the cash receipts journal.

a. ________ Sold merchandise for cash to Ree Co., invoice No. 1—$50.

b. ________ Sold merchandise on account to Flynn Co., invoice No. 2—$1,000.

c. ________ Issued credit memorandum No. 1 to Flynn Co. for defective merchandise—$25.

Single-Column Sales Journal

Entering basic sales invoices
❷ (10 min)

4. Enter each of the following invoices into a single-column sales journal. Total the entries and place appropriate general ledger account numbers below to show where the total would be posted. There is no need to record any details to individual customer accounts. The company uses 120 as their general ledger account number for Accounts Receivable, and the Sales account number is 400. Each sale carries terms of net 30 days.

2017
May 4 Invoice No. 801 Sold $200 to Francine Company on account.
7 Invoice No. 802 Sold $300 to Joshua Enterprises on account.
13 Invoice No. 803 Sold $100 to Charlize Company on account.
22 Invoice No. 804 Sold $350 to Francine Company on account.
25 Invoice No. 805 Sold $400 to Kirkhouse Consulting on account.
30 Invoice No. 806 Sold $250 to Charlize Company on account.

Multicolumn Sales Journal

Entering sales invoices in a multicolumn sales journal
❷ (18 min)

5. Enter each of the following invoices into a multicolumn sales journal. Driscoll Company sells two kinds of safety equipment: helmets (H) and safety shoes (S). Terms are all 2% 10 days, net 30. Total all the columns and cross-add the journal. Place appropriate account numbers at the bottom of each column to show where the totals would be posted. No need to record to individual accounts. Driscoll uses 1400 as their Accounts Receivable controlling account in the general ledger, 4100 for Helmet Sales, and 4200 for Safety Shoe Sales.

2016
Feb. 3 Invoice No. 301 Sold $200 (H) plus $100 (S) to Parkay Management.
7 Invoice No. 302 Sold $350 (H) plus $250 (S) to Ferlow Inspections.
11 Invoice No. 303 Sold $150 (H) plus $550 (S) to Merlet Waste Management.
15 Invoice No. 304 Sold $600 (H) plus $300 (S) to Parkay Management.
19 Invoice No. 305 Sold $700 (S) to Arkadia Company. (No helmet sales for this invoice.)
24 Invoice No. 306 Sold $400 (H) plus $150 (S) to Snake Creek & Co.
28 Invoice No. 307 Sold $500 (H) plus $250 (S) to Merlet Waste Management.

The Cash Receipts Journal

Entering transactions into the cash receipts journal
❹ (15 min)

6. Please refer to the information contained in question 5 above. During February 2016, Driscoll Company deposited four cheques as follows:

Feb. 5 Peter Driscoll wrote a personal cheque for $10,000 and deposited it in the company bank account. This is a contribution by owner.
12 Deposited a cheque from Parkay Management, paying invoice No. 301, taking discount.
20 Deposited a cheque from Merlet Waste Management, paying invoice No. 303, taking discount.
27 Deposited a cheque from Ferlow Inspections, paying invoice No. 302. No Discount.

Enter each deposit into a cash receipts journal, and cross-add the journal at month end. No need to record to individual customer accounts or to the general ledger accounts, but please insert the correct general ledger account numbers in the appropriate places as if the posting was done. Driscoll's Owner's Equity account number is 3000. The Sales Discounts account number is 4500. The Bank account number is 1000. The Accounts Receivable account number is 1200.

Preparing a Schedule of Accounts Receivable

Preparation of a schedule of accounts receivable
4 (10 min)

7. From the following, prepare a schedule of accounts receivable for AVE Co. for May 31, 2015:

Accounts Receivable Subsidiary Ledger

Bliss Co.

5/12	SJ1	50	5/25	CRJ1	20

Rowe Co.

5/18	SJ1	60			

Partial General Ledger

Accounts Receivable 1200

5/31	SJ1	110	5/31	CRJ1	20

Exercises

(The forms you need are on pages 6-9 to 6-14 of the *Study Guide with Working Papers.*)

Set A

Recording and posting from the sales journal
❷ ❹ (10 min)

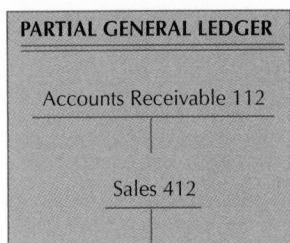

6-1A. From the sales journal below, record in the accounts receivable subsidiary ledger and post to the general ledger accounts as appropriate.

SALES JOURNAL

Page 1

Date		Account Debited	Invoice No.	PR	Dr. Accts. Receivable Cr. Sales
2016 April	18	Kevin Stone Co.	1		600 00
	19	Bill Valley Co.	2		900 00
		Total			1 500 00

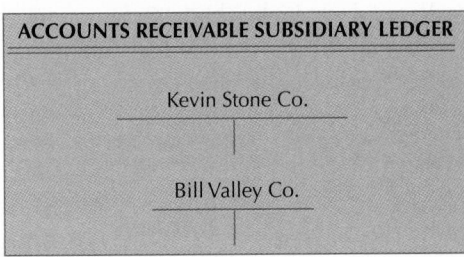

ACCOUNTS RECEIVABLE SUBSIDIARY LEDGER

Kevin Stone Co.

Bill Valley Co.

PARTIAL GENERAL LEDGER

Accounts Receivable 112

Sales 412

Journalizing, recording, and posting sales and cash receipts journal; schedule of accounts receivable
❶ ❷ ❸ ❹ (20 min)

6-2A. From the following transactions for Edna Co., when appropriate, journalize, record, post, and prepare a schedule of accounts receivable. Use the same journal headings (all page 1) and chart of accounts that Art's Clothing used in the text (use Edna Cares, Capital). You will have to set up your own accounts receivable subsidiary ledger and partial general ledger as needed. All sales terms are 2/10, n/30.

2017

June

2 Edna Cares invested $5,000 in the business.

3 Sold merchandise on account to Boston Co., invoice No. 218, $700.

3 Sold merchandise on account to Gary Co., invoice No. 219, $1,100.

6 Cash sale, $200.

9 Issued credit memorandum No. 24 to Boston Co. for defective merchandise, $200.

10 Received cheque from Boston Co. for invoice No. 218 less returns and discount.

16 Cash sale, $400.

17 Sold merchandise on account to Boston Co., invoice No. 220, $600.

Calculate net receipts, enter credit memo
❸ (5 min)

6-3A. From the following, calculate what amount Blue Co. can expect to receive from Frost Foundation with respect to invoice No. 6051, dated March 5, 2015. The total was $3,200 and terms are 3% 15 days, net 45 days. On March 7, credit memorandum No. 103 was issued to Frost Foundation in the amount of $400 for some minor damage to the items sold. Frost was expected to pay within the discount period. In addition, record the credit memorandum using the general journal. No need to post it or record to the accounts receivable sub-ledger.

Enter sales, credit memo, and cash receipts
❶ ❷ ❸ ❹ (18 min)

6-4A. On January 11, 2016, Glassiere Co. sold a Model 3146 home theatre equipment cabinet to the HLJ Company on invoice No. 3275. The unit has a list price of $4,600, and this customer receives a trade discount of 35%. All sales invoices are sold on terms of 2% 10 days, net 30. Due to a manufacturing defect, the colour of the stain used on this unit was slightly different from normal, and HLJ asked for and got a credit memorandum (No. 202) in the amount of $300 net, dated January 14 (which means this is deducted from the actual total of this invoice, not the list price). HLJ paid invoice No. 3275 less the trade discount and credit memorandum January 20. Record the sale, the credit memorandum, and the cash receipt in appropriate journals and record to the customer's account as necessary. Because the sales and cash receipts journals are only posted at month end, you may skip the general ledger postings for these two journals.

Entering sales into a multicolumn journal
❷ (20 min)

6-5A. Enter each of the following invoices into a multicolumn sales journal. Airwell Company sells three kinds of machining equipment: lathes (L), milling (M), and surfacing (S). Terms are all 2% 10 days, net 30. Total all columns and cross-add the journal. Place appropriate account numbers at the bottom of each column to show where the totals have been posted. Record to individual accounts in the accounts receivable sub-ledger as well as the general ledger accounts. Airwell uses 1200 as their Accounts Receivable controlling account in the general ledger, and 4010 for Lathes Sales; 4020 for Milling Sales, and 4030 for Surfacing Sales.

2017		
Aug.	2	Invoice No. 601 Sold $3,000 (L), $4,200 (M), and $2,500 (S) to Amaxe Engineering.
	5	Invoice No. 602 Sold $2,650 (L), $1,800 (M), and $900 (S) to Willow Productions.
	9	Invoice No. 603 Sold $4,100 (L), $3,600 (M), and $2,800 (S) to Stencle Machinery.
	11	Invoice No. 604 Sold $2,700 (M) and $4,300 (S) to Macro-El Holdings.
	14	Invoice No. 605 Sold $3,600 (L), $2,700 (M), and $1,700 (S) to Amaxe Engineering.
	19	Invoice No. 606 Sold $5,700 (L) and $6,200 (M) to Naroco Company.
	22	Invoice No. 607 Sold $3,300 (L), $3,500 (M), and $2,800 (S) to Willow Productions.
	24	Invoice No. 608 Sold $3,200 (L), $800 (M), and $2,700 (S) to Macro-El Holdings.
	29	Invoice No. 609 Sold $2,500 (M) and $2,900 (S) to Amaxe Engineering.

Recording to the cash receipts journal
❹ (15 min)

6-6A. Please refer to the information contained in the question 6-5A above. During August, 2017, Airwell Company deposited four cheques and made one additional deposit as follows:

Aug.	3	The owner arranged for a bank loan of $30,000 to finance inventory purchases. This amount was deposited in the company bank account.
	11	Deposited a cheque from Amaxe Engineering paying invoice No. 601, taking discount.
	19	Deposited a cheque from Stencle Machinery paying invoice No. 603, taking discount.

25 Deposited a cheque from Willow Productions paying invoice No. 602. No discount.

27 Deposited a cheque from Naroco Company paying invoice No. 606, taking discount.

Required: Enter each deposit into a cash receipts journal, and cross-add the journal at month end. Record to individual customer accounts as well as to the general ledger accounts, inserting the correct general ledger account numbers in the appropriate places as the posting is done. Airwell's Bank Loan Payable general ledger account number is 2200. The Sales Discounts account number is 4450. The Bank account number is 1100. Remember, the Accounts Receivable account number is 1200.

Set B

Recording and posting from the sales journal
❷ ❹ (10 min)

6-1B. From the sales journal below, record in the accounts receivable subsidiary ledger and post to the general ledger accounts as appropriate.

SALES JOURNAL

Page 1

Date		Account Debited	Invoice No.	PR	Dr. Accts. Receivable Cr. Sales
2016 April	18	Kevin Stone Co.	1		800 00
	19	Bill Valley Co.	2		700 00
		Total			1 500 00

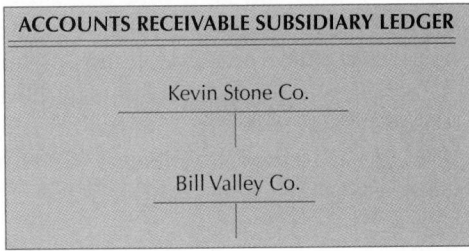

ACCOUNTS RECEIVABLE SUBSIDIARY LEDGER

Kevin Stone Co.

Bill Valley Co.

PARTIAL GENERAL LEDGER

Accounts Receivable 112

Sales 412

Journalizing, recording, and posting sales and cash receipts journal; schedule of accounts receivable
❶ ❷ ❸ ❹ (20 min)

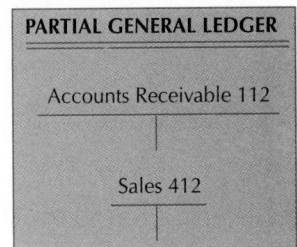

6-2B. From the following transactions for Edna Co., when appropriate, journalize, record, post, and prepare a schedule of accounts receivable. Use the same journal headings (all page 1) and chart of accounts that Art's Clothing used in the text (use Edna Cares, Capital). You will have to set up your own accounts receivable subsidiary ledger and partial general ledger as needed. All sales terms are 2/10, n/30.

2017
June

2 Edna Cares invested $6,000 in the business.

3 Sold merchandise on account to Boston Co., invoice No. 218, $800.

3 Sold merchandise on account to Gary Co., invoice No. 219, $1,200.

6 Cash sale, $300.

9 Issued credit memorandum No. 24 to Boston Co for defective merchandise, $150.

10 Received cheque from Boston Co. for invoice No. 218 less returns and discount.

16 Cash sale, $500.

17 Sold merchandise on account to Boston Co., invoice No. 220, $700.

Calculate net receipts, enter credit memo
❸ (5 min)

6-3B. From the following, calculate what amount Blue Co. can expect to receive from Frost Foundation with respect to invoice No. 6051, dated March 5, 2015. The total was $4,600 and terms are 3% 15 days, net 45 days. On March 7, credit memorandum No. 103 was issued to Frost Foundation in the amount of $500 for some minor damage to the items sold. Frost was expected to pay within the discount period. In addition, record this transaction using the general journal. No need to post it or record to the accounts receivable sub-ledger.

Enter sales, credit memo, and cash receipts
❶❷❸❹ (18 min)

6-4B. On January 11, 2016, Glassiere Co. sold a Model 3146 home theatre equipment cabinet to the HLJ Company on invoice No. 3275. The unit has a list price of $3,800 and this customer receives a trade discount of 40%. All sales invoices are sold on terms of 2% 10 days, net 30. Due to a manufacturing defect, the colour of the stain used on this unit was slightly different from normal, and KLJ asked for and got a credit memorandum (No. 202) in the amount of $200 net, dated January 14 (which means this is deducted from the actual total of this invoice, not the list price). HLJ Company paid the invoice less the trade discount and credit memorandum on January 20. Record the sale, the credit memorandum, and the cash receipt in appropriate journals and record to the customer's account as necessary. Because the sales and cash receipts journals are only posted at month end, you may skip the general ledger postings for these two journals.

Entering sales into a multicolumn journal
❷ (20 min)

6-5B. Enter each of the following invoices into a multicolumn Sales Journal. Airwell Company sells three kinds of machining equipment: lathes (L), milling (M), and surfacing (S). Terms are all 2% 10 days, net 30. Total all columns and cross-add the journal. Place appropriate account numbers at the bottom of each column to show where the totals have been posted. Record to individual accounts in the accounts receivable sub-ledger. Airwell uses 1200 as their Accounts Receivable controlling account in the general ledger; 4010 for Lathes Sales; 4020 for Milling Sales; and 4030 for Surfacing Sales.

2017

Aug. 2 Invoice No. 601 Sold $4,000 (L), $5,400 (M), and $1,900 (S) to Amaxe Engineering.

5 Invoice No. 602 Sold $3,850 (L), $2,700 (M), and $800 (S) to Willow Productions.

9 Invoice No. 603 Sold $3,700 (L), $5,600 (M), and $1,800 (S) to Stencle Machinery.

11 Invoice No. 604 Sold $3,600 (M) and $5,400 (S) to Macro-El Holdings.

14 Invoice No. 605 Sold $4,300 (L), $3,200 (M), and $2,500 (S) to Amaxe Engineering.

19 Invoice No. 606 Sold $4,800 (L) and $5,700 (M) to Naroco Company.

22 Invoice No. 607 Sold $4,200 (L), $2,900 (M), and $1,860 (S) to Willow Productions.

24 Invoice No. 608 Sold $4,400 (L), $2,300 (M), and $1,800 (S) to Macro-El Holdings.

29 Invoice No. 609 Sold $3,300 (M) and $2,700 (S) to Amaxe Engineering.

Recording to the cash receipts journal
❹ (15 min)

6-6B. Please refer to the information contained in the question 6-5B above. During August 2017, Airwell Company deposited four cheques and made one additional deposit as follows:

Aug.	3	The owner arranged for a bank loan of $25,000 to finance inventory purchases. This amount was deposited in the company bank account.
	11	Deposited a cheque from Amaxe Engineering paying invoice No. 601, taking discount.
	19	Deposited a cheque from Stencle Machinery paying invoice No. 603, taking discount.
	25	Deposited a cheque from Willow Productions paying invoice No. 602. No discount.
	27	Deposited a cheque from Naroco Company paying invoice No. 606, taking discount.

Required: Enter each deposit into a cash receipts journal, and cross-add the journal at month end. Record to individual customer accounts as well as to the general ledger accounts, inserting the correct general ledger account numbers in the appropriate places as the posting is done. Airwell's Bank Loan Payable general ledger account number is 2200. The Sales Discounts account number is 4450. The Bank account number is 1100. The Accounts Receivable account number is 1200.

Group A Problems

(The forms you need are on pages 6-15 to 6-30 of the *Study Guide with Working Papers.*)

Single-column journal: journalizing and posting to general ledger and recording to accounts receivable subsidiary ledger and preparing a schedule of accounts receivable
❶❷❸ (25 min)

Check Figure

Schedule of Accounts Receivable $3,230.00

6A-1. Rita Hayle has opened Food on the Go, a wholesale grocery and pizza company, in Edmonton. The following transactions occurred in June:

2016		
June	1	Sold merchandise to Joe Kase Co. on account, $400, invoice No. 702.
	4	Sold merchandise to Sue Moore Co. on account, $600, invoice No. 703.
	8	Sold merchandise to Long Co. on account, $700, invoice No. 704.
	11	Issued credit memorandum No. 34 to Joe Kase Co. for $150 worth of grocery merchandise returned because of spoilage.
	15	Sold merchandise to Sue Moore Co. on account, $180, invoice No. 705.
	18	Sold merchandise to Long Co. on account, $300, invoice No. 706.
	25	Sold merchandise to Joe Kase Co. on account, $1,200, invoice No. 707.

Required

a. Journalize the transactions in the appropriate journals.

b. Record in the accounts receivable subsidiary ledger and post to the general ledger as appropriate.

c. Prepare a schedule of accounts receivable.

Comprehensive problem: recording transactions in sales, cash receipts, and general journals; recording in accounts receivable subsidiary ledger and posting to general ledger; preparing a schedule of accounts receivable
❶❷❸❹ (70 min)

Check Figure

Schedule of Accounts Receivable $5,700.00

6A-2. Mark Peaker owns Peaker's Sneaker Shop of Dartmouth. (In your working papers, balances as of May 1 are provided for the accounts receivable and general ledger accounts.) The following transactions occurred in May:

2015		
May	1	Mark Peaker invested an additional $12,000 in the sneaker store.
	4	Sold $900 worth of merchandise on account to B. Dale, sales invoice No. 160, terms 1/10, n/30.
	4	Sold $500 worth of merchandise on account to Ron Lester, sales invoice No. 161, terms 1/10, n/30.
	8	Sold $200 worth of merchandise on account to Jim Zon, sales invoice No. 162, terms 1/10, n/30.
	11	Received cash from B. Dale in payment of May 4 transaction, sales invoice No. 160, less discount.
	21	Sold $3,000 worth of merchandise on account to Pam Pry, sales invoice No. 163, terms 1/10, n/30.
	22	Received cash payment from Ron Lester in payment of May 4 transaction, sales invoice No. 161.
	22	Collected cash sales, $3,000.
	25	Issued credit memorandum No. 31 to Pam Pry for $2,000 worth of merchandise returned from May 21 sales on account.
	25	Collected cash sales, $7,000.
	28	Received cash from Pam Pry in payment of May 21 sales invoice No. 163. (Don't forget about the credit memo and discount.)
	28	Sold sneaker rack equipment for $300 cash. (Beware.)
	29	Sold merchandise, priced at $4,000, on account to Ron Lester, sales invoice No. 164, terms 1/10, n/30.
	31	Issued credit memorandum No. 32 to Ron Lester for $700 worth of merchandise returned from May 29 transaction, sales invoice No. 164.

Required

a. Journalize the transactions.

b. Record in the accounts receivable subsidiary ledger and post to general ledger as needed.

c. Prepare a schedule of accounts receivable as of May 31.

Journalizing, recording, and posting sales and general journals; preparing a schedule of accounts receivable
❶❷❸ (45 min)

6A-3. Wilson Chan has just taken over a business started by his aunt in Sarnia, Ontario, and moved the company to Regina, Saskatchewan. The company is called Chan's Imported Technology (CIT for short) and has all new customers in the Regina region. CIT specializes in the sale of three types of advanced electronic devices: cell phones (CP), tablet computers (TC), and portable music players (MP). Wilson wants to keep track of each type of sale in total for each month of operations. Wilson employs two salespersons to oversee relations with their customers, and also wants to know the total of sales by salesperson each month. CIT's normal terms are 2% 10 days, net 30 days, but a couple of customers have been granted special terms of 3% 15 days, net 45 days. Here are the sales and sales-related transactions for CIT during their first month of operations in August 2016:

> *Check Figure*
>
> Total of Schedule of Accounts Receivable $69,165.00

2016

Aug. 2 Sold $4,000 (CP) and $5,500 (TC) to JIW Enterprises. Invoice No. 2001. Normal terms. Sold by Heidi Wong (HW hereafter).

4 Sold $3,200 (CP), $1,600 (TC). and $2,600 (MP) to Case-5 Electronics. Invoice No. 2002. Special terms. Sold by Paul Jeffries (PJ hereafter).

5 Sold $2,900 (TC) and $1,200 (MP) to Advanced Technologies in Motion. Invoice No. 2003. Normal terms. Sold by PJ.

6 JIW Enterprises messaged that there was a minor problem with the screens of two of the cell phones they purchased on August 2. Wilson agreed to a credit allowance of $150 and issued credit memorandum No. 101 dated this date. Wilson decided not to keep track of credits by product category or by salesperson.

10 Sold $3,000 (CP), $4,750 (TC), and $1,700 (MP) to Manfred Communications. Invoice No. 2004. Normal terms. Sold by HW.

13 Sold $1,400 (CP), $3,500 (TC), and $850 (MP) to JIW Enterprises. Invoice No. 2005. Normal terms. Sold by HW.

17 Sold $930 (CP), $1,400 (TC), and $1,100 (MP) to Advanced Technologies in Motion. Invoice No. 2006. Normal terms. Sold by PJ.

20 The purchasing manager for Manfred Communications dropped by to mention that there was a memory flaw in one of the portable music players sold to them on August 10. Manfred had already replaced the memory component with their own supply, and so an adjustment in price of $75 was agreed to. Issued credit memorandum No. 102 to Manfred Communications this date.

22 Sold $4,200 (CP), $3,800 (TC), and $1,300 (MP) to WMJ Sales. Invoice No. 2007. Special terms. Sold by HW.

26 Sold $6,200 (TC) to Case-5 Electronics. Invoice No. 2008. Special terms. Sold by PJ.

28 Sold $2,550 (CP), $4,400 (TC), and $1,780 (MP) to Manfred Communications. Invoice No. 2009. Normal terms. Sold by HW.

30 Sold $1,430 (CP), $2,800 (TC), and $1,300 (MP) to Advanced Technologies in Motion. Invoice No. 2010. Normal terms. Sold by PJ.

Required:

a. Enter the above transactions in both a 4-column sales journal and the general journal.

b. Record all transactions to the customers' accounts in the accounts receivable subsidiary ledger.

c. Ensure that the sales journal is completed (including details of salespersons) and cross-added for the month.

d. Post all transactions to the relevant general ledger accounts at month-end. See account numbers below.

e. Prepare a schedule of accounts receivable as of August 31. Please note—if you are also required to complete problem 6-A4 (see following), then you should only prepare this schedule once, after all cash receipts have been recorded.

Here are the general ledger account numbers used by CIT:

Accounts Receivable	1300	CP Sales	4100
Sales Returns and Allowances	4500	TC Sales	4200
Sales Discounts	4550	MP Sales	4300

Journalizing, recording, and posting a cash receipts journal; preparing a schedule of accounts receivable
4 (45 min)

6A-4. Please refer to problem 6-A3. The sales data listed there form the basis for much of this problem.

Check Figure

Total of Schedule of Accounts Receivable $25,110.00

The following cash was received by CIT during August, 2016:

2016		
Aug.	3	W. Chan contributed $50,000 and deposited this in the CIT bank account.
	11	JIW Enterprises paid Invoice No. 2001, less the credit memo, taking discount.
	14	Advanced Technologies in Motion paid Invoice No. 2003, taking discount.
	18	Case-5 Electronics paid Invoice No. 2002, taking their special discount.
	21	Manfred Communications dropped off a cheque in full payment of Invoice No. 2004, less the credit memo, and taking the discount. Although a day late, the discount was approved by W. Chan.
	23	JIW Enterprises paid Invoice No. 2005, taking discount.
	26	Advanced Technologies in Motion paid Invoice No. 2006, taking discount.
	31	WMJ Sales paid half of Invoice 2007, taking the special cash discount on the amount paid.

Required:

a. Enter the above transactions in the cash receipts journal.

b. Record all transactions to the customers' accounts in the AR subsidiary ledger.

c. Ensure that the cash receipts journal is completed and cross-added for the month.

d. Post all transactions to the relevant GL accounts at month-end. See account numbers below.

e. Prepare a schedule of accounts receivable as of Aug. 31, and ensure that the total agrees with GL account number 1300.

The company uses these additional GL account numbers:

Cash	1100
Owner's Equity, W. Chan	3000

Group B Problems

(The forms you need are on pages 6-15 to 6-30 of the *Study Guide with Working Papers.*)

Single-column journal: journalizing and posting to general ledger, recording in accounts receivable subsidiary ledger, and preparing a schedule of accounts receivable
❶ ❷ ❸ (25 min)

Check Figure
Schedule of Accounts Receivable $3,040.00

6B-1. The following transactions occurred for Food on the Go of Edmonton for the month of June:

2016
June
3 Sold merchandise to Joe Kase Co. on account, $800, invoice No. 1.
4 Sold merchandise to Sue Moore Co. on account, $550, invoice No. 2.
7 Sold merchandise to Long Co. on account, $900, invoice No. 3.
11 Issued credit memorandum No. 1 to Joe Kase Co. for $160 worth of merchandise returned because of spoilage.
14 Sold merchandise to Sue Moore Co. on account, $700, invoice No. 4.
18 Sold merchandise to Long Co. on account, $250, invoice No. 5.

Required

a. Journalize the transactions in the appropriate journals.
b. Record in the accounts receivable subsidiary ledger and post to the general ledger as appropriate.
c. Prepare a schedule of accounts receivable.

Comprehensive problem: recording transactions in sales, cash receipts, and general journals; recording in accounts receivable subsidiary ledger and posting to general ledger; preparing a schedule of accounts receivable
❶ ❷ ❸ ❹ (70 min)

Check Figure
Schedule of Accounts Receivable $8,000.00

6B-2. (In your working papers, all the beginning balances needed are provided for the accounts receivable subsidiary and general ledgers.) The following transactions occurred for Peaker's Sneaker Shop of Dartmouth:

2015
May
1 Mark Peaker invested an additional $14,000 in the sneaker store.
3 Sold $2,000 worth of merchandise on account to B. Dale, sales invoice No. 60, terms 1/10, n/30.
4 Sold $900 worth of merchandise on account to Ron Lester, sales invoice No. 61, terms 1/10, n/30.
8 Sold $600 worth of merchandise on account to Jim Zon, sales invoice No. 62, terms 1/10, n/30.
11 Received cash from B. Dale in payment of May 3 transaction, sales invoice No. 60, less discount.
18 Sold $4,000 worth of merchandise on account to Pam Pry, sales invoice No. 63, terms 1/10, n/30.
21 Received cash payment from Ron Lester in payment of May 4 transaction, sales invoice No. 61.
22 Collected cash sales, $6,000.
25 Issued credit memorandum No. 1 to Pam Pry for $500 worth of merchandise returned from May 18 sale.
25 Received cash from Pam Pry in payment of May 18 sales invoice No. 63. (Don't forget about the credit memo and discount.)
28 Collected cash sales, $12,000.
28 Sold sneaker rack equipment for $200 cash. (Beware.)
29 Sold $6,000 worth of merchandise on account to Ron Lester, sales invoice No. 64, terms 1/10, n/30.

May 31 Issued credit memorandum No. 32 to Ron Lester for $800 worth of merchandise returned from May 29 transaction, sales invoice No. 64.

Required

a. Journalize the transactions in the appropriate journals.

b. Record and post as appropriate.

c. Prepare a schedule of accounts receivable as of May 31.

Journalizing, recording, and posting sales and general journals; preparing a schedule of accounts receivable
❶❷❸ (45 min)

6B-3. Wilson Chan has just taken over a business started by his aunt in Sarnia, Ontario, and moved the company to Regina, Saskatchewan. The company is called Chan's Imported Technology (CIT for short) and has all new customers in the Regina region. CIT specializes in the sale of three types of advanced electronic devices: cell phones (CP), tablet computers (TC), and portable music players (MP). Wilson wants to keep track of each type of sale in total for each month of operations. Wilson employs two salespersons to oversee relations with their customers, and also wants to know the total of sales by salesperson each month. CIT's normal terms are 2% 10 days, net 30 days, but a couple of customers have been granted special terms of 3% 15 days, net 45 days. Here are the sales and sales-related transactions for CIT during their first month of operations in August 2016:

Check Figure

Total Schedule of Accounts Receivable $69,580.00

2016

Aug. 2 Sold $3,000 (CP) and $4,600 (TC) to JIW Enterprises. Invoice No. 4001. Normal terms. Sold by Heidi Wong (HW hereafter).

5 Sold $2,600 (CP), $3,600 (TC), and $800 (MP) to Case-5 Electronics. Invoice No. 4002. Special terms. Sold by Paul Jeffries (PJ hereafter).

6 Sold $3,700 (TC) and $1,400 (MP) to Advanced Technologies in Motion. Invoice No. 4003. Normal terms. Sold by PJ.

8 JIW Enterprises messaged that there was a minor problem with the screens of two of the cell phones they purchased on August 2. Wilson agreed to a credit allowance of $220 and issued credit memorandum No. 101 dated this date. Wilson decided not to keep track of credits by product category or by salesperson.

10 Sold $2,800 (CP), $4,800 (TC), and $1,200 (MP) to Manfred Communications. Invoice No. 4004. Normal terms. Sold by HW.

12 Sold $1,750 (CP), $2,900 (TC), and $960 (MP) to JIW Enterprises. Invoice No. 4005. Normal terms. Sold by HW.

16 Sold $1,700 (CP), $2,400 (TC), and $1,200 (MP) to Advanced Technologies in Motion. Invoice No. 4006. Normal terms. Sold by PJ.

21 The purchasing manager for Manfred Communications dropped by to mention that there was a memory flaw in one of the portable music players sold to them on August 10. Manfred had already replaced the memory component with their own supply, and so an adjustment in price of $60 was agreed to. Issued credit memorandum No. 102 to Manfred Communications this date.

23 Sold $3,700 (CP), $4,800 (TC), and $1,500 (MP) to WMJ Sales. Invoice No. 4007. Special terms. Sold by HW.
26 Sold $5,300 (TC) to Case-5 Electronics. Invoice No. 4008. Special terms. Sold by PJ.
29 Sold $3,150 (CP), $4,600 (TC), and $1,460 (MP) to Manfred Communications. Invoice No. 4009. Normal terms. Sold by HW.
30 Sold $1,840 (CP), $2,700 (TC), and $1,400 (MP) to Advanced Technologies in Motion. Invoice No. 4010. Normal terms. Sold by PJ.

Required:

a. Enter the above transactions in both a 4-column sales journal and the general journal.

b. Record all transactions to the customers' accounts in the accounts receivable subsidiary ledger.

c. Ensure that the sales journal is completed (including details of salespersons) and cross-added for the month.

d. Post all transactions to the relevant general ledger accounts at month-end. See account numbers below.

e. Prepare a schedule of accounts receivable as of August 31. Please note—if you are also required to complete problem 6-B4 (see following), then you should only prepare this schedule once, after all cash receipts have been recorded.

Here are the general ledger account numbers used by CIT:

Accounts Receivable	1300	CP Sales	4100
Sales Returns and Allowances	4500	TC Sales	4200
Sales Discounts	4550	MP Sales	4300

Journalizing, recording, and posting a cash receipts journal; preparing a schedule of accounts receivable
4 (45 min)

Check Figure

Total of Schedule of Accounts Receivable $25,450.00

6B-4. Please refer to problem 6-B3. The sales data listed there form the basis for much of this problem.

The following cash was received by CIT during August, 2016:

2016
Aug. 3 W. Chan contributed $40,000 and deposited this in the CIT bank account.
10 JIW Enterprises paid Invoice No. 4001, less the credit memo, taking discount.
14 Advanced Technologies in Motion paid Invoice No. 4003, taking discount.
18 Case-5 Electronics paid Invoice No. 4002, taking their special discount.
22 Manfred Communications dropped off a cheque in full payment of Invoice No. 4004, less the credit memo, and taking the discount. Although two days late, the discount was approved by W. Chan.
22 JIW Enterprises paid Invoice No. 4005, taking discount.
25 Advanced Technologies in Motion paid Invoice No. 4006, taking discount.
31 WMJ Sales paid half of Invoice No. 4007, taking the special cash discount on the amount paid.

Required:

a. Enter the above transactions in the cash receipts journal.

b. Record all transactions to the customers' accounts in the AR subsidiary ledger.

c. Ensure that the cash receipts journal is completed and cross-added for the month.

d. Post all transactions to the relevant GL accounts at month-end. See account numbers below.

e. Prepare a schedule of accounts receivable as of Aug. 31, and ensure that the total agrees with GL account number 1300.

The company uses these additional GL account numbers:

Cash	1100
Owner's Equity, W. Chan	3000

Group C Problems

(The forms you need are on pages 6-31 to 6-47 of the *Study Guide with Working Papers.*)

Multicolumn journal: journalizing and posting to the general ledger, recording in the accounts receivable ledger, and preparing a schedule of accounts receivable
❶❷❸ (50 min)

Check Figure

Schedule of Accounts Receivable $7,855.00

6C-1. The following transactions occurred for Lodge Co. of St. Albert for the month of July:

2016

July	2	Sold upholstery merchandise to Joan Timkins Co. on account, $1,600, invoice No. 115, terms: net 30 days.
	5	Sold carpet merchandise to Chris Cowan Co. on account, $825, invoice No. 116, terms: net 30 days.
	9	Sold upholstery merchandise to Cross & Co. on account, $1,950, invoice No. 117, terms: net 30 days.
	12	Issued credit memorandum No. 1 to Joan Timkins Co. for $400 worth of merchandise returned because of faulty colouring match.
	15	Sold carpet merchandise to Chris Cowan Co. on account, $925, invoice No. 118, terms: net 30 days.
	19	Sold upholstery merchandise to Cross & Co. on account, $930, invoice No. 119, terms: net 30 days.
	23	Sold carpet merchandise to Joan Timkins Co. on account, $2,025, invoice No. 120, terms: net 30 days.

Required

a. Journalize the transactions in the appropriate journals.

b. Record in the accounts receivable ledger and post to the general ledger as appropriate.

c. Prepare a schedule of accounts receivable as of July 31.

Comprehensive problem: recording transactions into sales, cash receipts, and general journals; recording to accounts receivable and posting to general ledger; preparing a schedule of accounts receivable
❶❷❸❹ (70 min)

6C-2. (In your working papers, all the beginning balances needed are provided for the accounts receivable and general ledger.) The following transactions occurred for Bedford Sausage Supply Co.:

2017

Sept.	2	Karen Blum, owner, invested an additional $15,000 in the business.
	3	Sold $1,850 worth of merchandise on account to Petra's Meat Market, sales invoice No. 460, terms 1/10, n/30.
	5	Sold $825 worth of merchandise on account to Chapman's Deli, sales invoice No. 461, terms 1/10, n/30.

Check Figure

Schedule of Accounts Receivable $6,084.60

Sept. 8 Sold $930 worth of merchandise on account to Valemont Variety Meats Co., sales invoice No. 462, terms 1/10, n/30.

12 Received cash from Petra's Meat Market in payment of September 3 transaction, sales invoice No. 460, less discount.

19 Sold $1,500 worth of merchandise on account to Discount Meats, sales invoice No. 463, terms 1/10, n/30.

22 Received cash payment from Chapman's Deli in payment of September 5 transaction, sales invoice No. 461.

23 Collected cash sale, $638.

23 Issued credit memorandum No. 101 to Discount Meats for $300 worth of merchandise returned from September 19 sales on account.

25 Received cash from Discount Meats in payment of September 19 sales invoice No. 463. (Don't forget about the credit memo and discount.)

Sept. 25 Collected cash sales, $813.

26 Sold meat cooling equipment for $900 cash. (Beware.)

29 Sold $1,620 worth of merchandise on account to Chapman's Deli, sales invoice No. 464, terms 1/10, n/30.

30 Issued credit memorandum No. 102 to Chapman's Deli for $420 worth of merchandise returned from September 29 transaction, sales invoice No. 464.

Required

a. Journalize the transactions in the appropriate journals.

b. Record and post as appropriate.

c. Prepare a schedule of accounts receivable as of Sept. 30.

Journalizing, recording, and posting sales and general journals; preparing a schedule of accounts receivable
❶ ❷ ❸ ❹ (45 min)

6C-3. Martha Kuerti has started up a new company called Calgary Camera Company (CCC for short) in the Calgary region. CCC specializes in the sale of four types of cameras to customers in "industrial" settings (means they usually buy several items at a time). The four categories of cameras that CCC sells are: point and shoot (PS), digital single-lens reflex (DS), surveillance cameras (SC), and video cameras (VC). Martha wants to keep track of each type of sale in total for each month of operations. She employs three salespersons to manage relations with customers, and also wants to know the total of sales by salesperson each month. CCC's normal terms are 2% 10 days, net 30 days, but a couple of customers have been granted special terms for selected purchases of 3% 12 days, net 36 days. Here are the sales and sales-related transactions for CCC during their first month of operations in November 2016:

Check Figure

Total of Schedule of Accounts Receivable $157,194.00

2016

Nov. 1 Sold $3,542 (PS), $3,670 (DS), and $5,734 (VC) to West Calgary Tribal Council. Invoice No. 5001. Normal terms. Sold by Fred Jacobs (FJ hereafter).

2 Sold $5,730 (PS), $2,825 (DS), $6,340 (SC), and $1,641 (VC) to KGC Investigations. Invoice No. 5002. Special terms. Sold by Chris Thomas (CT hereafter).

4 Sold $7,420 (PS) and $4,725 (DS) to South Calgary School District. Invoice No. 5003. Special terms. Sold by Grigov Mahlen (GM hereafter).

6 Sold $4,630 (DS) and $3,760 (VC) to Leisure Light Technologies. Invoice No. 5004. Normal terms. Sold by CT.

Nov. 8 KGC Investigations sent an e-mail that there was a minor problem with the lens of several surveillance cameras they purchased on November 2. Martha agreed to a credit allowance of $480 and issued credit memorandum No. 1001 dated this date. Martha decided not to keep track of sales returns by product or by salesperson.

10 Sold $3,742 (PS), $4,896 (DS), and $2,750 (VC) to West Calgary Tribal Council. Invoice No. 5005. Normal terms. Sold by FJ.

12 Sold $4,830 (PS), $3,764 (DS), and $2,467 (VC) to North Calgary College. Invoice No. 5006. Normal terms. Sold by GM.

14 Sold $2,418 (PS), $3,465 (DS), $3,480 (SC), and $1,837 (VC) to South Calgary School District. Invoice No. 5007. Special terms. Sold by GM.

16 Sold $2,830 (PS), $3,560 (DS), and $4,706 (VC) to Leisure Light Technologies. Invoice No. 5008. Normal terms. Sold by CT.

18 Sold $4,626 (PS), $2,416 (SC) and $1,825 (VC) to KGC Investigations. Invoice No. 5009. Normal terms. Sold by CT.

21 The Program Director for North Calgary College explained that there was a flaw in the GPS devices in a camera they purchased on November 12. The camera is otherwise useable, so an adjustment in price of $165 was agreed to. Issued credit memorandum No. 1002 this date.

23 Sold $2,840 (PS), $3,582 (DS), and $1,694 (VC) to SKH Management Company. Invoice No. 5010. Special terms. Sold by FJ.

25 Sold $4,608 (PS) and $6,448 (DS) to South Calgary School District. Invoice No. 5011. Special terms. Sold by GM.

26 Sold $4,006 (PS) and $4,376 (DS) to KGC Investigations. Invoice No. 5012. Special terms. Sold by CT.

29 Sold $7,836 (PS), $3,570 (DS), and $2,330 (VC) to West Calgary Tribal Council. Invoice No. 5013. Normal terms. Sold by FJ.

30 Sold $2,418 (PS), $4,660 (DS), $5,002 (SC), and $840 (VC) to Leisure Light Technologies. Invoice No. 5014. Normal terms. Sold by CT.

Required:

a. Enter the above transactions in both a 5-column sales journal and the general journal.

b. Record all transactions to the customers' accounts in the accounts receivable subsidiary ledger.

c. Ensure that the sales journal is completed (including details of salespersons) and cross-added for the month.

d. Post all transactions to the relevant general ledger accounts at month-end. See account numbers below.

e. Prepare a schedule of accounts receivable as of November 30. Please note—if you are also required to complete problem 6-C4 (see following), then you should only prepare this schedule once, after all cash receipts have been recorded.

Here are the general ledger account numbers used by CCC:

Accounts Receivable	1500	PS Sales	4000
Sales Returns and Allowances	4900	DS Sales	4100
Sales Discounts	4950	SC Sales	4200
		VC Sales	4300

Journalizing, recording, and posting a cash receipts journal and preparing a schedule of accounts receivable
❹ (45 min)

Check Figure

Total of Schedule of Accounts Receivable $65,572.01

6C-4. Please refer to problem 6-C3. The sales data listed there form the basis for much of this problem.

The following cash was received by CCC during November, 2016:

2016
Nov. 3 M. Kuerti contributed $45,000 and deposited this in the CCC bank account.
10 West Calgary Tribal Council paid Invoice No. 5001, taking discount.
11 KGC Investigations paid Invoice No. 5002, after deducting credit memo, taking discount.
16 South Calgary School District paid Invoice No. 5003, taking their special discount.
21 West Calgary Tribal Council paid Invoice No. 5005, taking the discount. Although a day late, the discount was approved by M. Kuerti.
22 North Calgary College paid Invoice No. 5006, less the credit memo, taking discount.
25 Leisure Light Technologies paid Invoice No. 5004 in full.
26 A major supplier, International Cameras, dropped off a cheque for $5,000. This is their agreed share of an advertising campaign. M. Kuerti agreed that the Advertising Expense account was to be credited.
28 South Calgary School District paid Invoice 5007, taking special discount.
30 KGC Investigations paid Invoice 5009 after deducting a discount of 3%. M. Kuerti did not approve the discount anyhow as it is two days late.

Required:

a. Enter the above transactions in the cash receipts journal.

b. Record all transactions to the customers' accounts in the AR subsidiary ledger.

c. Ensure that the cash receipts journal is completed and cross-added for the month.

d. Post all transactions to the relevant GL accounts at month-end. See account numbers below.

e. Prepare a schedule of accounts receivable as of Nov. 30, and ensure that the total agrees with GL account number 1500.

The company uses these additional GL account numbers:

Cash	1100
Owner's Equity, M. Kuerti	3300
Advertising Expense	5001

On-the-Job Training

(The forms you need are on page 6-48 of the *Study Guide with Working Papers.*)

The schedule of accounts receivable and the controlling account must match and the trial balance must balance
❶ ❸ (30 min)

T-1. The bookkeeper of Floore Company records credit sales in a sales journal and returns in a general journal. The bookkeeper did the following:

1. Recorded an $18 credit sale as $180 in the sales journal.
2. Correctly recorded a $40 sale in the sales journal but posted it to B. Blue's account as $400 in the accounts receivable ledger.
3. Made an addition error in determining the balance of J. B. Window Co. in the accounts receivable ledger.
4. Posted a sales return that was recorded in the general journal to the Sales Returns and Allowance account and the Accounts Receivable account but forgot to record it to the B. Katz Co.
5. Added the total of the sales column incorrectly.
6. Posted a sales return to the Accounts Receivable account but not to the Sales Returns and Allowances account. Accounts receivable ledger was recorded correctly.

Could you inform the bookkeeper in writing as to when each error will be discovered?

Comprehensive problem: journalizing and posting to the general and subsidiary ledgers.
❶ ❷ ❸ ❹ (120 min)

CONTINUING PROBLEM

This chapter will require you to record and post the sales and cash receipts transactions shown below.

A month has elapsed since Precision Computer Centre's year-end. Tony Freedman will use four specialized journals for recording business transactions in the month of September—two in this chapter, and two in Chapter 7. To assist you in recording the following transactions, the schedule of accounts receivable as of August 31 is shown below. An updated chart of accounts with the current balance listed for each account is provided on page 298.

The partial September transactions are as follows:

2016		
Sept.	3	Sold $700 worth of merchandise to Taylor Golf on credit, sales invoice No. 12680; terms are 2/10, n/30.
	9	Received from Taylor Golf balance owing as of August 31.
	10	Sold $3,000 worth of merchandise on account to Anthony Pitale, sales invoice No. 12681; terms are 2/10, n/30.
	10	Collected $12,000 for cash sales for the week of September 10.
	17	Collected balance in full from invoice No. 12681, Anthony Pitale.
	23	Sold $4,000 worth of merchandise on account to Vita Needle, sales invoice No. 12682; terms are 4/10, n/30.
	27	Issued credit memorandum to Taylor Golf for $400 worth of merchandise returned, invoice No. 12680.
	30	Sold $1,600 worth of merchandise to Anthony Pitale, invoice No. 12683; terms 2/10, n/30.
	30	Collected full payment from Vita Needle, invoice No. 12682.

Schedule of Accounts Receivable
Precision Computer Centre
August 31, 2016

Taylor Golf	$2,500.00
Carson Engineering	6,240.00
Total Amount Due	**$8,740.00**

Assignment:

(See pages 6-49 to 6-53 in your *Study Guide with Working Papers.*)

1. Journalize the transactions in the appropriate journals (cash receipts, sales, or general journal).
2. Record in the accounts receivable subsidiary ledger and post to the general ledger as appropriate. A partial general ledger is included in the *Study Guide with Working Papers.*
3. Prepare a schedule of accounts receivable, as of September 30, 2016.

PRECISION COMPUTER CENTRE CHART OF ACCOUNTS AND CURRENT BALANCES AS OF 8/31/2016			
Account #	**Account Name**	**Debit Balance**	**Credit Balance**
1000	Cash	1195 00	
1020	Accounts Receivable	8740 00	
1025	Prepaid Rent		
1030	Supplies	450 00	
1040	Merchandise Inventory	7100 00	
1080	Computer Shop Equipment	3800 00	
1081	Accumulated Amortization, Computer Shop Equipment		99 00
1090	Office Equipment	1050 00	
1091	Accumulated Amortization, Office Equipment		20 00
2000	Accounts Payable		1041 00
2030	Other Amounts Payable		1810 18
3000	T. Freedman, Capital		7406 00
3010	T. Freedman, Withdrawals		
3020	Income Summary	2015 00	
4000	Service Revenue		
4010	Sales		20149 82
4020	Sales Returns and Allowances		
4030	Sales Discounts		
5010	Advertising Expense	480 00	
5020	Rent Expense	400 00	
5030	Utilities Expense	95 00	
5040	Phone Expense	146 00	
5050	Supplies Expense		
5060	Insurance Expense		
5070	Postage Expense	25 00	
5080	Amortization Expense, Computer Shop Equipment		
5090	Amortization Expense, Office Equipment		
5100	Miscellaneous Expense	10 00	
5110	Wages Expense	5020 00	
5120	Payroll Benefits Expense	0 00	
5130	Interest Expense		
5140	Bad Debt Expense		
5600	Purchases		
5610	Purchases Returns and Allowances		
5620	Purchases Discounts		
5630	Freight-In		
	Totals	30526 00	30526 00

CHAPTER 7

Special Journals

THE BASICS, PART 2

LEARNING OBJECTIVES

- **LO 1** Entering transactions into the purchases journal, recording to the accounts payable sub-ledger and posting to general ledger accounts, and creating, recording, and posting a debit memorandum (p. 300)
- **LO 2** Understanding how the purchasing function of a business operates and the need for special journals in this area of operations (p. 304)
- **LO 3** Recording transactions in the cash payments journal (including payments to vendors after taking a cash discount), recording to the AP sub-ledger, posting to general ledger accounts, and preparing a schedule of accounts payable (p. 309)

Having a special journal for sales and cash received (see the previous chapter) is only part of the story. Most businesses also maintain special journals for things purchased (the purchases journal), as well as for cash expenditures (the cash disbursements journal, also called the cash payments journal).

This chapter explains how a business uses these two journals to ensure that their record keeping is completed efficiently and accurately. As with the previous chapter, most businesses—even some quite small ones—will use a computer and accounting software to perform these record-keeping tasks. All accounting students will benefit from knowing how these journals are handled in a manual system. That is the purpose of this chapter

DESIGNING AND UNDERSTANDING THE JOURNALS NEEDED FOR PURCHASING

In the previous chapter we saw why and how a business uses special journals to record its sales and cash receipts events, as well as how it handles credit memoranda and cash discounts taken when customers make payments within certain time periods.

It is certainly true that a company must maintain accurate and up-to-the-minute records of sales and credit events, since failing to do this can have serious consequences. It is just as important for a company to keep accurate and current track of their purchasing events, and what they owe to suppliers (sometimes also called vendors). To have products to sell, a merchandising company must pay strict attention to its purchasing processes, and this chapter discusses how accounting and bookkeeping can contribute to managing and keeping appropriate records of this crucial function.

While it might be true that a really small business could use a general journal to record transactions with suppliers, as any business grows it will become impossible to use this method of recording purchases and cash disbursements, for the same reasons that were mentioned in the previous chapter:

1. Using a general journal is very inefficient and results in too much time being taken to record transaction details, and
2. Only one person can use the general journal at a time, so this precludes the possibility of having more than one person recording transactions. Clearly, many businesses today are too large to manage with just a single bookkeeper.

Therefore, in this chapter we will show how most businesses manage the record-keeping functions relating to purchases and writing cheques by using special journals.

Before we take that step however, it will be helpful to mention some of the normal steps a business would take in managing the purchasing and payment functions. Note that some of these steps do not result in bookkeeping entries being made (for example, a purchase order, which will be described shortly), but a fuller appreciation of the major details will assist in understanding the overall process better, and allow students to better function in the business world.

LEARNING UNIT 7-1

Steps Taken in Purchasing Merchandise

LO 1

Entering transactions into the purchases journal, recording to the accounts payable sub-ledger and posting to general ledger accounts, and creating, recording, and posting a debit memorandum

Merchandising companies must take specific steps when they purchase goods for resale. Let's look at the steps Art's Clothing Company took when it ordered goods from Abby Blake Company on April 1.

STEPS TAKEN BY ART'S CLOTHING COMPANY WHEN ORDERING GOODS

Step 1: Prepare a Purchase Requisition at Art's Clothing

Authorized personnel initiate purchase requisitions. No example is shown here because this is strictly an internal form.

The inventory clerk notes a low inventory level of ladies' jackets for resale, so she sends a **purchase requisition** to the purchasing department. A duplicate copy is sent to the accounting department. A third copy remains with the department that initiated the request to allow follow-up on any late or missing shipments.

Step 2: Purchasing Department of Art's Clothing Prepares a Purchase Order

After checking various price lists and suppliers' catalogues, the purchasing department fills out a form called a **purchase order**. This form gives Abby Blake Company the authority to ship the ladies' jackets ordered by Art's Clothing Company (see Figure 7-1). Note that purchase orders do not result in any formal entries on the issuer's books. Most accounting software (such as Sage 50®) can easily handle the issuance of purchase orders. Purchase orders are usually pre-numbered so that they are easy to keep track of.

Figure 7-1
Purchase Order

> Most accounting software can easily create, print, and manage purchase orders. Even in programs such as *Sage 50®*, no accounts are debited or credited when a P.O. is created.

Purchase Order No. 41
Art's Clothing Company
1528 Belle Avenue
Toronto, Ontario M5A 2L4

Purchased From: Abby Blake Company
12 Foster Road
Quebec City, QC G1M 4H3

Date: April 1, 2016
Shipped Via: Freight truck
Terms: 2/10, n/60
FOB: Quebec City

Quantity	Description	Unit Price	Total
100	Ladies' Jackets Code 14-0	$50	$5,000

Art's Clothing
By: Bill Joy

Purchase order number must appear on all invoices.

> There are four copies of the purchase order: (1) (original) goes to supplier; (2) is sent to accounting department; (3) goes to department that initiated purchase requisition; (4) is filed in purchasing department.

Step 3: Sales Invoice Prepared by Abby Blake Company

Abby Blake Company receives the purchase order and prepares a sales invoice. The sales invoice for the seller is the **purchase invoice** for the buyer. A sales invoice is shown in Figure 7-2.

The invoice shows that the goods will be shipped F.O.B. Quebec City. This means that Art's Clothing Company must pay the shipping costs. The sales invoice shows this freight charge. This means that Abby Blake prepaid the shipping costs as a matter of convenience. Art's clothing will repay the freight charges when it pays the invoice.

If both the seller and buyer agree that the seller will pay the freight charges (without adding this cost to the invoice), the purchase order and invoice would say **F.O.B. destination**. **F.O.B.** is short for *Free On Board*, and the term has been in

Figure 7-2
Sales Invoice

Sales Invoice No. 228
Abby Blake Company
12 Foster Road
Quebec City, QC G1M 4H3

Sold to: Art's Clothing Co.
1528 Belle Avenue
Toronto, ON
M5A 2L4

Date: April 1, 2016
Shipped Via: Freight truck
Terms: 2/10, n/60
Your Order No.: 41
FOB: Quebec City

Quantity	Description	Unit Price	Total
100	Ladies' Jackets Code 14-0	$50	$5,000
	Freight		50
			$5,050

constant use for many decades. The term has a legal meaning as well, because if the agreed method of paying for freight is F.O.B. destination, then title to the goods shipped remains with the seller until they arrive and are received. This can have implications for the cost of lost or damaged goods, and can also have an influence on which goods are considered part of a company's ending inventory. If the parties agree that the purchaser will pay the shipping costs, the term is changed to **F.O.B. shipping point**. In many such cases, the purchaser will use a freight company that they have an account with, so no charges for freight will appear on the purchase invoice.

Goods shipped F.O.B. destination would not ordinarily be included in inventory unless they had been received by period end. Perhaps more important than whether goods are considered officially part of ending inventory is the critical matter of ensuring that only invoices for goods received (and therefore counted as inventory) should be entered as purchased (that is, shown as Accounts Payable) at period end. To ensure correct financial reporting, it is essential that proper attention is given to an accurate "cut-off" at period end. The rules are simple: if goods are considered to have been received at period end, then the related invoice must be entered in that period, otherwise, enter the invoice(s) in the following period.

Step 4: Receiving the Goods

When goods are received, Art's Clothing inspects the shipment and completes a **receiving report**. The receiving report verifies that the exact merchandise that was ordered was received in good condition.

Step 5: Verifying the Numbers

Before the invoice is approved for recording and payment, the accounting department must check the purchase order, invoice, and receiving report to make sure that all are in agreement and that no details have been omitted. The form used for checking and approval is an **invoice approval form** (see Figure 7-3). Employees will place their initials in the appropriate blank as they complete their part of the review process.

Remember that Art's Clothing Company does not record this purchase in its accounting records until the *invoice is approved for recording and payment.* However, Abby Blake Company records this transaction in its records when the sales invoice is prepared.

Step 6: Recording the Invoice

The next Learning Unit will discuss details of how invoices are entered, recorded, and posted.

Figure 7-3
Invoice Approval Form

INVOICE APPROVAL FORM	
Purchase order #	________
Requisition check	________
Purchase order check	________
Receiving report check	________
Invoice check	________
Approved for payment	________

This form can be rubber-stamped on invoices by some companies.

Step 7: Make appropriate entries for any goods returned or allowances received.

See Learning Unit 7-2.

Step 8: Make and record all payments due, being sure to take all available discounts.

Taking available discounts is usually a good idea, because the interest rate implicit in terms such as 2% 10, net 30 is equal to about 37% on an annual basis! See Learning Unit 7-3.

Step 9: Prepare a listing of all amounts owed at period end, and ensure that the total of this list agrees exactly with the total of the individual supplier accounts in the accounts payable subsidiary ledger.

Also covered in Learning Unit 7-3.

LEARNING UNIT 7-1 REVIEW

AT THIS POINT you should be able to:

- State the names of both special journals relating to the purchasing function. (p. 300)
- Say whether the sales function is more important than the purchasing function. (p. 299)
- Give at least two reasons for using special journals in purchasing (p. 300)
- State and explain first five steps in the purchasing process. (pp. 300–301)
- Explain the relationship between a purchase requisition, a purchase order, and a purchase invoice. (p. 300)
- Explain why a typical invoice approval form may be used. (p. 302)

Self-Review Quiz 7-1

(The forms you need are on page 7-1 of the *Study Guide with Working Papers*.)

Which of the following statements are true?

1. Recording purchase transactions in a general journal is considered efficient.
2. Most businesses will carefully enter all purchase orders using the purchase order journal.
3. A purchase requisition follows a purchase order.
4. It is important for a company to verify all numbers on a supplier's invoice.
5. In general, cash discounts are so minor they can be ignored.

Solution to Self-Review Quiz 7-1

Number 4 is true.

LEARNING UNIT 7-2

The Purchases Journal and Accounts Payable Subsidiary Ledger

LO 2

Understanding how the purchasing function of a business operates and the need for special journals in this area of operations

Let's look at how Art's Clothing Company journalizes, posts, and records to the accounts payable subsidiary ledger. We will also look at the **purchases journal**, a multicolumn special journal that Art's Clothing Company uses to record the buying of merchandise or other items on account, and the **accounts payable subsidiary ledger**, an alphabetical record of the amounts owed to creditors from purchases on account.

For example, on April 2, Art's Clothing Company records the following in its purchases journal:

- Date: April 2, 2016
- Account Credited: Abby Blake Company
- Date of Invoice: April 1, 2016
- Invoice Number: 228
- Terms: 2/10, n/60
- Accounts payable: $5,050; Purchases: $5,000; Freight-in, $50

As soon as the information is journalized in the purchases journal (see Figure 7-4), you should:

See Figure 7-4 for a complete purchases journal.

1. Record the transaction in the Abby Blake Co. account in the accounts payable subsidiary ledger to indicate that the amount owed is now $5,050. When this is complete, place a ✓ in the PR column of the purchases journal.
2. Post to Freight-In, account 514, in the general ledger right away. When this is complete, record 514 in the PR column under Sundry in the purchases journal.

Note that the normal balance in the accounts payable subsidiary ledger is a credit.

The posting and recording rules are similar to those shown previously in Chapter 6, but here we are looking at the buyer rather than the seller.

THE DEBIT MEMORANDUM

In Chapter 6 (page 259), Art's Clothing Company had to handle returned goods as a seller. It did this by issuing credit memoranda to customers who returned goods or received an allowance on the price. In this part of the chapter, Art's must also handle returns as a buyer. It does this by using debit memoranda. A **debit memorandum** is a piece of paper issued by a customer to a seller, which indicates that a return or allowance is required.

Suppose that, on April 6, Art's Clothing Company had purchased men's hats for $800 from Thorpe Company. On April 9, 20 hats valued at $200 were found to have defective brims. Art's issued a debit memorandum to Thorpe Company, as shown in Figure 7-5. At some point in the future, Thorpe will issue Art's a credit memorandum. Let's look at how Art's Clothing Company handles such a transaction in its accounting records.

Journalizing and Posting the Debit Memo

First, let's look at a transaction analysis chart.

Result of debit memo: debits or reduces Accounts Payable. On seller's books, accounts affected would include Sales Returns and Allowances and Accounts Receivable.

Accounts Affected	Category	↑ ↓	Rules
Accounts Payable	Liability	↓	Dr.
Purchases Returns and Allowances	Expense (Contra)	↑	Cr.

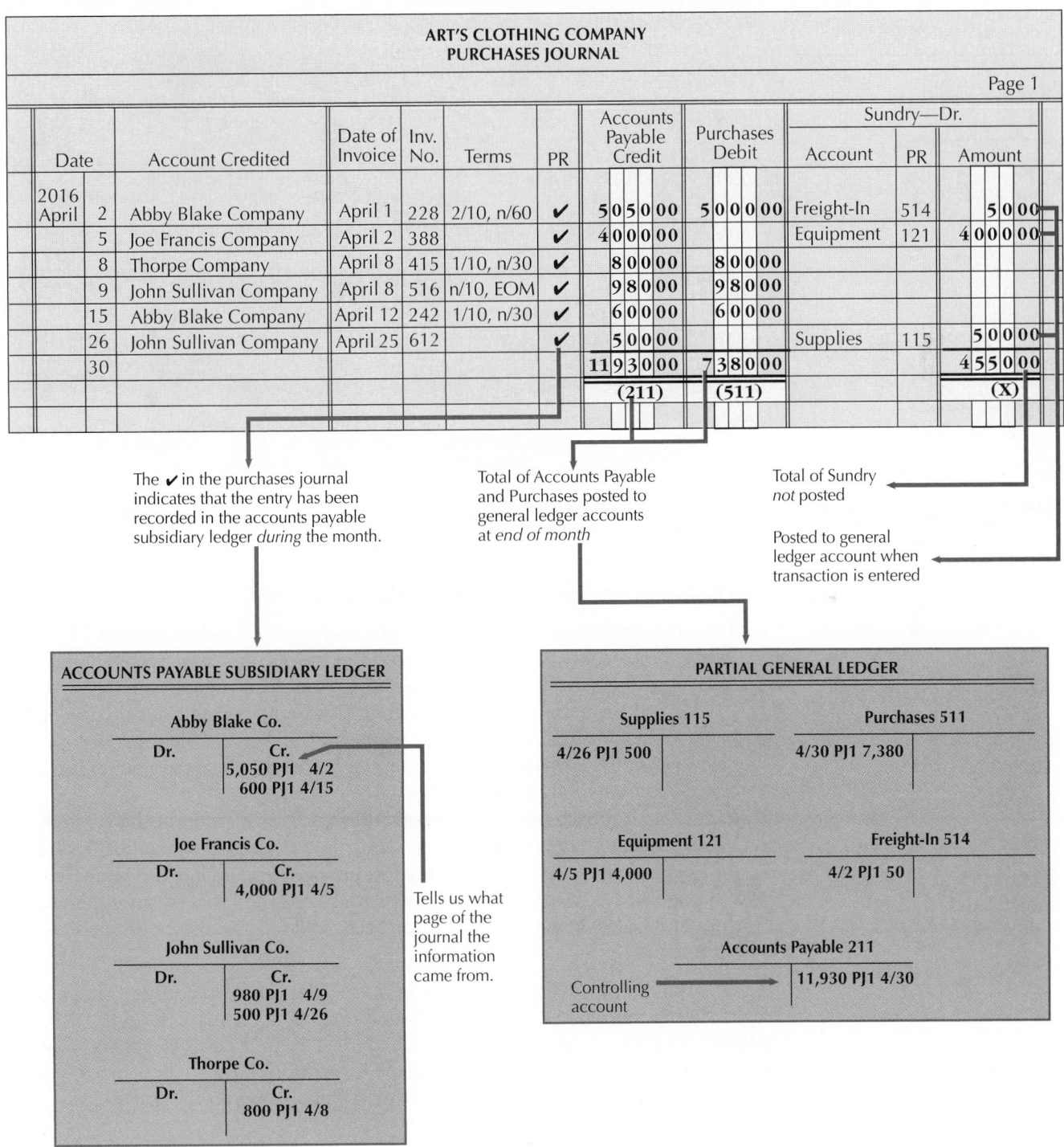

ART'S CLOTHING COMPANY
PURCHASES JOURNAL

Page 1

Date		Account Credited	Date of Invoice	Inv. No.	Terms	PR	Accounts Payable Credit	Purchases Debit	Sundry—Dr. Account	Sundry—Dr. PR	Sundry—Dr. Amount
2016 April	2	Abby Blake Company	April 1	228	2/10, n/60	✔	5050 00	5000 00	Freight-In	514	50 00
	5	Joe Francis Company	April 2	388		✔	4000 00		Equipment	121	4000 00
	8	Thorpe Company	April 8	415	1/10, n/30	✔	800 00	800 00			
	9	John Sullivan Company	April 8	516	n/10, EOM	✔	980 00	980 00			
	15	Abby Blake Company	April 12	242	1/10, n/30	✔	600 00	600 00			
	26	John Sullivan Company	April 25	612		✔	500 00		Supplies	115	500 00
	30						11930 00	7380 00			4550 00
							(211)	(511)			(X)

The ✔ in the purchases journal indicates that the entry has been recorded in the accounts payable subsidiary ledger *during* the month.

Total of Accounts Payable and Purchases posted to general ledger accounts at *end of month*

Total of Sundry *not* posted

Posted to general ledger account when transaction is entered

ACCOUNTS PAYABLE SUBSIDIARY LEDGER

Abby Blake Co.

Dr.	Cr.
	5,050 PJ1 4/2
	600 PJ1 4/15

Joe Francis Co.

Dr.	Cr.
	4,000 PJ1 4/5

John Sullivan Co.

Dr.	Cr.
	980 PJ1 4/9
	500 PJ1 4/26

Thorpe Co.

Dr.	Cr.
	800 PJ1 4/8

Tells us what page of the journal the information came from.

PARTIAL GENERAL LEDGER

Supplies 115

4/26 PJ1 500	

Purchases 511

4/30 PJ1 7,380	

Equipment 121

4/5 PJ1 4,000	

Freight-In 514

4/2 PJ1 50	

Accounts Payable 211

	11,930 PJ1 4/30

Controlling account

Figure 7-4
Purchases Journal

Figure 7-5
Debit Memorandum

Debit Memorandum			No. 1
Art's Clothing Company 1528 Belle Avenue Toronto, ON M5A 2L4			
To: Thorpe Company 3 Access Road Fredericton, NB E3B 4T3			April 9, 2016
WE DEBIT your account as follows:			
Quantity		Unit Cost	Total
20	Men's Hats Code 827—defective brims	$10	$200

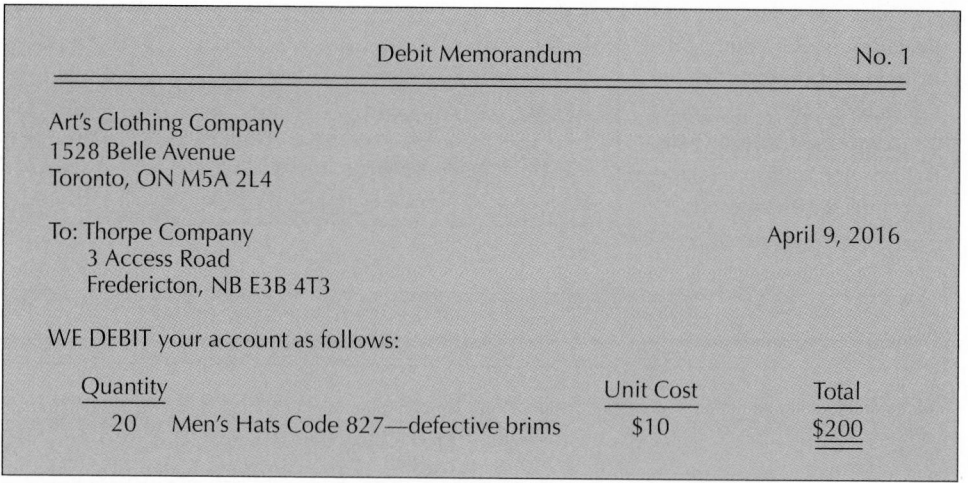

A debit memo shows that Art's does not owe as much money as was indicated in the company's purchases journal.

Next, let's examine the journal entry for the debit memorandum:

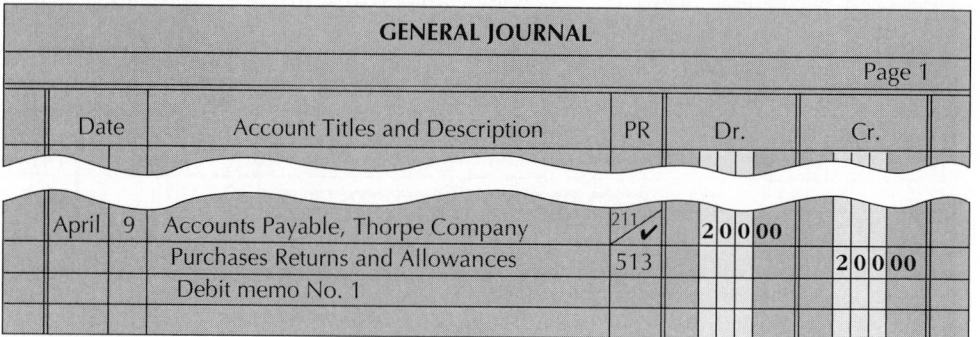

GENERAL JOURNAL

Page 1

Date		Account Titles and Description	PR	Dr.	Cr.
April	9	Accounts Payable, Thorpe Company	211/✓	200 00	
		Purchases Returns and Allowances	513		200 00
		Debit memo No. 1			

Purchases Returns and Allowances	
Dr.	Cr.
−	+

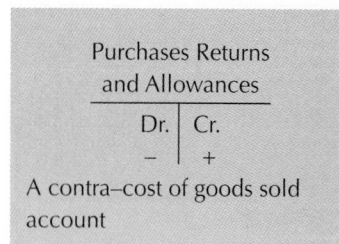

A contra–cost of goods sold account

The two postings and one recording are:

1. 211—Post to Accounts Payable as a debit in the general ledger account 211. When this is done, place in the PR column the account number, 211, above the diagonal on the same line as Accounts Payable in the journal.
2. ✓—Record the debit to Thorpe Co. in the accounts payable subsidiary ledger to show that Art's doesn't owe Thorpe as much money. When this is done, place a ✓ in the journal in the PR column below the diagonal line on the same line as Accounts Payable in the journal.
3. 513—Post to Purchases Returns and Allowances as a credit in the general ledger (account 513). When this is done, place the account number, 513, in the posting reference column of the journal on the same line as Purchases Returns and Allowances. (If equipment were returned that was not merchandise for resale, we would credit Equipment and not Purchases Returns and Allowances.)

It should be mentioned here that debit memos can be recorded using a dedicated special journal if the volume of such documents is high enough. Also, it is possible to enter debit memos into the purchases journal as negative amounts. Both of these methods of entry are almost identical to how a credit memo can be recorded, and since details of that treatment were shown in the last chapter, they are not shown here.

LEARNING UNIT 7-2 REVIEW

AT THIS POINT you should be able to:

- Journalize transactions in a purchases journal. (pp. 270 and 271)
- Explain how to record the accounts payable subsidiary ledger and post to the general ledger from a purchases journal. (p. 304)
- Explain a debit memorandum and be able to journalize an entry resulting from its issuance. (pp. 304–306)

Self-Review Quiz 7-2

(The forms you need are on pages 7-1 to 7-3 of the *Study Guide with Working Papers.*)

Journalize the following transactions in the purchases journal or general journal for Munroe Co. Record in the accounts payable subsidiary ledger and post to general ledger accounts as appropriate. Use the same journal headings that we used for Art's Clothing Company.

2017		
May	5	Bought merchandise on account from Flynn Co., invoice No. 512, dated May 2, terms 1/10, n/30, $900.
	6	Bought merchandise from John Butler Company, invoice No. 403, dated May 5, terms n/10, EOM, $1,000.
	13	Issued debit memo No. 1 to Flynn Co. for merchandise returned, $300, from invoice No. 512.
	16	Purchased $400 worth of equipment on account from John Butler Company, invoice No. 413, dated May 15.

Solution to Self-Review Quiz 7-2

Quiz Tip

Buyer	***Seller***
Issues Debit Memo	Receives Debit Memo
Receives Credit Memo	Issues Credit Memo
Dr. Accounts Payable	Dr. SRA
Cr. PRA	Cr. Accounts Receivable

MUNROE CO.
PURCHASES JOURNAL

Page 2

Date		Account Credited	Date of Invoice	Inv. No.	Terms	PR	Accounts Payable Credit	Purchases Debit	Sundry—Dr. Account	PR	Amount
2017 May	5	Flynn Co.	May 2	512	1/10, n/30	✔	900 00	900 00			
	6	John Butler	May 5	403	n/10, EOM	✔	1000 00	1000 00			
	16	John Butler	May 15	413		✔	400 00		Equip.	121	400 00
	31						2300 00	1900 00			400 00
							(212)	(512)			(X)

MUNROE CO.
GENERAL JOURNAL

Page 1

Date		Account Titles and Description	PR	Dr.	Cr.
2017 May	13	Accounts Payable, Flynn Co.	212/✔	300 00	
		Purchases Returns and Allowances	513		300 00
		Debit memo #1			

ACCOUNTS PAYABLE SUBSIDIARY LEDGER

JOHN BUTLER COMPANY
18 REED ROAD
WINNIPEG, MB R2B 8G6

Date		Explanation	PR	Debit	Credit	Cr. Balance
2017 May	6		PJ2		1000 00	1000 00
	16		PJ2		400 00	1400 00

FLYNN COMPANY
15 FOSS AVENUE
QUEBEC CITY, QC G1L 2W4

Date		Explanation	PR	Debit	Credit	Cr. Balance
2017 May	5		PJ2		900 00	900 00
	13		GJ1	300 00		600 00

PARTIAL GENERAL LEDGER

Equipment — Acct. No. 121

Date		Explanation	PR	Debit	Credit	Dr. or Cr.	Balance
2017 May	16		PJ2	400 00		Dr.	400 00

Accounts Payable — Acct. No. 212

Date		Explanation	PR	Debit	Credit	Dr. or Cr.	Balance
2017 May	13		GJ1	300 00		Dr.	300 00
	31		PJ2		2 300 00	Cr.	2 000 00

Purchases — Acct. No. 512

Date		Explanation	PR	Debit	Credit	Dr. or Cr.	Balance
2017 May	31		PJ2	1 900 00		Dr.	1 900 00

Purchases Returns and Allowances — Acct. No. 513

Date		Explanation	PR	Debit	Credit	Dr. or Cr.	Balance
2017 May	13		GJ1		300 00	Cr.	300 00

LEARNING UNIT 7-3

The Cash Payments Journal and Schedule of Accounts Payable

LO 3 Recording transactions in the cash payments journal (including payments to vendors after taking a cash discount), recording to the AP sub-ledger, posting to general ledger accounts, and preparing a schedule of accounts payable

Art's Clothing Company will record all payments made by cheque in a **cash payments journal** (also called a *cash disbursements journal*). In many ways, the structure of this journal resembles that of the cash receipts journal. Now, however, we are looking at the outward flow of cash instead of the inward flow.

Art's Clothing Company conducted the following cash transactions in April:

2016 April	2	Issued cheque No. 101 to Pete Blum for insurance paid in advance, $900.
	5	Issued cheque No. 102 to Joe Francis Company in payment of its April 2 invoice No. 388.
	9	Issued cheque No. 103 to Rick Flo Co. for merchandise purchased for cash, $800.
	12	Issued cheque No. 104 to Thorpe Company in payment of its April 5 invoice No. 415 less the return and discount.
	26	Issued cheque No. 105, $700, for salaries paid.

The diagram in Figure 7-6 shows the cash payments journal for the end of April, along with the recordings in the accounts payable subsidiary ledger and postings to the general ledger. Study the diagram; we will review it in a moment.

Figure 7-6
Cash Payments Journal Recording and Posting

CASH PAYMENTS JOURNAL

Page 1

Date		Chq. No.	Account Debited	PR	Sundry Accounts Dr.	Accounts Payable Dr.	Purchases Discounts Cr.	Cash Cr.
2016 April	2	101	Pete Blum, Insurance	116	900 00			900 00
	5	102	Joe Francis Company	✔		4000 00		4000 00
	9	103	Flo Co., Cash Purchases	511	800 00			800 00
	12	104	Thorpe Company	✔		600 00	6 00	594 00
	26	105	Salaries	611	700 00			700 00
	30				2400 00	4600 00	6 00	6994 00
					(X)	(211)	(512)	(111)

Posted daily

Individual debits to the accounts payable subsidiary ledger are posted daily. ✔ is placed in PR column when posted.

Total not posted

Individual items are posted during the month to the general ledger.

Total posted

Totals are posted to the general ledger at the end of the month.

ACCOUNTS PAYABLE SUBSIDIARY LEDGER

NAME Abby Blake Co.
ADDRESS 12 Foster Road, Quebec City, QC G1M 4H3

Date		Explanation	PR	Debit	Credit	Cr. Balance
2016 April	2		PJ1		5050 00	5050 00
	15		PJ1		600 00	5650 00

NAME Joe Francis Co.
ADDRESS 2 Roundy Road, Edmonton, AB T5H 2E7

Date		Explanation	PR	Debit	Credit	Cr. Balance
2016 April	5		PJ1		4000 00	4000 00
	5		CPJ1	4000 00		–0–

PARTIAL GENERAL LEDGER

Cash — Account No. 111

Date		Explanation	PR	Debit	Credit	Dr. or Cr.	Balance
2016 April	30		CRJ1	14324 00		Dr.	14324 00
	30		CPJ1		6994 00	Dr.	7330 00

Prepaid Insurance — Account No. 116

Date		Explanation	PR	Debit	Credit	Dr. or Cr.	Balance
2016 April	2		CPJ1	900 00		Dr.	900 00

Figure 7-6 (continued)

NAME John Sullivan Co.
ADDRESS 18 Print Street, Regina, SK S4P 2A6

Date		Explanation	PR	Debit	Credit	Cr. Balance
2016 April	9		PJ1		980 00	980 00
	26		PJ1		500 00	1 480 00

NAME Thorpe Co.
ADDRESS 3 Access Road, Fredericton, NB E3B 4T3

Date		Explanation	PR	Debit	Credit	Cr. Balance
2016 April	8		PJ1		800 00	800 00
	9		GJ1	200 00		600 00
	12		CPJ1	600 00		–0–

Note on Accounts Payable balance: Very occasionally (perhaps because of the return of defective goods after they have been paid for), a debit balance may be called for in Accounts Payable. Debit balances are opposite to the normal credit balance and are signified by placing the balance in brackets. For example, suppose we get a credit note from Joe Francis Co. for $400 after we have paid off its account completely. The account would then appear as follows:

NAME Joe Francis Co.
ADDRESS 2 Roundy Road, Edmonton, AB T5H 2E7

Date		Explanation	PR	Debit	Credit	Cr. Balance
2016 April	4		PJ1		4 000 00	4 000 00
	5		CPJ1	4 000 00		–0–
	15		GJ4	400 00		(400 00)

Controlling Account →

Accounts Payable — Account No. 211

Date		Explanation	PR	Debit	Credit	Dr. or Cr.	Balance
2016 April	9		GJ1	200 00		Dr.	200 00
	30		PJ1		11 930 00	Cr.	11 730 00
	30		CPJ1	4 600 00		Cr.	7 130 00

Purchases — Account No. 511

Date		Explanation	PR	Debit	Credit	Dr. or Cr.	Balance
2016 April	9		CPJ1	800 00		Dr.	800 00
	30		PJ1	7 380 00		Dr.	8 180 00

Purchases Discounts — Account No. 512

Date		Explanation	PR	Debit	Credit	Dr. or Cr.	Balance
2016 April	30		CPJ1		6 00	Cr.	6 00

Salaries Expense — Account No. 611

Date		Explanation	PR	Debit	Credit	Dr. or Cr.	Balance
2016 April	26		CPJ1	700 00		Dr.	700 00

JOURNALIZING, POSTING, AND RECORDING FROM THE CASH PAYMENTS JOURNAL TO THE ACCOUNTS PAYABLE SUBSIDIARY LEDGER AND THE GENERAL LEDGER

Posting and recording rules for this journal are similar to those for the cash receipts journal.

As explained in Chapter 6, Sundry is a miscellaneous accounts column that provides flexibility for reporting infrequent transactions that result in an outflow of cash.

Remember, there is no discount on sales tax or freight.

Figure 7-6 shows how Art's Clothing Company recorded the payment of cash on April 12 to Thorpe Company. The purchases journal (page 305) shows that Art's purchased $800 worth of merchandise from Thorpe on account on April 8. The amount Art's owes is discounted 1%. The amount paid ($800 − $200 returns) is recorded in the accounts payable subsidiary ledger as soon as the entry is made in the cash payments journal. The payment reduces the balance owing to Thorpe to zero. Art's Clothing Company receives a $6 purchases discount.

At the end of the month, the totals of the Cash, Purchases Discounts, and Accounts Payable accounts are posted to the general ledger. The total of Sundry is *not* posted. The accounts Prepaid Insurance, Purchases, and Salaries Expense are posted to the general ledger at the time the entry is put in the journal.

The cash payments journal of Art's Clothing Company can be crossadded as follows:

Debit Columns = Credit Columns

Sundry + Accounts Payable = Purchases Discounts + Cash

$2,400 + $4,600 = $6 + $6,994

$7,000 = $7,000

Schedule of Accounts Payable

Now let's prove that the sum of the accounts payable subsidiary ledger at the end of the month is equal to the controlling account, Accounts Payable, at the end of April for Art's Clothing Company. To do this, creditors with an ending balance in Art's accounts payable subsidiary ledger must be listed in the schedule of accounts payable (see Figure 7-7). At the end of the month, the total owed ($7,130) in Accounts Payable, the **controlling account** in the general ledger, should equal the sum of what is owed the individual creditors who are listed on the schedule of accounts payable. If it doesn't, the journalizing, posting, and recording must be checked to ensure that they are complete. Also, the balance of each account should be checked.

Figure 7-7
Schedule of Accounts Payable

ART'S CLOTHING COMPANY
SCHEDULE OF ACCOUNTS PAYABLE
APRIL 30, 2016

Abby Blake Co.	$5 6 5 0 00
John Sullivan Co.	1 4 8 0 00
Total Accounts Payable	$7 1 3 0 00

Trade Discounts

Trade discounts are not reflected on the books.

Trade discounts are reductions from the "official" selling price. Usually, they are given to customers who buy items to resell or use to produce other saleable goods.

Amount of Trade Discount = List Price − Net Price

Different trade discounts are available to different classes of customers. Often, trade discounts are listed in catalogues that contain the list price and the amount of trade discount available. Such catalogues usually are updated by discount sheets.

Trade discounts have *no relationship* to whether a customer is paying a bill early. Trade discounts and list prices are not shown in the accounts of either the purchaser or the seller. Cash discounts are not taken on the amount of trade discount.

For example, look at the following:

- List price, $800
- 30% trade discount
- 5% cash discount
- *Thus:* Invoice cost of $560 ($800 – $240) less the cash discount of $28 ($560 × 0.05) results in a final cost of $532 if the cash discount is taken.

The purchaser and the seller would record the invoice amount at $560.

At this point it is helpful to say that most companies focus on **net purchases**, which is the resulting amount after deducting **Purchases Discounts** and **Purchases Returns and Allowances** from gross **purchases**. The amounts in the following illustration are made-up:

Purchases		$11,111.11
Less:		
Purchases Discounts	$222.22	
Purchases Returns and Allowances	333.33	555.55
Net Purchases		$10, 555.56

Some companies also include freight in net purchases as well because freight is always a factor in arriving at the true cost of **merchandise** purchased for resale. Regardless whether freight is included in net purchases, it is always shown close to purchases in any financial statements.

LEARNING UNIT 7-3 REVIEW

AT THIS POINT you should be able to:

- Journalize, post, and record transactions utilizing a cash payments journal. (pp. 309–311)
- Prepare a schedule of accounts payable. (p. 312)
- Compare and contrast a cash discount with a trade discount. (pp. 312–313)

Self-Review Quiz 7-3

(The forms you need are on pages 7-3 and 7-5 of the *Study Guide with Working Papers.*)

Given the following information, journalize, cross-add, and, when appropriate, record and post the transactions of Melissa Company. Use the same headings as used for Art's Clothing Company. All purchases discounts are 2/12, n/30. The cash payments journal is page 2.

Accounts Payable Subsidiary Ledger

Name	*Balance*	*Invoice No.*
Bob Finkelstein	$300	488
Al Jeep	200	410

Partial General Ledger

Account No.	*Balance*
Cash 110	$700
Accounts Payable 210	500
Purchases Discounts 511	—
Advertising Expense 610	—

2015

June 1 Issued cheque No. 15 to Al Jeep in payment of its May 25 invoice No. 410, less purchases discount.

7 Issued cheque No. 16 to Moss Advertising Co. to pay advertising bill due, $75, no discount.

8 Issued cheque No. 17 to Bob Finkelstein in payment of his May 28 invoice No. 488, less purchases discounts.

Solution to Self-Review Quiz 7-3

MELISSA COMPANY
CASH PAYMENTS JOURNAL

Page 2

Date		Chq. No.	Account Debited	PR	Sundry Accounts Dr.	Accounts Payable Dr.	Purchases Discounts Cr.	Cash Cr.
2015 June	1	15	Al Jeep	✔		200 00	4 00	196 00
	7	16	Advertising Expense	610	75 00			75 00
	8	17	Bob Finkelstein	✔		300 00	6 00	294 00
					75 00	500 00	10 00	565 00
					(X)	(210)	(511)	(110)

$75 + $500 = $10 + $565

$575 = $575

ACCOUNTS PAYABLE SUBSIDIARY LEDGER

NAME Bob Finkelstein
ADDRESS 112 Flying Highway, Montreal, QC H1K 2H7

Date		Explanation	PR	Debit	Credit	Cr. Balance
2015 June	1	Balance	✔			300 00
	8		CPJ2	300 00		–0–

NAME Al Jeep
ADDRESS 118 Wang Road, London, ON N5X 2Y3

Date		Explanation	PR	Debit	Credit	Cr. Balance
2015 June	1	Balance	✔			200 00
	1		CPJ2	200 00		–0–

Quiz Tip

The balance of the accounts payable subsidiary ledger is zero.

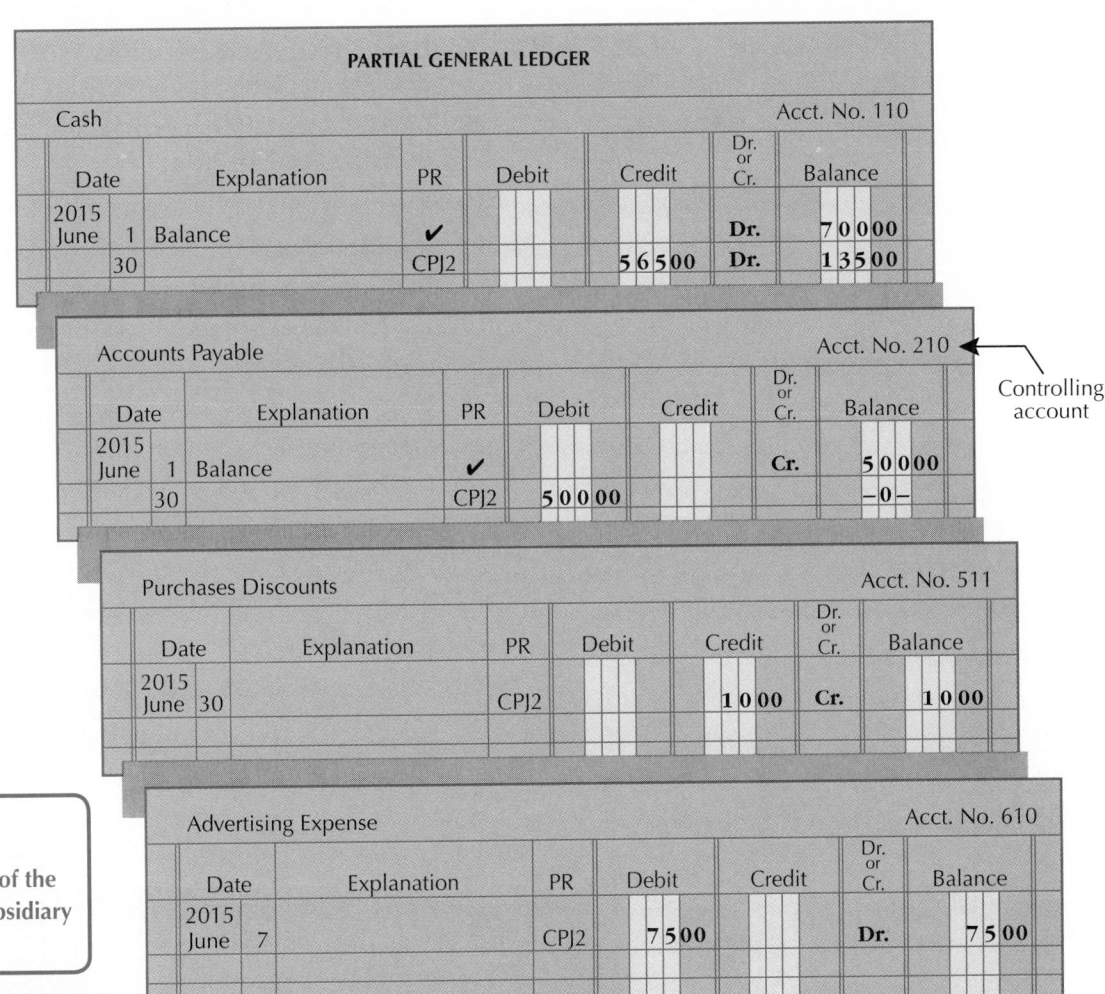

PARTIAL GENERAL LEDGER

Cash — Acct. No. 110

Date		Explanation	PR	Debit	Credit	Dr. or Cr.	Balance
2015 June	1	Balance	✔			Dr.	700 00
	30		CPJ2		565 00	Dr.	135 00

Accounts Payable — Acct. No. 210 ← Controlling account

Date		Explanation	PR	Debit	Credit	Dr. or Cr.	Balance
2015 June	1	Balance	✔			Cr.	500 00
	30		CPJ2	500 00			–0–

Purchases Discounts — Acct. No. 511

Date		Explanation	PR	Debit	Credit	Dr. or Cr.	Balance
2015 June	30		CPJ2		10 00	Cr.	10 00

Advertising Expense — Acct. No. 610

Date		Explanation	PR	Debit	Credit	Dr. or Cr.	Balance
2015 June	7		CPJ2	75 00		Dr.	75 00

! *Quiz Tip*

The normal balance of the accounts payable subsidiary ledger is a credit.

Chapter Assignments

COMPREHENSIVE DEMONSTRATION PROBLEM WITH SOLUTION TIPS*

(The forms you need are on pages 7-5 to 7-11 of the *Study Guide with Working Papers.*) Many instructors will ask students to complete this problem by handling both the material in this chapter and Chapter 6 at the same time. Reminder—the forms for both chapters are found in Chapter 7 pages of the *Study Guide with Working Papers.*

a. Journalize, record, and post the following transactions as needed to the sales, purchases, cash receipts, cash payments, and general journals. All terms are 2/10, n/30 on both sales and purchases.

b. Prepare a schedule of accounts receivable and accounts payable.

	2016		
CRJ	July	2	Walter Lantz invested $8,000 in the business.
PJ		3	Purchased $2,000 merchandise from Patel & Sons, their invoice No. 756.
SJ		4	Sold merchandise on account to Panda Co., invoice No. 1—$300.
SJ		5	Sold merchandise on account to Buzzard Co., invoice No. 2—$600.
CR		6	Cash sale—$400.

*Includes material from Chapters 6 & 7

GJ July 8 Issued credit memorandum No. 1 to Panda Co. for defective merchandise—$100.

9 Purchased $1,150 merchandise from Black Brothers, their invoice No. 2014.

10 Returned $400 defective merchandise to Patel & Sons.

CRJ 11 Received cheque from Panda Co. for invoice No. 1 less returns and discount.

12 Paid amount owing to Black Brothers, cheque 101.

CRJ 16 Cash sale—$500.

SJ 19 Sold merchandise on account to Panda Co.—$550, invoice No. 3.

22 Purchased $1,800 merchandise from Black Brothers, their invoice No. 2092.

24 Purchased $1,700 store display equipment from Adkins & Co., their invoice No. 1762.

26 Paid amount due to Adkins & Co., cheque 102.

29 Wrote cheque 103 for $250 to City News for ad.

31 Cheque 104 to Fern Supplies for cash purchase. Invoice No. 2178—$640.00.

Recorded immediately in subsidiary ledger.

WALTER LANTZ CO.
SALES JOURNAL

Page 1

Date		Account Debited	Terms	Invoice No.	PR	Dr. Accts. Rec. Cr. Sales
2016 July	4	Panda Co.	2/10, n/30	1	✔	300 00
	5	Buzzard Co.	2/10, n/30	2	✔	600 00
	19	Panda Co.	2/10, n/30	3	✔	550 00
	31					1 450 00
						(112) (411)

Total posted at end of month to general ledger accounts.

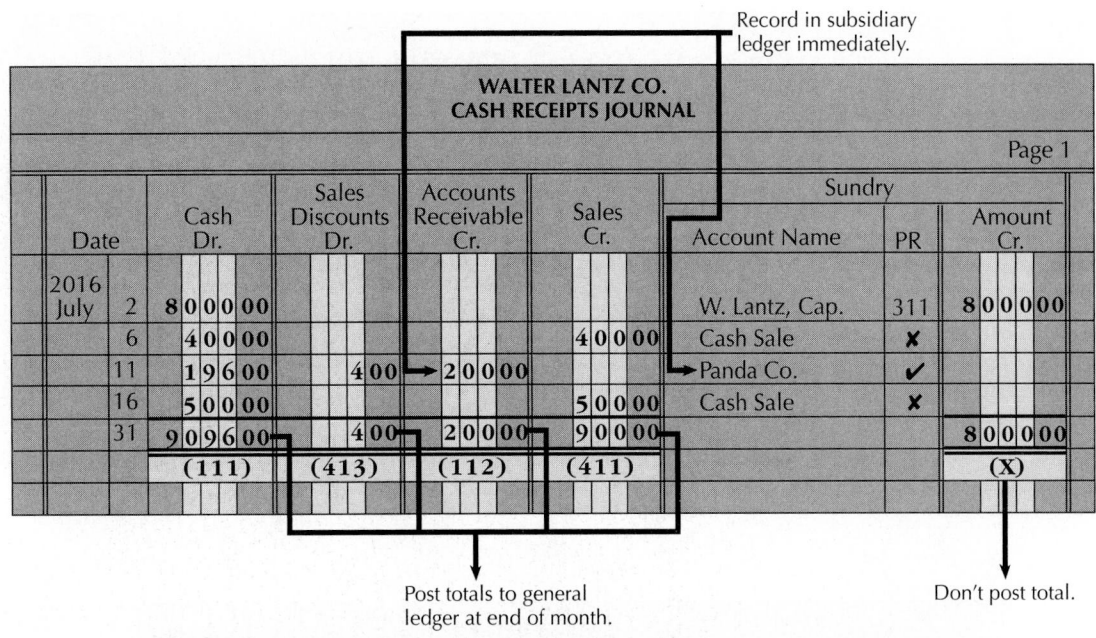

Record in subsidiary ledger immediately.

WALTER LANTZ CO.
CASH RECEIPTS JOURNAL

Page 1

Date		Cash Dr.	Sales Discounts Dr.	Accounts Receivable Cr.	Sales Cr.	Sundry Account Name	Sundry PR	Sundry Amount Cr.
2016 July	2	8,000 00				W. Lantz, Cap.	311	8,000 00
	6	400 00			400 00	Cash Sale	✘	
	11	196 00	4 00	200 00		Panda Co.	✔	
	16	500 00			500 00	Cash Sale	✘	
	31	9,096 00	4 00	200 00	900 00			8,000 00
		(111)	(413)	(112)	(411)			(X)

Post totals to general ledger at end of month.

Don't post total.

GENERAL JOURNAL Page 1

Date		Account Titles and Description	PR	Dr.	Cr.
2016 July	8	Sales Returns and Allowances	412	100 00	
		Accounts Receivable, Panda Co.	112/✔		100 00
		Issued credit memo			

Post immediately to general ledger.

Recorded immediately in subsidiary ledger.

Note: **It is acceptable to enter this CM as a negative amount in the Sales Journal, but this is not illustrated here**

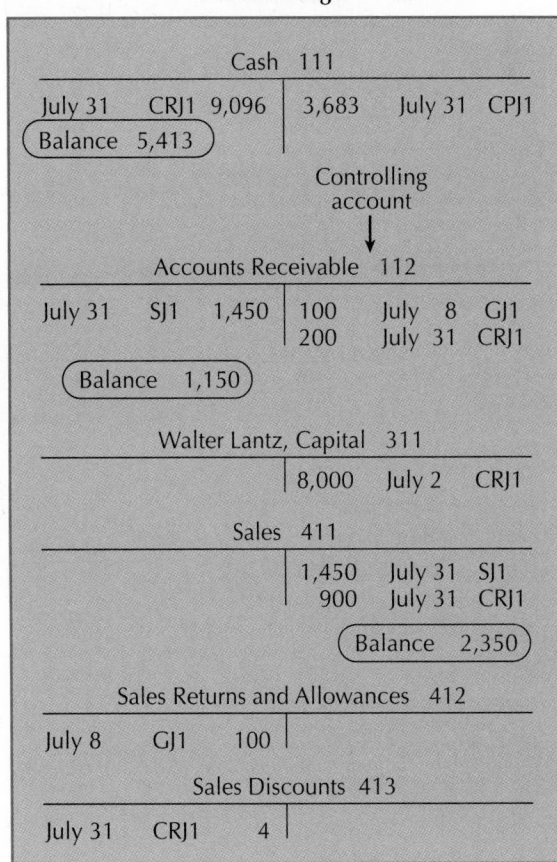

Accounts receivable subsidiary ledger usually contains accounts with debit balances

Accounts Receivable Subsidiary Ledger

Buzzard Co.

Date		PR	Debit	Credit	Dr. Balance
2016 July	5	SJ1	600 00		600 00

Panda Co.

Date		PR	Debit	Credit	Dr. Balance
2016 July	4	SJ1	300 00		300 00
	8	GJ1		100 00	200 00
	11	CRJ1		200 00	–0–
	19	SJ1	550 00		550 00

General Ledger

Cash 111

Debit			Credit		
July 31	CRJ1	9,096	3,683	July 31	CPJ1
Balance 5,413					

Controlling account

Accounts Receivable 112

Debit			Credit		
July 31	SJ1	1,450	100	July 8	GJ1
			200	July 31	CRJ1
Balance 1,150					

Walter Lantz, Capital 311

Debit			Credit		
			8,000	July 2	CRJ1

Sales 411

Debit			Credit		
			1,450	July 31	SJ1
			900	July 31	CRJ1
			Balance 2,350		

Sales Returns and Allowances 412

Debit			Credit
July 8	GJ1	100	

Sales Discounts 413

Debit			Credit
July 31	CRJ1	4	

WALTER LANTZ CO.
PURCHASES JOURNAL

Page 1

Date		Accounts Credited	Date of Invoice	Invoice Number	Terms	PR	Accounts Payable Cr.	Purchases Dr.	Sundry Dr. Account	Sundry Dr. PR	Sundry Dr. Amount
2016 July	3	Patel & Sons	July 3	756	2/10, N/30	✔	2000 00	2000 00			
	9	Black Brothers	July 7	2014	2/10, N/30	✔	1150 00	1150 00			
	22	Black Brothers	July 21	2092	2/10, N/30	✔	1800 00	1800 00			
	24	Adkins & Co.	July 24	1762	2/10, N/30	✔	1700 00		Equipment	141	17000 00
							6650 00	4950 00			17000 00
							(211)	(555)			(X)

Don't post this!

WALTER LANTZ CO.
CASH PAYMENTS JOURNAL

Page 1

Date		Chq. No.	Accounts Debited	PR	Sundry Dr.	Accounts Payable Dr.	Purchases Dr.	Purchases Discount Cr.	Cash Cr.
2016 July	12	101	Black Brothers	✔		1150 00		23 00	1127 00
	26	102	Adkins & Co.	✔		1700 00		34 00	1666 00
	29	103	City News - Adv.	601	250 00				250 00
	31	104	Fern Supplies				640 00		640 00
			Monthly Totals		250 00	2850 00	640 00	57 00	3683 00
					(X)	(211)	(555)	(558)	(111)

Total is not posted.

WALTER LANTZ CO.
GENERAL JOURNAL

Page 1

Date		Account Titles and Description	PR	Dr.	Cr.
2016 July	10	Accounts Payable—Patel & Sons	211/✔	400 00	
		Purchases Returns & Allowances	556		400 00
		Return of Goods—See Inv. 756			

Note: The above debit memo could be recorded as a negative amount in the Purchases Journal, but that treatment is not illustrated here.

WALTER LANTZ Co.
Accounts Payable Ledger

Patel & Sons

Date		Explanation	PR	Debit	Credit	Cr. Balance
2016 July	3		PJ1		2000 00	2000 00
	10		GJ1	400 00		1600 00

Black Brothers

Date		Explanation	PR	Debit	Credit	Cr. Balance
2016 July	9		PJ1		1150 00	1150 00
	12		CPJ1	1150 00		–0–
	22		PJ1		1800 00	1800 00

Adkins & Co.

Date		Explanation	PR	Debit	Credit	Cr. Balance
2016 July	24		PJ1		1700 00	1700 00
	26		CPJ1	1700 00		–0–

Partial General Ledger

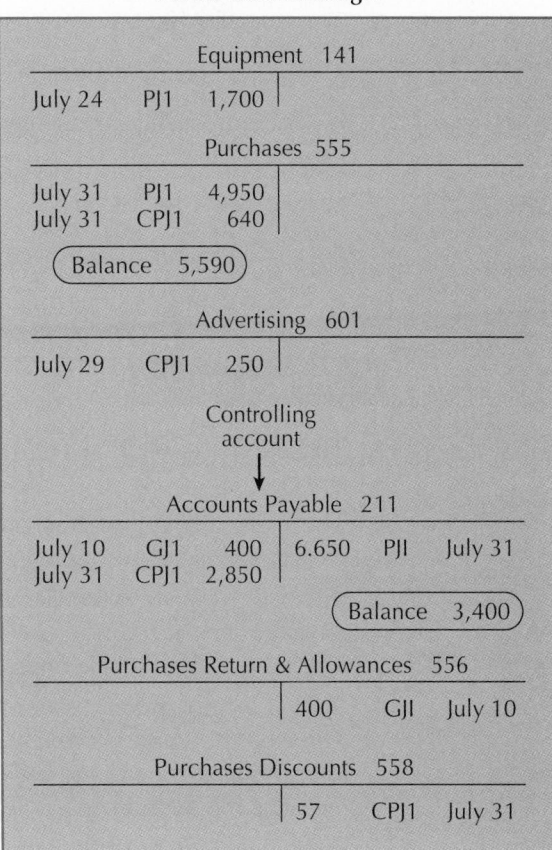

Equipment 141

Debit	Credit
July 24 PJ1 1,700	

Purchases 555

Debit	Credit
July 31 PJ1 4,950	
July 31 CPJ1 640	
Balance 5,590	

Advertising 601

Debit	Credit
July 29 CPJ1 250	

Controlling account ↓

Accounts Payable 211

Debit	Credit
July 10 GJ1 400	6.650 PJI July 31
July 31 CPJ1 2,850	
	Balance 3,400

Purchases Return & Allowances 556

Debit	Credit
	400 GJI July 10

Purchases Discounts 558

Debit	Credit
	57 CPJ1 July 31

The controlling accounts (Accounts Receivable and Accounts Payable) at the end of the month equal the sum of the accounts receivable and accounts payable subsidiary ledger.

WALTER LANTZ CO. SCHEDULE OF ACCOUNTS RECEIVABLE JULY 31, 2016	
Buzzard Co.	$ 600 00
Panda Co.	550 00
Total Accounts Receivable	$1150 00

WALTER LANTZ CO. SCHEDULE OF ACCOUNTS PAYABLE JULY 31, 2016	
Patel & Sons	$ 1600 00
Black Brothers	1800 00
Total Accounts Payable	$3400 00

SUMMARY OF KEY POINTS

Learning Unit 7-1

1. It is equally important to record purchasing and payment transactions as it is to record sales and receipts.
2. Using the General Journal to record these transactions is inefficient as well as impossible for larger firms.
3. The steps for buying merchandise from a company may include:
   - **a.** The requesting department prepares a purchase requisition.
   - **b.** The purchasing department prepares a purchase order.
   - **c.** The seller receives the order and prepares a sales invoice (a purchase invoice for the buyer).
   - **d.** The buyer receives the goods and prepares a receiving report.
   - **e.** The accounting department verifies and approves the invoice for payment.

Learning Unit 7-2

1. The purchases journal records the buying of merchandise or other items on account.
2. The accounts payable subsidiary ledger, organized in alphabetical order, is not in the same book as Accounts Payable, the controlling account in the general ledger.
3. Invoices from suppliers are entered in the Purchases Journal, and recorded to the supplier's account in the AP Subsidiary Ledger. The total of the Purchases Journal is posted to the controlling account at month-end.
4. A debit memorandum (issued by the buyer) indicates that the amount owed from a previous purchase is being reduced because some goods were defective or not up to a specific standard and thus were returned or an allowance was requested. On receiving the debit memorandum, the seller should issue a credit memorandum.
5. Debit Memos are both recorded to the individual supplier's account as well posted to the controlling account in the General Ledger.

Learning Unit 7-3

1. All payments by cheque are recorded in the cash payments journal.
2. At the end of the month, the schedule of accounts payable, a list of ending amounts owed to individual creditors, should equal the ending balance in Accounts Payable, the controlling account in the general ledger.
3. Trade discounts are deductions off the list price that have nothing to do with early payments (cash discounts). Invoice amounts are recorded after the trade discount is deducted. Cash discounts are calculated on the cost after deducting any trade discounts.

KEY TERMS

Accounts payable subsidiary ledger A book or file that contains the names of the creditors in alphabetical order and the amounts owed from purchases on account (p. 304)

Cash payments journal (cash disbursements journal) A special journal that records all transactions involving payment by cheque (p. 309)

Controlling account (AP) The account in the general ledger that summarizes or controls a subsidiary ledger. *Example:* The Accounts Payable account in the general ledger is the controlling account for the accounts payable subsidiary ledger. After postings are complete, it shows the total amount owed from purchases made on account. (p. 312)

Debit memorandum A memo issued by a purchaser to a seller, indicating that some purchases returns and allowances have occurred and therefore the purchaser now owes less money on account (p. 304)

F.O.B. "Free on board," which means without shipping charge to the buyer up to a specified location. The seller bears the cost up to the specified location and the buyer bears the cost from that location to the actual destination. (p. 301)

F.O.B. destination *Seller* pays or is responsible for the cost of freight to the destination or purchaser's location (p. 301)

F.O.B. shipping point *Purchaser* pays or is responsible for the shipping costs from the seller's shipping point to the purchaser's location (p. 302)

Invoice approval form The accounting department uses this form to check the invoice and finally approve it for recording and payment (p. 302)

Merchandise Goods brought into a store for resale to customers (p. 313)

Net purchases Gross purchases less purchases returns and allowances and purchases discounts (p. 313)

Purchase invoice The seller's sales invoice, which is sent to the purchaser (p. 301)

Purchase order A form used in business to place an order to buy goods from a seller (p. 300)

Purchase requisition A form used within a business by the requesting department asking the purchasing department of the business to buy specific goods (p. 300)

Purchases Merchandise bought for resale. It is an expense. (p. 313)

Purchases Discounts A contra-expense account in the general ledger that records discounts offered by suppliers of merchandise for prompt payment of purchases by buyers. Normally has a credit balance. (p. 313)

Purchases journal A multicolumn special journal that records the buying of merchandise or other items on account (p. 304)

Purchases Returns and Allowances A contra-expense account with a credit balance in the ledger that records the amount of defective or unacceptable merchandise returned to suppliers and/or price reductions given for defective items sold (p. 313)

Receiving report A business form used to notify purchasing and accounting of the ordered goods received, indicating the quantities and specific condition of the goods (p. 302)

Special journal A journal used to record similar groups of transactions. *Example:* the purchases journal, which records all purchases on account (p. 251)

Subsidiary ledger A ledger that contains accounts of a single type. *Example:* the accounts payable subsidiary ledger, which records all vendors that sell goods on account (p. 251)

Sundry accounts Miscellaneous accounts column(s) in a special journal, which records transactions that do not occur often (p. 259)

QUICK REVIEW

The following Tips are from Learning Units 7-1 to 7-3. Answer the Assess Your Progress questions and use the How Did You Do? at the bottom of the page to see how well you know the material. The Quick Review provides tips before each Assess Your Progress to help you avoid common accounting errors.

LU 7-1 Steps Taken in Purchasing Merchandise

Tips: Merchandise for resale to customers is called a purchase. The Purchases account is a cost that will be shown on the income statement. This cost works just like expenses but is directly related to bringing the goods for resale into the store. If shipping terms are F.O.B. destination, the seller will pay the cost of freight.

Assess Your Progress

Answer true or false to the following statements:

1. The first step in the Purchasing function is to create a Purchase Requisition.
2. Purchases Discounts is an expense.
3. F.O.B. shipping point means that the seller of the goods is responsible for covering the shipping costs.
4. Invoices received from a supplier should be carefully checked for a number of factors, including accuracy.
5. A credit memorandum received will result in an increase in Accounts Payable.

LU 7-2 The Purchases Journal and Accounts Payable Subsidiary Ledger

Tips: The accounts payable subsidiary ledger lists the amounts owed to each customer. It is just the opposite of the accounts receivable subsidiary ledger. The normal balance of the accounts payable subsidiary ledger is a credit. The controlling account, Accounts Payable, is located in the general ledger. The cost of freight is recorded in the Freight-In account. It has a debit balance. A debit memorandum means the buyer does not owe as much and thus Accounts Payable is reduced and a Purchases Returns and Allowances entry results. The debit memorandum also reduces what is owed to the customer in the subsidiary ledger.

Assess Your Progress

Answer true or false to the following statements:

1. Purchases Returns and Allowances is increased by a debit.
2. Freight-In is a cost that will be shown on the income statement.
3. The controlling account, Accounts Payable, is located in the subsidiary ledger.
4. The normal balance of each customer in the accounts payable subsidiary ledger is a credit.
5. Debit memoranda are issued by the seller.

LU 7-3 The Cash Payments Journal and Schedule of Accounts Payable

Tips: When a cash payment is made within the discount period from a charge purchase, the result is a debit to Accounts Payable and the subsidiary account and a credit to Purchases Discounts and Cash. Remember that Purchases Discounts is a contra-expense account with a normal credit balance. At the end of the month the total from the schedule of accounts payable should equal the ending balance in Accounts Payable, the controlling account.

Assess Your Progress

Answer true or false to the following statements:

1. Purchases Discounts is a contra-revenue account.
2. The schedule of accounts payable is listed by debits and credits.
3. An increase in Purchases Discounts is made by debiting the account.

4. Purchases Discounts are shown on the balance sheet.
5. The normal balance of each customer in the accounts payable subsidiary ledger is a debit.

How Did You Do? Answers to the Assess Your Progress Questions

LU 7-1

1. True.
2. False—Purchases Discounts is a contra-expense.
3. False—F.O.B. shipping point means that the buyer of the goods is responsible for covering the shipping costs.
4. True.
5. False—A credit memorandum received by the purchaser will result in a decrease in Accounts Payable.

LU 7-2

1. False—Purchases Returns and Allowances is increased by a credit.
2. True.
3. False—The controlling account, Accounts Payable, is located in the general ledger.
4. True.
5. False—Debit memoranda are issued by the buyer.

LU 7-3

1. False—Purchases Discounts is a contra-expense account.
2. False—The schedule of accounts payable contains no debits or credits.
3. False—An increase in Purchases Discounts is made by crediting the account.
4. False—Purchases Discounts are shown on the income statement.
5. False—The normal balance of each customer in the accounts payable subsidiary ledger is a credit.

BLUEPRINT OF PURCHASES AND CASH PAYMENTS JOURNALS

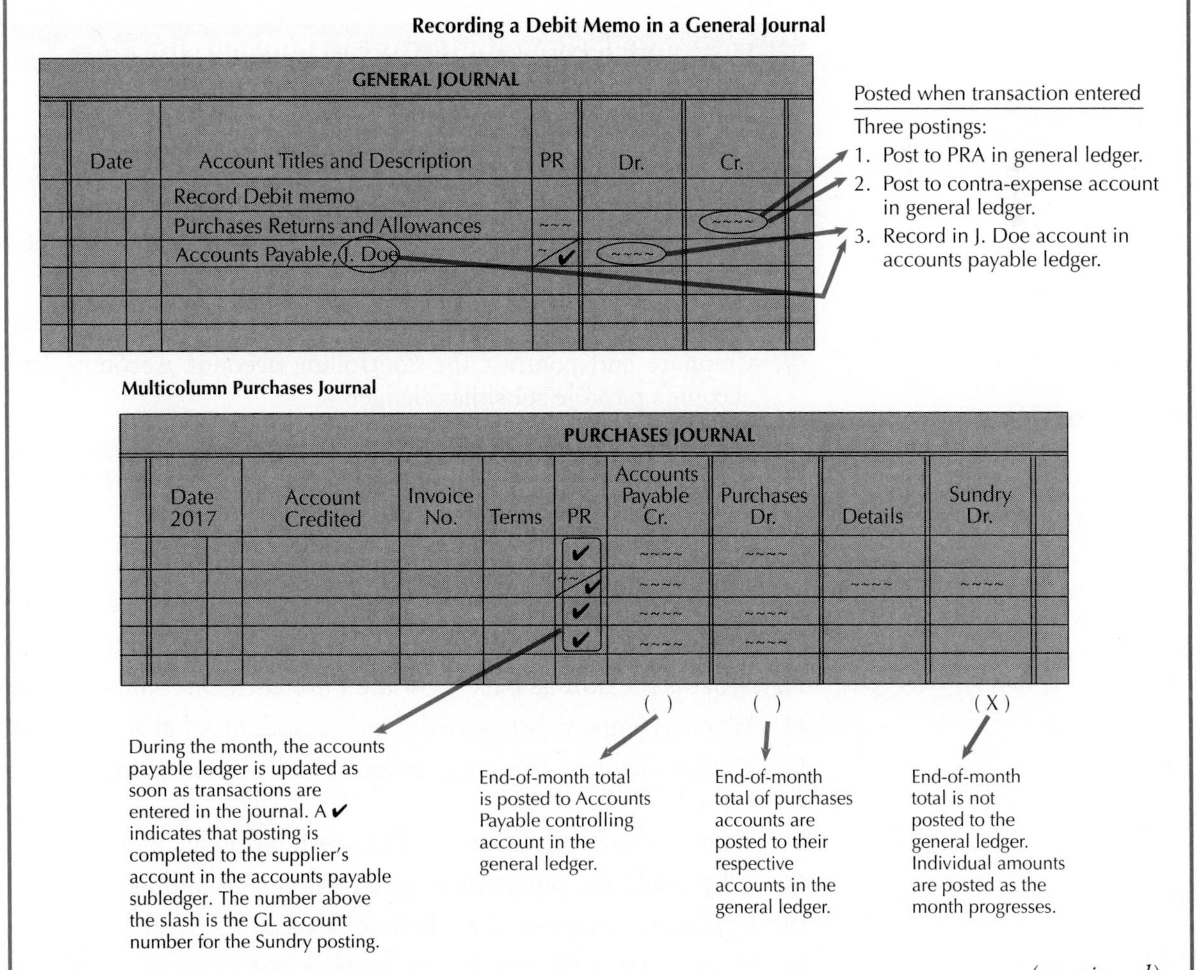

(continued)

Cash Payments Journal without GST

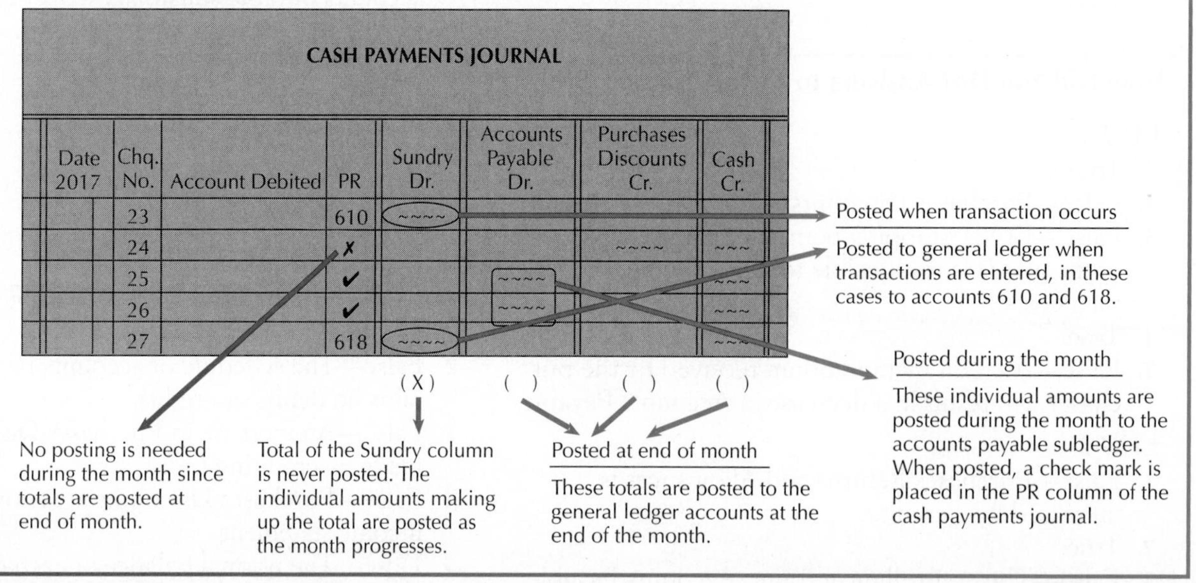

QUESTIONS, CLASSROOM DEMONSTRATION EXERCISES, EXERCISES, AND PROBLEMS

Discussion Questions and Critical Thinking/Ethical Case

1. Explain the purpose of a contra-expense account.
2. What is the normal balance of purchases discounts?
3. Give two examples of contra-expense accounts.
4. What is the difference between a discount period and a credit period?
5. Explain the terms (a) 2/10, n/30; (b) n/10, EOM.
6. If special journals are used, what purpose will a general journal serve?
7. Compare and contrast the controlling account Accounts Payable with the accounts payable subsidiary ledger.
8. Explain how to calculate net purchases.
9. Why is the accounts payable subsidiary ledger organized in alphabetical order?
10. When is a purchases journal used?
11. What is an invoice? What purpose does it serve?
12. Explain the difference between F.O.B. shipping point and F.O.B. destination.
13. Explain the relationship between a purchase requisition and a purchase order.
14. What is the normal balance of the Purchases Discounts account?
15. When a company issues a debit memorandum, what accounts will be affected?
16. Explain the main difference between a cash receipts journal and a cash payments journal.
17. When is the Sundry column of the cash payments journal posted?
18. Why would the purchaser issue a debit memorandum?
19. Explain the purpose of a schedule of accounts payable.
20. Frank Patel is the purchasing manager for Amazing Appliance Company of Edmonton. Near the year end he calls you into his office and suggests that there

are three large invoices from suppliers of merchandise the company has already received and will count in the year-end inventory. He asks you to not enter these invoices until the new year has begun. He reasons that this will help the "bottom line" this year by reducing the Purchases account, and this is necessary because the bank has shown some concern about falling profits in recent years, and may reduce the company's operating credit line, which Frank says would be a serious matter. Write down your response to Frank's suggestion.

MyAccountingLab

Make the grade with MyAccountingLab! The exercises and problems marked with ● can be found on MyAccountingLab. You can practise them as often as you want, and many of them feature step-by-step guided solutions to help you find the right answer.

Classroom Demonstration Exercises

(The forms you need are on pages 7-11 and 7-12 of the *Study Guide with Working Papers.*)

Overview

Recording transactions
❷ (10 min)

1. Complete the following table for Purchases Returns and Allowances, Purchases, and Purchases Discounts:

Accounts Affected	Category	↑ ↓	Rules	Temporary or Permanent

Calculating Net Purchases

Net purchases
❷ (10 min)

2. Given the following, calculate net purchases:

Gross purchases	$64
Purchases returns and allowances	7
Purchases discounts	3

Purchases Journal, General Journal, Recording, and Posting

Purchase transactions
❷ (10 min)

3. For each of the three transactions below, indicate which of these procedures should be used (more than one number can be used).

1. Journalize in purchases journal.
2. Record immediately in subsidiary ledger.
3. Post totals from the purchases journal (except Sundry total) at the end of the month to the general ledger.
4. Journalize in the general journal.
5. Immediately record in subsidiary ledgers and post to the general ledger.

   a. Bought merchandise on account from Also Co., invoice No. 12, $20.

   b. Bought equipment on account from Jones Co., invoice No. 13, $40.

   c. Issued debit memo No. 1 to Also Co. for merchandise returned, $4, from invoice No. 12.

Recording Transactions in Special Journals

Journalizing sales and purchases
❶ ❷ ❸ (10 min)

4. Indicate in which of these five journals each transaction described below will be journalized:

1. SJ
2. PJ
3. CRJ
4. CPJ
5. GJ

—— **a.** Issued credit memo No. 2, $13.
—— **b.** Cash sales, $20.
—— **c.** Received cheque from Blue Co., $50, less 3% discount.
—— **d.** Bought merchandise on account from Mel Co., $35, 1/10, n/30, invoice No. 20.
—— **e.** Cash purchase, $15.
—— **f.** Issued debit memo to Mel Co., $15 for merchandise returned from invoice No. 20.

Schedule of accounts payable
❸ (10 min)

5. From the following, prepare a schedule of accounts payable for AVE Co. for May 31, 2015:

Accounts Payable Subsidiary Ledger

Bloss Co.

5/25	CPJ1	10	5/19	PJ1	50

Rowe Co.

			5/8	PJ1	60

General Ledger

Accounts Payable

5/31	CPJ	10	5/31	PJ1	110

Business transactions of both the buyer and the seller
❶ ❷ (10 min)

6. Lois Long received $300 of merchandise from Blue Co. What would be the journal entry on the books of both the buyer and the seller?

Exercises

Set A

(The forms you need are on pages 7-13 and 7-16 of the *Study Guide with Working Papers.*)

Recording and posting from the purchases journal
❷ (10 min)

7-1A. From the purchases journal below, record in the accounts payable subsidiary ledger and post to the general ledger accounts as appropriate.

PURCHASES JOURNAL

Page 1

Date		Account Credited	Invoice No.	PR	Dr. Purchases Cr. Accounts Payable
2016					
April	14	Corrine Axell Co.	101		70000
	21	Mill Village Co.	102		50000
		Total			120000

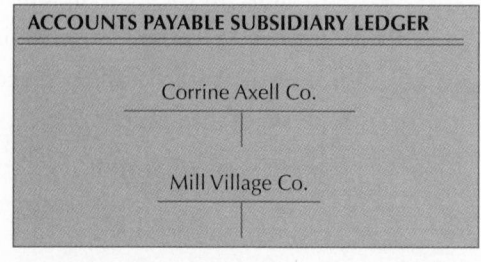

ACCOUNTS PAYABLE SUBSIDIARY LEDGER

Corrine Axell Co.

Mill Village Co.

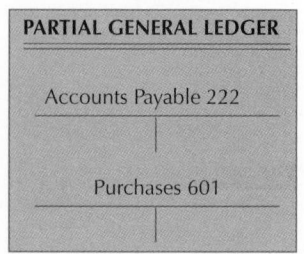

PARTIAL GENERAL LEDGER

Accounts Payable 222

Purchases 601

Journalizing, recording, and posting the purchases and cash payments journals; schedule of accounts payable
❷ ❸ (20 min)

7-2A. From the following transactions for Edna Co., when appropriate, journalize, record, post, and prepare a schedule of accounts payable. Use the same journal headings (all page 1) and chart of accounts that Art's Clothing Company used in the text. You will have to set up your own accounts payable subsidiary ledger and partial general ledger as needed.

2017		
June	2	Purchased merchandise on account from Regina Co., invoice No. 743. Terms 2% 10, net 30, $800.
	3	Purchased merchandise on account from Barstow Co., invoice No. 3118. Terms net 30 days, $700.
	4	Purchased merchandise on account from Garry Co., invoice No. 819. Terms 3% 15, n45, $1,400.
	6	Issued debit memorandum No. 101 to Regina Co. for damaged goods re: invoice No. 743, $200.
	9	Issued debit memorandum No. 102 to Barstow Co. for defective merchandise re: invoice No. 3118, $100.
	10	Sent cheque No. 831 to Regina Co. for invoice No. 743 less returns and discount.
	13	Purchased merchandise on account from Regina Co., invoice No. 784. Terms 2% 10, net 30, $1,200.
	14	Issued debit memorandum No. 103 to Garry Co. for defective merchandise re: invoice No. 819, $300.
	17	Sent cheque No. 832 to Garry Co. for invoice No. 819 less debit memorandum and discount.

Calculating net purchases
❷ (5 min)

7-3A. From the following facts, calculate what Adam Dell must pay Black Co. for the purchase of a bedroom set. Sale terms are 2/10, n/30.

a. Invoice price before tax, $3,000, dated April 5.

b. Returned one defective end table for credit of $200 on April 8.

c. Paid bill on April 13.

Journalizing, recording, and posting a debit memorandum
❷ (15 min)

7-4A. On July 8, 2017, Huston Co. issued debit memorandum No. 1 for $400 to Park Co. for merchandise returned from invoice No. 709. Your task is to journalize, record, and post this transaction as appropriate. Use the same account numbers as found in the text for Art's Clothing Company. The general journal page is page 1.

Journalizing, recording, and posting a cash payments journal
❸ (20 min)

7-5A. Journalize, record, and post when appropriate the following transactions into the cash payments journal (page 2) for Morgan's Clothing. Use the same headings as found in the text (page 310). All purchases discounts are 2/10, n/30.

Accounts Payable Subsidiary Ledger

Name	*Balance*	*Invoice No.*
B. Foss	$ 400	488
A. James	1,000	522
J. Ranch	900	562
B. Swanson	200	821

Partial General Ledger

Account	*Number*	*Balance*
Cash	110	$3,000
Accounts Payable	210	2,500
Purchases Discounts	511	—
Advertising Expense	610	—

2017
Apr. 2 Issued cheque No. 20 to A. James Company in payment of its March 29 invoice No. 522.

9 Issued cheque No. 21 to Flott Advertising in payment of its advertising bill, $100, no discount.

16 Issued cheque No. 22 to B. Foss in payment of its March 26 invoice No. 488.

Schedule of accounts payable
(3) (10 min)

7-6A. From Exercise 7-5A, prepare a schedule of accounts payable and verify that the total of the schedule equals the amount in the controlling account.

Trade and cash discounts
(2) (3) (10 min)

7-7A. Mary Rose Co. bought merchandise with a list price of $4,000. Mary's company was entitled to a 30% trade discount as well as a 3% cash discount. What was the actual cost of buying this merchandise after the cash discount?

Set B

(The forms you need are on pages 7-13 and 7-16 of the *Study Guide with Working Papers.*)

Recording and posting from the purchases journal
(2) (10 min)

7-1B. From the purchases journal below, record in the accounts payable subsidiary ledger and post to the general ledger accounts as appropriate.

PURCHASES JOURNAL

Page 1

Date		Account Credited	Invoice No.	PR	Dr. Purchases Cr. Accounts Payable
2016 April	12	Corrine Axell Co.	101		900 00
	25	Mill Village Co.	102		700 00
		Total			1600 00

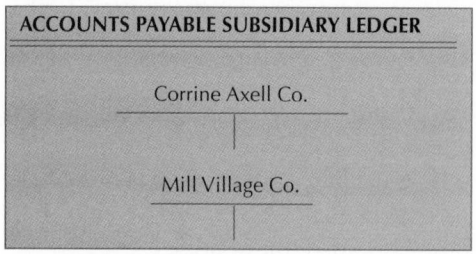

ACCOUNTS PAYABLE SUBSIDIARY LEDGER

Corrine Axell Co.

Mill Village Co.

PARTIAL GENERAL LEDGER

Accounts Payable 222

Purchases 601

Journalizing, recording, and posting purchases and cash payments journal; schedule of accounts payable
(2) (3) (20 min)

7-2B. From the following transactions for Edna Co., when appropriate, journalize, record, post, and prepare a schedule of accounts payable. Use the same journal headings (all page 1) and chart of accounts that Art's Clothing Company used in the text. You will have to set up your own accounts payable subsidiary ledger and partial general ledger as needed.

2017		
June	2	Purchased merchandise on account from Regina Co., invoice No. 743. Terms 2% 10, net 30, $900.
	3	Purchased merchandise on account from Barstow Co., invoice No. 3118. Terms net 30 days, $1,000.
	5	Purchased merchandise on account from Garry Co., invoice No. 819. Terms 3% 15, n45, $1,600.
	6	Issued debit memorandum No. 101 to Regina Co. for damaged goods re: invoice No. 743, $300
	8	Issued debit memorandum No. 102 to Barstow Co. for defective merchandise re: invoice No. 3118, $200.
	10	Sent cheque No. 831 to Regina Co. for invoice No. 743 less returns and discount.
	12	Purchased merchandise on account from Regina Co., invoice No. 784. Terms 2% 10, net 30, $1,500.
	13	Issued debit memorandum No. 103 to Garry Co. for defective merchandise re: invoice No. 819, $400.
	18	Sent cheque No. 832 to Garry Co. for invoice No. 819 less debit memorandum and discount.

Calculating net purchases
❷ (5 min)

7-3B. From the following facts, calculate what Adam Dell must pay Black Co. for the purchase of a bedroom set. Sale terms are 2/10, n/30.

a. Invoice price before tax, $5,000, dated April 5.

b. Returned one defective end table for credit of $400 on April 8.

c. Paid bill on April 13.

Journalizing, recording, and posting a debit memorandum
❷ (15 min)

7-4B. On July 10, 2017, Huston Co. issued debit memorandum No. 1 for $600 to Park Co. for merchandise returned from invoice No. 731. Your task is to journalize, record, and post this transaction as appropriate. Use the same account numbers as found in the text for Art's Clothing Company. The general journal page is page 1.

Journalizing, recording, and posting a cash payments journal
❸ (20 min)

7-5B. Journalize, record, and post when appropriate the following transactions into the cash payments journal (page 2) for Morgan's Clothing. Use the same headings as found in the text (page 276). All purchases discounts are 2/10, n/30.

Accounts Payable Subsidiary Ledger

Name	*Balance*	*Invoice No.*
B. Foss	$ 500	4823
A. James	1,300	5226
J. Ranch	800	5783
B. Swanson	300	8274

Partial General Ledger

Account	*Number*	*Balance*
Cash 110	110	$5,000
Accounts Payable 210	210	2,900
Purchases Discounts 511	511	—
Advertising Expense 610	610	—

2017

Apr. 3 Issued cheque No. 201 to A. James Company in payment of its March 29 invoice No. 5226.

10 Issued cheque No. 202 to Flott Advertising in payment of its advertising bill, $100, no discount.

17 Issued cheque No. 203 to B. Foss in payment of its March 26 invoice No. 4823.

Schedule of accounts payable
❸ (10 min)

7-6B. From Exercise 7-5B, prepare a schedule of accounts payable and verify that the total of the schedule equals the amount in the controlling account.

Trade and cash discounts
❷ ❸ (10 min)

7-7B. Mary Rose Co. bought merchandise with a list price of $6,000. Mary's company was entitled to a 30% trade discount as well as a 2% cash discount. What was the actual cost of buying this merchandise after the cash discount?

Group A Problems

(The forms you need are on pages 7-17 and 7-35 of the *Study Guide with Working Papers*.)

Journalizing, recording, and posting a purchases journal
❶ ❷ (30 min)

7A-1. Ely Goldman recently opened a specialty food store in Brantford. As the bookkeeper of his shop, journalize, record, and post when appropriate the following transactions (account numbers are: Store Supplies, 130; Store Equipment, 151; Accounts Payable, 210; Purchases, 510):

Check Figure
Total of Purchases column $3,110

2017

June 3 Bought merchandise on account from Bennet Co., invoice No. 7041, dated June 3, terms 2/10, n/30, $1,640.

4 Bought store equipment "on account" from Frank Co., invoice No. 672, dated June 4, $2,960.

8 Bought merchandise on account from Beamer Co., invoice No. 3710, dated June 7, terms 2/10, n/30, $1,470.

14 Bought store supplies on account from Bennet Co., invoice No. 7186, dated June 13, $950.

Journalizing, recording, and posting a purchases journal, as well as recording a debit memorandum and preparing a schedule of accounts
❶ ❷ ❸ (30 min)

7A-2. Sara's Cupcakes of Cold Lake uses a purchases journal (page 10) and a general journal (page 2) to record the following transactions (continued from April):

Check Figure
Total of Schedule of Accounts Payable $11,457

2016

May 8 Purchased merchandise on account from Stanton Co., invoice No. 1416, dated May 6, terms 2/10, n/60, $900.

11 Purchased merchandise on account from Kenn Co., invoice No. 618, dated May 11, terms 2/10, n/60, $1,540.

14 Purchased store supplies on account from Stacy Co., invoice No. 741, dated May 13, $1,050.

15 Issued debit memo No. 5 to Stanton Co. for merchandise returned, $300 from invoice No. 1416.

18 Purchased office equipment on account from King Co., invoice No. 1110, dated May 18, $1,837.

24 Purchased additional store supplies on account from Stacy Co., invoice No. 780, dated May 23, terms 2/10, n/30, $940.

The food store has decided to use a separate column for merchandise purchases and one for the purchase of supplies in the purchases journal.

Required

a. Journalize the transactions.

b. Post and record as appropriate.

c. Prepare a schedule of accounts payable.

Accounts Payable Ledger

Name	*Balance*
Stanton Co.	$790
Kenn Co.	1,240
Stacy Co.	2,615
King Co.	845

Partial General Ledger

Account	*Number*	*Balance*
Store Supplies	110	$720
Office Equipment	120	—
Accounts Payable	210	5,490
Purchases	510	21,410
Purchases Returns and Allowances	512	—

Journalizing, recording, and posting a cash payments journal; preparing a schedule of accounts payable
3 (40 min)

Check Figure

Total of Schedule of Accounts Payable $3,300

7A-3. Peter Daly operates a photo printing centre in Whitehorse. All transactions requiring the payment of cash are recorded in the cash payments journal (page 5). The account balances as of May 1, 2016, are as follows:

Accounts Payable Ledger

Name	*Balance*
Chedd Co.	$2,400
Marrk Co.	1,100
JNS Co.	700
P. Mark Co.	2,500

Partial General Ledger

Account	*Number*	*Balance*
Cash	110	$17,000
Delivery Truck	150	—
Accounts Payable	210	6,700
Purchases	510	—
Purchases Discount	512	—
Rent Expense	610	—
Utilities Expense	620	—

Required

a. Journalize the following transactions.

b. Record in the accounts payable ledger and post to the general ledger as appropriate.

c. Prepare a schedule of accounts payable.

2016		
May	3	Paid half the amount owed Marrk Co. from previous purchases on account, less a 2% purchases discount, cheque No. 211.
	3	Bought a used delivery truck for $8,000 cash, cheque No. 212, payable to Ring Motors Co.
	7	Bought merchandise for cash from Dart Co., cheque No. 213, $3,900.
	18	Bought additional merchandise from Tack Co., cheque No. 214, $1,800.
	24	Paid P. Mark Co. the amount owed—no purchases discount, cheque No. 215.
	27	Paid rent expense to Downtown Realty Trust, cheque No. 216, $1,800.
	28	Paid utilities to City Utility Co., cheque No. 217; $400.
	31	Paid half the amount owed JNS Co., no discount, cheque No. 218.

Comprehensive review problem: all special journals and the general journal; schedules of accounts payable and accounts receivable
❶ ❷ ❸ (120 min)

Check Figure

Total of Schedule of Accounts Receivable $7,900

7A-4. Mary James owns Mary's Card House in Halifax. As her newly hired accountant, your task is to:

a. Journalize the following transactions for the month of March.

b. Record in subsidiary ledgers and post to the general ledger as appropriate.

c. Total, rule, and cross-add the various journals.

d. Prepare a schedule of accounts receivable and a schedule of accounts payable at month-end.

The following is the partial chart of accounts for Mary's Card House:

Assets	**Revenue**
1100 Cash	4100 Card Sales
1200 Accounts Receivable	4120 Sales Returns and Allowances
1450 Prepaid Rent	4130 Sales Discounts
1620 Delivery Truck	
	Cost of Goods
Liabilities	5100 Card Purchases
2100 Accounts Payable	5120 Purchases Returns and Allowances
2200 Bank Loan Payable	5130 Purchases Discounts
Owner's Equity	**Expenses**
3000 M. James, Capital	6100 Salaries Expense
	6150 Cleaning Expense

2016

Mar. 1 Mary James invested $15,000 in the card store.

1 Paid three months' rent in advance to Harbour Realty, cheque No. 1001, $2,700.

1 Purchased merchandise from X-Card Company on account, $5,000. Invoice No. 710, dated March 1, terms 2/10, n/30.

2 Sold merchandise to Jas Investors on account, $1,800. Invoice No. 601, terms 2/10, n/30.

6 Sold merchandise to Paton Lee on account, $700. Invoice No. 602, terms 2/10, n/30.

8 Purchased merchandise from X-Card Company on account, $1,500. Invoice No. 716, dated March 7, terms 2/10, n/30.

9 Sold merchandise to Jas Investors on account, $900. Invoice No. 603, terms 2/10, n/30.

9 Paid Able Cleaning Service $360. Cheque No. 1002.

11 Paid X-Card Company invoice No. 710, dated March 1, cheque No. 1003, taking discount.

12 Paton Lee returned merchandise that cost $300 to Mary's Card House. Mary issued credit memorandum No. 1 to Paton Lee for $300.

12 Purchased merchandise from Kaelynn Imports on account, $4,000. Invoice No. 311, dated March 12, terms 1/15, n/60.

13 Arranged $20,000 bank loan with Royal Bank. Deposited today to the company's bank account.

14 Sold $1,300 worth of card merchandise for cash.

15 Paid casual salaries, $600, cheque No. 1004.

15 Returned merchandise to Kaelynn Imports in the amount of $1,000. Mary's Card House issued debit memorandum No. 1 to Kaelynn Imports.

16 Sold card merchandise for cash, $4,000.

16 Received payment from Paton Lee, invoice No. 602, (less returned merchandise), less discount.

16 Jas Investors paid invoice No. 601, no discount.

16 Sold card supplies to Gayle Herbert on account, $4,000. Invoice No. 604, terms 2/10, n/30.

19 Purchased used delivery truck on account from Halifax Auto, $14,000. Invoice No. 1471, dated March 19 (no discount terms).

22 Sold to Jas Investors card merchandise on account, $900. Invoice No. 605, terms 2/10, n/30.

23 Paid Kaelynn Imports balance owed, cheque No. 1005, taking discount.

23 Sold card merchandise on account to Gayle Herbert, $1,100. Invoice No. 606, terms 2/10, n/30.

24 Purchased for cash, card display supplies from AMR Supplies, $600. Cheque No. 1006.

26 Purchased card merchandise from Benson and McIntyre on account, $4,800. Invoice No. 211, dated March 26, terms 2/10, n/30.

Mar. 26 Jas Investors paid invoice No. 605, dated March 22, taking discount.

27 Gayle Herbert paid invoice No. 606, dated March 23, taking discount.

29 Purchased merchandise from X-Card Company, $1,400. Invoice No. 736, dated March 26, terms 2/10, n/30.

30 Paid half of the balance to Halifax Auto on their invoice No. 1471, cheque No. 1007.

31 Sold merchandise to Youville Company on account, $3,000. Invoice No. 607, terms 2/10, n/30.

Group B Problems

(The forms you need are on pages 7-17 and 7-35 of the *Study Guide with Working Papers.*)

Journalizing, recording, and posting a purchases journal
❶ ❷ (30 min)

7B-1. Ely Goldman recently opened a specialty food store in Brantford. As the bookkeeper of his shop, journalize, record, and post when appropriate the following transactions (account numbers are: Store Supplies, 130; Store Equipment, 151; Accounts Payable, 210; Purchases, 510):

Check Figure
Total of Purchases Column $4,825

2017
June 2 Bought merchandise on account from Beamer Co., invoice No. 3683, dated June 2, terms 2/10, n/30, $2,845.

4 Bought store equipment "on account" from Frank Co., invoice No. 653, dated June 4, $3,125.

7 Bought merchandise on account from Bennet Co., invoice No. 7089, dated June 7, terms 2/10, n/30, $1,980.

15 Bought store supplies on account from Beamer Co., invoice No. 3721, dated June 13, $750.

Journalizing, recording, and posting a purchases journal, as well as recording a debit memorandum and preparing a schedule of accounts
❶ ❷ ❸ (30 min)

7B-2. As the accountant of Sara's Cupcakes of Cold Lake (a) journalize the following transactions in the purchases journal (page 10) or the general journal (page 2), (b) record and post as appropriate, and (c) prepare a schedule of accounts payable. (Beginning balances are in your working papers and in Problem 7A-2.)

Check Figure
Total of Schedule of Accounts Payable $11,629

2016
May 7 Purchased merchandise on account from Kenn Co., invoice No. 589, dated May 7, terms 2/10, n/60, $750.

10 Purchased merchandise on account from Stanton Co., invoice No. 1475, dated May 10, terms 2/10, n/60, $1,050.

14 Purchased store supplies on account from Stacy Co., invoice No. 713, dated May 13, $1,145.

15 Issued debit memo No. 5 to Stanton Co. for merchandise returned, $250, from invoice No. 1475.

19 Purchased office equipment on account from King Co., invoice No. 1160, dated May 18, $2,569.

23 Purchased additional store supplies on account from Stacy Co., invoice No. 786, dated May 23, terms 2/10, n/30, $875.

The food store has decided to use a separate column for merchandise purchases and one for the purchase of supplies in the purchases journal.

Journalizing, recording, and posting a cash payments journal; preparing a schedule of accounts payable
❸ (40 min)

> *Check Figure*
> Total of Schedule of Accounts Payable $3,300

7B-3. Peter Daly operates a photo printing centre in Whitehorse. Peter has hired you as his bookkeeper to record the following transactions in the cash payments journal. He would like you to record and post as appropriate and supply him with a schedule of accounts payable. (Beginning balances are in your working papers and in Problem 7A-3.)

2016

May 3 Bought a used delivery truck for $8,500 cash, cheque No. 721, payable to Ring Motors Co.

3 Paid half the amount owed Marrk Co. from previous purchases on account, less a 3% purchases discount, cheque No. 722.

7 Bought merchandise from Dart Co., cheque No. 723, $2,780.

18 Bought additional merchandise from Tack Co., cheque No. 724, $500.

24 Paid P. Mark Co. the amount owed less a 3% purchases discount, cheque No. 725.

27 Paid rent expense to Downtown Realty Trust, cheque No. 726, $1,500.

28 Paid half the amount owed JNS Co., no discount, cheque No. 727.

31 Paid utilities to City Utility Co., cheque No. 728; $325.

Comprehensive review problem: all special journals and the general journal; schedules of accounts payable and accounts receivable
❶ ❷ ❸ (120 min)

> *Check Figure*
> Total of Schedule of Accounts Receivable $7,900
> Total of Schedule of Accounts Payable $15,100

7B-4. As the new accountant for Mary's Card House in Halifax, your task is to:

a. Journalize the transactions for the month of March.

b. Record in subsidiary ledgers and post to the general ledger as appropriate.

c. Total, rule, and cross-add the journals.

d. Prepare a schedule of accounts receivable and a schedule of accounts payable at month end.

(Use the same chart of accounts as in Problem 7A-4. Beginning balances are in your working papers.)

2016

Mar. 1 Mary James invested $12,000 in the card store.

1 Paid two months' rent in advance to Harbour Realty, cheque No. 1201, $1,800.

2 Purchased merchandise from X-Card Company on account, $3,500. Invoice No. 810, dated March 1, terms 2/10, n/30.

3 Sold merchandise to Jas Investors on account, $2,000. Invoice No. 401, terms 2/10, n/30.

6 Sold merchandise to Paton Lee on account, $900. Invoice No. 402, terms 2/10, n/30.

8 Purchased merchandise from X-Card Company on account, $1,750. Invoice No. 816, dated March 7, terms 2/10, n/30.

9 Sold merchandise to Jas Investors on account, $1,100. Invoice No. 403, terms 2/10, n/30.

9 Paid Able Cleaning Service $425. Cheque No. 1202.

Mar. 11 Paton Lee returned merchandise that cost $200 to Mary's Card House. Mary issued credit memorandum No. 1 to Paton Lee for $400.

12 Paid X-Card Company invoice No. 810, dated March 7, cheque No. 1203, taking discount.

13 Purchased merchandise from Kaelynn Imports on account, $4,200. Invoice No. 411, dated March 12, terms 1/15, n/60.

13 Arranged $15,000 bank loan with Royal Bank. Deposited today to the company's bank account.

14 Sold $1,500 worth of card supplies for cash.

15 Paid casual salaries, $800, cheque No. 1204.

15 Returned merchandise to Kaelynn Imports in the amount of $1,200. Mary's Card House issued debit memorandum No. 1 to Kaelynn Imports.

16 Sold merchandise for cash, $4,200.

16 Received payment from Paton Lee, invoice No. 402, (less returned merchandise), less discount.

16 Jas Investors paid invoice No. 401, no discount.

16 Sold card supplies to Gayle Herbert on account, $3,600. Invoice No. 404, terms 2/10, n/30.

19 Purchased used delivery truck on account from Halifax Auto, $13,500. Invoice No. 3211, dated March 19 (no discount terms).

22 Sold to Jas Investors merchandise on account, $1,100. Invoice No. 405, terms 2/10, n/30.

23 Paid Kaelynn Imports balance owed, cheque No. 1205, taking discount.

23 Sold card merchandise on account to Gayle Herbert, $1,300. Invoice No. 406, terms 2/10, n/30.

24 Purchased for cash, card display supplies from AMR Supplies, $500, cheque No. 1206.

26 Purchased card merchandise from Benson and McIntyre on account, $5,000. Invoice No. 311, dated March 26, terms 2/10, n/30.

26 Jas Investors paid invoice No. 405, dated March 22, taking discount.

26 Gayle Herbert paid invoice No. 406, dated March 23, taking discount.

29 Purchased merchandise from X-Card Company, $1,600. Invoice No. 836, dated March 26, terms 2/10, n/30.

30 Paid half of the balance to Halifax Auto on their invoice No. 3211, cheque No. 1207

31 Sold merchandise to Youville Company on account, $3,200. Invoice No. 407, terms 2/10, n/30.

Group C Problems

(The forms you need are on pages 7-36 and 7-54 of the *Study Guide with Working Papers.*)

Journalizing, recording, and posting a purchases journal
❶ ❷ (30 min)

Check Figure

Total of Purchases column $3,121

7C-1. Amy Burke recently opened a gift store in Shelburne. As the bookkeeper of her shop, journalize, record, and post when appropriate the following transactions (account numbers are: Store Supplies, 124; Store Equipment, 150; Accounts Payable, 211; Purchases, 500):

2016

Mar. 2 Bought merchandise on account from Whalen Co., invoice No. 6092, dated March 2, terms 2/10, n/30, $1,832.

5 Bought store equipment from Mega Gifts Co., invoice No. 672, dated March 4, $2,355.

9 Bought merchandise on account from Kelsey Co., invoice No. 3710, dated March 8, terms 2/10, n/30, $1,289.

17 Bought store supplies on account from Whalen Co., invoice No. 6136, dated March 16, $1.645.

Journalizing, recording, and posting a purchases journal, as well as recording a debit memorandum and preparing a schedule of accounts
❶ ❷ ❸ (30 min)

Check Figure

Total of Schedule of Accounts Payable $13,211.57

7C-2. Super Sweets of Edmonton, owned and operated by Jennifer Blanca, uses a purchases journal (page 15) and a general journal (page 3) to record the following transactions (continued from July):

2017

Aug. 5 Purchased merchandise on account from Bakker Co., invoice No. 2467, dated August 4, terms 2/10, n/60, $1,637.45.

9 Purchased merchandise on account from Holmes Co., invoice No. 1438, dated August 8, terms 2/10, n/60, $1,784.30.

12 Purchased store supplies on account from Genesis Co., invoice No. 5031, dated August 12, $1,478.25.

16 Issued debit memo No. 5 to Bakker Co. for merchandise returned, $245.00 from invoice No. 2467.

19 Purchased display equipment on account from Well-Equip Co., invoice No. 42784, dated August 18, $1,754.50.

25 Purchased additional store supplies on account from Genesis Co., invoice No. 5182, dated August 24, terms 2/10, n/30, $743.30.

The sweet store has decided to use a separate column for merchandise purchases and one for the purchase of supplies in the purchases journal.

Required

a. Journalize the transactions.

b. Post and record as appropriate.

c. Prepare a schedule of accounts payable.

Accounts Payable Ledger

Name	*Balance*
Bakker Co.	$1,469.40
Holmes Co.	2,705.15
Genesis Co.	1,468.37
Well-Equip Co.	415.85

Partial General Ledger

Account	*Number*	*Balance*
Store Supplies	110	$ 2,066.20
Display Equipment	120	4,380.00
Accounts Payable	210	6,058.77
Purchases	510	74,294.30
Purchases Returns and Allowances	512	683.28

Journalizing, recording, and posting a cash payments journal; preparing a schedule of accounts payable
❸ (45 min)

Check Figure

Total of Schedule of Accounts Payable $1,510.56

7C-3. June Devlin operates a Water Bottling Service in Yellowknife. All transactions requiring the payment of cash are recorded in the cash payments journal (page 14). The account balances as of May 1, 2016, are as follows:

Accounts Payable Ledger

Name	*Balance*
Mansard Co.	$3,278.40
Wolfe Co.	2,078.13
Frances Co.	925.00
Higgins Co.	2,745.75

Partial General Ledger

Account	*Number*	*Balance*
Cash	1110	$21,578.34
Delivery Truck	1500	—
Accounts Payable	2100	9.027.28
Purchases	5100	42,723.67
Purchases Discount	5150	634.88
Rent Expense	6400	800.00
Utilities Expense	6800	295.20

Required

a. Journalize the following transactions.

b. Record in the accounts payable ledger and post to the general ledger as appropriate.

c. Prepare a schedule of accounts payable.

2016		
May	4	Paid half the amount owed Wolfe Co. from previous purchases on account, less a 2% purchases discount, cheque No. 843.
	6	Bought a used delivery truck for $13,600.00 cash, cheque No. 844, payable to Northern Motors Co.
	8	Bought filter supplies for cash from Prime Filter Co., cheque No. 845, $3,465.00.
	9	Paid amount due to Mansard Co, less 3% discount; cheque No. 846.
	15	Bought containers from Excel Plastics Co., cheque No. 847, $1,945.00.
	25	Paid Higgins Co. the amount owed, no purchases discount, cheque No. 848.

May	28	Paid rent expense to Industrial Realty, cheque No. 849, $2,400.00.
	29	Paid utilities to Yellowknife Utilities Co., cheque No. 850; $174.37.
	31	Paid half the amount owed Frances Co., no discount, cheque No. 851.

Comprehensive review problem: all special journals and the general journal; schedules of accounts payable and accounts receivable
❶ ❷ ❸ (140 min)

Check Figure

Total of Schedule of Accounts Receivable $5,624.65

Total of Schedule of Accounts Payable $19,325.80

7C-4. Liz Ames owns Fancy Writing Supply Co. in Moncton. As her newly hired accountant, your task is to:

a. Journalize the following transactions for the month of May.
b. Record in subsidiary ledgers and post to the general ledger as appropriate.
c. Total, rule, and cross-add the various journals.
d. Prepare a schedule of accounts receivable and a schedule of accounts payable at month-end.

The following is the partial chart of accounts for Fancy Writing Supply Co.:

Assets
1000 Cash
1100 Accounts Receivable
1350 Prepaid Rent
1800 Printing Press

Liabilities
2150 Accounts Payable
2400 Bank Loan Payable

Owner's Equity
3000 E. Ames, Capital

Revenue
4000 Writing Supplies Sales
4020 Sales Returns and Allowances
4025 Sales Discounts

Cost of Goods
5000 Purchases
5100 Purchases Returns and Allowances
5125 Purchases Discounts

Expenses
6140 Cleaning Expense
6200 Display Supplies Expense
6500 Printing Supplies Expense
6800 Salaries Expense

2015		
May	1	Liz Ames invested $25,000.00 and a printing press worth $30,000.00 in the business.
	1	Paid three months' rent in advance to Riverfront Realty, cheque No. 3001, $2,100.00.
	2	Purchased merchandise from Gant Paper Co. on account, $5,247.25. Invoice No. 24388, dated May 1, terms 2/10, n/30.
	3	Sold merchandise to Dr. M. LaPeierre on account, $1,250.00. Invoice No. 801, terms 2/10, n/30.
	6	Sold merchandise to Hon. N. Marachee on account, $2,457.50. Invoice no. 802, terms 2/10, n/30.
	8	Purchased merchandise from Gant Paper Co. on account, $1,500. Invoice No. 24451, dated March 7, terms 2/10, n/30.
	9	Sold merchandise to Fern Michaels, LLB, on account, $1,250.00. Invoice No. 803, terms 2/10, n/30.

May	10	Paid Jenkins Cleaning Service $287.50. Cheque No. 3002.
	11	Paid Gant Paper Co. invoice No. 24388, dated May 2, cheque No. 3003, taking discount.
	12	Dr. M. LaPeirre returned letterhead that cost $175.00 because of a design flaw. Liz issued credit memorandum No. 101 to the customer for this amount.
	12	Purchased merchandise from Markham Inks on account, $985.25. Invoice No. 931, dated March 12, terms 3/15, n/60.
	13	Arranged $10,000.00 bank loan with Royal Bank. Deposited today to the company's bank account.
	14	Sold paper stock for cash, $585.00. Deposited today.
	15	Paid casual salaries to D. Lee, $970.00, cheque No. 3004.
	15	Returned merchandise to Markham Inks in the amount of $235.00. Liz issued debit memorandum No. 25 for this amount.
	16	Sold more paper stock for cash, $1,500.00. Deposited today.
	16	Received payment from Hon. N. Marachee, invoice No. 802, less discount.
	17	Dr. M. LaPeierre paid invoice No. 801, less return, no discount.
	18	Sold stationery supplies to B. Kirk, CA, on account, $2,765.50. Invoice No. 804, terms 2/10, n/30.
	19	Purchased used printing press on account from Maritime Equipment Sales, $21,500.00. Invoice No. 30275, dated May 19 (no discount terms).
	22	Sold to Dr. M. LaPeierre, additional stationery merchandise on account, $1,145.00. Invoice No. 805, terms 2/10, n/30.
	23	Paid Markham Inks balance owed, cheque No. 3005, taking discount.
	23	Sold merchandise on account to B. Kirk, CA, $724.65. Invoice No. 806, terms 2/10, n/30.
	24	Purchased for cash, display supplies from MDS Supplies, $387.50. Cheque No. 3006.
	26	Purchased envelope merchandise from Findlay and Fortune on account, $3,600.00. Invoice No. 6289, dated May 26, terms 2/10, n/30.
	26	Dr. M. LaPeierre paid invoice No. 805, dated May 22, taking discount.
	27	B. Kirk, CA, paid invoice No. 804, dated May 18, taking discount.
	29	Purchased merchandise from Gant Paper Co., $3,475.80. Invoice No. 24722, dated May 28, terms 2/10, n/30.
	30	Paid half of the balance to Maritime Equipment Sales on their invoice No. 30275, cheque No. 3007.
	31	Sold merchandise to Moncton Hospital on account, $3,650.00. Invoice No. 807, terms 2/10, n/30.

On-the-Job Training

(The forms you need are on page 7-55 of the *Study Guide with Working Papers.*)

Posting to the general ledger and the subsidiary ledger ❶❷❸

T-1. Jeff Ryan completed an Accounting I course and was recently hired as the bookkeeper of Spring Co. The special journals shown below have not been posted, nor are "Dr." and "Cr." used on the column headings. Please assist Jeff by posting to the general ledger and recording in the subsidiary ledger. (Only post or record the amounts since no chart of accounts is provided.) Make some written recommendations on how a new computer system may lessen the need for posting.

SALES JOURNAL

Account	PR	
Blue Co.		480000
Jon Co.		560000
Roff Co.		640000
Totals		1680000

PURCHASES JOURNAL

Account	PR	
Ralph Co.		400000
Sos Co.		600000
Jingle Co.		800000
Totals		1800000

GENERAL JOURNAL

Sales Returns and Allowances		160000	
Accounts Receivable, Jon Co.			160000
Customer returned merchandise			
Accounts Payable, Jingle Co.		80000	
Purchases Returns and Allowances			80000
Returned defective merchandise			

CASH RECEIPTS JOURNAL

Cash	Sales Discount	Accounts Receivable	Sales	Sundry Account Name	Sundry PR	Sundry Amount
470400	9600	480000		Blue Co.		
196000	4000	200000		Jon Co.		
500000			500000	Sales		
2000000				Notes Payable		2000000
313600	6400	320000		Roff Co.		
460000			460000	Sales		
3940000	20000	1000000	960000	Totals		2000000

CASH PAYMENTS JOURNAL

Account	PR	Sundry	Accounts Payable	Purchases Discounts	Cash
Sos Co.			300000	6000	294000
Salaries Expense		260000			260000
Jingle Co.			400000	8000	392000
Salaries Expense		260000			260000
Totals		520000	700000	14000	1206000

Comprehensive problem: journalizing and posting to the general and subsidiary ledgers
❶❷❸ (120 min)

CONTINUING PROBLEM

This chapter will require you to record and post the purchases and cash payments transactions.

A month has elapsed since Precision Computer Centre's year-end. Tony Freedman will use four specialized journals for recording business transactions in the month of September—you will find two in Chapter 6, and two in this chapter. To assist you in recording the transactions the Schedule of Accounts Payable as of August 31 is shown below. An updated chart of accounts with the current balance listed for each account is provided in Chapter 6 on page 298.

The partial September transactions are as follows:

2016		
Sep.	5	Paid amount due to Staples, $100, cheque No. 242.
	5	Bought merchandise on account from Multi Systems, purchase order No. 4010, $450; terms are 3/10, n/30.
	6	Bought office supplies on account from Staples, purchase order No. 4011, $250; terms are n/30.
	10	Purchased merchandise on account from Computer Connection, purchase order No. 4012, $500; terms are 1/30, n/60.
	13	Paid Multi Systems re September 5 purchase, less discount, cheque No. 243.
	13	Received West Bell phone bill for September, $70.00; terms n/30.
	13	Received and paid City Electric bill for September, $80, cheque No. 244.
	16	Remitted outstanding amount payable to Automated Payroll Service for September wages, $1,810.18, cheque No. 245.
	17	Issued debit memorandum No. 10 to Computer Connection for merchandise returned from purchase order No. 4012, $100.
	17	Paid net amount due to Computer Connection, less discount, cheque No. 246.
	23	Paid Alpha Office Co. the amount due from the end of August, cheque No. 247.
	25	Paid for office supplies, $50, cheque No. 248.
	27	Wrote cheque No. 249 to Able Holdings Inc. for September, October, and November rent, $1,200.00.
	30	Wrote cheque No. 250 to Automated Payroll Service for September wages, $3,740.20.
	30	Paid amount due to West Bell Canada as of August 31 plus the September phone bill received September 13, cheque No. 251. Total $216.00.

Schedule of Accounts Payable
Precision Computer Centre
August 31,2016

Alpha Office Co.	$ 420.00
City Newspaper	375.00
Staples	100.00
West Bell Canada	146.00
Total Amount Payable	**$1,041.00**

Assignment

The forms you need are on pages 7-56 and 7-62 of the *Study Guide with Working Papers*.

1. Journalize the transactions in the appropriate journals (cash payments, purchases, or general journal).
2. Record in the accounts payable subsidiary ledger and post to the general ledger as appropriate. A partial general ledger is included in the *Study Guide with Working Papers*.
3. Prepare a schedule of accounts payable as of September 30, 2016.

CHAPTER 8

Banking Procedures and Control of Cash

LEARNING OBJECTIVES

- LO 1 Depositing, writing, and endorsing cheques for a chequing account (p. 345)
- LO 2 Reconciling a bank statement (p. 351)
- LO 3 Establishing and replenishing a petty cash fund; setting up an auxiliary petty cash record (p. 362)
- LO 4 Establishing and replenishing a change fund (p. 366)
- LO 5 Handling transactions involving cash short and over (p. 366)

It is interesting to think about how the world of business has evolved over the decades and centuries. At one time all business transactions were carried out using actual coins made of gold, silver, and other valuable metals. Since those times, we have seen the almost complete shift to "paper money," whether official currency (like our new hard-to-counterfeit Canadian bills) or cheques. We still use coins of course, although the penny has now been discontinued. One is forced to wonder whether there will be a progressive loss of all of the coins we now take for granted.

We seem to be in the middle of another fundamental shift in the way business transactions take place. Increasingly, even paper money is being replaced by "electronic money." A large percentage of transactions are now made using only some electrons flowing through space. You have to wonder what the business world will look like in another 50 years or so—maybe even 25 years will produce significant changes!

With that said, it is still a requirement for accounting students to master the fundamental procedures of handling and accounting for business transactions made using paper money. This chapter largely deals with this topic and makes some mention of the important controls that will still be needed in the coming decades—whether we use paper money or not.

The internal control policies of a company will depend on things such as number of employees, company size, sources of cash, and usage of the Internet.

In the first five chapters of this book, we analyzed the accounting cycle for businesses that perform personal services (e.g., word processing or legal services). In this chapter, we turn our attention to Becca's Jewellery Store, a merchandising company that earns revenue by selling goods (or merchandise) to customers. When Becca's business began to increase, she became concerned that she was not monitoring the business's cash closely. She understood that a business with good **internal control systems** safeguards cash. Cash is the asset that is most easily stolen, lost, or mishandled. Therefore, it is important to protect all cash receipts and to control cash payments so that payments are made only for authorized business purposes.

After studying the situation carefully, Becca began a series of procedures to be followed by all company employees. The new company policies that Becca's Jewellery Store would put into place were as follows:

1. Responsibilities and duties of employees would be divided. For example, the person receiving the cash, whether at the register or by opening the mail, would not record this information into the accounting records. The accountant would not be handling the cash receipts.
2. All cash receipts of Becca's Jewellery Store would be deposited into the bank the same day they arrived except for unusual items such as a post-dated cheque, which would be kept on file and then deposited on the date it became negotiable.
3. All cash payments would be made by cheque (except petty cash, which is discussed later in this chapter).
4. Employees' jobs would be rotated. This change would allow workers to become acquainted with the work of others as well as to prepare for a possible changeover of jobs or to cover for employee absenteeism.
5. Becca Baker would sign all cheques after receiving authorization to pay from the departments concerned.
6. At time of payment, all supporting invoices or documents would be stamped paid. The stamp would show when the invoice or document is paid as well as the number of the cheque used.
7. All cheques would be prenumbered. Periodically, the number of the cheques that were issued and the numbers of the blank cheque forms remaining would be verified to make sure that all cheque numbers were accounted for. This change would control the use of cheques and make it difficult to use a cheque fraudulently without it being revealed at some point.
8. Monthly bank statements would be sent to and reconciled by someone other than the employees who handle, record, or deposit the cash.

LEARNING UNIT 8-1

Bank Procedures, Chequing Accounts, and Bank Reconciliation

LO 1

Depositing, writing, and endorsing cheques for a chequing account

Becca knew that a chequing account is one of the most useful and common banking services available, but she had many questions and decisions to make. She wanted to know about account options, monthly service charges, cheque printing charges, minimum balance requirements, interest paid on the account, availability of automatic teller machines (ATMs), and debit cards. Before Becca's Jewellery opened on April 1, 2016, she met with the manager at her local Royal Bank to discuss opening and using a chequing account for the company.

OPENING A CHEQUING ACCOUNT

A signature card is another safeguard.

The bank manager gave Becca a signature card to fill out. The bank uses the **signature card** to verify the authenticity of the signature on all cheques. Because Becca would be signing all the cheques for her company, she was the only person who needed to sign the card.

After Becca completed the initial paperwork, she received a set of cheques and deposit slips. A **deposit slip** is a form that is used when making deposits in a bank or credit union. When filling out a deposit slip, you list the total amount of currency, coins, and cheques that you are depositing (see Figure 8-1). You list each cheque you are depositing individually.

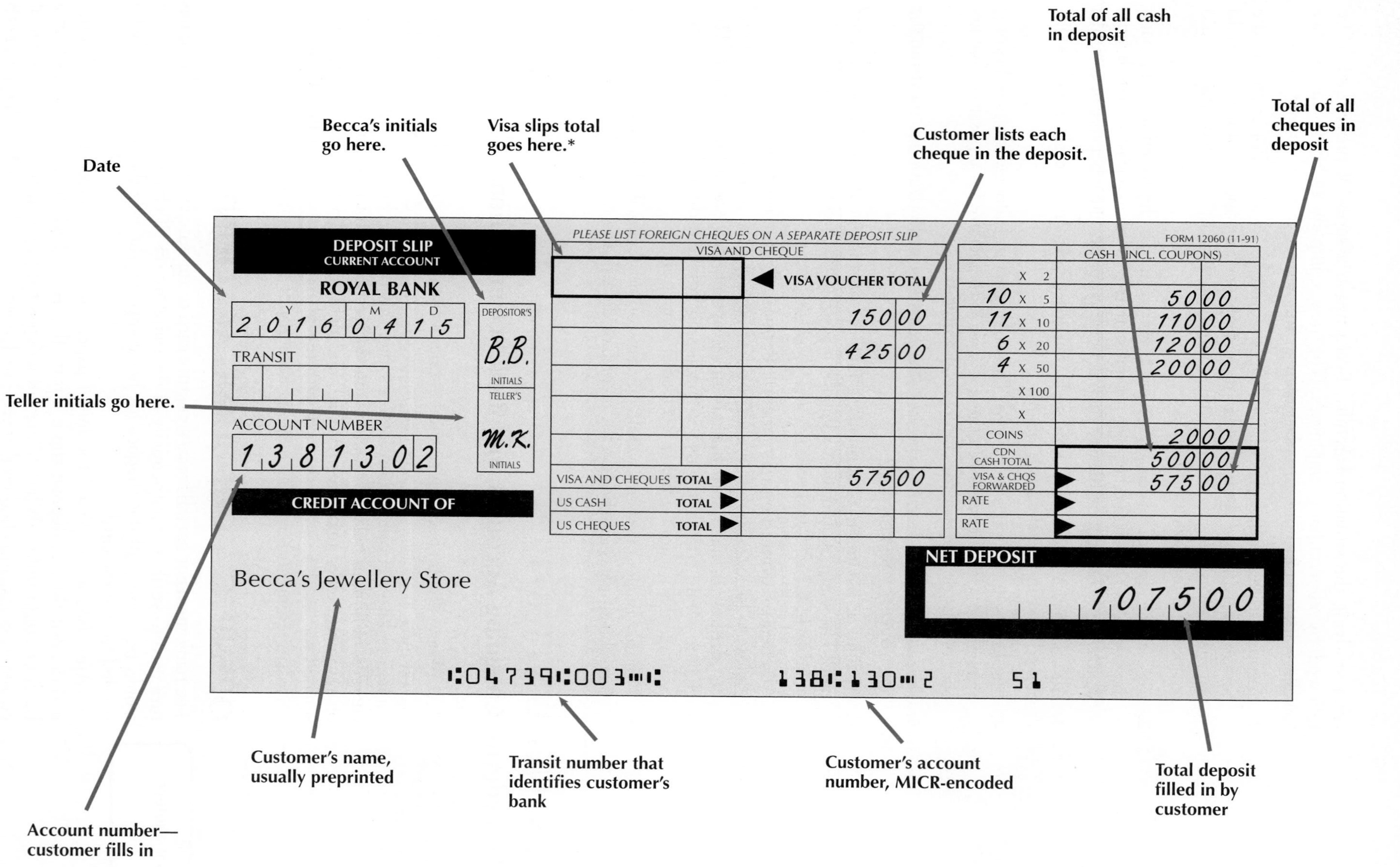

*Becca's company does not yet offer Visa as a payment method.

Figure 8-1 A Deposit Slip Example (This deposit is not part of the reconciliation that follows.)

When a deposit is completed, the depositor receives a copy of the deposit slip as a receipt or proof of the transaction. The deposit should also be recorded on the current cheque stub. The bank manager told Becca that she could give the deposits to a bank teller or she could use an automated teller machine (ATM). The ATM could also be used for withdrawing cash, transferring funds, or paying bills. For decades, ATM cards could be used only at ATM machines, but in recent years, they took on another function, a debit feature. The **debit card** can be used at many locations in a manner similar to a credit card. However, the amount of the purchase paid for with a debit card is deducted directly from your chequing account.

When a bank credits your account, it is increasing the balance.

Often, Becca makes her deposits after business hours, when the bank is closed. At those times, she puts the deposit into a sealed bag (provided by the bank) and places the bag in the night depository. The bank will credit Becca's account when the deposit is processed. Becca plans to make all business payments by written cheque (except petty cash) and deposit all money received (cash and cheques) in the bank account.

Many chequing accounts earn interest. For our purposes, however, we assume that the chequing account for Becca's Jewellery Store does not pay interest. Also, we assume that the chequing account has a monthly service charge but no individual charge for cheques written.

CHEQUE ENDORSEMENT

Endorsements can be made by using a rubber stamp instead of a handwritten signature.

Cheques have to be *endorsed* (signed) by the person to whom the cheque is made payable before they can be deposited or cashed. **Endorsement** is the signing or stamping of one's name at the top right side on the back of the cheque. This signature means that the payee has transferred the right to deposit or cash the cheque to someone else (the bank). The bank can then collect the money from the person or company that issued the cheque.

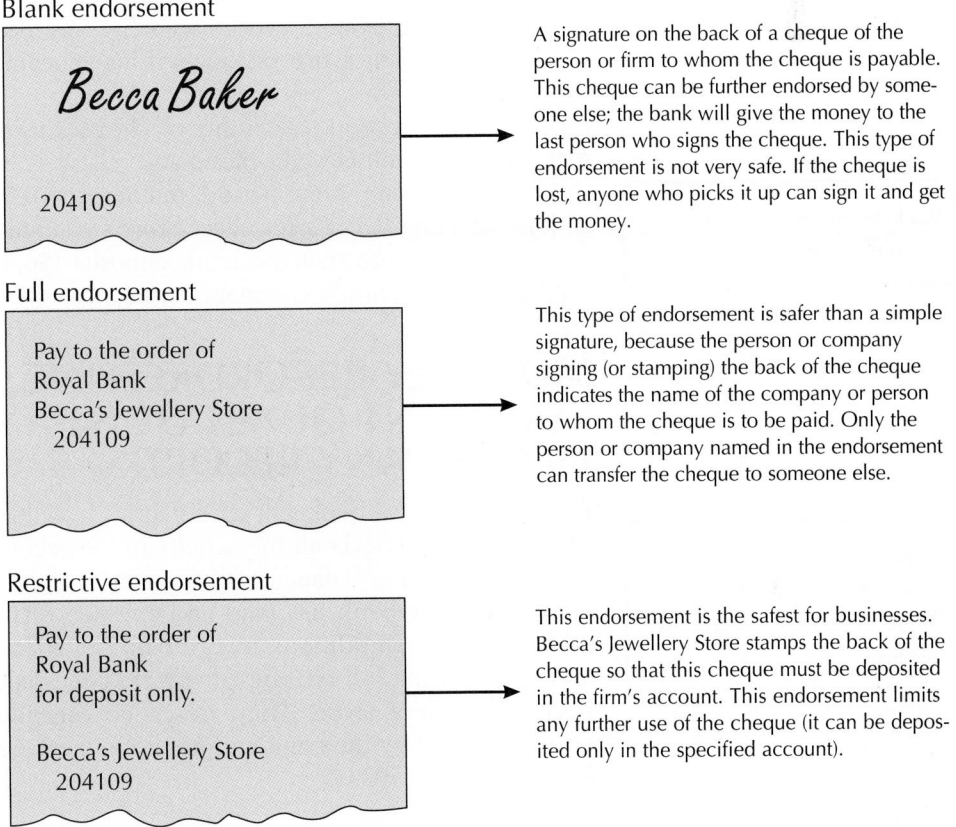

Three different types of endorsement can be used (see Figure 8-2). The first is a *blank endorsement*. A blank endorsement does not specify that a particular person

Figure 8-2
Types of Cheque Endorsement

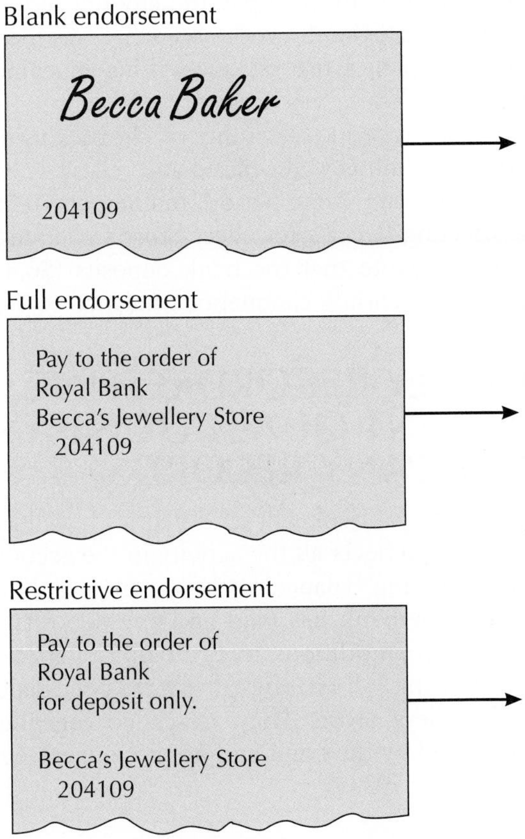

A signature on the back of a cheque of the person or firm to whom the cheque is payable. This cheque can be further endorsed by someone else; the bank will give the money to the last person who signs the cheque. This type of endorsement is not very safe. If the cheque is lost, anyone who picks it up can sign it and get the money.

This type of endorsement is safer than a simple signature, because the person or company signing (or stamping) the back of the cheque indicates the name of the company or person to whom the cheque is to be paid. Only the person or company named in the endorsement can transfer the cheque to someone else.

This endorsement is the safest for businesses. Becca's Jewellery Store stamps the back of the cheque so that this cheque must be deposited in the firm's account. This endorsement limits any further use of the cheque (it can be deposited only in the specified account).

or firm must endorse it. It can be further endorsed by someone else. The bank will pay the last person who signs the cheque. This type of endorsement is not very safe. If the cheque is lost, the person who finds it can sign it and get the money.

The second type of endorsement is a *full endorsement*. The person or company signing (or stamping) the back of the cheque indicates the name of the company or the person to whom the cheque is to be paid. Only the person or company named in the endorsement can transfer the cheque to someone else.

Bank regulations require the endorsement to be within the top 3.8 cm (1½ inches) to speed up the cheque-clearing process.

Restrictive endorsements, the third type of endorsement, are the safest for businesses. Becca's Jewellery Store stamps the back of the cheque so that it must be deposited in the firm's account. This stamp limits any further use of the cheque.

THE CHEQUEBOOK

When Becca opened her business's chequing account, she received cheques. These cheques could be used to buy things for the business or to pay bills or salaries.

A **cheque** is a written order signed by a **drawer** (the person who writes the cheque) instructing a **drawee** (the bank that pays the cheque) to pay a specific sum of money to the **payee** (the person to whom the cheque is payable). Figure 8-3 shows a cheque issued by Becca's Jewellery Store. Becca Baker is the drawer, Royal Bank is the drawee, and Ziegler Wholesalers is the payee.

Drawer: One who writes the cheque.

Drawee: One who pays money to payee.

Payee: One to whom the cheque is payable.

Look at the cheque in Figure 8-3. Notice that certain things, such as the company's name and address and the cheque number, are preprinted. You should also notice the line drawn after the amount, which is to fill up the empty space and ensure that the amount cannot be changed.

Figure 8-3 includes a cheque stub. The cheque stub is used to record transactions, and it is kept for future reference. The information found on the stub includes the beginning balance ($3,441), the amount of any deposits ($0), the total amount in the account ($3,441), the amount of the cheque being written ($580), and the ending balance ($2,861). The cheque stub should be filled out before the cheque is written.

If the written amount on the cheque does not match the amount expressed in figures, Royal Bank may pay the amount written in words, return the cheque unpaid, or contact the drawer to see what was meant.

Many companies use cheque-writing machines to type out the information on the cheque. These machines prevent people from making fraudulent changes on handwritten cheques. Printing of cheques using ink-jet printers is not recommended, as this ink is water-based and relatively easy to alter.

During the same time period, in-company records must be kept for all transactions affecting Becca's Jewellery Store's chequebook balance. Figure 8-4 shows these records. Note that the bank deposits ($6,446) minus the cheques written ($2,529) give an ending chequebook balance of $3,917.

Banking on the Internet is expanding rapidly.

MONTHLY RECORDKEEPING: THE BANK'S STATEMENT OF ACCOUNT AND IN-COMPANY RECORDS

Each month, Royal Bank will send Becca's Jewellery Store a Statement of Account. This statement reflects all the activity in the account during that period. It begins with the beginning balance of the account at the start of the month, along with the cheques the bank has paid and any deposits received (see Figure 8-5). Any other charges or additions to the bank balance are indicated by codes found on the statement. All cheques that have been paid by the bank are sent back to Becca's Jewellery Store. They are called **cancelled cheques** because they have been processed by the bank and are no longer negotiable. The ending balance in Figure 8-5 is $3,592.

Figure 8-5 shows one format for a bank statement. Different banks use different formats.

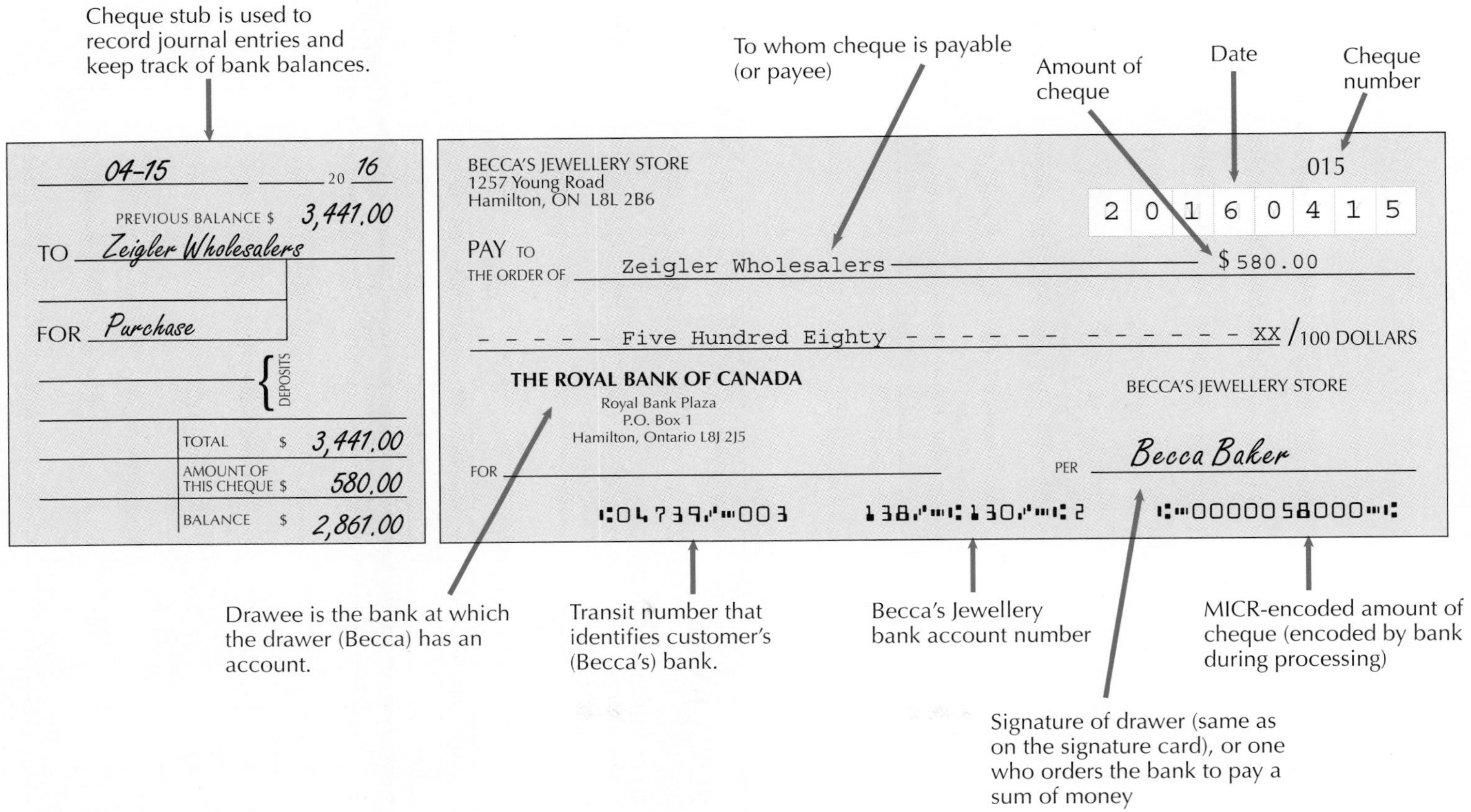
Cheque stub is used to record journal entries and keep track of bank balances.
To whom cheque is payable (or payee)
Amount of cheque
Date
Cheque number
04-15
20 16
PREVIOUS BALANCE $ 3,441.00
TO Zeigler Wholesalers
FOR Purchase
DEPOSITS
TOTAL $ 3,441.00
AMOUNT OF THIS CHEQUE $ 580.00
BALANCE $ 2,861.00
BECCA'S JEWELLERY STORE
1257 Young Road
Hamilton, ON L8L 2B6
015
2 0 1 6 0 4 1 5
PAY TO THE ORDER OF Zeigler Wholesalers
$ 580.00
Five Hundred Eighty XX/100 DOLLARS
THE ROYAL BANK OF CANADA
Royal Bank Plaza
P.O. Box 1
Hamilton, Ontario L8J 2J5
BECCA'S JEWELLERY STORE
FOR
PER Becca Baker
Drawee is the bank at which the drawer (Becca) has an account.
Transit number that identifies customer's (Becca's) bank.
Becca's Jewellery bank account number
MICR-encoded amount of cheque (encoded by bank during processing)
Signature of drawer (same as on the signature card), or one who orders the bank to pay a sum of money

Figure 8-3 A Typical Cheque and Cheque Stub

Figure 8-4 Transactions (In-Company Records) Affecting Chequebook Balance

Bank Deposits Made for April

Date of Deposit		Amount	Received from
April	1	$5,000	Becca Baker, Capital
	4	340	Jennifer Leung
	15	89	Mary Figueroa
	26	117	Carl Jones
	30	900	Cash Sales
	Total deposits for month:	$6,446	

Cheques Written for Month of April

Date		Cheque No.	Payment To:	Amount	Description
April	1	10	Quality Insurance	$ 500	Insurance paid in advance
	5	11	ABC Wholesalers	400	Merchandise
	8	12	Payroll	800	Salaries
	10	13	Times Newspaper	100	Advertising
	10	14	Verizon	99	Telephone
	15	15	Zeigler Wholesalers	580	Merchandise
	15		ATM Withdrawal	50	Postage
			Total amount of cheques written:	$2,529	

Cheques deposited	$6,446
Cheques paid	– 2,529
Balance in account	$3,917

ROYAL BANK

ACCOUNT NUMBER 138 130 2

BECCA'S JEWELLERY STORE
1257 Young Road
Hamilton ON L8L 2B6

CLOSING PERIOD 4/30/16

Address Correction on Reverse Side ☐

CHEQUING ACCOUNT							
On	Your Balance Was	No.	We Subtracted Cheques Totalling	Less Service Charge	No.	We Added Deposits Of	Making Your Present Balance
4/1	0	6	1,949.00	5.00	4	5,546.00	3,592.00

Date	Cheques • Withdrawals • Payment			Deposits • Interest • Advances	Balance
4/1				5,000.00	5,000.00
4/3	500.00				4,500.00
4/4				340.00	4,840.00
4/9	400.00				4,440.00
4/9	800.00				3,640.00
4/13	100.00				3,540.00
4/13	99.00				3,441.00
4/15				89.00	3,530.00
4/15	50.00 ATM				3,480.00
4/26				117.00	3,597.00
4/30	5.00 SC				3,592.00

Figure 8-5 Bank Statement

LO 2

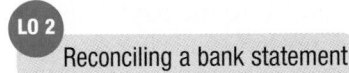

Reconciling a bank statement

THE BANK RECONCILIATION PROCESS

The problem is that the ending bank balance of $3,592 does not agree with the amount in Becca's chequebook, $3,917, or the balance in the cash amount in the ledger, $3,917. Such differences are caused partly by the time a bank takes to process a company's transactions. A company records a transaction when it occurs. A bank cannot record a deposit until it receives the funds, and it cannot pay a cheque until the cheque is presented by the payee. In addition, the bank statement will report fees and transactions that the company did not know about.

Online banking and computer software have made the reconciliation process even easier.

Becca's accountant has to find out why there is a $325 difference between the balances and how the records can be brought into balance. The process of reconciling the bank balance on the bank statement versus the company's chequebook balance is called a **bank reconciliation**. Bank reconciliations involve several steps, including calculating the deposits in transit and the outstanding cheques. The bank reconciliation often is done on the back of the **bank statement** (see Figure 8-6). It can also be done by computer software.

Deposits in Transit

In comparing the list of deposits received by the bank with the chequebook, the accountant notices that a deposit made on April 28 for $900 was not on the bank's statement. The accountant realizes that to prepare this statement, the bank included information about Becca's Jewellery Store only up to April 26. This deposit made by Becca was not shown on the monthly bank statement because it arrived at the bank after the statement was printed. Thus, timing becomes a consideration in the reconciliation process. Deposits not yet added to the bank balance

Figure 8-6
Bank Reconciliation Using the Back of the Bank Statement

Keep in mind that both the bank and the depositor can make mistakes that will not be discovered until the reconciliation process.

CHEQUES OUTSTANDING	
NUMBER	AMOUNT
15	580 00
TOTAL OF CHEQUES OUTSTANDING	580 00

1. Enter balance shown on this statement	3,592 00
2. If you have made deposits since the date of this statement add them to the above balance	900 00
3. SUBTOTAL	4,492 00
4. Deduct total of cheques outstanding	580 00
5. ADJUSTED BALANCE This should agree with your chequebook	3,912 00*

TO VERIFY YOUR CHEQUING BALANCE

1. Sort cheques by number or by date issued and compare with your cheque stubs and prior outstanding list. Make certain all cheques paid have been recorded in your chequebook. If any of your cheques were not included with this statement, list the numbers and amounts under "CHEQUES OUTSTANDING."
2. Deduct the Service Charge as shown on the statement from your chequebook balance.
3. Review copies of charge advices included with this statement and check for proper entry in your chequebook.

IF THE ADJUSTED BALANCE DOES NOT AGREE WITH YOUR CHEQUEBOOK BALANCE, THE FOLLOWING SUGGESTIONS ARE OFFERED FOR YOUR ASSISTANCE.

- Recheck additions and subtractions in your chequebook and figures to the left.
- Make certain chequebook balances have carried forward properly.
- Verify deposits recorded on statement against deposits entered in chequebook.
- Compare amount on each chequebook stub.

*Note the $5 service charge is included

Deposits in transit. These unrecorded deposits could result if a deposit were placed in a night depository on the last day of the month.

are called **deposits in transit**. This deposit needs to be added to the bank balance shown on the bank statement. Becca's chequebook is not affected, because the deposit has already been added to its balance. The bank has no way of knowing that the deposit is coming until it receives it.

Outstanding Cheques

Cheque No. 15 is outstanding.

The first thing the accountant does when the bank statement is received is put the cheques in numerical order (1, 2, 3, etc.). In doing so, the accountant notices that one payment was not made by the bank and cheque No. 15 was not returned by the bank.

Becca's books showed that this cheque had been deducted from the chequebook balance. The **outstanding cheque**, however, had not yet been presented to the bank for payment or deducted from the bank balance. When this cheque does reach the bank, the bank will reduce the amount of the balance.

Cheques outstanding are cheques drawn by the depositor but not yet presented to the bank for payment by the payee.

Service Charges

Becca's accountant also notices a bank **service charge** of $5. Becca's book balance will be lowered by $5.

Not Sufficient Funds

An **NSF (not sufficient funds)** cheque is a cheque that has been returned because the drawer did not have enough money in its account to pay the cheque. Accountants are continually on the lookout for NSF cheques. An NSF cheque means less money in the chequing account than was thought. Becca will have to (1) lower the chequebook balance and (2) try to collect the amount from the customer. The bank would notify Becca's Jewellery of an NSF cheque (or other deductions) by a **debit memorandum**. Think of a debit memorandum as a deduction from the depositor's balance.

Debit Memorandum:
↓
Deducted from balance.

If the bank acts as a collection agent for Becca's Jewellery, say in collecting notes, it will charge Becca a small fee and the net amount collected will be added to Becca's bank balance. The bank will send Becca a **credit memorandum** verifying the increase in her company's balance.

Credit memorandum:
Added to balance.

A journal entry is also needed to bring the ledger accounts of Cash and Service Charge expense up to date. Any adjustment to the chequebook balance results in a journal entry. The entry in Figure 8-7 was made to accomplish this step:

Figure 8-7
Service Charge Journalized

April	30	Service Charge Expense		5 00	
		Cash			5 00
		Bank service charge for April			

It is important for Becca to prepare a bank reconciliation when she receives her bank statement every month as part of the cash control procedure. It verifies the amount of cash in her chequing account. Another important reason to do a bank reconciliation is that it may uncover irregularities such as employee theft of funds.

Here are step-by-step instructions for preparing a bank reconciliation:

1. **Prepare a list of deposits in transit.** Compare the deposits listed on your bank statement with the bank deposits shown in your general ledger Cash account. On your bank reconciliation, list any deposits that have not appeared on (called "clearing") the bank statement. Also, take a look at the bank reconciliation you prepared last month. Did all of last month's deposits in transit show up on this month's bank statement? If not, you need to find out why not.

2. **Prepare a list of outstanding cheques.** In your general ledger Cash account, mark each cheque that cleared the bank statement this month. On your bank reconciliation, list all the recorded cheques that did not clear. Also, take a look at the bank reconciliation you prepared last month. Did any cheques outstanding from last month still not clear the bank? If so, be sure they are on your list of outstanding cheques this month. If a cheque is several months old and still has not cleared the bank, you may want to investigate further, and either replace it, or correct the company's book balance by making an adjusting entry.

> Adjustments to the cheque book balance must be journalized and posted. These steps keep the depositor's ledger accounts (especially Cash) up to date. This charge could be recorded as a miscellaneous expense, but most companies probably have a separate account for bank charges.

3. **Record any bank charges or credits.** Take a close look at your bank statement. Are all special charges made by the bank recorded in your books? If not, record them now as if you had just written a cheque for that amount. By the same token, any credits made to your account by the bank should be recorded as well. Post the entries to your general ledger.
4. **Compute the cash balance per your books.** This should be the general ledger Cash balance.
5. **Enter the bank balance on the reconciliation.** At the top of the bank reconciliation statement, enter the ending balance from the bank statement.
6. **Total the deposits in transit.** Add up the deposits in transit and enter the total on the reconciliation. Add the total deposits in transit to the bank balance to arrive at a subtotal.
7. **Total the outstanding cheques.** Add up the outstanding cheques, and enter the total on the reconciliation.
8. **Compute the balance per the reconciliation.** Subtract the total outstanding cheques from the subtotal in step 6. The result should equal the balance shown in your general ledger Cash account.

Before we look at a more comprehensive bank reconciliation, let's look at trends in banking.

TRENDS IN BANKING

Banking has changed a lot in the past several years, and additional changes are on the way as this is being written. It is still true that businesses make the usual deposits, and write the usual cheques, and those activities are described and illustrated in this chapter. However, even a small business needs to have the ability to handle and account for new methods of conducting everyday transactions that are becoming the mainstream way that many transactions are done.

Consider deposits. Most companies still accept cash, and therefore have the need to make daily deposits to the company bank account. But your author just returned from a family wedding outside Canada, and on the aircraft on the way there and back was a bit surprised to learn that although the airline sold a variety of food and other items they would no longer accept cash! All on-board purchases had to be made using a major credit card. Effectively, this means that, for that part of the airline's operations, there is no longer a need to handle actual cash, fill in a deposit slip, or make a deposit.

This trend is expected to continue and accelerate. Consider these other examples:

1. A company in Australia claims that it has re-invented the wallet. They distribute a special card that is easily read by a very weak radio signal. You simply wave the card (it can remain in a wallet or purse) close to a reader device and the entire transaction is completed in the blink of an eye. No need to remove the card from where it is kept, insert it into a reader, or enter a PIN—just wave your wallet past the special reader and you are done! No cash, no deposit slip, and no deposit to the company bank. Just some electrons moving through some very complex

circuitry. So far this is being used here in Canada for very small transactions, less than $25, although that limit can increase overnight, if the public becomes comfortable using it.

2. Credit cards are now being used in places that would be unthinkable just a few years ago. A small business can now accept payment in the form of a major credit card in almost every location imaginable. For example, your author bought a gift for his wife at a farmers' market in the middle of a field in Southern California using a major credit card. The payment was made by swiping the card through a small reader attached to the vendor's iPhone. During a recent wedding trip, his wife bought some new shoes at a major department store, and the clerk simply read her credit card with a portable reader that also scanned the code for the shoes, then e-mailed the receipt to her home in Edmonton. And many of us have paid a restaurant bill using their small portable card readers that print out a receipt once the transaction is approved.
3. Who has any idea where this all is heading? It seems easy to imagine that in just a few years many transactions could be completed using just a retina scan of a person's eye, since apparently every eye in the world is different, and therefore unique. One thing all of these new ways of conducting transactions have in common is the complete absence of cash.

However, cash will still remain an important part of the business world for a long time to come, so accounting students must still learn how to account for it.

Consider also how a business makes payments. Millions of cheques are still written in Canada each day, but a number of other forms of payment are becoming common. Most of these payments are made electronically, often by way of a secure Internet connection. It is getting to be quite easy to transfer funds to almost anyone using some form of **electronic funds transfer (EFT)**. Typically, a bank or other financial institution charges a premium for this service, so it tends to be used sparingly, but it is an extremely quick and efficient way to get funds to someone, especially when you need to make a payment in a hurry. This is especially true when sending funds to a person or company in a foreign country, where **SWIFT codes** exist to allow financial institutions across the globe to be uniquely identified. Use of SWIFT codes can result in moving money between individuals and companies anywhere on earth a painless and very quick matter.

It is also becoming common for a business to arrange for some routine expenses to be paid automatically using a pre-authorized debit. Many homeowners set up their finances to pay some routine monthly costs by automatic charge to a credit or debit card (utilities, cable, and cell phone charges, for instance). In the same way, a business can also arrange to have similar charges paid automatically, either by a charge to a credit card in the company name or by an automatic withdrawal from their bank using a debit card. Making these arrangements does give up some measure of control, but most of the monthly charges paid this way are not subject to much dispute, given that they vary only a little, if at all, from period to period. The savings in data processing can be substantial, and many businesses conclude that the savings in time alone is worth the slight increase in risk.

Many businesses are also making a corporate credit card part of their standard operating procedures. Especially for employees who travel a lot, this method of making payments can be very efficient and can greatly reduce the time needed to fill out expense claims as well as the wait to be reimbursed. From the company's point of view, this also saves a lot of time, because each month they get a summary of expenses by employee. It is becoming possible to integrate these monthly billings directly into the company's records, thus saving considerable time in record keeping.

A number of service companies have been created to facilitate payments between individuals and companies. PayPal is one such company, and it is becoming very common for a business to accept payments in this format, even though the system may have been initially created to help one individual get funds to another, such as when a payment must be made for a purchase from eBay.

It is also becoming rather common for many businesses to receive and send payments without the use of paper documents like cheques. Even quite small businesses using accounting software like Sage 50® can arrange their affairs to make this happen quickly and easily. Just a few years ago, it was likely that only very large companies with huge IT departments would make and receive money this way, but no longer. It is now rather common for a business to arrange their accounting to allow funds to be both received and sent using software, rather than pieces of paper. This trend will not only continue, but some predict that before long, actual pieces of paper will become a rarity, replaced by electrons flowing worldwide through the Internet.

It should also be mentioned here (although it might make a bit more sense after you study the next chapter on payroll) that many companies arrange to pay each employee using a form of EFT. The employer requires that each employee provide them with a blank cheque form for the account they wish to use to receive their wages or salary each period. At the end of each payroll the employer sends the net pay amount electronically to each employee. Not only is this efficient for the employer, but employees like the process as well, as their net pay shows up in their bank account without them having to do anything. This does not work in all situations, of course. Your author is aware of one company whose employees are sometimes given jobs despite having, shall we say, "shady" backgrounds. Several of these persons do not have a bank account, often because they are not literate and have never had an opportunity to establish themselves to the extent that would allow them to qualify for such an account. In addition, some companies are just too small, or have never shifted to using a computer or computer service to do their payroll. But many companies do use this method of paying their employees, and the number is certain to grow over time.

While all of these payment/receipt methods exist and are in daily use today, accounting students will need to account for funds being transferred in the more traditional way; by cheques sent and received. Therefore it is still necessary to learn the material in this chapter. Just do not be surprised when you are faced with these new technologies. Remember that money coming into a company's bank account is still a debit, while money going out is a credit, so making the necessary entries to record such transactions is little different from what you will learn in this chapter, although the references may not be as straightforward as just using a cheque or deposit number.

Here are a few more topics that relate to how banking is done today:

- ATMs **Automated teller machines** have been around for quite some time now, and hardly qualify any longer as a modern trend. It is very likely that every student has by now used one of these machines to either make a deposit to his or her bank account or withdraw funds. In fact it is probable that many students will only have visited an actual bank location to either set up their account in the first place (although this is now very easy to do online!), or arrange for a car or other bank loan. ATMs are now common throughout the world, and have largely supplanted traveller's cheques, which used to be the common and safe way to take funds along on a vacation or other trip. It remains as true today as it was in the beginning—do not share your PIN with anybody, and be cautious in accepting any help offered by a stranger when using an ATM.
- **Cheque Truncation** Banks no longer return cancelled cheques with their monthly bank statements as once was common. Today, the actual paid cheques are quickly scanned by the bank and an electronic copy kept on file in case it should ever be required for some legal or other purpose. Banks have different rules about such matters, but, for a monthly fee, many will send along a page or pages with miniature copies of all cheques paid. Often a law office will need

this feature, but many other businesses or individuals can make do without the actual copy of the paid cheque. This is another example of the disappearance of paper from the world of commerce!

- **International Banking** At one time it was very rare for a business or individual to need to do any banking outside the local country. Things are changing of course, and many companies are selling and purchasing goods and services on an international level. That means that banking must be responsive to this need. Many Canadian banks have offices in other countries, and when they do not have an actual branch, they can arrange for a customer to deal with an affiliated bank. International barriers are falling, and it is becoming quite easy to receive or send funds between countries. It is not yet really cheap to do this—not only do most banks charge significant fees to make these transactions, but they also make lots of money on foreign exchange conversion. As already mentioned, SWIF T codes are mandated for every branch of every bank in the world, and by using these codes, it is possible to transfer funds almost instantly across the globe. Pretty impressive, actually!
- **Electronic Integration** Today, even medium-sized or small companies can take advantage of the integration of electronic banking with their accounting records. Companies can issue purchase orders, track shipments, enter invoices, and make payments completely without any sort of written record at all (unless they choose to print any given document on a local printer). So it is not only funds that flow electronically, but the movement of goods can also be controlled by using appropriate accounting software along with special software used to ensure security and accuracy over the Internet. While these transactions are made electronically and even recorded the same way, accounting students must still understand the principles involved to ensure that a company's accounting records are accurate and current.

Example of a More Comprehensive Bank Statement

The bank reconciliation of Becca's Jewellery was not as complicated as it is for many companies, even using today's computer technology. Let's look at a reconciliation for Matty's Supermarket (Figures 8-8 and 8-9), which is based on the following:

Matty's Cash account balance		$13,176.84
Bank balance		23,726.04
Leased space to Subway—EFT receipt		8,456.00
Leased space to Dunkin' Donuts—EFT receipt		3,616.12
Matty pays a supplementary health insurance payment each month by electronic transfer		1,444.00
Deposits in transit 6/30		6,766.52
Cheques outstanding		
Chq. # 738	$1,144.00	
739	1,277.88	
740	332.00	
741	812.56	
742	1,834.12	
Cheque # 734 was overstated in company's books		1,440.00

Note in Figure 8-9 that each adjustment to Matty's chequebook is the reconciliation process that would result in general journal entries.

Figure 8-8
Bank Statement for Matty's Supermarket

ROYAL BANK
1 Left Street
Marblehead, NS B0T 6A4

ACCOUNT STATEMENT

Matty's Supermarket
20 Sullivan St.
Marblehead, NS B0T 7X3

Chequing Account: 775800061

Chequing Account Summary as of 6/30/15

Beginning Balance	Total Deposits	Total Withdrawals	Service Charge	Ending Balance
$26,224.48	**$17,410.56**	**$19,852.00**	**$57.00**	**$23,726.04**

Chequing Account Transactions

Deposits	Date	Amount
Deposit	6/05	4,000.00
Deposit	6/05	448.00
Deposit	6/08	778.40
EFT leasing: Dunkin' Donuts	6/18	3,616.12
EFT leasing: Subway	6/27	8,456.00
Interest	6/30	112.04

Charges	Date	Amount
Service charge: Cheque printing	6/30	57.00
EFT: Blue Cross/Blue Shield	6/21	1,444.00
NSF	6/21	208.00

Cheques

Number	Date	Amount
401	6/07	400.00
733	6/13	12,000.00
734	6/13	600.00
735	6/11	400.00
736	6/18	400.00
737	6/29	4,400.00

Daily Balance

Date	Balance	Date	Balance
5/31	26,224.48	6/18	21,267.00
6/05	30,672.48	6/21	19,615.00
6/07	30,272.48	6/27	28,071.00
6/09	30,050.88	6/30	23,726.04
6/11	30,650.88		
6/13	18,050.88		

Figure 8-9
Bank Reconciliation for Matty's Supermarket

MATTY'S SUPERMARKET
Bank Reconciliation as of June 30, 2015

General ledger balance			**Bank balance**		
Matty's general ledger balance		$13,176.84	Bank balance		$23,726.04
Add:			Add:		
EFT leasing: Dunkin' Donuts	$3,616.12		Deposits in transit, 6/30		6,766.52
EFT leasing: Subway	8,456,00				30,492.56
Interest	112.04				
Error: Overstated Cheque No. 734	1,440.00	13,624.16			
		26,801.00			
Deduct:			Deduct:		
Service charge	57.00		Outstanding cheques:		
NSF cheque	208.00		No. 738	$1,144.00	
EFT health insurance payment	1,444.00	1,709.00	No. 739	1,277.88	
			No. 740	332.00	
			No. 741	812.56	
			No. 742	1,834.12	5,400.56
Reconciled balance		$25,092.00	Reconciled balance		$25,092.00

LEARNING UNIT 8-1 REVIEW

AT THIS POINT you should be able to:

- Define and explain the need for a deposit slip. (p. 345)
- List as well as compare and contrast the three common types of cheque endorsement. (p. 347)
- Explain the structure of a cheque. (p. 349)
- Define and state the purpose of a bank statement. (p. 351)
- Explain deposits in transit, cheques outstanding, service charge, and NSF. (pp. 351–352)
- Explain the difference between a debit memorandum and a credit memorandum. (p. 352)
- Explain how to do a bank reconciliation. (pp. 351–353)
- Explain electronic funds transfer and cheque truncation. (pp. 354 and 355)
- Explain the advantages and disadvantages of online banking. (pp. 353–356)

Self-Review Quiz 8-1A

(The forms you need are on page 8-1 of the *Study Guide with Working Papers.*)

Indicate, by placing an X under it, the heading that describes the appropriate action for each of the following situations:

Situation	Add to Bank Balance	Deduct from Bank Balance	Add to Chequebook Balance	Deduct from Chequebook Balance
1. Cheque printing charge				
2. Deposits in transit				
3. NSF cheque				
4. A $50 cheque written and recorded by the company as $60				
5. Proceeds of a note collected by the bank				
6. Cheque outstanding				
7. Forgot to record direct deposit payroll payment				

Solution to Self-Review Quiz 8-1A

Quiz Tip

Deposits in transit are added to the bank balance, while cheques outstanding are subtracted from the bank balance.

Situation	Add to Bank Balance	Deduct from Bank Balance	Add to Chequebook Balance	Deduct from Chequebook Balance
1				X
2	X			
3				X
4			X	
5			X	
6		X		
7				X

Self-Review Quiz 8-1B

Maximum value from this review question will be obtained only when you make an honest attempt to complete it before looking at the solution provided.

KELLY'S TRAIL RIDES
OPENING BANK RECONCILIATION
MAY 31, 2017

Balance per Bank Statement—May 29, 2017			$8,543.86
Add: Deposit in Transit			1,253.48
			9,797.34
Less: Outstanding Cheques:	Chq. No.	Amount	
	814	$ 78.30	
	852	579.42	
	854	1,084.00	
	858	341.75	2,083.47
			$7,713.87
Balance per General Ledger—Account 1111			$7,756.37
Less: Bank Charges for May			42.50
			$7,713.87

KELLY'S TRAIL RIDES

Date Printed: July 7, 2017 Page: 1
G/L Listing: Account 1111 General Bank Account
General Ledger Listing for the period June 1 to June 30, 2017

Period	Source	Date	Description	Reference	Posting Sequence	Debits	Credits	Dr. Balance
6	GL-JE	Jun 1, 2017	Opening Balance					7,756.37
6	GL-JE	Jun 2, 2017	Syd Jenkins Tack Shop	CHQ 859	6-01		1,840.60	5,915.77
6	GL-JE	Jun 2, 2017	Municipal Utility Co.	CHQ 860	6-01		278.32	5,637.45
6	GL-JE	Jun 3, 2017	Deposit—CHRA	3827C	6-02	2,580.00		8,217.45
6	GL-JE	Jun 3, 2017	Atkin's Repairs	CHQ 861	6-03		650.00	7,567.45
6	GL-JE	Jun 6, 2017	Deposit—NS Group	3828C	6-04	3,295.00		10,862.45
6	GL-JE	Jun 6, 2017	Kelly Dean	CHQ 862	6-05		2,000.00	8,862.45
6	GL-JE	Jun 6, 2017	Chapperal Books	CHQ 863	6-05		245.75	8,616.70
6	GL-JE	Jun 6, 2017	NSF—R. Burke—CHRA	Royal DM	6-06		415.00	8,201.70
6	GL-JE	Jun 6, 2017	NSF Service Charge	Royal DM	6-06		25.00	8,176.70
6	GL-JE	Jun 6, 2017	MKP Properties	CHQ 864	6-07		1,465.50	6,711.20
6	GL-JE	Jun 9, 2017	Mary K. Madsen	CHQ 865	6-07		975.00	5,736.20
6	GL-JE	Jun 9, 2017	Bank Charges for May	ADJ 418	6-07		42.50	5,693.70
6	GL-JE	Jun 9, 2017	Deposit—KOH Group	3829C	6-08	4,250.00		9,943.70
6	GL-JE	Jun 10, 2017	Sandy's Quick Mart	CHQ 866	6-09		153.56	9,790.14
6	GL-JE	Jun 10, 2017	Canadian Map Company	CHQ 867	6-09		386.48	9,403.66
6	GL-JE	Jun 10, 2017	Merv Stringer	CHQ 868	6-09		845.00	8,558.66
6	GL-JE	Jun 10, 2017	Hunter Wholesale Co.	CHQ 869	6-09		218.60	8,340.06
6	GL-JE	Jun 13, 2017	Deposit—Manyberries	3830C	6-10	6,200.00		14,540.06
6	GL-JE	Jun 13, 2017	Mary K. Madsen	CHQ 870	6-11		1,140.00	13,400.06
6	GL-JE	Jun 13, 2017	Receiver General	CHQ 871	6-11		1,847.37	11,552.69
6	GL-JE	Jun 13, 2017	Renown Circulation	CHQ 872	6-11		74.50	11,478.19
6	GL-JE	Jun 13, 2017	Kelly Dean	CHQ 873	6-11		1,800.00	9,678.19
6	GL-JE	Jun 16, 2017	Deposit—Tanks a Lot	3831C	6-12	2,400.00		12,078.19
6	GL-JE	Jun 17, 2017	Carolyn Wolfsun	CHQ 874	6-13		750.00	11,328.19
6	GL-JE	Jun 17, 2017	Kendall Trailer Repairs	CHQ 875	6-14		1,547.50	9,780.69
6	GL-JE	Jun 20, 2017	Deposit—OFLR Group	3832C	6-15	3,865.00		13,645.69
6	GL-JE	Jun 20, 2017	Mary K. Madsen	CHQ 876	6-16		875.00	12,770.69
6	GL-JE	Jun 23, 2017	RBC—Loan Principal	Royal DM	6-17		745.20	12,025.49
6	GL-JE	Jun 23, 2017	RBC—Loan Interest	Royal DM	6-17		415.82	11,609.67
6	GL-JE	Jun 23, 2017	County Phone Company	CHQ 877	6-18		204.10	11,405.57
6	GL-JE	Jun 23, 2017	K. Simpson Feeds	CHQ 878	6-18		2,487.35	8,918.22
6	GL-JE	Jun 23, 2017	Bo Franklin	CHQ 879	6-18		377.43	8,540.79
6	GL-JE	Jun 23, 2017	Deposit—Acadian Group	3833C	6-20	2,545.00		11,085.79
6	GL-JE	Jun 23, 2017	Kelly Dean	CHQ 880	6-21		2,500.00	8,585.79
6	GL-JE	Jun 23, 2017	Phillip Madsen	CHQ 881	6-21		645.00	7,940.79
6	GL-JE	Jun 24, 2017	Covington Supplies Co.	CHQ 882	6-22		1,525.00	6,415.79
6	GL-JE	Jun 24, 2017	Bragg Creek High School	CHQ 883	6-22		250.00	6,165.79
6	GL-JE	Jun 24, 2017	OK Corral	CHQ 884	6-22		624.35	5,541.44
6	GL-JE	Jun 27, 2017	Deposit—Finchly Group	3834C	6-23	4,275.00		9,816.44
6	GL-JE	Jun 27, 2017	Deposit—Sundry Cash Sales	3834C	6-23	1,800.00		11,616.44
6	GL-JE	Jun 30, 2017	Mary K. Madsen	CHQ 885	6-24		1,150.00	10,466.44
6	GL-JE	Jun 30, 2017	Bearly's Bridles	CHQ 886	6-24		537.00	9,929.44
6	GL-JE	Jun 30, 2017	George Early Foods	CHQ 887	6-25		1,107.30	8,822.14
6	GL-JE	Jun 30, 2017	Riopan Milling	CHQ 888	6-25		2,176.64	6,645.50
6	GL-JE	Jun 30, 2017	Deposit—Epcor Group	3835C	6-26	5,250.00		11,895.50
6	GL-JE	Jun 30, 2017	Joan Fairfax—Salary	CHQ 889	6-27		2,156.44	9,739.06
6	GL-JE	Jun 30, 2017	Curly Adams—Salary	CHQ 890	6-27		1,984.23	7,754.83
6	GL-JE	Jun 30, 2017	Kelly Dean	CHQ 891	6-27		2,200.00	5,554.83

The above is a detailed printout of the bank account (account number 1111) for Kelly's Trail Rides. It looks a bit different from a hand-posted ledger account because it has been printed by accounting software, but the two versions are essentially the same. Note that this version shows somewhat more detail—a description and reference, for example.

ROYAL BANK OF CANADA

411 MAIN STREET
BRAGG CREEK
ALBERTA T8M 4G6

Account Statement

Account No.	
422-627-8	
Period	
From 29-May-17	To 28-Jun-17
Enclosures 28	Page 1

KELLY'S TRAIL RIDES
RR#5
Bragg Creek
Alberta T8J 6N3

Date	Transaction Description	Details Cheques	Details Deposits	Cheques & Debits	Deposits & Credits	Balance
	Balance Forward					8,543.86
May 30	Deposit				1,253.48	9,797.34
	Cheque	854		1,084.00		8,713.34
May 31	Cheque	852		579.42		8,133.92
Jun 2	Cheque	859		1,840.60		6,293.32
Jun 3	Deposit		3827C		2,580.00	8,873.32
Jun 3	Cheque	858		341.75		8,531.57
Jun 6	Deposit		3828C		3,295.00	11,826.57
	Cheque	860		278.32		11,548.25
	NSF R. Burke	DM		415.00		11,133.25
	NSF S/C	DM		25.00		11,108.25
Jun 7	Cheque	862		2,000.00		9,108.25
Jun 8	Cheque	861		650.00		8,458.25
	Cheque	863		245.75		8,212.50
Jun 9	Deposit		3829C		4,250.00	12,462.50
	Cheque	865		975.00		11,487.50
	Cheque	864		1,465.50		10,022.00
Jun 10	Cheque	868		845.00		9,177.00
Jun 13	Deposit		3830C		6,200.00	15,377.00
	Cheque	867		386.48		14,990.52
Jun 14	Cheque	866		153.56		14,836.96
	Cheque	869		218.60		14,618.36
Jun 15	Cheque	870		1,140.00		13,478.36
Jun 16	Deposit		3831C		2,400.00	15,878.36
	Cheque	873		1,800.00		14,078.36
Jun 17	Cheque	872		74.50		14,003.86
Jun 20	Deposit		3832C		3,865.00	17,868.86
	Cheque	871		1,847.37		16,021.49
	Cheque	876		875.00		15,146.49
Jun 23	Error in Jun 20 Deposit		CM		100.00	15,246.49
	Cheque	875		1,547.50		13,698.99
	Loan Principal	DM		745.20		12,953.79
	Loan Interest	DM		415.82		12,537.97
Jun 23	Deposit		3833C		2,545.00	15,082.97
	Cheque	877		204.10		14,878.87
	Cheque	878		2,487.35		12,391.52
Jun 24	Service Charges	DM		52.00		12,339.52
	Cheque	880		2,500.00		9,839.52
Jun 27	Deposit		3834C		6,075.00	15,914.52
	Cheque	881		645.00		15,269.52
	Cheque	874		750.00		14,519.52
Jun 30	Cheque	885		1,150.00		13,369.52
	Cheque	882		1,525.00		11,844.52
	Cheque	884		624.35		11,220.17

Solution to Self-Review Quiz 8-1B

Please be certain you have made an attempt at the quiz before looking at this solution.

KELLY'S TRAIL RIDES
BANK RECONCILIATION
JUNE 30, 2017

Balance per Bank Statement—June 30, 2017			$11,220.17
Add: Deposit in Transit			5,250.00
			16,470.17
Less: Outstanding Cheques:	Chq. No.	Amount	
	814	$ 78.30	
	879	377.43	
	883	250.00	
	886	537.00	
	887	1,107.30	
	888	2,176.64	
	889	2,156.44	
	890	1,984.23	
	891	2,200.00	10,867.34
			$ 5,602.83
Balance per General Ledger—Account 1111			$ 5,554.83
Add: Error in June 20 Deposit			100.00
			5,654.83
Less: Bank Charges—June 24—Bank Statement			52.00
			$ 5,602.83

LEARNING UNIT 8-2

The Establishment of Petty Cash and Change Funds

Petty cash is an asset on the balance sheet.

Petty cash is an asset that is established by drawing a new cheque. The Petty Cash account is debited only when established unless the amount of the petty cash fund is changed.

Becca realized how time-consuming and expensive it would be to write cheques for small amounts to pay for postage, small supplies, delivery charges, and so on. What was needed was a **petty cash fund**. It was estimated that, for any given month, Becca's Jewellery would need a fund of $60 to cover small expenditures. A cheque payable to the order of the *custodian* (one of Becca's employees responsible for overseeing the fund) was drawn and cashed to establish the fund. The cash was placed in a small metal box with a simple lock, which gave control of the fund to the custodian. A payment out of the fund was made only when a receipt or other supporting documentation was presented by the person requesting the money.

Similarly, Becca established a change fund to make cash transactions with customers more convenient. This unit will explain how to manage petty cash and change funds.

LO 3 Establishing and replenishing a petty cash fund; setting up an auxiliary petty cash record

SETTING UP THE PETTY CASH FUND

Shown here is the transaction analysis chart for the establishment of a $60 petty cash fund, which would be entered in the general journal (or the cash payments journal, as described in Chapter 7) on May 1, 2016.

1 Accounts Affected	2 Category	3 ⇅	4 Rules
Petty Cash	**Asset**	↑	**Dr.**
Cash (cheques)	**Asset**	↓	**Cr.**

GENERAL JOURNAL Page 1

Date		Account Titles and Description	PR	Dr.	Cr.
2016 May	1	Petty Cash		60 00	
		Cash			60 00
		Establishment of petty cash fund			

Note the new asset called *Petty Cash*; this new asset was created by writing cheque No. 16, thereby reducing the asset Cash. In reality, the total assets stay the same; what has occurred is a shift from the asset Cash (cheque No. 16) to a new asset account called Petty Cash.

The cheque for $60 is made payable to the custodian, Ted Sullivan, who endorses the cheque, cashes it, and uses the cash to operate the petty cash fund.

The Petty Cash account is not debited or credited again if the size of the fund is not changed. If the $60 fund is used up very quickly, the fund should be increased. If the fund is too large, the Petty Cash account should be reduced.

But who is responsible for controlling the petty cash fund? Becca gives her office manager, Ted Sullivan, the responsibility and the authority to make payments from the petty cash fund. In other companies, the cashier or secretary may be in charge of petty cash.

MAKING PAYMENTS FROM THE PETTY CASH FUND

Ted Sullivan has the responsibility for filling out a **petty cash voucher** for each cash payment made from the petty cash fund.

Note that the voucher (shown in Figure 8-11) when completed will include:

1. The voucher number (which will be in sequence): 1
2. The date: May 2
3. The person or organization to whom the payment was made: Al's Cleaners
4. The amount of payment: $3.00
5. The reason for payment: cleaning
6. The signature of the person who approved the payment: Ted Sullivan
7. The signature of the person who received the payment from petty cash: Becca Baker
8. The account to which the expense will be charged: 619

Voucher in box
+ Cash in box
= Original amount placed in petty cash&]

The completed vouchers are placed in the petty cash box. No matter how many vouchers Ted Sullivan fills out, *the total of (1) the vouchers in the box and (2) the cash on hand should equal the original amount of petty cash with which the fund was established ($60.00).*

Assume that at the end of May the following items are documented by petty cash vouchers in the petty cash box as having been paid by Ted Sullivan:

2016		
May	2	Cleaning package, $3.00
	6	Postage stamps, $9.00
	8	First-aid supplies, $15.00
	9	Delivery expense, $6.00
	14	Delivery expense, $15.00
	27	Postage stamps, $6.00

Figure 8-11
Petty Cash Voucher

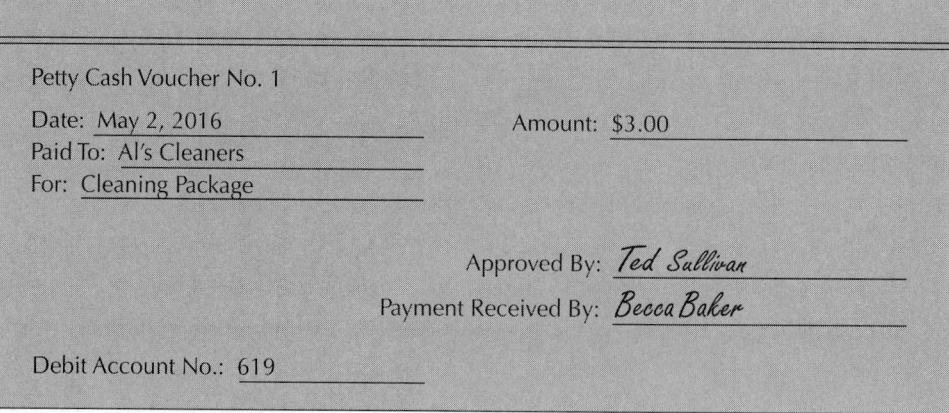

Petty Cash Voucher No. 1

Date: May 2, 2016   Amount: $3.00

Paid To: Al's Cleaners

For: Cleaning Package

Approved By: *Ted Sullivan*

Payment Received By: *Becca Baker*

Debit Account No.: 619

It is always a good idea to use Petty Cash Vouchers, but some companies think that the small amount of cash "at risk" is not large enough to require such formal controls. Such companies may not use these vouchers, and instead let the receipt submitted stand in for a formal voucher.

Ted records this information in the **auxiliary petty cash record** shown in Figure 8-12. It is not a special journal but an aid to Ted—an auxiliary record that is not essential but is quite helpful as part of the petty cash system. You may want to think of the auxiliary petty cash record as an optional worksheet. Let's look at how to replenish the petty cash fund.

Think of the auxiliary petty cash record as a worksheet that gathers information for the journal entry.

HOW TO REPLENISH THE PETTY CASH FUND

No postings will be done from the auxiliary book; it is not a journal. At some point, the summarized information found in the auxiliary petty cash record will be used as a basis for a journal entry in the cash payments journal and eventually posted to appropriate ledger accounts to reflect up-to-date balances.

Remember—the only time that the account *Petty Cash* is debited is when it is set up initially, or increased in amount at some later date. Never debit *Petty Cash* during replenishment.

The expenses of $54 (see Figure 8-12) are recorded in the general journal, debited to the appropriate accounts (Figure 8-13), and a new cheque, No. 17 for $54, is cashed and the proceeds given to Ted Sullivan for the petty cash fund. The petty cash box once again holds $60 cash. The old vouchers that were used are stamped to indicate they have been processed and the fund replenished. The expenses recorded in the general journal to cover the replenishment of the petty cash fund will subsequently be posted to the ledger.

Note that in the replenishment process, the debits in the general journal (Figure 8-13) are a summary of the totals of expenses (except sundry) or other items from the auxiliary petty cash record. Posting of these specific expenses will ensure that the expenses will not be understated on the income statement. The credit to

						Category of Payments			
Date		Voucher No.	Description	Receipts	Payments	Postage Expense	Delivery Expense	Sundry	
								Account	Amount
2016 May	1		Establishment	60 00					
	2	1	Cleaning		3 00			Cleaning	3 00
	6	2	Postage		9 00	9 00			
	8	3	First Aid		15 00			Misc.	15 00
	9	4	Delivery		6 00		6 00		
	14	5	Delivery		15 00		15 00		
	27	6	Postage		6 00	6 00			
			Total	60 00	54 00	15 00	21 00		18 00

Figure 8-12 Auxiliary Petty Cash Record

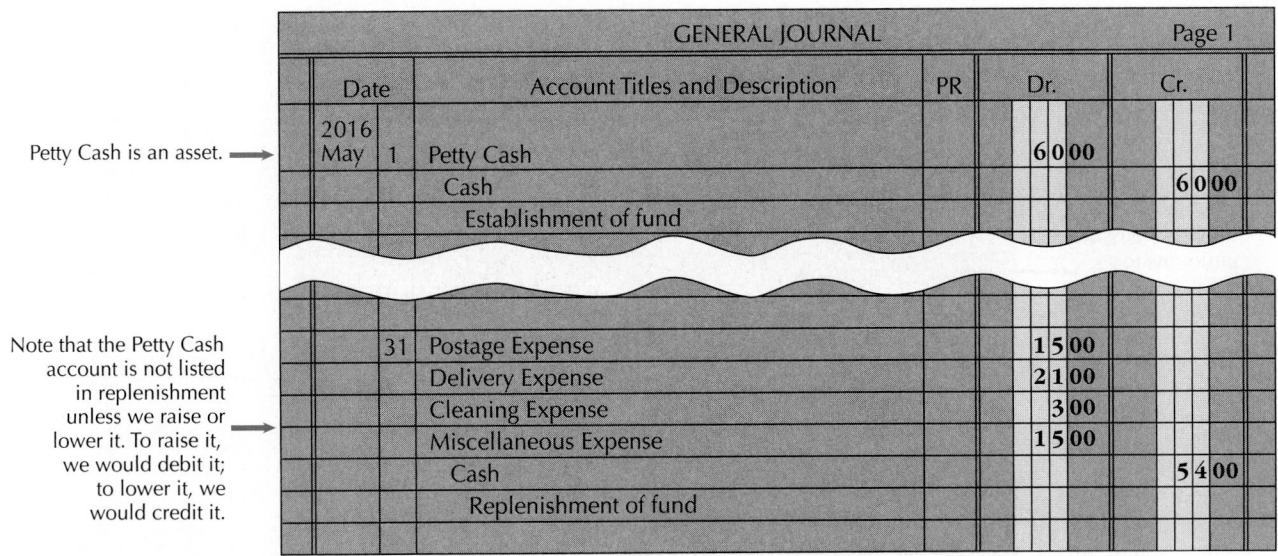

Petty Cash is an asset.

Note that the Petty Cash account is not listed in replenishment unless we raise or lower it. To raise it, we would debit it; to lower it, we would credit it.

GENERAL JOURNAL					Page 1
Date		Account Titles and Description	PR	Dr.	Cr.
2016 May	1	Petty Cash		60 00	
		Cash			60 00
		Establishment of fund			
	31	Postage Expense		15 00	
		Delivery Expense		21 00	
		Cleaning Expense		3 00	
		Miscellaneous Expense		15 00	
		Cash			54 00
		Replenishment of fund			

Figure 8-13 Establishment and Replenishment of Petty Cash Fund

cash is where we draw a cheque for $54 to put money back in the petty cash box. The $60 in the box now agrees with the petty cash account balance. *The end result is that our petty cash box is filled, and we have justified which accounts the petty cash money was spent for. Think of replenishment as a single, summarizing entry.*

A new cheque is written in the replenishment process, which is payable to the custodian, cashed by Sullivan, and the cash placed in the petty cash box.

Remember, if at some point the petty cash fund is to be greater than $60, a cheque can be written that will increase Petty Cash and decrease Cash. If the Petty Cash account balance is to be reduced, we can credit or reduce Petty Cash. However, for our present purpose, Petty Cash will remain at $60.

The auxiliary petty cash record after replenishment would look as shown in Figure 8-14. (Keep in mind that no postings are made from the auxiliary book.)

Figure 8-15 may help you put the sequence together.

Before concluding this unit, let's look at how Becca will handle setting up a change fund and at problems with cash shortages and overages.

AUXILIARY PETTY CASH RECORD

Date	Voucher No.	Description	Receipts	Payments	Category of Payments: Postage Expense	Delivery Expense	Sundry: Account	Amount
2016 May 1		Establishment	60 00					
2	1	Cleaning		3 00			Cleaning	3 00
6	2	Postage		9 00	9 00			
8	3	First Aid		15 00			Misc.	15 00
9	4	Delivery		6 00		6 00		
14	5	Delivery		15 00		15 00		
27	6	Postage		6 00	6 00			
		Totals	60 00	54 00	15 00	21 00		18 00
		Ending Balance		6 00				
			60 00	60 00				
		Ending Balance	6 00					
31		Replenishment	54 00					
31		Balance (New)	60 00					

Figure 8-14 Recording Replenishment in the Petty Cash Record

Have nothing to do with petty cash (amounts too great) → (points to May 2 row)

In this step, the old expenses are listed in the cash payments journal and a new cheque is written to replenish the fund. All old vouchers are removed from the petty cash box. → (points to May 29 row)

Date		Description	New Cheque Written	Recorded in Cash Payments Journal	Petty Cash Voucher Prepared	Recorded in Auxiliary Petty Cash Record	
2016 May	1	Establishment of petty cash for $60	X	X		X	Dr. Petty Cash Cr. Cash
	2	Paid salaries, $2,000	X	X			
	13	Paid $10 from petty cash for bandages			X	X	No journal entries
	20	Paid $8 from petty cash for postage			X	X	
	24	Paid light bill, $200	X	X			
	29	Replenishment of petty cash to $60	X	X		X	Dr. Individual Expenses Cr. Cash

Figure 8-15 Steps Involving Petty Cash

LO 4 Establishing and replenishing a change fund

Change fund is an asset on the balance sheet.

SETTING UP A CHANGE FUND AND INSIGHT INTO CASH SHORT AND OVER

If a company like Becca's Jewellery expects to have many cash transactions occurring, it may be a good idea to establish a **change fund** or float. This is a fund that is placed in the cash register drawer and used to make change for customers who pay cash. Becca decides to put $120 in the change fund, made up of various denominations of bills and coins. Let's look at a transaction analysis chart for this sort of procedure.

1 Accounts Affected	2 Category	3 ↑↓	4 Dr./Cr.
Change Fund	Asset	↑	Dr.
Cash	Asset	↓	Cr.

At the close of the business day, Becca will place the balance of the change fund back in the safe in the office. She will set up the change fund (the same amount of $120) in the appropriate denominations for the next business day. She will deposit the *remainder* of the cash taken in for the day in the bank.

Now let's look at how to record errors that are made in making change, called *cash short and over.*

LO 5 Handling transactions involving cash short and over

Beginning change fund
+ Cash register total
= Cash should have on hand
– Counted cash
= Shortage or overage of cash

Cash Short and Over

In a local pizza shop, the total sales for the day did not match the amount of cash on hand. Errors often happen in making change. To record and summarize the differences in cash, an expense account called **Cash Short and Over** is used. This account will record both overages (too much money) and shortages (not enough money). Let's first look at the account (in T account form).

Cash Short and Over	
Dr.	Cr.
Shortage	Overage

For one example of how other income items are shown, see page 591.

All shortages will be recorded as debits and all overages will be recorded as credits. This account is temporary. If the ending balance of the account is a debit (a shortage), it is considered a miscellaneous expense that would be reported on the income statement. If the balance of the account is a credit (an overage), it is considered as other income (or reduction of expense) reported on the income statement. Let's look at how the Cash Short and Over account could be used to record shortages or overages in sales as well as in the petty cash process.

Example 1: Shortages and Overages in Sales
On December 5, the pizza shop rang up sales of $560 for the day but had only $530 in cash.

1 Accounts Affected	2 Category	3 ↑↓	4 Dr./Cr.
Cash	Asset	↑	Debit $530
Cash Short and Over	Expense	↑	Debit $30
Sales	Revenue	↑	Credit $560

The journal entry would be as follows:

Dec.	5	Cash	530 00	
		Cash Short and Over	30 00	
		Sales		560 00
		Cash shortage		

Note that the shortage of $30 is a debit and would be recorded on the income statement as a miscellaneous expense.

What would the entry look like if the pizza shop showed a $50 overage?

1 Accounts Affected	2 Category	3 ↑↓	4 Dr./Cr.
Cash	Asset	↑	Debit $530
Cash Short and Over	Expense	↓	Debit $30
Sales	Revenue	↑	Credit $560

The journal entry would be as follows:

Dec.	5	Cash	610 00	
		Cash Short and Over		50 00
		Sales		560 00
		Cash overage		

Note that the Cash Short and Over account would be reported as other income on the income statement if it had a credit balance at year end. Now let's look at how to use this Cash Short and Over account to record petty cash transactions.

Example 2: Cash Short and Over in Petty Cash
A local computer company had established a $200 petty cash fund. Today, November 30, the petty cash box had $160 in vouchers as well as $32 in coin and currency. What would be the journal entry to replenish petty cash?

Assume the vouchers were made up of $90 for postage and $70 for supplies expense. If you add up the vouchers and cash in the box, cash is short by $8.

1 Accounts Affected	2 Category	3 ↑↓	4 Dr./Cr.
Postage Expense	**Expense**	↑	**Debit $90**
Supplies Expense	**Expense**	↑	**Debit $70**
Cash Short and Over	**Expense**	↑	**Debit $8**
Cash	**Asset**	↓	**Credit $168**

The journal entry would be as follows:

Nov.	8	Postage Expense	90 00	
		Supplies on Hand	70 00	
		Cash Short and Over	8 00	
		Cash		168 00
		Replenish petty cash		

If there had been an overage, the cash short and over would be a credit as other income. If an auxiliary petty cash record is used to record the cash short and over, it would be recorded as a payment of $8 under the category of payments in the sundry column. The Solution to Self-Review Quiz 8-2 shows how a fund shortage would be recorded in the auxiliary record.

LEARNING UNIT 8-2 REVIEW

AT THIS POINT you should be able to:

- State the purpose of a petty cash fund. (p. 362)
- Prepare a journal entry to establish a petty cash fund. (p. 363)
- Prepare a petty cash voucher. (pp. 363–364)
- Explain the relationship of the auxiliary petty cash record to the petty cash process. (p. 364)
- Prepare a journal entry to replenish Petty Cash to its original amount. (p. 364)
- Explain why individual expenses are debited in the replenishment process. (pp. 364–365)
- Explain how a change fund is established. (p. 366)
- Explain how Cash Short and Over could be a miscellaneous expense. (p. 367)

Self-Review Quiz 8-2

(The forms you need are on page 8-2 of the *Study Guide with Working Papers.*)

As the custodian of the petty cash fund, it is your task to prepare entries to establish the fund on October 1, 2016, as well as to replenish the fund on October 31. Please keep an auxiliary petty cash record.

Cheques to establish and replenish Petty Cash would be made out to the custodian.

2016		
Oct.	1	Establish petty cash fund for $90, cheque No. 8.
	4	Voucher 1, delivery expense, $21.
	8	Voucher 2, delivery expense, $15.

Oct.	11	Voucher 3, office repair expense, $24.
	18	Voucher 4, general expense, $12.
	29	Replenishment of petty cash fund, $78, cheque No. 108. (cheque would be payable to the custodian)

Solution to Self-Review Quiz 8-2

! ***Quiz Tip***

How to calculate shortage: $21 + $15 + $24 + $12 = $72 in vouchers replenished with $78 cheque; thus a $6 shortage.

Note that the amount for cash short and over was entered into the auxiliary petty cash record.

GENERAL JOURNAL — Page 6

Date		Account Titles and Description	PR	Dr.	Cr.
2016 Oct.	1	Petty Cash		90 00	
		Cash			90 00
		Establishment, Cheque No. 8			
	29	Delivery Expense		36 00	
		General Expense		12 00	
		Office Repair Expense		24 00	
		Cash Short and Over		6 00	
		Cash			78 00
		Replenishment, Cheque No. 108			

AUXILIARY PETTY CASH RECORD

Date		Voucher No.	Description	Receipts	Payments	Category of Payments: Delivery Expense	General Expense	Sundry: Account	Amount
2016 Oct.	1		Establishment	90 00					
	4	1	Delivery		21 00	21 00			
	8	2	Delivery		15 00	15 00			
	11	3	Repairs		24 00			Office Repairs	24 00
	18	4	General		12 00		12 00		
	31	5	Fund shortage		6 00			Cash S & O	6 00
			Totals	90 00	78 00	36 00	12 00		30 00
			Ending Balance		12 00				
				90 00	90 00				
	31		Ending Balance	12 00					
	31		Replenishment	78 00					
Nov.	1		Balance (New)	90 00					

Counting Down the Cash

Comprehensive question regarding internal controls
1 2 3 4 (20 min)

Subway now requires all of its franchisees to submit their weekly sales and inventory reports electronically using new point-of-sale (POS) touch-screen cash registers. With the new POS registers, clerks use a touch screen to punch in the number and type of items bought. Franchisees can quickly reconfigure prices and products to match new promotions. Not only is this POS method faster than using the old cash registers, but it also allows franchisees to view every transaction as it occurs—from their own back office computers or even from home. Also, individual POS terminals within the restaurant are linked, so franchisees are able to see consolidated data quickly.

The transition to electronic reporting and networked POS terminals, however, has not been without bumps, as Stan can testify. About six months before the deadline for all Subway franchisees to "go electronic," Stan attended a heated meeting on the topic at his local chapter of the North American Association of Subway Franchisees (NAASF). The NAASF is an independent organization of franchisees that serves as an advisory council on Subway policies and issues of common concern. Everyone seemed to be talking at once.

"I don't trust these machines. What am I supposed to do when the system crashes?" complained one man.

"Yeah, and I don't like the idea of a bunch of kids knowing more about how to run the software than I do," said one older franchisee.

"Don't be so quick to assume that our sandwich artists will love POS, " one woman said." I overheard one of my employees say to another, 'POS means Peeking Over Shoulders.' These young kids we hire have more reason to be resistant than we do!"

"I'll say they do!" rejoined Jay Harden, the president of Stan's local NAASF. "Employee theft is one of the largest problems that we face as franchisees. I, for one, really welcome the cash control we get with POS."

Stan had to agree with Jay. Training staff to record every sale and record it correctly is a critical component of a cash business like Subway. In Stan's view, the POS machines would make that training only easier. Cash control is built into the new system, which also provides the owners with information that will help them spot problems—such as employee theft—and track trends. Of course, thought Stan, the chore of counting down the cash at the end of a shift remained. No matter what type of computer program you install, cash still must be counted down and reconciled with the register tape at the end of each shift.

As the voices rang louder around him, Stan thought about what had happened that day when Ellen closed out her cash register drawer. He had spent hours figuring out a discrepancy between the cash in the drawer and the register tape. Ellen had forgotten to void a mistaken entry for $99.99. Stan had first suspected that she had made a huge error in counting change.

Thinking of errors in counting brought him back to the topic of the meeting. Stan raised his hand to speak. "One thing that concerns me is the potential for accounting errors. I still have to key in data from the POS into my accounting software. Every time I have to re-enter data, the potential for error multiplies."

"That shows some foresight, Stan," Jay Harden said. "We're actually exploring computer programs that will feed the data directly from the POS into our accounting programs."

Even some of the technophobes and POS skeptics in the group had to agree that that would be a great idea.

DISCUSSION QUESTIONS

1. What is an advisory council? Why do you think franchisees need one?
2. Why do you think some small business owners fear computerization?
3. How would Stan catch a discrepancy in the Cash account? How would he record a loss?
4. Why does Subway invest time, money, and effort in investigating new cash handling systems such as its new POS terminals?

Chapter Assignments

SUMMARY OF KEY POINTS

Learning Unit 8-1

1. Restrictive endorsement limits any further negotiation of a cheque.
2. Cheque stubs are filled out first before a cheque is written.
3. The payee is the person to whom the cheque is payable. The drawer is the one who orders the bank to pay a sum of money. The drawee is the bank where the drawer has an account.
4. The process of reconciling the bank statement balance with the company's cash balance is called bank reconciliation. The timing of deposits, when the bank statement was issued, and other factors often result in differences between the bank statement balance and the balance shown in the general ledger account.
5. Deposits in transit are added to the bank balance.
6. Cheques outstanding are subtracted from the bank balance.
7. NSF means that an account has insufficient funds to pay a cheque; therefore, the amount is not included in the recipient's bank balance and the chequing account balance is lowered.
8. When a bank debits your account, an amount is deducted from your balance. A credit to the account is an increase in your balance.
9. All adjustments to the chequebook balance require journal entries.

Learning Unit 8-2

1. Petty Cash is an asset found on the balance sheet.
2. The Auxiliary Petty Cash Record is an auxiliary book; thus no postings are done from this book. Think of it as an optional worksheet.
3. When a petty cash fund is established, the amount is entered as a debit to Petty Cash and a credit to Cash in the cash payments journal.
4. At the time of replenishment of the petty cash fund, all expenses are debited (by category) and a credit to Cash (a new cheque) results. This replenishment, when journalized and posted, updates the ledger from the journal.
5. The only time the Petty Cash account is used is to establish the fund to begin with or to bring the fund to a higher or lower level. If the petty cash level is deemed sufficient, all replenishments will debit specific expenses and credit Cash, and a new cheque will be written. The asset, Petty Cash account balance, will remain unchanged.
6. A change fund is an asset that is used to make change for customers on cash sales.
7. Cash Short and Over is an account that is either a miscellaneous expense or a miscellaneous income, depending on whether the ending balance is a shortage (a debit) or an overage (a credit).

KEY TERMS

Automated teller machine (ATM) A machine that permits customers to perform banking transactions without the assistance of a bank teller (p. 355)

Auxiliary petty cash record A supplementary record for summarizing petty cash information (p. 364)

Bank reconciliation The process of reconciling the chequebook balance with the bank balance given on the bank statement (p. 351)

Bank statement A report sent by a bank to a customer indicating the previous balance, individual cheques processed, individual deposits received, service charges, other sundry items, and ending bank balance (p. 351)

Cancelled cheques Cheques that have been processed by a bank and are no longer negotiable (p. 348)

Cash Short and Over The account that records cash shortages and overages. If the ending balance is a debit, it is recorded on the income statement as a miscellaneous expense; if it is a credit, it is recorded as miscellaneous income. (p. 366)

Change fund A fund made up of various denominations of bills and coins that is used to make change for customers (p. 366)

Cheque A form used to indicate a specific amount of money that is to be paid by the bank to a named person or company (p. 348)

Cheque truncation Procedure whereby cheques are not returned to the drawer with the bank statement but are instead kept at the bank for a certain length of time before being first scanned into electronic format and then destroyed (p. 355)

Credit memorandum Increase in depositor's balance (p. 352)

Debit card Similar to a credit card, but funds are deducted immediately from the cardholder's bank account (p. 347)

Debit memorandum Decrease in depositor's balance (p. 352)

Deposit slip Form provided by a bank for use in recording deposits of money or cheques into a bank account (p. 345)

Deposits in transit Deposits that were made by customers of a bank but did not reach or were not processed by the bank before the preparation of the bank statement (p. 352)

Drawee Bank with which the drawer has an account (p. 348)

Drawer Person who writes a cheque (p. 348)

Electronic funds transfer (EFT) An electronic system that transfers funds without the use of paper cheques (p. 354)

Electronic integration Close connection between companies' business records that greatly expedites business transactions—including funds transfer (p. 356)

Endorsement *Blank*—could be further endorsed. *Full*—restricts further endorsement to only the person or company named. *Restrictive*—restricts any further endorsement. (p. 347)

Internal control systems Systems of procedures and methods to control a firm's assets as well as monitor its operations (p. 344)

NSF (not sufficient funds) Notation indicating that a cheque has been written on an account that lacks sufficient funds to pay it (p. 352)

Outstanding cheques Cheques written by a company or person that were not received or not processed by the bank before the preparation of the bank statement (p. 352)

Payee The person or company the cheque is payable to (p. 348)

Petty cash fund A fund (source) that allows payment of small cash amounts without the writing of cheques (p. 362)

Petty cash voucher A petty cash form to be completed when money is taken out of petty cash (p. 363)

Service charge The fee charged by banks or other financial institutions to manage your bank account, such as receiving deposits and processing cheques (p. 352)

Signature card A form signed by a bank customer that the bank uses to verify signature authenticity on all cheques (p. 345)
SWIFT codes Numerical codes that identify banks worldwide, allowing safe and speedy transfer of funds (p. 354)

QUICK REVIEW

The following Tips are from Learning Units 8-1 to 8-2. Answer the Assess Your Progress questions and use the How Did You Do? at the bottom of the page to see how well you know the material. The Quick Review provides tips before each Assess Your Progress to help you avoid common accounting errors.

LU 8-1 Bank Procedures, Chequing Accounts, and Bank Reconciliations

Tips: When reconciling a bank statement, timing is a key consideration. Deposits in transit would be added to the bank balance while cheques outstanding would be subtracted. Sometimes on the bank statement, interest is shown and must be updated on the chequebook side. If you forget to record a withdrawal from an ATM, you must update your book balance. Keep in mind that any adjustments to the chequebook will require journal entries so the cash ledger account will be correct. Today, online banking (perhaps we should say, paperless banking) is taking over many of the manual tasks, but the accounting theory remains the same.

Assess Your Progress

Answer true or false to the following statements:

1. A credit memo from the bank means that it is decreasing your balance.
2. NSF results in an increase to your chequebook balance.
3. Blank endorsements are the safest type of endorsement.
4. The drawer is the one receiving a cheque.
5. A service charge must be adjusted on the bank balance.

LU 8-2 The Establishment of Petty Cash and Change Funds

Tips: Petty cash is an asset. When petty cash is replenished to the same level, all of the old expenses are shown and a new cheque is written. The account Petty Cash is not touched. When a higher total amount of petty cash is desired, the account Petty Cash will be debited to increase it (or credited to decrease it). Keep in mind that the account Cash Short and Over is a miscellaneous account found on the income statement. A debit balance on Cash Short and Over means that you have a shortage, and a credit balance means you have an overage.

Assess Your Progress

Answer true or false to the following statements:

1. Petty cash is an expense.
2. Increasing the Petty Cash account means that you have to credit it.
3. In the replenishment process, cash is not involved.
4. When petty cash is established, the Petty Cash account is debited.
5. A shortage in the Cash Short and Over account results in a credit balance.

How Did You Do? Answers to the Assess Your Progress Questions

LU 8-1

1. False—A credit memo from the bank means that it is increasing your balance.
2. False—NSF results in a decrease to your chequebook balance.
3. False—Restrictive endorsements are the safest type of endorsement.
4. False—The payee is to whom a cheque is payable.
5. False—A service charge must be adjusted on the chequebook balance.

LU 8-2

1. False—Petty Cash is an asset.
2. False—Increasing the Petty Cash account means that you have to debit it.
3. False—In the replenishment process, a new cheque (cash) needs to be written.
4. True.
5. False—A shortage in the Cash Short and Over account results in a debit balance.

BLUEPRINT OF A BANK RECONCILIATION

General Ledger Cash Balance		
Ending balance per books		$XXX
Add:		
Recording of errors that understate balance	XXX	
Proceeds of notes collected by bank or other items credited (added) by bank but not yet updated in chequebook	XXX	
		XXX
Deduct:		
Recording of errors that overstate balance	XXX	
Service charges	XXX	
Printing charges	XXX	
NSF cheques, or other items debited (charged) by bank but not yet updated in chequebook	XXX	
		XXX
Reconciled GL Balance (Adjusted Balance)		$XXX

Balance per Bank		
Ending bank statement balance (last figure on bank statement)		$XXX
Add:		
Deposits in transit (amount not yet credited by bank)	XXX	
Bank errors	XXX	
		XXX
Deduct:		
List of outstanding cheques (amount not yet debited by bank)	XXX	
Bank errors	XXX	
		XXX
Reconciled Bank Balance (Adjusted Balance)		$XXX

QUESTIONS, CLASSROOM DEMONSTRATION EXERCISES, EXERCISES, AND PROBLEMS

Discussion Questions and Critical Thinking/Ethical Case

1. What is the purpose of internal control?
2. What is the advantage of having preprinted deposit slips?
3. Explain the difference between a blank endorsement and a restrictive endorsement.
4. Explain the difference between payee, drawer, and drawee.
5. Why should cheque stubs be filled out first, before the cheque itself is written?
6. A bank statement is sent twice a month. True or false? Please explain.
7. Explain the end product of a bank reconciliation.
8. Why are cheques outstanding subtracted from the bank balance?
9. An NSF cheque results in a bank's issuing the depositor a credit memorandum. Agree or disagree. Support your response.

10. Why do adjustments to the chequebook balance in the reconciliation process need to be journalized?
11. What is EFT?
12. What are the major advantages and disadvantages of online banking?
13. What is meant by cheque truncation?
14. Petty cash is a liability. Accept or reject.
15. Explain the relationship of the auxiliary petty cash record to the cash payments journal.
16. At time of replenishment, why are the totals of individual expenses debited?
17. Explain the purpose of a change fund.
18. Explain how Cash Short and Over can be a miscellaneous expense.
19. Albert Ray, the bookkeeper of Logan Co. of Richmond, received a bank statement from Logan's bank. Albert noticed a $200 mistake made by the bank in the company's favour. Albert called his supervisor, who said that as long as it benefits the company, he should not tell the bank about the error. You make the call. Write your specific recommendations to Albert.

Classroom Demonstration Exercises

(The forms you need are on pages 8-3 and 8-4 in the *Study Guide with Working Papers.*)

Bank Reconciliation

Preparing a bank reconciliation
❷ (10 min)

1. Indicate which of the actions (**1** through **4**) listed below must be taken when doing a bank reconciliation for each of the six situations (**a** through **f**) described below.

1. Add to bank balance
2. Deduct from bank balance
3. Add to general ledger Cash balance
4. Deduct from general ledger Cash balance

___ **a.** $12 bank service charge
___ **b.** $300 deposit in transit
___ **c.** $162 NSF cheque
___ **d.** A $15 cheque was written and recorded as $25
___ **e.** Bank collected a $1,000 note less a $50 collection fee
___ **f.** Cheque No. 111 for the amount of $88 was outstanding

Journal Entries in Reconciliation Process

Recording items from the bank reconciliation
❷ (5 min)

2. Which of the transactions in question 1 above would require a journal entry?

Bank Reconciliation

Bank reconciliation
❷ (10 min)

3. From the following, construct a bank reconciliation for Woody Co. as of May 31, 2016.

GL Cash balance	$1,869.60	Outstanding cheques	427.80
Bank statement balance	1,951.20	Bank service charge	13.80
Deposits in transit	271.20	NSFcheque	61.20

Petty Cash

Setting up the petty cash fund and recording petty cash expenses
❸ (10 min)

4. Indicate which of the actions (**1** through **4**) listed would be necessary for each of the situations (**a** through **f**) described below.

1. New cheque written
2. Recorded in general journal
3. Petty cash voucher prepared
4. Recorded in auxiliary petty cash record

—— **a.** Established petty cash
—— **b.** Paid $1,000 bill for repairs
—— **c.** Paid $2 for bandages from petty cash
—— **d.** Paid $30 for stamps from petty cash
—— **e.** Paid electricity bill, $250
—— **f.** Replenished petty cash

Replenishment of Petty Cash

Replenishing the petty cash fund
❸ (15 min)

5. Petty cash was originally established with $20. During the month, $5 was paid out for bandages and $6 for stamps. During replenishment, the custodian discovered that the balance in petty cash was $8. Record, using a general journal entry, the replenishment of petty cash back to $20.

Increasing Petty Cash

Increasing the Petty Cash account
❸ (10 min)

6. In question 5 above, if the custodian decided to raise the level of petty cash to $30, what would be the journal entry to replenish (use a general journal entry)?

Exercises

Set A

(The forms you need are on pages 8-4 and 8-5 of the *Study Guide with Working Papers.*)

Bank reconciliation
❷ (15 min)

8-1A. From the following information, construct a bank reconciliation for Faith Co. as of July 31, 2016. Then prepare journal entries if needed.

Ending GL Cash balance	$445
Ending bank statement balance	300
Deposits (in transit)	200
Outstanding cheques	95
Bank service charge (debit memo)	15
NSF: Judith Wall's cheque returned	25

Establishing and replenishing petty cash
❸ (15 min)

8-2A. In general journal form, prepare journal entries to establish a petty cash fund on July 2 and replenish it on July 31.

2015		
July	2	A $100 petty cash fund is established.
	31	At the end of the month, $12 cash plus the following paid vouchers exist: donations expense, $20; postage expense, $18; office supplies expense, $25; miscellaneous expense, $25.

Cash shortage in replenishment
❸ (15 min)

8-3A. If, in Exercise 8-2A, cash on hand was $11, prepare the entry to replenish the petty cash on July 31.

Cash overage in replenishment
❸ (15 min)

8-4A. If, in Exercise 8-2A, cash on hand was $13, prepare the entry to replenish the petty cash on July 31.

Calculating cash shortage in a change fund
❺ (15 min)

8-5A. At the end of the day, the clerk for Pete's Variety Shop noticed an error in the amount of cash he had. Total cash sales from the sales tape were $1,200 while the total cash in the till was $1,156. Pete also keeps a $30 change fund in his shop. Prepare an appropriate general journal entry to record the cash sales as well as reveal the cash shortage.

Exercises

Set B

(The forms you need are on pages 8-4 and 8-5 of the *Study Guide with Working Papers.*)

Bank reconciliation
❷ (15 min)

8-1B. From the following information, construct a bank reconciliation for Faith Co. as of July 31, 2016. Then prepare journal entries if needed.

Ending GL Cash balance	$764
Ending bank statement balance	489
Deposits (in transit)	326
Outstanding cheques	148
Bank service charge (debit memo)	21
NSF: Judith Wall's cheque returned	76

Establishing and replenishing petty cash
❸ (15 min)

8-2B. In general journal form, prepare journal entries to establish a petty cash fund on July 2 and replenish it on July 31.

2015		
July	2	A $150 petty cash fund is established.
	31	At the end of the month, $15 cash plus the following paid vouchers exist: delivery expense, $55; postage expense, $34; office supplies expense, $18; miscellaneous expense, $28.

Cash shortage in replenishment
❸ (15 min)

8-3B. If, in Exercise 8-2B, cash on hand was $13, prepare the entry to replenish the petty cash on July 31.

Cash overage in replenishment
❸ (15 min)

8-4B. If, in Exercise 8-2B, cash on hand was $16, prepare the entry to replenish the petty cash on July 31.

Calculating cash shortage in a change fund
❺ (15 min)

8-5B. At the end of the day, the clerk for Pete's Variety Shop noticed an error in the amount of cash he had. Total cash sales from the sales tape were $1,700 while the total cash in the till was $1,726. As part of his cash, Pete keeps a $30 change fund in his shop. Prepare an appropriate general journal entry to record the cash sales as well as reveal the cash shortage.

Group A Problems

(The forms you need are on pages 8-6 to 8-11 of the *Study Guide with Working Papers.*)

Preparing a bank reconciliation, including collection of a note
❷ (20 min)

8A-1. Rose Company in Drumheller received a bank statement from TD Canada Trust indicating a bank balance of $7,100. Based on Rose's GL cash account, the balance was $5,700. Your task is to prepare a bank reconciliation for Rose Company as of July 31, 2017, from the following information (journalize entries as needed):

Check Figure
Reconciled balance $6,410

a. Cheques outstanding: No. 122, $800; No. 130, $1,000.

b. Deposits in transit, $1,110.

c. Rose Company forgot to record a $33 gasoline purchase made with a debit card.

d. Bank service charge, $60.

e. TD Canada Trust collected a note for Rose, $810, less a $7 collection fee.

Preparing a bank reconciliation with an NSF cheque, using the back of a bank statement
❷ (40 min)

8A-2. From the bank statement on the next page and the items below, please (a) complete the bank reconciliation for Rick's Deli of Regina found on the reverse of the bank statement and (b) journalize the appropriate entries as needed.

Check Figure
Reconciled balance $5,270

a. A deposit of $2,000 is in transit.

b. Rick's Deli has an ending GL cash balance of $5,600.

c. Cheques outstanding: No. 111, $600; No. 119, $1,200; No. 121, $330

d. Jim Rice's cheque for $300 bounced because of lack of sufficient funds.

Relationship to auxiliary petty cash record
❸ (30 min)

8A-3. The transactions on page 379 occurred in April and were related to the general journal and petty cash fund of Rick's Deli of Regina:

Check Figure
Cash replenishment $76

2016		
Apr.	1	Issued cheque No. 14 for $100 to establish a petty cash fund.
	5	Paid $15 from petty cash for postage, voucher No. 1.
	8	Paid $20 from petty cash for office supplies, voucher No. 2.
	16	Paid $18 from petty cash for office supplies, voucher No. 3.
	23	Paid $14 from petty cash for postage, voucher No. 4.
	26	Paid $9 from petty cash for local church donation, voucher No. 5 (this is a miscellaneous payment).
	29	Issued cheque No. 15 to Roy Kloon to pay for office equipment, $700.

The chart of accounts includes Cash, 100; Petty Cash, 120; Office Equipment, 130; Postage Expense, 610; Office Supplies Expense, 620; Miscellaneous Expense, 630. The headings of the auxiliary petty cash records are as follows:

AUXILIARY PETTY CASH RECORD

					Category of Payments			
							Sundry	
Date 2016	Voucher No.	Description	Receipts	Payments	Postage Expense	Office Supplies Expense	Account	Amount

BANK OF SASKATCHEWAN
10050–101 Street
Regina, Saskatchewan
S4J 6E2

03749

Account Statement

Account No.	
241 673 6	
Period From	To
Feb 01/18	Feb 28/18
Enclosures	Page
7	1

RICK'S DELI
8811–102 Street
Regina, SK
S4S 3G6

Date	Transaction Description		Cheques & Debits	Deposits & Credits	Balance
Feb 01	Balance Forward				6,000.00
Feb 02	Cheque -	108	90.00		
Feb 03	Cheque -	114	210.00		5,700.00
Feb 10	Deposit			300.00	
Feb 10	Cheque -	116	150.00		5,850.00
Feb 13	Deposit			600.00	6,450.00
Feb 16	Cheque -	113	600.00		5,850.00
Feb 20	Deposit			300.00	
Feb 20	NSF Returned Item		300.00		5,850.00
Feb 23	Deposit			1,200.00	7,050.00
Feb 24	Cheque -	117	1,200.00		5,850.00
Feb 26	Deposit			180.00	6,030.00
Feb 27	Cheque -	118	600.00		
Feb 28	Service Charge		30.00		5,400.00

No. of Debits	Total Amount	No. of Credits	Total Amount
8	3,180.00	5	2,580.00

Required

1. Record the appropriate entries in the general journal as well as in the auxiliary petty cash record as needed.
2. Be sure to replenish the petty cash fund on April 30 (cheque No. 16).

Establishing and replenishing petty cash, including handling a cash shortage
❸ ❹ ❺ **(40 min)**

8A-4. From the following, record the transactions in Logan's auxiliary petty cash record and general journal.

2015		
Oct. 1		A cheque was drawn (No. 444) payable to Roberta Floss, petty cashier, to establish a $150 petty cash fund.
	5	Paid $24 for postage stamps, voucher No. 1.
	9	Paid $12 for delivery charges on goods for resale, voucher No. 2.
	12	Paid $10 for donation to a mission (Miscellaneous Expense), voucher No. 3.
	15	Paid $9 for postage stamps, voucher No. 4.
	16	Paid $18 for delivery charges on goods for resale, voucher No. 5.
	26	Purchased computer supplies from petty cash for $25, voucher No. 6.
	29	Paid $14 for postage, voucher No. 7.
	30	Drew cheque No. 618 to replenish petty cash and cover a $3 shortage.

Check Figure

Cash replenishment $115

Preparing a bank reconciliation
❷ **(75 min)**

8A-5. Shown on pages 381 and 382 are the following for Casing Suppliers Ltd. of Oakville:

a. General ledger printout for March 2018.
b. Bank reconciliation as of February 28, 2018.
c. Bank statement for March 2018.

Required

Prepare a bank reconciliation at March 31, 2018.

Check Figure

Reconciled balance $3,236.76

Group B Problems

(The forms you need are on pages 8-6 to 8-11 of the *Study Guide with Working Papers.*)

Preparing a bank reconciliation, including collection of a note
❷ **(20 min)**

8B-1. As the bookkeeper of Rose Company of Drumheller, you received the bank statement from TD Canada Trust indicating a balance of $5,820. The ending chequebook balance was $6,321. Prepare the bank reconciliation for Rose Company as of July 31, 2017, and prepare journal entries as needed based on the following:

a. Deposits in transit, $2,875.
b. Bank service charges, $24.
c. Cheques outstanding: No. 111, $478; No. 115, $1,147.
d. TD Canada Trust collected a note for Rose, $1,770, less a $12 collection fee.
e. NSFcheque, $525.
f. Rose Company records cheque No. 107 as $900 to pay the month's rent. The cancelled cheque and bank statement show the actual cheque was $800.
g. The bank made an error by deducting a cheque for $560 issued by another business.

Check Figure

Reconciled balance $7,630

Preparing a bank reconciliation with an NSF cheque, using the back side of a bank statement.
❷ **(40 min)**

8B-2. Based on the account statement on page 383, (1) complete the bank reconciliation for Rick's Deli of Regina found on the reverse of the bank statement and (2) journalize the appropriate entries as needed.

a. Cheques outstanding: No. 110, $80; No. 116, $160; No. 118, $52.
b. A deposit of $416 is in transit.
c. The chequebook balance of Rick's Deli shows an ending balance of $798.
d. Jim Rice's cheque for $40 bounced because of lack of sufficient funds.

Check Figure

Reconciled balance $756

Casing Suppliers Ltd.
General Ledger Listing as of March 31, 2018

Period	Source	Date	Description	Reference	Posting Entry	Debits	Credits	Net Balance	Dr./Cr.
	1050		Royal Bank - Chequing		Balance Forward			4,741.34	Dr.
3	GL-GJ	2-Mar-18	WESTERN PROPERTIES LTD.	CHQ 3525	3 - 1		1,498.00	3,243.34	Dr.
3	GL-GJ	2-Mar-18	WALLY PIERCE - Deposit	1241	3 - 2	6,425.48		9,668.82	Dr.
3	GL-GJ	3-Mar-18	SANDY NESS - Deposit	1242	3 - 3	3,164.17		12,832.99	Dr.
3	GL-GJ	3-Mar-18	CARSON WHOLESALE INC.	CHQ 3526	3 - 4		3,614.85	9,218.14	Dr.
3	GL-GJ	4-Mar-18	QUICK COMPUTER REPAIRS LTD.	CHQ 3527	3 - 5		136.00	9,082.14	Dr.
3	GL-GJ	4-Mar-18	NIVENS QUALITY UPHOLSTERING	CHQ 3528	3 - 6		1,510.00	7,572.14	Dr.
3	GL-GJ	4-Mar-18	ALLEN MURRAY - Deposit	1243	3 - 7	8,742.00		16,314.14	Dr.
3	GL-GJ	5-Mar-18	A.F. KINGSLEY, ACCOUNTANT	CHQ 3529	3 - 8		749.00	15,565.14	Dr.
3	GL-GJ	6-Mar-18	BRENDA KELLY - Deposit	1244	3 - 9	1,756.25		17,321.39	Dr.
3	GL-GJ	6-Mar-18	EVANS CONTRACTING LTD.	CHQ 3530	3 - 10		5,248.95	12,072.44	Dr.
3	GL-GJ	6-Mar-18	CORRINTHIAN CONSULTING CO.	CHQ 3531	3 - 11		2,850.00	9,222.44	Dr.
3	GL-GJ	6-Mar-18	NANCY SNYDER	CHQ 3532	3 - 12		1,500.00	7,722.44	Dr.
3	GL-GJ	6-Mar-18	CITY PHONE COMPANY	CHQ 3535	3 - 13		168.45	7,553.99	Dr.
3	GL-GJ	9-Mar-18	LYCOS UTILITIES INC.	CHQ 3536	3 - 14		318.96	7,235.03	Dr.
3	GL-GJ	9-Mar-18	CASEY VALENCE	CHQ 3537	3 - 15		418.50	6,816.53	Dr.
3	GL-GJ	9-Mar-18	STATIONERY DEPOT LTD.	CHQ 3538	3 - 16		641.30	6,175.23	Dr.
3	GL-GJ	10-Mar-18	JAMIE DUPRE	CHQ 3539	3 - 17		365.00	5,810.23	Dr.
3	GL-GJ	11-Mar-18	WAN TSUI - Deposit	1245	3 - 18	1,616.82		7,427.05	Dr.
3	GL-GJ	11-Mar-18	LARRY MURDOCH - Salary	CHQ 3540	3 - 19		1,645.20	5,781.85	Dr.
3	GL-GJ	11-Mar-18	FREDA WANDERLING - Salary	CHQ 3541	3 - 20		1,586.45	4,195.40	Dr.
3	GL-GJ	12-Mar-18	RBC - Loan Interest	01 - 21	3 - 21		368.40	3,827.00	Dr.
3	GL-GJ	12-Mar-18	K CARDINAL - Deposit	1246	3 - 22	6,475.20		10,302.20	Dr.
3	GL-GJ	13-Mar-18	JAMISON SUPPLIERS LTD.	CHQ 3542	3 - 23		2,167.10	8,135.10	Dr.
3	GL-GJ	16-Mar-18	WORD WIZARDS LTD.	CHQ 3543	3 - 27		742.00	7,393.10	Dr.
3	GL-GJ	16-Mar-18	Canada Revenue Agency	CHQ 3544	3 - 28		1,684.52	5,708.58	Dr.
3	GL-GJ	16-Mar-18	RBC - Loan Repayment	01 - 24	3 - 29		3,000.00	2,708.58	Dr.
3	GL-GJ	16-Mar-18	JOY AMITY - Deposit	1247	3 - 30	648.00		3,356.58	Dr.
3	GL-GJ	16-Mar-18	THOMAS HUNT - Insurance	CHQ 3546	3 - 31		1,014.58	2,342.00	Dr.
3	GL-GJ	17-Mar-18	PEARSON HIGH SCHOOL ADVERT.	CHQ 3547	3 - 32		125.00	2,217.00	Dr.
3	GL-GJ	17-Mar-18	THE LOCAL TIMES	CHQ 3548	3 - 37		682.45	1,534.55	Dr.
3	GL-GJ	18-Mar-18	RBC - New cheques ordered	01 - 29	3 - 38		35.30	1,499.25	Dr.
3	GL-GJ	20-Mar-18	LINDA FRANKLIN - Deposit	1248	3 - 39	2,846.54		4,345.79	Dr.
3	GL-GJ	20-Mar-18	GRADY PURBOO - Deposit	1249	3 - 44	1,867.95		6,213.74	Dr.
3	GL-GJ	23-Mar-18	LARRY MURDOCH - Salary	CHQ 3549	3 - 45		1,645.20	4,568.54	Dr.
3	GL-GJ	23-Mar-18	FREDA WANDERLING - Salary	CHQ 3550	3 - 46		1,586.45	2,982.09	Dr.
3	GL-GJ	24-Mar-18	CRISPIN ROBICHAUD	CHQ 3551	3 - 47		1,256.75	1,725.34	Dr
3	GL-GJ	26-Mar-18	KEN CHARLES - Deposit	1250	3 - 48	1,648.65		3,373.99	Dr.
3	GL-GJ	27-Mar-18	WANDA GRIERSON - Deposit	1251	3 - 49	6,746.90		10,120.89	Dr.
3	GL-GJ	27-Mar-18	OREST FELDMAN - Deposit	1252	3 - 51	1,648.80		11,769.69	Dr.
3	GL-GJ	27-Mar-18	TIM EWASIUK - Deposit	1253	3 - 52	2,548.33		14,318.02	Dr.
3	GL-GJ	27-Mar-18	GRAHAM DENMANN	CHQ 3552	3 - 56		4,516.84	9,801.18	Dr.
3	GL-GJ	30-Mar-18	STILL PRODUCTIONS COMPANY	CHQ 3553	3 - 57		1,648.75	8,152.43	Dr.
3	GL-GJ	30-Mar-18	BRYANT WHOLESALE SUPPLIERS LTD	CHQ 3554	3 - 58		6,745.14	1,407.29	Dr.
3	GL-GJ	30-Mar-18	AGENCY RESTAURANT	CHQ 3555	3 - 62		158.76	1,248.53	Dr.
3	GL-GJ	30-Mar-18	COMPACT DESIGNS LTD.	CHQ 3556	3 - 65		253.60	994.93	Dr.
3	GL-GJ	31-Mar-18	AMY FIELDING - Deposit	1254	3 - 66	2,866.38		3,861.31	Dr.

Casing Suppliers Ltd.
Bank Reconciliation
February 28, 2018

Balance per Bank Statement			5,183.83
Add: Deposit in Transit			3,640.58
			8,824.41
Less: Outstanding Cheques:	3496	53.18	
	3523	1,685.25	
	3524	2,344.64	4,083.07
Balance per General Ledger			4,741.34

ROYAL BANK OF CANADA

Centreville Branch
Suite 410, Ambrose Gardens
Oakville, ON
M4W 7H2

Account Statement

Account No.	
765-432-8	
Period	
From Mar 1/18	To Mar 31/18
Enclosures 29	Page 1

CASING SUPPLIERS LTD.
1840 Rochester Road
Oakville, ON
M7J 4D6

Date		*Transaction Description*	*Cheques & Debits*	*Deposits & Credits*	*Balance*
Feb 28	Balance Forward				5,183.83
Mar 02	Deposit			3,640.58	8,824.41
Mar 02	Cheque	3524	2,344.64		6,479.77
Mar 02	Cheque	3525	1,498.00		4,981.77
Mar 02	Cheque	3523	1,685.25		3,296.52
Mar 02	Deposit			6,425.48	9,722.00
Mar 03	Deposit			3,164.17	12,886.17
Mar 04	Cheque	3526	3,614.85		9,271.32
Mar 04	Cheque	3527	136.00		9,135.32
Mar 04	Deposit			8,742.00	17,877.32
Mar 09	Cheque	3532	1,500.00		16,377.32
Mar 09	Cheque	3530	5,248.95		11,128.37
Mar 09	Deposit			1,756.25	12,884.62
Mar 09	Cheque	3529	749.00		12,135.62
Mar 09	Loan Interest Payment		368.40		11,767.22
Mar 10	Cheque	3528	1,510.00		10,257.22
Mar 11	Cheque	3536	318.96		9,938.26
Mar 11	Cheque	3531	2,850.00		7,088.26
Mar 11	Cheque	3535	168.45		6,919.81
Mar 11	Cheque	3538	641.30		6,278.51
Mar 11	Deposit			1,616.82	7,895.33
Mar 12	Cheque	3537	418.50		7,476.83
Mar 12	Deposit			6,475.20	13,952.03
Mar 12	Cheque	3541	1,586.45		12,365.58
Mar 12	Cheque	3540	1,645.20		10,720.38
Mar 16	Cheque	3542	2,167.10		8,553.28
Mar 16	Cheque	3543	742.00		7,811.28
Mar 16	Cheques Ordered		35.30		7,775.98
Mar 17	Cheque	3544	1,684.52		6,091.46
Mar 17	Cheque	3546	1,014.58		5,076.88
Mar 18	Cheque	3548	682.45		4,394.43
Mar 18	Deposit			648.00	5,042.43
Mar 18	Loan Principal Payment		3,000.00		2,042.43
Mar 20	Deposit			2,846.54	4,888.97
Mar 20	NSF Cheque - Joy Amity		648.00		4,240.97
Mar 20	NSF Service Charge		20.00		4,220.97
Mar 20	Deposit			1,867.95	6,088.92
Mar 22	Cheque	3550	1,586.45		4,502.47
Mar 24	Interest Earned			86.20	4,588.67
Mar 24	Cheque	3549	1,645.20		2,943.47
Mar 25	Cheque	3551	1,256.75		1,686.72
Mar 26	Deposit			1,648.65	3,335.37
Mar 27	Cheque	3552	4,516.84		(1,181.47)
Mar 27	Deposit			6,746.90	5,565.43
Mar 27	Deposit			1,648.80	7,214.23
Mar 30	Cheque	3553	1,648.75		5,565.48
Mar 30	Deposit			2,548.33	8,113.81
Mar 30	Bank Service Charge		42.75		8,071.06
Mar 30	Cheque	3555	158.76		7,912.30

BANK OF SASKATCHEWAN
10050–101 Street
Regina, Saskatchewan
S4J 6E2

Account Statement

Account No.	
241 673 6	
Period From	To
Apr 01/18	Apr 30/18
Enclosures	Page
7	1

03749

RICK'S DELI
8811–102 Street
Regina, SK
S3A 3G6

Date	Transaction Description		Cheques & Debits	Deposits & Credits	Balance
Apr 01	Balance Forward				718.00
Apr 02	Cheque -	108	12.00		
Apr 03	Cheque -	114	36.00		670.00
Apr 10	Deposit			40.00	
Apr 10	Cheque -	115	20.00		690.00
Apr 16	Deposit			80.00	770.00
Apr 17	Cheque -	113	80.00		690.00
Apr 20	Deposit			40.00	
Apr 20	NSF Returned Item		40.00		690.00
Apr 23	Deposit			160.00	850.00
Apr 24	Cheque -	117	160.00		690.00
Apr 27	Deposit			24.00	714.00
Apr 28	Cheque -	109	80.00		
Apr 30	Service Charge		2.00		632.00

No. of Debits	Total Amount	No. of Credits	Total Amount
8	430.00	5	344.00

Establishment and replenishment of petty cash

Relationship to auxiliary petty cash record

❸ (30 min)

8B-3. From the following transactions, (a) record the entries as needed in the general journal of Merry Co. of Lennoxville as well as the auxiliary petty cash record and (b) replenish the petty cash fund on April 30 (cheque No. 6).

2016		
Apr.	1	Issued cheque No. 4 for $80 to establish a petty cash fund.
	5	Paid $9 from petty cash for postage, voucher No. 1.
	8	Paid $12 from petty cash for office supplies, voucher No. 2.
	16	Paid $9 from petty cash for office supplies, voucher No. 3.
	23	Paid $6 from petty cash for postage, voucher No. 4.
	26	Paid $12 from petty cash for local charity donation, voucher No. 5 (this is a miscellaneous payment).
	29	Issued cheque No. 5 to Roy Kloon to pay for office equipment, $800.

Check Figure

Cash replenishment $48

Chart of accounts includes: Cash, 100; Petty Cash, 120; Office Equipment, 130; Postage Expense, 610; Office Supplies Expense, 620; Miscellaneous Expense, 630. Use the same headings as in Problem 8A-3.

Establishing and replenishing petty cash, and covering a cash shortage
❸ ❹ ❺ (40 min)

Check Figure

Cash replenishment $73

8B-4. From the following, record the transactions in Logan's auxiliary petty cash record and general journal:

2015		
Oct.	1	Roberta Floss, the petty cashier, cashed cheque No. 444 to establish a $100 petty cash fund.
	5	Paid $18 for postage stamps, voucher No. 1.
	9	Paid $12 for delivery charges on goods for resale, voucher No. 2.
	15	Paid $10 for donation to a homeless shelter (Miscellaneous Expense), voucher No. 3.
	15	Paid $14 for postage stamps, voucher No. 4.
	16	Paid $5 for delivery charges on goods for resale, voucher No. 5.
	26	Purchased computer supplies from petty cash for $7, voucher No. 6.
	29	Paid $4 for postage, voucher No. 7.
	30	Drew cheque No. 618 to replenish petty cash and cover a $3 shortage.

Preparing a bank reconciliation
❷ (75 min)

Check Figure

Reconciled balance $1,525.41

8B-5. Shown on pages 385 and 386 are the following for Casing Suppliers Ltd. of Oakville:

a. General ledger listing for March 2018
b. Bank reconciliation as of February 28, 2018
c. Bank statement for March 2018

Required

Prepare a bank reconciliation as of March 31, 2018.

Group C Problems

(The forms you need are on pages 8-12 to 8-18 of the *Study Guide with Working Papers.*)

Preparing a bank reconciliation, including collection of a note
❷ (20 min)

Check Figure

Reconciled balance $7,371

8C-1. Graham Company of Moncton received a bank statement from Royal Bank indicating a bank balance of $7,483. Based on Graham's cheque stubs, the ending chequebook balance was $6,919. Your task is to prepare a bank reconciliation for Graham Company as of May 31, 2016, from the following information (please journalize entries as needed):

a. Cheques outstanding: No. 354, $297; No. 356, $512; No. 347, $684.
b. Deposits in transit, $1,381.
c. Bank service charge, $39.
d. Royal Bank collected a note for Graham, $734, less a $14 collection fee.
e. Notice was received that a cheque from Harry Pride, a customer, was returned NSF, $151.
f. Bank recorded new cheques purchase, $78.

Preparing a bank reconciliation with an NSF cheque, using the back of a bank statement
❷ (40 min)

8C-2. From the following July 28, 2017, bank statement (p. 387), (a) complete a bank reconciliation for The Fresh Flower Shop of Halifax and (b) journalize the appropriate entries as needed.

a. A deposit of $2,122 is in transit.
b. The Fresh Flower Shop has an ending chequebook balance of $5,111.
c. Cheques outstanding: No. 231, $298; No. 245, $509; No. 246, $76; No. 247, $237.
d. Jane Yates's cheque for $225 bounced because of non-sufficient funds.

Casing Suppliers Ltd.
General Ledger Listing as of March 31, 2018

Period	Source	Date	Description	Reference	Posting Entry	Debits	Credits	Net Balance	Dr./Cr.
		1050	Royal Bank - Chequing		Balance Forward			4,328.94	Dr.
3	GL-GJ	2-Mar-18	WESTERN PROPERTIES LTD.	CHQ 2325	3 - 1		1,746.20	2,582.74	Dr.
3	GL-GJ	2-Mar-18	WALLY PIERCE - Deposit	942	3 - 2	6,186.42		8,769.16	Dr.
3	GL-GJ	2-Mar-18	SANDY NESS - Deposit	943	3 - 3	3,460.84		12,230.00	Dr.
3	GL-GJ	2-Mar-18	CARSON WHOLESALE INC.	CHQ 2326	3 - 4		3,477.16	8,752.84	Dr.
3	GL-GJ	5-Mar-18	QUICK COMPUTER REPAIRS LTD.	CHQ 2327	3 - 5		145.00	8,607.84	Dr.
3	GL-GJ	5-Mar-18	NIVENS QUALITY UPHOLSTERING	CHQ 2328	3 - 6		1,645.00	6,962.84	Dr.
3	GL-GJ	6-Mar-18	ALLEN MURRAY - Deposit	944	3 - 7	8,819.00		15,781.84	Dr.
3	GL-GJ	6-Mar-18	A.F. KINGSLEY, ACCOUNTANT	CHQ 2329	3 - 8		856.00	14,925.84	Dr.
3	GL-GJ	6-Mar-18	BRENDA KELLY - Deposit	945	3 - 9	1,614.25		16,540.09	Dr.
3	GL-GJ	6-Mar-18	EVANS CONTRACTING LTD.	CHQ 2330	3 - 10		5,584.15	10,955.94	Dr.
3	GL-GJ	6-Mar-18	CORRINTHIAN CONSULTING CO.	CHQ 2331	3 - 11		2,786.50	8,169.44	Dr.
3	GL-GJ	6-Mar-18	NANCY SNYDER	CHQ 2332	3 - 12		1,650.00	6,519.44	Dr.
3	GL-GJ	6-Mar-18	CITY PHONE COMPANY	CHQ 2335	3 - 13		166.42	6,353.02	Dr.
3	GL-GJ	9-Mar-18	LYCOS UTILITIES INC.	CHQ 2336	3 - 14		342.72	6,010.30	Dr.
3	GL-GJ	9-Mar-18	CASEY VALENCE	CHQ 2337	3 - 15		505.70	5,504.60	Dr.
3	GL-GJ	9-Mar-18	STATIONERY DEPOT LTD.	CHQ 2338	3 - 16		668.62	4,835.98	Dr.
3	GL-GJ	9-Mar-18	JAMIE DUPRE	CHQ 2339	3 - 17		376.00	4,459.98	Dr.
3	GL-GJ	10-Mar-18	WAN TSUI - Deposit	946	3 - 18	3,417.25		7,877.23	Dr.
3	GL-GJ	10-Mar-18	LARRY MURDOCH - Salary	CHQ 2340	3 - 19		1,864.20	6,013.03	Dr.
3	GL-GJ	10-Mar-18	FREDA WANDERLING - Salary	CHQ 2341	3 - 20		1,714.55	4,298.48	Dr.
3	GL-GJ	11-Mar-18	RBC - Loan Interest	01 - 21	3 - 21		326.42	3,972.06	Dr.
3	GL-GJ	11-Mar-18	K CARDINAL - Deposit	947	3 - 22	5,846.84		9,818.90	Dr.
3	GL-GJ	13-Mar-18	JAMISON SUPPLIERS LTD.	CHQ 2342	3 - 23		3,459.21	6,359.69	Dr.
3	GL-GJ	16-Mar-18	WORD WIZARDS LTD.	CHQ 2343	3 - 27		972.00	5,387.69	Dr.
3	GL-GJ	16-Mar-18	Canada Revenue Agency	CHQ 2344	3 - 28		1,742.36	3,645.33	Dr.
3	GL-GJ	16-Mar-18	RBC - Loan Repayment	01 - 24	3 - 29		2,000.00	1,645.33	Dr.
3	GL-GJ	16-Mar-18	JOY AMITY - Deposit	948	3 - 30	952.00		2,597.33	Dr.
3	GL-GJ	16-Mar-18	THOMAS HUNT - Insurance	CHQ 2346	3 - 31		753.24	1,844.09	Dr.
3	GL-GJ	17-Mar-18	PEARSON HIGH SCHOOL ADVERTISING	CHQ 2347	3 - 32		150.00	1,694.09	Dr.
3	GL-GJ	17-Mar-18	THE LOCAL TIMES	CHQ 2348	3 - 37		682.45	1,011.64	Dr.
3	GL-GJ	18-Mar-18	RBC - New cheques ordered	01 - 29	3 - 38		35.30	976.34	Dr.
3	GL-GJ	19-Mar-18	LINDA FRANKLIN - Deposit	949	3 - 39	2,456.38		3,432.72	Dr.
3	GL-GJ	20-Mar-18	GRADY PURBOO - Deposit	950	3 - 44	1,964.25		5,396.97	Dr.
3	GL-GJ	21-Mar-18	LARRY MURDOCH - Salary	CHQ 2349	3 - 45		1,864.20	3,532.77	Dr.
3	GL-GJ	23-Mar-18	FREDA WANDERLING - Salary	CHQ 2350	3 - 46		1,714.55	1,818.22	Dr.
3	GL-GJ	24-Mar-18	CRISPIN ROBICHAUD	CHQ 2351	3 - 47		1,256.75	561.47	Dr.
3	GL-GJ	25-Mar-18	KEN CHARLES - Deposit	951	3 - 48	1,906.72		2,468.19	Dr.
3	GL-GJ	27-Mar-18	WANDA GRIERSON - Deposit	952	3 - 49	3,868.46		6,336.65	Dr.
3	GL-GJ	27-Mar-18	OREST FELDMAN - Deposit	953	3 - 51	2,842.66		9,179.31	Dr.
3	GL-GJ	27-Mar-18	TIM EWASIUK - Deposit	954	3 - 52	2,442.91		11,622.22	Dr.
3	GL-GJ	27-Mar-18	GRAHAM DENMANN	CHQ 2352	3 - 56		4,458.78	7,163.44	Dr.
3	GL-GJ	30-Mar-18	STILL PRODUCTIONS COMPANY	CHQ 2353	3 - 57		1,594.34	5,569.10	Dr.
3	GL-GJ	30-Mar-18	BRYANT WHOLESALE SUPPLIERS LTD	CHQ 2354	3 - 58		5,840.60	–271.50	Cr.
3	GL-GJ	30-Mar-18	AGENCY RESTAURANT	CHQ 2355	3 - 62		162.70	–434.20	Cr.
3	GL-GJ	31-Mar-18	COMPACT DESIGNS LTD.	CHQ 2356	3 - 65		268.45	–702.65	Cr.
3	GL-GJ	31-Mar-18	AMY FIELDING - Deposit	955	3 - 66	3,148.62		2,445.97	Dr.

Casing Suppliers Ltd.
Bank Reconciliation
February 28, 2018

Balance per Bank Statement			5,183.83
Add: Deposit in Transit			2,856.32
			8,040.15
Less: Outstanding Cheques:	2296	87.26	
	2323	1,457.50	
	2324	2,166.45	3,711.21
Balance per General Ledger			4,328.94

ROYAL BANK OF CANADA
Centreville Branch
Suite 410, Ambrose Gardens
Oakville, ON
L4W 7H2

Account Statement

Account No.	
765-432-8	
Period	
From Mar 1/18	To Mar 31/18
Enclosures 29	Page 1

CASING SUPPLIERS LTD.
1840 Rochester Road
Oakville, ON
L7J 4D6

Date		*Transaction Description*	*Cheques & Debits*	*Deposits & Credits*	*Balance*
Feb 28	Balance Forward				5,183.83
Mar 02	Deposit			2,856.32	
Mar 02	Cheque	2324	2,166.45		5,873.70
Mar 02	Cheque	2325	1,746.20		
Mar 02	Cheque	2323	1,457.50		
Mar 02	Deposit			6,186.42	8,856.42
Mar 03	Deposit			3,460.84	12,317.26
Mar 04	Cheque	2326	3,477.16		8,840.10
Mar 06	Cheque	2327	145.00		
Mar 06	Deposit			8,819.00	17,514.10
Mar 06	Cheque	2332	1,650.00		15,864.10
Mar 09	Cheque	2330	5,584.15		
Mar 09	Deposit			1,614.25	
Mar 09	Cheque	2329	856.00		
Mar 09	Loan Interest Payment		326.42		10,711.78
Mar 10	Cheque	2328	1,645.00		9,066.78
Mar 10	Cheque	2336	342.72		
Mar 10	Cheque	2331	2,786.50		
Mar 10	Cheque	2335	166.42		
Mar 10	Cheque	2338	668.62		
Mar 10	Deposit			3,417.25	8,519.77
Mar 11	Cheque	2337	505.70		
Mar 11	Deposit			5,846.84	
Mar 12	Cheque	2341	1,714.55		
Mar 12	Cheque	2340	1,864.20		10,282.16
Mar 13	Cheque	2342	3,459.21		6,822.95
Mar 16	Cheque	2343	972.00		
Mar 16	Cheques Ordered		35.30		5,815.65
Mar 17	Cheque	2344	1,742.36		
Mar 17	Cheque	2346	753.24		3,320.05
Mar 18	Cheque	2348	682.45		
Mar 18	Deposit			952.00	
Mar 18	Loan Principal Payment		2,000.00		1,589.60
Mar 19	Deposit			2,456.38	4,045.98
Mar 20	NSF Cheque - Joy Amity		952.00		
Mar 20	NSF Service Charge		20.00		
Mar 20	Deposit			1,964.25	5,038.23
Mar 23	Cheque	2350	1,714.55		3,323.68
Mar 23	Interest Earned			86.20	3,409.88
Mar 24	Cheque	2349	1,864.20		1,545.68
Mar 25	Cheque	2351	1,256.75		288.93
Mar 26	Deposit			1,906.72	2,195.65
Mar 27	Cheque	2352	4,458.78		
Mar 27	Deposit			3,868.46	
Mar 27	Deposit			2,842.66	4,447.99
Mar 30	Cheque	2353	1,594.34		
Mar 30	Deposit			2,442.91	
Mar 31	Bank Service Charge		34.76		5,261.80
Mar 31	Cheque	2355	162.70		5,099.10

BANK OF INDUSTRY AND COMMERCE
48 JAMES STREET
HALIFAX, NOVA SCOTIA
B4T 2L0

08179

Account Statement

Account No.
914 817 2

Period	
From	To
Jun 29/17	Jul 28/17

Enclosures	Page
7	1

THE FRESH FLOWER SHOP
121 SPRING GARDEN ROAD
HALIFAX, NS
B5H 3E6

Date	Transaction Description		Cheques & Debits	Deposits & Credits	Balance
Jul 01	Balance Forward				2,824.00
Jul 02	Cheque -	241	385.00		2,439.00
Jul 03	Cheque -	240	410.00		2,029.00
Jul 10	Deposit			1,712.00	
Jul 10	Cheque -	243	250.00		3,491.00
Jul 14	Deposit			950.00	4,441.00
Jul 15	Cheque -	242	1,214.00		3,227.00
Jul 16	Deposit			225.00	3,452.00
Jul 21	NSF Returned Item		225.00		3,227.00
Jul 22	Deposit			1,260.00	4,487.00
Jul 24	Cheque -	248	1,410.00		3,077.00
Jul 25	Deposit			780.00	3,857.00
Jul 28	Cheque -	1126	607.00		
Jul 29	Service Charge		12.00		3,238.00

No. of Debits	Total Amount	No. of Credits	Total Amount
8	4,513.00	5	4,927.00

Check Figure

Reconciled balance $4,847

e. Cheque No. 241 for utilities expense was entered in the cash payments journal as $358.

f. The cheque for $607 shown by the bank as paid on July 28 was actually a cheque of the Active Automotive Repair. This error will be corrected by the bank next month. The bank apologized for the error.

Relationship to auxiliary petty cash record
3 (30 min)

8C-3. The following transactions occurred in March and were related to the general journal and petty cash fund of Samuel & Co. of St. John's.

2016		
Mar.	1	Issued cheque No. 314 for $200 to establish a petty cash fund.
	5	Paid $45 from petty cash for postage, voucher No. 1.
	8	Paid $39 from petty cash for office supplies, voucher No. 2.
	18	Paid $27 from petty cash for office supplies, voucher No. 3.
	25	Paid $47 from petty cash for postage, voucher No. 4.
	26	Paid $20 from petty cash to support a student walk event, voucher No. 5 (this is a miscellaneous payment).
	29	Issued cheque No. 315 to Klondike Office Equipment to pay for office equipment, $1,890.

Check Figure

Cash replenishment $178

The chart of accounts includes Cash, 100; Petty Cash, 105; Office Equipment, 170; Postage Expense, 645; Office Supplies Expense, 640;

Miscellaneous Expense, 630. The headings of the auxiliary petty cash records are the same as for Problem 8A-3.

Required

1. Record the appropriate entries in the general journal and the auxiliary petty cash record as needed.
2. Be sure to replenish the petty cash fund on March 31 (cheque No. 316).

Establishing and replenishing petty cash and covering a cash shortage
❸ ❹ ❺ (40 min)

Check Figure

Cash replenishment $212

8C-4. From the following, record the transactions in Caron Co.'s auxiliary petty cash record and general journal.

2015		
Oct.	1	A cheque was drawn, No. 772, payable to Herb Kiriak, petty cashier, to establish a $250 petty cash fund.
	5	Paid $41 for postage stamps, voucher No. 1.
	9	Paid $16 for delivery charges on goods for resale, voucher No. 2.
	12	Gave $30 donation to a church (Miscellaneous Expense), voucher No. 3.
	15	Paid $57 for postage stamps, voucher No. 4.
	16	Paid $13 for delivery charges on goods for resale, voucher No. 5.
	26	Purchased computer supplies from petty cash for $19, voucher No. 6.
	29	Paid $32 for postage, voucher No. 7.
	31	Drew cheque No. 813 to replenish petty cash (a $4 shortage was apparent when the cash was balanced).

Realistic bank reconciliation scenarios
❷ (90 min)

Check Figure

Reconciled balance $5,196.35

8C-5. Shown below and on pages 389 and 390 are the following for Northern Energy Consulting of Sinclair:

a. Bank reconciliation completed as of March 31, 2017
b. Bank statement for March 29 to April 29, 2017
c. General ledger listing for April 2017

Required

Reconcile the Balance per Bank Statement ($9,199.21) with the Balance per General Ledger ($5,648.15).

NORTHERN ENERGY CONSULTING
BANK RECONCILIATION
MARCH 31, 2017

Balance per Bank Statement			7,036.42
Add: Deposits in Transit		540.00	
		1,245.00	1,785.00
			8,821.42
Less: Outstanding cheques:			
	205	89.14	
	206	950.00	
	207	133.45	
	208	1,250.00	
	209	672.30	3,094.89
Balance per General Ledger			**5,726.53**

BANK OF ALBERTA
105 STREET BRANCH
4525–105 STREET
SINCLAIR, ALBERTA
T1Y 4P8

Account Statement

Account No.	
2361-445-99	
Period	
From	To
Mar 29/17	Apr 29/17
Enclosures	Page
14	50

NORTHERN ENERGY CONSULTING
5477–134 AVE.
SINCLAIR, ALBERTA
T2S 4G7

Date	Transaction Description		Cheques & Debits	Deposits & Credits	Balance
	Balance Forward				7,036.42
Mar 29	Error Correction		540.00		6,496.42
	Loan Proceeds			540.00	7,036.42
	Deposit			540.00	7,576.42
Apr 01	Deposit			1,245.00	8,821.42
	Cheque	0209	672.30		8,149.12
	Cheque	0205	89.14		8,059.98
	Cheque	0207	133.45		7,926.53
	Cheque	0210	208.25		7,718.28
	Cheque	0212	207.45		7,510.83
	NSF Returned		425.00		7,085.83
Apr 05	NSF Charge		15.00		7,070.83
Apr 05	Deposit			1,745.00	8,815.83
	Cheque	0208	1,250.00		7,565.83
	Cheque	0211	124.15		7,441.68
Apr 08	Deposit			428.00	7,869.68
Apr 08	Deposit			856.00	8,725.68
Apr 09	Deposit			968.27	9,693.95
	Cheque	0206	950.00		8,743.95
	Cheque	0213	642.00		8,101.95
	Cheque	0214	164.25		7,937.70
Apr 15	Deposit			254.36	8,192.06
	Cheque	0217	1,746.80		6,445.26
	Cheque	0218	1,254.35		5,190.91
Apr 15	Deposit			418.74	5,609.65
Apr 16	Deposit			366.05	5,975.70
Apr 19	Deposit			284.67	6,260.37
Apr 19	Deposit			200.60	6,460.97
Apr 19	Deposit			1,987.00	8,447.97
	Cheque	0215	65.70		8,382.27
Apr 20	Bank Service Charge		34.20		8,348.07
Apr 23	Deposit			502.46	8,850.53
Apr 26	Deposit			1,007.28	9,857.81
Apr 26	Loan Interest		37.50		9,820.31
	Loan Payment		317.50		9,502.81
	Cheque	0216	362.00		9,140.81
Apr 29	Interest Earned			58.40	9,199.21

No. of Debits	20	Total Amount Debits	9,239.04	Total Fees	34.20
No. of Credits	16	Total Amount Credits	11,401.83	Interest Paid	37.50

Date: May 12, 2017 2:34 pm
G/L listing for account 1100

NORTHERN ENERGY CONSULTING

General Ledger Listing as of April 30, 2017

Page: 1

Period	Source	Date	Description	Reference	Posting Entry	Debits	Credits	Net Balance
	1100 Bank of Alberta - Chequing							5,726.53
4	GL-GJ	01-Apr-17	ALBERTA PHONE CO.	CHQ 0210	4 - 1		208.25	5,518.28
4	GL-GJ	01-Apr-17	MAXIM OFFICE SUPPLIES	CHQ 0211	4 - 2		124.15	5,394.13
4	GL-GJ	02-Apr-17	CANADA POST	CHQ 0212	4 - 3		207.45	5,186.68
4	GL-GJ	02-Apr-17	HANDI PRINT AND GRAPHICS	CHQ 0213	4 - 4		642.00	4,544.68
4	GL-GJ	05-Apr-17	CITY TRUCK STOPS - Deposit	LT204	4 - 5	1,745.00		6.289.68
4	GL-GJ	08-Apr-17	PERFORMANCE OIL CHANGE - Deposit	LT298	4 - 6	428.00		6,717.68
4	GL-GJ	08-Apr-17	AUTO ROW SALES & SERVICE - Deposit	LT299	4 - 7	856.00		7,573.68
4	GL-GJ	08-Apr-17	SINCLAIR UTILITY	CHQ 0214	4 - 8		164.25	7,409.43
4	GL-GJ	08-Apr-17	KENYA COFFEE COMPANY	CHQ 0215	4 - 9		65.70	7,343.73
4	GL-GJ	09-Apr-17	THE CO-OPS OF MONTANA - Deposit	LT300	4 - 10	968.27		8,312.00
4	GL-GJ	09-Apr-17	RED'S GAS BAR - Deposit	LT303	4 - 11	254.36		8,566.36
4	GL-GJ	15-Apr-17	W/CANADA TRUCK STOPS - Deposit	LT296	4 - 12	418.74		8,895.10
4	GL-GJ	15-Apr-17	CITY NEWSPAPER	CHQ 0216	4 - 13		326.00	8,659.10
4	GL-GJ	15-Apr-17	CANADA REVENUE AGENCY - GST	CHQ 0217	4 - 14		1,746.80	6,912.30
4	GL-GJ	15-Apr-17	CANADA REVENUE AGENCY	CHQ 0218	4 - 15		1,254.35	5,657.95
4	GL-GJ	16-Apr-17	SUPER SAVE SERVICE - Deposit	LT290	4 - 16	366.05		6.024.00
4	GL-GJ	19-Apr-17	CARLY'S TRUCK WASH - Deposit	LT301	4 - 17	284.67		6,308.67
4	GL-GJ	19-Apr-17	APRIL'S MART - Deposit	LT302	4 - 18	200.60		6,509.27
4	GL-GJ	19-Apr-17	ELDORADO PETROLEUM - Deposit	LT295	4 - 19	1,987.00		8,496.27
4	GL-GJ	23-Apr-17	WEYBURN REFINERY	CHQ 0219	4 - 20		2,488.16	6,008.11
4	GL-GJ	23-Apr-17	TRI-CITY GAS - Deposit	LT305	4 - 21	502.46		6,510.57
4	GL-GJ	26-Apr-17	BENNY'S AUTO REPAIR - Deposit	LT306	4 - 22	1,007.28		7,517.85
4	GL-GJ	26-Apr-17	B OF A LOAN PAYMENT	4 - 23	4 - 23		317.50	7,200.85
4	GL-GJ	26-Apr-17	B OF A LOAN INTEREST	4 - 24	4 - 24		37.50	7,162.85
4	GL-GJ	26-Apr-17	LESLEY TRIPP - Salary	CHQ 0220	4 - 25		1,450.00	5,712.85
4	GL-GJ	26-Apr-17	ANDREW GALVOIR - Salary	CHQ 0221	4 - 26		1,220.00	4,492.85
4	GL-GJ	29-Apr-17	EDISON TUNE-UPS ALBERTA - Deposit	LT307	4 - 27	1,155.30		5,648.15

On-the-Job Training

(The forms you need are on pages 8-19 to 8-20 of the *Study Guide with Working Papers*.)

Replenishing the petty cash fund and increasing the petty cash account
3 (15 min)

T-1. Karen Johnson, the accountant of Hoop Co. of Nelson, has appointed Jim Pool as the petty cash custodian. The following transactions occurred in November:

2016		
Nov.	25	Cheque No. 441 was written and cashed to establish a $50 petty cash fund.
	26	Paid $8.50 delivery charge for goods purchased for resale.
	28	Purchased office supplies for $12 from petty cash.
	29	Purchased postage stamps for $15 from petty cash.

On December 3, Jim received the following internal memo:

> To: Jim Pool
>
> FROM: Karen Johnson
>
> RE: Petty Cash
>
> Jim, I'll need $5 for postage stamps. By the way, I noticed that our petty cash account seems to be too low. Increase its size to $100 please.

Help Jim replenish petty cash on December 3 by providing him with a general journal entry. Support your answer and indicate whether Karen was correct.

The bank reconciliation process
❷ (10 min)

T-2. Ginger Company of Bathurst has a policy of depositing all receipts and making all payments by cheque. On receiving the bank statement, Bill Free, a new bookkeeper, is quite upset that the balance in cash in the ledger is $4,209.50 while the ending bank balance is $4,440.50. Bill is convinced that the bank has made an error. Based on the following facts, is Bill's concern warranted? What other suggestions could you offer Bill in the bank reconciliation process?

a. The November 30 cash receipts, $611, had been placed in the bank's night depository after banking hours and consequently did not appear on the bank statement as a deposit.

b. Two debit memoranda and a credit memorandum were included with the returned cheques. None of the memoranda had been recorded at the time of the reconciliation. The first debit memorandum covered a $130 NSF cheque written by Abby Ellen. The second was a $6.50 debit memorandum for service charges. The credit memorandum was for $494 and represented the proceeds less a $6 collection fee from a $500 non-interest-bearing note collected for Ginger Company by the bank.

c. It was also found that cheques No. 942 for $71.50 and No. 947 for $206.50, both written and recorded on November 28, were not among the cancelled cheques returned.

d. Bill found that cheque No. 899 was correctly drawn for $1,094 as payment for a new cash register. However, this cheque had been recorded as though it were for $1,148.

e. The October bank reconciliation showed two cheques outstanding on September 30, No. 621 for $152.50 and No. 630 for $179.30. Cheque No. 630 was paid and returned with the November bank statement but cheque No. 621 was not.

Preparing a bank reconciliation
❷ (90 min)

T-3. On March 2, 2016, the accountant for Bergen Carpet Co. of Edmonton was injured in a skiing accident and was advised not to return to work for six weeks. The owners of the company are anxious to ensure that the company's bank statement is reconciled and have asked you to perform this task. You are presented with the following information:

a. Bank reconciliation prepared by the regular accountant at January 31, 2016:

Bergen Carpet Co.
Bank Reconciliation
January 31, 2016

Balance per Bank Statement		$ 8,364.02
Add: Deposit in Transit		2,576.03
		10,940.05
Less: Outstanding Cheques		
No. 417	$ 28.30	
419	1,043.25	
423	1,722.30	2,793.85
Balance per General Ledger		$ 8,146.20

b. General ledger listing of Bank Account (#110) for the month of February (see page 392).

c. Bank statement from the Royal Bank for the period ending February 26, 2016 (see page 393).

Required

Prepare the necessary reconciliation and any journal entries needed at February 28, 2016.

Date: 11 Mar. 2016 11:06 am — BERGEN CARPET CO. — Page: 1

G/L Listing

General Ledger Listing as of 28 Feb 2016

G/L listing for account [110] to [110]
for department [ ] to [222],
for fiscal period [2] 0 [2],
sorted by [Account] .

Last posting sequence number: 4

Acct. Dept.

Pd	Srce	Date	Description	Reference	Posting Entry	Batch Entry	Debits	Credits	Net Change/ Balance
	110	Bank							8,146.20
2	GL-GJ	01 Feb 16	KING PROPERTY	CHQ 404	2 - 1	2 - 1		974.15	
2	GL-GJ	01 Feb 16	SANDRA SMYTHE - Deposit	1007	2 - 2	2 - 2	8,145.38		
2	GL-GJ	04 Feb 16	INGRID LUNDREN - Deposit	1008	2 - 3	2 - 3	909.50		
2	GL-GJ	04 Feb 16	CAMPUS COPY SHOPPE	CHQ 424	2 - 4	2 - 4		133.75	
2	GL-GJ	04 Feb 16	BENJAMIN YEE	02 - 05	2 - 5	2 - 5	4,381.65		
2	GL-GJ	05 Feb 16	LITEMORE NEON SIGNS	CHQ 425	2 - 6	2 - 6		80.25	
2	GL-GJ	05 Feb 16	NORM & JANET TAYLOR - Deposit	1009	2 - 7	2 - 7	969.01		
2	GL-GJ	06 Feb 16	NAME - IT!	CHQ 426	2 - 9	2 - 9		240.75	
2	GL-GJ	06 Feb 16	JERRY SIMON - Deposit	1011	2 - 10	2 - 10	2,782.00		
2	GL-GJ	07 Feb 16	SAXONY WOOL MILLS	CHQ 427	2 - 11	2 - 11		4,559.11	
2	GL-GJ	07 Feb 16	QUALITY CARPET COMPANY	CHQ 428	2 - 12	2 - 12		6,829.28	
2	GL-GJ	07 Feb 16	JODY ARCHER	CHQ 429	2 - 13	2 - 13		25.00	
2	GL-GJ	08 Feb 16	CITY PHONE COMPANY	CHQ 430	2 - 14	2 - 14		121.75	
2	GL-GJ	08 Feb 16	CITY UTILITY COMPANY	CHQ 431	2 - 15	2 - 15		111.14	
2	GL-GJ	08 Feb 16	JOE'S GAS BAR	CHQ 432	2 - 16	2 - 16		94.66	
2	GL-GJ	08 Feb 16	WOOD'S STATIONERY	CHQ 433	2 - 17	2 - 17		1,091.40	
2	GL-GJ	04 Feb 16	CASH	CHQ 434	2 - 18	2 - 18		100.00	
2	GL-GJ	08 Feb 16	IVY LEUNG - Deposit	1012	2 - 19	2 - 19	2,169.96		
2	GL-GJ	08 Feb 16	EMILY BERGEN - Salary	CHQ 435	2 - 20	2 - 20		697.35	
2	GL-GJ	08 Feb 16	JAMES BERGEN - Salary	CHQ 436	2 - 21	2 - 21		697.35	
2	GL-GJ	08 Feb 16	RBC/TERMPLAN LOAN PAYMENT	02 - 22	2 - 22	2 - 22		601.87	
2	GL-GJ	08 Feb 16	RBC/DEMAND LOAN INTEREST	02 - 23	2 - 23	2 - 23		695.20	
2	GL-GJ	13 Feb 16	PAT HARPER - Deposit	1013	2 - 27	2 - 27	404.46		
2	GL-GJ	13 Feb 16	CITY LIGHTING	CHQ 437	2 - 29	2 - 29		112.50	
2	GL-GJ	13 Feb 16	FREDDY DUNCAN	CHQ 438	2 - 30	2 - 30		2,010.40	
2	GL-GJ	13 Feb 16	RECEIVER GENERAL FOR CANADA	CHQ 439	2 - 31	2 - 31		993.04	
2	GL-GJ	15 Feb 16	VOID	CHQ 440	2 - 32	2 - 32	0.00		
2	GL-GJ	18 Feb 16	WILSON INSURANCE AGENCY	CHQ 441	2 - 33	2 - 33		802.50	
2	GL-GJ	18 Feb 16	COMMUNITY CALENDAR	CHQ 442	2 - 34	2 - 34		246.10	
2	GL-GJ	18 Feb 16	STANDARD NEWS	CHQ 443	2 - 35	2 - 35		909.50	
2	GL-GJ	18 Feb 16	T C CHURCHILL - Deposit	1015	2 - 36	2 - 36	3,610.18		
2	GL-GJ	18 Feb 16	RBC/LOAN PROCESSING CHARGE	02 - 37	2 - 37	2 - 37		40.00	
2	GL-GJ	25 Feb 16	BEATRICE DAY - Deposit	1016	2 - 38	2 - 38	4,068.68		
2	GL-GJ	25 Feb 16	JOAN ANDERSON - Deposit	02 - 44	2 - 44	2 - 44	2,569.07		
2	GL-GJ	25 Feb 16	EMILY BERGEN - Salary	CHQ 444	2 - 46	2 - 46		697.35	
2	GL-GJ	25 Feb 16	JAMES BERGEN - Salary	CHQ 445	2 - 47	2 - 47		697.35	
2	GL-GJ	24 Feb 16	BOB JONES	CHQ 446	2 - 49	2 - 49		240.00	
2	GL-GJ	26 Feb 16	MICHEL ROBICHAUD - Deposit	02 - 53	2 - 53	2 - 53	3,456.10		
2	GL-GJ	26 Feb 16	JUDY CARMICHAEL - Deposit	1022	2 - 54	2 - 54	1,218.20		
2	GL-GJ	28 Feb 16	DMJ CONSTRUCTION - Deposit	02 - 55	2 - 55	2 - 55	1,786.90		
2	GL-GJ	28 Feb 16	FREDDY DUNCAN	CHQ 447	2 - 56	2 - 56		1,950.90	
2	GL-GJ	28 Feb 16	GEORGE BETTS	CHQ 448	2 - 57	2 - 57		1,213.20	
2	GL-GJ	28 Feb 16	GREENBRIAR RESTAURANT	CHQ 449	2 - 58	2 - 58		76.15	9,429.09
			Acct 110 - Balance, Feb 28, 2016						17,575.29

ROYAL BANK
MAIN BRANCH
10107 JASPER AVENUE
EDMONTON AB
T5J 1W9 03749

Account Statement

Account No.	
124-629-7	
Period	
From	To
Jan 27/16	Feb 26/16
Enclosures	Page
	1

BERGEN CARPET CO.
BAY 215
10620 - 104 AVENUE
EDMONTON AB
T5J 3G2

Date	Transaction Description		Cheques & Debits	Deposits & Credits	Balance
	Balance Forward				8,364.02
Jan 28	Deposit			2,576.03	10,940.05
Jan 28	Cheque -	404	974.15		
	Cheque -	419	1,043.25		8,922.65
Jan 29	Cheque -	423	1,722.30		7,200.35
Jan 30	Cheque -	424	133.75		7,066.60
Feb 01	Deposit			8,145.38	15,211.98
Feb 04	Deposit			5,291.15	
	Cheque -	434	100.00		20,403.13
Feb 05	Deposit			969.01	21,372.14
Feb 06	Deposit			2,782.00	
	Cheque -	425	80.25		
	Loan Payment - Principal		601.87		
	Loan Interest		695.20		22,776.82
Feb 07	Cheque -	430	121.75		
	Cheque -	436	697.35		
	Cheque -	435	697.35		21,260.37
Feb 08	Deposit			2,169.96	
	Cheque -	431	111.14		23,319.19
Feb 10	Cheque -	433	1,091.40		
	Cheque -	432	94.66		
	Cheque -	428	6,829.28		
	Cheque -	426	240.75		15,063.10
Feb 13	Deposit			404.46	
	Loan Management Fee		40.00		
	Cheque -	438	2,010.40		
	Cheque -	427	4,559.11		
	Cheque -	437	112.50		8,745.55
Feb 18	Deposit			3,610.18	12,355.73
Feb 18	Deposit			4,068.68	
	Cheque -	429	25.00		16,399.41
Feb 18	Cheque -	441	802.50		15,596.91
Feb 18	Cheque -	442	246.10		
	NSF Returned		404.46		14,946.35
Feb 21	NSF Charge		15.00		14,931.35
Feb 24	Cheque -	444	697.35		
	Cheque -	445	697.35		13,536.65
Feb 25	Deposit			2,569.07	
	Cheque -	439	993.04		15,112.68
Feb 26	Deposit			4,674.30	
	Cheque -	446	240.00		
	Service Charge		18.45		19,528.53

No. of Debits	Total Amount	No. of Credits	Total Amount
30	26,095.71	11	37,260.22

Recording and posting transactions; preparing a trial balance; and preparing a bank reconciliation
❷ ❸ (60 min)

CONTINUING PROBLEM

Following is a list of transactions for the month of October. Petty Cash Account (1010) and Miscellaneous Expense Account (5100) have been added to the chart of accounts.

Assignment

(See pages 8-21 to 8-29 in your *Study Guide with Working Papers.*)

1. Record the transactions in appropriate journals or petty cash format.
2. Post the transactions to the general ledger accounts.
3. Prepare a trial balance.

2016		
Oct.	1	Paid cleaning contract for October, November, and December, $900, cheque No. 252.
	4	Established a petty cash fund for $100, cheque No. 253.
	4	Collected $3,600 from a cash customer for building three systems.
	4	Invoiced (invoice No. 12684) and received $1,600 from Anthony Pitale.
	8	Purchased $25 worth of stamps, using petty cash voucher No. 101.
	8	Withdrew $2,000 (cheque No. 254) for personal use.
	9	Purchased $22 worth of supplies, using petty cash voucher No. 102.
	11	Paid the newspaper carrier $10, using petty cash voucher No. 103.
	15	Paid the amount due for October phone bill to West Bell Canada, $65, cheque No. 255.
	15	Paid the amount due for the October electric bill to City Electric, $95, cheque No. 256.
	22	Performed computer services for Taylor Golf; billed the client $4,200, invoice No. 12685.
	25	Paid $20 for computer paper, using petty cash voucher No. 104.
	28	Took $15 out of petty cash for lunch, voucher No. 105.
	29	Replenished the petty cash, cheque No. 257. Coin and currency in drawer $8.

Since Tony was so busy trying to close his books, he forgot to reconcile the May, June, and July bank statements. What follows on pages 395 and 396 is a list of all deposits and cheques written for these three months (each entry is identified by chapter, transaction date, or transaction letter) and bank statements for May through July. Reconciliations for August and September are not part of this problem.

Precision Computer Centre summary of deposits and cheques

Chapter	Transaction	Payor/Payee	Amount
		DEPOSITS	
1	(a)	Tony Freedman	$4,500
1	(f)	Cash customer	250
1	(g)	Cash customer	200
1	(i)	Taylor Golf	1,200
2	(p)	Cash customer	900
3	July 5	Tonya Parker Jones	325
3	July 8	Summer Lipe	220
3	July 12	Jeannine Sparks	850
3	July 26	Mike Hammer	140

Chapter	Transaction	Cheque No.	Payor/Payee	Amount
			CHEQUES	
1	(b)	201	Multi Systems, Inc.	$1,200
1	(c)	202	Office Furniture, Inc.	600
1	(e)	203	Capital Management	400
1	(j)	204	Tony Freedman	100
2	(l)	205	Insurance Protection, Inc.	150
2	(m)	206	Office Depot	200
2	(n)	207	Computer Edge Magazine	1,400
2	(q)	208	City Electric	85
2	(r)	209	Canada Post	50
3	July 3	210	Capital Management	1,200
3	July 10	211	West Bell Canada	155
3	July 15	212	Computer Connection	200
3	July 17	213	Multi Systems, Inc.	1,200

BANK STATEMENT

Royal Bank of Canada 322 Glen Avenue, Edmonton, AB T5P 2T9

Precision Computer Centre   Statement Date: May 21, 2016

Cheques Paid:			***Deposits and Credits:***	
Date paid	***Number***	***Amount***	***Date received***	***Amount***
5-5	***201***	***1,200.00***	***5-3***	***4,500.00***
5-7	***202***	***600.00***	***5-10***	***250.00***
5-14	***203***	***400.00***	***5-20***	***200.00***
			5-21	***1,200.00***
Total 3 cheques paid for $2,200.00			***Total Deposits***	***$6,150.00***

Ending Balance on May 21—$3,950.00

Received Statement May 28, 2016.

BANK STATEMENT

Royal Bank of Canada 322 Glen Avenue, Edmonton, AB T5P 2T9

Precision Computer Centre   Statement Date: June 18, 2016

Cheques Paid:			***Deposits and Credits:***	
Date paid	***Number***	***Amount***	***Date received***	***Amount***
6-2	***204***	***100.00***	***6-11***	***900.00***
6-7	***205***	***150.00***		
6-9	***206***	***200.00***		
6-16	***207***	***1,400.00***		
6-21	***208***	***85.00***		
Total 5 cheques paid for $1,935.00			***Total Deposits***	***$900.00***
Beginning balance on May 21—$3,950.00			***Ending balance on June 18—$2,915.00***	

Received Statement June 28, 2016.

BANK STATEMENT
Royal Bank of Canada 322 Glen Avenue, Edmonton, AB T5P 2T9

Precision Computer Centre ***Statement Date: July 23, 2016***

Cheques Paid:			*Deposits and Credits:*	
Date paid	*Number*	*Amount*	*Date received*	*Amount*
7-2	*209*	*50.00*	*7-8*	*325.00*
7-6	*210*	*1,200.00*	*7-10*	*220.00*
7-13	*211*	*155.00*	*7-13*	*850.00*
Total 3 cheques paid for $1,405.00			***Total Deposits***	***$1,395.00***
Beginning balance on June 18 $2,915.00			***Ending balance on July 23 $2,905.00***	

Received Statement July 28, 2016.

Assignment

Compare Precision Computer Centre's deposits and cheques with the bank statements, and complete a bank reconciliation as of July 31.

CHAPTER 9

Payroll Procedures

THE EMPLOYEES' PERSPECTIVE

LEARNING OBJECTIVES

- LO 1 Calculating gross pay, routine deductions, and net pay for an employee (p. 398)
- LO 2 Preparing a company's payroll summary (p. 408)
- LO 3 Recording a typical payroll from a summary (p. 410)
- LO 4 Maintaining an individual's earnings record (p. 412)

Think for a moment about the fact that the vast majority of Canadian businesses have employees and therefore need to "do the payroll" on a regular basis. Some do their payroll weekly, some twice a month, others every two weeks and of course a large number do their payroll monthly. There are even a few companies that pay their employees daily!

In theory, completing a payroll is a simple enough task. After all, it is just a matter of applying our federal or provincial laws to amounts that are likely set out clearly enough in written form—an employment contract, or something like that. The thing is, the laws and regulations we have in our country are lengthy and very complex, and contracts are often written in challenging legal jargon, so it often turns out that completing the payroll is anything but simple.

So, here's a thought: Employees who have the skills, knowledge, and experience to deal effectively with creating a payroll on a regular basis are always considered a valuable resource to a company. Often, such individuals receive a salary that is somewhat higher than they might otherwise be able to enjoy. This chapter describes in some detail how a payroll works and is constructed. If you find the material interesting and challenging, possibly you may want to learn more and pursue at least part of your career in this area.

Becoming an expert in the subject of payroll and related issues can take a long time because:

1. There are many federal and provincial laws that affect payroll and they change periodically.
2. Sometimes employers and employees view each other with suspicion in matters concerning payroll. This requires special care to get the figures correct.
3. The actual computation and payment of a payroll is quite detailed, leaving room for a number of mistakes to occur.

In Canada today, a company has two common alternatives to processing a payroll manually:

- Use a computer with appropriate software, such as Sage 50®.
- Contract with a payroll service (either an independent service or one connected with a chartered bank).

Either alternative is attractive to medium- or large-sized companies. Some smaller companies continue to process their payroll manually, thus avoiding the costs of the more sophisticated alternatives. Programs such as Sage 50® can also help in processing a payroll for smaller companies with simple payroll needs.

In this chapter, we will examine the details of a payroll for ABC Company for the first week in March. We will stress those things that affect individual employees. The next chapter examines the same subject from the employer's point of view.

In this chapter and the next, many deductions, maximum amounts, and minimum amounts are obtained from Canada Revenue Agency's recently published figures. Students should be aware that these will change at least annually. Your instructor may supply you with the most up-to-date figures, but remember that you should concentrate on learning the principles involved, not on matching the exact figures illustrated in this chapter and the next.

The tables that are included in the appendices at the end of this chapter for CPP and EI have been somewhat condensed to save space. If you use these condensed tables, your figures will differ by a few cents from the "official" tables. This is not a problem for classroom use, but you should not use the textbook tables for any business-world payroll taxes–use the official tables for that.

LEARNING UNIT 9-1

Important Laws and How They Affect Payroll

LO 1

Calculating gross pay, routine deductions, and net pay for an employee

A number of laws and regulations at the federal and provincial levels govern payroll. We will look at several of them here.

MINIMUM WAGE LAWS

Every province has a law that sets the lowest hourly wage that can legally be paid to an employee. The actual **minimum wage laws** vary somewhat from province to province and have a very small effect on the subject of payroll.

However, such laws also set out the maximum number of hours an employee can be asked to work per day and per week before an *overtime* premium must be paid. A typical requirement (and the one we shall adopt) is that employees who work more than 8 hours on any day or 40 hours in a week must be paid at time-and-a-half for the overtime hours. If Janet Johnson worked 4 hours on Monday, 8 hours on Tuesday, 11 hours on Wednesday, 8 hours on Friday, and 4 hours on Saturday, she would have worked only 35 hours during the week but would have earned 3 hours of overtime premium because she worked 11 hours on Wednesday.

Now suppose that Janet worked the following hours during a sample week:

Monday	7 hours	
Tuesday	8 hours	
Wednesday	11 hours	
Thursday	8 hours	
Friday	7 hours	
Saturday	4 hours	
Total	45 hours	for the week

If Janet's hourly rate were $10 per hour, her gross wages for the week would be computed as follows:

Regular time	40 h @ $10.00/h	$400
Overtime	5 h @ $15.00/h	75
Total earnings		$475

Note that the three hours of overtime worked on Wednesday are included in the total overtime of five hours.

Sometimes employers arrive at the same total by a slightly different calculation:

Regular rate	45 h @ $10.00/h	$450
Overtime rate (or premium)	5 h @ $5.00/h	25
Total earnings		$475

This second approach stresses the cost of overtime. A manager can more easily recognize the added cost of asking employees to work longer hours. We will use the first approach in this chapter since it reflects the point of view of the employee.

FEDERAL AND PROVINCIAL INCOME TAX

The federal and provincial governments each require employees to pay a tax based on the income that they earn. The details of our income tax system are not covered here, but we need to know a few essentials:

1. Taxes are *calculated* once a year: Employees must file a tax return by April 30 for the year ended on the previous December 31. However, the tax is *collected* from employees by payroll deductions each pay period.
2. In all provinces and territories in Canada (except Quebec), income tax must be determined and deducted by using the method called **TONI** (Tax on Income). Prior to TONI, provinces and territories typically based their income tax on the amount of federal tax. Since this percentage was easily determined for each province, only a single amount had to be looked up (or computed) for each employee per pay period. Because many provinces have introduced their own rules for income tax, this procedure no longer works, and now two amounts need to be looked up per employee per pay period; however, these amounts can then be combined for all other purposes.

These two deductions can be looked up in tables contained in a booklet called *Payroll Deductions Tables* (T4032). There is a separate booklet for each province and territory, and they can be obtained from **Canada Revenue Agency (CRA)**. You can pick up a copy from a local federal building, phone to have a copy delivered (1-800-959-2221), or go on the Internet and obtain the booklets and tables that way (www.cra-arc.gc.ca). The government also distributes the tables in electronic form. From the same website, you can download and use the Payroll Deductions Online Calculator (PDOC). In this chapter, we will refer you to the printed tables, since this is arguably the clearest procedure, but in the business world, one or more of the other approaches may work better.

Appendices 9-1F and 9-1P at the end of this chapter reproduce portions of the June 30, 2013, Ontario tables* for student use. The complete tables include sections for biweekly, semi-monthly, monthly, and other pay periods. These have not been reproduced because we are restricting our coverage to a weekly pay period. The procedures for other pay periods are nearly identical.

Please take a brief look at the federal tables (see pages 433 through 438). Notice that there are ranges of earnings shown on the left and various deduction figures in the 11 columns to the right of the earnings amounts. These deduction amounts get

*These tables were effective as of January 1, 2013, and include the changes made necessary by the introduction of the Ontario Health Premium. Note that this is not the same as the Employer Health Tax. The new tables (see the end of this chapter) include the new premium already—no special steps are necessary.

The employer is not responsible for verifying the claims made by employees on their TD1 forms, except that obviously incorrect TD1 forms should be investigated, possibly with the help of a local tax service office.

smaller as the claim code categories increase from 0 to 10. Each employee's **claim code** is determined by filling in **TD1 forms**. Since TONI has been introduced, there are now two TD1 forms to be completed by each new employee. The federal TD1 form is shown in Figure 9-1. Each province also has its own TD1 form, and the most current example from Ontario is shown as part b of Figure 9-1. In both the federal and provincial forms, only the first page is illustrated, as this contains most of the important information needed to determine a Total Claim Amount, which is then compared to a table (shown as part c of Figure 9-1) to choose a claim code for an employee. Notice that there are similarities as well as differences between the two TD1 forms. Each begins with a Basic personal amount, although these amounts are different, and also lists several specific factors that help calculate the Total Claim Amount. The federal form includes as item 2 a "Child amount," which the provincial form does not, and many of the specific amounts differ between the two forms as well. Students will be especially interested to note that the treatment of tuition, and especially textbooks, differs a lot between the two forms. Also worthy of mentioning is that page 2 of these forms contains a section that allows an employee to ask that some additional amount of tax be deducted each pay period. Such a request might seem strange at first, but many taxpayers work two or sometimes three jobs at the same time, and if no extra amounts of tax were deducted, they would end up paying a significant amount of extra tax when they file their tax return each year. This is because our Canadian tax laws, like most other countries, state that the rate of tax you pay goes up as the total amount you earn gets higher.

Despite the differences, the intent of the forms is the same—to calculate a dollar amount, which, when compared to a table (see part c of Figure 9-1), will arrive at a claim code number, which ranges from 1 through 10. It is this claim code number that governs how much tax an employer deducts from each employee when calculating a payroll. This procedure may seem very complicated, and it can be a bit hard to understand, but most employers will assist their employees in completing these forms if asked, so a full understanding of all of the many implications is probably not necessary. Certainly for the purposes of this text, we can say that the completion of both TD1 forms is the responsibility of each employee, and leave it at that. Do note, however, that the more dollar amounts entered into each form (for dependents, tuition, etc.), the higher the Total Claim Amount will be, and this leads to a higher claim code as well. As you will see, a higher claim code leads to a reduced amount of federal and provincial tax being deducted, which is as it should be.

Janet Johnson's TD1 forms show that she is claiming only the Basic Personal Amount as her Total Claim Amount. Many if not most Canadians will do the same, generally because they are single, or, if married, their spouse also works. If you compare Janet's Total Claim Amount with the chart shown as part c of Figure 9-1, you will see that she has a claim code of 1 for both the federal and provincial tax deduction. The great majority of Canadian employees will also have the same Claim Code for federal and provincial purposes, but as time goes by, this might change as differences between the two tax systems become more pronounced. Naturally, this will depend to a large extent on which province you are working in, but in any event, there is only a minor difference in looking up the amount of tax to be deducted—you just need to be careful to look in the column that corresponds to the claim code arrived at using the federal TD1 and its provincial counterpart. This is a good place to emphasize that everyone should be careful, in looking up tax deduction amounts, that they ignore the first column, labelled as Claim Code 0. This column is not used too often, as it deals almost exclusively with non-resident employees, a subject that is not covered in our discussion of payroll topics.

Employees do not have to fill out a new TD1 each time the tax laws change, unless they are claiming a new type of exemption (such as an education deduction or start supporting a new dependant). The old TD1 figures are automatically

Canada Revenue Agency / Agence du revenu du Canada

2013 Personal Tax Credits Return

TD1

Your employer or payer will use this form to determine the amount of your tax deductions.

Read the back before completing this form. Complete this form based on the best estimate of your circumstances.

Last name	First name and initial(s)	Date of birth (YYYY/MM/DD)	Employee number
JOHNSON	JANET	1966/03/12	N/A
Address including postal code		For non-residents only – Country of permanent residence	Social insurance number
602, 805 Fifth Street, Any City, Ontario M1X 2X2			111 222 333

1. Basic personal amount – Every resident of Canada can claim this amount. If you will have more than one employer or payer at the same time in 2013, see "More than one employer or payer at the same time" on the next page. If you are a non-resident, see "Non-residents" on the next page.	**11,038**
2. Child amount – Either parent (but not both), may claim $2,234 for each child born in 1996 or later, that resides with both parents throughout the year. If the child is **infirm, add $2,040** to the claim for that child. Any unused portion can be transferred to that parent's spouse or common-law partner. If the child does not reside with both parents throughout the year, the parent who is entitled to claim the "Amount for an eligible dependant" on line 8 may also claim the child amount for that same child.	
3. Age amount – If you will be 65 or older on December 31, 2013, and your net income for the year from all sources will be $34,562 or less, enter $6,854. If your net income for the year will be between $34,562 and $80,256 and you want to calculate a partial claim, get the TD1-WS, *Worksheet for the 2013 Personal Tax Credits Return*, and complete the appropriate section.	
4. Pension income amount – If you will receive regular pension payments from a pension plan or fund (excluding Canada Pension Plan, Quebec Pension Plan, Old Age Security, or Guaranteed Income Supplement payments), enter $2,000 or your estimated annual pension income, whichever is less.	
5. Tuition, education, and textbook amounts (full time and part time) – If you are a student enrolled at a university or college, or an educational institution certified by Human Resources and Skills Development Canada, and you will pay more than $100 per institution in tuition fees, complete this section. If you are enrolled full time, or if you have a mental or physical disability and are enrolled part time, enter the total of the tuition fees you will pay, plus $400 for each month that you will be enrolled, plus $65 per month for textbooks. If you are enrolled part time and do not have a mental or physical disability, enter the total of the tuition fees you will pay, plus $120 for each month that you will be enrolled part time, plus $20 per month for textbooks.	
6. Disability amount – If you will claim the disability amount on your income tax return by using Form T2201, *Disability Tax Credit Certificate*, enter $7,697.	
7. Spouse or common-law partner amount – If you are supporting your spouse or common-law partner who lives with you, and whose net income for the year will be less than $11,038 ($13,078 if he or she is **infirm**) enter the difference between this amount and his or her estimated net income for the year. If your spouse's or common-law partner's net income for the year will be $11,038 or more ($13,078 or more if he or she is **infirm**), you cannot claim this amount.	
8. Amount for an eligible dependant – If you do not have a spouse or common-law partner and you support a dependent relative who lives with you, and whose net income for the year will be less than $11,038 ($13,078 if he or she is **infirm** and you **did not claim the child amount** for this dependant), enter the difference between this amount and his or her estimated net income. If your eligible dependant's net income for the year will be $11,038 or more ($13,078 or more if he or she is **infirm**), you cannot claim this amount.	
9. Caregiver amount – If you are taking care of a dependant who lives with you, whose net income for the year will be $15,334 or less, and who is either your or your spouse's or common-law partner's: • parent or grandparent (aged 65 or older), enter $4,490 ($6,530 if he or she is **infirm**); or • relative (aged 18 or older) who is dependent on you because of an infirmity, enter $6,530. If the dependant's net income for the year will be between $15,334 and $19,824 ($15,334 and $21,864 if he or she is **infirm**) and you want to calculate a partial claim, get the TD1-WS, and complete the appropriate section.	
10. Amount for infirm dependants age 18 or older – If you support an infirm dependant age 18 or older who is your or your spouse's or common-law partner's relative, who lives in Canada, and whose net income for the year will be $6,548 or less, enter $6,530. You cannot claim an amount for a dependant you claimed on line 9. If the dependant's net income for the year will be between $6,548 and $13,078 and you want to calculate a partial claim, get the TD1-WS, and complete the appropriate section.	
11. Amounts transferred from your spouse or common-law partner – If your spouse or common-law partner will not use all of his or her age amount, pension income amount, tuition, education and textbook amounts, disability amount or child amount on his or her income tax return, enter the unused amount.	
12. Amounts transferred from a dependant – If your dependant will not use all of his or her **disability amount** on his or her income tax return, enter the unused amount. If your or your spouse's or common-law partner's dependent child or grandchild will not use all of his or her **tuition, education, and textbook amounts** on his or her income tax return, enter the unused amount.	
13. TOTAL CLAIM AMOUNT – Add lines 1 through 12. Your employer or payer will use this amount to determine the amount of your tax deductions.	$11,038

Continue on the next page ➔

TD1 E (13) (Vous pouvez obtenir ce formulaire en français à **www.arc.gc.ca/formulaires** ou au **1-800-959-3376**.) Canada

Figure 9-1(a) Federal TD1 Form, Page 1

Ontario

2013 Ontario
Personal Tax Credits Return

TD1ON

Your employer or payer will use this form to determine the amount of your provincial tax deductions.
Read the back before completing this form. Complete this form based on the best estimate of your circumstances.

Last name	First name and initial(s)	Date of birth (YYYY/MM/DD)	Employee number
JOHNSON	JANET	1966/03/12	N/A
Address including postal code		**For non-residents only –** Country of permanent residence	Social insurance number
602, 805 Fifth Street, Any City, Ontario M1X 2X2			111 222 333

1. Basic personal amount – Every person employed in Ontario and every pensioner residing in Ontario can claim this amount. If you will have more than one employer or payer at the same time in 2013, see "Will you have more than one employer or payer at the same time?" on the next page.	**9,574**
2. Age amount – If you will be 65 or older on December 31, 2013, and your net income from all sources will be $34,798, or less, enter $4,674. If your net income for the year will be between $34,798 and $65,958 and you want to calculate a partial claim, get the TD1ON-WS, *Worksheet for the 2013 Ontario Personal Tax Credits Return*, and complete the appropriate section.	
3. Pension income amount – If you will receive regular pension payments from a pension plan or fund (excluding Canada Pension Plan, Quebec Pension Plan, Old Age Security, or Guaranteed Income Supplement payments), enter $1,324, or your estimated annual pension income, whichever is less.	
4. Tuition and education amounts (full time and part time) – If you are a student enrolled at a university, college, or educational institution certified by Human Resources and Skills Development Canada, and you will pay more than $100 per institution in tuition fees, complete this section. If you are enrolled full time, or if you have a mental or physical disability and are enrolled part time, enter the total of the tuition fees you will pay, plus $515 for each month that you will be enrolled. If you are enrolled part time and do not have a mental or physical disability, enter the total of the tuition fees you will pay, plus $154 for each month that you will be enrolled part time.	
5. Disability amount – If you will claim the disability amount on your income tax return by using Form T2201, *Disability Tax Credit Certificate*, enter $7,735.	
6. Spouse or common-law partner amount – If you are supporting your spouse or common-law partner who lives with you, and whose net income for the year will be $813 or less, enter $8,129. If his or her net income for the year will be between $813 and $8,942 and you want to calculate a partial claim, get the TD1ON-WS, and complete the appropriate section.	
7. Amount for an eligible dependant – If you do not have a spouse or common-law partner and you support a dependent relative who lives with you, and whose net income for the year will be $813 or less, enter $8,129. If his or her net income for the year will be between $813 and $8,942 and you want to calculate a partial claim, get the TD1ON-WS, and complete the appropriate section.	
8. Caregiver amount – If you are taking care of a dependant who lives with you, whose net income for the year will be $15,438 or less, and who is either your or your spouse's or common-law partner's: • parent or grandparent (aged 65 or older); or • relative (aged 18 or older) who is dependent on you because of an infirmity, enter $4,513. If the dependant's net income for the year will be between $15,438 and $19,951 and you want to calculate a partial claim, get the TD1ON-WS, and complete the appropriate section.	
9. Amount for infirm dependants age 18 or older – If you are supporting an infirm dependant aged 18 or older who is your or your spouse's or common-law partner's relative, who lives in Canada, and whose net income for the year will be $6,414 or less, enter $4,513. You cannot claim an amount for a dependant you claimed on line 8. If the dependant's net income for the year will be between $6,414 and $10,927 and you want to calculate a partial claim, get the TD1ON-WS, and complete the appropriate section.	
10. Amounts transferred from your spouse or common-law partner – If your spouse or common-law partner will not use all of his or her age amount, pension income amount, tuition and education amounts, or disability amount on his or her income tax return, enter the unused amount.	
11. Amounts transferred from a dependant – If your dependant will not use all of his or her **disability amount** on his or her income tax return, enter the unused amount. If your or your spouse's or common-law partner's dependent child or grandchild will not use all of his or her **tuition and education amounts** on his or her income tax return, enter the unused amount.	
12. TOTAL CLAIM AMOUNT – Add lines 1 through 11. Your employer or payer will use your claim amount to determine the amount of your provincial tax deductions.	$9,574

Continue on the next page →

TD1ON E (13)

(Vous pouvez obtenir ce formulaire en français à **www.arc-cra.gc.ca** ou en composant le **1-800-959-3376**.)

Canada

Figure 9-1(b) Provincial TD1 ON Form, Page 1

Figure 9-1(c)
Federal and Ontario Claim Codes

Chart 3 – 2013 Federal claim codes	
Total claim amount ($)	**Claim code**
No claim amount	0
11,038.00	1
11,038.01 to 13,147.00	2
13,147.01 to 15,256.00	3
15,256.01 to 17,365.00	4
17,365.01 to 19,474.00	5
19,474.01 to 21,583.00	6
21,583.01 to 23,692.00	7
23,692.01 to 25,801.00	8
25,801.01 to 27,910.00	9
27,910.01 to 30,019.00	10
30,019.01 and over	X The employer has to calculate the tax manually
No withholding	E

Chart 4 – 2013 Ontario claim codes	
Total claim amount ($)	**Claim code**
No claim amount	0
9,574.00	1
9,574.01 to 11,637.00	2
11,637.01 to 13,700.00	3
13,700.01 to 15,763.00	4
15,763.01 to 17,826.00	5
17,826.01 to 19,889.00	6
19,889.01 to 21,952.00	7
21,952.01 to 24,015.00	8
24,015.01 to 26,078.00	9
26,078.01 to 28,141.00	10
28,141.01 and over	X The employer has to calculate to the manually
No withholding	E

updated by most accounting software programs, and even the government tables (such as those at the end of the chapter) automatically include the effects of **indexing**—the automatic increases in claim amounts to include inflation.

Payroll periods can be:

Weekly: 52 pay periods/year
Biweekly: 26 pay periods/year
Semi-monthly: 24 pay periods/year
Monthly: 12 pay periods/year

Notice that the procedure for deducting income tax is not very precise. The actual tax that Janet will have to pay for the year will depend on dozens of factors, some of them quite personal (such as whether she has paid any allowable medical fees during the taxation year, or whether she has charitable donations or medical expenses). The purpose of the deduction tables is to ensure that wage earners pay about as much tax as they would owe on their earnings for the week. Sometimes employees have to pay extra tax when they file their annual tax returns, but usually they get a refund. This is because the tables tend to ignore many allowable tax deductions.

In our example on pages 398-399, Janet will have $31.70 deducted as federal income tax (from Appendix 9-1F) and $18.65 as provincial income tax (from Appendix 9-1P). This is a total of $50.35, and it is this total amount that will be used in the steps that follow. Remember that while you must look up (or compute) two amounts, they are combined for all further steps in the payroll process.

In practice, there are several modifications sometimes made to the amount of income tax deducted. Some employees (perhaps because they have more than one place of employment) ask that additional income tax be deducted. There is a place on the TD1 form to request this, and it is a fairly common event in determining income tax deduction amounts. There are also several less common reasons why the actual deduction for income tax may differ from the amounts in the official tables. A detailed study of these adjustments is not considered to be a part of this book.

In an effort to conserve resources, the government has begun to publish the various tables of deductions in computer-readable format. Your instructor may arrange to supply you with a copy, or make a copy available for the duration of the course.

You may also use the Internet to access these tables. Set your browser to: www.cra-arc.gc.ca/payroll.

CANADA OR QUEBEC PENSION PLAN

In the mid-1960s, the **Canada and Quebec Pension Plans** were introduced. Their purpose was to provide a pension benefit (as well as certain other benefits) for Canadians at retirement. The law requires a deduction of 4.95% from the earnings of each taxpayer in Canada who is at least 18 years of age but not 70 years or older and who is not in receipt of a disability or retirement pension from CPP. (The first $67.30 of earnings in a week are not subject to this deduction. Likewise, earnings in excess of $47,600 per year are not subject to the 4.95% levy.)

It is possible to compute the necessary deduction for the Canada Pension Plan (CPP) for each employee, but the federal government has provided detailed tables in the booklet *Payroll Deductions Tables (T4032)* to make this unnecessary (see Appendix 9-2 and Learning Unit 9-2). As you can see, Janet Johnson should have a CPP deduction of $20.18—($475 – $67.30) × 0.0495—taken from her wages this pay period. However, since the tables we are using show $20.16, that is the amount we shall use in the illustration. The federal government maintains a precise record of the CPP payments made by each Canadian because the benefits that we will receive are related to the contributions we make plus the amounts contributed by our employers on our behalf—by law, the same amount as is deducted. There are more details on this in the next chapter. Remember that the tables shown in Appendix 9-2 as well as Appendix 9-3 are not as precise as the actual tables as supplied by the CRA, so expect to see minor differences in the amounts deducted for CPP (and EI—see the following page).

A summary of CPP earnings and contributions is available online through Services Canada. Once you set up a My Service Canada account you can log in to see the contributions summary as well as estimated monthly CPP benefits.

EMPLOYMENT INSURANCE PLAN

The EI deduction rate is subject to change from year to year. However, the $43,200 maximum insurable earnings is fixed until it is changed by legislation.

It is a requirement for virtually all employees, regardless of age, to participate in Canada's **Employment Insurance (EI) plan**. (There are some exceptions.) This plan entitles workers to a certain level of income if they become unemployed. The details are very complex and a full discussion of the plan is beyond the scope of this text.

In each pay period, an amount of 1.88% is deducted from an employee's wages. This deduction applies only to the first $47,400 per year. Fortunately, the deductions are rather straightforward for most employees and can be found in the same booklet as the CPP deductions (see Appendix 9-3 at the end of this chapter). In Janet Johnson's case, she will have an EI deduction of $8.94 (approximately $475.00 × 0.0188) made from her wages for this week.

CPP AND EI: SOME ADDITIONAL INFORMATION

Students should be aware that unique CPP deduction tables are supplied for weekly, biweekly, semi-monthly, and monthly pay periods. In calculating the CPP deduction per pay period, there is no maximum contribution per period—just an annual upper limit ($2,356.20 for 2013).

The EI deduction, however, is different. A single table is used for all pay periods. As shown at the bottom of any EI table, there is a maximum deduction for each annual period. Since the maximum insurable earning is $47,400, the annual maximum premium is $891.12 (47,400 × 0.0188).

WORKERS' COMPENSATION PLANS

In all provinces, workers' incomes are protected in the event of an injury that occurs on the job. Since the cost of this **workers' compensation** is typically paid by the employer, no deductions are made from employees' wages. We will not pursue this matter further in this chapter, except to note that computer programs such as Sage 50® need to know what rate to use (the rate varies by category of employment and from province to province) to calculate payroll expenses properly.

VARIOUS UNION AGREEMENTS

Most unions operate under laws that are enacted provincially or federally. In many businesses, workers have been organized into bargaining units, or unions. Normally, the union and the employer agree that **union dues** are to be deducted from the employees' wages and forwarded to the union treasurer, usually monthly. In our example, the ABC Company does not have unionized employees and therefore no deductions are shown.

OTHER DEDUCTIONS

Other deductions are sometimes made from an employee's earnings. Details will vary from one employer to another, but the following deductions are common in Canada:

1. Medical and dental insurance premiums
2. Company pension plan—current service
3. Company pension plan—past service
4. Charitable donations
5. Canada Savings Bonds installments
6. Parking charges
7. Social fund charges
8. Repayment of loans or advances
9. Long-term income replacement premiums
10. Life insurance premiums
11. Garnishees

OTHER INCOME AMOUNTS

In Chapter 6, brief mention was made of the details kept by some companies regarding records of sales made per period by salesperson. This information is valuable in itself, as a sales manager can monitor which of her employees are performing well and which ones are underperforming. In some companies where records are kept of sales by salesperson, part of that individual's income is determined by their sales record. Sometimes this is a simple process—a straight percentage of this week's sales, for instance. In other cases, the calculation can be quite complex, with attention paid to longer-term rolling averages, as well as previous period's performance. The payment of a **commission**, however complicated it might be, is for the purpose of rewarding good performance and signalling where added effort is needed.

We will not discuss the theory of compensation further at this point. Any student interested in this challenging and worthwhile topic can easily find details in other textbooks, and a lot of popular books as well. Our task is to see how the accountant should handle the work of adding commission income to an employee's payroll details. As with many things relating to payroll, it is not the bookkeeping details that are the challenge—it can be difficult to interpret management's policies with regard to commissions. It is all too often true that a particular customer is served by two or more salespeople, thereby making the determination of who gets what commission a difficult task. It is generally not the task of the accounting staff to make these judgments, so we will focus our attention on the computational aspects of paying commissions to employees.

For our example we are going to assume that XYZ Company in Toronto sells fashion wear and has three salespeople. Each receives a weekly "salary" that increases somewhat as time passes, plus a commission of 3% of the retail value of their net sales for a week. Here are the details of what happened last week:

Salesperson	Net Sales	Base Salary	Commission	Total Pay
June Halperson	$18,450	$300.00	$553.50	$ 853.50
Winnie Mason	14,300	350.00	429.00	779.00
Molly Tunis	20,600	400.00	618.00	1,018.00

XYZ Company also has a number of other employees as well, but their rates of pay are either entirely salary, or hourly, and are determined in the usual way. The above information has all the details needed to calculate the net pay for each of the three salespeople. You simply use the amount in the right-most column as their gross pay for the week. All of the other rules you already know about payroll apply equally to these employees as well. It is the same thing as calculating an hourly-paid employee's gross pay when overtime hours are involved. You add the overtime to the hourly-pay amount, and the result is gross pay. For XYZ Company, the commissions earned are added to the base salary to determine the gross pay for that employee for a given week.

Some companies also give employees a bonus at certain times throughout the year. A bonus is often paid at or near the end of December each year, and some other companies pay out bonuses based on how well the company performs during the fiscal year. It is impossible to predict the timing of these types of payments, but when they happen, it is usually the case that they get added to whatever the employee usually earns in the period, and all the usual deductions are then based on the total amount. Sometimes, however, a bonus is so large that it would cause the usual tax rules to distort the amount of tax deducted. If this is the case, there is a special way of calculating the tax on the bonus itself. This is not covered in this chapter, as it is a very rare event, and is well covered in the payroll documents provided by the CRA.

LEARNING UNIT 9-1 REVIEW

AT THIS POINT you should be able to:

- Calculate regular and overtime earnings. (pp. 398–399)
- Calculate regular and commission earnings. (p. 406)
- Explain the purpose of a TD1 form. (p. 400)
- Determine income tax deductions given a completed TD1 form and total earnings. (p. 403)
- Determine a deduction for CPP from tables supplied. (p. 404)
- Determine a deduction for EI from tables supplied. (p. 404)
- Explain the operation of maximum deductions for both CPP and EI. (p. 404)
- Describe in general terms the nature of certain other routine deductions. (p. 405)

Self-Review Quiz 9-1

(The forms you need are on page 9-1 of the *Study Guide with Working Papers.*)

Using the tables in Appendices 9-1, 9-2, and 9-3, determine the gross pay and deductions for income tax, CPP, and EI for Norma Fry, a single taxpayer (claim code 1) who worked 42 hours last week at a wage rate of $12 per hour.

Solution to Self-Review Quiz 9-1

Gross pay:		
40 h @ $12/h		$480.00
2 h @ $18/h (overtime)		36.00
Gross pay		$516.00
Deductions:		
Income tax (from Appendices 9-1F and 9-1P)*	$58.70	
CPP (from Appendix 9-2)	22.16	
EI (from Appendix 9-3)	9.69	
Total deductions		90.55
Net pay ($516 – $90.55)		$425.45

*Federal amount = $37.85; provincial amount = $20.85.

LEARNING UNIT 9-2

A Typical Payroll

LO 2

Preparing a company's payroll summary

The ABC Company has six employees to be paid for the first week of March 2016. They are listed below, together with the number of hours each worked and their rates of pay:

Name	*Hours*	*Rate*
Janet Johnson	45	$ 10/h
Peter Black	42	18/h
John Chernochan	44	17/h
Tony Chui	41	12/h
Beth Madora	38	15/h
Elaine Dumont, Manager	40	900/wk

Employees are paid weekly at the ABC Company. The **payroll summary** in Figure 9-2 has been prepared based upon tables and calculations covered earlier in this chapter. Don't worry if the summary appears a bit complicated—we will deal with each column in turn. Note that all deductions are based on the 2013 rates shown in the appendices to this chapter, not the actual federal amounts.

THE PAYROLL SUMMARY IN DETAIL

Many medium- to large-sized companies use a computer to help prepare their payroll. The data output from a computerized payroll are often remarkably similar to the illustrations in this chapter.

A. Claim Code The law requires all employees to complete and sign TD1 exemption forms at the beginning of employment and whenever there is a change in the employee's circumstances. As shown in Figure 9-1, this form allows employees to specify their exemption status so that an appropriate amount of income tax can be deducted. The claim code for each employee is shown in this column. You can see that four of the employees are claiming a claim code of 1, resulting in the maximum **income tax deduction** at their earnings level. The other two employees (John and Elaine) presumably have dependants, who allow each of them to specify a higher claim code, with a lower income tax deduction at that earnings level. New TD1 forms can be filed at any time, and until new forms are filed the old claim code continues. If a form is not filed, each employee is treated as if he or she has a claim code of 1.

Claim code 0 is used for non-resident taxpayers. Be careful using the tax tables—you can always ignore the first deduction column when using this textbook.

B. Hours Worked Each employee may work a different number of hours in each week. Remember that *overtime rates* will apply to hours in excess of 40 per week or 8 in one day. Notice also that Elaine's hours are shown even though she is not paid according to the number of hours that she worked. It is not unusual to record the hours worked daily by each employee. A weekly total is then transferred to this column in the payroll summary.

C. Rate of Pay The rates of pay are as set out above. Notice that all employees except Elaine are paid on an hourly basis. Elaine, as manager, receives a weekly salary, but this fact does not change subsequent payroll steps.

D. Regular Earnings Regular earnings are computed based upon regular hours per week—or, as in Elaine's case, a salary.

E. Overtime Earnings The segregation of overtime earnings helps the ABC Company to control this expensive use of employees' time. A common practice is to hire an additional employee when this figure becomes too high.

F. Gross Pay Each employee earns a total amount per week. It is this figure that governs the legally required deductions. Gross pay may mean regular earnings plus overtime, or salary plus commissions.

G, H, I. Income Tax Deductions From Appendices 9-1F and 9-1P, we have already seen that Janet's income tax deduction totals $50.35. Make sure that you can find the

Figure 9-2
Payroll Summary

ABC Company
Payroll Summary Sheet
For the Week Ending March 7, 2016

Employee	Claim Code*	Total Hrs. Reg.	Total Hrs. O/T	Reg. Rate Pay/Hr	Earnings Regular	Earnings Overtime	Earnings Gross Pay
Janet Johnson	1	40	5	$10.00	400 00	75 00	475 00
Peter Black	1	40	2	$18.00	720 00	54 00	774 00
John Chernochan	4	40	4	$17.00	680 00	102 00	782 00
Tony Chui	1	40	1	$12.00	480 00	18 00	498 00
Beth Madora	1	38	0	$15.00	570 00	0 00	570 00
Elaine Dumont	3	40	–	900/Wk	900 00	0 00	900 00
					3 750 00	249 00	3 999 00
	(A)	(B)		(C)	(D)	(E)	(F)

Above is Part a

*-We are assuming that the claim codes are the same for federal and provincial tax deduction purposes. This is not always true, and will depend on the details of each employee's Federal and Provincial TD-1 forms.

Memo only FIT	Memo only PIT	Deductions Total Tax	Deductions CPP	Deductions EI	Deductions Medical	Deductions Charitable	Net Pay	Chq. No.
31 70	18 65	50 35	20 16	8 94	0 00	5 00	390 55	1407
73 35	36 60	109 95	34 93	14 55	18 00	5 00	591 57	1408
59 25	32 30	91 55	35 33	14 72	38 00	5 00	597 40	1409
35 05	20 10	55 15	21 29	9 35	0 00	5 00	407 21	1410
45 10	23 50	68 60	24 83	10 71	18 00	5 00	442 86	1411
86 45	44 15	130 60	41 09	16 92	38 00	5 00	668 39	1412
		506 20	177 63	75 19	112 00	30 00	3 097 98	
(G)	(H)	(I)	(J)	(K)	(L)	(M)	(N)	(O)

Above is Part b

amounts deducted for the other employees in Appendices 9-1F and 9-1P. Note that there is no need to total columns G and H. Only the I column total is used below.

J. CPP Deduction Appendix 9-2 is the source for these CPP deductions.

K. EI Deduction See Appendix 9-3 to trace each employee's EI deduction.

L. Medical Deduction The law regarding medical deductions varies from one province to another. Some provinces do not require a deduction for provincial health care plans. In our example, a deduction is required for each household. This explains why no deductions are made from Janet's and Tony's wages. We may assume that they are covered by their spouses' deductions.

M. Charitable Deduction Each employee has agreed to a weekly deduction to support a charitable cause—perhaps Operation Eyesight.

N. Net Pay This is each employee's gross pay less all deductions, often known as *take-home pay.*

O. Cheque Number A cheque is issued to each employee for the exact amount due. When the cheques are issued, their numbers are written here. If a direct deposit scheme were used by the ABC Company, they might insert a transfer code here instead.

LEARNING UNIT 9-2 REVIEW

AT THIS POINT you should be able to:

- Calculate earnings, deductions, and net pay for an employee. (pp. 408–409)
- Describe the preparation of a payroll summary. (pp. 408–409)
- Explain the purpose of each column in a payroll summary. (pp. 408–409)

Self-Review Quiz 9-2

(The forms you need are on page 9-1 of the *Study Guide with Working Papers.*)

If a new employee, Robert Meade, begins employment next week, calculate his gross and net pay assuming a TD1 claim code of 3, 40 hours worked, a wage of \$11/h, and no medical or charitable deduction.

Solution to Self-Review Quiz 9-2

Did you calculate a net pay of \$384.02? Details are:

Gross pay: 40 h @ \$11/h		\$440.00
Deductions:		
Income tax (from Appendices 9-1F and 9-1P)*	\$29.30	
CPP (from Appendix 9-2)	18.42	
EI (from Appendix 9-3)	8.26	
Medical	0.00	
Charitable	0.00	
Total deductions		55.98
Net pay (\$440.00 – \$55.98)		\$384.02

*Federal tax = \$17.50; provincial tax = \$11.80.

LEARNING UNIT 9-3

Recording and Payment

LO 3 Recording a typical payroll from a summary

The details in Figure 9-2 are used to make the journal entry shown below, which records the payroll for the first week in March for the ABC Company:

			Dr.	Cr.
2016				
March	7	Salaries and Wages Expense	3999 00	
		Income Taxes Payable		506 20
		CPP Payable		177 63
		EI Payable		75 19
		Medical Plan Payable		112 00
		Charitable Contributions Payable		30 00
		Salaries and Wages Payable		3097 98
		To record payroll for first week in March		

Some companies keep track of different salary or wage expenses separately. For instance, it is useful to separate Elaine's salary from the wages of the other workers. The owners can then separate the cost of management from the cost of labour.

It is also useful to further break down the labour cost into more detail. Consider the additional information available to the owners if we assume that Tony and Beth are sales personnel. The debit to Sales Wages Expense would be $1,068 ($498 + $570). Instead of the single debit of $3,999 to an account called Salaries and Wages Expense, we would now have three debits:

Date		Account	PR	Debit	Credit
2016					
March	7	Management Salaries Expense		900 00	
		Sales Wages Expense		1 068 00	
		Wages Expense		2 031 00	

(The credit side of the entry would not change.)

If we assume that the ABC Company uses this more detailed method, then the entry would be posted to the ledger accounts summarized as follows (opening balances are ignored):

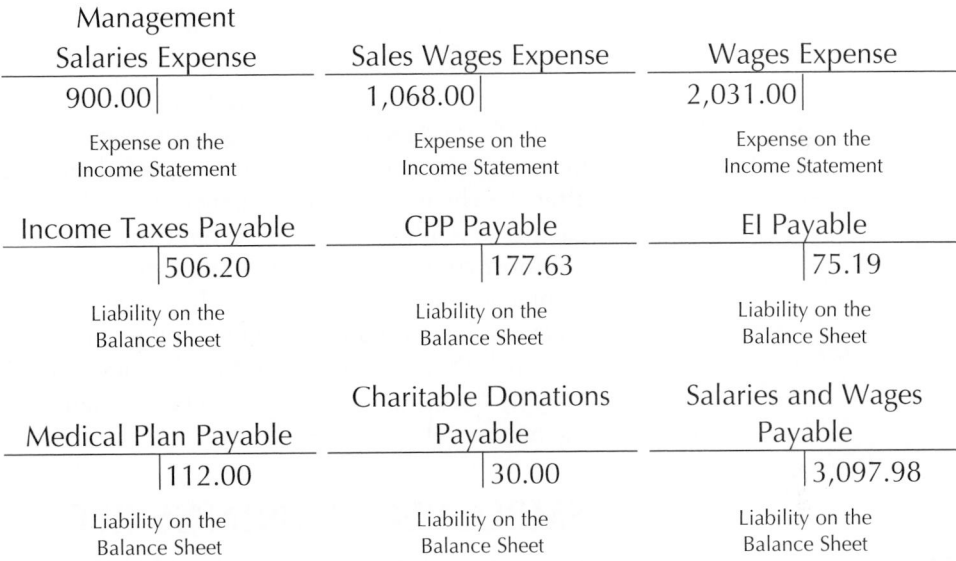

Management Salaries Expense	
900.00	

Expense on the Income Statement

Sales Wages Expense	
1,068.00	

Expense on the Income Statement

Wages Expense	
2,031.00	

Expense on the Income Statement

Income Taxes Payable	
	506.20

Liability on the Balance Sheet

CPP Payable	
	177.63

Liability on the Balance Sheet

EI Payable	
	75.19

Liability on the Balance Sheet

Medical Plan Payable	
	112.00

Liability on the Balance Sheet

Charitable Donations Payable	
	30.00

Liability on the Balance Sheet

Salaries and Wages Payable	
	3,097.98

Liability on the Balance Sheet

Figure 9-3 summarizes the main elements of the payroll process.

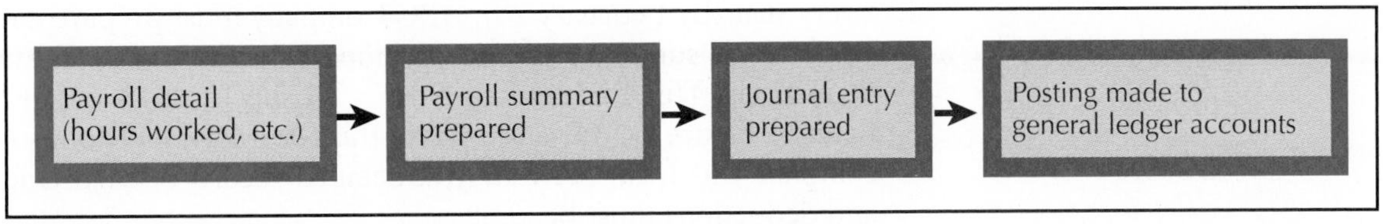

Figure 9-3 The Payroll Recording and Posting Process

LAST STEP DIRECTLY AFFECTING EMPLOYEES

From the employees' point of view, the best part of the payroll process is receiving their net pay each week. The ABC Company writes a cheque to each employee in payment of his or her weekly *take-home pay* (see columns N and O, Figure 9-2). As each cheque is written, it is recorded in the *cash disbursements journal*, as shown in Figure 9-4.

When the cash payments journal is posted, the balance in the Salaries and Wages Payable account will be reduced to zero. The exact same thing will be true when all of the general journal entries are posted if a cash payments journal is not used. This is as it should be since the amount recorded as payable, $3,097.98, has

Date		Chq. No.	Accounts Payment To:	PR	Sundry Dr.	Accounts Payable Dr.	Salaries and Wages Payable Dr.	Purchases Discount Cr.	Cash Cr.
2016									
Mar.	8	1407	Janet Johnson				390 55		390 55
		1408	Peter Black				591 57		591 57
		1409	John Chernochan				597 40		597 40
		1410	Tony Chui				407 21		407 21
		1411	Beth Madora				442 86		442 86
		1412	Elaine Dumont				668 39		668 39

CASH PAYMENTS JOURNAL

Figure 9-4 Cash Payments Journal (also called Cash Disbursements Journal)

been paid by cheques numbered 1407–1412 and the amount remaining to be paid is nil. Please remember that the cash payments journal is posted at the end of the month. The general journal may be posted more often than once a month. It is only after the cheques have been issued, recorded, and posted that the balance in the Salaries and Wages Payable account will be zero.

Most companies pay their employees by cheque although, in a very few cases, companies pay out actual cash. Many large companies transfer wages directly to their employees' bank accounts. Some companies have a separate bank account on which they issue their payroll cheques. The main reason for this practice is to simplify the payment process and reconciliation of bank accounts, especially when the number of employees is large.

EMPLOYEE EARNINGS RECORD

LO 4

Maintaining an individual's earnings record

To meet legal requirements, the ABC Company must keep a separate record of each employee's earnings. This **employee earnings record** is essential for the following reasons:

1. Every year (by February 28), ABC Company must prepare and deliver to each employee a summary of the previous calendar year's earnings and related deductions. This form is known as a **T4 slip** (or **T4A** or **T4 Supplementary**). Refer to Figure 9-5 for a sample of this form for Janet Johnson. Notice that to complete this form accurately, a detailed record of each employee's earnings and deductions must be kept.
2. When an employee leaves his or her employment for any reason, a special form is required to comply with the employment insurance laws. This form is called a **Record of Employment**.
3. In deducting CPP, it is necessary to keep deducting only as long as an employee's earnings are below a certain level. CPP is payable up to a maximum of $2,356.20 for 2013. Therefore, it is necessary to stop making deductions when this amount is reached. For EI there is no maximum per pay period, but the total per year cannot exceed $891.12 (for 2013).

Figure 9-6 shows a partial employee earnings record for Janet Johnson for the latest year. Each employee will have his or her own earnings record. Such records are often part of a computer file.

Figure 9-5
T4 Slip

Employer's name – Nom de l'employeur

ABC Company
123 Main Street
Any City, Ontario X1X 1X1

Canada Revenue Agency / Agence du revenu du Canada

T4

STATEMENT OF REMUNERATION PAID
ÉTAT DE LA RÉMUNÉRATION PAYÉE

Year / Année: 2016

14	Employment income – line 101 / Revenus d'emploi – ligne 101	21,480.00
22	Income tax deducted – line 437 / Impôt sur le revenu retenu – ligne 437	2,229.36
54	Payroll Account Number (15 characters) / Numéro de compte de retenues (15 caractères)	111222333RP0001
10	Province of employment / Province d'emploi	
16	Employee's CPP contributions – line 308 / Cotisations de l'employé au RPC – ligne 308	1,019.70
24	EI insurable earnings / Gains assurables d'AE	
12	Social insurance number / Numéro d'assurance sociale	123 456 789
28	Exempt – Exemption: CPP/QPP, EI, PPIP / RPC/RRQ, AE, RPAP	
29	Employment code / Code d'emploi	
17	Employee's QPP contributions – line 308 / Cotisations de l'employé au RRQ – ligne 308	
26	CPP/QPP pensionable earnings / Gains ouvrant droit à pension – RPC/RRQ	
18	Employee's EI premiums – line 312 / Cotisations de l'employé à l'AE – ligne 312	455.15
44	Union dues – line 212 / Cotisations syndicales – ligne 212	
20	RPP contributions – line 207 / Cotisations à un RPA – ligne 207	
46	Charitable donations – see over / Dons de bienfaisance – voir au verso	260.00
52	Pension adjustment – line 206 / Facteur d'équivalence – ligne 206	
50	RPP or DPSP registration number / N° d'agrément d'un RPA ou d'un RPDB	
55	Employee's PPIP premiums – see over / Cotisations de l'employé au RPAP – voir au verso	
56	PPIP insurable earnings / Gains assurables du RPAP	

Employee's name and address – Nom et adresse de l'employé
Last name (in capital letters) – Nom de famille (en lettres moulées) | First name – Prénom | Initials – Initiales

JOHNSON JANET

602, 805 Fifth Street
Any City, Ontario M1X 2X2

Other information (see over) / Autres renseignements (voir au verso): Box – Case | Amount – Montant | Box – Case | Amount – Montant | Box – Case | Amount – Montant

T4 (09)

Source: Revenue Canada. Reproduced with permission of the Minister of Public Works and Government Services Canada, 2013.

LEARNING UNIT 9-3 REVIEW

AT THIS POINT you should be able to:

- Record a payroll from a payroll summary. (pp. 410–411)
- Break down gross wages into more detail. (p. 411)
- Post the entry recording the payroll into appropriate ledger accounts. (p. 411)
- Demonstrate the payment of net pay to employees by cheque. (pp. 411–412)
- Record the cheques to employees in the cash disbursements journal. (p. 412)
- Illustrate the employee's earnings record. (p. 414)
- State the upper limit of EI and CPP deductions. (p. 412)

Self-Review Quiz 9-3

(The forms you need are on page 9-1 of the *Study Guide with Working Papers.*)

Indicate whether the following statements are true or false:

1. All payroll registers are special journals. This means no payroll entry is ever needed.
2. Income Tax Payable is a liability on the balance sheet.
3. Salaries and Wages Expense has a normal balance of a debit.
4. Employee earnings records are optional for an employer.
5. The Record of Employment form must be completed annually for each employee.
6. All wages must be paid by cheque.
7. Cheques paying wages must be recorded in the cash disbursements journal.

Figure 9-6 Employee Earnings Record

Name of Employee	*Janet Johnson*	ABC Company	Employee Address:
Social Insurance Number	*123 456 789*	Employee's Earnings Record	*602,805 Fifth Street*
Date of Birth	*03/12/87*	For the Calendar Year 2016	*AnyCity, ON M1X 2X2*

				Earnings			Deductions						
Week	Net Claim Code	Rate of Pay	Hours Worked	Regular	Overtime	Gross Pay	Total Tax	CPP	EI	Medical	Charitable	Net Pay	Chq. No.
1	1	$10/Hr.	40	400 00		400 00	31 55	16 44	7 51		5 00	339 50	1061
2			42	400 00	30 00	430 00	39 50	17 93	8 07		5 00	359 50	1102
3			43	400 00	45 00	445 00	42 95	18 67	8 38		5 00	370 00	1150
4			40	400 00		400 00	31 55	16 44	7 51		5 00	339 50	1194
5			46	400 00	90 00	490 00	53 65	20 90	9 20		5 00	401 25	1237
6			40	400 00		400 00	31 55	16 44	7 51		5 00	339 50	1291
7			41	400 00	15 00	415 00	35 50	17 19	7 81		5 00	349 50	1352
8			45	400 00	75 00	475 00	50 35	20 16	8 94		5 00	390 55	1407
9			40	400 00		400 00	31 55	16 44	7 51		5 00	339 50	1448
10			40	400 00		400 00	31 55	16 44	7 51		5 00	339 50	1492
11			42	400 00	30 00	430 00	39 50	17 93	8 07		5 00	359 50	1540
Weeks 12 through 48 are omitted here to save some space.													
49		$12/Hr.	46	480 00	108 00	588 00	71 85	25 73	11 05		5 00	474 37	3021
50			40	480 00		480 00	51 30	20 40	9 01		5 00	394 29	3191
51			48	480 00	144 00	624 00	78 15	27 51	11 72		5 00	501 62	3154
52			40	480 00		480 00	51 30	20 40	9 01		5 00	394 29	3214
				21 480 00	2 730 00	24 210 00	2 229 36	1 019 70	455 15		260 00	20 245 79	

Solution to Self-Review Quiz 9-3

1. False
2. True
3. True
4. False
5. False. The Record of Employment is required only when an employee leaves.
6. False. Cash or automatic bank transfers are also normal.
7. True, in general, although other possibilities exist, such as special payroll journals or even the general journal (for very small companies).

Payroll Records: A Full-Time Job

Comprehensive payroll question ❶ ❷ ❸ (30 min)

Like every Subway restaurant owner, Stan needs to keep a master file of important employee information. This file contains every employee's name, address, phone number, social insurance number, rate of pay, hours worked per week, and other forms.

Stan employs two part-time "sandwich artists" and no full-time managers—yet. If his sales continue to be high, he'll need to hire someone to manage operations so that he can spend more time analyzing the financials—with Lila's help—and growing his business. A majority of restaurants hire mostly part-timers with a core of full-time employees, but the numbers vary from restaurant to restaurant. Benefits vary too. Stan, for instance, plans to offer health and dental benefits when he hires a manager. He knows what a great incentive these benefits are with health costs so high. He pays his sandwich artists, Rashid and Ellen, the minimum wage since they both have less than a year's experience. However, he's talking to Mariah Washington about creating some incentives to keep them motivated. If Rashid and Ellen are with him for a full year, they'll see a nice raise in their biweekly paycheques.

Stan must record all this vital information and report it to the various provincial and federal authorities. In addition, Stan includes total payroll expenses on the weekly sales and inventory report, which he submits electronically to headquarters from his POS screen.

Scheduling workers and keeping payroll records are the bane of Stan's existence. These tasks are incredibly time-consuming. He was pleased to hear, then, at the last meeting of his local North American Association of Subway Franchisees (NAASF) that the new point of sale (POS) terminals will soon offer an electronic scheduling package.

"Wow! That will really help," said Stan cheerfully to another franchisee. "No more differently coloured ink just to keep track of who will work when! Now I can plan around Rashid and Ellen's exam schedules without a hassle. Scheduling might just become my favourite module in the new system."

"Sure," said Javier Gonzalez, another owner. "Now you can concentrate on payroll records. What fun!"

"Ay. Que lata," Stan groaned. What a drag!

DISCUSSION QUESTIONS

1. What payroll records does Stan need to keep for his Subway restaurant?
2. What other information might Stan want so as to schedule working hours for each employee?
3. How does the payroll register help Stan prepare the payroll? Consult the process outlined on pages 410-411.

Chapter Assignments

SUMMARY OF KEY POINTS

Learning Unit 9-1

1. The minimum-wage law sets the lowest hourly wage that can be paid to an employee and establishes the maximum number of hours per day and per week that an employee may work before an overtime premium must be paid.
2. Employers may calculate overtime pay separately from regular pay to highlight the cost of having employees work overtime.
3. Each pay period, employees are required to pay federal and provincial income tax and to contribute to the Canada Pension Plan and the Employment Insurance plan according to their level of earnings. The amount to be deducted for each employee is found in tables published by the federal government.
4. A TD1 form specifies the claim code for each employee. This in turn governs the income tax deducted each pay period. There are separate TD1 forms for both federal and provincial use.
5. CPP and EI have a maximum contribution of $2,356.20 per year and $891.12 per year, respectively. (These maximums will change annually.)
6. Other deductions (e.g., union dues or company-related matters) may also be made from an employee's earnings.
7. Commission earnings may be added to a base salary to calculate gross earnings for a period.

Learning Unit 9-2

1. Each pay period, a payroll summary is prepared. It includes the following information for each employee: claim code; rate of pay; hours worked; regular earnings; overtime earnings; gross pay; income tax deductions; CPP deduction; EI deduction; other deductions such as medical and charitable; net pay; and cheque number.
2. Gross pay determines the level of deductions.
3. Gross pay less deductions equals net, or take-home, pay.

Learning Unit 9-3

1. The payroll register is completed each pay period and provides basic data for recording the payroll.
2. The Salaries and Wages Expense entry is made and posted to ledger accounts. In addition to summarizing the deductions payable, the ledger accounts are used to classify wage expenses by type.
3. Each payroll cheque written is recorded in the cash disbursements journal (or the general journal). Journal amounts or totals are posted to the general ledger monthly.
4. Employers must maintain an employee earnings record for each employee. The source of the information summarized here is the payroll register.
5. Each year, employers must prepare and deliver to each employee a T4 or T4A form that summarizes the employee's earnings and deductions for the calendar year.
6. When an employee leaves, is laid off, or is terminated, the employer must complete a Record of Employment form.

KEY TERMS

Canada and Quebec Pension Plans Provide a retirement benefit for all Canadians who contribute to the plans during their employment years. Requires a payroll deduction from each employee until a yearly maximum is reached (The maximum that we are using is $2,356.20, but a new maximum is used each year.) (p. 404)

Canada Revenue Agency (CRA) The Canada Revenue Agency is the body that oversees the collection of income tax as well as CPP and EI. Formerly called Canada Customs and Revenue Agency (CCRA), the Customs function is now part of another federal agency. (p. 399)

Claim code A number from 0 to 10 that determines the amount of income tax deducted each pay period. The appropriate claim code is based on information provided by the employee when completing a TD1 form. (p. 400)

Commissions Earnings made by some employees in certain circumstances may be added to a base salary to arrive at gross earnings for a period. (p. 406)

Employee earnings record A page, or sheet, or computer file that records and totals the details concerning an employee's earnings, deductions, net pay, and identification details for a calendar year. Used in preparing T4 slips (p. 412)

Employment Insurance (EI) plan A plan to which all employees must contribute and which provides a certain level of income for those workers who are unemployed. Contributions are made up to a maximum of $891.12 for 2013 (based on 1.88 percent of the maximum insurable earnings of $47,400). (p. 404)

Income tax deductions The amount withheld from employees' wages each period and sent (on behalf of the employees) to the federal government. The amount of the deduction is determined by tables published by the federal government, customized for each province. (p. 408)

Indexing A procedure whereby the personal exemption claim amounts are increased each year by the government to allow for the effects of inflation (p. 403)

Minimum wage laws Laws that govern the lowest wage legally payable in a province. Such a law also states the province's rules about overtime premiums and maximum weekly working hours. (p. 398)

Other deductions Most employees have a variety of items for which a deduction is required. The exact type and amount of these deductions will vary a great deal from one employer to another. Common examples are union dues and provincial health care premiums. (p. 405)

Payroll summary Sometimes known as the payroll journal or payroll register, this document lists in considerable detail the income, deductions, net pay, and other information for each employee for a given pay period. A total for all employees per category is always shown. This summary forms the basis for posting to appropriate ledger accounts. (p. 408)

Record of Employment A special form to be completed for each employee at the end of his or her employment. Used in helping to determine the level of employment insurance payments a taxpayer is eligible for (p. 412)

TD1 forms Forms completed by an employee upon commencement of employment (and periodically thereafter) that set out the deductions claimed by the employee. A claim code determined by this form affects the amount of income tax deducted. There are separate federal and provincial forms. (p. 400)

TONI Tax on Income is a way of determining provincial income-tax deductions. Instead of being a percentage of federal tax, each province bases its amount of income tax on the amount of income earned by a taxpayer. (p. 399)

T4 slip or T4A or T4 Supplementary A special form issued annually to each employee summarizing annual earnings and deductions and used by an employee as a basic document in filing an annual income tax return (p. 412)

Union dues Fees deducted from an employee's wages and forwarded to the union treasurer, usually monthly (p. 405)

Workers' Compensation Provincial plans, paid by employers, designed to assist employees who are injured (p. 405)

QUICK REVIEW

The following Tips are from Learning Units 9-1 to 9-3. Answer the Assess Your Progress questions and use the How Did You Do? at the bottom of the page to see how well you know the material. The Quick Review provides tips before each Assess Your Progress to help you avoid common accounting errors.

LU 9-1 Calculating Gross Pay, Routine Deductions, and Net Pay

Tips: An employee's gross pay is generally quite easy, as it is based on an agreement of some kind. Often it is necessary to calculate gross pay based on hours worked. Provincial laws govern when and how overtime rates are to be applied. Deductions are based on a combination of federal laws, provincial laws and also agreements between a company and its employees. Income tax deductions are required by both the federal and provincial governments, while CPP and EI are paid only to the federal government. Several deductions may be necessary due to a company's policies (insurance, health care, parking, and many others). Each pay period, an employee's net pay is the gross amount less all deductions.

Assess Your Progress

Answer true or false to the following statements:

1. All employees must pay CPP each pay period.
2. Employees cease paying EI after a limit is reached.
3. Overtime is usually paid on hours worked in excess of 40 per week.
4. The federal government controls the deductions for health care.
5. All employees pay income tax at the same rate.

LU 9-2 Preparing a Typical Payroll Summary

Tips: A payroll summary consists of a row for each employee, and a column for any data item applicable to that employee for the pay period. Typically, there are columns for name, SIN, claim code, gross pay, overtime, deductions of each type, net pay and a cheque number. The summary must be carefully generated, with proper attention paid to accuracy. It is critical to ensure that the summary balances, both across each row, and the totals at the bottom of each column. Any errors causing the column totals to not cross-add must be investigated and corrected. If the payroll is being done manually, it can be a big help to use spreadsheet software like Excel to ensure mathematical accuracy.

Assess Your Progress

Answer true or false to the following statements:

1. The payroll summary shows gross pay, deductions, and net pay for each employee.
2. It is legally necessary to include a claim code column in the summary.
3. Separate amounts for federal and provincial income taxes must be shown in the summary.
4. A separate total for provincial and for federal tax is required.
5. A column for charitable deductions is always necessary.

LU 9-3 Recording and Paying the Payroll from a Summary. Employee's Earnings Record

Tips: The journal entry to record a payroll is based on the totals at the bottom of the payroll summary. It is not necessary to enter details for each employee separately into the general journal, providing the summary is kept as a permanent record. Some companies will enter the payroll details directly from the payroll summary into the general ledger. This turns the summary into a journal in a formal bookkeeping sense. A cheque is usually prepared to each employee based on the details in the summary, and is in the amount of the net pay for that employee. The cheques can be entered into the general journal individually, but that is not too efficient. Generally it is most appropriate for these cheques to be entered in the Cash Payments journal. Some companies make a direct deposit to each employee's bank account, thereby skipping the step of generating and recording each cheque. Companies are required to maintain a record of all payroll details for each employee. This record is always for a calendar year: January 1 to December 31.

Assess Your Progress

Answer true or false to the following statements:

1. There is always a single debit amount to wages expense each payroll period.
2. The total deducted for CPP is credited to a liability account each pay period.
3. A separate credit entry is needed each pay period for federal and provincial income taxes deducted.
4. It is common for the Salaries and Wages Payable account to have a small balance after posting the cheques made out to each employee for a given pay period.
5. It is sometimes helpful to maintain the employee's earnings record based on the company's fiscal year.

How Did You Do? Answers to the Assess Your Progress Questions

LU 9-1

1. Generally true—but some do not pay at all based on age, and there are annual limits.
2. True—The limit at the time of writing this edition is $891.12, but this will likely change yearly.
3. True—but each province has its own set of rules and regulations concerning this matter.
4. False—Health care is administered provincially, and in addition, the cost (if any) can be shared between employers and employees.
5. False—For at least two reasons. One, income tax rates are progressive: they go up as income rises. Second, each employee's tax deduction depends on the TD-1 form that he or she completes, resulting in different claim codes for each person.

LU 9-2

1. True.
2. False—It might be helpful, but is not required.
3. False—It might be helpful, but only a total for both taxes combined is really needed.
4. False—Since this detail is not needed in subsequent steps, these totals are left off the summary.
5. False—Not all employers have this deduction. In general, employees have a column for each deduction needed in each company. For the most part, each employer will have a unique set of columns.

LU 9-3

1. False—Many companies will keep track of each major category of wages/salaries, and may have many different debits each payroll period.
2. True.
3. False—Only a single total for both is needed.
4. False—If there is a small balance, it needs to be investigated to see what went wrong.
5. False—Never! This record must be maintained on a calendar-year basis to allow the annual T4 forms to be accurately prepared.

BLUEPRINT FOR RECORDING, POSTING, AND PAYING THE PAYROLL

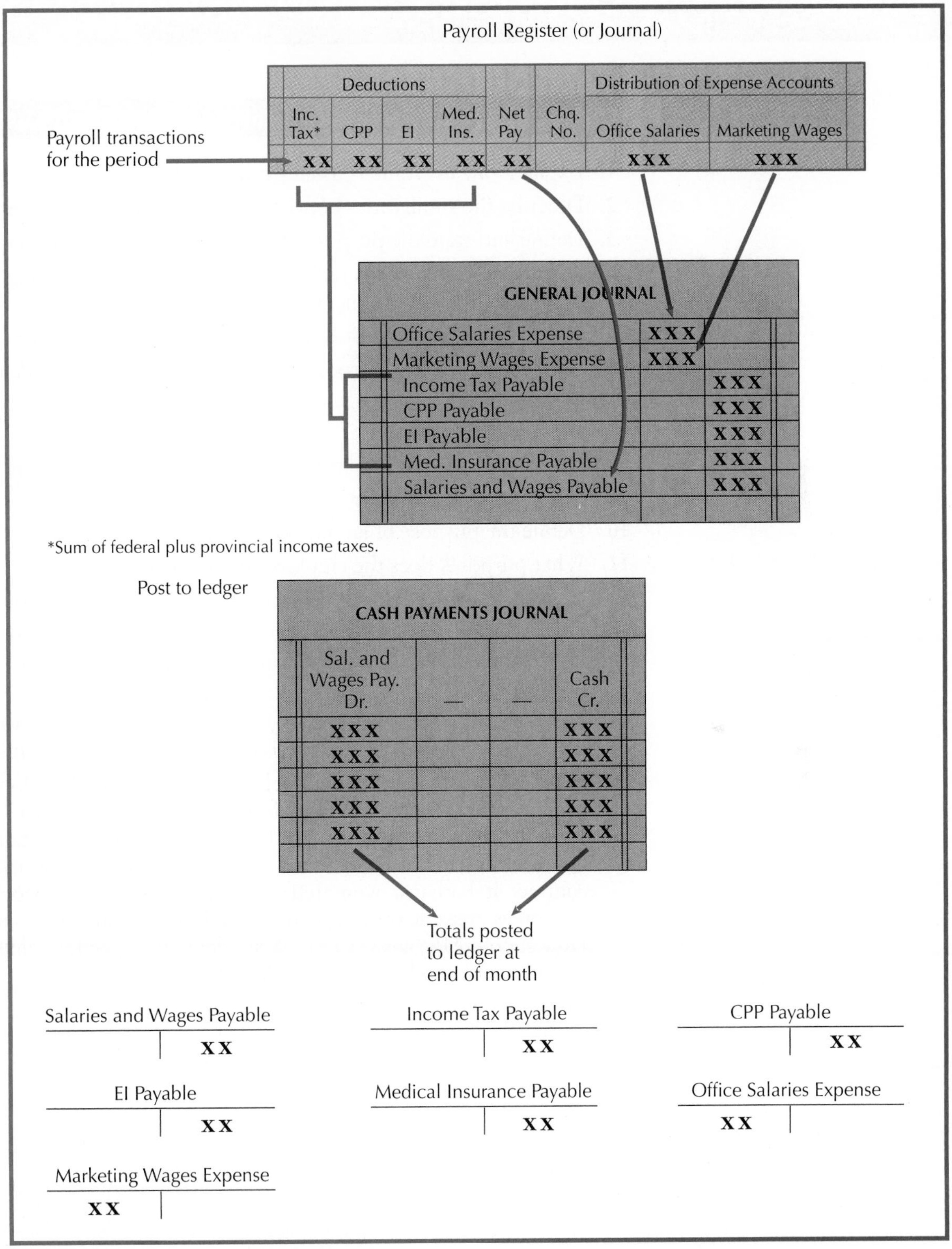

Payroll Register (or Journal)
Deductions
Inc. Tax*
CPP
EI
Med. Ins.
Net Pay
Chq. No.
Distribution of Expense Accounts
Office Salaries
Marketing Wages
Payroll transactions for the period
XX XX XX XX XX
XXX XXX
GENERAL JOURNAL
Office Salaries Expense XXX
Marketing Wages Expense XXX
Income Tax Payable XXX
CPP Payable XXX
EI Payable XXX
Med. Insurance Payable XXX
Salaries and Wages Payable XXX
*Sum of federal plus provincial income taxes.
Post to ledger
CASH PAYMENTS JOURNAL
Sal. and Wages Pay. Dr.
—
—
Cash Cr.
XXX XXX
XXX XXX
XXX XXX
XXX XXX
XXX XXX
Totals posted to ledger at end of month
Salaries and Wages Payable
XX
Income Tax Payable
XX
CPP Payable
XX
EI Payable
XX
Medical Insurance Payable
XX
Office Salaries Expense
XX
Marketing Wages Expense
XX

QUESTIONS, CLASSROOM DEMONSTRATION EXERCISES, EXERCISES, AND PROBLEMS

Discussion Questions and Critical Thinking/Ethical Case

1. Explain how overtime is usually calculated.
2. Describe the similiarities between overtime and commission income.
3. Define and state the purpose of completing a T4 Supplementary.
4. Usually, claiming more credits on a TD1 results in receiving more money per paycheque. Please comment.
5. All payroll registers must be special journals. True or false?
6. Define and state the purpose of the Canada and Quebec Pension Plans.
7. The employer doesn't have to contribute to the Canada Pension Plan. Agree or disagree?
8. Explain how federal and provincial income tax withholdings are determined.
9. What is a calendar year?
10. Define the purpose of an income-tax deduction.
11. What purposes does the employee earnings record serve?
12. Explain the differences in determining CPP and EI deductions.
13. Draw a diagram showing how the following relate: (a) weekly payroll, (b) payroll register, (c) individual earnings, (d) journal entries, (e) cash disbursements journal.
14. If you earned $80,000 this year, you would pay more CPP than your brother, who earned $60,000. Agree or disagree, and explain your answer.
15. Meg Lentz completes the payroll each month for the Monarch Machining Company in Moncton. Just before the end of last month the owner, Jeff Harding, directed her to "cut at least 30%" from the amounts owed to CRA, because the firm needed the money to purchase a new lathe for a special contract it had just won. Jeff explained that the cut would be made up as soon as possible once revenue started to come in from using the new asset. How should Meg answer Jeff? Write down the specific points you think Meg should present to her boss regarding this matter.

MyAccountingLab

Make the grade with MyAccountingLab! The exercises and problems marked with ● can be found on MyAccountingLab. You can practise them as often as you want, and many of them feature step-by-step guided solutions to help you find the right answer.

Classroom Demonstration Exercises

(The forms you need are on page 9-2 of the *Study Guide with Working Papers.*)

Calculating Gross Earnings

Calculating wages overtime
❶ (10 min)

1. Calculate the total wages earned (assume an overtime rate of time-and-a-half over 40 hours):

Employee	*Hourly Rate*	*No. of Hours Worked*
a. Marina Lizunova	$10	37
b. Jill Jones	12	50

CPP and EI

Calculating CPP and EI
❶ (15 min)

2. Pete Martin, married and claiming code 1, has cumulative earnings before this weekly pay period of $48,700. Assuming that he is paid $1,200 this week, what will his deduction be for CPP and EI?

Net Pay

Calculating net pay
❶ (15 min)

3. Calculate Pete's net pay from question 2 above. Income tax is $247.25 and supplemental health insurance is $40.

Payroll Register

The payroll summarized
❷ (10 min)

4. For each of the six items listed below, indicate which of these three descriptions applies:

a. Total of gross pay—comes from distribution of expense accounts

b. A deduction

c. Net pay

1. Office Salaries Expense and Wages Expense
2. CPP Payable
3. EI Payable
4. Federal Income Tax Payable
5. Medical Insurance Payable
6. Salaries and Wages Payable

Payroll Account

Categorizing accounts
❷ (15 min)

5. Indicate for each of the accounts listed below which of the following apply:

a. An asset

b. A liability

c. An expense

d. Appears in the income statement

e. Appears on the balance sheet

1. CPP Payable
2. Office Salaries Expense
3. Federal Income Tax Payable
4. EI Payable
5. Salaries and Wages Payable

Exercises

Set A

(The forms you need are on page 9-3 of the *Study Guide with Working Papers.*)

Calculating wages with overtime
❶ (15 min)

9-1A. Calculate the total wages earned for each employee (assume an overtime rate of time-and-a-half over 40 hours):

Employee	*Hourly Rate*	*Hours Worked*
Jean Knott	$13.20	36
Abe Janzen	15.00	44
Mike Toth	16.00	46

Calculating net pay
❶ ❷ (20 min)

9-2A. Compute the net pay for each employee for the first week of February using the tables in the text.

Employee	*Status*	*Claim Code*	*This Week's Pay*
Ben Smith	Married	4	$610
May Cheung	Single	1	820

The only deductions are for income tax, CPP, and EI.

Categorizing accounts
❷ (10 min)

9-3A. Complete the table.

	Account Category	Dr./Cr.	Financial Statement on Which Account Appears
CPP Payable			
Income Tax Payable			
Medical Insurance Payable			
Wages and Salaries Payable			
Office Salaries Expense			
Marketing Wages Expense			

Payroll register and the journal entry
❷ (10 min)

9-4A. The following weekly payroll journal entry was prepared by Moore Co. Explain from which columns of the payroll register the data have come.

			Debit	Credit
Jan.	7	Shop Expense	6,000.00	
		Factory Wages Expense	4,000.00	
		CPP Payable		485.00
		EI Payable		173.00
		Income Tax Payable		3,600.00
		Union Dues Payable		210.00
		Salaries and Wages Payable		5,522.00

Paying the payroll
❷ (15 min)

If you are a student from a province other than Ontario, you may be supplied by your instructor with provincial tax tables. Otherwise, please use the tax tables supplied in the appendices at the end of this chapter.

9-5A. From Exercise 9-4A, prepare the entries in the cash payments journal to record payment of the payroll, given the following data for January 7:

Employee	*Employee's Net Pay*	*Cheque No.*
Nina Smith	$2,050	111
Jean Logan	1,329	112
Fred Singer	2,143	113

Exercises

Set B

(The forms you need are on page 9-3 of the *Study Guide with Working Papers.*)

Calculating wages with overtime
❶ (15 min)

9-1B. Calculate the total wages earned for each employee (assume an overtime rate of time-end-a-half over 40 hours):

Employee	*Hourly Rate*	*Hours Worked*
Jean Knott	$14.50	38
Abe Janzen	16.00	42
Mike Toth	17.50	45

Calculating net pay
❶ ❷ (20 min)

9-2B. Compute the net pay for each employee for the first week of February using the tables in the text.

Employee	*Status*	*Claim Code*	*This Week's Pay*
Ben Smith	Married	3	$685
May Cheung	Single	1	920

The only deductions are for income tax, CPP, and EI.

Categorizing accounts
❷ (10 min)

9-3B. Complete the table.

	Account Category	**Dr./Cr.**	**Financial Statement on Which Account Appears**
EI Payable			
Income Tax Payable			
Employee Donations Payable			
Wages and Salaries Payable			
Office Salaries Expense			
Sales Wages Expense			

Payroll register and the journal entry
❷ (10 min)

9-4B. The following monthly payroll journal entry was prepared by Moore Co. Explain from which columns of the payroll register the data have come.

Jan.	31	Shop Expense	5 200 00	
		Factory Wages Expense	4 800 00	
		CPP Payable		452 00
		EI Payable		189 00
		Income Tax Payable		3 152 00
		Union Dues Payable		180 00
		Salaries and Wages Payable		6 027 00

Paying the payroll
❸ (15 min)

If you are a student from a province other than Ontario, you may be supplied by your instructor with provincial tax tables. Otherwise, please use the tax tables supplied in the appendices at the end of this chapter.

9-5B. From Exercise 9-4B, prepare the entries in the cash payments journal to record payment of the payroll, given the following data for January 31:

Employee	*Employee's Net Pay*	*Cheque No.*
Nina Smith	$2,190	1604
Jean Logan	1,540	1605
Fred Singer	2,297	1606

Group A Problems

(The forms you need are on pages 9-4 to 9-10 of the *Study Guide with Working Papers.*)

Calculating gross earnings with overtime
❶ (20 min)

Check Figure

Tony Lee Gross Earnings $990.00

9A-1. From the following information, please complete the chart for gross earnings for the week. (Assume an overtime rate of time-and-a-half over 40 hours.)

Employee	*Hourly Rate*	*Number of Hours Worked*	*Gross Earnings*
Stephen Post	$12.00	45	
Jean Nicola	13.50	38	
Maria Cardinal	14.00	43	
Tony Lee	18.00	50	

Completing a payroll register
❶ ❸ (30 min)

Check Figure

Net Pay $3,122.68

9A-2. Nickels Company of Windsor has five salaried employees. Your task is to record the following information for the last week of March in a payroll register.

Employee	*Department*	*Claim Code*	*Weekly Salary*
Jenny Quan	Sales	3	$950
Frank Sloan	Sales	1	620
Alberta Nobel	Office	1	980
Jeremy Gold	Office	4	650
Nancy James	Sales	1	820

Assume that each employee contributes $12 per week for union dues.

Completing a payroll register and journalizing the payroll entry
❶ ❷ ❸ ❹ (50 min)

Check Figure

Net Pay $2,506.98

9A-3. The bookkeeper for Pinto Co. of Peterborough gathered the following data from employee earnings records as well as daily time cards. Your task is (a) to complete a payroll register on November 5 and (b) to journalize the appropriate entry to record the weekly payroll.

Assumptions

1. Income tax (federal and provincial), CPP, and EI are from tables at the end of this chapter (see Appendices 9-1 to 9-3).
2. Each employee contributes $20 per week for health insurance.
3. Overtime is paid at a rate of time-and-a-half over 40 hours per week, or 8 hours in any given day.

Employee	Claim Code	Daily Time M	T	W	T	F	Hourly Rate	Dept.	Cum. CPP Before This Payroll
Mary Cardinal*	1	6	4	8	12	7	$23	Sales	$2,184.60
Bill Smith	3	7	9	11	9	4	15	Office	1,201.46
Joe Kingle*	2	8	10	7	12	10	24	Sales	2,316.14
Anita Tsui	4	8	8	6	8	8	12	Office	579.00

*Both of these employees reached the EI maximum last pay period.

Completing a payroll register, journalizing, posting, and recording the payment of net pay
❶ ❷ ❸ (50 min)

Check Figure

Net Pay $3,279.83

9A-4. Brenda Oakes, the accountant for Byscane Co. of Shelburne, has gathered the following data for the September 23 weekly payroll:

Employee	Net Claim Code	Salary	Cheque. No.	Cum. CPP Before This Payroll	Department
Jim Ryan	5	$ 940	47	$1,059.80	Factory
Emma LaPierre	1	975	48	2,108.42	Office
Jean Arnold	1	1,140	49	1,722.80	Factory
Bob Sylvan*	4	1,410	50	2,304.72	Office

*This employee has been paid more than $47,400 already this year.

Assumptions

1. Income taxes, CPP, and EI are calculated from tables in the text.
2. Union dues are $15 per week.
3. Medical coverage is $24 per week (except for Bob, whose wife pays the family premium).

Required

a. Prepare a payroll register for September 23.
b. Journalize and post the payroll entry.
c. Record the payment of the payroll on September 26 to each employee using a cash payments journal.

Group B Problems

(The forms you need are on pages 9-4 to 9-10 of the *Study Guide with Working Papers*.)

Calculating gross earnings with overtime
❶ (20 min)

Check Figure

Tony Lee Gross Earnings $988.00

9B-1. From the following information, complete the chart for gross earnings for the week. (Assume an overtime rate of time-and-a-half over 40 hours.)

	Hourly Rate	Number of Hours Worked	Gross Earnings
Stephen Post	$13.00	46	
Jean Nicola	14.50	40	
Maria Cardinal	16.00	36	
Tony Lee	19.00	48	

Completing the payroll register
❶ ❷ (30 min)

> *Check Figure*
> Net Pay $2,993.29

9B-2. Nickels Company of Windsor has five salaried employees. Your task is to record the following information in a payroll register for the last week of March.

Employee	*Department*	*Claim Code*	*Weekly Salary*
Jenny Quan	Office	1	$ 920
Frank Sloan	Sales	2	580
Alberta Nobel	Office	1	1,130
Jeremy Gold	Office	1	690
Nancy James	Sales	4	560

Assume that each employee contributes $14 per week for union dues.

Completing the payroll register and journalizing the payroll entry
❶ ❷ ❸ ❹ (50 min)

> *Check Figure*
> Net Pay $677.65

9B-3. The bookkeeper for Pinto Co. of Peterborough gathered the following data from employee earnings records as well as daily time cards. Your task is (1) to complete a payroll register on November 5 and (2) to journalize the appropriate entry to record the payroll.

Employee	*Claim Code*	*Daily Time* M	T	W	T	F	*Hourly Rate*	*Dept.*	*Cum. CPP Before This Payroll*
Mary Cardinal*	2	8	6	9	10	8	$22	Sales	$2,206.48
Bill Smith	4	9	10	9	10	7	14	Office	1,380.00
Joe Kingle*	3	8	10	12	8	9	25	Sales	2,332.14
Anita Tsui	1	9	7	8	10	8	12	Office	942.54

*Both of these employees reached the EI maximum last period.

Assumptions

1. Income taxes, CPP, and EI are from tables at the end of this chapter. (See Appendices 9-1 to 9-3.)
2. Each employee contributes $12 per week for health insurance.
3. Overtime is paid at a rate of time-and-a-half over 40 hours per week or over 8 hours in any day.

Payroll register completion, journalizing, posting, and paying the payroll
❶ ❷ ❸ (50 min)

> *Check Figure*
> Net Pay $3,017.35

9B-4. Brenda Oakes, the accountant for Byscane Co. of Shelburne, has gathered the following data for the September 23 payroll:

Employee	*Net Claim Code*	*Salary*	*Cheque. No.*	*Cum. CPP Before This Payroll*	*Department*
Jim Ryan	4	$ 870	57	$1,692.40	Factory
Emma LaPierre	1	960	58	1,871.42	Office
Jean Arnold	1	980	59	1,879.66	Office
Bob Sylvan*	2	1,240	60	2,338.18	Factory

*This employee has already reached the EI maximum in August.

Assumptions

1. Income taxes, CPP, and EI are calculated from tables in the text.
2. Union dues are $14 per week.
3. Medical coverage is $28 per week (except for Bob, whose wife pays the family premium).

Required

a. Prepare a payroll register on September 23.

b. Journalize and post the payroll entry.

c. Record the payment of the payroll on September 25 to each employee using a cash payments journal.

Group C Problems

(The forms you need are on pages 9-11 to 9-20 of the *Study Guide with Working Papers.*)

Calculating gross earnings with overtime
➊ **(20 min)**

Check Figure
Erika Hance Gross Earnings $875.75

9C-1. From the following data, calculate the gross earnings for each of the five employees who are entitled to time-and-a-half for the greater of any hours exceeding 40 for the week or 8 in any given day.

Employee	*M*	*T*	*W*	*T*	*F*	*S*	*Total Hours*	*Hourly Rate*
A. Al Topping	6	8	8	9	8	5	44	$23.00
B. Barb Frank	6	7	8	8	7	5	41	21.00
C. Amos Ng	8	7	8	10	9	—	42	14.00
D. Carl Holdman	9	6	8	11	7	6	47	18.50
E. Erika Hance	8	7	9	13	8	6	51	15.50

Completing the payroll register
➊ ➌ **(30 min)**

Check Figure
Net Pay $3,136.59

9C-2. The employees mentioned in Problem 9C-1 work for Waylon Company of Thunder Bay. Complete a payroll register for the second week of February using the gross earnings you obtained in answering 9C-1. Cheque numbers begin at 1424. Assume the following additional information:

Employee	*Claim Code*	*Union Dues*	*Medical Plan*
A	2	$16	$32.00
B	1	16	48.00
C	3	16	32.00
D	4	16	32.00
E	1	16	48.00

Completing the payroll register (alternative problem)
➊ ➌ **(40 min)**

Check Figure
Net Pay $2,775.52

9C-3. (Alternative to 9C-2) Assume the following gross earnings for the employees of Waylon Company of Thunder Bay for the third week of February. Other information remains the same as in 9C-2. Cheque numbers begin at 1443. Complete the payroll register for the third week of February.

Employee	*Gross Earnings*
A	$978.00
B	800.00
C	680.00
D	792.00
E	558.00

Recording the payroll entry
➋ **(10 min)**

9C-4. Refer to the payroll register that you completed in 9C-2. Prepare the journal entry necessary to record the payroll for the second week of February.

Recording the payroll entry (alternative problem)
➋ **(10 min)**

9C-5. (Alternative to 9C-4) Refer to the payroll register you completed in 9C-3. Prepare the journal entry necessary to record the payroll for the third week of February.

Completing the payroll register and journalizing the payroll entry
➊ ➋ ➌ **(40 min)**

9C-6. The payroll clerk for the Marlin Company of Armstrong assembled the following data for the company's five employees before suddenly becoming quite ill. You have been approached to complete the payroll register so that the employees can receive their cheques in a timely fashion. You must (a) complete the payroll register for the week ending October 20 and (a) prepare the entry necessary to record the payroll. Hours in excess of 40 in any given week are paid at time-and-a-half.

Check Figure

Net Pay $3,576.62

	Claim	*Daily Time*								*CPP to*	*Union*	
Employee	*Code*	*M*	*T*	*W*	*T*	*F*	*S*	*Rate*	*Dept.*	*Date*	*Dues*	*Medical*
Fred Mora	2	—	8	8	10	12	5	$ 24.00	Sales	$2,294.38	$9	$26
Pat Samuels	1	9	—	7	10	7	8	20.00	Sales	1,084.59	9	48
Emilia Leung	3	8	9	8	9	8	6	14.50	Admin.	692.30	9	26
Keith Jones	5	8	8	8	8	8	—	18.00	Admin.	727.40	9	48
David Jarvic*	1	9	8	7	11	8	8	1,400.00*	Mgr.	2,356.20	—	48

* Weekly salary, no overtime. This employee has already earned $58,800 so far this year.

Comprehensive payroll problem—completing payroll registers, journalizing payrolls, and recording cheques issued
❶ ❷ ❸ (75 min)

Check Figure

Net Pay $5,783.61

9C-7. Comet Engineering of Delta is a consulting firm that employs four professional staff, two casual clerks, and you as office manager (accountant). Everyone except the clerks is paid a weekly salary. The clerks are paid an hourly rate and receive time-and-a-half for hours worked in excess of 8 per day or 40 per week. Using the information below, complete the payroll register for the week ending August 20; make the necessary entry to record the payroll for that week; and record the issuance of cheques to each employee. Daily hours for the clerks are shown at the end.

Employee	*Claim Code*	*Rate or Salary*	*Life Ins.*	*Disab.*	*Med.*	*Donations*	*CPP to Date*	*Chq. No.*
Donna Alvarez	3	$1,640.00	$19	$32	$36.00	$25.00	$2,287.46	574
Joan Kemp	4	1,490.00	12	28	36.00	25.00	2,340.92	575
John Harper	1	1,290.00	10	24	18.00	18.00	1,630.72	576
Tim Culver	2	1,340.00	8	25	36.00	18.00	984.37	577
May Silver	1	18.00	—	—	18.00	—	645.23	578
Joe Polemko	4	15.00	—	—	36.00	5.00	1,020.84	579
Yourself	2	875.00	6	18	18.00	5.00	823.65	580

Hourly employees worked:

	M	*T*	*W*	*T*	*F*	*S*	*Total*
May Silver	8	8	9	10	5	8	48
Joe Polemko	10	8	12	8	5	—	43

Hourly workers receive time-and-a-half rate for more than 40 hours in a week, or more than 8 hours in any given day. Two of the employees (Donna Alvarez and Joan Kemp) reached the EI maximum the last pay period.

On-the-Job Training

(The forms you need are on page 9-21 of the *Study Guide with Working Papers.*)

Gross pay including overtime and sole proprietorship
❶ (20 min)

T-1. Small Co., a sole proprietorship based in Truro, has two employees, Jim Roy and Janice Alter. The owner of Small Co. is Bert Ryan. During the current pay period, Jim has worked 48 hours and Janice 56. The reason for these extra hours is that both Jim and Janice worked their regular 40-hour work week plus Jim worked 8 extra hours on Sunday while Janice worked 8 extra hours on Saturday as well as Sunday. Their contract with Small Co. is that they are each paid an hourly rate of $14 per hour with all hours over 40 per week to be at time-and-a-half and all hours on Sunday to be paid at double time. Bert, the owner, believes he is also entitled to a salary since he works many hours. He plans to pay himself $750 per week.

As the accountant of Small Co., calculate the gross pay for Jim and Janice and offer some advice to Bert regarding his salary.

CPP and EI deductions
❶ ❸ ❹ (20 min)

T-2. Marcy Moore recently moved to your city from another large Canadian centre. She was employed as an engineer by a large oil company and was rather well paid. She now works as a senior engineer for a newly established consulting firm. When she moved in October, Marcy had contributed the yearly maximum CPP premiums of $2,356.20 as well as the limit of $891.12 for EI while employed at the oil company. She feels that is unfair of her new employer to continue to deduct CPP and EI from her salary. She has heard that you are taking an accounting course and has asked you for your opinion. What advice can you give her?

CONTINUING PROBLEM

Comprehensive problem: recording and posting transactions, including preparing the payroll register and preparing a trial balance
❶ ❷ ❸ (20 min)

In preparing for next year, Tony Freedman has hired two employees to work on an hourly basis assisting with some troubleshooting and repair work.

Assume the following details:

a. The following accounts have been added to the chart of accounts: Wages Expense, 5110; Income Taxes Payable, 2020; CPP Payable, 2030; EI Payable, 2040; and Wages Payable, 2010.

b. CPP is deducted according to the tables in Appendix 9-2.

c. EI is deducted according to Appendix 9-3.

d. Both employees have claim codes of 1.

e. Each employee earns $20 an hour and is paid time-and-a-half for hours worked in excess of 40 weekly.

Assignment

(See pages 9-22 to 9-35 in your *Study Guide with Working Papers*.)

1. Record the partial transactions listed below in the appropriate journal and post to the general ledger.

2. Prepare a payroll register.

3. Prepare a trial balance as of November 30, 2016.

Nov.	1	Billed Vita Needle Company $6,800, invoice No. 12686, for services rendered.
	4	Billed Accu Pac, Inc. $3,900, invoice No. 12687, for services rendered.
	5	Purchased new shop benches, $1,400 on account from System Design Furniture (invoice No. 8771) (purchase order No. 4013).
	8	Paid the two employees' wages: Lance Klumm, 38 hours, and Aurelle Hall, 42 hours (cheques No. 258 and No. 259).
	11	Received the phone bill, $150.
	12	Collected $500 of the amount due from Taylor Golf.
	15	Paid the two employees' wages: Lance Klumm, 34 hours, and Aurelle Hall, 36 hours (cheques No. 260 and No. 261).
	18	Collected $800 of the amount due from Taylor Golf.
	19	Purchased a fax machine for the office from Multi Systems Inc. on credit, $450 (invoice No. 1784) (purchase order No. 4014).
	22	Paid the two employees' wages: Lance Klumm, 32 hours and Aurelle Hall, 35 hours (cheques No. 262 and No. 263).
	25	Collected half of the amount due from Vita Needle Company re Nov. 1 transaction.
	29	Paid the two employees wages: Lance Klumm, 38 hours, and Aurelle Hall, 44 hours (cheques No. 264 and No. 265).
	29	Rent expired for October and November, $800.

Schedule of Accounts Receivable
Precision Computer Centre
October 31, 2016

Carson Engineering	$ 6,240.00
Antony Pitale	1,600.00
Taylor Golf	4,500.00
Total Amount Due	$12,340.00

Schedule of Accounts Payable
Precision Computer Centre
October 31, 2016

City Newspaper	$375.00
Staples	250.00
Total Amount Payable	$625.00

Appendices

Employee payroll deductions (extracted): Income taxes, CPP, EI

Appendix 9-1F—Federal Taxes

Federal tax deductions
Effective January 1, 2013
Weekly (52 pay periods a year)
Also look up the tax deductions in the provincial table

Pay												
From	Less than	CC 0	CC 1	CC 2	CC 3	CC 4	CC 5	CC 6	CC 7	CC 8	CC 9	CC 10
	248	* (1)	.00									
248 -	250	32.10	.25									
250 -	252	32.35	.50									
252 -	254	32.65	.80									
254 -	256	32.90	1.05									
256 -	258	33.20	1.35									
258 -	260	33.45	1.65									
260 -	262	33.75	1.90									
262 -	264	34.05	2.20									
264 -	266	34.30	2.45									
266 -	268	34.60	2.75									
268 -	270	34.85	3.05									
270 -	272	35.15	3.30	.25								
272 -	274	35.45	3.60	.55								
274 -	276	35.70	3.85	.85								
276 -	278	36.00	4.15	1.10								
278 -	280	36.25	4.45	1.40								
280 -	282	36.55	4.70	1.65								
282 -	284	36.85	5.00	1.95								
284 -	286	37.10	5.25	2.25								
286 -	288	37.40	5.55	2.50								
288 -	290	37.65	5.85	2.80								
290 -	292	37.95	6.10	3.05								
292 -	294	38.25	6.40	3.35								
294 -	296	38.50	6.65	3.60								
296 -	298	38.80	6.95	3.90								
298 -	300	39.05	7.20	4.20								
300 -	302	39.35	7.50	4.45								
302 -	304	39.60	7.80	4.75								
304 -	306	39.90	8.05	5.00								
306 -	308	40.20	8.35	5.30								
308 -	310	40.45	8.60	5.60								
310 -	312	40.75	8.90	5.85								
312 -	314	41.00	9.20	6.15	.05							
314 -	316	41.30	9.45	6.40	.35							
316 -	318	41.60	9.75	6.70	.60							
318 -	320	41.85	10.00	7.00	.90							
320 -	322	42.15	10.30	7.25	1.15							
322 -	324	42.40	10.60	7.55	1.45							
324 -	326	42.70	10.85	7.80	1.75							
326 -	328	43.00	11.15	8.10	2.00							
328 -	330	43.25	11.40	8.35	2.30							
330 -	332	43.55	11.70	8.65	2.55							
332 -	334	43.80	12.00	8.95	2.85							
334 -	336	44.10	12.25	9.20	3.15							
336 -	338	44.40	12.55	9.50	3.40							
338 -	340	44.65	12.80	9.75	3.70							
340 -	342	44.95	13.10	10.05	3.95							
342 -	344	45.20	13.35	10.35	4.25							
344 -	346	45.50	13.65	10.60	4.55							
346 -	348	45.75	13.95	10.90	4.80							
348 -	350	46.05	14.20	11.15	5.10							
350 -	352	46.35	14.50	11.45	5.35							
352 -	354	46.60	14.75	11.75	5.65							
354 -	356	46.90	15.05	12.00	5.90							

D-1

(1) You normally use claim code "0" only for non-resident employees. However, if you have non-resident employees who earn less than the minimum amount shown in the "Pay" column, you may not be able to use these tables. Instead, refer to the "Step-by-step calculation of tax deductions" in Section "A" of this publication.

Federal tax deductions

Effective January 1, 2013

Weekly (52 pay periods a year)

Also look up the tax deductions in the provincial table

Pay												
From	Less than	CC 0	CC 1	CC 2	CC 3	CC 4	CC 5	CC 6	CC 7	CC 8	CC 9	CC 10
356	360	47.30	15.45	12.45	6.35	.25						
360	364	47.85	16.05	13.00	6.90	.80						
364	368	48.45	16.60	13.55	7.45	1.40						
368	372	49.00	17.15	14.10	8.00	1.95						
372	376	49.55	17.70	14.65	8.60	2.50						
376	380	50.10	18.25	15.20	9.15	3.05						
380	384	50.65	18.80	15.80	9.70	3.60						
384	388	51.20	19.40	16.35	10.25	4.15						
388	392	51.80	19.95	16.90	10.80	4.75						
392	396	52.35	20.50	17.45	11.40	5.30						
396	400	52.90	21.05	18.00	11.95	5.85						
400	404	53.45	21.60	18.60	12.50	6.40	.35					
404	408	54.00	22.20	19.15	13.05	6.95	.90					
408	412	54.60	22.75	19.70	13.60	7.55	1.45					
412	416	55.15	23.30	20.25	14.15	8.10	2.00					
416	420	55.70	23.85	20.80	14.75	8.65	2.55					
420	424	56.25	24.40	21.35	15.30	9.20	3.10					
424	428	56.80	24.95	21.95	15.85	9.75	3.70					
428	432	57.35	25.55	22.50	16.40	10.30	4.25					
432	436	57.95	26.10	23.05	16.95	10.90	4.80					
436	440	58.50	26.65	23.60	17.50	11.45	5.35					
440	444	59.05	27.20	24.15	18.10	12.00	5.90					
444	448	59.60	27.75	24.75	18.65	12.55	6.50	.40				
448	452	60.15	28.35	25.30	19.20	13.10	7.05	.95				
452	456	60.75	28.90	25.85	19.75	13.70	7.60	1.50				
456	460	61.30	29.45	26.40	20.30	14.25	8.15	2.05				
460	464	61.85	30.00	26.95	20.90	14.80	8.70	2.65				
464	468	62.40	30.55	27.50	21.45	15.35	9.25	3.20				
468	472	62.95	31.10	28.10	22.00	15.90	9.85	3.75				
472	476	63.50	31.70	28.65	22.55	16.45	10.40	4.30				
476	480	64.10	32.25	29.20	23.10	17.05	10.95	4.85				
480	484	64.65	32.80	29.75	23.65	17.60	11.50	5.40				
484	488	65.20	33.35	30.30	24.25	18.15	12.05	6.00				
488	492	65.75	33.90	30.90	24.80	18.70	12.60	6.55	.45			
492	496	66.30	34.50	31.45	25.35	19.25	13.20	7.10	1.00			
496	500	66.90	35.05	32.00	25.90	19.85	13.75	7.65	1.60			
500	504	67.45	35.60	32.55	26.45	20.40	14.30	8.20	2.15			
504	508	68.00	36.15	33.10	27.05	20.95	14.85	8.80	2.70			
508	512	68.55	36.70	33.65	27.60	21.50	15.40	9.35	3.25			
512	516	69.10	37.25	34.25	28.15	22.05	16.00	9.90	3.80			
516	520	69.65	37.85	34.80	28.70	22.60	16.55	10.45	4.35			
520	524	70.25	38.40	35.35	29.25	23.20	17.10	11.00	4.95			
524	528	70.80	38.95	35.90	29.80	23.75	17.65	11.55	5.50			
528	532	71.35	39.50	36.45	30.40	24.30	18.20	12.15	6.05			
532	536	71.90	40.05	37.00	30.95	24.85	18.75	12.70	6.60	.50		
536	540	72.45	40.65	37.60	31.50	25.40	19.35	13.25	7.15	1.10		
540	544	73.00	41.20	38.15	32.05	26.00	19.90	13.80	7.70	1.65		
544	548	73.60	41.75	38.70	32.60	26.55	20.45	14.35	8.30	2.20		
548	552	74.15	42.30	39.25	33.20	27.10	21.00	14.95	8.85	2.75		
552	556	74.70	42.85	39.80	33.75	27.65	21.55	15.50	9.40	3.30		
556	560	75.25	43.40	40.40	34.30	28.20	22.15	16.05	9.95	3.90		
560	564	75.80	44.00	40.95	34.85	28.75	22.70	16.60	10.50	4.45		
564	568	76.40	44.55	41.50	35.40	29.35	23.25	17.15	11.10	5.00		
568	572	76.95	45.10	42.05	35.95	29.90	23.80	17.70	11.65	5.55		
572	576	77.50	45.65	42.60	36.55	30.45	24.35	18.30	12.20	6.10	.05	

D-2

Federal tax deductions

Effective January 1, 2013

Weekly (52 pay periods a year)

Also look up the tax deductions in the provincial table

Pay From	Pay Less than	CC 0	CC 1	CC 2	CC 3	CC 4	CC 5	CC 6	CC 7	CC 8	CC 9	CC 10
576	584	78.35	46.50	43.45	37.35	31.30	25.20	19.10	13.05	6.95	.85	
584	592	79.45	47.60	44.55	38.50	32.40	26.30	20.25	14.15	8.05	2.00	
592	600	80.55	48.75	45.70	39.60	33.50	27.45	21.35	15.25	9.20	3.10	
600	608	81.70	49.85	46.80	40.70	34.65	28.55	22.45	16.40	10.30	4.20	
608	616	82.80	50.95	47.95	41.85	35.75	29.65	23.60	17.50	11.40	5.35	
616	624	83.95	52.10	49.05	42.95	36.90	30.80	24.70	18.65	12.55	6.45	.35
624	632	85.05	53.20	50.15	44.10	38.00	31.90	25.85	19.75	13.65	7.60	1.50
632	640	86.15	54.30	51.30	45.20	39.10	33.05	26.95	20.85	14.80	8.70	2.60
640	648	87.30	55.45	52.40	46.30	40.25	34.15	28.05	22.00	15.90	9.80	3.75
648	656	88.40	56.55	53.50	47.45	41.35	35.25	29.20	23.10	17.00	10.95	4.85
656	664	89.50	57.70	54.65	48.55	42.45	36.40	30.30	24.20	18.15	12.05	5.95
664	672	90.65	58.80	55.75	49.65	43.60	37.50	31.40	25.35	19.25	13.15	7.10
672	680	91.75	59.90	56.85	50.80	44.70	38.60	32.55	26.45	20.35	14.30	8.20
680	688	92.85	61.05	58.00	51.90	45.80	39.75	33.65	27.55	21.50	15.40	9.30
688	696	94.00	62.15	59.10	53.00	46.95	40.85	34.75	28.70	22.60	16.50	10.45
696	704	95.10	63.25	60.20	54.15	48.05	41.95	35.90	29.80	23.70	17.65	11.55
704	712	96.20	64.40	61.35	55.25	49.15	43.10	37.00	30.90	24.85	18.75	12.65
712	720	97.35	65.50	62.45	56.40	50.30	44.20	38.15	32.05	25.95	19.85	13.80
720	728	98.45	66.60	63.60	57.50	51.40	45.35	39.25	33.15	27.10	21.00	14.90
728	736	99.60	67.75	64.70	58.60	52.55	46.45	40.35	34.30	28.20	22.10	16.05
736	744	100.70	68.85	65.80	59.75	53.65	47.55	41.50	35.40	29.30	23.25	17.15
744	752	101.80	69.95	66.95	60.85	54.75	48.70	42.60	36.50	30.45	24.35	18.25
752	760	102.95	71.10	68.05	61.95	55.90	49.80	43.70	37.65	31.55	25.45	19.40
760	768	104.05	72.20	69.15	63.10	57.00	50.90	44.85	38.75	32.65	26.60	20.50
768	776	105.15	73.35	70.30	64.20	58.10	52.05	45.95	39.85	33.80	27.70	21.60
776	784	106.30	74.45	71.40	65.30	59.25	53.15	47.05	41.00	34.90	28.80	22.75
784	792	107.40	75.55	72.50	66.45	60.35	54.25	48.20	42.10	36.00	29.95	23.85
792	800	108.50	76.70	73.65	67.55	61.45	55.40	49.30	43.20	37.15	31.05	24.95
800	808	109.65	77.80	74.75	68.65	62.60	56.50	50.40	44.35	38.25	32.15	26.10
808	816	110.75	78.90	75.90	69.80	63.70	57.65	51.55	45.45	39.35	33.30	27.20
816	824	111.90	80.05	77.00	70.90	64.85	58.75	52.65	46.60	40.50	34.40	28.35
824	832	113.00	81.15	78.10	72.05	65.95	59.85	53.80	47.70	41.60	35.55	29.45
832	840	114.10	82.25	79.25	73.15	67.05	61.00	54.90	48.80	42.75	36.65	30.55
840	848	115.70	83.85	80.80	74.70	68.65	62.55	56.45	50.40	44.30	38.20	32.10
848	856	117.35	85.50	82.45	76.40	70.30	64.20	58.15	52.05	45.95	39.90	33.80
856	864	119.05	87.20	84.15	78.05	72.00	65.90	59.80	53.75	47.65	41.55	35.50
864	872	120.70	88.85	85.85	79.75	73.65	67.60	61.50	55.40	49.35	43.25	37.15
872	880	122.40	90.55	87.50	81.40	75.35	69.25	63.15	57.10	51.00	44.90	38.85
880	888	124.05	92.25	89.20	83.10	77.00	70.95	64.85	58.75	52.70	46.60	40.50
888	896	125.75	93.90	90.85	84.80	78.70	72.60	66.55	60.45	54.35	48.30	42.20
896	904	127.40	95.60	92.55	86.45	80.35	74.30	68.20	62.10	56.05	49.95	43.85
904	912	129.10	97.25	94.20	88.15	82.05	75.95	69.90	63.80	57.70	51.65	45.55
912	920	130.80	98.95	95.90	89.85	83.75	77.65	71.55	65.50	59.40	53.30	47.25
920	928	132.50	100.65	97.60	91.55	85.45	79.35	73.25	67.20	61.10	55.00	48.95
928	936	134.20	102.35	99.30	93.25	87.15	81.05	75.00	68.90	62.80	56.70	50.65
936	944	135.90	104.05	101.00	94.95	88.85	82.75	76.70	70.60	64.50	58.45	52.35
944	952	137.60	105.75	102.70	96.65	90.55	84.45	78.40	72.30	66.20	60.15	54.05
952	960	139.30	107.45	104.40	98.35	92.25	86.15	80.10	74.00	67.90	61.85	55.75
960	968	141.00	109.15	106.10	100.05	93.95	87.85	81.80	75.70	69.60	63.55	57.45
968	976	142.70	110.85	107.80	101.75	95.65	89.55	83.50	77.40	71.30	65.25	59.15
976	984	144.40	112.55	109.50	103.45	97.35	91.25	85.20	79.10	73.00	66.95	60.85
984	992	146.15	114.30	111.25	105.15	99.10	93.00	86.90	80.85	74.75	68.65	62.60
992	1000	147.90	116.05	113.00	106.95	100.85	94.75	88.70	82.60	76.50	70.45	64.35
1000	1008	149.65	117.80	114.75	108.70	102.60	96.50	90.45	84.35	78.25	72.20	66.10
1008	1016	151.40	119.60	116.55	110.45	104.35	98.30	92.20	86.10	80.05	73.95	67.85

D-3

Federal tax deductions
Effective January 1, 2013
Weekly (52 pay periods a year)
Also look up the tax deductions in the provincial table

Pay From - Less than	CC 0	CC 1	CC 2	CC 3	CC 4	CC 5	CC 6	CC 7	CC 8	CC 9	CC 10
1016 - 1028	153.60	121.80	118.75	112.65	106.55	100.50	94.40	88.30	82.25	76.15	70.05
1028 - 1040	156.25	124.40	121.35	115.30	109.20	103.10	97.05	90.95	84.85	78.80	72.70
1040 - 1052	158.90	127.05	124.00	117.95	111.85	105.75	99.70	93.60	87.50	81.45	75.35
1052 - 1064	161.55	129.70	126.65	120.55	114.50	108.40	102.30	96.25	90.15	84.05	78.00
1064 - 1076	164.20	132.35	129.30	123.20	117.15	111.05	104.95	98.90	92.80	86.70	80.60
1076 - 1088	166.80	135.00	131.95	125.85	119.75	113.70	107.60	101.50	95.45	89.35	83.25
1088 - 1100	169.45	137.60	134.55	128.50	122.40	116.30	110.25	104.15	98.05	92.00	85.90
1100 - 1112	172.10	140.25	137.20	131.15	125.05	118.95	112.90	106.80	100.70	94.65	88.55
1112 - 1124	174.75	142.90	139.85	133.75	127.70	121.60	115.50	109.45	103.35	97.25	91.20
1124 - 1136	177.40	145.55	142.50	136.40	130.35	124.25	118.15	112.10	106.00	99.90	93.80
1136 - 1148	180.00	148.20	145.15	139.05	132.95	126.90	120.80	114.70	108.65	102.55	96.45
1148 - 1160	182.65	150.80	147.75	141.70	135.60	129.50	123.45	117.35	111.25	105.20	99.10
1160 - 1172	185.30	153.45	150.40	144.35	138.25	132.15	126.10	120.00	113.90	107.85	101.75
1172 - 1184	187.95	156.10	153.05	146.95	140.90	134.80	128.70	122.65	116.55	110.45	104.40
1184 - 1196	190.60	158.75	155.70	149.60	143.55	137.45	131.35	125.30	119.20	113.10	107.00
1196 - 1208	193.20	161.40	158.35	152.25	146.15	140.10	134.00	127.90	121.85	115.75	109.65
1208 - 1220	195.85	164.00	160.95	154.90	148.80	142.70	136.65	130.55	124.45	118.40	112.30
1220 - 1232	198.50	166.65	163.60	157.55	151.45	145.35	139.30	133.20	127.10	121.05	114.95
1232 - 1244	201.15	169.30	166.25	160.15	154.10	148.00	141.90	135.85	129.75	123.65	117.60
1244 - 1256	203.80	171.95	168.90	162.80	156.75	150.65	144.55	138.50	132.40	126.30	120.20
1256 - 1268	206.40	174.60	171.55	165.45	159.35	153.30	147.20	141.10	135.05	128.95	122.85
1268 - 1280	209.05	177.20	174.15	168.10	162.00	155.90	149.85	143.75	137.65	131.60	125.50
1280 - 1292	211.70	179.85	176.80	170.75	164.65	158.55	152.50	146.40	140.30	134.25	128.15
1292 - 1304	214.35	182.50	179.45	173.35	167.30	161.20	155.10	149.05	142.95	136.85	130.80
1304 - 1316	217.00	185.15	182.10	176.00	169.95	163.85	157.75	151.70	145.60	139.50	133.40
1316 - 1328	219.60	187.80	184.75	178.65	172.55	166.50	160.40	154.30	148.25	142.15	136.05
1328 - 1340	222.25	190.40	187.35	181.30	175.20	169.10	163.05	156.95	150.85	144.80	138.70
1340 - 1352	224.90	193.05	190.00	183.95	177.85	171.75	165.70	159.60	153.50	147.45	141.35
1352 - 1364	227.55	195.70	192.65	186.55	180.50	174.40	168.30	162.25	156.15	150.05	144.00
1364 - 1376	230.20	198.35	195.30	189.20	183.15	177.05	170.95	164.90	158.80	152.70	146.60
1376 - 1388	232.80	201.00	197.95	191.85	185.75	179.70	173.60	167.50	161.45	155.35	149.25
1388 - 1400	235.45	203.60	200.55	194.50	188.40	182.30	176.25	170.15	164.05	158.00	151.90
1400 - 1412	238.10	206.25	203.20	197.15	191.05	184.95	178.90	172.80	166.70	160.65	154.55
1412 - 1424	240.75	208.90	205.85	199.75	193.70	187.60	181.50	175.45	169.35	163.25	157.20
1424 - 1436	243.40	211.55	208.50	202.40	196.35	190.25	184.15	178.10	172.00	165.90	159.80
1436 - 1448	246.00	214.20	211.15	205.05	198.95	192.90	186.80	180.70	174.65	168.55	162.45
1448 - 1460	248.65	216.80	213.75	207.70	201.60	195.50	189.45	183.35	177.25	171.20	165.10
1460 - 1472	251.30	219.45	216.40	210.35	204.25	198.15	192.10	186.00	179.90	173.85	167.75
1472 - 1484	253.95	222.10	219.05	212.95	206.90	200.80	194.70	188.65	182.55	176.45	170.40
1484 - 1496	256.60	224.75	221.70	215.60	209.55	203.45	197.35	191.30	185.20	179.10	173.00
1496 - 1508	259.20	227.40	224.35	218.25	212.15	206.10	200.00	193.90	187.85	181.75	175.65
1508 - 1520	261.85	230.00	226.95	220.90	214.80	208.70	202.65	196.55	190.45	184.40	178.30
1520 - 1532	264.50	232.65	229.60	223.55	217.45	211.35	205.30	199.20	193.10	187.05	180.95
1532 - 1544	267.15	235.30	232.25	226.15	220.10	214.00	207.90	201.85	195.75	189.65	183.60
1544 - 1556	269.80	237.95	234.90	228.80	222.75	216.65	210.55	204.50	198.40	192.30	186.20
1556 - 1568	272.40	240.60	237.55	231.45	225.35	219.30	213.20	207.10	201.05	194.95	188.85
1568 - 1580	275.05	243.20	240.15	234.10	228.00	221.90	215.85	209.75	203.65	197.60	191.50
1580 - 1592	277.70	245.85	242.80	236.75	230.65	224.55	218.50	212.40	206.30	200.25	194.15
1592 - 1604	280.35	248.50	245.45	239.35	233.30	227.20	221.10	215.05	208.95	202.85	196.80
1604 - 1616	283.00	251.15	248.10	242.00	235.95	229.85	223.75	217.70	211.60	205.50	199.40
1616 - 1628	285.60	253.80	250.75	244.65	238.55	232.50	226.40	220.30	214.25	208.15	202.05
1628 - 1640	288.25	256.40	253.35	247.30	241.20	235.10	229.05	222.95	216.85	210.80	204.70
1640 - 1652	290.90	259.05	256.00	249.95	243.85	237.75	231.70	225.60	219.50	213.45	207.35
1652 - 1664	293.55	261.70	258.65	252.55	246.50	240.40	234.30	228.25	222.15	216.05	210.00
1664 - 1676	296.20	264.35	261.30	255.20	249.15	243.05	236.95	230.90	224.80	218.70	212.60

D-4

Federal tax deductions
Effective January 1, 2013
Weekly (52 pay periods a year)
Also look up the tax deductions in the provincial table

Pay From	Pay Less than	CC 0	CC 1	CC 2	CC 3	CC 4	CC 5	CC 6	CC 7	CC 8	CC 9	CC 10
1676	1692	299.60	267.75	264.70	258.65	252.55	246.45	240.40	234.30	228.20	222.15	216.05
1692	1708	303.75	271.90	268.85	262.80	256.70	250.60	244.55	238.45	232.35	226.30	220.20
1708	1724	307.90	276.10	273.05	266.95	260.85	254.80	248.70	242.60	236.55	230.45	224.35
1724	1740	312.10	280.25	277.20	271.10	265.05	258.95	252.85	246.80	240.70	234.60	228.55
1740	1756	316.25	284.40	281.35	275.25	269.20	263.10	257.00	250.95	244.85	238.75	232.70
1756	1772	320.40	288.55	285.50	279.45	273.35	267.25	261.20	255.10	249.00	242.95	236.85
1772	1788	324.55	292.70	289.65	283.60	277.50	271.40	265.35	259.25	253.15	247.10	241.00
1788	1804	328.70	296.90	293.85	287.75	281.65	275.60	269.50	263.40	257.35	251.25	245.15
1804	1820	332.90	301.05	298.00	291.90	285.85	279.75	273.65	267.60	261.50	255.40	249.35
1820	1836	337.05	305.20	302.15	296.05	290.00	283.90	277.80	271.75	265.65	259.55	253.50
1836	1852	341.20	309.35	306.30	300.25	294.15	288.05	282.00	275.90	269.80	263.75	257.65
1852	1868	345.35	313.50	310.45	304.40	298.30	292.20	286.15	280.05	273.95	267.90	261.80
1868	1884	349.50	317.70	314.65	308.55	302.45	296.40	290.30	284.20	278.15	272.05	265.95
1884	1900	353.70	321.85	318.80	312.70	306.65	300.55	294.45	288.40	282.30	276.20	270.15
1900	1916	357.85	326.00	322.95	316.85	310.80	304.70	298.60	292.55	286.45	280.35	274.30
1916	1932	362.00	330.15	327.10	321.05	314.95	308.85	302.80	296.70	290.60	284.55	278.45
1932	1948	366.15	334.30	331.25	325.20	319.10	313.00	306.95	300.85	294.75	288.70	282.60
1948	1964	370.30	338.50	335.45	329.35	323.25	317.20	311.10	305.00	298.95	292.85	286.75
1964	1980	374.50	342.65	339.60	333.50	327.45	321.35	315.25	309.20	303.10	297.00	290.95
1980	1996	378.65	346.80	343.75	337.65	331.60	325.50	319.40	313.35	307.25	301.15	295.10
1996	2012	382.80	350.95	347.90	341.85	335.75	329.65	323.60	317.50	311.40	305.35	299.25
2012	2028	386.95	355.10	352.05	346.00	339.90	333.80	327.75	321.65	315.55	309.50	303.40
2028	2044	391.10	359.30	356.25	350.15	344.05	338.00	331.90	325.80	319.75	313.65	307.55
2044	2060	395.30	363.45	360.40	354.30	348.25	342.15	336.05	330.00	323.90	317.80	311.75
2060	2076	399.45	367.60	364.55	358.45	352.40	346.30	340.20	334.15	328.05	321.95	315.90
2076	2092	403.60	371.75	368.70	362.65	356.55	350.45	344.40	338.30	332.20	326.15	320.05
2092	2108	407.75	375.90	372.85	366.80	360.70	354.60	348.55	342.45	336.35	330.30	324.20
2108	2124	411.90	380.10	377.05	370.95	364.85	358.80	352.70	346.60	340.55	334.45	328.35
2124	2140	416.10	384.25	381.20	375.10	369.05	362.95	356.85	350.80	344.70	338.60	332.55
2140	2156	420.25	388.40	385.35	379.25	373.20	367.10	361.00	354.95	348.85	342.75	336.70
2156	2172	424.40	392.55	389.50	383.45	377.35	371.25	365.20	359.10	353.00	346.95	340.85
2172	2188	428.55	396.70	393.65	387.60	381.50	375.40	369.35	363.25	357.15	351.10	345.00
2188	2204	432.70	400.90	397.85	391.75	385.65	379.60	373.50	367.40	361.35	355.25	349.15
2204	2220	436.90	405.05	402.00	395.90	389.85	383.75	377.65	371.60	365.50	359.40	353.35
2220	2236	441.05	409.20	406.15	400.05	394.00	387.90	381.80	375.75	369.65	363.55	357.50
2236	2252	445.20	413.35	410.30	404.25	398.15	392.05	386.00	379.90	373.80	367.75	361.65
2252	2268	449.35	417.50	414.45	408.40	402.30	396.20	390.15	384.05	377.95	371.90	365.80
2268	2284	453.50	421.70	418.65	412.55	406.45	400.40	394.30	388.20	382.15	376.05	369.95
2284	2300	457.70	425.85	422.80	416.70	410.65	404.55	398.45	392.40	386.30	380.20	374.15
2300	2316	461.85	430.00	426.95	420.85	414.80	408.70	402.60	396.55	390.45	384.35	378.30
2316	2332	466.00	434.15	431.10	425.05	418.95	412.85	406.80	400.70	394.60	388.55	382.45
2332	2348	470.15	438.30	435.25	429.20	423.10	417.00	410.95	404.85	398.75	392.70	386.60
2348	2364	474.30	442.50	439.45	433.35	427.25	421.20	415.10	409.00	402.95	396.85	390.75
2364	2380	478.50	446.65	443.60	437.50	431.45	425.35	419.25	413.20	407.10	401.00	394.95
2380	2396	482.65	450.80	447.75	441.65	435.60	429.50	423.40	417.35	411.25	405.15	399.10
2396	2412	486.80	454.95	451.90	445.85	439.75	433.65	427.60	421.50	415.40	409.35	403.25
2412	2428	490.95	459.10	456.05	450.00	443.90	437.80	431.75	425.65	419.55	413.50	407.40
2428	2444	495.10	463.30	460.25	454.15	448.05	442.00	435.90	429.80	423.75	417.65	411.55
2444	2460	499.30	467.45	464.40	458.30	452.25	446.15	440.05	434.00	427.90	421.80	415.75
2460	2476	503.45	471.60	468.55	462.45	456.40	450.30	444.20	438.15	432.05	425.95	419.90
2476	2492	507.60	475.75	472.70	466.65	460.55	454.45	448.40	442.30	436.20	430.15	424.05
2492	2508	511.75	479.90	476.85	470.80	464.70	458.60	452.55	446.45	440.35	434.30	428.20
2508	2524	515.90	484.10	481.05	474.95	468.85	462.80	456.70	450.60	444.55	438.45	432.35
2524	2540	520.10	488.25	485.20	479.10	473.05	466.95	460.85	454.80	448.70	442.60	436.55
2540	2556	524.25	492.40	489.35	483.25	477.20	471.10	465.00	458.95	452.85	446.75	440.70

Federal tax deductions

Effective January 1, 2013

Weekly (52 pay periods a year)

Also look up the tax deductions in the provincial table

Pay From	Pay Less than	CC 0	CC 1	CC 2	CC 3	CC 4	CC 5	CC 6	CC 7	CC 8	CC 9	CC 10
2556	2576	528.90	497.10	494.05	487.95	481.85	475.80	469.70	463.60	457.55	451.45	445.35
2576	2596	534.10	502.30	499.25	493.15	487.05	481.00	474.90	468.80	462.75	456.65	450.55
2596	2616	539.55	507.75	504.70	498.60	492.50	486.45	480.35	474.25	468.20	462.10	456.00
2616	2636	545.35	513.55	510.50	504.40	498.30	492.25	486.15	480.05	474.00	467.90	461.80
2636	2656	551.15	519.35	516.30	510.20	504.10	498.05	491.95	485.85	479.80	473.70	467.60
2656	2676	556.95	525.15	522.10	516.00	509.90	503.85	497.75	491.65	485.60	479.50	473.40
2676	2696	562.75	530.95	527.90	521.80	515.70	509.65	503.55	497.45	491.40	485.30	479.20
2696	2716	568.55	536.75	533.70	527.60	521.50	515.45	509.35	503.25	497.20	491.10	485.00
2716	2736	574.35	542.55	539.50	533.40	527.30	521.25	515.15	509.05	503.00	496.90	490.80
2736	2756	580.15	548.35	545.30	539.20	533.10	527.05	520.95	514.85	508.80	502.70	496.60
2756	2776	585.95	554.15	551.10	545.00	538.90	532.85	526.75	520.65	514.60	508.50	502.40
2776	2796	591.75	559.95	556.90	550.80	544.70	538.65	532.55	526.45	520.40	514.30	508.20
2796	2816	597.55	565.75	562.70	556.60	550.50	544.45	538.35	532.25	526.20	520.10	514.00
2816	2836	603.35	571.55	568.50	562.40	556.30	550.25	544.15	538.05	532.00	525.90	519.80
2836	2856	609.15	577.35	574.30	568.20	562.10	556.05	549.95	543.85	537.80	531.70	525.60
2856	2876	614.95	583.15	580.10	574.00	567.90	561.85	555.75	549.65	543.60	537.50	531.40
2876	2896	620.75	588.95	585.90	579.80	573.70	567.65	561.55	555.45	549.40	543.30	537.20
2896	2916	626.55	594.75	591.70	585.60	579.50	573.45	567.35	561.25	555.20	549.10	543.00
2916	2936	632.35	600.55	597.50	591.40	585.30	579.25	573.15	567.05	561.00	554.90	548.80
2936	2956	638.15	606.35	603.30	597.20	591.10	585.05	578.95	572.85	566.80	560.70	554.60
2956	2976	643.95	612.15	609.10	603.00	596.90	590.85	584.75	578.65	572.60	566.50	560.40
2976	2996	649.75	617.95	614.90	608.80	602.70	596.65	590.55	584.45	578.40	572.30	566.20
2996	3016	655.55	623.75	620.70	614.60	608.50	602.45	596.35	590.25	584.20	578.10	572.00
3016	3036	661.35	629.55	626.50	620.40	614.30	608.25	602.15	596.05	590.00	583.90	577.80
3036	3056	667.15	635.35	632.30	626.20	620.10	614.05	607.95	601.85	595.80	589.70	583.60
3056	3076	672.95	641.15	638.10	632.00	625.90	619.85	613.75	607.65	601.60	595.50	589.40
3076	3096	678.75	646.95	643.90	637.80	631.70	625.65	619.55	613.45	607.40	601.30	595.20
3096	3116	684.55	652.75	649.70	643.60	637.50	631.45	625.35	619.25	613.20	607.10	601.00
3116	3136	690.35	658.55	655.50	649.40	643.30	637.25	631.15	625.05	619.00	612.90	606.80
3136	3156	696.15	664.35	661.30	655.20	649.10	643.05	636.95	630.85	624.80	618.70	612.60
3156	3176	701.95	670.15	667.10	661.00	654.90	648.85	642.75	636.65	630.60	624.50	618.40
3176	3196	707.75	675.95	672.90	666.80	660.70	654.65	648.55	642.45	636.40	630.30	624.20
3196	3216	713.55	681.75	678.70	672.60	666.50	660.45	654.35	648.25	642.20	636.10	630.00
3216	3236	719.35	687.55	684.50	678.40	672.30	666.25	660.15	654.05	648.00	641.90	635.80
3236	3256	725.15	693.35	690.30	684.20	678.10	672.05	665.95	659.85	653.80	647.70	641.60
3256	3276	730.95	699.15	696.10	690.00	683.90	677.85	671.75	665.65	659.60	653.50	647.40
3276	3296	736.75	704.95	701.90	695.80	689.70	683.65	677.55	671.45	665.40	659.30	653.20
3296	3316	742.55	710.75	707.70	701.60	695.50	689.45	683.35	677.25	671.20	665.10	659.00
3316	3336	748.35	716.55	713.50	707.40	701.30	695.25	689.15	683.05	677.00	670.90	664.80
3336	3356	754.15	722.35	719.30	713.20	707.10	701.05	694.95	688.85	682.80	676.70	670.60
3356	3376	759.95	728.15	725.10	719.00	712.90	706.85	700.75	694.65	688.60	682.50	676.40
3376	3396	765.75	733.95	730.90	724.80	718.70	712.65	706.55	700.45	694.40	688.30	682.20
3396	3416	771.55	739.75	736.70	730.60	724.50	718.45	712.35	706.25	700.20	694.10	688.00
3416	3436	777.35	745.55	742.50	736.40	730.30	724.25	718.15	712.05	706.00	699.90	693.80
3436	3456	783.15	751.35	748.30	742.20	736.10	730.05	723.95	717.85	711.80	705.70	699.60
3456	3476	788.95	757.15	754.10	748.00	741.90	735.85	729.75	723.65	717.60	711.50	705.40
3476	3496	794.75	762.95	759.90	753.80	747.70	741.65	735.55	729.45	723.40	717.30	711.20
3496	3516	800.55	768.75	765.70	759.60	753.50	747.45	741.35	735.25	729.20	723.10	717.00
3516	3536	806.35	774.55	771.50	765.40	759.30	753.25	747.15	741.05	735.00	728.90	722.80
3536	3556	812.15	780.35	777.30	771.20	765.10	759.05	752.95	746.85	740.80	734.70	728.60
3556	3576	817.95	786.15	783.10	777.00	770.90	764.85	758.75	752.65	746.60	740.50	734.40
3576	3596	823.75	791.95	788.90	782.80	776.70	770.65	764.55	758.45	752.40	746.30	740.20
3596	3616	829.55	797.75	794.70	788.60	782.50	776.45	770.35	764.25	758.20	752.10	746.00
3616	3636	835.35	803.55	800.50	794.40	788.30	782.25	776.15	770.05	764.00	757.90	751.80
3636	3656	841.15	809.35	806.30	800.20	794.10	788.05	781.95	775.85	769.80	763.70	757.60

D-6

Appendix 9-1P—Ontario Tax Tables

Ontario provincial tax deductions

Effective January 1, 2013
Weekly (52 pay periods a year)

Also look up the tax deductions in the federal table

Pay From	Pay Less than	CC 0	CC 1	CC 2	CC 3	CC 4	CC 5	CC 6	CC 7	CC 8	CC 9	CC 10
	285	* (1)	.00									
285 -	287	13.60	.15									
287 -	289	13.70	.35									
289 -	291	13.80	.55									
291 -	293	13.90	.70									
293 -	295	14.00	.90									
295 -	297	14.10	1.10									
297 -	299	14.20	1.30									
299 -	301	14.30	1.45									
301 -	303	14.40	1.65									
303 -	305	14.45	1.85									
305 -	307	14.55	2.05	.05								
307 -	309	14.65	2.20	.20								
309 -	311	14.75	2.40	.40								
311 -	313	14.85	2.60	.60								
313 -	315	14.95	2.80	.80								
315 -	317	15.05	3.00	.95								
317 -	319	15.15	3.15	1.15								
319 -	321	15.20	3.35	1.35								
321 -	323	15.30	3.55	1.55								
323 -	325	15.40	3.75	1.75								
325 -	327	15.50	3.90	1.90								
327 -	329	15.60	4.10	2.10								
329 -	331	15.70	4.30	2.30								
331 -	333	15.80	4.50	2.50								
333 -	335	15.90	4.65	2.65								
335 -	337	16.00	4.85	2.85								
337 -	339	16.05	5.05	3.05								
339 -	341	16.15	5.25	3.25								
341 -	343	16.25	5.40	3.40								
343 -	345	16.35	5.60	3.60								
345 -	347	16.45	5.80	3.80								
347 -	349	16.55	6.00	4.00								
349 -	351	16.65	6.20	4.15	.15							
351 -	353	16.75	6.35	4.35	.35							
353 -	355	16.80	6.55	4.55	.55							
355 -	357	16.90	6.75	4.75	.75							
357 -	359	17.00	6.95	4.95	.90							
359 -	361	17.10	7.10	5.10	1.10							
361 -	363	17.20	7.30	5.30	1.30							
363 -	365	17.30	7.50	5.50	1.50							
365 -	367	17.40	7.70	5.70	1.65							
367 -	369	17.50	7.85	5.85	1.85							
369 -	371	17.60	8.05	6.05	2.05							
371 -	373	17.65	8.25	6.25	2.25							
373 -	375	17.75	8.45	6.45	2.40							
375 -	377	17.85	8.55	6.60	2.60							
377 -	379	17.95	8.65	6.80	2.80							
379 -	381	18.05	8.75	7.00	3.00							
381 -	383	18.15	8.85	7.20	3.20							
383 -	385	18.25	8.95	7.35	3.35							
385 -	387	18.40	9.10	7.65	3.65	.10	.10	.10	.10	.10	.10	.10
387 -	389	18.65	9.35	7.95	3.95	.20	.20	.20	.20	.20	.20	.20
389 -	391	18.85	9.55	8.25	4.25	.30	.30	.30	.30	.30	.30	.30
391 -	393	19.05	9.75	8.55	4.55	.55	.45	.45	.45	.45	.45	.45

E-1

(1) You normally use claim code "0" only for non-resident employees. However, if you have non-resident employees who earn less than the minimum amount shown in the "Pay" column, you may not be able to use these tables. Instead, refer to the "Step-by-step calculation of tax deductions" in Section "A" of this publication.

Ontario provincial tax deductions

Effective January 1, 2013

Weekly (52 pay periods a year)

Also look up the tax deductions in the federal table

Pay From - Less than	CC 0	CC 1	CC 2	CC 3	CC 4	CC 5	CC 6	CC 7	CC 8	CC 9	CC 10
393 - 397	19.40	10.10	9.05	5.00	1.00	.60	.60	.60	.60	.60	.60
397 - 401	19.80	10.50	9.50	5.65	1.65	.85	.85	.85	.85	.85	.85
401 - 405	20.25	10.95	9.95	6.25	2.25	1.10	1.10	1.10	1.10	1.10	1.10
405 - 409	20.65	11.35	10.35	6.85	2.85	1.35	1.35	1.35	1.35	1.35	1.35
409 - 413	21.10	11.80	10.80	7.50	3.50	1.60	1.60	1.60	1.60	1.60	1.60
413 - 417	21.50	12.20	11.20	8.10	4.10	1.80	1.80	1.80	1.80	1.80	1.80
417 - 421	21.95	12.65	11.65	8.70	4.70	2.05	2.05	2.05	2.05	2.05	2.05
421 - 425	22.35	13.10	12.05	9.35	5.35	2.30	2.30	2.30	2.30	2.30	2.30
425 - 429	22.80	13.50	12.50	9.95	5.95	2.55	2.55	2.55	2.55	2.55	2.55
429 - 433	23.25	13.95	12.95	10.55	6.55	2.80	2.80	2.80	2.80	2.80	2.80
433 - 437	23.65	14.35	13.35	11.20	7.20	3.15	3.00	3.00	3.00	3.00	3.00
437 - 441	24.10	14.80	13.80	11.80	7.80	3.80	3.25	3.25	3.25	3.25	3.25
441 - 445	24.50	15.20	14.20	12.20	8.40	4.40	3.50	3.50	3.50	3.50	3.50
445 - 449	24.95	15.65	14.65	12.65	9.05	5.00	3.75	3.75	3.75	3.75	3.75
449 - 453	25.35	16.05	15.05	13.05	9.65	5.65	4.00	4.00	4.00	4.00	4.00
453 - 457	25.80	16.50	15.50	13.50	10.25	6.25	4.20	4.20	4.20	4.20	4.20
457 - 461	26.25	16.95	15.95	13.90	10.90	6.85	4.45	4.45	4.45	4.45	4.45
461 - 465	26.65	17.35	16.35	14.35	11.50	7.50	4.70	4.70	4.70	4.70	4.70
465 - 469	27.10	17.80	16.80	14.80	12.10	8.10	4.95	4.95	4.95	4.95	4.95
469 - 473	27.50	18.20	17.20	15.20	12.75	8.70	5.20	5.20	5.20	5.20	5.20
473 - 477	27.95	18.65	17.65	15.65	13.35	9.35	5.40	5.40	5.40	5.40	5.40
477 - 481	28.35	19.05	18.05	16.05	13.95	9.95	5.95	5.65	5.65	5.65	5.65
481 - 485	28.65	19.35	18.35	16.35	14.35	10.45	6.45	5.75	5.75	5.75	5.75
485 - 489	28.85	19.55	18.55	16.55	14.55	10.80	6.80	5.75	5.75	5.75	5.75
489 - 493	29.05	19.75	18.75	16.75	14.75	11.20	7.20	5.75	5.75	5.75	5.75
493 - 497	29.25	19.95	18.95	16.90	14.90	11.55	7.55	5.75	5.75	5.75	5.75
497 - 501	29.40	20.10	19.10	17.10	15.10	11.95	7.95	5.75	5.75	5.75	5.75
501 - 505	29.60	20.30	19.30	17.30	15.30	12.30	8.30	5.75	5.75	5.75	5.75
505 - 509	29.80	20.50	19.50	17.50	15.50	12.70	8.70	5.75	5.75	5.75	5.75
509 - 513	30.00	20.70	19.70	17.70	15.65	13.05	9.05	5.75	5.75	5.75	5.75
513 - 517	30.15	20.85	19.85	17.85	15.85	13.45	9.45	5.75	5.75	5.75	5.75
517 - 521	30.35	21.05	20.05	18.05	16.05	13.80	9.80	5.80	5.75	5.75	5.75
521 - 525	30.55	21.25	20.25	18.25	16.25	14.20	10.20	6.20	5.75	5.75	5.75
525 - 529	30.75	21.45	20.45	18.45	16.45	14.40	10.55	6.55	5.75	5.75	5.75
529 - 533	30.90	21.60	20.60	18.60	16.60	14.60	10.95	6.95	5.75	5.75	5.75
533 - 537	31.10	21.80	20.80	18.80	16.80	14.80	11.30	7.30	5.75	5.75	5.75
537 - 541	31.30	22.00	21.00	19.00	17.00	15.00	11.70	7.70	5.75	5.75	5.75
541 - 545	31.50	22.20	21.20	19.20	17.20	15.20	12.10	8.05	5.75	5.75	5.75
545 - 549	31.65	22.40	21.35	19.35	17.35	15.35	12.45	8.45	5.75	5.75	5.75
549 - 553	31.85	22.55	21.55	19.55	17.55	15.55	12.85	8.80	5.75	5.75	5.75
553 - 557	32.05	22.75	21.75	19.75	17.75	15.75	13.20	9.20	5.75	5.75	5.75
557 - 561	32.25	22.95	21.95	19.95	17.95	15.95	13.60	9.55	5.75	5.75	5.75
561 - 565	32.45	23.15	22.15	20.10	18.10	16.10	13.95	9.95	5.95	5.75	5.75
565 - 569	32.60	23.30	22.30	20.30	18.30	16.30	14.30	10.35	6.30	5.75	5.75
569 - 573	32.80	23.50	22.50	20.50	18.50	16.50	14.50	10.70	6.70	5.75	5.75
573 - 577	33.00	23.70	22.70	20.70	18.70	16.70	14.70	11.10	7.05	5.75	5.75
577 - 581	33.20	23.90	22.90	20.90	18.85	16.85	14.85	11.45	7.45	5.75	5.75
581 - 585	33.35	24.05	23.05	21.05	19.05	17.05	15.05	11.85	7.85	5.75	5.75
585 - 589	33.55	24.25	23.25	21.25	19.25	17.25	15.25	12.20	8.20	5.75	5.75
589 - 593	33.75	24.45	23.45	21.45	19.45	17.45	15.45	12.60	8.60	5.75	5.75
593 - 597	33.95	24.65	23.65	21.65	19.65	17.60	15.60	12.95	8.95	5.75	5.75
597 - 601	34.10	24.80	23.80	21.80	19.80	17.80	15.80	13.35	9.35	5.75	5.75
601 - 605	34.30	25.00	24.00	22.00	20.00	18.00	16.00	13.70	9.70	5.75	5.75
605 - 609	34.50	25.20	24.20	22.20	20.20	18.20	16.20	14.10	10.10	6.10	5.75
609 - 613	34.70	25.40	24.40	22.40	20.40	18.40	16.35	14.35	10.45	6.45	5.75

E-2

Ontario provincial tax deductions
Effective January 1, 2013
Weekly (52 pay periods a year)
Also look up the tax deductions in the federal table

Pay From - Less than	CC 0	CC 1	CC 2	CC 3	CC 4	CC 5	CC 6	CC 7	CC 8	CC 9	CC 10
613 - 621	34.95	25.65	24.65	22.65	20.65	18.65	16.65	14.65	11.05	7.00	5.75
621 - 629	35.35	26.05	25.05	23.05	21.05	19.05	17.05	15.05	11.80	7.75	5.75
629 - 637	35.70	26.40	25.40	23.40	21.40	19.40	17.40	15.40	12.55	8.50	5.75
637 - 645	36.10	26.80	25.80	23.80	21.80	19.80	17.80	15.80	13.30	9.30	5.75
645 - 653	36.45	27.20	26.15	24.15	22.15	20.15	18.15	16.15	14.05	10.05	6.00
653 - 661	36.85	27.55	26.55	24.55	22.55	20.55	18.55	16.55	14.55	10.80	6.80
661 - 669	37.25	27.95	26.95	24.90	22.90	20.90	18.90	16.90	14.90	11.55	7.55
669 - 677	37.60	28.30	27.30	25.30	23.30	21.30	19.30	17.30	15.30	12.30	8.30
677 - 685	38.00	28.70	27.70	25.70	23.65	21.65	19.65	17.65	15.65	13.05	9.05
685 - 693	38.35	29.05	28.05	26.05	24.05	22.05	20.05	18.05	16.05	13.80	9.80
693 - 701	39.00	29.70	28.70	26.70	24.70	22.70	20.70	18.70	16.70	14.70	10.80
701 - 709	39.85	30.55	29.55	27.55	25.55	23.55	21.55	19.55	17.55	15.55	12.05
709 - 717	40.75	31.45	30.45	28.40	26.40	24.40	22.40	20.40	18.40	16.40	13.30
717 - 725	41.60	32.30	31.30	29.30	27.30	25.25	23.25	21.25	19.25	17.25	14.50
725 - 733	42.45	33.15	32.15	30.15	28.15	26.15	24.15	22.10	20.10	18.10	15.75
733 - 741	43.30	34.00	33.00	31.00	29.00	27.00	25.00	23.00	21.00	18.95	16.95
741 - 749	43.90	34.60	33.60	31.55	29.55	27.55	25.55	23.55	21.55	19.55	17.55
749 - 757	44.25	34.95	33.95	31.95	29.95	27.95	25.95	23.95	21.95	19.95	17.90
757 - 765	44.65	35.35	34.35	32.30	30.30	28.30	26.30	24.30	22.30	20.30	18.30
765 - 773	45.20	35.90	34.90	32.90	30.90	28.90	26.90	24.90	22.90	20.90	18.90
773 - 781	45.90	36.60	35.60	33.60	31.60	29.60	27.60	25.60	23.60	21.60	19.60
781 - 789	46.60	37.30	36.30	34.30	32.30	30.30	28.30	26.30	24.30	22.30	20.30
789 - 797	47.30	38.00	37.00	35.00	33.00	31.00	29.00	27.00	25.00	23.00	21.00
797 - 805	48.00	38.75	37.70	35.70	33.70	31.70	29.70	27.70	25.70	23.70	21.70
805 - 813	48.75	39.45	38.45	36.45	34.40	32.40	30.40	28.40	26.40	24.40	22.40
813 - 821	49.45	40.15	39.15	37.15	35.15	33.10	31.10	29.10	27.10	25.10	23.10
821 - 829	50.15	40.85	39.85	37.85	35.85	33.85	31.80	29.80	27.80	25.80	23.80
829 - 837	50.85	41.55	40.55	38.55	36.55	34.55	32.55	30.50	28.50	26.50	24.50
837 - 845	51.55	42.25	41.25	39.25	37.25	35.25	33.25	31.25	29.25	27.20	25.20
845 - 853	52.25	42.95	41.95	39.95	37.95	35.95	33.95	31.95	29.95	27.95	25.90
853 - 861	52.95	43.65	42.65	40.65	38.65	36.65	34.65	32.65	30.65	28.65	26.65
861 - 869	53.65	44.35	43.35	41.35	39.35	37.35	35.35	33.35	31.35	29.35	27.35
869 - 877	54.35	45.05	44.05	42.05	40.05	38.05	36.05	34.05	32.05	30.05	28.05
877 - 885	55.05	45.75	44.75	42.75	40.75	38.75	36.75	34.75	32.75	30.75	28.75
885 - 893	55.75	46.45	45.45	43.45	41.45	39.45	37.45	35.45	33.45	31.45	29.45
893 - 901	56.50	47.20	46.20	44.15	42.15	40.15	38.15	36.15	34.15	32.15	30.15
901 - 909	57.20	47.90	46.90	44.90	42.85	40.85	38.85	36.85	34.85	32.85	30.85
909 - 917	57.90	48.60	47.60	45.60	43.60	41.60	39.55	37.55	35.55	33.55	31.55
917 - 925	58.60	49.30	48.30	46.30	44.30	42.30	40.30	38.30	36.30	34.30	32.25
925 - 933	60.80	51.50	50.50	48.50	46.50	44.50	42.50	40.45	38.45	36.45	34.45
933 - 941	62.90	53.60	52.60	50.60	48.60	46.60	44.60	42.60	40.60	38.60	36.60
941 - 949	63.60	54.30	53.30	51.30	49.30	47.30	45.30	43.30	41.30	39.30	37.30
949 - 957	64.35	55.05	54.05	52.05	50.05	48.00	46.00	44.00	42.00	40.00	38.00
957 - 965	65.05	55.75	54.75	52.75	50.75	48.75	46.75	44.75	42.70	40.70	38.70
965 - 973	65.75	56.45	55.45	53.45	51.45	49.45	47.45	45.45	43.45	41.45	39.45
973 - 981	66.45	57.15	56.15	54.15	52.15	50.15	48.15	46.15	44.15	42.15	40.15
981 - 989	67.20	57.90	56.90	54.90	52.90	50.90	48.85	46.85	44.85	42.85	40.85
989 - 997	67.90	58.60	57.60	55.60	53.60	51.60	49.60	47.60	45.60	43.60	41.60
997 - 1005	68.65	59.35	58.35	56.35	54.35	52.35	50.35	48.35	46.35	44.35	42.30
1005 - 1013	69.40	60.10	59.10	57.10	55.05	53.05	51.05	49.05	47.05	45.05	43.05
1013 - 1021	70.10	60.80	59.80	57.80	55.80	53.80	51.80	49.80	47.80	45.80	43.80
1021 - 1029	70.85	61.55	60.55	58.55	56.55	54.55	52.55	50.55	48.50	46.50	44.50
1029 - 1037	71.60	62.30	61.30	59.25	57.25	55.25	53.25	51.25	49.25	47.25	45.25
1037 - 1045	72.30	63.00	62.00	60.00	58.00	56.00	54.00	52.00	50.00	48.00	46.00
1045 - 1053	73.05	63.75	62.75	60.75	58.75	56.75	54.75	52.70	50.70	48.70	46.70

E-3

Ontario provincial tax deductions

Effective January 1, 2013
Weekly (52 pay periods a year)

Also look up the tax deductions in the federal table

Pay From - Less than	CC 0	CC 1	CC 2	CC 3	CC 4	CC 5	CC 6	CC 7	CC 8	CC 9	CC 10
1053 - 1065	73.95	64.65	63.65	61.65	59.65	57.65	55.65	53.65	51.65	49.65	47.65
1065 - 1077	75.05	65.75	64.75	62.75	60.75	58.75	56.75	54.75	52.75	50.75	48.75
1077 - 1089	76.15	66.85	65.85	63.85	61.85	59.85	57.85	55.85	53.85	51.85	49.80
1089 - 1101	77.25	67.95	66.95	64.95	62.95	60.95	58.95	56.95	54.95	52.95	50.90
1101 - 1113	78.35	69.05	68.05	66.05	64.05	62.05	60.05	58.05	56.05	54.00	52.00
1113 - 1125	79.45	70.15	69.15	67.15	65.15	63.15	61.15	59.15	57.15	55.10	53.10
1125 - 1137	80.55	71.25	70.25	68.25	66.25	64.25	62.25	60.25	58.20	56.20	54.20
1137 - 1149	81.65	72.35	71.35	69.35	67.35	65.35	63.35	61.35	59.30	57.30	55.30
1149 - 1161	82.75	73.45	72.45	70.45	68.45	66.45	64.45	62.40	60.40	58.40	56.40
1161 - 1173	83.85	74.55	73.55	71.55	69.55	67.55	65.55	63.50	61.50	59.50	57.50
1173 - 1185	84.95	75.65	74.65	72.65	70.65	68.65	66.60	64.60	62.60	60.60	58.60
1185 - 1197	86.05	76.75	75.75	73.75	71.75	69.70	67.70	65.70	63.70	61.70	59.70
1197 - 1209	87.15	77.85	76.85	74.85	72.85	70.80	68.80	66.80	64.80	62.80	60.80
1209 - 1221	88.25	78.95	77.95	75.95	73.90	71.90	69.90	67.90	65.90	63.90	61.90
1221 - 1233	89.35	80.05	79.05	77.05	75.00	73.00	71.00	69.00	67.00	65.00	63.00
1233 - 1245	90.45	81.15	80.15	78.10	76.10	74.10	72.10	70.10	68.10	66.10	64.10
1245 - 1257	91.50	82.25	81.20	79.20	77.20	75.20	73.20	71.20	69.20	67.20	65.20
1257 - 1269	92.60	83.30	82.30	80.30	78.30	76.30	74.30	72.30	70.30	68.30	66.30
1269 - 1281	93.70	84.40	83.40	81.40	79.40	77.40	75.40	73.40	71.40	69.40	67.40
1281 - 1293	95.00	85.50	84.50	82.50	80.50	78.50	76.50	74.50	72.50	70.50	68.50
1293 - 1305	96.30	86.60	85.60	83.60	81.60	79.60	77.60	75.60	73.60	71.60	69.60
1305 - 1317	97.60	87.70	86.70	84.70	82.70	80.70	78.70	76.70	74.70	72.70	70.70
1317 - 1329	98.95	88.80	87.80	85.80	83.80	81.80	79.80	77.80	75.80	73.80	71.80
1329 - 1341	100.25	89.90	88.90	86.90	84.90	82.90	80.90	78.90	76.90	74.90	72.90
1341 - 1353	101.55	91.00	90.00	88.00	86.00	84.00	82.00	80.00	78.00	76.00	74.00
1353 - 1365	102.90	92.10	91.10	89.10	87.10	85.10	83.10	81.10	79.10	77.10	75.10
1365 - 1377	104.20	93.20	92.20	90.20	88.20	86.20	84.20	82.20	80.20	78.20	76.20
1377 - 1389	105.50	94.35	93.30	91.30	89.30	87.30	85.30	83.30	81.30	79.30	77.25
1389 - 1401	109.45	98.30	97.05	95.00	93.00	91.00	89.00	87.00	85.00	82.95	80.95
1401 - 1413	111.05	99.90	98.70	96.40	94.40	92.35	90.35	88.35	86.35	84.35	82.35
1413 - 1425	112.35	101.20	100.00	97.60	95.45	93.45	91.45	89.45	87.45	85.45	83.45
1425 - 1437	113.65	102.50	101.30	98.90	96.55	94.55	92.55	90.55	88.55	86.55	84.55
1437 - 1449	115.00	103.85	102.65	100.25	97.80	95.65	93.65	91.65	89.65	87.65	85.65
1449 - 1461	116.30	105.15	103.95	101.55	99.15	96.75	94.75	92.75	90.75	88.75	86.75
1461 - 1473	117.65	106.45	105.25	102.85	100.45	98.05	95.85	93.85	91.85	89.85	87.85
1473 - 1485	118.95	107.80	106.60	104.20	101.80	99.35	96.95	94.95	92.95	90.95	88.95
1485 - 1497	120.25	109.10	107.90	105.50	103.10	100.70	98.30	96.05	94.05	92.05	90.05
1497 - 1509	121.60	110.40	109.20	106.80	104.40	102.00	99.60	97.20	95.15	93.15	91.15
1509 - 1521	122.90	111.75	110.55	108.15	105.75	103.35	100.90	98.50	96.25	94.25	92.25
1521 - 1533	124.20	113.05	111.85	109.45	107.05	104.65	102.25	99.85	97.45	95.35	93.35
1533 - 1545	126.15	114.65	113.45	111.05	108.65	106.25	103.80	101.40	99.00	96.65	94.65
1545 - 1557	128.25	116.25	115.05	112.65	110.25	107.85	105.45	103.05	100.60	98.20	96.00
1557 - 1569	130.35	117.85	116.65	114.25	111.85	109.45	107.05	104.65	102.25	99.80	97.40
1569 - 1581	132.45	119.45	118.25	115.85	113.45	111.05	108.65	106.25	103.85	101.45	99.05
1581 - 1593	134.50	121.05	119.85	117.45	115.05	112.65	110.25	107.85	105.45	103.05	100.65
1593 - 1605	136.60	122.70	121.50	119.05	116.65	114.25	111.85	109.45	107.05	104.65	102.25
1605 - 1617	138.70	124.30	123.10	120.70	118.25	115.85	113.45	111.05	108.65	106.25	103.85
1617 - 1629	140.80	126.30	124.70	122.30	119.90	117.50	115.05	112.65	110.25	107.85	105.45
1629 - 1641	142.85	128.35	126.80	123.90	121.50	119.10	116.70	114.30	111.85	109.45	107.05
1641 - 1653	144.95	130.45	128.90	125.75	123.10	120.70	118.30	115.90	113.50	111.05	108.65
1653 - 1665	147.05	132.55	131.00	127.85	124.75	122.30	119.90	117.50	115.10	112.70	110.30
1665 - 1677	149.15	134.65	133.05	129.95	126.80	123.90	121.50	119.10	116.70	114.30	111.90
1677 - 1689	151.25	136.75	135.15	132.05	128.90	125.80	123.10	120.70	118.30	115.90	113.50
1689 - 1701	153.30	138.80	137.25	134.15	131.00	127.90	124.75	122.30	119.90	117.50	115.10
1701 - 1713	155.40	140.90	139.35	136.20	133.10	129.95	126.85	123.90	121.50	119.10	116.70

E-4

Ontario provincial tax deductions

Effective January 1, 2013

Weekly (52 pay periods a year)

Also look up the tax deductions in the federal table

Pay From - Less than	CC 0	CC 1	CC 2	CC 3	CC 4	CC 5	CC 6	CC 7	CC 8	CC 9	CC 10
1713 - 1729	157.85	143.35	141.80	138.65	135.55	132.40	129.30	126.15	123.40	121.00	118.60
1729 - 1745	160.65	146.15	144.55	141.45	138.30	135.20	132.05	128.95	125.80	123.15	120.70
1745 - 1761	163.40	148.90	147.35	144.20	141.10	137.95	134.85	131.70	128.60	125.45	122.85
1761 - 1777	166.20	151.70	150.15	147.00	143.90	140.75	137.65	134.50	131.40	128.25	125.15
1777 - 1793	169.00	154.50	152.90	149.80	146.65	143.55	140.40	137.30	134.15	131.05	127.90
1793 - 1809	171.75	157.25	155.70	152.60	149.45	146.35	143.20	140.10	136.95	133.85	130.70
1809 - 1825	174.55	160.05	158.50	155.35	152.25	149.10	146.00	142.85	139.75	136.60	133.50
1825 - 1841	177.35	162.85	161.30	158.15	155.05	151.90	148.80	145.65	142.50	139.40	136.25
1841 - 1857	180.15	165.65	164.05	160.95	157.80	154.70	151.55	148.45	145.30	142.20	139.05
1857 - 1873	182.90	168.40	166.85	163.70	160.60	157.45	154.35	151.20	148.10	144.95	141.85
1873 - 1889	185.70	171.20	169.65	166.50	163.40	160.25	157.15	154.00	150.90	147.75	144.65
1889 - 1905	188.50	174.00	172.40	169.30	166.15	163.05	159.90	156.80	153.65	150.55	147.40
1905 - 1921	191.25	176.75	175.20	172.10	168.95	165.85	162.70	159.60	156.45	153.35	150.20
1921 - 1937	194.05	179.55	178.00	174.85	171.75	168.60	165.50	162.35	159.25	156.10	153.00
1937 - 1953	196.85	182.35	180.80	177.65	174.50	171.40	168.25	165.15	162.00	158.90	155.75
1953 - 1969	199.65	185.10	183.55	180.45	177.30	174.20	171.05	167.95	164.80	161.70	158.55
1969 - 1985	202.40	187.90	186.35	183.20	180.10	176.95	173.85	170.70	167.60	164.45	161.35
1985 - 2001	205.20	190.70	189.15	186.00	182.90	179.75	176.65	173.50	170.40	167.25	164.15
2001 - 2017	208.00	193.50	191.90	188.80	185.65	182.55	179.40	176.30	173.15	170.05	166.90
2017 - 2033	210.75	196.25	194.70	191.60	188.45	185.35	182.20	179.10	175.95	172.85	169.70
2033 - 2049	213.55	199.05	197.50	194.35	191.25	188.10	185.00	181.85	178.75	175.60	172.50
2049 - 2065	216.35	201.85	200.25	197.15	194.00	190.90	187.75	184.65	181.50	178.40	175.25
2065 - 2081	219.15	204.60	203.05	199.95	196.80	193.70	190.55	187.45	184.30	181.20	178.05
2081 - 2097	221.90	207.40	205.85	202.70	199.60	196.45	193.35	190.20	187.10	183.95	180.85
2097 - 2113	224.70	210.20	208.65	205.50	202.40	199.25	196.15	193.00	189.90	186.75	183.65
2113 - 2129	227.50	213.00	211.40	208.30	205.15	202.05	198.90	195.80	192.65	189.55	186.40
2129 - 2145	230.25	215.75	214.20	211.10	207.95	204.85	201.70	198.60	195.45	192.30	189.20
2145 - 2161	233.05	218.55	217.00	213.85	210.75	207.60	204.50	201.35	198.25	195.10	192.00
2161 - 2177	235.85	221.35	219.75	216.65	213.50	210.40	207.25	204.15	201.00	197.90	194.75
2177 - 2193	238.65	224.10	222.55	219.45	216.30	213.20	210.05	206.95	203.80	200.70	197.55
2193 - 2209	241.40	226.90	225.35	222.20	219.10	215.95	212.85	209.70	206.60	203.45	200.35
2209 - 2225	244.20	229.70	228.15	225.00	221.90	218.75	215.65	212.50	209.40	206.25	203.15
2225 - 2241	247.00	232.50	230.90	227.80	224.65	221.55	218.40	215.30	212.15	209.05	205.90
2241 - 2257	249.75	235.25	233.70	230.60	227.45	224.30	221.20	218.05	214.95	211.80	208.70
2257 - 2273	252.55	238.05	236.50	233.35	230.25	227.10	224.00	220.85	217.75	214.60	211.50
2273 - 2289	255.35	240.85	239.25	236.15	233.00	229.90	226.75	223.65	220.50	217.40	214.25
2289 - 2305	258.15	243.60	242.05	238.95	235.80	232.70	229.55	226.45	223.30	220.20	217.05
2305 - 2321	260.90	246.40	244.85	241.70	238.60	235.45	232.35	229.20	226.10	222.95	219.85
2321 - 2337	263.70	249.20	247.65	244.50	241.40	238.25	235.15	232.00	228.90	225.75	222.65
2337 - 2353	266.50	252.00	250.40	247.30	244.15	241.05	237.90	234.80	231.65	228.55	225.40
2353 - 2369	269.25	254.75	253.20	250.05	246.95	243.80	240.70	237.55	234.45	231.30	228.20
2369 - 2385	272.05	257.55	256.00	252.85	249.75	246.60	243.50	240.35	237.25	234.10	231.00
2385 - 2401	274.85	260.35	258.75	255.65	252.50	249.40	246.25	243.15	240.00	236.90	233.75
2401 - 2417	277.60	263.10	261.55	258.45	255.30	252.20	249.05	245.95	242.80	239.70	236.55
2417 - 2433	280.40	265.90	264.35	261.20	258.10	254.95	251.85	248.70	245.60	242.45	239.35
2433 - 2449	283.20	268.70	267.15	264.00	260.90	257.75	254.65	251.50	248.35	245.25	242.10
2449 - 2465	286.00	271.50	269.90	266.80	263.65	260.55	257.40	254.30	251.15	248.05	244.90
2465 - 2481	288.75	274.25	272.70	269.55	266.45	263.30	260.20	257.05	253.95	250.80	247.70
2481 - 2497	291.55	277.05	275.50	272.35	269.25	266.10	263.00	259.85	256.75	253.60	250.50
2497 - 2513	294.35	279.85	278.25	275.15	272.00	268.90	265.75	262.65	259.50	256.40	253.25
2513 - 2529	297.10	282.60	281.05	277.95	274.80	271.70	268.55	265.45	262.30	259.20	256.05
2529 - 2545	299.90	285.40	283.85	280.70	277.60	274.45	271.35	268.20	265.10	261.95	258.85
2545 - 2561	302.70	288.20	286.65	283.50	280.40	277.25	274.10	271.00	267.85	264.75	261.60
2561 - 2577	305.50	290.95	289.40	286.30	283.15	280.05	276.90	273.80	270.65	267.55	264.40
2577 - 2593	308.25	293.75	292.20	289.05	285.95	282.80	279.70	276.55	273.45	270.30	267.20

Ontario provincial tax deductions

Effective January 1, 2013

Weekly (52 pay periods a year)

Also look up the tax deductions in the federal table

Pay From - Less than	CC 0	CC 1	CC 2	CC 3	CC 4	CC 5	CC 6	CC 7	CC 8	CC 9	CC 10
2593 - 2613	311.40	296.90	295.35	292.20	289.10	285.95	282.85	279.70	276.60	273.45	270.35
2613 - 2633	314.90	300.40	298.80	295.70	292.55	289.45	286.30	283.20	280.05	276.95	273.80
2633 - 2653	318.35	303.85	302.30	299.15	296.05	292.90	289.80	286.65	283.55	280.40	277.30
2653 - 2673	321.85	307.35	305.80	302.65	299.55	296.40	293.30	290.15	287.00	283.90	280.75
2673 - 2693	325.35	310.80	309.25	306.15	303.00	299.90	296.75	293.65	290.50	287.40	284.25
2693 - 2713	328.80	314.30	312.75	309.60	306.50	303.35	300.25	297.10	294.00	290.85	287.75
2713 - 2733	332.30	317.80	316.20	313.10	309.95	306.85	303.70	300.60	297.45	294.35	291.20
2733 - 2753	335.75	321.25	319.70	316.60	313.45	310.35	307.20	304.10	300.95	297.85	294.70
2753 - 2773	339.25	324.75	323.20	320.05	316.95	313.80	310.70	307.55	304.45	301.30	298.20
2773 - 2793	342.75	328.25	326.65	323.55	320.40	317.30	314.15	311.05	307.90	304.80	301.65
2793 - 2813	346.20	331.70	330.15	327.00	323.90	320.75	317.65	314.50	311.40	308.25	305.15
2813 - 2833	349.70	335.20	333.65	330.50	327.40	324.25	321.15	318.00	314.90	311.75	308.65
2833 - 2853	353.20	338.70	337.10	334.00	330.85	327.75	324.60	321.50	318.35	315.25	312.10
2853 - 2873	356.65	342.15	340.60	337.45	334.35	331.20	328.10	324.95	321.85	318.70	315.60
2873 - 2893	360.15	345.65	344.10	340.95	337.85	334.70	331.60	328.45	325.35	322.20	319.05
2893 - 2913	363.65	349.10	347.55	344.45	341.30	338.20	335.05	331.95	328.80	325.70	322.55
2913 - 2933	367.10	352.60	351.05	347.90	344.80	341.65	338.55	335.40	332.30	329.15	326.05
2933 - 2953	370.60	356.10	354.50	351.40	348.25	345.15	342.00	338.90	335.75	332.65	329.50
2953 - 2973	374.05	359.55	358.00	354.90	351.75	348.65	345.50	342.40	339.25	336.15	333.00
2973 - 2993	377.55	363.05	361.50	358.35	355.25	352.10	349.00	345.85	342.75	339.60	336.50
2993 - 3013	381.05	366.55	364.95	361.85	358.70	355.60	352.45	349.35	346.20	343.10	339.95
3013 - 3033	384.50	370.00	368.45	365.35	362.20	359.10	355.95	352.80	349.70	346.55	343.45
3033 - 3053	388.00	373.50	371.95	368.80	365.70	362.55	359.45	356.30	353.20	350.05	346.95
3053 - 3073	391.50	377.00	375.40	372.30	369.15	366.05	362.90	359.80	356.65	353.55	350.40
3073 - 3093	394.95	380.45	378.90	375.75	372.65	369.50	366.40	363.25	360.15	357.00	353.90
3093 - 3113	398.45	383.95	382.40	379.25	376.15	373.00	369.90	366.75	363.65	360.50	357.40
3113 - 3133	401.95	387.40	385.85	382.75	379.60	376.50	373.35	370.25	367.10	364.00	360.85
3133 - 3153	405.40	390.90	389.35	386.20	383.10	379.95	376.85	373.70	370.60	367.45	364.35
3153 - 3173	408.90	394.40	392.80	389.70	386.55	383.45	380.30	377.20	374.05	370.95	367.80
3173 - 3193	412.35	397.85	396.30	393.20	390.05	386.95	383.80	380.70	377.55	374.45	371.30
3193 - 3213	415.85	401.35	399.80	396.65	393.55	390.40	387.30	384.15	381.05	377.90	374.80
3213 - 3233	419.35	404.85	403.25	400.15	397.00	393.90	390.75	387.65	384.50	381.40	378.25
3233 - 3253	422.80	408.30	406.75	403.65	400.50	397.40	394.25	391.15	388.00	384.85	381.75
3253 - 3273	426.30	411.80	410.25	407.10	404.00	400.85	397.75	394.60	391.50	388.35	385.25
3273 - 3293	429.80	415.30	413.70	410.60	407.45	404.35	401.20	398.10	394.95	391.85	388.70
3293 - 3313	433.25	418.75	417.20	414.05	410.95	407.80	404.70	401.55	398.45	395.30	392.20
3313 - 3333	436.75	422.25	420.70	417.55	414.45	411.30	408.20	405.05	401.95	398.80	395.70
3333 - 3353	440.25	425.70	424.15	421.05	417.90	414.80	411.65	408.55	405.40	402.30	399.15
3353 - 3373	443.70	429.20	427.65	424.50	421.40	418.25	415.15	412.00	408.90	405.75	402.65
3373 - 3393	447.20	432.70	431.15	428.00	424.90	421.75	418.60	415.50	412.35	409.25	406.10
3393 - 3413	450.70	436.15	434.60	431.50	428.35	425.25	422.10	419.00	415.85	412.75	409.60
3413 - 3433	454.15	439.65	438.10	434.95	431.85	428.70	425.60	422.45	419.35	416.20	413.10
3433 - 3453	457.65	443.15	441.55	438.45	435.30	432.20	429.05	425.95	422.80	419.70	416.55
3453 - 3473	461.10	446.60	445.05	441.95	438.80	435.70	432.55	429.45	426.30	423.20	420.05
3473 - 3493	464.60	450.10	448.55	445.40	442.30	439.15	436.05	432.90	429.80	426.65	423.55
3493 - 3513	468.10	453.60	452.00	448.90	445.75	442.65	439.50	436.40	433.25	430.15	427.00
3513 - 3533	471.55	457.05	455.50	452.35	449.25	446.10	443.00	439.85	436.75	433.60	430.50
3533 - 3553	475.05	460.55	459.00	455.85	452.75	449.60	446.50	443.35	440.25	437.10	434.00
3553 - 3573	478.55	464.05	462.45	459.35	456.20	453.10	449.95	446.85	443.70	440.60	437.45
3573 - 3593	482.00	467.50	465.95	462.80	459.70	456.55	453.45	450.30	447.20	444.05	440.95
3593 - 3613	485.50	471.00	469.45	466.30	463.20	460.05	456.95	453.80	450.65	447.55	444.40
3613 - 3633	489.00	474.45	472.90	469.80	466.65	463.55	460.40	457.30	454.15	451.05	447.90
3633 - 3653	492.45	477.95	476.40	473.25	470.15	467.00	463.90	460.75	457.65	454.50	451.40
3653 - 3673	495.95	481.45	479.85	476.75	473.60	470.50	467.35	464.25	461.10	458.00	454.85
3673 - 3693	499.40	484.90	483.35	480.25	477.10	474.00	470.85	467.75	464.60	461.50	458.35

E-6

Appendix 9-2—Simulated Canada Pension Plan Contributions

Weekly (52 Pay periods a year)

Page 1 of 2

Students are advised to use this table for classroom purposes only. Although accurate for 2013, it has fewer categories of pay amounts than the official table.

Pay				Pay				Pay				Pay				Pay			
From		To	CPP	From		To	CPP	From		To	CPP	From		To	CPP	From		To	CPP
-	~	67.30	-	134.01	~	135.00	3.33	206.01	~	207.00	6.89	278.01	~	279.00	10.45	350.01	~	351.00	14.02
67.31	~	67.61	0.01	135.01	~	136.00	3.38	207.01	~	208.00	6.94	279.01	~	280.00	10.50	351.01	~	352.00	14.07
67.62	~	67.83	0.02	136.01	~	137.00	3.43	208.01	~	209.00	6.99	280.01	~	281.00	10.55	352.01	~	353.00	14.12
67.84	~	68.04	0.03	137.01	~	138.00	3.47	209.01	~	210.00	7.04	281.01	~	282.00	10.60	353.01	~	354.00	14.17
68.05	~	68.25	0.04	138.01	~	139.00	3.52	210.01	~	211.00	7.09	282.01	~	283.00	10.65	354.01	~	355.00	14.22
68.26	~	68.47	0.05	139.01	~	140.00	3.57	211.01	~	212.00	7.14	283.01	~	284.00	10.70	355.01	~	356.00	14.27
68.48	~	68.68	0.06	140.01	~	141.00	3.62	212.01	~	213.00	7.19	284.01	~	285.00	10.75	356.01	~	357.00	14.32
68.69	~	68.89	0.07	141.01	~	142.00	3.67	213.01	~	214.00	7.24	285.01	~	286.00	10.80	357.01	~	358.00	14.36
68.90	~	69.10	0.08	142.01	~	143.00	3.72	214.01	~	215.00	7.29	286.01	~	287.00	10.85	358.01	~	359.00	14.41
69.11	~	70.00	0.11	143.01	~	144.00	3.77	215.01	~	216.00	7.34	287.01	~	288.00	10.90	359.01	~	360.00	14.46
71.01	~	72.00	0.21	144.01	~	145.00	3.82	216.01	~	217.00	7.39	288.01	~	289.00	10.95	360.01	~	361.00	14.51
72.01	~	73.00	0.26	145.01	~	146.00	3.87	217.01	~	218.00	7.43	289.01	~	290.00	11.00	361.01	~	362.00	14.56
73.01	~	74.00	0.31	146.01	~	147.00	3.92	218.01	~	219.00	7.48	290.01	~	291.00	11.05	362.01	~	363.00	14.61
74.01	~	75.00	0.36	147.01	~	148.00	3.97	219.01	~	220.00	7.53	291.01	~	292.00	11.10	363.01	~	364.00	14.66
75.01	~	76.00	0.41	148.01	~	149.00	4.02	220.01	~	221.00	7.58	292.01	~	293.00	11.15	364.01	~	365.00	14.71
76.01	~	77.00	0.46	149.01	~	150.00	4.07	221.01	~	222.00	7.63	293.01	~	294.00	11.20	365.01	~	366.00	14.76
77.01	~	78.00	0.50	150.01	~	151.00	4.12	222.01	~	223.00	7.68	294.01	~	295.00	11.25	366.01	~	367.00	14.81
78.01	~	80.00	0.58	151.01	~	152.00	4.17	223.01	~	224.00	7.73	295.01	~	296.00	11.30	367.01	~	368.00	14.86
80.01	~	81.00	0.65	152.01	~	153.00	4.22	224.01	~	225.00	7.78	296.01	~	297.00	11.35	368.01	~	369.00	14.91
81.01	~	82.00	0.70	153.01	~	154.00	4.27	225.01	~	226.00	7.83	297.01	~	298.00	11.39	369.01	~	370.00	14.96
82.01	~	83.00	0.75	154.01	~	155.00	4.32	226.01	~	227.00	7.88	298.01	~	299.00	11.44	370.01	~	371.00	15.01
83.01	~	84.00	0.80	155.01	~	156.00	4.37	227.01	~	228.00	7.93	299.01	~	300.00	11.49	371.01	~	372.00	15.06
84.01	~	85.00	0.85	156.01	~	157.00	4.42	228.01	~	229.00	7.98	300.01	~	301.00	11.54	372.01	~	373.00	15.11
85.01	~	86.00	0.90	157.01	~	158.00	4.46	229.01	~	230.00	8.03	301.01	~	302.00	11.59	373.01	~	374.00	15.16
86.01	~	87.00	0.95	158.01	~	159.00	4.51	230.01	~	231.00	8.08	302.01	~	303.00	11.64	374.01	~	375.00	15.21
87.01	~	88.00	1.00	159.01	~	160.00	4.56	231.01	~	232.00	8.13	303.01	~	304.00	11.69	375.01	~	376.00	15.26
88.01	~	89.00	1.05	160.01	~	161.00	4.61	232.01	~	233.00	8.18	304.01	~	305.00	11.74	376.01	~	377.00	15.31
89.01	~	90.00	1.10	161.01	~	162.00	4.66	233.01	~	234.00	8.23	305.01	~	306.00	11.79	377.01	~	378.00	15.35
90.01	~	91.00	1.15	162.01	~	163.00	4.71	234.01	~	235.00	8.28	306.01	~	307.00	11.84	378.01	~	379.00	15.40
91.01	~	92.00	1.20	163.01	~	164.00	4.76	235.01	~	236.00	8.33	307.01	~	308.00	11.89	379.01	~	380.00	15.45
92.01	~	93.00	1.25	164.01	~	165.00	4.81	236.01	~	237.00	8.38	308.01	~	309.00	11.94	380.01	~	381.00	15.50
93.01	~	94.00	1.30	165.01	~	166.00	4.86	237.01	~	238.00	8.42	309.01	~	310.00	11.99	381.01	~	382.00	15.55
94.01	~	95.00	1.35	166.01	~	167.00	4.91	238.01	~	239.00	8.47	310.01	~	311.00	12.04	382.01	~	383.00	15.60
95.01	~	96.00	1.40	167.01	~	168.00	4.96	239.01	~	240.00	8.52	311.01	~	312.00	12.09	383.01	~	384.00	15.65
96.01	~	97.00	1.45	168.01	~	169.00	5.01	240.01	~	241.00	8.57	312.01	~	313.00	12.14	384.01	~	385.00	15.70
97.01	~	98.00	1.49	169.01	~	170.00	5.06	241.01	~	242.00	8.62	313.01	~	314.00	12.19	385.01	~	386.00	15.75
98.01	~	99.00	1.54	170.01	~	171.00	5.11	242.01	~	243.00	8.67	314.01	~	315.00	12.24	386.01	~	387.00	15.80
99.01	~	100.00	1.59	171.01	~	172.00	5.16	243.01	~	244.00	8.72	315.01	~	316.00	12.29	387.01	~	388.00	15.85
100.01	~	101.00	1.64	172.01	~	173.00	5.21	244.01	~	245.00	8.77	316.01	~	317.00	12.34	388.01	~	389.00	15.90
101.01	~	102.00	1.69	173.01	~	174.00	5.26	245.01	~	246.00	8.82	317.01	~	318.00	12.38	389.01	~	390.00	15.95
102.01	~	103.00	1.74	174.01	~	175.00	5.31	246.01	~	247.00	8.87	318.01	~	319.00	12.43	390.01	~	391.00	16.00
103.01	~	104.00	1.79	175.01	~	176.00	5.36	247.01	~	248.00	8.92	319.01	~	320.00	12.48	391.01	~	392.00	16.05
104.01	~	105.00	1.84	176.01	~	177.00	5.41	248.01	~	249.00	8.97	320.01	~	321.00	12.53	392.01	~	393.00	16.10
105.01	~	106.00	1.89	177.01	~	178.00	5.45	249.01	~	250.00	9.02	321.01	~	322.00	12.58	393.01	~	394.00	16.15
106.01	~	107.00	1.94	178.01	~	179.00	5.50	250.01	~	251.00	9.07	322.01	~	323.00	12.63	394.01	~	395.00	16.20
107.01	~	108.00	1.99	179.01	~	180.00	5.55	251.01	~	252.00	9.12	323.01	~	324.00	12.68	395.01	~	396.00	16.25
108.01	~	109.00	2.04	180.01	~	181.00	5.60	252.01	~	253.00	9.17	324.01	~	325.00	12.73	396.01	~	397.00	16.30
109.01	~	110.00	2.09	181.01	~	182.00	5.65	253.01	~	254.00	9.22	325.01	~	326.00	12.78	397.01	~	398.00	16.34
110.01	~	111.00	2.14	182.01	~	183.00	5.70	254.01	~	255.00	9.27	326.01	~	327.00	12.83	398.01	~	399.00	16.39
111.01	~	112.00	2.19	183.01	~	184.00	5.75	255.01	~	256.00	9.32	327.01	~	328.00	12.88	399.01	~	400.00	16.44
112.01	~	113.00	2.24	184.01	~	185.00	5.80	256.01	~	257.00	9.37	328.01	~	329.00	12.93	400.01	~	401.00	16.49
113.01	~	114.00	2.29	185.01	~	186.00	5.85	257.01	~	258.00	9.41	329.01	~	330.00	12.98	401.01	~	402.00	16.54
114.01	~	115.00	2.34	186.01	~	187.00	5.90	258.01	~	259.00	9.46	330.01	~	331.00	13.03	402.01	~	403.00	16.59
115.01	~	116.00	2.39	187.01	~	188.00	5.95	259.01	~	260.00	9.51	331.01	~	332.00	13.08	403.01	~	404.00	16.64
116.01	~	117.00	2.44	188.01	~	189.00	6.00	260.01	~	261.00	9.56	332.01	~	333.00	13.13	404.01	~	405.00	16.69
117.01	~	118.00	2.48	189.01	~	190.00	6.05	261.01	~	262.00	9.61	333.01	~	334.00	13.18	405.01	~	406.00	16.74
118.01	~	119.00	2.53	190.01	~	191.00	6.10	262.01	~	263.00	9.66	334.01	~	335.00	13.23	406.01	~	407.00	16.79
119.01	~	120.00	2.58	191.01	~	192.00	6.15	263.01	~	264.00	9.71	335.01	~	336.00	13.28	407.01	~	408.00	16.84
120.01	~	121.00	2.63	192.01	~	193.00	6.20	264.01	~	265.00	9.76	336.01	~	337.00	13.33	408.01	~	409.00	16.89
121.01	~	122.00	2.68	193.01	~	194.00	6.25	265.01	~	266.00	9.81	337.01	~	338.00	13.37	409.01	~	410.00	16.94
122.01	~	123.00	2.73	194.01	~	195.00	6.30	266.01	~	267.00	9.86	338.01	~	339.00	13.42	410.01	~	411.00	16.99
123.01	~	124.00	2.78	195.01	~	196.00	6.35	267.01	~	268.00	9.91	339.01	~	340.00	13.47	411.01	~	412.00	17.04
124.01	~	125.00	2.83	196.01	~	197.00	6.40	268.01	~	269.00	9.96	340.01	~	341.00	13.52	412.01	~	413.00	17.09
125.01	~	126.00	2.88	197.01	~	198.00	6.44	269.01	~	270.00	10.01	341.01	~	342.00	13.57	413.01	~	414.00	17.14
126.01	~	127.00	2.93	198.01	~	199.00	6.49	270.01	~	271.00	10.06	342.01	~	343.00	13.62	414.01	~	415.00	17.19
127.01	~	128.00	2.98	199.01	~	200.00	6.54	271.01	~	272.00	10.11	343.01	~	344.00	13.67	415.01	~	416.00	17.24
128.01	~	129.00	3.03	200.01	~	201.00	6.59	272.01	~	273.00	10.16	344.01	~	345.00	13.72	416.01	~	417.00	17.29
129.01	~	130.00	3.08	201.01	~	202.00	6.64	273.01	~	274.00	10.21	345.01	~	346.00	13.77	417.01	~	418.00	17.33
130.01	~	131.00	3.13	202.01	~	203.00	6.69	274.01	~	275.00	10.26	346.01	~	347.00	13.82	418.01	~	419.00	17.38
131.01	~	132.00	3.18	203.01	~	204.00	6.74	275.01	~	276.00	10.31	347.01	~	348.00	13.87	419.01	~	420.00	17.43
132.01	~	133.00	3.23	204.01	~	205.00	6.79	276.01	~	277.00	10.36	348.01	~	349.00	13.92	420.01	~	421.00	17.48
133.01	~	134.00	3.28	205.01	~	206.00	6.84	277.01	~	278.00	10.40	349.01	~	350.00	13.97	421.01	~	422.00	17.53

Maximum CPP contributions for the 2013 year total $2,356.20. This will probably increase from year to year.

Simulated Canada Pension Plan Contributions

Weekly (52 Pay periods a year) Page 2 of 2

Students are advised to use this table for classroom purposes only. Although accurate for 2013, it has fewer categories of pay amounts than the official table.

Pay				Pay				Pay				Pay				Pay			
From		To	CPP	From		To	CPP	From		To	CPP	From		To	CPP	From		To	CPP
422.01	~	423.00	17.58	495.01	~	496.00	21.20	636.01	~	638.00	28.20	782.01	~	784.00	35.43	1,120.01	~	1,125.00	52.23
423.01	~	424.00	17.63	496.01	~	497.00	21.25	638.01	~	640.00	28.30	784.01	~	786.00	35.53	1,125.01	~	1,130.00	52.48
424.01	~	425.00	17.68	497.01	~	498.00	21.29	640.01	~	642.00	28.40	786.01	~	788.00	35.63	1,130.01	~	1,135.00	52.73
425.01	~	426.00	17.73	498.01	~	499.00	21.34	642.01	~	644.00	28.50	788.01	~	790.00	35.72	1,135.01	~	1,140.00	52.97
426.01	~	427.00	17.78	499.01	~	500.00	21.39	644.01	~	646.00	28.60	790.01	~	792.00	35.82	1,140.01	~	1,145.00	53.22
427.01	~	428.00	17.83	500.01	~	502.00	21.47	646.01	~	648.00	28.70	792.01	~	794.00	35.92	1,145.01	~	1,150.00	53.47
428.01	~	429.00	17.88	502.01	~	504.00	21.57	648.01	~	650.00	28.79	794.01	~	796.00	36.02	1,150.01	~	1,155.00	53.72
429.01	~	430.00	17.93	504.01	~	506.00	21.67	650.01	~	652.00	28.89	796.01	~	798.00	36.12	1,155.01	~	1,160.00	53.96
430.01	~	431.00	17.98	506.01	~	508.00	21.77	652.01	~	654.00	28.99	798.01	~	800.00	36.22	1,160.01	~	1,165.00	54.21
431.01	~	432.00	18.03	508.01	~	510.00	21.86	654.01	~	656.00	29.09	800.01	~	805.00	36.39	1,165.01	~	1,170.00	54.46
432.01	~	433.00	18.08	510.01	~	512.00	21.96	656.01	~	658.00	29.19	805.01	~	810.00	36.64	1,170.01	~	1,175.00	54.71
433.01	~	434.00	18.13	512.01	~	514.00	22.06	658.01	~	660.00	29.29	810.01	~	815.00	36.89	1,175.01	~	1,180.00	54.95
434.01	~	435.00	18.18	514.01	~	516.00	22.16	660.01	~	662.00	29.39	815.01	~	820.00	37.13	1,180.01	~	1,185.00	55.20
435.01	~	436.00	18.23	516.01	~	518.00	22.26	662.01	~	664.00	29.48	820.01	~	825.00	37.38	1,185.01	~	1,190.00	55.45
436.01	~	437.00	18.28	518.01	~	520.00	22.36	664.01	~	666.00	29.59	825.01	~	830.00	37.63	1,190.01	~	1,195.00	55.70
437.01	~	438.00	18.32	520.01	~	522.00	22.46	666.01	~	668.00	29.69	830.01	~	835.00	37.88	1,195.01	~	1,200.00	55.94
438.01	~	439.00	18.37	522.01	~	524.00	22.56	668.01	~	670.00	29.78	835.01	~	840.00	38.12	1,200.01	~	1,205.00	56.19
439.01	~	440.00	18.42	524.01	~	526.00	22.66	670.01	~	672.00	29.88	840.01	~	845.00	38.37	1,205.01	~	1,210.00	56.44
440.01	~	441.00	18.47	526.01	~	528.00	22.76	672.01	~	674.00	29.98	845.01	~	850.00	38.62	1,210.01	~	1,215.00	56.69
441.01	~	442.00	18.52	528.01	~	530.00	22.85	674.01	~	676.00	30.08	850.01	~	855.00	38.87	1,215.01	~	1,220.00	56.93
442.01	~	443.00	18.57	530.01	~	532.00	22.95	676.01	~	678.00	30.18	855.01	~	860.00	39.11	1,220.01	~	1,225.00	57.18
443.01	~	444.00	18.62	532.01	~	534.00	23.05	678.01	~	680.00	30.28	860.01	~	865.00	39.36	1,225.01	~	1,230.00	57.43
444.01	~	445.00	18.67	534.01	~	536.00	23.15	680.01	~	682.00	30.38	865.01	~	870.00	39.61	1,230.01	~	1,235.00	57.68
445.01	~	446.00	18.72	536.01	~	538.00	23.25	682.01	~	684.00	30.48	870.01	~	875.00	39.86	1,235.01	~	1,240.00	57.92
446.01	~	447.00	18.77	538.01	~	540.00	23.35	684.01	~	686.00	30.58	875.01	~	880.00	40.10	1,240.01	~	1,245.00	58.17
447.01	~	448.00	18.82	540.01	~	542.00	23.45	686.01	~	688.00	30.68	880.01	~	885.00	40.35	1,245.01	~	1,250.00	58.42
448.01	~	449.00	18.87	542.01	~	544.00	23.55	688.01	~	690.00	30.77	885.01	~	890.00	40.60	1,250.01	~	1,255.00	58.67
449.01	~	450.00	18.92	544.01	~	546.00	23.65	690.01	~	692.00	30.87	890.01	~	895.00	40.85	1,255.01	~	1,260.00	58.91
450.01	~	451.00	18.97	546.01	~	548.00	23.75	692.01	~	694.00	30.97	895.01	~	900.00	41.09	1,260.01	~	1,265.00	59.16
451.01	~	452.00	19.02	548.01	~	550.00	23.84	694.01	~	696.00	31.07	900.01	~	905.00	41.34	1,265.01	~	1,270.00	59.41
452.01	~	453.00	19.07	550.01	~	552.00	23.94	696.01	~	698.00	31.17	905.01	~	910.00	41.59	1,270.01	~	1,275.00	59.66
453.01	~	454.00	19.12	552.01	~	554.00	24.04	698.01	~	700.00	31.27	910.01	~	915.00	41.84	1,275.01	~	1,280.00	59.90
454.01	~	455.00	19.17	554.01	~	556.00	24.14	700.01	~	702.00	31.37	915.01	~	920.00	42.08	1,280.01	~	1,285.00	60.15
455.01	~	456.00	19.22	556.01	~	558.00	24.24	702.01	~	704.00	31.47	920.01	~	925.00	42.33	1,285.01	~	1,290.00	60.40
456.01	~	457.00	19.27	558.01	~	560.00	24.34	704.01	~	706.00	31.57	925.01	~	930.00	42.58	1,290.01	~	1,295.00	60.65
457.01	~	458.00	19.31	560.01	~	562.00	24.44	706.01	~	708.00	31.67	930.01	~	935.00	42.83	1,295.01	~	1,300.00	60.89
458.01	~	459.00	19.36	562.01	~	564.00	24.54	708.01	~	710.00	31.76	935.01	~	940.00	43.07	1,300.01	~	1,305.00	61.14
459.01	~	460.00	19.41	564.01	~	566.00	24.64	710.01	~	712.00	31.86	940.01	~	945.00	43.32	1,305.01	~	1,310.00	61.39
460.01	~	461.00	19.46	566.01	~	568.00	24.74	712.01	~	714.00	31.96	945.01	~	950.00	43.57	1,310.01	~	1,315.00	61.64
461.01	~	462.00	19.51	568.01	~	570.00	24.83	714.01	~	716.00	32.06	950.01	~	955.00	43.82	1,315.01	~	1,320.00	61.88
462.01	~	463.00	19.56	570.01	~	572.00	24.93	716.01	~	718.00	32.16	955.01	~	960.00	44.06	1,320.01	~	1,325.00	62.13
463.01	~	464.00	19.61	572.01	~	574.00	25.03	718.01	~	720.00	32.26	960.01	~	965.00	44.31	1,325.01	~	1,330.00	62.38
464.01	~	465.00	19.66	574.01	~	576.00	25.13	720.01	~	722.00	32.36	965.01	~	970.00	44.56	1,330.01	~	1,335.00	62.63
465.01	~	466.00	19.71	576.01	~	578.00	25.23	722.01	~	724.00	32.46	970.01	~	975.00	44.81	1,335.01	~	1,340.00	62.87
466.01	~	467.00	19.76	578.01	~	580.00	25.33	724.01	~	726.00	32.56	975.01	~	980.00	45.05	1,340.01	~	1,345.00	63.12
467.01	~	468.00	19.81	580.01	~	582.00	25.43	726.01	~	728.00	32.66	980.01	~	985.00	45.30	1,345.01	~	1,350.00	63.37
468.01	~	469.00	19.86	582.01	~	584.00	25.53	728.01	~	730.00	32.75	985.01	~	990.00	45.55	1,350.01	~	1,355.00	63.62
469.01	~	470.00	19.91	584.01	~	586.00	25.63	730.01	~	732.00	32.85	990.01	~	995.00	45.80	1,355.01	~	1,360.00	63.86
470.01	~	471.00	19.96	586.01	~	588.00	25.73	732.01	~	734.00	32.95	995.01	~	1,000.00	46.04	1,360.01	~	1,365.00	64.11
471.01	~	472.00	20.01	588.01	~	590.00	25.82	734.01	~	736.00	33.05	1,000.01	~	1,005.00	46.29	1,365.01	~	1,370.00	64.36
472.01	~	473.00	20.06	590.01	~	592.00	25.92	736.01	~	738.00	33.15	1,005.01	~	1,010.00	46.54	1,370.01	~	1,375.00	64.61
473.01	~	474.00	20.11	592.01	~	594.00	26.02	738.01	~	740.00	33.25	1,010.01	~	1,015.00	46.79	1,375.01	~	1,380.00	64.85
474.01	~	475.00	20.16	594.01	~	596.00	26.12	740.01	~	742.00	33.35	1,015.01	~	1,020.00	47.03	1,380.01	~	1,385.00	65.10
475.01	~	476.00	20.21	596.01	~	598.00	26.22	742.01	~	744.00	33.45	1,020.01	~	1,025.00	47.28	1,385.01	~	1,390.00	65.35
476.01	~	477.00	20.26	598.01	~	600.00	26.32	744.01	~	746.00	33.55	1,025.01	~	1,030.00	47.53	1,390.01	~	1,395.00	65.60
477.01	~	478.00	20.30	600.01	~	602.00	26.42	746.01	~	748.00	33.65	1,030.01	~	1,035.00	47.78	1,395.01	~	1,400.00	65.84
478.01	~	479.00	20.35	602.01	~	604.00	26.52	748.01	~	750.00	33.74	1,035.01	~	1,040.00	48.02	1,400.01	~	1,405.00	66.09
479.01	~	480.00	20.40	604.01	~	606.00	26.62	750.01	~	752.00	33.84	1,040.01	~	1,045.00	48.27	1,405.01	~	1,410.00	66.34
480.01	~	481.00	20.45	606.01	~	608.00	26.72	752.01	~	754.00	33.94	1,045.01	~	1,050.00	48.52	1,410.01	~	1,415.00	66.59
481.01	~	482.00	20.50	608.01	~	610.00	26.81	754.01	~	756.00	34.04	1,050.01	~	1,055.00	48.77	1,415.01	~	1,420.00	66.83
482.01	~	483.00	20.55	610.01	~	612.00	26.91	756.01	~	758.00	34.14	1,055.01	~	1,060.00	49.01	1,420.01	~	1,425.00	67.08
483.01	~	484.00	20.60	612.01	~	614.00	27.01	758.01	~	760.00	34.24	1,060.01	~	1,065.00	49.26	1,425.01	~	1,430.00	67.33
484.01	~	485.00	20.65	614.01	~	616.00	27.11	760.01	~	762.00	34.34	1,065.01	~	1,070.00	49.51	1,430.01	~	1,435.00	67.58
485.01	~	486.00	20.70	616.01	~	618.00	27.21	762.01	~	764.00	34.44	1,070.01	~	1,075.00	49.76	1,435.01	~	1,440.00	67.82
486.01	~	487.00	20.75	618.01	~	620.00	27.31	764.01	~	766.00	34.54	1,075.01	~	1,080.00	50.00	1,440.01	~	1,445.00	68.07
487.01	~	488.00	20.80	620.01	~	622.00	27.41	766.01	~	768.00	34.64	1,080.01	~	1,085.00	50.25	1,445.01	~	1,450.00	68.32
488.01	~	489.00	20.85	622.01	~	624.00	27.51	768.01	~	770.00	34.73	1,085.01	~	1,090.00	50.50	1,450.01	~	1,455.00	68.57
489.01	~	490.00	20.90	624.01	~	626.00	27.61	770.01	~	772.00	34.83	1,090.01	~	1,095.00	50.75	1,455.01	~	1,460.00	68.81
490.01	~	491.00	20.95	626.01	~	628.00	27.71	772.01	~	774.00	34.93	1,095.01	~	1,100.00	50.99	1,460.01	~	1,465.00	69.06
491.01	~	492.00	21.00	628.01	~	630.00	27.80	774.01	~	776.00	35.03	1,100.01	~	1,105.00	51.24	1,465.01	~	1,470.00	69.31
492.01	~	493.00	21.05	630.01	~	632.00	27.90	776.01	~	778.00	35.13	1,105.01	~	1,110.00	51.49	1,470.01	~	1,475.00	69.56
493.01	~	494.00	21.10	632.01	~	634.00	28.00	778.01	~	780.00	35.23	1,110.01	~	1,115.00	51.74	1,475.01	~	1,480.00	69.80
494.01	~	495.00	21.15	634.01	~	636.00	28.10	780.01	~	782.00	35.33	1,115.01	~	1,120.00	51.98	1,480.01	~	1,485.00	70.05

Maximum CPP contributions for the 2013 year total $2,356.20. This will probably increase from year to year.

Appendix 9-3—Simulated Employment Insurance Premium Calculations

Any number of pay periods a year

Students are advised to use this table for classroom purposes only. Although accurate for 2013, it has fewer categories of Insurable Earnings than the official table.

Insurable Earnings From	To	EI Premium
- ~	0.68	0.01
0.69 ~	1.13	0.02
1.14 ~	1.59	0.03
1.60 ~	2.04	0.03
2.05 ~	2.49	0.04
2.50 ~	2.95	0.05
2.96 ~	3.40	0.06
3.41 ~	3.85	0.07
3.86 ~	4.31	0.08
4.32 ~	4.77	0.09
4.78 ~	5.22	0.09
5.23 ~	5.68	0.10
5.69 ~	6.13	0.11
6.14 ~	6.59	0.12
6.60 ~	7.04	0.13
7.05 ~	7.49	0.14
7.50 ~	7.95	0.15
7.96 ~	8.40	0.15
8.41 ~	8.86	0.16
8.87 ~	9.31	0.17
9.32 ~	9.77	0.18
9.78 ~	10.22	0.19
10.23 ~	10.68	0.20
10.69 ~	11.13	0.21
11.14 ~	11.59	0.21
11.60 ~	12.04	0.22
12.05 ~	12.50	0.23
12.51 ~	12.95	0.24
12.96 ~	13.41	0.25
13.42 ~	13.86	0.26
13.87 ~	14.32	0.26
14.33 ~	14.77	0.27
14.78 ~	15.23	0.28
15.24 ~	15.68	0.29
15.69 ~	16.14	0.30
16.15 ~	16.59	0.31
16.60 ~	17.05	0.32
17.06 ~	17.50	0.32
17.51 ~	17.96	0.33
17.97 ~	18.41	0.34
18.42 ~	18.87	0.35
18.88 ~	19.32	0.36
19.33 ~	19.78	0.37
19.79 ~	20.23	0.38
20.24 ~	20.69	0.38
20.70 ~	21.14	0.39
21.15 ~	21.60	0.40
21.61 ~	22.05	0.41
22.06 ~	22.51	0.42
22.52 ~	22.96	0.43
22.97 ~	23.42	0.44
23.43 ~	23.87	0.44
23.88 ~	24.33	0.45
24.34 ~	24.78	0.46
24.79 ~	25.24	0.47
25.25 ~	25.69	0.48
25.70 ~	26.15	0.49
26.16 ~	26.60	0.50
26.61 ~	27.06	0.50
27.07 ~	27.51	0.51
27.52 ~	27.97	0.52
27.98 ~	28.42	0.53
28.43 ~	28.88	0.54
28.89 ~	29.33	0.55
29.34 ~	29.79	0.56
29.80 ~	30.24	0.56
30.25 ~	30.70	0.57
30.71 ~	31.15	0.58
31.16 ~	31.61	0.59
31.62 ~	32.06	0.60
32.07 ~	32.52	0.61
32.53 ~	32.97	0.62

Insurable Earnings From	To	EI Premium
32.98 ~	33.50	0.62
33.51 ~	34.50	0.64
34.51 ~	35.50	0.66
35.51 ~	36.50	0.68
36.51 ~	37.50	0.70
37.51 ~	38.50	0.71
38.51 ~	39.50	0.73
39.51 ~	40.50	0.75
40.51 ~	41.50	0.77
41.51 ~	42.50	0.79
42.51 ~	43.50	0.81
43.51 ~	44.50	0.83
44.51 ~	45.50	0.85
45.51 ~	46.50	0.86
46.51 ~	47.50	0.88
47.51 ~	48.50	0.90
48.51 ~	49.50	0.92
49.51 ~	50.50	0.94
50.51 ~	51.50	0.96
51.51 ~	52.50	0.98
52.51 ~	53.50	1.00
53.51 ~	54.50	1.02
54.51 ~	55.50	1.03
55.51 ~	56.50	1.05
56.51 ~	57.50	1.07
57.51 ~	58.50	1.09
58.51 ~	59.50	1.11
59.51 ~	60.50	1.13
60.51 ~	61.50	1.15
61.51 ~	62.50	1.17
62.51 ~	63.50	1.18
63.51 ~	64.50	1.20
64.51 ~	65.50	1.22
65.51 ~	66.50	1.24
66.51 ~	67.50	1.26
67.51 ~	68.50	1.28
68.51 ~	69.50	1.30
69.51 ~	70.50	1.32
70.51 ~	71.50	1.33
71.51 ~	72.50	1.35
72.51 ~	73.50	1.37
73.51 ~	74.50	1.39
74.51 ~	75.50	1.41
75.51 ~	76.50	1.43
76.51 ~	77.50	1.45
77.51 ~	78.50	1.47
78.51 ~	79.50	1.49
79.51 ~	80.50	1.50
80.51 ~	81.50	1.52
81.51 ~	82.50	1.54
82.51 ~	83.50	1.56
83.51 ~	84.50	1.58
84.51 ~	85.50	1.60
85.51 ~	86.50	1.62
86.51 ~	87.50	1.64
87.51 ~	88.50	1.65
88.51 ~	89.50	1.67
89.51 ~	90.50	1.69
90.51 ~	91.50	1.71
91.51 ~	92.50	1.73
92.51 ~	93.50	1.75
93.51 ~	94.50	1.77
94.51 ~	95.50	1.79
95.51 ~	96.50	1.80
96.51 ~	97.50	1.82
97.51 ~	98.50	1.84
98.51 ~	99.50	1.86
99.51 ~	100.50	1.88
100.51 ~	101.50	1.90
101.51 ~	102.50	1.92
102.51 ~	103.50	1.94
103.51 ~	104.50	1.96

Insurable Earnings From	To	EI Premium
104.51 ~	105.50	1.97
105.51 ~	106.50	1.99
106.51 ~	107.50	2.01
107.51 ~	108.50	2.03
108.51 ~	109.50	2.05
109.51 ~	110.50	2.07
110.51 ~	111.50	2.09
111.51 ~	112.50	2.11
112.51 ~	113.50	2.12
113.51 ~	114.50	2.14
114.51 ~	115.50	2.16
115.51 ~	116.50	2.18
116.51 ~	117.50	2.20
117.51 ~	118.50	2.22
118.51 ~	119.50	2.24
119.51 ~	120.50	2.26
120.51 ~	121.50	2.27
121.51 ~	122.50	2.29
122.51 ~	123.50	2.31
123.51 ~	124.50	2.33
124.51 ~	125.50	2.35
125.51 ~	126.50	2.37
126.51 ~	127.50	2.39
127.51 ~	128.50	2.41
128.51 ~	129.50	2.43
129.51 ~	130.50	2.44
130.51 ~	131.50	2.46
131.51 ~	132.50	2.48
132.51 ~	133.50	2.50
133.51 ~	134.50	2.52
134.51 ~	135.50	2.54
135.51 ~	136.50	2.56
136.51 ~	137.50	2.58
137.51 ~	138.50	2.59
138.51 ~	139.50	2.61
139.51 ~	140.50	2.63
140.51 ~	141.50	2.65
141.51 ~	142.50	2.67
142.51 ~	143.50	2.69
143.51 ~	144.50	2.71
144.51 ~	145.50	2.73
145.51 ~	146.50	2.74
146.51 ~	147.50	2.76
147.51 ~	148.50	2.78
148.51 ~	149.50	2.80
149.51 ~	150.50	2.82
150.51 ~	151.50	2.84
151.51 ~	152.50	2.86
152.51 ~	153.50	2.88
153.51 ~	154.50	2.90
154.51 ~	155.50	2.91
155.51 ~	156.50	2.93
156.51 ~	157.50	2.95
157.51 ~	158.50	2.97
158.51 ~	159.50	2.99
159.51 ~	160.50	3.01
160.51 ~	161.50	3.03
161.51 ~	162.50	3.05
162.51 ~	163.50	3.06
163.51 ~	164.50	3.08
164.51 ~	165.50	3.10
165.51 ~	166.50	3.12
166.51 ~	167.50	3.14
167.51 ~	168.50	3.16
168.51 ~	169.50	3.18
169.51 ~	170.50	3.20
170.51 ~	171.50	3.21
171.51 ~	172.50	3.23
172.51 ~	173.50	3.25
173.51 ~	174.50	3.27
174.51 ~	175.50	3.29
175.51 ~	176.50	3.31

Insurable Earnings From	To	EI Premium
176.51 ~	177.50	3.33
177.51 ~	178.50	3.35
178.51 ~	179.50	3.37
179.51 ~	180.50	3.38
180.51 ~	181.50	3.40
181.51 ~	182.50	3.42
182.51 ~	183.50	3.44
183.51 ~	184.50	3.46
184.51 ~	185.50	3.48
185.51 ~	186.50	3.50
186.51 ~	187.50	3.52
187.51 ~	188.50	3.53
188.51 ~	189.50	3.55
189.51 ~	190.50	3.57
190.51 ~	191.50	3.59
191.51 ~	192.50	3.61
192.51 ~	193.50	3.63
193.51 ~	194.50	3.65
194.51 ~	195.50	3.67
195.51 ~	196.50	3.68
196.51 ~	197.50	3.70
197.51 ~	198.50	3.72
198.51 ~	199.50	3.74
199.51 ~	200.50	3.76
200.51 ~	201.50	3.78
201.51 ~	202.50	3.80
202.51 ~	203.50	3.82
203.51 ~	204.50	3.84
204.51 ~	205.50	3.85
205.51 ~	206.50	3.87
206.51 ~	207.50	3.89
207.51 ~	208.50	3.91
208.51 ~	209.50	3.93
209.51 ~	210.50	3.95
210.51 ~	211.50	3.97
211.51 ~	212.50	3.99
212.51 ~	213.50	4.00
213.51 ~	214.50	4.02
214.51 ~	215.50	4.04
215.51 ~	216.50	4.06
216.51 ~	217.50	4.08
217.51 ~	218.50	4.10
218.51 ~	219.50	4.12
219.51 ~	220.50	4.14
220.51 ~	221.50	4.15
221.51 ~	222.50	4.17
222.51 ~	223.50	4.19
223.51 ~	224.50	4.21
224.51 ~	225.50	4.23
225.51 ~	226.50	4.25
226.51 ~	227.50	4.27
227.51 ~	228.50	4.29
228.51 ~	229.50	4.31
229.51 ~	230.50	4.32
230.51 ~	231.50	4.34
231.51 ~	232.50	4.36
232.51 ~	233.50	4.38
233.51 ~	234.50	4.40
234.51 ~	235.50	4.42
235.51 ~	236.50	4.44
236.51 ~	237.50	4.46
237.51 ~	238.50	4.47
238.51 ~	239.50	4.49
239.51 ~	240.50	4.51
240.51 ~	241.50	4.53
241.51 ~	242.50	4.55
242.51 ~	243.50	4.57
243.51 ~	244.50	4.59
244.51 ~	245.50	4.61
245.51 ~	246.50	4.62
246.51 ~	247.50	4.64
247.51 ~	248.50	4.66

Insurable Earnings From	To	EI Premium
248.51 ~	249.50	4.68
249.51 ~	250.50	4.70
250.51 ~	251.50	4.72
251.51 ~	252.50	4.74
252.51 ~	253.50	4.76
253.51 ~	254.50	4.78
254.51 ~	255.50	4.79
255.51 ~	256.50	4.81
256.51 ~	257.50	4.83
257.51 ~	258.50	4.85
258.51 ~	259.50	4.87
259.51 ~	260.50	4.89
260.51 ~	261.50	4.91
261.51 ~	262.50	4.93
262.51 ~	263.50	4.94
263.51 ~	264.50	4.96
264.51 ~	265.50	4.98
265.51 ~	266.50	5.00
266.51 ~	267.50	5.02
267.51 ~	268.50	5.04
268.51 ~	269.50	5.06
269.51 ~	270.50	5.08
270.51 ~	271.50	5.09
271.51 ~	272.50	5.11
272.51 ~	273.50	5.13
273.51 ~	274.50	5.15
274.51 ~	275.50	5.17
275.51 ~	276.50	5.19
276.51 ~	277.50	5.21
277.51 ~	278.50	5.23
278.51 ~	279.50	5.25
279.51 ~	280.50	5.26
280.51 ~	281.50	5.28
281.51 ~	282.50	5.30
282.51 ~	283.50	5.32
283.51 ~	284.50	5.34
284.51 ~	285.50	5.36
285.51 ~	286.50	5.38
286.51 ~	287.50	5.40
287.51 ~	288.50	5.41
288.51 ~	289.50	5.43
289.51 ~	290.50	5.45
290.51 ~	291.50	5.47
291.51 ~	292.50	5.49
292.51 ~	293.50	5.51
293.51 ~	294.50	5.53
294.51 ~	295.50	5.55
295.51 ~	296.50	5.56
296.51 ~	297.50	5.58
297.51 ~	298.50	5.60
298.51 ~	299.50	5.62
299.51 ~	300.50	5.64
300.51 ~	301.50	5.68
301.51 ~	302.50	5.68
302.51 ~	303.50	5.70
303.51 ~	304.50	5.72
304.51 ~	305.50	5.73
305.51 ~	306.50	5.75
306.51 ~	307.50	5.77
307.51 ~	308.50	5.79
308.51 ~	309.50	5.81
309.51 ~	310.50	5.83
310.51 ~	311.50	5.85
311.51 ~	312.50	5.87
312.51 ~	313.50	5.89
313.51 ~	314.50	5.90
314.51 ~	315.50	5.92
315.51 ~	316.50	5.94
316.51 ~	317.50	5.96
317.51 ~	318.50	5.98
318.51 ~	319.50	6.00
319.51 ~	320.50	6.02

Simulated Employment Insurance Premiums

Any number of pay periods a year

Students are advised to use this table for classroom purposes only. Although accurate for 2013, it has fewer categories of pay amounts than the official table.

Insurable Earnings From	To	EI Premium	Insurable Earnings From	To	EI Premium	Insurable Earnings From	To	EI Premium	Insurable Earnings From	To	EI Premium	Insurable Earnings From	To	EI Premium
320.51	321.50	6.03	436.51	438.50	8.23	582.56	584.50	10.97	728.51	730.50	13.71	946.51	949.50	17.82
321.51	322.50	6.05	438.51	440.50	8.26	584.51	586.50	11.01	730.51	733.50	13.76	949.51	954.50	17.90
322.51	323.50	6.07	440.51	442.50	8.30	586.51	588.50	11.05	733.51	736.50	13.82	954.51	959.50	17.99
323.51	324.50	6.09	442.51	444.50	8.34	588.51	590.50	11.08	736.51	739.50	13.87	959.51	964.50	18.09
324.51	325.50	6.11	444.51	446.50	8.38	590.51	592.50	11.12	739.51	742.50	13.93	964.51	969.50	18.18
325.51	326.50	6.13	446.51	448.50	8.41	592.51	594.50	11.16	742.51	745.50	13.99	969.51	974.50	18.27
326.51	327.50	6.15	448.51	450.50	8.45	594.51	596.50	11.20	745.51	748.50	14.04	974.51	979.50	18.37
327.51	328.50	6.17	450.51	452.50	8.49	596.51	598.50	11.23	748.51	751.50	14.10	979.51	984.50	18.46
328.51	329.50	6.19	452.51	454.50	8.53	598.51	600.50	11.27	751.51	754.50	14.16	984.51	989.50	18.56
329.51	330.50	6.20	454.51	456.50	8.56	600.51	602.50	11.31	754.51	757.50	14.21	989.51	994.50	18.65
330.51	331.50	6.22	456.51	458.50	8.60	602.51	604.50	11.35	757.51	760.50	14.27	994.51	999.50	18.74
331.51	332.50	6.24	458.51	460.50	8.64	604.51	606.50	11.38	760.51	763.50	14.33	999.51	1,004.50	18.84
332.51	333.50	6.26	460.51	462.50	8.68	606.51	608.50	11.42	763.51	766.50	14.38	1,004.51	1,009.50	18.93
333.51	334.50	6.28	462.51	464.50	8.71	608.51	610.50	11.46	766.51	769.50	14.44	1,009.51	1,014.50	19.03
334.51	335.50	6.30	464.51	466.50	8.75	610.51	612.50	11.50	769.51	772.50	14.49	1,014.51	1,019.50	19.12
335.51	336.50	6.32	466.51	468.50	8.79	612.51	614.50	11.53	772.51	775.50	14.55	1,019.51	1,024.50	19.21
336.51	337.50	6.34	468.51	470.50	8.83	614.51	616.50	11.57	775.51	778.50	14.61	1,024.51	1,029.50	19.31
337.51	338.50	6.35	470.51	472.50	8.86	616.51	618.50	11.61	778.51	781.50	14.66	1,029.51	1,034.50	19.40
338.51	339.50	6.37	472.51	474.50	8.90	618.51	620.50	11.65	781.51	784.50	14.72	1,034.51	1,039.50	19.50
339.51	340.50	6.39	474.51	476.50	8.94	620.51	622.50	11.68	784.51	787.50	14.78	1,039.51	1,044.50	19.59
340.51	341.50	6.41	476.51	478.50	8.98	622.51	624.50	11.72	787.51	790.50	14.83	1,044.51	1,049.50	19.68
341.51	342.50	6.43	478.51	480.50	9.01	624.51	626.50	11.76	790.51	793.50	14.89	1,049.51	1,054.50	19.78
342.51	343.50	6.45	480.51	482.50	9.05	626.51	628.50	11.80	793.51	796.50	14.95	1,054.51	1,059.50	19.87
343.51	344.50	6.47	482.51	484.50	9.09	628.51	630.50	11.83	796.51	799.50	15.00	1,059.51	1,064.50	19.97
344.51	345.50	6.49	484.51	486.50	9.13	630.51	632.50	11.87	799.51	802.50	15.06	1,064.51	1,069.50	20.06
345.51	346.50	6.50	486.51	488.50	9.17	632.51	634.50	11.91	802.51	805.50	15.12	1,069.51	1,074.50	20.15
346.51	347.50	6.52	488.51	490.50	9.20	634.51	636.50	11.95	805.51	808.50	15.17	1,074.51	1,079.50	20.25
347.51	348.50	6.54	490.51	492.50	9.24	636.51	638.50	11.99	808.51	811.50	15.23	1,079.51	1,084.50	20.34
348.51	349.50	6.56	492.51	494.50	9.28	638.51	640.50	12.02	811.51	814.50	15.28	1,084.51	1,089.50	20.44
349.51	350.50	6.58	494.51	496.50	9.32	640.51	642.50	12.06	814.51	817.50	15.34	1,089.51	1,094.50	20.53
350.51	352.50	6.61	496.51	498.50	9.35	642.51	644.50	12.10	817.51	820.50	15.40	1,094.51	1,099.50	20.62
352.51	354.50	6.65	498.51	500.50	9.39	644.51	646.50	12.14	820.51	823.50	15.45	1,099.51	1,104.50	20.72
354.51	356.50	6.68	500.51	502.50	9.43	646.51	648.50	12.17	823.51	826.50	15.51	1,104.51	1,109.50	20.81
356.51	358.50	6.72	502.51	504.50	9.47	648.51	650.50	12.21	826.51	829.50	15.57	1,109.51	1,114.50	20.91
358.51	360.50	6.76	504.51	506.50	9.50	650.51	652.50	12.29	829.51	832.50	15.62	1,114.51	1,119.50	21.00
360.51	362.50	6.80	506.51	508.50	9.54	652.51	654.50	12.32	832.51	835.50	15.68	1,119.51	1,124.50	21.09
362.51	364.50	6.83	508.51	510.50	9.58	654.51	656.50	12.36	835.51	838.50	15.74	1,124.51	1,129.50	21.19
364.51	366.50	6.87	510.51	512.50	9.62	656.51	658.50	12.40	838.51	841.50	15.79	1,129.51	1,134.50	21.29
366.51	368.50	6.91	512.51	514.50	9.65	658.51	660.50	12.44	841.51	844.50	15.85	1,134.51	1,139.50	21.38
368.51	370.50	6.95	514.51	516.50	9.69	660.51	662.50	12.47	844.51	847.50	15.90	1,139.51	1,144.50	21.47
370.51	372.50	6.98	516.51	518.50	9.73	662.51	664.50	12.51	847.51	850.50	15.96	1,144.51	1,149.50	21.56
372.51	374.50	7.02	518.51	520.50	9.77	664.51	666.50	12.55	850.51	853.50	16.02	1,149.51	1,154.50	21.66
374.51	376.50	7.06	520.51	522.50	9.80	666.51	668.50	12.59	853.51	856.50	16.07	1,154.51	1,159.50	21.75
376.51	378.50	7.10	522.51	524.50	9.84	668.51	670.50	12.62	856.51	859.50	16.13	1,159.51	1,164.50	21.85
378.51	380.50	7.13	524.51	526.50	9.88	670.51	672.50	12.66	859.51	862.50	16.19	1,164.51	1,174.50	21.99
380.51	382.50	7.17	526.51	528.50	9.92	672.51	674.50	12.70	862.51	865.50	16.24	1,174.51	1,184.50	22.17
382.51	384.50	7.21	528.51	530.50	9.95	674.51	676.50	12.74	865.51	868.50	16.30	1,184.51	1,194.50	22.36
384.51	386.50	7.25	530.51	532.50	9.99	676.51	678.50	12.77	868.51	871.50	16.36	1,194.51	1,204.50	22.55
386.51	388.50	7.29	532.51	534.50	10.03	678.51	680.50	12.81	871.51	874.50	16.41	1,204.51	1,214.50	22.74
388.51	390.50	7.32	534.51	536.50	10.07	680.51	682.50	12.85	874.51	877.50	16.47	1,214.51	1,224.50	22.93
390.51	392.50	7.36	536.51	538.50	10.11	682.51	684.50	12.89	877.51	880.50	16.53	1,224.51	1,234.50	23.11
392.51	394.50	7.40	538.51	540.50	10.14	684.51	686.50	12.93	880.51	883.50	16.58	1,234.51	1,244.50	23.30
394.51	396.50	7.44	540.51	542.50	10.18	686.51	688.50	12.96	883.51	886.50	16.64	1,244.51	1,254.50	23.49
396.51	398.50	7.47	542.51	544.50	10.22	688.51	690.50	13.00	886.51	889.50	16.69	1,254.51	1,264.50	23.68
398.51	400.50	7.51	544.51	546.50	10.26	690.51	692.50	13.04	889.51	892.50	16.75	1,264.51	1,274.50	23.87
400.51	402.50	7.55	546.51	548.50	10.29	692.51	694.50	13.08	892.51	895.50	16.81	1,274.51	1,284.50	24.05
402.51	404.50	7.59	548.51	550.50	10.33	694.51	696.50	13.11	895.51	898.50	16.86	1,284.51	1,294.50	24.24
404.51	406.50	7.62	550.51	552.50	10.37	696.51	698.50	13.15	898.51	901.50	16.92	1,294.51	1,304.50	24.43
406.51	408.50	7.66	552.51	554.50	10.41	698.51	700.50	13.19	901.51	904.50	16.98	1,304.51	1,314.50	24.62
408.51	410.50	7.70	554.51	556.50	10.44	700.51	702.50	13.23	904.51	907.50	17.03	1,314.51	1,324.50	24.81
410.51	412.50	7.74	556.51	558.50	10.48	702.51	704.50	13.26	907.51	910.50	17.09	1,324.51	1,334.50	24.99
412.51	414.50	7.77	558.51	560.50	10.52	704.51	706.50	13.30	910.51	913.50	17.15	1,334.51	1,344.50	25.18
414.51	416.50	7.81	560.51	562.50	10.56	706.51	708.50	13.34	913.51	916.50	17.20	1,344.51	1,354.50	25.37
416.51	418.50	7.85	562.51	564.50	10.59	708.51	710.50	13.38	916.51	919.50	17.26	1,354.51	1,364.50	25.56
418.51	420.50	7.89	564.51	566.50	10.63	710.51	712.50	13.41	919.51	922.50	17.31	1,364.51	1,374.50	25.75
420.51	422.50	7.92	566.51	568.50	10.67	712.51	714.50	13.45	922.51	925.50	17.37	1,374.51	1,384.50	25.93
422.51	424.50	7.96	568.51	570.50	10.71	714.51	716.50	13.49	925.51	928.50	17.43	1,384.51	1,394.50	26.12
424.51	426.50	8.00	570.51	572.50	10.74	716.51	718.50	13.53	928.51	931.50	17.48	1,394.51	1,404.50	26.31
426.51	428.50	8.04	572.51	574.50	10.78	718.51	720.50	13.56	931.51	934.50	17.54	1,404.51	1,414.50	26.50
428.51	430.50	8.07	574.51	576.50	10.82	720.51	722.50	13.60	934.51	937.50	17.60	1,414.51	1,424.50	26.69
430.51	432.50	8.11	576.51	578.50	10.86	722.51	724.50	13.64	937.51	940.50	17.65	1,424.51	1,434.50	26.87
432.51	434.50	8.15	578.51	580.50	10.89	724.51	726.50	13.68	940.51	943.50	17.71	1,434.51	1,444.50	27.06
434.51	436.50	8.19	580.51	582.50	10.93	726.51	728.50		943.51	946.50	17.77	1,444.51	1,454.50	27.25

To obtain deductions for amounts over $1454.50, (or to calculate exact deductions), multiply the earnings amount by 0.0188

Note - Yearly maximum employee premiums are $891.12 (maximum insurable earnings are $47,400)

CHAPTER 10

The Employer's Tax Responsibilities

PRINCIPLES AND PROCEDURES

LEARNING OBJECTIVES

- **LO 1** How to calculate and record the employer's expenses associated with payroll (p. 450)
- **LO 2** How employers remit and record their employees' deductions to the Canada Revenue Agency (p. 454)
- **LO 3** Employers' annual responsibilities for filing the T4 Summary form (p. 459)

Most students will by now have received at least one payroll cheque. Listed on part of the document is a section often called the "pay stub". Listed there are the many details about how much was earned, and no doubt several deductions. Have you ever wondered what happens to these deductions from the company's viewpoint?

At least monthly, each employer in Canada must make a report of all deductions made from employees' pay slips, and send along any funds owing to the federal government. The government is very strict about this, in part because they never want to see the situation where an employee "loses" some amounts from his or her pay cheque, and the monies never show up in their account in the federal records.

This chapter details how this report is made, and how a business accounts for its share of payroll expenses each period. The chapter also shows the annual report that all businesses must file with the government called the T4 Summary.

Detailed information about how a business must deal with payroll remittances can be found by downloading form (or file) T4001, Employer's Guide—Payroll Deductions and Remittances from the CRA website: www.cra-arc.gc.ca

In the previous chapter, we examined how ABC Company calculates its weekly payroll and maintains a record of each employee's earnings. In Canada, many employers must remit to the government monthly the totals deducted from their employees in the previous month. Certain employers (those who have more than $15,000 to remit monthly) must send in their withholdings more often, while some very small employers may now remit only every quarter (only if there are withholdings of less than $1,000 per month). In the balance of this chapter, we will assume an employer who remits monthly.

An important fact in our country is that employers share the total cost of CPP and EI with their employees. The cost of workers' compensation is borne by the employer alone. The employer's share of these payments is considered an expense of doing business and is accounted for as such. In this chapter, we will examine how this expense is calculated and illustrate the forms that need to be completed (and sent to the government) as part of the payroll process. We will also examine the accounting procedures that must be followed.

LEARNING UNIT 10-1

Employer's Expenses Associated with Payroll

> If you take over another employer's business, you must still obtain a new identification number (unless the business is a corporation).

> While the remittance cheque goes to the federal government, a part of the tax deducted is forwarded to the provinces.

> Notice that the income tax amount is sent by the employer, but it is not an expense because the employees are paying it.

Employers must apply for a remittance number (called a **business number**) to handle their responsibilities for payroll correctly. A special form called a Request for a Business Number (Form RC1(E)) must be submitted, which asks the employer to answer several questions about the business's operations. Once this form is processed, the employer is issued a permanent unique identification number. This number is used to ensure that the amounts of money sent (we often say *remitted*) to the government each month are recorded correctly; that is, in the right company's account. The same number is also used for GST/HST remittances and other purposes.

The actual amount sent to the federal government (concerning payroll) each month depends on three deductions taken from employees' wages:

1. Income tax (total of federal plus provincial)
2. Canada (or Quebec) Pension Plan
3. Employment Insurance

A simple **remittance formula** can be used to ensure that the correct figure is remitted each period:

Income tax deducted × 1.0	= $XXX.XX
CPP deducted × 2.0	= XXX.XX
EI deducted × 2.4	= XXX.XX
Total	= $XXX.XX

We will soon see in more detail how this formula works. Before we look at the details, however, a word of caution: the employer should ensure that the required remittance is made by the due date (usually the 15th day of the month following the payroll deductions). Failure to remit on time usually results in a penalty of 10% of the amount due over $500. This penalty is harsh and should be avoided. Not only is the amount high, but it is not deductible as a business expense for tax purposes.

> **LO 1** How to calculate and record the employer's expenses associated with payroll

HOW TO CALCULATE EMPLOYER'S REMITTANCE

Income Tax

> Some provinces levy higher tax rates than others. As this is written, a single taxpayer earning $2,000 weekly will have the following amounts deducted for provincial tax:
>
> In Ontario—$204.40
> In Alberta—$162.35

Remember that all employees pay an amount of income tax based upon their level of earnings. We saw in Chapter 9 that the ABC Company deducted income tax from each employee's earnings. This amount must now be sent to the government. Notice that the amount sent is exactly the same as the amount deducted since the employer does not contribute to the employee's tax. This part of the required remittance is therefore quite simple: Each month employers must send in the exact amount of income tax deducted from employees in the previous month. In our simple formula, that is why we multiply by 1.0—the result is exactly the amount deducted.

Canada (Quebec) Pension Plan

> Note that federal tax rates are the same for all taxpayers.

Almost all employees contribute an amount every pay period to CPP (at least until the maximum is reached). In Canada, the employer must match the employee's contribution to CPP. This means that the amount of CPP remitted is exactly double the amount deducted. In our simple formula, that is why we multiply by 2.0—the result is double the amount deducted.

If an employee commences a job with a new employer partway through a calendar year, the deduction of CPP is calculated without regard to the CPP already paid while employed by the former company. If the employee pays more than the yearly maximum, then a refund of CPP contributions can be claimed by the individual when he or she files an income tax return for the year. The employer's share is not refundable and cannot be recovered.

Employment Insurance

Recall that employees contribute an amount every pay period for Employment Insurance. Employers also contribute to EI by paying an amount that is 140% of the deductions made from employees' wages. The effect is that the employer must remit 2.4 times the amount deducted from the employees. In our simple formula, that is why we multiply by 2.4—1.0 for the employees' deduction, plus 1.4 for the employer's share. This 1.4 employer's portion can be reduced if the employer has an approved wage-loss replacement plan, but in this chapter, we are assuming no reduction. Also note that the rules for overpayment of EI are almost exactly the same as for CPP: the employee can recover his or her overpayment at tax time while there is no refund to an employer.

In Chapter 9, the employer made the following journal entry for the payroll in the first week in March:

GENERAL JOURNAL

Date		Account Titles and Description	PR	Dr.	Cr.
2016 Mar.	7	Management Salaries Expense		900.00	
		Sales Wages Expense		1,068.00	
		Wages Expense		2,031.00	
		Income Taxes Payable			506.20
		CPP Payable			177.63
		EI Payable			75.19
		Medical Plan Payable			112.00
		Charitable Contributions Payable			30.00
		Salaries and Wages Payable			3,097.98
		To record payroll for the first week in March			

ABC Company must now make the following additional entry to record its liability correctly:

GENERAL JOURNAL

Date		Account Titles and Description	PR	Dr.	Cr.
2016 Mar.	7	Employee Benefits Expense		282.90	
		CPP Payable (1 × 177.63)			177.63
		EI Payable (1.4 × 75.19)			105.27
		To record employer portion of CPP and EI for week 1, March			

Note: This expense—employee benefits expense—is also known by many different names—payroll taxes expense, for example. Some employers separate it into EI and CPP portions, but this is not usually necessary.

After the above entry is posted, the following T accounts would be changed as shown:

Employee Benefits Expense		CPP Payable		EI Payable	
282.90*			177.63**		75.19**
			177.63*		105.27*
Expense on the Income Statement		Liability on the Balance Sheet		Liability on the Balance Sheet	

*New entry made above.
**Original entry from Chapter 9.

Students should be aware that employers sometimes share or pay entirely for the cost of other employee benefits, such as extended health care, long-term disability insurance, and dental plans. These costs would also be recorded by journal entry at the same time CPP and EI are recorded. For example, if ABC Company agreed it would charge its employees only half the cost of health care, it would make the following entry instead of the one illustrated previously:

GENERAL JOURNAL

Page 4

Date		Account Titles and Description	PR	Dr.	Cr.
2016					
Mar.	7	Employee Benefits Expense		338 90	
		CPP Payable			177 63
		EI Payable			105 27
		Medical Plan Payable*			56 00
		To record employer's portion of CPP, EI,			
		and medical insurance for week 1, March			

*Note that the employees' deductions would go down by 50%.

Workers' Compensation

Most companies are also required to bear another expense related to salaries and wages: workers' compensation. This expenditure is typically paid to a provincial government (usually its Workers' Compensation Board, or **WCB** for short) once or several times per year, depending on how large the employer is, how many employees it has, the salaries/wages earned, and the likelihood of injury while on the job. Naturally, the rates charged are higher for relatively risky tasks such as steelworking, and a lot lower for most office workers. Assuming for this illustration that ABC Company in the province of Ontario has an average WCB rate of 2.5%, the company would make an additional journal entry for the first payroll to record the amount payable to the WCB of Ontario. Please note that the amounts payable will not go to the federal government along with income taxes, CPP, and EI, but will instead be paid to the provincial WCB at a time that differs a lot among the provinces. We will assume that ABC Company will remit these payments once every three months. Here is the entry the company would make for the first payroll in March:

GENERAL JOURNAL					
Date		Account Titles and Description	PR	Dr.	Cr.
2016 Mar.	7	WCB Expense		9998	
		Accrued WCB Payable (a current liability)			9998
		To record WCB expense for this payroll			

The company would make a similar entry for each payroll, based on 2.5% of the amounts earned by the employees, but we will not show these entries for each of the four payrolls in March. The actual payment of WCB amounts is covered later in the chapter (see page 459).

LEARNING UNIT 10-1 REVIEW

AT THIS POINT you should be able to:

- Explain one purpose of form RC1(E). (p. 450)
- Calculate the employer's share of CPP and EI. (pp. 450–451)
- Explain when employee deductions must be remitted. (p. 450)
- Journalize the employer's employee benefits expense, including Workers' Compensation Board. (pp. 451–453)
- Post the above WCB journal entry to appropriate ledger accounts (p. 453)

Self-Review Quiz 10-1

(The forms you need are on page 10-1 of the *Study Guide with Working Papers.*)

Given the following journal entry for the payroll totals of the second week in March 2016, prepare the entry to record ABC Company's portion of CPP and EI:

GENERAL JOURNAL					
Date		Account Titles and Description	PR	Dr.	Cr.
2016 Mar.	14	Management Salaries Expense		90000	
		Sales Wages Expense		106800	
		Wages Expense		206700	
		Income Taxes Payable			51740
		CPP Payable			17942
		EI Payable			7586
		Medical Plan Payable			11200
		Charitable Contributions Payable			3000
		Salaries and Wages Payable			312032
		To record payroll for week 2 in March			

Solution to Self-Review Quiz 10-1

GENERAL JOURNAL

Date		Account Titles and Description	PR	Dr.	Cr.
2016					
Mar.	14	Employee Benefits Expense		285 62	
		CPP Payable (1 × 179.42)			179 42
		EI Payable (1.4 × 75.86)			106 20
		To record employer portion of CPP and			
		EI for week 2, March			

LEARNING UNIT 10-2

Completing the Monthly Remittance Form

LO 2

How employers remit and record their employees' deductions to the Canada Revenue Agency

Most smaller companies are required to remit the total amounts due with respect to their payrolls each month by the 15th of the following month. Payment may be made at most financial institutions in Canada or a cheque can be mailed, as long as it reaches the government by the appropriate deadline.

We have already seen the ABC Company's entries for the first two weeks in March*. Let us assume the following payroll data for the third and fourth weeks:

Income tax × 1
+ CPP × 2
+ EI × 2.4 = Amount remitted

CPP × 1
+ EI × 1.4 = Employer's expense

GENERAL JOURNAL

Date		Account Titles and Description	PR	Dr.	Cr.
2016					
Mar.	21	Management Salaries Expense		900 00	
		Sales Wages Expense		1068 00	
		Wages Expense		2145 00	
		Income Taxes Payable			538 10
		CPP Payable			183 27
		EI Payable			77 32
		Medical Plan Payable			112 00
		Charitable Contributions Payable			30 00
		Salaries and Wages Payable			3172 31
		To record payroll for week 3, March—new data			

GENERAL JOURNAL

Date		Account Titles and Description	PR	Dr.	Cr.
2016					
Mar.	28	Management Salaries Expense		900 00	
		Sales Wages Expense		1068 00	
		Wages Expense		2120 00	
		Income Taxes Payable			531 82
		CPP Payable			182 04
		EI Payable			76 85
		Medical Plan Payable			112 00
		Charitable Contributions Payable			30 00
		Salaries and Wages Payable			3155 29
		To record payroll for week 4, March—new data			

After posting, the relevant liability T accounts would appear as shown:

	Income Taxes Payable		CPP Payable		EI Payable	
Week 1: Employees		506.20*		177.63*		75.19*
Employer				177.63**		105.27**
Week 2: Employees		517.40*		179.42*		75.86*
Employer				179.42**		106.20**
Week 3: Employees		538.10*		183.27*		77.32*
Employer				183.27**		108.25**
Week 4: Employees		531.82*		182.04*		76.85*
Employer				182.04**		107.59**
Balance (March)		2,093.52		1,444.72		732.53

*Original payroll entry.

**Benefits entry. (Week 1 amounts from Chapter 9. Weeks 2, 3, and 4 amounts from this chapter. See page 454 for weeks 3 and 4.)

GENERAL JOURNAL

Date		Account Titles and Description	PR	Dr.	Cr.
2016 Mar.	21	Employee Benefits Expense		291.52	
		CPP Payable (1 × 183.27)			183.27
		EI Payable (1.4 × 77.32)			108.25
		To record employer portion of CPP and			
		EI for the third week of March—new data			

GENERAL JOURNAL

Date		Account Titles and Description	PR	Dr.	Cr.
2016 Mar.	28	Employee Benefits Expense		289.63	
		CPP Payable (1 × 182.04)			182.04
		EI Payable (1.4 × 76.85)			107.59
		To record employer portion of CPP and			
		EI for the fourth week of March—new data			

Since these liability accounts contain the total amounts due, ABC Company can complete a required **(Monthly) Remittance Form (PD7A)**.

ABC Company will issue a cheque for $4,270.77, dated April 15, payable to Canada Revenue Agency (CRA), specifically to the Receiver General. This cheque will be entered in the cash disbursements journal in April. When this cheque is entered, the following accounts will be affected:

GENERAL JOURNAL					
Date		Account Titles and Description	PR	Dr.	Cr.
2016					
Apr.	15	Income Taxes Payable		2093 52	
		CPP Payable		1444 72	
		EI Payable		732 53	
		Cash			4270 77
		To record payment of withholdings			

After these amounts are posted, the liability accounts at the end of March will all be paid.

Remember that by April 15 there will be two new weekly payrolls (in April) to contend with, so the ledger accounts may not ever have a balance of exactly zero. The amount payable at the end of any month, however, will be accurate when all postings have been made.

So far in these chapters, we have been illustrating the use of three separate liability accounts, as is obvious from the journal entry above. Many companies prefer to operate a single account called, not surprisingly, Due to CRA. While some detail may be obscured by using just one account, it is true that a single cheque is written each month, so this practice is justified.

Whether one liability account or three are used is much less important than keeping proper track of the amounts owed to the CRA. Many businesses must remit the appropriate amounts monthly, and this is so regardless of whether the payroll is completed daily, weekly, semi-monthly, bi-weekly, or monthly. The penalties for failing to remit the appropriate amounts are costly and every attempt should be made to avoid them.

Students will recall that employers sometimes pay part or all of the cost of other benefits. These costs are not sent to the CRA; instead, they are remitted (usually monthly) to the provincial health care plan, the Workers' Compensation Board authority, and/or private insurance companies that provide the benefits. These details of payroll are handled in a manner similar to the remittance to the CRA and are not illustrated here.

LEARNING UNIT 10-2 REVIEW

AT THIS POINT you should be able to:

- Explain the balances in the following ledger accounts before the monthly remittance to the CRA is made. (p. 455)
  - **a.** Income Tax Payable
  - **b.** CPP Payable
  - **c.** EI Payable
- Issue and record the cheque that would accompany form PD7A. (pp. 455–456)
- Explain how the balances in the ledger accounts listed in **a.** to **c.** above would change after posting the remittance cheque. (p. 456)

Self-Review Quiz 10-2

(The forms you need are on pages 10-1 and 10-2 of the *Study Guide with Working Papers.*)

Given the two semi-monthly payrolls for June 2015, summarized by the journal entries below, answer the following:

1. What journal entries would be made to record the employer's share of CPP and EI for the month?
2. Post the original entries and the entries that you suggested in question 1 to the T accounts shown. (Not all T accounts are shown; ignore the ones not shown.)
3. What amount would the employer remit to the CRA by the 15th of July 2015?

Here are the semi-monthly journal entries:

GENERAL JOURNAL

Date		Account Titles and Description	PR	Dr.	Cr.
2015					
Jun.	15	Sales Salaries Expense		2850 00	
		Office Salaries Expense		3240 00	
		Income Taxes Payable			1239 60
		CPP Payable			284 12
		EI Payable			114 49
		Salaries and Wages Payable			4451 79
		To record payroll data for the first half			
		of the month			

GENERAL JOURNAL

Date		Account Titles and Description	PR	Dr.	Cr.
2015					
Jun.	30	Sales Salaries Expense		2850 00	
		Office Salaries Expense		3175 00	
		Income Taxes Payable			1234 56
		CPP Payable			280 90
		EI Payable			113 27
		Salaries and Wages Payable			4396 27
		To record payroll data for the second half			
		of the month			

Here are the T accounts to use in question 2 of Self-Review Quiz 9-2 (opening balances are ignored):

Income Tax Payable	CPP Payable	EI Payable

Solutions to Self-Review Quiz 10-2

1.

GENERAL JOURNAL

Date		Account Titles and Description	PR	Dr.	Cr.
2015					
Jun.	15	Employee Benefits Expense		444 41	
		CPP Payable			284 12
		EI Payable (114.49 × 1.4)			160 29
		To record benefits expense for the			
		first half of the month			

GENERAL JOURNAL

Date		Account Titles and Description	PR	Dr.	Cr.
2015					
Jun.	30	Employee Benefits Expense		439 48	
		CPP Payable			280 90
		EI Payable (113.27 × 1.4)			158 58
		To record benefits expense for the			
		second half of the month			

2. Your T accounts should appear as follows:

Income Tax Payable		CPP Payable		EI Payable	
	1,239.60		284.12		114.49
	1,234.56		284.12		160.29
	2,474.16 Balance		280.90		113.27
			280.90		158.58
			1,130.04 Balance		546.63 Balance

3. The employer would remit $4,150.83, calculated as follows:

Income Tax Payable (balance)	$2,474.16
CPP Payable (balance)	1,130.04
EI Payable (balance)	546.63
	$4,150.83

LEARNING UNIT 10-3

Employer's Annual T4 Summary

LO 3

Employers' annual responsibilities for filing the T4 Summary form

Every year, employers are required to file an annual return called a **T4 Summary** (see Figure 10-1). This return summarizes the information provided to employees on their T4 slips (see Chapter 9, Figure 9-5).

Careful, accurate work helps ensure that the filing of the T4-T4A Summary is not an unpleasant task.

		Deductions		
Employee Name	**Total Wages**	**Income Tax**	**CPP**	**EI**
Janet Johnson	$24,210.00	$2,229.36	$1,019.70	$455.15
Peter Black	41,700.00	6,764.86	1,890.90	783.96
John Chernochan	38,620.00	2,715.40	1,738.44	726.06
Tony Chui	31,480.00	4,087.54	1,385.01	591.82
Beth Madora	35,090.00	4,685.32	1,563.71	659.69
Elaine Dumont	48,086.00	6,740.72	2,207.01	904.02
Casual Employees	20,696.00	1,625.84	497.40	389.12
(Total)	$239,882.00	$28,849.04	$10,302.16	$4,509.82

It is important to note that the form illustrated in Figure 10-1 is completed for a calendar year. Even if the fiscal year ends on September 30, the T4 Summary must be filed for the calendar year (January 1 to December 31). The deadline for submitting this form to the government and the T4 forms to the employees is February 28 each year for the calendar year ended the previous December 31.

The completion of this form can be a difficult task because any errors made during the year in completing the payroll register, and any errors made in preparing the employees' individual T4 slips, will be discovered in this final step. The totals shown for CPP, EI, and income tax as illustrated in the table above must also agree with the totals remitted according to the monthly PD7A form or any deficiency remitted.

It is not unusual to find intelligent, hard-working, successful employers who find this aspect of payroll processing very difficult. Some computer firms selling payroll software are successful because they promise employers relief from the manual balancing procedures each February 28. In actual fact, the task is not too difficult—provided the payroll register is completed with neatness and accuracy and all subsequent steps are done with care.

WORKERS' COMPENSATION INSURANCE

ABC Company is required to have workers' compensation insurance to insure its employees against losses due to accidental injury or death incurred while on the job. The company is required to estimate the cost of this insurance and to pay the premium in advance.

The premium for workers' compensation insurance is based on the total estimated gross payroll, and in that company's province, the rate is calculated per $100 of weekly payroll. At year-end, the actual payroll is compared with the estimated payroll, and ABC will either receive credit for overpayment or be responsible for paying additional premiums.

These are the facts on which ABC Company's insurance cost was calculated:

1. Estimated payroll: $230,000.
2. Two grades of workers: General Workers and Managers.
3. Rate per $100 of payroll: General Workers, $2.90; Managers, $0.68.
4. Estimated payroll: General Workers, $190,000; Managers, $40,000.

Canada Revenue Agency | Agence du revenu du Canada

0505 **T4** Summary / Sommaire

For the year ending December 31, / Pour l'année se terminant le 31 décembre **20** 16

SUMMARY OF REMUNERATION PAID
SOMMAIRE DE LA RÉMUNÉRATION PAYÉE

You have to file your T4 information return on or before the last day of **February**. See the information on the back of this form.

Vous devez produire votre déclaration de renseignements T4 au plus tard le dernier jour de **février**. Lisez les renseignements au verso de ce formulaire.

Payroll Account Number (15 characters) – Numéro de compte de retenues (15 caractères)
1112222333RP000

Name and address of employer – Nom et adresse de l'employeur

ABC Company
123 Main Street
Any City, Ontario
X1X 1X1

88	Total number of T4 slips filed – Nombre total de feuillets T4 produits	12
14	Employment income – Revenus d'emploi	239,882.00
20	Registered pension plan (RPP) contributions / Cotisations à un régime de pension agréé (RPA)	
52	Pension adjustment – Facteur d'équivalence	
16	Employees' CPP contributions – Cotisations des employés au RPC	10,302.16
27	Employer's CPP contributions – Cotisations de l'employeur au RPC	10,302.16
18	Employees' EI premiums – Cotisations des employés à l'AE	4,509.82
19	Employer's EI premiums – Cotisations de l'employeur à l'AE	6,313.75
22	Income tax deducted – Impôt sur le revenu retenu	28,849.04
80	Total deductions reported (16 + 27 + 18 + 19 + 22) / Total des retenues déclarées (16 + 27 + 18 + 19 + 22)	60,276.93
82	**Minus:** remittances – **Moins :** versements	60,276.93

Generally, we do not charge or refund a difference of $2 or less.

Généralement, une différence de 2 $ ou moins n'est ni exigée ni remboursée.

Difference – Différence: 0.00

84	Overpayment – Paiement en trop	0.00
86	Balance due – Solde dû	0.00
	Amount enclosed – Somme jointe	0.00

Do not use this area
N'inscrivez rien ici

90 Last to current / Précédente à courante: 1, 2; Other / Autre: 3
91 Pro Forma: 1, 2
93 Y – A, D – J
94 PD15-1
96 POF / PSF
97 NLFP / APPT
Memo – Note
Prepared by – Établi par
Date

SIN of the proprietor(s) or principal owner(s) – NAS du ou des propriétaires

Canadian-controlled private corporations or unincorporated employers
Sociétés privées sous contrôle canadien ou employeurs non constitués
74 | 75

Person to contact about this return – Personne avec qui communiquer au sujet de cette déclaration
76 Elaine Dumont

Area code / Indicatif régional; Telephone number / Numéro de téléphone; Extension / Poste
78 900 123-4567

Certification – Attestation

I certify that the information given in this T4 return (T4 Summary and related T4 slips) is, to the best of my knowledge, correct and complete.
J'atteste que les renseignements fournis dans cette déclaration T4 (le T4 *Sommaire* et les feuillets T4 connexes) sont, à ma connaissance, exacts et complets.

Date (Y-A / M / D-J)	Signature of authorized person – Signature d'une personne autorisée	Position or office – Titre ou poste
2017 02 24	E. Dumont	Manager

Privacy Act, personal information bank number CRA PPU 005
Loi sur la protection des renseignements personnels fichier de renseignements personnels numéro ARC PPU 005
T4 Summary – Sommaire (09)

Canada

Figure 10-1 Summary of Remuneration Paid

Source: Canada Revenue Agency. Reproduced with permission of the Minister of Public Works and Government Services Canada, 2013.

The estimated premium was calculated as follows:

General Workers:	\$190,000/\$100 = 1,900; 1,900 × \$2.90	=	\$5,510
Managers:	\$40,000/\$100 = 400; 400 × \$0.68	=	272
	Total Estimated Premium:		\$5,782

Accounts Affected	Category	↑↓	Dr./Cr.
Prepaid Insurance, Worker's Compensation	Asset	↑	Dr.
Cash	Asset	↓	Cr.

ABC Company would have to pay \$5,782 in advance. At the end of the year, records show that the total payroll was \$239,882.00. The Manager's payroll was \$48,086 (see page 459).

Given those amounts, the company's actual premium should be \$5,889.06, calculated as follows:

General Workers:	\$191,796/\$100 = 1,918; 1,918 × \$2.90	=	\$5,562.08
Managers:	\$48,086/\$100 = 481; 481 × \$0.68	=	326.98
	Total Premium:		\$5,889.06

Because the actual premium is \$107.06 higher than the estimate, ABC must pay this amount in early 2017 together with the estimated premium for the 2017 year.

The \$107.06 adjustment takes place on December 31 by debiting Workers' Compensation Insurance Expense and crediting Workers' Compensation Insurance Payable.

Accounts Affected	Category	↑↓	Dr./Cr.
Workers' Compensation Insurance Expense	Expense	↑	Dr.
Workers' Compensation Insurance Payable	Liability	↑	Cr.

LEARNING UNIT 10-3 REVIEW

AT THIS POINT you should be able to:

- Describe the process of filing an annual T4 Summary. (p. 459)
- Illustrate the completion of the T4 Summary. (p. 460)
- Calculate workers' compensation insurance. (p. 461)

Self-Review Quiz 10-3

(The form you need is on page 10-2 of the *Study Guide with Working Papers.*)

Respond true or false to the following:

1. A T4 Summary must be filed each year by February 28.
2. A T4 Summary is sent to each employee by February 28 each year.
3. The completion of the T4 forms can be a difficult task.
4. The total of the individual amounts on all T4 Supplementary forms must equal the totals on the T4 Summary.

Solutions to Self-Review Quiz 10-3

1. True **2.** False **3.** True **4.** True

SUBWAY

Hold the Lettuce, Withhold the Taxes

Payroll tax responsibilities
❶ ❷ ❸ (30 min)

"As an employer, Stan, what are your tax responsibilities?" asked Angel Tavarez, president of the local Kiwanis Club. They were at one of the luncheons sponsored by the club every month, and Stan had been asked to join a discussion on the Role of Small Business in Our Local Economy. Fortunately, Angel had told the panelists the questions in advance so Stan had his answers ready.

"Well, of course, I pay provincial and federal government taxes myself. I also have to file provincial and federal withholding taxes for each of my two employees. I have to withhold federal and provincial income taxes as well as CPP and EI for each of them. I pay CPP, EI, and workers' compensation premiums too," said Stan.

"That's strange," said a voice from the audience. "My brother-in-law has a Subway restaurant in the U.S. and he pays city taxes as well as state and federal taxes. What's going on here?"

"Naturally, the situation is slightly different for Subway owners in different locations—and certainly in different countries," said Stan confidently. "Some U.S. cities have city income taxes. Different states have different regulations about workers' compensation, as well, just as different provinces do."

"Oh, right," said the voice, sounding embarrassed.

"So, Stan, how often do you have to pay taxes," asked Angel Tavarez, shifting the topic diplomatically.

Stan picked up a piece of chalk and drew twelve large circles on the blackboard. Then he wrote the word "ASPIRIN" in each of the circles. A murmur of "Huhs" and "Whats" went around the room.

"The average employee working for a company pays tax once a year on April 30 and has one big tax headache. As an employer," Stan said, "I file tax returns on a monthly basis, so I have twelve big tax headaches a year! Each month I complete Form PD7A, the Employer's Monthly Remittance Report, to report and pay payroll taxes to the CRA. Along with that, I have to deposit the tax money into a chartered bank once a month. In addition, I have to file the T4 Summary at the end of each year. Then, for each employee, I must give them a T4 slip . . . ."

"Stan," Angel interrupted, "I'm afraid time is running out for your segment of the panel discussion. We'll move on to Pamela Pudelle who is going to tell us about advertising her new pet-grooming parlour."

Stan suppressed a chuckle as a woman who looked amazingly like a poodle took the microphone. Later, during the reception, he tapped Angel on the shoulder and said, "Sorry I went over my time limit."

"You didn't really go over," said Angel, "but you were getting a little too technical for the audience."

While Stan was sorry to have let the discussion veer off course, he felt a burst of pride. Who would have thought a year ago that he would be willing—and able—to expound on the tax burden of a small business owner!

DISCUSSION QUESTIONS

1. What are the taxes called federal and provincial income taxes? How much do they cost Stan?
2. Why is Stan classified as a monthly depositor of withholdings?
3. Assume Stan owed $2,069.90 in total withholdings for March. When would it be due? What would happen if that day were Sunday?

Chapter Assignments

SUMMARY OF KEY POINTS

Learning Unit 10-1

1. The employer's remittance to the CRA includes (a) income tax (employees' deductions), (b) CPP (both employees' and employer's shares), and (c) EI (again, both employees' and employer's shares).
2. The employee benefits expense is made up of both CPP (same amount as deducted from employees) and EI (1.4 times the amount deducted from employees).
3. Journal entries are made to record the payroll and then to record the employer's share of CPP and EI.
4. Employers sometimes share or pay entirely for the cost of other employee benefits (health care, insurance, etc.). These costs would also be recorded by journal entry at the same time as CPP and EI. Workers' compensation is paid entirely by the employer.

Learning Unit 10-2

1. Employers must complete form PD7A and submit it with their remittance to the CRA by the 15th day of the month following the month in which the salary payment was made. (Larger employers remit more often.)
2. A significant penalty is paid by any employer remitting after the due date.
3. Employers sometimes pay part or all of the costs of health care, insurance plans, etc., on behalf of their employees. These costs are not sent to the CRA; instead, they are remitted (usually monthly) to the provincial health care plan and/or private companies that provide the benefits.

Learning Unit 10-3

1. Once every year, by February 28, employers must file an annual T4 Summary (for the previous calendar year) with the federal government.
2. On or before the same date, each employee must be given a copy of his or her individual earnings summary form (T4 Supplementary). This form summarizes all relevant payroll information for each employee for the previous calendar year.
3. Unless care is taken in preparing the payroll records throughout the year, the completion of the T4 forms can be a challenging task.
4. Workers' compensation is a business expense for all companies having employees. An estimated amount is usually paid early in the calendar year. The exact amount is then calculated more precisely after the year's details of payroll are known. This results in a refund or additional payment.

KEY TERMS

Business number A number given by the federal government that uniquely identifies each employer who is required to forward deductions made from employees. Used to keep track of the exact remittance each employer sends on behalf of its employees. (p. 450)

(Monthly) Remittance Form (PD7A) A form used to identify the employer and the amounts of money sent to the CRA periodically on behalf of employees (p. 455)

Remittance formula A formula that can be used to double-check the amount of money being sent in each month on behalf of the employees. Computed as:

Income tax deducted × 1.0	=	XXX.XX
CPP deducted × 2.0	=	XX.XX
EI deducted × 2.4	=	XX.XX
Total		XXX.XX

(p. 450)

T4 Summary A form sent to the federal government once each year showing the totals of income tax, CPP, and EI deducted from all employees during the last calendar year. The totals on this form must agree exactly with the totals submitted on the various T4 Supplementary forms. (p. 459)

T4 Supplementary A form given to each employee by February 28 every year that gives the totals of wages earned, income tax, CPP, and EI deducted, and other similar information for the past calendar year. Total of all T4 Supplementary slips must agree with the totals reported on the T4 Summary. (Refer to p. 413 in Chapter 9.)

WCB expense The cost to the employer of insuring employees against accidents in the workplace (p. 453)

QUICK REVIEW

The following Tips are from Learning Units 10-1 to 10-3. Answer the Assess Your Progress questions and use the How Did You Do? at the bottom of the page to see how well you know the material. The Quick Review provides tips before each Assess Your Progress to help you avoid common accounting errors.

LU 10-1 Calculating the Employer's Expenses Associated with a Payroll

Tips: In general, an employer's payroll expense consists of all costs made necessary by paying employees each pay period. Some expenses are mandated by the government: CPP, EI, and WCB. Other expenses are related to agreements made with employees: sharing pension costs, health-care costs, or life insurance, etc. There is no cost associated with the deduction of income tax, because employees pay 100% of these amounts. A short formula can be used to compute the remittance an employer needs to make to the Receiver General of Canada: 1 × tax deducted + 2 × CPP deducted + 2.4 × EI deducted. WCB is a provincial matter, and is calculated and paid without reference to any particular payroll amount, except that some employers may accrue the expense amounts as each payroll is completed.

Assess Your Progress

Answer true or false to the following statements:

1. All employees must pay WCB each pay period.
2. Employer's expense contains more EI than CPP in a normal payroll.
3. Recording employer payroll expense always involves a credit to a liability account.
4. The entry to record payroll expense each period always contains a credit to Income Taxes Payable.
5. Income Taxes Payable, CPP Payable, and EI Payable are all current liability accounts on the balance sheet.

LU 10-2 Completing the Monthly Remittance Form

Tips: Most employers in Canada are responsible for reporting payroll details on a monthly basis, and also for sending along to the Receiver General any monies due for the reporting month. Failure to remit all monies due within the allowed time limits can have costly consequences. Since companies can choose to create a payroll weekly, semi-monthly, every two weeks, or monthly (or, even a combination of these, say weekly for hourly-paid workers and monthly for salaried employees), it is necessary to carefully track all amounts payable and compute the amounts due on a monthly basis. Following this, it is of course necessary to send along to the Receiver General all amounts due in respect of payroll for any given month.

Assess Your Progress

Answer true or false to the following statements:

1. Payroll amounts due each month consist of Income taxes, CPP, and EI deducted from each employee for each payroll during the month.
2. Remittances are due by the 15th of the month following the payroll month.
3. In a properly-run payroll there will always be a zero balance in the payroll liability account(s) at the end of each month.
4. A separate liability account is required for Income taxes, CPP, and EI.
5. A separate cheque must be sent to the province each payroll period for provincial income taxes deducted each payroll period.

LU 10-3 Employer's Annual T4 Summary

Tips: Before the end of February each year, all employers must submit an annual summary of all payroll details to the government by way of completing a form called the T4 Summary. The summary form goes to the federal government, while each employee receives an individual T4 slip that shows details of all relevant payroll amounts for the previous calendar year. Employees then use this T4 slip as one of the fundamental documents in preparing their annual income tax return. Preparing the T4 detailed reports can be a challenge for many companies because of the large volume of detail required to be maintained, and the zero tolerance for any errors. Many companies either use a computer to generate their payrolls each period, or take advantage of one of the many payroll services offered on a fee-for-service basis across the country, often due entirely to the need to keep proper track of T4 amounts.

Assess Your Progress

Answer true or false to the following statements:

1. A T4 Summary form is needed for each employee.
2. Amounts shown on the T4 Summary must agree with the total submitted to the Canada Revenue Agency for the previous calendar year.
3. Each employee's name is listed on the T4 Summary form.
4. The T4 Summary form must be signed by a responsible company official.
5. The T4 Summary permits a company to ignore small differences of $50 or less.

How Did You Do? Answers to the Assess Your Progress Questions

LU 10-1

1. False—Employees are not responsible for WCB deductions at all. These are paid entirely by employers.
2. True—Employers pay 1.4 times the EI deducted, but only 1.0 times the CPP.
3. True.
4. False—The entire liability is not changed. All income taxes are as deducted from employees.
5. True—Some companies will only maintain a single liability account, however.

LU 10-2

1. True.
2. True.
3. False—There will usually be a balance remaining in this account, because the payment is not made until the 15th of the next month.
4. False—Some companies have three accounts, some have only one. There is no law about this at all.
5. False—Provincial income taxes are sent to the federal government and then re-distributed to the provinces on a routine basis.

LU 10-3

1. False—Each employee gets a T4 slip, but only one summary form is needed.
2. True—apart from minor errors.
3. False—Each employee's name is on his or her T4 slip, a copy of which is sent to the government by the end of February each year, but no names are on the Summary form.
4. True.
5. False—A difference of less than $2 is neither refunded or collected.

BLUEPRINT OF THE TAX CALENDAR

A Sampling of Dates Involving Employer's Tax Responsibilities

January 15 (and the 15th of each month)	PD7A form	Remit the monthly amount to the CRA. Remember the formula: 1 × tax deducted + 2 × CPP deducted + 2.4 × EI deducted = Total amount to be remitted
February 28	T4 form	Complete these forms and send or deliver them to all persons employed during the year.
February 28	T4 Summary	Send this form, together with copies of the individual T4 forms, to the government. The totals on this form must match the sum of all individual T4 slips and, as well, must agree with the employer's accounting records.

Certain other forms may be required throughout the year, although they are not subject to an exact timetable:

RC1 form	Every employer needs to obtain a permanent number that permits the government to keep an accurate record of funds remitted. Since this number is permanent, employers will need to submit this form only once.
Record of Employment	Whenever an employee ceases his or her employment, this form must be completed and a copy given to the former employee within one week. A copy goes to the government to assist in the fair and efficient administration of the Employment Insurance Act.

QUESTIONS, CLASSROOM DEMONSTRATION EXERCISES, EXERCISES, AND PROBLEMS

Discussion Questions and Critical Thinking/Ethical Case

1. What makes up employee benefits expense?
2. All employers must remit their payroll deductions once a month (by the 15th of the following month). Please comment.
3. The only payroll-related costs borne by employers are CPP and EI. Please comment.
4. An RC1 form must be submitted annually by all employers. True or false?
5. Why could failure to remit employees' deductions on time be costly?
6. Each employer doubles the amount of income tax deducted from employees each month when remitting to the CRA. True or false?
7. Which of the following accurately summarizes the correct formula for determining the monthly remittance to the CRA? (IT = income tax)

   a. (2 × IT) + (2.4 × CPP) + (2 × EI)
   b. (1 × IT) + (2 × CPP) + (2.4 × EI)
   c. (1 × IT) + (2.4 × CPP) + (2 × EI)
   d. (2 × IT) + (2 × CPP) + (2.4 × EI)

8. A remittance form (PD7A) must be sent to the federal government once every pay period. True or false?
9. Why do some computer firms do good business selling payroll software to employers?
10. Employers must complete their T4 Summaries no later than two months after the end of their fiscal year. True or false?
11. Abby Ross works in the Payroll Department for Lange Co. as a junior accountant. Abby also is going to school for an advanced degree in accounting. After work each day, she uses the company's photocopy machine to make extra copies of her assignments. Should she be photocopying personal material on a company machine? You make the call. Write down your specific recommendations to Abby.

Classroom Demonstration Exercises

(The forms you need are on page 10-3 of the *Study Guide with Working Papers.*)

Employee benefits expense
❶ (15 min)

1. The Fisher Company had two employees for the week ended July 24. On the basis of the following information, prepare a general journal entry to record the employee benefits expense for that payroll.

		Deductions			
Employee	*Salary*	*IT*	*CPP*	*EI*	*Net Pay*
Brett Pym	900	165	41	16	678
Carmen Flynn	1,000	176	46	18	760

Calculating amounts to remit to CRA
❷ (15 min)

2. Assume that the Fisher Company (see above) had five payrolls in the month of July, all identical to the one shown above. What amount would the company send to the CRA in August to meet its legal obligation for payroll remittance?

CPP and EI deductions
❶ (30 min)

3. For the payroll week ending on October 9 (the 41st payroll period of the year), the three following employees had gross earnings as indicated. Each had been employed at the same salary since January 1:

Beth Hudson	$1,100
John Wong	975
Ida Hastings	850

Without using tables, compute the amount of CPP and EI to be deducted from each employee for payroll No. 41.

CPP and EI deductions
❶ (30 min)

4. Fred Blake has agreed to work for the Cummings Foundation at a total annual salary of $54,000. He is uncertain whether he should be paid biweekly or semimonthly and has asked for your assistance. Calculate the typical deductions for CPP and EI that must be taken from Fred's salary under either alternative. Will the choice affect the total EI or CPP Fred pays during the year?

Exercises

Set A

(The forms you need are on pages 10-3 and 10-4 of the *Study Guide with Working Papers.*)

Recording employee benefits expense
❶ (15 min)

10-1A. From the following information, prepare a general journal entry to record the employee benefits expense for Jones Company for the weekly payroll of July 9:

		Deductions			
Employee	*Total Salary*	*Tax*	*CPP*	*EI*	*Net Pay*
Troy Ness	900	183	41	17	659
Jay Young	600	95	26	11	468
Tim Wyatt	800	152	36	15	597

Recording employee benefits expense
❶ **(20 min)**

10-2A. From the following information, prepare a general journal entry to record the employee benefits expense of Windsor Company for the monthly payroll for April:

		Deductions			
Employee	*Total Salary*	*Tax*	*CPP*	*EI*	*Net Pay*
Bert Lamont	2,500	364	109	47	1,980
Joan Quan	2,300	334	99	43	1,824
Mark Totem	1,700	188	70	32	1,410
Jean Dzurko	1,800	205	75	34	1,486

Remittance calculation
❷ **(10 min)**

10-3A. What amount will the Windsor Company send to the CRA in the month of May (for the April payroll)? See Exercise 10-2A above.

Recording employee benefits expense, stage 1
❶ **(15 min)**

10-4A. For the first two weeks of March, the Star Company had payroll details as shown below:

				Deductions			
Employee	*Hours*	*Rate*	*Total Pay*	*Tax*	*CPP*	*EI*	*Net Pay*
Pam Tifford	80	16	1,280	196	57	24	1,003
Isaac Gold	70	17	1,190	179	52	22	937
Bob Boudreau	80	14	1,120	160	49	21	890

Prepare the general journal entry to record the employee benefits expense for the two-week period.

Recording employee benefits expense, stage 2
❶ **(15 min)**

10-5A. For the last two weeks in March, the Star Company had the following payroll details:

				Deductions			
Employee	*Hours*	*Rate*	*Total Pay*	*Tax*	*CPP*	*EI*	*Net Pay*
Pam Tifford	75	16	1,200	169	53	23	955
Isaac Gold	85	17	1,445	239	65	27	1,114
Jim Francis	80	14	1,120	152	49	21	898

Prepare the general journal entry to record the employee benefits expense for the last two-week period.

Calculating a remittance—multiple periods
❷ **(10 min)**

10-6A. There are only four payroll weeks in March. Calculate the total remittance that Star Company would make to the CRA in the month of April based on its March payroll activities. Refer to Exercises 10-4A and 10-5A.

Workers' compensation premium
❶ **(30 min)**

10-7A. For this exercise, please assume a province that has three rates for worker's compensation: General Office Workers, \$1.75 per \$100; Sales Staff, \$2.55 per \$100; Management Personnel, \$1.20 per \$100.

In this province, DSK Enterprises operates a business that has workers in each of these categories. The company has projected the following salary expense for each category of employee for the 2017 calendar year:

General Office Worker	$254,000
Sales Staff	$347,000
Management Personnel	$418,000

Required

a. Calculate the WCB premium that DSK would submit to its provincial WCB for the 2017 year.

b. Given that actual salary expenses turned out to be as shown below, calculate the refund or added premium that the company receives from, or has to send to, its WCB early in January 2018.

General Office Worker	$249,800
Sales Staff	$354,600
Management Personnel	$416,000

Exercises

Set B

(The forms you need are on pages 10-3 and 10-4 of the *Study Guide with Working Papers.*)

Recording employee benefits expense
❶ (15 min)

10-1B. From the following information, prepare a general journal entry to record the employee benefits expense for Jones Company for the weekly payroll of July 9:

		Deductions			
Employee	*Total Salary*	*Tax*	*CPP*	*EI*	*Net Pay*
Troy Ness	980	215	45	18	702
Jay Young	700	120	31	13	536
Tim Wyatt	850	168	39	16	627

Recording employee benefits expense
❶ (20 min)

10-2B. From the following information, prepare a general journal entry to record the employee benefits expense of Windsor Company for the monthly payroll for April:

		Deductions			
Employee	*Total Salary*	*Tax*	*CPP*	*EI*	*Net Pay*
Bert Lamont	2,600	395	114	49	2,042
Joan Quan	2,400	361	104	45	1,890
Mark Totem	1,800	214	75	34	1,477
Jean Dzurko	2,000	256	85	38	1,621

Remittance calculation
❷ (10 min)

10-3B. What amount will the Windsor Company send to the CRA in the month of May (for the April payroll)? See Exercise 10-2B above.

Recording employee benefits expense, stage 1
❶ (15 min)

10-4B. For the first two weeks of March, the Star Company had payroll details as shown below:

				Deductions			
Employee	*Hours*	*Rate*	*Total Pay*	*Tax*	*CPP*	*EI*	*Net Pay*
Pam Tifford	80	18	1,440	231	65	27	1,117
Isaac Gold	70	19	1,330	210	59	25	1,036
Bob Boudreau	76	15	1,140	161	50	21	908

Prepare the general journal entry to record the employee benefits expense for the two-week period.

Recording employee benefits expense, stage 2
❷ (15 min)

10-5B. For the last two weeks in March, the Star Company had the following payroll details:

				Deductions			
Employee	*Hours*	*Rate*	*Total Pay*	*Tax*	*CPP*	*EI*	*Net Pay*
Pam Tifford	78	18	1,404	222	63	26	1,093
Isaac Gold	80	19	1,520	260	69	29	1,162
Jim Francis	74	16	1,184	172	52	22	938

Prepare the general journal entry to record the employee benefits expense for the last two-week period.

Calculating a remittance—multiple periods
❷ (10 min)

10-6B. There are only four payroll weeks in March. Calculate the total remittance that Star Company would make to the CRA in the month of April based on its March payroll activities. Refer to Exercises 10-4B and 10-5B.

Workers' Compensation premium
❶ (30 min)

10-7B. For this exercise, please assume a province that has three rates for worker's compensation: General Office Workers, $1.85 per $100; Sales Staff, $2.45 per $100; Management Personnel, $1.25 per $100.

In this province, DSK Enterprises operates a business that has workers in each of these categories. The company has projected the following salary expense for each category of employee for the 2017 calendar year:

General Office Worker	$286,000
Sales Staff	375,000
Management Personnel	460,000

Required

a. Calculate the WCB premium that DSK would submit to its provincial WCB for the 2017 year.

b. Given that actual salary expenses turned out to be as shown below, calculate the refund or added premium that the company receives from, or has to send to, its WCB early in January 2018.

General Office Worker	$292,000
Sales Staff	374,000
Management Personnel	468,000

Group A Problems

(The forms you need are on pages 10-5 to 10-9 of the *Study Guide with Working Papers.*)

Recording Employee Benefits Expense and subsequent entries
❶ ❷ (40 min)

10A-1. The payroll register for Rice Company of Sackville is summarized below for the month of April, 2015:

		Deductions						
Employee	*Total Salary*	*Tax*	*CPP*	*EI*	*Medical*	*Union Dues*	*Net Pay*	*Chq. No.*
Bob Roberts	3,100	432	139	58	28	21	2,422	474
Robin Case	2,750	457	122	52	56	21	2,042	475
Bailey Tropp	2,400	226	104	45	56	21	1,948	476
Ishma Blumen	2,650	339	117	50	56	21	2,067	477
	10,900	1,454	482	205	196	84	8,479	

Check Figure

Employee Benefits Expense $965.00

The union dues are remitted to the treasurer of the union by the 10th day of the next month. Rice Company matches its employees' contributions to the medical plan. Assume that the information in the above table has been recorded and cheques No. 474 to 477 were issued.

Required

a. Record the company's benefits expense, assuming no such entry was made when cheques No. 474 to No. 477 were recorded.

b. In May, the Rice Company issued the following three cheques:

1. May 10, 2015, to the Employees' Union, cheque No. 495.
2. May 15, 2015, to the CRA, cheque No. 502.
3. May 20, 2015, to the Provincial Health Care Insurance Company, cheque No. 531.

How much was each cheque for?

c. What journal entries would be made to record the three cheques in **b.** above?

Recording Employee Benefits Expense and subsequent calculations
❶ ❷ (30 min)

10A-2. Gibraltor Co. of Sussex recorded the following payroll details in its payroll journal for the month of March, 2016:

		Deductions							
Employee	*Total Salary*	*Tax*	*CPP*	*EI*	*LTD*	*Medical*	*Union Dues*	*Net Pay*	*Chq. No.*
Fred Jones	3,200	458	144	60	26	38	24	2,450	716
May George	2,600	394	114	49	50	65	24	1,904	717
Bren Morley	2,700	316	119	51	50	38	24	2,102	718
Joyce Fisher	2,400	282	104	45	26	–	24	1,919	719
Pat Sailer	2,300	227	99	43	26	38	24	1,843	720
	13,200	1,677	580	248	178	179	120	10,218	

Union dues are remitted by the end of the following month to the employees' union treasurer. Employees pay 100% of the long-term disability (LTD). Gibraltor Co. matches its employees' contributions to the medical plan and remits by the 20th of the following month.

Required

Check Figure

Employee Benefits Expense $1,106.20

a. Assume that there was no employee benefits expense recognized as the payroll register was recorded. Give the general journal entry necessary to record this employee benefits expense for March 2016.

b. List the cheques, together with their amounts and dates, that Gibraltor Co. would issue in April 2016 with respect to the above payroll data.

Recording Employee Benefits Expense—a more comprehensive example
❶ ❷ (45 min)

10A-3. The Candy Co. of Lethbridge pays its workers twice each month. Data for the two pay periods on June, 2016 are shown below:

First half of June 2016:

		Deductions						
Employee	*Total Salary*	*Tax*	*CPP*	*EI*	*Union*	*Charitable*	*Net Pay*	*Chq. No.*
Ann Wyatt	1,600	194	72	30	14	18	1,272	312
Jim Elliott	1,520	201	68	29	14	18	1,190	313
Bren Stairs	1,245	138	54	23	14	18	998	314
Becky Holmes	1,306	163	57	25	14	18	1,029	315
	5,671	696	251	107	56	72	4,489	

Second half of June 2016:

		Deductions						
Employee	*Total Salary*	*Tax*	*CPP*	*EI*	*Union*	*Charitable*	*Net Pay*	*Chq. No.*
Ann Wyatt	1,640	197	74	31	14	18	1,306	387
Jim Elliott	1,520	201	68	29	14	18	1,190	388
Bren Stairs	1,245	138	54	23	14	18	998	389
Becky Holmes	1,492	204	67	28	14	18	1,161	390
	5,897	740	263	111	56	72	4,655	

Union dues must be remitted to the union treasurer by the 15th of the following month. Candy Co. matches the employees' charitable contributions to Save the Children Canada on a 2-to-1 basis. Donations are mailed to this organization semi-annually. A cheque will be sent for the first half of the year on July 5, 2016. Employee deductions for Charitable have remained consistent since January 1, 2016.

Required

Check Figure

Employee Benefits Expense, June $1,107.20

a. Assuming that the payroll register has been posted, but no entries have been made for employee benefits expense for June, make the two journal entries that are necessary to record this expense of Candy Co. for June 2016.

b. Give details of the various cheques that will be issued in July 2016 based on Candy Co.'s payroll activities for the year so far.

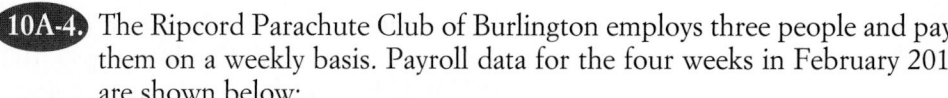

10A-4. The Ripcord Parachute Club of Burlington employs three people and pays them on a weekly basis. Payroll data for the four weeks in February 2015 are shown below:

Week 1–February

		Deductions							
Employee	*Weekly Salary*	*Tax*	*CPP*	*EI*	*LTD*	*Pension*	*Medical*	*Net Pay*	*Chq. No.*
Phil Lesage	800	135	36	15	14	41	24	535	205
Linda Barry	800	115	36	15	14	41	16	563	206
Howard Post	1,000	173	46	19	18	52	24	668	207

Week 2–February

		Deductions							
Employee	*Weekly Salary*	*Tax*	*CPP*	*EI*	*LTD*	*Pension*	*Medical*	*Net Pay*	*Chq. No.*
Phil Lesage	900	162	41	17	16	48	24	592	216
Linda Barry	800	115	36	15	14	41	16	563	217
Howard Post	1,000	173	46	19	18	52	24	668	218

Week 3–February

		Deductions							
Employee	*Weekly Salary*	*Tax*	*CPP*	*EI*	*LTD*	*Pension*	*Medical*	*Net Pay*	*Chq. No.*
Phil Lesage	900	162	41	17	16	48	24	592	221
Linda Barry	800	115	36	15	14	41	16	563	222
Howard Post	1,000	173	46	19	18	52	24	668	223

Week 4–February

		Deductions							
Employee	*Weekly Salary*	*Tax*	*CPP*	*EI*	*LTD*	*Pension*	*Medical*	*Net Pay*	*Chq. No.*
Phil Lesage	900	162	41	17	16	48	24	592	244
Linda Barry	800	115	36	15	14	41	16	563	245
Howard Post	1,250	260	59	24	22	63	24	798	246

Check Figure

Cheque to CRA in March is $3,356.80

Assumptions

Employees pay 100% of the cost of long-term disability (LTD). Employees contribute just over 5% of their salary to the pension plan; the employer contributes 6% of the employees' salary to the plan. Medical cost is split 50/50 by employees and employer. All payroll-related deductions are paid on the 15th of March, 2015.

Recording Employee Benefits Expense—multiple periods

Required

a. While recording in the payroll journal for February, the Ripcord Parachute Club bookkeeper did not record any expense for employee benefits. Give the four journal entries that should be made for the month to record this expense.

Posting routine entries for a monthly period

b. Post the entries from the payroll journal and the entries in **a.** to the T accounts shown as follows. (You may ignore the accounts that are not shown.)

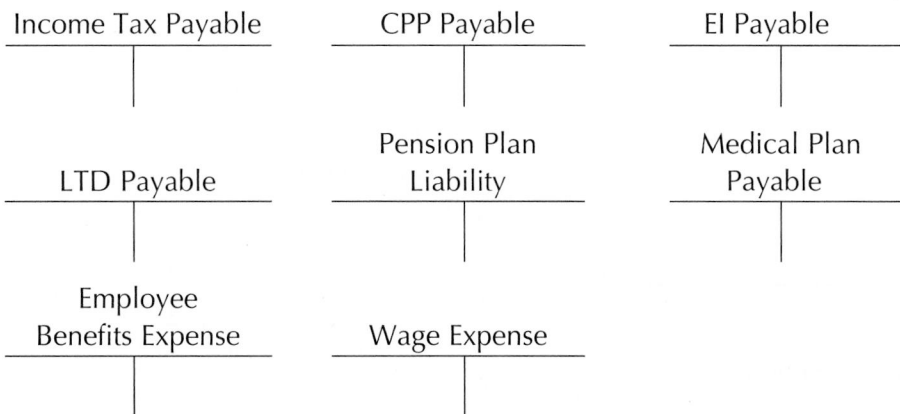

Income Tax Payable	CPP Payable	EI Payable

LTD Payable	Pension Plan Liability	Medical Plan Payable

Employee Benefits Expense	Wage Expense

Calculating remittances
❶ ❷ (60 min)

c. List the cheques and the amounts of the cheques that will be issued on March 15 for the February payroll.

Group B Problems

(The forms you need are on pages 10-5 to 10-9 of the *Study Guide with Working Papers*.)

Recording Employee Benefits Expense and subsequent entries
❶ ❷ (40 min)

Check Figure

Employee Benefits Expense $995.20

10B-1. The payroll register for Rice Company of Sackville is summarized below for the month of April 2015:

		Deductions						
Employee	*Total Salary*	*Tax*	*CPP*	*EI*	*Medical*	*Union Dues*	*Net Pay*	*Chq. No.*
Bob Roberts	3,250	454	146	61	28	21	2,540	514
Robin Case	2,800	433	124	53	56	21	2,113	515
Bailey Tropp	2,450	336	107	46	56	21	1,884	516
Ishma Blumen	2,800	392	124	53	56	21	2,154	517
	11,300	1,615	501	213	196	84	8,691	

The union dues are remitted to the treasurer of the union by the 10th day of the next month. Rice Company matches its employees' contributions to the medical plan. Assume that the information in the above table has been recorded and cheques No. 514 to No. 517 were issued.

Required

a. Record the company's benefits expense, assuming no such entry was made when cheques No. 514 to No. 517 were recorded.

b. In May, Rice Company issued the following three cheques:

1. May 10, to the Employees' Union, cheque No. 533.
2. May 15, to the CRA, cheque No. 550.
3. May 20, to the Provincial Health Care Insurance Company, cheque No. 565.

How much was each cheque for?

c. What entries would be made to record the three cheques in **b.** above?

Recording Employee Benefits Expense and subsequent calculations
❶ ❷ (30 min)

10B-2. Gibraltor Co. of Sussex recorded the following payroll details in its payroll journal for the month of March 2016:

		Deductions							
Employee	*Total Salary*	*Tax*	*CPP*	*EI*	*LTD*	*Medical*	*Union Dues*	*Net Pay*	*Chq. No.*
Fred Jones	3,350	492	151	63	26	38	24	2,556	853
May George	2,800	430	124	53	50	65	24	2,054	854
Bren Morley	2,900	352	129	55	50	38	24	2,252	855
Joyce Fisher	2,500	274	109	47	26	–	24	2,020	856
Pat Sailer	2,500	256	109	47	26	38	24	2,000	857
	14,050	1,804	622	265	178	179	120	10,882	

Check Figure

Employee Benefits Expense $1,172.00

Union dues are remitted by the end of the following month to the employees' union treasurer. Employees pay 100% of the long-term disability (LTD). Gibraltor Co. matches its employees' contributions to the medical plan and remits by the 20th of the following month.

Required

a. Assume that there was no employee benefits expense recognized as the payroll register was recorded. Give the general journal entry necessary to record this employee benefits expense for March 2016.

b. List the cheques, together with their amounts and dates, that Gibraltor Co. would issue in April 2016 with respect to the above payroll data.

Recording Employee Benefits Expense—a more comprehensive example
❶ ❷ (45 min)

10B-3. The Candy Co. of Lethbridge pays its workers twice each month. Data for the two pay periods on June 2016 are shown below:

First half of June 2016:

		Deductions						
Employee	*Total Salary*	*Tax*	*CPP*	*EI*	*Union*	*Charitable*	*Net Pay*	*Chq. No.*
Ann Wyatt	1,640	202	74	31	14	18	1,301	526
Jim Elliott	1,565	210	70	29	14	18	1,224	527
Bren Stairs	1,300	150	57	24	14	18	1,037	528
Becky Holmes	1,508	194	67	28	14	18	1,187	529
	6,013	756	268	112	56	72	4,749	

Second half of June 2016:

Employee	Total Salary	Deductions Tax	CPP	EI	Union	Char-itable	Net Pay	Chq. No.
Ann Wyatt	1,640	202	74	31	14	18	1,301	589
Jim Elliott	1,595	214	72	30	14	18	1,247	590
Bren Stairs	1,300	150	57	24	14	18	1,037	591
Becky Holmes	1,610	202	72	30	14	18	1,274	592
	6,145	768	275	115	56	72	4,859	

Union dues must be remitted to the union treasurer by the 15th of the following month. Candy Co. matches the employees' charitable contributions to Save the Children Canada on a 2-to-1 basis. Donations are mailed to this organization semi-annually. Deductions from all employees to May 31 this year have totalled $580. A cheque will be sent for the first half of the year on July 5, 2016.

Check Figure

Employee Benefits Expense, June $1,148.80

Required

a. Assuming that the payroll register has been posted, but no entries have been made for employee benefits expense for June, make the two journal entries that are necessary to record this expense for Candy Co. for June 2016.

b. Give details of the various cheques that will be issued in July 2016 based on Candy Co.'s payroll activities for the year so far.

10B-4. The Ripcord Parachute Club of Burlington employs three people and pays them on a weekly basis. Payroll data for the four weeks in February 2015 are shown below:

Check Figure

Cheque to CRA in March is $3,835.00

Week 1–February

Employee	Weekly Salary	Deductions Tax	CPP	EI	LTD	Pen.	Med.	Net Pay	Chq. No.
Phil Lesage	975	165	45	18	18	49	22	658	342
Linda Barry	900	158	41	17	16	46	14	608	343
Howard Post	1,125	204	52	21	22	59	22	745	344

Week 2–February

Employee	Weekly Salary	Deductions Tax	CPP	EI	LTD	Pen.	Med.	Net Pay	Chq. No.
Phil Lesage	975	165	45	18	18	49	22	658	358
Linda Barry	950	162	44	18	17	48	14	647	359
Howard Post	1,125	204	52	21	22	59	22	745	360

Week 3–February

Employee	Weekly Salary	Deductions: Tax	CPP	EI	LTD	Pen.	Med.	Net Pay	Chq. No.
Phil Lesage	975	165	45	18	18	49	22	658	374
Linda Barry	950	162	44	18	17	48	14	647	375
Howard Post	1,185	216	55	22	23	61	22	786	376

Week 4–February

Employee	Weekly Salary	Deductions: Tax	CPP	EI	LTD	Pen.	Med.	Net Pay	Chq. No.
Phil Lesage	1,000	168	46	19	18	51	22	676	392
Linda Barry	950	162	44	18	17	48	14	647	393
Howard Post	1,185	216	55	22	23	61	22	786	394

Assumptions

Employees pay 100% of the cost of long-term disability (LTD). Employees contribute just over 5% of their salary to the pension plan; the employer contributes 6% of the employees' salary to the plan. Medical cost is split 50/50 by employees and employer. All payroll-related deductions are paid on the 15th of March, 2015.

Required

Recording Employee Benefits Expense—multiple periods

a. While recording the payroll journal in February 2015, the bookkeeper for the Ripcord Parachute Club did not record any expense for employee benefits. Give the four journal entries that should be made for the month to record this expense.

Posting routine entries for a monthly period

b. Post the entries from the payroll journal and the entries in **a.** above to the T accounts shown below. (You may ignore the accounts that are not shown.)

Income Tax Payable	CPP Payable	EI Payable
LTD Payable	Pension Plan Liability	Medical Plan Payable
Employee Benefits Expense	Wage Expense	

Calculating remittances
❶ ❷ (60 min)

c. List the cheques and the amounts of the cheques that will be issued on March 15, 2015, for the February 2015 payroll.

Group C Problems

(The forms you need are on pages 10-10 to 10-15 of the *Study Guide with Working Papers*.)

Recording benefits expense and computing and entering cheques issued re payroll
❶ ❷ (45 min)

10C-1. The payroll register for Bawlf Hardware Co. of Creston for the month of May 2015 is shown below:

		Deductions							
Employee	*Salary*	*IT*	*CPP*	*EI*	*Health*	*LTD*	*Union Dues*	*Net Pay*	*Chq. No.*
Jake Jacobson	2,800	374	124	53	45	48	25	2,131	514
Mary Hind	2,350	286	102	44	68	42	25	1,783	515
Kyle Good	2,200	232	94	41	45	40	25	1,723	516
Lily Chau	2,750	314	122	52	68	47	25	2,122	517
Roy Verhagen	2,100	209	90	39	68	38	25	1,631	518
	12,200	1,415	532	229	294	215	125	9,390	

Check Figure

Employee Benefits Expense $1,067.60

Union dues must be submitted to the treasurer of the union by the 20th day of the next month. Bawlf Hardware matches the employees' contributions to the LTD plan, and the total must be sent to the insurance company by the 10th of the month following the payroll. Assume that all payroll information except benefits has been recorded and cheques No. 514 to No. 518 were issued.

Required

a. Record Bawlf's benefits expense for the month of May 2015.

b. In June 2015 Bawlf Hardware issued the following three cheques:

1. Cheque No. 543, June 10, to ABC Insurance Company for the LTD
2. Cheque No. 551, June 15, to the CRA for employee deductions
3. Cheque No. 567, June 15, to the Hardware Employees Union, Local 471, for union dues

How much was each cheque for?

c. What entry would be made in the general journal to record each cheque in **b.** above?

Recording benefits expense and liabilities; calculating dates and amounts of cheques to be issued
❶ ❷ (45 min)

10C-2. Counterpoint Counselling Co. of Edmonton recorded the following details in its professional payroll journal for July 2017:

		Deductions								
Employee	*Salary*	*IT*	*CPP*	*EI*	*Chari-table*	*Life Ins.*	*Assn. Dues*	*Health*	*Net Pay*	*Chq. No.*
Paula Amer	5,350	1,126	250	101	25	36	42	112	3,658	1274
Mike Steeves	5,900	1,275	278	111	50	39	42	112	3,993	1275
Pat Melvor	5,140	1,096	240	97	40	32	42	74	3,519	1276
Debbie Chan	6,350	1,475	300	104	60	44	42	112	4,213	1277
Boris Hecht	7,200	1,854	154	56	75	48	42	74	4,897	1278
Kim Gere	6,250	1,462	295	118	55	43	42	112	4,123	1279
	36,190	8,288	1,517	587	305	242	252	596	24,403	

Note that some of the above deductions reflect the fact that annual maximums were reached in July 31, 2017.

Check Figure

Employee Benefits Expense $2,643.80

Counterpoint matches the charitable donation of each employee and forwards the total on the 25th of each month to the Canadian Centre for Counselling Research. Association dues are sent to the Provincial Counsellors Society on the 20th of each month. Life insurance premiums are remitted to ABCD Insurance Company Ltd. by the 20th day of the following month. Health insurance premiums are remitted to the Provincial Health Care Organization by the 15th of the next month, at the same time as the employee deductions are sent to the CRA.

Required

a. Give the general journal entry necessary to complete the recording of this payroll, assuming no entry was made for benefits or related expenses when the payroll was recorded.

b. List the cheques, along with their amounts and dates, that Counterpoint would issue in the month of August 2017 with respect to this payroll.

Recording benefits expense and liabilities
❶ (15 min)

Check Figure

Employee Benefits Expense $312.99

10C-3. Refer to Problem 9C-2 (page 429).

Required

a. Give the general journal entry necessary to recognize all payroll benefits expense arising from that payroll, given the entry you made in Chapter 9.

Recording benefits expense and liabilities
❶ (15 min)

Check Figure

Employee Benefits Expense $271.81

10C-4. Refer to Problem 9C-3 (page 429).

Required

a. Give the general journal entry necessary to recognize all payroll benefits expenses arising from that payroll, given the entry you made in Problem 9C-3.

Recording benefits expense and related liabilities for two pay periods, plus calculating details of payroll benefits cheques to be issued
❶ ❷ (45 min)

Check Figure

Employee Benefits Expense total $1,368.00 for the month

10C-5. Munchkin Bakery Co. of Timmins pays its employees every two weeks (26 pay periods each year). There are two pay periods for March of 2016, and the details for each payroll are shown below:

March 15 Payroll:

		Deductions						
Employee	*Total Salary*	*Tax*	*CPP*	*EI*	*Health*	*Union*	*Net Pay*	*Chq. No.*
Holly Wilson	1,950	305	90	37	22	8	1,488	358
Reg Black	1,375	168	61	26	22	8	1,090	359
Amos Troy	1,450	162	65	27	38	8	1,150	360
Bernie Dyck	1,150	129	50	22	38	8	903	361
Cindy Nishimura	1,600	211	73	30	22	8	1,256	362
Totals	7,525	975	339	142	142	40	5,887	

March 29 Payroll:

		Deductions						
Employee	*Total Salary*	*Tax*	*CPP*	*EI*	*Health*	*Union*	*Net Pay*	*Chq. No.*
Holly Wilson	1,950	305	90	37	22	7	1,489	386
Reg Black	1,400	174	63	26	22	8	1,107	387
Amos Troy	1,450	162	65	27	38	8	1,150	388
Bernie Dyck	1,240	148	55	23	38	8	968	389
Cindy Nishimura	1,600	211	73	30	22	8	1,256	390
Totals	7,640	1,000	346	143	142	39	5,970	

Union dues must be remitted to the union treasurer by the 28th of the following month, while health premiums are matched by Munchkin and remitted to the provincial treasurer by the 10th of the month following. A cheque is sent to the CRA by the 15th of each following month as well.

Required

a. Assuming that the payroll register has been journalized, but no other related entries made, prepare the two journal entries necessary to record the benefits expense for March 2016.

b. Give the details of all cheques that Munchkin will issue in April 2016 with respect to payroll deductions.

Recording benefits expense and related liabilities for five pay periods in a month, plus calculating details of payroll benefits cheques to be issued ❶ ❷ (90 min)

Check Figure

Cheque to CRA is $6,188.44.

10C-6. The Grierson Auto Repair Company pays each of its employees weekly every Friday. During the month of May 2017, there were five pay periods, which are detailed as follows. (Note that employees pay 100% of the cost of health and dental plans.)

Week 1–May 2, 2017:

		Deductions							
Employee	*Weekly Earnings*	*IT*	*CPP*	*EI*	*Union Dues*	*Health Plan*	*Dental Plan*	*Net Pay*	*Chq. No.*
Hal Dyer	785.00	122.40	35.53	14.76	6.32	16.40	8.40	581.19	1475
Carol James	820.00	117.50	37.26	15.42	6.32	10.56	8.40	624.54	1476
LeRoy Cohen	904.00	160.30	41.42	17.00	6.32	10.56	8.40	660.00	1477
Peter Tsui	948.00	160.45	43.59	17.82	6.32	16.40	8.40	695.02	1478
Wendy Sage	758.00	118.45	34.19	14.25	6.32	16.40	8.40	559.99	1479
Weekly Totals	4,215.00	679.10	191.99	79.25	31.60	70.32	42.00	3,120.74	

Week 2–May 9, 2017:

		Deductions							
Employee	*Weekly Earnings*	*IT*	*CPP*	*EI*	*Union Dues*	*Health Plan*	*Dental Plan*	*Net Pay*	*Chq. No.*
Hal Dyer	765.00	118.60	34.54	14.38	6.32	16.40	8.40	566.36	1512
Carol James	780.00	108.75	35.28	14.66	6.32	10.56	8.40	596.03	1513
LeRoy Cohen	902.00	161.40	41.32	16.96	6.32	10.56	8.40	657.04	1514
Peter Tsui	942.00	159.70	43.30	17.71	6.32	16.40	8.40	690.17	1515
Wendy Sage	752.00	115.60	33.89	14.14	6.32	16.40	8.40	557.25	1516
Weekly Totals	4,141.00	664.05	188.33	77.85	31.60	70.32	42.00	3,066.85	

Week 3–May 16, 2017:

		Deductions							
Employee	*Weekly Earnings*	*IT*	*CPP*	*EI*	*Union Dues*	*Health Plan*	*Dental Plan*	*Net Pay*	*Chq. No.*
Hal Dyer	812.00	125.90	36.86	15.27	6.32	16.40	8.40	602.85	1577
Carol James	804.00	113.65	36.47	15.12	6.32	10.56	8.40	613.48	1578
LeRoy Cohen	884.00	154.00	40.43	16.62	6.32	10.56	8.40	647.67	1579
Peter Tsui	964.00	164.20	44.39	18.12	6.32	16.40	8.40	706.17	1580
Wendy Sage	756.00	117.15	34.09	14.21	6.32	16.40	8.40	559.43	1581
Weekly Totals	4,220.00	674.90	192.24	79.34	31.60	70.32	42.00	3,129.60	

Week 4–May 23, 2017:

		Deductions							
Employee	*Weekly Earnings*	*IT*	*CPP*	*EI*	*Union Dues*	*Health Plan*	*Dental Plan*	*Net Pay*	*Chq. No.*
Hal Dyer	840.00	131.60	38.25	15.79	6.52	16.40	8.40	623.04	1604
Carol James	780.00	108.75	35.28	14.66	6.52	10.56	8.40	595.83	1605
LeRoy Cohen	914.00	163.90	41.91	17.18	6.52	10.56	8.40	665.53	1606
Peter Tsui	840.00	132.10	38.25	15.79	6.52	16.40	8.40	622.54	1607
Wendy Sage	754.00	116.50	33.99	14.18	6.52	16.40	8.40	558.01	1608
Weekly Totals	4,128.00	652.85	187.68	77.60	32.60	70.32	42.00	3,064.95	

Week 5–May 30, 2017:

		Deductions							
Employee	*Weekly Earnings*	*IT*	*CPP*	*EI*	*Union Dues*	*Health Plan*	*Dental Plan*	*Net Pay*	*Chq. No.*
Hal Dyer	764.00	118.47	34.49	14.36	6.52	16.40	8.40	565.36	1638
Carol James	804.00	113.65	36.47	15.12	6.52	10.56	8.40	613.28	1639
LeRoy Cohen	902.00	161.40	41.32	16.96	6.52	10.56	8.40	656.84	1640
Peter Tsui	932.00	162.40	42.80	17.52	6.52	16.40	8.40	677.96	1641
Wendy Sage	769.00	119.62	34.73	14.46	6.52	16.40	8.40	568.87	1642
Weekly Totals	4,171.00	675.54	189.81	78.42	32.60	70.32	42.00	3,082.31	

Required

a. Assuming that the payroll register has been journalized, but no other related entries have been made, prepare the five journal entries necessary to record the benefits expense for May 2017.

b. Give the details of all cheques that Grierson will issue in June 2017 with respect to payroll deductions.

On-the-Job Training

(The forms you need are on page 10-15 of the *Study Guide with Working Papers.*)

Calculating employer's expenses
❶ ❷ (30 min)

T-1. The Tidy Tax Return Co. employs 50 extra people for the period February 1 through April 30 each year to process a large volume of tax returns. Each employee receives $10 per hour and works 40 hours a week (for 14 weeks). Early in May, all 50 additional workers are laid off.

A personnel service has offered to supply the needed 50 workers at a cost of $12 per hour. The managers of Tidy Tax Return Co. are not sure whether to accept the new offer.

Please prepare a memo to the management outlining the advantages of using the personnel service bureau and also the advantages of continuing with the present arrangement. Do not restrict your answer to financial considerations only.

Preparing and recording journal entries and the payroll registry; posting; and filing the T4 Summary
❶ ❷ ❸ (150 min)

CONTINUING PROBLEM

Because it is the end of the calendar year, Tony Freedman knows that, in addition to recording the normal entries for December 2016, he will need to complete certain tasks that relate to payroll. Specifically, he will need to prepare T4 slips for his two employees, and then complete the T4 Summary for the year (remember that he has had employees for only two months).

Assignment

(See pages 10-16 to 10-32 in your *Study Guide with Working Papers*.)

Nov. 30 Record the employer's share of payroll benefits for the previous month of November. Refer to the work that you completed for the end of November (Chapter 9) for the details you need to complete this task.

Dec. 6 Paid the two employees their wages: L. Klumm, 43 hours, and A. Hall, 34 hours (cheques No. 266 and No. 267).

9 Received the balance of the amount due from Vita Needle Company, November 1, 2016, invoice No. 12685.

10 Received invoice No. 4668 from *City Newspaper* re advertising seasonal specials, due in 30 days, $480.

11 Received December telephone bill from West Bell Canada, $165.

13 Paid the two employees their wages: L. Klumm, 40 hours, and A. Hall, 42 hours (cheques No. 268 and No. 269).

13 Paid telephone bill received November 9, $150 (cheque No. 270).

13 Collected amount owing by Accu Pac, Inc., re November 4 invoice No. 12687.

13 Purchased the remaining goods for resale of a friend's computer sales operation for cash, $7,000 (cheque No. 271).

13 Paid amount due to CRA re November wages, $1,668.43 (cheque No. 272).

16 Paid amount due to System Design Furniture re November 4 purchase (its invoice No. 8771), $1,400 (cheque No. 273).

17 Paid amount due to Multi Systems for November 19 purchase (its invoice No. 1784), $450 (cheque No. 274).

17 Purchased on account from Alpha Office Co., supplies totalling $318, its invoice No. 8161 (purchase order No. 4015), due within 30 days.

20 Paid the two employees their wages: L. Klumm, 34 hours, and A. Hall, 36 hours (cheques No. 275 and No. 276).

20 Billed Carson Engineering Corp. for major project involving 28 of its computers, $8,750, invoice No. 12688.

23 Paid utilities bill for November and December, $486, to City Electric (cheque No. 277).

24 Paid the two employees their wages to noon today: L. Klumm, 32 hours, and A. Hall, 38 hours (cheques No. 278 and No. 279). Because of seasonal factors, these are their final cheques this calendar year (office closed until January 2, 2017).

Dec.	30	Received $5,495 cash from Augustana Co. for services. Invoice No. 12689.
	31	Record the employer's share of payroll benefits for the month of December. Refer to the details of your payroll journal to complete this task.

MINI PRACTICE SET

Estimated time 2 hours

Pete's Market
Completing Payroll Requirements

This Mini Practice Set will aid in putting the pieces of payroll together. In this project, you are the bookkeeper and will have the responsibility of recording payroll in the payroll register, paying the payroll, recording the employer's tax responsibilities, and making payment according to the CRA's requirements.

Pete's Market, owned by Pete Reel, is located at 33 Riel Drive, Your Town, Ontario, M5W 2A4. His business number is 12345 6789 RP. The following are the employees of Pete's Market, along with their salaries, exemptions, etc.

Weekly Salaries

Date	*Name*	*Claim Code*	*Weekly Salary*
Sept. 7, 2018	Fred Flynn	5	$1,190
Sept. 14, 2018	Fred Flynn	5	1,190
Sept. 21, 2018	Fred Flynn	5	1,265
Sept. 28, 2018	Fred Flynn	5	1,265

Note: Fred Flynn receives a salary increase September 17, 2018.

Sept. 7, 2018	Mary Jones	1	$1,265
Sept. 14, 2018	Mary Jones	1	1,265
Sept. 21, 2018	Mary Jones	1	1,265
Sept. 28, 2018	Mary Jones	1	1,265

Note: On September 21, 2018, Mary reaches her CPP maximum of $2,356.20. Deduct only $34.67 CPP for Mary in that payroll, then no further CPP is deducted in September. Also note that Mary reached her maximum deduction for EI in August, so no EI deduction is made from her pay in September.

Sept. 7, 2018	Lilly Vron	1	$940
Sept. 14, 2018	Lilly Vron	1	940
Sept. 21, 2018	Lilly Vron	1	940
Sept. 28, 2018	Lilly Vron	3	940

Source deductions payable at August 31, 2018 (employer portion already recorded):

CPP Payable	*EI Payable*	*Income Taxes Payable*
$1,576.80	$592.08	$3,268.75

Required

(The forms you need are on pages 10-33 to 10-36 of the *Study Guide with Working Papers.*)

Using the general journal and payroll register provided, complete the following for the month of September 2018:

2018		
Sept.	7	Complete payroll register for September 7 payroll, journalize payroll entry, and journalize entry for all employer's expenses related to payroll.
	7	Transfer cash for September 7 payroll net pay from operating account to payroll account.
	14	Process payroll (follow the same procedures as for September 7 payroll).
	14	Transfer cash for September 14 payroll net pay from operating account to payroll account.
	14	Pay CRA for prior month's source deductions payable.
	21	Process payroll for September 21. Note change in Fred Flynn's salary.
	21	Transfer cash for September 21 payroll net pay from operating account to payroll account.
	28	Process payroll for September 28. Note change in Lilly Vron's claim code.
	28	Transfer cash for September 28 payroll net pay from operating account to payroll account.

COMPREHENSIVE REVIEW

Estimated time 1.5 hours

Verdunn Company
Payroll Project

Verdunn Company has four salaried employees as well as a couple of hourly workers who receive overtime at 1.5 times their normal rate for any hours worked over 40 in a week. On the payroll register (provided in the *Study Guide with Working Papers*), record the employees' payroll for the month of February of the current year. You may use current deduction tables found on the CRA website, since the text only has weekly deduction tables (or, you might use the proper formula to calculate the CPP and EI instead of using tables, but you will need the tables for the tax deductions). A solution to this comprehensive problem is available to instructors based on the rules for the province of Ontario, so you may be asked to use that province's tax tables for completing the exercise. On the other hand, your instructor may ask you to use the tables for another province—in which case slightly different solution will be needed to assure your answers match exactly. Be sure you know what the requirements are before proceeding.

Use the following data:

Employee	*Net Claim Code*	*Hours Worked, or Biweekly Salary (first two weeks of February)*	*Hours Worked, or Biweekly Salary (last two weeks of February)*
Adams, Taylor	1	$ 1,245	$ 1,245
Evans, Chelsea	3	1,475	1,525
Johnson, Quinn	2	1,550	1,550
Winston, Jammeel	4	980	1,050
Chan, Jeffery*	1	Wk1 – 38, Wk2 – 43	Wk3 – 42, Wk4 – 45
Lovejoy, Katherine**	2	Wk1 – 42, Wk2 – 35	Wk3 – 40, Wk4 – 46

*Rate is $14.00 per hour **Rate is $16.00 per hour

Each employee contributes $16 biweekly to a supplementary health insurance plan and $11 biweekly to group insurance. This small company is sponsoring a young man in Africa to get an education, and each of the six employees agree to have $5.00 deducted from his or her payroll each pay period. The employer matches contributions to the supplemental health plan, remits exactly the group insurance premiums deducted, and doubles the charitable deductions, making the necessary payments by the 15th of the following month. Jeffery Chan has worked at the company only since mid-January and does not become eligible to participate in either the supplemental health or the group insurance until the coming April payroll. He has agreed to the charitable deduction, however.

Journalize the following:
(The blank forms you need are on pages 10-37 to 10-44 of the *Study Guide with Working Papers.*)

1. The payroll for the biweekly pay periods ending February 14 and February 28 of the current year. Remember to use biweekly CPP and Income Tax deduction tables. The EI tables are not sensitive to the payroll period being used. You can calculate both CPP and EI if that is easier.
2. Employee benefits expense resulting from each payroll.
3. Payment of net pay to employees on February 14 and February 28. (Cheques 370–375 and then 419–424)

4. Remittance to the Receiver General (Cheque 465) on March 15.
5. Remittance to Ontario Supplementary Medical (Cheque 466) on March 15.
6. Remittance of group insurance to Mayfair Financial (Cheque 467) on March 15.
7. Remittance to African Educational Fund (Cheque 468) on March 15.

Once the journals are completed, post all necessary amounts to appropriate GL accounts using the account forms provided in the *Study Guide with Working Papers*. Except for the Cash account, all opening balances have been removed for simplicity.

For the first two items above, use the General Journal (forms provided in the *Study Guide with Working Papers*). All cheques should be recorded using a Cash Payments Journal (also provided in the *Study Guide with Working Papers*).

Thanks to Imelda Engels in Cranbrook, BC, for the inspiration and much of the details for this assignment.

CHAPTER 11

Special Journals with Taxes

LEARNING OBJECTIVES

LO 1 Recording sales that include PST, GST, or HST in the sales journal (p. 490)

LO 2 Creating, recording, and posting a credit memorandum for returned sales when PST, GST, or HST is included (p. 492)

LO 3 Recording cash received using a cash receipts journal when PST, GST, or HST is included (p. 501)

LO 4 Preparing schedules of accounts receivable and accounts payable, and balancing to control accounts (p. 504)

LO 5 Journalizing purchase transactions that include GST or HST in the purchases journal (p. 507)

LO 6 Creating, recording, and posting a debit memorandum for purchase returns when GST or HST is included (p. 510)

LO 7 Accounting for GST or HST using the simplified approach. (p. 511)

LO 8 Recording cash paid out in the cash payments journal when GST or HST is included (p. 512)

The use of special journals makes recording business transactions much more efficient, and details of their use were covered in Chapters 6 and 7. However, to allow students to focus on the principles involved, both Chapters 6 and 7 avoided the complexities of taxes on goods and services sold or purchased.

Of course the reality in the business world, almost regardless of nationality, is that taxes are ever present and all accounting students must become familiar with the proper accounting procedures needed to deal with them. This chapter extends the topic of special journals to include both provincial sales taxes (PST) as well as GST/HST. Please bear in mind that in the world of taxation, there is nothing so permanent as change. Not only do tax rates change from time to time (Nova Scotia recently raised their HST rate to 15%, for example), but the basis for retail taxation itself is subject to change, as the citizens of British Columbia know full well. That province recently rejected paying HST and voted to return to paying PST and GST. So think of this chapter as showing the principles of taxation in the business world. Details may change, but the principles of the accounting treatment of taxes charged and paid remain pretty much constant.

Chapters 5, 6 and 7 introduced the topic of special journals and how using them can simplify and speed up the work that bookkeepers and accountants need to do, whether this be daily, weekly, or monthly. This chapter builds on that material and expands it to cover how special journals must be designed and used to account for taxes. After all, and as much as we all may regret it, taxes are a reality in the business world and are not going to go away any time soon. Before working through a comprehensive example, we first present separate sections showing how taxes are included in each of the four main journals: sales, cash receipts, purchases, and cash payments. We will also show how both sales and purchase returns are recorded and posted correctly when taxes are included.

INTRODUCTION TO GST AND HST

With very few exceptions, all Canadians and Canadian companies must pay either GST (currently 5%) or HST (currently mostly 13%) on their purchases, including most services, such as legal fees. Since businesses both pay GST/HST and charge GST/HST to their customers, this is a subject that is essential for anyone who plans to make all or part of their career in bookkeeping or accounting.

Some of the things that Canadians buy are not subject to GST/HST. Financial services such as insurance and bank fees are not taxed, and neither are most food products. One often-mentioned example is the fact that if a Canadian buys one or two doughnuts, GST/HST is applied because they are considered a snack. However, if that same Canadian buys a half-dozen of the identical doughnuts, they are considered a foodstuff and are exempt! Some find this situation amusing, but the reality is that if exemptions are to be allowed from GST/HST rates, then definitions need to be in place to ensure that the tax is applied consistently. No doubt some changes will be made to the list of taxable items as time goes on and political priorities change. Two classes of taxable items that have often been mentioned as possibly subject to change are textbooks (indeed, books in general) and clothing (especially for children). While these changes may take place, they are details easily managed by accountants, if the accountants have a proper understanding of how the tax is supposed to work and the methods used to account for it. This chapter will cover all the critical details to ensure that students are capable of carrying out their duties involving this set of taxes.

As you read this, it is likely true for most students that they have never known Canada without the GST. The **Goods and Services Tax (GST)** was introduced in 1991, with the **Harmonized Sales Tax (HST)** coming into effect in 1997. These two taxes are essentially identical, apart from the difference in rates, and, as you will discover, are accounted for in the same way. In five provinces (Nova Scotia, New Brunswick, Ontario, Prince Edward Island, and Newfoundland and Labrador), HST has replaced a combination of GST and a Provincial Sales Tax (PST). In 2013 British Columbia's citizens voted to opt out of the HST and revert to a GST + PST option.

The trend toward HST now appears to be unstoppable, with the possible exception of Alberta, Nunavut, Yukon, and the Northwest Territories, which have no PST to replace. Provinces moving to HST have made a sharing agreement with the federal government that provides, among many other things, that the tax will be administered by the federal government, and most of the provinces will receive 8/13 (8%) of the tax, with the federal portion equalling 5/13 (5%). This means that the same 5% GST is paid by all Canadians, and in addition an extra 8% is also added on in three of the provinces (Nova Scotia is 10% and and Prince Edward Island is 9%). For this edition, we illustrate HST at 13% for the most part, but have also included some material that refers to GST at 5%. Depending on where you are studying this chapter, your instructor may alter any of the problems to ensure that your educational experience is as realistic as possible.

Since some provinces still charge a PST, this chapter will illustrate, explain, and present test material on this form of taxation, since it is a fact that many students will face PST as a reality in their routine bookkeeping and accounting duties. We cover PST in Learning Unit 1, along with GST/HST on sales, since PST is applied only at the retail level, and it is accounted for in much the same way as GST/HST.

Since PST is generally considered a retail tax, businesses do not pay (technically, they receive an exemption from) PST on their purchases. From time to time, a business will pay some minor amount of PST, mostly because it is too much trouble to apply for an exemption. An example is the occasional purchase of minor office supplies for cash. Regular purchases of office supplies are often done by phone or e-mail with a familiar supplier, and that business relationship is likely to include having a sales tax exemption certificate or number on file—so no PST gets charged in most cases involving office supplies. However, from time to time some "critical" office supply item needs to be replaced—often by a staff member on his or her lunch break—and so PST gets charged. In this chapter, we do not take the time to fully explain or illustrate this process, since almost by definition it is a minor matter for most businesses. Most companies just write off this tax as an expense, often including it as part of the cost of office supplies or whatever. A very few companies might charge the PST to a separate expense account—PST on Purchases, for example—but it hardly seems a useful procedure in most cases.

LEARNING UNIT 11-1

Chou's Toy Shop: Seller's View of a Merchandising Company

LO 1

Recording sales that include PST, GST, or HST in the sales journal

There is no PST in Alberta, Nunavut, the Northwest Territories, or the Yukon.

PROVINCIAL SALES TAX CHARGED

Chou must charge PST to his customers and send it to the province. Sales tax payable represents a liability to Chou's business.

Assume that Chou's business is located in a province that charges an 8% provincial sales tax. Chou's sales on July 18 were $3,000. Chou must figure out the PST on the sales. For this purpose, let's assume that there were only two sales on that date: a cash sale ($1,800) and a charge sale ($1,200).

The PST on the cash sale is calculated as follows:

$$\$1{,}800 \times 0.08 = \$144 \text{ tax}$$

$$\$1{,}800 + \$144 \text{ tax} = \$1{,}944 \text{ cash received from customer}$$

Here is how the PST on the charge sale is computed:

$$\$1{,}200 \times 0.08 = \$96 \text{ tax}$$

$$\$96 \text{ tax} + \$1{,}200 \text{ charge} = \$1{,}296 \text{ Total Accounts Receivable}$$

This is how it would be recorded:

Accounts Affected	Category	↑↓	Rules	T Account Update
Cash	Asset	↑	Dr.	Cash — Dr.: 1,944; Cr.:
Accounts Receivable	Asset	↑	Dr.	Accounts Receivable — Dr.: 1,296; Cr.:
Sales Tax Payable	Liability	↑	Cr.	Sales Tax Payable — Dr.: ; Cr.: 144, 96
Sales	Revenue	↑	Cr.	Sales — Dr.: ; Cr.: 3,000

Notice that the amount of Sales does not change when sales tax is charged. It is still $3,000.

Date		Account Titles and Description	PR	Dr.	Cr.
July	18	Cash		1944 00	
		Accounts Receivable		1296 00	
		Sales Tax Payable			240 00
		Sales			3000 00
		July 18 Sales			

Later in this chapter, we will show you how to record a credit memorandum with sales tax. Notice that in either case (cash or credit), it is the customer who pays the PST, not Chou's business.

Also note that only a very small business would use the general journal to record sales that include PST. Most would use a special journal (the sales journal) to record such sales. We illustrate this below.

Let's look at how Munroe Menswear Company, a retailer, handles PST at 8% on a sale made to Jones. Figure 11-1 shows Munroe's Sales Journal.

Sales Tax Payable

	XXX

A liability in the general ledger

Also, a new account, **Provincial Sales Tax (PST) Payable**, must be created. This account is a liability account in the general ledger with a credit balance. The customer owes Munroe the sale amount plus the tax.

Keep in mind that if sales discounts are available, they are not normally calculated on the sales tax. The discount is on the selling price less any returns before the tax. For example, if Jones receives a 2% discount, he pays the following:

	\$5,400	Total owed (tax is \$400)
\$5,000 × 0.02 = \$100 savings →	− 100	Savings (discount)
	\$5,300	Amount paid

Figure 11-1
Munroe Sales Journal

MUNROE MENSWEAR COMPANY
SALES JOURNAL

Page 3

Date		Account Debited	PR	Accounts Receivable Dr.	Sales Tax Payable Cr.	Sales Cr.
2016						
June	1	Jones	✔	5400 00	400 00	5000 00
	4	Roe	✔	108 00	8 00	100 00
	30	Totals		19440 00	1440 00	18000 00
				(113)	(215)	(411)

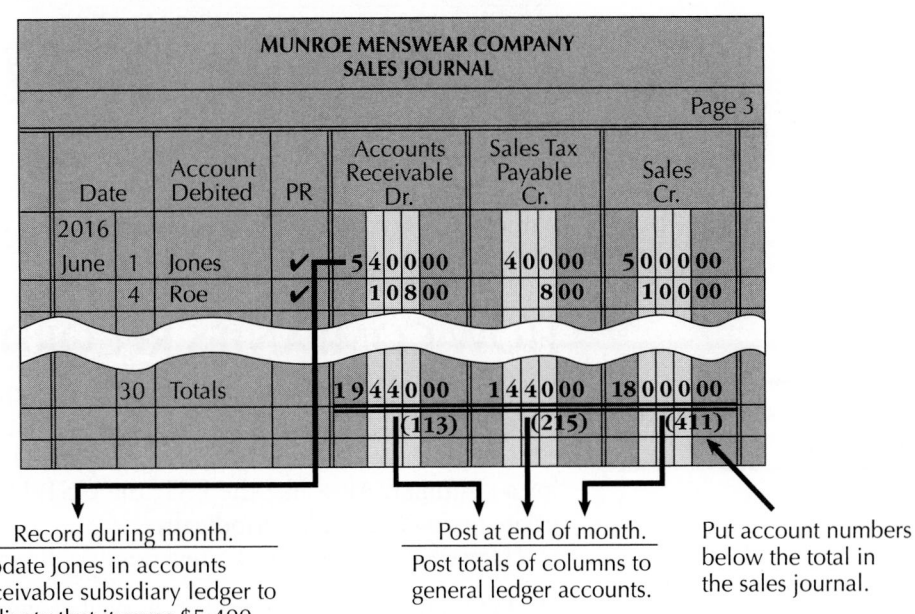

Record during month.
Update Jones in accounts receivable subsidiary ledger to indicate that it owes \$5,400 to Munroe.

Post at end of month.
Post totals of columns to general ledger accounts.

Put account numbers below the total in the sales journal.

LO 2

Creating, recording, and posting a credit memorandum for returned sales when PST, GST, or HST is included

THE CREDIT MEMORANDUM WITH PROVINCIAL SALES TAX

Figure 11-1 shows the sales journal for Munroe Menswear Company. Remember, since Munroe is a retail company, its customers must pay PST if they are in a province that charges PST. Let's assume that on June 8 Roe returns $50 worth of the $100 worth of merchandise he bought earlier in the month. Let's analyze and journalize the credit memo that Munroe issued. Keep in mind that the customer is no longer responsible for paying for either the returned merchandise or the 8% tax on it.

Accounts Affected	Category	↑↓	Rules	T Account Update
Sales Returns and Allowances	Revenue (Contra)	↑	Dr.	Sales Returns and Allowances: Dr. 50 | Cr.
Provincial Sales Tax Payable ($8 tax on $100) ($4 tax on $50)	Liability	↓	Dr.	Provincial Sales Tax Payable: Dr. 4,00 | Cr.
Accounts Receivable, Roe	Asset	↓	Cr.	Accounts Rec.: Dr. | Cr. 54; Roe: Dr. 108 | Cr. 54

Date		Account	Dr.	Cr.
June	8	Sales Returns and Allowances	50 00	
		Provincial Sales Tax Payable	4 00	
		Accounts Receivable, Roe		54 00
		Issued credit memo		

This journal entry requires three postings to the general ledger and one recording for Roe in the accounts receivable subsidiary ledger. Note that since Roe returned half of his merchandise, he was able to reduce what he pays for PST by half (from $8 to $4).

HOW COMPANIES RECORD GST AND HST

Similarities and differences between PST and GST

Before illustrating the normal accounting treatment of the GST/HST, notice that there are both similarities and differences between the GST and PST (covered earlier). Like the PST, the GST/HST is added to the total of each invoice prepared for a customer. Also, like the PST, the GST/HST must be remitted to the appropriate taxing authority periodically.

However, there are also a few notable differences:

1. GST/HST applies to services as well as goods (e.g., a lawyer will add 5% (or 13%) to each invoice for professional services).
2. GST/HST applies at all levels in the economy—not just the retail level, as in the case of PST.
3. GST/HST is paid by businesses to their suppliers as well as charged by them to their customers. The difference between the tax charged from customers and the tax paid to suppliers is the amount sent to (or recovered from) the federal government each period.

4. GST/HST might result in a business receiving a refund in some periods. Since GST/HST is payable on large asset purchases (e.g., a delivery van), a business may claim this amount against the GST/HST it owes. In the long run, if a business is successful, it should remit more GST/HST than it receives as a refund; however, in a particular period it may be eligible to receive a refund.

GST/HST CHARGED ON SALES

To illustrate the basic accounting treatment for **GST/HST charged**, we will refer to an example you have already seen. Figure 6-3 (sales invoice) showed what an invoice would look like before GST/HST. Figure 11-2 shows the same invoice with HST added.

> *Note:* **There are more similarities with than differences from the bookkeeping procedures described previously.**

You should notice two things about this invoice. First, HST is added at 13% (GST would be added at 5%) of the total price of the goods. Second, the invoice shows a registration (or business) number. Each business in Canada (*except very small ones*) must be registered for GST/HST by the federal government and use the number in all its dealings with the federal government.

This invoice is recorded in the sales journal of Art's Clothing Company. The main difference is that now the bookkeeping task is made slightly longer because of the need to keep track of the HST. Figure 6-2 on page 254 showed the sales journal before HST. Figure 11-3 shows how this new invoice, and some others not illustrated individually, are recorded with HST. Posting to the various ledger accounts is also illustrated. Figure 11-3a shows how a multicolumn sales journal would look. It also shows CM1 entered as a negative. This CM is discussed next.

The total invoice amounts are recorded during the month in the individual customers' accounts in the accounts receivable subsidiary ledger. This process is identical to the pre-GST/HST method except that the totals are higher.

At the end of the month, instead of posting a single amount as *both* a credit (to Sales) and a debit (to Accounts Receivable), there are three totals to post. A new account is now required—HST Payable, No. 212. This is a liability account in the general ledger with a credit balance. Notice that the totals of the two credits (Sales and HST) equal the single debit (Accounts Receivable).

Figure 11-2
Sales Invoice with HST

Sales Invoice No. 1001

Art's Clothing Company
1528 Belle Avenue
Toronto, Ontario M5A 2L4

Sold to: Hal's Clothing
91 Century Avenue
Winnipeg, MB R2C 4X7

Date: April 2, 2016
Your purchase order No: 430
Ship via: Acme Truck Co.

Shipped to: Same
Terms: 2/10, n/30

Sold by: J.L.

Quantity	Description	Unit Price	Total
20	Men's dress shirts—code 16B	$20.00	$400.00
10	Ladies' designer jeans—code 18C	35.00	350.00
10	Baseball caps—code 22D	5.00	50.00
		Subtotal	$800.00
	Add:	HST	104.00
		TOTAL	$904.00

Business No. 109309799

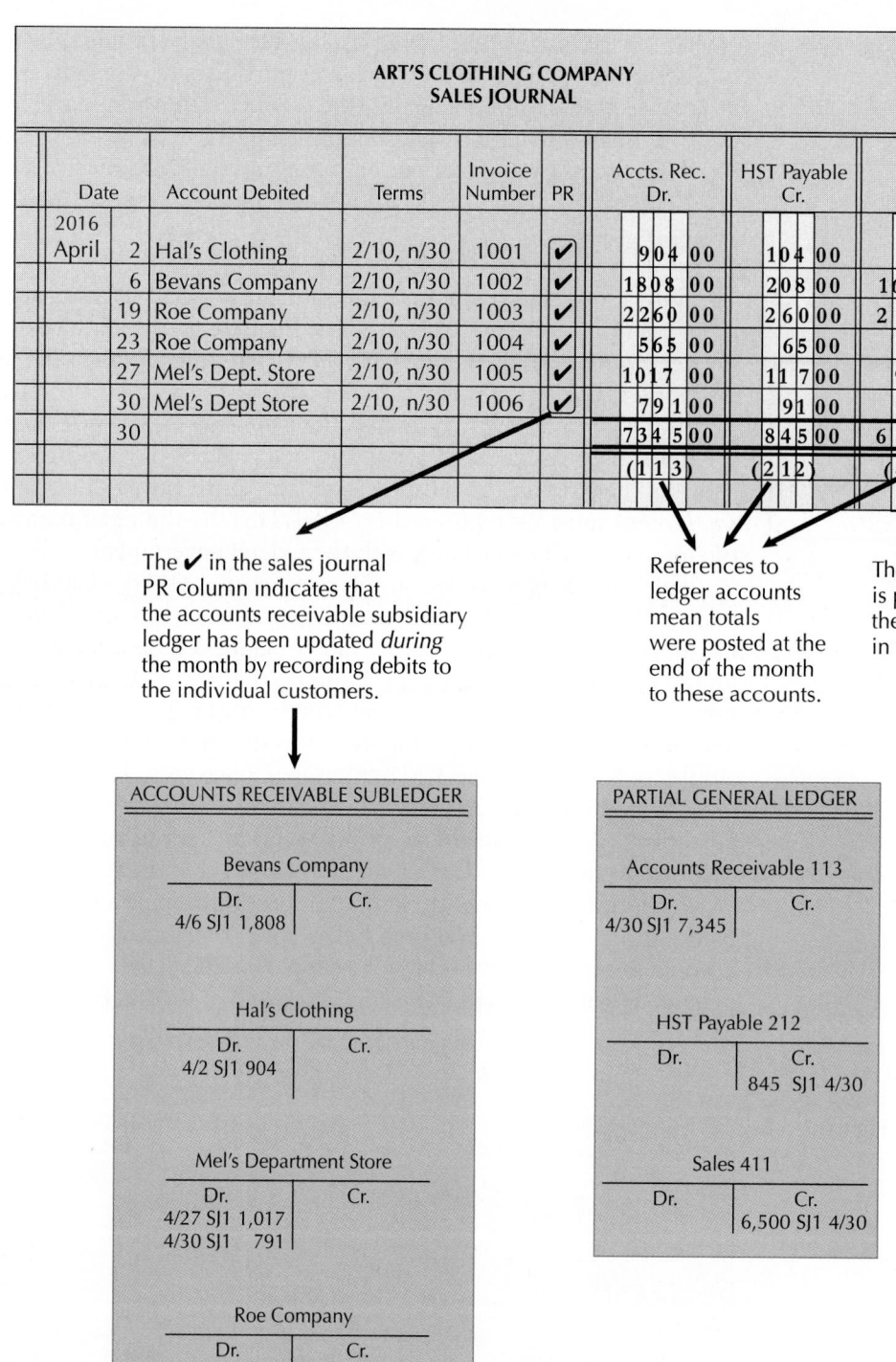

ART'S CLOTHING COMPANY
SALES JOURNAL

Page 1

Date		Account Debited	Terms	Invoice Number	PR	Accts. Rec. Dr.	HST Payable Cr.	Sales Cr.
2016								
April	2	Hal's Clothing	2/10, n/30	1001	✔	904 00	104 00	800 00
	6	Bevans Company	2/10, n/30	1002	✔	1808 00	208 00	1600 00
	19	Roe Company	2/10, n/30	1003	✔	2260 00	260 00	2000 00
	23	Roe Company	2/10, n/30	1004	✔	565 00	65 00	500 00
	27	Mel's Dept. Store	2/10, n/30	1005	✔	1017 00	117 00	900 00
	30	Mel's Dept Store	2/10, n/30	1006	✔	791 00	91 00	700 00
	30					7345 00	845 00	6500 00
						(113)	(212)	(411)

The ✔ in the sales journal PR column indicates that the accounts receivable subsidiary ledger has been updated *during* the month by recording debits to the individual customers.

References to ledger accounts mean totals were posted at the end of the month to these accounts.

The total of $6,500 is posted at the end of the month to Sales (Cr.) in the general ledger.

ACCOUNTS RECEIVABLE SUBLEDGER

Bevans Company

Dr.	Cr.
4/6 SJ1 1,808	

Hal's Clothing

Dr.	Cr.
4/2 SJ1 904	

Mel's Department Store

Dr.	Cr.
4/27 SJ1 1,017	
4/30 SJ1 791	

Roe Company

Dr.	Cr.
4/19 SJ1 2,260	
4/23 SJ1 565	

PARTIAL GENERAL LEDGER

Accounts Receivable 113

Dr.	Cr.
4/30 SJ1 7,345	

HST Payable 212

Dr.	Cr.
	845 SJ1 4/30

Sales 411

Dr.	Cr.
	6,500 SJ1 4/30

Figure 11-3 Sales Journal and Postings with HST

ART'S CLOTHING COMPANY SALES JOURNAL										
										Page 1
Date		Customer's Account	Sold By	Invoice Number	PR	Invoice Total Dr.	13% HST	Men's Clothing Sales Cr.	Ladies' Clothing Sales Cr.	Other Sales Cr.
2016 April	2	Hal's Clothing	JL	1001	✔	904 00	104 00	400 00	350 00	50 00
	6	Bevan Company	MC	1002	✔	1 808 00	208 00	600 00	800 00	200 00
	12	Bevan Company		CM-1	✔	(678 00)	(78 00)	(600 00)		
	19	Roe Company	PK	1003	✔	2 260 00	260 00	1 100 00	750 00	150 00
	23	Roe Company	PK	1004	✔	565 00	65 00	200 00	200 00	100 00
	27	Mel's Department Store	JL	1005	✔	1 017 00	117 00	460 00	380 00	60 00
	29	Mel's Department Store	JL	1006	✔	791 00	91 00	310 00	350 00	40 00
	30	Monthly Totals			✔	6 667 00	767 00	2 470 00	2 830 00	830 00
						(113)	(224)	(411)	(412)	(413)
Sales by Salesperson: See Note 1 below										
			JL			2 400 00		<<<See Note 2 Below>>>		
			MC			1 600 00				
			PK			2 500 00				
		Total Sales				6 500 00				

Note: 1. The sales amounts by salesperson do not include the GST. Since a sales tax results entirely from a governmental decision, no individual should be "credited with" the tax amounts. The CM is not deducted from the amounts either.

2. The number of column totals to be posted has increased from three to five, because we now have three sales categories instead of the original one. The only difference is that postings now go to accounts 411, 412, and 413 instead of just to account 411 when a single sales account was used. All other postings and recordings are as before.

Figure 11-3a Multicolumn Sales Journal with HST and a Credit Memo

The credit memorandum with HST is very similar to an invoice with HST except that the amounts are opposite in meaning and effect, and often smaller.

GST/HST AND THE CREDIT MEMORANDUM

As you already know, a business occasionally finds it necessary to issue a customer a **credit memorandum** (often called a credit note). The pre-HST form of a credit memorandum is shown in Figure 6-4 on page 256. The new form of credit memorandum showing HST is shown in Figure 11-4.

Figure 11-4 Credit Memorandum with HST

Art's Clothing Company
1528 Belle Avenue
Toronto, ON M5A 2L4

Credit Memorandum No. 1

Date: April 12, 2016

Credit to: Bevans Company
110 Aster Road
Amherst, NS B4H 3A5

We credit your account as follows:

Merchandise returned—60 model 8B men's dress gloves	$600.00
Plus HST	78.00
Total Credit	$678.00

Business No. 109309799

Figure 11-5
Postings for the Credit Memorandum with HST

ART'S CLOTHING COMPANY
GENERAL JOURNAL

Page 1

Date		Account Titles and Description	PR	Debit	Credit
2016					
April	12	HST Payable	212	78 00	
		Sales Returns and Allowances	412	600 00	
		Accounts Receivable, Bevans Co.	113/✔		678 00

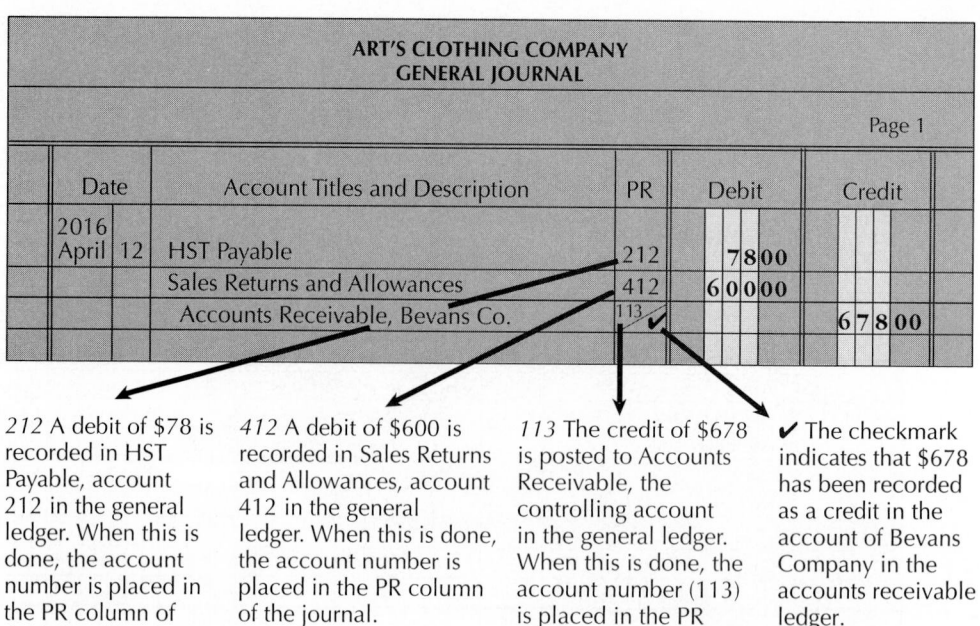

212 A debit of $78 is recorded in HST Payable, account 212 in the general ledger. When this is done, the account number is placed in the PR column of the journal.

412 A debit of $600 is recorded in Sales Returns and Allowances, account 412 in the general ledger. When this is done, the account number is placed in the PR column of the journal.

113 The credit of $678 is posted to Accounts Receivable, the controlling account in the general ledger. When this is done, the account number (113) is placed in the PR column of the journal, above the /.

✔ The checkmark indicates that $678 has been recorded as a credit in the account of Bevans Company in the accounts receivable ledger.

As before, we will assume that the volume of credit notes is low and that Art's Clothing Company uses the general journal to record these notes. The journal entry will appear as shown in Figure 11-5.

Remember that the $78 debit posting will reduce the amount of HST owed to the federal government and must be taken into account when preparing a cheque for the amount owed at period-end. The customer, Bevans Company, now receives a credit totalling $678. This includes the extra 13% for HST. Since the original invoice included this 13% tax as an addition, it is proper that any refund for returned or damaged goods also include the 13% tax. The amount owed to Art's Clothing Company by Bevans Company is reduced by $678.

As was the case in Chapter 6, a credit memorandum can be recorded in three different ways. If the volume of CMs is very high, a special journal can be employed. In any province that charges PST, this journal would have four headings:

1. Sales Returns and Allowances (Dr.)
2. PST Payable (Dr.)
3. GST Payable (Dr.)
4. Accounts Receivable (Cr.)

In a province that does not charge PST (apart from the portion combined with GST), there would be only three columns; the PST column would not be needed. Of course, if a company keeps track of their sales using a multicolumn sales journal, then the credit memo journal might be designed to also include the relevant sales categories as well.

In addition to the above, and as shown in Chapter 6, a company can just enter any credit memos directly into the sales journal as negative amounts. As stated in Chapter 6, this approach is very efficient, but needs to be carefully monitored so that abuses are avoided. Refer to Figure 11-3a to see how this would look.

PROVINCIAL SALES TAX WITH GST/HST

In many provinces (not in Ontario, Nova Scotia, New Brunswick, Prince Edward Island, Newfoundland and Labrador, or Alberta), when a sale is made to a customer at the retail level, PST is added to the invoice. Since 1991, it has been necessary to also add GST to these invoices. A typical invoice in a province with a 8% PST might look like Figure 11-6.

In provinces that charge HST, the invoice would look like Figure 11-2.

SALES INVOICE WITH PST AND GST

The Munroe Menswear Company would record this invoice along with other invoices for June 2017 in its sales journal. This recording and posting process is illustrated in Figure 11-7. Note that, apart from the addition of one more column (for the GST), this is similar to the illustration shown in Figure 11-3.

No sales discount is taken on GST/HST or PST amounts because the monies are charged on behalf of the government.

It is worth repeating that if sales discounts are available, they are usually taken on the *sales amount only*, not the GST/HST or PST. If Jones receives a 2% discount on invoice No. 1420 (see Figure 11-6), it would pay the following amount:

Original sales amount of invoice No. 1420	$1,500
Less: 2% discount	30
	1,470
Plus: PST as originally computed	120
Plus: GST as originally computed	75
Amount paid	$1,665

Figure 11-6
Sales Invoice with PST and GST

Assume the PST rate in this province is 8%.

Munroe Menswear Company
147 Main Street
Saskatoon, Saskatchewan
S8A 2G7

To: Jones Company
228 Market Street
Saskatoon, Saskatchewan
S8J 2P2

Invoice # 1420
June 01, 2017

10 Company Blazers with logo @ $150.00 each		$1,500.00
	PST @ 8%	120.00
		1,620.00
	GST @ 5%	75.00
	Total	$1,695.00

Business No. 142716491

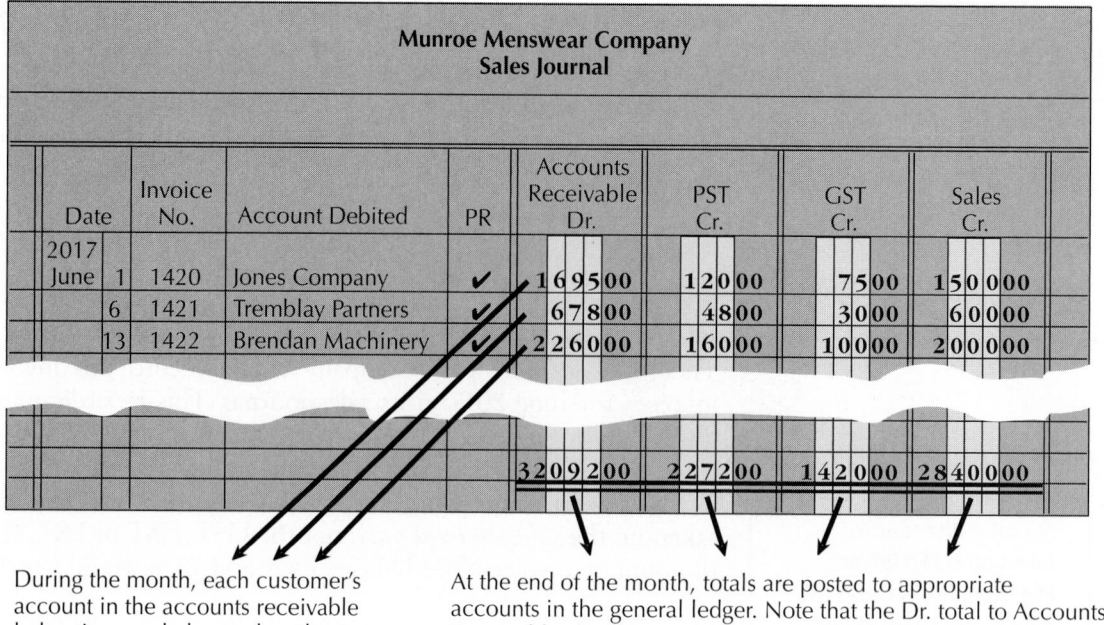

Munroe Menswear Company
Sales Journal

Date		Invoice No.	Account Debited	PR	Accounts Receivable Dr.	PST Cr.	GST Cr.	Sales Cr.
2017								
June	1	1420	Jones Company	✔	1695 00	120 00	75 00	1500 00
	6	1421	Tremblay Partners	✔	678 00	48 00	30 00	600 00
	13	1422	Brendan Machinery	✔	2260 00	160 00	100 00	2000 00
					32092 00	2272 00	1420 00	28400 00

During the month, each customer's account in the accounts receivable ledger is recorded to update the amount owed. Note that these figures include the PST and GST.

At the end of the month, totals are posted to appropriate accounts in the general ledger. Note that the Dr. total to Accounts Receivable ($32,092) equals the total of the three Cr. postings to PST, GST, and Sales ($2,272 + $1,420 + $28,400 = $32,092).

Figure 11-7 Munroe's Sales Journal with GST

CREDIT MEMORANDUM WITH PST AND GST/HST

Let us assume that Jones receives permission to return some of the goods billed on invoice No. 1420 (Figure 11-6). The result is in a credit memorandum (or credit note) being prepared by Munroe Menswear Company. This credit memo would appear as shown in Figure 11-8.

The credit memo would be recorded by Munroe Company in its general journal (unless there was a large number of returns, in which case a special journal could be used). The entry to record credit note No. 104 is as shown in Figure 11-9.

This entry is posted in a similar fashion to the entry in Figure 11-5. The only change is that there is also a posting of a debit to PST Payable (account No. 210) as well as to GST Payable (account No. 212). It is often useful to use a multicolumn sales journal to record sales that include both PST and GST. This is very similar to what was illustrated in Figure 11-3a, except there are now two Tax Payable columns, not one. Also note that it is possible to record credit memos in the multicolumn journal as was shown in Figure 11-3a.

The credit memorandum with PST and GST is very similar to an invoice with PST and GST except that the amounts are opposite in meaning and effect, and often smaller.

Figure 11-8
Credit Memo with PST and GST

Munroe Menswear Company
147 Main Street
Saskatoon, Saskatchewan
S8A 2G7

To: Jones Company
228 Market Street
Saskatoon, Saskatchewan
S8J 2P2

Credit Memo # 104
July 15, 2017

Returned 2 Blazers—Ref. Invoice 1420, June 1, 2017—@ $150.00 each

	$300.00
PST @ 8%	24.00
	324.00
GST @ 5%	15.00
Total	$339.00

Business No. 142716491

Figure 11-9
Recording Credit Memo with PST and GST

MUNROE MENSWEAR COMPANY
GENERAL JOURNAL

Page 1

Date		Account Titles and Description	PR	Debit	Credit
2017 July	15	Sales Returns and Allowances	412	300 00	
		GST Payable	212	15 00	
		PST Payable	210	24 00	
		Accounts Receivable, Jones Co.	113/✔		339 00
		To record credit memo number 104			

LEARNING UNIT 11-1 REVIEW

AT THIS POINT you should be able to:

- Explain the basics of GST/HST and PST added to sales invoices in Canada. (pp. 489–490)
- Explain, journalize, and post an invoice that includes both GST/HST and PST. (pp. 497–498)
- Explain, journalize, and post a credit memorandum that includes both GST and PST. (pp. 498–499)

Self-Review Quiz 11-1

(The forms you need are on pages 11-1 and 11-2 of the *Study Guide with Working Papers.*)

Journalize the following transactions in the sales journal or the general journal for Moss Company. Post to the accounts receivable and general ledger accounts as appropriate. Use the same journal headings and general ledger account numbers that were used in Figures 11-7 and 11-9.

2015
May 1 Sold merchandise to Jane Company, invoice No. 101—$400 plus PST $32 plus GST $20—total $452.00. Terms 2/10, n/30
4 Sold merchandise to Ralph Company, invoice No. 102—$3,000 plus PST $240 plus GST $150—total $3,390.00. Terms 2/10, n/30
21 Issued credit memorandum No. 4 to Ralph Company, $500 plus PST $40 plus GST $25—total $565.00. Reason—defective goods

Solution to Self-Review Quiz 11-1

MOSS COMPANY
SALES JOURNAL

Page 1

Date		Account Debited	Invoice Number	PR	Accts. Rec. Dr.	PST Payable Cr.	GST Payable Cr.	Sales Cr.
2015 May	1	Jane Company	101	✔	452 00	32 00	20 00	400 00
	4	Ralph Company	102	✔	3390 00	240 00	150 00	3000 00
					3842 00	272 00	170 00	3400 00
					(112)	(210)	(212)	(411)

MOSS COMPANY
GENERAL JOURNAL

Date		Account Titles and Description	PR	Debit	Credit
2015					
May	21	Sales Returns and Allowances	412	500 00	
		GST Payable	212	25 00	
		PST Payable	210	40 00	
		Accounts Receivable, Ralph Co.	112/✓		565 00
		To record credit memo No. 4			

PARTIAL GENERAL LEDGER

Accounts Receivable — Acct. No. 112

Date		Explanation	PR	Debit	Credit	Dr. or Cr.	Balance
2015							
May	21		GJ1		565 00	Cr.	565 00
	31		SJ1	3842 00		Dr.	3277 00

PST Payable — Acct. No. 210

Date		Explanation	PR	Debit	Credit	Dr. or Cr.	Balance
2015							
May	21		GJ1	40 00		Dr.	40 00
	31		SJ1		272 00	Cr.	232 00

GST Payable — Acct. No. 212

Date		Explanation	PR	Debit	Credit	Dr. or Cr.	Balance
2015							
May	21		GJ1	25 00		Dr.	25 00
	31		SJ1		170 00	Cr.	145 00

Sales — Acct. No. 411

Date		Explanation	PR	Debit	Credit	Dr. or Cr.	Balance
2015							
May	31		SJ1		3400 00	Cr.	3400 00

Sales Returns and Allowances — Acct. No. 412

Date		Explanation	PR	Debit	Credit	Dr. or Cr.	Balance
2015							
May	21		GJ1	500 00		Dr.	500 00

PARTIAL ACCOUNTS RECEIVABLE SUBLEDGER

NAME Jane Company
ADDRESS 1218 Broadview Avenue, Toronto, ON M5X 2A1

Date		Explanation	PR	Debit	Credit	Dr. Balance
2015 May	1		SJ1	452 00		452 00

NAME Ralph Company
ADDRESS 1300 Marine Drive, West Vancouver, BC V6P 9B6

Date		Explanation	PR	Debit	Credit	Dr. Balance
2015 May	4		SJ1	3390 00		3390 00
	21		GJ1		565 00	2825 00

LEARNING UNIT 11-2

Cash Receipts Journal and Schedule of Accounts Receivable

LO 3

Recording cash received using a cash receipts journal when PST, GST, or HST is included

Besides the sales journal, another special journal often used in a merchandising operation is the cash receipts journal. The cash receipts journal records the receipt of cash (or cheques) from any source. The number of columns a cash receipts journal will have depends on how frequently certain types of transactions occur. For example, in the cash receipts journal for Art's Clothing Company, the accountant has developed the headings shown in Figure 11-10. Note that a column for HST (on cash sales only) has been included. HST on credit sales is recorded in the sales journal as already described. Below each heading is a description of the purpose of that column and when to update the accounts receivable subsidiary ledger as well as the general ledger.

The following transactions occurred in April for Art's Clothing Company and affected the cash receipts journal:

2016		
Apr.	1	Art Newner invested $8,000 in the business.
	5	Received cheque from Hal's Clothing for payment of invoice No. 1 less discount.
	12	Cash sales for first half of April, $900 plus HST.
	16	Received cheque from Bevans Company in settlement of invoice No. 2 less returns and discount.
	22	Received cheque from Roe Company for payment of invoice No. 3 less discount.
	26	Sold store equipment, $500.
	30	Cash sales for second half of April, $1,200 plus HST.

Figure 11-11 shows the cash receipts journal for the end of April along with the recordings to the accounts receivable subsidiary ledger and posting to the general ledger. Study the diagram; we will review it in a moment.

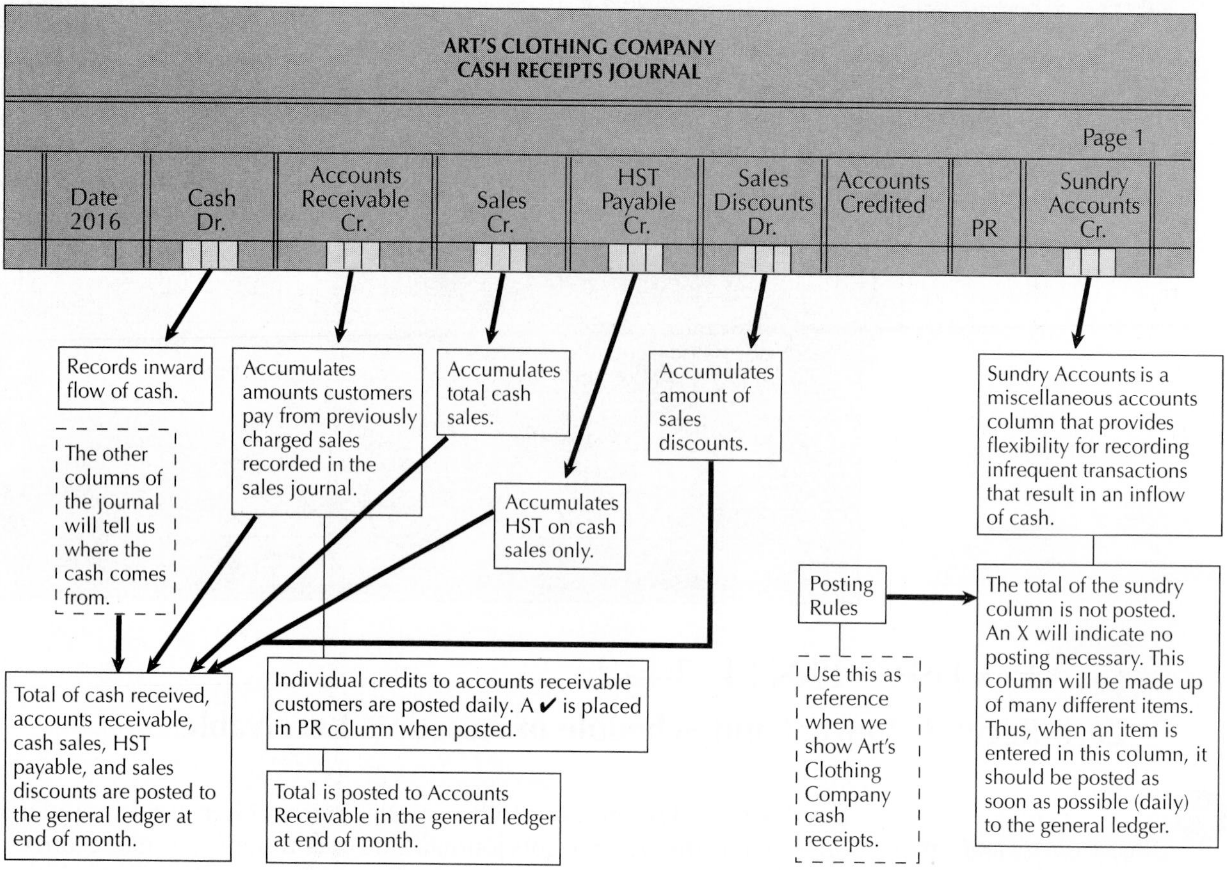
ART'S CLOTHING COMPANY
CASH RECEIPTS JOURNAL
Page 1
Date 2016
Cash Dr.
Accounts Receivable Cr.
Sales Cr.
HST Payable Cr.
Sales Discounts Dr.
Accounts Credited
PR
Sundry Accounts Cr.
Records inward flow of cash.
Accumulates amounts customers pay from previously charged sales recorded in the sales journal.
Accumulates total cash sales.
Accumulates amount of sales discounts.
Sundry Accounts is a miscellaneous accounts column that provides flexibility for recording infrequent transactions that result in an inflow of cash.
The other columns of the journal will tell us where the cash comes from.
Accumulates HST on cash sales only.
Posting Rules
The total of the sundry column is not posted. An X will indicate no posting necessary. This column will be made up of many different items. Thus, when an item is entered in this column, it should be posted as soon as possible (daily) to the general ledger.
Use this as reference when we show Art's Clothing Company cash receipts.
Total of cash received, accounts receivable, cash sales, HST payable, and sales discounts are posted to the general ledger at end of month.
Individual credits to accounts receivable customers are posted daily. A ✔ is placed in PR column when posted.
Total is posted to Accounts Receivable in the general ledger at end of month.

Figure 11-10 Cash Receipts Journal with HST

JOURNALIZING, RECORDING, AND POSTING FROM THE CASH RECEIPTS JOURNAL

On April 5, Art's Clothing Company received a cheque from Hal's Clothing for payment of invoice No. 1 less discount. Remember, it was in the sales journal that this transaction was first recorded (Figure 11-3). At that time, we updated the accounts receivable ledger, indicating that Hal's Clothing owed Art $904. Since Hal's Clothing is paying within the 10-day discount period, Art's Clothing Company offers a $16 sales discount ($800 × 0.02). (Remember, all credit sales carried terms of 2/10, n/30.)

Now, when payment is received, Art's Clothing Company updates the cash receipts journal (page 503) by entering the date (April 5), cash debit of $888, sales discounts debit of $16, credit to accounts receivable of $904, and which account name (Hal's Clothing) is to be credited. The terms of sale indicate that Hal's Clothing is entitled to the discount and no longer owes Art's Clothing Company the $904 balance. *As soon as this line is entered into the cash receipts journal, Art's Clothing Company will update the ledger account of Hal's Clothing.* Note, in the accounts receivable ledger of Hal's Clothing, how the date (April 5), posting reference (CRJ1), and credit amount ($904) account are recorded. The balance in Hal's accounts receivable ledger is zero. The last step of this transaction is to go back to the cash receipts journal and put a ✓ in the posting reference column.

The last step is to put a check mark in the PR column of the cash receipts journal to show the accounts receivable ledger is up to date.

In studying this cash receipts journal, note that:

1. All totals of cash receipts in the journal columns except sundry were posted to the general ledger at the end of the month.
2. Art Newner, Capital, and Store Equipment were posted to the general ledger when entered in the sundry column. It is assumed that the equipment account had a beginning balance of $4,000 in the general ledger. There is no HST on the owner's capital contribution.

CASH RECEIPTS JOURNAL

Page 1

Date		Cash Dr.	Accounts Receivable Cr.	Sales Cr.	HST Payable Cr.	Sales Discount Dr.	Accounts Credited	PR	Sundry Accounts Cr.
2016 April	1	8000 00					Art Newner, Capital	311	8000 00
	5	888 00	904 00			16 00	Hal's Clothing	✔	
	12	1017 00		900 00	117 00		Cash Sales	✗	
	16	1110 00	1130 00			20 00	Bevans Company	✔	
	22	2220 00	2260 00			40 00	Roe Company	✔	
	26	565 00			65 00		Store Equipment	121	500 00
	30	1356 00		1200 00	156 00		Cash Sales	✗	
	30	15156 00	4294 00	2100 00	338 00	76 00			8500 00
		(111)	(113)	(411)	(212)	(413)			(X)

Totals posted to general ledger at end of month

Total not posted

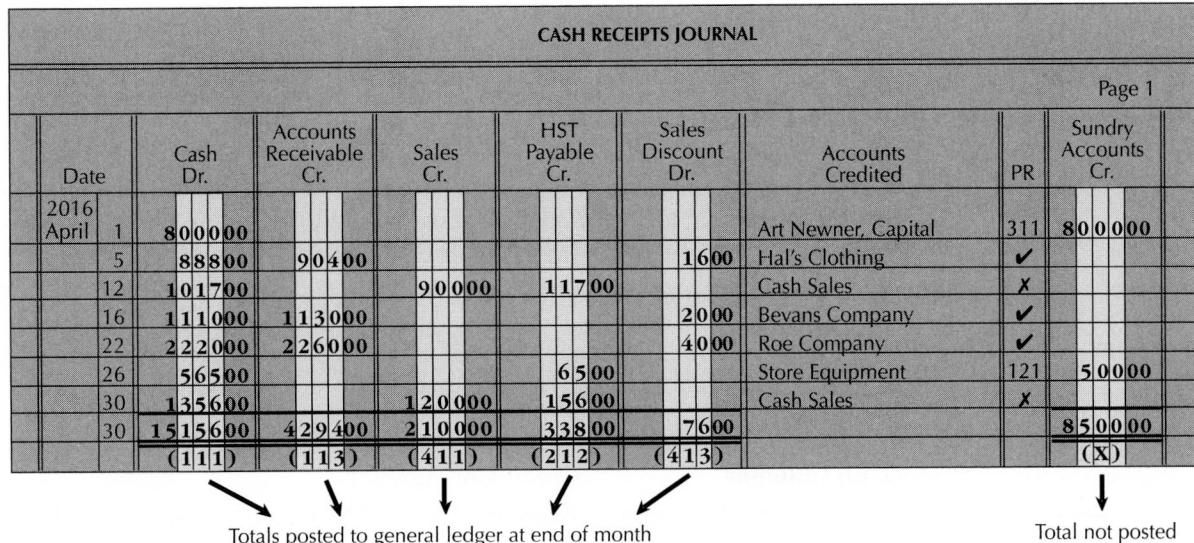

Figure 11-11 Cash Receipts Journal and Posting with HST

ACCOUNTS RECEIVABLE SUBSIDIARY LEDGER

NAME Bevans Company
ADDRESS 110 Aster Road, Amherst, NS B4H 3A5

Date		Explanation	PR	Debit	Credit	Dr. Balance
2016 April	6		SJ1	1808 00		1808 00
	12		GJ1		678 00	1130 00
	16		CRJ1		1130 00	-0-

NAME Hal's Clothing
ADDRESS 91 Century Avenue, Winnipeg, MB R2C 4X7

Date		Explanation	PR	Debit	Credit	Dr. Balance
2016 April	2		SJ1	904 00		904 00
	5		CRJ1		904 00	-0-

NAME Mel's Department Store
ADDRESS 181 Foss Road, Fredericton, NB E3A 2N8

Date		Explanation	PR	Debit	Credit	Dr. Balance
2016 April	26		SJ1	1017 00		1017 00
			SJ1	791 00		1808 00

NAME Roe Company
ADDRESS 18 Rantool Street, Regina, SK S4P 3J7

Date		Explanation	PR	Debit	Credit	Dr. Balance
2016 April	19		SJ1	2260 00		2260 00
	22		CRJ1		2260 00	-0-
	23		SJ1	565 00		565 00

Note on accounts receivable: Very occasionally (because of an error, e.g., when a customer pays twice for the same invoice), a credit balance may be called for. Credit balances are opposite to the normal debit balance and are signified by placing the balance in brackets. For example, suppose that Hal's Clothing (see above) mistakenly paid its invoice twice. The account would then appear as follows:

NAME Hal's Clothing
ADDRESS 91 Century Avenue, Winnipeg, MB R2C 4X7

Date		Explanation	PR	Debit	Credit	Dr. Balance
2016 April	2		SJ1	904 00		904 00
	5		CRJ1		904 00	-0-
	10		CRJ1		904 00	(904 00)

PARTIAL GENERAL LEDGER

Cash — Acct. No. 111

Date		Explanation	PR	Debit	Credit	Dr. or Cr.	Balance
2016 April	30		CRJ1	15156 00		Dr.	15156 00

Accounts Receivable — Acct. No. 113

Date		Explanation	PR	Debit	Credit	Dr. or Cr.	Balance
2016 April	12		GJ1		678 00	Cr.	678 00
	30		SJ1	7345 00		Dr.	6667 00
	30		CRJ1		4294 00	Dr.	2373 00

Store Equipment — Acct. No. 121

Date		Explanation	PR	Debit	Credit	Dr. or Cr.	Balance
2016 April	1	Balance				Dr.	4000 00
	26		CRJ1		500 00	Dr.	3500 00

HST Payable — Acct. No. 212

Date		Explanation	PR	Debit	Credit	Dr. or Cr.	Balance
2016 April	12		GJ1	78 00		Dr.	78 00
	30		SJ1		845 00	Cr.	767 00
	30		CRJ1		338 00	Cr.	1105 00

Art Newner Capital — Acct. No. 311

Date		Explanation	PR	Debit	Credit	Dr. or Cr.	Balance
2016 April	1		CRJ1		8000 00	Cr.	8000 00

Sales — Acct. No. 411

Date		Explanation	PR	Debit	Credit	Dr. or Cr.	Balance
2016 April	30		SJ1		6500 00	Cr.	6500 00
	30		CRJ1		2100 00	Cr.	8600 00

Sales Returns and Allowances — Acct. No. 412

Date		Explanation	PR	Debit	Credit	Dr. or Cr.	Balance
2016 April	12		GJ1	600 00		Dr.	600 00

Sales Discounts — Acct. No. 413

Date		Explanation	PR	Debit	Credit	Dr. or Cr.	Balance
2016 April	30		CRJ1	76 00		Dr.	76 00

3. The cash sales were not posted when entered (hence the X to show no posting is needed). The sales and cash totals are posted at the end of the month.
4. A ✓ means information was recorded daily to the accounts receivable ledger.
5. The Accounts Credited column describes each transaction.

We can prove the accuracy of recording transactions of the cash receipts journal by totalling the columns with debit balances and the columns with credit balances. Cross-adding is done before the totals are posted. Also, if a bookkeeper were using more than one page for the cash receipts journal, the balances on the bottom of one page would be brought forward to the top of the next page. This verifying of totals would result in less work when trying to find journalizing or posting errors at a later date. Let's see how to cross-add the cash receipts journal of Art's Clothing Company (Figure 11-11).

Proving the cash receipts journal

Debit Columns	= **Credit Columns**
Cash + Sales Discounts	= **Accounts Receivable + Sales + Sundry + HST**
$15,156 + $76	= **$4,294 + $2,100 + $8,500 + $338**
$15,232	= **$15,232**

Now let's take a moment to see what PST would look like in the cash receipts journal of a business that would need to record sales tax as well as HST. A typical cash receipts journal might look as follows:

CASH RECEIPTS JOURNAL

Page 1

Date 2016	Cash Dr.	Accounts Receivable Cr.	Sales Cr.	PST Payable Cr.	HST Payable Cr.	Sales Discounts Dr.	Accounts Credited	PR	Sundry Accounts Cr.

The total of sales tax payable would be posted to Sales Tax Payable in the general ledger at the end of the month.

The total of the sales tax as a result of cash sales would be posted to Sales Tax Payable in the general ledger at the end of the month. It represents a liability of the merchant to forward the tax to the provincial government. Remember, cash discounts are not usually taken on the sales tax (or GST/HST).

Now let's prove the accounts receivable ledger to the controlling account—Accounts Receivable—at the end of April for Art's Clothing Company.

LO 4

Preparing schedules of accounts receivable and accounts payable, and balancing to control accounts

SCHEDULE OF ACCOUNTS RECEIVABLE

From Figure 11-11, let's list the customers that have an ending balance in the accounts receivable ledger of Art's Clothing Company. As mentioned in Chapter 6, this listing is called a schedule of accounts receivable. The balance of the controlling account, Accounts Receivable ($2,373), in the general ledger (see above) does indeed equal the sum of the individual customer balances in the accounts receivable ledger ($2,373) as shown below in the schedule of accounts receivable. The schedule of accounts receivable can help forecast potential cash inflows as well as possible credit and chargeion decisions.

Schedule is listed in alphabetical order.

Art's Clothing Company
Schedule of Accounts Receivable
April 30, 2016

Mel's Department Store	$1,808.00
Roe Company	565.00
Total Accounts Receivable	$2,373.00

LEARNING UNIT 11-2 REVIEW

AT THIS POINT you should be able to:

- Journalize, record, and post transactions with sales tax using a cash receipts journal (pp. 502–504)
- Prepare a schedule of accounts receivable (p. 504)

Self-Review Quiz 11-2

(The forms you need are on pages 11-3 to 11-5 of the *Study Guide with Working Papers.*)

Journalize, cross-foot, record, and post when appropriate the following transactions into the cash receipts journal of Moore Co. Use the same headings as for Art's Clothing Company.

Accounts Receivable Ledger

Name	*Balance*	*Invoice No.*
Irene Welch	$565	1
Chantel Simard	226	2

Partial General Ledger

Account	*Account No.*	*Balance*
Cash	110	$600
Accounts Receivable	120	791
Store Equipment	130	600
HST Payable	212	91
Sales	410	700
Sales Discounts	420	—

2016

May 3 Received cheque from Irene Welch for invoice No. 1 less 2% discount.

7 Cash sales, $400 plus HST of $20.

14 Received cheque from Chantel Simard for invoice No. 2 less 2% discount.

20 Sold store equipment at cost, $300 (plus HST).

Solution to Self-Review Quiz 11-2

MOORE COMPANY
CASH RECEIPTS JOURNAL

Page 2

Date	Cash Dr.	Accounts Receivable Cr.	Sales Cr.	HST Payable Cr.	Sales Discounts Dr.	Description of Receipt	PR	Sundry Accounts Cr.
2016 May 3	55500	56500			1000	Irene Welch	✔	
7	45200		40000	5200		Cash Sales	✗	
14	22200	22600			400	Chantel Simard	✔	
20	33900			3900		Store Equipment	130	30000
31	156800	79100	40000	9100	1400			30000
	(110)	(120)	(410)	(212)	(420)			(X)

Cross-adding: $1,582.00 = $1,582.00

PARTIAL GENERAL LEDGER

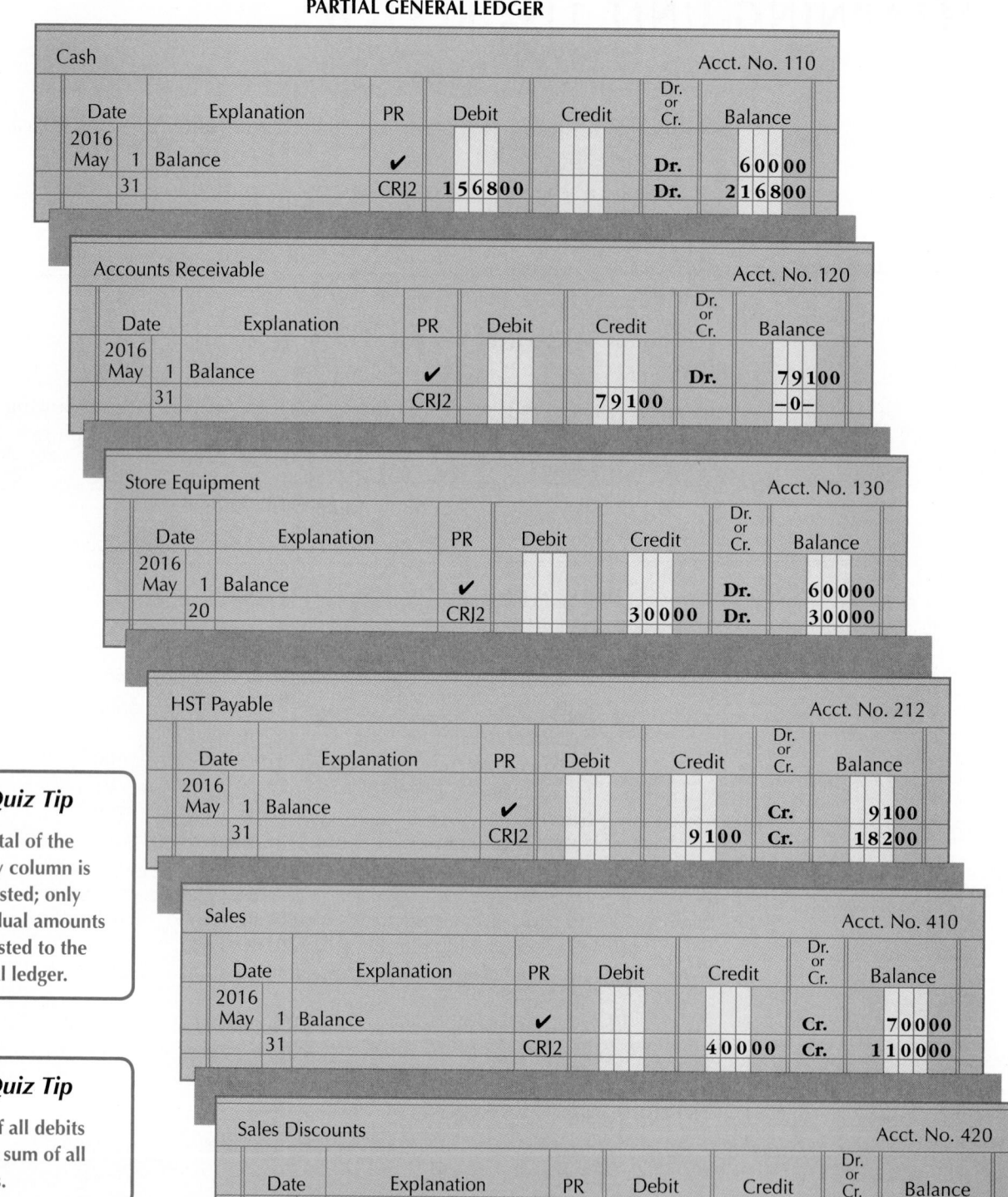

Cash — Acct. No. 110

Date		Explanation	PR	Debit	Credit	Dr. or Cr.	Balance
2016 May	1	Balance	✔			Dr.	60000
	31		CRJ2	156800		Dr.	216800

Accounts Receivable — Acct. No. 120

Date		Explanation	PR	Debit	Credit	Dr. or Cr.	Balance
2016 May	1	Balance	✔			Dr.	79100
	31		CRJ2		79100		–0–

Store Equipment — Acct. No. 130

Date		Explanation	PR	Debit	Credit	Dr. or Cr.	Balance
2016 May	1	Balance	✔			Dr.	60000
	20		CRJ2		30000	Dr.	30000

HST Payable — Acct. No. 212

Date		Explanation	PR	Debit	Credit	Dr. or Cr.	Balance
2016 May	1	Balance	✔			Cr.	9100
	31		CRJ2		9100	Cr.	18200

Sales — Acct. No. 410

Date		Explanation	PR	Debit	Credit	Dr. or Cr.	Balance
2016 May	1	Balance	✔			Cr.	70000
	31		CRJ2		40000	Cr.	110000

Sales Discounts — Acct. No. 420

Date		Explanation	PR	Debit	Credit	Dr. or Cr.	Balance
2016 May	31		CRJ2	1400		Dr.	1400

Quiz Tip

The total of the Sundry column is not posted; only individual amounts are posted to the general ledger.

Quiz Tip

Sum of all debits equals sum of all credits.

ACCOUNTS RECEIVABLE LEDGER

NAME Irene Welch
ADDRESS 10 Rong Road, Timmins, ON P4N 4M3

Date		Explanation	PR	Debit	Credit	Dr. Balance
2016 May	1	Balance	✔			525 00
	3		CRJ2		525 00	–0–

NAME Chantel Simard
ADDRESS 9017 Robitaille Road, Montreal, QC H1K 4R3

Date		Explanation	PR	Debit	Credit	Dr. Balance
2016 May	1	Balance	✔			210 00
	14		CRJ2		210 00	–0–

LEARNING UNIT 11-3

GST/HST Paid on Purchases

LO 5 Journalizing purchase transactions that include GST or HST in the purchases journal

OVERVIEW

In the previous learning unit, we learned that GST or HST charged on sales needs to be sent to the federal government periodically. No surprises here—this is very similar to PST. However, the GST/HST is what we refer to as a value-added tax. Without getting overly technical, each business in effect adds a net tax to the "improvement" in value that it adds to the goods and/or services it provides or sells. If a company buys some merchandise (to resell) for $1,000 and actually sells it for $1,500, then the GST/HST is applicable only to the $500 difference.

While that is true, the tax works in the following manner:

- First, the business charges the GST at 5% on the selling price of $1,500. This would amount to $75 (5% × $1,500) (covered in Learning Unit 11-1).
- Second, the business pays the 5% GST on the $1,000 for which the merchandise was purchased. This amounts to $50 (5% × $1,000) (covered in this learning unit).
- Companies remit the net difference between the GST that they charge on sales and the GST that they pay on purchases.
- Finally, the tax sent to the federal government in the case of 5% GST is only $25 (5% × $500 or $75 less $50) because the business gets a credit for the tax it paid on the purchase.

Summary

5% GST charged on sale of merchandise: 5% × $1,500.00 =	$75
5% GST paid on purchase of merchandise: 5% × $1,000.00 =	$50
Net tax to be remitted (5% of difference of $500.00)	$25

If HST were involved instead of GST, the Summary would look like this:

HST charged	$195
HST paid	130
HST to remit	$ 65

Businesses do not keep track of GST/HST separately on each item of inventory they sell, of course. However, the above example makes it plain that companies must keep track of the total GST/HST that they pay so they can claim a refund when they calculate the tax that they must periodically send to the federal government.

This learning unit details the accounting tasks that must be handled properly to record GST/HST accurately.

RECORDING PURCHASES WITH GST/HST

> *Note:* **Recording purchases with GST is very similar to recording purchases with no GST—just one extra column is needed.**

In the earlier learning units, we discussed purchases and cash payments without GST/HST. In Figure 7-1 on page 301 of Chapter 7, a typical purchase order was illustrated. Some companies have not changed their purchase orders to include GST/HST since it is now the law for GST/HST to be included even if the purchase order says nothing. Other companies may refer to the fact that the specified price does not include GST/HST. They expect that 5% GST or 13% HST will be added. Still other companies specify and calculate the tax. These companies produce a purchase order that would look like the one shown below in Figure 11-12 (assuming HST at 13%).

When the supplier fills the purchase order, an invoice will be prepared that includes GST/HST. In Figure 7-2 on page 301, a sales invoice before HST was illustrated. The same sales invoice incorporating HST is shown in Figure 11-13. Note that HST is charged on the shipping charges as well as the amount charged for the goods.

This invoice is recorded (as others) by the purchaser in a manner similar to the original example shown earlier in Chapter 7. The major change is that now the purchases journal has one additional column—**Prepaid HST**. Figure 11-14 shows how the purchases journal would appear with HST included.

Figure 11-12
Purchase Order with HST

Purchase Order No. 41
Art's Clothing Company
1528 Belle Avenue
Toronto, Ontario M5A 2L4

Purchased From: Abby Blake Company
12 Foster Road
Quebec City, QC G1M 4H3

Date: April 1, 2016
Shipped VIA: Freight truck
Terms: 2/10, n/60
FOB: Quebec City

Quantity	Description	Unit Price	Total
100	Ladies' Jackets Code 14-0	$50	$5,000.00
		Add HST	650.00
		Total Price before Shipping	$5,650.00

Purchase order number must appear on all invoices.

Art's Wholesale
By: Bill Joy

Figure 11-13
Sales Invoice with HST

Sales Invoice No. 228
Abby Blake Company
12 Foster Road
Quebec City, QC G1M 4H3

Sold to: Art's Clothing Co.
1528 Belle Avenue
Toronto, ON
M5A 2L4

Date: April 1, 2016
Shipped VIA: Freight truck
Terms: 2/10, n/60
Your Order No: 41
FOB: Quebec City

Quantity	Description	Unit Price	Total
100	Ladies' Jackets Code 14-0	$50	$5,000.00
	Freight		50.00
	Sub-total		$5,050.00
	HST (13%)		656.50
	Total		$5,706.50
	Business No. 142714982		

ART'S CLOTHING COMPANY
PURCHASES JOURNAL

Page 1

Date			Date of Invoice	Inv. No.	Terms	PR	Accounts Payable Credit	Purchases Debit	Prepaid HST Dr.	Sundry—Dr. Account Name	PR	Amount
2016 April	2	Abby Blake Company	April 01	228	2/10, n/60	✔	5706 50	5000 00	656 50	Freight-In	514	50 00
	5	Joe Francis Company	April 02	388		✔	4520 00		520 00	Equipment	121	4000 00
	8	Thorpe Company	April 05	415	1/10, n/30	✔	904 00	800 00	104 00			
	9	John Sullivan Company	April 06	516	n/10, EOM	✔	1107 40	980 00	127 40			
	15	Abby Blake Company	April 12	242	1/10, n/30	✔	678 00	600 00	78 00			
	29	John Sullivan Company	April 26	612		✔	565 00		65 00	Supplies	115	500 00
	30						13480 90	7380 00	1550 90			4550 00
							(211)	(511)	(125)			(X)

The ✔ in the posting reference column indicates that the accounts payable ledger has been updated during the month.

Total Accounts Payable, Prepaid HST, and Purchases are posted to general ledger accounts at end of month.

Posted to general ledger account when transaction is entered.

Total of Sundry is not posted—the individual items are posted instead.

ACCOUNTS PAYABLE SUBSIDIARY LEDGER

Tells us what page of journal information came from.

Abby Blake Co.

Dr.	Cr.
	5,706.50 PJ1 4/2
	678.00 PJ1 4/15

Joe Francis Co.

Dr.	Cr.
	4,520.00 PJ1 4/5

John Sullivan Co.

Dr.	Cr.
	1,107.40 PJ1 4/9
	565.00 PJ1 4/29

Thorpe Co.

Dr.	Cr.
	904.00 PJ1 4/8

PARTIAL GENERAL LEDGER

Supplies 115

4/29 PJ1 500.00	

Accounts Payable 211

	13,480.90 PJ1 4/30

Equipment 121

4/5 PJ1 4,000.00	

Purchases 511

4/30 PJ1 7,380.00	

Prepaid HST 125

4/30 PJ1 1,550.90	

Freight-In 514

4/2 PJ1 50.00	

Many companies prefer to record GST/HST in a "liability" account that is placed close to the GST/HST Payable account. This helps to underscore the fact that GST/HST paid on purchases is deducted from any such taxes charged, with only the net amount sent to the government.

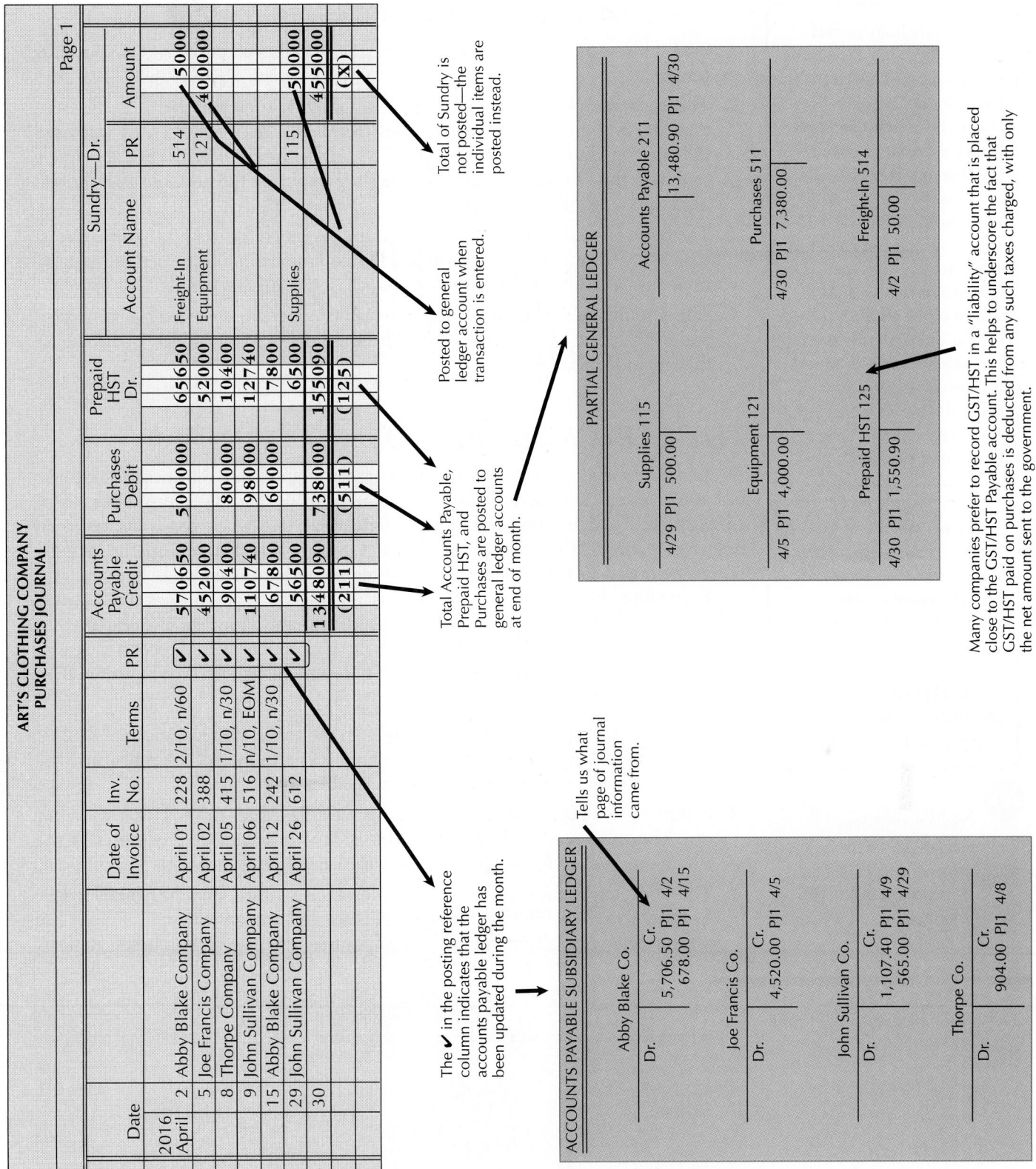

Figure 11-14 Purchases Journal with HST

A more technically correct term for the credit a company receives for the GST/HST it pays is *Input Tax Credit*. Do not be confused by the use of the word *Credit*; these GST/HST amounts are debits in a formal bookkeeping sense. This is logical since GST/HST on purchases is considered an asset. However, it is sometimes treated as a contra-liability since it offsets the GST/HST payable on sales made. Some companies record this "asset" in an account that follows GST/HST Payable in the current liabilities section of the chart of accounts.

Note the following while you review Figure 11-14:

1. GST/HST is paid on equipment purchases as well as on purchases of goods for resale.
2. The account (No. 125) used to record GST/HST on purchases is different than the account used to record sales (recall that account No. 212 was used in Learning Unit 11-2 for recording GST/HST on sales). While not absolutely required, this procedure can make the preparation of the periodic governmental returns less of a burden.
3. The basic operation of the purchases journal is much the same as before. Cross-adding reveals that the addition of an HST column has not disturbed the equality of debits ($7,380 + $4,550 + $1,550.90 = $13,480.90) and credits ($13,480.90).
4. The amounts posted to the accounts payable ledger are posted at the same time and in the same way as previously. The amounts are now higher, of course, as they include HST at 13%.

THE DEBIT MEMORANDUM

Remember that five provinces (Ontario, Prince Edward Island Nova Scotia, New Brunswick, and Newfoundland and Labrador) charge and charge HST at 13% to 15% rather than GST at 5% and PST at an individual provincial rate. The HST replaces both PST and GST in those five provinces.

As already discussed, from time to time, purchased goods are returned to suppliers because of insufficient quality, defective manufacturing, and the like. We have seen an example of a **debit memorandum**, which is prepared when goods are returned (refer to Figure 7-5 on page 306). When GST/HST is charged on the original purchase, it must also be added to the debit memorandum, as shown in Figure 11-15.

Recording this debit memorandum is usually done in the general journal, although a specialized journal could be used if a large number of debit memos were common in a given business. Art's Clothing Company would record the debit memorandum (illustrated in Figure 11-15) in its general journal (see Figure 11-16).

The four postings are:

LO 6

Creating, recording, and posting a debit memorandum for purchase returns when GST or HST is included

1. 211—Post to Accounts Payable as a debit in the general ledger account No. 211. When this is done, place the account number, 211, in the PR column, above the diagonal on the same line as Accounts Payable.
2. ✓ Record to Thorpe Co. in the accounts payable ledger to show that we don't owe Thorpe as much money. When this is done, place a ✓ in the journal in the PR column below the diagonal line on the same line as Accounts Payable.
3. 513—Post to Purchases, Returns and Allowances as a credit in the general ledger (account No. 513). When this is done, place the account number, 513, in the posting reference column of the journal on the same line as Purchases, Returns

Figure 11-15
Debit Memorandum with HST

Debit Memorandum — No. 1

Art's Clothing Company
1528 Belle Avenue
Toronto, ON M5A 2L4

To: Thorpe Company
3 Access Road
Fredericton, NB E3B 4T3

April 9, 2016

WE DEBIT your account as follows:

Quantity		Unit Cost	Total
20	Men's Hats Code 827—defective brims	$10.00	$200.00
	Add HST @ 13%		26.00
	Total Adjustment		$226.00

Figure 11-16
Posting the Debit Memo with HST

GENERAL JOURNAL

Page 1

Date		Account Titles and Description	PR	Dr.	Cr.
2016 April	9	Accounts Payable, Thorpe Company	211/✔	226 00	
		Purchases, Returns and Allowances	513		200 00
		Prepaid HST	125		26 00
		To record debit memo No. 1			

A debit memorandum with GST/HST is very similar to a supplier's invoice with GST/HST except that the amounts are opposite in meaning and effect, and often smaller.

and Allowances (if equipment was returned that was not merchandise for resale, we would credit Equipment and not Purchases, Returns and Allowances).

4. 125—Post to Prepaid HST as a credit. This causes an increase in the amount of GST/HST owed to the federal government because it decreases the amount that is claimable to offset the liability recorded in account No. 212 (see Learning Objective 11-2 for details of this account).

QUICK METHOD OF ACCOUNTING FOR GST/HST

L 07

Accounting for GST or HST using the simplified approach.

This chapter provides details of how most companies in Canada should manage the accounting/recordkeeping for GST/HST. Basically, a business sends along to the federal government any GST/HST it charges after subtracting any GST/HST it pays. This is simple enough in concept, but it does mean that a lot of record-keeping is needed.

If your company qualifies (the main consideration is that the volume of sales cannot exceed $400,000 for a year), it is possible to use the quick method of accounting for GST/HST. Details of how this works are contained in form RC4058, which you can obtain from the CRA or download from their website.

The quick method can save on some record-keeping, because a company no longer needs to keep track of most GST/HST that they pay. However, this method still requires a business to keep detailed records of their sales, all of which must include GST or HST charged at whatever rates are normal for their location. Put another way: even a small business cannot get any relief from charging GST or HST by using the quick method of accounting. They also must pay the cost of accounting for this tax.

The way the quick method operates is reasonably simple. The business keeps track of the GST/HST that they charge, but remits only part of that amount to the government. The amount remitted is a choice of two rates:

- Rate 1 applies if the business buys things and then re-sells them. The best example here might be a small store selling basic groceries.
- Rate 2 applies if the business mostly sells a service. Examples include a dry-cleaning operation or a taxi service.

Not too surprisingly, the applicable rates vary a lot from province to province. Not only that, but the rules may change if a business has their main location in one province, but sells goods or services to residents in another. However, many businesses will not need to pay attention to these complexities, and can just use the rates that are applicable to their situation. By way of illustration, here are two rates for a business that does not sell goods:

The business is in Ontario, selling to Ontarians—8.8%

The business is in Nova Scotia, selling to Nova Scotians—10.0%

Let's assume that a dry-cleaning business in Halifax, Nova Scotia, charges $300,000 in fees from its customers in a year. In that province it is necessary to charge 15% HST, so the total cash received in the year will be $345,000—or $300,000 plus 15%. If that business uses the quick method of accounting, it needs to send 10% of its revenue to the federal government, or $30,000. The difference of $15,000 ($45,000 less $30,000) is its to keep, and is intended to reflect the HST the business would have paid on their purchases for the year. Remember that most businesses will need to pay rent, do some advertising, and purchase some necessary supplies, etc., and all of these will have HST charged on them.

Whether a small business is better off to use the quick method is impossible to say with precision. The government has made one rather large concession that helps justify using this approach. If a business makes a major asset purchase in a year, it is allowed to claim a refund on the GST/HST they pay. So, for example if our dry-cleaning business in Halifax buys a delivery van for $40,000, it will pay an additional $6,000 in HST on that purchase. However, the business permitted to claim that amount back because it is a major capital purchase.

Some businesses are probably better off to avoid the quick method. One excellent example is a new venture in its first few years of operation. It is rather common for such a business to lose money during the early years. The sales volume may be small, but the rent is not, for instance, or the business may pay out large amounts for advertising or promotion to help gain a positive reputation. If this is the case, then the business should avoid using the quick method, because it will likely be paying out more GST/HST than it charges, and therefore would receive a refund if it employs the usual method of accounting as detailed in this chapter.

The bottom line is- Check with a professional before committing to a choice of method. It may cost the business some professional fees, but it is a shame to pay more in taxes than necessary.

The Cash Payments Journal

LO 8

Recording cash paid out in the cash payments journal when GST or HST is included

The addition of HST does not alter the fact that Art's Clothing Company will record all payments made by cash (or most likely by cheque) in a cash payments journal. However, as you probably suspect, this journal now has a separate column for Prepaid HST, which the original illustration shown in Figure 7-6 on page 310 did not have.

Trace the following cash disbursements through Figure 11-17. The following (revised) transactions affected the cash disbursements journal:

Note that even though the cash payments journal has a column for HST, it is never used when paying a regular supplier. The GST/HST on these purchases is recorded when the original entries are made in the Purchases Journal. Do not record the GST/HST on these purchases twice!

April	2	Issued cheque No. 101 to Pete Blum for insurance paid in advance, $900. (***Note:*** Insurance is not subject to GST/HST.)
	5	Issued cheque No. 102 to Joe Francis Company in payment of its April 2 invoice No. 388.
	9	Issued cheque No. 103 to Flo Co. for merchandise purchased for cash $800 plus HST $104, total $904.
	12	Issued cheque No. 104 to Thorpe Company in payment of its April 6 invoice No. 415, less the return and discount.
	26	Issued cheque No. 105, $700 salaries paid.

In tracing the cash payments to the payments journal, a few points may be of interest:

1. There is no HST on the insurance payment of $900. Insurance premiums are classified as financial services and no HST is paid on these services.
2. Similarly, no HST is paid on salaries of $700 on April 26.
3. HST does not affect the $6 purchase discount allowed when payment is made to the Thorpe Company on April 12. This discount is calculated only on the $600 (net) purchase, not on the $678 that is the total amount payable because of the extra 13% HST. The actual amount paid is $672 because the $678 is reduced by $6 due to the allowed purchase discount.

CASH PAYMENTS JOURNAL

Page 1

Date		Chq. No.	Account Debited	PR	Sundry Accounts Dr.	Accounts Payable Dr.	Purchases Dr.	Prepaid HST Dr.	Purchases Discounts Cr.	Cash Cr.
2016 April	2	101	Pete Blum, Insurance	116	900 00					900 00
	5	102	Joe Francis Company	✔		4 520 00				4 520 00
	9	103	Flo Co., Cash Purchases				800 00	104 00		904 00
	12	104	Thorpe Company	✔		678 00			6 00	672 00
	26	105	Salaries	611	700 00					700 00
					1 600 00	5 198 00	800 00	104 00	6 00	7 696 00
					(X)	(211)	(511)	(125)	(512)	(111)

Total not posted.

Total posted to general ledger at end of month.

ACCOUNTS PAYABLE SUBSIDIARY LEDGER

NAME Abby Blake Co.
ADDRESS 12 Foster Road, Quebec City, QC G1M 4H3

Date		Explanation	PR	Debit	Credit	Cr. Balance
2016 April	2		PJ1		5 706 50	5 706 50
	15		PJ1		678 00	6 384 50

NAME Joe Francis Co.
ADDRESS 2 Roundy Road, Edmonton, AB T5H 2E7

Date		Explanation	PR	Debit	Credit	Cr. Balance
2016 April	5		PJ1		4 520 00	4 520 00
	5		CPJ1	4 520 00		–0–

PARTIAL GENERAL LEDGER

Cash — Acct. No. 111

Date		Explanation	PR	Debit	Credit	Dr. or Cr.	Balance
2016 April	30		CRJ1	15 156 00		Dr.	15 156 00
	30		CPJ1		7 696 00	Dr.	7 460 00

Prepaid Insurance — Acct. No. 116

Date		Explanation	PR	Debit	Credit	Dr. or Cr.	Balance
2016 April	2		CPJ1	900 00		Dr.	900 00

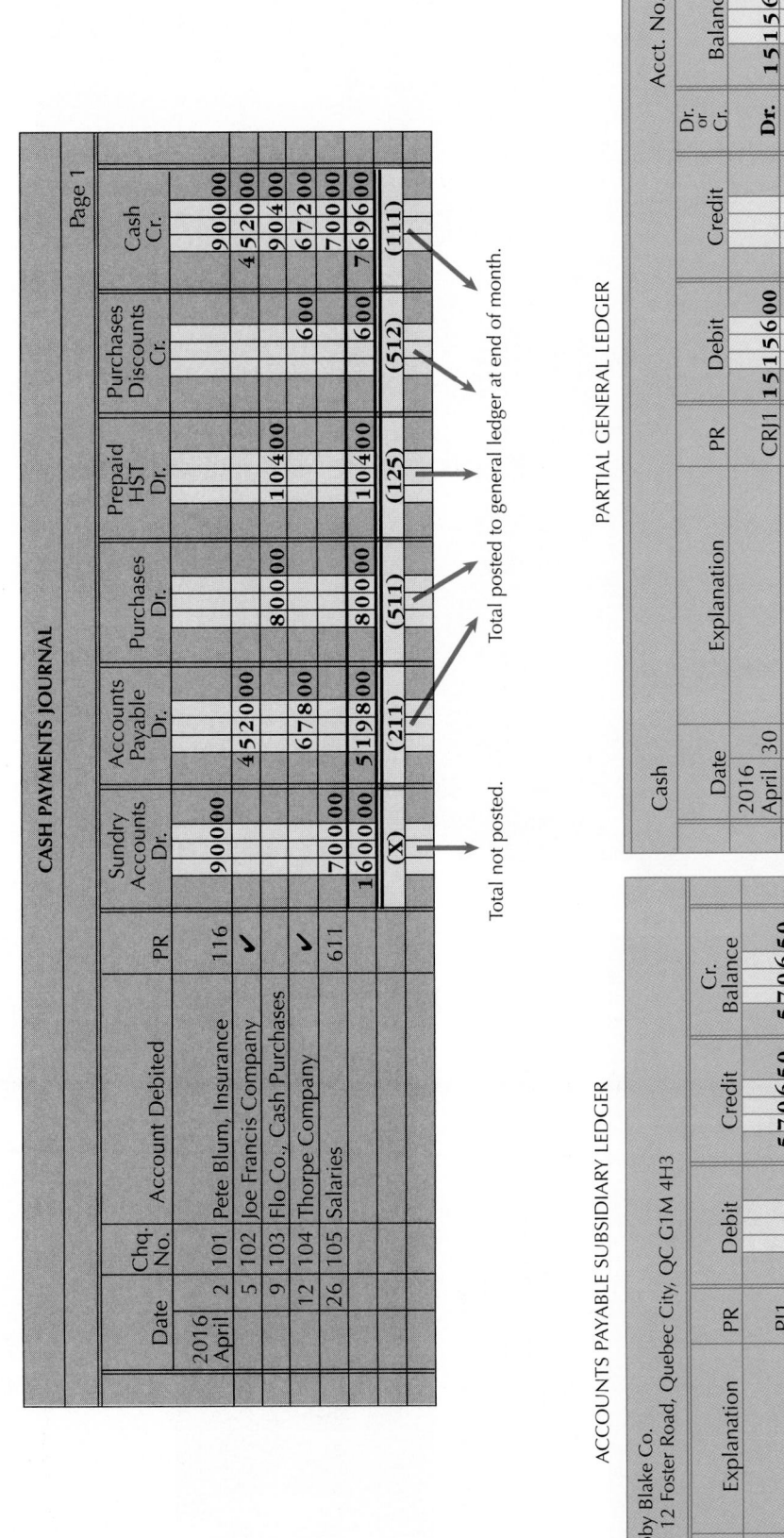

Figure 11-17 Cash Payments Journal and Posting with HST

NAME John Sullivan Co.
ADDRESS 18 Print Street, Regina, SK S4P 2A6

Date		Explanation	PR	Debit	Credit	Cr. Balance
2016						
April	9		PJ1		1107 40	1107 40
	26		PJ1		565 00	1672 40

NAME Thorpe Company
ADDRESS 3 Access Road, Fredericton, NB E3B 4T3

Date		Explanation	PR	Debit	Credit	Cr. Balance
2016						
April	8		PJ1		904 00	904 00
	9		GJ1	226 00		678 00
	12		CPJ1	678 00		–0–

Note on Accounts Payable balance: Very occasionally (perhaps because of the return of defective goods after they have been paid for), a debit balance may be called for on Accounts Payable. Debit balances are opposite to the normal credit balance and are signified by placing the balance in brackets. For example, suppose we get a credit note from Joe Francis Co. for $420.00 after we have paid off its account completely. The account would then appear as follows:

NAME Joe Francis Co.
ADDRESS 2 Roundy Road, Edmonton, AB T5H 2E7

Date		Explanation	PR	Debit	Credit	Cr. Balance
2016						
April	5		PJ1		4520 00	4520 00
	5		CPJ1	4520 00		–0–
	13		GJ4	452 00		(452 00)

Controlling account

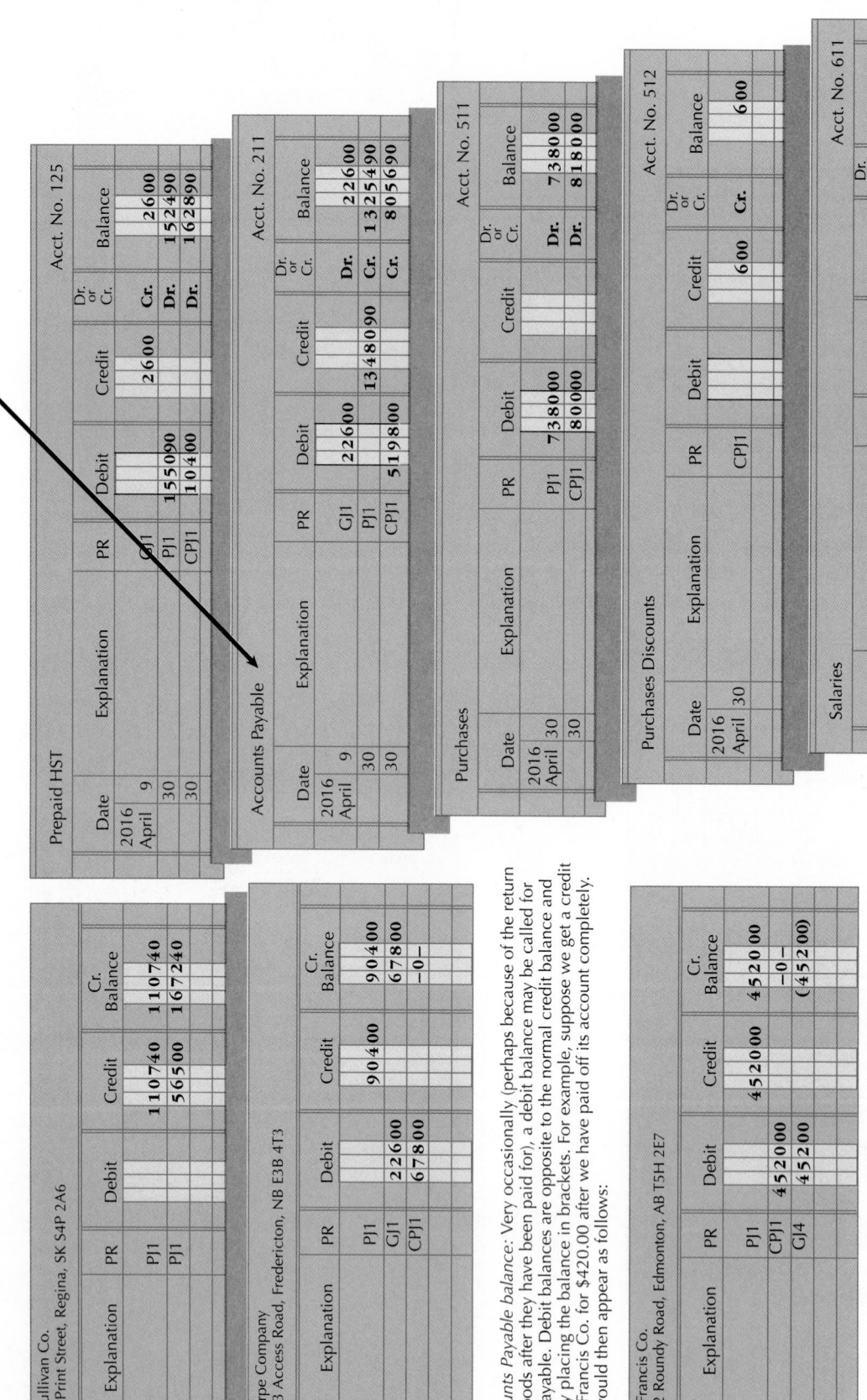

Prepaid HST — Acct. No. 125

Date		Explanation	PR	Debit	Credit	Dr. or Cr.	Balance
2016							
April	9		GJ1		26 00	Cr.	26 00
	30		PJ1	1550 90		Dr.	1524 90
	30		CPJ1	104 00		Dr.	1628 90

Accounts Payable — Acct. No. 211

Date		Explanation	PR	Debit	Credit	Dr. or Cr.	Balance
2016							
April	9		GJ1	226 00		Dr.	226 00
	30		PJ1		13480 90	Cr.	13254 90
	30		CPJ1	5198 00		Cr.	8056 90

Purchases — Acct. No. 511

Date		Explanation	PR	Debit	Credit	Dr. or Cr.	Balance
2016							
April	30		PJ1	7380 00		Dr.	7380 00
	30		CPJ1	800 00		Dr.	8180 00

Purchases Discounts — Acct. No. 512

Date		Explanation	PR	Debit	Credit	Dr. or Cr.	Balance
2016							
April	30		CPJ1		6 00	Cr.	6 00

Salaries — Acct. No. 611

Date		Explanation	PR	Debit	Credit	Dr. or Cr.	Balance
2016							
April	26		CPJ1	700 00		Dr.	700 00

Figure 11-17 Cash Payments Journal and Posting with HST (continued)

Schedule of Accounts Payable

Notice that it is not difficult to prepare a schedule of accounts payable at month-end from Figure 11-17. This schedule would look like:

Art's Clothing Company
Schedule of Accounts Payable
April 30, 2016

Abby Blake Co.	$6,384.50
John Sullivan Co.	1,672.40
Total Accounts Payable	$8,056.90

If you refer again to Figure 11-17, you can see that $8,056.90 is exactly the balance in account No. 211—Accounts Payable. Hence, the subsidiary ledger accounts are in agreement with the controlling account in the general ledger. As always, if the total of the individual accounts in the accounts payable ledger does not agree with the controlling account, it will be necessary to double-check all postings and the mathematical computations of balances in each supplier's account to find the difference. Also, be sure that any entries made in the general journal are posted to the general ledger accounts.

LEARNING UNIT 11-3 REVIEW

AT THIS POINT you should be able to:

- Describe the nature of the GST/HST. (p. 507)
- Record the GST/HST on purchases. (pp. 508–510)
- Record the GST/HST on returned purchases. (pp. 510– 511)
- Describe and calculate GST/HST using the Quick Method. (p. 511)
- Record the GST/HST on other cash payments. (pp. 512– 514)
- Prepare a schedule of accounts payable at period-end. (p. 515)

Self-Review Quiz 11-3

(The forms you need are on pages 11-6 and 11-7 of the *Study Guide with Working Papers.*)

Journalize the following transactions in the purchases journal (page 2) or general journal (page 1) for Munroe Co. Post or record to the accounts payable ledger and general ledger accounts as appropriate. Use the same journal headings as we used for Art's Clothing Company.

2017		
May	5	Bought merchandise on account from Flynn Co., invoice No. 512, dated May 2, terms 1/10, n/30, $900 plus GST $45. Total $945.
	6	Bought merchandise from John Butler Company, invoice No. 403, dated May 6, terms n/10, EOM, $1,000 plus GST $50. Total $1,050.
	13	Issued debit memo No. 1 to Flynn Co. for merchandise returned, $300, from invoice No. 512, plus GST $15. Total $315.
	16	Purchased $400 worth of equipment on account from John Butler Company, invoice No. 413, dated May 16, plus GST $20. Total $420.

Solution to Self-Review Quiz 11-3

MUNROE CO.
PURCHASES JOURNAL

Page 2

Date		Description	Date of Invoice	Inv. No.	Terms	PR	Accounts Payable Credit	Purchases Debit	GST Prepaid Debit	Sundry—Debit Account Name	Sundry—Debit PR	Sundry—Debit Amount
2017 May	5	Flynn Co.	May 2	512	1/10, n/30	✔	945 00	900 00	45 00			
	6	John Butler Co.	May 6	403	n/10, EOM	✔	1050 00	1000 00	50 00			
	16	John Butler Co.	May 16	413		✔	420 00		20 00	Equipment	121	400 00
	31						2415 00	1900 00	115 00			400 00
							(212)	(512)	(125)			(X)

MUNROE CO.
GENERAL JOURNAL

Page 1

Date		Account Titles and Description	PR	Dr.	Cr.
2017 May	13	Accounts Payable, Flynn Co.	212/✔	315 00	
		Purchases Returns and Allowances	513		300 00
		GST Prepaid	125		15 00

ACCOUNTS PAYABLE SUBSIDIARY LEDGER

NAME Flynn Co.
ADDRESS 15 Foss Avenue, Quebec City, QC G1L 2W4

Date		Explanation	PR	Debit	Credit	Cr. Balance
2017 May	5		PJ2		945.00	945.00
	13		GJ1	315.00		630.00

NAME John Butler Co.
ADDRESS 18 Reed Road, Winnipeg, MB R2B 8G6

Date		Explanation	PR	Debit	Credit	Cr. Balance
2017 May	6		PJ2		1,050.00	1,050.00
	16		PJ2		420.00	1,470.00

PARTIAL GENERAL LEDGER

Equipment — Acct. No. 121

Date		Explanation	PR	Debit	Credit	Dr. or Cr.	Balance
2017 May	16		PJ2	400.00		Dr.	400.00

GST Prepaid — Acct. No. 125

Date		Explanation	PR	Debit	Credit	Dr. or Cr.	Balance
2017 May	13		GJ1		15.00	Cr.	15.00
	31		PJ2	115.00		Dr.	100.00

Accounts Payable — Acct. No. 212

Date		Explanation	PR	Debit	Credit	Dr. or Cr.	Balance
2017 May	13		GJ1	315.00		Dr.	315.00
	31		PJ2		2,415.00	Cr.	2,100.00

Purchases — Acct. No. 512

Date		Explanation	PR	Debit	Credit	Dr. or Cr.	Balance
2017 May	31		PJ2	1,900.00		Dr.	1,900.00

Purchase Returns and Allowances — Acct. No. 513

Date		Explanation	PR	Debit	Credit	Dr. or Cr.	Balance
2017 May	13		GJ1		300.00	Cr.	300.00

Chapter Assignments

COMPREHENSIVE DEMONSTRATION PROBLEM WITH SOLUTION TIPS—INCLUDING HST AT 13%

(The forms you need are on pages 11-8 to 11-10 of the *Study Guide with Working Papers.*)

Record the following transactions in special or general journals. Record and post as appropriate.

Note: All credit sales are 2/10, n/30. All merchandise purchased on account has 3/10, n/30 credit terms.

	2015		
CRJ	Mar.	1	J. Ling invested $3,000 in the business.
PJ		2	Purchased merchandise on account from Case Co., $600 plus HST, invoice No. 222.
SJ		2	Sold merchandise on account to Balder Co., $500 plus HST, invoice No. 1.
CRJ		6	Sold $2,000 worth of merchandise plus HST for cash.
CPJ		6	Paid Case Co. for previous purchases on account, cheque No. 1.
SJ		8	Sold merchandise on account to Lewis Co., $1,000 plus HST, invoice No. 2.
CRJ		9	Received payment from Balder for invoice No. 1.
GJ		12	Issued a credit memorandum to Lewis Co. for $200 plus HST for faulty merchandise.
CRJ		13	Received payment from Lewis Co.
PJ		16	Purchased merchandise on account from Noone Co., $1,000 plus HST, invoice No. 555.
PJ		19	Purchased equipment on account from Case Co., $300 plus HST, invoice No. 226.
GJ		20	Issued a debit memorandum to Noone Co. for $500 plus HST for defective merchandise.
CPJ		20	Paid salaries, $300, cheque No. 2. (No HST on salaries!)
CPJ		23	Paid Noone balance owed, cheque No. 3.
CPJ		27	Paid Bowler Co. $400 plus HST for advertising, cheque No. 4.

Record accounts receivable subsidiary ledger immediately.

J. LING CO.
SALES JOURNAL

Page 1

Date		Inv. No.	Customer's Name	Terms	PR	Accounts Receivable Dr.	HST Payable Cr.	Sales Cr.
2015								
Mar.	2	1	Balder Co.	2/10, n/30	✔	565 00	65 00	500 00
	8	2	Lewis Co.	2/10, n/30	✔	1130 00	130 00	1000 00
	31					1695 00	195 00	1500 00
						(112)	(225)	(410)

Total posted at end of month to these accounts

J. LING CO.
CASH RECEIPTS JOURNAL

Page 1

Date		Cash Dr.	Accounts Receivable Cr.	Sales Cr.	HST Payable Cr.	Sales Discounts Dr.	Description of Receipt	PR	Sundry Cr.
2015 Mar.	1	3000 00					J. Ling, Capital	310	3000 00
	6	2260 00		2000 00	260 00		Cash Sales	✘	
	9	555 00	565 00			10 00	Balder Co.	✔	
	13	888 00	4000 00			16 00	Lewis Co.	✔	
	31	6703 00	1469 00	2000 00	260 00	26 00			3000 00
		(111)	(112)	(410)	(225)	(430)			(X)

J. LING CO.
PURCHASES JOURNAL

Page 1

Date		Account Credited	Date of Inv.	Inv. No.	Terms	PR	Accounts Payable Cr.	Purchases Dr.	Prepaid HST Dr.	Sundry Dr. Account	Sundry Dr. PR	Sundry Dr. Amount
2015 Mar.	2	Case Co.	Mar. 2	222	3%10, Net 30	✔	678 00	600 00	78 00			
	16	Noone Co.	Mar. 16	555	3%10, Net 30	✔	1130 00	1000 00	130 00			
	19	Case Co.	Mar. 17	226	3%10, Net 30	✔	339 00		39 00	Equipment	116	300 00
	31						2147 00	1600 00	247 00			300 00
							(210)	(510)	(114)			(X)

J. LING CO.
CASH PAYMENTS JOURNAL

Page 1

Date		Chq. No.	Account Debited	PR	Sundry Dr.	Accounts Payable Dr.	Prepaid HST Dr.	Purchases Dr.	Purchases Discount Cr.	Cash Cr.
2015 Mar.	6	1	Case Co.	✔		678 00			18 00	660 00
	20	2	Salaries	610	300 00					300 00
	23	3	Noone Co.	✔		565 00			15 00	550 00
	27	4	Bowler Co.	601	400 00		52 00			452 00
	31				700 00	1243 00	52 00		33 00	1962 00
					(X)	(210)	(114)		(530)	(111)

GENERAL JOURNAL					Page 1
Date		Account Titles and Description	PR	Dr.	Cr.
2015 Mar.	12	Sales Returns and Allowances	420	200 00	
		HST Payable	225	26 00	
		Accounts Receivable, Lewis Co.	112/✔		226 00
		Issued credit memo (including HST)	225		
	20	Accounts Payable, Noone Co.	210/✔	565 00	
		Purchases Returns and Allowances	520		500 00
		HST Prepaid	114		65 00
		Issued debit memo			

Record and post immediately to subsidiary and general ledgers.

ACCOUNTS RECEIVABLE SUBSIDIARY LEDGER

Balder Co.

Date	PR	Dr.	Cr.	Dr. Bal.
2015 3/2	SJ1	565		565
3/9	CRJ1		565	—

Lewis Co.

Date	PR	Dr.	Cr.	Dr. Bal.
2015 3/8	SJ1	1,130		1,130
3/12	GJ1		226	904
3/13	CRJ1		904	—

ACCOUNTS PAYABLE SUBSIDIARY LEDGER

Case Co.

Date	PR	Dr.	Cr.	Cr. Bal.
2015 3/2	PJ1		678	678
3/6	CPJ1	678		—
3/19	PJ1		339	339

Noone Co.

Date	PR	Dr.	Cr.	Cr. Bal.
2015 3/16	PJ1		1,130	1,130
3/20	GJ1	565		565
3/23	CPJ1	565		—

GENERAL LEDGER

Cash 111

3/31 CRJ1 6,703	1,962 3/31 CPJ1
Balance 4,741	

Accounts Receivable 112

3/31 SJ1 1,695	226 3/12 GJ1
	1,469 3/31 CRJ1

HST Prepaid 114

3/31 PJ1 247	65 3/20 GJ1
3/31 CPJ1 52	
Balance 234	

Equipment 116

3/19 PJ1 300	

Accounts Payable 210

3/20 GJ1 565	2,147 3/31 PJ1
3/31 CPJ1 1243	
	339 Balance

J. Ling, Capital 310

	3,000 3/1 CRJ1

Advertising 601

3/27 CPJ1 400	

HST Payable 225

3/12 GJ 26	195 3/31 SJ1
	260 3/31 CRJ1
	429 Balance

Sales 410

	1,500 3/31 SJ1
	2,000 3/31 CRJ1
	3,500 Balance

Sales Returns and Allowances 420

3/12 GJ1 200	

Sales Discounts 430

3/31 CRJ1 26	

Purchases 510

3/31 PJ1 1,600	

Purchases Ret. and Allow. 520

	500 3/20 GJ1

Purchases Discounts 530

	33 3/31 CPJ1

Salaries Expense 610

3/20 CPJ1 300	

Summary of Solution Tips

Learning Unit 11-2—Seller	Learning Unit 11-3—Buyer
Sales journal	Purchases journal
Cash receipts journal	Cash payments journal
Accounts receivable subsidiary ledger	Accounts payable subsidiary ledger
Sales (Cr.)	Purchases (Dr.)
Sales Returns and Allowances (Dr.)	Purchase Returns and Allowances (Cr.)
Sales Discounts (Dr.)	Purchases Discounts (Cr.)
Accounts Receivable (Dr.)	Accounts Payable (Cr.)
GST(HST) Payable (Cr.)	GST(HST) Prepaid (Dr.)
Issue a credit memo	Receive a credit memo
or	*or*
Receive a debit memo	Issue a debit memo
Schedule of accounts receivable	Schedule of accounts payable

When Do I Do What? — A Step-by-Step Walk-Through of This Comprehensive Demonstration Problem

Transaction   *What to Do Step by Step*

2015

Mar. 1 *Money received:* Record in cash receipts journal. Post immediately to J. Ling, Capital since it is in Sundry. There is no HST on cash to or from an owner.

2 *Bought merchandise on account:* Record in purchases journal. Record to Case Co. immediately in the accounts payable subsidiary ledger. Total is $678, including HST.

2 *Sale on account:* Record in sales journal. Record immediately to Balder Co. in accounts receivable subsidiary ledger. Place a ✓ in PR column of sales journal when subsidiary is updated. Total is $565, including HST.

6 *Money in:* Record in cash receipts journal. No posting needed (put an X in PR column.) Note that total includes $260 of HST.

6 *Money out:* Record in cash payments journal. Save $18 ($600 × 0.03), which is a Purchases Discount. Record immediately to Case Co. in accounts payable subsidiary ledger (the full amount of $678).

8 *Sale on account:* Record in sales journal. Update immediately to Lewis in accounts receivable subsidiary ledger. Total to include HST.

9 *Money in:* Record in cash receipts journal. Since Balder paid within 10 days, they get a $10 discount. Record immediately to Balder in the accounts receivable subsidiary ledger the full amount of $565. Cash is $565 − $10 = $555.

12 *Returns:* Record in general journal. Seller issues credit memo resulting in higher sales returns and customers owing less. All postings and recordings are done immediately. Note the HST amount of $26 ($200 × 0.13).

13 *Money in:* Record in cash receipts journal:

$$\begin{array}{rr} \$1{,}000 - \$200 \text{ returns} = & \$800 \\ & \underline{\times\ 0.02} \\ & \$\ \ 16 \text{ discount} \end{array}$$

Record the $904 ($1,130 − $226) immediately to Lewis in the accounts receivable subsidiary ledger. Cash received is $904 less $16 = $888.

Mar. 16 *Buy now, pay later:* Record in purchases journal. Record immediately to Noone Co. in the accounts payable subsidiary ledger. Note HST at 13%

19 *Buy now, pay later:* Record in purchases journal under Sundry. This is not merchandise for resale, but HST still applies. Record and post immediately.

20 *Returns:* Record in general journal. Buyer issues a debit memo, reducing its accounts payable because of Purchases Returns and Allowances. Post and record immediately. HST is included at 13%.

20 *Salaries:* Record in cash payments journal, Sundry column. There is no HST on salaries.

23 *Money out:* Record in cash payments journal. Save 3% ($15), a purchases discount. Record immediately in accounts payable subsidiary ledger, reducing Noone by $565.

27 *Money out:* Record in cash payments journal. (No discount is mentioned.) Debit advertising expense in the Sundry Accounts column and post immediately. Note the HST amount of $52 that is entered in the Prepaid HST column. Total amount paid is $400 + 13%, or $452.

At the end of the month: Post totals (except Sundry) of special journals to the general ledger.

Note: In this problem, at the end of the month: (1) Accounts Receivable in the general ledger, the controlling account, has a zero balance as does each title in the accounts receivable subsidiary ledger. (2) The balance in Accounts Payable (the controlling account) is $339. In the accounts payable subsidiary ledger, Case is owed $339. The sum of the subsidiary ledger accounts does equal the balance in the controlling account at the end of the month.

SUMMARY OF KEY POINTS

Learning Unit 11-1

1. Recording GST/HST in the sales journal requires the addition of one new column. Other procedures are not changed.
2. Often both PST and GST will appear on the same invoice. Recording this in the sales journal requires the use of two extra columns, but again, the basic procedures are little changed.
3. When a sales discount is allowed, it is taken on the pre-PST and pre-GST/HST amount only, not on the total invoice.
4. Recording a credit memorandum with PST and GST/HST requires an extra line in the general journal for each. The credit to the customer's account includes the invoice amount plus PST and GST/HST.

Learning Unit 11-2

1. The cash receipts journal records receipt of cash from any source.
2. The sundry column records the credit part of a transaction that does not occur frequently. Never post the *total* of sundry. Post items in the sundry column to the general ledger when entered.
3. A ✔ in the posting reference column of the cash receipts journal means that the accounts receivable subsidiary ledger has been updated (recorded) with a credit.

4. An ✘ in the cash receipts journal posting-reference column means no posting was necessary since the totals of these columns will be posted at the end of the month.
5. Cross-adding means proving that the total of debits and the total of credits are equal in the special journal, thus verifying the accuracy of recording.
6. A schedule of accounts receivable is a listing of the ending balances of customers in the accounts receivable subsidiary ledger. This total should be the same balance as found in the controlling account, Accounts Receivable, in the general ledger.

Learning Unit 11-3

1. GST/HST is paid on most purchases of goods and services in Canada. It is very important for businesses to keep proper track of the GST/HST that they pay because they can deduct this from the GST/HST otherwise payable on their own sales.
2. All payments by cheque are recorded in the cash payments journal. Record any GST/HST paid on cash purchases in this journal as well.
3. At the end of the month, the schedule of accounts payable, a list of ending amounts owed to individual creditors, must equal the ending balance in Accounts Payable, the controlling account in the general ledger.
4. Trade discounts are deductions off the list price that have nothing to do with early payments (cash discounts). Invoice amounts are recorded after the trade discount is deducted. Cash discounts are not taken on trade discounts.
5. Cash discounts are not taken on GST/HST amounts.
6. A separate column is added to the purchases journal and to the cash payments journal to record the GST/HST on items purchased either on account or for cash.
7. When a debit note is issued for a purchases return or allowance, the GST/HST is always added to the total. When the debit note is recorded in the general journal, the GST/HST amount is credited to the same account as that used to track the GST/HST amounts paid for the period. This increases the amount owed to the federal government. Other postings are done in the same way as described earlier.
8. GST/HST may be reported to the federal government using the quick method of accounting. For certain Canadian businesses with relatively low sales volume (currently $400,000 or less though this will likely change form time to time) this simplified method may be a faster and cheaper way from them to manage their GST/HST remittance.

KEY TERMS

Credit memorandum A document sent by the seller to a customer who has returned merchandise previously purchased on credit. The credit memorandum indicates to the customer that the seller is reducing the amount owed by the customer. The total will include GST/HST (or even PST) if that was charged on the original invoice. (p. 495)

Debit memorandum A memo issued by a purchaser to a seller, indicating that some purchases returns and allowances have occurred and therefore the purchaser now owes less money on account. The total will include GS, HST, or PST if that was charged on the original invoice. (p. 510)

Goods and Services Tax (GST) A "value added" tax introduced in Canada in 1991. It is added to most sales of goods and services. Currently it is calculated at 5%. (p. 489)

GST/HST charged The tax amount billed to customers and due to be sent to the federal government. It is a liability account with a credit balance. See also the next chapter for a fuller explanation of the net amount payable. (p. 493)

Harmonized Sales Tax (HST) A 13% to 15% tax identical to GST, charged in Ontario, Prince Edward Island, Nova Scotia, New Brunswick, and Newfoundland and Labrador. It replaces both the PST and GST in those provinces. (p. 489)

Prepaid GST/HST An asset account used to accumulate the GST/HST paid (or payable) to suppliers on goods or services purchased. It is an asset because it can be deducted from the amount otherwise payable to the federal government. This is sometimes shown with current liabilities (but is still a debit-balance account). (p. 508)

Provincial Sales Tax (PST) Payable A liability account in the general ledger that accumulates the amount of provincial sales tax owed. It has a credit balance. (p. 491)

QUICK REVIEW

The following Tips are from Learning Units 11-1 to 11-3. Answer the Assess Your Progress questions and use the How Did You Do? at the bottom of the next page to see how well you know the material. The Quick Review provides tips before each Assess Your Progress to help you avoid common accounting errors.

LU 11-1 Seller's View of a Merchandise Company; Recording Sales and Sales Returns

Tips: There are two main sorts of sales taxes at the retail level in Canada. All provinces must charge GST on sales of goods and services, and this current rate is 5%, but it may change—it started out at 7%, after all. In addition, most provinces also levy a provincial sales tax, at varying percentages, and this tax, when levied by itself, does not usually apply to services. Several provinces have decided to combine their PST with GST, and now charge a combined rate in exactly the same way as GST is charged. This combined tax is the HST (Harmonized Sales Tax). In all cases, any retail tax is entered as a credit to a liability account, and must be paid to the appropriate taxing authority on a regular basis. In general, the sales journal and even the cash receipts journal are designed with a column for any tax charged. In provinces that charge PST and GST there will always be two added columns. Provinces charging only GST or HST will need only one added column.

Assess Your Progress

Answer true or false to the following statements:

1. Sales Tax Payable is an asset.
2. The Provincial Sales Tax (PST) Payable account has a credit balance.
3. When a sales discount is taken, remember to take the discount on the HST as well.
4. British Columbia has returned to charging PST along with GST.
5. Alberta has only GST to be charged.

LU 11-2 Cash Receipts Journal and Schedule of Accounts Receivable

Tips: The HST/GST column in the cash receipts journal is used mostly for cash sales. GST/HST on credit sales is recorded in the sales journal. As in Chapter 6, the CRJ will contain all routine cash received by a company. Many times cash receipts are from credit customers, but the CRJ needs the ability to record certain non-standard cash receipts, and uses the sundry column for such purposes. The CRJ is posted almost exactly like the CRJ in Chapter 6, apart from any possible GST/HST on cash sales (or a few other transactions, such as the sale of an asset, or miscellaneous revenue such as rental income). Such amounts would be included in that column's total and posted to the GST/HST Payable account at period end. At the end of each month, a schedule of accounts receivable is prepared and the total compared to the A/R account in the GL. Any differences must be investigated and corrections made at the earliest possible date. As was the case in Chapter 6, this schedule can be constructed so it shows details of how long each amount owing has been outstanding. The only difference is that the amounts are higher because of the amount of the taxes included. This more detailed schedule is a big help in maintaining control over accounts receivable, and ensuring that the maximum possible amounts are charged from customers.

Assess Your Progress

Answer true or false to the following statements:

1. The HST Payable column in the cash receipts journal is posted daily.
2. There is a column for GST/HST on the schedule of accounts receivable at month end.
3. All miscellaneous receipts of cash are recorded using the general journal.
4. GST/HST on cash sales is recorded in the CRJ.
5. If an owner contributes more money to a company, there is HST on that amount.

LU 11-3 GST Paid on Purchases

Tips: GST/HST on purchases is recorded in the purchases journal when an invoice is initially received from a supplier. It is not recorded when that invoice is paid using the cash payments journal. It is important to make certain that all GST/HST paid is recorded properly as a debit, since all such amounts are used to reduce the amount otherwise payable as recorded in the sales and cash receipts journals. PST on goods purchased is not usually an issue, as PST applies mainly at the retail level, and most goods purchased for resale do not attract PST.

Debit memos are used to record reductions in amounts payable for invoices recorded, and may be recorded in the general journal, a separate special journal or as a negative amount in the purchases journal. At month-end a listing of all amounts payable is prepared from the details and balances in the A/P subsidiary ledger, and that list's total must agree with the accounts payable control account in the general ledger. The list of accounts payable may be prepared with details of how long individual balances have remained unpaid, and this detail helps manage the flow of funds to suppliers. One very important issue when managing the amounts payable to suppliers, is to take all available discounts that are offered. Especially with the low interest rates that are currently in effect, it may be an excellent idea to borrow any funds needed to finance the early payment of invoices, thus taking any available discounts. The interest rates inherent in most of the terms available in the normal course of business greatly exceeds the cost of borrowing.

Assess Your Progress

Answer true or false to the following statements:

1. When defective merchandise is sent back and a debit memorandum is issued, remember to include the GST or HST charged on that defective merchandise when recording this document.
2. Always remember to calculate purchases discounts on the total bill including taxes.
3. Debit memos can be entered in three different ways.
4. It is nice, but not too critical, to enter GST/HST paid on purchases.
5. The implied interest rate in "2% 10, net 30" terms exceeds 30%.

How Did You Do? Answers to the Assess Your Progress Questions

LU 11-1

1. False—Sales Tax Payable is a liability.
2. True.
3. False—No sales discount is taken on GST/HST or PST because these monies are charged on behalf of the government.
4. True, as of Spring, 2013.
5. True—no PST at all in this province

LU 11-2

1. False—The HST Payable is posted to the general ledger at the end of the month.
2. False—These details are not shown on this document—just the gross amounts are shown.
3. False—The CRJ has a column called Sundry that can be used for this purpose.
4. True.
5. False—There is no GST/HST on transactions between owners and companies.

LU 11-3

1. True.
2. False—Do not include the HST/GST amount when calculating the purchases discount.
3. True.
4. False—Always remember to record these amounts.
5. True—About 37.4%.

BLUEPRINT OF SALES AND CASH RECEIPTS JOURNALS

Posting and Recording: Multicolumn Sales Journal

SALES JOURNAL

Date	Description	PR	Accounts Receivable Dr.	Provincial Sales Tax Payable Cr.	GST Payable Cr.	Sales Cr.
		✔	~~~~	~~~~	~~~~	~~~~
		✔	~~~~	~~~~	~~~~	~~~~
		✔	~~~~	~~~~	~~~~	~~~~
		✔	~~~~	~~~~	~~~~	~~~~
		✔	~~~~	~~~~	~~~~	~~~~
			( )	( )	( )	( )

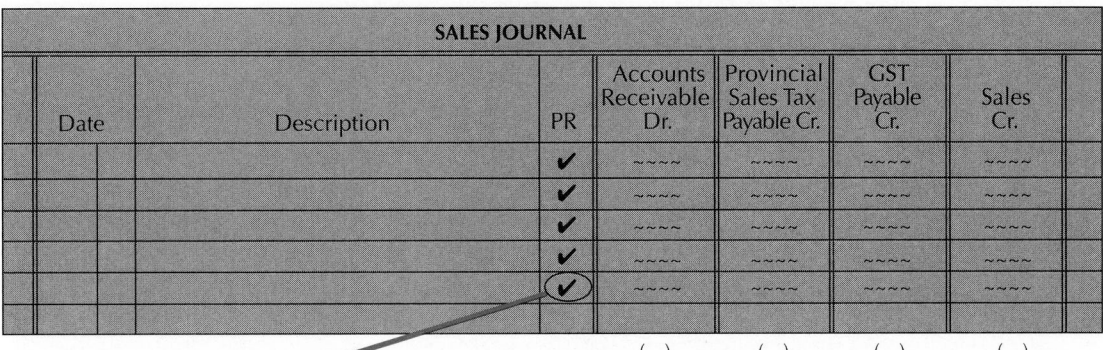

During the month, the accounts receivable ledger is updated as soon as transactions are entered in the journal. A check mark indicates that recording is completed to the customer's account in the accounts receivable subledger.

End of month total is posted to Accounts Receivable control account in the general ledger.

End of month totals of both taxes payable are posted to their respective accounts in the general ledger.

End of month total of sales is posted to the general ledger.

Recording a Credit Memo with Sales Tax and GST/HST in a General Journal

GENERAL JOURNAL

Date	Account Titles and Description	PR	Dr.	Cr.
	Sales Returns and Allowances	~~~	~~~~	
	Provincial Sales Tax Payable		~~~~	
	GST Payable		~~~~	
	Accounts Receivable, J. Doe	~~/✓		~~~~
	Issued credit memo			

Posted when transactions entered

Four postings:

1. Post to SRA in general ledger.
2. Post to liability accounts in general ledger.
3. Post to Accounts Receivable in general ledger.
4. Record in J. Doe account in accounts receivable ledger.

Cash Receipts Journal with PST and GST/HST

CASH RECEIPTS JOURNAL

PR	Sundry Cr.	Sales Cr.	Accounts Receivable Cr.	Provincial Sales Tax Payable Cr.	GST Payable Cr.	Sales Discount Dr.	Cash Dr.
510	~~~						~~~
(X)		~~~		~~~	~~~		~~~
✓			~~~				~~~
✓			~~~				~~~
	(X)	( )	( )	( )	( )	( )	( )

Posted when transaction occurs

Posted to general ledger account when transaction is entered. In this case, it was account No. 510.

Recorded during the month

These individual amounts are recorded during the month to the accounts receivable subledger. When they are recorded, a check mark is placed in the PR column of the cash receipts journal.

Posted at end of month

These totals are posted to the general ledger accounts at the end of the month.

No posting needed during month since totals of sales, GST, PST, and cash are posted at end of month.

Total of the Sundry column is never posted. The individual amounts making up the total are posted as the month progresses.

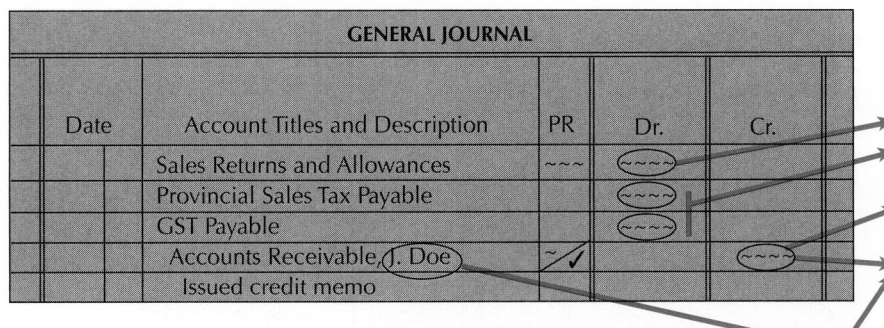

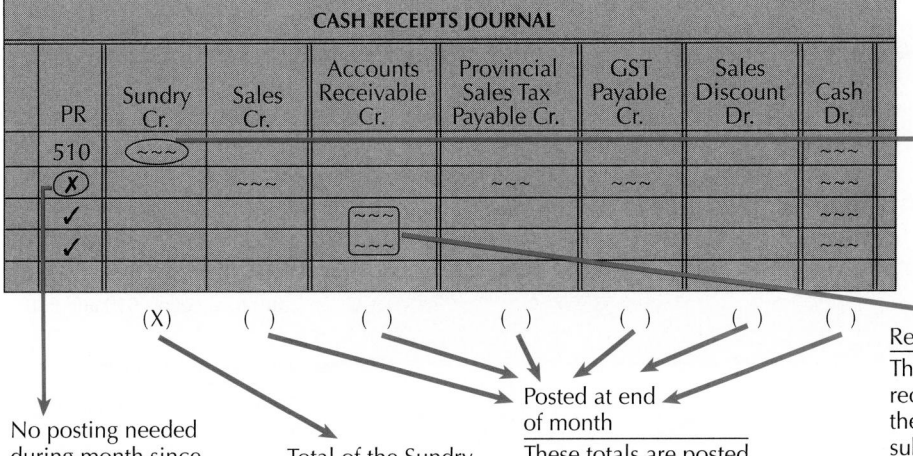

BLUEPRINT OF PURCHASES AND CASH PAYMENTS JOURNALS

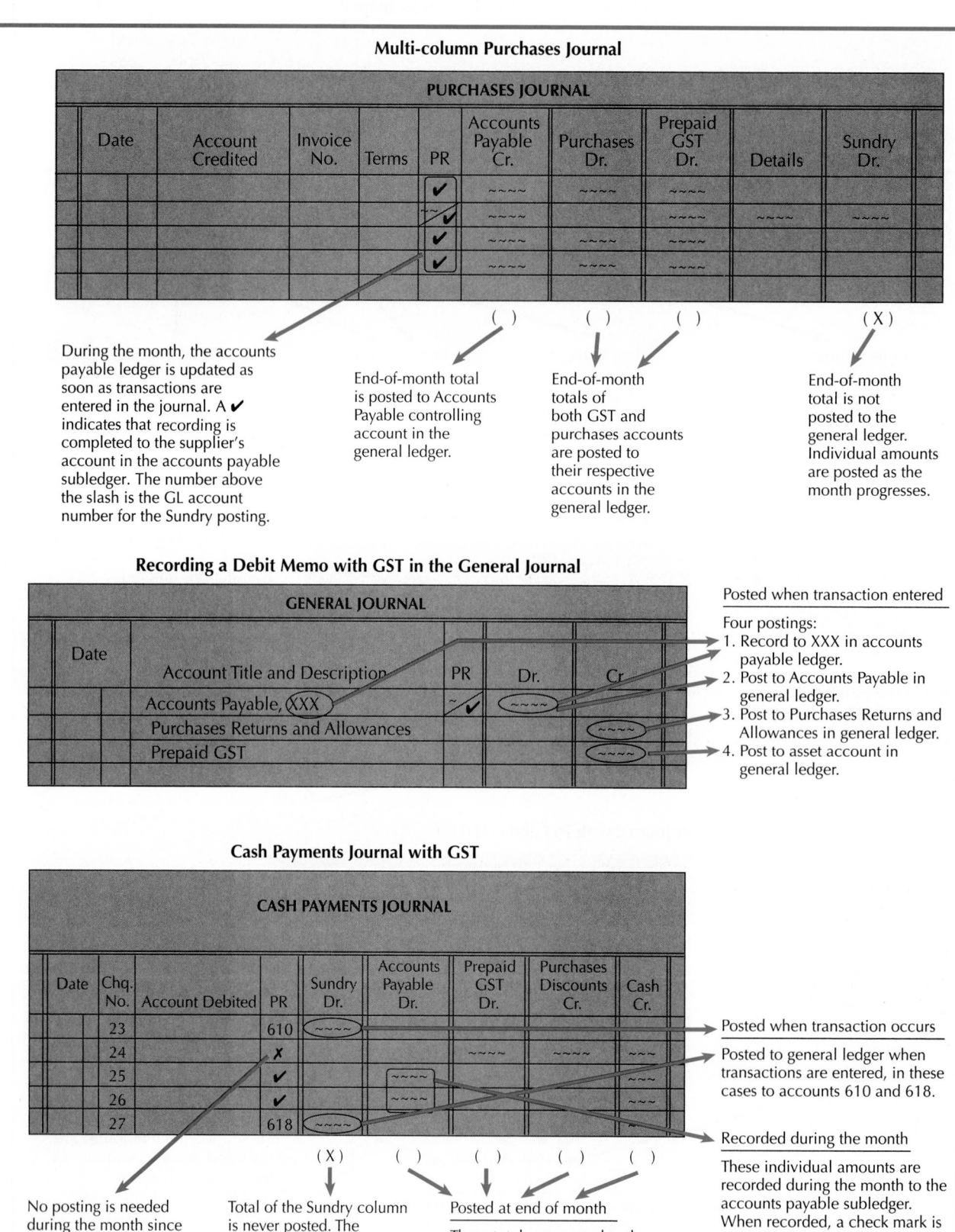

Multi-column Purchases Journal

PURCHASES JOURNAL

Date	Account Credited	Invoice No.	Terms	PR	Accounts Payable Cr.	Purchases Dr.	Prepaid GST Dr.	Details	Sundry Dr.
				✔	~~~~	~~~~	~~~~		
				~~/✔	~~~~		~~~~	~~~~	~~~~
				✔	~~~~	~~~~	~~~~		
				✔	~~~~	~~~~	~~~~		
					( )	( )	( )		(X)

During the month, the accounts payable ledger is updated as soon as transactions are entered in the journal. A ✔ indicates that recording is completed to the supplier's account in the accounts payable subledger. The number above the slash is the GL account number for the Sundry posting.

End-of-month total is posted to Accounts Payable controlling account in the general ledger.

End-of-month totals of both GST and purchases accounts are posted to their respective accounts in the general ledger.

End-of-month total is not posted to the general ledger. Individual amounts are posted as the month progresses.

Recording a Debit Memo with GST in the General Journal

GENERAL JOURNAL

Date	Account Title and Description	PR	Dr.	Cr.
	Accounts Payable, XXX	~/✔	~~~~	
	Purchases Returns and Allowances			~~~~
	Prepaid GST			~~~~

Posted when transaction entered

Four postings:

1. Record to XXX in accounts payable ledger.
2. Post to Accounts Payable in general ledger.
3. Post to Purchases Returns and Allowances in general ledger.
4. Post to asset account in general ledger.

Cash Payments Journal with GST

CASH PAYMENTS JOURNAL

Date	Chq. No.	Account Debited	PR	Sundry Dr.	Accounts Payable Dr.	Prepaid GST Dr.	Purchases Discounts Cr.	Cash Cr.
	23		610	~~~~				
	24		✗			~~~~	~~~~	~~~
	25		✔		~~~~			~~~
	26		✔		~~~~			~~~
	27		618	~~~~				~
				(X)	( )	( )	( )	( )

Posted when transaction occurs

Posted to general ledger when transactions are entered, in these cases to accounts 610 and 618.

Recorded during the month

These individual amounts are recorded during the month to the accounts payable subledger. When recorded, a check mark is placed in the PR column of the cash payments journal.

No posting is needed during the month since totals of purchases, GST, PST, and cash are posted at end of month.

Total of the Sundry column is never posted. The individual amounts making up the total are posted as the month progresses.

Posted at end of month

These totals are posted to the general ledger accounts at the end of the month.

QUESTIONS, CLASSROOM DEMONSTRATION EXERCISES, EXERCISES, AND PROBLEMS

Discussion Questions and Critical Thinking/Ethical Case

1. Explain how PST differs from GST/HST.
2. What is the normal balance of the Sales Discounts account?
3. What is a value-added tax?
4. (Tricky) Why doesn't the purchase requisition generally mention GST/HST?
5. Explain why a retail business includes a column for PST in its Sales Journal, but does not include a similar column in its Purchases Journal.
6. What effect on the liability account "PST Payable" does a credit memorandum have?
7. State the differences between a cash receipts journal and a cash payments journal. Assume taxes are included, and give a brief comment on each difference.
8. When a seller issues a credit memorandum with both PST and GST included, what accounts are affected?
9. Sales discounts are taken on GST or PST amounts. Agree or disagree and say why.
10. In any given reporting period (assume a month) a successful business will always owe some GST or HST. Agree or disagree and explain your answer.
11. Why would a purchaser issue a debit memorandum? Wouldn't it include any PST?
12. Explain the relationship between a purchases journal and a cash payments journal with respect to the extra column(s) needed to account for taxes.
13. State why it is so important for firms to keep track of the GST/HST that they pay each period.
14. Why does GST/HST on a debit note act to increase the net amount of GST/HST payable?
15. Spring Co. bought merchandise from All Co. with terms 2/10, n/30. Joanne Ring, the bookkeeper, forgot to pay the bill within the first 10 days. She went to Mel Ryan, Head Accountant, who told her to backdate the cheque so it would look as though the bill was paid within the discount period. Joanne told Mel that she thought they could get away with it. Should Joanne and Mel backdate the cheque to take advantage of the discount? You make the call. Write down your specific recommendations to Joanne.

MyAccountingLab

Make the grade with MyAccountingLab! The exercises and problems marked with ● can be found on MyAccountingLab. You can practise them as often as you want, and many of them feature step-by-step guided solutions to help you find the right answer.

Classroom Demonstration Exercises

(The forms you need are on pages 11-11 and 11-12 of the *Study Guide with Working Papers.*)

Overview

Categorizing accounts
❶ ❷ ❺ ❻ (10 min)

1. Complete the following table for Sales, Sales Returns and Allowances, and Sales Discounts, PST Payable, and HST Payable.

Accounts Affected	Category	↑ ↓	Rules	Temporary or Permanent

Calculating Net Sales

Net sales
❶ ❷ (10 min)

2. Given the following, calculate net sales:

Gross sales	\$100
PST rate	8%
GST rate	5%
Sales returns and allowances	12
Sales discounts	2%

Credit Memorandum

Analyzing a return transaction
❷ (10 min)

3. Draw a transaction analysis box for the following credit memorandum: Issued credit memorandum to North Corp. for defective merchandise—\$315, including GST.

Calculating net purchases
❺ ❻ (10 min)

4. Calculate net purchases from the following: Purchases, \$100; Purchase Returns and Allowances, \$12; Purchase Discounts, \$2; and GST on Purchases, \$5.

Sales and Cash Receipts Journal

Analyzing transactions
❶ ❷ (10 min)

5. Beside each of the four transactions at the top of the next page, enter the number of any of the following six treatments that apply. (A number can be used more than once.)

1. Journalize into sales journal.
2. Journalize into cash receipts journal.
3. Record immediately to subsidiary ledger.
4. Totals of special journals will be posted at end of month (except Sundry column).
5. Post to general ledger immediately.
6. Journalize into general journal.

a. ________ Sold merchandise on account to Ally Co., invoice No. 10—$40, plus GST.

b. ________ Received cheque from Moore Co.—$105, including GST, less 2% discount.

c. ________ Cash Sales—$100, plus GST.

d. ________ Issued credit memorandum No. 2 to Ally Co. for defective merchandise—$20, plus GST.

Schedule of accounts receivable
4 (10 min)

6. From the following, prepare a schedule of accounts receivable for Blue Co. for May 31, 2015.

Accounts Receivable Subsidiary Ledger

Bon Co.

5/6 SJ1 105	

Peke Co.

5/20 SJ1 63	21 5/27 CRJ1

Green Co.

5/8 SJ1 84	

General Ledger

Accounts Receivable

5/31 SJ1 252	5/31 CRJ1 21

Exercises

Set A

(The forms you need are on pages 11-13 to 11-16 of the *Study Guide with Working Papers.*)

Recording and posting from the sales journal
1 (15 min)

11-1A. From the sales journal below, record in the accounts receivable subsidiary ledger and post to the general ledger accounts as appropriate.

SALES JOURNAL

Page 1

Date		Account Debited	Invoice No.	PR	Accts. Receivable Dr.	GST Payable Cr.	Sales Cr.
2016 April	19	Kevin Stone Co.	1		630 00	30 00	600 00
	20	Bill Valley Co.	2		945 00	45 00	900 00
					1575 00	75 00	1500 00

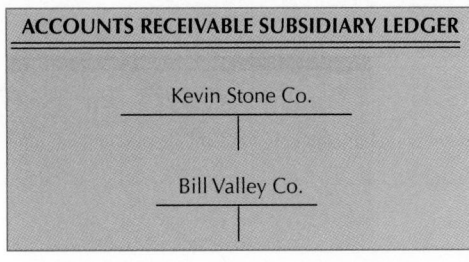

ACCOUNTS RECEIVABLE SUBSIDIARY LEDGER

Kevin Stone Co.

Bill Valley Co.

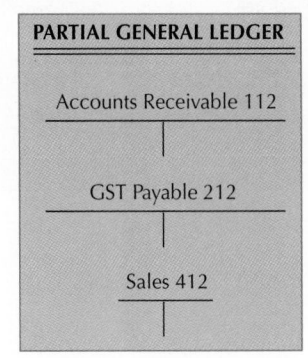

PARTIAL GENERAL LEDGER

Accounts Receivable 112

GST Payable 212

Sales 412

Journalizing, recording, and posting that includes credit memorandum
❶ ❷ (15 min)

11-2A. Journalize, record, and post when appropriate the following transactions into the sales journal (same headings as Exercise 11-1A) and general journal (page 1). All sales carry terms of 2/10, n/30.

2016
May 17 Sold merchandise on account to Ronald Co., invoice No. 147, $1,200, plus 5% GST.
18 Sold merchandise on account to Bass Co., invoice No. 148, $1,900, plus 5% GST.
21 Issued credit memorandum No. 12 to Bass Co. for defective merchandise, $700, plus 5% GST.

Use the following account numbers: Accounts Receivable, 112; GST Payable, 225; Sales, 411; Sales Returns and Allowances, 412.

Journalizing transaction into cash receipts journal
❸ (15 min)

11-3A. From Exercise 11-2A, journalize the receipt of a cheque from Ronald Co. for payment of invoice No. 147 on May 25, 2016, in the cash receipts journal. Use the same headings as for Walter Lantz Co. (on page 270 of Chapter 6).

Journalizing, recording, and posting sales and cash receipts journal; schedule of accounts receivable
❶ ❷ ❸ ❹ (45 min)

11-4A. From the following transactions for Edna Co., when appropriate, journalize, record, post, and prepare a schedule of accounts receivable. Use the same journal headings (all page 1) and chart of accounts that Art's Clothing Company used in the text (use Edna Cares, Capital). You will have to set up your own accounts receivable subsidiary ledger and partial general ledger as needed. All sales terms are 2/10, n/30.

2017
June 2 Edna Cares invested $5,000 in the business.
3 Sold merchandise on account to Boston Co., invoice No. 218, $700, plus 13% HST.
3 Sold merchandise on account to Gary Co., invoice No. 219, $1,100, plus 13% HST.
6 Cash sale, $200, plus 13% HST.
9 Issued credit memorandum No. 24 to Boston Co. for defective merchandise, $200, plus 13% HST.
10 Received cheque from Boston Co. for invoice No. 218 less returns and discount.
16 Cash sale, $400, plus 13% HST.
17 Sold merchandise on account to Boston Co., invoice No. 220, $600, plus 13% HST.

11-5A. From the accompanying purchases journal, record in the accounts payable subsidiary ledger and post to general ledger accounts as appropriate.

PURCHASES JOURNAL Page 1

Date		Account Credited	Date of Invoice	Terms	PR	Accounts Payable Credit	GST Prepaid Debit	Purchases Debit	Sundry—Dr. Account	Sundry—Dr. PR	Sundry—Dr. Amount
2017 June	3	Barr Co.	June 3	1/10, n/30		42000	2000	40000			
	6	Jess Co.	June 6	n/10, EOM		84000	4000	80000			
	9	Rey Co.	June 9			63000	3000		Equipment		60000

Recording in the accounts payable subsidiary ledger and posting to the general ledger from a purchases journal
4 5 (15 min)

Partial Accounts Payable Subsidiary Ledger	Partial General Ledger
Barr Co.	Equipment 120
Jess Co.	GST Prepaid 125
Rey Co.	Accounts Payable 210
	Purchases 510

Journalizing, recording, and posting a debit memorandum
6 (15 min)

11-6A. On July 8, 2017, Aster Co. issued debit memorandum No. 1 for $400 to Reel Co. for merchandise returned from invoice No. 312, which originally included GST at 5%. Your task is to journalize, record, and post this transaction as appropriate. Use the same account numbers as found in the text for Art's Clothing Company. The general journal page is page 1.

Journalizing, recording, and posting a cash payments journal
8 (20 min)

11-7A. Journalize, record, and post when appropriate the following transactions into the cash payments journal (page 2) for Morgan's Clothing. Use the same headings as found in the text for Art's Clothing Company (page 310 of Chapter 7). All purchases discounts are 2/10, n/30, and the amounts shown include GST at 5%.

Accounts Payable Subsidiary Ledger

Name	*Balance*	*Invoice No.*
B. Foss	$ 420	488
A. James	1,050	522
J. Ranch	945	562
B. Swanson	210	821

Partial General Ledger

Account	*Number*	*Balance*
Cash	110	$3,000
GST Prepaid	125	
Accounts Payable	210	2,625
Purchases Discounts	511	
Advertising Expense	610	

2016

Apr. 2 Issued cheque No. 20 to A. James Company in payment of its March 29 invoice No. 522.

9 Issued cheque No. 21 to Flott Advertising in payment of its advertising bill, $100, plus GST at 5%, no discount.

16 Issued cheque No. 22 to B. Foss in payment of its March 26 invoice No. 488.

Schedule of accounts payable
4 (10 min)

11-8A. From Exercise 11-7A, prepare a schedule of accounts payable and verify that the total of the schedule equals the amount in the controlling account.

Quick method of HST
7 (5 min)

11-9A. Sudbury Outdoor Wear sells a line of specialized clothing to customers in their local area. For the calendar year 2016, the company sold $325,000 worth of clothing before taxes. HST in Ontario is 13%. The company has elected to use the quick method of accounting for HST, and the applicable rate for Ontario is 4.4%. How much HST must the company send to the federal government for this year?

Exercises

Set B

(The forms you need are on pages 11-13 to 11-16 of the *Study Guide with Working Papers.*)

Recording and posting from the sales journal
❶ (15 min)

11-1B. From the sales journal below, record in the accounts receivable subsidiary ledger and post to the general ledger accounts as appropriate.

SALES JOURNAL

Page 1

Date		Account Debited	Invoice No.	PR	Accts. Receivable Dr.	GST Payable Cr.	Sales Cr.
2016 April	19	Kevin Stone Co.	1		735 00	35 00	700 00
	20	Bill Valley Co.	2		840 00	40 00	800 00
					1575 00	75 00	1500 00

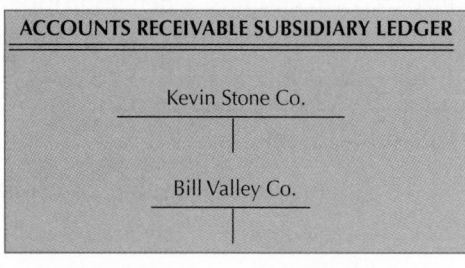

ACCOUNTS RECEIVABLE SUBSIDIARY LEDGER

Kevin Stone Co.

Bill Valley Co.

PARTIAL GENERAL LEDGER

Accounts Receivable 112

GST Payable 212

Sales 412

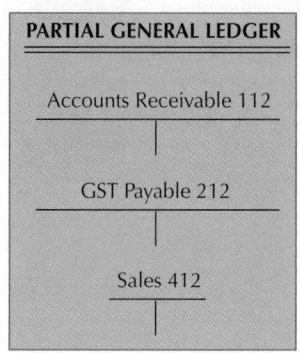

Journalizing, recording, and posting that includes credit memorandum
❶ ❷ (15 min)

11-2B. Journalize, record, and post when appropriate the following transactions into the sales journal (same headings as Exercise 11-1B) and general journal (page 1). All sales terms are 2/10, n/30.

2016
May 15 Sold merchandise on account to Ronald Co., invoice No. 246, $1,500, plus 5% GST.
19 Sold merchandise on account to Bass Co., invoice No. 247, $2,200, plus 5% GST.
23 Issued credit memorandum No. 12 on account to Bass Co. for defective merchandise, $400, plus 5% GST.

Use the following account numbers: Accounts Receivable, 112; GST Payable, 225; Sales, 411; Sales Returns and Allowances, 412.

Journalizing transaction into cash receipts journal
❷ (15 min)

11-3B. From Exercise 11-2B, journalize the receipt of a cheque from Ronald Co. for payment of invoice No. 246 on May 24, 2016, in the cash receipts journal. Use the same headings as for Walter Lantz Co. (on page 270 of Chapter 6).

Journalizing, recording, and posting sales and cash receipts journals; schedule of accounts receivable
❶ ❷ ❸ ❹ (45 min)

11-4B. From the following transactions for Edna Co., when appropriate, journalize, record, post, and prepare a schedule of accounts receivable. Use the same journal headings (all page 1) and chart of accounts that Art's Clothing Company used in the text (use Edna Cares, Capital). You will have to set up your own accounts receivable subsidiary ledger and partial general ledger as needed. All sales terms are 2/10, n/30.

2017		
June	2	Edna Cares invested $8,000 in the business.
	3	Sold merchandise on account to Boston Co., invoice No. 218, $900, plus 13% HST.
	3	Sold merchandise on account to Gary Co., invoice No. 219, $1,200, plus 13% HST.
	6	Cash sale, $300, plus 13% HST.
	9	Issued credit memorandum No. 24 to Boston Co. for defective merchandise, $150, plus 13% HST.
	10	Received cheque from Boston Co. for invoice No. 218 less returns and discount.
	16	Cash sale, $350, plus 13% HST.
	17	Sold merchandise on account to Boston Co., invoice No. 220, $1,100, plus 13% HST.

Recording in the accounts payable subsidiary ledger and posting to the general ledger from the purchases journal
❹ ❺ (15 min)

11-5B. From the accompanying purchases journal, record in the accounts payable subsidiary ledger and post to general ledger accounts as appropriate.

PURCHASES JOURNAL — Page 1

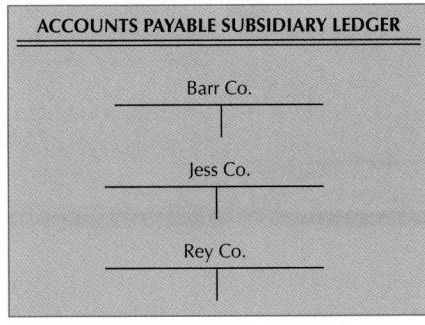

Date		Account Credited	Date of Invoice	Terms	PR	Accounts Payable Cr.	Prepaid GST Dr.	Purchases Dr.	Sundry—Dr. Account	Sundry—Dr. PR	Sundry—Dr. Amount
2017 June	3	Barr Co.	June 3	1/10, n/30		525 00	25 00	500 00			
	6	Jess Co.	June 6	n/10, EOM		945 00	45 00	900 00			
	9	Rey Co.	June 9			420 00	20 00		Equipment		400 00

ACCOUNTS PAYABLE SUBSIDIARY LEDGER

Barr Co.

Jess Co.

Rey Co.

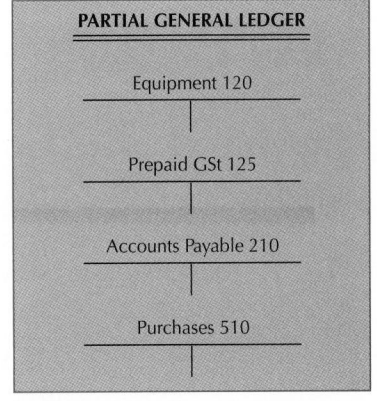

PARTIAL GENERAL LEDGER

Equipment 120

Prepaid GSt 125

Accounts Payable 210

Purchases 510

Journalizing, recording, and posting a debit memorandum
❻ (15 min)

11-6B. On July 7, 2017, Aster Co. issued debit memorandum No. 3 for $250 to Reel Co. for merchandise returned from invoice No. 632, which originally included GST at 5%. Your task is to journalize, record, and post this transaction as appropriate. Use the same account numbers as found in the text for Art's Clothing Company. The general journal page is page 1.

Journalizing, recording, and posting a cash payments journal
❽ (20 min)

11-7B. Journalize, record, and post when appropriate the following transactions into the cash payments journal (page 2) for Morgan's Clothing. Use the same headings as found in the text for Art's Clothing Company (page 310 of Chapter 7). All purchases discounts are 2/10, n/30, and the amounts shown include GST at 5%.

Accounts Payable Subsidiary Ledger

Name	*Balance*	*Invoice No.*
B. Foss	$ 630	452
A. James	1,155	567
J. Ranch	840	587
B. Swanson	315	659

Partial General Ledger

Account	*Number*	*Balance*
Cash	110	$2,000
Prepaid GST	125	
Accounts Payable	210	2,940
Purchases Discounts	511	
Advertising Expense	610	

2017

Apr. 3 Issued cheque No. 200 to A. James Company in payment of its March 29 invoice No. 567.

8 Issued cheque No. 201 to Flott Advertising in payment of its advertising bill, $100, plus GST at 5%, no discount.

15 Issued cheque No. 202 to B. Foss in payment of its March 26 invoice No. 452.

Schedule of accounts payable
❹ (10 min)

11-8B. From Exercise 11-7B, prepare a schedule of accounts payable and verify that the total of the schedule equals the amount in the controlling account.

Quick method of HST
❼ (5 min)

11-9B. Sudbury Outdoor Wear sells a line of specialized clothing to customers in their local area. For the calendar year 2016, the company sold $280,000 worth of clothing before taxes. HST in Ontario is 13%. The company has elected to use the quick method of accounting for HST, and the applicable rate for Ontario is 4.4%. How much HST must the company send to the federal government for this year?

Group A Problems

(The forms you need are on pages 11-17 to 11-43 of the *Study Guide with Working Papers.*)

Comprehensive problem: using GST and PST in recording transactions in sales, cash receipts, and general journals; recording in accounts receivable subsidiary ledger and posting to general ledger; cross-adding and preparing a schedule of accounts receivable
❶❷❸❹ (90 min)

Check Figure
Schedule of Accounts Receivable $1,977.50

11A-1. Bill Murray opened Bill's Cosmetic Market in London on April 1. Bill offers no sales discount, and 8% PST and 5% GST is charged on all cosmetic sales. The following transactions occurred in April:

2016

Apr. 2 Bill Murray invested $6,000 in the cosmetic market from his personal savings account.

5 From the cash register tapes, lipstick cash sales were $5,000 plus taxes.

5 From the cash register tapes, eyeshadow cash sales were $2,000 plus taxes.

8 Sold lipstick on account to Alice Koy Co., $300, sales invoice No. 1001, plus taxes.

9 Sold eyeshadow on account to Marika Sanchez Co., $1,000, sales invoice No. 1002, plus taxes.

12 Issued credit memorandum No. 10 to Alice Koy Co. for $150 for lipstick returned. (Be sure to reduce taxes payable for Bill's.)

19 Marika Sanchez Co. paid half the amount owed from sales invoice No. 1002, dated April 9.

22 Sold lipstick on account to Jeff Tong Co., $500, sales invoice No. 1003, plus taxes.

23 Sold eyeshadow on account to Rusty Neal Co., $800, sales invoice No. 1004, plus taxes.

Apr.	23	Issued credit memorandum No. 11 to Jeff Tong Co. for $200 (plus taxes) for lipstick returned from sales invoice No. 1003, dated April 22.
	26	Cash sales taken from the cash register tape showed: **1.** Lipstick—$1,000 + taxes **2.** Eyeshadow—$3,000 + taxes
	29	Sold lipstick on account to Marika Sanchez Co., $400, sales invoice No. 1005, plus taxes.
	30	Received payment from Marika Sanchez Co. of sales invoice No. 1005, dated April 29.

Required

a. Journalize the above in the sales journal, cash receipts journal, or general journal.

b. Record in the accounts receivable subsidiary ledger and post to the general ledger when appropriate.

c. Prepare a schedule of accounts receivable for the end of April 2016.

Comprehensive problem: using HST in recording transactions in sales, cash receipts, and general journals; recording in accounts receivable and posting to general ledger; cross-adding and preparing a schedule of accounts receivable
❶ ❷ ❸ ❹ (90 min)

Check Figure

Schedule of Accounts Receivable $7,090.75

11A-2. Mary Parker owns Parker's SCUBA Shop of Bathurst. (In your *Study Guide with Working Papers*, balances as of April 1 are provided for the accounts receivable and general ledger accounts.) In Mary's province, it is necessary to add HST of 13% to arrive at the final invoice amount. The following transactions occurred in April:

2017		
Apr.	1	Mary Parker invested an additional $15,000 in the business.
	3	Sold $500 worth of merchandise (plus 13% HST) on account to J. Simpson, sales invoice No. 614, terms 2/10, n/30.
	7	Sold $1,200 worth of merchandise (plus HST) on account to R. Langley, sales invoice No. 615, terms 2/10, n/30.
	8	Sold $300 worth of merchandise (plus HST) on account to J. Fellowes, sales invoice No. 616, terms 2/10, n/30.
	11	Received cash from J. Simpson in payment of April 3 transaction, sales invoice No. 614, less discount.
	14	Sold $2,000 worth of merchandise (plus HST) on account to Phyllis Leung, sales invoice No. 617, terms 2/10, n/30.
	15	Received cash, less discount, from R. Langley in payment of April 7 transaction, sales invoice No. 615.
	18	Charged cash sales, $1,600 (plus HST).
	18	Issued credit memorandum No. 101 to Phyllis Leung for $500 (plus HST) worth of merchandise returned from April 14 sales.
	21	Received payment from Roland Doncaster of the amount due from previous month, $904.00.
	22	Received cash from Phyllis Leung in payment of April 14 sales invoice No. 617. (Don't forget about the credit memo, HST, and discount.)
	25	Charged cash sales, $4,000 (plus necessary HST).
	28	Sold merchandise priced at $5,000 (plus HST), on account, to Roland Doncaster, sales invoice No. 618, terms 2/10, n/30.
	29	Issued credit memorandum No. 102 to Roland Doncaster for $800 worth of merchandise (plus HST) returned from April 28 transaction, sales invoice No. 618.

Required

a. Journalize the transactions.

b. Record in the accounts receivable ledger and post to the general ledger as needed.

c. Prepare a schedule of accounts receivable as of April 30.

Journalizing, recording, and posting a purchases journal, as well as recording a debit memorandum and preparing a schedule of accounts payable
4 5 6 (45 min)

Check Figure

Total Schedule of Accounts Payable $6,310.50

11A-3. Mabel's Natural Food Store of Cold Lake uses a purchases journal (page 10) and a general journal (page 2) to record the following transactions (continued from April):

2015		
May	8	Purchased merchandise on account from Aton Co., invoice No. 400, dated May 7, terms 2/10, n/60, $600, plus 5% GST.
	11	Purchased merchandise on account from Broward Co., invoice No. 120, dated May 11, terms 2/10, n/60, $1,200, plus GST.
	14	Purchased store supplies on account from Midden Co., invoice No. 510, dated May 14, $700, plus GST.
	15	Issued debit memo No. 8 to Aton Co. for merchandise returned, $400 (plus GST) from invoice No. 400.
	18	Purchased office equipment on account from Relar Co., invoice No. 810, dated May 18, $560, plus GST.
	25	Purchased additional store supplies on account from Midden Co., invoice No. 516, dated May 25, terms 2/10, n/30, $650, plus GST.

The food store has decided to use a separate column for the purchases of supplies in the purchases journal, which also has a separate column for GST.

Required

a. Journalize the transactions.

b. Post and record as appropriate.

c. Prepare a schedule of accounts payable as of May 31, 2015.

Accounts Payable Subsidiary Ledger

Name	*Balance*
Aton Co.	$ 420
Broward Co.	630
Midden Co.	1,260
Relar Co.	525

Partial General Ledger

Account	*Number*	*Balance*
Store Supplies	110	$ —
Prepaid GST	112	471
Office Equipment	120	—
Accounts Payable	210	2,835
Purchases	510	16,000
Purchases Returns and Allowances	512	—

Journalizing, recording, and posting a cash payments journal with GST; preparing a schedule of accounts payable
4 8 (45 min)

Check Figure

Total of Schedule of Accounts Payable $1,995.00

11A-4. Wendy Jones operates a wholesale computer centre in Whitehorse. All transactions requiring the payment of cash are recorded in the cash payments journal (page 5). The account balances for Jones' Computer Centre as of May 1, 2016, are as follows:

Accounts Payable Subsidiary Ledger

Name	*Balance*	*GST Included*
Alvin Co.	$1,260	$60
Henry Co.	630	30
Soy Co.	840	40
Xon Co.	1,470	70

Partial General Ledger

Account	*Number*	*Balance*
Cash	110	$17,000
Prepaid GST	132	920
Delivery Truck	150	—
Accounts Payable	210	4,200
Computer Purchases	510	—
Computer Purchases Discount	511	—
Rent Expense	610	—
Utilities Expense	620	—

Required

a. Journalize the following transactions.

b. Record in the accounts payable ledger and post to the general ledger as appropriate.

c. Prepare a schedule of accounts payable.

2016		
May	3	Paid half the amount owed Henry Co. from previous purchases of computers on account, less a 2% purchases discount, cheque No. 21.
	3	Bought a delivery truck for $8,000 cash, plus GST of $400, cheque No. 22, payable to Bill Ring Co.
	7	Bought computer merchandise from Lectro Co., cheque No. 23, $3,900, plus GST.
	17	Bought additional computer merchandise from Pulse Co., cheque No. 24, $800, plus GST.
	24	Paid Xon Co. the amount owed less a 2% purchases discount, cheque No. 25.
	27	Paid rent expense to King's Realty Trust, cheque No. 26, $2,000, plus GST.
	28	Paid utilities expense to Stone Utility Co., cheque No. 27, $300, plus GST.
	31	Paid half the amount owed Soy Co., no discount, cheque No. 28.

Comprehensive review problem with GST (or HST): all special journals and the general journal; schedules of accounts payable and accounts receivable
1 2 3 4 5 6 8 (120 min)

11A-5. Abby Ellen owns Abby's Toy House in Halifax. As her newly hired accountant, your task is to:

a. Journalize the transactions for the month of March.

b. Record in subsidiary ledgers and post to the general ledger as appropriate.

c. Total, rule, and cross-add the journals.

d. Prepare a schedule of accounts receivable and a schedule of accounts payable, as of March 31, 2016.

Check Figures

Total of Schedule of Accounts Receivable $7,980.00 (GST 5%) or $8,588.00 (HST 13%)

Total of Schedule of Accounts Payable $9,450.00 (GST 5%) or $10,170.00 (HST 13%)

Note: Please substitute HST at 13% for GST at 5% if your instructor so directs.

The following is the partial chart of accounts for Abby's Toy House:

Assets	**Revenue**
110 Cash	410 Toy Sales
112 Accounts Receivable	412 Sales Returns and Allowances
114 Prepaid Rent	414 Sales Discounts
116 Prepaid GST/HST	
121 Delivery Truck	**Cost of Goods**
	510 Toy Purchases
Liabilities	512 Purchases Returns and Allowances
210 Accounts Payable	514 Purchases Discounts
218 GST/HST Payable	
	Expenses
Owner's Equity	610 Salaries Expense
310 A. Ellen, Capital	612 Cleaning Expense

2016

Mar. 1 Abby Ellen invested $10,000 in the toy store.

1 Paid three months' rent in advance, cheque No. 1, $3,000, plus GST.

1 Purchased merchandise from Earl Miller Company on account, $4,000, plus GST. Invoice No. 410, dated March 1, terms 2/10, n/30.

4 Sold merchandise to Bill Burton on account, $1,000, plus GST. Invoice No. 1, terms 2/10, n/30.

6 Sold merchandise to Jim Rex on account, $700, plus GST. Invoice No. 2, terms 2/10, n/30.

8 Purchased merchandise from Earl Miller Co. on account, $1,200, plus GST. Invoice No. 415, dated March 8, terms 2/10, n/30.

8 Sold merchandise to Bill Burton on account, $600, plus GST. Invoice No. 3, terms 2/10, n/30.

11 Paid cleaning service $300, plus GST. Cheque No. 2.

11 Paid Earl Miller Co. invoice No. 410, dated March 1, cheque No. 3.

12 Jim Rex returned merchandise that cost $300 (before GST) to Abby's Toy House. Abby issued credit memorandum No. 1 to Jim Rex for $300, plus GST.

12 Purchased merchandise from Minnie Katz on account, $4,000, plus GST. Invoice No. 311, dated March 12, terms 1/15, n/60.

13 Sold $1,300 (plus GST) worth of toy merchandise for cash.

15 Paid salaries, $600, cheque No. 4.

15 Returned merchandise to Minnie Katz in the amount of $1,000, plus GST. Abby's Toy House issued debit memorandum No. 1 to Minnie Katz.

15 Sold merchandise for cash, $4,000, plus GST.

15 Received payment from Jim Rex, invoice No. 2 (less returned merchandise), less discount.

18 Bill Burton paid invoice No. 1.

18 Sold toy merchandise to Amy Rose on account, $4,000, plus GST. Invoice No. 4, terms 2/10, n/30.

Mar.	19	Purchased delivery truck on account from Sam Katz's Garage, \$3,000, plus GST. Invoice No. 111, dated March 19 (no discount).
	22	Sold to Bill Burton merchandise on account, \$900, plus GST. Invoice No. 5, terms 2/10, n/30.
	22	Paid Minnie Katz balance owed, cheque No. 5.
	22	Sold toy merchandise on account to Amy Rose, \$1,100, plus GST. Invoice No. 6, terms 2/10, n/30.
	25	Purchased toy merchandise, \$600, plus GST. Cheque No. 6.
	26	Purchased toy merchandise from Woody Smith on account, \$4,800, plus GST. Invoice No. 211, dated March 26, terms 2/10, n/30.
	26	Bill Burton paid invoice No. 5, dated March 22.
	26	Amy Rose paid invoice No. 6, dated March 22.
	28	Abby invested an additional \$5,000 in the business.
	28	Purchased merchandise from Earl Miller Co., \$1,400, plus GST. Invoice No. 436, dated March 26, terms 2/10, n/30.
	29	Paid Earl Miller Co. invoice No. 436, cheque No. 7.
	29	Sold merchandise to Bonnie Flow Company on account, \$3,000, plus GST. Invoice No. 7, terms 2/10, n/30

Group B Problems

(The forms you need are on pages 11-17 to 11-43 of the *Study Guide with Working Papers.*)

Comprehensive problem: using sales taxes in recording transactions in sales, cash receipts, and general journals; recording in accounts receivable subsidiary ledger and posting to general ledger; preparing a schedule of accounts receivable
❶ ❷ ❸ ❹ ❺ ❽ (90 min)

Check Figure
Schedule of Accounts Receivable \$2,203.50

11B-1. Bill's Cosmetic Market of Brandon began operating in April. There is 8% PST and 5% GST on all cosmetic sales. Bill offers no discounts. The following transactions occurred in April:

2016		
Apr.	2	Bill Murray invested \$10,000 in the cosmetic market from his personal account.
	3	From the cash register tapes, lipstick cash sales were \$5,000 plus taxes.
	4	From the cash register tapes, eyeshadow cash sales were \$3,000 plus taxes.
	5	Sold lipstick on account to Alice Koy Co., \$400, sales invoice No. 1001, plus taxes.
	9	Sold eyeshadow on account to Marika Sanchez Co., \$900, sales invoice No. 1002, plus taxes.
	16	Issued credit memorandum No. 30 to Alice Koy Co. for lipstick returned, \$200. (Be sure to reduce taxes payable.)
	18	Marika Sanchez Co. paid half the amount owed from sales invoice No. 1002, dated April 9.
	19	Sold lipstick on account to Jeff Tong Co., \$600 sales invoice No. 1003, plus taxes.
	22	Sold eyeshadow on account to Rusty Neal Co., \$1,000, sales invoice No. 1004, plus taxes.
	23	Issued credit memorandum No. 31 to Jeff Tong Co. for \$300 (plus taxes), for lipstick returned from sales invoice No. 1003, dated April 20.

Apr. 26 Sold lipstick on account to Marika Sanchez Co., $900, sales invoice No. 1005, plus taxes.

29 Cash sales taken from the cash register tape showed:
1. Lipstick—$4,000 + taxes
2. Eyeshadow—$2,000 + taxes

30 Received payment from Marika Sanchez Co. of sales invoice No. 1005, dated April 26.

Required

a. Journalize, record, and post as appropriate.

b. Prepare a schedule of accounts receivable for the end of April 2016.

Comprehensive problem: using sales taxes in recording transactions in sales, cash receipts, and general journals; recording in accounts receivable subsidiary ledger and posting to general ledger; preparing a schedule of accounts receivable
❶❷❸❹ (90 min)

Check Figure

Schedule of Accounts Receivable $8,333.75

11B-2. Mary Parker owns Parker's SCUBA Shop in Bathurst. (In your *Study Guide with Working Papers*, balances as of April 1 are provided for the accounts receivable and general ledger accounts.) In Mary's province, it is necessary to add HST of 13% to the sales total to arrive at the final invoice amount. The following transactions occurred in April:

2017

Apr. 1 Mary Parker invested an additional $14,000 in the business.

4 Sold $800 worth of merchandise (plus HST at 13%) on account to J. Simpson, sales invoice No. 614, terms 2/10, n/30.

4 Sold $1,600 worth of merchandise (plus HST) on account to R. Langley, sales invoice No. 615, terms 2/10, n/30.

8 Sold $600 worth of merchandise (plus HST) on account to J. Fellowes, sales invoice No. 616, terms 2/10, n/30.

11 Received cash from J. Simpson in payment of April 4 transaction, sales invoice No. 614, less discount (pre-HST amount).

14 Sold $3,000 worth of merchandise (plus HST) on account to Phyllis Leung, sales invoice No. 617, terms 2/10, n/30.

18 Received cash payment from R. Langley in payment of April 4 transaction, sales invoice No. 615.

18 Charged cash sales, $2,500 (plus HST).

21 Issued credit memorandum No. 101 to Phyllis Leung for $900 (plus HST) of merchandise returned from April 14 sales on account.

21 Received payment from Roland Doncaster of the amount due from the previous month, $904.00.

21 Received cash from Phyllis Leung in payment of April 14 sales invoice No. 617. (Don't forget the credit memo, HST, and discount.)

22 Charged cash sales, $3,200 plus HST.

25 Sold merchandise priced at $6,000 (plus HST) on account to Roland Doncaster, sales invoice No. 618, terms 2/10, n/30.

29 Issued credit memorandum No. 102 to Roland Doncaster for $1,000 worth of merchandise (plus HST) returned from April 25 transaction, sales invoice No. 618.

Required

a. Journalize the transactions.

b. Record in the accounts receivable ledger and post to the general ledger as needed.

c. Prepare a schedule of accounts receivable as of April 30, 2017.

Journalizing, recording, and posting a purchases journal with GST, as well as recording the issuing of a debit memorandum and preparing a schedule of accounts payable
4 5 6 (45 min)

Check Figure

Total of Schedule of Accounts Payable $6,405.00

11B-3. As the accountant of Mabel's Natural Food Store of Cold Lake, (a) journalize the following transactions in the purchases (page 10) or general journal (page 2), (b) record and post as appropriate, and (c) prepare a schedule of accounts payable as of May 31, 2015. Beginning balances are in your *Study Guide with Working Papers.*

2015
May 8 Purchased merchandise on account from Broward Co., invoice No. 420, dated May 7, terms 2/10, n/60, $500, plus 5% GST.
11 Purchased merchandise on account from Aton Co., invoice No. 400, dated May 11, terms 2/10, n/60, $900, plus GST.
14 Purchased store supplies on account from Midden Co., invoice No. 510, dated May 11, $800, plus GST.
15 Issued debit memo No. 7 to Aton Co. for merchandise returned, $400, plus GST (from invoice No. 400).
18 Purchased office equipment on account from Relar Co., invoice No. 810, dated May 18, $750, plus GST.
25 Purchased additional store supplies on account from Midden Co., invoice No. 516, dated May 22, terms 2/10, n/30, $850, plus GST.

Journalizing, recording, and posting a cash payments journal with GST; preparing a schedule of accounts payable
4 8 (45 min)

Check Figure

Total of Schedule of Accounts Payable $1,995.00

11B-4. Wendy Jones of Whitehorse has hired you as her bookkeeper to record the following transactions in the cash payments journal. She would like you to record and post as appropriate and supply her with a schedule of accounts payable as of May 31, 2016. (Beginning balances are in your *Study Guide with Working Papers* and in Problem 11A-4.)

2016
May 3 Bought a delivery truck for $8,000 cash, plus GST, cheque No. 21, payable to Randy Rosse Co.
3 Paid half the amount owed Henry Co. from previous purchases of computer merchandise on account, less a 5% purchases discount, cheque No. 22.
7 Bought computer merchandise from Jane Co. for $900 cash, plus GST, cheque No. 23.
17 Bought additional computer merchandise from Jane Co., cheque No. 24, $1,000, plus GST.
24 Paid Xon Co. the amount owed less a 5% purchases discount, cheque No. 25.
27 Paid rent expense to Regan Realty Trust, cheque No. 26, $3,000, plus GST.
28 Paid half the amount owed Soy Co., no discount, cheque No. 27.
31 Paid utilities expense to County Utility, cheque No. 28, $425, plus GST.

Comprehensive review problem with GST (or HST): all special journals and the general journal; schedules of accounts payable and accounts receivable
❶ ❷ ❸ ❹ ❺ ❻ ❽ (120 min)

11B-5. As the new accountant for Abby's Toy House in Halifax, your task is to:

a. Journalize the transactions for the month of March.

b. Record in subsidiary ledgers and post to the general ledger as appropriate.

c. Total, rule, and cross-foot the journals.

d. Prepare a schedule of accounts receivable and a schedule of accounts payable as of March 31, 2016.

Note: Please substitute HST at 13% for GST at 5% if your instructor so directs.

(Use the same chart of accounts as in Problem 11A-5. Your *Study Guide with Working Papers* has all the forms you need to complete this problem.)

2016

Mar.
1 Abby invested $8,000 in the new toy store.
1 Paid two months' rent in advance, cheque No. 1, $1,000, plus GST.
1 Purchased merchandise from Earl Miller Company, invoice No. 410, dated March 1, terms 2/10, n/30; $6,000, plus GST.
4 Sold merchandise to Bill Burton on account, $1,600, plus GST. Invoice No. 1, terms 2/10, n/30.
6 Sold merchandise to Jim Rex on account, $800, plus GST, invoice No. 2, terms 2/10, n/30.
7 Purchased merchandise from Earl Miller Company, $800, plus GST. Invoice No. 415, dated March 7, terms 2/10, n/30.
9 Sold merchandise to Bill Burton on account, $700, plus GST. Invoice No. 3, terms 2/10, n/30.
9 Paid cleaning service, $400, plus GST, cheque No. 2.
10 Jim Rex returned merchandise that cost $200 (plus GST) to Abby. Abby issued credit memorandum No. 1 to Jim Rex for $200, plus GST.
10 Purchased merchandise from Minnie Katz, $7,000, plus GST. Invoice No. 311, dated March 9, terms 1/15, n/60.
11 Paid Earl Miller Co. invoice No. 410, dated March 1, cheque No. 3.
13 Sold $1,500 (plus GST) worth of toy merchandise for cash.
15 Paid salaries, $700, cheque No. 4.
15 Returned merchandise to Minnie Katz in the amount of $500, plus GST. Abby issued debit memorandum No. 1 to Minnie Katz.
15 Sold merchandise for cash, $4,800, plus GST.
15 Received payment from Jim Rex for invoice No. 2 (less returned merchandise) less discount.
18 Bill Burton paid invoice No. 1.
18 Sold toy merchandise to Amy Rose on account, $6,000, plus GST. Invoice No. 4, terms 2/10, n/30.
19 Purchased delivery truck on account from Sam Katz's Garage, $2,500, plus GST. Invoice No. 111, dated March 19 (no discount).
21 Sold merchandise on account to Bill Burton, $2,000, plus GST. Invoice No. 5, terms 2/10, n/30.
22 Paid Minnie Katz balance owed, cheque No. 5.
22 Sold toy merchandise on account to Amy Rose, $2,000, plus GST. Invoice No. 6, terms 2/10, n/30.

Check Figures

Total of Schedule of Accounts Receivable $10,395.00 (GST 5%) or $11,187.00 (HST 13%)
Total of Schedule of Accounts Payable $9,660.00 (GST 5%) or $10,396.00 (HST 13%)

Mar. 26 Purchased toy merchandise, $800, plus GST, cheque No. 6.
26 Purchased toy merchandise from Woody Smith on account, $5,900, plus GST. Invoice No. 211, dated March 26, terms 2/10, n/30.
26 Bill Burton paid invoice No. 5, dated March 21.
26 Amy Rose paid invoice No. 6, dated March 22.
27 Abby invested an additional $3,000 in the business.
28 Purchased merchandise from Earl Miller Co., $4,200, plus GST. Invoice No. 436, dated March 26, terms 2/10, n/30.
29 Paid Earl Miller Co. invoice No. 436, cheque No. 7.
29 Sold merchandise to Bonnie Flow Company on account, $3,200, plus GST. Invoice No. 7, terms 2/10, n/30.

Group C Problems

(The forms you need are on pages 11-44 to 11-75 of the *Study Guide with Working Papers*.)

Multicolumn sales journal: use of sales tax; journalizing and posting to the general ledger and recording in the accounts receivable subledger; and preparing a schedule of accounts receivable
❻ ❽ (45 min)

Check Figure

Schedule of Accounts Receivable $37,432.50

11C-1. In September, the following transactions occurred for Forrest Equipment Supply of Regina (your *Study Guide with Working Papers* has balances as of September 1 for certain general ledger and accounts receivable ledger accounts):

2017
Sept. 2 Sold merchandise to Ray Fortuna on account, $9,500, invoice No. 703, plus 5% PST.
5 Sold merchandise to Wilma Jorge on account, $3,000, invoice No. 704, plus 5% PST.
8 Sold merchandise to Cassie Ho on account, $15,800, invoice No. 705, plus 5% PST.
9 Issued credit memorandum No. 14 to Ray Fortuna for $1,200 for defective merchandise returned from September 2 transaction. (Be careful to record the reduction in PST payable as well.)
12 Sold merchandise to Wilma Jorge on account, $4,650, invoice No. 706, plus 5% PST.

Required

a. Journalize the transactions in the appropriate journals.
b. Record in the accounts receivable ledger and post to the general ledger as appropriate.
c. Prepare a schedule of accounts receivable as of September 30, 2017.

Comprehensive problem: using sales taxes in recording transactions into sales, cash receipts, and general journals; recording in the accounts receivable subledger and posting to the general ledger; and preparing a schedule of accounts receivable
❶ ❷ ❸ ❹ (90 min)

11C-2. Royce's Communication Sales Co. began operating in August. Royce's offers no discounts (all terms are net 30 days), and 8% PST and 5% GST is charged on all sales. The following transactions occurred in August:

2016
Aug. 1 Royce Lamoureux invested $32,000 in Royce's Communication Sales Co. from his personal account.
2 From the cash register tapes, cellular cash sales were $5,400 plus taxes.
6 From the cash register tapes, radio cash sales were $8,150 plus taxes.

Check Figure

Schedule of Accounts Receivable $17,311.60

Aug. 7 Sold cellular equipment on account to Kelly's Real Estate Co., $4,260, sales invoice No. 1201, plus taxes.
9 Sold radio equipment on account to Well's Hotshot Service Co., $3,100, sales invoice No. 1202, plus taxes.
13 Issued credit memorandum No. 1 to Kelly's Real Estate Co. for cellular equipment returned, $800. (Be sure to reduce taxes payable.)
16 Well's Hotshot Service Co. paid half the amount owed from sales invoice No. 1202, dated August 9.
20 Sold cellular equipment on account to Mountain Explorations Co., $5,770, sales invoice No. 1203, plus taxes.
20 Received proceeds of loan from the Business Development Bank of Canada, $50,000.
22 Sold radio equipment on account to Walkin's Safety Supply Co., $5,820. Sales invoice No. 1204, plus taxes.
23 Issued credit memorandum No. 2 to Mountain Explorations Co. for $1,420 for equipment returned from sales invoice No. 1203, dated August 20. Remember to include taxes!
26 Received payment of net amount due from Kelly's Real Estate Co. on sales invoice No. 1201, less the credit allowed.
27 Cash sales taken from the cash register tape showed:
1. Cellular—$8,400 + taxes
2. Radio—$7,600 + taxes
30 Sold cellular equipment on account to Well's Hotshot Service Co., $5,150 sales invoice, No. 1205, plus taxes.
31 Received balance from Well's Hotshot Service Co. for sales invoice No. 1202, dated August 9.

Required

a. Journalize, record, and post as appropriate.

b. Prepare a schedule of accounts receivable for the end of August.

Comprehensive problem: using HST in recording transactions in sales, cash receipts, and general journals; recording in the accounts receivable subledger and posting to the general ledger; and preparing a schedule of accounts receivable ❶❷❸❹ (90 min)

11C-3. Martha Worth owns and operates Rarity Collectibles Shop in St. John's. (In your *Study Guide with Working Papers*, balances as of January 1 are provided for the accounts receivable and general ledger accounts.) In this province, it is necessary to add HST of 13% to the sales total to arrive at the final invoice amount. The following transactions occurred in January:

2017
Jan. 2 Martha Worth invested $42,000 in the business.
3 Sold $2,600 worth of merchandise (plus HST) on account to Starcraft Reproductions, sales invoice No. 344, terms 2/10, n/30.
6 Sold $3,200 worth of merchandise (plus HST) on account to Burgess Fancys, sales invoice No. 345, terms 2/10, n/30.
8 Sold $3,800 worth of merchandise (plus HST) on account to Hard-To-Find Co., sales invoice No. 346, terms 2/10, n/30.
10 Received cash from Starcraft Reproductions in payment of January 3 transaction, sales invoice No. 344, less discount.
14 Sold $2,480 worth of merchandise (plus HST) on account to Georgina's Collections, sales invoice No. 347, terms 2/10, n/30.
16 Received cash payment from Burgess Fancys in payment of January 6 transaction, sales invoice No. 345.
17 Charged cash sales, $4,125 plus HST.

Check Figure

Schedule of Accounts Receivable $14,371.34

Jan. 20 Issued credit memorandum No. 10 to Georgina's Collections for $500 worth of merchandise (plus HST) returned from January 14 sales on account.

21 Received cash from Georgina's Collections in payment of January 14 sales invoice No. 347. (Don't forget about the credit memo, HST, and discount.)

24 Charged cash sales, $4,720, plus HST.

27 Sold merchandise priced at $6,000 (plus HST) on account to Perfect Sales Co., sales invoice No. 348, terms 2/10, n/30.

31 Issued credit memorandum No. 11 to Perfect Sales Co. for $1,200 (plus HST) of merchandise returned from January 27 transaction, sales invoice No. 348.

Required

a. Journalize the transactions.

b. Record in the accounts receivable ledger and post to the general ledger as needed.

c. Prepare a schedule of accounts receivable as of January 31, 2017.

Journalizing, recording, and posting a purchases journal with GST, as well as recording the issuing of a debit memorandum and preparing a schedule of accounts payable
4 5 6 (45 min)

Check Figure

Total of Schedule of Accounts Payable $22,053.15

11C-4. Farber's Fabric Co. of Yellowknife uses a purchases journal (page 21) and a general journal (page 32) to record the following transactions (continued from July). The GST rate is 5%:

2015

Aug. 3 Purchased fabric for resale from European Import Fabrics Co., invoice No. 653, dated August 2, terms net 15 days, $1,362 plus GST.

7 Purchased merchandise on account from Eddyn Co., invoice No. 250, dated August 7, terms 2/10, n/60, $920, plus GST.

10 Purchased merchandise on account from Forward Co., invoice No. 1124, dated August 7, terms 1/10, n/60, $1,626, plus GST.

13 Purchased store supplies on account from Lavoy Co., invoice No. 712, dated August 13, $2,680, plus GST.

14 Issued debit memo No. 8 to Eddyn Co. for merchandise returned, $160, plus GST, from invoice No. 250.

17 Purchased office equipment on account from Reliant Co., invoice No. 873, dated August 14, $2,610, plus GST.

24 Purchased additional store supplies on account from Lavoy Co., invoice No. 816, dated August 24, terms 2/10, n/30, $725, plus GST.

28 Purchased fabric for resale from European Import Fabrics Co., invoice No. 713, dated August 27, terms net 15 days, $2,740, plus GST.

The fabric store has decided to keep a separate column for the purchases of supplies in the purchases journal and also has a separate column for GST. The account balances as of August 1, 2015, are as follows:

Accounts Payable Subsidiary Ledger

Name	*Balance*
Eddyn Co.	$ 840
European Import	3,255
Forward Co.	1,575
Lavoy Co.	525
Reliant Co.	2,730

Partial General Ledger

Account	*Number*	*Balance*
Store Supplies	130	$ —
Prepaid GST	142	2,795
Office Equipment	180	—
Accounts Payable	220	8,925
Purchases	500	86,340
Purchases Returns and Allowances	510	1,374

Required

a. Journalize the transactions.

b. Post and record as appropriate.

c. Prepare a schedule of accounts payable as of August 31, 2015.

Journalizing, recording, and posting a cash payments journal with GST; preparing a schedule of accounts payable
4 8 (60 min)

> *Check Figure*
>
> **Total of Schedule of Accounts Payable $2,261.18**

11C-5. Jim Stokes owns and operates a welding supplies company in Fort Liard. All transactions requiring the payment of cash are recorded in the cash payments journal (page 45). The account balances as of May 1, 2017, are as follows:

Accounts Payable Subsidiary Ledger

Name	*Balance*	*GST Included*
Dominion Gases Co.	$1,454.25	$ 69.25
Glover Gauges Co.	865.23	41.20
Marker Gloves Co.	1,812.95	86.33
Prism Accessories Co.	3,869.17	184.25
Vertal Rod Co.	2,434.06	115.91

Partial General Ledger

Account	*Number*	*Balance*
Cash	100	$22,941.18
Prepaid GST	145	2,418.12*
Delivery Truck	170	—
Accounts Payable	200	10,435.66
Welding Purchases	500	56,422.29
Welding Purchases Discounts	510	506.20
Rent Expense	670	3,730.00
Utilities Expense	690	1,204.66

*Will not agree with the amounts included in the accounts payable balances.

Required

a. Journalize the following transactions.

b. Record in the accounts payable ledger and post to the general ledger as appropriate.

c. Prepare a schedule of accounts payable as of May 31, 2017.

2017

May 1 Paid half the amount owed Dominion Gases Co. from previous purchases on account, less a 2% purchases discount, cheque No. 464.

2 Bought a delivery truck for $21,400 cash, plus GST of $1,070, cheque No. 465, payable to City Truck Sales Co.

5 Paid the amount owing to Glover Gauges Co., cheque No. 466.

May	6	Bought welding merchandise (cash purchase) from Vericon Canada Co., cheque No. 467, $1,846, plus GST.
	13	Paid the balance due to Prism Accessories Co. after deducting a 5% discount as per usual terms for this company, cheque No. 468.
	19	Bought additional welding merchandise (cash purchase) from Pulse Co., cheque No. 469, $850, plus GST.
	23	Paid Marker Gloves Co. the amount owed less a 2% purchases discount, cheque No. 470.
	27	Paid rent expense to Abbott Properties Co., cheque No. 471, $1,720, plus GST.
	29	Paid utilities expense to Stony Plain Utility Co., cheque No. 472, $364, plus GST.
	30	Paid $900.00 to Vertal Rod Co., no discount, cheque No. 473.

Comprehensive review problem with GST (or, optionally, HST): all special journals and the general journal, schedules of accounts payable, and accounts receivable

❶ ❷ ❸ ❹ ❺ ❻ ❼ **(140 min)**

Check Figures

Total of Schedule of Accounts Receivable $7,839.30 (GST 5%) or $8,436.58 (HST 13%)

Total of Schedule of Accounts Payable $28,728.00 (GST 5%) or $30,916.80 (HST 13%)

11C-6. Betty Cardinal runs Cardinal's Book Shop in a downtown location. As her newly hired accountant, your task is to do the following (substituting HST at 13% for GST at 5% if your instructor so directs):

a. Journalize the transactions for the month of October.

b. Record to subsidiary ledgers and post to the general ledger as appropriate.

c. Total, rule, and cross-add the journals.

d. Prepare a schedule of accounts receivable and a schedule of accounts payable as of October 31, 2016.

The following is the partial chart of accounts for Cardinal's Book Shop:

Assets	**Revenue**
110 Cash	410 Book Sales
120 Accounts Receivable	412 Sales Returns and Allowances
135 Prepaid Rent	414 Sales Discounts
138 Prepaid GST/HST	
180 Delivery Truck	**Cost of Goods**
	510 Book Purchases
Liabilities	512 Purchases Returns and Allowances
210 Accounts Payable	514 Purchases Discounts
218 GST/HST Payable	
	Expenses
Owner's Equity	615 Cleaning Expense
310 B. Cardinal, Capital	650 Salaries Expense

2016		
Oct.	1	Betty Cardinal invested $20,000 in the bookstore.
	1	Paid three months' rent in advance, cheque No. 121, $2,700, plus GST.
	3	Purchased merchandise from Milligan Book Company on account, $4,270, plus GST. Invoice No. 410, dated October 2, terms 2/10, n/30.
	3	Sold merchandise to First City Library on account, $2,465, plus GST. Invoice No. 781, terms 2/10, n/30.
	7	Sold merchandise to District College on account, $3,160, plus GST. Invoice No. 782, terms 2/10, n/30.
	8	Purchased merchandise from Milligan Book Co. on account, $2,940, plus GST. Invoice No. 415, dated October 8, terms 2/10, n/30.

Oct.	8	Sold merchandise to First City Library on account, \$1,856, plus GST. Invoice No. 783, terms 2/10, n/30.
	8	Paid cleaning service \$280, plus GST, cheque No. 122.
	11	District College returned merchandise that cost \$312 (before GST) to Cardinal's Book Shop. Cardinal issued credit memorandum No. 1 to District College for \$312, plus GST.
	11	Purchased merchandise from Winnipeg Book Supply on account, \$1,852, plus GST. Invoice No. 311, dated October 8, terms 1/15, n/60.
	11	Paid Milligan Book Co. invoice No. 410, dated October 2, cheque No. 123.
	14	Sold \$2,420, plus GST, worth of book merchandise for cash.
	15	Paid salaries, \$920, cheque No. 124.
	15	Returned merchandise to Winnipeg Book Supply in the amount of \$362 plus GST. Cardinal's Book Shop issued debit memorandum No. 18 to Winnipeg Book Supply.
	15	Sold merchandise for cash, \$1,047, plus GST.
	15	Received payment from District College, invoice No. 782 (less returned merchandise), less discount.
	18	First City Library paid invoice No. 781.
	18	Sold book merchandise to Rural Bookmobile Co. on account, \$2,484, plus GST. Invoice No. 784, terms 2/10, n/30.
	21	Purchased delivery truck on account from Suburban Auto Sales Co., \$18,600, plus GST. Invoice No. 111, dated October 19 (no discount).
	22	Sold merchandise to First City Library on account, \$2,694, plus GST. Invoice No. 785, terms 2/10, n/30.
	22	Paid Winnipeg Book Supply balance owed, cheque No. 125.
	25	Sold book merchandise on account to Rural Bookmobile Co., \$2,412, plus GST. Invoice No. 786, terms 2/10, n/30.
	25	Purchased used book merchandise for cash, \$3,200, plus GST, cheque No. 126.
	28	Purchased book merchandise from Smithsonian Book Co. on account, \$5,820, plus GST. Invoice No. 211, dated October 25, terms 2/10, n/30.
	28	Sold merchandise for cash, \$940, plus GST.
	29	First City Library paid invoice No. 785, dated October 22.
	29	Rural Bookmobile Co. paid invoice No. 786, dated October 25.
	30	Betty invested an additional \$12,000 in the business.
	30	Purchased merchandise from Milligan Book Co., \$3,120 plus GST. Invoice No. 436, dated October 26, terms 2/10, n/30.
	31	Paid Milligan Book Co. invoice No. 436, cheque No. 127.
	31	Sold merchandise to Flower & Company on account, \$3,126, plus GST. Invoice No. 787, terms 2/10, n/30.

On-the-Job Training

(The forms you need are on pages 11-76 and 11-77 of the *Study Guide with Working Papers.*)

Cash discounts
5 8 (20 min)

Hint: $R = \frac{1}{PT}$

T-1. Angie Co. bought merchandise for \$1,000 with credit terms of 2/10, n/30. Because of the bookkeeper's incompetence, the 2% cash discount was missed. The bookkeeper told Pete Angie, the owner, not to get excited.

After all, it was a $20 discount that was missed—not hundreds of dollars. Act as Mr. Angie's assistant and show the bookkeeper that his $20 represents a sizeable equivalent interest cost. In your calculation, assume a 360-day year. Make some written recommendations so that this will not happen again.

Working backwards to reconstruct journals
❶ ❷ ❸ ❹ (60 min)

T-2. Ronald Howard has been hired by Green Company to help reconstruct the sales journal, general journal, and cash receipts journal, which were recently destroyed in a fire. The owner of Green has supplied him with the data shown below. Enter the entries into the reconstructed sales journal, general journal, and cash receipts journal. (Don't worry about dates, invoice numbers, etc.) What written recommendation should Ron make so that reconstruction will not be needed in the future?

Accounts Receivable Subsidiary Ledger

P. Bond

Balance	100	150	CRJ
SJ	150	Entitled to 2% discount	

M. Raff

Balance	200		
SJ	100		

J. Smooth

Balance	300	1,000	GJ
SJ	2,000	1,000	CRJ
SJ	1,000	500	GJ
		Entitled to 1% discount (refers to 1,000 CRJ)	

R. Venner

Balance	200	400	CRJ
SJ	400		

Partial General Ledger

Cash

	12,737		

Accounts Receivable

Balance	800	1,000	GJ
SJ	3,650	500	GJ
		1,550	CRJ

Shelving Equipment

Balance	200	200	CRJ

M. Rang, Capital

		1,000	Balance
		5,000	(Additional investment this month)

Sales

		800	Balance
		6,000	CRJ ← 5,000 and 1,000
		3,650	SJ

Sales Discounts

CRJ	13		

Sales Returns and Allowances

GJ	1,000		
GJ	500		

Recording sales and purchases with HST transactions
4 6 8 (60 min)

CONTINUING PROBLEM

Tony Freedman was very happy to see the progress made by using the specialized journals. Effective January 1, 2017, the company obtains an HST number* and so begins to charge HST at 13% on all sales made. The company also pays HST from January 1 on all purchases. The special journals used in Tony's company have been modified to include columns for HST, and these can be found in the *Study Guide with Working Papers*, pages 11-78 to 11-91.

The partial January transactions are as follows:

2017

Jan.

3 Received cheque from Carson Engineering Corp. for amount outstanding.

3 Wrote cheque No. 280 to Able Holdings for December, January, and February rent, $1,200 (HST exempt).

3 Bought merchandise on account from Computer Connection (purchase order No. 4016), $2,500, plus HST, terms 3/10, n/30.

3 Paid amount due to Staples (cheque No. 281).

3 Sold $900, plus HST, worth of merchandise to Taylor Golf on credit, sales invoice No. 12690; terms are 2/10, n/30.

3 Charged $5,085, including HST, for cash sales for the week of January 3.

6 Bought merchandise on account from Multi Systems (purchase order No. 4017), $300, plus HST; terms are 3/10, n/30.

6 Bought office supplies on account from Staples (purchase order No. 4018), $200, plus HST; terms are n/30.

9 Issued debit memorandum No. 11 to Computer Connection for merchandise returned from purchase order No. 4016, $300 (remember the HST).

9 Paid *City Newspaper* amount owing from December 31, cheque No. 282.

10 Received electric bill for January, $250, plus HST.

10 Received from Taylor Golf balance owing as of December 31.

10 Purchased merchandise on account from Computer Connection (purchase order No. 4019), $500, plus HST, terms are 1/30, n/60.

10 Paid West Bell Canada December 11 bill, cheque No. 283.

10 Sold $3,500, plus HST, worth of merchandise on account to Digital Prints Co., invoice 12691, terms are 2/10, n/30.

10 Charged $13,560, including HST, for cash sales for the week of January 10.

13 Paid net amount due to Computer Connection (purchase order No. 4016), less discount, cheque No. 284.

13 Paid amount due to CRA re December wages, cheque No. 285.

13 Received January phone bill, $110, plus HST.

13 Paid Multi Systems re January 6 purchase, less discount, cheque No. 286.

17 Charged $15,820, including HST, for cash sales for the week of January 17.

*Please ignore the fact that in Alberta there is only GST at 5%. This makes the Continuing Problem more relevant to a greater number of students.

17 Paid Alpha Office Co. the amount owing from December, cheque No. 287.

23 Sold $4,000, plus HST, worth of merchandise on account to Noel Aberhart, sales invoice No. 12692; terms are 4/10, n/30.

24 Charged $13,560, including HST, for cash sales for the week of January 24.

27 Issued credit memorandum to Digital Prints Co. for $400 worth of merchandise returned (remember the HST), invoice No. 12691.

27 Charged amount owing (less discount) from Noel Aberhart, invoice No. 12692.

30 Sold $1,600, plus HST, worth of merchandise to Anthony Pitale, invoice No. 12693; terms 2/10, n/30.

30 Charged full payment from Digital Prints (remember the credit memorandum), invoice No. 12691.

31 Charged $12,430, including HST, for cash sales for the week of January 31.

31 Wrote cheque No. 288 to Automated Payroll Service for January covering January wages, $8,740.20. Tony has decided to spend his time doing repairs and making sales rather than preparing payroll records like he did in November and December. The company issues cheques to all employees weekly but obtains one cheque monthly from Tony's company for wages, benefits, and its own charges at month-end.

Schedule of Accounts Receivable
Precision Computer Centre
December 31, 2016

Anthony Pitale	$ 1,600.00
Taylor Golf	3,200.00
Carson Engineering	14,990.00
Total Amount Due	$19,790.00

Schedule of Accounts Payable
Precision Computer Centre
December 31, 2016

Alpha Office Co.	$ 318.00
City Newspaper	855.00
Staples	250.00
West Bell Canada	165.00
Total Amount Payable	$1,588.00

Assignment

(See pages 11-78 to 11-91 in your *Study Guide with Working Papers*.)

1. Journalize the transactions in the appropriate journals (cash receipts, sales, cash payments, purchases, or general journal).
2. Record in the accounts receivable subsidiary ledger and accounts payable subsidiary ledger and post to the general ledger as appropriate. A partial general ledger is included in the *Study Guide with Working Papers*.
3. Prepare a schedule of accounts receivable, and a schedule of accounts payable as of January 31, 2017.

CHAPTER 12

Preparing a Worksheet for a Merchandising Company

LEARNING OBJECTIVES

LO 1 Figuring adjustments for merchandise inventory, unearned rent, supplies used, insurance expired, amortization expense, and salaries accrued (p. 555)

LO 2 Preparing a worksheet for a merchandising company (p. 558)

All students are now familiar with how to prepare a worksheet and the three typical financial statements for a company that does not buy and sell things—many times this is a service company of some kind. In most countries there are a vast number of companies that are in the business of selling goods of one sort or another. Most students can probably name at least six such companies in less than a minute: Canadian Tire, Best Buy, Sears, Rona, Target, Michaels, etc.—The list is a very long one.

Each of these business firms share one notable thing: they all own stocks of the things they sell, that is, merchandise inventory. Most service firms carry no inventory, so there is nothing more to learn about completing their worksheets and statements. However, when a business owns a lot of inventory (and most of these businesses own a *lot* of inventory) then the worksheet and financial statements need a little more work than you may be familiar with. Not a big change, mind you, but there are a few things that are different. That is the purpose of this chapter, plus it covers an additional adjustment for unearned revenue.

In Chapters 6, 7 and 10, we discussed the special journals and subsidiary ledgers of a merchandising company. Appendix material on MyAccountingLab provides an introduction to perpetual inventory. Now our attention will shift to recording adjustments and completing a worksheet for a merchandising company. Learning Unit 12-1 will introduce two new adjustments that we have not yet discussed, Merchandise Inventory and Unearned Rent. Learning Unit 12-2 will show how to complete the worksheet with these new adjustments, while the Chapter 12 appendix, located on MyAccountingLab, shows worksheets for a perpetual inventory system.

LEARNING UNIT 12-1

Adjustments for Merchandise Inventory and Unearned Rent

LO 1

Figuring adjustments for merchandise inventory, unearned rent, supplies used, insurance expired, amortization expense, and salaries accrued

An important item in a merchandising company worksheet and financial records is *Merchandise Inventory*. This means the goods that a company has available to sell to customers. There are several ways of keeping track of the cost of goods sold and the quantity of inventory that a company has on hand. At the end of Auxiliary Chapter 19 (which is on MyAccountingLab), another system, called a **perpetual inventory system**, will be discussed. In this system, businesses with large inventories can have current information about inventory on hand and the actual cost of goods sold. Most such companies use a computer to keep track of their inventory records.

In this chapter, we will discuss the **periodic inventory system** in which the balance of the inventory account is updated only at the end of the accounting period. This system is used by smaller companies that sell a variety of merchandise with low unit prices. The number of companies using this system of accounting for inventory is still significant but is declining. This decline is due to the increasing availability of computers and software that together encourage the use of the more useful and informative perpetual system.

Let's take the merchandise inventory of Art's Clothing Company as an example. Let's assume Art's Clothing Company started the year with $19,000 worth of merchandise; this is called **beginning merchandise inventory** or simply **beginning inventory**. During the period, the cost of beginning inventory does not change; instead, all purchases of merchandise are recorded in the Purchases account. During the period, $52,000 worth of merchandise was purchased and recorded in the Purchases account.

Cost of goods sold
Beginning inventory
+ Net purchases
– Ending inventory
= Cost of goods sold

At the end of the period, the company takes a physical count of the merchandise in stock; this amount is **ending merchandise inventory** or simply **ending inventory** and is calculated on an inventory sheet as shown in Figure 12-1.

This $4,000, which is the ending inventory for this period, will be the beginning inventory for the next period.

When the income statement is prepared, the cost of goods sold section will require two distinct numbers for inventory. The beginning inventory adds to the cost of goods sold, while the ending inventory reduces the cost of goods sold.

Remember that the two figures for beginning and ending inventory were calculated months apart. Thus they cannot merely be combined to come up with one inventory figure; that would not be accurate.

First adjustment transfers amount in beginning inventory from Merchandise Inventory to Income Summary.

ADJUSTMENT FOR MERCHANDISE INVENTORY

Adjusting the Merchandise Inventory account is a two-step process because we want to keep both beginning inventory and ending inventory amounts separate; we cannot simply combine them. So the first step deals with beginning merchandise inventory.

Figure 12-1
Ending Inventory Sheet

ART'S CLOTHING COMPANY
ENDING INVENTORY SHEET
AS OF DECEMBER 31, 2016

Amount	Explanation	Unit Cost	Total
20	Ladies' Jackets code 14-0	$50	$1,000
10	Men's Hats code 827	10	100
90	Men's Shirts code 423	10	900
100	Ladies' Blouses code 481	20	2,000
			$4,000

Counted by ________ Checked and priced by ________

Note that Income Summary has no normal balance of debit or credit.

Given: Beginning Inventory, $19,000 Our first adjustment removes the beginning inventory amount from the asset account (Merchandise Inventory) and transfers it to Income Summary. We do this by crediting Merchandise Inventory for $19,000 and debiting Income Summary for the same amount. This is shown below in T account form and on a transaction analysis chart:

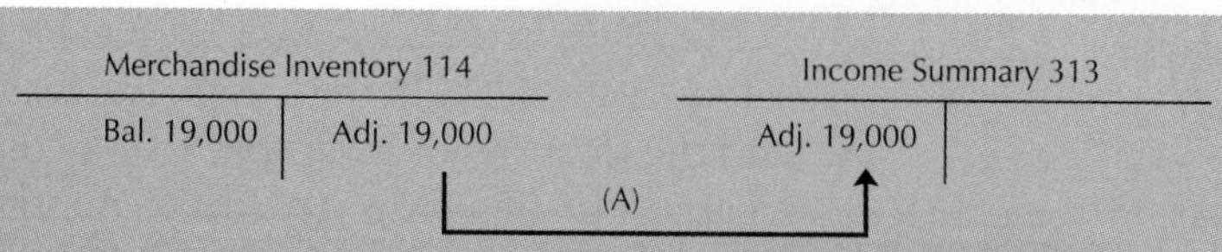

Accounts Affected	Category	↑↓	Rules
Income Summary	Equity	N/A	Dr.
Merchandise Inventory	Asset	↓	Cr.

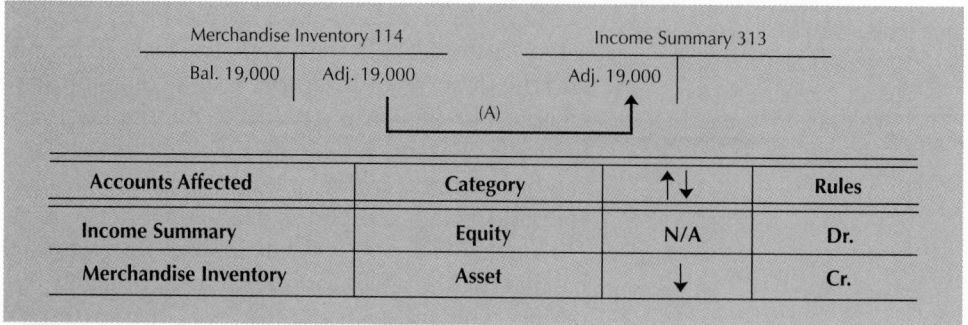

(The adjusting entries would be first entered on the worksheet and then formally recorded in the general journal, then posted.)

Second adjustment updates inventory account with a figure for ending inventory.

The second step is to enter the amount of ending inventory ($4,000) in the Merchandise Inventory account. This is done to record the amount of goods on hand at the end of the period as an asset and to reduce the cost of goods sold (since we have not sold this inventory yet). To do this, we debit Merchandise Inventory for $4,000 and credit Income Summary for the same amount. This is shown below in T account form and on a transaction analysis chart:

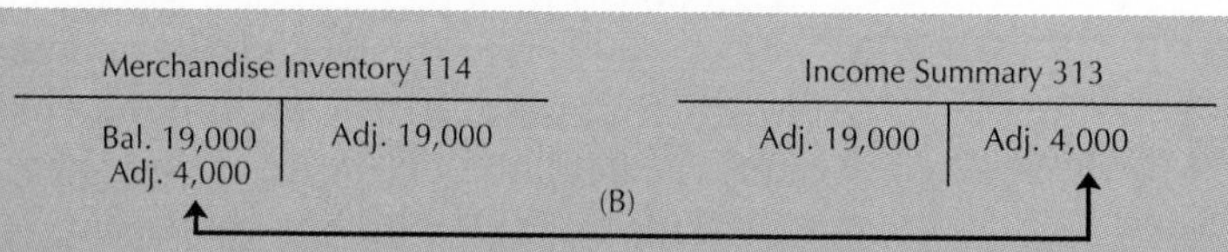

Accounts Affected	Category	↑↓	Rules
Merchandise Inventory	Asset	↑	Dr.
Income Summary	Equity	N/A	Cr.

Note: If freight-in were involved, it would have been added to the net cost of purchases.

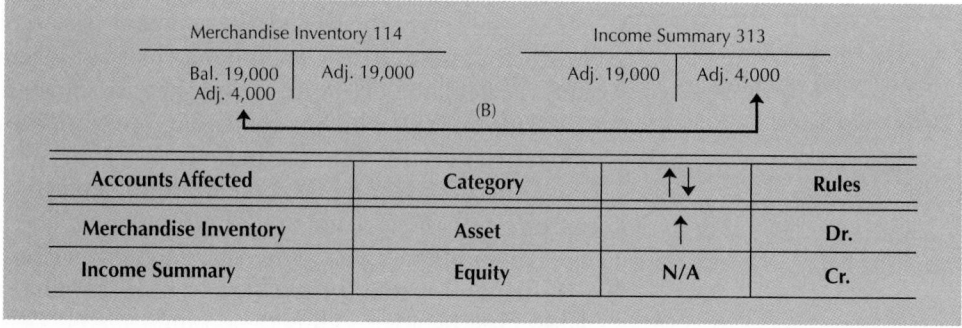

Let's look at how this method of recording merchandise inventory is reflected in the balance sheet and income statement (see Figure 12-2). Note that the $19,000 worth of beginning inventory is assumed sold and is shown on the income statement as part of the cost of goods sold. The ending inventory of $4,000 has not been sold and reduces the cost of goods sold on the income statement. The ending inventory for this period becomes the next period's beginning inventory. When the income

Figure 12-2
Recording Inventory on a Partial Balance Sheet and Income Statement

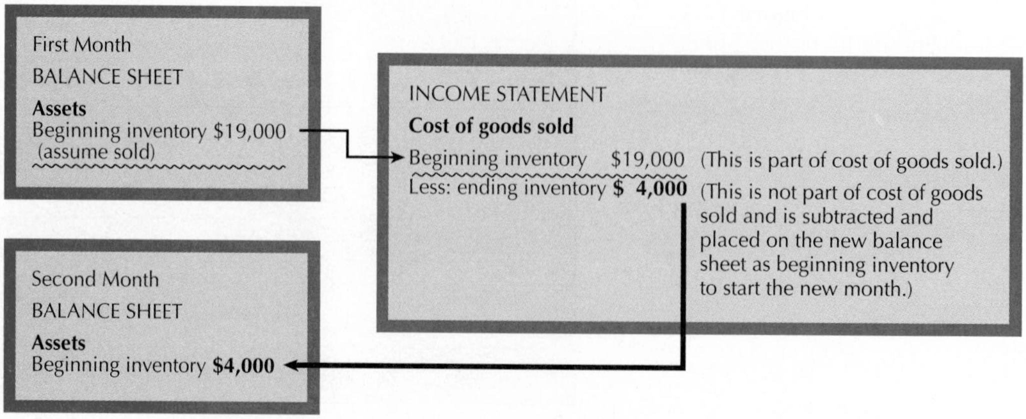

statement is prepared, we will need a figure for beginning inventory as well as a figure for ending inventory.

The second adjustment we will discuss in this unit concerns an account that we have never dealt with before, Unearned Rent.

ADJUSTMENT FOR UNEARNED RENT

A new account that we have not seen before is a liability called Unearned Rent. This account records the amount collected for rent before the service has been provided (renting the space). For example, Art's Clothing Company is subletting some unneeded space to Jesse Company for $200 per month. Jesse Company sends Art a cheque for $600 for three months' rent paid in advance. This unearned rent ($600) is also often called Rent Received in Advance. Regardless of the actual name, it is a liability on the balance sheet because Art's Clothing Company owes Jesse Company three months' worth of occupancy.

Received cash for renting space in future

Cash	A	↑	Dr.
Unearned Rent	Liab.	↑	Cr.

When Art's Clothing Company fulfills a portion of the rental agreement (when Jesse Company has been in the space for a period of time), this liability account will be reduced and the account called Rental Income will be increased because Art's Clothing Company will have earned the rent. Rental Income is another type of revenue for Art's Clothing Company in addition to its revenue earned from sales of merchandise.

The adjustment when rental income is earned

Unearned Rent	Liab.	↓	Dr.
Rental Income	Other Rev.	↑	Cr.

There are other types of unearned revenue besides unearned rent—examples would be subscriptions for magazines, legal fees collected before the work is performed, and season tickets to the local symphony. The key point is that revenue, under accrual accounting, is recognized when it is *earned*, whether money is received then or not. Here Art's Clothing Company collected cash in advance for a service that it has not performed yet. Thus a liability called Unearned Rent is the result. Art's Clothing Company may have the cash, but no Rental Income is recorded until it is *earned*.

In the next learning unit, we will show how to record the adjustment to Rental Income when the worksheet is completed.

LEARNING UNIT 12-1 REVIEW

AT THIS POINT you should be able to:

- Define the periodic method of inventory accounting. (p. 555)
- Explain why beginning and ending inventory are two separate figures in the cost of goods sold section on the income statement. (p. 555)
- Show how to calculate a figure for ending inventory. (p. 556)
- Explain why unearned rent is a liability account. (p. 557)

Self-Review Quiz 12-1

(The form you need is on page 12-1 in the *Study Guide with Working Papers.*)

Given the following, prepare the two adjusting entries for Merchandise Inventory on 12/31/16:

Merchandise Inventory, 01/01/16	$ 8,000
Purchases	9,000
Purchases Returns and Allowances	3,000
Merchandise Inventory, 12/31/16	4,000
Cost of Goods Sold	10,000
Unearned Magazine Subscriptions	5,000

Quiz Tip

Note that Unearned Magazine Subscriptions is a liability and not involved in the adjustment for Merchandise Inventory.

Solution to Self-Review Quiz 12-1

2016				
Dec.	31	Income Summary	8 0 0 0 00	
		Merchandise Inventory		8 0 0 0 00
	31	Merchandise Inventory	4 0 0 0 00	
		Income Summary		4 0 0 0 00
		To record opening and closing inventories		

LEARNING UNIT 12-2

Completing the Worksheet

LO 2

Preparing a worksheet for a merchandising company

In this unit, we prepare a worksheet for Art's Clothing Company. For convenience, we reproduce the company's chart of accounts in Figure 12-3.

Figure 12-4 shows the trial balance that was prepared on December 31, 2016, from the general ledger of Art's Clothing Company. (***Note:*** It is recorded directly in the first two columns of the worksheet.)

In looking at the trial balance, we see many new titles that have appeared since we completed a trial balance for a service company back in Chapter 5. Let's look specifically at these new titles in the summary in Table 12-1.

Figure 12-3
Art's Clothing Company
Chart of Accounts

Chart of Accounts

Assets 100–199
111 Cash
112 Petty Cash
113 Accounts Receivable
114 Merchandise Inventory
115 Supplies
116 Prepaid Insurance
121 Store Equipment
122 Accumulated Amortization, Store Equipment

Liabilities 200–299
211 Accounts Payable
212 Salaries Payable
213 Income Tax Payable
214 CPP Payable
215 EI Payable
218 Unearned Rent
220 Mortgage Payable

Owner's Equity 300–399
311 Art Newner, Capital
312 Art Newner, Withdrawals
313 Income Summary

Revenue 400–499
411 Sales
412 Sales Returns and Allowances
413 Sales Discounts
414 Rental Income

Cost of Goods Sold 500–599
511 Purchases
512 Purchases Discounts
513 Purchases Returns and Allowances
514 Freight-In

Expenses 600–699
611 Salaries Expense
612 Payroll Tax Expense
613 Amortization Expense, Store Equipment
614 Supplies Expense
615 Insurance Expense
616 Postage Expense
617 Miscellaneous Expense
618 Interest Expense
619 Cleaning Expense
620 Delivery Expense

Figure 12-4
Trial Balance Section of the Worksheet

ART'S CLOTHING COMPANY
WORKSHEET
FOR THE YEAR ENDED DECEMBER 31, 2016

Account Titles	Trial Balance Dr.	Trial Balance Cr.
Cash	12920 00	
Petty Cash	100 00	
Accounts Receivable	14500 00	
Merchandise Inventory	19000 00	
Supplies	800 00	
Prepaid Insurance	900 00	
Store Equipment	4000 00	
Accumulated Amortization, Store Equip.		400 00
Accounts Payable		17900 00
Income Tax Payable		1240 00
CPP Payable		260 00
EI Payable		200 00
Unearned Rent		600 00
Mortgage Payable		2320 00
Art Newner, Capital		7905 00
Art Newner, Withdrawals	8600 00	
Income Summary		
Sales		95000 00
Sales Returns and Allowances	950 00	
Sales Discounts	670 00	
Purchases	52000 00	
Purchases Discounts		860 00
Purchases Returns and Allowances		680 00
Freight-In	450 00	
Salaries Expense	11700 00	
Payroll Tax Expense	420 00	
Postage Expense	25 00	
Miscellaneous Expense	30 00	
Interest Expense	300 00	
	127365 00	127365 00

Note the following:

1. **Mortgage Payable** is a liability account that records the increases and decreases in the amount of debt owed on a mortgage. We will discuss this more in the next chapter when financial reports are prepared.
2. **Interest Expense** represents a non-operating expense for Art's Clothing Company and thus is categorized as "miscellaneous expense." The interest would be a regular expense if it were incurred for business purposes. We will also be looking at this in the next chapter.
3. **Unearned Revenue** is a liability account that records receipt of payment for goods and services in advance of delivery. Unearned Rent is a particular example of this general type of account.

Adjustments We have already discussed Adjustments A and B (page 543), which make up the two-step process involved in adjusting Merchandise Inventory at the end of the accounting period. Now we will go on to show T accounts and transaction analysis charts for some more adjustments that need to be made at this point in a merchandising firm, just as they do in a service company.

TABLE 12-1 Summary of New Account Titles

Title	Category	Report(s) Found on	Normal Balance	Temporary/ Permanent
Petty Cash	Asset	Balance sheet	Dr.	Permanent
Merchandise Inventory* (Beginning)	Asset	Balance sheet prior period	Dr.	Permanent
	Expense	Income statement of current period		
Income Tax Payable	Liability	Balance sheet	Cr.	Permanent
CPP Payable	Liability	Balance sheet	Cr.	Permanent
EI Payable	Liability	Balance sheet	Cr.	Permanent
Unearned Rent**	Liability	Balance sheet	Cr.	Permanent
Mortgage Payable	Liability	Balance sheet	Cr.	Permanent
Sales	Revenue	Income statement	Cr.	Temporary
Sales Returns and Allowances	Revenue (contra)	Income statement	Dr.	Temporary
Sales Discounts	Revenue (contra)	Income statement	Dr.	Temporary
Purchases	Expense	Income statement	Dr.	Temporary
Purchases Discounts	Expense (contra)	Income statement	Cr.	Temporary
Purchases Returns and Allowances	Expense (contra)	Income statement	Cr.	Temporary
Freight-In	Expense	Income statement	Dr.	Temporary
Payroll Tax Expense	Expense	Income statement	Dr.	Temporary
Postage Expense	Expense	Income statement	Dr.	Temporary
Interest Expense	Expense	Income statement	Dr.	Temporary

* The ending inventory of the current period is a contra-expense on the income statement and will be an asset on the balance sheet for next period.
** Referred to as Unearned Revenue.
Note: Students may benefit from a brief look at the Blueprint on page 606.

Adjustment C: Rental Income Earned by Art's Clothing Company, $200 A month ago, Cash was increased by $600, as was a liability, Unearned Rent. Art's Clothing Company received payment in advance but had not earned the rental income. Now, since $200 has been earned, the liability is reduced and Rental Income can be recorded for the $200.

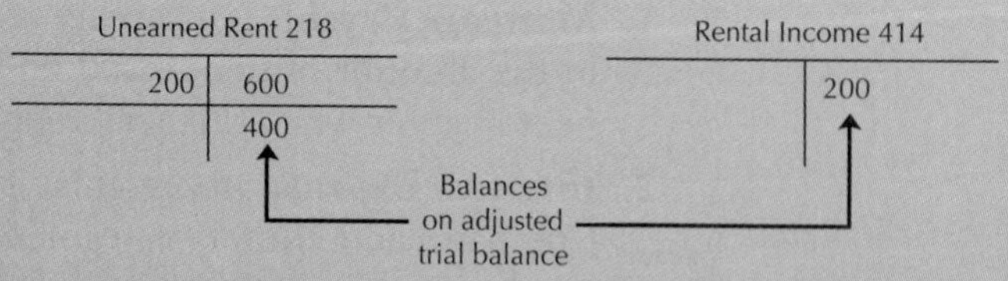

Unearned Rent	**Liability**	↓	**Dr.**	**$200**
Rental Income	**Revenue**	↑	**Cr.**	**$200**

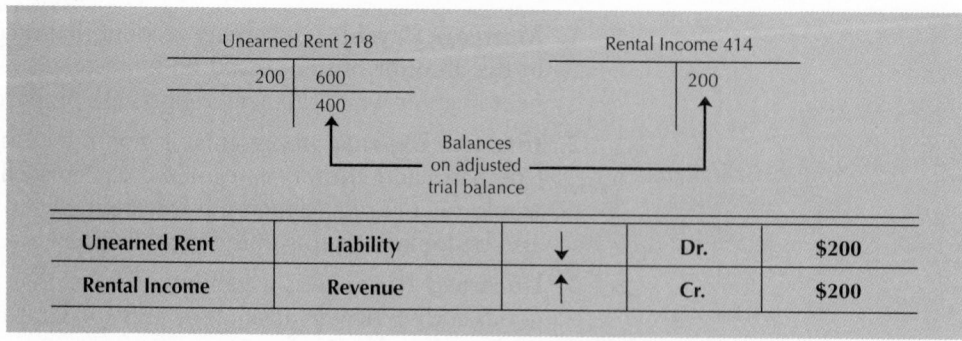

Adjustment D: Supplies Used Up, $500 $500 worth of supplies has been used up; thus there is a need to increase Supplies Expense and decrease the asset, Supplies.

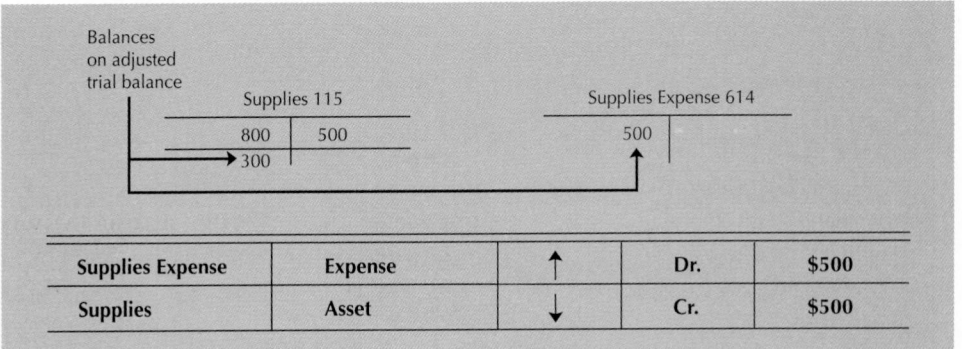

Supplies Expense	**Expense**	↑	**Dr.**	**$500**
Supplies	**Asset**	↓	**Cr.**	**$500**

Adjustment E: Insurance Expired, $300 Since $300 worth of insurance has expired, Insurance Expense is increased by $300 and the asset, Prepaid Insurance, is decreased by $300.

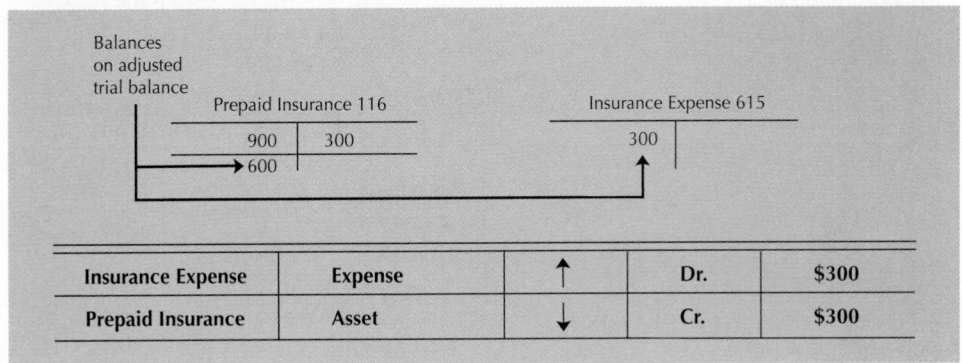

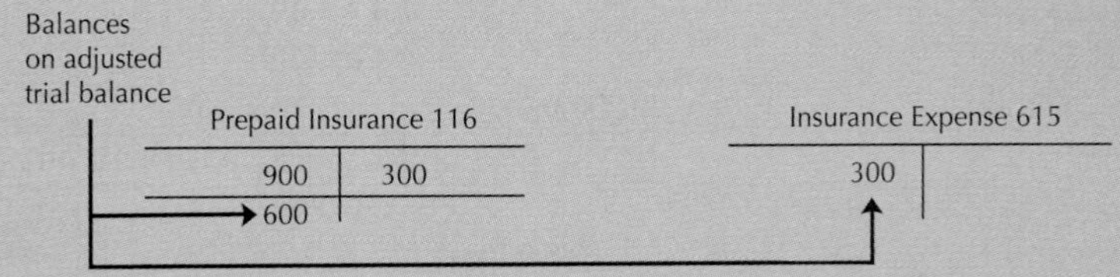

Insurance Expense	**Expense**	↑	**Dr.**	**$300**
Prepaid Insurance	**Asset**	↓	**Cr.**	**$300**

Adjustment F: Depreciation Expense, $50 When depreciation is taken, Depreciation Expense and Accumulated Depreciation are both increased by $50. Note that the cost of the store equipment remains the same.

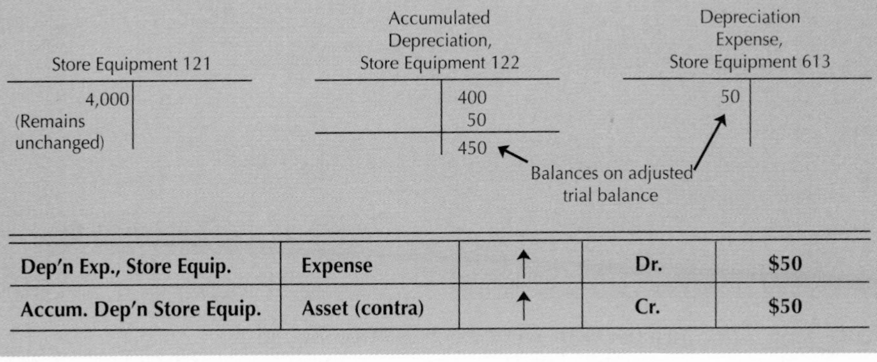

Dep'n Exp., Store Equip.	**Expense**	↑	**Dr.**	**$50**
Accum. Dep'n Store Equip.	**Asset (contra)**	↑	**Cr.**	**$50**

Adjustment G: Accrued Salaries, $600 The $600 in Accrued Salaries causes an increase in Salaries Expense and Accrued Salaries Payable.

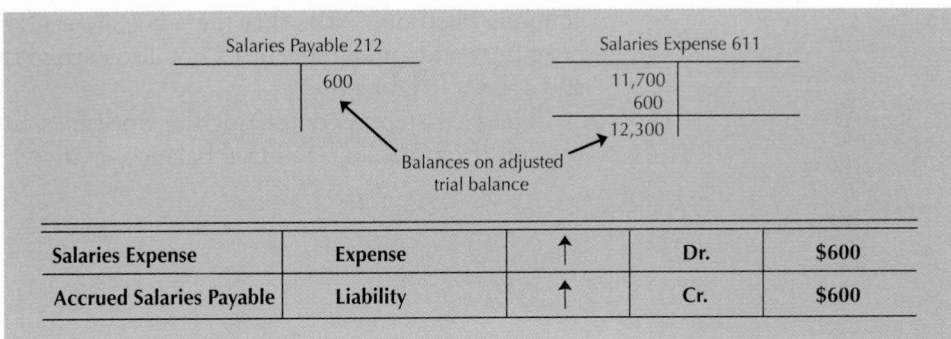

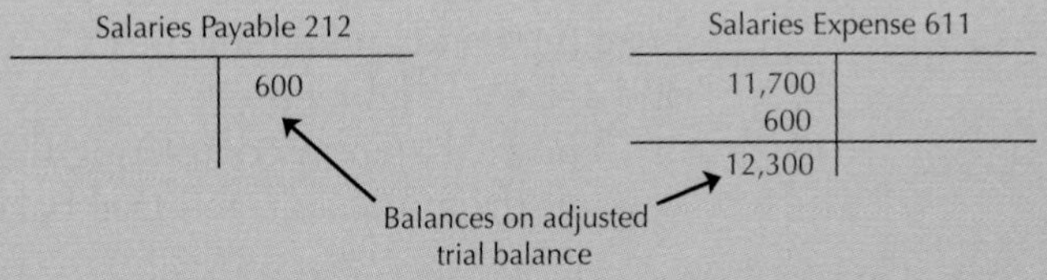

Salaries Expense	**Expense**	↑	**Dr.**	**$600**
Accrued Salaries Payable	**Liability**	↑	**Cr.**	**$600**

Account Titles	Trial Balance Dr.	Trial Balance Cr.	Adjustments Dr.	Adjustments Cr.	Adjusted Trial Balance Dr.	Adjusted Trial Balance Cr.
Cash	12920 00				12920 00	
Petty Cash	100 00				100 00	
Accounts Receivable	14500 00				14500 00	
Merchandise Inventory	19000 00		(B) 4000 00	(A) 19000 00	4000 00	
Supplies	800 00			(D) 500 00	300 00	
Prepaid Insurance	900 00			(E) 300 00	600 00	
Store Equipment	4000 00				4000 00	
Accumulated Depreciation, Store Equip.		400 00		(F) 50 00		450 00
Accounts Payable		17900 00				17900 00
Income Tax Payable		1240 00				1240 00
CPP Payable		260 00				260 00
EI Payable		200 00				200 00
Unearned Rent		600 00	(C) 200 00			400 00
Mortgage Payable		2320 00				2320 00
Art Newner, Capital		7905 00				7905 00
Art Newner, Withdrawals	8600 00				8600 00	
Income Summary			(A) 19000 00	(B) 4000 00	19000 00	4000 00
Sales		95000 00				95000 00
Sales Returns and Allowances	950 00				950 00	
Sales Discounts	670 00				670 00	
Purchases	52000 00				52000 00	
Purchases Discounts		860 00				860 00
Purchases Returns and Allowances		680 00				680 00
Freight-In	450 00				450 00	
Salaries Expense	11700 00		(G) 600 00		12300 00	
Payroll Tax Expense	420 00				420 00	
Postage Expense	25 00				25 00	
Miscellaneous Expense	30 00				30 00	
Interest Expense	300 00				300 00	
	127365 00	127365 00				
Rental Income				(C) 200 00		200 00
Supplies Expense			(D) 500 00		500 00	
Insurance Expense			(E) 300 00		300 00	
Depreciation Expense, Store Equipment			(F) 50 00		50 00	
Accrued Salaries Payable				(G) 600 00		600 00
			24650 00	24650 00	132015 00	132015 00

Figure 12-5 Worksheet with Three Sections Completed

Figure 12-5 shows the worksheet with the adjustments and adjusted trial balance columns filled out. Note that the adjustment numbers in Income Summary from beginning and ending inventory are also carried over to the adjusted trial balance and are *not* combined.

The next step in completing the worksheet is to fill out the income statement columns from the adjusted trial balance, as shown in Figure 12-6.

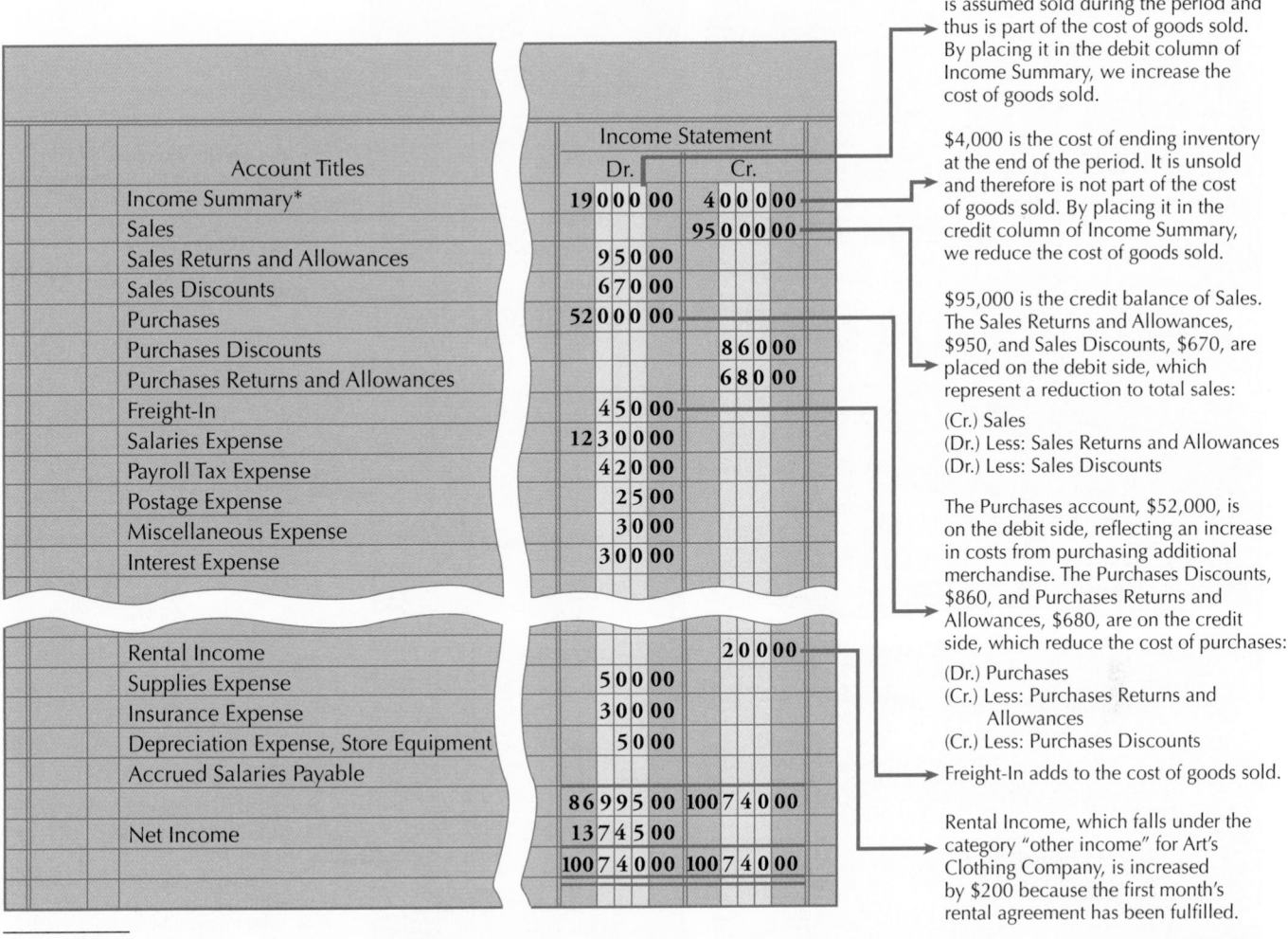

Account Titles	Income Statement Dr.	Income Statement Cr.
Income Summary*	19000 00	4000 00
Sales		95000 00
Sales Returns and Allowances	950 00	
Sales Discounts	670 00	
Purchases	52000 00	
Purchases Discounts		860 00
Purchases Returns and Allowances		680 00
Freight-In	450 00	
Salaries Expense	12300 00	
Payroll Tax Expense	420 00	
Postage Expense	25 00	
Miscellaneous Expense	30 00	
Interest Expense	300 00	
Rental Income		200 00
Supplies Expense	500 00	
Insurance Expense	300 00	
Depreciation Expense, Store Equipment	50 00	
Accrued Salaries Payable		
	86995 00	100740 00
Net Income	13745 00	
	100740 00	100740 00

$19,000 worth of beginning inventory is assumed sold during the period and thus is part of the cost of goods sold. By placing it in the debit column of Income Summary, we increase the cost of goods sold.

$4,000 is the cost of ending inventory at the end of the period. It is unsold and therefore is not part of the cost of goods sold. By placing it in the credit column of Income Summary, we reduce the cost of goods sold.

$95,000 is the credit balance of Sales. The Sales Returns and Allowances, $950, and Sales Discounts, $670, are placed on the debit side, which represent a reduction to total sales:

(Cr.) Sales
(Dr.) Less: Sales Returns and Allowances
(Dr.) Less: Sales Discounts

The Purchases account, $52,000, is on the debit side, reflecting an increase in costs from purchasing additional merchandise. The Purchases Discounts, $860, and Purchases Returns and Allowances, $680, are on the credit side, which reduce the cost of purchases:

(Dr.) Purchases
(Cr.) Less: Purchases Returns and Allowances
(Cr.) Less: Purchases Discounts

Freight-In adds to the cost of goods sold.

Rental Income, which falls under the category "other income" for Art's Clothing Company, is increased by $200 because the first month's rental agreement has been fulfilled.

*Remember, we do not combine the $19,000 and $4,000 in Income Summary. When we prepare the cost of goods sold section for the formal financial report, we will need both a beginning and an ending figure for inventory.

Figure 12-6 Income Statement Section of the Worksheet

The last step in completing the worksheet is to fill out the balance sheet columns (Figure 12-7). Note that only the ending inventory is carried over to the balance sheet from the adjusted trial balance column. Take time also to look at the placement of the payroll tax liabilities as well as Unearned Rent on the worksheet.

Figure 12-8 is the completed worksheet.

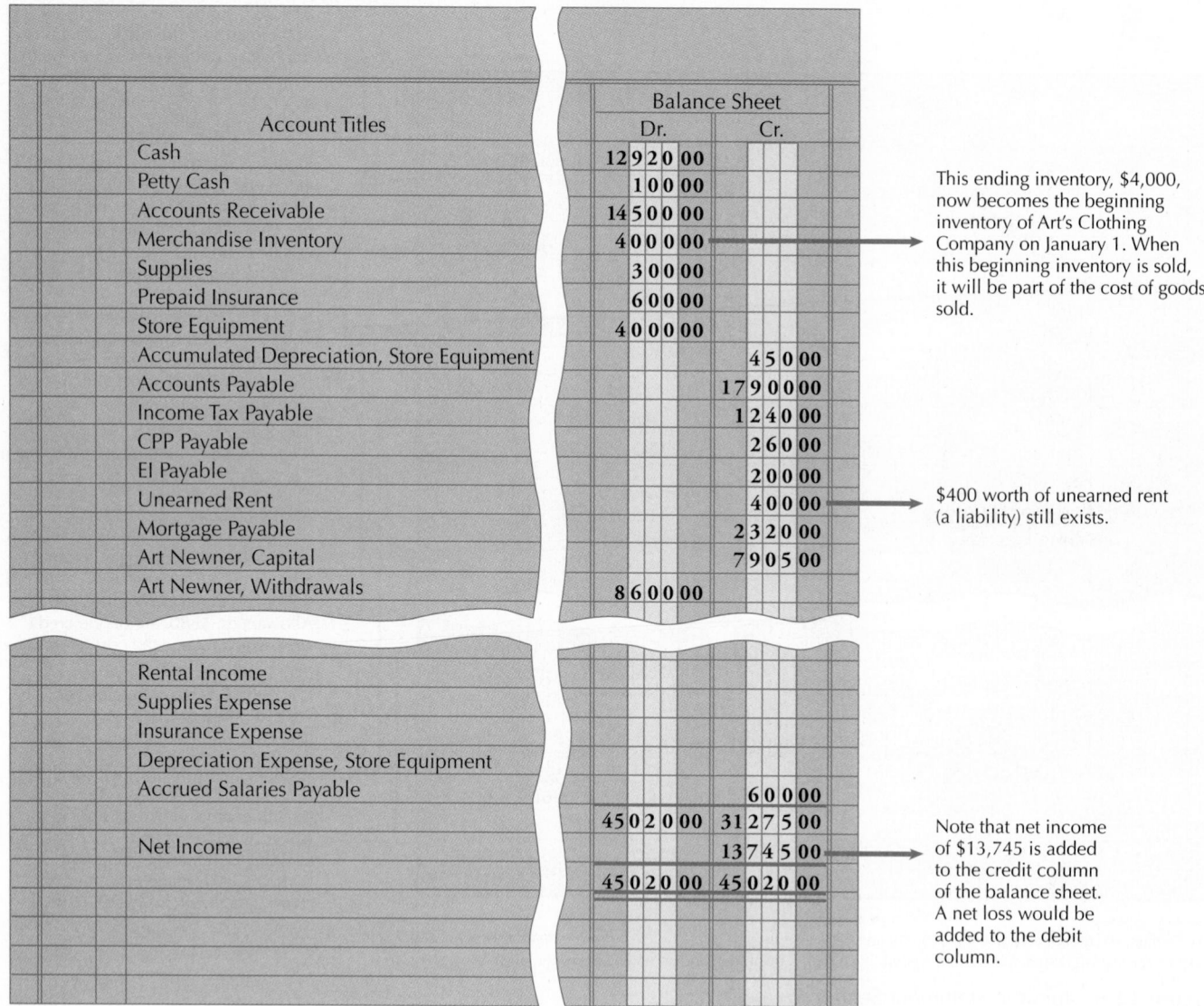

Account Titles	Balance Sheet Dr.	Balance Sheet Cr.
Cash	12920 00	
Petty Cash	100 00	
Accounts Receivable	14500 00	
Merchandise Inventory	4000 00	
Supplies	300 00	
Prepaid Insurance	600 00	
Store Equipment	4000 00	
Accumulated Depreciation, Store Equipment		450 00
Accounts Payable		17900 00
Income Tax Payable		1240 00
CPP Payable		260 00
EI Payable		200 00
Unearned Rent		400 00
Mortgage Payable		2320 00
Art Newner, Capital		7905 00
Art Newner, Withdrawals	8600 00	
Rental Income		
Supplies Expense		
Insurance Expense		
Depreciation Expense, Store Equipment		
Accrued Salaries Payable		600 00
	45020 00	31275 00
Net Income		13745 00
	45020 00	45020 00

This ending inventory, $4,000, now becomes the beginning inventory of Art's Clothing Company on January 1. When this beginning inventory is sold, it will be part of the cost of goods sold.

$400 worth of unearned rent (a liability) still exists.

Note that net income of $13,745 is added to the credit column of the balance sheet. A net loss would be added to the debit column.

Figure 12-7 Balance Sheet Section of the Worksheet

ART'S CLOTHING COMPANY WORKSHEET FOR THE YEAR ENDED DECEMBER 31, 2016										
Account Titles	Trial Balance		Adjustments		Adjusted Trial Balance		Income Statement		Balance Sheet	
	Dr.	Cr.	Dr.	Cr.	Dr.	Cr.	Dr.	Cr.	Dr.	Cr.
Cash	12920 00				12920 00				12920 00	
Petty Cash	100 00				100 00				100 00	
Accounts Receivable	14500 00				14500 00				14500 00	
Merchandise Inventory	19000 00		(B) 4000 00	(A) 19000 00	4000 00				4000 00	
Supplies	800 00			(D) 500 00	300 00				300 00	
Prepaid Insurance	900 00			(E) 300 00	600 00				600 00	
Store Equipment	4000 00				4000 00				4000 00	
Accumulated Depreciation, Store Equipment		400 00		(F) 50 00		450 00				450 00
Accounts Payable		17900 00				17900 00				17900 00
Income Tax Payable		1240 00				1240 00				1240 00
CPP Payable		260 00				260 00				260 00
EI Payable		200 00				200 00				200 00
Unearned Rent		600 00	(C) 200 00			400 00				400 00
Mortgage Payable		2320 00				2320 00				2320 00
Art Newner, Capital		7905 00				7905 00				7905 00
Art Newner, Withdrawals	8600 00				8600 00				8600 00	
Income Summary			(A) 19000 00	(B) 4000 00	19000 00	4000 00	19000 00	4000 00		
Sales		95000 00				95000 00		95000 00		
Sales Returns and Allowances	950 00				950 00		950 00			
Sales Discounts	670 00				670 00		670 00			
Purchases	52000 00				52000 00		52000 00			
Purchases Discounts		860 00				860 00		860 00		
Purchases Returns and Allowances		680 00				680 00		680 00		
Freight-In	450 00				450 00		450 00			
Salaries Expense	11700 00		(G) 600 00		12300 00		12300 00			
Payroll Tax Expense	420 00				420 00		420 00			
Postage Expense	25 00				25 00		25 00			
Miscellaneous Expense	30 00				30 00		30 00			
Interest Expense	300 00				300 00		300 00			
	127365 00	127365 00								
Rental Income				(C) 200 00		200 00		200 00		
Supplies Expense			(D) 500 00		500 00		500 00			
Insurance Expense			(E) 300 00		300 00		300 00			
Depreciation Expense, Store Equipment			(F) 50 00		50 00		50 00			
Accrued Salaries Payable				(G) 600 00		600 00				600 00
			24650 00	24650 00	132015 00	132015 00	86995 00	100740 00	45020 00	31275 00
Net Income							13745 00			13745 00
							100740 00	100740 00	45020 00	45020 00

Figure 12-8 Completed Worksheet

LEARNING UNIT 12-2 REVIEW

AT THIS POINT you should be able to:

- Complete adjustments for a merchandising company. (pp. 558–562)
- Complete a worksheet. (pp. 562–565)

Self-Review Quiz 12-2

(The form you need is a blank, fold-out worksheet at the end of the *Study Guide with Working Papers*.)

From the trial balance shown here, complete a worksheet for Ray Company. Additional data includes: (a) and (b) On December 31, 2012, ending inventory was calculated as $200; (c) storage fees earned, $516; (d) rent expired, $100; (e) depreciation expense, office equipment, $60; (f) salaries accrued, $200.

RAY COMPANY
TRIAL BALANCE
DECEMBER 31, 2015

Account Titles	Trial Balance Dr.	Trial Balance Cr.
Cash	2486 00	
Merchandise Inventory	824 00	
Prepaid Rent	1152 00	
Prepaid Insurance	60 00	
Office Equipment	2160 00	
Accumulated Depreciation, Office Equipment		560 00
Unearned Storage Fees		2516 00
Accounts Payable		100 00
B. Ray, Capital		1932 00
Income Summary	—	—
Sales		11040 00
Sales Returns and Allowances	546 00	
Sales Discounts	216 00	
Purchases	5256 00	
Purchases Returns and Allowances		168 00
Purchases Discounts		102 00
Salaries Expense	2016 00	
Insurance Expense	1392 00	
Utilities Expense	96 00	
Plumbing Expense	214 00	
	16418 00	16418 00

Quiz Tip

The ending inventory of $200 becomes next year's beginning inventory.

Solution to Self-Review Quiz 12-2

The solution is shown on page 567.

RAY COMPANY
WORKSHEET
FOR THE YEAR ENDED DECEMBER 31, 2015

Account Titles	Trial Balance		Adjustments		Adjusted Trial Balance		Income Statement		Balance Sheet	
	Dr.	Cr.	Dr.	Cr.	Dr.	Cr.	Dr.	Cr.	Dr.	Cr.
Cash	2486 00				2486 00				2486 00	
Merchandise Inventory	824 00		(B) 200 00	(A) 824 00	200 00				200 00	
Prepaid Rent	1152 00			(D) 100 00	1052 00				1052 00	
Prepaid Insurance	60 00				60 00				60 00	
Office Equipment	2160 00				2160 00				2160 00	
Accum. Dep'n Office Equipment		560 00		(E) 60 00		620 00				620 00
Unearned Storage Fees		2516 00	(C) 516 00			2000 00				2000 00
Accounts Payable		100 00				100 00				100 00
B. Ray, Capital		1932 00				1932 00				1932 00
Income Summary			(A) 824 00	(B) 200 00	824 00	200 00	824 00	200 00		
Sales		11040 00				11040 00		11040 00		
Sales Returns and Allowances	546 00				546 00		546 00			
Sales Discounts	216 00				216 00		216 00			
Purchases	5256 00				5256 00		5256 00			
Purchases Returns and Allowances		168 00				168 00		168 00		
Purchases Discounts		102 00				102 00		102 00		
Salaries Expense	2016 00		(F) 200 00		2216 00		2216 00			
Insurance Expense	1392 00				1392 00		1392 00			
Utilities Expense	96 00				96 00		96 00			
Plumbing Expense	214 00				214 00		214 00			
	16418 00	16418 00								
Storage Fees Earned				(C) 516 00		516 00		516 00		
Rent Expense			(D) 100 00		100 00		100 00			
Depreciation Expense, Equipment			(E) 60 00		60 00		60 00			
Accrued Salaries Payable				(F) 200 00		200 00				200 00
			1900 00	1900 00	16878 00	16878 00	10920 00	12026 00	5958 00	4852 00
Net Income							1106 00			1106 00
							12026 00	12026 00	5958 00	5958 00

Chapter Assignments

SUMMARY OF KEY POINTS

Learning Unit 12-1

1. The periodic inventory system updates the record of goods on hand only at the end of the accounting period. This system is used by companies with a variety of merchandise with low unit prices.
2. In the periodic inventory system, additional purchases of merchandise during the accounting period will be recorded in the Purchases account. The amount of beginning inventory will remain unchanged during the accounting period. At the end of the period, a new figure for ending inventory will be calculated.
3. At the end of the accounting period, beginning inventory is added to the cost of goods sold, while ending inventory reduces the cost of goods sold.
4. The perpetual inventory system keeps a continuous record of inventory. It is used by companies with a low volume of sales and high unit prices and often utilizes a computer system.
5. Unearned Revenue is a liability account that accumulates revenue that has not been earned yet, although the cash has been received. It represents a liability to the seller until the service or product is performed or delivered.

Learning Unit 12-2

1. Two important adjustments in the accounting for a merchandising company deal with the Merchandise Inventory account and with the Unearned Revenue account (unearned rent).
2. Figures for beginning and ending inventory on the Income Summary line on the worksheet are never combined; they are also carried over separately to the adjusted trial balance and income statement columns of the worksheet. In the balance sheet column, the figure for ending inventory becomes the beginning inventory figure for the new accounting period.
3. When a company delivers goods or services for which it has been paid in advance, an adjustment is made to reduce the liability account Unearned Revenue and to increase a revenue account.

KEY TERMS

Beginning merchandise inventory (beginning inventory) The cost of goods on hand in a company at the beginning of an accounting period (p. 555)

Ending merchandise inventory (ending inventory) The cost of goods that remain unsold at the end of the accounting period. It is an asset on the balance sheet. (p. 555)

Mortgage Payable A liability account showing the amount owed on a mortgage (p. 559)

Periodic inventory system An inventory system that, at the end of each accounting period, calculates the cost of the unsold goods on hand by taking the cost of each unit times the number of units of each product on hand (p. 555)

Perpetual inventory system An inventory system that keeps continual track of each type of inventory by recording units on hand at the beginning, units purchased and sold, and the balance after each sale or purchase (p. 555)

Unearned Revenue A liability account that records receipt of payment for goods or services in advance of delivery. When the goods or services are delivered, an adjustment is made to reduce Unearned Revenue and increase earned revenue. (The example we used in this chapter is Unearned Rent.) (p. 559)

QUICK REVIEW

The following Tips are from Learning Units 12-1 to 12-2. Answer the Assess Your Progress questions and use the How Did You Do? at the bottom of the page to see how well you know the material. The Quick Review provides tips before each Assess Your Progress to help you avoid common accounting errors.

LU 12-1 Adjustments for Merchandise Inventory and Unearned Rent

Tips: The purpose of the adjustment for Merchandise Inventory is to wipe out the beginning inventory and bring on the ending inventory. We assume that the beginning inventory is sold and is part of the cost of goods sold. The ending inventory is not sold and is not part of the cost of goods sold. The ending inventory becomes the new figure for beginning inventory in the next period. Unearned Rent is not a revenue account. It is a liability. Revenue will be recognized when it is earned, and that is when an entry is made reducing the Unearned Rent and crediting Rental Revenue.

Assess Your Progress

Answer true or false to the following statements:

1. Freight-In is a cost of goods sold account.
2. Beginning Inventory is subtracted from cost of goods sold.
3. Income Summary is not used to adjust Merchandise Inventory.
4. When unearned rent is earned, the liability will go up.
5. The ending inventory of one period can never be the new inventory of the next period.

LU 12-2 Completing the Worksheet

Tips: Before you complete the worksheet, make sure you review this table:

Sales	**Revenue**	**Credit Balance**	**Income Statement**
Sales Returns and Allowances	Revenue (contra)	Debit Balance	Income Statement
Unearned Rent/Unearned Revenue	Liability	Credit Balance	Balance Sheet
Purchases	Expense	Debit Balance	Income Statement
Purchases Returns and Allowances	Expense (contra)	Credit Balance	Income Statement

Assess Your Progress

Answer true or false to the following statements:

1. Ending inventory goes in the credit column of the balance sheet section of the worksheet.
2. Freight-In goes in the debit column of the balance sheet section of the worksheet.
3. Unearned Rent goes in the debit column of the balance sheet section of the worksheet.
4. Accumulated Depreciation goes in the credit column of the balance sheet section of the worksheet.
5. Income Summary for the beginning inventory goes in the credit column of the income statement.

How Did You Do? Answers to the Assess Your Progress Questions

LU 12-1

1. True.
2. False—Beginning inventory is added to cost of goods sold.
3. False—Income Summary is used to adjust Merchandise Inventory.
4. False—When unearned rent is earned, the liability will go down.
5. False—The ending inventory of one period always becomes new inventory of the next period.

LU 12-2

1. False—Ending inventory goes in the debit column of the balance sheet section of the worksheet.
2. True.
3. False—Unearned Rent goes in the credit column of the balance sheet section of the worksheet.
4. True.
5. True.

BLUEPRINT OF A WORKSHEET FOR A MERCHANDISING COMPANY

WORKSHEET

Account Titles	Adjustments		Adjusted Trial Balance		Income Statement		Balance Sheet	
	Dr.	Cr.	Dr.	Cr.	Dr.	Cr.	Dr.	Cr.
Cash			X				X	
Petty Cash			X				X	
Accounts Receivable			X				X	
Merchandise Inventory	X-E	X-B	X-E				X-E	
Supplies			X				X	
Equipment			X				X	
Accumulated Depreciation, Store Equipment				X				X
Accounts Payable				X				X
Income Tax Payable				X				X
CPP Payable				X				X
EI Payable				X				X
Unearned Sales				X				X
Mortgage Payable				X				X
A. Flynn, Capital				X				X
A. Flynn, Withdrawals			X				X	
Income Summary*	X-B	X-E	X-B	X-E	X-B	X-E		
Sales				X		X		
Sales Returns and Allowances			X		X			
Sales Discounts			X		X			
Purchases			X		X			
Purchases Returns and Allowances				X		X		
Purchases Discounts				X		X		
Freight-In			X		X			
Salaries Expense			X		X			
Payroll Tax Expense			X		X			
Insurance Expense			X		X			
Depreciation Expense			X		X			
Accrued Salaries				X				X
Rental Income				X		X		

*Note that the figures for beginning inventory (X-B) and ending inventory (X-E) are never combined on the Income Summary line of the worksheet. When the formal income statement is prepared, two distinct figures for inventory will be used to explain and calculate cost of goods sold. Beginning inventory adds to cost of goods sold; ending inventory reduces cost of goods sold.

QUESTIONS, CLASSROOM DEMONSTRATION EXERCISES, EXERCISES, AND PROBLEMS

Discussion Questions and Critical Thinking/Ethical Case

1. When would a company consider using a periodic inventory system?
2. What is the function of the Purchases account?
3. A low-volume, high-unit-price inventory requires a company to use a periodic inventory system. Accept or reject this statement and support your answer.
4. Explain why unearned revenue is a liability account.
5. In a periodic system of inventory, the balance of beginning inventory will remain unchanged during the period. True or false?
6. What is the purpose of an inventory sheet?
7. Why do many unearned revenue accounts have to be adjusted?
8. Explain why figures for beginning and ending inventory are not combined on the Income Summary line of the worksheet.
9. Jim Heary is the custodian of petty cash. Jim, who is short of personal cash, decided to pay his home electrical and telephone bills from petty cash. He plans to pay it back next month. Do you believe Jim should do this? You make the call. Write down your specific recommendations to Jim.

MyAccountingLab

Make the grade with MyAccountingLab! The exercises and problems marked with ● can be found on MyAccountingLab. You can practise them as often as you want, and many of them feature step-by-step guided solutions to help you find the right answer.

Classroom Demonstration Exercises

(The forms you need are on page 12-2 of the *Study Guide with Working Papers.*)

Adjustment for Merchandise Inventory

Journalizing adjustments for merchandise inventory
❶ (10 min)

1. Given the following, journalize the adjusting entries for merchandise inventory. Note that ending inventory has a balance of $18,000.

Merchandise Inventory 114		Income Summary 313	
60,000			

Adjustment for Unearned Fees

Journalizing adjustments for unearned fees
❶ (15 min)

2. **a.** Given the following, journalize the adjusting entry. By December 31, 2017, $210 worth of the unearned dog-walking fees were earned.

Unearned Dog-Walking Fees 225		Earned Dog-Walking Fees 441	
	900 12/1/17		5,000 12/1/17

b. What is the account category of unearned dog-walking fees?

The Income Statement and Balance Sheet columns of a worksheet
❷ (10 min)

3. Match each of the six items listed below with one of the following locations:

1. Located on the Income Statement debit column of the worksheet
2. Located on the Income Statement credit column of the worksheet
3. Located on the Balance Sheet debit column of the worksheet
4. Located on the Balance Sheet credit column of the worksheet

_____ a. Beginning Merchandise Inventory
_____ b. Sales Returns and Allowances
_____ c. Accrued Salaries
_____ d. Sales
_____ e. Ending Merchandise Inventory
_____ f. Accounts Receivable

Merchandise Inventory Adjustment on Worksheet

Adjustments for merchandise inventory
❶ (10 min)

4. Given beginning merchandise inventory of $2,000 and ending merchandise inventory of $50, what would be the adjusting entries?

Income Summary on the Worksheet

Adjustments for merchandise inventory
❷ (10 min)

5.

	Adjustments		Adjusted Trial Balance		Income Statement	
	Dr.	Cr.	Dr.	Cr.	Dr.	Cr.
Income Summary	A	B	C	D	E	F

Given a figure for Beginning Inventory of $400 and a $900 figure for Ending Inventory, place these numbers on the Income Summary line of this partial worksheet.

Exercises

Set A

(The forms you need are on page 12-3 of the *Study Guide with Working Papers.*)

Categorizing account titles
❶ (10 min)

12-1A. Indicate the normal balance and category of each of the following accounts:

a. Purchases Returns and Allowances
b. Merchandise Inventory (beginning of period)
c. Freight-In
d. Payroll Tax Expense
e. Purchases Discounts
f. Sales Discount
g. CPP Payable
h. Unearned Revenue

Calculating net sales, cost of goods sold, gross profit, and net income
❶ (15 min)

12-2A. From the following, calculate (a) net sales, (b) cost of goods sold, (c) gross profit, and (d) net income:

Data Sales, $22,000; Sales Discounts, $500; Sales Returns and Allowances, $250; Beginning Inventory, $650; Net Purchases, $13,200; Ending Inventory, $510; Operating Expenses, $3,600.

Unearned revenue
❶ (10 min)

12-3A. Allan Co. had the following balances on December 31, 2015:

Cash	
2,100	

Unearned Janitorial Service Revenue	
	600

Janitorial Service Revenue	
	7,200

The accountant for Allan has asked you to make an adjustment since $400 worth of janitorial services have just been performed for customers who had paid in advance. Construct a transaction analysis chart.

Calculating cost of goods sold
❶ ❷ (15 min)

12-4A. Lesan Co. purchased merchandise costing $400,000. Calculate the cost of goods sold under the following different situations:

a. Beginning inventory of $40,000 and no ending inventory

b. Beginning inventory of $50,000 and a $60,000 ending inventory

c. No beginning inventory and a $30,000 ending inventory

Preparing a worksheet
❷ (20 min)

12-5A. Prepare a worksheet from the following information:

(A and B) Merchandise Inventory—ending	$13
(C) Store Supplies on Hand	4
(D) Depreciation on Store Equipment	4
(E) Accrued Salaries	2

MOORE CO.
TRIAL BALANCE
DECEMBER 31, 2015

	Dr.	Cr.
Cash	8 00	
Accounts Receivable	5 00	
Merchandise Inventory	11 00	
Store Supplies	10 00	
Store Equipment	20 00	
Accumulated Depreciation, Store Equipment		6 00
Accounts Payable		5 00
J. Moore, Capital		34 00
Income Summary	—	—
Sales		64 00
Sales Returns and Allowances	9 00	
Purchases	23 00	
Purchases Discounts		3 00
Freight-In	3 00	
Salaries Expense	10 00	
Advertising Expense	13 00	
Totals	112 00	112 00

Set B

(The forms you need are on page 12-3 of the *Study Guide with Working Papers.*)

Categorizing account titles
❶ (10 min)

12-1B. Indicate the normal balance and category of each of the following accounts:

a. Sales Returns and Allowances

b. Merchandise Inventory (end of period)

c. Miscellaneous Income

d. Payroll Tax Expense
e. Sales Discounts
f. Purchases Returns and Allowances
g. Income Tax Payable
h. Prepaid Expenses

Calculating net sales, cost of goods sold, gross profit, and net income
❶ (15 min)

12-2B. From the following, calculate (a) net sales, (b) cost of goods sold, (c) gross profit, and (d) net income:

Data Sales, $35,000; Sales Discounts, $800; Sales Returns and Allowances, $5,000; Beginning Inventory, $900; Net Purchases, $13,700; Ending Inventory, $650; Operating Expenses, $4,900.

Unearned revenue
❶ (10 min)

12-3B. Allan Co. had the following balances on December 31, 2015:

Cash	
2,400	

Unearned Janitorial Service Revenue	
	700

Janitorial Service Revenue	
8,400	

The accountant for Allan has asked you to make an adjustment since $500 worth of janitorial services have just been performed for customers who had paid in advance. Construct a transaction analysis chart.

Calculating cost of goods sold
❶ ❷ (15 min)

12-4B. Lesan Co. purchased merchandise costing $400,000. Calculate the cost of goods sold under the following different situations:

a. Beginning inventory of $34,000 and no ending inventory
b. Beginning inventory of $45,000 and $55,000 ending inventory
c. No beginning inventory and $42,000 ending inventory

Preparing a worksheet
❷ (20 min)

12-5B. Prepare a worksheet from the following information:

(A and B) Merchandise Inventory—ending	$15
(C) Store Supplies on Hand	5
(D) Depreciation on Store Equipment	7
(E) Accrued Salaries Payable	3

MOORE CO.
TRIAL BALANCE
DECEMBER 31, 2015

	Dr.	Cr.
Cash	900	
Accounts Receivable	800	
Merchandise Inventory	1200	
Store Supplies	900	
Store Equipment	2400	
Accumulated Depreciation, Store Equipment		700
Accounts Payable		600
J. Moore, Capital		3800
Income Summary	—	—
Sales		6700
Sales Returns and Allowances	700	
Purchases	2700	
Purchases Discounts		500
Freight-In	400	
Salaries Expense	1200	
Advertising Expense	1100	
Totals	12300	12300

Group A Problems

(The forms you need are on page 12-4 of the *Study Guide with Working Papers.*)

Calculating net sales, cost of goods sold, gross profit, and net income
❶ (30 min)

12A-1. On the basis of the accounts listed below, calculate:

a. Net sales
b. Cost of goods sold
c. Gross profit
d. Net income

Accounts Payable	$ 6,000
Operating Expenses	2,000
J. Jensen, Capital	19,400
Purchases	4,450
Freight-In	80
Ending Merchandise Inventory, December 31, 2016	1,250
Sales	10,210
Accounts Receivable	1,489
Cash	756
Purchases Discounts	142
Sales Returns and Allowances	275
Beginning Merchandise Inventory, January 1, 2016	1,565
Purchases Returns and Allowances	251
Sales Discounts	394

Check Figure

Net Income $3,089

Comprehensive problem: Completing a worksheet for a merchandising company
❶ ❷ (60 min)

12A-2. From the following trial balance, complete a worksheet for Jim's Hardware of Halifax:

JIM'S HARDWARE
TRIAL BALANCE
DECEMBER 31, 2015

	Dr.	Cr.
Cash	78600	
Accounts Receivable	115200	
Merchandise Inventory	60000	
Prepaid Insurance	68400	
Store Equipment	216000	
Accumulated Depreciation, Store Equipment		66000
Accounts Payable		51600
Jim Spool, Capital		163200
Income Summary	—	—
Sales		1104000
Sales Returns and Allowances	54600	
Sales Discounts	21600	
Purchases	525600	
Purchases Discounts		16800
Purchases Returns and Allowances		10200
Wages Expense	171600	
Rent Expense	79200	
Telephone Expense	11400	
Miscellaneous Expense	9600	
	1411800	1411800

Check Figure

Net Income $1,989

Assumptions

a. and **b.** Ending inventory on December 31, $315

c. Insurance expired, $150

d. Depreciation expense on store equipment, $60

e. Accrued wages, $90

Comprehensive problem: Completing a worksheet
❶ ❷ (60 min)

12A-3. The owner of Waltz Company in Fairview has asked you to prepare a worksheet from the following trial balance and additional data:

Check Figure

Net Income $5,300

WALTZ COMPANY
TRIAL BALANCE
DECEMBER 31, 2017

	Dr.	Cr.
Cash	540800	
Petty Cash	24000	
Accounts Receivable	251200	
Beginning Merchandise Inventory, January 1	509200	
Prepaid Rent	61600	
Office Supplies	94400	
Office Equipment	928000	
Accumulated Depreciation, Office Equipment		760000
Accounts Payable		596400
K. Waltz, Capital		547600
K. Waltz, Withdrawals	480000	
Income Summary	—	—
Sales		5248400
Sales Returns and Allowances	9600	
Sales Discounts	240000	
Purchases	2931600	
Purchases Discounts		1600
Purchases Returns and Allowances		34800
Office Salaries Expense	740800	
Insurance Expense	240000	
Advertising Expense	80000	
Utilities Expense	57600	
	7188800	7188800

Additional Data

a. and **b.** Ending merchandise inventory on December 31, $1,805

c. Office supplies used up, $210

d. Rent expired, $195

e. Depreciation expense on office equipment, $550

f. Office salaries earned but not paid, $310

Comprehensive problem: Completing a worksheet with payroll and unearned revenue
❶ ❷ (60 min)

12A-4. From the following trial balance and additional data, complete the worksheet for Ron's Wholesale Clothing Company of Winnipeg.

Check Figure

Net Loss $824

RON'S WHOLESALE CLOTHING COMPANY
TRIAL BALANCE
DECEMBER 31, 2016

	Dr.	Cr.
Cash	4 460 00	
Petty Cash	300 00	
Accounts Receivable	7 500 00	
Merchandise Inventory	9 000 00	
Supplies	1 000 00	
Prepaid Insurance	850 00	
Store Equipment	2 500 00	
Accumulated Depreciation, Store Equipment		1 500 00
Accounts Payable		10 635 00
Income Tax Payable		1 060 00
CPP Payable		108 00
EI Payable		150 00
Unearned Storage Fees		357 00
Ron Win, Capital		12 500 00
Ron Win, Withdrawals	4 300 00	
Income Summary	—	—
Sales		45 000 00
Sales Returns and Allowances	1 475 00	
Sales Discounts	1 335 00	
Purchases	26 000 00	
Purchases Discounts		550 00
Purchases Returns and Allowances		400 00
Freight-In	225 00	
Salaries Expense	12 000 00	
Payroll Tax Expense	420 00	
Interest Expense	895 00	
	72 260 00	72 260 00

Additional Data

a. and **b.** Ending merchandise inventory on December 31, $6,000
c. Supplies on hand, $400
d. Insurance expired, $600
e. Depreciation expense on store equipment, $400
f. Storage fees earned, $176

Group B Problems

(The forms you need are on page 12-4 of the *Study Guide with Working Papers*.)

Calculating net sales, cost of goods sold, gross profit, and net income
❶ (30 min)

Check Figure

Net Income $1,273

12B-1. From the following accounts, calculate (a) net sales, (b) cost of goods sold, (c) gross profit, and (d) net income.

Sales Discounts	$ 500
Purchases Returns and Allowances	64
Beginning Merchandise Inventory, January 1, 2016	79

Sales Returns and Allowances	$ 191
Purchases Discounts	42
Cash	3,895
Accounts Receivable	441
Sales	3,950
Ending Merchandise Inventory, December 31, 2016	75
Freight-In	41
Purchases	1,152
R. Roland, Capital	1,950
Operating Expenses	895
Accounts Payable	129

Comprehensive problem: Completing a worksheet for a merchandising company
❶ ❷ (60 min)

Check Figure

Net Income $1,336

12B-2. As the accountant for Jim's Hardware of Halifax, you have been asked to complete a worksheet from the following trial balance as well as additional data.

JIM'S HARDWARE
TRIAL BALANCE
DECEMBER 31, 2015

	Dr.	Cr.
Cash	96000	
Accounts Receivable	160000	
Merchandise Inventory	73600	
Prepaid Insurance	111200	
Store Equipment	320000	
Accumulated Depreciation, Store Equipment		168000
Accounts Payable		140800
J. Spool, Capital		257600
Income Summary	—	—
Sales		1480000
Sales Returns and Allowances	72800	
Sales Discounts	68800	
Purchases	708800	
Purchases Discounts		24000
Purchases Returns and Allowances		24800
Wages Expense	230400	
Rent Expense	184000	
Telephone Expense	55200	
Miscellaneous Expense	14400	
	2095200	2095200

Additional Data

a. and **b.** Cost of ending inventory on December 31, $480
c. Insurance expired, $112
d. Depreciation expense on store equipment, $90
e. Accrued wages, $150

Comprehensive problem: Completing a worksheet
❶ ❷ (60 min)

12B-3. From the following, complete a worksheet for Waltz Company of Fairview.

Check Figure

Net Income $6,740

WALTZ COMPANY
TRIAL BALANCE
DECEMBER 31, 2017

	Dr.	Cr.
Cash	3800 00	
Petty Cash	100 00	
Accounts Receivable	3400 00	
Merchandise Inventory	5204 00	
Prepaid Rent	1200 00	
Office Supplies	1360 00	
Office Equipment	9680 00	
Accumulated Depreciation, Office Equipment		4040 00
Accounts Payable		7964 00
K. Waltz, Capital		5476 00
K. Waltz, Withdrawals	5000 00	
Income Summary	—	—
Sales		52462 00
Sales Returns and Allowances	116 00	
Sales Discounts	2200 00	
Purchases	29296 00	
Purchases Discounts		1208 00
Purchases Returns and Allowances		1350 00
Office Salaries Expense	7408 00	
Insurance Expense	2200 00	
Advertising Expense	800 00	
Utilities Expense	736 00	
	72500 00	72500 00

Additional Data

a. and **b.** Ending merchandise inventory on December 31, $1,600
c. Office supplies on hand, $470
d. Rent expired, $600
e. Depreciation expense on office equipment, $250
f. Salaries accrued, $180

Comprehensive problem: Completing a worksheet with payroll and unearned revenue
❶ ❷ (60 min)

Check Figure

Net Income $3,636

12B-4. From the following trial balance and additional data, complete the worksheet for Ron's Wholesale Clothing Company of Winnipeg.

RON'S WHOLESALE CLOTHING COMPANY
TRIAL BALANCE
DECEMBER 31, 2016

	Dr.	Cr.
Cash	2600 00	
Petty Cash	30 00	
Accounts Receivable	3000 00	
Beginning Merchandise Inventory, January 1	3600 00	
Supplies	270 00	
Prepaid Insurance	180 00	
Store Equipment	1000 00	
Accumulated Depreciation, Store Equipment		496 00
Accounts Payable		4590 00
Income Tax Payable		590 00
CPP Payable		74 00
EI Payable		100 00
Unearned Storage Fees		350 00
Ron Win, Capital		2734 00
Ron Win, Withdrawals	1800 00	
Income Summary	—	—
Sales		19400 00
Sales Returns and Allowances	560 00	
Sales Discounts	480 00	
Purchases	8600 00	
Purchases Discounts		240 00
Purchases Returns and Allowances		160 00
Freight-In	100 00	
Salaries Expense	6000 00	
Payroll Tax Expense	194 00	
Interest Expense	320 00	
	28734 00	28734 00

Additional Data

a. and **b.** Ending merchandise inventory on December 31, $3,950
c. Supplies on hand, $50
d. Insurance expired, $55
e. Depreciation expense on store equipment, $100
f. Storage fees earned, $115

Group C Problems

(The forms you need are on page 12-5 of the *Study Guide with Working Papers*.)

Calculating net sales, cost of goods sold, gross profit, and net income
❶ (30 min)

12C-1. On the basis of the accounts listed below, calculate:

a. Net sales
b. Cost of goods sold
c. Gross profit
d. Net income

Accounts Payable	$ 3,800
Operating Expenses	1,150
P. Juarez, Capital	12,460
Purchases	6,785
Freight-In	157
Ending Merchandise Inventory, December 31, 2015	1,670
Sales	13,730
Accounts Receivable	2,675
Cash	1,456
Purchases Discounts	262
Sales Returns and Allowances	208
Beginning Merchandise Inventory, January 1, 2015	1,940
Purchases Returns and Allowances	466
Sales Discounts	424

Check Figure

Net Income $5,464

Comprehensive problem: Completing a worksheet for a merchandising company
❶ ❷ (75 min)

Check Figure

Net Income $1,544.09

12C-2. From the following trial balance and additional data, complete a worksheet for Corocan Tile Company of Cranbrook for the 12-month period ending October 31, 2016.

COROCAN TILE COMPANY
TRIAL BALANCE
OCTOBER 31, 2016

	Dr.	Cr.
Cash	171040	
Petty Cash	20000	
Accounts Receivable	431670	
Beginning Merchandise Inventory, November 1	1346700	
Supplies	73300	
Prepaid Insurance	91400	
GST Prepaid	74852	
Tile Cutting Equipment	782000	
Accumulated Depreciation, Equipment		175555
Accounts Payable		1678240
GST Collected		167358
Income Tax Payable		177100
CPP Payable		24620
EI Payable		37380
Winnie Corocan, Capital		639544
Winnie Corocan, Withdrawals	633800	
Income Summary	—	—
Sales		6906673
Sales Returns and Allowances	138824	
Sales Discounts	71542	
Purchases	4277264	
Purchases Discounts		88230
Purchases Returns and Allowances		51286
Freight-In	42570	
Salaries Expense	1587000	
Payroll Taxes Expense	142600	
Interest Expense	61424	
	9945986	9945986

Additional Data

a. and **b.** Ending merchandise inventory on October 31, $11,416

c. Supplies on hand, $357.10

d. Insurance expired, $609.33

e. Depreciation expense on equipment for the year ending October 31, 2016, is calculated assuming a life of six years, residual value of $1,500, straight-line method.

f. Advertising bill received, $500, plus GST of $25

g. Employees had worked for 62 hours at an average of $18 per hour at fiscal year-end but will receive this pay in November.

Comprehensive problem: Completing a worksheet
❶ ❷ (75 min)

12C-3. The owner of Patel Antique Clock Company of Churchill has asked you to prepare a worksheet from the following trial balance and additional data:

Check Figure

Net Income $6,681.87

PATEL ANTIQUE CLOCK COMPANY
TRIAL BALANCE
MAY 31, 2017

	Dr.	Cr.
Cash	762 40	
Petty Cash	150 00	
Accounts Receivable	2715 96	
Beginning Clock Inventory, June 1	10766 42	
Repair Supplies	624 30	
Prepaid Insurance	753 76	
GST Prepaid	696 12	
Clock Repair Equipment	4300 00	
Accumulated Depreciation, Repair Equipment		1480 00
Accounts Payable		8686 92
GST Collected		912 48
Income Tax Payable		1155 40
CPP Payable		167 70
EI Payable		278 60
Mike Patel, Capital		5566 08
Mike Patel, Withdrawals	4380 00	
Income Summary	—	—
Sales		57014 08
Sales Returns and Allowances	267 10	
Sales Discounts	176 42	
Purchases	30488 92	
Purchases Discounts		277 44
Purchases Returns and Allowances		512 86
Freight-In	1096 33	
Salaries Expense	13475 00	
Payroll Taxes Expense	1276 40	
Advertising Expense	721 68	
Rent Expense	2788 00	
Utilities Expense	612 75	
	76051 56	76051 56

Additional Data

a. and **b.** Ending clock inventory on May 31, 2017, $12,488.92

c. Supplies on hand at May 31 totalled $376.40

d. Insurance expired, $502.51

e. Depreciation expense on equipment for the year ending May 31, 2017, is calculated using the straight-line method, 10-year life with a residual value of $600.

f. Advertising bill received, $300, plus GST of $15

g. Employees had worked but not been paid for 43.5 hours at $12 per hour at year-end.

Comprehensive problem: Completing a worksheet with payroll and unearned revenue ❶ ❷ (75 min)

12C-4. From the following trial balance and additional data, complete the worksheet for Gwendolyn's Archery Sales Company of Moncton.

Check Figure

Net Income $3,943.73

GWENDOLYN'S ARCHERY SALES COMPANY
TRIAL BALANCE
APRIL 30, 2016

	Dr.	Cr.
Cash	2 467 93	
Petty Cash	75 00	
Accounts Receivable	764 82	
Beginning Merchandise Inventory, May 1	17 368 44	
Supplies on Hand	896 26	
Prepaid Insurance	1 158 20	
GST Prepaid	1 458 76	
Equipment	8 975 00	
Accumulated Depreciation, Equipment		5 762 14
Accounts Payable		21 479 50
GST Collected		2 444 70
Income Tax Payable		974 70
CPP Payable		367 12
EI Payable		190 08
Gwen Sterling, Capital		11 373 06
Gwen Sterling, Withdrawals	8 450 00	
Income Summary	—	—
Sales		78 422 76
Sales Returns and Allowances	467 13	
Sales Discounts	472 38	
Purchases	56 381 58	
Purchases Discounts		782 40
Purchases Returns and Allowances		1 328 37
Freight-In	376 82	
Salaries Expense	14 762 80	
Payroll Taxes Expense	1 812 61	
Advertising Expense	2 572 84	
Rent Expense	3 720 00	
Utilities Expense	944 26	
	123 124 83	123 124 83

Additional Data

a. and **b.** Ending merchandise inventory on April 30, 2016, $26,407.30

c. Supplies on hand at end of April, $412.68

d. A calculation showed that $531.40 of prepaid insurance was the correct amount at year-end.

e. Depreciation expense on equipment for the year ending April 30, 2016, was calculated using the straight-line method, seven-year life with a residual value of $450.

f. Utilities bill received, $110, plus GST of $5.50

g. At year-end, employees had worked but not been paid for a total of 120 hours at an average of $14 per hour.

On-the-Job Training

(The forms you need are on page 12-6 of the *Study Guide with Working Papers.*)

Professional fees on the accrual basis
1 (20 min)

T-1. Kim Andrews prepared the following income statement on a cash basis for Ed Sloan, M.D.:

ED SLOAN, M.D. INCOME STATEMENT FOR THE YEAR ENDED DECEMBER 31, 2015	
Professional Fees Earned	5000000
Expenses	1800000
Net Income	3200000

Ed Sloan has requested information from Kim as to what his professional fees earned would be under the accrual-basis system of accounting. Kim has asked you to provide Dr. Sloan with this information, basing it on the following facts that Kim ignored in the original preparation of the financial report:

	2014	*2015*
Accrued Professional Fees	$4,200	$5,300
Unearned Professional Fees	6,200	4,250

Merchandise inventory in relation to net income/loss
1 (20 min)

T-2. Abby Jay is having a difficult time understanding the relationships among sales, cost of goods sold, gross profit, and net income for a merchandising company. As the accounting lab tutor, you have been asked to sit down with Abby and explain how to calculate the missing amounts in each situation listed below. Keep in mind that each situation is a distinct and separate business problem.

	Sales	Beginning Inventory	Purchases	Ending Inventory	Cost of Goods Sold	Gross Profit	Expense	Net Income or Loss
Sit. 1	320,000	200,000	160,000	?	260,000	?	80,000	?
Sit. 2	380,000	140,000	?	180,000	200,000	?	100,000	80,000
Sit. 3	480,000	200,000	?	160,000	?	220,000	140,000	80,000
Sit. 4	?	160,000	280,000	140,000	?	160,000	140,000	?
Sit. 5	440,000	160,000	260,000	?	240,000	?	100,000	?
Sit. 6	280,000	120,000	?	140,000	160,000	?	?	40,000
Sit. 7	?	160,000	200,000	120,000	?	160,000	?	–20,000
Sit. 8	320,000	?	200,000	140,000	?	160,000	?	40,000

Recording adjustments and completing a worksheet
❶ ❷ (60 min)

CONTINUING PROBLEM

Another six months have passed and the fiscal year has concluded for Precision Computer Centre. Tony Freedman wants to make the necessary adjustments to his company's accounts to prepare accurate financial statements at July 31, 2017.

Assignment

(The worksheet you require is at the end of the *Study Guide with Working Papers.*)

To prepare the necessary adjustments, use the trial balance shown on the next page and the information below.

Complete the 10-column worksheet for the 12 months ended July 31, 2017.

Inventory

Tony took inventory at the end of July and determined that there was $17,400 worth of merchandise left in stock on July 31.

Amortization of Computer Equipment

Computer depreciates at $33 a month—purchased May 6, 2016.

Computer workstations depreciate at $20 per month—purchased July 17, 2016.

Shop benches depreciate at $25 per month—purchased November 5, 2016.

Amortization of Office Equipment

Office equipment depreciates at $10 per month—purchased May 16, 2016.

Fax machine depreciates at $10 per month—purchased November 19, 2016.

Remember: If any long-term asset is purchased in the first 15 days of the month, Freedman will record depreciation for the full month. If an asset is purchased later than the 15th, he will not record depreciation in the month when it was purchased.

Additional Information

Rent for six months, at $400 per month, has expired.

Supplies on hand at year-end amounted to $530.

A portion of the insurance paid for in February has expired. Remember that the entire premium was debited to Prepaid Insurance.

The balance in Unearned Service Revenue (account 2050) was received from a new customer on June 1, 2017. It represents a prepayment to cover all necessary service on 10 computers for the 12 months ending May 31, 2018.

PRECISION COMPUTER CENTRE
TRIAL BALANCE AS OF JULY 31, 2017

Account #	Account Name	Debit Balance	Credit Balance
1000	Cash	39,574.72	
1010	Petty Cash	100.00	
1020	Accounts Receivable	21,620.00	
1025	Prepaid Rent	2,400.00	
1030	Supplies	1,860.52	
1035	Prepaid Insurance	1,846.00	
1040	Merchandise Inventory	7,100.00	
1080	Computer Shop Equipment	5,200.00	
1081	Accumulated Depreciation, Computer Shop Equipment		99.00
1090	Office Equipment	1,500.00	
1091	Accumulated Depreciation, Office Equipment		20.00
2000	Accounts Payable		4,362.00
2010	Wages Payable		
2015	Due to CRA		
2050	Unearned Service Revenue		4,800.00
2060	HST Payable		3,149.83
2066	HST Recoverable	2,818.64	
3000	T. Freedman, Capital		7,406.00
3010	T. Freedman, Withdrawals	18,735.00	
3020	Income Summary		
4000	Service Revenue		96,806.00
4010	Sales		146,448.00
4020	Sales Returns and Allowances	1,350.00	
4030	Sales Discounts	590.00	
4050	Service Contracts Sold		
5010	Advertising Expense	2,716.37	
5015	Cleaning Expense	900.00	
5020	Rent Expense	2,400.00	
5030	Utilities Expense	2,482.15	
5040	Phone Expense	1,980.04	
5050	Supplies Expense	286.00	
5060	Insurance Expense		
5070	Postage Expense	176.11	
5080	Depreciation Expense, Computer Shop Equipment		
5090	Depreciation Expense, Office Equipment		
5100	Miscellaneous Expense	143.12	
5110	Wages Expense	77,964.89	
5120	Payroll Benefits Expense	835.37	
5140	Bad Debts Expense		
5600	Purchases	68,414.06	
5610	Purchases Returns and Allowances		822.18
5620	Purchases Discounts		245.80
5630	Freight-In	1,165.82	
	Totals	264,158.81	264,158.81

CHAPTER 13

Completion of the Accounting Cycle for a Merchandising Company

LEARNING OBJECTIVES

Many Canadian companies engage in merchandising—buying and selling goods to individuals or companies. As we saw in the last chapter, their somewhat unique structure means that some small changes are needed to the process of completing their worksheets and preparing their statements.

For similar reasons there are a few differences in how the accounting cycle is completed for these merchandising entities. This chapter covers the final few topics and will help students learn how to do all of the remaining steps in the accounting cycle.

In this chapter, we discuss the steps involved in completing the accounting cycle for a merchandising company: preparing financial statements, journalizing and posting adjusting and closing entries, preparing a post-closing trial balance, and reversing entries. First, we will deal with preparing financial statements at the close of the accounting cycle.

LEARNING UNIT 13-1

Preparing Financial Statements

LO 1 Preparing financial statements for a merchandising company

As we discussed in Chapter 5, the three financial statements can be prepared from the worksheet. Let's begin by looking at how Art's Clothing Company prepares the income statement.

THE INCOME STATEMENT

Art is interested in knowing how well his business performed for the year ended December 31, 2016. What were its net sales? Were there many returns of goods from dissatisfied customers? What was the cost of the goods brought into the store versus the selling price received? How many goods were returned to suppliers? What is the cost of the goods that have not been sold? What was the cost of the freight-in? The income statement in Figure 13-1 is prepared from the income statement columns of the worksheet. (Review it first, and then we will explain each section of the income statement and where the information came from on the worksheet.)

Note that there are no debit or credit columns on the formal income statement—the inside columns on financial reports are used for subtotalling, not for debit and credit.

Note also that the income statement is broken down into several sections. Remembering the sections can help you make sense of the statement and set it up correctly on your own. Basically what it presents is this:

Net Sales
− Cost of Goods Sold
= Gross Profit
− Operating Expenses
= Net Income from Operations
+ Other Income
− Other Expenses
= Net Income

Let's take these sections one at a time and see where the figures come from on the worksheet.

Revenue Section

Sales
− Sales Returns and Allowances
− Sales Discounts
= Net Sales

Net Sales The first major category of the income statement shows net sales. The figure here of $93,380 is *not* found on the worksheet—the accountant must take the individual amounts for gross sales, sales returns and allowances, and sales discounts found on the worksheet and *combine* them to arrive at a figure for net sales. Thus, although the worksheet has the individual components, it is not until the formal income statement that these individual amounts are summarized in one figure for net sales.

Cost of Goods Sold Section

Beginning Inventory
+ Net Cost of Purchases
− Ending Inventory
= Cost of Goods Sold

On the worksheet, we separate figures for Merchandise Inventory. The $19,000 represents the beginning inventory of the period while the $4,000, calculated from an inventory sheet, is the ending inventory. Note on the financial report that the cost of goods sold section uses two separate figures for inventory. Remember in the periodic system that goods brought in during the accounting period are added to the Purchases account, not to the Merchandise Inventory account.

Note that the following numbers are not found on the worksheet but are shown on the formal income statement (they are combined by the accountant in preparing the income statement):

- **Net Purchases:** $50,460 (Purchases – Purchases Discounts – Purchases Returns and Allowances)
- **Net Cost of Purchases:** $50,910 (Net Purchases + Freight-In)

ART'S CLOTHING COMPANY
PARTIAL WORKSHEET
FOR THE YEAR ENDED DECEMBER 31, 2016

Account Titles	Income Statement Dr.	Income Statement Cr.
Income Summary	19000 00	4000 00
Sales		95000 00
Sales Returns and Allowances	950 00	
Sales Discounts	670 00	
Purchases	52000 00	
Purchases Discounts		860 00
Purchases Returns and Allowances		680 00
Freight-In	450 00	
Salaries Expense	12300 00	
Payroll Tax Expense	420 00	
Postage Expense	25 00	
Miscellaneous Expense	30 00	
Interest Expense	300 00	
Rental Income		200 00
Supplies Expense	500 00	
Insurance Expense	300 00	
Depreciation Expense, Store Equip.	50 00	
Accrued Salaries		
	86995 00	100740 00
Net Income	13745 00	
	100740 00	100740 00

ART'S CLOTHING COMPANY
INCOME STATEMENT
FOR THE YEAR ENDED DECEMBER 31, 2016

Revenue				
Gross Sales				$95000 00
Less: Sales Ret. and Allow.			$950 00	
Sales Discounts			670 00	1620 00
Net Sales				93380 00
Cost of Goods Sold				
Merchandise Inventory, 1/1/16			19000 00	
Purchases		$52000 00		
Less: Pur. Discounts	$860 00			
Pur. Ret. and Allow.	680 00	1540 00		
Net Purchases		50460 00		
Add: Freight-In		450 00		
Net Cost of Purchases			50910 00	
Cost of Goods Available for Sale			69910 00	
Less: Merch. Inv., 12/31/16			4000 00	
Cost of Goods Sold				65910 00
Gross Profit				27470 00
Operating Expenses				
Salaries Expense			12300 00	
Payroll Tax Expense			420 00	
Dep'n. Exp., Store Equip.			50 00	
Supplies Expense			500 00	
Insurance Expense			300 00	
Postage Expense			25 00	
Miscellaneous Expense			30 00	
Total Operating Expenses				13625 00
Net Income from Operations				13845 00
Other Income				
Rental Income			200 00	
Other Expenses				
Interest Expense			300 00	100 00
Net Income				$13745 00

Figure 13-1
Partial Worksheet and Income Statement

- **Cost of Goods Available for Sale:** $69,910 (Beginning Inventory + Net Cost of Purchases)
- **Cost of Goods Sold:** $65,910 (Cost of Goods Available for Sale – Ending Inventory)

Gross Profit

Net Sales
– Cost of Goods Sold
= Gross Profit

The figure for gross profit ($27,470) is arrived at by subtracting cost of goods sold from net sales ($93,380 – $65,910). The gross profit figure of $27,470 is not found by itself on the worksheet but, like others we have discussed, it is calculated by the accountant from separate figures on the worksheet.

Operating Expenses Section

The total of the operating expenses does not appear on its own on the worksheet; to get this figure of $13,625, the accountant adds up all the expenses on the worksheet that resulted from doing business.

Many companies break expenses down into those directly related to the selling activity of the company (**selling expenses**) and those related to administrative or office activity (**administrative expenses** or **general expenses**). Here's a sample list broken down into these two categories:

Operating Expenses

Selling Expenses	*Administrative Expenses*
Sales Salaries Expense	Rent Expense
Delivery Expense	Office Salaries Expense
Advertising Expense	Utilities Expense
Depreciation Expense, Store Equipment	Supplies Expense
Insurance Expense	Depreciation Expense, Office Equipment
Total Selling Expenses	Total Administrative Expenses

Other Income (or Other Revenue) Section

This section will record any **other income** or revenue besides revenue from sales. For example, Art's Clothing Company makes a profit from subletting a portion of a building and earning rental income of $200 and that income goes in this section.

Other Expenses Section

This section will record **other expenses**, non-operating expenses—those not related to the main operating activities of the business. For example, Art's Clothing Company has paid or owes $300 interest on money it has borrowed.

STATEMENT OF OWNER'S EQUITY

Statement of owner's equity is the same for a merchandising business as for a service firm.

The information used to complete the statement of owner's equity comes from the balance sheet columns of the worksheet. Keep in mind that the capital account in the ledger should be checked to see if any additional investments have occurred during the period. Note in the following diagram that the worksheet aids in this.

The ending figure of $13,050 for Art Newner, Capital, will be carried over to the balance sheet, which is the final report we will look at in this chapter.

Any additional investment by the owner would be added to his or her beginning capital amount. The illustration at the right does not show this however.

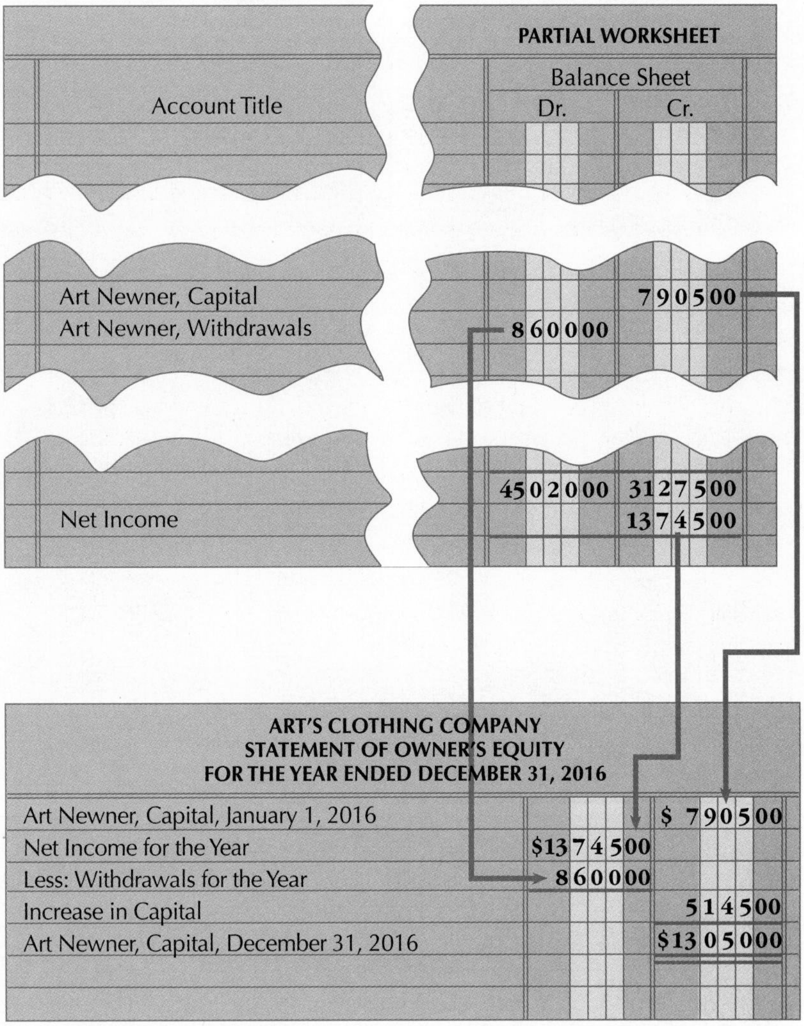

PARTIAL WORKSHEET
Balance Sheet
Account Title
Dr.
Cr.
Art Newner, Capital
Art Newner, Withdrawals
7905 00
8600 00
4502000
3127500
Net Income
1374500
ART'S CLOTHING COMPANY
STATEMENT OF OWNER'S EQUITY
FOR THE YEAR ENDED DECEMBER 31, 2016
Art Newner, Capital, January 1, 2016
Net Income for the Year
Less: Withdrawals for the Year
Increase in Capital
Art Newner, Capital, December 31, 2016
$ 790500
$1374500
860000
514500
$1305000

THE BALANCE SHEET

Figure 13-2 shows how a worksheet is used to aid in the preparation of a **classified balance sheet**. A classified balance sheet breaks down the assets and liabilities into more detail. Classified balance sheets provide management, owners, creditors, and suppliers with more information about the company's ability to pay current and long-term debts. They also provide a more complete financial picture of the firm.

The categories on the classified balance sheet are as follows.

Current assets are defined as cash and assets that will be converted into cash or used up during the normal operating cycle of the company or one year, whichever is longer. (Think of the **operating cycle** as the time period it takes a company to buy and sell merchandise and then collect accounts receivable.)

Accountants list current assets in order of how easily they can be converted into cash (this is called *liquidity*). In most cases, Accounts Receivable can be turned into cash more quickly than Merchandise Inventory—for example, it can be quite difficult to sell an outdated computer in a computer store or to sell last year's model car this year.

Capital assets are long-lived assets used in the production or sale of goods or services. Art's Clothing Company has only one capital asset, store equipment;

ART'S CLOTHING COMPANY
WORKSHEET
FOR THE YEAR ENDED DECEMBER 31, 2016

Account Titles	Balance Sheet Dr.	Balance Sheet Cr.
Cash	12 920 00	
Petty Cash	100 00	
Accounts Receivable	14 500 00	
Merchandise Inventory	4 000 00	
Supplies	300 00	
Prepaid Insurance	600 00	
Store Equipment	4 000 00	
Accum. Dep'n., Store Equipment		450 00
Accounts Payable		17 900 00
Income Tax Payable		1 240 00
CPP Payable		260 00
EI Payable		200 00
Unearned Rent		400 00
Mortgage Payable		2 320 00
Accrued Salaries		600 00
	45 020 00	31 275 00
Net Income		13 745 00
	45 020 00	45 020 00

ART'S CLOTHING COMPANY
CLASSIFIED BALANCE SHEET
DECEMBER 31, 2016

Assets		
Current Assets		
Cash	$12 920 00	
Petty Cash	100 00	
Accounts Receivable	14 500 00	
Merchandise Inventory	4 000 00	
Supplies	300 00	
Prepaid Insurance	600 00	
Total Current Assets		$32 420 00
Capital Assets		
Store Equipment	4 000 00	
Less: Accumulated Depreciation	450 00	3 550 00
Total Assets		$ 35 970 00
Liabilities		
Current Liabilities		
Accounts Payable	$17 900 00	
Income Tax Payable	1 240 00	
CPP Payable	260 00	
EI Payable	200 00	
Accrued Salaries	600 00	
Mortgage Payable (current portion)	320 00	
Unearned Rent	400 00	
Total Current Liabilities		$20 920 00
Long-Term Liabilities		
Mortgage Payable		2 000 00
Total Liabilities		22 920 00
Owner's Equity		
Art Newner, Capital		13 050 00
Total Liabilities and Owner's Equity		$35 970 00

Note: The figure of $13,050 for Art Newner, Capital, comes from the statement of owner's equity.

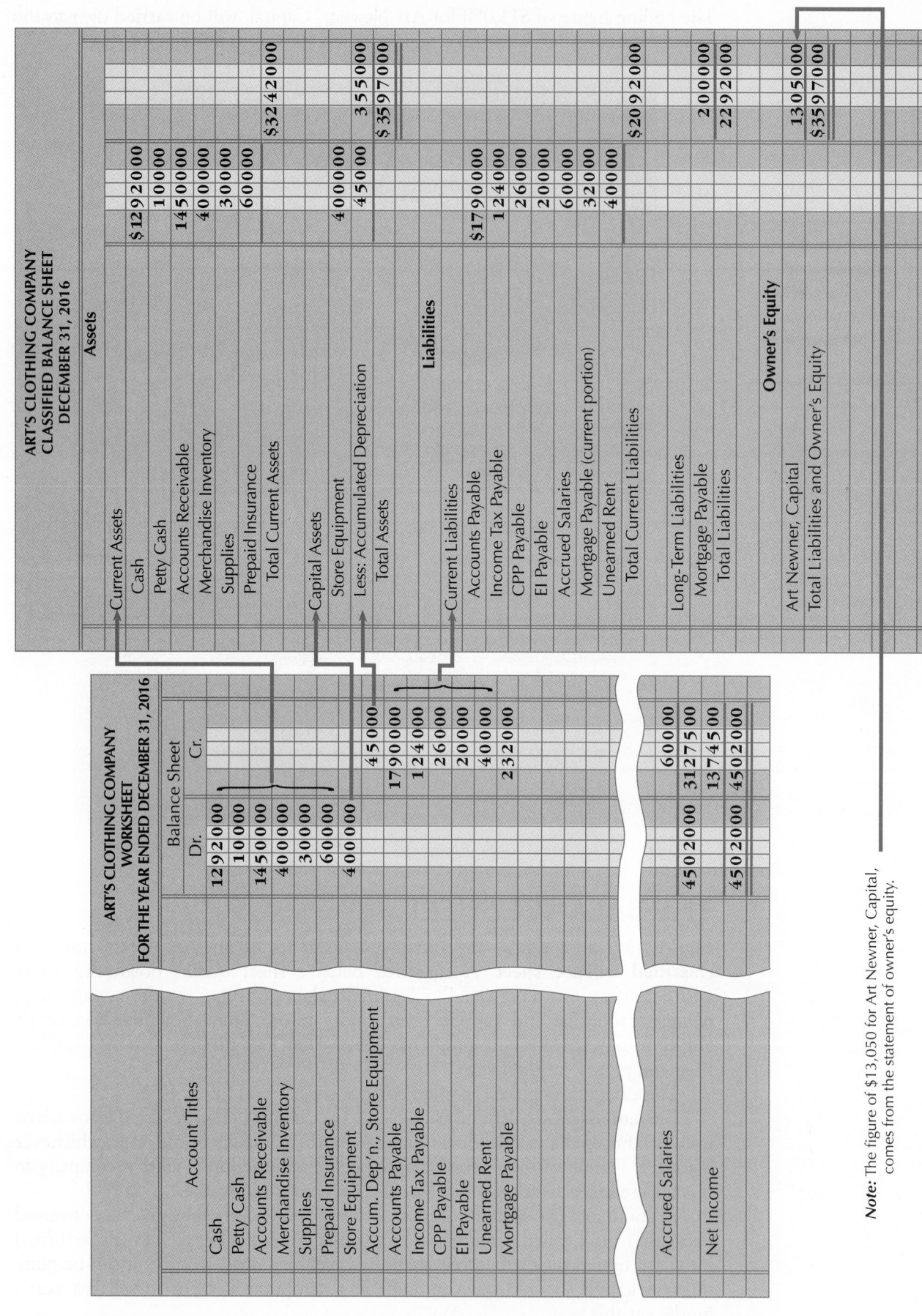

Figure 13-2 Partial Worksheet and Balance Sheet

Mortgage payable	$2,320
Current portion	− 320
Long-term	$2,000

The current portion of a long-term liability is the amount of principal to be repaid during the next year. Do not include any interest to be paid next year.

other capital assets could include buildings and land. The assets are usually listed in order of how long they will last; the longest-lived assets are listed first. Land would usually be the first asset listed (and land is never amortized). Note that we still show the cost of the asset less its accumulated amortization.

Current liabilities are the debts or obligations of Art's Clothing Company that must be paid within one year or one operating cycle. The order of listing accounts in this section is not always the same—many times companies will list their liabilities in the order in which they expect to pay them off. Note that the current portion of the mortgage, $320 (that portion due within one year), is listed toward the end of the list since that is paid off over the year.

Long-term liabilities are debts or obligations not due and payable for a comparatively long period, usually for more than one year. For Art's Clothing Company there is only one long-term liability—Mortgage Payable. The long-term portion of the mortgage is listed here; the current portion, due within one year, is listed under Current Liabilities.

A classified balance sheet (when examined along with the income statement) can provide management, owners, creditors, and suppliers with more information about the company's ability to pay debts, both current and long-term. As well, it provides a more complete financial picture of the firm than a standard balance sheet would.

LEARNING UNIT 13-1 REVIEW

AT THIS POINT you should be able to:

- Prepare a detailed income statement from the worksheet. (pp. 588–590)
- Explain the difference between selling and administrative expenses. (p. 590)
- Explain which columns of the worksheet are used in preparing a statement of owner's equity. (pp. 590– 591)
- Prepare a classified balance sheet from a worksheet. (pp. 591–593)
- Explain as well as compare current assets and capital assets. (p. 591)
- Using Mortgage Payable as an example, explain the difference between current and long-term liabilities. (p. 593)

Self-Review Quiz 13-1

(The forms you need are on pages 13-2 and 13-3 of the *Study Guide with Working Papers*.)

Using the worksheet from Self-Review Quiz 12-2 (page 566), prepare in proper form (1) an income statement, (2) a statement of owner's equity, and (3) a classified balance sheet for Ray Company.

> **Quiz Tip**
> Note that the cost of goods sold has separate figures for beginning inventory and ending inventory.

Solutions to Self-Review Quiz 13-1

1.

RAY COMPANY
INCOME STATEMENT
FOR THE YEAR ENDED DECEMBER 31, 2015

Revenue				
Sales				$11040 00
Less: Sales Returns and Allowances			$546 00	
Sales Discounts			216 00	762 00
Net Sales				10278 00
Cost of Goods Sold				
Merchandise Inventory, 1/1/15			824 00	
Purchases		$5256 00		
Less: Pur. Ret. and Allowances	$168 00			
Purchases Discounts	102 00	270 00		
Net Purchases			4986 00	
Cost of Goods Available for Sale			5810 00	
Less: Merchandise Inv., 12/31/15			200 00	
Cost of Goods Sold				5610 00
Gross Profit				4668 00
Operating Expenses				
Salaries Expense			2216 00	
Insurance Expense			1392 00	
Utilities Expense			96 00	
Plumbing Expense			214 00	
Rent Expense			100 00	
Depreciation Expense, Equipment			60 00	
Total Operating Expenses				4078 00
Net Income from Operations				590 00
Other Income				
Storage Fees				516 00
Net Income				$1106 00

2.

RAY COMPANY
STATEMENT OF OWNER'S EQUITY
FOR THE YEAR ENDED DECEMBER 31, 2015

B. Ray, Capital, 1/1/15	$1932 00
Net Income for the Year	1106 00
B. Ray, Capital, 12/31/15	$3038 00

3.

RAY COMPANY BALANCE SHEET DECEMBER 31, 2015		
Assets		
Current Assets		
Cash	$2 4 8 6 00	
Merchandise Inventory	2 0 0 00	
Prepaid Rent	1 0 5 2 00	
Prepaid Insurance	6 0 00	
Total Current Assets		$3 7 9 8 00
Capital Assets		
Office Equipment	$2 1 6 0 00	
Less: Accumulated Depreciation	6 2 0 00	1 5 4 0 00
Total Assets		$5 3 3 8 00
Liabilities		
Current Liabilities		
Accounts Payable	$ 1 0 0 00	
Accrued Salaries	2 0 0 00	
Unearned Storage Fees	2 0 0 0 00	
Total Liabilities		$2 3 0 0 00
Owner's Equity		
B. Ray, Capital		3 0 3 8 00
Total Liabilities and Owner's Equity		$5 3 3 8 00

LEARNING UNIT 13-2

Journalizing and Posting Adjusting and Closing Entries; Preparing the Post-Closing Trial Balance

LO 2

Recording adjusting and closing entries

JOURNALIZING AND POSTING ADJUSTING ENTRIES

From the worksheet of Art's Clothing Company, repeated here as Figure 13-3 for your convenience, the adjusting entries can be journalized from the adjustments column and posted to the ledger. Keep in mind that the adjustments have been recorded only on the worksheet, not in the journal or in the ledger—at this point the journal does not reflect adjustments, and the ledger still contains only unadjusted amounts.

ART'S CLOTHING COMPANY
WORKSHEET
FOR THE YEAR ENDED DECEMBER 31, 2016

Account Titles	Trial Balance		Adjustments		Adjusted Trial Balance		Income Statement		Balance Sheet	
	Dr.	Cr.	Dr.	Cr.	Dr.	Cr.	Dr.	Cr.	Dr.	Cr.
Cash	12920 00				12920 00				12920 00	
Petty Cash	100 00				100 00				100 00	
Accounts Receivable	14500 00				14500 00				14500 00	
Merchandise Inventory	19000 00		(B) 4000 00	(A) 19000 00	4000 00				4000 00	
Supplies	800 00			(D) 500 00	300 00				300 00	
Prepaid Insurance	900 00			(E) 300 00	600 00				600 00	
Store Equipment	4000 00				4000 00				4000 00	
Accum. Dep'n., Store Equipment		400 00		(F) 50 00		450 00				450 00
Accounts Payable		17900 00				17900 00				17900 00
Income Tax Payable		1240 00				1240 00				1240 00
CPP Payable		260 00				260 00				260 00
EI Payable		200 00				200 00				200 00
Unearned Rent		600 00	(C) 200 00			400 00				400 00
Mortgage Payable		2320 00				2320 00				2320 00
Art Newner, Capital		7905 00				7905 00				7905 00
Art Newner, Withdrawals	8600 00				8600 00				8600 00	
Income Summary			(A) 19000 00	(B) 4000 00	19000 00	4000 00	19000 00	4000 00		
Sales		95000 00				95000 00		95000 00		
Sales Returns and Allowances	950 00				950 00		950 00			
Sales Discounts	670 00				670 00		670 00			
Purchases	52000 00				52000 00		52000 00			
Purchases Discounts		860 00				860 00		860 00		
Purchases Returns and Allowances		680 00				680 00		680 00		
Freight-In	450 00				450 00		450 00			
Salaries Expense	11700 00		(G) 600 00		12300 00		12300 00			
Payroll Tax Expense	420 00				420 00		420 00			
Postage Expense	25 00				25 00		25 00			
Miscellaneous Expense	30 00				30 00		30 00			
Interest Expense	300 00				300 00		300 00			
	127365 00	127365 00								
Rental Income				(C) 200 00		200 00		200 00		
Supplies Expense			(D) 500 00		500 00		500 00			
Insurance Expense			(E) 300 00		300 00		300 00			
Depreciation Expense, Store Equip.			(F) 50 00		50 00		50 00			
Accrued Salaries Payable				(G) 600 00		600 00				600 00
			24650 00	24650 00	132015 00	132015 00	86995 00	100740 00	45020 00	31275 00
Net Income							13745 00			13745 00
							100740 00	100740 00	45020 00	45020 00

Figure 13-3 Completed Worksheet

The journalized and posted adjusting entries are shown below. Note that the liability Unearned Rent is reduced by $200 and Rental Income has increased by $200.

ART'S CLOTHING COMPANY
GENERAL JOURNAL

Page 2

Date		Account Titles and Description	PR	Dr.	Cr.
		Adjusting Entries			
2016					
Dec.	31	Income Summary	313	19 000 00	
		Merchandise Inventory	114		19 000 00
		Transferred beginning inventory			
		to Income Summary			
	31	Merchandise Inventory	114	4 000 00	
		Income Summary	313		4 000 00
		Records cost of ending inventory			
	31	Unearned Rent	218	200 00	
		Rental Income	414		200 00
		Rental income earned			
	31	Supplies Expense	614	500 00	
		Supplies	115		500 00
		Supplies consumed			
	31	Insurance Expense	615	300 00	
		Prepaid Insurance	116		300 00
		Insurance expired			
	31	Depreciation Exp., Store Equipment	613	50 00	
		Acc. Depreciation, Store Equipment	122		50 00
		Depreciation on equipment			
	31	Salaries Expense	611	600 00	
		Accrued Salaries	212		600 00
		Accrued salary			

Partial General Ledger

Merchandise Inventory 114	
19,000	19,000
4,000	

Accum. Dep'n., Store Equipment 122	
	400
	50

Income Summary 313	
19,000	4,000

Dep'n. Expense, Store Equipment 613	
50	

Supplies 115	
800	500

Accrued Salaries 212	
	600

Rental Income 414	
	200

Supplies Expense 614	
500	

Prepaid Insurance 116	
900	300

Unearned Rent 218	
200	600

Salaries Expense 611	
11,700	
600	

Insurance Exp. 615	
300	

JOURNALIZING AND POSTING CLOSING ENTRIES

In Chapter 5, we discussed the closing process for a service company. The goals of closing have not changed. They are to clear all temporary accounts in the ledger to zero and to update capital in the ledger to its latest balance. A merchandising company will also use the worksheet and the following steps to complete the closing process:

1. Close all balances in the income statement credit column of the worksheet, *except* Income Summary, by debits. Then credit the total to the Income Summary account.
2. Close all balances in the income statement debit column of the worksheet, *except* Income Summary, by credits. Then debit the total to the Income Summary account.
3. Transfer the balance of the Income Summary account to the Capital account.
4. Transfer the balance of the owner's Withdrawal account to the Capital account.

Let's look now at the journalized closing entries in Figure 13-4. When these entries are posted, all the temporary accounts will have zero balances in the ledger and the Capital account will be updated with a new balance.

Let's take a moment to look at the Income Summary account in T account form as it would exist after step 2 above:

Income Summary 313

	Adj.	19,000	4,000	Adj.
	Clos.	67,995	96,740	Clos.
		86,995	100,740	
Net income →	Clos.	13,745		

Note that Income Summary before the closing process contains the adjustments for Merchandise Inventory. Sometimes accountants include the inventory adjustments as part of the closing. This is not illustrated in this text; *it is not very important which procedure is used*, just that it is made accurately. The end result is that the net income of $13,745 is closed to the Capital account.

THE POST-CLOSING TRIAL BALANCE

LO 3 Preparing a post-closing trial balance

The post-closing trial balance (often referred to as an opening trial balance) shown on page 600 is prepared from the general ledger. Note first that all temporary accounts have been closed and thus are not shown on this post-closing trial balance. Note also that the ending inventory figure of the last accounting period, $4,000, becomes the beginning inventory figure on January 1, 2017.

Figure 13-4
General Journal

ART'S CLOTHING COMPANY
GENERAL JOURNAL

Page 2

Date		Account Titles and Description	PR	Dr.	Cr.
		Closing Entries			
2016 Dec.	31	Sales	411	9500000	
		Rental Income	414	20000	
		Purchases Discounts	512	86000	
		Purchases Returns and Allowances	513	68000	
		Income Summary	313		9674000
		To transfer credit account balances on income statement column of worksheet to Income Summary			
	31	Income Summary	313	6799500	
		Sales Returns and Allowances	412		95000
		Sales Discounts	413		67000
		Purchases	511		5200000
		Freight-In	514		45000
		Salaries Expense	611		1230000
		Payroll Tax Expense	612		42000
		Postage Expense	616		2500
		Miscellaneous Expense	617		3000
		Interest Expense	618		30000
		Supplies Expense	614		50000
		Insurance Expense	615		30000
		Depreciation Expense, Store Equip.	613		5000
		To transfer all expenses and other debit balances in the income statement column of the worksheet to Income Summary			
	31	Income Summary	313	1374500	
		A. Newner, Capital	311		1374500
		To transfer net income to Capital from Income Summary			
	31	A. Newner, Capital	311	860000	
		A. Newner, Withdrawals	312		860000
		Closes withdrawals to Capital account			

Notice that the adjustments to inventory are not included in these closing entries although some accountants do include them here.

Quiz Tip

Note in the first closing entry that the four account titles (now listed as debits) were found on the worksheet as credits in the Income Statement column.

ART'S CLOTHING COMPANY POST-CLOSING TRIAL BALANCE DECEMBER 31, 2016		
	Dr.	Cr.
Cash	12 9 2 0 00	
Petty Cash	1 0 0 00	
Accounts Receivable	14 5 0 0 00	
Merchandise Inventory	4 0 0 0 00	
Supplies	3 0 0 00	
Prepaid Insurance	6 0 0 00	
Store Equipment	4 0 0 0 00	
Accumulated Depreciation, Store Equipment		4 5 0 00
Accounts Payable		17 9 0 0 00
Income Tax Payable		1 2 4 0 00
CPP Payable		2 6 0 00
EI Payable		2 0 0 00
Accrued Salaries		6 0 0 00
Unearned Rent		4 0 0 00
Mortgage Payable		2 3 2 0 00
Art Newner, Capital		13 0 5 0 00
	36 4 2 0 00	36 4 2 0 00

LEARNING UNIT 13-2 REVIEW

AT THIS POINT you should be able to:

- Journalize and post adjusting entries for a merchandising company. (pp. 595–597)
- Explain the relationship of the worksheet to the adjusting and closing process. (p. 598)
- Complete the closing process for a merchandising company. (p. 598)
- Prepare a post-closing trial balance and explain why ending Merchandise Inventory is not a temporary account. (pp. 598–600)

Self-Review Quiz 13-2

(The form you need is on page 13-4 of the *Study Guide with Working Papers.*)

Using the worksheet from Self-Review Quiz 12-2 (page 566), journalize the closing entries.

Solution to Self-Review Quiz 13-2

Page 2

Date		Account Titles and Description	PR	Dr.	Cr.
		Closing			
Dec.	31	Sales		11040 00	
		Storage Fees Earned		516 00	
		Purchases Returns and Allowances		168 00	
		Purchases Discounts		102 00	
		Income Summary			11826 00
	31	Income Summary		10096 00	
		Sales Returns and Allowances			546 00
		Sales Discounts			216 00
		Purchases			5256 00
		Salaries Expense			2216 00
		Insurance Expense			1392 00
		Utilities Expense			96 00
		Plumbing Expense			214 00
		Rent Expense			100 00
		Depreciation Expense, Equipment			60 00
	31	Income Summary		1106 00	
		B. Ray, Capital			1106 00

LEARNING UNIT 13-3

Reversing Entries *(Optional Section)*

LO 4 Dealing with reversing entries

Reversing entries are not mandatory.

Now that we have completed the accounting cycle for Art's Clothing Company, let's look at an optional way of handling some adjusting entries—it is called making reversing entries. **Reversing entries** are general journal entries that are the opposite of adjusting entries. Reversing entries help reduce potential errors and simplify the record-keeping process. Let's look at how Art's bookkeeper handles the closing entry for salaries at the end of the year (see Figure 13-5).

Note that the permanent account, Accrued Salaries carries a $600 balance over to the new accounting period. ***Remember:*** The $600 was an expense of the prior year.

Figure 13-5 Closing Entries

Adjusting Journal Entry

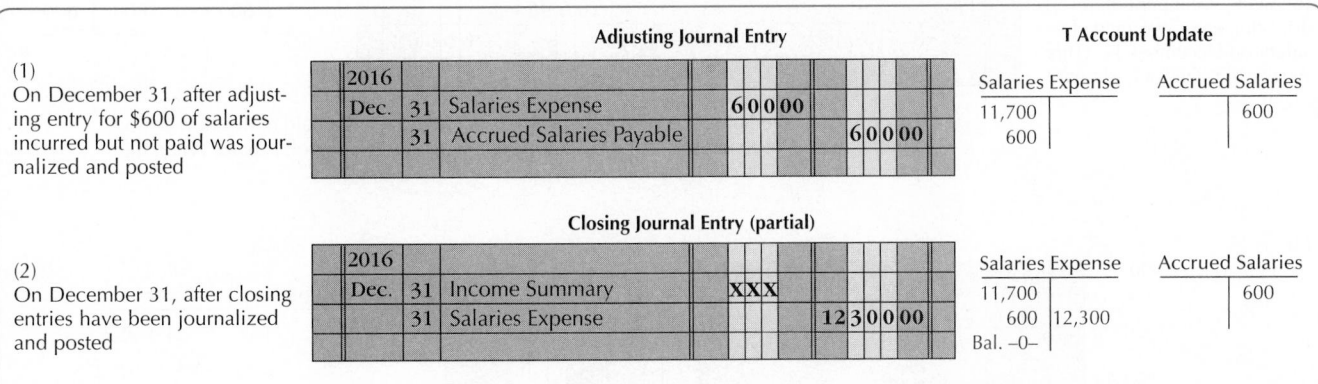

(1)
On December 31, after adjusting entry for $600 of salaries incurred but not paid was journalized and posted

2016					
Dec.	31	Salaries Expense		600 00	
	31	Accrued Salaries Payable			600 00

T Account Update

Salaries Expense		Accrued Salaries	
11,700			600
600			

Closing Journal Entry (partial)

(2)
On December 31, after closing entries have been journalized and posted

2016					
Dec.	31	Income Summary		XXX	
	31	Salaries Expense			12300 00

Salaries Expense		Accrued Salaries	
11,700			600
600	12,300		
Bal. –0–			

On January 8 of the new year (2017), the payroll to be paid is $2,000. If the optional reversing entry is *not* used, the bookkeeper makes the following journal entry:

2017				
Jan.	8	Accrued Salaries Payable	600 00	
	8	Salaries Expense	1 400 00	
	8	Cash		2 000 00

Salaries Expense	
1,400	

Accrued Salaries Payable	
600	600

Cash	
	2,000

To do this, the bookkeeper has to refer to the adjustment on December 31 to determine how much of the $2,000 of salary is indeed a new salary expense and what portion was shown in the old year although not paid then. It is easy to see how errors can result if the bookkeeper pays the payroll but forgets about the adjustment in the previous year. For this reason, reversing entries can help avoid errors.

Figure 13-6 shows the four steps the bookkeeper would take if reversing entries were used. Note that steps 1 and 2 are the same whether the accountant uses reversing entries or not.

Note that the balance of Salaries Expense is indeed only $1,400, the *true* expense in the new year. Reversing results in switching the adjustment on the first day of the new period. Also note that each of the accounts ends up with the same balance no matter which method is chosen. However, using a reversing entry for salaries allows the accountant to make the normal entry when it is time to pay salaries.

One should be careful with reversing entries since not all adjustments can be reversed. Here is a list of the types of adjustments that can be reversed:

1. When there is an increase in an asset account (no previous balance)
Example: Interest Receivable
Interest Income

Figure 13-6 Reversing Entries

(1)
On December 31, adjustment for salary was recorded.

Salaries Expense	
11,700	
600	

Accrued Salaries Payable	
	600

(2)
Closing entry on December 31

Salaries Expense	
11,700	12,300
600	

Accrued Salaries Payable	
	600

(3)
On January 1 (first day of the following fiscal period), reverse adjusting entry was made for salary on December 31. (This means "flipping" adjustment.)

2017				
Jan.	1	Accrued Salaries	600 00	
		Salaries Expense		600 00

Salaries Expense	
	600

Accrued Salaries Payable	
600	600

By doing this, the liability is reduced to zero. We know it will be paid in this new period, but the salaries expense has a credit balance of $600 until the payroll is paid. When the payroll of $2,000 is paid, the following happens:

(4)
Paid payroll, $2,000

2017				
Jan.	8	Salaries Expense	2 000 00	
		Cash		2 000 00

Salaries Expense	
2,000	600

Cash	
	2,000

2. When there is an increase in a liability account (no previous balance)

Example: Wages Expense
Accrued Wages

Except in the case of businesses in their first year of operation, accounts such as Accumulated Depreciation or Inventory will have previous balances and thus will *not* be reversed.

The increasing use of computers in accounting has changed the role and purpose of reversing entries somewhat. Most accounting software packages allow users to establish recurring entries that can be entered into the accounting records more or less automatically each month. Also, many accounting programs permit a given entry to be automatically reversed in the next period by simply checking a box on a screen.

In this chapter we illustrate reversing entries as being done manually. Students are encouraged to discover what features are present in the software they are using (or have access to) that modify the nature, purpose, and usefulness of reversing entries.

LEARNING UNIT 13-3 REVIEW

AT THIS POINT you should be able to:

- Explain the purpose of reversing entries. (p. 601)
- Complete a reversing entry. (p. 602)
- Explain when reversing entries can be used. (pp. 603–604)

Self-Review Quiz 13-3

(The form you need is on page 13-4 of the *Study Guide with Working Papers.*)

Explain which of the following situations could be reversed:

1.

Supplies Expense	
200	

Supplies	
800	200

2.

Wages Expense	
3,000	
200	

Accrued Wages	
	200

3.

Sales	
	4,000
	50

Unearned Sales	
50	200

Solution to Self-Review Quiz 13-3

1. Not reversed—Asset, Supplies is decreasing, not increasing.
2. Reversed—Liability is increasing and no previous balance exists.
3. Not reversed—Liability is decreasing and a previous balance exists.

Chapter Assignments

SUMMARY OF KEY POINTS

Learning Unit 13-1

1. The formal income statement can be prepared from the income statement columns of the worksheet.
2. There are no debit or credit columns on the formal income statement.
3. The cost of goods sold section has a figure for beginning inventory and a separate figure for ending inventory.
4. Operating expenses could be broken down into selling and administrative expenses.
5. The ending figure for capital is not found on the worksheet. It comes from the statement of owner's equity.
6. A classified balance sheet breaks assets down into current and capital. Liabilities are broken down into current and long-term.

Learning Unit 13-2

1. The information for journalizing adjusting and closing entries can be obtained from the worksheet.
2. In the closing process, all temporary accounts will be zero and the capital account is brought up to its new balance.
3. Inventory is not a temporary account. The ending inventory, along with other permanent accounts, will be listed in the post-closing trial balance.

Learning Unit 13-3

1. Reversing entries are optional and could aid in reducing potential errors and also simplify the record-keeping process.
2. The reversing entry "flips" the adjustment on the first day of the new fiscal period. Thus, the bookkeeper need not look back at what happened in the old year when recording the current year's transactions.
3. Reversing entries are used only if (a) assets are increasing and have no previous balance or (b) liabilities are increasing and have no previous balance.

KEY TERMS

Administrative expenses (general expenses) Expenses such as general office expenses that are incurred indirectly in the selling of goods (p. 590)

Capital assets Long-lived assets such as buildings or land that are used in the production or sale of goods or services (p. 591)

Classified balance sheet A balance sheet that categorizes assets as current or capital and groups liabilities as current or long-term (p. 591)

Current assets Assets that can be converted into cash or used within one year or the normal operating cycle of the business, whichever is longer (p. 591)

Current liabilities Obligations that will come due within one year or within the operating cycle, whichever is longer (p. 593)

Long-term liabilities Obligations that are not due or payable for a long time, usually for more than a year (p. 593)

Operating cycle Average time it takes to buy and sell merchandise and then collect accounts receivable (p. 591)

Other expenses Non-operating expenses that do not relate to the main operating activities of the business; they appear in a separate section on the income statement. One example given in the text is Interest Expense—interest owed on money borrowed by the company. (p. 590)

Other income This includes any revenue other than revenue from sales and appears in a separate section on the income statement. Examples would be Rental Income and Storage Fees. (p. 590)

Reversing entries Year-end optional bookkeeping technique in which certain adjusting entries are reversed or switched on the first day of the new accounting period so that transactions in the new period can be recorded without referring to prior adjusting entries (p. 601)

Selling expenses Expenses directly related to the sale of goods (p. 590)

QUICK REVIEW

The following Tips are from Learning Units 13-1 to 13-3. Answer the Assess Your Progress questions and use the How Did You Do? at the bottom of the page to see how well you know the material. The Quick Review provides tips before each Assess Your Progress to help you avoid common accounting errors.

LU 13-1 Preparing Financial Statements

Tips: The financial statements do not show debits or credits. The inside columns are for subtotalling. The totals on the financial statements will not always equal the same total amounts on the worksheet. Net Income will always be the same on the worksheet and income statement.

Purchases along with Beginning Merchandise Inventory will be added to Cost of Goods Sold, while Ending Inventory will be subtracted. Revenue less Cost of Goods Sold equals Gross Profit. To get Net Income from Operations, we subtract from Gross Profit the Operating Expenses.

Assess Your Progress

Answer true or false to the following statements:

1. Freight-In is subtracted from Net Purchases.
2. Sales on the formal income statement has a credit balance.
3. Rental Income is shown on the balance sheet.
4. Accumulated Depreciation is a contra-asset on the balance sheet.
5. Unearned Rent is a revenue on the income statement.

LU 13-2 Journalizing and Posting Adjusting and Closing Entries; Preparing the Post-Closing Trial Balance

Tips: All adjustments are taken from the adjustments column on the worksheet. Keep in mind that we adjust Inventory through Income Summary. We assume that old inventory is sold and is a cost and that the ending inventory is not a cost until it is sold. Another way to state this is to say that the cost of any inventory at year end is "held back" and becomes an expense next year. Income Summary is a temporary account and will not appear on the post-closing trial balance. The closing process transfers all temporary accounts through Income Summary except Withdrawals, which is closed directly to Owner's Equity (Capital).

Assess Your Progress

Answer true or false to the following statements:

1. Some temporary accounts will go on the post-closing trial balance.
2. Merchandise Inventory (ending) is listed as a debit on the post-closing trial balance.
3. Unearned Rent is a permanent account.
4. The Capital amount on the post-closing trial balance is listed before the closing process.
5. Purchases is listed on the post-closing trial balance.

LU 13-3 Reversing Entries *(Optional Section)*

Tips: Reversing entries is a way of handling some adjusting entries. By making a reversing entry in the new period, the accountant does not have to worry about the past adjustment and will make the normal entry when a transaction occurs. Reversing entries can be done when an increase occurs in an asset (no previous balance) or when an increase occurs in a liability account (no previous balance).

Assess Your Progress

Answer true or false to the following statements:

1. Reversing entries are required.
2. Interest Income and Interest Receivables may sometimes use a reversing entry.
3. Reversing entries are made in the old year, not the new.

4. Reversing entries for Salary will show true salary expense in the new year.
5. Regardless of whether reversing entries are used, the same balances will end up in each account.

How Did You Do? Answers to the Assess Your Progress Questions

LU 13-1

1. False—Freight-In is added to Net Purchases.
2. False—Sales on the formal income statement has no debits or credits.
3. False—Rental Income is shown on the income statement.
4. True.
5. False—Unearned Rent is a liability on the balance sheet.

LU 13-2

1. False—No temporary accounts will go on the post-closing trial balance.
2. True.
3. True.
4. False—The Capital account on the post-closing trial balance is listed after the closing process.
5. False—Purchases is a temporary account and will not appear on the post-closing trial balance.

LU 13-3

1. False—Reversing entries are optional.
2. True.
3. False—Reversing entries are made in the new year.
4. True.
5. True.

BLUEPRINT OF FINANCIAL STATEMENTS

(1) INCOME STATEMENT

Revenue				
Sales				$ XXX
Less: Sales Ret. and Allow.			$ XXX	
Sales Discounts			XXX	XXX
Net Sales				XXXX
Cost of Goods Sold				
Merchandise Inventory, 1/1/16			XXX	
Purchases		$XXX		
Less: Pur. Ret. and Allow.	$XXX			
Purchases Discounts	XXX	XXX		
Net Purchases		XXX		
Add: Freight-In		XXX		
Net Cost of Purchases			XXX	
Cost of Goods Available for Sale			XXXX	
Less: Merch. Inv., 12/31/16			XXX	
Cost of Goods Sold				XXXX
Gross Profit				XXXX
Operating Expenses				
~~			XXX	
~~			XXX	
~~			XXX	
Total Operating Expenses				XXX
Net Income from Operations				XXX
Other Income				
Rental Income			XXX	
Storage Fees Income			XXX	
Total Other Income				XXX
Other Expenses				
Interest Expense			XXX	XXX
Net Income				$ XXX

(2) STATEMENT OF OWNER'S EQUITY

Beginning Capital		$ XXX
Additional Investments		XXX
Total Investment		XXX
Net Income*	$ XXX	
Less: Withdrawals	XXX	
Increase (Decrease) in Capital		XXX
Ending Capital		$ XXX

*From the income statement.

(3) BALANCE SHEET

Assets			
Current Assets			
Cash		$ XXXX	
Accounts Receivable		XXXX	
Merchandise Inventory		XXXX	
Prepaid Insurance		XXX	
Total Current Assets			$ XXXX
Capital Assets			
Store Equipment	$ XXXX		
Less: Accumulated Depreciation	XXX	XXXX	
Office Equipment	XXXX		
Less: Accumulated Depreciation	XXX	XXXX	
Total Capital Assets			XXXX
Total Assets			$ XXXX
Liabilities			
Current Liabilities			
Accounts Payable		$ XXX	
Accrued Salaries		XXX	
Income Taxes Payable		XXX	
Unearned Revenue		XX	
Mortgage Payable (current portion)		XX	
Total Current Liabilities			$ XXX
Long-Term Liabilities			
Mortgage Payable			XXX
Total Liabilities			XXXX
Owner's Equity			
Capital*			XXXX
Total Liabilities and Owner's Equity			$ XXXX

*From statement of owner's equity.

QUESTIONS, CLASSROOM DEMONSTRATION EXERCISES, EXERCISES, AND PROBLEMS

Discussion Questions and Critical Thinking/Ethical Case

1. Which columns of the worksheet aid in the preparation of the income statement?
2. Explain the components of cost of goods sold.
3. Explain how operating expenses can be broken down into different categories.
4. What is the difference between current assets and capital assets?
5. What is an operating cycle?
6. Why journalize adjusting entries after the formal reports have been prepared?
7. Explain the steps in closing for a merchandising company.
8. Temporary accounts could appear on a post-closing trial balance. Agree or disagree with this statement.
9. What is the purpose of using reversing entries? Are they mandatory? When should they be used?
10. Janet Flynn, owner of Reel Company, plans to apply for a bank loan at Canadian National Bank. Since the company has a lot of debt on its balance sheet, Janet does not plan to show the loan officer the balance sheet. She plans only to take the income statement. Do you feel that this is a sound financial move by Janet? You make the call. Write down your specific recommendations to Janet.

Classroom Demonstration Exercises

(The forms you need are on page 13-5 of the *Study Guide with Working Papers.*)

Calculate Net Sales

The revenue section of the income statement
❶ (5 min)

1. From the following, calculate net sales:

Purchases	$100
Gross Sales	180
Sales Returns and Allowances	5
Sales Discounts	2
Operating Expenses	15

Calculate Cost of Goods Sold

The cost of goods sold section of the income statement
❶ (5 min)

2. From the following, calculate cost of goods sold:

Freight-In	$ 5
Beginning Inventory	20
Ending Inventory	15
Net Purchases	50

Calculate Gross Profit and Net Income

Gross profit and net income on the income statement
❶ (10 min)

3. Using Classroom Demonstration Exercises 1 and 2, calculate:

a. Gross profit

b. Net income or net loss

Classification of Accounts

Analyzing accounts for the balance sheet
❶ ❷ (15 min)

4. Indicate in which of the following four categories each of the 10 accounts listed below belongs:

a. Current assets

b. Capital assets

c. Current liabilities

d. Long-term liabilities

____ **1.** Merchandise Inventory

____ **2.** Unearned Rent

____ **3.** Prepaid Insurance

____ **4.** CPP Payable

____ **5.** Store Equipment

____ **6.** Mortgage Payable (Not Current)

____ **7.** Income Tax Payable

____ **8.** Accumulated Amortization

____ **9.** EI Payable

____ **10.** Petty Cash

Reversing Entries

Preparing a reversing entry
❹ (10 min)

5.

December 31, 2015

Salary Expense

Debit	Credit
900	1,200 closing
Adj. 300	

Accrued Salaries

Debit	Credit
	300 Adj.

a. On January 1, 2016, prepare a reversing entry. On January 8, 2016, journalize the entry to record the payment of salary expense, $900.

b. What will be the balance in Salary Expense on January 8 (after posting)?

Exercises

Set A

(The forms you need are on pages 13-6 and 13-7 of the *Study Guide with Working Papers.*)

Preparing cost of goods sold section
❶ (15 min)

13-1A. From the following account information, prepare an income statement cost of goods sold section in proper form: Freight-In, $300; Merchandise Inventory, 12/31/17, $9,000; Purchases Discounts, $900; Merchandise Inventory, 12/1/17, $4,000; Purchases, $58,000; Purchases Returns and Allowances, $1,100.

Categorizing and classifying account titles
❶ (10 min)

13-2A. Give the category, the classification, and the report(s) on which each of the following appears (e.g., **Cash**—asset, current asset, balance sheet):

a. Accrued Salaries
b. Accounts Payable
c. Mortgage Payable
d. Unearned Legal Fees
e. Income Tax Payable
f. Office Equipment
g. Land

Journalizing closing entries
❷ (10 min)

13-3A. From the following partial worksheet, journalize the closing entries of December 31 for A. Slow Co.

A. SLOW CO.
WORKSHEET
FOR THE YEAR ENDED DECEMBER 31, 2016

	Income Statement		Balance Sheet	
Account Titles	Dr.	Cr.	Dr.	Cr.
Cash			193 00	
Merchandise Inventory			450 00	
Prepaid Advertising			561 00	
Prepaid Insurance			30 00	
Office Equipment			1080 00	
Accum. Dep'n., Office Equip.				210 00
Accounts Payable				258 00
A. Slow, Capital				966 00
Income Summary	362 00	450 00		
Sales		5520 00		
Sales Returns and Allowances	223 00			
Sales Discounts	108 00			
Purchases	2628 00			
Purchases Returns and Allow.		34 00		
Purchases Discounts		51 00		
Salaries Expense	1083 00			
Insurance Expense	696 00			
Utilities Expense	48 00			
Plumbing Expense	57 00			
Advertising Expense	15 00			
Dep'n. Expense, Office Equip.	30 00			
Accrued Salaries				75 00
	5250 00	6055 00	2314 00	1509 00
Net Income	805 00			805 00
	6055 00	6055 00	2314 00	2314 00

Preparing a partially completed balance sheet ❶ **(15 min)**

13-4A. From the worksheet in Exercise 13-3A, prepare the assets section of a classified balance sheet.

Reversing entry ❷ ❹ **(30 min)**

13-5A. On December 31, 2016, $300 of salaries has been accrued. (Salaries before accrued amount totalled $26,000.) The next payroll to be paid will be on February 3, 2017, for $6,000. Do the following:

a. Journalize and post the adjusting entry (use T accounts).
b. Journalize and post the reversing entry on January 1.
c. Journalize and post the payment of the payroll. Cash has a balance of $15,000 before the payment of payroll on February 3, 2017.

Set B

(The forms you need are on pages 13-6 and 13-7 of the *Study Guide with Working Papers.*)

Preparing cost of goods sold section ❶ **(15 min)**

13-1B. From the following account information, prepare an income statement cost of goods sold section in proper form: Freight-In, $400; Merchandise Inventory, 12/31/17, $9,500; Purchases Discounts, $800; Merchandise Inventory, 12/1/17, $7,600; Purchases, $61,000; Purchases Returns and Allowances, $1,300.

Categorizing and classifying account titles ❶ **(10 min)**

13-2B. Give the category, the classification, and the report(s) on which each of the following appears (e.g., **Cash**—asset, current asset, balance sheet):

a. Mortgage Payable—current portion
b. Accounts Receivable
c. Rent Paid in Advance
d. Unearned Accounting Fees
e. CPP Payable
f. Vehicles
g. Accumulated Depreciation, Vehicles

Journalizing closing entries
❷ **(10 min)**

13-3B. From the following partial worksheet, journalize the closing entries of December 31 for A. Slow Co.

A. SLOW CO.
WORKSHEET
FOR THE YEAR ENDED DECEMBER 31, 2016

Account Titles	Income Statement Dr.	Income Statement Cr.	Balance Sheet Dr.	Balance Sheet Cr.
Cash			203 00	
Merchandise Inventory			650 00	
Prepaid Advertising			680 00	
Prepaid Insurance			360 00	
Office Equipment			1980 00	
Accum. Dep'n., Office Equip.				360 00
Accounts Payable				548 00
A. Slow, Capital				1366 00
Income Summary	575 00	650 00		
Sales		7720 00		
Sales Returns and Allowances	364 00			
Sales Discounts	277 00			
Purchases	3726 00			
Purchases Returns and Allow.		304 00		
Purchases Discounts		280 00		
Salaries Expense	1576 00			
Insurance Expense	578 00			
Utilities Expense	135 00			
Plumbing Expense	88 00			
Advertising Expense	56 00			
Dep'n. Expense, Office Equip.	65 00			
Accrued Salaries				85 00
	7440 00	8954 00	3873 00	2359 00
Net Income	1514 00			1514 00
	8954 00	8954 00	3873 00	3873 00

Preparing a partially completed balance sheet
❶ **(15 min)**

13-4B. From the worksheet in Exercise 13-3B, prepare the assets section of a classified balance sheet.

Reversing entry
❷ ❹ **(30 min)**

13-5B. On December 31, 2016, $700 of salaries have been accrued. (Salaries before accrued amount totalled $29,000.) The next payroll to be paid will be on February 3, 2017, for $7,500. Do the following:

a. Journalize and post the adjusting entry (use T accounts).
b. Journalize and post the reversing entry on January 1.
c. Journalize and post the payment of the payroll. Cash has a balance of $16,000 before the payment of payroll on February 3, 2017.

Group A Problems

(The forms you need are on pages 13-8 to 13-25 of the *Study Guide with Working Papers.*)

Preparing an income statement from a worksheet
❶ (40 min)

13A-1. Prepare a formal income statement from the following partial worksheet for Porter's Pants Co. of Hantsport.

PORTER'S PANTS CO.
PARTIAL WORKSHEET
FOR THE YEAR ENDED DECEMBER 31, 2015

Account Titles	Income Statement Dr.	Income Statement Cr.
Income Summary	370 00	260 00
Sales		2800 00
Sales Returns and Allow.	119 00	
Sales Discounts	64 00	
Purchases	870 00	
Purchases Returns and Allow.		167 00
Purchases Discounts		129 00
Freight-In	102 00	
Salaries Expense	300 00	
Insurance Expense	200 00	
Advertising Expense	155 00	
Rental Income		200 00
Rent Expense	215 00	
Depreciation Exp., Store Equip.	200 00	
Accrued Salaries		
	2595 00	3556 00
Net Income	961 00	
	3556 00	3556 00

Check Figure
Net Income from operations $761

Check Figure
(for P13A-2)Total Assets $18,340

Completing the worksheet; preparing financial reports; journalizing adjusting and closing entries
❶ ❷ (90 min)

13A-2. Prepare a statement of owner's equity and a classified balance sheet from the partial worksheet for James Company of Penticton (page 614). ***Note:*** Of the Mortgage Payable, $200 is due within one year.

13A-3.
a. Complete the partial worksheet for Jay's Supplies of Sarnia (p. 615).
b. Prepare an income statement, a statement of owner's equity, and a classified balance sheet. ***Note:*** The amount of the mortgage due the first year is $800.
c. Journalize the adjusting and closing entries.

Check Figure (for p13A-3)
Net Income $4,340

Comprehensive problem: preparing the worksheet; preparing financial reports; journalizing and posting adjusting and closing entries; preparing a post-closing trial balance; journalizing a reversing entry
❶ ❷ ❸ ❹ (150 min)

13A-4. Using the ledger balances and additional data shown on the next two pages, do the following for Callahan Lumber of Hinton for the year ended December 31, 2016:

a. Prepare the worksheet.
b. Prepare the income statement, statement of owner's equity, and balance sheet.
c. Journalize and post adjusting and closing entries. (Be sure to put beginning balances in the ledger first.)
d. Prepare a post-closing trial balance.
e. Journalize the reversing entry for wages.

Check Figure
Net Income $4,841

Preparing statement of owner's equity and a classified balance sheet from a worksheet
❶ (40 min)

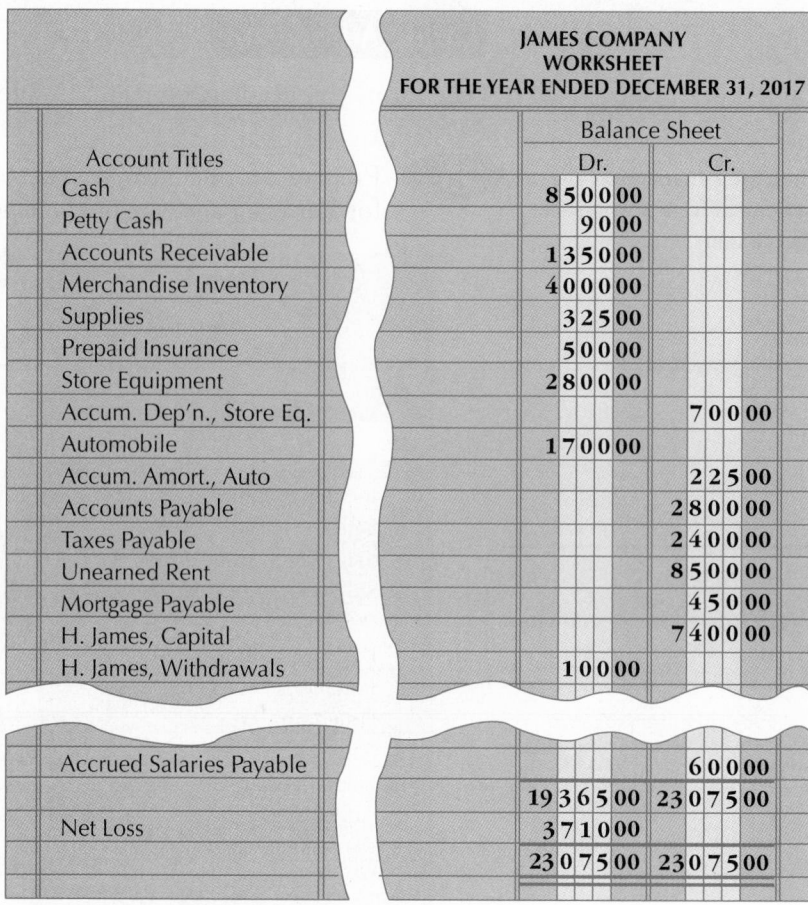

JAMES COMPANY
WORKSHEET
FOR THE YEAR ENDED DECEMBER 31, 2017

Account Titles	Balance Sheet Dr.	Balance Sheet Cr.
Cash	8500 00	
Petty Cash	90 00	
Accounts Receivable	1350 00	
Merchandise Inventory	4000 00	
Supplies	325 00	
Prepaid Insurance	500 00	
Store Equipment	2800 00	
Accum. Dep'n., Store Eq.		700 00
Automobile	1700 00	
Accum. Amort., Auto		225 00
Accounts Payable		2800 00
Taxes Payable		2400 00
Unearned Rent		8500 00
Mortgage Payable		450 00
H. James, Capital		7400 00
H. James, Withdrawals	100 00	
Accrued Salaries Payable		600 00
	19365 00	23075 00
Net Loss	3710 00	
	23075 00	23075 00

Additional Data (for Problem 13A-4)

Account No.		
110	Cash	$ 1,680
111	Accounts Receivable	960
112	Merchandise Inventory	4,550
113	Lumber Supplies	269
114	Prepaid Insurance	218
121	Lumber Equipment	3,000
122	Accumulated Depreciation, Lumber Equipment	490
220	Accounts Payable	1,160
221	Accrued Wages	—
330	J. Callahan, Capital	7,352
331	J. Callahan, Withdrawals	3,000
332	Income Summary	—
440	Sales	22,800
441	Sales Returns and Allowances	200
550	Purchases	14,800
551	Purchases Discounts	285
552	Purchases Returns and Allowances	300
660	Wages Expense	2,480
661	Advertising Expense	400
662	Rent Expense	830
663	Amortization Expense, Lumber Equipment	—
664	Lumber Supplies Expense	—
665	Insurance Expense	—

JAY'S SUPPLIES
WORKSHEET
FOR THE YEAR ENDED DECEMBER 31, 2016

Account Titles	Trial Balance Dr.	Trial Balance Cr.	Adjustments Dr.	Adjustments Cr.	
Cash	2000 00				
Accounts Receivable	3000 00				
Merchandise Inventory	11000 00		(B) 10400 00	11000 00	(A)
Prepaid Insurance	1880 00			500 00	(E)
Equipment	3400 00				
Accum. Dep'n., Equipment		1080 00		400 00	(D)
Accounts Payable		5080 00			
Unearned Training Fees		2120 00	(C) 320 00		
Mortgage Payable		1200 00			
P. Jay, Capital		10560 00			
P. Jay, Withdrawals	4280 00				
Income Summary			(A) 11000 00	10400 00	(B)
Sales		95800 00			
Sales Returns and Allowances	3200 00				
Sales Discounts	2600 00				
Purchases	63600 00				
Purchases Returns and Allow.		13600 00			
Purchases Discounts		3200 00			
Freight-In	2680 00				
Advertising Expense	11400 00				
Rent Expense	10000 00				
Salaries Expense	13600 00				
	132640 00	132640 00			
Training Fees Earned				320 00	(C)
Dep'n. Exp., Equipment			(D) 400 00		
Insurance Expense			(E) 500 00		
			22620 00	22620 00	

Additional Data (for Problem 13A-4)

a. and **b.** Merchandise inventory, December 31	$5,420
c. Lumber supplies on hand, December 31	110
d. Insurance expired	120
e. Depreciation for the year	300
f. Accrued wages on December 31	125

Group B Problems

(The forms you need are on pages 13-8 to 13-25 of the *Study Guide with Working Papers.*)

Preparing an income statement from a worksheet
1 (40 min)

Check Figure

Net Income from operations $845

13B-1. From the partial worksheet shown below, prepare a formal income statement.

PORTER'S PANTS CO.
PARTIAL WORKSHEET
FOR THE YEAR ENDED DECEMBER 31, 2015

Account Titles	Income Statement Dr.	Income Statement Cr.
Income Summary	300 00	295 00
Sales		4100 00
Sales Returns and Allowances	145 00	
Sales Discounts	175 00	
Purchases	2000 00	
Purchases Returns and Allowances		175 00
Purchases Discounts		85 00
Freight-In	50 00	
Salaries Expense	360 00	
Insurance Expense	275 00	
Advertising Expense	165 00	
Rental Income		230 00
Rent Expense	225 00	
Depreciation Exp., Store Equipment	115 00	
Accrued Salaries		
	3810 00	4885 00
Net Income	1075 00	
	4885 00	4885 00

Preparing a statement of owner's equity and a classified balance sheet from a worksheet
1 (40 min)

Check Figure

Total Assets $28,294

13B-2. From the partial worksheet for James Company of Penticton shown on page 617, complete:

a. Statement of owner's equity

b. Classified balance sheet

Note: Of the Mortgage Payable, $3,000 is due within one year.

Completing the worksheet; preparing financial reports; journalizing adjusting and closing entries
1 2 (90 min)

Check Figure

Net Loss $12,050

13B-3. Using the information provided on the partial worksheet for Jay's Supplies of Sarnia shown on page 618, your task is to:

a. Complete the worksheet.

b. Prepare the income statement, statement of owner's equity, and classified balance sheet. The amount of the mortgage due the first year is $800.

c. Journalize the adjusting and closing entries.

JAMES COMPANY
WORKSHEET
FOR THE YEAR ENDED DECEMBER 31, 2017

Account Titles	Balance Sheet Dr.	Balance Sheet Cr.
Cash	2500 00	
Petty Cash	50 00	
Accounts Receivable	1300 00	
Merchandise Inventory	4250 00	
Supplies	344 00	
Prepaid Insurance	600 00	
Store Equipment	18000 00	
Accum. Dep'n., Store Eq.		750 00
Automobile	2500 00	
Accum. Amort., Auto		500 00
Accounts Payable		3450 00
Taxes Payable		2100 00
Unearned Rent		11000 00
Mortgage Payable		8000 00
H. James, Capital		10500 00
H. James, Withdrawals	4000 00	
Accrued Salaries Payable		100 00
	33544 00	36400 00
Net Loss	2856 00	
	36400 00	36400 00

Comprehensive problem: preparing the worksheet; preparing financial reports, journalizing and posting adjusting and closing entries; preparing a post-closing trial balance; journalizing reversing entry
❶ ❷ ❸ ❹ (150 min)

Check Figure

Net Income $3,480

13B-4. From the following ledger balances and additional data on page 602, do the following for Callahan Lumber of Hinton:

a. Prepare the worksheet.

b. Prepare the income statement, statement of owner's equity, and balance sheet.

c. Journalize and post adjusting and closing entries. (Be sure to put beginning balances in the ledger first.)

d. Prepare a post-closing trial balance.

e. Journalize the reversing entry for wages.

Account No.		
110	Cash	$ 1,140
111	Accounts Receivable	1,270
112	Merchandise Inventory	5,600
113	Lumber Supplies	260
114	Prepaid Insurance	117
121	Lumber Equipment	2,600
122	Accumulated Depreciation, Lumber Equipment	340
220	Accounts Payable	1,330
221	Accrued Wages	—
330	J. Callahan, Capital	7,562
331	J. Callahan, Withdrawals	3,500
332	Income Summary	—
440	Sales	23,000
441	Sales Returns and Allowances	400
550	Purchases	14,700

JAY'S SUPPLIES
WORKSHEET
FOR THE YEAR ENDED DECEMBER 31, 2016

Account Titles	Trial Balance Dr.	Trial Balance Cr.	Adjustments Dr.	Adjustments Cr.
Cash	3000 00			
Accounts Receivable	3000 00			
Merchandise Inventory	11700 00		(B) 8000 00	11700 00 (A)
Prepaid Insurance	1000 00			350 00 (E)
Equipment	5000 00			
Accum. Dep'n., Equipment		1900 00		500 00 (D)
Accounts Payable		2100 00		
Unearned Training Fees		1450 00	(C) 400 00	
Mortgage Payable		2400 00		
P. Jay, Capital		27750 00		
P. Jay, Withdrawals	4000 00			
Income Summary			(A) 11700 00	8000 00 (B)
Sales		100800 00		
Sales Returns and Allowances	4100 00			
Sales Discounts	2800 00			
Purchases	70000 00			
Purchases Returns and Allow.		2000 00		
Purchases Discounts		1400 00		
Freight-In	2700 00			
Advertising Expense	8000 00			
Rent Expense	8500 00			
Salaries Expense	16000 00			
	139800 00	139800 00		
Training Fees Earned				400 00 (C)
Depreciation Exp., Equipment			(D) 500 00	
Insurance Expense			(E) 350 00	
			20950 00	20950 00

Additional Data (for Problem 13B-4)

551	Purchases Discounts	$ 440
552	Purchases Returns and Allowances	545
660	Wages Expense	2,390
661	Advertising Expense	400
662	Rent Expense	840
663	Depreciation Expense, Lumber Equipment	—
664	Lumber Supplies Expense	—
665	Insurance Expense	—

Additional Data

a. and **b.** Merchandise inventory, December 31	$ 4,700
c. Lumber supplies on hand, December 31	80
d. Insurance expired	70
e. Depreciation for the year	460
f. Accrued wages on December 31	165

Group C Problems

(The forms you need are on pages 13-26 to 13-43 of the *Study Guide with Working Papers.*)

Preparing an income statement from a worksheet
❶ (40 min)

> *Check Figure*
>
> **Net Income from Operations $6,278.13**

13C-1. From the partial worksheet shown below, prepare a formal income statement for Kate's Pie and Kite Shop of Yarmouth:

KATE'S PIE AND KITE SHOP
PARTIAL WORKSHEET
FOR THE YEAR ENDED SEPTEMBER 30, 2015

Account Titles	Income Statement Dr.	Income Statement Cr.
Income Summary	425782	547726
Sales		5356825
Sales Returns and Allowances	83450	
Sales Discounts	34475	
Purchases	2145834	
Purchases Returns and Allowances		55830
Purchases Discounts		23876
Freight-In	47158	
Rental Income		180000
Advertising Expense	135250	
Depreciation Expense, Equipment	87500	
Cleaning Expense	240000	
Insurance Expenses	36875	
Rent Expense	720000	
Salaries Expense	1145860	
Utilities Expense	254260	
	5356444	6164257
Net Income	807813	
	6164257	6164257

Preparing a statement of owner's equity and a classified balance sheet from a worksheet
❶ (40 min)

> *Check Figure*
>
> **Total Assets $84,105.35**

13C-2. Using the information provided on the partial worksheet of Toronto's Castell Ceramics Co. shown on page 620, complete:

a. Statement of owner's equity

b. Classified balance sheet

Note: Of the Mortgage Payable, $1,800 is due within one year.

Completing the worksheet; preparing financial reports; journalizing adjusting and closing entries
❶ ❷ (90 min)

> *Check Figure*
>
> **Net Income $15,193.86**

13C-3. From the partial worksheet of Mikolaski Modern Design Company of Brandon, shown on page 621, your task is to:

a. Complete the worksheet.

b. Prepare the income statement, statement of owner's equity, and a classified balance sheet. The amount of the mortgage due the first year is $3,600.

c. Journalize the adjusting and closing entries.

CASTELL CERAMICS CO. PARTIAL WORKSHEET FOR THE YEAR ENDED AUGUST 31, 2017		
	Balance Sheet	
Account Titles	Dr.	Cr.
Petty Cash	75.00	
Cash	11,538.62	
Accounts Receivable	18,976.30	
Merchandise Inventory	22,766.28	
Supplies on Hand	1,268.75	
Prepaid Insurance	875.40	
Prepaid GST	2,137.64	
Cutting Equipment	18,760.00	
Accumulated Depreciation, Cutting Equipment		7,250.00
Delivery Van	21,875.00	
Accumulated Depreciation, Delivery Van		4,780.00
Accounts Payable		27,648.36
GST Collected		2,874.62
Unearned Rent		1,750.00
Chattel Mortgage Payable, Van		15,742.37
B. Castell, Capital		42,675.98
B. Castell, Withdrawals	14,670.00	
Accrued Salaries		860.00
Net Income		9,361.66
	112,942.99	112,942.99

Comprehensive problem: preparing the worksheet; preparing financial reports; journalizing and posting adjusting and closing entries; preparing a post-closing trial balance; journalizing reversing entry
❶ ❷ ❸ ❹ (180 min)

> ***Check Figure***
>
> **Net Income $3,868**

13C-4. Using the ledger balances and additional data shown below and on the next two pages, do the following for Brennan Sales Co. as of December 31, 2015:

a. Prepare the worksheet.

b. Prepare the income statement, statement of owner's equity, and balance sheet.

c. Journalize and post adjusting and closing entries. (Be sure to put beginning balances in the ledger first.)

d. Prepare a post-closing trial balance.

e. Journalize the reversing entry for wages.

Account No.		
1100	Cash	$ 720
1110	Accounts Receivable	1,620
1120	Merchandise Inventory	5,910
1130	Supplies	430
1140	Prepaid Insurance	238
1150	Prepaid GST	647
1210	Equipment	8,500
1220	Accumulated Depreciation, Equipment	1,640

MIKOLASKI MODERN DESIGN COMPANY
WORKSHEET
FOR THE YEAR ENDED NOVEMBER 30, 2016

Account Titles	Trial Balance Dr.	Trial Balance Cr.	Adjustments Dr.	Adjustments Cr.
Cash in Bank	3465 78			
Petty Cash	50 00			
Accounts Receivable	11575 20			
Merchandise Inventory	16479 22		(B)25672 44	16479 22 (A)
Prepaid Insurance	765 85			257 75 (E)
Prepaid GST	1653 45			
Equipment	21575 00			
Accum. Depreciation, Equipment		14762 40		1357 60 (D)
Building	28700 00			
Accum. Depreciation, Building		21653 70		647 82 (D)
Accounts Payable		8400 00		
Mortgage Payable		11446 52		
Unearned Rent		2400 00	(C) 800 00	
GST Collected		2167 85		
L. Mikolaski, Capital		32420 22		
L. Mikolaski, Withdrawals	16450 00			
Income Summary			(A) 16479 22	25672 44 (B)
Sales		77327 56		
Sales Discounts and Allowances	358 92			
Purchases	42649 04			
Purchases Returns and Allowances		455 72		
Purchases Discounts		576 22		
Freight-In	632 88			
Advertising Expense	1245 00			
Cleaning Expense	2605 60			
Repair Expense	876 20			
Salaries Expense	21575 60			
Utilities Expense	952 45			
	171610 19	171610 19		
Rental Income Earned				800 00 (C)
Dep'n. Exp., on Equip. and Building			(D) 2005 42	
Insurance Expense			(E) 257 75	
			45214 83	45214 83

Additional Data (for Problem 13C-4)

2200	Accounts Payable	$ 1,660
2210	Accrued Wages	—
2220	GST Collected	897
3300	W. Brennan, Capital	12,012
3310	W. Brennan, Withdrawals	4,700
3320	Income Summary	—
4400	Sales	31,000
4410	Sales Returns and Allowances	630
5500	Purchases	18,400
5510	Purchases Discounts	730
5520	Purchases Returns and Allowances	276
6600	Wages Expense	4,530
6610	Advertising Expense	690

Additional Data (for Problem 13C-4)

6620	Rent Expense	$1,200
6630	Depreciation Expense, Equipment	—
6640	Supplies Expense	—
6650	Insurance Expense	—

a. and **b.** Merchandise inventory, December 31	$ 4,875
c. Supplies on hand, December 31	$ 190
d. Insurance expired	$ 68
e. Amortization for the year	$ 750
f. Accrued wages on December 31	$ 395
g. Advertising bill received—due next year (add Prepaid GST of $10)	$ 200

On-the-Job Training

(The forms you need are on pages 13-44 to 13-45 of the *Study Guide with Working Papers.*)

Reconstructing an income statement
❶ ❷ (60 min)

T-1. Chan Company recently had most of its records destroyed in a fire. The information for 2017 was discovered by the bookkeeper.

Beg. Inv. $1,400
End. Inv. 1,000

CHAN COMPANY
GENERAL JOURNAL

Page 2

Date		Account Titles and Description	PR	Dr.	Cr.
2017					
Dec.	31	Income Summary	312	3630 00	
		Sales Returns and Allowances	420		140 00
		Sales Discounts	430		30 00
		Purchases	500		2400 00
		Delivery Expense	600		90 00
		Salaries Expense	610		840 00
		Rent Expense	620		30 00
		Office Supplies Expense	630		50 00
		Advertising Expense	640		10 00
		Depreciation Exp., Store Equipment	650		40 00
	31	Sales	410	5542 00	
		Purchases Discounts	510	120 00	
		Purchases Returns and Allowances	520	100 00	
		Income Summary	312		5762 00
	31	Income Summary	312	1732 00	
		J. Chan, Capital	310		1732 00

Assist the bookkeeper in reconstructing an income statement for 2017.

Preparing a classified balance sheet
❶ ❷ (60 min)

T-2. Hope Lang, a junior accountant, has the December 31, 2015, trial balance of Gregot Company sitting on her desk. Attached is a memo from her supervisor requesting that a classified balance sheet be prepared. Hope gathers the following data:

a. A physical inventory at December 31 showed $70,000 on hand.

b. The cost of office supplies on hand was $600.

c. Insurance unexpired was $750.

d. Depreciation (straight-line) is based on a 25-year life.

Using the following trial balance of Gregot Co., assist Hope with this project. ***Hint:*** Ending figure for capital is $105,850.

GREGOT COMPANY
TRIAL BALANCE
DECEMBER 31, 2015

Account Titles and Description	Dr.	Cr.
Cash	11000 00	
Accounts Receivable	38000 00	
Inventory, January 1	80000 00	
Prepaid Insurance	2000 00	
Office Supplies	1000 00	
Land	17500 00	
Building	50000 00	
Accumulated Depreciation, Building		10000 00
Notes Payable		40000 00
Accounts Payable		30000 00
G. Gregot, Capital		98400 00
G. Gregot, Withdrawals	13000 00	
Income Summary	—	
Retail Sales		32900 00
Sales Returns and Allowances	21000 00	—
Sales Discounts	8000 00	
Purchases	215500 00	
Purchases Returns and Allowances		11600 00
Purchases Discounts		4000 00
Transportation-In	5000 00	
Advertising Expense	2500 00	
Wage Expense	55000 00	
Utilities Expense	3500 00	
	523000 00	523000 00

CONTINUING PROBLEM

Journalizing and posting adjusting entries; preparing the financial statements from a worksheet
❶ ❷ (60 min)

Using the worksheet in Chapter 12 for Precision Computer Centre, journalize and post the adjusting entries and prepare the financial statements.

(See pages 13-46 to 13-56 in your *Study Guide with Working Papers*.)

MINI PRACTICE SET

Estimated time 5 hours

The Corner Dress Shop

This Mini Practice Set will help you review all the key concepts of the accounting cycle for a merchandising company along with the integration of payroll.

Betty Loeb took over the business now known as The Corner Dress Shop on January 1, 2016. Betty purchased the business name and all assets except cash from her Aunt Marion, who had run it for over 10 years. Certain liabilities were assumed by Betty's new business as part of the deal.

You are the bookkeeper of The Corner Dress Shop and have gathered the following information. It is your task to complete the accounting cycle for March 2016.

THE CORNER DRESS SHOP
TRIAL BALANCE
FEBRUARY 28, 2016

Account Titles and Description	Dr.	Cr.
Cash	30775 31	
Petty Cash	50 00	
Accounts Receivable	8291 85	
Office Supplies	624 30	
Prepaid Rent	1800 00	
Prepaid Insurance	1000 00	
GST Prepaid	436 34	
Inventory	8309 00	
Computer and Office Equipment	5000 00	
Acc. Dep'n—Computer & Office Equipment		261 12
Computer Software	739 00	
Acc. Dep'n—Computer Software		61 58
Delivery Truck	12000 00	
Acc. Dep'n—Delivery Truck		340 00
Accounts Payable		4788 99
Income Taxes Payable		1108 82
EI Payable		408 79
CPP Payable		810 30
Medical Plan Payable		112 00
Charitable Donations Payable		180 00
GST Collected		2313 65
Rent Received in Advance		600 00
Betty Loeb, Capital		48078 80
Betty Loeb, Withdrawals	7300 00	
Sales		59865 05
Cost of Goods Sold	19073 38	
Wages Expense	18120 00	
CPP Expense	810 30	
EI Expense	476 92	
Insurance Expense	200 00	
Rent Expense	1800 00	
Dep'n Expense—Computer & Office Equipment	261 12	
Dep'n Expense—Software	61 58	
Dep'n Expense—Delivery Truck	340 00	
Accounting Expense	1460 00	
	118929 10	118929 10

Balances in subsidiary ledgers as of February 28:

*Accounts Receivable**		*Accounts Payable**	
Ronald Co.	$5,538.00	Blew Co.	$2,543.77
Sally's Store	2,753.85	Dresses by Shelley	1,510.22
		Silk Magic	735.00

*Includes 5% GST.

Payroll is paid monthly and employee claim codes are unchanged.

The payroll register for January and February is provided on page 627. In March, salaries are as follows (all deductions are the same unless indicated):

Mel Case	$ 1,960	New income tax = $58.24 ($58.24 + 0.00)
Jane Holl	2,900	For CPP and EI use 0.0495 and 0.0188
Jackie Moore	4,300	respectively (remember no CPP on amounts less than $291.67 in a month).

Required

(The forms you need are on pages 13-59 to 13-81 of the *Study Guide with Working Papers.*)

a. Set up a general ledger, accounts receivable ledger, accounts payable ledger, auxiliary petty cash record, and payroll register. (Before beginning, be sure to update the ledger accounts on the basis of information given in the trial balance for February 28.)

b. Journalize all transactions during March. Your instructor may ask you to use an inventory ledger and the perpetual method. The practice set can be completed using either method of accounting for inventory. If no specific method is indicated, use the periodic method and change the name of the "Cost of Goods Sold" account to "Purchases."

c. Prepare the payroll register for March.

d. Update the accounts payable and accounts receivable subsidiary ledgers for March.

e. Post to the general ledger.

f. Prepare a trial balance on a worksheet and complete the worksheet as of March 31, 2016.

g. Prepare an income statement, statement of owner's equity, and classified balance sheet.

h. Journalize the adjusting and closing entries.

i. Post the adjusting and closing entries to the ledger.

j. Prepare a post-closing trial balance.

The chart of accounts for The Corner Dress Shop is provided on the next page.:

Chart of Accounts

Assets		Liabilities	
1110	Cash	2100	Accounts Payable
1115	Petty Cash	2200	Accrued Wages
1120	Accounts Receivable	2330	Income Taxes Payable
1135	Office Supplies	2335	EI Payable
1140	Prepaid Rent	2340	CPP Payable
1145	Prepaid Insurance	2350	Medical Plan Payable
1150	GST Prepaid	2360	Charitable Donations Payable
1210	Inventory	2400	GST Collected
1330	Computer and Office Equipment	2500	Rent Received in Advance
1335	Acc. Dep'n.—Computer & Office Equipment		
1340	Computer Software		
1345	Acc. Dep'n.—Computer Software		
1350	Delivery Truck		
1355	Acc. Dep'n.—Delivery Truck		
Owner's Equity		**Revenue**	
3110	Betty Loeb, Capital	4110	Sales
3120	Betty Loeb, Withdrawals	4140	Sales Discounts
		4150	Sales Returns & Allowances
Cost of Goods Sold		**Expenses**	
5040	Cost of Goods Sold	5400	Wages Expense
5140	Purchases Discounts	5430	EI Expense
5150	Purchases Returns and Allowances	5440	CPP Expense
		5500	Postage Expense
		5510	Insurance Expense
		5520	Cleaning Expense
		5530	Rent Expense
		5540	Delivery Expense
		5550	Dep'n. Expense—Computer and Office Equipment
		5560	Dep'n. Expense—Software
		5570	Dep'n. Expense—Delivery Truck
		5590	Accounting Expense
		5595	Miscellaneous Expense

Transactions

2016

Mar. 1 Paid rent cheque No. 121 to Smithstone Realty, $900.00 + GST of 5%.

4 Purchased merchandise from Jones Company, invoice No. JC 59087:
CT-01 50 @ $10 each + GST
CY-01 50 @ $10 each + GST

4 Paid $6 from petty cash fund for doughnuts, voucher No. 01 (miscellaneous expense, NO GST).

4 Sold merchandise on account to Morris Company, invoice No. CD 1081:
PO-01 5 @ $39.99 each + GST
PO-02 5 @ $39.99 each + GST
SK-01 6 @ $89 each + GST

5 Paid Dresses by Shelley $1,510.22 (invoice No. DS 12895), cheque No. 122.

PAYROLL JOURNAL—JANUARY

Employee	Federal Claim	Provincial Claim	Gross Earnings	Cumulative CPP	IT—Fed	IT—Prov	IT—Total
Mel Case	4	4	1860.00	–	44.27	0.00	44.27
Jane Holl	1	1	2900.00	–	255.52	125.03	380.55
Jackie Moore	3	3	4300.00	–	459.84	224.16	684.00
							1108.82
			9060.00				

JANUARY (continued)

Deductions				Net Pay	Cheque No.
CPP	EI	Health	Charitable		
77.63	34.97	28.00	20.00	1655.13	
129.11	54.52	42.00	30.00	2263.82	
198.41	80.84	42.00	40.00	3254.75	
405.15	170.33	112.00	90.00	7173.70	

PAYROLL JOURNAL—FEBRUARY

Employee	Federal Claim	Provincial Claim	Gross Earnings	Cumulative CPP	IT—Fed	IT—Prov	IT—Total
Mel Case	4	4	1860.00	–	44.27	0.00	44.27
Jane Holl	1	1	2900.00	–	255.52	125.03	380.55
Jackie Moore	3	3	4300.00	–	459.84	224.16	684.00
							1108.82
			9060.00				

FEBRUARY (continued)

Deductions				Net Pay	Cheque No.
CPP	EI	Health	Charitable		
77.63	34.97	28.00	20.00	1655.13	
129.11	54.52	42.00	30.00	2263.82	
198.41	80.84	42.00	40.00	3254.75	
405.15	170.33	112.00	90.00	7173.70	

Mar. 5 Received payment from Ronald Company, $5,538.00 (invoice No. CD 1078).

7 Paid $12.60 from petty cash fund for postage, voucher No. 02.

8 Paid Blew Company $2,543.77, cheque No. 123 (invoice No. BC 1795).

8 Received payment from Sally's Store (invoice No. CD 1076), $2,753.85.

11 Paid $5 for delivery expense from petty cash fund, voucher No. 03.

12 Received amount due from Morris Company, less 2% discount.

Mar.	12	Purchased from Dresses by Shelley, invoice No. DS 12947: CD-01 75 @ $19 each + GST CD-02 75 @ $19 each + GST
	12	Paid cleaning service $300 + GST, cheque No. 124 (cheque was issued to Cleaners Inc.).
	13	Purchased from Blew Company, invoice No. BC 1896: DI-01 20 @ $48 each + GST DS-01 20 @ $80 each + GST PO-01 75 @ $12.50 each + GST PO-02 75 @ $12.50 each + GST
	15	Sold to Bing Company, invoice No. CD 1082: SD-01 5 @ $29.99 each + GST
	15	Paid CRA for income tax, CPP, and EI for February, cheque No. 125. (***Note:*** Record as a compound entry in the cash payments journal.)
	15	Paid CRA for GST due (net) end of February, cheque No. 126.*
	15	Paid the Government of Ontario for medical premiums due for the month of February, cheque No. 127.
	18	Cash sales, summarized on invoice No. CD 1083: CD-01 30 @ $59.95 each + GST CD-02 45 @ $59.95 each + GST CT-01 15 @ $30 each + GST CY-01 21 @ $30 each + GST DI-01 10 @ $150 each + GST DS-01 6 @ $250 each + GST SK-01 4 @ $89 each + GST WD-01 5 @ $750 each + GST
	18	Paid Jones Company amount owed (invoice No. JC 59087), cheque No. 128.
	19	Bing Company returns dresses purchased on invoice No. CD 1082. Credit memo No. 001 was issued.
	19	Paid Dresses by Shelley amount due, less 2% discount (invoice No. DS 12947), cheque No. 129.
	20	Betty Loeb withdrew $1,000 for her personal use, cheque No. 130.
	21	Sold to Sally's Store, invoice No. CD 1084: DI-01 10 @ $150 each + GST CD-01 10 @ $59.95 each + GST
	26	Purchased from Dresses by Shelley, invoice No. DS 13062: CD-01 50 @ $19 each + GST CD-02 50 @ $19 each + GST
	28	Paid $10 from the petty cash fund for first aid emergency, voucher No. 04.
	29	Recorded and paid employees, cheques No. 131, No. 132, and No. 133 (cash payments journal).
	29	Issued cheque to Jane Holl for replenishment of petty cash fund, cheque No. 134 (compound entry in cash payments journal).

*Two steps are usually needed here. Step 1 (done in the G/L) is to transfer the debit balance in the GST Prepaid account to the GST Collected liability account. The net credit balance, then, is reduced by posting the cheque (recorded in the cash payments journal) that pays this net amount (step 2).

Additional Data

a. and **b.** Ending merchandise inventory is $13,424.

c. Rental income earned, $300 (one month's rent from subletting. Received in advance in February).

d. Depreciation (straight-line):

Delivery truck	Residual value = $1,800, expected life of 5 years
Computer	Residual value = $ 300, expected life of 3 years
Computer Software	Residual value = $ 0, expected life of 2 years

e. One month of insurance has expired.

Appendix 12

A Worksheet for Art's Clothing Company Using a Perpetual Inventory System

What's New:

The Merchandise Inventory account does not need to be adjusted. The $4,000 figure for merchandise is the up-to-date balance in the account. The difference between beginning inventory and ending inventory will be part of a new account called *Cost of Goods Sold* on the worksheet.

How the $65,910 of Cost of Goods Sold was calculated from a periodic setup:

	Purchases	**$52,000**	←	**Assumed sold; part of cost**
+	**Merchandise Inventory**	**15,000**	←	**Beg. Inv. – Ending Inv. $19,000 – $4,000**
–	**Purchases Discount**	**860**	→	**Reduces costs**
–	**Purchases Returns and Allowances**	**680**	↗	
+	**Freight-In**	**450**	→	**Adds to cost**
		$65,910		**Cost of Goods Sold**

What's deleted from the periodic worksheet: Account titles for Purchases, Purchases Discounts, Purchases Returns and Allowances, and Freight-In.

Note: Net income is the same on the periodic and the perpetual worksheets.

PROBLEM FOR APPENDIX

Using the completed worksheet on page 567 in the text, convert this worksheet to a perpetual inventory system worksheet. (The worksheet is at the end of the *Study Guide with Working Papers.*)

ART'S CLOTHING COMPANY WORKSHEET
DECEMBER 31, 2013

	Trial Balance		Adjustments		Adjusted Trial Balance		Income Statement		Balance Sheet	
	Dr.	Cr.	Dr.	Cr.	Dr.	Cr.	Dr.	Cr.	Dr.	Cr.
Cash	12420 00				12420 00				12420 00	
Petty Cash	100 00				100 00				100 00	
Accounts Receivable	14500 00				14500 00				14500 00	
Merchandise Inventory	4000 00				4000 00				4000 00	
Supplies	800 00			(B) 500 00	300 00				300 00	
Prepaid Insurance	900 00			(C) 300 00	600 00				600 00	
Prepaid HST	500 00				500 00				500 00	
Store Equipment	4000 00				4000 00				4000 00	
Accumulated Amortization, Store Equipment		400 00		(D) 50 00		450 00				450 00
Accounts Payable		17900 00				17900 00				17900 00
Income Tax Payable		1240 00				1240 00				1240 00
CPP Payable		260 00				260 00				260 00
EI Payable		200 00				200 00				200 00
HST Payable		700 00				700 00				700 00
Unearned Rent		600 00	(A) 200 00			400 00				400 00
Mortgage Payable		1620 00				1620 00				1620 00
Art Newner, Capital		7905 00				7905 00				7905 00
Art Newner, Withdrawals	8600 00				8600 00				8600 00	
Sales		95000 00				95000 00		95000 00		
Sales Returns and Allowances	950 00				950 00		950 00			
Sales Discounts	670 00				670 00		670 00			
Cost of Goods Sold	65910 00				65910 00		65910 00			
Salary Expense	11700 00		(E) 600 00		12300 00		12300 00			
Payroll Tax Expense	420 00				420 00		420 00			
Postage Expense	25 00				25 00		25 00			
Miscellaneous Expense	30 00				30 00		30 00			
Interest Expense	300 00		(G) 600 00		300 00		300 00			
	125825 00	125825 00								
Rental Income				(A) 200 00		200 00		200 00		
Supplies Expense			(B) 500 00		500 00		500 00			
Insurance Expense			(C) 300 00		300 00		300 00			
Amortization Expense, Equipment			(D) 50 00		50 00		50 00			
Salaries Payable				(E) 600 00		600 00				600 00
			1650 00	1650 00	126475 00	126475 00	81455 00	95200 00		
							13745 00			13745 00
							95200 00	95200 00	45020 00	45020 00

List of Auxiliary Chapters

Index

C

D

E

H

I

J

L

M

N

O

P

R

U

V

W